CLOSE IMAGINING
An Introduction *to* Literature

Other books by Benjamin DeMott

NOVELS

The Body's Cage
A Married Man

ESSAYS

Hells & Benefits
You Don't Say
Supergrow
Surviving the 70's
Scholarship for Society
America in Literature
    (with Alan Tractenberg)

CLOSE IMAGINING
An Introduction *to* Literature

BENJAMIN DeMOTT
Amherst College

A BEDFORD BOOK

St. Martin's Press • NEW YORK

Library of Congress Catalog Card Number: 87–060600

Manufactured in the United States of America

1   0   9   8   7
f   e   d   c   b   a

For information, write St. Martin's Press, Inc.,
175 Fifth Avenue, New York, NY 10010

Editorial Offices: Bedford Books *of* St. Martin's Press,
29 Commonwealth Avenue, Boston, MA 02116

ISBN: 0–312–00336–6

Book design: Sandra Rigney, The Book Department, Inc.
Cover design: Hannus Design Associates.
The cover illustration is Will Barnett's *Silent Seasons — Fall*. 1967.
Oil on Canvas. 43 ½ × 33 inches.
Collection of the Whitney Museum of American Art.
Purchased with funds from Mr. and Mrs. Daniel H. Silberberg. 73.48

Acknowledgments

Renata Adler. "Brownstone" from *Speedboat* by Renata Adler. Copyright © 1976 by Renata Adler. Reprinted by permission of Random House, Inc.

A. R. Ammons. "Cascadilla Falls" and "I went out to the sun" reprinted from *Collected Poems*, 1951–1971, by A. R. Ammons, by permission of W. W. Norton & Company, Inc. Copyright © 1972 by A. R. Ammons.

John Ashbery. "The Instruction Manual" from *Some Trees* by John Ashbery. Copyright © 1956 by John Ashbery. Reprinted by permission of Georges Borchardt, Inc. and the author.

Margaret Atwood. "Landcrab" from *Field* #22, Spring 1980. Reprinted by permission.

(Continued on page 1429)

To the memory of Mina Shaughnessy

. . . the process of reading is not a half-sleep, but, in highest sense, an exercise, a gymnast's struggle . . . The reader is to do something for himself, must be on the alert, must himself or herself construct indeed the poem, argument, history, metaphysical essay—the text furnishing the hints, the clue, the start or framework. Not the book needs so much to be the complete thing, but the reader of the book does.

—Walt Whitman, *Democratic Vistas*

Preface for Instructors

Close Imagining is a book not about what writers do but about what readers do. It's conceived as an extended response to a question that is urgent in an age when reading is beleaguered: What are we studying literature for in the first place? Why bother with reading stories and poems and plays? What's the point? What does anybody get out of such reading? Why should anybody want to be "introduced" to literature?

The emphasis in *Close Imagining* is upon reading as an enterprise offering students opportunities to improve their performance in a variety of significant human activities. Connections are drawn between powers developed through the study of imaginative literature and abilities that figure in the conduct of personal, social, and civic life. The powers in question are those brought into play as readers enter into active collaboration with writers in constructing literary experiences.

Two different kinds of texts are collected in these pages: (1) imaginative works created by story writers, poets, and playwrights; and (2) responses to those works created by students, teachers, and literary critics. In Part One, Acts of Construction, where the stress is on the referential dimensions of texts, questions are aimed at strengthening the student's capacity to construct life situations, to probe for the content of moments of human feeling, to define ways in which evoking this or that particular moment of feeling works to deepen or complicate familiar beliefs and assumptions. In Part Two, The Experience of Language, the concern is more directly with language, but the emphasis remains on literature as a resource for human development. Questions and responses strive to clarify the uses of literary ways of thinking — thinking by analogy and comparison, thinking and feeling through the perspective of irony, and so on.

The book is not organized in a traditional pattern, but topics are introduced with an eye to the convenience of teachers whose usual practice is to deal separately with such matters as point of view, figures of speech, symbol, and metrics. Instructors accustomed to teaching *Antigone* and *Hamlet* — together with the best-known English ballads; stories by Hawthorne, Hemingway, Faulkner, and Updike; and familiar poems by Hardy, Dickinson, Marvell, and others — will find their favorites well represented in the book's contents. The selections balance older classics with contemporary classics (poems by Philip Larkin, for example) and with new writing by Caryl Churchill, Deborah Eisenberg, and other young writers. But, to repeat, the book's primary goal is to help individual readers achieve awareness of their powers as active collaborators with writers and to develop and refine those powers. Its further aim is to enable individual readers to participate fully in a community of lively interpreters of texts — people seeking understanding, both of literature and life, through their own activity as writers.

The book's approach has a history, naturally. As a teacher of literature I have discovered over the years that discussions of what writers do tend to be short, teacher dominated, and unchallenging. When what happens in the literature classroom dwindles into instruction in the difference between metaphor and simile (the writer uses *like* or *as* in simile), or between a story and poem, I and everybody else in the room wish we were elsewhere, even out in the snow. I've also learned that the most interesting discussions in literature class have to do with how readers work, how they bring to life the works we read together, how they arrive at and express their versions of the works — their interpretations and criticisms. My attention as a teacher has come to focus on the ways in which students and I myself construct texts as experiences we can talk about, write about, and share with others.

But obviously nobody's preferences as a teacher exist in a vacuum. They are directly affected by what is taking place in the field of study. During the past three decades or so the emphasis in literary studies in colleges and universities has shifted from the pursuit, through canny explication, of perfected accounts of *the* meaning of individual literary texts. A more recent focus has been upon the roles readers play in shaping their experience of texts, and upon the social and historical influences shaping those roles. Instead of asking, What exactly is the writer's meaning in this text? or, What exactly did the writer do to bring this meaning across? theorists and critics are inquiring directly into such matters as: What do readers do in arriving at their own versions of the texts they read? When readers express to themselves, in their own words, the "point" of a story, poem, or play as they experience it, where are those words coming from? How are they generated?

Many significant assumptions lie behind this shift of focus. One is that not only are texts experienced differently by different readers within the same historical period but that what people make of a work in one period will be different from what is made of it in another. A second assumption is that the activities of reading and writing are more tightly interconnected than was once thought. As we read we are constantly translating the words on the page into our own words — in a sense, rewriting the work into our own language. A third assumption is that in a media age wherein efforts to persuade and manipulate are of unprecedented intensity and range, a special need exists for understanding of the role of readers. When everything from beer to political and religious causes is marketed in language, readers cannot afford to be submissive; they *must* become active and questioning.

Some theorists and critics who, in varying degrees, accept these and related assumptions are grouped as specialists in what is called "reader response." *Close Imagining* is not an introduction to the reader response school of criticism and only very occasionally addresses any of the pivotal issues in the broad area of literary theory. (Among those issues are the problematic nature of human perception, the ambiguous status of language as an instrument for representing reality, and the nature and functions of the codes used by readers in organizing meanings as they work their way through texts.) But obviously there are important links between this book and the general movement away from the idea of the sacred, autonomous, inviolable text. It's fair to say, in short, that *Close Imagining* is a product both of practical experience and personal preference and of the influence of several late-twentieth-century trends in the profession of literature teaching.

Acknowledgments

Although I owe many debts to critics, scholars, and theorists who have helped me think through critical issues, I hesitate to cite writers individually because few would recognize — or perhaps approve — what is made of their guidance in these pages. I must nevertheless mention by name Louise Rosenblatt, Edward Said, and the late Roland Barthes. I've written elsewhere, at length, in appreciation of my undergraduate teacher Fred Tupper; I seldom read a Shakespeare play without remembering one or another of his ways of bringing lines to life. Theodore Baird began teaching me thirty-five years ago, when I was an instructor of English at Amherst. One of his many contributions was to show me how to secure oral and written responses from students that drew more directly on their actual reading experience than did conventional classroom questions or standard assignments for literary essays. Mina Shaughnessy, whose death at an early age was surely among the severest losses to the community of teachers of reading and writing in my time, taught me that reading student responses well — and assisting students to do the same — is exceptionally demanding work. (As Shaughnessy herself performed it, the work sometimes qualified as an art.)

I am particularly grateful to Richard Rorty, who heard me out one morning in Palo Alto in the early 1980s on the subject of the summoning reader of books and life; he knew nothing of the work I had in progress, but his response clarified my direction and rekindled my enthusiasm for what I was launching.

The first concrete support for *Close Imagining* came from the Fund for the Improvement of Post-Secondary Education in the U.S. Department of Education, which made me a member of the first generation of Mina Shaughnessy scholars. Long conversations with fund staff members — especially Rusty Garth — who read and probed drafts of my proposals strengthened my grasp of what I was about. When the ideas were under sufficient control to be laid out at an editorial lunch table, I was lucky in my audience — Charles Christensen and Joan Feinberg of Bedford Books. They saw immediately what kind of book I had in mind, knew that risk was entailed, yet backed me unhesitatingly.

Early drafts were commented upon helpfully by a team of reviewers who approached the assignment with intensity and scrupulosity that I can't believe authors of introductory texts customarily receive: Robert Atwan; Sylvan Barnet; Marion Copeland, Holyoke Community College; William J. Gracie, Jr., Miami University; X. J. Kennedy; Carol MacKay, University of Texas at Austin; Donald McQuade, University of California at Berkeley; Stephen Mailloux, Syracuse University; Janet S. Marting, University of Akron; Shirley Morahan, Northeast Missouri State University; Ross Murfin, University of Miami; David Richter, Queens College; Mike Rose, University of California at Los Angeles; Hephzibah Roskelly, University of Massachusetts at Boston; Susan Schweik, University of California at Berkeley; Margaret J. Webb, Eastern Michigan University; Jack H. White, Mississippi State University; Eve Zarin, Lehman College of the City University of New York. Special thanks go to William E. Sheidley, University of Connecticut, a reviewer who began commenting on this project at the prospectus stage and made countless suggestions at every stage thereafter (of which I followed many). His way of living into the evolving text kept me in direct touch with my theme — the active reader creating the text in collaboration with the writer.

Editorial and other staff members at Bedford Books are by now accustomed to effusive thanks from authors guilty about the state of their dependency. But they must listen once more. Karen Henry's firm understanding of my basic purposes and fine feeling for structure and organization made her proposals for revision consistently valuable. Susan M. S. Brown, copy editor, and Elizabeth Schaaf and Mary Lou Wilshaw in production coped with me as though it weren't a trial, and everybody at Bedford who worked on the project buoyed me with their enthusiasm and cheer. I am grateful to Wilhelmina Eaton, my typist.

It remains for me to name my largest debt, which is, of course, to my students. (I am afraid that now there are not fewer than thousands of them.) Some of their written work is printed in these pages, and I remember many individual classes that they brought to life as we worked together, exchanging our separate versions of texts, surprising each other, doubting each other, straightening each other out, absorbing each other's contributions, moving on. I hope that any of my former students who happen upon *Close Imagining* will recognize it for what it is — a grateful effort at payback.

Contents

FICTION   732

Alternate Contents by Genre

FICTION

DRAMA

CLOSE IMAGINING
An Introduction *to* Literature

Introduction
for Students

Bringing Literature
to Life

The good reader of a poem, story, or play is a full partner with the author of the work. Good readers work with authors to bring poems and stories to life. *Close Imagining* focuses on *active reading* — on how we as readers bring imaginative writing to life.

In our partnership with authors we have a lot to do. For one thing, we have to feel out "character." This means deciding for ourselves about the nature of the strangers whose thoughts and behavior are being presented.

> In the day we sweat it out in the streets of a runaway American
>   dream
> At night we ride through mansions of glory in suicide machines
> Sprung from cages out on Highway 9
> Chrome wheeled, fuel injected
> And steppin' out over the line
> Baby this town rips the bones from your back
> It's a death trap, it's a suicide rap
> We gotta get out while we're young
> 'Cause tramps like us, baby we were born to run

What sort of person is talking here? Only when we build up a clear idea of the human being in Bruce Springsteen's lyric, making the person real to ourselves, do the words begin to come vigorously alive.

It's the same with the life situations in which characters like and unlike ourselves find themselves, and the same with the feelings stirring inside them. Acting in partnership with the author, we use our imaginations to bring the situations close. And we enter personally into the feelings that those situations arouse.

1

LOUISE GLÜCK   (b. 1943)

Labor Day

Requiring something lovely on his arm
Took me to Stamford, Connecticut, a quasi-farm,
His family's; later picking up the mammoth
Girlfriend of Charlie, meanwhile trying to pawn me off
On some third guy also up for the weekend.   5
But Saturday we still were paired; spent
It sprawled across that sprawling acreage
Until the grass grew limp
With damp. Like me. Johnston-baby, I can still see
The pelted clover, burrs' prickle fur and gorged   10
Pastures spewing infinite tiny bells. You pimp.

The character talking in this poem offers a clipped account of a holiday weekend, ending with a direct address to "Johnston-baby." As we imagine for ourselves the situation of being carelessly used and dropped, we draw closer to her feelings, live inside her defensive cynicism, share the stony bitterness behind "You pimp."

In bringing imaginative literature to life we are nearly always concerned with evoking characters, situations, and feelings. But the collaboration with authors involves many other activities. Through unique acts of patterning and molding, writers transform language into a medium of art. Good readers respond to — become involved in — these acts of patterning. Even as they are reading, they ask and answer questions about moral and other options open to individual characters dealing with families, work, loves. And good readers arrive at conclusions about humanity, nature, or the world of spirit based on their study of what happens to particular people in particular stories.

WHY WRITERS CAN'T DO IT ALL

It's fair to ask at this point: Why should we as readers have so much to do? Don't authors have obligations? Shouldn't their work be complete and alive in itself, totally independent of us?

Authors do have obligations, but there are clear limits on what they can do for us, their readers. They can point us in the direction of other people; they can teach us how to ask intelligent questions about other people's feelings, situations, hopes. But the actual deed of bringing lives that are separate and distant near enough so that we genuinely care about them — so that we're moved by the happiness or sorrow or guilt or confusion of strangers — can't be performed for us by anyone else. Our sympathy is among our most intimate possessions. A writer can introduce us to circumstances deserving our concern, but control of our sympathy remains with us from start to finish.

The same holds for control of our decision-making faculties — the faculties we rely on when making up our minds about the meaning of statements and events. Poems, stories, and plays may be filled with knowledge, but tact — respect for the intelligence of the reader — tends to lead authors away from explicitness. And this adds to our responsibilities. We must render personal judgment on people, and draw conclusions about the meaning of sequences of events. We're given guidance by the poet, storyteller, or playwright, but we are *not* given correct answers, partly because writers know that most of us neither want them nor believe they exist.

One more reason why readers must be continuously active is that reading a poem, story, or play is an experience, and nobody can have our experience for us. Each person passes through adolescence and young adulthood, middle age and old age in a distinct way, and, while these phases of life are often theorized about, and reduced to formula, the difference between the formula and the actual living through of a phase of life is as great as the difference between the air we breathe and the shorthand sign for its chemical composition. Authors can give interviews telling people what they had in mind in writing one or another text. Reviewers can summarize plots. But these are abstract formulas, remote from the feel of the work as known by somebody passing through it as an experience. Living *into* a story — living it through — is necessarily a personal act. Reading well means being on intimate terms with the story, poem, or play, possessing it, inhabiting it as we inhabit our own lives.

And always we are working *with* writers, in a state of vital interdependency. Without the poem and the poet, the novel and the novelist, the play and the playwright, we are powerless to focus our imaginations. But without readers to bring their texts to life — readers who transform plot into felt anticipations and anxieties within themselves — writers are equally powerless. Our sympathies as readers, our activities and skills, are pivotal to the process of imaginative bringing-to-life that lies at the heart of literature.

INFLUENCES ON READERS

Sympathies differ from reader to reader, and so, too, do the influences affecting us as we bring works to life. As good readers we try to stay alert to those influences, finding ways of using them to broaden our responses. We know that our maleness or femaleness can affect our reading, influencing the direction of our sympathy when we're reading about, say, a conflict between a man and a woman. Age as well as gender has an impact; a love poem in which we hear the voice of somebody portrayed as entering old age will sound different to readers in their twenties than to readers in their fifties and sixties.

Religious faith and national and ethnic heritage are major factors in shaping our responses; Jews and non-Jews, Roman Catholics and Christian Scientists, don't hear poems addressed to the Virgin Mary in the same way. Native Americans respond differently from others to the great invocations of sacred places that nineteenth-century tribal leaders addressed to the White Fathers in Washington who were dispossessing them of their burial grounds. Money and social class also affect our ways of reading; the famous command in the Communist Manifesto ("Workers of the world, unite!") has different meanings for coal miners than for millionaires.

And beyond all this, shaping our responses directly and indirectly, are the special circumstances and character of our education. People whose early learning was book oriented and took place at home and in classrooms feel differently about the world of writing than do those whose early learning centered on street smarts and survival. People with lengthy exposure to any of the major contemporary systems of interpretation of human behavior, such as Marxism or Freudianism, explain the behavior of characters in stories, poems, and plays in different terms from those used by readers unfamiliar with, or hostile to, those systems.

And always the extent of our reading experience conditions our activity as readers. Not surprisingly, writers — even those who specialize in action and adventure — are usually avid, experienced readers. When they approach any of a variety of subjects — from the death of a fellow artist to the beginning or end of a love affair — they're fully conscious that they're joining the company of many others who, down through the centuries, have written on similar themes. They also know the conventions that those earlier writers have observed — for example, the convention of claiming, in a love poem, that the poem can make the beloved immortal, or the convention of imagining, in an elegy, some kind of rebirth for the departed. Sometimes they follow the conventions, sometimes they argue with them — and our awareness or unawareness of this background affects our ways of reading. The more stories, poems, plays, and novels we've read, the more likely we are to think of texts first in terms of their relation to each other — the similarities and contrasts in their treatment of similar materials, and so on.

Thousands of poems have been written about the coming of spring; readers familiar with a fair share of them tend to approach a new one with questions in mind about how it connects with the tradition created by earlier spring poems and about whether (and how) it offers us something fresh to justify adding another such poem to the total. Readers unfamiliar with the body of poetry about spring will obviously not begin by comparing the new poem with older poems.

But wherever we start, it's important that we know ourselves as readers and strive for alertness to the elements of our nature, position in life, and education that are likely to shape our initial response to what we're reading. We don't do this in order to make light of those initial responses; the strength of first reactions is the strength of our individuality and seldom warrants disrespect. We seek awareness of the influences on us because we want to be able to reach beyond our own preoccupations, standard beliefs, habitual ways of dealing either with literature or with life. That need for enlarged perspectives is no less genuine for the experienced, trained reader than for the reader without extensive literary knowledge. (Eccentric responses and readings — reactions in which it's difficult for others to participate — are traceable almost invariably to influences about which the reader isn't adequately conscious.)

Our goal is to stretch ourselves — to work out from our personal starting points to positions and perspectives that allow us to see more and feel more than we can if we don't move freely in our imaginations. Reading is "broadening" only if, working in collaboration with writers, we seek a degree of release from the limits imposed by gender, class, clan, education, and the rest, confronting our own natures and finding the elements in what we are that can help us bridge gaps between ourselves and others. (For instance, the experience of reverence, as known by a person of one particular religious faith, can provide access to meanings and dimensions of reality known to members of other, wholly different faiths.) How far we can go, how various we can become — how open in our sympathies — depends partly on our personal gift for flexibility, partly on how energetically and successfully we develop our skills as readers.

HOW TO IMPROVE AS A READER

How can active readers improve their skills? Better imaginative reading requires time and practice. It also requires that we separate the phases of a complex emotional and intellectual process and concentrate on one at a time. And it requires that, even while we separate phases of our activity, we bear in mind that such separation is *only* a method of practice. Athletes and musicians often bear down on one or another technical aspect of their pursuit. Tennis players will decide to take their game apart — to work, say, on the service toss. Golfers reexamine their swing. Pianists concentrate at one moment on fingering techniques and at the next on picking up their pace as sight readers. But everybody knows that athletic and musical performances exist as wholes, not as parts, and it's the same with performances in reading. We practice one phase of the overall activity at a time but can't afford to forget that good reading fuses all those separable phases into one unified experience.

When we're reading well, we're in touch simultaneously with the traits and nature of characters in a story, poem, or play *and* with an imagined person's approach to a moment of crisis, *and* with broader meanings that are asking for definition, *and* with the special qualities of the language in and through which all the rest is organized.

But focusing on parts of the process can be immensely help-ful. Skills that are honed individually can be trusted to energize each other when brought together. The exercises in *Close Imagining* aim at sharpening the essentials of imaginative reading through questions that deal with one activity at a time. Each chapter title describes what kind of practice is under way, what activities of the reader are up for scrutiny and development.

WHY IMPROVE AS A READER?

Why is working to become a better reader of imaginative writing a worthwhile undertaking? For longer than thirty-five years I've been teaching literature to college students in public and private institutions, in small colleges and large universities, in the United States and overseas. For me the phrase *teaching literature* means helping students grow as readers who bring poems, plays, and stories to life *for themselves*.

A good many of the happiest moments I remember in my life have taken place — amazingly — in a classroom, as one of my students, working with a writer, brought to bear a personal re-sponse that lighted up a line or a scene or a whole story in such a way that all of us, at that moment, could feel ourselves chal-lenged, stretched, enlivened. There's been so much entertain-ment and stimulation in literature classes for me that I some-times find it hard to understand why anybody would ask why studying the subject is worthwhile.

On the other hand, I have heard many statements about the value of reading that seem to me wrongheaded. On some occa-sions, enthusiasts of great literature speak as though ignorance of Shakespeare — or whatever writer happens to be in high fash-ion — was proof of bad manners. Nice people don't eat with their fingers. Nice people read John Keats and *Macbeth*. Enthusi-asts of poetry, drama, and fiction also speak on occasion as though we should seek acquaintance with great works of imagina-tive writing solely for direct experience of beauty. And there are many lovers of literature who have found its significance ex-clusively in the ethical lessons it teaches, whether explicitly or obliquely.

It's easy to agree that the experience of beauty is invaluable. It's true that many works of literary art can be evoked — by good

readers — as experiences of truth: noble, practical, or discon-
certing. And although the idea that it's a sign of good breeding to
have read the great writers is offensive, I believe that the reading
of imaginative writing does have a significant social dimension.
For generations Jane Austen and Charles Dickens, Anton Chekhov and William Wordsworth, Miguel de Cervantes and Mo-
lière — and scores of others — have lived in the minds of intelligent men and women, and held a place in their conversation.
One way of connecting ourselves with the humanity preceding
our own, thereby clarifying both our location and our identity, is
by having in our heads not just the news of the present age but a
portion of what earlier ages regarded as interesting and ponder-
able. At the level of dress codes and the like, keeping up tradition
can be pointless, but knowing what the smart people of an earlier
day considered worth remembering clearly makes sense. So, too,
does knowing the work of living writers — from Ralph Ellison
and Adrienne Rich to James Merrill and Gwendolyn Brooks —
that future generations are likely to remember.

And all this makes stronger sense when we reflect on the uses
of an educated imagination. This, for me, is what reading is all
about. Without an educated imagination nobody is likely to be
much good at raising children, succeeding in business, even
persuading another person to share life with him or her for
longer than a month at a time. Adeptness at bringing experience
to life, shrewdness at speculating about what is taking place from
moment to moment in other creatures, responsiveness to imagined feelings, thoughts, reactions — these are qualities without
which most days of most lives would be extremely thin. The state
of development of our gifts in these areas affects our tastes, our
ambitions, and our capacity to realize our ambitions. It affects
our ability to care about the spectrum of human life from sports
to politics, our aptitude for learning to love (not to mention
becoming worthy of affection), and our readiness to provide
leadership and, where appropriate, to accept leadership. The
very act of perception itself — taking in the reality around us —
depends on our power to animate, to bring the world fully to life.
"We animate what we see," said the great American thinker and
poet Ralph Waldo Emerson, "we see only what we animate."

It's this power that we nourish and enlarge when we improve
ourselves as readers of imaginative literature. And it's for this

reason, in my opinion, that the work is profoundly worthwhile. Animating these poems, stories, and plays is, in itself, a superbly enjoyable occupation. And knowing how to bring stories, poems, and plays to vivid life adds significantly to our range and force as human beings.

PART ONE

Acts *of* Construction

Each of the five chapters that make up Part One of *Close Imagining* deals with a particular mode of imaginative activity in which readers engage. And each of these activities can be thought of as a kind of building — an act of construction. The building materials with which we work are various. We begin with words on the page, of course — the words with which the author composed the poem or story or play. We use in addition the knowledge that we bring to these words — the information, expertise, book learning, and personal memories that enable us to interpret the words on the page. We also use our immediate experience as readers of the author's words — remembered responses, that is, to specific words, phrases, lines, and sentences we encountered during the actual reading.

What we construct out of these materials is, finally, a reading experience — a personal experience, a personal version, of the particular text. Invariably this reading experience is multidimensional. In achieving it we create clarity for ourselves about the feelings and reactions that other human beings are having to their special situations. We build up a sense of what one or another imagined person is like, hammering together details of appearance and temperament, faults and virtues. We also build up a sense of changes taking place — sometimes lasting, sometimes temporary — within imagined persons. (Most human beings are fascinated by their own processes of development at each period — and at crisis moments — of their lives; writers share that fascination.) And always we're seeking to frame some kind of understanding — some structure of ideas that will enable us to express the meaning of the totality of the activities we have been engaged in as readers of the text. The first three chapters of Part One deal with our acts of construction as imaginers of feeling, character, and change; the fourth and fifth chapters concern what we do when we construct ideas.

The questions in Part One — and elsewhere in *Close Imagining* — are accompanied by responses: excerpts from papers written by students and from commentaries by the editor or literary critics addressing the questions. One purpose of the responses is to illustrate differences in reading experiences — varying ways in which readers of the same text construct the characters, feelings, and ideas they see as central in that text. A more significant purpose is to provide opportunities for becoming more alert, attentive readers by observing how others attend to their own reading experiences.

It's impossible to exaggerate the importance of this matter of paying attention to — of growing increasingly conscious *as we read* of — our own moment-to-moment reactions and responses. And the example of others can be extremely helpful as we sharpen this attentiveness. Seeing what others have to say about the texts we ourselves have written about is usually interesting — but there's much more to be done besides checking out overall agreements or disagreements, or deciding whether this or that reader is or isn't smarter than we are. What we're looking for, at bottom, is evidence about *where* other readers have focused their attention, *how* they kept track of their own responses, and *why* they arrived at their interpretive decisions. What exactly did they notice that we didn't? Why did they ignore what we took to be pivotal? Do some of them bring to bear on their remembered experience as readers an intensity or clarity that seems enviable? Where do we notice a limitation on a reader's attentiveness that can function, for us, as a warning?

It will be clearer as we go along that practicing many different kinds of activity is essential for readers whose goal is to improve their imaginative performance. At every step of the way much can be learned from scrutinizing the performances of others who share that goal.

1

Imagining Feeling

Bringing works of literature to life almost invariably means entering quickly into another person's thoughts and feelings. We step outside ourselves, and seem — for a short stretch of time — as close to another's nerves, moods, shifts of mood as we are to our own.

WENDELL BERRY   (b. 1934)
The Peace of Wild Things

When despair for the world grows in me
and I wake in the night at the least sound
in fear of what my life and my children's lives may be,
I go and lie down where the wood drake
rests in his beauty on the water, and the great heron feeds.   5
I come into the peace of wild things
who do not tax their lives with forethought
of grief. I come into the presence of still water.
And I feel above me the day-blind stars
waiting with their light. For a time   10
I rest in the grace of the world, and am free.

We may or may not have children about whose future we worry, we may or may not be haunted by despair — but we can slip easily into the experience of momentary release that's the core of this poem.

Many times when the language of a poem looks hard or eccentric or confusing, the best move we can make is to ask who is speaking, what that person feels, and why.

13

E. E. CUMMINGS   (1894–1962)
a salesman

a salesman is an it that stinks Excuse

Me whether it's president of the you were say
or a jennelman name misder finger isn't
important whether it's millions of other punks
or just a handful absolutely doesn't   5
matter and whether it's in lonjewray

or shrouds is immaterial it stinks

a salesman is an it that stinks to please

but whether to please itself or someone else
makes no more difference than if it sells   10
hate condoms education snakeoil vac
uumcleaners terror strawberries democ
ra(caveat emptor)cy superfluous hair

Or Think We've Met subhuman rights Before

    Reading e. e. cummings's "a salesman" for the first time, most of us are confused a little by the crazy-seeming spelling, absence of punctuation, lame puns, made-up words, and so on. Once we begin focusing on feeling, though, things open up. We move into the protest of a person who's had it up to here with oily insincerity — the slick manners of hucksters whose use of different strokes for different folks is based on the belief that everybody can be suckered. When we feel *with* cummings's words, we feel itchiness to the point of anger. We know — freshly — what it's like to be a customer who hates being treated as a bosom friend by strangers whose only real interest is often in our money or our vote. We know what it's like to detest being trapped into reciprocal niceness by the oh-so-personal concern of smoothie fakers, whether in malls or used-car lots or TV commercials. We know what it's like to want to be able to fight off hypocritical politeness by using rude words ("stinks"), and what it's like to want to mock mealymouthedness by imitating it ("Excuse/Me . . . Think We've Met . . . Before").

    Most people don't walk around constantly feeling this resentful about commercial con men and women. But now and then the whole atmosphere of sham and hoax and hype can get to us, and cummings's poem makes us live inside the feelings of a human being who, at this particular moment, has reached the limits of tolerance for con.

How is it possible for us to make this movement from our own more or less casual daily acceptance of commercial dissimulation to this consumer's impatience and hostility? Why are we able to construct somebody else's insides, feel the beat of somebody else's pulse? One part of the answer lies in the gift of the literary creator — the artist's mastery of suggestiveness. That pell-mell unpunctuated list of huckstered products starting in line 11 — "hate condoms education snakeoil vac/uumcleaners" et cetera — helps us create the sense of uncontrollably mounting edginess. In the second part of this book we'll look at how the organization of words on the page helps direct our feelings. But here our focus is our own sympathy — our instinct of fellow feeling, our ability to use our experience and our powers of inference to make shrewd guesses about what's taking place in a mind different from our own.

In daily life some of our guesses are better than others, naturally. At times we're rightly confident about our knowledge of someone else's feelings. The baby cries and, knowing that he or she must be wet or hungry or in need of cuddling, we act at once to meet the need. A blind person without a Seeing Eye dog waits uncertainly at a traffic light; grasping his or her need, we quickly offer a hand. A friend receives a bad grade or loses a sports or political contest or suffers the collapse of a relationship, and we try to find words to ease the unhappiness. We often understand things at a glance, and the appropriate comforting action comes almost automatically.

Not all feelings, however, are as quickly recognizable or easy to diagnose as these. Our own as well as other people's feelings can confuse and mystify us. (How easy would it be for a salesman to understand someone who was claiming that "a salesman is an it that stinks"?) We lose our way in complications and contradictions and wind up guessing wrong.

But our mistakes don't mean that the resources we lean on are insignificant. Sympathy, sensitivity to others, and the power of inference are essential to the daily effort to function well in human society. They are also central resources for the active reader. They're indispensable when we begin bringing to life the state of mind and feeling of the person who's sore at hucksters in cummings's poem. And these resources can be strengthened by practice in the imaginative collaboration of writers and readers. The combination of the writer's form and language and our energizing imagination allows us to hold the person and moment before us — to step nearer to them and step back, to sympathize and criticize. We can invent the provocations and frustrations that lie behind feelings. By using both our intuition and our reason, by thinking feelingly and feeling thoughtfully, we can construct a full experience from within. This act of constructing-from-within — building up the interiors of events and situations — is crucial to what we do in bringing imaginative literature to life.

ASKING THE RIGHT QUESTIONS

The building materials with which we work come in the form of responses to questions that we ourselves pose from the moment we start reading. What is being talked about here? How do we make sense of this reaction? What caused this particular moment of feeling? What would it be like to be the person who's experiencing this feeling? What's it like to be so sick of salesmen you feel like abusing all of them as stinkers to their faces? Sometimes the responses come quickly; sometimes they don't. Depending on the poem, story, or play, we may find it necessary to keep redefining the questions with which we began, filling out our knowledge of the causes in greater detail, framing new queries. What's going on here? What's happening to this person? What happened a moment ago? Does the person in view understand what just occurred? Does the person understand his or her feelings here and now? Why? Why not? Is the person about to commit some action? How will the person explain this moment of feeling and action in the future?

Often when trying to clarify "What's going on here?" we have to begin at or near the beginning of the text, asking questions that at first glance may seem remote from feelings, and allowing the answers to nudge us along gradually into the flow of the feeling. With cummings's "a salesman" we might start, for instance, with questions about the word *it* in the first line. Why is the salesman called an "it"? Is the implication that some aspect of the salesman causes him to stop being human — turns him into a thing or an animal? But if so, *what* aspect? The fact that the "it" is said to "stink" adds to the abuse but doesn't in itself give us much of an answer. Nor do the six lines that follow.

Ah, but the *eighth* line of the poem — "a salesman is an it that stinks to please" — here we get something that may have a bearing on the question. It's hard to think of a thing or an animal that "stinks to please," although skunks stink to defend themselves. And when skunks exude a substance to have an effect on another creature, they don't do this selectively, with an eye to the nature or individuality of the dog, cat, or whatever. It's a more or less automatic reaction to *any* member of a foreign species. Whereas human beings in their interactions with each other are supposed to be heedful of, interested in, respectful toward each other's individuality. They're supposed to assume that personal differences exist and matter. Maybe what turns the salesman into a nonhuman creature — an "it" — is the fact that his pretended concern for us, his effusions, are as automatic, as heedless of our own special identity, as the emissions of a skunk. As the skunk responds to the genus *dog*, the salesman responds to the genus *customer*. We resent this denial of our individuality. And is it perhaps our awareness that his extravagant politeness — his "Excuse Me's" and "Think We've Met Before's" — also has nothing to do with us as individuals that makes it obnoxious?

Once we've moved this far — to the beginnings of a response to our first question about why the poem calls the salesman "it" instead of "him" — we've begun to edge our way into the flow of the feeling, and toward a sense of "what's going on here."

The process of creating new questions — intermediary questions — usually involves focusing on an aspect of what's being said that seems to invite closer scrutiny. We grasp that we need to probe a little to "get" the full meaning of the detail. And as we pursue this work of clarification, we begin to notice dimensions that we missed the first time through, such as the implicit link between the manners of salesmen to customers and skunks to other species. We push the door open and enter into a fresh set of questions (What's the specific link between man and animal here?).

The process is roughly the same for all readers. But each reader is likely to generate his or her own set of specific intermediary questions. Another reader might have started, for example, with an intermediary question about why the identity of neither the salesman ("whether it's president . . . or . . . misder finger") nor the product ("hate" or "vac*l*uum cleaners") seems to matter. Middle-level questions are bound to differ from reader to reader. And as we multiply them, they can become dense enough to make it worthwhile for a reader to jot notes on a scrap of paper in order to keep track of the responses. But time is always on our side: the poem, story, or play won't go away. It stays bright and visible, allowing itself to be called back for a fresh look, lived through for yet another reading. If we're unable to reach into its insides the minute we "finish" its last word, we can start over: begin verbalizing our questions, framing in the interiors that will help us see and feel each moment with clarity and assurance.

THE PROBLEM OF "RIGHT RESPONSES"

Writing responses to blunt questions about stories, poems, and plays isn't most people's idea of a great night out. In the first place, how can there be a "right response" to such questions? In the second place, why isn't it enough simply to think hard about a work without having to produce a full-dress essay?

Fair questions. When we guess about other people's responses, we're drawing on individual funds of knowledge and experience, and that knowledge is shaped — as we said in the introduction — by a huge variety of forces: sex, race, class, religion, educational background, many more. We can teach ourselves to become more aware of the way in which our guesses are molded by personal experience. And when we work together in a classroom setting, we can often achieve greater clarity about the reasons for major differences among human guesses. But even that sharper consciousness of the forces shaping our own and other people's responses is unlikely ever to make any of us comfortable with a person who claims he or she has *the* single, definitive, right answer. The best we can do is compare responses — guesses — with other responses, working to uncover the reasons for the differences, and working also to develop more clearly the standards on which our preferences among guesses are based.

It's exactly these twin purposes — making comparisons and developing and articulating personal standards — that we serve by writing responses to poems, stories, and plays. The first part of *Close Imagining* includes a variety of responses that should be helpful for comparison — excerpts from student papers and observations by the editor and others. At least once in each chapter of this book responses will be provided. (Some readers will choose to look over these responses before writing their own; others will do the opposite.) The range of these responses will establish that a narrow concept of "right answers" is irrelevant to the work in progress. To repeat, the good reader's aim is to develop and sharpen personal standards of judgment.

ASKING QUESTIONS ABOUT FEELING

The following selections call for the evoking of three different moments of feeling, one from the life of a newly married couple in their twenties, the second from the life of a mature rural housewife, and the third from the life of an infant. The first moment occurs in a story, the second and third in poems. The job is to live into these moments in such a way as to bring them fully to life. And the question we'll work with will be quite simple — as simple as this: *What's going on here?* At the end of each text that blunt question is presented together with a passage from the text.

JOHN UPDIKE (b. 1932)
Snowing in Greenwich Village

The Maples had moved just the day before to West Thirteenth Street, and that evening they had Rebecca Cune over, because now they were so close. A tall, always slightly smiling girl with an absent manner, she allowed Richard Maple to slip off her coat and scarf even as she stood gently greeting Joan. Richard, moving with an extra precision and grace because of the smoothness with which the business had been managed — though he and Joan had been married nearly two years, he was still so young-looking that people did not instinctively lay upon him hostly duties; their reluctance worked in him a corresponding hesitancy, so that often it was his wife who poured the drinks, while he sprawled on the sofa in the attitude of a favored and wholly delightful guest — entered the dark bedroom, entrusted the bed with Rebecca's clothes, and returned to the living room. Her coat had seemed weightless.

Rebecca, seated beneath the lamp, on the floor, one leg tucked under her, one arm up on the Hide-a-Bed that the previous tenants had not as yet removed, was saying, "I had known her, you know, just for the day she taught me the job, but I said okay. I was living in an awful place called a hotel for ladies. In the halls they had typewriters you put a quarter in."

Joan, straight-backed on a Hitchcock chair from her parents' home in Vermont, a damp handkerchief balled in her hand, turned to Richard and explained, "Before her apartment now, Becky lived with this girl and her boy friend."

"Yes, his name was Jacques," Rebecca said.

Richard asked, "You lived with them?" The arch composure ₅ of his tone was left over from the mood aroused in him by his successful and, in the dim bedroom, somewhat poignant — as if he were with great tact delivering a disappointing message — disposal of their guest's coat.

"Yes, and he insisted on having his name on the mailbox. He was terribly afraid of missing a letter. When my brother was in the Navy and came to see me and saw on the mailbox" — with three parallel movements of her fingers she set the names beneath one another —

"Georgene Clyde,
Rebecca Cune,
Jacques Zimmerman,

he told me I had always been such a nice girl. Jacques wouldn't even move out so my brother would have a place to sleep. He had to sleep on the floor." She lowered her lids and looked in her purse for a cigarette.

"Isn't that wonderful?" Joan said, her smile broadening helplessly as she realized what an inane thing it had been to say. Her cold worried Richard. It had lasted seven days without improving. Her face was pale, mottled pink and yellow; this accentuated the Modiglianiesque quality established by her long neck and oval blue eyes and her habit of sitting to her full height, her head quizzically tilted and her hands palm downward in her lap.

Rebecca, too, was pale, but in the consistent way of a drawing, perhaps — the weight of her lids and a certain virtuosity about the mouth suggested it — by da Vinci.

"Who would like some sherry?" Richard asked in a deep voice, from a standing position.

"We have some hard stuff if you'd rather," Joan said to   10
Rebecca; from Richard's viewpoint the remark, like those advertisements which from varying angles read differently, contained the quite legible declaration that this time *he* would have to mix the Old Fashioneds.

"The sherry sounds fine," Rebecca said. She enunciated her words distinctly, but in a faint, thin voice that disclaimed for them any consequence.

"I think, too," Joan said.

"Good." Richard took from the mantel the eight-dollar bottle of Tio Pepe that the second man on the Spanish sherry account had stolen for him. So all could share in the drama of it, he uncorked the bottle in the living room. He posingly poured out three glasses, half-full, passed them around, and leaned against the mantel (the Maples had never had a mantel before), swirling the liquid, as the agency's wine expert had told him to do, thus liberating the esters and ethers, until his wife said, as she always did, it being the standard toast in her parents' home, "Cheers, dears!"

Rebecca continued the story of her first apartment. Jacques had never worked. Georgene never held a job more than three weeks. The three of them contributed to a kitty, to which all enjoyed equal access. Rebecca had a separate bedroom. Jacques and Georgene sometimes worked on television scripts; they pinned the bulk of their hopes onto a serial titled *The IBI*   "I" for Intergalactic, or Interplanetary, or something — *in Space and Time*. One of their friends was a young Communist who never washed and always had money because his father owned half of the West Side. During the day, when the two girls were off working, Jacques flirted with a young Swede upstairs who kept dropping her mop onto the tiny balcony outside their window. "A real bombardier," Rebecca said. When Rebecca moved into a single apartment for herself and was all settled and happy, Georgene and Jacques offered to bring a mattress and sleep on her floor. Rebecca felt that the time had come for her to put her foot down. She said no. Later, Jacques married a girl other than Georgene.

"Cashews, anybody?" Richard said. He had bought a can at   15
the corner delicatessen, expressly for this visit, though if Rebecca

had not been coming, he would have bought something else there on some other excuse, just for the pleasure of buying his first thing at the store where in the coming years he would purchase so much.

"No thank you," Rebecca said. Richard was so far from expecting refusal that out of momentum he pressed them on her again, exclaiming, "Please! They're so good for you." She took two and bit one in half.

He offered the dish, a silver porringer given to the Maples as a wedding present and which they had never before had the space to unpack, to his wife, who took a greedy handful and looked so pale that he asked, "How do you feel?" not so much forgetting the presence of their guest as parading his concern, quite genuine at that, before her.

"Fine," Joan said edgily, and perhaps she did.

Though the Maples told some stories — how they had lived in a log cabin in a Y.M.C.A. camp for the first three months of their married life, how Bitsy Flaner, a mutual friend, was the only girl enrolled in Bentham Divinity School, how Richard's advertising work brought him into contact with Yogi Berra — they did not regard themselves (that is, each other) as raconteurs, and Rebecca's slight voice dominated the talk. She had a gift for odd things.

Her rich uncle lived in a metal house, furnished with auditorium chairs. He was terribly afraid of fire. Right before the depression he had built an enormous boat to take himself and some friends to Polynesia. All his friends lost their money in the crash. He did not. He made money. He made money out of everything. But he couldn't go on the trip alone, so the boat was still waiting in Oyster Bay, a huge thing, rising thirty feet out of water. The uncle was a vegetarian. Rebecca had not eaten turkey for Thanksgiving until she was thirteen years old because it was the family custom to go to the uncle's house on that holiday. The custom was dropped during the war, when the children's synthetic heels made black marks all over his asbestos floor. Rebecca's family had not spoken to the uncle since. "Yes, what got me," Rebecca said, "was the way each new wave of vegetables would come in as if it were a different course."

Richard poured the sherry around again and, because this made him the center of attention anyway, said, "Don't some vegetarians have turkeys molded out of crushed nuts for Thanksgiving?"

After a stretch of silence, Joan said, "I don't know." Her

voice, unused for ten minutes, cracked on the last syllable. She cleared her throat, scraping Richard's heart.

"What would they stuff them with?" Rebecca asked, dropping an ash into the saucer beside her.

Beyond and beneath the window there arose a clatter. Joan reached the windows first, Richard next, and lastly Rebecca, standing on tiptoe, elongating her neck. Six mounted police, standing in their stirrups, were galloping two abreast down Thirteenth Street. When the Maples' exclamations had subsided, Rebecca remarked, "They do it every night at this time. They seem awfully jolly, for policemen."

"Oh, and it's snowing!" Joan cried. She was pathetic about 25 snow; she loved it so much, and in these last years had seen so little. "On our first night here! Our first *real* night." Forgetting herself, she put her arms around Richard, and Rebecca, where another guest might have turned away, or smiled too broadly, too encouragingly, retained without modification her sweet, absent look and studied, through the embracing couple, the scene outdoors. The snow was not taking on the wet street; only the hoods and tops of parked automobiles showed an accumulation.

"I think I'd best go," Rebecca said.

"Please don't," Joan said with an urgency Richard had not expected; clearly she was very tired. Probably the new home, the change in the weather, the good sherry, the currents of affection between herself and her husband that her sudden hug had renewed, and Rebecca's presence had become in her mind the inextricable elements of one enchanting moment.

"Yes, I think I'll go because you're so snuffly and peaked."

"Can't you just stay for one more cigarette? Dick, pass the sherry around."

"A teeny bit," Rebecca said, holding out her glass. "I guess I 30 told you, Joan, about the boy I went out with who pretended to be a headwaiter."

Joan giggled expectantly. "No, honestly, you never did." She hooked her arm over the back of the chair and wound her hand through the slats, like a child assuring herself that her bedtime has been postponed. "What did he do? He imitated headwaiters?"

"Yes, he was the kind of guy who, when we get out of a taxi and there's a grate giving out steam, crouches down" — Rebecca lowered her head and lifted her arms — "and pretends he's the Devil."

The Maples laughed, less at the words themselves than at the way Rebecca had evoked the situation by conveying, in her understated imitation, both her escort's flamboyant attitude and her own undemonstrative nature. They could see her standing by the taxi door, gazing with no expression as her escort bent lower and lower, seized by his own joke, his fingers writhing demonically as he felt horns sprout through his scalp, flames lick his ankles, and his feet shrivel into hoofs. Rebecca's gift, Richard realized, was not that of having odd things happen to her but that of representing, through the implicit contrast with her own sane calm, all things touching her as odd. This evening too might appear grotesque in her retelling: "Six policemen on horses galloped by and she cried "It's snowing!" and hugged him. He kept telling her how sick she was and filling us full of sherry."

"What else did he do?" Joan asked.

"At the first place we went to — it was a big night club on the 35 roof of somewhere — on the way out he sat down and played the piano until a woman at a harp asked him to stop."

Richard asked, "Was the woman *playing* the harp?"

"Yes, she was strumming away." Rebecca made circular motions with her hands.

"Well, did he play the tune she was playing? Did he *accompany* her?" Petulance, Richard realized without understanding why, had entered his tone.

"No, he just sat down and played something else. I couldn't tell what it was."

"Is this *really* true?" Joan asked, egging her on. 40

"And then at the next place we went to, we had to wait at the bar for a table and I looked around and he was walking among the tables asking people if everything was all right."

"Wasn't it *aw*ful?" said Joan.

"Yes. Later he played the piano there, too. We were sort of the main attraction. Around midnight he thought we ought to go out to Brooklyn to his sister's house. I was exhausted. We got off the subway two stops too early, under the Manhattan Bridge. It was deserted, with nothing going by except black limousines. Miles above our head" — she stared up, as though at a cloud, or the sun — "was the Manhattan Bridge and he kept saying it was the el. We finally found some steps and two policemen who told us to go back to the subway."

"What does this amazing man do for a living?" Richard asked.

"He teaches school. He's quite bright." She stood up, extend- 45 ing in stretch a long, silvery white arm. Richard got her coat and said he'd walk her home.

"It's only three-quarters of a block," Rebecca protested in a voice free of any insistent inflection.

"You must walk her home, Dick," Joan said. "Pick up a pack of cigarettes." The idea of his walking in the snow seemed to please her, as if she were anticipating how he would bring back with him, in the snow on his shoulders and the coldness of his face, all the sensations of the walk she was not well enough to risk.

"You should stop smoking for a day or two," he told her.

Joan waved them goodbye from the head of the stairs.

The snow, invisible except around street lights, exerted a   50 fluttering romantic pressure on their faces. "Coming down hard now," he said.

"Yes."

At the corner, where the snow gave the green light a watery blueness, her hesitancy in following him as he turned to walk with the light across Thirteenth Street led him to ask, "It is this side of the street you live on, isn't it?"

"Yes."

"I thought I remembered from the time we drove you down from Boston." The Maples had lived in the West Eighties then. "I remember I had an impression of big buildings."

"The church and the butcher's school," Rebecca said. "Every   55 day about ten when I'm going to work the boys learning to be butchers come out for an intermission all bloody and laughing."

Richard looked up at the church; the steeple was fragmentarily silhouetted against the scattered lit windows of a tall improvement on Seventh Avenue. "Poor church," he said. "It's hard in this city for a steeple to be the tallest thing."

Rebecca said nothing, not even her habitual "Yes." He felt rebuked for being preachy. In his embarrassment he directed her attention to the first next thing he saw, a poorly lettered sign above a great door. "Food Trades Vocational High School," he read aloud. "The people upstairs told us that the man before the man before *us* in our apartment was a wholesale meat salesman who called himself a Purveyor of Elegant Foods. He kept a woman in the apartment."

"Those big windows up there," Rebecca said, pointing up at the third story of a brownstone, "face mine across the street. I can look in and feel we are neighbors. Someone's always there; I don't know what they do for a living."

After a few more steps they halted, and Rebecca, in a voice that Richard imagined to be slightly louder than her ordinary one, said, "Do you want to come up and see where I live?"

"Sure." It seemed implausible to refuse.   60

They descended four concrete steps, opened a shabby orange door, entered an overheated half-basement lobby, and began to climb four flights of wooden stairs. Richard's suspicion on the street that he was trespassing beyond the public gardens of courtesy turned to certain guilt. Few experiences so savor of the illicit as mounting stairs behind a woman's fanny. Three years ago, Joan had lived in a fourth-floor walkup, in Cambridge. Richard never took her home, even when the whole business, down to the last intimacy, had become formula, without the fear that the landlord, justifiably furious, would leap from his door and devour him as they passed.

Opening her door, Rebecca said, "It's hot as hell in here," swearing for the first time in his hearing. She turned on a weak light. The room was small; slanting planes, the underside of the building's roof, intersecting the ceiling and walls, cut large prismatic volumes from Rebecca's living space. As he moved further forward, toward Rebecca, who had not yet removed her coat, Richard perceived, on his right, an unexpected area created where the steeply slanting roof extended itself to the floor. Here a double bed was placed. Tightly bounded on three sides, the bed had the appearance not so much of a piece of furniture as of a permanently installed, blanketed platform. He quickly took his eyes from it and, unable to face Rebecca at once, stared at two kitchen chairs, a metal bridge lamp around the rim of whose shade plump fish and helm wheels alternated, and a four-shelf bookcase — all of which, being slender and proximate to a tilting wall, had an air of threatened verticality.

"Yes, here's the stove on top of the refrigerator I told you about," Rebecca said. "Or did I?"

The top unit overhung the lower by several inches on all sides. He touched his fingers to the stove's white side. "This room is quite sort of nice," he said.

"Here's the view," she said. He moved to stand beside her at 65 the windows, lifting aside the curtains and peering through tiny flawed panes into the apartment across the street.

"That guy *does* have a huge window," Richard said.

She made a brief agreeing noise of n's.

Though all the lamps were on, the apartment across the street was empty. "Looks like a furniture store," he said. Rebecca had still not taken off her coat. "The snow's keeping up."

"Yes. It is."

"Well" — this word was too loud; he finished the sentence   70
too softly — "thanks for letting me see it. I — have you read
this?" He had noticed a copy of *Auntie Mame* lying on a hassock.

"I haven't had the time," she said.

"I haven't read it either. Just reviews. That's all I ever read."

This got him to the door. There, ridiculously, he turned. It
was only at the door, he decided in retrospect, that her conduct
was quite inexcusable: not only did she stand unnecessarily close,
but, by shifting the weight of her body to one leg and leaning her
head sidewise, she lowered her height several inches, placing him
in a dominating position exactly fitted to the broad, passive
shadows she must have known were on her face.

"Well — " he said.

"Well." Her echo was immediate and possibly meaningless.   75

"Don't, don't let the b-butchers get you." The stammer of
course ruined the joke, and her laugh, which had begun as soon
as she had seen by his face that he would attempt something
funny, was completed ahead of his utterance.

As he went down the stairs she rested both hands on the
banister and looked down toward the next landing. "Good
night," she said.

"Night." He looked up; she had gone into her room. Oh but
they were close.

Question

What's going on at "Rebecca had still not taken off her coat"
(para. 68)? Write your response and compare it with those that
follow.

Responses

COLLEGE SOPHOMORE: In his state of confusion, Richard looks to
Rebecca for an answer. If she takes off her coat she will signal to
him that she will take control. She will show she wants him. If she
does not take off her coat, he will know she views him as a
husband. His anxieties and doubts concerning his wife, marriage, and personal actions will be dispelled, having survived the
night's encounter.

However, when Rebecca does not take off her coat, Richard
does not admit that he has been treated as the husband of a
friend. Because he is unable to accept the consequences of his

marriage, he feels rejected. The combination of this rejection with the anxieties he feels Rebecca has caused him to experience heightens his self-consciousness.

Instead of understanding why Rebecca does not encourage him, Richard takes her seeming rejection as another blow caused by her. He is doing something very common to people who are made uncomfortable by another: judging that person to be wrong, weird, or different. Richard fails to realize that Rebecca has not caused the anxiety he feels but is somehow making him more aware of it. He decides that Rebecca's actions are strange: "It was only at the door, he decided in retrospect, that her conduct was quite inexcusable: . . . she . . . [placed] him in a dominating position" (para. 73).

Choosing to ignore his own doubts about his marriage, wife, and personal situation, and the reasons behind Rebecca's rejection of him, he becomes the desired in his mind and he attacks Rebecca for desiring him. Thus he creates a rationalization that is acceptable to him. Richard is unable to solve the confusion and complexity of his situation, and therefore he denies it by attacking what he believes to be the source of these troubles.

COLLEGE FRESHMAN:　Why was Richard so preoccupied with that coat? So what if she hadn't taken her coat off. Maybe she just forgot. Why was *he* making such a big deal out of it? Oh, but to *him*, it was a big deal. Updike informs us in the very beginning that Richard is fascinated by the coat and that touching it evoked in him desirous feelings toward Rebecca. He blew out of proportion the whole incident with the coat precisely because of the way it had made him feel before.

Another reason his attention was focused on the coat was that, as soon as Rebecca walked in the door, she specifically said she was hot as hell, swearing for the first time in his presence for emphasis. This provoked Richard to think to himself, why did she *want* me to hear her say that? Why hasn't she taken the coat off if it's so hot in here? My God, she must be waiting for me to offer to take it off. It is as if he would have felt less threatened by her if she had just taken it off right away, but he felt that as long as she kept that coat on, she was continuing to lure him into her trap.

At this moment, as Richard is feeling himself sinking deeper and deeper and letting his attraction toward her start to get the best of him, we reach the climax of the story. By deciding not to take off her coat, he is actually subduing his desirous feelings rather than feebly giving in to them. He is able to leave a guiltless man. However, had he decided to offer to remove her coat right then, it would have been just as shameful an act as sleeping with her *would have been*, because he would have been yielding to his purely physical desires and allowing himself to reexperience the pleasurable feelings that the coat had evoked in him just a few hours before.

COLLEGE FRESHMAN: I do not believe that Rebecca ever intends during the evening to have any involvement with Richard. She is not truly torn between two choices. She is a sensitive woman, someone who notices the absurdity of situations and turns them into funny stories. She is a reserved woman but also a woman of mood. She is not embarrassed by Joan's affectionate gesture toward Richard at the window; she simply accepts it as part of the moment. She looks out the window. Perhaps she is thinking how pretty it looks; perhaps she is wishing she had someone to share this moment with, as Joan has Richard. When he offers to walk her home, she accepts. On the street it is snowing and the mood is romantic. She asks him up to her apartment, and at the door she lowers her face flatteringly and submissively. She stands close to him. But she has not taken off her coat. Why? Because she does not intend to make a pass at him, nor does she want him to make a pass at her. To take off her coat would be to suggest this as a more concrete possibility. As long as her coat is on, it acts as a shield. Nothing will happen, but the possibility is still there.

I believe this is what she is enjoying. The snow, the street-lights, the romance, the possibility of something sexual between her and Richard — all contribute to a mood that appeals to her, and to him. But she does not really want to have Richard. He loves Joan and she likes Joan, and I doubt that either of them would really want to change that. The last line, "Oh but they were close," is very important. This is the point to the encounter. The feeling that they were close to it is like a special warmth in the blood that he can carry back to the street and then to Joan and that Rebecca can carry to bed with her. That is the essence of the moment, the essence of the snow in Greenwich Village. If Rebecca had taken off her coat, the moment would have been different, too heavy for a snowfall.

COLLEGE FRESHMAN: Although Rebecca would like to seduce Richard, and although she realizes Richard might enjoy being seduced, she is hesitant to act. She asks Richard up to her apartment in a voice "slightly louder than her ordinary one" (para. 59), thus showing her uneasiness and hesitancy even to hint at anything sexual. She realizes that Richard, although possibly attracted to her, is ultimately faithful to his wife, and thus she fears rejection. Richard has shown his loyalty to Joan by parading his concern for her health in front of Rebecca, and by embracing Joan, which "renews" his "currents of affection" (27) — currents that temporarily lapsed in Rebecca's presence. Rebecca is also friends with Joan, and any pass at Richard would be an abasement of their friendship.

So Rebecca decides to leave the decision to Richard. She asks him up — a seemingly innocent and friendly invitation were it not for the nervousness behind it — and once there she plays a passive role. She has remained on safe ground thus far, and she hopes that Richard will capitalize on her opening by making the next move. She feels that removing her jacket would be too cozy, too intimate, and too sexually suggestive. At the door his curious desire for Rebecca temporarily overwhelms his loyalty to Joan, and he turns "ridiculously" (73). He is tempted, yet as afraid to act as Rebecca is. Rebecca does not take advantage of this last chance. She continues to use her strategy of passiveness — this time less subtly — to show him that she is willing. She is, however, still putting the burden of decision on him. She will not "take off her coat" (in other words, make a move), and Richard leaves.

COLLEGE FRESHMAN: Richard is extremely nervous. He is desperately trying to make the right impression. Rebecca is experiencing the same emotions. She wants to please him, to flatter his ego, to become the dominated female. For Rebecca as well, overanxiousness and nervousness play their parts. "And her laugh, which had begun as soon as she had seen by his face that he would attempt something funny, was completed ahead of his utterance" (para. 76). Their every move is calculated, but each step seems to become fumbled. Both Richard and Rebecca search for opportunities to make a pass, but like those of inexperienced teenagers, the passes become bumbling faux pas.

She lowered her height several inches, placing him in a dominating position exactly fitted to broad passive shadows she must have known were on her face.

"Well — " he said.

"Well." Her echo was immediate and possibly meaningless. (paras. 73–75)

For the two of them the courting ritual has begun. The air is rife with sexual excitement. At the same time, however, another sensation exists in both of them. On a completely different level, the emotion of guilt thrives. Both Richard and Rebecca are filled with it. Richard's guilty feelings begin at precisely the same moment as does his sexual excitement. "Richard's suspicion . . . that he was trespassing beyond the public gardens of courtesy turned to certain guilt" (61). After studying her bed, he is unable even to face her.

EDITOR: We learn from the coat-slipping-off and bottle-opening routines in the opening pages that Dick Maple is a rather vain young man — keen on thinking of himself as smooth and graceful, inclined to do things "posingly" (para. 13). He's also eager, as someone comparatively new to Manhattan and engaged in a worldly line of work (advertising), to master gestures and knowledge that he associates with sophisticated urban life (swirling the sherry, for instance). There are many suggestions that Rebecca Cune takes for granted styles of behavior far more daring than those to which Dick is accustomed. Dick's name, the details of his nervousness about the landlord during his courting days, his stay in a YMCA log cabin, and other details suggest that a strict Protestant upbringing could be part of his background. He chides his wife about smoking. He speaks half-disapprovingly about a previous tenant who "kept a woman in the apartment" (57).

But nearly everything we pick up about Rebecca points toward the exotic and liberated. Her first name and the "virtuosity" of her mouth (8). Her absent, unshockable way of responding to practically everything. The facts that she lived for a stretch with an unmarried couple, went out with a man who pretended to be the Devil.

And, close to this coat moment, there's her sense of Dick (he *thinks* it's her sense) as somebody "preachy" (57), her lack of hesitation about asking up a married man, her "swearing . . . in his hearing" (62), and her choice of reading matter (*Auntie Mame* was, in its time, a somewhat naughty best-seller).

Add all this up and it seems reasonable to say that during the tiny interval of time wherein objects have "an air of threatened verticality" (63), Dick believes he's in the presence of a young woman who's game for anything — a woman who, if not on the verge of making an outright sexual advance, is at least bent on behaving as though she wouldn't reject one. Dick also thinks that he himself — despite scruples, upbringing, and innocence — may be on the verge of making that advance. What else but the thought of the terribly immediate availability of the bed or the even more shocking thought of Rebecca lying in it — accounts for his looking away so quickly from the bed or for his inability to look at her?

So there's a lot to be evoked here besides the feeling of impatience. Dick sees Rebecca's coat as a challenge and a predic-ament. He wants to think of himself as sophisticated and pol-ished, and a little while earlier it was precisely the ease with which he took Rebecca's things that made him see himself that way. But would it be sophisticated to make this same move again? Rebecca is in her own home now; shouldn't she take her coat off unassisted? How else does it come off when she gets home from work? But maybe she assumes that he's about to offer to help her with it, or perhaps it was gauche of him not to have offered help the second they came in the door, or maybe she wants the coat on because she's just been out in the snow, or . . . What's the best way to resolve these quandaries?

But we can't stop yet in our imagining. We have to deal with another complication inside Dick; namely, What will happen if he touches Rebecca? What will she do? What will he do? Will she fling herself at him, misinterpreting his gentlemanly, urbane ac-tion? Isn't there a chance that his courtesy will turn instantly into a pass at her? Would that be hateful or delicious? Should he be ashamed of himself or proud of his daring or what?

We have to imagine impatience here — and guilt, uncer-tainty, fear, confusion, and ambition. But we have to imagine sexual desire as well, even though the author himself is wary on this point. Updike leaves open the possibility that, with a person who — at this stage in his life — is as self-involved, vain, and inexperienced as Dick Maple, desire might well not be in the picture at all.

Continuing the Discussion

1. Reader 3 doubts that "Rebecca ever intends . . . to have any involvement with Richard." How do you explain this reading of Rebecca's feelings? Can a basis for it be found in the story itself? Where?
2. Reader 4 says that "Rebecca would like to seduce Richard." How do you explain this reading of Rebecca's feelings? Can a basis for it be found in the story itself? Where?
3. Differences such as those between readers 3 and 4 obviously have something to do with differences between the readers themselves. Without knowing the people in question, it's impossible to be certain about such differences — but still we can guess. Make a guess of your own about possible personal reasons for the contrast between these readings of Rebecca's feelings.

THOMAS HARDY   (1840–1928)
The Slow Nature
(An incident of Froom Valley)

"Thy husband — poor, poor Heart! — is dead —
    Dead, out by Moreford Rise;
A bull escaped the barton-shed,
    Gored him, and there he lies!"

— "Ha, ha — go away! 'Tis a tale, methink,   5
    Thou joker Kit!" laughed she.
"I've known thee many a year, Kit Twink,
    And ever hast thou fooled me!"

— "But, Mistress Damon — I can swear
    Thy goodman John is dead!   10
And soon th'lt hear their feet who bear
    His body to his bed."

So unwontedly sad was the merry man's face —
    That face which had long deceived —

That she gazed and gazed; and then could trace   15
    The truth there; and she believed.

She laid a hand on the dresser-ledge,
    And scanned far Egdon-side;
And stood; and you heard the wind-swept sedge
    And the rippling Froom; till she cried: 20

"O my chamber's untidied, unmade my bed,
    Though the day has begun to wear;
'What a slovenly hussif!' it will be said,
    When they all go up my stair!"

She disappeared; and the joker stood   25
    Depressed by his neighbour's doom,
And amazed that a wife struck to widowhood
    Thought first of her unkempt room.

But a fortnight thence she could take no food,
    And she pined in a slow decay;   30
While Kit soon lost his mournful mood
    And laughed in his ancient way.

Question

What's going on in lines 17–24?

    She laid a hand on the dresser-ledge,
        And scanned far Egdon-side;
    And stood; and you heard the wind-swept sedge
        And the rippling Froom; till she cried:

    "O my chamber's untidied, unmade my bed,
        Though the day has begun to wear;
    'What a slovenly hussif!' it will be said,
        When they all go up my stair!"

Write your response and compare it with those that follow.

Responses

COLLEGE FRESHMAN: Mistress Damon has finally realized the harsh reality that her husband is indeed dead. For the first time in her life she knows that Kit is truly sincere in telling her that her husband has been killed. She slowly begins to place her hand on the dresser ledge and look out the window in the distance. As she searches in vain she knows that she will never again see her husband.

> She disappeared; and the joker stood
>   Depressed by his neighbour's doom,
> And amazed that a wife struck to widowhood
>   Thought first of her unkempt room. (25–28)

This quotation tends to make the reader believe that Mistress Damon never loved her husband as a human being but rather as an expendable object. Thus the only reason that she begins to cry is that she no longer has a "security blanket" from which she may receive warmth. Without her husband she slowly begins to crumble like a building without a foundation.

COLLEGE FRESHMAN: As she "laid a hand on the dresser-ledge" and stared out at the countryside, Mistress Damon was doing two things. First, she was giving herself a sort of mental pep talk; arguing to herself that in fact she was a brave person and this unfortunate event could not conquer her composure. She was setting up her game plan of how to act around all of the people she would be forced to see as they came to express their regrets. Ultimately she decided to proceed with everyday tasks such as tidying her room, hoping to forget her misfortune.

Second, I believe the widow was taking one last silent moment to say good-bye to her husband. The dresser she touched certainly had been touched by him also, and every aspect of the countryside, I am sure, seemed to wear some memory of him. So there in the silence she stood, determined to ignore her intense sorrow, while at the same time she was engulfed by the recollections of her lost love. Her supposed need to tend to the state of her room overtook her thoughtfulness, although eventually she had to dust the shelf where she left reality.

COLLEGE SENIOR: Lines 17–24 bring to the reader a very peculiar, very painful, and very difficult human moment — an awful moment to contemplate. As she lays "a hand on the dresser-ledge," Mistress Damon's mind becomes cloudy and her thoughts race as they search for a place to settle — she becomes distant from the world. The instant her mind registers the dreadful news, her thoughts invade and flood her emotions. As she scans "far Egdon-side" her feelings swell and quickly enter and occupy her physicality — her head becomes foggy and only the memory of her beloved husband lives; the room and all around her ceases to exist. A sickening feeling swells up from her stomach and clutches her throat — her throat hurts, and she cries.

The next lines show the woman's fragile constitution. She goes into shock as her mind refuses to ponder or accept such debilitating news; she becomes concerned with what people will think of her untidy room. The particulars of her fate are disturbing and unsettling. Her distance from the world would not lessen and she is unable to forget. Her unutterable sadness refuses to retreat from her mind and body. Her deterioration comes from her inability to feel forward, to launch her psyche out of the present, at least for quick moments.

EDITOR: The only possible answer to this question might seem to be that Mistress Damon is taking in "the truth" that her husband is gone. But this answer says both too much and too little. The next few lines indicate that she hasn't digested "the truth" in any genuine sense. Mistress Damon responds to the terrible news by worrying about what her neighbors will say about her as a housekeeper. But this isn't because she doesn't care about her husband. The closing stanza shows that she does.

Probably what is happening in these lines is that Mistress Damon becomes a person almost trapped at the brink of the unknowable, a person barely bringing off an escape from an abyss. The countrywoman is asked to take in an event whose meanings are beyond her capacity to fathom. The magnitude of the loss, the enormous changes that are imminent, the absence of a lifetime companion of meals and evenings — the person whose impression may still be visible in the dents of a chair cushion or a sweater hanging on a peg — the stilling of a voice more familiar than one's own . . . Mistress Damon's consciousness may move for an instant in those directions, but it can't sustain the movement, can't find a way to breathe.

But then suddenly there's an opening. Her mind races toward it — toward a different, lesser panic. This panic isn't a response to the unthinkable or unknowable. It's a response to the fear of being bad-mouthed as a poor housekeeper. The inexpressible anguish of loss is remade in the space of a few lines into a very concrete anxiety about being regarded as "slovenly." An unendurable fear — a fear that simply paralyzes, renders her incapable of thought or action — is replaced by a fear that can be coped with by acting, working, cleaning, neatening.

This brief passage of time can be brought to life as a movement from helplessness to release from helplessness — the release that other bereaved human beings have found, time and again, in the complicated rituals and errands of funeral arrangements. The mind that finds such release can't fully realize the brevity of the comfort, can't begin to acknowledge that the loss, now an abstraction rather than a sense of emptiness renewed each day, must in time be felt in all its weight. It is even possible to imagine that some quiver of thankfulness might wake in Mistress Damon for a second — gratitude for her escape from panic, "happiness" that some clear, hard, immediate, tangible task exists into which her thoughts and energies can be plunged.

SYLVIA PLATH   (1932–1963)
Balloons

Since Christmas they have lived with us,
Guileless and clear,
Oval soul-animals,
Taking up half the space,
Moving and rubbing on the silk   5

Invisible air drifts,
Giving a shriek and pop
When attacked, then scooting to rest, barely trembling.
Yellow cathead, blue fish ——
Such queer moons we live with   10

Instead of dead furniture!
Straw mats, white walls
And these traveling
Globes of thin air, red, green,
Delighting   15

The heart like wishes or free
Peacocks blessing
Old ground with a feather
Beaten in starry metals.
Your small   20

Brother is making
His balloon squeak like a cat.
Seeming to see
A funny pink world he might eat on the other side of it,
He bites,   25

Then sits
Back, fat jug
Contemplating a world clear as water.
A red
Shred in his little fist.   30

Question

What's going on in line 28 — "Contemplating a world clear
as water"? Write your response and compare it to those that
follow.

Responses

EDITOR: An infant boy has been playing with the balloon in the
living room, making it "squeak like a cat" (line 30). Peering
through it he sees a "funny pink world" (32). Suddenly he bites it
and it bursts. End of balloon.

That's the event as observed from outside. It's not, however,
the experience we possess if we bring this moment to life — life
as lived by the child. *Our* minds tend to fit events out with
beginnings, middles, and ends. Events thereby become completely intelligible to us. Child plays with toy, child bites toy, toy
is destroyed. Obvious cause; obvious effect. But this infant's
world is, for him, empty of cause and effect. It has color in it, and
changes of color, and, in addition, a few impulses (to bite, to eat).
But it lacks orderly sequences, has no reasons, doesn't even have
puzzles. For an event to be puzzling to a grown-up, the grown-up
has to be able to see it as occurring for no evident reason;
nobody unaware that things happen for reasons can take in the
absence of reasons. Living into the moment of the popped balloon as known by the little boy means living into a simple, abrupt
change of sensation — from having one's eyes filled with a
"funny pink world" to having them filled with "a world clear as
water."

And it also means living into a world much less buttoned up and hooked together, much less mapped and anchored, than the one we know. Is a sound connected, by the baby, to his shift of color at the second the balloon pops? Not likely: That sound isn't part of this particular configuration, this swift change of scene. If we see with the child, we see an *x* that flows in an unorganized, unschematized manner. We live briefly in a world without tenses, without before and after, and — most notably — without any sense of *without*. Our grown-up assumption that the sound of a popped balloon is surprising is off the mark. So too is our assumption that the first feeling accompanying the popping of the balloon is — in the child — regret at the loss. The infant's world isn't ours; to see with him we must change ourselves, shed our learned ways of organizing experience. What's going on here at this moment? A set of events that grown-ups can only begin to imagine if they're willing to unmake their conventional styles of perception. Bringing the moment to life requires us to make real to ourselves the difference between vision that's almost pattern-less, and our own vision, which is dense with structures of every sort.

There's a lot more to do with "Balloons" in order to arrive at a full active reading; we haven't said anything about the observer in the poem, for instance — the person who's describing the infant's play with the balloon. But just now our focus is simply upon clarifying a distinct moment of feeling — finding out how to bring to life, in the imagination, a human feeling or sensation different from our own. Writing or talking about another way of seeing is, of course, not the same as experiencing that kind of perception. But by finding a language for what is happening, launching our own imagining and animating, we can take a step closer to the insides of the experience — toward the kind of newly dawning reality that imaginative writing often seeks to create.

ANOTHER RESPONSE: A reader of Plath's "Balloons" and of the preceding commentary remarked that in her opinion the feelings that need to be imagined in the last two stanzas are those of the mother of the children playing with the balloons. If we explore the mother's feelings, said this reader, instead of the reactions of the "small/Brother," we sense the contrast between the mother's delight in the Christmas balloons and the small brother's "more destructive image-making." The brother, "in biting the balloon, clarifies his world and destroys her lively, lovely images."

To bring the poem to life in this way requires a much more strongly developed interest in — and sensitivity to — masculine-feminine differences than the editor possesses. That interest and sensitivity put a charge on phrases such as "A red/Shred in his little fist" (lines 29–30) — catch a suggestion of careless male brutality — that came as a surprise to the editor. And that is by no means the only difference between these two responses to the poem. The second reader herself observed that the reason she keeps "returning to the mother's rich responses to living with the balloons" is that she "prefers imagination to innocence as a way to view the world."

As is evident, readers create literary experiences reflecting their nature, background, gifts, tastes. The fundamental activity for close imaginers isn't that of disputing "other readings" or arriving at decisions about which version of a text is authoritative. It is, instead, enlarging the range of our responsiveness so that we learn not only from the text as we experience it but as it's experienced by others whose perceptions are different — and often richer and deeper than our own.

FOR FURTHER STUDY

PHILIP LARKIN   (1922–1985)
Coming

On longer evenings,
Light, chill and yellow,
Bathes the serene
Foreheads of houses.
A thrush sings,   5
Laurel-surrounded
In the deep bare garden,
Its fresh-peeled voice
Astonishing the brickwork.
It will be spring soon,   10

It will be spring soon —
And I, whose childhood
Is a forgotten boredom,
Feel like a child
Who comes on a scene   15
Of adult reconciling,
And can understand nothing
But the unusual laughter,
And starts to be happy.

WILLIAM WORDSWORTH   (1770–1850)
Composed upon Westminster Bridge
September 3, 1802

Earth has not anything to show more fair;
Dull would he be of soul who could pass by
A sight so touching in its majesty:
This City now doth, like a garment, wear
The beauty of the morning; silent, bare,   5
Ships, towers, domes, theaters, and temples lie
Open unto the fields, and to the sky;
All bright and glittering in the smokeless air.
Never did sun more beautifully steep
In his first splendor, valley, rock, or hill;   10
Ne'er saw I, never felt, a calm so deep!
The river glideth at his own sweet will:
Dear God! the very houses seem asleep;
And all that mighty heart is lying still!

DEBORAH EISENBERG   (b. 1945)
What It Was Like, Seeing Chris

While I sit with all the other patients in the waiting room, I always think that I will ask Dr. Wald what exactly is happening to my eyes, but when I go into his examining room alone it is dark, with a circle of light on the wall, and the doctor is standing with his back to me arranging silver instruments on a cloth. The big chair is empty for me to go sit in, and each time then I feel as if I have gone into a dream straight from being awake, the way you do sometimes at night, and I go to the chair without saying anything.

The doctor prepares to look at my eyes through a machine. I put my forehead and chin against the metal bands and look into the tiny ring of blue light while the doctor dabs quickly at my eye with something, but my head starts to feel numb, and I have to lift it back. "Sorry," I say. I shake my head and put it back against the metal. Then I stare into the blue light and try to hold my head still and to convince myself that there is no needle coming toward my eye, that my eye is not anesthetized.

"Breathe," Dr. Wald says. "Breathe." But my head always goes numb again, and I pull away, and Dr. Wald has to wait for me to resettle myself against the machine. "Nervous today, Laurel?" he asks, not interested.

One Saturday after I had started going to Dr. Wald, Maureen and I walked around outside our old school. We dangled on the little swings with our knees bunched while the dry leaves blew around us, and Maureen told me she was sleeping with Kevin. Kevin is a sophomore, and to me he had seemed much older than we were when we'd begun high school in September. "What is it like?" I asked.

"Fine." Maureen shrugged. "Who do you like these days, any- 5 how? I notice you haven't been talking much about Dougie."

"No one," I said. Maureen stopped her swing and looked at me with one eyebrow raised, so I told her — although I was sorry as soon as I opened my mouth — that I'd met someone in the city.

"In the city?" she said. Naturally she was annoyed. "How did you get to meet someone in the city?"

It was just by accident, I told her, because of going to the eye doctor, and anyway it was not some big thing. That was what I told Maureen, but I remembered the first time I had seen Chris as surely as if it were a stone I could hold in my hand.

It was right after my first appointment with Dr. Wald. I had taken the train into the city after school, and when the doctor was finished with me I was supposed to take a taxi to my sister Penelope's dancing school, which was on the east side of the Park, and do homework there until Penelope's class was over and Mother picked us up. Friends of my parents ask me if I want to be a dancer, too, but they are being polite.

Across the street from the doctor's office, I saw a place called 10 Jake's. I stared through the window at the long shining bar and mirrors and round tables, and it seemed to me I would never be inside a place like that, but then I thought how much I hated sitting outside Penelope's class and how much I hated the doctor's office, and I opened the door and walked right in.

I sat down at a table near the wall, and I ordered a Coke. I looked around at all the people with their glasses of colored liquids, and I thought how happy they were — vivid and free and sort of the same, as if they were playing.

I watched the bartender as he gestured and talked. He was really putting on a show telling a story to some people I could only see from the back. There was a man with shiny, straight hair that shifted like a curtain when he laughed, and a man with curly blond hair, and between them a girl in a fluffy sweater. The men — or boys (I couldn't tell, and still don't know) — wore shirts with seams on the back that curved up from their belts to their shoulders. I watched their shirts, and I watched in the mirror behind the bar as their beautiful goldish faces settled from laughing. I looked at them in the mirror, and I particularly noticed the one with the shiny hair, and I watched his eyes get like crescents, as if he were listening to another story, but then I saw he was smiling. He was smiling into the mirror in front of him, and in the mirror I was just staring, staring at him, and he was smiling back into the mirror at me.

The next week I went back to Dr. Wald for some tests, and when I was finished, although I'd planned to go do homework at Penelope's dancing school, I went straight to Jake's instead. The same two men were at the bar, but a different girl was with them. I pretended not to notice them as I went to the table I had sat at before.

I had a Coke, and when I went up to the bar to pay, the one with the shiny hair turned right around in front of me. "Clothes-abuse squad," he said, prizing my wadded-up coat out of my arms. He shook it out and smiled at me. "I'm Chris," he said, "and this is Mark." His friend turned to me like a soldier who has been waiting, but the girl with them only glanced at me and turned to talk to someone else.

Chris helped me into my coat, and then he buttoned it up, as 15 if I were a little child. "Who are you?" he said.

"Laurel," I said.

Chris nodded slowly. "Laurel," he said. And when he said that, I felt a shock on my face and hands and front as if I had pitched against flat water.

"So you are going out with this guy, or what?" Maureen asked me.

"Maureen," I said. "He's just a person I met." Maureen looked at me again, but I just looked back at her. We twisted our swings up and let ourselves twirl out.

"So what's the matter with your eyes?" Maureen said. "Can't 20 you just wear glasses?"

"Well, the doctor said he couldn't tell exactly what was wrong yet," I said. "He says he wants to keep me under observation, because there might be something happening to my retina." But I realized then that I didn't understand what that meant at all, and I also realized that I was really, but really, scared.

Maureen and I wandered over to the school building and looked in the window of the fourth-grade room, and I thought how strange it was that I used to fit in those miniature chairs, and that a few years later Penelope did, and that my little brother, Paul, fit in them now. There was a sickly old turtle in an aquarium on the sill just like the one we'd had. I wondered if it was the same one. I think they're sort of prehistoric, and some of them live to be a hundred or two hundred years old.

"I bet your mother is completely hysterical," Maureen said.

I smiled. Maureen thinks it's hilarious the way my mother expects everything in her life (*her* life) to be perfect. "I had to bring her with me last week," I said.

"Ick," Maureen said sympathetically, and I remembered how 25 awful it had been, sitting and waiting next to Mother. Whenever Mother moved — to cross her legs or smooth out her skirt or pick up a magazine — the clean smell of her perfume came over to me. Mother's perfume made a nice little space for her there in the stale office. We didn't talk at all, and it seemed like a long time before an Asian woman took me into a small white room and turned off the light. The woman had a serious face, like an angel, and she wore a white hospital coat over her clothes. She didn't seem to speak much English. She sat me down in front of something which looked like a map of planets drawn in white on black, hanging on the wall.

The woman moved a wand across the map, and the end of the wand glimmered. "You say when you see light," she told me. In the silence I made myself say "Now" over and over as I saw the light blinking here and there upon the planet map. Finally the woman turned on the light in the room and smiled at me. She rolled up the map and put it with the wand into a cupboard.

"Where are you from?" I asked her, to shake off the sound of my voice saying "Now."

She hesitated, and I felt sick, because I thought I had said something rude, but finally the meaning of the question seemed to reach her. "Japanese," she said. She put the back of her hand against my hair. "Very pretty," she said. "Very pretty."

Then Dr. Wald looked at my eyes, and after that Mother and I were brought into his consulting room. We waited, facing the huge desk, and eventually the doctor walked in. There was just a tiny moment when he saw Mother, but then he sat right down and explained, in a sincere, televisionish voice I had never heard him use before, that he wanted to see me once a month. He told my mother there might or might not be "cause for concern," and he spoke right to her, with a little frown as she looked down at her clasped hands. Men always get important like that when they're talking to her, and she and the doctor both looked extra serious, as if they were reminding themselves that it was me they were talking about, not each other. While Mother scheduled me for the last week of each month (on Thursday because of Penelope's class), the cross-looking receptionist seemed to be figuring out how much Mother's clothes cost.

When Mother and I parked in front of Penelope's dancing 30 school, Penelope was just coming out with some of the other girls. They were in jeans, but they all had their hair still pulled up tightly on top of their heads, and Penelope had the floaty, peaceful look she gets after class. Mother smiled at her and waved, but then she looked suddenly at me. "Poor Laurel," she said. Tears had come into her eyes, and answering tears sprang into my own, but mine were tears of unexpected rage. I saw how pleased Mother was, thinking that we were having that moment together, but what I was thinking, as we looked at each other, was that even though I hadn't been able to go to Jake's that afternoon because of her, at least now I would be able to go back once a month and see Chris.

"And all week," I told Maureen, "Mother has been saying I got it from my father's family, and my father says it's glaucoma in his family and his genes have nothing to do with retinas."

"Really?" Maureen asked. "Is something wrong with your dad?"

Maureen is always talking about my father and saying how "attractive" he is. If she only knew the way he talks about her! When she comes over, he sits down and tells her jokes. A few weeks ago when she came by for me, he took her outside in back to show her something and I had to wait a long time. But when she isn't at our house, he acts as if she's just some stranger. Once he said to me that she was cheap.

Of course, there was no reason for me to think that Chris would be at Jake's the next time I went to the doctor's, but he was.

He and Mark were at the bar as if they'd never moved. I went to my little table, and while I drank my Coke I wondered whether Chris could have noticed that I was there. Then I realized that he might not remember me at all.

I was stalling with the ice in the bottom of my glass when 35 Chris sat down next to me. I hadn't even seen him leave the bar. He asked me a lot of things — all about my family and where I lived, and how I came to be at Jake's.

"I go to a doctor right near here," I told him.

"Psychiatrist?" he asked.

All I said was no, but I felt my face stain red.

"I'm twenty-seven," he said. "Doesn't that seem strange to you?"

"Well, some people are," I said. 40

I was hoping Chris would assume I was much older than I was. People usually did, because I was tall. And it was usually a problem, because they were disappointed in me for not acting older (even if they knew exactly how old I was, like my teachers). But what Chris said was, "I'm much, much older than you. Probably almost twice as old." And I understood that he wanted me to see that he knew perfectly well how old I was. He wanted me to see it, and he wanted me to think it was strange.

When I had to leave, Chris walked me to the bar to say hello to Mark, who was talking to a girl.

"Look," the girl said. She held a lock of my hair up to Mark's, and you couldn't tell whose pale curl was whose. Mark's eyes, so close, also looked just like mine, I saw.

"We could be brother and sister," Mark said, but his voice sounded like a recording of a voice, and for a moment I forgot how things are divided up, and I thought Mark must be having trouble with his eyes, too.

From then on, I always went straight to Jake's after leaving 45 the doctor, and when I passed by the bar I could never help glancing into the mirror to see Chris's face. I would just sit at my table and drink my Coke and listen for his laugh, and when I heard it I felt completely still, the way you do when you have a fever and someone puts his hand on your forehead. And sometimes Chris would come sit with me and talk.

At home and at school, I thought about all the different girls who hung around with Chris and Mark. I thought about them one by one, as if they were little figurines I could take down from a glass case to inspect. I thought about how they looked, and I thought about the girls at school and about Penelope, and I looked in the mirror.

I looked in the mirror over at Maureen's house while Maureen put on nail polish, and I tried to make myself see my sister. We are both pale and long, but Penelope is beautiful, as everyone has always pointed out, and I, I saw, just looked unsettled.

"You could use some makeup," Maureen said, shaking her hands dry, "but you look fine. You're lucky that you're tall. It means you'll be able to wear clothes."

I love to go over to Maureen's house. Maureen is an only child, and her father lives in California. Her mother is away a lot, too, and when she is, Carolina, the maid, stays over. Carolina was there that night, and she let us order in pizza for dinner.

"Maureen is my girl. She is my girl," Carolina said after 50 dinner, putting her arms around Maureen. Maureen almost always has some big expression on her face, but when Carolina does that she just goes blank.

Later I asked Maureen about Chris. I was afraid of talking about him because it seemed as if he might dissolve if I did, but I needed Maureen's advice badly. I told her it was just like French class, where there were two words for "you." Sometimes when Chris said "you" to me I would turn red, as if he had used some special word. And I could hardly say "you" to him. It seemed amazing to me sometimes when I was talking to Chris that a person could just walk up to another person and say "you."

"Does that mean something about him?" I asked. "Or is it just about me?"

"It's just you," Maureen said. "It doesn't count. It's just like when you sit down on a bus next to a stranger and you know that your knee is touching his but you pretend it isn't."

Of course Maureen was almost sure to be right. Why wouldn't she be? Still, I kept thinking that it was just possible that she might be wrong, and the next time I saw Chris something happened to make me think she was.

My vision had fuzzed up a lot during that week, and when Dr. 55 Wald looked at my eyes he didn't get up. "Any trouble lately with that sensation of haziness?" he asked.

I got scorching hot when he said that, and I felt like lying. "Not really," I said. "Yes, a bit."

He put some drops in my eyes and sent me to the waiting room, where I looked at bust exercises in *Redbook* till the drops started to work and the print melted on the page. I had never noticed before how practically no one in the waiting room was even pretending to read. One woman had bandages over her eyes, and most people were just staring and blinking. A little boy was halfheartedly moving a stiff plastic horse on the floor in front of him, but he wasn't even looking at it.

The doctor examined my eyes with the light so bright it made the back of my head sting. "Good," he said. "I'll see you in — what is it? — a month."

I was out on the street before I realized that I still couldn't see. My vision was like a piece of loosely woven cloth that was pulling apart. In the street everything seemed to be moving off, and all the lights looked like huge haloed globes, bobbing and then dipping suddenly into the pocketed air. The noises were one big pool of sound — horns and brakes and people yelling — and to cross the street I had to plunge into a mob of people and rush along wherever it was they were going.

When I finally got through to Jake's my legs were trembling 60 badly, and I just went right up to Chris at the bar, where he was listening to his friend Sherman tell a story. Without even glancing at me, Chris put his hand around my wrist, and I just stood there next to him, with my wrist in his hand, and I listened, too.

Sherman was telling how he and his band had been playing at some club the night before and during a break, when he'd been sitting with his girlfriend, Candy, a man had come up to their table. "He's completely destroyed," Sherman said, "and Candy and I are not exactly on top of things ourselves. But the guy keeps waving this ring, and the basic idea seems to be that it's his wife's wedding ring. He's come home earlier and his wife isn't there, but the ring is, and he's sure his wife's out screwing around. So the guy keeps telling me about it over and over, and I can't get him to shut up, but finally he notices Candy and he says, 'That your old lady?' 'Yeah,' I tell him. 'Good-looking broad,' the guy says, and he hands me the ring. 'Keep it,' the guy says. 'It's for you — not for this bitch with you.'"

One of the girls at the bar reached over and touched the flashing ring that was on a chain around Sherman's neck. "Pretty," she said. "Don't you want it, Candy?" But the girl she had spoken to remained perched on her barstool, with her legs crossed, smiling down at her drink.

"So what did you think of that?" Chris said as he walked me over to my table and sat down with me. I didn't say anything. "Sherman can be sort of disgusting. But it's not an important thing," Chris said.

The story had made me think about the kids at school — that we don't know yet what our lives are really going to be like. It made me feel that anything might be a thing that's important, and I started to cry, because I had never noticed that I was always lonely in my life until just then, when Chris had understood how much the story had upset me, and had said something to make me feel better.

Chris dipped a napkin into a glass of water and mopped off 65 my face, but I was clutching a pencil in my pocket so hard I broke it, and that started me crying again.

"Hey," Chris said. "Look. It's not dead." He grabbed another napkin and scribbled on it with each half of the pencil. "It's fine, see? Look. That's just how they reproduce. Don't they teach you anything at school? Here," he said. "We'll just tuck them under this, and we'll have two very happy little pencils."

And then, after a while, when I was laughing and talking, all at once he stood up. "I'm sorry to have to leave you like this," he said, "but I promised Mark I'd help him with something." And I saw that Mark and a girl were standing at the bar, looking at us. "Ready," Chris called over to them. "Honey," he said, and a waitress materialized next to him. "Get this lady something to drink and put it on my tab. Thanks," he said. And then he walked out, with Mark and the girl.

But the strange thing was that I don't think Mark had actually been waiting for Chris. I don't think Chris had promised Mark anything. I think Mark and the girl had only been looking at us to look, because I could see that they were surprised when Chris called over to them, and also the three of them stood talking on the sidewalk before they went on together. And right then was when I thought for a minute that Maureen had been wrong about me and Chris. It was not when Chris held my wrist, and not when Chris understood how upset I was, and not when Chris dried off my tears, but it was when Chris left, that I thought Maureen was wrong.

My grades were getting a lot worse, and my father decided to help me with my homework every night after dinner. "All right," he would say, standing behind my chair and leaning over me. "Think. If you want to make an equation out of this question, how do you have to start? We've talked about how to do this, Laurel." But I hated his standing behind me like that so much all I could do was try to send out rays from my back that would make him stand farther away. Too bad I wasn't Maureen. She would have loved it.

For me, every day pointed forward or backward to the last 70 Thursday of each month, but those Thursdays came and went without anything really changing, either at the doctor's or at

Jake's, until finally in the spring. Everyone else in my class had spent most of a whole year getting excited or upset about classes and parties and exams and sports, but all those things were one thing to me — a nasty fog that was all around me while I waited.

And then came a Thursday when Chris put his arm around me as soon as I walked into Jake's. "I have to do an errand," he said. "Want a Coke first?"

"I'm supposed to be at my sister's class by six," I said. In case he hadn't been asking me to go with him, I would just seem to be saying something factual.

"I'll get you there," Chris said. He stood in back of me and put both arms around my shoulders, and I could feel exactly where he was touching me. Chris's friends had neutral expressions on their faces as if nothing was happening, and I tried to look as if nothing was happening, too.

As we were going out the door, a girl coming in grabbed Chris. "Are you leaving?" she said.

"Yeah," Chris told her.   75

"Well, when can I talk to you?" she asked.

"I'll be around later, honey," Chris said, but he just kept walking. "Christ, what a bimbo," he said to me, shaking his head, and I felt ashamed for no reason.

When Chris drove his fast little bright car it seemed like part of him, and there I was, inside it, too. I felt that we were inside a shell together, and we could see everything that was outside it, and we drove and drove and Chris turned the music loud. And suddenly Chris said, "I'd really like to see you a lot more. It's too bad you can't come into the city more often." I didn't know what to say, but I gathered that he didn't expect me to say anything.

We parked in a part of the city where the buildings were huge and squat. Chris rang a bell and we ran up flights of wooden stairs to where a man in white slacks and an unbuttoned shirt was waiting.

"Joel, this is Laurel," Chris said.   80

"Hello, Laurel," Joel said. He seemed to think there was something funny about my name, and he looked at me the way I've noticed grown men often do, as if I couldn't see them back perfectly well.

Inside, Chris and Joel went through a door, leaving me in an enormous room with white sofas and floating mobiles. The room was immaculate except for a silky purple-and-gold kimono lying on the floor. I picked up the kimono and rubbed it against my cheek and put it on over my clothes. Then I went and looked out the window at the city stretching on and on. In a building across the street, figures moved slowly behind dirty glass. They were making things, I suppose.

After a while Chris and Joel burst back into the room. Chris's eyes were shiny, and he was grinning like crazy.

"Hey," Joel said, grabbing the edges of the kimono I was wearing. "That thing looks better on her than on me."

"What wouldn't?" Chris said. Joel stepped back as Chris put 85 his arms around me from behind again.

"I resent that, I resent that! But I don't deny it!" Joel said. Chris was kissing my neck and my ears, and both he and Joel were giggling.

I wondered what would happen if Chris and I were late and Mother saw me drive up in Chris's car, but we darted around in the traffic and shot along the avenues and pulled up near Penelope's dancing school with ten minutes to spare. Then, instead of saying anything, Chris just sat there with one hand still on the wheel and the other on the shift, and he didn't even look at me. When I just experimentally touched his sleeve and he still didn't move, I more or less flung myself on top of him and started crying into his shirt. I was in his lap, all tangled up, and I was kissing him and kissing him, and my hands were moving by themselves.

Suddenly I thought of all the people outside the car walking their bouncy little dogs, and I thought how my mother might pull up at any second, and I sat up fast and opened my eyes. Everything looked slightly different from the way it had been looking inside my head — a bit smaller and farther away — and I realized that Chris had been sitting absolutely still, and he was staring straight ahead.

"Goodbye," I said, but Chris still didn't move or even look at me. I couldn't understand what had happened to Chris.

"Wait," Chris said, still without looking at me. "Here's my 90 phone number." He shook himself and wrote it out slowly.

At the corner I looked back and saw that Chris was still there, leaning back and staring out the windshield.

"Why did he give me his phone number, do you think?" I asked Maureen. We were at a party in Peter Klingeman's basement.

"I guess he wants you to call him," Maureen said. I know she didn't really feel like talking. Kevin was standing there, with his hand under her shirt, and she was sort of jumpy. "Frankly,

Laurel, he sounds a bit weird to me, if you don't mind my saying," Maureen said. I felt ashamed again. I wanted to talk to Maureen more, but Kevin was pulling her off to the Klingemans' TV room.

Then Dougie Pfeiffer sat down next to me. "I think Maureen and Kevin have a really good relationship," he said.

I was wondering how I ever could have had a crush on him in 95 eighth grade when I realized it was my turn to say something. "Did you ever notice," I said, "how some people say 'in eighth grade' and other people say 'in *the* eighth grade'?"

"Laurel," Dougie said, and he grabbed me, shoving his tongue into my mouth. Then he took his tongue back out and let me go. "God, I'm sorry, Laurel," he said.

I didn't really care what he did with his tongue. I thought how his body, under his clothes, was just sort of an outline, like a kid's drawing, and I thought of the long zipper on Chris's leather jacket, and a little rip I noticed once in his jeans, and the weave of the shirt that I'd cried on.

I carried Chris's phone number around with me everywhere, and finally I asked my mother if I could go into the city after school on Thursday and then meet her at Penelope's class.

"No," Mother said.

"Why not?" I said. 100

"We needn't discuss this, Laurel," my mother said.

"You let me go in to see Dr. Wald," I said.

"Don't," Mother said. "Anyhow, you can't just . . . wander around in New York."

"I have to do some shopping," I said idiotically.

Mother started to say something, but then she stopped, and 105 she looked at me as if she couldn't quite remember who I was. "Oh, who cares?" she said, not especially to me.

There was a permanent little line between Mother's eyebrows, I noticed, and suddenly I felt I was seeing her through a window. I went up to my room and cried and cried, but later I couldn't get to sleep, thinking about Chris.

I called him Thursday.

"What time is it?" he said with his blistery laugh. "I just woke up." He told me he had gone to a party the night before and when he came out his car had been stolen. He was stoned, and he thought the sensible thing was to walk over to Mark's place, which is miles from his, but on the way he found his car parked out on the street. "I should've reported it, but I figured, hey, what a great opportunity, so I just stole it back."

Chris didn't mention anything about our seeing each other.
"I've got to come into the city today to do some stuff," I said. 110
"Yeah," Chris said. "I've got a lot to do today myself."

Well, that was that, obviously, unless I did something drastic.
"I thought I'd stop in and say hi, if you're going to be around,"
I said. My heart was jumping so much it almost knocked me
down.

"Great," Chris said. "That's really sweet." But his voice
sounded muted, and I wasn't at all surprised when I got to Jake's
and he wasn't there. I was on my third Coke when Chris walked
in, but a girl wearing lots of bracelets waylaid him at the bar, and
he sat down with her.

I didn't dare finish my Coke or ask for my check. All I could
do was stay put and do whatever Chris made me do. Finally the
girl at the bar left, giving Chris a big, meaty kiss, and he wandered over and sat down with me.

"God. Did you see that girl who was sitting with me?" he said. 115
"That girl is so crazy. There's nothing she won't put in her mouth.
I was at some party a few weeks ago, and I walk in through this
door, 'cause I'm looking for the john, and there's Beverly, lying
on the floor stark naked. So you know what she does?"

"No," I said.

"She says, 'Excuse me,' and instead of putting something on
she reaches up and turns out the light. Now, that's thinkin', huh?"
He laughed. "Have you finished all those things you had to do?"
he asked me.

"Yes," I said.

"That's great," Chris said. "I'm really running around like a
chicken today. Honey," he said to a waitress, "put that on my tab,
will you?" He pointed at my watery Coke.

"Sandra was looking for you," the waitress said. "Did she 120
find you?"

"Yeah, thanks," Chris said. He gave me a kiss on the cheek,
which was the first time he had kissed me at all, except at Joel's,
and he left.

I knew I had made some kind of mistake, but I couldn't
figure out what it was. I would only be able to figure it out from
Chris, but it would be two weeks until I saw him again. Every
night, I looked out the window at the red glow of the city beyond
all the quiet little houses and yards, and every night after I got
into bed I felt it draw nearer and nearer, hovering just beyond
my closed eyes, with Chris inside it. While I slept, it receded
again; but by morning, when I woke up and put on my school
clothes, I had come one day closer.

After my next appointment with Dr. Wald, Chris wasn't at Jake's. For the first time since I had gone to Jake's, Chris didn't come at all.

On the way home it was all I could do not to cry in front of Mother and Penelope. And I wondered what I was going to do from that afternoon on.

"And how was Dr. Wald today?" my father said when we sat down for dinner. 125

"I didn't ask," I said.

My father paused to acknowledge my little joke.

"What I meant," he said, "was how is my lovely daughter?"

I knew he was trying to say something nice, but he could have picked something sincere for once. I hated the way he had taken off his jacket and opened up his collar and rolled up his sleeves, and I thought I would be sick if he stood behind my chair later. "Penelope is your lovely daughter," I said, and threw my silverware onto the table.

From upstairs I listened. I knew that Penelope would have 130 frozen, the way she does when someone says in front of me how pretty she is, but no one said anything about me that I could hear.

Later, Penelope and Paul and I made up a story together, the way we had when we were younger. Paul fell asleep suddenly in the middle with little tears in the corners of his eyes, and I tucked Penelope into bed. When I smoothed out the covers, a shadow of relief crossed her face.

That Saturday, Mother took me shopping in the city without Penelope or Paul. "I thought we should get you a present," Mother said. "Something pretty." She smiled at me in a strange, stiff way.

"Thank you," I said. I felt good that we were driving together, but I was sad, too, that Mother was trying to bring me into the clean, bright, fancy, daytime part of New York that Penelope's dancing school was in, because when would she accept that there was no place there for me? I wondered if Mother wanted to say something to me, but we just drove silently, except for once, when Mother pointed out a lady in a big, white, flossy fur coat.

At Bonwit's, Mother picked out an expensive dress for me. "What do you think?" she said when I tried it on.

I was glad that Mother had chosen it, because it was very 135 pretty, and it was white, and it was expensive, but in the mirror I just looked skinny and dazed. "I like it," I said. "But don't you think it looks wrong on me?"

"Well, it seems fine to me, but it's up to you," Mother said. "You can have it if you want."

"But look, Mother," I said. "Look. Do you think it's all right?"

"If you don't like it, don't get it," she said. "It's your present."

At home after dinner I tried the white dress on again and stared at myself in the mirror, and I thought maybe it looked a little better.

I went down to the living room, where Mother was stretched out on the sofa with her feet on my father's lap. When I walked in he started to get up, but Mother didn't move. "My God," my father said. "It's Lucia."   140

My mother giggled. "Wedding scene or mad scene?" she said.

Upstairs I folded the dress back into the box for Bonwit's to pick up. At night I watched bright dancing patterns in the dark and I dreaded going back to Dr. Wald.

The doctor didn't seem to notice anything unusual at my next appointment. I still had to face walking the short distance to Jake's, though. I practically fell over from relief when I saw Chris at the bar, and he reached out as I went by and reeled me in, smiling. He was talking to Mark and some other friends, and he stood me with my back to him and rubbed my shoulders and temples. I tried to smile hello to Mark, who was staring at me with his pale eyes, but he just kept staring, listening to Chris. I closed my eyes and leaned back against Chris, who folded his arms around me. When Chris finished his story, everyone laughed except me. Chris blew a little stream of air into my hair, ruffling it up. "Want to take a ride?" he said.

We drove for a while, fast, circling the city, and Chris slammed tapes into the tape deck. Then we parked and Chris turned and looked at me.

"What do you want to do?" Chris asked me.   145

"Now?" I said, but he just looked at me, and I didn't know what he meant. "Nothing," I said.

"Have I seemed preoccupied to you lately, honey?" he asked.

"I guess maybe a little," I said, even though I hadn't really ever thought about how he seemed. He just seemed like himself. But he told me that yes, he had been preoccupied. He had borrowed some money to start an audio business, but he had to help out a cousin, too. I couldn't make any sense of what he was talking about, and I didn't really care, either. I was thinking that now he had finally called me "honey." It made me so happy, so happy, even though "honey" was what he called everyone, and I had been the only Laurel.

Chris talked and talked, and I watched his mouth as the words came out. "I know you wonder what's going on with me," he said. "What it is is I worry that you're so young. I'm a difficult person. There are a lot of strange things about me. I'm really crazy about you, you know. I'm really crazy about you, but I can't ask you to see me."

"Why don't I come in and stay over with you a week from Friday," I said. "Can I?" 150

Chris blinked. "Terrific, honey," he said cautiously. "That's a date."

I arranged it with Maureen that I would say I was staying at her house. "Don't wear underwear," Maureen told me. "That really turns guys on."

Chris and I met at Jake's, but we didn't stay there long. We drove all over the city, stopping at different places. Chris knew people everywhere, and we would sit down at the bar and talk to them. We went to an apartment with some of the people we ran into, where everyone lay around listening to tapes. And once we went to a club and watched crowds of people change like waves with the music, under flashing lights.

Chris didn't touch me, not once, not even accidentally, all during that time.

Sometime between things we stopped for food. I couldn't eat, 155 but Chris seemed starving. He ate his cheeseburger and French fries, and then he ate mine. And then he had a big piece of pecan pie.

Late, very late, we climbed into the car again, but there was nothing left to do. "Home?" Chris said without turning to me.

Chris's apartment seemed so strange, and maybe that was just because it was real. But I had surely never been inside such a small, plain place to live before, and Chris hardly seemed to own anything. There were a few books on a shelf, and a little kitchen off in the corner, with a pot on the stove. It was up several flights of dark stairs, in a brick building, and it must have been on the edge of the city, because I could see water out of the window, and ribbons of highway elevated on huge concrete pillars, and dark piers.

Chris's bed, which was tightly made with the sheet turned back over the blanket, looked very narrow. All the music we had been hearing all night was rocketing around in my brain, and I felt jittery and a bit sick. Chris passed a joint to me, and he lay down with his hands over his eyes. I sat down on the edge of the bed next to him and waited, but he didn't move. "Remember when I asked you a while ago what you wanted to do and you said 'Nothing'?" Chris asked me.

"But that was —" I started to say, and then the funny sound of Chris's voice caught up with me, and all the noise in my head shut off.

"I remember," Chris said. Then a long time went by.   160

"Why did you come here, Laurel?" Chris said.

When I didn't answer, he said, "Why? Why did you come here? You're old enough now to think about what you're doing." And I remembered I had never been alone with him before, except in his car.

"Yes," I said into the dead air. Whatever I'd been waiting for all that time had vanished. "It's all right."

"It's all right?" Chris said furiously. "Well, good. It's all right, then." He was still lying on his back with his hands over his eyes, and neither of us moved. I thought I might shatter.

Sometime in the night Chris spoke again. "Why are you   165
angry?" he said. His voice was blurred, as if he'd been asleep. I wanted to tell him I wasn't angry, but it seemed wrong, and I was afraid of what would happen if I did. I put my arms around him and started kissing him. He didn't move a muscle, but I kept right on. I knew it was my only chance, and I thought that if I stopped I would have to leave. "Don't be angry," he said.

Sometime in the night I sprang awake. Chris was holding my wrists behind my back with one hand and unbuttoning my shirt with the other, and his body felt very tense. "Don't!" I said, before I understood.

"'Don't!'" echoed Chris, letting go of me. He said it just the way I had, sounding just as frightened. He fell asleep immediately then, sprawled out, but I couldn't sleep anymore, and later, when Chris spoke suddenly into the dark, I felt I'd been expecting him to. "Your parents are going to worry," he said deliberately, as if he were reading.

"No," I said. I wondered how long he had been awake. "They think I'm at Maureen's." And then I realized how foolish it was for me to have said that.

"They'll worry," he said. "They will worry. They'll be very frightened."

And then I was so frightened myself that the room bulged   170
and there was a sound in my ears like ball bearings rolling

around wildly. I put my hands against my hot face, and my skin felt to me as if it belonged to a stranger. It felt like a marvel — brand-new and slightly moist — and I wondered if anyone else would ever touch it and feel what I had felt.

"Look — " Chris said. He sounded blurry again, and help-less and sad. "Look — see how bad I am for you, Laurel? See how I make you cry?" Then he put his arms around me, and we lay there on top of the bed for a long, long time, and sometimes we kissed each other. My shirt sleeve was twisted and it hurt against my arm, but I didn't move.

When the night red began finally to bleach out of the sky, I touched Chris's wrist. "I have to go now," I said. That wasn't true, of course. My parents would expect me to stay at Maureen's till at least noon. "I have to be home when it gets light."

"Do you?" Chris said, but his eyes were closed.

I stood up and buttoned my shirt.

"I'll take you to the train," Chris said.   175

At first he didn't move, but finally he stood up, too. "I need some coffee," he said. And when he looked at me my heart sank. He was smiling. He looked as if he wanted to start it up — start it all again.

I went into the bathroom, so I wouldn't be looking at Chris. There was a tub and a sink and a toilet. Chris uses them, I thought, as if that would explain something to me, but the thought was like a sealed package. Stuck in the corner of the mirror over the sink was a picture of a man's face torn from a magazine. It was a handsome face, but I didn't like it.

"That's a guy I went to high school with," Chris said from behind me. "He's a very successful actor now."

"That's nice," I said, and waited as long as I could. "Look — it's almost light."

And in the instant that Chris glanced at the window, where in   180 fact the faintest dawn was showing, I stepped over to the door and opened it.

In the car, Chris seemed the way he usually did. "I'm sorry I'm so tired, honey," he said. "I've been having a rough time lately. We'll get together another time, when I'm not so hassled."

"Yes," I said. "Good." I don't think he really remembered the things we had said in the dark.

When we stopped at the station, Chris put his arm across me, but instead of opening the door he just held the handle. "You think I'm really weird, don't you?" he said, and smiled at me.

"I think you're tired," I said, making myself smile back. And Chris released the handle and let me out.

I took the train through the dawn and walked from the 185
station, pausing carefully if it looked as though someone was
awake inside a house I was passing. Once a dog barked, and I
stood absolutely still for minutes.

I threw chunks from the lawn at Maureen's window, so Carolina wouldn't wake up, but I was afraid the whole town would be
out by the time Maureen heard.

Maureen came down the back way and got me. We each put
on one of her bathrobes, and we made a pot of coffee, which is
something I'm not allowed to drink.

"What happened?" Maureen asked.

"I don't know," I said.

"What do you mean, you don't know?" Maureen said. "You 190
were there."

Even though my face was in my hands, I could tell Maureen
was staring at me. "Well," she said after a while. "Hey. Want to
play some Clue?" She got the Clue board down from her room,
and we played about ten games.

The next week I really did stay over at Maureen's.

"Again?" my mother said. "We must do something for Mrs.
MacIntyre. She's been so nice to you."

Dougie and Kevin showed up together after Maureen and
Carolina and I had eaten a barbecued chicken from the deli and
Carolina had gone to her room to watch the little TV that Mrs.
MacIntyre had put there. I figured it was no accident that Dougie
had shown up with Kevin. It had to be a brainstorm of Maureen's, and I thought, Well, so what. So after Maureen and Kevin
went up to Maureen's room I went into the den with Dougie. We
pretty much knew from classes and books and stuff what to do,
so we did it. The thing that surprised me most was that you
always read in books about "stained sheets," "stained sheets,"
and I never knew what that meant, but I guess I thought it would
be pretty interesting. But the little stuff on the sheet just looked
completely innocuous, like Elmer's glue, and it seemed that it
might even dry clear like Elmer's glue. At any rate, it didn't seem
like anything that Carolina would have to absolutely kill herself
about when she did the laundry.

We went back into the living room to wait, and I sat while 195
Dougie walked around poking at things on the shelves. "Look,"
Dougie said, "Clue." But I just shrugged, and after a while
Maureen and Kevin came downstairs looking pretty pleased with
themselves.

I sat while Dr. Wald finished at the machine, and I waited for him to say something, but he didn't.

"Am I going to go blind?" I asked him finally, after all those months.

"What?" he said. Then he remembered to look at me and smile. "Oh, no, no. We won't let it come to that."

I knew what I would find at Jake's, but I had to go anyway, just to finish. "Have you seen Chris?" I asked one of the wait-resses. "Or Mark?"

"They haven't been around for a while," she said. "Sheila," she called over to another waitress, "where's Chris these days?" 200

"Don't ask me," Sheila said sourly, and both of them stared at me.

I could feel my blood traveling in its slow loop, carrying a heavy proudness through every part of my body. I had known Chris could injure me, and I had never cared how much he could injure me, but it had never occurred to me until this moment that I could do anything to him.

Outside, it was hot. There were big bins of things for sale on the sidewalk, and horns were honking, and the sun was yellow and syrupy. I noticed two people who must have been mother and daughter, even though you couldn't really tell how old either of them was. One of them was sort of crippled, and the other was very peculiar looking, and they were all dressed up in stiff, cheap party dresses. They looked so pathetic with their sweaty, eager faces and ugly dresses that I felt like crying. But then I thought that they might be happy, much happier than I was, and that I just felt sorry for them because I thought I was better than they were. And I realized that I wasn't really different from them anyhow — that every person just had one body or another, and some of them looked right and worked right and some of them didn't — and I thought maybe it was myself I was feeling sorry for, because of Chris, or maybe because it was obvious even to me, a total stranger, how much that mother loved her homely daughter in that awful dress.

When Mother and Penelope and I got back home, I walked over to Maureen's house, but I decided not to stop. I walked by the playground and looked in at the fourth-grade room and the turtle that was still lumbering around its dingy aquarium, and it came into my mind how even Paul was older now than the kids who would be sitting in those tiny chairs in the fall, and I thought about all the millions and billions of people in the world, all getting older, all trapped in things that had already happened to them.

When I was a kid, I used to wonder (I bet everyone did) whether there was somebody somewhere on the earth, or even in the universe, or ever had been in all of time, who had had exactly the same experience that I was having at that moment, and I hoped so badly that there was. But I realized then that that could never occur, because every moment is all the things that have happened before and all the things that are going to happen, and every moment is just the way all those things look at one point on their way along a line. And I thought how maybe once there was, say, a princess who lost her mother's ring in a forest, and how in some other galaxy a strange creature might fall, screaming, on the shore of a red lake, and how right that second there could be a man standing at a window overlooking a busy street, aiming a loaded revolver, but how it was just me, there, after Chris, staring at that turtle in the fourth-grade room and wondering if it would die before I stopped being able to see it.

205

HENRIK IBSEN   (1828–1906)

A Doll's House

TRANSLATED BY MICHAEL MEYER

CHARACTERS
Torvald Helmer, *a lawyer*
Nora, *his wife*
Dr. Rank
Mrs. Linde
Nils Krogstad, *also a lawyer*

The Helmers' three small children
Anne-Marie, *their nurse*
Helen, *the maid*
A Porter

SCENE: *The action takes place in the Helmers' apartment.*

ACT I

A comfortably and tastefully, but not expensively furnished room. Backstage right a door leads out to the hall; backstage left, another door to Helmer's study. Between these two doors stands a piano. In the middle of the left-hand wall is a door, with a window downstage of it. Near the window, a round table with armchairs and a small sofa. In the right-hand wall, slightly upstage, is a door; downstage of this, against the same wall, a stove lined with porcelain tiles, with a couple of arm-chairs and a rocking-chair in front of it. Between the stove and the side door is a small table. Engravings on the wall. A what-not with china and other bric-a-brac;

a small bookcase with leather-bound books. A carpet on the floor; a fire in the stove. A winter day.

A bell rings in the hall outside. After a moment, we hear the front door being opened. Nora enters the room, humming contentedly to herself. She is wearing outdoor clothes and carrying a lot of parcels, which she puts down on the table right. She leaves the door to the hall open; through it, we can see a Porter carrying a Christmas tree and a basket. He gives these to the Maid, who has opened the door for them.

Nora: Hide that Christmas tree away, Helen. The children mustn't see it before I've decorated it this evening. (*To the Porter, taking out her purse.*) How much — ?

Porter: A shilling.

Nora: Here's half a crown. No, keep it.

The Porter touches his cap and goes. Nora closes the door. She continues to laugh happily to herself as she removes her coat, etc. She takes from her pocket a bag containing macaroons and eats a couple. Then she tiptoes across and listens at her husband's door.

Nora: Yes, he's here. (*Starts humming again as she goes over to the table, right.*)

Helmer (from his room): Is that my skylark twittering out there?

Nora (opening some of the parcels): It is!

Helmer: Is that my squirrel rustling?

Nora: Yes!

Helmer: When did my squirrel come home?

Nora: Just now. (*Pops the bag of macaroons in her pocket and wipes her mouth.*) Come out here, Torvald, and see what I've bought.

Helmer: You mustn't disturb me! (*Short pause; then he opens the door and looks in, his pen in his hand.*) Bought, did you say? All that? Has my little squanderbird been overspending again?

Nora: Oh, Torvald, surely we can let ourselves go a little this year! It's the first Christmas we don't have to scrape.

Helmer: Well, you know, we can't afford to be extravagant.

Nora: Oh yes, Torvald, we can be a little extravagant now. Can't we? Just a tiny bit? You've got a big salary now, and you're going to make lots and lots of money.

Helmer: Next year, yes. But my new salary doesn't start till April.

Nora: Pooh; we can borrow till then.

Helmer: Nora! (*Goes over to her and takes her playfully by the ear.*) What a little spendthrift you are! Suppose I were to borrow fifty pounds today, and you spent it all over Christmas, and then on New Year's Eve a tile fell off a roof on to my head —

Nora (puts her hand over his mouth): Oh, Torvald! Don't say such dreadful things!

Helmer: Yes, but suppose something like that did happen? What then?

Nora: If anything as frightful as that happened, it wouldn't make much difference whether I was in debt or not.

Helmer: But what about the people I'd borrowed from?

Nora: Them? Who cares about them? They're strangers.

Helmer: Oh, Nora, Nora, how like a woman! No, but seriously, Nora, you know how I feel about this. No debts! Never borrow! A home that is founded on debts can never be a place of freedom and beauty. We two have stuck it out bravely up to now; and we shall continue to do so for the short time we still have to.

Nora (goes over towards the stove): Very well, Torvald. As you say.

Helmer (follows her): Now, now! My little songbird mustn't droop her wings. What's this? Is little squirrel sulking? (*Takes out his purse.*) Nora; guess what I've got here!

Nora (turns quickly): Money!

Helmer: Look. (*Hands her some banknotes.*) I know how these small expenses crop up at Christmas.

Nora (counts them): One — two — three — four. Oh, thank you, Torvald, thank you! I should be able to manage with this.

Helmer: You'll have to.

Nora: Yes, yes, of course I will. But come over here, I want to show you everything I've bought. And so cheaply! Look, here are new clothes for Ivar — and a sword. And a horse and a trumpet for Bob. And a doll and a cradle for Emmy — they're nothing much, but she'll pull them apart in a few days. And some bits of material and handkerchiefs for the maids. Old Anne-Marie ought to have had something better, really.

Helmer: And what's in that parcel?

Nora (cries): No. Torvald, you mustn't see that before this evening!

Helmer: Very well. But now, tell me, you little spendthrift, what do you want for Christmas?

Nora: Me? Oh, pooh, I don't want anything.

Helmer: Oh, yes, you do. Now tell me, what, within reason, would you most like?

Nora: No, I really don't know. Oh, yes — Torvald — !

Helmer: Well?

Nora (plays with his coat-buttons; not looking at him): If you really want to give me something, you could — you could —

Helmer: Come on, out with it.

Nora (quickly): You could give me money, Torvald. Only as much as you feel you can afford; then later I'll buy something with it.

Helmer: But, Nora —

Nora: Oh yes, Torvald dear, please! Please! Then I'll wrap up the notes in pretty gold paper and hang them on the Christmas tree. Wouldn't that be fun?

Helmer: What's the name of that little bird that can never keep any money?

Nora: Yes, yes, squanderbird; I know. But let's do as I say, Torvald; then I'll have time to think about what I need most. Isn't that the best way? Mm?

Helmer (smiles): To be sure it would be, if you could keep what I give you and really buy yourself something with it. But you'll spend it on all sorts of useless things for the house, and then I'll have to put my hand in my pocket again.

Nora: Oh, but Torvald —

Helmer: You can't deny it, Nora dear. (*Puts his arm round her waist.*) The squanderbird's a pretty little creature, but she gets through an awful lot of money. It's incredible what an expensive pet she is for a man to keep.

Nora: For shame! How can you say such a thing? I save every penny I can.

Helmer (laughs): That's quite true. Every penny you can. But you can't.

Nora (hums and smiles, quietly gleeful): Hm. If you only knew how many expenses we larks and squirrels have, Torvald.

Helmer: You're a funny little creature. Just like your father used to be. Always on the look-out for some way to get money, but as soon as you have any it just runs through your fingers, and you never know where it's gone. Well, I suppose I must take you as you are. It's in your blood. Yes, yes, yes, these things are hereditary, Nora.

Nora: Oh, I wish I'd inherited more of Papa's qualities.

Helmer: And I wouldn't wish my darling little songbird to be any different from what she is. By the way, that reminds me. You look awfully — how shall I put it? — awfully guilty today.

Nora: Do I?

Helmer: Yes, you do. Look me in the eyes.

Nora (looks at him): Well?

Helmer (wags his finger): Has my little sweet-tooth been indulging herself in town today, by any chance?

Nora: No, how can you think such a thing?

Helmer: Not a tiny little digression into a pastry shop?

Nora: No, Torvald, I promise —

Helmer: Not just a wee jam tart?

Nora: Certainly not.

Helmer: Not a little nibble at a macaroon?

Nora: No, Torvald — I promise you, honestly —

Helmer: There, there. I was only joking.

Nora (goes over to the table, right): You know I could never act against your wishes.

Helmer: Of course not. And you've given me your word — (*Goes over to her.*) Well, my beloved Nora, you keep your little Christmas secrets to yourself. They'll be revealed this evening, I've no doubt, once the Christmas tree has been lit.

Nora: Have you remembered to invite Dr. Rank?

Helmer: No. But there's no need; he knows he'll be dining with us. Anyway, I'll ask him when he comes this morning. I've ordered some good wine. Oh, Nora, you can't imagine how I'm looking forward to this evening.

Nora: So am I. And, Torvald, how the children will love it!

Helmer: Yes, it's a wonderful thing to know that one's position is assured and that one has an ample income. Don't you agree? It's good to know that, isn't it?

Nora: Yes, it's almost like a miracle.

Helmer: Do you remember last Christmas? For three whole weeks you shut yourself away every evening to make flowers for the Christmas tree, and all those other things you were going to surprise us with. Ugh, it was the most boring time I've ever had in my life.

Nora: I didn't find it boring.

Helmer (smiles): But it all came to nothing in the end, didn't it?

Nora: Oh, are you going to bring that up again? How could I help the cat getting in and tearing everything to bits?

Helmer: No, my poor little Nora, of course you couldn't. You simply wanted to make us happy, and that's all that matters. But it's good that those hard times are past.

Nora: Yes, it's wonderful.

Helmer: I don't have to sit by myself and be bored. And you don't have to tire your pretty eyes and your delicate little hands —

Nora (claps her hands): No, Torvald, that's true, isn't it — I don't have to any longer? Oh, it's really all just like a miracle. (*Takes his arm.*) Now, I'm going to tell you what I thought we might do, Torvald. As soon as Christmas is over — (*A bell rings in the hall.*) Oh, there's the doorbell. (*Tidies up one or two things in the room.*) Someone's coming. What a bore.

Helmer: I'm not at home to any visitors. Remember!

Maid (in the doorway): A lady's called, madam. A stranger.

Nora: Well, ask her to come in.

Maid: And the doctor's here too, sir.

Helmer: Has he gone to my room?

Maid: Yes, sir.

Helmer goes into his room. The Maid shows in Mrs. Linde, who is dressed in traveling clothes, and closes the door.

Mrs. Linde (shyly and a little hesitantly): Good evening, Nora.

Nora (uncertainly): Good evening —

Mrs. Linde: I don't suppose you recognize me.

Nora: No, I'm afraid I — Yes, wait a minute — surely — (*Exclaims.*) Why, Christine! Is it really you?

Mrs. Linde: Yes, it's me.

Nora: Christine! And I didn't recognize you! But how could I — ? (*More quietly.*) How you've changed, Christine!

Mrs. Linde: Yes, I know. It's been nine years — nearly ten —

Nora: Is it so long? Yes, it must be. Oh, these last eight years have been such a happy time for me! So you've come to town? All that way in winter! How brave of you!

Mrs. Linde: I arrived by the steamer this morning.

Nora: Yes, of course — to enjoy yourself over Christmas. Oh, how splendid! We'll have to celebrate! But take off your coat. You're not cold, are you? (*Helps her off with it.*) There! Now let's sit down here by the stove and be comfortable. No, you take the armchair. I'll sit here in the rocking-chair. (*Clasps Mrs. Linde's hands.*) Yes, now you look like your old self. It was just at first that — you've got a little paler, though, Christine. And perhaps a bit thinner.

Mrs. Linde: And older, Nora. Much, much older.

Nora: Yes, perhaps a little older. Just a tiny bit. Not much. (*Checks herself suddenly and says earnestly.*) Oh, but how thoughtless of me to sit here and chatter away like this! Dear, sweet Christine, can you forgive me?

Mrs. Linde: What do you mean, Nora?

Nora (quietly): Poor Christine, you've become a widow.

Mrs. Linde: Yes. Three years ago.

Nora: I know, I know — I read it in the papers. Oh, Christine, I meant to write to you so often, honestly. But I always put it off, and something else always cropped up.

Mrs. Linde: I understand, Nora dear.

Nora: No, Christine, it was beastly of me. Oh, my poor darling, what you've gone through! And he didn't leave you anything?

Mrs. Linde: No.

Nora: No children, either?

Mrs. Linde: No.

Nora: Nothing at all, then?

Mrs. Linde: Not even a feeling of loss or sorrow.

Nora (looks incredulously at her): But, Christine, how is that possible?

Mrs. Linde (smiles sadly and strokes Nora's hair): Oh, these things happen, Nora.

Nora: All alone. How dreadful that must be for you. I've three lovely children. I'm afraid you can't see them now, because they're out with nanny. But you must tell me everything —

Mrs. Linde: No, no, no. I want to hear about you.

Nora: No, you start. I'm not going to be selfish today, I'm just going to think about you. Oh, but there's one thing I *must* tell you. Have you heard of the wonderful luck we've just had?

Mrs. Linde: No. What?

Nora: Would you believe it — my husband's just been made manager of the bank!

Mrs. Linde: Your husband? Oh, how lucky — !

Nora: Yes, isn't it? Being a lawyer is so uncertain, you know, especially if one isn't prepared to touch any case that isn't — well — quite nice. And of course Torvald's been very firm about that — and I'm absolutely with him. Oh, you can imagine how happy we are! He's joining the bank in the New Year, and he'll be getting a big salary, and lots of percentages too. From now on we'll be able to live quite differently — we'll be able to do whatever we want. Oh, Christine, it's such a relief! I feel so happy! Well, I mean, it's lovely to have heaps of money and not to have to worry about anything. Don't you think?

Mrs. Linde: It must be lovely to have enough to cover one's needs, anyway.

Nora: Not just our needs! We're going to have heaps and heaps of money!

Mrs. Linde (smiles): Nora, Nora, haven't you grown up yet? When we were at school you were a terrible little spendthrift.

Nora (laughs quietly): Yes, Torvald still says that. (*Wags her finger.*) But "Nora, Nora" isn't as silly as you think. Oh, we've been in no position for me to waste money. We've both had to work.

Mrs. Linde: You too?

Nora: Yes, little things — fancy work, crocheting, embroidery and so forth. (*Casually.*) And other things too. I suppose you know Torvald left the Ministry when we got married? There were no prospects of promotion in his department, and of course he needed more money. But the first year he over-worked himself quite dreadfully. He had to take on all sorts of extra jobs, and worked day and night. But it was too much for him, and he became frightfully ill. The doctors said he'd have to go to a warmer climate.

Mrs. Linde: Yes, you spent a whole year in Italy, didn't you?

Nora: Yes. It wasn't easy for me to get away, you know. I'd just had Ivar. But of course we had to do it. Oh, it was a marvelous trip! And it saved Torvald's life. But it cost an awful lot of money, Christine.

Mrs. Linde: I can imagine.

Nora: Two hundred and fifty pounds. That's a lot of money, you know.

Mrs. Linde: How lucky you had it.

Nora: Well, actually, we got it from my father.

Mrs. Linde: Oh, I see. Didn't he die just about that time?

Nora: Yes, Christine, just about then. Wasn't it dreadful, I couldn't go and look after him. I was expecting little Ivar any day. And then I had my poor Torvald to care for — we really didn't think he'd live. Dear, kind Papa! I never saw him again, Christine. Oh, it's the saddest thing that's happened to me since I got married.

Mrs. Linde: I know you were very fond of him. But you went to Italy —

Nora: Yes. Well, we had the money, you see, and the doctors said we mustn't delay. So we went the month after Papa died.

Mrs. Linde: And your husband came back completely cured?

Nora: Fit as a fiddle!

Mrs. Linde: But — the doctor?

Nora: How do you mean?

Mrs. Linde: I thought the maid said that the gentleman who arrived with me was the doctor.

Nora: Oh yes, that's Doctor Rank, but he doesn't come because anyone's ill. He's our best friend, and he looks us up at least once every day. No, Torvald hasn't had a moment's illness since we went away. And the children are fit and healthy and so am I. (*Jumps up and claps her hands.*) Oh God, oh God, Christine, isn't it a wonderful thing to be alive and happy!

Oh, but how beastly of me! I'm only talking about myself. (*Sits on a footstool and rests her arms on Mrs. Linde's knee.*) Oh, please don't be angry with me! Tell me, is it really true you didn't love your husband? Why did you marry him, then?

Mrs. Linde: Well, my mother was still alive; and she was helpless and bedridden. And I had my two little brothers to take care of. I didn't feel I could say no.

Nora: Yes, well, perhaps you're right. He was rich then, was he?

Mrs. Linde: Quite comfortably off, I believe. But his business was unsound, you see, Nora. When he died it went bankrupt, and there was nothing left.

Nora: What did you do?

Mrs. Linde: Well, I had to try to make ends meet somehow, so I started a little shop, and a little school, and anything else I could turn my hand to. These last three years have been just one endless slog for me, without a moment's rest. But now it's over, Nora. My poor dear mother doesn't need me any more; she's passed away. And the boys don't need me either; they've got jobs now and can look after themselves.

Nora: How relieved you must feel —

Mrs. Linde: No, Nora. Just unspeakably empty. No one to live for any more. (*Gets up restlessly.*) That's why I couldn't bear to stay out there any longer, cut off from the world. I thought it'd be easier to find some work here that will exercise and occupy my mind. If only I could get a regular job — office work of some kind —

Nora: Oh but, Christine, that's dreadfully exhausting; and you look practically finished already. It'd be much better for you if you could go away somewhere.

Mrs. Linde (*goes over to the window*): I have no Papa to pay for my holidays, Nora.

Nora (*gets up*): Oh, please don't be angry with me.

Mrs. Linde: My dear Nora, it's I who should ask you not to be angry. That's the worst thing about this kind of situation — it makes one so bitter. One has no one to work for; and yet one has to be continually sponging for jobs. One has to live; and so one becomes completely egocentric. When you told me about this luck you've just had with Torvald's new job — can you imagine? — I was happy not so much on your account, as on my own.

Nora: How do you mean? Oh, I understand. You mean Torvald might be able to do something for you?

Mrs. Linde: Yes, I was thinking that.

Nora: He will too, Christine. Just you leave it to me. I'll lead up to it so delicately, so delicately; I'll get him in the right mood. Oh, Christine, I do so want to help you.

Mrs. Linde: It's sweet of you to bother so much about me, Nora. Especially since you know so little of the worries and hardships of life.

Nora: I? You say *I* know little of — ?

Mrs. Linde (smiles): Well, good heavens — those bits of fancy work of yours — well, really — ! You're a child, Nora.

Nora (tosses her head and walks across the room): You shouldn't say that so patronizingly.

Mrs. Linde: Oh?

Nora: You're like the rest. You all think I'm incapable of getting down to anything serious —

Mrs. Linde: My dear —

Nora: You think I've never had any worries like the rest of you.

Mrs. Linde: Nora dear, you've just told me about all your difficulties —

Nora: Pooh — that! (*Quietly.*) I haven't told you about the big thing.

Mrs. Linde: What big thing? What do you mean?

Nora: You patronize me, Christine; but you shouldn't. You're proud that you've worked so long and so hard for your mother.

Mrs. Linde: I don't patronize anyone, Nora. But you're right — I am both proud and happy that I was able to make my mother's last months on earth comparatively easy.

Nora: And you're also proud of what you've done for your brothers.

Mrs. Linde: I think I have a right to be.

Nora: I think so too. But let me tell you something, Christine. I too have done something to be proud and happy about.

Mrs. Linde: I don't doubt it. But — how do you mean?

Nora: Speak quietly! Suppose Torvald should hear! He mustn't, at any price — no one must know, Christine — no one but you.

Mrs. Linde: But what is this?

Nora: Come over here. (*Pulls her down on to the sofa beside her.*) Yes, Christine — I too have done something to be happy and proud about. It was I who saved Torvald's life.

Mrs. Linde: Saved his — ? How did you save it?

Nora: I told you about our trip to Italy. Torvald couldn't have lived if he hadn't managed to get down there —

Mrs. Linde: Yes, well — your father provided the money —

Nora (smiles): So Torvald and everyone else thinks. But —

Mrs. Linde: Yes?

Nora: Papa didn't give us a penny. It was I who found the money.

Mrs. Linde: You? All of it?

Nora: Two hundred and fifty pounds. What do you say to that?

Mrs. Linde: But Nora, how could you? Did you win a lottery or something?

Nora (scornfully): Lottery? (*Sniffs.*) What would there be to be proud of in that?

Mrs. Linde: But where did you get it from, then?

Nora (hums and smiles secretively): Hm; tra-la-la-la!

Mrs. Linde: You couldn't have borrowed it.

Nora: Oh? Why not?

Mrs. Linde: Well, a wife can't borrow money without her husband's consent.

Nora (tosses her head): Ah, but when a wife has a little business sense, and knows how to be clever —

Mrs. Linde: But Nora, I simply don't understand —

Nora: You don't have to. No one has said I borrowed the money. I could have got it in some other way. (*Throws herself back on the sofa.*) I could have got it from an admirer. When a girl's as pretty as I am —

Mrs. Linde: Nora, you're crazy!

Nora: You're dying of curiosity now, aren't you, Christine?

Mrs. Linde: Nora dear, you haven't done anything foolish?

Nora (sits up again): Is it foolish to save one's husband's life?

Mrs. Linde: I think it's foolish if without his knowledge you —

Nora: But the whole point was that he mustn't know! Great heavens, don't you see? He hadn't to know how dangerously ill he was. I was the one they told that his life was in danger and that only going to a warm climate could save him. Do you suppose I didn't try to think of other ways of getting him down there? I told him how wonderful it would be for me to go abroad like other young wives; I cried and prayed; I asked him to remember my condition, and said he ought to be nice and tender to me; and then I suggested he might quite easily borrow the money. But then he got almost angry with me, Christine. He said I was frivolous, and that it was his duty as a husband not to pander to my moods and caprices — I think that's what he called them. Well, well, I thought, you've got to be saved somehow. And then I thought of a way —

Mrs. Linde: But didn't your husband find out from your father that the money hadn't come from him?

Nora: No, never. Papa died just then. I'd thought of letting him into the plot and asking him not to tell. But since he was so ill — ! And as things turned out, it didn't become necessary.

Mrs. Linde: And you've never told your husband about this?

Nora: For heaven's sake, no! What an idea! He's frightfully strict about such matters. And besides — he's so proud of being a *man* — it'd be so painful and humiliating for him to know that he owed anything to me. It'd completely wreck our relationship. This life we have built together would no longer exist.

Mrs. Linde: Will you never tell him?

Nora (thoughtfully, half-smiling): Yes — some time, perhaps. Years from now, when I'm no longer pretty. You mustn't laugh! I mean of course, when Torvald no longer loves me as he does now; when it no longer amuses him to see me dance and dress up and play the fool for him. Then it might be useful to have something up my sleeve. (*Breaks off.*) Stupid, stupid, stupid! That time will never come. Well, what do you think of my big secret, Christine? I'm not completely useless, am I? Mind you, all this has caused me a frightful lot of worry. It hasn't been easy for me to meet my obligations punctually. In case you don't know, in the world of business there are things called quarterly installments and interest, and they're a terrible problem to cope with. So I've had to scrape a little here and save a little there as best I can. I haven't been able to save much on the housekeeping money, because Torvald likes to live well; and I couldn't let the children go short of clothes — I couldn't take anything out of what he gives me for them. The poor little angels!

Mrs. Linde: So you've had to stint yourself, my poor Nora?

Nora: Of course. Well, after all, it was my problem. Whenever Torvald gave me money to buy myself new clothes, I never used more than half of it; and I always bought what was cheapest and plainest. Thank heaven anything suits me, so that Torvald's never noticed. But it made me a bit sad sometimes, because it's lovely to wear pretty clothes. Don't you think?

Mrs. Linde: Indeed it is.

Nora: And then I've found one or two other sources of income. Last winter I managed to get a lot of copying to do. So I shut myself away and wrote every evening, late into the night. Oh, I often got so tired, so tired. But it was great fun, though, sitting there working and earning money. It was almost like being a man.

Mrs. Linde: But how much have you managed to pay off like this?

Nora: Well, I can't say exactly. It's awfully difficult to keep an exact check on these kind of transactions. I only know I've paid everything I've managed to scrape together. Sometimes I really didn't know where to turn. (*Smiles.*) Then I'd sit here and imagine some rich old gentleman had fallen in love with me —

Mrs. Linde: What! What gentleman?

Nora: Silly! And that now he'd died and when they opened his will it said in big letters: "Everything I possess is to be paid forthwith to my beloved Mrs. Nora Helmer in cash."

Mrs. Linde: But, Nora dear, who was this gentleman?

Nora: Great heavens, don't you understand? There wasn't any old gentleman; he was just something I used to dream up as I sat here evening after evening wondering how on earth I could raise some money. But what does it matter? The old bore can stay imaginary as far as I'm concerned, because now I don't have to worry any longer! (*Jumps up.*) Oh, Christine, isn't it wonderful? I don't have to worry any more! No more troubles! I can play all day with the children, I can fill the house with pretty things, just the way Torvald likes. And, Christine, it'll soon be spring, and the air'll be fresh and the skies blue, — and then perhaps we'll be able to take a little trip somewhere. I shall be able to see the sea again. Oh, yes, yes, it's a wonderful thing to be alive and happy!

The bell rings in the hall.

Mrs. Linde (gets up): You've a visitor. Perhaps I'd better go.

Nora: No, stay. It won't be for me. It's someone for Torvald —

Maid (in the doorway): Excuse me, madam, a gentleman's called who says he wants to speak to the master. But I didn't know — seeing as the doctor's with him —

Nora: Who is this gentleman?

Krogstad (in the doorway): It's me, Mrs. Helmer.

Mrs. Linde starts, composes herself, and turns away to the window.

Nora (takes a step toward him and whispers tensely): You? What is it? What do you want to talk to my husband about?

Krogstad: Business — you might call it. I hold a minor post in the bank, and I hear your husband is to become our new chief —

Nora: Oh — then it isn't — ?

Krogstad: Pure business, Mrs. Helmer. Nothing more.

Nora: Well, you'll find him in his study.

Nods indifferently as she closes the hall door behind him. Then she walks across the room and sees to the stove.

Mrs. Linde: Nora, who was that man?

Nora: A lawyer called Krogstad.

Mrs. Linde: It was him, then.

Nora: Do you know that man?

Mrs. Linde: I used to know him — some years ago. He was a solicitor's clerk in our town, for a while.

Nora: Yes, of course, so he was.

Mrs. Linde: How he's changed!

Nora: He was very unhappily married, I believe.

Mrs. Linde: Is he a widower now?

Nora: Yes, with a lot of children. Ah, now it's alight.

She closes the door of the stove and moves the rocking-chair a little to one side.

Mrs. Linde: He does — various things now, I hear?

Nora: Does he? It's quite possible — I really don't know. But don't let's talk about business. It's so boring.

Dr. Rank enters from Helmer's study.

Rank (still in the doorway): No, no, my dear chap, don't see me out. I'll go and have a word with your wife. (*Closes the door and notices Mrs. Linde.*) Oh, I beg your pardon. I seem to be *de trop* here too.

Nora: Not in the least. (*Introduces them.*) Dr. Rank. Mrs. Linde.

Rank: Ah! A name I have often heard in this house. I believe I passed you on the stairs as I came up.

Mrs. Linde: Yes. Stairs tire me; I have to take them slowly.

Rank: Oh, have you hurt yourself?

Mrs. Linde: No, I'm just a little run down.

Rank: Ah, is that all? Then I take it you've come to town to cure yourself by a round of parties?

Mrs. Linde: I have come here to find work.

Rank: Is that an approved remedy for being run down?

Mrs. Linde: One has to live, Doctor.

Rank: Yes, people do seem to regard it as a necessity.

Nora: Oh, really, Dr. Rank. I bet you want to stay alive.

Rank: You bet I do. However miserable I sometimes feel, I still want to go on being tortured for as long as possible. It's the same with all my patients; and with people who are morally sick, too. There's a moral cripple in with Helmer at this very moment —

Mrs. Linde (softly): Oh!

Nora: Whom do you mean?

Rank: Oh, a lawyer fellow called Krogstad — you wouldn't know him. He's crippled all right; morally twisted. But even he started off by announcing, as though it were a matter of enormous importance, that he had to live.

Nora: Oh? What did he want to talk to Torvald about?

Rank: I haven't the faintest idea. All I heard was something about the bank.

Nora: I didn't know that Krog — that this man Krogstad had any connection with the bank.

Rank: Yes, he's got some kind of job down there. (*To Mrs. Linde.*) I wonder if in your part of the world you too have a species of human being that spends its time fussing around trying to smell out moral corruption? And when they find a case they give him some nice, comfortable position so that they can keep a good watch on him. The healthy ones just have to lump it.

Mrs. Linde: But surely it's the sick who need care most?

Rank (shrugs his shoulders): Well, there we have it. It's that attitude that's turning human society into a hospital.

Nora, lost in her own thoughts, laughs half to herself and claps her hands.

Rank: Why are you laughing? Do you really know what society is?

Nora: What do I care about society? I think it's a bore. I was laughing at something else — something frightfully funny. Tell me, Dr. Rank — will everyone who works at the bank come under Torvald now?

Rank: Do you find that particularly funny?

Nora (smiles and hums): Never you mind! Never you mind! (*Walks around the room.*) Yes, I find it very amusing to think that we — I mean, Torvald — has obtained so much influence over so many people. (*Takes the paper bag from her pocket.*) Dr. Rank, would you like a small macaroon?

Rank: Macaroons! I say! I thought they were forbidden here.

Nora: Yes, well, these are some Christine gave me.

Mrs. Linde: What? I — ?

Nora: All right, all right, don't get frightened. You weren't to know Torvald had forbidden them. He's afraid they'll ruin my teeth. But, dash it — for once — ! Don't you agree, Dr. Rank? Here! (*Pops a macaroon into his mouth.*) You too, Christine. And I'll have one too. Just a little one. Two at the most.

(*Begins to walk round again.*) Yes, now I feel really, really happy. Now there's just one thing in the world I'd really love to do.

Rank: Oh? And what is that?

Nora: Just something I'd love to say to Torvald.

Rank: Well, why don't you say it?

Nora: No, I daren't. It's too dreadful.

Mrs. Linde: Dreadful?

Rank: Well, then, you'd better not. But you can say it to us. What is it you'd so love to say to Torvald?

Nora: I've the most extraordinary longing to say: "Bloody hell!"

Rank: Are you mad?

Mrs. Linde: My dear Nora — !

Rank: Say it. Here he is.

Nora (hiding the bag of macaroons): Ssh! Ssh!

Helmer, with his overcoat on his arm and his hat in his hand, enters from his study.

Nora (goes to meet him): Well, Torvald dear, did you get rid of him?

Helmer: Yes, he's just gone.

Nora: May I introduce you — ? This is Christine. She's just arrived in town.

Helmer: Christine — ? Forgive me, but I don't think —

Nora: Mrs. Linde, Torvald dear. Christine Linde.

Helmer: Ah. A childhood friend of my wife's, I presume?

Mrs. Linde: Yes, we knew each other in earlier days.

Nora: And imagine, now she's traveled all this way to talk to you.

Helmer: Oh?

Mrs. Linde: Well, I didn't really —

Nora: You see, Christine's frightfully good at office work, and she's mad to come under some really clever man who can teach her even more than she knows already —

Helmer: Very sensible, madam.

Nora: So when she heard you'd become head of the bank — it was in her local paper — she came here as quickly as she could and — Torvald, you will, won't you? Do a little something to help Christine? For my sake?

Helmer: Well, that shouldn't be impossible. You are a widow, I take it, Mrs. Linde?

Mrs. Linde: Yes.

Helmer: And you have experience of office work?

Mrs. Linde: Yes, quite a bit.

Helmer: Well then, it's quite likely I may be able to find some job for you —

Nora (claps her hands): You see, you see!

Helmer: You've come at a lucky moment, Mrs. Linde.

Mrs. Linde: Oh, how can I ever thank you — ?

Helmer: There's absolutely no need. (*Puts on his overcoat.*) But now I'm afraid I must ask you to excuse me —

Rank: Wait. I'll come with you.

He gets his fur coat from the hall and warms it at the stove.

Nora: Don't be long, Torvald dear.

Helmer: I'll only be an hour.

Nora: Are you going too, Christine?

Mrs. Linde (puts on her outdoor clothes): Yes, I must start to look round for a room.

Helmer: Then perhaps we can walk part of the way together.

Nora (helps her): It's such a nuisance we're so cramped here — I'm afraid we can't offer to —

Mrs. Linde: Oh, I wouldn't dream of it. Goodbye, Nora dear, and thanks for everything.

Nora: Au revoir. You'll be coming back this evening, of course. And you too, Dr. Rank. What? If you're well enough? Of course you'll be well enough. Wrap up warmly, though.

They go out, talking, into the hall. Children's voices are heard from the stairs.

Nora: Here they are! Here they are!

She runs out and opens the door. Anne-Marie, the nurse, enters with the children.

Nora: Come in, come in! (*Stoops down and kisses them.*) Oh, my sweet darlings — ! Look at them, Christine! Aren't they beautiful?

Rank: Don't stand here chattering in this draught!

Helmer: Come, Mrs. Linde. This is for mothers only.

Dr. Rank, Helmer, and Mrs. Linde go down the stairs. The nurse brings the children into the room. Nora follows, and closes the door to the hall.

Nora: How well you look! What red cheeks you've got! Like apples and roses! (*The children answer her inaudibly as she talks to them.*) Have you had fun? That's splendid. You gave Emmy and Bob a ride on the sledge? What, both together? I say! What a clever boy you are, Ivar! Oh, let me hold her for a moment, Anne-Marie! My sweet little baby doll! (*Takes the smallest child from the nurse and dances with her.*) Yes, yes, Mummy will dance with Bob too. What? Have you been throwing snowballs? Oh,

I wish I'd been there! No, don't — I'll undress them myself,
Anne-Marie. No, please let me; it's such fun. Go inside and
warm yourself; you look frozen. There's some hot coffee on
the stove. (*The nurse goes into the room on the left. Nora takes off
the children's outdoor clothes and throws them anywhere while they
all chatter simultaneously.*) What? A big dog ran after you? But
he didn't bite you? No, dogs don't bite lovely little baby dolls.
Leave those parcels alone, Ivar. What's in them? Ah, wouldn't
you like to know! No, no; it's nothing nice. Come on, let's play
a game. What shall we play? Hide and seek. Yes, let's play
hide and seek. Bob shall hide first. You want me to? All right,
let me hide first.

*Nora and the children play around the room, and in the adjacent room to the left,
laughing and shouting. At length Nora hides under the table. The children rush
in, look, but cannot find her. Then they hear her half-stifled laughter, run to the
table, lift up the cloth, and see her. Great excitement. She crawls out as though to
frighten them. Further excitement. Meanwhile, there has been a knock on the door
leading from the hall, but no one has noticed it. Now the door is half-opened and
Krogstad enters. He waits for a moment; the game continues.*

Krogstad: Excuse me, Mrs. Helmer —
Nora (turns with a stifled cry and half jumps up): Oh! What do you
want?
Krogstad: I beg your pardon; the front door was ajar. Someone
must have forgotten to close it.
Nora (gets up): My husband is not at home, Mr. Krogstad.
Krogstad: I know.
Nora: Well, what do want here, then?
Krogstad: A word with you.
Nora: With — ? (*To the children, quietly.*) Go inside to Anne-Marie.
What? No, the strange gentleman won't do anything to hurt
Mummy. When he's gone we'll start playing again.

She takes the children into the room on the left and closes the door behind them.

Nora (uneasy, tense): You want to speak to me?
Krogstad: Yes.
Nora: Today? But it's not the first of the month yet.
Krogstad: No, it is Christmas Eve. Whether or not you have a
merry Christmas depends on you.
Nora: What do you want? I can't give you anything today —
Krogstad: We won't talk about that for the present. There's some-
thing else. You have a moment to spare?
Nora: Oh, yes. Yes, I suppose so; though —

Krogstad: Good. I was sitting in the café down below and I saw your husband cross the street —

Nora: Yes.

Krogstad : With a lady.

Nora: Well?

Krogstad: Might I be so bold as to ask: was not that lady a Mrs. Linde?

Nora: Yes.

Krogstad: Recently arrived in town?

Nora: Yes, today.

Krogstad: She is a good friend of yours, is she not?

Nora: Yes, she is. But I don't see —

Krogstad: I used to know her too once.

Nora: I know.

Krogstad: Oh? You've discovered that. Yes, I thought you would. Well then, may I ask you a straight question: is Mrs. Linde to be employed at the bank?

Nora: How dare you presume to cross-examine me, Mr. Krogstad? You, one of my husband's employees? But since you ask, you shall have an answer. Yes, Mrs. Linde is to be employed by the bank. And I arranged it, Mr. Krogstad. Now you know.

Krogstad: I guessed right, then.

Nora (walks up and down the room): Oh, one has a little influence, you know. Just because one's a woman it doesn't necessarily mean that — When one is in a humble position, Mr. Krogstad, one should think twice before offending someone who — hm —

Krogstad: — who has influence?

Nora: Precisely.

Krogstad (changes his tone): Mrs. Helmer, will you have the kindness to use your influence on my behalf?

Nora: What? What do you mean?

Krogstad: Will you be so good as to see that I keep my humble position at the bank?

Nora: What do you mean? Who is thinking of removing you from your position?

Krogstad: Oh, you don't need to play innocent with me. I realize it can't be very pleasant for your friend to risk bumping into me; and now I also realize whom I have to thank for being hounded out like this.

Nora: But I assure you —

Krogstad: Look, let's not beat about the bush. There's still time, and I'd advise you to use your influence to stop it.

Nora: But, Mr. Krogstad, I have no influence!

Krogstad: Oh? I thought you just said —

Nora: But I didn't mean it like that! I? How on earth could you imagine that I would have any influence over my husband?

Krogstad: Oh, I've known your husband since we were students together. I imagine he has his weaknesses like other married men.

Nora: If you speak impertinently of my husband, I shall show you the door.

Krogstad: You're a bold woman, Mrs. Helmer.

Nora: I'm not afraid of you any longer. Once the New Year is in, I'll soon be rid of you.

Krogstad (more controlled): Now listen to me, Mrs. Helmer. If I'm forced to, I shall fight for my little job at the bank as I would fight for my life.

Nora: So it sounds.

Krogstad: It isn't just the money; that's the last thing I care about. There's something else — well, you might as well know. It's like this, you see. You know of course, as everyone else does, that some years ago I committed an indiscretion.

Nora: I think I did hear something —

Krogstad: It never came into court; but from that day, every opening was barred to me. So I turned my hand to the kind of business you know about. I had to do something; and I don't think I was one of the worst. But now I want to give up all that. My sons are growing up; for their sake, I must try to regain what respectability I can. This job in the bank was the first step on the ladder. And now your husband wants to kick me off that ladder back into the dirt.

Nora: But my dear Mr. Krogstad, it simply isn't in my power to help you.

Krogstad: You say that because you don't want to help me. But I have the means to make you.

Nora: You don't mean you'd tell my husband that I owe you money?

Krogstad: And if I did?

Nora: That'd be a filthy trick! (*Almost in tears.*) This secret that is my pride and my joy — that he should hear about it in such a filthy, beastly way — hear about it from you! It'd involve me in the most dreadful unpleasantness —

Krogstad: Only — unpleasantness?

Nora (vehemently): All right, do it! You'll be the one who'll suffer. It'll show my husband the kind of man you are, and then you'll never keep your job.

Krogstad: I asked you whether it was merely domestic unpleasantness you were afraid of.

Nora: If my husband hears about it, he will of course immediately
pay you whatever is owing. And then we shall have nothing
more to do with you.

Krogstad (takes a step closer): Listen, Mrs. Helmer. Either you've a
bad memory or else you know very little about financial
transactions. I had better enlighten you.

Nora: What do you mean?

Krogstad: When your husband was ill, you came to me to borrow
two hundred and fifty pounds.

Nora: I didn't know anyone else.

Krogstad: I promised to find that sum for you —

Nora: And you did find it.

Krogstad: I promised to find that sum for you on certain conditions. You were so worried about your husband's illness
and so keen to get the money to take him abroad that I
don't think you bothered much about the details. So it won't
be out of place if I refresh your memory. Well — I promised
to get you the money in exchange for an I.O.U., which I
drew up.

Nora: Yes, and which I signed.

Krogstad: Exactly. But then I added a few lines naming your
father as security for the debt. This paragraph was to be
signed by your father.

Nora: Was to be? He did sign it.

Krogstad: I left the date blank for your father to fill in when he
signed this paper. You remember, Mrs. Helmer?

Nora: Yes, I think so.

Krogstad: Then I gave you back this I.O.U. for you to post to your
father. Is that not correct?

Nora: Yes.

Krogstad: And of course you posted it at once; for within five or
six days you brought it along to me with your father's signature on it. Whereupon I handed you the money.

Nora: Yes, well. Haven't I repaid the installments as agreed?

Krogstad: Mm — yes, more or less. But to return to what we were
speaking about — that was a difficult time for you just then,
wasn't it, Mrs. Helmer?

Nora: Yes, it was.

Krogstad: And your father was very ill, if I am not mistaken.

Nora: He was dying.

Krogstad: He did in fact die shortly afterwards?

Nora: Yes.

Krogstad: Tell me, Mrs. Helmer, do you by any chance remember the date of your father's death? The day of the month, I mean.

Nora: Papa died on the twenty-ninth of September.

Krogstad: Quite correct; I took the trouble to confirm it. And that leaves me with a curious little problem — (*Takes out a paper.*) — which I simply cannot solve.

Nora: Problem? I don't see —

Krogstad: The problem, Mrs. Helmer, is that your father signed this paper three days after his death.

Nora: What? I don't understand —

Krogstad: Your father died on the twenty-ninth of September. But look at this. Here your father has dated his signature the second of October. Isn't that a curious little problem, Mrs. Helmer? (*Nora is silent.*) Can you suggest any explanation? (*She remains silent.*) And there's another curious thing. The words "second of October" and the year are written in a hand which is not your father's, but which I seem to know. Well, there's a simple explanation to that. Your father could have forgotten to write in the date when he signed, and someone else could have added it before the news came of his death. There's nothing criminal about that. It's the signature itself I'm wondering about. It *is* genuine, I suppose, Mrs. Helmer? It was your father who wrote his name here?

Nora (after a short silence, throws back her head and looks defiantly at him): No, it was not. It was I who wrote Papa's name there.

Krogstad: Look, Mrs. Helmer, do you realize this is a dangerous admission?

Nora: Why? You'll get your money.

Krogstad: May I ask you a question? Why didn't you send this paper to your father?

Nora: I couldn't. Papa was very ill. If I'd asked him to sign this, I'd have had to tell him what the money was for. But I couldn't have told him in his condition that my husband's life was in danger. I couldn't have done that!

Krogstad: Then you would have been wiser to have given up your idea of a holiday.

Nora: But I couldn't! It was to save my husband's life. I couldn't put it off.

Krogstad: But didn't it occur to you that you were being dishonest towards me?

Nora: I couldn't bother about that. I didn't care about you. I hated you because of all the beastly difficulties you'd put in my way when you knew how dangerously ill my husband was.

Krogstad: Mrs. Helmer, you evidently don't appreciate exactly what you have done. But I can assure you that it is no bigger nor worse a crime than the one I once committed, and thereby ruined my whole social position.

Nora: You? Do you expect me to believe that you would have taken a risk like that to save your wife's life?

Krogstad: The law does not concern itself with motives.

Nora: Then the law must be very stupid.

Krogstad: Stupid or not, if I show this paper to the police, you will be judged according to it.

Nora: I don't believe that. Hasn't a daughter the right to shield her father from worry and anxiety when he's old and dying? Hasn't a wife the right to save her husband's life? I don't know much about the law, but there must be something somewhere that says that such things are allowed. You ought to know about that, you're meant to be a lawyer, aren't you? You can't be a very good lawyer, Mr. Krogstad.

Krogstad: Possibly not. But business, the kind of business we two have been transacting — I think you'll admit I understand something about that? Good. Do as you please. But I tell you this. If I get thrown into the gutter for a second time, I shall take you with me.

He bows and goes out through the hall.

Nora (stands for a moment in thought, then tosses her head): What nonsense! He's trying to frighten me! I'm not that stupid. (*Busies herself gathering together the children's clothes; then she suddenly stops.*) But — ? No, it's impossible. I did it for love, didn't I?

Children (in the doorway, left). Mummy, the strange gentleman's gone out into the street.

Nora: Yes, yes, I know. But don't talk to anyone about the strange gentleman. You hear? Not even to Daddy.

Children: No, Mummy. Will you play with us again now?

Nora: No, no. Not now.

Children: Oh but, Mummy, you promised!

Nora: I know, but I can't just now. Go back to the nursery. I've a lot to do. Go away, my darlings, go away. (*She pushes them gently into the other room, and closes the door behind them. She sits on the sofa, takes up her embroidery, stitches for a few moments, but soon stops.*) No! (*Throws the embroidery aside, gets up, goes to the door leading to the hall, and calls.*) Helen! Bring in the Christmas tree! (*She goes to the table on the left and opens the drawer in it; then pauses again.*) No, but it's utterly impossible!

Maid (enters with the tree): Where shall I put it, madam?

Nora: There, in the middle of the room.
Maid: Will you be wanting anything else?
Nora: No, thank you, I have everything I need.

The maid puts down the tree and goes out.

Nora (busy decorating the tree): Now — candles here — and flowers here. That loathsome man! Nonsense, nonsense, there's nothing to be frightened about. The Christmas tree must be beautiful. I'll do everything that you like, Torvald. I'll sing for you, dance for you —

Helmer, with a bundle of papers under his arm, enters.

Nora: Oh — are you back already?
Helmer: Yes. Has anyone been here?
Nora: Here? No.
Helmer: That's strange. I saw Krogstad come out of the front door.
Nora: Did you? Oh yes, that's quite right — Krogstad was here for a few minutes.
Helmer: Nora, I can tell from your face, he's been here and asked you to put in a good word for him.
Nora: Yes.
Helmer: And you were to pretend you were doing it of your own accord? You weren't going to tell me he'd been here? He asked you to do that too, didn't he?
Nora: Yes, Torvald. But —
Helmer: Nora, Nora! And you were ready to enter into such a conspiracy? Talking to a man like that, and making him promises — and then, on top of it all, to tell me an untruth!
Nora: An untruth?
Helmer: Didn't you say no one had been here? (*Wags his finger.*) My little songbird must never do that again. A songbird must have a clean beak to sing with; otherwise she'll start twittering out of tune. (*Puts his arm round her waist.*) Isn't that the way we want things? Yes, of course it is. (*Lets go of her.*) So let's hear no more about that. (*Sits down in front of the stove.*) Ah, how cozy and peaceful it is here. (*Glances for a few moments at his papers.*)
Nora (busy with the tree; after a short silence): Torvald.
Helmer: Yes.
Nora: I'm terribly looking forward to that fancy dress ball at the Stenborgs on Boxing Day.
Helmer: And I'm terribly curious to see what you're going to surprise me with.

Nora: Oh, it's so maddening.

Helmer: What is?

Nora: I can't think of anything to wear. It all seems so stupid and meaningless.

Helmer: So my little Nora's come to that conclusion, has she?

Nora (behind his chair, resting her arms on its back): Are you very busy, Torvald?

Helmer: Oh —

Nora: What are those papers?

Helmer: Just something to do with the bank.

Nora: Already?

Helmer: I persuaded the trustees to give me authority to make certain immediate changes in the staff and organization. I want to have everything straight by the New Year.

Nora: Then that's why this poor man Krogstad —

Helmer: Hm.

Nora (still leaning over his chair, slowly strokes the back of his head): If you hadn't been so busy, I was going to ask you an enormous favor, Torvald.

Helmer: Well, tell me. What was it to be?

Nora: You know I trust your taste more than anyone's. I'm so anxious to look really beautiful at the fancy dress ball. Torvald, couldn't you help me to decide what I shall go as, and what kind of costume I ought to wear?

Helmer: Aha! So little Miss Independent's in trouble and needs a man to rescue her, does she?

Nora: Yes, Torvald. I can't get anywhere without your help.

Helmer: Well, well, I'll give the matter thought. We'll find something.

Nora: Oh, how kind of you! (*Goes back to the tree. Pause.*) How pretty these red flowers look! But, tell me, is it so dreadful, this thing that Krogstad's done?

Helmer: He forged someone else's name. Have you any idea what that means?

Nora: Mightn't he have been forced to do it by some emergency?

Helmer: He probably just didn't think — that's what usually happens. I'm not so heartless as to condemn a man for an isolated action.

Nora: No, Torvald, of course not!

Helmer: Men often succeed in re-establishing themselves if they admit their crime and take their punishment.

Nora: Punishment?

Helmer: But Krogstad didn't do that. He chose to try and trick his way out of it; and that's what has morally destroyed him.

Nora: You think that would — ?

Helmer: Just think how a man with that load on his conscience must always be lying and cheating and dissembling; how he must wear a mask even in the presence of those who are dearest to him, even his own wife and children! Yes, the children. That's the worst danger, Nora.

Nora: Why?

Helmer: Because an atmosphere of lies contaminates and poisons every corner of the home. Every breath that the children draw in such a house contains the germs of evil.

Nora (comes closer behind him): Do you really believe that?

Helmer: Oh, my dear, I've come across it so often in my work at the bar. Nearly all young criminals are the children of mothers who are constitutional liars.

Nora: Why do you say mothers?

Helmer: It's usually the mother; though of course the father can have the same influence. Every lawyer knows that only too well. And yet this fellow Krogstad has been sitting at home all these years poisoning his children with his lies and pretenses. That's why I say that, morally speaking, he is dead. (*Stretches out his hands towards her.*) So my pretty little Nora must promise me not to plead his case. Your hand on it. Come, come, what's this? Give me your hand. There. That's settled, now. I assure you it'd be quite impossible for me to work in the same building as him. I literally feel physically ill in the presence of a man like that.

Nora (draws her hand from his and goes over to the other side of the Christmas tree): How hot it is in here! And I've so much to do.

Helmer (gets up and gathers his papers): Yes, and I must try to get some of this read before dinner. I'll think about your costume too. And I may even have something up my sleeve to hang in gold paper on the Christmas tree. (*Lays his hand on her head.*) My precious little songbird!

He goes into his study and closes the door.

Nora (softly, after a pause): It's nonsense. It must be. It's impossible. It *must* be impossible!

Nurse (in the doorway, left): The children are asking if they can come in to Mummy.

Nora: No, no, no; don't let them in! You stay with them, Anne-Marie.

Nurse: Very good, madam. (*Closes the door.*)

Nora (pale with fear): Corrupt my little children — ! Poison my

home! (*Short pause. She throws back her head.*) It isn't true! It
couldn't be true!

ACT II

*The same room. In the corner by the piano the Christmas tree stands, stripped and
disheveled, its candles burned to their sockets. Nora's outdoor clothes lie on the
sofa. She is alone in the room, walking restlessly to and fro. At length she stops by
the sofa and picks up her coat.*

Nora (*drops the coat again*): There's someone coming! (*Goes to the
door and listens.*) No, it's no one. Of course — no one'll come
today, it's Christmas Day. Nor tomorrow. But perhaps — !
(*Opens the door and looks out.*) No. Nothing in the letter-box.
Quite empty. (*Walks across the room.*) Silly, silly. Of course he
won't do anything. It couldn't happen. It isn't possible. Why,
I've three small children.

The Nurse, carrying a large cardboard box, enters from the room on the left.

Nurse: I found those fancy dress clothes at last, madam.
Nora: Thank you. Put them on the table.
Nurse (*does so*): They're all rumpled up.
Nora: Oh, I wish I could tear them into a million pieces!
Nurse: Why, madam! They'll be all right. Just a little patience.
Nora: Yes, of course. I'll go and get Mrs. Linde to help me.
Nurse: What, out again? In this dreadful weather? You'll catch a
    chill, madam.
Nora: Well, that wouldn't be the worst. How are the children?
Nurse: Playing with their Christmas presents, poor little dears.
    But —
Nora: Are they still asking to see me?
Nurse: They're so used to having their Mummy with them.
Nora: Yes, but, Anne-Marie, from now on I shan't be able to
    spend so much time with them.
Nurse: Well, children get used to anything in time.
Nora: Do you think so? Do you think they'd forget their mother if
    she went away from them — for ever?
Nurse: Mercy's sake, madam! For ever!
Nora: Tell me, Anne-Marie — I've so often wondered. How could
    you bear to give your child away — to strangers?
Nurse: But I had to when I came to nurse my little Miss Nora.
Nora: Do you mean you wanted to?
Nurse: When I had the chance of such a good job? A poor girl

what's got into trouble can't afford to pick and choose. That good-for-nothing didn't lift a finger.

Nora: But your daughter must have completely forgotten you.

Nurse: Oh no, indeed she hasn't. She's written to me twice, once when she got confirmed and then again when she got married.

Nora (hugs her): Dear old Anne-Marie, you were a good mother to me.

Nurse: Poor little Miss Nora, you never had any mother but me.

Nora: And if my little ones had no one else, I know you would — no, silly, silly, silly! (*Opens the cardboard box.*) Go back to them, Anne-Marie. Now I must — Tomorrow you'll see how pretty I shall look.

Nurse: Why, there'll be no one at the ball as beautiful as my Miss Nora.

She goes into the room, left.

Nora (begins to unpack the clothes from the box, but soon throws them down again): Oh, if only I dared to go out! If I could be sure no one would come, and nothing would happen while I was away! Stupid, stupid! No one will come. I just mustn't think about it. Brush this muff. Pretty gloves, pretty gloves! Don't think about it, don't think about it! One, two, three, four, five, six — (*Cries.*) Ah — they're coming — !

She begins to run toward the door, but stops uncertainly. Mrs. Linde enters from the hall, where she has been taking off her outdoor clothes.

Nora: Oh, it's you, Christine. There's no one else out there, is there? Oh, I'm so glad you've come.

Mrs. Linde: I hear you were at my room asking for me.

Nora: Yes, I just happened to be passing. I want to ask you to help me with something. Let's sit down here on the sofa. Look at this. There's going to be a fancy dress ball tomorrow night upstairs at Consul Stenborg's, and Torvald wants me to go as a Neapolitan fisher-girl and dance the tarantella. I learned it on Capri.

Mrs. Linde: I say, are you going to give a performance?

Nora: Yes, Torvald says I should. Look, here's the dress. Torvald had it made for me in Italy; but now it's all so torn, I don't know —

Mrs. Linde: Oh, we'll soon put that right; the stitching's just come away. Needle and thread? Ah, here we are.

Nora: You're being awfully sweet.

Mrs. Linde (sews): So you're going to dress up tomorrow, Nora? I must pop over for a moment to see how you look. Oh, but I've completely forgotten to thank you for that nice evening yesterday.

Nora (gets up and walks across the room): Oh, I didn't think it was as nice as usual. You ought to have come to town a little earlier, Christine. . . . Yes, Torvald understands how to make a home look attractive.

Mrs. Linde: I'm sure you do, too. You're not your father's daughter for nothing. But, tell me. Is Dr. Rank always in such low spirits as he was yesterday?

Nora: No, last night it was very noticeable. But he's got a terrible disease; he's got spinal tuberculosis, poor man. His father was a frightful creature who kept mistresses and so on. As a result Dr. Rank has been sickly ever since he was a child — you understand —

Mrs. Linde (puts down her sewing): But, my dear Nora, how on earth did you get to know about such things?

Nora (walks about the room): Oh, don't be silly, Christine — when one has three children, one comes into contact with women who — well, who know about medical matters, and they tell one a thing or two.

Mrs. Linde (sews again; a short silence): Does Dr. Rank visit you every day?

Nora: Yes, every day. He's Torvald's oldest friend, and a good friend to me too. Dr. Rank's almost one of the family.

Mrs. Linde: But, tell me — is he quite sincere? I mean, doesn't he rather say the sort of thing he thinks people want to hear?

Nora: No, quite the contrary. What gave you that idea?

Mrs. Linde: When you introduced me to him yesterday, he said he'd often heard my name mentioned here. But later I noticed your husband had no idea who I was. So how could Dr. Rank — ?

Nora: Yes, that's quite right, Christine. You see, Torvald's so hopelessly in love with me that he wants to have me all to himself — those were his very words. When we were first married, he got quite jealous if I as much as mentioned any of my old friends back home. So naturally, I stopped talking about them. But I often chat with Dr. Rank about that kind of thing. He enjoys it, you see.

Mrs. Linde: Now listen, Nora. In many ways you're still a child; I'm a bit older than you and have a little more experience of the world. There's something I want to say to you. You ought to give up this business with Dr. Rank.

Nora: What business?

Mrs. Linde: Well, everything. Last night you were speaking about this rich admirer of yours who was going to give you money —

Nora: Yes, and who doesn't exist — unfortunately. But what's that got to do with — ?

Mrs. Linde: Is Dr. Rank rich?

Nora: Yes.

Mrs. Linde: And he has no dependents?

Nora: No, no one. But —

Mrs. Linde: And he comes here to see you every day?

Nora: Yes, I've told you.

Mrs. Linde: But how dare a man of his education be so forward?

Nora: What on earth are you talking about?

Mrs. Linde: Oh, stop pretending, Nora. Do you think I haven't guessed who it was who lent you that two hundred pounds?

Nora: Are you out of your mind? How could you imagine such a thing? A friend, someone who comes here every day! Why, that'd be an impossible situation!

Mrs. Linde: Then it really wasn't him?

Nora: No, of course not. I've never for a moment dreamed of — anyway, he hadn't any money to lend then. He didn't come into that till later.

Mrs. Linde: Well, I think that was a lucky thing for you, Nora dear.

Nora: No, I could never have dreamed of asking Dr. Rank — Though I'm sure that if I ever did ask him —

Mrs. Linde: But of course you won't.

Nora: Of course not. I can't imagine that it should ever become necessary. But I'm perfectly sure that if I did speak to Dr. Rank —

Mrs. Linde: Behind your husband's back?

Nora: I've got to get out of this other business; and *that's* been going on behind his back. I've *got* to get out of it.

Mrs. Linde: Yes, well, that's what I told you yesterday. But —

Nora (walking up and down): It's much easier for a man to arrange these things than a woman —

Mrs. Linde: One's own husband, yes.

Nora: Oh, bosh. (*Stops walking.*) When you've completely repaid a debt, you get your I.O.U. back, don't you?

Mrs. Linde: Yes, of course.

Nora: And you can tear it into a thousand pieces and burn the filthy, beastly thing!

Mrs. Linde (looks hard at her, puts down her sewing, and gets up slowly): Nora, you're hiding something from me.

Nora: Can you see that?

Mrs. Linde: Something has happened since yesterday morning. Nora, what is it?

Nora (goes toward her): Christine! (*Listens.*) Ssh! There's Torvald. Would you mind going into the nursery for a few minutes? Torvald can't bear to see sewing around. Anne-Marie'll help you.

Mrs. Linde (gathers some of her things together): Very well. But I shan't leave this house until we've talked this matter out.

She goes into the nursery, left. As she does so, Helmer enters from the hall.

Nora (runs to meet him): Oh, Torvald dear, I've been so longing for you to come back!

Helmer: Was that the dressmaker?

Nora: No, it was Christine. She's helping me mend my costume. I'm going to look rather splendid in that.

Helmer: Yes, that was quite a bright idea of mine, wasn't it?

Nora: Wonderful! But wasn't it nice of me to give in to you?

Helmer (takes her chin in his hand): Nice — to give in to your husband? All right, little silly, I know you didn't mean it like that. But I won't disturb you. I expect you'll be wanting to try it on.

Nora: Are you going to work now?

Helmer: Yes. (*Shows her a bundle of papers.*) Look at these. I've been down to the bank — (*Turns to go into his study.*)

Nora: Torvald.

Helmer (stops): Yes.

Nora: If little squirrel asked you really prettily to grant her a wish —

Helmer: Well?

Nora: Would you grant it to her?

Helmer: First I should naturally have to know what it was.

Nora: Squirrel would do lots of pretty tricks for you if you granted her wish.

Helmer: Out with it, then.

Nora: Your little skylark would sing in every room —

Helmer: My little skylark does that already.

Nora: I'd turn myself into a little fairy and dance for you in the moonlight, Torvald.

Helmer: Nora, it isn't that business you were talking about this morning?

Nora (comes closer): Yes, Torvald — oh, please! I beg of you!

Helmer: Have you really the nerve to bring that up again?

Nora: Yes, Torvald, yes, you must do as I ask! You must let Krogstad keep his place at the bank!

Helmer: My dear Nora, his is the job I'm giving to Mrs. Linde.

Nora: Yes, that's terribly sweet of you. But you can get rid of one of the other clerks instead of Krogstad.

Helmer: Really, you're being incredibly obstinate. Just because you thoughtlessly promised to put in a word for him, you expect me to —

Nora: No, it isn't that, Helmer. It's for your own sake. That man writes for the most beastly newspapers — you said so yourself. He could do you tremendous harm. I'm so dreadfully frightened of him —

Helmer: Oh, I understand. Memories of the past. That's what's frightening you.

Nora: What do you mean?

Helmer: You're thinking of your father, aren't you?

Nora: Yes, yes. Of course. Just think what those dreadful men wrote in the papers about Papa! The most frightful slanders. I really believe it would have lost him his job if the Ministry hadn't sent you down to investigate, and you hadn't been so kind and helpful to him.

Helmer: But my dear little Nora, there's a considerable difference between your father and me. Your father was not a man of unassailable reputation. But I am; and I hope to remain so all my life.

Nora: But no one knows what spiteful people may not dig up. We could be so peaceful and happy now, Torvald — we could be free from every worry — you and I and the children. Oh, please, Torvald, please — !

Helmer: The very fact of your pleading his cause makes it impossible for me to keep him. Everyone at the bank already knows that I intend to dismiss Krogstad. If the rumor got about that the new manager had allowed his wife to persuade him to change his mind —

Nora: Well, what then?

Helmer: Oh, nothing, nothing. As long as my little Miss Obstinate gets her way — Do you expect me to make a laughing-stock of myself before my entire staff — give people the idea that I am open to outside influence? Believe me, I'd soon feel the consequences! Besides — there's something else that makes it impossible for Krogstad to remain in the bank while I am its manager.

Nora: What is that?

Helmer: I might conceivably have allowed myself to ignore his moral obloquies —

Nora: Yes, Torvald, surely?

Helmer: And I hear he's quite efficient at his job. But we — well, we were schoolfriends. It was one of those friendships that one enters into over-hastily and so often comes to regret later in life. I might as well confess the truth. We — well, we're on Christian name terms. And the tactless idiot makes no attempt to conceal it when other people are present. On the contrary, he thinks it gives him the right to be familiar with me. He shows off the whole time, with "Torvald this," and "Torvald that." I can tell you, I find it damned annoying. If he stayed, he'd make my position intolerable.

Nora: Torvald, you can't mean this seriously.

Helmer: Oh? And why not?

Nora: But it's so petty.

Helmer: What did you say? Petty? You think *I* am petty?

Nora: No, Torvald dear, of course you're not. That's just why —

Helmer: Don't quibble! You call my motives petty. Then I must be petty too. Petty! I see. Well, I've had enough of this. (*Goes to the door and calls into the hall.*) Helen!

Nora: What are you going to do?

Helmer (searching among his papers): I'm going to settle this matter once and for all. (*The Maid enters.*) Take this letter downstairs at once. Find a messenger and see that he delivers it. Immediately! The address is on the envelope. Here's the money.

Maid: Very good, sir. (*Goes out with the letter.*)

Helmer (putting his papers in order): There now, little Miss Obstinate.

Nora (tensely): Torvald — what was in that letter?

Helmer: Krogstad's dismissal.

Nora: Call her back, Torvald! There's still time. Oh, Torvald, call her back! Do it for my sake — for your own sake — for the children! Do you hear me, Torvald? Please do it! You don't realize what this may do to us all!

Helmer: Too late.

Nora: Yes. Too late.

Helmer: My dear Nora, I forgive you this anxiety. Though it is a bit of an insult to me. Oh, but it is! Isn't it an insult to imply that I should be frightened by the vindictiveness of a depraved hack journalist? But I forgive you, because it so charmingly testifies to the love you bear me. (*Takes her in his arms.*) Which is as it should be, my own dearest Nora. Let what will happen, happen. When the real crisis comes, you will not find me lacking in strength or courage. I am man enough to bear the burden for us both.

Nora (fearfully): What do you mean?

Helmer: The whole burden, I say —

Nora (calmly): I shall never let you do that.

Helmer: Very well. We shall share it, Nora — as man and wife. And that is as it should be. (*Caresses her.*) Are you happy now? There, there, there; don't look at me with those frightened little eyes. You're simply imagining things. You go ahead now and do your tarantella, and get some practice on that tambourine. I'll sit in my study and close the door. Then I won't hear anything, and you can make all the noise you want. (*Turns in the doorway.*) When Dr. Rank comes, tell him where to find me. (*He nods to her, goes into his room with his papers, and closes the door.*)

Nora (desperate with anxiety, stands as though transfixed, and whispers): He said he'd do it. He will do it. He will do it, and nothing'll stop him. No, never that. I'd rather anything. There must be some escape — Some way out — ! (*The bell rings in the hall.*) Dr. Rank — ! Anything but that! Anything, I don't care — !

She passes her hand across her face, composes herself, walks across, and opens the door to the hall. Dr. Rank is standing there, hanging up his fur coat. During the following scene, it begins to grow dark.

Nora: Good evening, Dr. Rank. I recognized your ring. But you mustn't go to Torvald yet. I think he's busy.

Rank: And — you?

Nora (as he enters the room and she closes the door behind him): Oh, you know very well I've always time to talk to you.

Rank: Thank you. I shall avail myself of that privilege as long as I can.

Nora: What do you mean by that? As long as you *can?*

Rank: Yes. Does that frighten you?

Nora: Well, it's rather a curious expression. Is something going to happen?

Rank: Something I've been expecting to happen for a long time. But I didn't think it would happen quite so soon.

Nora (seizes his arm): What is it? Dr. Rank, you must tell me!

Rank (sits down by the stove): I'm on the way out. And there's nothing to be done about it.

Nora (sighs with relief): Oh, it's you — ?

Rank: Who else? No, it's no good lying to oneself. I am the most wretched of all my patients, Mrs. Helmer. These last few days I've been going through the books of this poor body of mine, and I find I am bankrupt. Within a month I may be rotting up there in the churchyard.

Nora: Ugh, what a nasty way to talk!

Rank: The facts aren't exactly nice. But the worst is that there's so much else that's nasty to come first. I've only one more test to make. When that's done I'll have a pretty accurate idea of when the final disintegration is likely to begin. I want to ask you a favor. Helmer's a sensitive chap, and I know how he hates anything ugly. I don't want him to visit me when I'm in hospital —

Nora: Oh but, Dr. Rank —

Rank: I don't want him there. On any pretext. I shan't have him allowed in. As soon as I know the worst, I'll send you my visiting card with a black cross on it, and then you'll know that the final filthy process has begun.

Nora: Really, you're being quite impossible this evening. And I did hope you'd be in a good mood.

Rank: With death on my hands? And all this to atone for someone else's sin? Is there justice in that? And in every single family, in one way or another, the same merciless law of retribution is at work —

Nora (holds her hands to her ears): Nonsense! Cheer up! Laugh!

Rank: Yes, you're right. Laughter's all the damned thing's fit for. My poor innocent spine must pay for the fun my father had as a gay young lieutenant.

Nora (at the table, left): You mean he was too fond of asparagus and *foie gras?*

Rank: Yes, and truffles too.

Nora: Yes, of course, truffles, yes. And oysters too, I suppose?

Rank: Yes, oysters, oysters. Of course.

Nora: And all that port and champagne to wash them down. It's too sad that all those lovely things should affect one's spine.

Rank: Especially a poor spine that never got any pleasure out of them.

Nora: Oh yes, that's the saddest thing of all.

Rank (looks searchingly at her): Hm —

Nora (after a moment): Why did you smile?

Rank: No, it was you who laughed.

Nora: No, it was you who smiled, Dr. Rank!

Rank (gets up): You're a worse little rogue than I thought.

Nora: Oh, I'm full of stupid tricks today.

Rank: So it seems.

Nora (puts both her hands on his shoulders): Dear, dear Dr. Rank, you mustn't die and leave Torvald and me.

Rank: Oh, you'll soon get over it. Once one is gone, one is soon forgotten.

Nora (looks at him anxiously): Do you believe that?

Rank: One finds replacements, and then —

Nora: Who will find a replacement?

Rank: You and Helmer both will, when I am gone. You seem to have made a start already, haven't you? What was this Mrs. Linde doing here yesterday evening?

Nora: Aha! But surely you can't be jealous of poor Christine?

Rank: Indeed I am. She will be my successor in this house. When I have moved on, this lady will —

Nora: Ssh — don't speak so loud! She's in there!

Rank: Today again? You see!

Nora: She's only come to mend my dress. Good heavens, how unreasonable you are! (*Sits on the sofa.*) Be nice now, Dr. Rank. Tomorrow you'll see how beautifully I shall dance; and you must imagine that I'm doing it just for you. And for Torvald of course; obviously. (*Takes some things out of the box.*) Dr. Rank, sit down here and I'll show you something.

Rank (sits): What's this?

Nora: Look here! Look!

Rank: Silk stockings!

Nora: Flesh-colored. Aren't they beautiful? It's very dark in here now, of course, but tomorrow — No, no, no; only the soles. Oh well, I suppose you can look a bit higher if you want to.

Rank: Hm —

Nora: Why are you looking so critical? Don't you think they'll fit me?

Rank: I can't really give you a qualified opinion on that.

Nora (looks at him for a moment): Shame on you! (*Flicks him on the ear with the stockings.*) Take that. (*Puts them back in the box.*)

Rank: What other wonders are to be revealed to me?

Nora: I shan't show you anything else. You're being naughty.

She hums a little and looks among the things in the box.

Rank (after a short silence): When I sit here like this being so intimate with you, I can't think — I cannot imagine what would have become of me if I had never entered this house.

Nora (smiles): Yes, I think you enjoy being with us, don't you?

Rank (more quietly, looking into the middle distance): And now to have to leave it all —

Nora: Nonsense. You're not leaving us.

Rank (as before): And not to be able to leave even the most wretched token of gratitude behind; hardly even a passing sense of loss; only an empty place, to be filled by the next comer.

Nora: Suppose I were to ask you to — ? No —

Rank: To do what?

Nora: To give me proof of your friendship —

Rank: Yes, yes?

Nora: No, I mean — to do me a very great service —

Rank: Would you really for once grant me that happiness?

Nora: But you've no idea what it is.

Rank: Very well, tell me, then.

Nora: No, but, Dr. Rank, I can't. It's far too much — I want your help and advice, and I want you to do something for me.

Rank: The more the better. I've no idea what it can be. But tell me. You do trust me, don't you?

Nora: Oh, yes, more than anyone. You're my best and truest friend. Otherwise I couldn't tell you. Well then, Dr. Rank — there's something you must help me to prevent. You know how much Torvald loves me — he'd never hesitate for an instant to lay down his life for me —

Rank (leans over towards her): Nora — do you think he is the only one — ?

Nora (with a slight start): What do you mean?

Rank: Who would gladly lay down his life for you?

Nora (sadly): Oh, I see.

Rank: I swore to myself I would let you know that before I go. I shall never have a better opportunity. . . . Well, Nora, now you know that. And now you also know that you can trust me as you can trust nobody else.

Nora (rises; calmly and quietly): Let me pass, please.

Rank (makes room for her but remains seated): Nora —

Nora (in the doorway to the hall): Helen, bring the lamp. (*Goes over to the stove.*) Oh, dear Dr. Rank, this was really horrid of you.

Rank (gets up): That I have loved you as deeply as anyone else has? Was that horrid of me?

Nora: No — but that you should go and tell me. That was quite unnecessary —

Rank: What do you mean? Did you know, then — ?

The Maid enters with the lamp, puts it on the table, and goes out.

Rank: Nora — Mrs. Helmer — I am asking you, did you know this?

Nora: Oh, what do I know, what did I know, what didn't I know — I really can't say. How could you be so stupid, Dr. Rank? Everything was so nice.

Rank: Well, at any rate now you know that I am ready to serve you, body and soul. So — please continue.

Nora (looks at him): After this?

Rank: Please tell me what it is.

Nora: I can't possibly tell you now.

Rank: Yes, yes! You mustn't punish me like this. Let me be allowed to do what I can for you.

Nora: You can't do anything for me now. Anyway, I don't need any help. It was only my imagination — you'll see. Yes, really. Honestly. (*Sits in the rocking-chair, looks at him, and smiles.*) Well, upon my word you *are* a fine gentleman, Dr. Rank. Aren't you ashamed of yourself, now that the lamp's been lit?

Rank: Frankly, no. But perhaps I ought to say — *adieu?*

Nora: Of course not. You will naturally continue to visit us as before. You know quite well how Torvald depends on your company.

Rank: Yes, but you?

Nora: Oh, I always think it's enormous fun having you here.

Rank: That was what misled me. You're a riddle to me, you know. I'd often felt you'd just as soon be with me as with Helmer.

Nora: Well, you see, there are some people whom one loves, and others whom it's almost more fun to be with.

Rank: Oh yes, there's some truth in that.

Nora: When I was at home, of course I loved Papa best. But I always used to think it was terribly amusing to go down and talk to the servants; because they never told me what I ought to do; and they were such fun to listen to.

Rank: I see. So I've taken their place?

Nora (jumps up and runs over to him): Oh, dear, sweet Dr. Rank, I didn't mean that at all. But I'm sure you understand — I feel the same about Torvald as I did about Papa.

Maid (enters from the hall): Excuse me, madam. (*Whispers to her and hands her a visiting card.*)

Nora (glances at the card): Oh! (*Puts it quickly in her pocket.*)

Rank: Anything wrong?

Nora: No, no, nothing at all. It's just something that — it's my new dress.

Rank: What? But your costume is lying over there.

Nora: Oh — that, yes — but there's another — I ordered it specially — Torvald mustn't know —

Rank: Ah, so that's your big secret?

Nora: Yes, yes. Go in and talk to him — he's in his study — keep
him talking for a bit —

Rank: Don't worry. He won't get away from me. (*Goes into Helmer's
study.*)

Nora (to the Maid): Is he waiting in the kitchen?

Maid: Yes, madam, he came up the back way —

Nora: But didn't you tell him I had a visitor?

Maid: Yes, but he wouldn't go.

Nora: Wouldn't go?

Maid: No, madam, not until he'd spoken with you.

Nora: Very well, show him in; but quietly. Helen, you mustn't tell
anyone about this. It's a surprise for my husband.

Maid: Very good, madam. I understand. (*Goes.*)

Nora: It's happening. It's happening after all. No, no, no, it can't
happen, it mustn't happen.

*She walks across and bolts the door of Helmer's study. The Maid opens the door
from the hall to admit Krogstad, and closes it behind him. He is wearing an
overcoat, heavy boots, and a fur cap.*

Nora (goes towards him): Speak quietly. My husband's at home.

Krogstad: Let him hear.

Nora: What do you want from me?

Krogstad: Information.

Nora: Hurry up, then. What is it?

Krogstad: I suppose you know I've been given the sack.

Nora: I couldn't stop it, Mr Krogstad. I did my best for you, but it
didn't help.

Krogstad: Does your husband love you so little? He knows what I
can do to you, and yet he dares to —

Nora: Surely you don't imagine I told him?

Krogstad: No. I didn't really think you had. It wouldn't have been
like my old friend Torvald Helmer to show that much courage —

Nora: Mr. Krogstad, I'll trouble you to speak respectfully of my
husband.

Krogstad: Don't worry, I'll show him all the respect he deserves.
But since you're so anxious to keep this matter hushed up, I
presume you're better informed than you were yesterday of
the gravity of what you've done?

Nora: I've learned more than you could ever teach me.

Krogstad: Yes, a bad lawyer like me —

Nora: What do you want from me?

Krogstad: I just wanted to see how things were with you, Mrs. Helmer. I've been thinking about you all day. Even duns and hack journalists have hearts, you know.

Nora: Show some heart, then. Think of my little children.

Krogstad: Have you and your husband thought of mine? Well, let's forget that. I just wanted to tell you, you don't need to take this business too seriously, I'm not going to take any action, for the present.

Nora: Oh, no — you won't, will you? I knew it.

Krogstad: It can all be settled quite amicably. There's no need for it to become public. We'll keep it among the three of us.

Nora: My husband must never know about this.

Krogstad: How can you stop him? Can you pay the balance of what you owe me?

Nora: Not immediately.

Krogstad: Have you any means of raising the money during the next few days?

Nora: None that I would care to use.

Krogstad: Well, it wouldn't have helped anyway. However much money you offered me now I wouldn't give you back that paper.

Nora: What are you going to do with it?

Krogstad: Just keep it. No one else need ever hear about it. So in case you were thinking of doing anything desperate —

Nora: I am.

Krogstad: Such as running away —

Nora: I am.

Krogstad: Or anything more desperate —

Nora: How did you know?

Krogstad: — just give up the idea.

Nora: How did you know?

Krogstad: Most of us think of that at first. I did. But I hadn't the courage —

Nora (dully): Neither have I.

Krogstad (relieved): It's true, isn't it? You haven't the courage either?

Nora: No. I haven't. I haven't.

Krogstad: It'd be a stupid thing to do anyway. Once the first little domestic explosion is over. . . . I've got a letter in my pocket here addressed to your husband —

Nora: Telling him everything?

Krogstad: As delicately as possible.

Nora (quickly): He must never see that letter. Tear it up. I'll find the money somehow —

Krogstad: I'm sorry, Mrs. Helmer, I thought I'd explained —

Nora: Oh, I don't mean the money I owe you. Let me know how much you want from my husband, and I'll find it for you.

Krogstad: I'm not asking your husband for money.

Nora: What do you want, then?

Krogstad: I'll tell you. I want to get on my feet again, Mrs. Helmer. I want to get to the top. And your husband's going to help me. For eighteen months now my record's been clean. I've been in hard straits all that time; I was content to fight my way back inch by inch. Now I've been chucked back into the mud, and I'm not going to be satisfied with just getting back my job. I'm going to get to the top, I tell you. I'm going to get back into the bank, and it's going to be higher up. Your husband's going to create a new job for me —

Nora: He'll never do that!

Krogstad: Oh, yes he will. I know him. He won't dare to risk a scandal. And once I'm in there with him, you'll see! Within a year I'll be his right-hand man. It'll be Nils Krogstad who'll be running that bank, not Torvald Helmer!

Nora: That will never happen.

Krogstad: Are you thinking of — ?

Nora: Now I *have* the courage.

Krogstad: Oh, you can't frighten me. A pampered little pretty like you —

Nora: You'll see! You'll see!

Krogstad: Under the ice? Down in the cold, black water? And then, in the spring, to float up again, ugly, unrecognizable, hairless — ?

Nora: You can't frighten me.

Krogstad: And you can't frighten me. People don't do such things, Mrs. Helmer. And anyway, what'd be the use? I've got him in my pocket.

Nora: But afterwards? When I'm no longer — ?

Krogstad: Have you forgotten that then your reputation will be in my hands? (*She looks at him speechlessly.*) Well, I've warned you. Don't do anything silly. When Helmer's read my letter, he'll get in touch with me. And remember, it's your husband who's forced me to act like this. And for that I'll never forgive him. Goodbye, Mrs. Helmer. (*He goes out through the hall.*)

Nora (runs to the hall door, opens it a few inches, and listens): He's going. He's not going to give him the letter. Oh, no, no, it couldn't possibly happen. (*Opens the door a little wider.*) What's he doing? Standing outside the front door. He's not going downstairs. Is he changing his mind? Yes, he — !

A letter falls into the letter-box. Krogstad's footsteps die away down the stairs.

Nora (with a stifled cry, runs across the room towards the table by the sofa. A pause): In the letter-box. (*Steals timidly over towards the hall door.*) There it is! Oh, Torvald, Torvald! Now we're lost!

Mrs. Linde (enters from the nursery with Nora's costume): Well, I've done the best I can. Shall we see how it looks — ?

Nora (whispers hoarsely): Christine, come here.

Mrs. Linde (throws the dress on the sofa): What's wrong with you? You look as though you'd seen a ghost!

Nora: Come here. Do you see that letter? There — look — through the glass of the letter-box.

Mrs. Linde: Yes, yes, I see it.

Nora: That letter's from Krogstad —

Mrs. Linde: Nora! It was Krogstad who lent you the money!

Nora: Yes. And now Torvald's going to discover everything.

Mrs. Linde: Oh, believe me, Nora, it'll be best for you both.

Nora: You don't know what's happened. I've committed a forgery —

Mrs. Linde: But, for heaven's sake — !

Nora: Christine, all I want is for you to be my witness.

Mrs. Linde: What do you mean? Witness what?

Nora: If I should go out of my mind — and it might easily happen —

Mrs. Linde: Nora!

Nora: Or if anything else should happen to me — so that I wasn't here any longer —

Mrs. Linde: Nora, Nora, you don't know what you're saying!

Nora: If anyone should try to take the blame, and say it was all his fault — you understand — ?

Mrs. Linde: Yes, yes — but how can you think — ?

Nora: Then you must testify that it isn't true, Christine. I'm not mad — I know exactly what I'm saying — and I'm telling you, no one else knows anything about this. I did it entirely on my own. Remember that.

Mrs. Linde: All right. But I simply don't understand —

Nora: Oh, how could you understand? A — miracle — is about to happen.

Mrs. Linde: Miracle?

Nora: Yes. A miracle. But it's so frightening, Christine. It *mustn't* happen, not for anything in the world.

Mrs. Linde: I'll go over and talk to Krogstad.

Nora: Don't go near him. He'll only do something to hurt you.

Mrs. Linde: Once upon a time he'd have done anything for my sake.

Nora: He?

Mrs. Linde: Where does he live?

Nora: Oh, how should I know — ? Oh, yes, wait a moment — ! (*Feels in her pocket.*) Here's his card. But the letter, the letter — !

Helmer (from his study, knocks on the door): Nora!

Nora (cries in alarm): What is it?

Helmer: Now, now, don't get alarmed. We're not coming in; you've closed the door. Are you trying on your costume?

Nora: Yes, yes — I'm trying on my costume. I'm going to look so pretty for you, Torvald.

Mrs. Linde (who has been reading the card): Why, he lives just around the corner.

Nora: Yes; but it's no use. There's nothing to be done now. The letter's lying there in the box.

Mrs. Linde: And your husband has the key?

Nora: Yes, he always keeps it.

Mrs. Linde: Krogstad must ask him to send the letter back unread. He must find some excuse —

Nora: But Torvald always opens the box at just about this time —

Mrs. Linde: You must stop him. Go in and keep him talking. I'll be back as quickly as I can.

She hurries out through the hall.

Nora (goes over to Helmer's door, opens it and peeps in): Torvald!

Helmer (offstage): Well, may a man enter his own drawing-room again? Come on, Rank, now we'll see what — (*In the doorway.*) But what's this?

Nora: What, Torvald dear?

Helmer: Rank's been preparing me for some great transformation scene.

Rank (in the doorway): So I understood. But I seem to have been mistaken.

Nora: Yes, no one's to be allowed to see me before tomorrow night.

Helmer: But, my dear Nora, you look quite worn out. Have you been practicing too hard?

Nora: No, I haven't practiced at all yet.

Helmer: Well, you must.

Nora: Yes, Torvald, I must, I know. But I can't get anywhere without your help. I've completely forgotten everything.

Helmer: Oh, we'll soon put that to rights.

Nora: Yes, help me, Torvald. Promise me you will? Oh, I'm so nervous. All those people — ! You must forget everything except me this evening. You mustn't think of business — I won't even let you touch a pen. Promise me, Torvald?

Helmer: I promise. This evening I shall think of nothing but you — my poor, helpless little darling. Oh, there's just one thing I must see to — (*Goes towards the hall door.*)

Nora: What do you want out there?

Helmer: I'm only going to see if any letters have come.

Nora: No, Torvald, no!

Helmer: Why, what's the matter?

Nora: Torvald, I beg you. There's nothing there.

Helmer: Well, I'll just make sure.

He moves towards the door. Nora runs to the piano and plays the first bars of the tarantella.

Helmer (at the door, turns): Aha!

Nora: I can't dance tomorrow if I don't practice with you now.

Helmer (goes over to her): Are you really so frightened, Nora dear?

Nora: Yes, terribly frightened. Let me start practicing now, at once — we've still time before dinner. Oh, do sit down and play for me, Torvald dear. Correct me, lead me, the way you always do.

Helmer: Very well, my dear, if you wish it.

He sits down at the piano. Nora seizes the tambourine and a long multi-colored shawl from the cardboard box, wraps the latter hastily around her, then takes a quick leap into the center of the room.

Nora: Play for me! I want to dance!

Helmer plays and Nora dances. Dr. Rank stands behind Helmer at the piano and watches her.

Helmer (as he plays): Slower, slower!

Nora: I can't!

Helmer: Not so violently, Nora.

Nora: I must!

Helmer (stops playing): No, no, this won't do at all.

Nora (laughs and swings her tambourine): Isn't that what I told you?

Rank: Let me play for her.

Helmer (gets up): Yes, would you? Then it'll be easier for me to show her.

Rank sits down at the piano and plays. Nora dances more and more wildly. Helmer has stationed himself by the stove and tries repeatedly to correct her, but she seems not to hear him. Her hair works loose and falls over her shoulders; she ignores it and continues to dance. Mrs. Linde enters.

Mrs. Linde (stands in the doorway as though tongue-tied): Ah — !

Nora (as she dances): Oh, Christine, we're having such fun!

Helmer: But, Nora darling, you're dancing as if your life depended on it.

Nora: It does.

Helmer: Rank, stop it! This is sheer lunacy. Stop it, I say!

Rank ceases playing. Nora suddenly stops dancing.

Helmer (goes over to her): I'd never have believed it. You've forgotten everything I taught you.

Nora (throws away the tambourine): You see!

Helmer: I'll have to show you every step.

Nora: You see how much I need you! You must show me every step of the way. Right to the end of the dance. Promise me you will, Torvald?

Helmer: Never fear, I will.

Nora: You mustn't think about anything but me — today or tomorrow. Don't open any letters — don't even open the letterbox —

Helmer: Aha, you're still worried about that fellow —

Nora: Oh, yes, yes, him too.

Helmer: Nora, I can tell from the way you're behaving, there's a letter from him already lying there.

Nora: I don't know. I think so. But you mustn't read it now. I don't want anything ugly to come between us till it's all over.

Rank (quietly, to Helmer): Better give her her way.

Helmer (puts his arm round her): My child shall have her way. But tomorrow night, when your dance is over —

Nora: Then you will be free.

Maid (appears in the doorway, right): Dinner is served, madam.

Nora: Put out some champagne, Helen.

Maid: Very good, madam. (*Goes.*)

Helmer: I say! What's this, a banquet?

Nora: We'll drink champagne until dawn! (*Calls.*) And, Helen! Put out some macaroons! Lots of macaroons — for once!

Helmer (takes her hands in his): Now, now, now. Don't get so excited. Where's my little songbird, the one I know?

Nora: All right. Go and sit down — and you too, Dr. Rank. I'll be with you in a minute. Christine, you must help me put my hair up.

Rank (quietly, as they go): There's nothing wrong, is there? I mean, she isn't — er — expecting — ?

Helmer: Good heavens no, my dear chap. She just gets scared like a child sometimes — I told you before —

They go out right.

Nora: Well?

Mrs. Linde: He's left town.

Nora: I saw it from your face.

Mrs. Linde: He'll be back tomorrow evening. I left a note for him.

Nora: You needn't have bothered. You can't stop anything now. Anyway, it's wonderful really, in a way — sitting here and waiting for the miracle to happen.

Mrs. Linde: Waiting for what?

Nora: Oh, you wouldn't understand. Go in and join them. I'll be with you in a moment.

Mrs. Linde goes into the dining-room.

Nora (stands for a moment as though collecting herself. Then she looks at her watch): Five o'clock. Seven hours till midnight. Then another twenty-four hours till midnight tomorrow. And then the tarantella will be finished. Twenty-four and seven? Thirty-one hours to live.

Helmer (appears in the doorway, right): What's happened to my little songbird?

Nora (runs to him with her arms wide): Your songbird is here!

ACT III

The same room. The table which was formerly by the sofa has been moved into the center of the room; the chairs surround it as before. The door to the hall stands open. Dance music can be heard from the floor above. Mrs. Linde is seated at the table, absent-mindedly glancing through a book. She is trying to read, but seems unable to keep her mind on it. More than once she turns and listens anxiously towards the front door.

Mrs. Linde (looks at her watch): Not here yet. There's not much time left. Please God he hasn't — ! (*Listens again.*) Ah, here he is. (*Goes out into the hall and cautiously opens the front door. Footsteps can be heard softly ascending the stairs. She whispers.*) Come in. There's no one here.

Krogstad (in the doorway): I found a note from you at my lodgings. What does this mean?

Mrs. Linde: I must speak with you.

Krogstad: Oh? And must our conversation take place in this house?

Mrs. Linde: We couldn't meet at my place; my room has no separate entrance. Come in. We're quite alone. The maid's asleep, and the Helmers are at the dance upstairs.

Krogstad (comes into the room): Well, well! So the Helmers are dancing this evening? Are they indeed?

Mrs. Linde: Yes. why not?

Krogstad: True enough. Why not?

Mrs. Linde: Well, Krogstad. You and I must have a talk together.

Krogstad: Have we two anything further to discuss?

Mrs. Linde: We have a great deal to discuss.

Krogstad: I wasn't aware of it.

Mrs. Linde: That's because you've never really understood me.

Krogstad: Was there anything to understand? It's the old story, isn't it — a woman chucking a man because something better turns up?

Mrs. Linde: Do you really think I'm so utterly heartless? You think it was easy for me to give you up?

Krogstad: Wasn't it?

Mrs. Linde: Oh, Nils, did you really believe that?

Krogstad: Then why did you write to me the way you did?

Mrs. Linde: I had to. Since I had to break with you, I thought it my duty to destroy all the feelings you had for me.

Krogstad (clenches his fists): So that was it. And you did this for money!

Mrs. Linde: You mustn't forget I had a helpless mother to take care of, and two little brothers. We couldn't wait for you, Nils. It would have been so long before you'd had enough to support us.

Krogstad: Maybe. But you had no right to cast me off for someone else.

Mrs. Linde: Perhaps not. I've often asked myself that.

Krogstad (more quietly): When I lost you, it was just as though all solid ground had been swept from under my feet. Look at me. Now I am a shipwrecked man, clinging to a spar.

Mrs. Linde: Help may be near at hand.

Krogstad: It was near. But then you came, and stood between it and me.

Mrs. Linde: I didn't know, Nils. No one told me till today that this job I'd found was yours.

Krogstad: I believe you, since you say so. But now you know, won't you give it up?

Mrs. Linde: No — because it wouldn't help you even if I did.

Krogstad: Wouldn't it? I'd do it all the same.

Mrs. Linde: I've learned to look at things practically. Life and poverty have taught me that.

Krogstad: And life has taught me to distrust fine words.

Mrs. Linde: Then it's taught you a useful lesson. But surely you still believe in actions?

Krogstad: What do you mean?

Mrs. Linde: You said you were like a shipwrecked man clinging to a spar.

Krogstad: I have good reason to say it.

Mrs. Linde: I'm in the same position as you. No one to care about, no one to care for.

Krogstad: You made your own choice.

Mrs. Linde: I had no choice — then.

Krogstad: Well?

Mrs. Linde: Nils, suppose we two shipwrecked souls could join hands?

Krogstad: What are you saying?

Mrs. Linde: Castaways have a better chance of survival together than on their own.

Krogstad: Christine!

Mrs. Linde: Why do you suppose I came to this town?

Krogstad: You mean — you came because of me?

Mrs. Linde: I must work if I'm to find life worth living. I've always worked, for as long as I can remember; it's been the greatest joy of my life — my only joy. But now I'm alone in the world, and I feel so dreadfully lost and empty. There's no joy in working just for oneself. Oh, Nils, give me something — someone — to work for.

Krogstad: I don't believe all that. You're just being hysterical and romantic. You want to find an excuse for self-sacrifice.

Mrs. Linde: Have you ever known me to be hysterical?

Krogstad: You mean you really — ? Is it possible? Tell me — you know all about my past?

Mrs. Linde: Yes.

Krogstad: And you know what people think of me here?

Mrs. Linde: You said just now that with me you might have become a different person.

Krogstad: I know I could have.

Mrs. Linde: Couldn't it still happen?

Krogstad: Christine — do you really mean this? Yes — you do —
   I see it in your face. Have you really the courage — ?
Mrs. Linde: I need someone to be a mother to; and your children
   need a mother. And you and I need each other. I believe in
   you, Nils. I am afraid of nothing — with you.
Krogstad (clasps her hands): Thank you, Christine — thank you!
   Now I shall make the world believe in me as you do! Oh —
   but I'd forgotten —
Mrs. Linde (listens): Ssh! The tarantella! Go quickly, go!
Krogstad: Why? What is it?
Mrs. Linde: You hear that dance? As soon as it's finished, they'll
   be coming down.
Krogstad: All right, I'll go. It's no good, Christine. I'd forgotten —
   you don't know what I've just done to the Helmers.
Mrs. Linde: Yes, Nils. I know.
Krogstad: And yet you'd still have the courage to — ?
Mrs. Linde: I know what despair can drive a man like you to.
Krogstad: Oh, if only I could undo this!
Mrs. Linde: You can. Your letter is still lying in the box.
Krogstad: Are you sure?
Mrs. Linde: Quite sure. But —
Krogstad (looks searchingly at her): Is that why you're doing this?
   You want to save your friend at any price? Tell me the truth.
   Is that the reason?
Mrs. Linde: Nils, a woman who has sold herself once for the sake
   of others doesn't make the same mistake again.
Krogstad: I shall demand my letter back.
Mrs. Linde: No, no.
Krogstad: Of course I shall. I shall stay here till Helmer comes
   down. I'll tell him he must give me back my letter — I'll say
   it was only to do with my dismissal, and that I don't want him
   to read it —
Mrs. Linde: No, Nils, you mustn't ask for that letter back.
Krogstad: But — tell me — wasn't that the real reason you asked
   me to come here?
Mrs. Linde: Yes — at first, when I was frightened. But a day has
   passed since then, and in that time I've seen incredible things
   happen in this house. Helmer must know the truth. This
   unhappy secret of Nora's must be revealed. They must come
   to a full understanding; there must be an end of all these
   shiftings and evasions.
Krogstad: Very well. If you're prepared to risk it. But one thing I
   can do — and at once —

Mrs. Linde (listens): Hurry! Go, go! The dance is over. We aren't safe here another moment.

Krogstad: I'll wait for you downstairs.

Mrs. Linde: Yes, do. You can see me home.

Krogstad: I've never been so happy in my life before!

He goes out through the front door. The door leading from the room into the hall remains open.

Mrs. Linde (tidies the room a little and gets her hat and coat): What a change! Oh, what a change! Someone to work for — to live for! A home to bring joy into! I won't let this chance of happiness slip through my fingers. Oh, why don't they come? (*Listens.*) Ah, here they are. I must get my coat on.

She takes her hat and coat. Helmer's and Nora's voices become audible outside. A key is turned in the lock and Helmer leads Nora almost forcibly into the hall. She is dressed in an Italian costume with a large black shawl. He is in evening dress, with a black cloak.

Nora (still in the doorway, resisting him): No, no, no — not in here! I want to go back upstairs. I don't want to leave so early.

Helmer: But my dearest Nora —

Nora: Oh, please, Torvald, please! Just another hour!

Helmer: Not another minute, Nora, my sweet. You know what we agreed. Come along, now. Into the drawing-room. You'll catch cold if you stay out here.

He leads her, despite her efforts to resist him, gently into the room.

Mrs. Linde: Good evening.

Nora: Christine!

Helmer: Oh, hullo, Mrs. Linde. You still here?

Mrs. Linde: Please forgive me. I did so want to see Nora in her costume.

Nora: Have you been sitting here waiting for me?

Mrs. Linde: Yes. I got here too late, I'm afraid. You'd already gone up. And I felt I really couldn't go back home without seeing you.

Helmer (takes off Nora's shawl): Well, take a good look at her. She's worth looking at, don't you think? Isn't she beautiful, Mrs. Linde?

Mrs. Linde: Oh, yes, indeed —

Helmer: Isn't she unbelievably beautiful? Everyone at the party said so. But dreadfully stubborn she is, bless her pretty little heart. What's to be done about that? Would you believe it, I practically had to use force to get her away!

Nora: Oh, Torvald, you're going to regret not letting me stay — just half an hour longer.

Helmer: Hear that, Mrs. Linde? She dances her tarantella — makes a roaring success — and very well deserved — though possibly a trifle too realistic — more so than was aesthetically necessary, strictly speaking. But never mind that. Main thing is — she had a success — roaring success. Was I going to let her stay on after that and spoil the impression? No, thank you. I took my beautiful little Capri signorina — my capricious little Capricienne, what? — under my arm — a swift round of the ballroom, a curtsey to the company, and, as they say in novels, the beautiful apparition disappeared! An exit should always be dramatic, Mrs. Linde. But unfortunately that's just what I can't get Nora to realize. I say, it's hot in here. (*Throws his cloak on a chair and opens the door to his study.*) What's this? It's dark in here. Ah, yes, of course — excuse me. (*Goes in and lights a couple of candles.*)

Nora (whispers swiftly, breathlessly): Well?

Mrs. Linde (quietly): I've spoken to him.

Nora: Yes?

Mrs. Linde: Nora — you must tell your husband everything.

Nora (dully): I knew it.

Mrs. Linde: You've nothing to fear from Krogstad. But you must tell him.

Nora: I shan't tell him anything.

Mrs. Linde: Then the letter will.

Nora: Thank you, Christine. Now I know what I must do. Ssh!

Helmer (returns): Well, Mrs. Linde, finished admiring her?

Mrs. Linde: Yes. Now I must say good night.

Helmer: Oh, already? Does this knitting belong to you?

Mrs. Linde (takes it): Thank you, yes. I nearly forgot it.

Helmer: You knit, then?

Mrs. Linde: Why, yes.

Helmer: Know what? You ought to take up embroidery.

Mrs. Linde: Oh? Why?

Helmer: It's much prettier. Watch me, now. You hold the embroidery in your left hand, like this, and then you take the needle in your right hand and go in and out in a slow, easy movement — like this. I am right, aren't I?

Mrs. Linde: Yes, I'm sure —

Helmer: But knitting, now — that's an ugly business — can't help it. Look — arms all huddled up — great clumsy needles going up and down — makes you look like a damned China-man. I say, that really was a magnificent champagne they served us.

Mrs. Linde: Well, good night, Nora. And stop being stubborn. Remember!

Helmer: Quite right, Mrs. Linde!

Mrs. Linde: Good night, Mr. Helmer.

Helmer (accompanies her to the door): Good night, good night! I hope you'll manage to get home all right? I'd gladly — but you haven't far to go, have you? Good night, good night. (*She goes. He closes the door behind her and returns.*) Well, we've got rid of her at last. Dreadful bore that woman is!

Nora: Aren't you very tired, Torvald?

Helmer: No, not in the least.

Nora: Aren't you sleepy?

Helmer: Not a bit. On the contrary, I feel extraordinarily exhila-rated. But what about you? Yes, you look very sleepy and tired.

Nora: Yes, I am very tired. Soon I shall sleep.

Helmer: You see, you see! How right I was not to let you stay longer!

Nora: Oh, you're always right, whatever you do.

Helmer (kisses her on the forehead): Now my little songbird's talking just like a real big human being. I say, did you notice how cheerful Rank was this evening?

Nora: Oh? Was he? I didn't have a chance to speak with him.

Helmer: I hardly did. But I haven't seen him in such a jolly mood for ages. (*Looks at her for a moment, then comes closer.*) I say, it's nice to get back to one's home again, and be all alone with you. Upon my word, you're a distractingly beautiful young woman.

Nora: Don't look at me like that, Torvald!

Helmer: What, not look at my most treasured possession? At all this wonderful beauty that's mine, mine alone, all mine.

Nora (goes round to the other side of the table): You mustn't talk to me like that tonight.

Helmer (follows her): You've still the tarantella in your blood, I see. And that makes you even more desirable. Listen! Now the other guests are beginning to go. (*More quietly.*) Nora — soon the whole house will be absolutely quiet.

Nora: Yes, I hope so.

Helmer: Yes, my beloved Nora, of course you do! Do you know — when I'm out with you among other people like we were tonight, do you know why I say so little to you, why I keep so aloof from you, and just throw you an occasional glance? Do you know why I do that? It's because I pretend to myself that you're my secret mistress, my clandestine little sweetheart, and that nobody knows there's anything at all between us.

Nora: Oh, yes, yes, yes — I know you never think of anything but me.

Helmer: And then when we're about to go, and I wrap the shawl round your lovely young shoulders, over this wonderful curve of your neck — then I pretend to myself that you are my young bride, that we've just come from the wedding, that I'm taking you to my house for the first time — that, for the first time, I am alone with you — quite alone with you, as you stand there young and trembling and beautiful. All evening I've had no eyes for anyone but you. When I saw you dance the tarantella, like a huntress, a temptress, my blood grew hot, I couldn't stand it any longer! That was why I seized you and dragged you down here with me —

Nora: Leave me, Torvald! Get away from me! I don't want all this.

Helmer: What? Now, Nora, you're joking with me. Don't want, don't want — ? Aren't I your husband — ?

There is a knock on the front door.

Nora (starts): What was that?

Helmer (goes towards the hall): Who is it?

Rank (outside): It's me. May I come in for a moment?

Helmer (quietly, annoyed): Oh, what does he want now? (*Calls.*) Wait a moment. (*Walks over and opens the door.*) Well! Nice of you not to go by without looking in.

Rank: I thought I heard your voice, so I felt I had to say goodbye. (*His eyes travel swiftly around the room.*) Ah, yes — these dear rooms, how well I know them. What a happy, peaceful home you two have.

Helmer: You seemed to be having a pretty happy time yourself upstairs.

Rank: Indeed I did. Why not? Why shouldn't one make the most of this world? As much as one can, and for as long as one can. The wine was excellent —

Helmer: Especially the champagne.

Rank: You noticed that too? It's almost incredible how much I managed to get down.

Nora: Torvald drank a lot of champagne too, this evening.

Rank: Oh?

Nora: Yes. It always makes him merry afterwards.

Rank: Well, why shouldn't a man have a merry evening after a well-spent day?

Helmer: Well-spent? Oh, I don't know that I can claim that.

Rank (slaps him across the back): I can, though, my dear fellow!

Nora: Yes, of course, Dr. Rank — you've been carrying out a scientific experiment today, haven't you?

Rank: Exactly.

Helmer: Scientific experiment! Those are big words for my little Nora to use!

Nora: And may I congratulate you on the finding?

Rank: You may indeed.

Nora: It was good, then?

Rank: The best possible finding — both for the doctor and the patient. Certainty.

Nora (quickly): Certainty?

Rank: Absolute certainty. So aren't I entitled to have a merry evening after that?

Nora: Yes, Dr. Rank. You were quite right to.

Helmer: I agree. Provided you don't have to regret it tomorrow.

Rank: Well, you never get anything in this life without paying for it.

Nora: Dr. Rank — you like masquerades, don't you?

Rank: Yes, if the disguises are sufficiently amusing.

Nora: Tell me. What shall we two wear at the next masquerade?

Helmer: You little gadabout! Are you thinking about the next one already?

Rank: We two? Yes, I'll tell you. You must go as the Spirit of Happiness —

Helmer: You try to think of a costume that'll convey that.

Rank: Your wife need only appear as her normal, everyday self —

Helmer: Quite right! Well said! But what are you going to be? Have you decided that?

Rank: Yes, my dear friend. I have decided that.

Helmer: Well?

Rank: At the next masquerade, I shall be invisible.

Helmer: Well, that's a funny idea.

Rank: There's a big, black hat — haven't you heard of the invisible hat? Once it's over your head, no one can see you any more.

Helmer (represses a smile): Ah yes, of course.

Rank: But I'm forgetting what I came for. Helmer, give me a cigar. One of your black Havanas.

Helmer: With the greatest pleasure. (*Offers him the box.*)

Rank (takes one and cuts off the tip): Thank you.

Nora (strikes a match): Let me give you a light.

Rank: Thank you. (*She holds out the match for him. He lights his cigar.*) And now — goodbye.

Helmer: Goodbye, my dear chap, goodbye.

Nora: Sleep well, Dr. Rank.

Rank: Thank you for that kind wish.

Nora: Wish me the same.

Rank: You? Very well — since you ask. Sleep well. And thank you for the light. (*He nods to them both and goes.*)

Helmer (quietly): He's been drinking too much.

Nora (abstractedly): Perhaps.

Helmer takes his bunch of keys from his pocket and goes out into the hall.

Nora: Torvald, what do you want out there?

Helmer: I must empty the letter-box. It's absolutely full. There'll be no room for the newspapers in the morning.

Nora: Are you going to work tonight?

Helmer: You know very well I'm not. Hullo, what's this? Some-one's been at the lock.

Nora: At the lock — ?

Helmer: Yes, I'm sure of it. Who on earth — ? Surely not one of the maids? Here's a broken hairpin. Nora, it's yours —

Nora (quickly): Then it must have been the children.

Helmer: Well, you'll have to break them of that habit. Hm, hm. Ah, that's done it. (*Takes out the contents of the box and calls into the kitchen.*) Helen! Put out the light on the staircase. (*Comes back into the drawing-room with the letters in his hand and closes the door to the hall.*) Look at this! You see how they've piled up? (*Glances through them.*) What on earth's this?

Nora (at the window): The letter! Oh, no, Torvald, no!

Helmer: Two visiting cards — from Rank.

Nora: From Dr. Rank?

Helmer (looks at them): Peter Rank, M.D. They were on top. He must have dropped them in as he left.

Nora: Has he written anything on them?

Helmer: There's a black cross above his name. Look. Rather grue-some, isn't it? It looks just as though he was announcing his death.

Nora: He is.

Helmer: What? Do you know something? Has he told you anything?

Nora: Yes. When these cards come, it means he's said goodbye to us. He wants to shut himself up in his house and die.

Helmer: Ah, poor fellow. I knew I wouldn't be seeing him for much longer. But so soon — ! And now he's going to slink away and hide like a wounded beast.

Nora: When the time comes, it's best to go silently. Don't you think so, Torvald?

Helmer (walks up and down): He was so much a part of our life. I can't realize that he's gone. His suffering and loneliness seemed to provide a kind of dark background to the happy sunlight of our marriage. Well, perhaps it's best this way. For him, anyway. (*Stops walking.*) And perhaps for us too, Nora. Now we have only each other. (*Embraces her.*) Oh, my beloved wife — I feel as though I could never hold you close enough. Do you know, Nora, often I wish some terrible danger might threaten you, so that I could offer my life and my blood, everything, for your sake.

Nora (tears herself loose and says in a clear, firm voice): Read your letters now, Torvald.

Helmer: No, no. Not tonight. Tonight I want to be with you, my darling wife —

Nora: When your friend is about to die — ?

Helmer: You're right. This news has upset us both. An ugliness has come between us; thoughts of death and dissolution. We must try to forget them. Until then — you go to your room; I shall go to mine.

Nora (throws her arms round his neck): Good night, Torvald! Good night!

Helmer (kisses her on the forehead): Good night, my darling little songbird. Sleep well, Nora. I'll go and read my letters.

He goes into the study with the letters in his hand, and closes the door.

Nora (wild-eyed, fumbles around, seizes Helmer's cloak, throws it round herself and whispers quickly, hoarsely): Never see him again. Never. Never. Never. (*Throws the shawl over her head.*) Never see the children again. Them too. Never. Never. Oh — the icy black water! Oh — that bottomless — that — ! Oh, if only it were all over! Now he's got it — he's reading it. Oh, no, no! Not yet! Goodbye, Torvald! Goodbye, my darlings!

She turns to run into the hall. As she does so, Helmer throws open his door and stands there with an open letter in his hand.

Helmer: Nora!

Nora (shrieks): Ah — !

Helmer: What is this? Do you know what is in this letter?

Nora: Yes, I know. Let me go! Let me go!

Helmer (holds her back): Go? Where?

Nora (tries to tear herself loose): You mustn't try to save me, Torvald!

Helmer (staggers back): Is it true? Is it true, what he writes? Oh, my God! No, no — it's impossible, it can't be true!

Nora: It *is* true. I've loved you more than anything else in the world.

Helmer: Oh, don't try to make silly excuses.

Nora (takes a step towards him): Torvald —

Helmer: Wretched woman! What have you done?

Nora: Let me go! You're not going to suffer for my sake. I won't let you!

Helmer: Stop being theatrical. (*Locks the front door.*) You're going to stay here and explain yourself. Do you understand what you've done? Answer me! Do you understand?

Nora (looks unflinchingly at him and, her expression growing colder, says): Yes. Now I am beginning to understand.

Helmer (walking around the room): Oh, what a dreadful awakening! For eight whole years — she who was my joy and my pride — a hypocrite, a liar — worse, worse — a criminal! Oh, the hideousness of it! Shame on you, shame!

Nora is silent and stares unblinkingly at him.

Helmer (stops in front of her): I ought to have guessed that something of this sort would happen. I should have foreseen it. All your father's recklessness and instability — be quiet! — I repeat, all your father's recklessness and instability he has handed on to you. No religion, no morals, no sense of duty! Oh, how I have been punished for closing my eyes to his faults! I did it for your sake. And now you reward me like this.

Nora: Yes. Like this.

Helmer: Now you have destroyed all my happiness. You have ruined my whole future. Oh, it's too dreadful to contemplate! I am in the power of a man who is completely without scruples. He can do what he likes with me, demand what he pleases, order me to do anything — I dare not disobey him. I am condemned to humiliation and ruin simply for the weakness of a woman.

Nora: When I am gone from this world, you will be free.

Helmer: Oh, don't be melodramatic. Your father was always ready with that kind of remark. How would it help me if you were "gone from this world," as you put it? It wouldn't assist me in the slightest. He can still make all the facts public; and if he does, I may quite easily be suspected of having been an accomplice in your crime. People may think that I was behind it — that it was I who encouraged you! And for all this I have to thank you, you whom I have carried on my hands through all the years of our marriage! Now do you realize what you've done to me?

Nora (coldly calm): Yes.

Helmer: It's so unbelievable I can hardly credit it. But we must try to find some way out. Take off that shawl. Take it off, I say! I must try to buy him off somehow. This thing must be hushed up at any price. As regards our relationship — we must appear to be living together just as before. Only *appear*, of course. You will therefore continue to reside here. That is understood. But the children shall be taken out of your hands. I dare no longer entrust them to you. Oh, to have to say this to the woman I once loved so dearly — and whom I still — ! Well, all that must be finished. Henceforth there can be no question of happiness; we must merely strive to save what shreds and tatters — (*The front door bell rings. Helmer starts.*) What can that be? At this hour? Surely not — ? He wouldn't — ? Hide yourself, Nora. Say you're ill.

Nora does not move. Helmer goes to the door of the room and opens it. The Maid is standing half-dressed in the hall.

Maid: A letter for madam.

Helmer: Give it to me. (*Seizes the letter and shuts the door.*) Yes, it's from him. You're not having it. I'll read this myself.

Nora: Read it.

Helmer (by the lamp): I hardly dare to. This may mean the end for us both. No, I must know. (*Tears open the letter hastily; reads a few lines; looks at a piece of paper which is enclosed with it; utters a cry of joy.*) Nora! (*She looks at him questioningly.*) Nora! No — I must read it once more. Yes, yes, it's true! I am saved! Nora, I am saved!

Nora: What about me?

Helmer: You too, of course. We're both saved, you and I. Look! He's returning your I.O.U. He writes that he is sorry for what has happened — a happy accident has changed his life — oh, what does it matter what he writes? We are saved, Nora! No one can harm you now. Oh, Nora, Nora — no, first let me destroy this filthy thing. Let me see — ! (*Glances at the I.O.U.*) No, I don't want to look at it. I shall merely regard the whole business as a dream. (*He tears the I.O.U. and both letters into pieces, throws them into the stove, and watches them burn.*) There. Now they're destroyed. He wrote that ever since Christmas Eve you've been — oh, these must have been three dreadful days for you, Nora.

Nora: Yes. It's been a hard fight.

Helmer: It must have been terrible — seeing no way out except — no, we'll forget the whole sordid business. We'll just be happy and go on telling ourselves over and over again: "It's over! It's over!" Listen to me, Nora. You don't seem to realize. It's over! Why are you looking so pale? Ah, my poor little Nora, I understand. You can't believe that I have forgiven you. But I have, Nora. I swear it to you. I have forgiven you everything. I know that what you did you did for your love of me.

Nora: That is true.

Helmer: You have loved me as a wife should love her husband. It was simply that in your inexperience you chose the wrong means. But do you think I love you any the less because you don't know how to act on your own initiative? No, no. Just lean on me. I shall counsel you. I shall guide you. I would not be a true man if your feminine helplessness did not make you doubly attractive in my eyes. You mustn't mind the hard words I said to you in those first dreadful moments when my whole world seemed to be tumbling about my ears. I have forgiven you, Nora. I swear it to you; I have forgiven you.

Nora: Thank you for your forgiveness.

She goes out through the door, right.

Helmer: No, don't go — (*Looks in.*) What are you doing there?

Nora (offstage): Taking off my fancy dress.

Helmer (by the open door): Yes, do that. Try to calm yourself and get your balance again, my frightened little songbird. Don't be afraid. I have broad wings to shield you. (*Begins to walk around near the door.*) How lovely and peaceful this little home of ours is, Nora. You are safe here; I shall watch over you like a

hunted dove which I have snatched unharmed from the claws
of the falcon. Your wildly beating little heart shall find peace
with me. It will happen, Nora; it will take time, but it will
happen, believe me. Tomorrow all this will seem quite different. Soon everything will be as it was before. I shall no
longer need to remind you that I have forgiven you; your own
heart will tell you that it is true. Do you really think I could
ever bring myself to disown you, or even to reproach you?
Ah, Nora, you don't understand what goes on in a husband's
heart. There is something indescribably wonderful and satisfying for a husband in knowing that he has forgiven his
wife — forgiven her unreservedly, from the bottom of his
heart. It means that she has become his property in a double
sense; he has, as it were, brought her into the world anew; she
is now not only his wife but also his child. From now on that
is what you shall be to me, my poor, helpless, bewildered
little creature. Never be frightened of anything again, Nora.
Just open your heart to me. I shall be both your will and your
conscience. What's this? Not in bed? Have you changed?

Nora (in her everyday dress): Yes, Torvald. I've changed.

Helmer: But why now — so late — ?

Nora: I shall not sleep tonight.

Helmer: But, my dear Nora —

Nora (looks at her watch): It isn't that late. Sit down here, Torvald.
You and I have a lot to talk about.

She sits down on one side of the table.

Helmer: Nora, what does this mean? You look quite drawn —

Nora: Sit down. It's going to take a long time. I've a lot to say to
you.

Helmer (sits down on the other side of the table): You alarm me, Nora. I
don't understand you.

Nora: No, that's just it. You don't understand me. And I've never
understood you — until this evening. No, don't interrupt
me. Just listen to what I have to say. You and I have got to face
facts, Torvald.

Helmer: What do you mean by that?

Nora (after a short silence): Doesn't anything strike you about the
way we're sitting here?

Helmer: What?

Nora: We've been married for eight years. Does it occur to you
that this is the first time that we two, you and I, man and wife,
have ever had a serious talk together?

Helmer: Serious? What do you mean, serious?

Nora: In eight whole years — no, longer — ever since we first met — we have never exchanged a serious word on a serious subject.

Helmer: Did you expect me to drag you into all my worries — worries you couldn't possibly have helped me with?

Nora: I'm not talking about worries. I'm simply saying that we have never sat down seriously to try to get to the bottom of anything.

Helmer: But, my dear Nora, what on earth has that got to do with you?

Nora: That's just the point. You have never understood me. A great wrong has been done to me, Torvald. First by Papa, and then by you.

Helmer: What? But we two have loved you more than anyone in the world!

Nora (shakes her head): You have never loved me. You just thought it was fun to be in love with me.

Helmer: Nora, what kind of a way is this to talk?

Nora: It's the truth, Torvald. When I lived with Papa, he used to tell me what he thought about everything, so that I never had any opinions but his. And if I did have any of my own, I kept them quiet, because he wouldn't have liked them. He called me his little doll, and he played with me just the way I played with my dolls. Then I came here to live in your house —

Helmer: What kind of a way is that to describe our marriage?

Nora (undisturbed): I mean, then I passed from Papa's hands into yours. You arranged everything the way you wanted it, so that I simply took over your taste in everything — or pretended I did — I don't really know — I think it was a little of both — first one and then the other. Now I look back on it, it's as if I've been living here like a pauper, from hand to mouth. I performed tricks for you, and you gave me food and drink. But that was how you wanted it. You and Papa have done me a great wrong. It's your fault that I have done nothing with my life.

Helmer: Nora, how can you be so unreasonable and ungrateful? Haven't you been happy here?

Nora: No; never. I used to think I was; but I haven't ever been happy.

Helmer: Not — not happy?

Nora: No. I've just had fun. You've always been very kind to me. But our home has never been anything but a playroom. I've been your doll-wife, just as I used to be Papa's doll-child. And the children have been my dolls. I used to think it was fun when you came in and played with me, just as they think it's fun when I go in and play games with them. That's all our marriage has been, Torvald.

Helmer: There may be a little truth in what you say, though you exaggerate and romanticize. But from now on it'll be different. Playtime is over. Now the time has come for education.

Nora: Whose education? Mine or the children's?

Helmer: Both yours and the children's, my dearest Nora.

Nora: Oh, Torvald, you're not the man to educate me into being the right wife for you.

Helmer: How can you say that?

Nora: And what about me? Am I fit to educate the children?

Helmer: Nora!

Nora: Didn't you say yourself a few minutes ago that you dare not leave them in my charge?

Helmer: In a moment of excitement. Surely you don't think I meant it seriously?

Nora: Yes. You were perfectly right. I'm not fitted to educate them. There's something else I must do first. I must educate myself. And you can't help me with that. It's something I must do by myself. That's why I'm leaving you.

Helmer (jumps up): What did you say?

Nora: I must stand on my own feet if I am to find out the truth about myself and about life. So I can't go on living here with you any longer.

Helmer: Nora, Nora!

Nora: I'm leaving you now, at once. Christine will put me up for tonight—

Helmer: You're out of your mind! You can't do this! I forbid you!

Nora: It's no use your trying to forbid me any more. I shall take with me nothing but what is mine. I don't want anything from you, now or ever.

Helmer: What kind of madness is this?

Nora: Tomorrow I shall go home — I mean, to where I was born. It'll be easiest for me to find some kind of a job there.

Helmer: But you're blind! You've no experience of the world —

Nora: I must try to get some, Torvald.

Helmer: But to leave your home, your husband, your children! Have you thought what people will say?

Nora: I can't help that. I only know that I must do this.

Helmer: But this is monstrous! Can you neglect your most sacred duties?

Nora: What do you call my most sacred duties?

Helmer: Do I have to tell you? Your duties towards your husband, and your children.

Nora: I have another duty which is equally sacred.

Helmer: You have not. What on earth could that be?

Nora: My duty towards myself.

Helmer: First and foremost you are a wife and a mother.

Nora: I don't believe that any longer. I believe that I am first and foremost a human being, like you — or anyway, that I must try to become one. I know most people think as you do, Torvald, and I know there's something of the sort to be found in books. But I'm no longer prepared to accept what people say and what's written in books. I must think things out for myself, and try to find my own answer.

Helmer: Do you need to ask where your duty lies in your own home? Haven't you an infallible guide in such matters — your religion?

Nora: Oh, Torvald, I don't really know what religion means.

Helmer: What are you saying?

Nora: I only know what Pastor Hensen told me when I went to confirmation. He explained that religion meant this and that. When I get away from all this and can think things out on my own, that's one of the questions I want to look into. I want to find out whether what Pastor Hensen said was right — or anyway, whether it is right for me.

Helmer: But it's unheard of for so young a woman to behave like this! If religion cannot guide you, let me at least appeal to your conscience. I presume you have some moral feelings left? Or — perhaps you haven't? Well, answer me.

Nora: Oh, Torvald, that isn't an easy question to answer. I simply don't know. I don't know where I am in these matters. I only know that these things mean something quite different to me from what they do to you. I've learned now that certain laws are different from what I'd imagined them to be; but I can't accept that such laws can be right. Has a woman really not the right to spare her dying father pain, or save her husband's life? I can't believe that.

Helmer: You're talking like a child. You don't understand how society works.

Nora: No, I don't. But now I intend to learn. I must try to satisfy myself which is right, society or I.

Helmer: Nora, you're ill; you're feverish. I almost believe you're out of your mind.

Nora: I've never felt so sane and sure in my life.

Helmer: You feel sure that it is right to leave your husband and your children?

Nora: Yes, I do.

Helmer: Then there is only one possible explanation.

Nora: What?

Helmer: That you don't love me any longer.

Nora: No, that's exactly it.

Helmer: Nora! How can you say this to me?

Nora: Oh, Torvald, it hurts me terribly to have to say it, because you've always been so kind to me. But I can't help it. I don't love you any longer.

Helmer (controlling his emotions with difficulty): And you feel quite sure about this too?

Nora: Yes, absolutely sure. That's why I can't go on living here any longer.

Helmer: Can you also explain why I have lost your love?

Nora: Yes, I can. It happened this evening, when the miracle failed to happen. It was then that I realized you weren't the man I'd thought you to be.

Helmer: Explain more clearly. I don't understand you.

Nora: I've waited so patiently, for eight whole years — well, good heavens, I'm not such a fool as to suppose that miracles occur every day. Then this dreadful thing happened to me, and then I *knew:* "Now the miracle will take place!" When Krogstad's letter was lying out there, it never occurred to me for a moment that you would let that man trample over you. I *knew* that you would say to him: "Publish the facts to the world." And when he had done this —

Helmer: Yes, what then? When I'd exposed my wife's name to shame and scandal —

Nora: I was certain that you would step forward and take all the blame on yourself, and say: "I am the one who is guilty!"

Helmer: Nora!

Nora: You're thinking I wouldn't have accepted such a sacrifice from you? No, of course I wouldn't! But what would my world have counted for against yours? That was the miracle I was hoping for, and dreading. And it was to prevent it happening that I wanted to end my life.

Helmer: Nora, I would gladly work for you night and day, and endure sorrow and hardship for your sake. But no man can be expected to sacrifice his honor, even for the person he loves.

Nora: Millions of women have done it.

Helmer: Oh, you think and talk like a stupid child.

Nora: That may be. But you neither think nor talk like the man I could share my life with. Once you'd got over your fright — and you weren't frightened of what might threaten me, but only of what threatened you — once the danger was past, then as far as you were concerned it was exactly as though nothing had happened. I was your little songbird just as before — your doll whom henceforth you would take particular care to protect from the world because she was so weak and fragile. (*Gets up.*) Torvald, in that moment I realized that for eight years I had been living here with a complete stranger, and had borne him three children — ! Oh, I can't bear to think of it! I could tear myself to pieces!

Helmer (sadly): I see it, I see it. A gulf has indeed opened between us. Oh, but Nora — couldn't it be bridged?

Nora: As I am now, I am no wife for you.

Helmer: I have the strength to change.

Nora: Perhaps — if your doll is taken from you.

Helmer: But to be parted — to be parted from you! No, no, Nora, I can't conceive of it happening!

Nora (goes into the room, right): All the more necessary that it should happen.

She comes back with her outdoor things and a small traveling bag, which she puts down on a chair by the table.

Helmer: Nora, Nora, not now! Wait till tomorrow!

Nora (puts on her coat): I can't spend the night in a strange man's house.

Helmer: But can't we live here as brother and sister, then — ?

Nora (fastens her hat): You know quite well it wouldn't last. (*Puts on her shawl.*) Goodbye, Torvald. I don't want to see the children. I know they're in better hands than mine. As I am now, I can be nothing to them.

Helmer: But some time, Nora — some time — ?

Nora: How can I tell? I've no idea what will happen to me.

Helmer: But you are my wife, both as you are and as you will be.

Nora: Listen, Torvald. When a wife leaves her husband's house, as I'm doing now, I'm told that according to the law he is freed of any obligations towards her. In any case, I release you from any such obligations. You mustn't feel bound to me in any way, however small, just as I shall not feel bound to you. We must both be quite free. Here is your ring back. Give me mine.

Helmer: That too?

Nora: That too.

Helmer: Here it is.

Nora: Good. Well, now it's over. I'll leave the keys here. The servants know about everything to do with the house — much better than I do. Tomorrow, when I have left town, Christine will come to pack the things I brought here from home. I'll have them sent on after me.

Helmer: This is the end then! Nora, will you never think of me any more?

Nora: Yes, of course. I shall often think of you and the children and this house.

Helmer: May I write to you, Nora?

Nora: No, never. You mustn't do that.

Helmer: But at least you must let me send you —

Nora: Nothing. Nothing.

Helmer: But if you should need help — ?

Nora: I tell you, no. I don't accept things from strangers.

Helmer: Nora — can I never be anything but a stranger to you?

Nora (picks up her bag): Oh, Torvald! Then the miracle of miracles would have to happen.

Helmer: The miracle of miracles?

Nora: You and I would both have to change so much that — oh, Torvald, I don't believe in miracles any longer.

Helmer: But I want to believe in them. Tell me. We should have to change so much that — ?

Nora: That life together between us two could become a marriage. Goodbye.

She goes out through the hall.

Helmer (sinks down on a chair by the door and buries his face in his hands): Nora! Nora! (*Looks round and gets up.*) Empty! She's gone! (*A hope strikes him.*) The miracle of miracles — ?

The street door is slammed shut downstairs.

2

Imagining Character

In Chapter 1 our point of focus was *feeling*. We worked at constructing feelings, imagining what was taking place in human beings caught up in sharply defined human situations. In this chapter we'll continue to construct feelings but begin practicing another, closely related activity as well. It's the activity of deciding what to make of the imagined human beings who speak or are spoken of in literary texts.

DENISE LEVERTOV   (b. 1923)
The Dogwood

The sink is full of dishes. Oh well.
Ten o'clock, there's no
hot water.
The kitchen floor is unswept, the broom
has been shedding straws. Oh well.   5

The cat is sleeping, Nikolai is sleeping,
Mitch is sleeping, early to bed,
aspirin for a cold. Oh well.

No school tomorrow, someone for lunch,
4 dollars left from the 10 — how did that go?   10
Mostly on food. Oh well.

I could decide
to hear some chamber music
and today I saw — what?
Well, some huge soft deep   15

blackly gazing purple
and red (and pale)
anemones. Does that
take my mind off the dishes?
And dogwood besides.   20
Oh well. Early to bed, and I'll get up
early and put
a shine on everything and write
a letter to Duncan later that will shine too
with moonshine. Can I make it? Oh well.   25

Most of us are pretty well acquainted with the "Oh well" feeling — the inner decision to relax, let up on ourselves, stop stewing about our problems. There's nothing especially tricky about constructing the state of mind behind each of the first four "Oh wells" in Levertov's "The Dogwood." But to bring to life the feeling in the last fourteen lines of the poem, we need a more particularized sense of the person who's talking — awareness of differences between her and others who shrug and say "Oh well."

One noticeable difference is that this person seems a bit more conscious of "Oh well" as a ploy — a mode of escape — than most of us tend to be. The repetitions of the phrase suggest that she sees what she's up to when she uses it, sees that "Oh well" helps her to shed guilt about dishes in the sink or vanished dollars or whatever. A sort of self-serving game, "Oh well" is a means of saying it's better to be easygoing than to be a person full of hang-ups about doing every little job promptly. Realizing that the character in the poem knows all this both about herself and about her own words, we get a clearer sense of her as a person.

But of course there's more to her nature than simply her attitude toward her use of a standard phrase. Several details help us fill out her picture. She's a person who talks to herself. (This poem isn't addressed to outsiders; if it were, we might expect the writer to introduce us to Nikolai, Mitch, and Duncan by specifying her relationship to them.) She's a person who's at once down to earth (can't forget the dishes), highly responsive to beauty (the chamber music, the finely evoked anemones, the dogwood), and inclined to postpone unpleasant jobs (it's ten o'clock and still the sink awaits). She's a person who questions her life not on a global

or highly intense scale, but in terms of daily trade-offs. (Is remembering the dogwood and anemones really enough to pay me
for doing the damned dishes?) And she's a person who, through
her quiet monologue, can manage to cheer herself up, producing
a fresh-start mentality with which to face tomorrow.

A private person, all in all: intelligent, sensitive, modest, not
terribly demanding of others, self-aware, humorous (the self-
teasing "moonshine" in line 25), a shade anxious (but not
driven), a shade flighty (but not scatterbrained). With this much
in the way of a sketch, we can grasp both the resemblances and
the differences between the feelings accompanying an ordinary
"Oh well" and her feelings. By clarifying feeling and character
simultaneously, we decide for ourselves who this person is.

JOHN BERRYMAN   (1914–1972)
Dream Song 14

Life, friends, is boring. We must not say so.
After all, the sky flashes, the great sea yearns,
we ourselves flash and yearn,
and moreover my mother told me as a boy
(repeatingly) "Ever to confess you're bored   5
    means you have no

Inner Resources." I conclude now I have no
inner resources, because I am heavy bored.
Peoples bore me,
literature bores me, especially great literature,   10
Henry bores me, with his plights & gripes
as bad as achilles,

Who loves people and valiant art, which bores me.
And the tranquil hills, & gin, look like a drag
and somehow a dog   15
has taken itself & its tail considerably away
into mountains or sea or sky, leaving
behind: me, wag.

One way of constructing the speaker of this poem is by
comparing his gestures and ways of speaking with those in "The
Dogwood." This speaker is conscious of us, the audience, and

addresses us directly. He deals in grand concepts and large conclusions about "life." He's a self-dramatizer and self-mocker, aggressive and impatient. His self-depreciation ("me, wag" at the
end) is a good deal less gentle than that of the speaker in "The
Dogwood," and he seems, on balance, a critically demanding,
wittily self-important presence. Both these speakers have problems. Both have a developed capacity to see themselves. (Berryman's way in his long series of "Dream Songs" is by projecting
himself as several voices — among them "I," "Henry," and "Mr.
Bore.")

But these speakers' senses of themselves — their ways of taking themselves — are utterly different, as different as Mistress
Damon's (in Hardy's "The Slow Nature," p. 33) is from Richard
Maple's (in Updike's "Snowing in Greenwich Village," p. 19). To
put ourselves in touch with the life of feeling in each poem, we
have to construct the separate, distinct being of each character.

MARSHALING AND
ORGANIZING THE DETAILS

The two essentials for bringing character to life are marshaling the details, images, facts out of which we make up a person
and organizing those details into a pattern expressing our convictions about what the details mean. In the case of "The Dogwood," the facts and details range from the consciously repeated
"Oh wells" to the intimate, just-talking-to-myself manner, from
the heightened language describing the anemones to the carefully stated hour, "ten o'clock." Marshaling the details simply
means choosing — and bringing together for reflection — those
parts of the text that we can read as evidence bearing on character. Organizing the details means connecting them, one or more
at a time, with the hunches that come to us, as we concentrate on
them, about the nature of the person. In making the connections
and filling out a pattern, we supply interpretive language of our
own. It's with the help of this language that we arrive at an
account of a distinct human being: "intelligent, sensitive, not
terribly demanding of others, self-aware, humorous," and so on.

The key to the process is the calling up of interpretive words from within ourselves. Often a poem, story, or play provides us with terms describing the appearance or voice, the gestures or manners of a figure. Sometimes it presents figures solely through depicted deeds or through their own words. But always we, as animators, must move from the author's language to our own. We must find our own labels for the person being introduced to us.

Why so? Why can't we settle for the poet's words? Why do we need to invent our own terms?

There are two reasons, one rooted in common sense, the other suggested by the results of recent scientific research. We'll look at the common-sense reason in detail in the next section. The research, which deals with reading comprehension, indicates that when reading, we seem to be engaged at every point in translating the words in print into words of our own. As we move from sentence to sentence, line to line, down the page, we never stop restating and renaming. Instead of dealing purely with the words that are offered, we ceaselessly generate hypotheses, predictions, and patterns in our own lingo, mingling the author's words with our own knowledge and assumptions. Reading a poem, story, or play isn't, then, a matter of comprehending the author's words alone but of understanding those words as continuously combined with the language we ourselves ante up in deciding what's taking place at any given moment. We haven't any option as readers except to summon our own terms for the people who are introduced to us.

POSSESSING A TEXT

The common-sense answer to why we have to find our own labels has to do with the nature of closeness and possession. What belongs to us has heightened reality for us. Speaking back to a poem, making it talk our language, brings it closer, makes it momentarily part of us. When we suddenly hear on the radio the first notes of an old favorite, when we see, at an affordable price, the stamp or coin or spare part that's eluded us for months, or when we see, in a crowd of people waiting for arrivals, the one face that has deep meaning for us, that face or object or song *leaps out.* It lives and breathes because of our investment of care in it.

Likewise with stories, poems, or plays, it takes the use of our own labels for imagined figures and feelings to make those figures our own. Nothing except the measure of substance and energy we add to them makes them radiate significance. Nobody knows even the simplest of our possessions — our winter coat, our beat-up car — as we know it; nobody can name its relations to our life, to our sense of self, our sacrifice, our dreams and frustrations, as well as we can. And to a degree this is true of people in a work of literature, once we have succeeded in bringing them to life. After we've made them ours, by finding the words within ourselves that best link them to our personal understandings, they, too, become unique possessions. Nobody can know them quite as we do, and nothing can vivify them more than the special knowledge that we bring to bear upon them.

There are limits, naturally, to how fully and exclusively we can claim to possess a text or a character. We're accountable for the uses we make of any of our possessions. We're accountable for the language we use in setting up personal relationships between ourselves and imagined people on a page. This means that we want to be able to show other readers why we think this or that label for a character's behavior or traits seems to us appropriate — why we claim that the speaker in "The Dogwood" is modest and the speaker in "Dream Song 14" is aggressive and self-important. It's essential that we, as summoners of the life of a story, poem, or play, be able to explain and convincingly justify our personal descriptions of characters or feelings. Total eccentricity is as troubling in readers as in drivers.

But the existence of limits on our freedom to choose labels for characters doesn't for a minute imply that people of intelligence and good will come inevitably to the same conclusions about which labels are appropriate. As we've said several times before, we're all individuals; we have different stocks of experience and different words for expressing that experience. What matters isn't universal agreement but our determination to do all that we can to show others why we settled on our chosen terms. The discussion that results rarely fails to enrich the responses of everybody who participates in it, even though agreement remains out of reach.

SEEING FOR OURSELVES

One other point is worth keeping in mind as we launch into the work of naming characteristics. Our need to come up with labels of our own for imagined persons in a text links up with our way of dealing with living people in the world around us. Nothing is clearer, in life, than that our friends' versions of themselves, although useful in telling us what they think they are, can't be the last word on what they are for us. The questions are unavoidable: What do *I* think of the person? What does he or she add up to for me? It's when we don't care about another person that we tend to be accepting — in a bored, uninterested way — of that person's self-characterization. Let him run on, we think. It doesn't matter to me. But when either our own interest or our own need obliges us to pay serious attention to other human beings, we're likely to find ourselves looking for terms that will bring them into focus: terms that they might not use for themselves or might even fail to appreciate.

Genuine human encounter involves, in other words, *independent* effort at understanding and interpreting. If our encounters are to be more than perfunctory — mere ritual exchanges of politeness — we have to energize them by inquiry. We have to listen to what people say about themselves. We have to imagine how they see themselves. We have to consider what others say about them. We have to check these and other kinds of information against our own impressions.

Entering into this kind of activity requires the use of knowledge and language that belong uniquely to us; often the effort to come up with appropriate terms is a struggle, even when we are offered much guidance from outside. Pollsters who try to assess voters' impressions of potential political candidates usually offer a set of terms with which to work: Which of the following words best describes your reaction to Senator X? But even when terms are provided, most interviewees take their time choosing among them and often insist on inserting terms of their own. It's not easy to sort out impressions of another human being, to put them in order and reach conclusions about what's more and what's less important.

And the demands are obviously much greater when the whole task of coming up with fresh labels for our impressions falls to us. But taking another person in requires that we do just this — move beyond the terms that are offered to language of our own that registers exactly what we personally make of the character out there. As it is in life, so it is, more or less, with stories, poems, and plays.

ASKING QUESTIONS ABOUT CHARACTER

The three figures with which we begin constructing character in this chapter are an elderly New Englander, a contemporary working woman who is also a wife and mother, and a sharecropper in the American South: central personages in two poems and a story. The overarching question in these exercises is again very simple: What do you make of _____ here? And again we move toward a response by framing and answering more particular, intermediary questions.

Suppose we were working on the question, What do you make of Kit Twink? (he was the bearer of bad tidings to Mistress Damon in Hardy's "The Slow Nature" on page 33).

We might start by asking what the poem tells us about his personality: what kind of relationships he tends to have with other people (teasing, joking), whether he is sensitive or heavy-handed (he blurts his story to Mistress Damon without any attempt to ease her into the tragedy; he doesn't offer her any gesture of comfort), where we see him as kind or good-natured, where we see him as a person of limited intelligence and imagination, and so on.

The "right questions" about character are always those that help us take the two steps necessary to *evoking* a character: marshaling the details in the text that have a bearing on character and finding interpretive language that adds those details up in accordance with a personal understanding of their meaning. The task is to dwell on each imaginative creation — to interrogate them thoughtfully and intensely enough, moving back and forth from the general question to helpfully particular questions — to bring them fully to life.

EDWIN ARLINGTON ROBINSON (1869–1935)

Mr. Flood's Party

Old Eben Flood, climbing alone one night
Over the hill between the town below
And the forsaken upland hermitage
That held as much as he should ever know
On earth again of home; paused warily.   5
The road was his with not a native near;
And Eben, having leisure, said aloud,
For no man else in Tilbury Town to hear:

"Well, Mr. Flood, we have the harvest moon
Again, and we may not have many more;   10
The bird is on the wing, the poet says,
And you and I have said it here before.
Drink to the bird." He raised up to the light
The jug that he had gone so far to fill,
And answered huskily: "Well, Mr. Flood,   15
Since you propose it, I believe I will."

Alone, as if enduring to the end
A valiant armor of scarred hopes outworn,
He stood there in the middle of the road
Like Roland's ghost winding a silent horn.°   20
Below him, in the town among the trees,
Where friends of other days had honored him,
A phantom salutation of the dead
Rang thinly till old Eben's eyes were dim.

Then, as a mother lays her sleeping child   25
Down tenderly, fearing it may awake,
He set the jug down slowly at his feet
With trembling care, knowing that most things break;
And only when assured that on firm earth
It stood, as the uncertain lives of men   30
Assuredly did not, he paced away,
And with his hand extended paused again:

"Well, Mr. Flood, we have not met like this
In a long time; and many a change has come

20 *Roland's ghost . . . horn:* Roland, the hero of several major medieval romances, had an ivory
horn whose sound was so powerful that it threw the enemy army into a panic.

To both of us, I fear, since last it was   35
We had a drop together. Welcome home!"
Convivially returning with himself,
Again he raised the jug up to the light;
And with an acquiescent quaver said:
"Well, Mr. Flood, if you insist, I might.   40

"Only a very little, Mr. Flood —
For auld lang syne. No more, sir; that will do."
So, for the time, apparently it did,
And Eben evidently thought so too;
For soon amid the silver loneliness   45
Of night he lifted up his voice and sang,
Secure, with only two moons listening,
Until the whole harmonious landscape rang —

"For auld lang syne." The weary throat gave out,
The last word wavered; and the song being done,   50
He raised again the jug regretfully
And shook his head, and was again alone.
There was not much that was ahead of him,
And there was nothing in the town below —
Where strangers would have shut the many doors   55
That many friends had opened long ago.

Question

What do you make of Eben Flood in lines 51–52?

He raised again the jug regretfully
And shook his head, and was again alone.

Write your response and compare it with the one that follows.

Response

EDITOR: Among the pertinent facts about Eben Flood are these:
He's old; he's outlived many friends he once had in the valley
town called Tilbury; when he travels from his fairly distant
upland home to the valley town, he goes on foot; he drinks; on
the evening during which we watch him, he's made a trip to town
to buy some jug liquor; he samples this liquor more than once on

his way home; and he has been induced to break into a song that for years ranked as the favorite at communal sings.

What we make of Eben Flood in lines 51–52 depends in good measure on how we read the shake of the head that he gives after his song is done and he's "again alone." Such a gesture can bespeak puzzlement, bewilderment, frustration, or even anger, but to know what kind of puzzlement or anger we're dealing with, we need to decide for ourselves what kind of person we take Eben Flood to be. Does he shake his head at the world — at the erratic patterns of longevity that can bring on fearful loneliness and render long life a curse rather than a blessing? Or does he shake his head at himself, at the absurd force of his longing for company, which not only leads him to invent a drinking companion and give voice to a song rarely sung except in boozy unison with others, but also persuades him, for a minute, that other voices are joined with his and that he's not really by himself on his journey home?

Or do we say that Eben Flood shakes his head at both the world and himself? If we take up this third view of the man, we necessarily see him as an aged person whose feeling for the pathos of his own life situation has in it a trace of wry self-consciousness. And, as it happens, there's justification for that view of old Flood. Nobody entirely lacking in wit could fabricate the little split-personality drama that Flood does, as though to add something to the solace provided by the jug.

Mr. Flood 1 and Mr. Flood 2 contrive grimly amusing "reasons" for drinking. Flood 1 presents himself as concerned to toast the turning of the season, the closing off of the growth cycle, the passage of time ("The bird is on the wing," line 11). Flood 2 presents himself as ordinarily reluctant to tipple but willing to share in this toast out of deference to the person offering it ("Since you propose it, I believe I will," 16). The person offering the toast seems at moments to tease the somewhat grandiose language old parties have been known to indulge in when coming together to speak of the past ("many a change has come," 34). And there's some humor in the mockery of the reluctant tippler in stanzas 5 and 6 ("if you insist . . . only a very little . . . No more, sir"). It takes wit to play out one's lonely drinking session as a kind of contest of wills between two characters: one rather sniffishly abstemious, the other hearty and encouraging.

It would be a mistake, of course, to allow awareness of Eben Flood as a man of humor to hide the poignancy of his situation. It would also be a mistake to make the man out to be a deep thinker. It's not in Mr. Flood to advance from pondering the fact of his solitary survival to ripe philosophical reflection on the meaning of time, mutability, and the like. Neither is it in him to find much ground for an optimistic view of the human condition. I see a character who's wry and tough and salty, possessing a fine clear eye for the way other human beings — both the piously abstemious and the sternly distant who shut their door to him in town — deceive themselves. Flood knows that human life is not well arranged, that the pattern of living and dying has a good deal of dumb accident in it. And he knows that there is absolutely nothing to be done about that.

A grim, bitten survivor heedful of the unfairness of the world, he has wit enough to see a trace of ironic comedy in his own survival, and he hasn't gone fully cold to life. He remembers the pleasures of fraternal bonds and, while the booze-blurred moon goes double on him, he sings — and recovers briefly both the illusion of companionship and the illusion of the natural world ("the whole harmonious landscape," 48) as friendly to humanity. But that shake of the head in line 52 does shake the illusion off. It shows us a not quite sober realist — a man who wishes for better comforters than fantasy and a jug but knows that, for him, they don't exist.

AMY CLAMPITT   (b. 1924)
A New Life

Autonomy these days — surprise! — is moving up
in the corporate structure. She's thrown over
the old laid-back lifestyle, repudiated its
green-haired prophets, and gotten married

(pre-Raphaelite red velvet, a sheaf of roses,   5
hair falling in two long blond tresses). She's
now at home on a rural route, its row of mailboxes
a mile and a half from the Freeway. Not-quite-

two-year-old Autonomy Junior spends long days
with the sitter, can count up to five, and sees   10
the world moving past so fast, he delivers daily
not slow words but quick, predicated word-clusters.

Up before dawn three days out of five, at the
bathroom mirror Autonomy swiftly, with brush and
hairdryer, concocts a frame for her face of that   15
temporal gold, like the gilding of the aspens

in the Rockies, like every prototypical true
blonde who began as some other color; puts on
her boardroom clothes — flounced denim with
boots and weskit, or spiked sandals and pallid   20

executive knit — to drive off into the just-
stirred mother-of-pearl of the day, the velour
of hoarfrost's transient platinum on the blacktop
of a piece with the pristine pale upholstery

of the brand-new Brougham — into the ductile   25
realm of the Freeway, that reentry into the mystery
of being betweenwheres, alone in the effortless
anteroom of the Machine, of the Many. The Company

these days is paying her way to an earlybird
course in Econ at the University. At eight   30
thirty, while her wedded bedfellow, in the other
car, the red Toyota, drops off their offspring

with the sitter, her class over, she'll be taking
the Freeway again to headquarters. These days
she's in Quality Circles, a kind of hovering   35
equipoise between Management and not-Management,

precarious as the lake-twinned tremor of aspens,
as the lingering of the ash-blond arcade of foliage
completing itself as it leans to join its own inversion.
Whatever fabrication, whatever made thing   40

she is thus vertiginously linked to, there's no
disconnecting the image of Autonomy contained but
still moving — toward what is unclear — up through
the heady apertures of the Gross National Product,

from that thing, the ambiguous offspring of the Company —   45
through whose dense mansions, burbling with unheard

melodies of the new, her pal and bedfellow is moving up too.
Evenings, while he heads for *his* course at the University,

she collects the not-yet-two-year-old from the sitter,
kicks off her stiltwalker's footgear, peels away   50
the layers of the persona she takes to Quality Circles,
and slides into irontight jeans, the time-honored

armor of mellowing out; picks up yesterday's litter
around the playpen, puts together a quick concoction
via the microwave oven, and resumes — her charge,   55
all the while, voluble at her hip or underfoot —

the improbable game of move-and-countermove-between-
mother-and-child. Whether, back at headquarters,
back there in the winking imaginary map that leaps
from the minds of the computer programmers, there's   60

a mother-lode of still smarter bombs, the germ
of an even cleverer provocation to instability
within the neutron or of God knows what other, yet
inviolate speck at the core of the cosmos, who knows —

or whether playing at mothering, the mirage of a   65
rise into ethereal realms of the managerial — of
hoarfrost at dawn along the edge of the Freeway,
the hurtled ease of finding oneself betweenwheres,

alone in the evolving anteroom of the Machine, of
that artifice of the pursuit of happiness — will be,   70
as the green-haired prophets of punk would have it,
a total, or only partial
                        apocalyptic freakout.

Question

   What do you make of Autonomy in lines 55–58?

      . . . and resumes — her charge,
      all the while, voluble at her hip or underfoot —

      the improbable game of move-and-countermove-between-
      mother-and-child. . . .

Write your response and compare it with the one that follows.

Response

EDITOR: In deciding what to make of Autonomy here we need first to assemble the facts and details provided about her nature and life — evidence concerning her appearance, possessions, and attitudes as a working woman, mother, wife, and homemaker. Much of the evidence is organized, in the poem itself, in terms of a contrast between the central character's past and present, her old life and new life.

In the old life Autonomy's behavior was the kind associated with "green-haired prophets"(line 4) — far-out, alternative, hippie influenced, anti-Establishment. But she's now "thrown over" (2) that life-style, switched to a mode of living that is resolutely conventional — obedient to corporate requirements for "moving up" (1), enthusiastic about "The Company" (28), fascinated by precisely the schemes to improve worker productivity ("Quality Circles," 35) that the hippie or flower-power crowd of yesteryear would have despised as manipulative and totalitarian. Autonomy in the 1980s dresses with care in careerist uniforms and owns a variety of objects (from a "brand-new Brougham," 25, to a microwave oven, 55) that her former self would doubtless have spurned. Her relationships are respectably sanctioned by formal marriage vows, the future that interests her is the one that professional economists, not "green-haired prophets," claim to understand; her daily schedule is rigidly ordered from dawn to dusk, nothing "laid-back" (3) about it.

Our first hint about how to organize and interpret the poem's upcoming details of character arrives in the first word, which gives us Autonomy's name. The name suggests that the poet won't be offering us a photographic likeness of a real-life contemporary woman. Abstract nouns expressing parental aspirations for their offspring have often been used as names (Patience, Hope, Charity), but, until the advent of this poem, Autonomy had probably never been imagined as anybody's first name. More important, the name carries an edge of hostility. The aspirations it implies are rather less selfless than those proclaimed by Patience or Charity, and as we connect those aspirations with other information about Autonomy's nature and life, we find added ground for suspecting that Clampitt doesn't mean for us to see the person bearing the name as admirable.

We notice especially the stress laid on the artificial, mechanical, contrived aspects of Autonomy's behavior. This woman doesn't simply put on makeup in the morning; she "concocts a frame for her face" (15). The supper she cooks isn't a meal but a radiated "quick concoction" (54). The self she displays at work is ungenuine (once she's home Autonomy "peels away/the layers of the persona she takes to Quality Circles," 50–51). And the self that appears at home seems equally phony. Not only does she merely play at mothering but the play resembles chess — a "game of move-and-countermove" (57) — filled with guile rather than relaxed and comfortably affectionate. And Autonomy never does speak in her own voice, expressing thoughts or feelings in a direct, personal manner.

A negative portrait, in sum. Autonomy seems to represent total capitulation to the will of a corporation — a system that, in this case, invades and shapes every aspect of an individual's life, from clothes to education to meals to child rearing. Her acquiescence in domination exactly parallels her husband's and foreshadows what will happen to her son, who bears her name and can apparently be expected to be trapped like his parents in mindless climbing of corporate ladders.

Given the evidence and the implicit and explicit directions about how she should be interpreted, we have to conclude that Autonomy is to be understood as a counterfeit human being who could as easily be male as female — someone who spends her days passing herself off in one guise after another: alternative-life-styler, Victorian maiden (the "pre-Raphaelite red velvet" in line 5 alludes to a color and texture much favored by late-nineteenth-century romantic painters of remote, mysterious-seeming young women), executive go-getter, efficient wife and mother, and so on. An observer different from the author of this poem might look at similar behavior and present it differently, emphasizing energy, hard work, pride, and longing for independence rather than "artifice" (70), "fabrication" (40), and moral vacancy. But while the former qualities do surface here and there in the poem, they aren't perceived positively. Autonomy as we make her out doesn't even qualify as a figure of pathos; she comes across as slick, abstract, unloving, and, in the end, incapable of being true to herself.

WILLIAM FAULKNER   (1897–1962)
Barn Burning

The store in which the Justice of the Peace's court was sitting smelled of cheese. The boy, crouched on his nail keg at the back of the crowded room, knew he smelled cheese, and more: from where he sat he could see the ranked shelves close-packed with the solid, squat, dynamic shapes of tin cans whose labels his stomach read, not from the lettering which meant nothing to his mind but from the scarlet devils and the silver curve of fish — this, the cheese which he knew he smelled and the hermetic meat which his intestines believed he smelled coming in intermittent gusts momentary and brief between the other constant one, the smell and sense just a little of fear because mostly of despair and grief, the old fierce pull of blood. He could not see the table where the Justice sat and before which his father and his father's enemy (*our enemy* he thought in that despair; *ourn! mine and hisn both! He's my father!*) stood, but he could hear them, the two of them that is, because his father had said no word yet:

"But what proof have you, Mr. Harris?"

"I told you. The hog got into my corn. I caught it up and sent it back to him. He had no fence that would hold it. I told him so, warned him. The next time I put the hog in my pen. When he came to get it I gave him enough wire to patch up his pen. The next time I put the hog up and kept it. I rode down to his house and saw the wire I gave him still rolled on to the spool in his yard. I told him he could have the hog when he paid me a dollar pound fee. That evening a nigger came with the dollar and got the hog. He was a strange nigger. He said, 'He say to tell you wood and hay kin burn.' I said, 'What?' 'That whut he say to tell you,' the nigger said. 'Wood and hay kin burn.' That night my barn burned. I got the stock out but I lost the barn."

"Where is the nigger? Have you got him?"

"He was a strange nigger, I tell you. I don't know what became of him."

"But that's not proof. Don't you see that's not proof?"

"Get that boy up here. He knows." For a moment the boy thought too that the man meant his older brother until Harris said, "Not him. The little one. The boy," and, crouching, small for his age, small and wiry like his father, in patched and faded jeans even too small for him, with straight, uncombed, brown hair and eyes gray and wild as storm scud, he saw the men between himself and the table part and become a lane of grim faces, at the end of which he saw the Justice, a shabby, collarless, graying man in spectacles, beckoning him. He felt no floor under his bare feet; he seemed to walk beneath the palpable weight of the grim turning faces. His father, stiff in his black Sunday coat donned not for the trial but for the moving, did not even look at him. *He aims for me to lie,* he thought, again with that frantic grief and despair. *And I will have to do hit.*

"What's your name, boy?" the Justice said.

"Colonel Sartoris Snopes," the boy whispered.

"Hey?" the Justice said. "Talk louder. Colonel Sartoris? I reckon anybody named for Colonel Sartoris in this country can't help but tell the truth, can they?" The boy said nothing. *Enemy! Enemy!* he thought; for a moment he could not even see, could not see that the Justice's face was kindly nor discern that his voice was troubled when he spoke to the man named Harris: "Do you want me to question this boy?" But he could hear, and during those subsequent long seconds while there was absolutely no sound in the crowded little room save that of quiet and intent breathing it was as if he had swung outward at the end of a grape vine, over a ravine, and at the top of the swing had been caught in a prolonged instant of mesmerized gravity, weightless in time.

"No!" Harris said violently, explosively. "Damnation! Send him out of here!" Now time, the fluid world, rushed beneath him again, the voices coming to him again through the smell of cheese and sealed meat, the fear and despair and the old grief of blood:

"This case is closed. I can't find against you, Snopes, but I can give you advice. Leave this country and don't come back to it."

His father spoke for the first time, his voice cold and harsh, level, without emphasis: "I aim to. I don't figure to stay in a country among people who . . ." he said something unprintable and vile, addressed to no one.

"That'll do," the Justice said. "Take your wagon and get out of this country before dark. Case dismissed."

His father turned, and he followed the stiff black coat, the wiry figure walking a little stiffly from where a Confederate provost's man's musket ball had taken him in the heel on a stolen horse thirty years ago, followed the two backs now, since his older brother had appeared from somewhere in the crowd, no taller than the father but thicker, chewing tobacco steadily, between the two lines of grim-faced men and out of the store and across

10

15

the worn gallery and down the sagging steps and among the dogs and half-grown boys in the mild May dust, where as he passed a voice hissed:

"Barn burner!"

Again he could not see, whirling; there was a face in a red haze, moonlike, bigger than the full moon, the owner of it half again his size, he leaping in the red haze toward the face, feeling no blow, feeling no shock when his head struck the earth, scrabbling up and leaping again, feeling no blow this time either and tasting no blood, scrabbling up to see the other boy in full flight and himself already leaping into pursuit as his father's hand jerked him back, the harsh, cold voice speaking above him: "Go get in the wagon."

It stood in a grove of locusts and mulberries across the road. His two hulking sisters in their Sunday dresses and his mother and her sister in calico and sunbonnets were already in it, sitting on and among the sorry residue of the dozen and more movings which even the boy could remember — the battered stove, the broken beds and chairs, the clock inlaid with mother-of-pearl, which would not run, stopped at some fourteen minutes past two o'clock of a dead and forgotten day and time, which had been his mother's dowry. She was crying, though when she saw him she drew her sleeve across her face and began to descend from the wagon. "Get back," the father said.

"He's hurt. I got to get some water and wash his . . ."

"Get back in the wagon," his father said. He got in too, over the tail-gate. His father mounted to the seat where the older brother already sat and struck the gaunt mules two savage blows with the peeled willow, but without heat. It was not even sadistic; it was exactly that same quality which in later years would cause his descendants to over-run the engine before putting a motor car into motion, striking and reining back in the same movement. The wagon went on, the store with its quiet crowd of grimly watching men dropped behind; a curve in the road hid it. *Forever* he thought. *Maybe he's done satisfied now, now that he has . . .* stopping himself, not to say it aloud even to himself. His mother's hand touched his shoulder.

"Does hit hurt?" she said.

"Naw," he said. "Hit don't hurt. Lemme be."

"Can't you wipe some of the blood off before hit dries?"

"I'll wash to-night," he said. "Lemme be, I tell you."

The wagon went on. He did not know where they were going. None of them ever did or ever asked, because it was always somewhere, always a house of sorts waiting for them a day or two days or even three days away. Likely his father had already arranged to make a crop on another farm before he . . . Again he had to stop himself. He (the father) always did. There was something about his wolflike independence and even courage when the advantage was at least neutral which impressed strangers, as if they got from his latent ravening ferocity not so much a sense of dependability as a feeling that his ferocious conviction in the rightness of his own actions would be of advantage to all whose interest lay with his.

That night they camped, in a grove of oaks and beeches where a spring ran. The nights were still cool and they had a fire against it, of a rail lifted from a nearby fence and cut into lengths — a small fire, neat, niggard almost, a shrewd fire; such fires were his father's habit and custom always, even in freezing weather. Older, the boy might have remarked this and wondered why not a big one; why should not a man who had not only seen the waste and extravagance of war, but who had in his blood an inherent voracious prodigality with material not his own, have burned everything in sight? Then he might have gone a step farther and thought that that was the reason: that niggard blaze was the living fruit of nights passed during those four years in the woods hiding from all men, blue or gray, with his strings of horses (captured horses, he called them). And older still, he might have divined the true reason: that the element of fire spoke to some deep mainspring of his father's being, as the element of steel or of powder spoke to other men, as the one weapon for the preservation of integrity, else breath were not worth the breathing, and hence to be regarded with respect and discretion.

But he did not think this now and he had seen those same niggard blazes all his life. He merely ate his supper beside it and was already half asleep over his iron plate when his father called him, and once more he followed the stiff back, the stiff and ruthless limp, up the slope and on to the starlit road where, turning, he could see his father against the stars but without face or depth — a shape black, flat, and bloodless as though cut from tin in the iron folds of the frockcoat which had not been made for him, the voice harsh like tin and without heat like tin:

"You were fixing to tell them. You would have told him."

He didn't answer. His father struck him with the flat of his hand on the side of the head, hard but without heat, exactly as he had struck the two mules at the store, exactly as he would strike either of them with any stick in order to kill a horse fly, his voice still without heat or anger. "You're getting to be a man. You got to learn. You got to learn to stick to your own blood or you ain't going to have any blood to stick to you. Do you think either of them, any man there this morning, would? Don't you know all they wanted was a chance to get at me because they knew I had them beat? Eh?" Later, twenty years later, he was to tell himself, "If I had said they wanted only truth, justice, he would have hit me again." But now he said nothing. He was not crying. He just stood there. "Answer me," his father said.

"Yes," he whispered. His father turned.   30

"Get on to bed. We'll be there tomorrow."

Tomorrow they were there. In the early afternoon the wagon stopped before a paintless two-room house identical almost with the dozen others it had stopped before even in the boy's ten years, and again, as on the other dozen occasions, his mother and aunt got down and began to unload the wagon, although his two sisters and his father and brother had not moved.

"Likely it ain't fitten for hawgs," one of the sisters said.

"Nevertheless, fit it will and you'll hog it and like it," his father said. "Get out of them chairs and help your Ma unload."

The two sisters got down, big, bovine, in a flutter of cheap   35
ribbons; one of them drew from the jumbled wagon bed a battered lantern, the other a worn broom. His father handed the reins to the older son and began to climb stiffly over the wheel. "When they get unloaded, take the team to the barn and feed them." Then he said, and at first the boy thought he was still speaking to his brother. "Come with me."

"Me?" he said.

"Yes," his father said. "You."

"Abner," his mother said. His father paused and looked back — the harsh level stare beneath the shaggy, graying, irascible brows.

"I reckon I'll have a word with the man that aims to begin tomorrow owning me body and soul for the next eight months."

They went back up the road. A week ago — or before last   40
night, that is — he would have asked where they were going, but not now. His father had struck him before last night but never before had he paused afterward to explain why; it was as if the blow and the following calm, outrageous voice still rang, repercussed, divulging nothing to him save the terrible handicap of being young, the light weight of his few years, just heavy enough to prevent his soaring free of the world as it seemed to be

ordered but not heavy enough to keep him footed solid in it, to resist it and try to change the course of its events.

Presently he could see the grove of oaks and cedars and the other flowering trees and shrubs where the house would be, though not the house yet. They walked beside a fence massed with honeysuckle and Cherokee roses and came to a gate swinging open between two brick pillars, and now, beyond a sweep of drive, he saw the house for the first time and at that instant he forgot his father and the terror and despair both, and even when he remembered his father again (who had not stopped) the terror and despair did not return. Because, for all the twelve movings, they had sojourned until now in a poor country, a land of small farms and fields and houses, and he had never seen a house like this before. *Hit's big as a courthouse* he thought quietly, with a surge of peace and joy whose reason he could not have thought into words, being too young for that: *They are safe from him. People whose lives are a part of this peace and dignity are beyond his touch, he no more to them than a buzzing wasp: capable of stinging for a little moment but that's all; the spell of this peace and dignity rendering even the barns and stable and cribs which belong to it impervious to the puny flames he might contrive* . . . this, the peace and joy, ebbing for an instant as he looked again at the stiff black back, the stiff and implacable limp of the figure which was not dwarfed by the house, for the reason that it had never looked big anywhere and which now, against the serene columned backdrop, had more than ever that impervious quality of something cut ruthlessly from tin, depthless, as though, sidewise to the sun, it would cast no shadow. Watching him, the boy remarked the absolutely undeviating course which his father held and saw the stiff foot come squarely down in a pile of fresh droppings where a horse had stood in the drive and which his father could have avoided by a simple change of stride. But it ebbed only for a moment, though he could not have thought this into words either, walking on in the spell of the house, which he could even want but without envy, without sorrow, certainly never with that ravening and jealous rage which unknown to him walked in the ironlike black coat before him: *Maybe he will feel it too. Maybe it will even change him now from what maybe he couldn't help but be.*

They crossed the portico. Now he could hear his father's stiff foot as it came down on the boards with clocklike finality, a sound out of all proportion to the displacement of the body it bore and which was not dwarfed either by the white door before it, as though it had attained to a sort of vicious and ravening minimum not to be dwarfed by anything — the flat, wide, black hat, the formal coat of broadcloth which had once been black but which had now that friction-glazed greenish cast of the bodies of old house flies, the lifted sleeve which was too large, the lifted hand like a curled claw. The door opened so promptly that the boy knew the Negro must have been watching them all the time, an old man with neat grizzled hair, in a linen jacket, who stood barring the door with his body, saying, "Wipe yo foots, white man, fo you come in here. Major ain't home nohow."

"Get out of my way, nigger," his father said, without heat too, flinging the door back and the Negro also and entering, his hat still on his head. And now the boy saw the prints of the stiff foot on the doorjamb and saw them appear on the pale rug behind the machinelike deliberation of the foot which seemed to bear (or transmit) twice the weight which the body compassed. The Negro was shouting "Miss Lula! Miss Lula!" somewhere behind them, then the boy, deluged as though by a warm wave by a suave turn of the carpeted stair and a pendant glitter of chandeliers and a mute gleam of gold frames, heard the swift feet and saw her too, a lady — perhaps he had never seen her like before either — in a gray, smooth gown with lace at the throat and an apron tied at the waist and the sleeves turned back, wiping cake or biscuit dough from her hands with a towel as she came up the hall, looking not at his father at all but at the tracks on the blond rug with an expression of incredulous amazement.

"I tried," the Negro cried. "I tole him to . . ."

"Will you please go away?" she said in a shaking voice. 45 "Major de Spain is not at home. Will you please go away?"

His father had not spoken again. He did not speak again. He did not even look at her. He just stood stiff in the center of the rug, in his hat, the shaggy iron-gray brows twitching slightly above the pebble-colored eyes as he appeared to examine the house with brief deliberation. Then with the same deliberation he turned; the boy watched him pivot on the good leg and saw the stiff foot drag round the arc of the turning, leaving a final long and fading smear. His father never looked at it, he never once looked down at the rug. The Negro held the door. It closed behind them, upon the hysteric and indistinguishable woman-wail. His father stopped at the top of the steps and scraped his boot clean on the edge of it. At the gate he stopped again. He stood for a moment, planted stiffly on the stiff foot, looking back at the house. "Pretty and white, ain't it?" he said. "That's sweat. Nigger sweat. Maybe it ain't white enough yet to suit him. Maybe he wants to mix some white sweat with it."

Two hours later the boy was chopping wood behind the

house within which his mother and aunt and the two sisters (the mother and aunt, not the two girls, he knew that; even at this distance and muffled by walls the flat loud voices of the two girls emanated an incorrigible idle inertia) were setting up the stove to prepare a meal; when he heard the hooves and saw the linen-clad man on a fine sorrel mare, whom he recognized even before he saw the rolled rug in front of the Negro youth following on a fat bay carriage horse — a suffused, angry face vanishing, still at full gallop, beyond the corner of the house where his father and brother were sitting in the two tilted chairs; and a moment later, almost before he could have put the axe down, he heard the hooves again and watched the sorrel mare go back out of the yard, already galloping again. Then his father began to shout one of the sisters' names, who presently emerged backward from the kitchen door dragging the rolled rug along the ground by one end while the other sister walked behind it.

"If you ain't going to tote, go on and set up the wash pot," the first said.

"You, Sarty!" the second shouted. "Set up the wash pot!" His father appeared at the door, framed against that shabbiness, as he had been against that other bland perfection, impervious to either, the mother's anxious face at his shoulder.

"Go on," the father said. "Pick it up." The two sisters 50 stooped, broad, lethargic; stooping, they presented an incredible expanse of pale cloth and a flutter of tawdry ribbons.

"If I thought enough of a rug to have to git hit all the way from France I wouldn't keep hit where folks coming in would have to tromp on hit," the first said. They raised the rug.

"Abner," the mother said. "Let me do it."

"You go back and git dinner," his father said. "I'll tend to this."

From the woodpile through the rest of the afternoon the boy watched them, the rug spread flat in the dust beside the bubbling wash pot, the two sisters stooping over it with that profound and lethargic reluctance, while the father stood over them in turn, implacable and grim, driving them though never raising his voice again. He could smell the harsh homemade lye they were using; he saw his mother come to the door once and look toward them with an expression not anxious now but very like despair; he saw his father turn, and he fell to with the axe and saw from the corner of his eye his father raise from the ground a flattish fragment of field stone and examine it and return to the pot, and this time his mother actually spoke: "Abner. Abner. Please don't. Please, Abner."

Then he was done too. It was dusk; the whippoorwills had   55
already begun. He could smell coffee from the room where they
would presently eat the cold food remaining from the mid-
afternoon meal, though when he entered the house he realized
they were having coffee again probably because there was a
fire on the hearth, before which the rug now lay spread over the
backs of the two chairs. The tracks of his father's foot were gone.
Where they had been were now long, water-cloudy scoriations
resembling the sporadic course of a lilliputian mowing machine.

It still hung there while they ate the cold food and then went
to bed, scattered without order or claim up and down the two
rooms, his mother in one bed, where his father would later lie,
the older brother in the other, himself, the aunt, and the two
sisters on pallets on the floor. But his father was not in bed yet.
The last thing the boy remembered was the depthless, harsh
silhouette of the hat and coat bending over the rug and it seemed
to him that he had not even closed his eyes when the silhouette
was standing over him, the fire almost dead behind it, the stiff
foot prodding him awake. "Catch up the mule," his father said.

When he returned with the mule his father was standing in
the black door, the rolled rug over his shoulder. "Ain't you going
to ride?" he said.

"No. Give me your foot."

He bent his knee into his father's hand, the wiry, surprising
power flowed smoothly, rising, he rising with it, on to the mule's
bare back (they had owned a saddle once; the boy could remember it though not when or where) and with the same effortless
ness his father swung the rug up in front of him. Now in the
starlight they retraced the afternoon's path, up the dusty road
rife with honeysuckle, through the gate and up the black tunnel
of the drive to the lightless house, where he sat on the mule and
felt the rough warp of the rug drag across his thighs and vanish.

"Don't you want me to help?" he whispered. His father did   60
not answer and now he heard again that stiff foot striking the
hollow portico with that wooden and clocklike deliberation, that
outrageous overstatement of the weight it carried. The rug,
hunched, not flung (the boy could tell that even in the darkness)
from his father's shoulder struck the angle of wall and floor with
a sound unbelievably loud, thunderous, then the foot again,
unhurried and enormous; a light came on in the house and the
boy sat, tense, breathing steadily and quietly and just a little fast,
though the foot itself did not increase its beat at all, descending
the steps now; now the boy could see him.

"Don't you want to ride now?" he whispered. "We kin both

ride now," the light within the house altering now, flaring up and sinking. *He's coming down the stairs now*, he thought. He had already ridden the mule up beside the horse block; presently his father was up behind him and he doubled the reins over and slashed the mule across the neck, but before the animal could begin to trot the hard, thin arm came around him, the hard, knotted hand jerking the mule back to a walk.

In the first red rays of the sun they were in the lot, putting plow gear on the mules. This time the sorrel mare was in the lot before he heard it at all, the rider collarless and even bareheaded, trembling, speaking in a shaking voice as the woman in the house had done, his father merely looking up once before stooping again to the hame he was buckling, so that the man on the mare spoke to his stooping back:

"You must realize you have ruined that rug. Wasn't there anybody here, any of your women . . ." he ceased, shaking, the boy watching him, the older brother leaning now in the stable door, chewing, blinking slowly and steadily at nothing apparently. "It cost a hundred dollars. But you never had a hundred dollars. You never will. So I'm going to charge you twenty bushels of corn against your crop. I'll add it in your contract and when you come to the commissary you can sign it. That won't keep Mrs. de Spain quiet but maybe it will teach you to wipe your feet off before you enter her house again."

Then he was gone. The boy looked at his father, who still had not spoken or even looked up again, who was now adjusting the logger-head in the hame.

"Pap," he said. His father looked at him — the inscrutable 65 face, the shaggy brows beneath which the gray eyes glinted coldly. Suddenly the boy went toward him, fast, stopping as suddenly. "You done the best you could!" he cried. "If he wanted hit done different why didn't he wait and tell you how? He won't git no twenty bushels! He won't git none! We'll gether hit and hide hit! I kin watch . . ."

"Did you put the cutter back in that straight stock like I told you?"

"No, sir," he said.

"Then go do it."

That was Wednesday. During the rest of that week he worked steadily, at what was within his scope and some which was beyond it, with an industry that did not need to be driven nor even commanded twice; he had this from his mother, with the difference that some at least of what he did he liked to do, such as splitting wood with the half-size axe which his mother and aunt had earned, or saved money somehow, to present him with at Christmas. In company with the two older women (and on one afternoon, even one of the sisters), he built pens for the shoat and the cow which were a part of his father's contract with the landlord, and one afternoon, his father being absent, gone somewhere on one of the mules, he went to the field.

They were running a middle buster now, his brother holding 70 the plow straight while he handled the reins, and walking beside the straining mule, the rich black soil shearing cool and damp against his bare ankles, he thought *Maybe this is the end of it. Maybe even that twenty bushels that seems hard to have to pay for just a rug will be a cheap price for him to stop forever and always from being what he used to be*; thinking, dreaming now, so that his brother had to speak sharply to him to mind the mule: *Maybe he even won't collect the twenty bushels. Maybe it will all add up and balance and vanish — corn, rug, fire; the terror and grief; the being pulled two ways like between two teams of horses — gone, done with for ever and ever.*

Then it was Saturday; he looked up from beneath the mule he was harnessing and saw his father in the black coat and hat. "Not that," his father said. "The wagon gear." And then, two hours later, sitting in the wagon bed behind his father and brother on the seat, the wagon accomplished a final curve, and he saw the weathered paintless store with its tattered tobacco- and patent medicine posters and the tethered wagons and saddle animals below the gallery. He mounted the gnawed steps behind his father and brother, and there again was the lane of quiet, watching faces for the three of them to walk through. He saw the man in spectacles sitting at the plank table and he did not need to be told this was a Justice of the Peace; he sent one glare of fierce, exultant, partisan defiance at the man in collar and cravat now, whom he had seen but twice before in his life, and that on a galloping horse, who now wore on his face an expression not of rage but of amazed unbelief which the boy could not have known was at the incredible circumstance of being sued by one of his own tenants, and came and stood against his father and cried at the Justice: "He ain't done it! He ain't burnt . . ."

"Go back to the wagon," his father said.

"Burnt?" the Justice said. "Do I understand this rug was burned too?"

"Does anybody here claim it was?" his father said. "Go back to the wagon." But he did not, he merely retreated to the rear of the room, crowded as that other had been, but not to sit down this time, instead, to stand pressing among the motionless bodies, listening to the voices:

"And you claim twenty bushels of corn is too high for the 75 damage you did to the rug?"

"He brought the rug to me and said he wanted the tracks washed out of it. I washed the tracks out and took the rug back to him."

"But you didn't carry the rug back to him in the same condition it was in before you made the tracks on it."

His father did not answer, and now for perhaps half a minute there was no sound at all save that of breathing, the faint, steady suspiration of complete and intent listening.

"You decline to answer that, Mr. Snopes?" Again his father did not answer. "I'm going to find against you, Mr. Snopes. I'm going to find that you were responsible for the injury to Major de Spain's rug and hold you liable for it. But twenty bushels of corn seems a little high for a man in your circumstances to have to pay. Major de Spain claims it cost a hundred dollars. October corn will be worth about fifty cents. I figure that if Major de Spain can stand a ninety-five dollar loss on something he paid cash for, you can stand a five-dollar loss you haven't earned yet. I hold you in damages to Major de Spain to the amount of ten bushels of corn over and above your contract with him, to be paid to him out of your crop at gathering time. Court adjourned."

It had taken no time hardly, the morning was but half begun. 80 He thought they would return home and perhaps back to the field, since they were late, far behind all other farmers. But instead his father passed on behind the wagon, merely indicating with his hand for the older brother to follow with it, and crossed the road toward the blacksmith shop opposite, pressing on after his father, overtaking him, speaking, whispering up at the harsh, calm face beneath the weathered hat: "He won't git no ten bushels neither. He won't git one. We'll . . ." until his father glanced for an instant down at him, the face absolutely calm, the grizzled eyebrows tangled above the cold eyes, the voice almost pleasant, almost gentle:

"You think so? Well, we'll wait till October anyway."

The matter of the wagon — the setting of a spoke or two and the tightening of the tires — did not take long either, the business of the tires accomplished by driving the wagon into the spring branch behind the shop and letting it stand there, the mules nuzzling into the water from time to time, and the boy on the seat with the idle reins, looking up the slope and through the sooty tunnel of the shed where the slow hammer rang and where his father sat on an upended cypress bolt, easily, either talking or listening, still sitting there when the boy brought the dripping wagon up out of the branch and halted it before the door.

"Take them on to the shade and hitch," his father said. He did so and returned. His father and the smith and a third man squatting on his heels inside the door were talking, about crops and animals; the boy, squatting too in the ammoniac dust and hoof-parings and scales of rust, heard his father tell a long and unhurried story out of the time before the birth of the older brother even when he had been a professional horsetrader. And then his father came up beside him where he stood before a tattered last year's circus poster on the other side of the store, gazing rapt and quiet at the scarlet horses, the incredible poisings and convolutions of tulle and tights and the painted leers of comedians, and said, "It's time to eat."

But not at home. Squatting beside his brother against the front wall, he watched his father emerge from the store and produce from a paper sack a segment of cheese and divide it carefully and deliberately into three with his pocket knife and produce crackers from the same sack. They all three squatted on the gallery and ate, slowly, without talking; then in the store again, they drank from a tin dipper tepid water smelling of the cedar bucket and of living beech trees. And still they did not go home. It was a horse lot this time, a tall rail fence upon and along which men stood and sat and out of which one by one horses were led, to be walked and trotted and then cantered back and forth along the road while the slow swapping and buying went on and the sun began to slant westward, they — the three of them — watching and listening, the older brother with his muddy eyes and his steady, inevitable tobacco, the father commenting now and then on certain of the animals, to no one in particular.

It was after sundown when they reached home. They ate 85 supper by lamplight, then, sitting on the doorstep, the boy watched the night fully accomplish, listening to the whippoor-wills and the frogs, when he heard his mother's voice: "Abner! No! No! Oh, God. Oh, God. Abner!" and he rose, whirled, and saw the altered light through the door where a candle stub now burned in a bottle neck on the table and his father, still in the hat and coat, at once formal and burlesque as though dressed carefully for some shabby and ceremonial violence, emptying the reservoir of the lamp back into the five-gallon kerosene can from which it had been filled, while the mother tugged at his arm until he shifted the lamp to the other hand and flung her back, not savagely or viciously, just hard, into the wall, her hands flung out against the wall for balance, her mouth open and in her face the same quality of hopeless despair as had been in her voice. Then his father saw him standing in the door.

"Go to the barn and get that can of oil we were oiling the wagon with," he said. The boy did not move. Then he could speak.

"What . . ." he cried. "What are you . . ."

"Go get that oil," his father said. "Go."

Then he was moving, running, outside the house, toward the stable: this the old habit, the old blood which he had not been permitted to choose for himself, which had been bequeathed him willy nilly and which had run for so long (and who knew where, battening on what of outrage and savagery and lust) before it came to him. *I could keep on,* he thought. *I could run on and on and never look back, never need to see his face again. Only I can't. I can't,* the rusted can in his hand now, the liquid sploshing in it as he ran back to the house and into it, into the sound of his mother's weeping in the next room, and handed the can to his father.

"Ain't you going to even send a nigger?" he cried. "At least 90 you sent a nigger before!"

This time his father didn't strike him. The hand came even faster than the blow had, the same hand which had set the can on the table with almost excruciating care flashing from the can toward him too quick for him to follow it, gripping him by the back of his shirt and on to tiptoe before he had seen it quit the can, the face stooping at him in breathless and frozen ferocity, the cold, dead voice speaking over him to the older brother who leaned against the table, chewing with that steady, curious, side-wise motion of cows:

"Empty the can into the big one and go on. I'll catch up with you."

"Better tie him up to the bedpost," the brother said.

"Do like I told you," the father said. Then the boy was moving, his bunched shirt and the hard, bony hand between his shoulder-blades, his toes just touching the floor, across the room and into the other one, past the sisters sitting with spread heavy thighs in the two chairs over the cold hearth, and to where his mother and aunt sat side by side on the bed, the aunt's arms about his mother's shoulders.

"Hold him," the father said. The aunt made a startled move- 95
ment. "Not you," the father said. "Lennie. Take hold of him. I
want to see you do it." His mother took him by the wrist. "You'll
hold him better than that. If he gets loose don't you know what he
is going to do? He will go up yonder." He jerked his head toward
the road. "Maybe I'd better tie him."

"I'll hold him," his mother whispered.

"See you do then." Then his father was gone, the stiff foot
heavy and measured upon the boards, ceasing at last.

Then he began to struggle. His mother caught him in both
arms, he jerking and wrenching at them. He would be stronger in
the end, he knew that. But he had no time to wait for it. "Lemme
go!" he cried. "I don't want to have to hit you!"

"Let him go!" the aunt said. "If he don't go, before God, I am
going up there myself!"

"Don't you see I can't?" his mother cried. "Sarty! Sarty! No! 100
No! Help me, Lizzie!"

Then he was free. His aunt grasped at him but it was too late.
He whirled, running, his mother stumbled forward on to her
knees behind him, crying to the nearer sister. "Catch him, Net!
Catch him!" But that was too late too, the sister (the sisters were
twins, born at the same time, yet either of them now gave the
impression of being, encompassing as much living meat and
volume and weight as any other two of the family) not yet having
begun to rise from the chair, her head, face, alone merely turned,
presenting to him in the flying instant an astonishing expanse of
young female features untroubled by any surprise even, wearing
only an expression of bovine interest. Then he was out of the
room, out of the house, in the mild dust of the starlit road and the
heavy rifeness of honeysuckle, the pale ribbon unspooling with
terrific slowness under his running feet, reaching the gate at last
and turning in, running, his heart and lungs drumming, on up
the drive toward the lighted house, the lighted door. He did not
knock, he burst in, sobbing for breath, incapable for the moment
of speech; he saw the astonished face of the Negro in the linen
jacket without knowing when the Negro had appeared.

"De Spain!" he cried, panted. "Where's . . ." then he saw the
white man too emerging from a white door down the hall.
"Barn!" he cried. "Barn!"

"What?" the white man said. "Barn?"

"Yes!" the boy cried. "Barn!"

"Catch him!" the white man shouted. 105

But it was too late this time too. The Negro grasped his shirt, but the entire sleeve, rotten with washing, carried away, and he was out that door too and in the drive again, and had actually never ceased to run even while he was screaming into the white man's face.

Behind him the white man was shouting, "My horse! Fetch my horse!" and he thought for an instant of cutting across the park and climbing the fence into the road, but he did not know the park nor how high the vine-massed fence might be and he dared not risk it. So he ran on down the drive, blood and breath roaring; presently he was in the road again though he could not see it. He could not hear either: the galloping mare was almost upon him before he heard her, and even then he held his course, as if the very urgency of his wild grief and need must in a moment more find him wings, waiting until the ultimate instant to hurl himself aside and into the weed-choked roadside ditch as the horse thundered past and on, for an instant in furious silhouette against the stars, the tranquil early summer night sky which, even before the shape of the horse and rider vanished, strained abruptly and violently upward: a long, swirling roar incredible and soundless, blotting the stars, and he springing up and into the road again, running again, knowing it was too late yet still running even after he heard the shot and, an instant later, two shots, pausing now without knowing he had ceased to run, crying "Pap! Pap!," running again before he knew he had begun to run, stumbling, tripping over something and scrabbling up again without ceasing to run, looking backward over his shoulder at the glare as he got up, running on among the invisible trees, panting, sobbing, "Father! Father!"

At midnight he was sitting on the crest of a hill. He did not know it was midnight and he did not know how far he had come. But there was no glare behind him now and he sat now, his back toward what he had called home for four days anyhow, his face toward the dark woods which he would enter when breath was strong again, small, shaking steadily in the chill darkness, hugging himself into the remainder of his thin, rotten shirt, the grief and despair now no longer terror and fear but just grief and despair. *Father. My father*, he thought. "He was brave!" he cried suddenly, aloud but not loud, no more than a whisper: "He was! He was in the war! He was in Colonel Sartoris' cav'ry!" not knowing that his father had gone to that war a private in the fine old European sense, wearing no uniform, admitting the authority of and giving fidelity to no man or army or flag, going to war as Malbrouck himself did: for booty — it meant nothing and less than nothing to him if it were enemy booty or his own.

The slow constellations wheeled on. It would be dawn and then sun-up after a while and he would be hungry. But that would be tomorrow and now he was only cold, and walking would cure that. His breathing was easier now and he decided to get up and go on, and then he found that he had been asleep because he knew it was almost dawn, the night almost over. He could tell that from the whippoorwills. They were everywhere now among the dark trees below him, constant and inflectioned and ceaseless, so that, as the instant for giving over to the day birds drew nearer and nearer, there was no interval at all between them. He got up. He was a little stiff, but walking would cure that too as it would the cold, and soon there would be the sun. He went on down the hill, toward the dark woods within which the liquid silver voices of the birds called unceasing — the rapid and urgent beating of the urgent and quiring heart of the late spring night. He did not look back.

Question

What do you make of Ab Snopes here?

"Pretty and white, ain't it?" he said. "That's sweat. Nigger sweat. Maybe it ain't white enough yet to suit him. Maybe he wants to mix some white sweat with it." (para. 46)

Write your response and compare it with those that follow.

Responses

EDITOR: We know that Ab Snopes is harsh to his wife, his sons, and his daughters, and that he is particularly cruel to his stock. We know that his hatred of the planters with whom he enters into sharecropping agreements repeatedly issues in acts of wanton destruction. We know that he's ridden with suspicion of his own closest kin, expecting them to betray him. And we know that — worse than any of this — he often behaves with fearful coldness to those who try desperately to communicate the loving respect they feel for him.

Given such a combination of racism, destructiveness, and blank insensitivity, it's tempting to imagine Ab as a figure in whom ignorance and brutality obliterate every sympathetic impulse, every normative response to peace, dignity, or beauty.

Major de Spain seems to reach something close to that conclusion after the rug-laundering episode ("Wasn't there anybody
here, any of your women, . . ." 63). And although Ab's son is
intensely loyal to his father and indignant at the injustice of the
Major's twenty-bushel "charge" for the destruction of the rug,
Sarty clearly has a conviction that "peace and dignity" are somehow "*beyond his [father's] touch, he no more to them than a buzzing
wasp*" (41). Is there anything to be made of Ab Snopes except a
person whose raging malevolence has badly stunted if not crippled his humanity?

Denying the force of the malevolence is impossible — but
tracing it solely to ignorance and insensitivity falsifies Ab's nature. Uneducated, probably illiterate, schooled in none of the
revolutionary traditions which, in urban settings, were shaping
popular protests against "economic injustice" when this story
was written in the late 1930s, Ab nevertheless has managed,
through the exercise of his own primitive intelligence, to make
sense of his world, to arrive at a vision of the relations between
labor, money, and the beautiful. It's a vision that's miles away
from transforming itself into a broadly historical account of
capital accumulation. Ab Snopes can't frame a theory to himself
about, say, proletarian enslavement; he has no language in which
to imagine a class solidarity leading to political action aimed at
securing justice and truth. Indeed, he would explode at the
notion that considerations of truth and justice have any perti-
nence either to the interests of the authorities opposing him or
to his own interests in defying them. ("Later, twenty years later,
[Sarty] was to tell himself, 'If I had said they wanted only truth,
justice, he would have hit me again,'" 29.) For Ab Snopes the only
principle lending significance to his war with the de Spains of
this world is that of blood loyalty — determination to beat your
personal enemy if you can and keep faith, at all costs, with your
clan.

Yet despite all this, Ab does see that part of the power of the
beautiful and the orderly to command our respect depends upon
our refusal to remind ourselves that they have been brought into
existence by other people's labor — by effort that often in history has been slave labor and has seldom been fairly recom-
pensed. Sarty Snopes, grown up, presumably arrives finally at an

understanding both that his father's situation was one of economic oppression and that the oppressors, when sitting in a court of law, are capable of attempting to reach beyond selfishness to a decent distribution of justice. But his father had, at the time, no grip on any of this.

Yet Ab is not a fool, and brutality and insensitivity are not the only features of character that we can make out in him. What we need also to summon is the terrible frustration of an undeveloped mind — aware of the weight of an immense unfairness, aware of the habit of the weak perpetually to behave as though the elegance, grace, beauty, and order found often in the neighborhoods of the rich somehow were traceable exclusively to the superior nature of the rich — and yet unable to move forward from either awareness to anything approaching rational protest. His rage cannot become a force leading toward any positive principle; it has no way to express itself except in viciousness to those closest at hand. It can't begin to make a serious bid for admiration, because whatever inclination we might have to admire it is instantly crossed by repugnance at the cruelty inherent in it.

But it remains true that, together with the ignorance and brutality in Ab Snopes, there is a ferocious, primitive undeceivedness in his reading of the terms of the relationship between rich and poor, lucky and unlucky, advantaged and disadvantaged. Ab Snopes has seen a portion of the truth of the world that many on his level, and most who are luckier, never see. We can damn him for allowing that truth to wreck his humanity, but when we fully bring him to life as a character, it's impossible not to include with our indictment a sense of pity.

CLEANTH BROOKS: Ab Snopes . . . is a hard-bitten sharecropper who has become soured on the world. . . . Being landless, Ab arranges with a landowner to occupy a cabin or tenant's house and is furnished with food and perhaps other supplies through the winter, in return for planting and raising a crop on certain specified acres of land. At harvest time, Ab shares with the landowner half or perhaps two-thirds of what has been gathered, and out of his share pays his bill for supplies. It was not a good system for the tenant, often not for the landowner either, and certainly not for the land. For a sharecropper had little incentive to try to improve the land. Too often, the temporary tenant fell out with the landowner because he had been defrauded, or thought he had been defrauded, of his fair share, and after living a year or two at one place, moved on.

Ab Snopes became so embittered that he retaliated against the last landowner by setting fire to his barn. But it was hard to prove that Ab committed arson, and so he was not jailed but allowed to move on to another part of the country where, late in the season, he took up a tenancy on land belonging to Major de Spain.

Ab arrives with a chip on his shoulder, practically picks a disagreement with de Spain, and almost before his family has settled in the paintless two-room house, prepares to burn de Spain's barn. It is a desperate act as well as criminal, and little Sarty Snopes finds himself caught between loyalty to his father, with whose rage and despair he sympathizes, and his own sense of honor and decency.

He is thoroughly aware that Major de Spain is not at fault and that it is wrong wantonly to destroy his property. This knowledge would prove a considerable burden for an adult to bear, but the Snopes boy has an additional burden: as Faulkner describes it, "the terrible handicap of being young" [para. 40]. Sarty has been impressed by the "peace and dignity" of the de Spain mansion. He is not envious of it. He simply recognizes in it a desirable orderliness that casts a spell over him. He thinks that perhaps it will cast such a spell over his father. As he walks beside him he thinks: "*Maybe he will feel it too. Maybe it will even change him now from what maybe he couldn't help but be*"[41].

What enchants the boy, though, stirs the embittered man to jealous rage.

William Faulkner: First Encounters (1983), pp. 16–17.

Continuing the Discussion

Cleanth Brooks, a literary critic, sees "jealous rage" as the key to Ab Snopes's character; the editor emphasizes Snopes's "frustration." How might this difference in the reading of character be explained?

FOR FURTHER STUDY

T. S. ELIOT   (1888–1965)

The Love Song of J. Alfred Prufrock

S'io credessi che mia risposta fosse
A persona che mai tornasse al mondo,
Questa fiamma staria senza piu scosse.
Ma perciocche giammai di questo fondo
Non torno vivo alcun, s'i'odo il vero,
Senza tema d'infamia ti rispondo.°

Let us go then, you and I,
When the evening is spread out against the sky
Like a patient etherized upon a table;
Let us go, through certain half-deserted streets,
The muttering retreats   5
Of restless nights in one-night cheap hotels
And sawdust restaurants with oyster-shells:
Streets that follow like a tedious argument
Of insidious intent
To lead you to an overwhelming question . . .   10
Oh, do not ask, "What is it?"
Let us go and make our visit.

In the room the women come and go
Talking of Michelangelo.

The yellow fog that rubs its back upon the window-panes,   15
The yellow smoke that rubs its muzzle on the window-panes
Licked its tongue into the corners of the evening,
Lingered upon the pools that stand in drains,
Let fall upon its back the soot that falls from chimneys,
Slipped by the terrace, made a sudden leap,   20
And seeing that it was a soft October night,
Curled once about the house, and fell asleep.

Epigraph. S'io credessi . . . rispondo: From Dante's *Inferno*, canto 27, lines 58–63. The speaker, Guido da Montefeltro, is wrapped in an endless flame for having given false counsel. He begins his life story with these lines: "If I believed that my reply were made to one who could ever climb to the world again, this flame would shake no more. But since no shade ever returned — if what I am told is true — from this blind world into the living light, without fear of dishonor I answer you."

And indeed there will be time°
For the yellow smoke that slides along the street,
Rubbing its back upon the window-panes;   25
There will be time, there will be time
To prepare a face to meet the faces that you meet;
There will be time to murder and create,
And time for all the works and days of hands
That lift and drop a question on your plate;   30
Time for you and time for me,
And time yet for a hundred indecisions,
And for a hundred visions and revisions,
Before the taking of a toast and tea.

In the room the women come and go   35
Talking of Michelangelo.

And indeed there will be time
To wonder, "Do I dare?" and, "Do I dare?"
Time to turn back and descend the stair,
With a bald spot in the middle of my hair —   40
(They will say: "How his hair is growing thin!")
My morning coat, my collar mounting firmly to the chin,
My necktie rich and modest, but asserted by a simple pin —
(They will say: "But how his arms and legs are thin!")
Do I dare   45
Disturb the universe?
In a minute there is time
For decisions and revisions which a minute will reverse.

For I have known them all already, known them all: —
Have known the evenings, mornings, afternoons,   50
I have measured out my life with coffee spoons;
I know the voices dying with a dying fall
Beneath the music from a farther room.
    So how should I presume?

And I have known the eyes already, known them all —   55
The eyes that fix you in a formulated phrase,
And when I am formulated, sprawling on a pin,
When I am pinned and wriggling on the wall,
Then how should I begin
To spit out all the butt-ends of my days and ways?   60
    And how should I presume?

23 *there will be time*: An allusion to Ecclesiastes 3:1–8: "For everything there is a season and a time for every matter under heaven. . . ."

And I have known the arms already, known them all —
Arms that are braceleted and white and bare
(But in the lamplight, downed with light brown hair!)
Is it perfume from a dress   65
That makes me so digress?
Arms that lie along a table, or wrap about a shawl.
   And should I then presume?
   And how should I begin?

     . . . . .

Shall I say, I have gone at dusk through narrow streets   70
And watched the smoke that rises from the pipes
Of lonely men in shirt-sleeves, leaning out of windows? . . .

I should have been a pair of ragged claws
Scuttling across the floors of silent seas.

     . . . . .

And the afternoon, the evening, sleeps so peacefully!   75
Smoothed by long fingers,
Asleep . . . tired . . . or it malingers,
Stretched on the floor, here beside you and me.
Should I, after tea and cakes and ices,
Have the strength to force the moment to its crisis?   80
But though I have wept and fasted, wept and prayed,
Though I have seen my head (grown slightly bald) brought in
   upon a platter,°
I am no prophet — and here's no great matter;
I have seen the moment of my greatness flicker,
And I have seen the eternal Footman hold my coat, and
   snicker,   85
And in short, I was afraid.

And would it have been worth it, after all,
After the cups, the marmalade, the tea,
Among the porcelain, among some talk of you and me,
Would it have been worth while,   90
To have bitten off the matter with a smile,
To have squeezed the universe into a ball°
To roll it toward some overwhelming question,
To say: "I am Lazarus, come from the dead,
Come back to tell you all, I shall tell you all" —   95

---

82 *head . . . upon a platter*: An allusion to John the Baptist, whose head Salome demanded that
Herod deliver to her on a platter (see Matthew 14:1–12 and Mark 6:17–29).   92 *squeezed . . .
a ball*: An allusion to Marvell's "To His Coy Mistress," lines 41–42 (see p. 607).

If one, settling a pillow by her head,
    Should say: "That is not what I meant at all.
    That is not it, at all."

And would it have been worth it, after all,
Would it have been worth while,   100
After the sunsets and the dooryards and the sprinkled streets,
After the novels, after the teacups, after the skirts that trail
    along the floor —
And this, and so much more? —
It is impossible to say just what I mean!
But as if a magic lantern threw the nerves in patterns on a
    screen: 105
Would it have been worth while
If one, settling a pillow or throwing off a shawl,
And turning toward the window, should say:
    "That is not it at all,
    That is not what I meant, at all."   110
          · · · · ·

No! I am not Prince Hamlet, nor was meant to be;
Am an attendant lord,° one that will do
To swell a progress, start a scene or two,
Advise the prince; no doubt, an easy tool,
Deferential, glad to be of use;   115
Politic, cautious, and meticulous;
Full of high sentence, but a bit obtuse;
At times, indeed, almost ridiculous —
Almost, at times, the Fool.

I grow old . . . I grow old . . .   120
I shall wear the bottoms of my trousers rolled.

Shall I part my hair behind? Do I dare to eat a peach?
I shall wear white flannel trousers, and walk upon the beach.
I have heard the mermaids singing, each to each.

I do not think that they will sing to me.   125

I have seen them riding seaward on the waves
Combing the white hair of the waves blown back
When the wind blows the water white and black.

We have lingered in the chambers of the sea
By sea-girls wreathed with seaweed red and brown   130
Till human voices wake us, and we drown.

112 *an attendant lord*: Like Polonius in Shakespeare's *Hamlet* (p. 175).

ROBERT BROWNING   (1812–1889)
Soliloquy of the Spanish Cloister

Gr-r-r — there go, my heart's abhorrence!
   Water your damned flower-pots, do!
If hate killed men, Brother Lawrence,
   God's blood, would not mine kill you!
What? your myrtle-bush wants trimming?   5
   Oh, that rose has prior claims —
Needs its leaden vase filled brimming?
   Hell dry you up with its flames!

At the meal we sit together;
   Salve tibi!° I must hear   *Hail to thee!*   10
Wise talk of the kind of weather,
   Sort of season, time of year:
Not a plenteous cork-crop: scarcely
   Dare we hope oak-galls, I doubt;
What's the Latin name for "parsley"?   15
   What's the Greek name for "swine's snout"?

Whew! We'll have our platter burnished,
   Laid with care on our own shelf!
With a fire-new spoon we're furnished,
   And a goblet for ourself,   20
Rinsed like something sacrificial
   Ere 'tis fit to touch our chaps —
Marked with L. for our initial!
   (He-he! There his lily snaps!)

Saint, forsooth! While Brown Dolores   25
   Squats outside the Convent bank
With Sanchicha, telling stories,
   Steeping tresses in the tank,
Blue-black, lustrous, thick like horsehairs,
   — Can't I see his dead eye glow,   30
Bright as 'twere a Barbary corsair's?
   (That is, if he'd let it show!)

When he finishes refection,
   Knife and fork he never lays
Cross-wise, to my recollection,   35
   As I do, in Jesu's praise.
I the Trinity illustrate,
   Drinking watered orange-pulp —

In three sips the Arian° frustrate;
  While he drains his at one gulp!   40

Oh, those melons! if he's able
  We're to have a feast; so nice!
One goes to the Abbot's table,
  All of us get each a slice.
How go on your flowers? None double?   45
  Not one fruit-sort can you spy?
Strange! — And I, too, at such trouble,
  Keep them close-ripped on the sly!

There's a great text in Galatians,
  Once you trip on it, entails   50
Twenty-nine distinct damnations,
  One sure, if another fails;
If I trip him just a-dying,
  Sure of heaven as sure can be,
Spin him round and send him flying   55
  Off to hell, a Manichee°?

Or, my scrofulous French novel
  On grey paper with blunt type!
Simply glance at it, you grovel
  Hand and foot in Belial's° gripe;   *the Devil's*   60
If I double down its pages
  At the woeful sixteenth print,
When he gathers his greengages,
  Ope a sieve and slip it in't?

Or, there's Satan!—one might venture   65
  Pledge one's soul to him, yet leave
Such a flaw in the indenture
  As he'd miss till, past retrieve,
Blasted lay that rose-acacia
  We're so proud of! *Hy, Zy, Hine.* . . .   70
'St, there's Vespers! *Plena gratia*
Ave, Virgo!° Gr-r-r — you swine!   *Hail, Virgin, full of grace!*

---

39 *Arian*: A follower of Arius, a third- or fourth-century heretic who rejected the doctrine of the Trinity.   56 *Manichee*: A follower of the third-century Persian philosopher Manes, another heretic in the eyes of Brother Lawrence's church.

KATHERINE MANSFIELD   (1888–1923)
Miss Brill

Although it was so brilliantly fine — the blue sky powdered
with gold and great spots of light like white wine splashed over
the Jardins Publiques — Miss Brill was glad that she had decided
on her fur. The air was motionless, but when you opened your
mouth there was just a faint chill, like a chill from a glass of
iced water before you sip, and now and again a leaf came drifting
— from nowhere, from the sky. Miss Brill put up her hand and
touched her fur. Dear little thing! It was nice to feel it again. She
had taken it out of its box that afternoon, shaken out the moth
powder, given it a good brush, and rubbed the life back into the
dim little eyes. "What has been happening to me?" said the sad
little eyes. Oh, how sweet it was to see them snap at her again
from the red eiderdown! . . . But the nose, which was of some
black composition, wasn't at all firm. It must have had a knock,
somehow. Never mind — a little dab of black sealing-wax when
the time came — when it was absolutely necessary . . . Little
rogue! Yes, she really felt like that about it. Little rogue biting its
tail just by her left ear. She could have taken it off and laid it on
her lap and stroked it. She felt a tingling in her hands and arms,
but that came from walking, she supposed. And when she
breathed, something light and sad — no, not sad, exactly —
something gentle seemed to move in her bosom.

There were a number of people out this afternoon, far more
than last Sunday. And the band sounded louder and gayer. That
was because the Season had begun. For although the band played
all the year round on Sundays, out of season it was never the
same. It was like some one playing with only the family to listen;
it didn't care how it played if there weren't any strangers present.
Wasn't the conductor wearing a new coat, too? She was sure it was
new. He scraped with his foot and flapped his arms like a rooster
about to crow, and the bandsmen sitting in the green rotunda
blew out their cheeks and glared at the music. Now there came a
little "flutey" bit — very pretty! — a little chain of bright drops.
She was sure it would be repeated. It was; she lifted her head and
smiled.

Only two people shared her "special" seat: a fine old man in
a velvet coat, his hands clasped over a huge carved walking-stick,
and a big old woman, sitting upright, with a roll of knitting on
her embroidered apron. They did not speak. This was disap-

pointing, for Miss Brill always looked forward to the conversation. She had become really quite expert, she thought, at listening as though she didn't listen, at sitting in other people's lives just for a minute while they talked round her.

She glanced, sideways, at the old couple. Perhaps they would go soon. Last Sunday, too, hadn't been as interesting as usual. An Englishman and his wife, he wearing a dreadful Panama hat and she button boots. And she'd gone on the whole time about how she ought to wear spectacles; she knew she needed them; but that it was no good getting any; they'd be sure to break and they'd never keep on. And he'd been so patient. He'd suggested everything — gold rims, the kind that curved round your ears, little pads inside the bridge. No, nothing would please her. "They'll always be sliding down my nose!" Miss Brill had wanted to shake her.

The old people sat on the bench, still as statues. Never mind, 5 there was always the crowd to watch. To and fro, in front of the flower beds and the band rotunda, the couples and groups paraded, stopped to talk, to greet, to buy a handful of flowers from the old beggar who had his tray fixed to the railings. Little children ran among them, swooping and laughing; little boys with big white silk bows under their chins, little girls, little French dolls, dressed up in velvet and lace. And sometimes a tiny staggerer came suddenly rocking into the open from under the trees, stopped, stared, as suddenly sat down "flop," until its small high-stepping mother, like a young hen, rushed scolding to its rescue. Other people sat on the benches and green chairs, but they were nearly always the same, Sunday after Sunday, and — Miss Brill had often noticed — there was something funny about nearly all of them. They were odd, silent, nearly all old, and from the way they stared they looked as though they'd just come from dark little rooms or even — even cupboards!

Behind the rotunda the slender trees with yellow leaves down drooping, and through them just a line of sea, and beyond the blue sky with gold-veined clouds.

Tum-tum-tum tiddle-um! tiddle-um! tum tiddley-um tum ta! blew the band.

Two young girls in red came by and two young soldiers in blue met them, and they laughed and paired and went off arm-in-arm. Two peasant women with funny straw hats passed, gravely, leading beautiful smoke-colored donkeys. A cold, pale nun hurried by. A beautiful woman came along and dropped her bunch of violets, and a little boy ran after to hand them to her, and she took them and threw them away as if they'd been poisoned. Dear me! Miss Brill didn't know whether to admire that or not! And now an ermine toque and a gentleman in gray met just in front of her. He was tall, stiff, dignified, and she was wearing the ermine toque she'd bought when her hair was yellow. Now everything, her hair, her face, even her eyes, was the same color as the shabby ermine, and her hand, in its cleaned glove, lifted to dab her lips, was a tiny yellowish paw. Oh, she was so pleased to see him — delighted! She rather thought they were going to meet that after-noon. She described where she'd been — everywhere, here, there, along by the sea. The day was so charming — didn't he agree? And wouldn't he, perhaps? . . . But he shook his head, lighted a cigarette, slowly breathed a great deep puff into her face, and, even while she was still talking and laughing, flicked the match away and walked on. The ermine toque was alone; she smiled more brightly than ever. But even the band seemed to know what she was feeling and played more softly, played ten-derly, and the drum beat, "The Brute! The Brute!" over and over. What would she do? What was going to happen now? But as Miss Brill wondered, the ermine toque turned, raised her hand as though she'd seen some one else, much nicer, just over there, and pattered away. And the band changed again and played more quickly, more gayly than ever, and the old couple on Miss Brill's seat got up and marched away, and such a funny old man with long whiskers hobbled along in time to the music and was nearly knocked over by four girls walking abreast.

Oh, how fascinating it was! How she enjoyed it! How she loved sitting here, watching it all! It was like a play. It was exactly like a play. Who could believe the sky at the back wasn't painted? But it wasn't till a little brown dog trotted on solemn and then slowly trotted off, like a little "theater" dog, a little dog that had been drugged, that Miss Brill discovered what it was that made it so exciting. They were all on the stage. They weren't only the audience, not only looking on; they were acting. Even she had a part and came every Sunday. No doubt somebody would have noticed if she hadn't been there; she was part of the performance after all. How strange she'd never thought of it like that before! And yet it explained why she made such a point of starting from home at just the same time each week — so as not to be late for the performance — and it also explained why she had quite a queer, shy feeling at telling her English pupils how she spent her Sunday afternoons. No wonder! Miss Brill nearly laughed out loud. She was on the stage. She thought of the old invalid gentle-

man to whom she read the newspaper four afternoons a week
while he slept in the garden. She had got quite used to the frail
head on the cotton pillow, the hollowed eyes, the open mouth
and the high pinched nose. If he'd been dead she mightn't have
noticed for weeks; she wouldn't have minded. But suddenly he
knew he was having the paper read to him by an actress! "An
actress!" The old head lifted; two points of light quivered in the
old eyes. "An actress — are ye?" And Miss Brill smoothed the
newspaper as though it were the manuscript of her part and said
gently: "Yes, I have been an actress for a long time."

The band had been having a rest. Now they started again. 10
And what they played was warm, sunny, yet there was just a faint
chill — a something, what was it? — not sadness — no, not sadness — a something that made you want to sing. The tune lifted,
lifted, the light shone; and it seemed to Miss Brill that in another
moment all of them, all the whole company, would begin singing.
The young ones, the laughing ones who were moving together,
they would begin, and the men's voices, very resolute and brave,
would join them. And then she too, she too, and the others on the
benches — they would come in with a kind of accompaniment —
something low, that scarcely rose or fell, something so beautiful — moving . . . And Miss Brill's eyes filled with tears and she
looked smiling at all the other members of the company. Yes, we
understand, we understand, she thought — though what they
understood she didn't know.

Just at that moment a boy and a girl came and sat down
where the old couple had been. They were beautifully dressed;
they were in love. The hero and heroine, of course, just arrived
from his father's yacht. And still soundlessly singing, still with
that trembling smile, Miss Brill prepared to listen.

"No, not now," said the girl. "Not here, I can't."

"But why? Because of that stupid old thing at the end there?"
asked the boy. "Why does she come here at all — who wants her?
Why doesn't she keep her silly old mug at home?"

"It's her fu-fur which is so funny," giggled the girl. "It's
exactly like a fried whiting."

"Ah, be off with you!" said the boy in an angry whisper. 15
Then: "Tell me, ma petite chère —

"No, not here," said the girl. "Not *yet*."

On her way home she usually bought a slice of honeycake at
the baker's. It was her Sunday treat. Sometimes there was an
almond in her slice, sometimes not. It made a great difference. If
there was an almond it was like carrying home a tiny present — a

surprise — something that might very well not have been there. She hurried on the almond Sundays and struck the match for the kettle in quite a dashing way.

But today she passed the baker's by, climbed the stairs, went into the little dark room — her room like a cupboard — and sat down on the red eiderdown. She sat there for a long time. The box that the fur came out of was on the bed. She unclasped the necklet quickly; quickly, without looking, laid it inside. But when she put the lid on she thought she heard something crying.

RANDALL JARRELL   (1914–1965)
The Lost Children

Two little girls, one fair, one dark,
One alive, one dead, are running hand in hand
Through a sunny house. The two are dressed
In red and white gingham, with puffed sleeves and sashes.
They run away from me . . . But I am happy;   5
When I wake I feel no sadness, only delight.
I've seen them again, and I am comforted
That, somewhere, they still are.

It is strange
To carry inside you someone else's body;   10
To know it before it's born;
To see at last that it's a boy or girl, and perfect;
To bathe it and dress it; to watch it
Nurse at your breast, till you almost know it
Better than you know yourself — better than it knows itself.   15
You own it as you made it.
You are the authority upon it.

But as the child learns
To take care of herself, you know her less.
Her accidents, adventures are her own,   20
You lose track of them. Still, you know more
About her than anyone *except* her.

Little by little the child in her dies.
You say, "I have lost a child, but gained a friend."
You feel yourself gradually discarded.   25
She argues with you or ignores you
Or is kind to you. She who begged to follow you

Anywhere, just so long as it was you,
Finds follow the leader no more fun.
She makes few demands; you are grateful for the few.   30

The young person who writes once a week
Is the authority upon herself.
She sits in my living room and shows her husband
My albums of her as a child. He enjoys them
And makes fun of them. I look too   35
And I realize the girl in the matching blue
Mother-and-daughter dress, the fair one carrying
The tin lunch box with the half-pint thermos bottle
Or training her pet duck to go down the slide
Is lost just as the dark one, who is dead, is lost.   40
But the world in which the two wear their flared coats
And the hats that match, exists so uncannily
That, after I've seen its pictures for an hour,
I believe in it: the bandage coming loose
One has in the picture of the other's birthday,   45
The castles they are building, at the beach for asthma.
I look at them and all the old sure knowledge
Floods over me, when I put the album down
I keep saying inside: "I *did* know those children.
I braided those braids. I was driving the car   50
The day that she stepped in the can of grease
We were taking to the butcher for our ration points.
I *know* those children. I know all about them.
Where are they?"

I stare at her and try to see some sign   55
Of the child she was. I can't believe there isn't any.
I tell her foolishly, pointing at the picture,
That I keep wondering where she is.
She tells me, "Here I am."
                            Yes, and the other   60
Isn't dead, but has everlasting life . . .

The girl from next door, the borrowed child,
Said to me the other day, "You like children so much,
Don't you want to have some of your own?"
I couldn't believe that she could say it.   65
I thought: "Surely you can look at me and see them."

When I see them in my dreams I feel such joy.
If I could dream of them every night!

When I think of my dream of the little girls

It's as if we were playing hide-and-seek.   70
The dark one
Looks at me longingly, and disappears;
The fair one stays in sight, just out of reach
No matter where I reach. I am tired
As a mother who's played all day, some rainy day.   75
I don't want to play it any more, I don't want to,
But the child keeps on playing, so I play.

WILLIAM SHAKESPEARE (1564–1616)
Hamlet, Prince of Denmark

EDITED BY WILLARD EDWARD FARNHAM

NAMES OF THE ACTORS

Claudius, *King of Denmark*
Hamlet, *son to the late, and nephew
   to the present, King*
Polonius, *Lord Chamberlain*
Horatio, *friend to Hamlet*
Laertes, *son to Polonius*
Voltemand ⎫
Cornelius ⎪
Rosencrantz ⎬ *courtiers*
Guildenstern ⎪
Osric   ⎪
A Gentleman ⎭
A Priest
Marcellus ⎫ *officers*
Bernardo ⎭

Francisco, *a soldier*
Reynaldo, *servant to Polonius*
Players
Two Clowns, *gravediggers*
Fortinbras, *Prince of Norway*
A Norwegian Captain
English Ambassadors
Gertrude, *Queen of Denmark, mother
   to Hamlet*
Ophelia, *daughter to Polonius*
Ghost of Hamlet's Father
Lords, Ladies, Officers, Soldiers,
   Sailors, Messengers, Atten-
   dants

SCENE: *Elsinore Castle, Denmark*

ACT I

SCENE I. *A sentry-post.*

Enter Bernardo and Francisco, two sentinels.

Bernardo: Who's there?
Francisco: Nay, answer me. Stand and unfold yourself.
Bernardo: Long live the king!
Francisco: Bernardo?
Bernardo: He.   5

Francisco: You come most carefully upon your hour.
Bernardo: 'Tis now struck twelve. Get thee to bed, Francisco.
Francisco: For this relief much thanks. 'Tis bitter cold,
  And I am sick at heart.
Bernardo: Have you had quiet guard?
Francisco: Not a mouse stirring.   10
Bernardo: Well, good night.
  If you do meet Horatio and Marcellus,
  The rivals° of my watch, bid them make haste.

Enter Horatio and Marcellus.

Francisco: I think I hear them. Stand, ho! Who is there?
Horatio: Friends to this ground.
Marcellus: And liegemen to the Dane.°   15
Francisco: Give you good night.
Marcellus: O, farewell, honest soldier.
  Who hath relieved you?
Francisco: Bernardo hath my place.
  Give you good night.   *Exit Francisco.*
Marcellus: Holla, Bernardo!
Bernardo: Say —
  What, is Horatio there?
Horatio: A piece of him.
Bernardo: Welcome, Horatio. Welcome, good Marcellus.   20
Horatio: What, has this thing appeared again to-night?
Bernardo: I have seen nothing.
Marcellus: Horatio says 'tis but our fantasy,
  And will not let belief take hold of him
  Touching this dreaded sight twice seen of us.   25
  Therefore I have entreated him along
  With us to watch the minutes of this night,
  That, if again this apparition come,
  He may approve° our eyes and speak to it.
Horatio: Tush, tush, 'twill not appear.
Bernardo: Sit down awhile,   30
  And let us once again assail your ears,
  That are so fortified against our story,
  What we two nights have seen.
Horatio: Well, sit we down,
  And let us hear Bernardo speak of this.
Bernardo: Last night of all,   35

ACT I, SCENE I. 13 *rivals:* Sharers.   15 *Dane:* King of Denmark.   29 *approve:* Confirm.

When yond same star that's westward from the pole°
Had made his course t'illume that part of heaven
Where now it burns, Marcellus and myself,
The bell then beating one —

Enter Ghost.

Marcellus: Peace, break thee off. Look where it comes again.   40
Bernardo: In the same figure like the king that's dead.
Marcellus: Thou art a scholar; speak to it, Horatio.
Bernardo: Looks 'a not like the king? Mark it, Horatio.
Horatio: Most like. It harrows me with fear and wonder.
Bernardo: It would be spoke to.
Marcellus: Speak to it, Horatio.   45
Horatio: What art thou that usurp'st this time of night
    Together with that fair and warlike form
    In which the majesty of buried Denmark°
    Did sometimes° march? By heaven I charge thee, speak.
Marcellus: It is offended.
Bernardo: See, it stalks away.   50
Horatio: Stay. Speak, speak. I charge thee, speak.   *Exit Ghost.*
Marcellus: 'Tis gone and will not answer.
Bernardo: How now, Horatio? You tremble and look pale.
    Is not this something more than fantasy?
    What think you on't?   55
Horatio: Before my God, I might not this believe
    Without the sensible and true avouch
    Of mine own eyes.
Marcellus: Is it not like the king?
Horatio: As thou art to thyself.
    Such was the very armor he had on   60
    When he th' ambitious Norway° combated.
    So frowned he once when, in an angry parle,°
    He smote the sledded Polacks on the ice.
    'Tis strange.
Marcellus: Thus twice before, and jump° at this dead hour,   65
    With martial stalk hath he gone by our watch.
Horatio: In what particular thought to work I know not;
    But, in the gross and scope° of my opinion,
    This bodes some strange eruption to our state.

---

36 *pole*: Polestar.   48 *buried Denmark*: The buried King of Denmark.   49 *sometimes*: Formerly.   61 *Norway*: King of Norway.   62 *parle*: Parley.   65 *jump*: Just, exactly.   68 *gross and scope*: Gross scope, general view.

Marcellus: Good now, sit down, and tell me he that knows,   70
    Why this same strict and most observant watch
    So nightly toils° the subject° of the land,
    And why such daily cast of brazen cannon
    And foreign mart° for implements of war,
    Why such impress° of shipwrights, whose sore task   75
    Does not divide the Sunday from the week.
    What might be toward° that this sweaty haste
    Doth make the night joint-laborer with the day?
    Who is't that can inform me?
Horatio: That can I.
    At least the whisper goes so. Our last king,   80
    Whose image even but now appeared to us,
    Was as you know by Fortinbras of Norway,
    Thereto pricked on by a most emulate° pride,
    Dared to the combat; in which our valiant Hamlet
    (For so this side of our known world esteemed him)   85
    Did slay this Fortinbras; who, by a sealed compact
    Well ratified by law and heraldry,°
    Did forfeit, with his life, all those his lands
    Which he stood seized° of to the conqueror;
    Against the which a moiety competent°   90
    Was gagèd° by our king, which had returned
    To the inheritance of Fortinbras
    Had he been vanquisher, as, by the same comart°
    And carriage° of the article designed,
    His fell to Hamlet. Now, sir, young Fortinbras,   95
    Of unimprovèd° mettle hot and full,
    Hath in the skirts of Norway here and there
    Sharked° up a list of lawless resolutes°
    For food and diet to some enterprise
    That hath a stomach° in't; which is no other,   100
    As it doth well appear unto our state,
    But to recover of us by strong hand
    And terms compulsatory those foresaid lands
    So by his father lost; and this, I take it,
    Is the main motive of our preparations,   105

---

72 *toils*: Makes toil; *subject*: Subjects.   74 *mart*: Trading.   75 *impress*: Conscription.
77 *toward*: In preparation.   83 *emulate*: Jealously rivaling.   87 *law and heraldry*: Law of
heralds regulating combat.   89 *seized*: Possessed.   90 *moiety competent*: Sufficient portion.
91 *gagèd*: Engaged, staked.   93 *comart*: Joint bargain.   94 *carriage*: Purport.   96 *unimpro-
vèd*: Unused.   98 *Sharked*: Snatched indiscriminately as the shark takes prey; *resolutes*:
Desperadoes.   100 *stomach*: Show of venturesomeness.

The source of this our watch, and the chief head°
Of this posthaste and romage° in the land.
Bernardo: I think it be no other but e'en so.
Well may it sort° that this portentous figure
Comes armèd through our watch so like the king   110
That was and is the question of these wars.
Horatio: A mote° it is to trouble the mind's eye.
In the most high and palmy state of Rome,
A little ere the mightiest Julius fell,
The graves stood tenantless and the sheeted° dead   115
Did squeak and gibber in the Roman streets;
As° stars with trains of fire and dews of blood,
Disasters° in the sun; and the moist star°
Upon whose influence Neptune's empire stands
Was sick almost to doomsday with eclipse.   120
And even the like precurse° of feared events,
As harbingers° preceding still° the fates
And prologue to the omen° coming on,
Have heaven and earth together demonstrated
Unto our climatures° and countrymen.   125

Enter Ghost.

But soft, behold, lo where it comes again!
I'll cross it,° though it blast me. — Stay, illusion.

He spreads his arms.

If thou hast any sound or use of voice,
Speak to me.
If there be any good thing to be done   130
That may to thee do ease and grace to me,
Speak to me.
If thou art privy to thy country's fate,
Which happily° foreknowing may avoid,
O, speak!   135
Or if thou hast uphoarded in thy life
Extorted treasure in the womb of earth,
For which, they say, you spirits oft walk in death,

---

106 *head*: Fountainhead, source.   107 *romage*: Intense activity.   109 *sort*: Suit.   112 *mote*:
Speck of dust.   115 *sheeted*: In shrouds.   117 *As*: Something is obviously wrong with the
transition of thought. The conjecture that some preceding matter has been left out of the text
is perhaps as good as any.   118 *Disasters*: Ominous signs; *moist star*: Moon.   121 *precurse*:
Foreshadowing.   122 *harbingers*: Forerunners; *still*: Constantly.   123 *omen*: Calamity.
125 *climatures*: Regions.   127 *cross it*: Cross its path.   134 *happily*: Haply, perchance.

The cock crows.

      Speak of it. Stay and speak. Stop it, Marcellus.

Marcellus: Shall I strike at it with my partisan?°   140

Horatio: Do, if it will not stand.

Bernardo: 'Tis here.

Horatio: 'Tis here.   *Exit Ghost.*

Marcellus: 'Tis gone.

    We do it wrong, being so majestical,

    To offer it the show of violence,

    For it is as the air invulnerable,   145

    And our vain blows malicious mockery.

Bernardo: It was about to speak when the cock crew.

Horatio: And then it started, like a guilty thing

    Upon a fearful summons. I have heard

    The cock, that is the trumpet to the morn,   150

    Doth with his lofty and shrill-sounding throat

    Awake the god of day, and at his warning,

    Whether in sea or fire, in earth or air,

    Th' extravagant° and erring° spirit hies

    To his confine; and of the truth herein   155

    This present object made probation.°

Marcellus: It faded on the crowing of the cock.

    Some say that ever 'gainst° that season comes

    Wherein our Saviour's birth is celebrated,

    This bird of dawning singeth all night long,   160

    And then, they say, no spirit dare stir abroad,

    The nights are wholesome, then no planets strike,°

    No fairy takes,° nor witch hath power to charm.

    So hallowed and so gracious is that time.

Horatio: So have I heard and do in part believe it.   165

    But look, the morn in russet mantle clad

    Walks o'er the dew of yon high eastward hill.

    Break we our watch up, and by my advice

    Let us impart what we have seen to-night

    Unto young Hamlet, for upon my life   170

    This spirit, dumb to us, will speak to him.

    Do you consent we shall acquaint him with it,

    As needful in our loves, fitting our duty?

Marcellus: Let's do't, I pray, and I this morning know

    Where we shall find him most conveniently.   *Exeunt.* 175

---

140 *partisan*: Pike.   154 *extravagant*: Wandering beyond bounds; *erring*: Wandering.
156 *probation*: Proof.   158 *'gainst*: Just before.   162 *strike*: Work evil by influence.
163 *takes*: Bewitches.

SCENE II. *A room of state.*

Flourish. Enter Claudius, King of Denmark, Gertrude the Queen, Councillors, Polonius and his son Laertes, Hamlet, cum aliis° including Voltemand and Cornelius.

King: Though yet of Hamlet our dear brother's death
    The memory be green, and that it us befitted
    To bear our hearts in grief, and our whole kingdom
    To be contracted in one brow of woe,
    Yet so far hath discretion fought with nature   5
    That we with wisest sorrow think on him
    Together with remembrance of ourselves.
    Therefore our sometime sister, now our queen,
    Th' imperial jointress° to this warlike state,
    Have we, as 'twere with a defeated joy,   10
    With an auspicious and a dropping eye,
    With mirth in funeral and with dirge in marriage,
    In equal scale weighing delight and dole,
    Taken to wife. Nor have we herein barred°
    Your better wisdoms, which have freely gone   15
    With this affair along. For all, our thanks.
    Now follows, that you know, young Fortinbras,
    Holding a weak supposal of our worth,
    Or thinking by our late dear brother's death
    Our state to be disjoint and out of frame,   20
    Colleaguèd° with this dream of his advantage,
    He hath not failed to pester us with message
    Importing the surrender of those lands
    Lost by his father, with all bands of law,
    To our most valiant brother. So much for him.   25
    Now for ourself and for this time of meeting.
    Thus much the business is: we have here writ
    To Norway, uncle of young Fortinbras —
    Who, impotent and bedrid, scarcely hears
    Of this his nephew's purpose — to suppress   30
    His further gait° herein, in that the levies,
    The lists, and full proportions° are all made
    Out of his subject; and we here dispatch
    You, good Cornelius, and you, Voltemand,
    For bearers of this greeting to old Norway,   35
    Giving to you no further personal power

SCENE II. *cum aliis*: With others.   9 *jointress*: A woman who has a jointure, or joint tenancy of an estate.   14 *barred*: Excluded.   21 *Colleaguèd*: United.   31 *gait*: Going.   32 *proportions*: Amounts of forces and supplies.

> To business with the king, more than the scope
> Of these delated° articles allow.
> Farewell, and let your haste commend your duty.

Cornelius: ⎱
Voltemand: ⎰ In that, and all things, will we show our duty.   40

King: We doubt it nothing. Heartily farewell.

Exeunt Voltemand and Cornelius.

> And now, Laertes, what's the news with you?
> You told us of some suit. What is't, Laertes?
> You cannot speak of reason to the Dane°
> And lose your voice.° What wouldst thou beg, Laertes,   45
> That shall not be my offer, not thy asking?
> The head is not more native° to the heart,
> The hand more instrumental° to the mouth,
> Than is the throne of Denmark to thy father.
> What wouldst thou have, Laertes?

Laertes: My dread lord,   50
> Your leave and favor to return to France,
> From whence though willingly I came to Denmark
> To show my duty in your coronation,
> Yet now I must confess, that duty done,
> My thoughts and wishes bend again toward France   55
> And bow them to your gracious leave and pardon.

King: Have you your father's leave? What says Polonius?

Polonius: He hath, my lord, wrung from me my slow leave
> By laborsome petition, and at last
> Upon his will I sealed my hard consent.   60
> I do beseech you give him leave to go.

King: Take thy fair hour, Laertes. Time be thine,
> And thy best graces spend it at thy will.
> But now, my cousin° Hamlet, and my son —

Hamlet (aside): A little more than kin,° and less than kind!°   65

King: How is it that the clouds still hang on you?

Hamlet: Not so, my lord. I am too much in the sun.°

Queen: Good Hamlet, cast thy nighted color off,
> And let thine eye look like a friend on Denmark.

---

38 *delated*: Detailed.   44 *Dane*: King of Denmark.   45 *lose your voice*: Speak in vain.
47 *native*: Joined by nature.   48 *instrumental*: Serviceable.   64 *cousin*: Kinsman more
distant than parent, child, brother, or sister.   65 *kin*: Related as nephew; *kind*: Kindly in
feeling, as by kind, or nature, a son would be to his father.   67 *sun*: Sunshine of the king's
undesired favor (with the punning additional meaning of "place of a son").

Do not for ever with thy vailèd° lids   70
Seek for thy noble father in the dust.
Thou know'st 'tis common. All that lives must die,
Passing through nature to eternity.
Hamlet: Ay, madam, it is common.
Queen: If it be,
Why seems it so particular with thee?   75
Hamlet: Seems, madam? Nay, it is. I know not "seems."
'Tis not alone my inky cloak, good mother,
Nor customary suits of solemn black,
Nor windy suspiration of forced breath,
No, nor the fruitful river in the eye,   80
Nor the dejected havior of the visage,
Together with all forms, moods, shapes of grief,
That can denote me truly. These indeed seem,
For they are actions that a man might play,
But I have that within which passeth show —   85
These but the trappings and the suits of woe.
King: 'Tis sweet and commendable in your nature, Hamlet,
To give these mourning duties to your father,
But you must know your father lost a father,
That father lost, lost his, and the survivor bound   90
In filial obligation for some term
To do obsequious° sorrow. But to persever°
In obstinate condolement is a course
Of impious stubbornness. 'Tis unmanly grief.
It shows a will most incorrect to heaven,   95
A heart unfortified, a mind impatient,
An understanding simple and unschooled.
For what we know must be and is as common
As any the most vulgar thing to sense,
Why should we in our peevish opposition   100
Take it to heart? Fie, 'tis a fault to heaven,
A fault against the dead, a fault to nature,
To reason most absurd, whose common theme
Is death of fathers, and who still hath cried,
From the first corse till he that died to-day,   105
"This must be so." We pray you throw to earth
This unprevailing woe, and think of us
As of a father, for let the world take note

---

70 *vailèd*: Downcast.   92 *obsequious*: Proper to obsequies or funerals; *persever*: Persevere
(accented on the second syllable, as always in Shakespeare).

You are the most immediate to our throne,
And with no less nobility of love   110
Than that which dearest father bears his son
Do I impart toward you. For your intent
In going back to school in Wittenberg,
It is most retrograde° to our desire,
And we beseech you, bend you to remain   115
Here in the cheer and comfort of our eye,
Our chiefest courtier, cousin, and our son.
Queen: Let not thy mother lose her prayers, Hamlet.
I pray thee stay with us, go not to Wittenberg.
Hamlet: I shall in all my best obey you, madam.   120
King: Why, 'tis a loving and a fair reply.
Be as ourself in Denmark. Madam, come.
This gentle and unforced accord of Hamlet
Sits smiling to my heart, in grace whereof
No jocund health that Denmark drinks to-day   125
But the great cannon to the clouds shall tell,
And the king's rouse° the heaven shall bruit° again,
Respeaking earthly thunder. Come away.

Flourish. Exeunt all but Hamlet.

Hamlet: O that this too too sullied° flesh would melt,
Thaw, and resolve itself into a dew,   130
Or that the Everlasting had not fixed
His canon° 'gainst self-slaughter. O God, God,
How weary, stale, flat, and unprofitable
Seem to me all the uses of this world!
Fie on't, ah, fie, 'tis an unweeded garden   135
That grows to seed. Things rank and gross in nature
Possess it merely.° That it should come to this,
But two months dead, nay, not so much, not two,
So excellent a king, that was to this
Hyperion° to a satyr, so loving to my mother   140
That he might not beteem° the winds of heaven

114 *retrograde:* Contrary.   127 *rouse:* Toast drunk in wine; *bruit:* Echo.   129 *sullied:* Use of
this emendation of the "sallied" of the 1604–5 quarto instead of the widely accepted "solid"
of the 1623 folio is strongly recommended by: (1) the implications of the interestingly
corrupt "too much grieu'd and sallied flesh" of the 1603 quarto, into which the intrusive
participle "grieu'd" cannot be thought to have come at the call of an original "solid"
standing in the place of "sallied"; (2) the example of the "sallies" in a later passage of
the 1604–5 quarto (II.i.39), which in its context is most certainly to be taken as "sullies"
and which in the folio appears as "sulleyes."   132 *canon:* Law.   137 *merely:* Completely.
140 *Hyperion:* The sun god.   141 *beteem:* Allow.

Visit her face too roughly. Heaven and earth,
Must I remember? Why, she would hang on him
As if increase of appetite had grown
By what it fed on, and yet within a month — 145
Let me not think on't; frailty, thy name is woman —
A little month, or ere those shoes were old
With which she followed my poor father's body
Like Niobe,° all tears, why she, even she —
O God, a beast that wants discourse° of reason 150
Would have mourned longer — married with my uncle,
My father's brother, but no more like my father
Than I to Hercules. Within a month,
Ere yet the salt of most unrighteous tears
Had left the flushing in her gallèd° eyes, 155
She married. O, most wicked speed, to post
With such dexterity to incestuous sheets!
It is not nor it cannot come to good.
But break my heart, for I must hold my tongue.

Enter Horatio, Marcellus, and Bernardo.

Horatio: Hail to your lordship!
Hamlet: I am glad to see you well. 160
     Horatio — or I do forget myself.
Horatio: The same, my lord, and your poor servant ever.
Hamlet: Sir, my good friend, I'll change° that name with you.
     And what make° you from Wittenberg, Horatio?
     Marcellus? 165
Marcellus: My good lord!
Hamlet: I am very glad to see you. (*To Bernardo.*) Good even, sir.
     But what, in faith, make you from Wittenberg?
Horatio: A truant disposition, good my lord.
Hamlet: I would not hear your enemy say so, 170
     Nor shall you do my ear that violence
     To make it truster of your own report
     Against yourself. I know you are no truant.
     But what is your affair in Elsinore?
     We'll teach you to drink deep ere you depart. 175
Horatio: My lord, I came to see your father's funeral.
Hamlet: I prithee do not mock me, fellow student.
     I think it was to see my mother's wedding.

149 *Niobe*: The proud mother who boasted of having more children than Leto and was
punished when they were slain by Apollo and Artemis, children of Leto; the grieving Niobe
was changed by Zeus into a stone, which continually dropped tears.   150 *discourse*: Logical
power or process.   155 *gallèd*: Irritated.   163 *change*: Exchange.   164 *make*: Do.

Horatio: Indeed, my lord, it followed hard upon.

Hamlet: Thrift, thrift, Horatio. The funeral baked meats   180
    Did coldly furnish forth the marriage tables.
    Would I had met my dearest° foe in heaven
    Or ever I had seen that day, Horatio!
    My father — methinks I see my father.

Horatio: Where, my lord?

Hamlet: In my mind's eye, Horatio.   185

Horatio: I saw him once. 'A was a goodly king.

Hamlet: 'A was a man, take him for all in all,
    I shall not look upon his like again.

Horatio: My lord, I think I saw him yesternight.

Hamlet: Saw? who?   190

Horatio: My lord, the king your father.

Hamlet: The king my father?

Horatio: Season your admiration° for a while
    With an attent ear till I may deliver
    Upon the witness of these gentlemen
    This marvel to you.

Hamlet: For God's love let me hear!   195

Horatio: Two nights together had these gentlemen,
    Marcellus and Bernardo, on their watch
    In the dead waste and middle of the night
    Been thus encountered. A figure like your father,
    Armèd at point° exactly, cap-a-pe,°   200
    Appears before them and with solemn march
    Goes slow and stately by them. Thrice he walked
    By their oppressed and fear-surprisèd eyes
    Within his truncheon's° length, whilst they, distilled
    Almost to jelly with the act of fear,   205
    Stand dumb and speak not to him. This to me
    In dreadful secrecy impart they did,
    And I with them the third night kept the watch,
    Where, as they had delivered, both in time,
    Form of the thing, each word made true and good,   210
    The apparition comes. I knew your father.
    These hands are not more like.

Hamlet: But where was this?

Marcellus: My lord, upon the platform where we watched.

Hamlet: Did you not speak to it?

---

182 *dearest:* Direst, bitterest.   192 *Season your admiration:* Control your wonder.   200 *at point:* Completely; *cap-a-pe:* From head to foot.   204 *truncheon:* Military commander's baton.

Horatio: My lord, I did,
    But answer made it none. Yet once methought   215
    It lifted up it° head and did address
    Itself to motion like as it would speak.
    But even then the morning cock crew loud,
    And at the sound it shrunk in haste away
    And vanished from our sight.
Hamlet: 'Tis very strange.   220
Horatio: As I do live, my honored lord, 'tis true,
    And we did think it writ down in our duty
    To let you know of it.
Hamlet: Indeed, indeed, sirs, but this troubles me.
    Hold you the watch to-night?
All: We do, my lord.   225
Hamlet: Armed, say you?
All: Armed, my lord.
Hamlet: From top to toe?
All: My lord, from head to foot.
Hamlet: Then saw you not his face?
Horatio: O, yes, my lord. He wore his beaver° up.   230
Hamlet: What, looked he frowningly?
Horatio: A countenance more in sorrow than in anger.
Hamlet: Pale or red?
Horatio: Nay, very pale.
Hamlet: And fixed his eyes upon you?
Horatio: Most constantly.
Hamlet: I would I had been there.   235
Horatio: It would have much amazed you.
Hamlet: Very like, very like. Stayed it long?
Horatio: While one with moderate haste might tell° a hundred.
Both: Longer, longer.
Horatio: Not when I saw't.
Hamlet: His beard was grizzled,° no?   240
Horatio: It was as I have seen it in his life,
    A sable silvered.°
Hamlet: I will watch to-night.
    Perchance 'twill walk again.
Horatio: I warr'nt it will.
Hamlet: If it assume my noble father's person,
    I'll speak to it though hell itself should gape   245

---

216 *it*: Its.   230 *beaver*: Visor or movable face-guard of the helmet.   238 *tell*: Count.
240 *grizzled*: Grey.   242 *sable silvered*: Black mixed with white.

And bid me hold my peace. I pray you all,
If you have hitherto concealed this sight,
Let it be tenable° in your silence still,
And whatsomever else shall hap to-night,
Give it an understanding but no tongue.   250
I will requite your loves. So fare you well.
Upon the platform, 'twixt eleven and twelve
I'll visit you.
All: Our duty to your honor.
Hamlet: Your loves, as mine to you. Farewell.
                                        Exeunt all but Hamlet.
My father's spirit — in arms? All is not well.   255
I doubt° some foul play. Would the night were come!
Till then sit still, my soul. Foul deeds will rise,
Though all the earth o'erwhelm them, to men's eyes.   *Exit.*

SCENE III. *The chambers of Polonius.*

Enter Laertes and Ophelia, his sister.

Laertes: My necessaries are embarked. Farewell.
     And, sister, as the winds give benefit
     And convoy° is assistant, do not sleep,
     But let me hear from you.
Ophelia: Do you doubt that?
Laertes: For Hamlet, and the trifling of his favor,   5
     Hold it a fashion and a toy in blood,
     A violet in the youth of primy° nature,
     Forward, not permanent, sweet, not lasting,
     The perfume and suppliance° of a minute,
     No more.
Ophelia: No more but so?
Laertes: Think it no more.   10
     For nature crescent° does not grow alone
     In thews and bulk, but as this temple° waxes
     The inward service of the mind and soul
     Grows wide withal. Perhaps he loves you now,
     And now no soil nor cautel° doth besmirch   15
     The virtue of his will,° but you must fear,
     His greatness weighed,° his will is not his own.

---

248 *tenable*: Held firmly.   256 *doubt*: Suspect, fear.   SCENE III. 3 *convoy*: Means of transport.
7 *primy*: Of the springtime.   9 *perfume and suppliance*: Filling sweetness.   11 *crescent*:
Growing.   12 *this temple*: The body.   15 *cautel*: Deceit.   16 *will*: Desire.   17 *greatness
weighed*: High position considered.

For he himself is subject to his birth.
He may not, as unvalued persons do,
Carve for himself, for on his choice depends   20
The safety and health of this whole state,
And therefore must his choice be circumscribed
Unto the voice and yielding° of that body
Whereof he is the head. Then if he says he loves you,
It fits your wisdom so far to believe it   25
As he in his particular act and place
May give his saying deed, which is no further
Than the main voice of Denmark goes withal.
Then weigh what loss your honor may sustain
If with too credent° ear you list his songs,   30
Or lose your heart, or your chaste treasure open
To his unmastered importunity.
Fear it, Ophelia, fear it, my dear sister,
And keep you in the rear of your affection,°
Out of the shot and danger of desire.   35
The chariest maid is prodigal enough
If she unmask her beauty to the moon.
Virtue itself scapes not calumnious strokes.
The canker° galls° the infants of the spring
Too oft before their buttons° be disclosed,   40
And in the morn and liquid dew of youth
Contagious blastments° are most imminent.
Be wary then; best safety lies in fear.
Youth to itself rebels, though none else near.
Ophelia: I shall the effect of this good lesson keep   45
As watchman to my heart, but, good my brother,
Do not as some ungracious pastors do,
Show me the steep and thorny way to heaven,
Whiles like a puffed and reckless libertine
Himself the primrose path of dalliance treads   50
And recks° not his own rede.°
Enter Polonius.
Laertes: O, fear me not.
I stay too long. But here my father comes.
A double blessing is a double grace;
Occasion smiles upon a second leave.
Polonius: Yet here, Laertes? Aboard, aboard, for shame!   55

---

23 *yielding:* Assent.   30 *credent:* Credulous.   34 *affection:* Feelings, which rashly lead forward into dangers.   39 *canker:* Rose worm; *galls:* Injures.   40 *buttons:* Buds.   42 *blastments:* Blights.   51 *recks:* Regards; *rede:* Counsel.

The wind sits in the shoulder of your sail,
And you are stayed for. There — my blessing with thee,
And these few precepts in thy memory
Look thou character.° Give thy thoughts Ems no tongue,
Nor any unproportioned° thought his act.   60
Be thou familiar, but by no means vulgar.
Those friends thou hast, and their adoption tried,
Grapple them unto thy soul with hoops of steel,
But do not dull thy palm with entertainment
Of each new-hatched, unfledged courage.° Beware   65
Of entrance to a quarrel; but being in,
Bear't that th' opposèd may beware of thee.
Give every man thine ear, but few thy voice;
Take each man's censure,° but reserve thy judgment.
Costly thy habit as thy purse can buy,   70
But not expressed in fancy; rich, not gaudy,
For the apparel oft proclaims the man,
And they in France of the best rank and station
Are of a most select and generous chief° in that.
Neither a borrower nor a lender be,   75
For loan oft loses both itself and friend,
And borrowing dulleth edge of husbandry.°
This above all, to thine own self be true,
And it must follow as the night the day
Thou canst not then be false to any man.   80
Farewell. My blessing season° this in thee!
Laertes: Most humbly do I take my leave, my lord.
Polonius: The time invites you. Go, your servants tend.°
Laertes: Farewell, Ophelia, and remember well
What I have said to you.
Ophelia: 'Tis in my memory locked,   85
And you yourself shall keep the key of it.
Laertes: Farewell.   *Exit Laertes.*
Polonius: What is't, Ophelia, he hath said to you?
Ophelia: So please you, something touching the Lord Hamlet.
Polonius: Marry,° well bethought.   90
'Tis told me he hath very oft of late
Given private time to you, and you yourself
Have of your audience been most free and bounteous.

---

59 *character*: Inscribe.   60 *unproportioned*: Unadjusted to what is right.   65 *courage*: Man of
spirit, young blood.   69 *censure*: Judgment.   74 *chief*: Eminence.   77 *husbandry*: Thrifti-
ness.   81 *season*: Ripen and make fruitful.   83 *tend*: Wait.   90 *Marry*: By Mary.

If it be so — as so 'tis put on me,
And that in way of caution — I must tell you   95
You do not understand yourself so clearly
As it behooves my daughter and your honor.
What is between you? Give me up the truth.

Ophelia: He hath, my lord, of late made many tenders°
Of his affection to me.   100

Polonius: Affection? Pooh! You speak like a green girl,
Unsifted° in such perilous circumstance.
Do you believe his tenders, as you call them?

Ophelia: I do not know, my lord, what I should think.

Polonius: Marry, I will teach you. Think yourself a baby   105
That you have ta'en these tenders° for true pay
Which are not sterling. Tender yourself more dearly,
Or (not to crack the wind of° the poor phrase,
Running it thus) you'll tender me a fool.

Ophelia: My lord, he hath importuned me with love   110
In honorable fashion.

Polonius: Ay, fashion you may call it. Go to,° go to.

Ophelia: And hath given countenance to his speech, my lord,
With almost all the holy vows of heaven.

Polonius: Ay, springes° to catch woodcocks.° I do know,   115
When the blood burns, how prodigal the soul
Lends the tongue vows. These blazes, daughter,
Giving more light than heat, extinct in both
Even in their promise, as it is a-making,
You must not take for fire. From this time   120
Be something scanter of your maiden presence.
Set your entreatments° at a higher rate
Than a command to parley.° For Lord Hamlet,
Believe so much in him that he is young,
And with a larger tether may he walk   125
Than may be given you. In few, Ophelia,
Do not believe his vows, for they are brokers,°

---

99 *tenders*: Offers.   102 *Unsifted*: Untested.   106–09 *tenders . . . Tender . . . tender*: Offers . . .
hold in regard . . . present (a word play going through three meanings, the last use of the
word yielding further complexity with its valid implications that she will show herself to him
as a fool, will show him to the world as a fool, and may go so far as to present him with a baby,
which would be a fool because "fool" was an Elizabethan term of endearment especially
applicable to an infant as a "little innocent").   108 *crack . . . of*: Make wheeze like a horse
driven too hard.   112 *Go to*: Go away, go on (expressing impatience).   115 *springes*:
Snares; *woodcocks*: Birds believed foolish.   122 *entreatments*: Military negotiations for surrender.   123 *parley*: Confer with a besieger.   127 *brokers*: Middlemen, panders.

Not of that dye which their investments° show,
But mere implorators of unholy suits,
Breathing like sanctified and pious bawds,   130
The better to beguile. This is for all:
I would not, in plain terms, from this time forth
Have you so slander° any moment° leisure
As to give words or talk with the Lord Hamlet.
Look to't, I charge you. Come your ways.   135

Ophelia: I shall obey, my lord.   *Exeunt.*

SCENE IV. *The sentry-post.*

Enter Hamlet, Horatio, and Marcellus.

Hamlet: The air bites shrewdly;° it is very cold.
Horatio: It is a nipping and an eager° air.
Hamlet: What hour now?
Horatio: I think it lacks of twelve.
Marcellus: No, it is struck.
Horatio: Indeed? I heard it not. It then draws near the season   5
    Wherein the spirit held his wont to walk.

A flourish of trumpets, and two pieces goes off.

    What does this mean, my lord?
Hamlet: The king doth wake to-night and takes his rouse,°
    Keeps wassail, and the swaggering upspring° reels,
    And as he drains his draughts of Rhenish° down   10
    The kettledrum and trumpet thus bray out
    The triumph° of his pledge.
Horatio: Is it a custom?
Hamlet: Ay, marry, is't,
    But to my mind, though I am native here
    And to the manner born, it is a custom   15
    More honored in the breach than the observance.°
    This heavy-headed revel east and west
    Makes us traduced and taxed of° other nations.
    They clepe° us drunkards and with swinish phrase
    Soil our addition,° and indeed it takes   20

---

128 *investments*: Clothes.   133 *slander*: Use disgracefully; *moment*: Momentary.   SCENE IV.
1 *shrewdly*: Wickedly.   2 *eager*: Sharp.   8 *rouse*: Carousal.   9 *upspring*: A German dance.
10 *Rhenish*: Rhine wine.   12 *triumph*: Achievement, feat (in downing a cup of wine at one
draught).   16 *More . . . observance*: Better broken than observed.   18 *taxed of*: Censured by.
19 *clepe*: Call.   20 *addition*: Reputation, title added as a distinction.

From our achievements, though performed at height,
The pith and marrow of our attribute.°
So oft it chances in particular men
That (for some vicious mole° of nature in them,
As in their birth, wherein they are not guilty,   25
Since nature cannot choose his° origin)
By the o'ergrowth of some complexion,°
Oft breaking down the pales° and forts of reason,
Or by some habit that too much o'erleavens°
The form of plausive° manners — that (these men   30
Carrying, I say, the stamp of one defect,
Being nature's livery,° or fortune's star°)
Their virtues else, be they as pure as grace,
As infinite as man may undergo,
Shall in the general censure take corruption   35
From that particular fault. The dram of evil
Doth all the noble substance of a doubt,°
To his own scandal.

Enter Ghost.

Horatio: Look, my lord, it comes.
Hamlet: Angels and ministers of grace defend us!
Be thou a spirit of health° or goblin° damned,   40
Bring with thee airs from heaven or blasts from hell,
Be thy intents wicked or charitable,
Thou com'st in such a questionable shape
That I will speak to thee. I'll call thee Hamlet,
King, father, royal Dane. O, answer me!   45
Let me not burst in ignorance, but tell
Why thy canonized° bones, hearsèd in death,
Have burst their cerements,° why the sepulchre
Wherein we saw thee quietly interred

---

22 *attribute*: Reputation, what is attributed.   24 *mole*: Blemish, flaw.   26 *his*: Its.
27 *complexion*: Part of the makeup, combination of humors.   28 *pales*: Barriers, fences.
29 *o'erleavens*: Works change throughout, as yeast ferments dough.   30 *plausive*: Pleasing.
32 *livery*: Characteristic equipment or provision; *star*: Makeup as formed by stellar influence.
37 *Doth . . . doubt*: This difficult and often altered line is here printed without emendation. In
the famous crux of which it is a key part the intent of what Hamlet is saying had perhaps best
be taken as a close rewording of what he has just been saying; he may be taken to say that the
dram of evil imparts a doubtful quality to all the noble human substance, to his (its) own
scandal, i.e., to the detriment of the nobility itself because of the general censure that he has
mentioned before in developing at involved length what he offers here with the emphasis of
brevity.   40 *of health*: Sound, good; *goblin*: Fiend.   47 *canonized*: Buried with the established rites of the Church.   48 *cerements*: Waxed grave-cloths.

Hath oped his ponderous and marble jaws   50
To cast thee up again. What may this mean
That thou, dead corse, again in complete steel,
Revisits thus the glimpses of the moon,
Making night hideous, and we fools of nature°
So horridly to shake our disposition   55
With thoughts beyond the reaches of our souls?
Say, why is this? wherefore? what should we do?

Ghost beckons.

Horatio: It beckons you to go away with it,
    As if it some impartment did desire
    To you alone.
Marcellus: Look with what courteous action   60
    It waves you to a more removèd ground.
    But do not go with it.
Horatio: No, by no means.
Hamlet: It will not speak. Then will I follow it.
Horatio: Do not, my lord.
Hamlet: Why, what should be the fear?
    I do not set my life at a pin's fee,   65
    And for my soul, what can it do to that,
    Being a thing immortal as itself?
    It waves me forth again. I'll follow it.
Horatio: What if it tempt you toward the flood, my lord,
    Or to the dreadful summit of the cliff   70
    That beetles° o'er his base into the sea,
    And there assume some other horrible form,
    Which might deprive° your sovereignty of reason°
    And draw you into madness? Think of it.
    The very place puts toys° of desperation,   75
    Without more motive, into every brain
    That looks so many fathoms to the sea
    And hears it roar beneath.
Hamlet: It waves me still.
    Go on. I'll follow thee.
Marcellus: You shall not go, my lord.
Hamlet: Hold off your hands.   80
Horatio: Be ruled. You shall not go.

---

54 *fools of nature*: Men made conscious of natural limitations by a supernatural manifestation.
71 *beetles*: Juts out.   73 *deprive*: Take away; *sovereignty of reason*: State of being ruled by reason.
75 *toys*: Fancies.

Hamlet: My fate cries out
And makes each petty artere° in this body
As hardy as the Nemean lion's° nerve.°
Still am I called. Unhand me, gentlemen.
By heaven, I'll make a ghost of him that lets° me!   85
I say, away! Go on. I'll follow thee.

                                        Exit Ghost, and Hamlet.

Horatio: He waxes desperate with imagination.
Marcellus: Let's follow. 'Tis not fit thus to obey him.
Horatio: Have after. To what issue will this come?
Marcellus: Something is rotten in the state of Denmark.   90
Horatio: Heaven will direct it.
Marcellus: Nay, let's follow him.   *Exeunt.*

SCENE V. *Another part of the fortifications.*

Enter Ghost and Hamlet.

Hamlet: Whither wilt thou lead me? Speak. I'll go no further.
Ghost: Mark me.
Hamlet: I will.
Ghost: My hour is almost come,
When I to sulph'rous and tormenting flames°
Must render up myself.
Hamlet: Alas, poor ghost!
Ghost: Pity me not, but lend thy serious hearing   5
To what I shall unfold.
Hamlet: Speak. I am bound to hear.
Ghost: So art thou to revenge, when thou shalt hear.
Hamlet: What?
Ghost: I am thy father's spirit,
Doomed for a certain term to walk the night,   10
And for the day confined to fast° in fires,
Till the foul crimes done in my days of nature
Are burnt and purged away. But that I am forbid
To tell the secrets of my prison house,
I could a tale unfold whose lightest word   15
Would harrow up thy soul, freeze thy young blood,
Make thy two eyes like stars start from their spheres,°
Thy knotted and combinèd locks to part,

---

82 *artere*: Artery.   83 *Nemean lion*: A lion slain by Hercules in the performance of one of his twelve labors; *nerve*: Sinew.   85 *lets*: Hinders.   SCENE V. 3 *flames*: Sufferings in purgatory (not hell).   11 *fast*: Do penance.   17 *spheres*: Transparent revolving shells in each of which, according to the Ptolemaic astronomy, a planet or other heavenly body was placed.

And each particular hair to stand an° end
Like quills upon the fretful porpentine.°   20
But this eternal blazon° must not be
To ears of flesh and blood. List, list, O, list!
If thou didst ever thy dear father love —

Hamlet: O God!

Ghost: Revenge his foul and most unnatural murder.   25

Hamlet: Murder?

Ghost: Murder most foul, as in the best it is,
But this most foul, strange, and unnatural.

Hamlet: Haste me to know't, that I, with wings as swift
As meditation° or the thoughts of love,   30
May sweep to my revenge.

Ghost: I find thee apt,
And duller shouldst thou be than the fat weed
That roots itself in ease on Lethe° wharf,
Wouldst thou not stir in this. Now, Hamlet, hear.
'Tis given out that, sleeping in my orchard,   35
A serpent stung me. So the whole ear of Denmark
Is by a forgèd process° of my death
Rankly abused. But know, thou noble youth,
The serpent that did sting thy father's life
Now wears his crown.

Hamlet: O my prophetic soul!   40
My uncle?

Ghost: Ay, that incestuous, that adulterate° beast,
With witchcraft of his wit, with traitorous gifts —
O wicked wit and gifts, that have the power
So to seduce! — won to his shameful lust   45
The will of my most seeming-virtuous queen.
O Hamlet, what a falling-off was there,
From me, whose love was of that dignity
That it went hand in hand even with the vow
I made to her in marriage, and to decline   50
Upon a wretch whose natural gifts were poor
To those of mine!
But virtue, as it never will be moved,
Though lewdness court it in a shape of heaven,°
So lust, though to a radiant angel linked,   55

---

19 *an*: On.   20 *porpentine*: Porcupine.   21 *eternal blazon*: Revelation of eternity.
30 *meditation*: Thought.   33 *Lethe*: The river in Hades which brings forgetfulness of past life
to a spirit who drinks of it.   37 *forgèd process*: Falsified official report.   42 *adulterate*:
Adulterous.   54 *shape of heaven*: Angelic disguise.

Will sate itself in a celestial bed
And prey on garbage.
But soft, methinks I scent the morning air.
Brief let me be. Sleeping within my orchard,
My custom always of the afternoon,   60
Upon my secure° hour thy uncle stole
With juice of cursed hebona° in a vial,
And in the porches of my ears did pour
The leperous distilment, whose effect
Holds such an enmity with blood of man   65
That swift as quicksilver it courses through
The natural gates and alleys of the body,
And with a sudden vigor it doth posset°
And curd, like eager° droppings into milk,
The thin and wholesome blood. So did it mine,   70
And a most instant tetter° barked° about
Most lazar-like° with vile and loathsome crust
All my smooth body.
Thus was I sleeping by a brother's hand
Of life, of crown, of queen at once dispatched,   75
Cut off even in the blossoms of my sin,
Unhouseled,° disappointed,° unaneled,°
No reck'ning made, but sent to my account
With all my imperfections on my head.
O, horrible! O, horrible! most horrible!   80
If thou hast nature in thee, bear it not.
Let not the royal bed of Denmark be
A couch for luxury° and damnèd incest.
But howsomever thou pursues this act,
Taint not thy mind, nor let thy soul contrive   85
Against thy mother aught. Leave her to heaven
And to those thorns that in her bosom lodge
To prick and sting her. Fare thee well at once.
The glowworm shows the matin° to be near
And gins to pale his uneffectual fire.   90
Adieu, adieu, adieu. Remember me.   *Exit.*
Hamlet: O all you host of heaven! O earth! What else?
And shall I couple hell? O fie! Hold, hold, my heart,
And you, my sinews, grow not instant old,

---

61 *secure*: Carefree, unsuspecting.   62 *hebona*: Some poisonous plant.   68 *posset*: Curdle.
69 *eager*: Sour.   71 *tetter*: Eruption; *barked*: Covered as with a bark.   72 *lazar-like*: Leper-
like.   77 *Unhouseled*: Without the Sacrament; *disappointed*: Unprepared spiritually; *unaneled*:
Without extreme unction.   83 *luxury*: Lust.   89 *matin*: Morning.

But bear me stiffly up. Remember thee? 95
Ay, thou poor ghost, while memory holds a seat
In this distracted globe.° Remember thee?
Yea, from the table° of my memory
I'll wipe away all trivial fond records,
All saws° of books, all forms,° all pressures° past 100
That youth and observation copied there,
And thy commandment all alone shall live
Within the book and volume of my brain,
Unmixed with baser matter. Yes, by heaven!
O most pernicious woman! 105
O villain, villain, smiling, damnèd villain!
My tables — meet it is I set it down
That one may smile, and smile, and be a villain.
At least I am sure it may be so in Denmark.

Writes.

So, uncle, there you are. Now to my word: 110
It is "Adieu, adieu, remember me."
I have sworn't.

Enter Horatio and Marcellus.

Horatio: My lord, my lord!
Marcellus: Lord Hamlet!
Horatio: Heavens secure him!
Hamlet: So be it!
Marcellus: Illo, ho, ho,° my lord! 115
Hamlet: Hillo, ho, ho, boy! Come, bird, come.
Marcellus: How is't, my noble lord?
Horatio: What news, my lord?
Hamlet: O, wonderful!
Horatio: Good my lord, tell it.
Hamlet: No, you will reveal it.
Horatio: Not I, my lord, by heaven.
Marcellus: Nor I, my lord. 120
Hamlet: How say you then? Would heart of man once think it?
    But you'll be secret?
Both: Ay, by heaven, my lord.
Hamlet: There's never a villain dwelling in all Denmark
    But he's an arrant knave.

97 *globe*: Head.   98 *table*: Writing tablet, record book.   100 *saws*: Wise sayings; *forms*: Mental images, concepts; *pressures*: Impressions.   115 *Illo, ho, ho*: Cry of the falconer to summon his hawk.

Horatio: There needs no ghost, my lord, come from the grave   125
    To tell us this.
Hamlet: Why, right, you are in the right,
    And so, without more circumstance° at all,
    I hold it fit that we shake hands and part:
    You, as your business and desires shall point you,
    For every man hath business and desire   130
    Such as it is, and for my own poor part,
    Look you, I'll go pray.
Horatio: These are but wild and whirling words, my lord.
Hamlet: I am sorry they offend you, heartily;
    Yes, faith, heartily.
Horatio: There's no offense, my lord.   135
Hamlet: Yes, by Saint Patrick, but there is, Horatio,
    And much offense too. Touching this vision here,
    It is an honest° ghost, that let me tell you.
    For your desire to know what is between us,
    O'ermaster't as you may. And now, good friends,   140
    As you are friends, scholars, and soldiers,
    Give me one poor request.
Horatio: What is't, my lord? We will.
Hamlet: Never make known what you have seen to-night.
Both: My lord, we will not.
Hamlet: Nay, but swear't.
Horatio: In faith,   145
    My lord, not I.
Marcellus: Nor I, my lord — in faith.
Hamlet: Upon my sword.°
Marcellus: We have sworn, my lord, already.
Hamlet: Indeed, upon my sword, indeed.

Ghost cries under the stage.

Ghost: Swear.
Hamlet: Ha, ha, boy, say'st thou so? Art thou there, truepenny?°   150
    Come on. You hear this fellow in the cellarage.
    Consent to swear.
Horatio: Propose the oath, my lord.
Hamlet: Never to speak of this that you have seen,
    Swear by my sword.
Ghost (beneath): Swear.   155

---

127 *circumstance*: Ceremony.   138 *honest*: Genuine (not a disguised demon).   147 *sword*:
I.e., upon the cross formed by the sword hilt.   150 *truepenny*: Honest old fellow.

Hamlet: Hic et ubique?° Then we'll shift our ground.
 Come hither, gentlemen,
 And lay your hands again upon my sword.
 Swear by my sword
 Never to speak of this that you have heard.   160
Ghost (beneath): Swear by his sword.
Hamlet: Well said, old mole! Canst work i' th' earth so fast?
 A worthy pioner!° Once more remove, good friends.
Horatio: O day and night, but this is wondrous strange!
Hamlet: And therefore as a stranger give it welcome.   165
 There are more things in heaven and earth, Horatio,
 Than are dreamt of in your philosophy.°
 But come:
 Here as before, never, so help you mercy,
 How strange or odd some'er I bear myself   170
 (As I perchance hereafter shall think meet
 To put an antic° disposition on),
 That you, at such times seeing me, never shall,
 With arms encumb'red° thus, or this head-shake,
 Or by pronouncing of some doubtful phrase,   175
 As "Well, well, we know," or "We could, an if° we would,"
 Or "If we list to speak," or "There be, an if they might,"
 Or such ambiguous giving out, to note
 That you know aught of me — this do swear,
 So grace and mercy at your most need help you.   180
Ghost (beneath): Swear.

They swear.

Hamlet: Rest, rest, perturbèd spirit! So, gentlemen,
 With all my love I do commend° me to you,
 And what so poor a man as Hamlet is
 May do t' express his love and friending to you,   185
 God willing, shall not lack. Let us go in together,
 And still° your fingers on your lips, I pray.
 The time is out of joint. O cursèd spite
 That ever I was born to set it right!
 Nay, come, let's go together.   *Exeunt.* 190

156 *Hic et ubique*: Here and everywhere.   163 *pioner*: Pioneer, miner.   167 *your philosophy*:
This philosophy one hears about.   172 *antic*: Grotesque, mad.   174 *encumb'red*: Folded.
176 *an if*: If.   183 *commend*: Entrust.   187 *still*: Always.

ACT II

SCENE I. *The chambers of Polonius.*

Enter old Polonius, with his man Reynaldo.

Polonius: Give him this money and these notes, Reynaldo.
Reynaldo: I will, my lord.
Polonius: You shall do marvellous wisely, good Reynaldo,
    Before you visit him, to make inquire
    Of his behavior.
Reynaldo: My lord, I did intend it.   5
Polonius: Marry, well said, very well said. Look you, sir,
    Enquire me first what Danskers° are in Paris,
    And how, and who, what means,° and where they keep,°
    What company, at what expense; and finding
    By this encompassment° and drift of question   10
    That they do know my son, come you more nearer
    Than your particular demands° will touch it.
    Take you as 'twere some distant knowledge of him,
    As thus, "I know his father and his friends,
    And in part him" — do you mark this, Reynaldo?   15
Reynaldo: Ay, very well, my lord.
Polonius: "And in part him, but," you may say, "not well,
    But if't be he I mean, he's very wild
    Addicted so and so." And there put on him
    What forgeries° you please; marry, none so rank   20
    As may dishonor him — take heed of that —
    But, sir, such wanton, wild, and usual slips
    As are companions noted and most known
    To youth and liberty.
Reynaldo: As gaming, my lord.
Polonius: Ay, or drinking, fencing, swearing, quarrelling,   25
    Drabbing.° You may go so far.
Reynaldo: My lord, that would dishonor him.
Polonius: Faith, no, as you may season° it in the charge.
    You must not put another scandal on him,
    That he is open to incontinency.°   30

ACT II, SCENE I. 7 *Danskers*: Danes.   8 *what means*: What their wealth; *keep*: Dwell.
10 *encompassment*: Circling about.   12 *particular demands*: Definite questions.   20 *forgeries*:
Invented wrongdoings.   26 *Drabbing*: Whoring.   28 *season*: Soften.   30 *incontinency*: Extreme sensuality.

That's not my meaning. But breathe his faults so quaintly°
That they may seem the taints of liberty,
The flash and outbreak of a fiery mind,
A savageness in unreclaimèd° blood,
Of general assault.°
Reynaldo: But, my good lord —   35
Polonius: Wherefore should you do this?
Reynaldo: Ay, my lord,
I would know that.
Polonius: Marry, sir, here's my drift,
And I believe it is a fetch of warrant.°
You laying these slight sullies on my son
As 'twere a thing a little soiled i' th' working,   40
Mark you,
Your party in converse, him you would sound,
Having ever° seen in the prenominate° crimes
The youth you breathe of guilty, be assured
He closes with you° in this consequence:°   45
"Good sir," or so, or "friend," or "gentleman" —
According to the phrase or the addition°
Of man and country —
Reynaldo: Very good, my lord.
Polonius: And then, sir, does 'a this — 'a does —
What was I about to say? By the mass, I was about to   50
say something! Where did I leave?
Reynaldo: At "closes in the consequence," at "friend or
so," and "gentleman."
Polonius: At "closes in the consequence" — Ay, marry!
He closes thus: "I know the gentleman;   55
I saw him yesterday, or t' other day,
Or then, or then, with such or such, and, as you say,
There was 'a gaming, there o'ertook° in's rouse,°
There falling out° at tennis"; or perchance,
"I saw him enter such a house of sale,"   60
Videlicet,° a brothel, or so forth.
See you now —
Your bait of falsehood takes this carp of truth,
And thus do we of wisdom and of reach,°

31 *quaintly*: Expertly, gracefully.   34 *unreclaimèd*: Untamed.   35 *Of general assault*: Assailing
all young men.   38 *fetch of warrant*: Allowable trick.   43 *Having ever*: If he has ever;
prenominate: Aforementioned.   45 *closes with you*: Follows your lead to a conclusion; *consequence*: Following way.   47 *addition*: Title.   58 *o'ertook*: Overcome with drunkenness; *rouse*:
Carousal.   59 *falling out*: Quarrelling.   61 *Videlicet*: Namely.   64 *reach*: Far-reaching
comprehension.

With windlasses° and with assays of bias,°   65
By indirections find directions° out.
So, by my former lecture and advice,
Shall you my son. You have me, have you not?
Reynaldo: My lord, I have.
Polonius: Good bye ye,° fare ye well.
Reynaldo: Good my lord.   70
Polonius: Observe his inclination in yourself.
Reynaldo: I shall, my lord.
Polonius: And let him ply his music.
Reynaldo: Well, my lord.
Polonius: Farewell.   *Exit Reynaldo.*

Enter Ophelia.

                How now, Ophelia, what's the matter?
Ophelia: O my lord, my lord, I have been so affrighted!   75
Polonius: With what, i' th' name of God?
Ophelia: My lord, as I was sewing in my closet,°
    Lord Hamlet, with his doublet° all unbraced,°
    No hat upon his head, his stockings fouled,
    Ungartered, and down-gyvèd° to his ankle,   80
    Pale as his shirt, his knees knocking each other,
    And with a look so piteous in purport
    As if he had been loosèd out of hell
    To speak of horrors — he comes before me.
Polonius: Mad for thy love?
Ophelia: My lord, I do not know,   85
    But truly I do fear it.
Polonius: What said he?
Ophelia: He took me by the wrist and held me hard.
    Then goes he to the length of all his arm,
    And with his other hand thus o'er his brow
    He falls to such perusal of my face   90
    As 'a would draw it. Long stayed he so.
    At last, a little shaking of mine arm
    And thrice his head thus waving up and down,
    He raised a sigh so piteous and profound
    As it did seem to shatter all his bulk   95
    And end his being. That done, he lets me go,

---

65 *windlasses*: Roundabout courses; *assays of bias*: Devious attacks.   66 *directions*: Ways of
procedure.   69 *God bye ye*: God be with you, good-bye.   77 *closet*: Private living-room.
78 *doublet*: Jacket; *unbraced*: Unlaced.   80 *down-gyvèd*: Fallen down like gyves or fetters on a
prisoner's legs.

And with his head over his shoulder turned
He seemed to find his way without his eyes,
For out o'doors he went without their helps
And to the last bended their light on me.   100
Polonius: Come, go with me. I will go seek the king.
    This is the very ecstasy° of love,
    Whose violent property° fordoes° itself
    And leads the will to desperate undertakings
    As oft as any passion under heaven   105
    That does afflict our natures. I am sorry.
    What, have you given him any hard words of late?
Ophelia: No, my good lord; but as you did command
    I did repel his letters and denied
    His access to me.
Polonius: That hath made him mad.   110
    I am sorry that with better heed and judgment
    I had not quoted° him. I feared he did but trifle
    And meant to wrack thee; but beshrew° my jealousy.
    By heaven, it is as proper to our age
    To cast beyond ourselves° in our opinions   115
    As it is common for the younger sort
    To lack discretion. Come, go we to the king.
    This must be known, which, being kept close,° might move°
    More grief to hide than hate to utter love.°
    Come.   *Exeunt.* 120

SCENE **II.** *A chamber in the castle.*

Flourish. Enter King and Queen, Rosencrantz, and Guildenstern with others.

King: Welcome, dear Rosencrantz and Guildenstern.
    Moreover that° we much did long to see you,
    The need we have to use you did provoke
    Our hasty sending. Something have you heard
    Of Hamlet's transformation — so call it,   5
    Sith° nor th' exterior nor the inward man
    Resembles that it was. What it should be,
    More than his father's death, that thus hath put him
    So much from th' understanding of himself,

---

102 *ecstasy:* Madness.   103 *property:* Quality; *fordoes:* Destroys.   112 *quoted:* Observed.
113 *beshrew:* Curse.   115 *cast beyond ourselves:* Find by calculation more significance in
something than we ought to.   118 *close:* Secret; *move:* cause.   119 *to hide . . . love:* By such
hiding of love than there would be hate moved by a revelation of it (a violently condensed
putting of the case which is a triumph of special statement for Polonius).   SCENE II.
2 *Moreover that:* Besides the fact that.   6 *Sith:* Since.

I cannot dream of. I entreat you both   10
That, being of so young days brought up with him,
And sith so neighbored to his youth and havior,°
That you vouchsafe your rest here in our court
Some little time, so by your companies
To draw him on to pleasures, and to gather   15
So much as from occasion you may glean,
Whether aught to us unknown afflicts him thus,
That opened° lies within our remedy.

Queen: Good gentlemen, he hath much talked of you,
And sure I am two men there are not living   20
To whom he more adheres.° If it will please you
To show us so much gentry° and good will
As to expend your time with us awhile
For the supply and profit of our hope,
Your visitation shall receive such thanks   25
As fits a king's remembrance.

Rosencrantz: Both your majesties
Might, by the sovereign power you have of us,
Put your dread pleasures more into command
Than to entreaty.

Guildenstern: But we both obey,
And here give up ourselves in the full bent°   30
To lay our service freely at your feet,
To be commanded.

King: Thanks, Rosencrantz and gentle Guildenstern.
Queen: Thanks, Guildenstern and gentle Rosencrantz.
And I beseech you instantly to visit   35
My too much changèd son. — Go, some of you,
And bring these gentlemen where Hamlet is.

Guildenstern: Heavens make our presence and our practices
Pleasant and helpful to him!

Queen: Ay, amen!

*Exeunt Rosencrantz and Guildenstern
with some Attendants.*

Enter Polonius.

Polonius: Th' ambassadors from Norway, my good lord,   40
Are joyfully returned.

King: Thou still° hast been the father of good news.

---

12 *youth and havior*: Youthful ways of life.   18 *opened*: Revealed.   21 *more adheres*: Is more
attached.   22 *gentry*: Courtesy.   30 *in the full bent*: At the limit of bending (of a bow), to
full capacity.   42 *still*: Always.

Polonius: Have I, my lord? Assure you, my good liege,
    I hold my duty as I hold my soul,
    Both to my God and to my gracious king,   45
    And I do think — or else this brain of mine
    Hunts not the trail of policy so sure
    As it hath used to do — that I have found
    The very cause of Hamlet's lunacy.
King: O, speak of that! That do I long to hear.   50
Polonius: Give first admittance to th' ambassadors.
    My news shall be the fruit° to that great feast.
King: Thyself do grace° to them and bring them in.   *Exit Polonius.*
    He tells me, my dear Gertrude, he hath found
    The head and source of all your son's distemper.   55
Queen: I doubt° it is no other but the main,
    His father's death and our o'erhasty marriage.
King: Well, we shall sift him.

Enter Ambassadors Voltemand and Cornelius, with Polonius.

                           Welcome, my good friends.
    Say, Voltemand, what from our brother Norway?
Voltemand: Most fair return of greetings and desires.   60
    Upon our first,° he sent out to suppress
    His nephew's levies, which to him appeared
    To be a preparation 'gainst the Polack,
    But better looked into, he truly found
    It was against your highness, whereat grieved,   65
    That so his sickness, age, and impotence
    Was falsely borne in hand,° sends out arrests
    On Fortinbras; which he in brief obeys,
    Receives rebuke from Norway, and in fine°
    Makes vow before his uncle never more   70
    To give th' assay° of arms against your majesty.
    Whereon old Norway, overcome with joy,
    Gives him threescore thousand crowns in annual fee
    And his commission to employ those soldiers,
    So levied as before, against the Polack,   75
    With an entreaty, herein further shown,

(Gives a paper.)

    That it might please you to give quiet pass
    Through your dominions for this enterprise,

---

52 *fruit*: Dessert.   53 *grace*: Honor.   56 *doubt*: Suspect.   61 *our first*: Our first words about the matter.   67 *borne in hand*: Deceived.   69 *in fine*: In the end.   71 *assay*: Trial.

On such regards° of safety and allowance
As therein are set down.

King: It likes us well;   80
And at our more considered time° we'll read,
Answer, and think upon this business.
Meantime we thank you for your well-took labor.
Go to your rest; at night we'll feast together.
Most welcome home!   *Exeunt Ambassadors.*

Polonius: This business is well ended.   85
My liege and madam, to expostulate°
What majesty should be, what duty is,
Why day is day, night night, and time is time,
Were nothing but to waste night, day, and time.
Therefore, since brevity is the soul of wit,°   90
And tediousness the limbs and outward flourishes,
I will be brief. Your noble son is mad.
Mad call I it, for, to define true madness,
What is't but to be nothing else but mad?
But let that go.

Queen: More matter, with less art.   95
Polonius: Madam, I swear I use no art at all.
That he is mad, 'tis true: 'tis true 'tis pity,
And pity 'tis 'tis true — a foolish figure.°
But farewell it, for I will use no art.
Mad let us grant him then, and now remains   100
That we find out the cause of this effect —
Or rather say, the cause of this defect,
For this effect defective comes by cause.
Thus it remains, and the remainder thus.
Perpend.°   105
I have a daughter (have while she is mine),
Who in her duty and obedience, mark,
Hath given me this. Now gather, and surmise.

(Reads the letter.)

"To the celestial, and my soul's idol, the most beautified
Ophelia," —   110
That's an ill phrase, a vile phrase; "beautified" is a vile
phrase. But you shall hear. Thus:

(Reads.)

---

79 *regards*: Terms.   81 *considered time*: Convenient time for consideration.   86 *expostulate*:
Discuss.   90 *wit*: Understanding.   98 *figure*: Figure in rhetoric.   105 *Perpend*: Ponder.

"In her excellent white bosom, these, &c."

Queen: Came this from Hamlet to her?

Polonius: Good madam, stay awhile. I will be faithful.   115

(Reads.)

>   "Doubt° thou the stars are fire;
>   Doubt that the sun doth move;
>   Doubt truth to be a liar;
>   But never doubt I love.
>   "O dear Ophelia, I am ill at these numbers.° I have not   120
> art to reckon my groans, but that I love thee best, O
> most best, believe it. Adieu.
>   "Thine evermore, most dear lady,
>   whilst this machine° is to° him, Hamlet."

This in obedience hath my daughter shown me,   125
And more above° hath his solicitings,
As they fell out by time, by means, and place,
All given to mine ear.

King: But how hath she
Received his love?

Polonius: What do you think of me?

King: As of a man faithful and honorable.   130

Polonius: I would fain prove so. But what might you think,
When I had seen this hot love on the wing
(As I perceived it, I must tell you that,
Before my daughter told me), what might you,
Or my dear majesty your queen here, think,   135
If I had played the desk or table book,°
Or given my heart a winking,° mute and dumb,
Or looked upon this love with idle sight?
What might you think? No, I went round° to work
And my young mistress thus I did bespeak: 140
"Lord Hamlet is a prince, out of thy star.°
This must not be." And then I prescripts° gave her,
That she should lock herself from his resort,
Admit no messengers, receive no tokens.
Which done, she took the fruits of my advice,   145
And he, repellèd, a short tale to make,

---

116 *Doubt:* Suspect.   120 *numbers:* Verses.   124 *machine:* Body; *to:* Attached to.
126 *above:* Besides.   136 *desk or table book:* I.e., silent receiver.   137 *winking:* Closing of the
eyes.   139 *round:* Roundly, plainly.   141 *star:* Condition determined by stellar influence.
142 *prescripts:* Instructions.

Fell into a sadness, then into a fast,
Thence to a watch,° thence into a weakness,
Thence to a lightness,° and, by this declension,
Into the madness wherein now he raves,   150
And all we mourn for.
King: Do you think 'tis this?
Queen: It may be, very like.
Polonius: Hath there been such a time — I would fain know that —
That I have positively said "'Tis so,"
When it proved otherwise?
King: Not that I know.   155
Polonius (pointing to his head and shoulder):
Take this from this, if this be otherwise.
If circumstances lead me, I will find
Where truth is hid, though it were hid indeed
Within the center.°
King: How may we try it further?
Polonius: You know sometimes he walks four hours together   160
Here in the lobby.
Queen: So he does indeed.
Polonius: At such a time I'll loose my daughter to him.
Be you and I behind an arras° then.
Mark the encounter. If he love her not,
And be not from his reason fallen thereon,°   165
Let me be no assistant for a state
But keep a farm and carters.
King: We will try it.

Enter Hamlet reading on a book.

Queen: But look where sadly the poor wretch comes reading.
Polonius: Away, I do beseech you both, away.

                              Exit King and Queen with Attendants.

I'll board° him presently.° O, give me leave.   170
How does my good Lord Hamlet?
Hamlet: Well, God-a-mercy.°
Polonius: Do you know me, my lord?
Hamlet: Excellent well. You are a fishmonger.°

---

148 *watch*: Sleepless state.   149 *lightness*: Lightheadedness.   159 *center*: Center of the earth
and also of the Ptolemaic universe.   163 *arras*: Hanging tapestry.   165 *thereon*: On that
account.   170 *board*: Accost; *presently*: At once.   172 *God-a-mercy*: Thank you (literally,
"God have mercy!").   174 *fishmonger*: Seller of harlots, procurer (a cant term used here with
a glance at the fishing Polonius is doing when he offers Ophelia as bait).

Polonius: Not I, my lord.   175
Hamlet: Then I would you were so honest a man.
Polonius: Honest, my lord?
Hamlet: Ay, sir. To be honest, as this world goes, is to be one man
    picked out of ten thousand.
Polonius: That's very true, my lord.   180
Hamlet: For if the sun breed maggots in a dead dog, being a good
    kissing carrion° — Have you a daughter?
Polonius: I have, my lord.
Hamlet: Let her not walk i' th' sun. Conception is a blessing, but
    as your daughter may conceive, friend, look to't.   185
Polonius (aside): How say you by that? Still harping on my daugh-
    ter. Yet he knew me not at first. 'A said I was a fishmonger. 'A
    is far gone, far gone. And truly in my youth I suffered much
    extremity for love, very near this. I'll speak to him again. —
    What do you read, my lord?   190
Hamlet: Words, words, words.
Polonius: What is the matter, my lord?
Hamlet: Between who?°
Polonius: I mean the matter that you read, my lord.
Hamlet: Slanders, sir, for the satirical rogue says here that old   195
    men have grey beards, that their faces are wrinkled, their
    eyes purging thick amber and plum-tree gum, and that they
    have a plentiful lack of wit, together with most weak hams.
    All which, sir, though I most powerfully and potently believe,
    yet I hold it not honesty to have it thus set down, for you   200
    yourself, sir, should be old as I am if, like a crab, you could go
    backward.
Polonius (aside): Though this be madness, yet there is method
    in't. — Will you walk out of the air, my lord?
Hamlet: Into my grave?   205
Polonius: Indeed, that's out of the air. (*Aside.*) How pregnant°
    sometimes his replies are! a happiness° that often madness
    hits on, which reason and sanity could not so prosperously be
    delivered of. I will leave him and suddenly contrive the
    means of meeting between him and my daughter. — My   210
    honorable lord, I will most humbly take my leave of you.
Hamlet: You cannot, sir, take from me anything that I will more
    willingly part withal° — except my life, except my life, ex-
    cept my life.

---

182 *good kissing carrion*: Good bit of flesh for kissing.   193 *Between who*: Matter for a quarrel
between what persons (Hamlet's willful misunderstanding).   206 *pregnant*: Full of meaning.
207 *happiness*: Aptness of expression.   213 *withal*: With.

Enter Guildenstern and Rosencrantz.

Polonius: Fare you well, my lord.   215
Hamlet: These tedious old fools!
Polonius: You go to seek the Lord Hamlet. There he is.
Rosencrantz (to Polonius): God save you, sir!   *Exit Polonius.*
Guildenstern: My honored lord!
Rosencrantz: My most dear lord!   220
Hamlet: My excellent good friends! How dost thou, Guilden-
   stern? Ah, Rosencrantz! Good lads, how do ye both?
Rosencrantz: As the indifferent° children of the earth.
Guildenstern: Happy in that we are not over-happy.
   On Fortune's cap we are not the very button.   225
Hamlet: Nor the soles of her shoe?
Rosencrantz: Neither, my lord.
Hamlet: Then you live about her waist, or in the middle of her
   favors?
Guildenstern: Faith, her privates° we.   230
Hamlet: In the secret parts of Fortune? O, most true! she is a
   strumpet. What news?
Rosencrantz: None, my lord, but that the world's grown honest.
Hamlet: Then is doomsday near. But your news is not true. Let
   me question more in particular. What have you, my good   235
   friends, deserved at the hands of fortune that she sends you
   to prison hither?
Guildenstern: Prison, my lord?
Hamlet: Denmark's a prison.
Rosencrantz: Then is the world one.   240
Hamlet: A goodly one; in which there are many confines,° wards,°
   and dungeons, Denmark being one o' th' worst.
Rosencrantz: We think not so, my lord.
Hamlet: Why, then 'tis none to you, for there is nothing either
   good or bad but thinking makes it so. To me it is a prison.   245
Rosencrantz: Why, then your ambition makes it one. 'Tis too nar-
   row for your mind.
Hamlet: O God, I could be bounded in a nutshell and count
   myself a king of infinite space, were it not that I have bad
   dreams.   250
Guildenstern: Which dreams indeed are ambition, for the very
   substance of the ambitious is merely the shadow of a dream.

---

223 *indifferent*: Average.   230 *privates*: Ordinary men in private, not public, life (with
obvious play upon the sexual term "private parts").   241. *confines*: Places of imprisonment;
wards: Cells.

Hamlet: A dream itself is but a shadow.

Rosencrantz: Truly, and I hold ambition of so airy and light a quality that it is but a shadow's shadow.   255

Hamlet: Then are our beggars bodies,° and our monarchs and outstretched° heroes the beggars' shadows. Shall we to th' court? for, by my fay,° I cannot reason.

Both: We'll wait upon° you.

Hamlet: No such matter. I will not sort you with the rest of my   260
servants, for, to speak to you like an honest man, I am most dreadfully attended. But in the beaten way of friendship, what make° you at Elsinore?

Rosencrantz: To visit you, my lord; no other occasion.

Hamlet: Beggar that I am, I am even poor in thanks, but I thank   265
you; and sure, dear friends, my thanks are too dear a half-penny.° Were you not sent for? Is it your own inclining? Is it a free visitation? Come, come, deal justly with me. Come, come. Nay, speak.

Guildenstern: What should we say, my lord?   270

Hamlet: Why, anything — but to th' purpose. You were sent for, and there is a kind of confession in your looks, which your modesties have not craft enough to color. I know the good king and queen have sent for you.

Rosencrantz: To what end, my lord?   275

Hamlet: That you must teach me. But let me conjure you by the rights of our fellowship, by the consonancy° of our youth, by the obligation of our ever-preserved love, and by what more dear a better proposer° can charge you withal,° be even° and direct with me whether you were sent for or no.   280

Rosencrantz (aside to Guildenstern): What say you?

Hamlet (aside): Nay then, I have an eye of you. — If you love me, hold not off.

Guildenstern: My lord, we were sent for.

Hamlet: I will tell you why. So shall my anticipation prevent°   285
your discovery,° and your secrecy to the king and queen moult no feather.° I have of late — but wherefore I know not — lost all my mirth, forgone all custom of exercises; and indeed, it goes so heavily with my disposition that this goodly

---

256 *bodies*: Solid substances, not shadows (because beggars lack ambition).   257 *outstretched*: Elongated as shadows (with a corollary implication of far-reaching with respect to the ambitions that make both heroes and monarchs into shadows).   258 *fay*: Faith.   259 *wait upon*: Attend.   263 *make*: Do.   267 *a halfpenny*: At a halfpenny.   277 *consonancy*: Accord (in sameness of age).   279 *proposer*: Propounder;   *withal*: With; *even*: Straight.   285 *prevent*: forestall.   286 *discovery*: Disclosure.   287 *moult no feather*: Be left whole.

frame the earth seems to me a sterile promontory; this most 290
excellent canopy, the air, look you, this brave o'erhanging
firmament,° this majestical roof fretted° with golden fire —
why, it appeareth nothing to me but a foul and pestilent
congregation of vapors. What a piece of work is a man, how
noble in reason, how infinite in faculties; in form and mov- 295
ing how express° and admirable, in action how like an angel,
in apprehension how like a god: the beauty of the world, the
paragon of animals! And yet to me what is this quintessence°
of dust? Man delights not me — nor woman neither, though
by your smiling you seem to say so. 300

Rosencrantz: My lord, there was no such stuff in my thoughts.

Hamlet: Why did ye laugh then, when I said "Man delights not
me"?

Rosencrantz: To think, my lord, if you delight not in man, what
lenten° entertainment the players shall receive from you. We 305
coted° them on the way, and hither are they coming to offer
you service.

Hamlet: He that plays the king shall be welcome — his majesty
shall have tribute of me — , the adventurous knight shall use
his foil and target,° the lover shall not sigh gratis, the hu- 310
morous man° shall end his part in peace, the clown shall
make those laugh whose lungs are tickle o' th' sere,° and the
lady shall say her mind freely, or the blank verse shall halt°
for't. What players are they?

Rosencrantz: Even those you were wont to take such delight in, the 315
tragedians of the city.

Hamlet: How chances it they travel? Their residence,° both in
reputation and profit, was better both ways.

Rosencrantz: I think their inhibition° comes by the means of the
late innovation.° 320

Hamlet: Do they hold the same estimation they did when I was in
the city? Are they so followed?

Rosencrantz: No indeed, are they not.

Hamlet: How comes it? Do they grow rusty?

---

292 *firmament*: Sky; *fretted*: Decorated with fretwork. 296 *express*: Well framed.
298 *quintessence*: Fifth or last and finest essence (an alchemical term). 305 *lenten*: Scanty.
306 *coted*: Overtook. 310 *foil and target*: Sword and shield. 311 *humorous man*: Eccentric
character dominated by one of the humours. 312 *tickle o' th' sere*: Hair-triggered for the
discharge of laughter ("sere": part of a gunlock). 313 *halt*: Go lame. 317 *residence*:
Residing at the capital. 319 *inhibition*: Impediment to acting in residence (formal prohibi-
tion?). 320 *innovation*: New fashion of having companies of boy actors play on the "private" stage (?), political upheaval (?).

214 IMAGINING CHARACTER

Rosencrantz: Nay, their endeavor keeps in the wonted pace, but 325
there is, sir, an eyrie° of children, little eyases,° that cry out
on the top of question° and are most tyrannically clapped
for't. These are now the fashion, and so berattle° the common stages° (so they call them) that many wearing rapiers
are afraid of goosequills° and dare scarce come thither. 330

Hamlet: What, are they children? Who maintains 'em? How are
they escoted?° Will they pursue the quality° no longer than
they can sing?° Will they not say afterwards, if they should
grow themselves to common players (as it is most like, if their
means are no better), their writers do them wrong to make 355
them exclaim against their own succession?

Rosencrantz: Faith, there has been much to do on both sides, and
the nation holds it no sin to tarre° them to controversy.
There was, for a while, no money bid for argument° unless
the poet and the player went to cuffs in the question. 340

Hamlet: Is't possible?

Guildenstern: O, there has been much throwing about of brains.

Hamlet: Do the boys carry it away?

Rosencrantz: Ay, that they do, my lord — Hercules and his load°
too. 345

Hamlet: It is not very strange, for my uncle is King of Denmark,
and those that would make mows° at him while my father
lived give twenty, forty, fifty, a hundred ducats apiece for his
picture in little. 'Sblood,° there is something in this more
than natural, if philosophy could find it out. 350

A flourish.

Guildenstern: There are the players.

Hamlet: Gentlemen, you are welcome to Elsinore. Your hands,
come then. Th' appurtenance of welcome is fashion and
ceremony. Let me comply with you in this garb,° lest my
extent° to the players (which I tell you must show fairly 355
outwards) should more appear like entertainment than

326 *eyrie*: Nest; *eyases*: nestling hawks. 327 *on the top of question*: Above others on matter of dispute. 328 *berattle*: Berate. 329 *common stages*: "Public" theatres of the "common" players, who were organized in companies mainly composed of adult actors (allusion being made to the "War of the Theatres" in Shakespeare's London). 330 *goosequills*: Pens (of satirists who made out that the London public stage showed low taste). 332 *escoted*: Supported; *quality*: Profession of acting. 333 *sing*: I.e., with unchanged voices. 338 *tarre*: Incite. 339 *argument*: Matter of a play. 343 *load*: I.e., the whole world (with a topical reference to the sign of the Globe Theatre, a representation of Hercules bearing the world on his shoulders). 347 *mows*: Grimaces. 349 *'Sblood*: By God's blood. 354 *garb*: Fashion. 355 *extent*: Showing of welcome.

yours. You are welcome. But my uncle-father and aunt-mother are deceived.

Guildenstern: In what, my dear lord?

Hamlet: I am but mad north-north-west. When the wind is south- 360
erly I know a hawk° from a handsaw.°

Enter Polonius.

Polonius: Well be with you, gentlemen.

Hamlet: Hark you, Guildenstern — and you too — at each ear a
hearer. That great baby you see there is not yet out of his
swaddling clouts.° 365

Rosencrantz: Happily° he is the second time come to them, for
they say an old man is twice a child.

Hamlet: I will prophesy he comes to tell me of the players. Mark
it. — You say right, sir; a Monday morning, 'twas then indeed. 370

Polonius: My lord, I have news to tell you.

Hamlet: My lord, I have news to tell you. When Roscius° was an
actor in Rome —

Polonius: The actors are come hither, my lord.

Hamlet: Buzz, buzz. 375

Polonius: Upon my honor —

Hamlet: Then came each actor on his ass —

Polonius: The best actors in the world, either for tragedy, comedy,
history, pastoral, pastoral-comical, historical-pastoral, tragi-
cal-historical, tragical-comical-historical-pastoral, scene indi- 380
vidable,° or poem unlimited.° Seneca° cannot be too heavy,
nor Plautus° too light. For the law of writ° and the liberty,°
these are the only men.

Hamlet: O Jephtha,° judge of Israel, what a treasure hadst thou!

Polonius: What treasure had he, my lord? 385

Hamlet: Why,

> "One fair daughter, and no more,
> The which he lovèd passing° well."

---

361 *hawk*: Mattock or pickaxe (also called "hack"; here used apparently with a play on
"hawk": a bird); *handsaw*: Carpenter's tool (apparently with a play on some corrupt form of
"hernshaw"; heron, a bird often hunted with the hawk).   365 *clouts*: Clothes.   366 *Happily*: Haply, perhaps.   372 *Roscius*: The greatest of Roman comic actors.   380–81 *scene
individable*: Drama observing the unities; *poem unlimited*: Drama not observing the unities;
Seneca: Roman writer of tragedies.   382 *Plautus*: Roman writer of comedies; *law of writ*:
Orthodoxy determined by critical rules of the drama; *liberty*: Freedom from such orthodoxy.
384 *Jephtha*: The compelled sacrificer of a dearly beloved daughter (Judges 11).
388 *passing*: Surpassingly (verses are from a ballad on Jephthah).

Polonius (aside): Still on my daughter.
Hamlet: Am I not i' th' right, old Jephtha?   390
Polonius: If you call me Jephtha, my lord, I have a daughter that I
  love passing well.
Hamlet: Nay, that follows not.
Polonius: What follows then, my lord?
Hamlet: Why,
                "As by lot, God wot,"   395
          and then, you know,
                "It came to pass, as most like it was."
      The first row° of the pious chanson° will show you more, for
      look where my abridgment° comes.

Enter the Players.

      You are welcome, masters, welcome, all. — I am glad to see   400
      thee well. — Welcome, good friends. — O, old friend, why,
      thy face is valanced° since I saw thee last. Com'st thou to
      beard me in Denmark? — What, my young lady° and mis-
      tress? By'r Lady, your ladyship is nearer to heaven than when
      I saw you last by the altitude of a chopine.° Pray God your 405
      voice, like a piece of uncurrent° gold, be not cracked within
      the ring.° — Masters, you are all welcome. We'll e'en to't like
      French falconers, fly at anything we see. We'll have a speech
      straight. Come, give us a taste of your quality. Come, a pas-
      sionate speech.   410
Player: What speech, my good lord?
Hamlet: I heard thee speak me a speech once, but it was never
      acted, or if it was, not above once, for the play, I remember,
      pleased not the million; 'twas caviary° to the general,° but it
      was (as I received it, and others, whose judgments in such   415
      matters cried in the top of° mine) an excellent play, well
      digested in the scenes, set down with as much modesty as
      cunning. I remember one said there were no sallets° in the
      lines to make the matter savory, nor no matter in the phrase
      that might indict the author of affectation, but called it an 420
      honest method, as wholesome as sweet, and by very much
      more handsome than fine. One speech in't I chiefly loved.

---

398 *row*: Stanza; *chanson*: Song.   399 *my abridgment*: That which shortens my talk.
402 *valanced*: Fringed (with a beard).   403 *young lady*: Boy who plays women's parts.
405 *chopine*: Women's thick-soled shoe.   406 *uncurrent*: Not legal tender.   407 *within the
ring*: From the edge through the line circling the design on the coin (with a play on "ring": a
sound).   414 *caviary*: Caviar; *general*: Multitude.   416 *in the top of*: More authoritatively
than.   418 *sallets*: Salads, highly seasoned passages.

'Twas Aeneas' tale to Dido, and thereabout of it especially
where he speaks of Priam's slaughter.° If it live in your
memory, begin at this line — let me see, let me see: 425
    "The rugged Pyrrhus, like th' Hyrcanian beast° —"
'Tis not so; it begins with Pyrrhus:
    "The rugged Pyrrhus, he whose sable° arms,
    Black as his purpose, did the night resemble
    When he lay couchèd in the ominous° horse,°   430
    Hath now this dread and black complexion smeared
    With heraldry more dismal.° Head to foot
    Now is he total gules,° horridly tricked°
    With blood of fathers, mothers, daughters, sons,
    Baked and impasted with the parching° streets,   435
    That lend a tyrannous and a damnèd light
    To their lord's murder. Roasted in wrath and fire,
    And thus o'ersizèd° with coagulate° gore,
    With eyes like carbuncles, the hellish Pyrrhus
    Old grandsire Priam seeks."   440
So, proceed you.
Polonius: Fore God, my lord, well spoken, with good accent and
good discretion.
Player: "Anon he finds him,
    Striking too short at Greeks. His antique sword,   445
    Rebellious to his arms, lies where it falls,
    Repugnant to command. Unequal matched,
    Pyrrhus at Priam drives, in rage strikes wide,
    But with the whiff and wind of his fell° sword
    Th' unnervèd father falls. Then senseless° Ilium,   450
    Seeming to feel this blow, with flaming top
    Stoops to his° base, and with a hideous crash
    Takes prisoner Pyrrhus' ear. For lo! his sword,
    Which was declining on the milky head
    Of reverend Priam, seemed i' th' air to stick.   455
    So as a painted° tyrant Pyrrhus stood,
    And like a neutral to his will and matter°
    Did nothing.

---

424 *Priam's slaughter*: I.e., at the fall of Troy (Aeneid II, 506 ff.).   426 *Hyrcanian beast*: Tiger.
428 *sable*: Black.   430 *ominous*: Fateful; *horse*: The wooden horse by which the Greeks gained
entrance to Troy.   432 *dismal*: Ill-omened.   433 *gules*: Red (heraldic term); *tricked*: Decorated in color (heraldic term).   435 *parching*: I.e., because Troy was burning.   438 *o'er-
sizèd*: Covered as with size, a glutinous material used for filling pores of plaster, etc.; *coagulate*:
Clotted.   449 *fell*: Cruel.   450 *senseless*: Without feeling.   452 *his*: Its.   456 *painted*:
Pictured.   457 *will and matter*: Purpose and its realization (between which he stands motionless).

But as we often see, against° some storm,
A silence in the heavens, the rack° stand still,   460
The bold winds speechless, and the orb below
As hush as death, anon the dreadful thunder
Doth rend the region,° so after Pyrrhus' pause,
Arousèd vengeance sets him new awork,
And never did the Cyclops'° hammers fall   465
On Mars' armor, forged for proof eterne,°
With less remorse than Pyrrhus' bleeding sword
Now falls on Priam.
Out, out, thou strumpet Fortune! All you gods,
In general synod take away her power,   470
Break all the spokes and fellies° from her wheel,
And bowl the round nave° down the hill of heaven,
As low as to the fiends."

Polonius: This is too long.

Hamlet: It shall to the barber's, with your beard. — Prithee say 475
    on. He's for a jig° or a tale of bawdry, or he sleeps. Say on;
    come to Hecuba.

Player: "But who (ah woe!) had seen the mobled° queen —"

Hamlet: "The mobled queen"?

Polonius: That's good. "Mobled queen" is good.   480

Player: "Run barefoot up and down, threat'ning the flames
    With bisson rheum;° a clout° upon that head
    Where late the diadem stood, and for a robe,
    About her lank and all o'erteemèd° loins,
    A blanket in the alarm of fear caught up —   485
    Who this had seen, with tongue in venom steeped
    'Gainst Fortune's state° would treason have pronounced.
    But if the gods themselves did see her then,
    When she saw Pyrrhus make malicious sport
    In mincing with his sword her husband's limbs,   490
    The instant burst of clamor that she made
    (Unless things mortal move them not at all)
    Would have made milch° the burning eyes° of heaven
    And passion in the gods."

---

457 *against:* Just before.   458 *rack:* Clouds.   461 *region:* Sky.   463 *Cyclops:* Giant work-men who made armor in the smithy of Vulcan.   464 *proof eterne:* Eternal protection.   469 *fellies:* Segments of the rim.   470 *nave:* Hub.   474 *Jig:* Short comic piece with singing and dancing often presented after a play.   476 *mobled:* Muffled.   480 *bisson rheum:* Blind-ing tears; *clout:* Cloth.   482 *o'erteemèd:* Overproductive of children.   485 *state:* Govern-ment of worldly events.   491 *milch:* Tearful (milk-giving); *eyes:* I.e., stars.

Polonius: Look, whe'r° he has not turned his color, and has tears   495
in's eyes. Prithee no more.

Hamlet: 'Tis well. I'll have thee speak out the rest of this soon. —
Good my lord, will you see the players well bestowed?° Do
you hear? Let them be well used, for they are the abstract and
brief chronicles of the time. After your death you were better   500
have a bad epitaph than their ill report while you live.

Polonius: My lord, I will use them according to their desert.

Hamlet: God's bodkin,° man, much better! Use every man after
his desert, and who shall scape whipping? Use them after
your own honor and dignity. The less they deserve, the more   505
merit is in your bounty. Take them in.

Polonius: Come, sirs.

Hamlet: Follow him, friends. We'll hear a play to-morrow. *(Aside to
Player.)* Dost thou hear me, old friend? Can you play "The
Murder of Gonzago"?   510

Player: Ay, my lord.

Hamlet: We'll ha't to-morrow night. You could for a need study a
speech of some dozen or sixteen lines which I would set
down and insert in't, could you not?

Player: Ay, my lord.   515

Hamlet: Very well. Follow that lord, and look you mock him
not. — My good friends, I'll leave you till night. You are welcome to Elsinore.   *Exeunt Polonius and Players.*

Rosencrantz: Good my lord.   *Exeunt Rosencrantz and Guildenstern.*

Hamlet: Ay, so, God bye to you. — Now I am alone.   520
O, what a rogue and peasant slave am I!
Is it not monstrous that this player here,
But in a fiction, in a dream of passion,
Could force his soul so to his own conceit°
That from her working all his visage wanned,   525
Tears in his eyes, distraction in his aspect,
A broken voice, and his whole function° suiting
With forms to his conceit? And all for nothing,
For Hecuba!
What's Hecuba to him, or he to Hecuba,   530
That he should weep for her? What would he do
Had he the motive and the cue for passion
That I have? He would drown the stage with tears

---

495 *whe'r*: Whether.   498 *bestowed*: Lodged.   503 *God's bodkin*: By God's little body.
524 *conceit*: Conception, idea.   527 *function*: Action of bodily powers.

And cleave the general ear with horrid speech,
Make mad the guilty and appal the free,   535
Confound the ignorant, and amaze indeed
The very faculties of eyes and ears.
Yet I,
A dull and muddy-mettled° rascal, peak°
Like John-a-dreams,° unpregnant° of my cause,   540
And can say nothing. No, not for a king,
Upon whose property and most dear life
A damned defeat was made. Am I a coward?
Who calls me villain? breaks my pate across?
Plucks off my beard and blows it in my face?   545
Tweaks me by the nose? gives me the lie i' th' throat
As deep as to the lungs? Who does me this?
Ha, 'swounds,° I should take it, for it cannot be
But I am pigeon-livered° and lack gall
To make oppression bitter, or ere this   550
I should ha' fatted all the region kites°
With this slave's offal.° Bloody, bawdy villain!
Remorseless, treacherous, lecherous, kindless° villain!
O, vengeance!
Why, what an ass am I! This is most brave,   555
That I, the son of a dear father murdered,
Prompted to my revenge by heaven and hell,
Must like a whore unpack my heart with words
And fall a-cursing like a very drab,
A stallion!° Fie upon 't, foh! About, my brains.   560
Hum —
I have heard that guilty creatures sitting at a play
Have by the very cunning of the scene
Been struck so to the soul that presently°
They have proclaimed their malefactions.   565
For murder, though it have no tongue, will speak
With most miraculous organ. I'll have these players
Play something like the murder of my father
Before mine uncle. I'll observe his looks.
I'll tent° him to the quick. If 'a do blench,°   570
I know my course. The spirit that I have seen

---

539 *muddy-mettled*: Dull-spirited; *peak*: Mope.   540 *John-a-dreams*: A sleepy dawdler; *unpregnant*: Barren of realization.   548 *'swounds*: By God's wounds.   549 *pigeon-livered*: Of dove-like gentleness.   551 *region kites*: Kites of the air.   552 *offal*: Guts.   553 *kindless*: Unnatural.   560 *stallion*: Prostitute (male or female).   564 *presently*: Immediately.   570 *tent*: Probe; *blench*: Flinch.

May be a devil, and the devil hath power
T' assume a pleasing shape, yea, and perhaps
Out of my weakness and my melancholy,
As he is very potent with such spirits,   575
Abuses° me to damn me. I'll have grounds
More relative° than this. The play's the thing
Wherein I'll catch the conscience of the king.   *Exit.*

ACT III

SCENE I. *A chamber in the castle.*

Enter King, Queen, Polonius, Ophelia, Rosencrantz, Guildenstern, Lords.

King: And can you by no drift of conference°
    Get from him why he puts on this confusion,
    Grating so harshly all his days of quiet
    With turbulent and dangerous lunacy?
Rosencrantz: He does confess he feels himself distracted,   5
    But from what cause 'a will by no means speak.
Guildenstern: Nor do we find him forward to be sounded,
    But with a crafty madness keeps aloof
    When we would bring him on to some confession
    Of his true state.
Queen: Did he receive you well?   10
Rosencrantz: Most like a gentleman.
Guildenstern: But with much forcing of his disposition.
Rosencrantz: Niggard of question, but of our demands
    Most free in his reply.
Queen: Did you assay° him
    To any pastime?   15
Rosencrantz: Madam, it so fell out that certain players
    We o'erraught° on the way. Of these we told him,
    And there did seem in him a kind of joy
    To hear of it. They are here about the court,
    And, as I think, they have already order   20
    This night to play before him.
Polonius: 'Tis most true,
    And he beseeched me to entreat your majesties
    To hear and see the matter.

---

576 *Abuses:* Deludes.   577 *relative:* Pertinent.   ACT III, SCENE I. 1 *drift of conference:* Direction of conversation.   14 *assay:* Try to win.   17 *o'erraught:* Overtook.

King: With all my heart, and it doth much content me
    To hear him so inclined.   25
    Good gentlemen, give him a further edge°
    And drive his purpose into these delights.
Rosencrantz: We shall, my lord.   *Exeunt Rosencrantz and Guildenstern.*
King: Sweet Gertrude, leave us too,
    For we have closely° sent for Hamlet hither,
    That he, as 'twere by accident, may here   30
    Affront° Ophelia.
    Her father and myself (lawful espials°)
    Will so bestow ourselves that, seeing unseen,
    We may of their encounter frankly judge
    And gather by him, as he is behaved,   35
    If't be th' affliction of his love or no
    That thus he suffers for.
Queen: I shall obey you. —
    And for your part, Ophelia, I do wish
    That your good beauties be the happy cause
    Of Hamlet's wildness. So shall I hope your virtues   40
    Will bring him to his wonted way again,
    To both your honors.
Ophelia: Madam, I wish it may.   *Exit Queen.*
Polonius: Ophelia, walk you here. — Gracious, so please you,
    We will bestow ourselves. —
(To Ophelia.)   Read on this book,
    That show of such an exercise° may color°   45
    Your loneliness. We are oft to blame in this,
    'Tis too much proved, that with devotion's visage
    And pious action we do sugar o'er
    The devil himself.
King (aside):   O, 'tis too true.
    How smart a lash that speech doth give my conscience!   50
    The harlot's cheek, beautied with plast'ring art,
    Is not more ugly to° the thing that helps it
    Than is my deed to my most painted word.
    O heavy burthen!
Polonius: I hear him coming. Let's withdraw, my lord.   55

                         Exeunt King and Polonius.

26 *edge*: Keenness of desire.   29 *closely*: Privately.   31 *Affront*: Come face to face with.
32 *espials*: Spies.   45 *exercise*: Religious exercise (the book being obviously one of devotion);
color: Give an appearance of naturalness to.   52 *to*: Compared to.

Enter Hamlet.

Hamlet: To be, or not to be — that is the question:
Whether 'tis nobler in the mind to suffer
The slings and arrows of outrageous fortune
Or to take arms against a sea of troubles
And by opposing end them. To die, to sleep —   60
No more — and by a sleep to say we end
The heartache, and the thousand natural shocks
That flesh is heir to. 'Tis a consummation
Devoutly to be wished. To die, to sleep —
To sleep — perchance to dream: ay, there's the rub,°   65
For in that sleep of death what dreams may come
When we have shuffled off° this mortal coil,°
Must give us pause. There's the respect°
That makes calamity of so long life.°
For who would bear the whips and scorns of time,   70
Th' oppressor's wrong, the proud man's contumely
The pangs of despised love, the law's delay,
The insolence of office, and the spurns
That patient merit of th' unworthy takes,
When he himself might his quietus° make   75
With a bare bodkin?° Who would fardels° bear,
To grunt and sweat under a weary life,
But that the dread of something after death,
The undiscovered country, from whose bourn°
No traveller returns, puzzles the will,   80
And makes us rather bear those ills we have
Than fly to others that we know not of?
Thus conscience does make cowards of us all,
And thus the native hue of resolution
Is sicklied o'er with the pale cast of thought,   85
And enterprises of great pitch° and moment
With this regard° their currents turn awry
And lose the name of action. — Soft you now,
The fair Ophelia! — Nymph, in thy orisons°
Be all my sins remembered.

---

65 *rub*: Obstacle (literally, obstruction encountered by a bowler's ball).   67 *shuffled off*: Cast off as an encumbrance; *coil*: To-do, turmoil.   68 *respect*: Consideration.   69 *of so long life*: So long-lived.   75 *quietus*: Settlement (literally, release from debt).   76 *bodkin*: Dagger; *fardels*: Burdens.   79 *bourn*: Confine, region.   86 *pitch*: Height (of a soaring falcon's flight).   87 *regard*: Consideration.   89 *orisons*: Prayers (because of the book of devotion she reads).

Ophelia: Good my lord,   90
    How does your honor for this many a day?
Hamlet: I humbly thank you, well, well, well.
Ophelia: My lord, I have remembrances of yours
    That I have longèd long to re-deliver.
    I pray you, now receive them.
Hamlet: No, not I,   95
    I never gave you aught.
Ophelia: My honored lord, you know right well you did,
    And with them words of so sweet breath composed
    As made the things more rich. Their perfume lost,
    Take these again, for to the noble mind   100
    Rich gifts wax poor when givers prove unkind.
    There, my lord.
Hamlet: Ha, ha! Are you honest?°
Ophelia: My lord?
Hamlet: Are you fair?   105
Ophelia: What means your lordship?
Hamlet: That if you be honest and fair, your honesty should ad-
    mit no discourse to your beauty.
Ophelia: Could beauty, my lord, have better commerce° than with
    honesty?   110
Hamlet: Ay, truly; for the power of beauty will sooner transform
    honesty from what it is to a bawd than the force of honesty
    can translate beauty into his likeness. This was sometime
    a paradox,° but now the time gives it proof. I did love you
    once.   115
Ophelia: Indeed, my lord, you made me believe so.
Hamlet: You should not have believed me, for virtue cannot so
    inoculate° our old stock but we shall relish° of it. I loved you
    not.
Ophelia: I was the more deceived.   120
Hamlet: Get thee to a nunnery. Why wouldst thou be a breeder of
    sinners? I am myself indifferent honest,° but yet could ac-
    cuse me of such things that it were better my mother had not
    borne me: I am very proud, revengeful, ambitious, with more
    offenses at my beck than I have thoughts to put them in, 125
    imagination to give them shape, or time to act them in. What
    should such fellows as I do crawling between earth and

---

103 *honest*: Chaste.   109 *commerce*: Intercourse.   114 *paradox*: Idea contrary to common
opinion.   118 *inoculate*: Graft; *relish*: Have a flavor (because of original sin).   122 *indifferent honest*: Moderately respectable.

heaven? We are arrant knaves all; believe none of us. Go thy
ways to a nunnery. Where's your father?

Ophelia: At home, my lord.   130

Hamlet: Let the doors be shut upon him, that he may play the
fool nowhere but in's own house. Farewell.

Ophelia: O, help him, you sweet heavens!

Hamlet: If thou dost marry, I'll give thee this plague for thy
dowry: be thou as chaste as ice, as pure as snow, thou shalt   135
not escape calumny. Get thee to a nunnery. Go, farewell. Or
if thou wilt needs marry, marry a fool, for wise men know
well enough what monsters° you make of them. To a nunnery, go, and quickly too. Farewell.

Ophelia: O heavenly powers, restore him!   140

Hamlet: I have heard of your paintings too, well enough. God
hath given you one face, and you make yourselves another.
You jig, you amble, and you lisp; you nickname God's creatures and make your wantonness° your ignorance.° Go to,
I'll no more on't; it hath made me mad. I say we will have no   145
more marriage. Those that are married already — all but
one — shall live. The rest shall keep as they are. To a nunnery, go.   *Exit.*

Ophelia: O, what a noble mind is here o'erthrown!
The courtier's, soldier's, scholar's, eye, tongue, sword,   150
Th' expectancy and rose° of the fair state,
The glass° of fashion and the mold of form,
Th' observed of all observers, quite, quite down!
And I, of ladies most deject and wretched,
That sucked the honey of his music vows,   155
Now see that noble and most sovereign reason
Like sweet bells jangled, out of time and harsh,
That unmatched form and feature of blown youth
Blasted with ecstasy.° O, woe is me
T' have seen what I have seen, see what I see!   160

Enter King and Polonius.

King: Love? his affections° do not that way tend,
Nor what he spake, though it lacked form a little,
Was not like madness. There's something in his soul

---

138 *monsters*: I.e., unnatural combinations of wisdom and uxorious folly.   144 *wantonness*:
Affectation; *your ignorance*: A matter for which you offer the excuse that you don't know any
better.   151 *expectancy and rose*: Fair hope.   152 *glass*: Mirror.   159 *ecstasy*: Madness.
161 *affections*: Emotions.

O'er which his melancholy sits on brood,
and I do doubt° the hatch and the disclose   165
Will be some danger; which for to prevent,
I have in quick determination
Thus set it down: he shall with speed to England
For the demand of our neglected tribute.
Haply the seas, and countries different,   170
With variable objects, shall expel
This something-settled° matter in his heart,
Whereon his brains still beating puts him thus
From fashion of himself. What think you on't?
Polonius: It shall do well. But yet do I believe   175
The origin and commencement of his grief
Sprung from neglected love. — How now, Ophelia?
You need not tell us what Lord Hamlet said.
We heard it all. — My lord, do as you please,
But if you hold it fit, after the play   180
Let his queen mother all alone entreat him
To show his grief. Let her be round° with him,
And I'll be placed, so please you, in the ear
Of all their conference. If she find him not,
To England send him, or confine him where   185
Your wisdom best shall think.
King: It shall be so.
Madness in great ones must not unwatched go.   *Exeunt.*

SCENE II. *The hall of the castle.*

Enter Hamlet and three of the Players.

Hamlet: Speak the speech, I pray you, as I pronounced it to you,
trippingly° on the tongue. But if you mouth it, as many of
our players do, I had as lief the town crier spoke my lines.
Nor do not saw the air too much with your hand, thus, but
use all gently, for in the very torrent, tempest, and (as I may 5
say) whirlwind of your passion, you must acquire and beget a
temperance that may give it smoothness. O, it offends me to
the soul to hear a robustious° periwig-pated° fellow tear a
passion to tatters, to very rags, to split the ears of the groundlings,° who for the most part are capable of nothing but   10

---

165 *doubt:* Fear.   172 *something-settled:* Somewhat settled.   182 *round:* Plain-spoken.
SCENE II. 2 *trippingly:* Easily.   8 *robustious:* Boisterous; *periwig-pated:* Wig-wearing (after the
custom of actors).   9–10 *groundlings:* Spectators who paid least and stood on the ground in
the pit or yard of the theatre.

inexplicable dumb shows° and noise. I would have such a
fellow whipped for o'erdoing Termagant.° It out-herods
Herod.° Pray you avoid it.

Player: I warrant your honor.

Hamlet: Be not too tame neither, but let your own discretion be   15
your tutor. Suit the action to the word, the word to the action,
with this special observance, that you o'erstep not the modesty of nature. For anything so overdone is from° the purpose of playing, whose end, both at the first and now, was
and is, to hold, as 'twere, the mirror up to nature, to show   20
virtue her own feature, scorn her own image, and the very
age and body of the time his form and pressure.° Now this
overdone, or come tardy off,° though it make the unskillful
laugh, cannot but make the judicious grieve, the censure of
the which one° must in your allowance o'erweigh a whole   25
theatre of others. O, there be players that I have seen play,
and heard others praise, and that highly (not to speak it
profanely), that neither having th' accent of Christians, nor
the gait of Christian, pagan, nor man, have so strutted and
bellowed that I have thought some of Nature's journeymen°   30
had made men, and not made them well, they imitated humanity so abominably.

Player: I hope we have reformed that indifferently° with us, sir.

Hamlet: O, reform it altogether! And let those that play your
clowns speak no more than is set down for them, for there be   35
of them° that will themselves laugh, to set on some quantity
of barren spectators to laugh too, though in the mean time
some necessary question of the play be then to be considered. That's villainous and shows a most pitiful ambition in
the fool that uses it. Go make you ready.   *Exeunt Players.*   40

Enter Polonius, Guildenstern, and Rosencrantz.

How now, my lord? Will the king hear this piece of work?

Polonius: And the queen too, and that presently.°

Hamlet: Bid the players make haste.   *Exit Polonius.*
Will you two help to hasten them?

---

11 *dumb shows:* Brief actions without words, forecasting dramatic matter to follow (the play
presented later in this scene giving an old-fashioned example).   12 *Termagant:* A Saracen
"god" in medieval romance and drama.   13 *Herod:* The raging tyrant of old Biblical plays.
18 *from:* Apart from.   22 *pressure:* Impressed or printed character.   23 *come tardy off:*
Brought off slowly and badly.   25 *the censure of the which one:* The judgment of even one of
whom.   30 *journeymen:* Workmen not yet masters of their trade.   33 *indifferently:* Fairly
well.   36 *of them:* Some of them.   42 *presently:* At once.

Rosencrantz: Ay, my lord.   *Exeunt they two.* 45
Hamlet: What, ho, Horatio!

Enter Horatio.

Horatio: Here, sweet lord, at your service.
Hamlet: Horatio, thou art e'en as just a man
  As e'er my conversation coped withal.°
Horatio: O, my dear lord —
Hamlet: Nay, do not think I flatter.   50
  For what advancement may I hope from thee,
  That no revenue hast but thy good spirits
  To feed and clothe thee? Why should the poor be flattered?
  No, let the candied tongue lick absurd pomp,
  And crook the pregnant° hinges of the knee   55
  Where thrift° may follow fawning. Dost thou hear?
  Since my dear soul was mistress of her choice
  And could of men distinguish her election,
  S' hath sealed° thee for herself, for thou hast been
  As one in suff'ring all that suffers nothing,   60
  A man that Fortune's buffets and rewards
  Hast ta'en with equal thanks; and blest are those
  Whose blood° and judgment are so well commeddled°
  That they are not a pipe for Fortune's finger
  To sound what stop she please. Give me that man   65
  That is not passion's slave, and I will wear him
  In my heart's core, ay, in my heart of heart,
  As I do thee. Something too much of this —
  There is a play to-night before the king.
  One scene of it comes near the circumstance   70
  Which I have told thee, of my father's death.
  I prithee, when thou seest that act afoot,
  Even with the very comment of thy soul°
  Observe my uncle. If his occulted° guilt
  Do not itself unkennel in one speech,   75
  It is a damnèd ghost° that we have seen,
  And my imaginations are as foul
  As Vulcan's stithy.° Give him heedful note,
  For I mine eyes will rivet to his face,

---

49 *conversation coped withal*: Intercourse with men encountered.   55 *pregnant*: Quick to move.   56 *thrift*: Profit.   59 *sealed*: Marked.   63 *blood*: Passion; *commeddled*: Mixed together.   73 *the very . . . soul*: Thy deepest sagacity.   74 *occulted*: Hidden.   76 *damnèd ghost*: Evil spirit, devil (as thought of in II.ii.569–574).   78 *stithy*: Smithy.

And after we will both our judgments join   80
In censure of° his seeming.
Horatio: Well, my lord.
If 'a steal aught the while this play is playing,
And scape detecting, I will pay the theft.

Enter Trumpets and Kettledrums, King, Queen, Polonius, Ophelia, Rosencrantz,
Guildenstern, and other Lords attendant.

Hamlet: They are coming to the play. I must be idle.°
Get you a place.   85
King: How fares our cousin° Hamlet?
Hamlet: Excellent, i' faith, of the chameleon's dish.° I eat the air,
promise-crammed. You cannot feed capons so.
King: I have nothing with this answer, Hamlet. These words are
not mine.°   90
Hamlet: No, nor mine now. (*To Polonius.*) My lord, you played once
i' th' university, you say?
Polonius: That did I, my lord, and was accounted a good actor.
Hamlet: What did you enact?
Polonius: I did enact Julius Caesar. I was killed i' th' Capitol;   95
Brutus killed me.
Hamlet: It was a brute part of him to kill so capital a calf there. Be
the players ready?
Rosencrantz: Ay, my lord. They stay upon your patience.°
Queen: Come hither, my dear Hamlet, sit by me.   100
Hamlet: No, good mother. Here's metal more attractive.
Polonius (to the King): O ho! do you mark that?
Hamlet: Lady, shall I lie in your lap?

He lies at Ophelia's feet.

Ophelia: No, my lord.
Hamlet: I mean, my head upon your lap?   105
Ophelia: Ay, my lord.
Hamlet: Do you think I meant country matters?°
Ophelia: I think nothing, my lord.
Hamlet: That's a fair thought to lie between maids' legs.
Ophelia: What is, my lord?   110

---

81 *censure of*: Sentence upon.   84 *be idle*: Be foolish, act the madman.   86 *cousin*: Nephew.
87 *chameleon's dish*: I.e., air (which was believed the chameleon's food; Hamlet willfully takes
fares in the sense of "feeds").   90 *not mine*: Not for me as the asker of my question.
99 *stay upon your patience*: Await your indulgence.   107 *country matters*: Rustic goings-on,
barnyard mating (with a play upon a sexual term).

Hamlet: Nothing.

Ophelia: You are merry, my lord.

Hamlet: Who, I?

Ophelia: Ay, my lord.

Hamlet: O God, your only jig-maker!° What should a man do but   115
be merry? For look you how cheerfully my mother looks, and
my father died within's two hours.

Ophelia: Nay, 'tis twice two months, my lord.

Hamlet: So long? Nay then, let the devil wear black, for I'll have a
suit of sables.° O heavens! die two months ago, and not   120
forgotten yet? Then there's hope a great man's memory may
outlive his life half a year. But, by'r Lady, 'a must build
churches then, or else shall 'a suffer not thinking on, with the
hobby-horse,° whose epitaph is "For O, for O, the hobby-
horse is forgot!"   125

*The trumpets sound. Dumb show follows: Enter a King and Queen very lovingly,
the Queen embracing him, and he her. She kneels; and makes show of protestation
unto him. He takes her up, and declines his head upon her neck. He lies him down
upon a bank of flowers. She, seeing him asleep, leaves him. Anon come in another
man: takes off his crown, kisses it, pours poison in the sleeper's ears, and leaves
him. The Queen returns, finds the King dead, makes passionate action. The
poisoner, with some three or four, come in again, seem to condole with her. The
dead body is carried away. The poisoner woos the Queen with gifts; she seems
harsh awhile, but in the end accepts love.   Exeunt.*

Ophelia: What means this, my lord?

Hamlet: Marry, this is miching mallecho;° it means mischief.

Ophelia: Belike this show imports the argument of the play.

Enter Prologue.

Hamlet: We shall know by this fellow. The players cannot keep
counsel; they'll tell all.   130

Ophelia: Will 'a tell us what this show meant?

Hamlet: Ay, or any show that you'll show him. Be not you ashamed
to show, he'll not shame to tell you what it means.

Ophelia: You are naught,° you are naught. I'll mark the play.

Prologue: For us and for our tragedy,   135
    Here stooping to your clemency,
    We beg your hearing patiently.   *Exit.*

---

115 *jig-maker:* Writer of jigs (see II.ii.474).   120 *sables:* Black furs (luxurious garb, not for
mourning).   124 *hobby-horse:* Traditional figure strapped round the waist of a performer in
May games and morris dances.   127 *miching mallecho:* Sneaking iniquity.   134 *naught* In-
decent.

Hamlet: Is this a prologue, or the posy° of a ring?°
Ophelia: 'Tis brief, my lord.
Hamlet: As woman's love.   140

Enter two Players as King and Queen.

King: Full thirty times hath Phoebus' cart° gone round
    Neptune's salt wash and Tellus'° orbèd ground,
    And thirty dozen moons with borrowed° sheen
    About the world have times twelve thirties been,
    Since love our hearts, and Hymen° did our hands,   145
    Unite commutual° in most sacred bands.
Queen: So many journeys may the sun and moon
    Make us again count o'er ere love be done!
    But woe is me, you are so sick of late,
    So far from cheer and from your former state,   150
    That I distrust you.° Yet, though I distrust,
    Discomfort you, my lord, it nothing must.
    For women fear too much, even as they love,
    And women's fear and love hold quantity,°
    In neither aught, or in extremity.   155
    Now what my love is, proof hath made you know,
    And as my love is sized, my fear is so.
    Where love is great, the littlest doubts are fear;
    Where little fears grow great, great love grows there.
King: Faith, I must leave thee, love, and shortly too;   160
    My operant powers° their functions leave to do.
    And thou shalt live in this fair world behind,
    Honored, beloved, and haply one as kind
    For husband shalt thou —
Queen: O, confound the rest!
    Such love must needs be treason in my breast.   165
    In second husband let me be accurst!
    None wed the second but who killed the first.
Hamlet (aside): That's wormwood.°
Queen: The instances° that second marriage move
    Are base respects of thrift, but none of love.   170
    A second time I kill my husband dead
    When second husband kisses me in bed.

---

138 *posy*: Brief motto in rhyme ("poesy"); *ring*: Finger ring.   141 *Phoebus' cart*: The sun's
chariot.   142 *Tellus*: Roman goddess of the earth.   143 *borrowed*: I.e., taken from the sun.
145 *Hymen*: Greek god of marriage.   146 *commutual*: Mutually.   151 *distrust you*: Fear for
you.   154 *quantity*: Proportion.   161 *operant powers*: Active bodily forces.   168 *wormwood*: A bitter herb.   169 *instances*: Motives.

King: I do believe you think what now you speak,
    But what we do determine oft we break.
    Purpose is but the slave to° memory,   175
    Of violent birth, but poor validity,°
    Which now like fruit unripe sticks on the tree,
    But fall unshaken when they mellow be.
    Most necessary 'tis that we forget
    To pay ourselves what to ourselves is debt.   180
    What to ourselves in passion we propose,
    The passion ending, doth the purpose lose.
    The violence of either grief or joy
    Their own enactures° with themselves destroy.
    Where joy most revels, grief doth most lament;   185
    Grief joys, joy grieves, on slender accident.
    This world is not for aye, nor 'tis not strange
    That even our loves should with our fortunes change,
    For 'tis a question left us yet to prove,
    Whether love lead fortune, or else fortune love.   190
    The great man down, you mark his favorite flies,
    The poor advanced makes friends of enemies;
    And hitherto doth love on fortune tend,
    For who not needs shall never lack a friend,
    And who in want a hollow friend doth try,   195
    Directly seasons him° his enemy.
    But, orderly to end where I begun,
    Our wills and fates do so contrary run
    That our devices still° are overthrown;
    Our thoughts are ours, their ends none of our own.   200
    So think thou wilt no second husband wed,
    But die thy thoughts when thy first lord is dead.
Queen: Nor earth to me give food, nor heaven light,
    Sport and repose lock from me day and night,
    To desperation turn my trust and hope,   205
    An anchor's° cheer in prison be my scope,
    Each opposite that blanks° the face of joy
    Meet what I would have well, and it destroy,
    Both here and hence° pursue me lasting strife,
    If, once a widow, ever I be wife!   210
Hamlet: If she should break it now!

---

175 *slave to*: I.e., dependent upon for life.   176 *validity*: Strength.   184 *enactures*: Fulfill-
ments.   196 *seasons him*: Ripens him into.   199 *still*: Always.   206 *anchor's*: Hermit's.
207 *blanks*: Blanches, makes pale.   209 *hence*: In the next world.

King: 'Tis deeply sworn. Sweet, leave me here awhile.
My spirits grow dull, and fain I would beguile
The tedious day with sleep.
Queen: Sleep rock thy brain,

He sleeps.

And never come mischance between us twain!   *Exit.* 215
Hamlet: Madam, how like you this play?
Queen: The lady doth protest too much, methinks.
Hamlet: O, but she'll keep her word.
King: Have you heard the argument?° Is there no offense in't?
Hamlet: No, no, they do but jest, poison in jest; no offense i' th' 220
world.
King: What do you call the play?
Hamlet: "The Mousetrap." Marry, how? Tropically.° This play is
the image of a murder done in Vienna. Gonzago is the duke's
name; his wife, Baptista. You shall see anon. 'Tis a knavish 225
piece of work, but what o' that? Your majesty, and we that
have free° souls, it touches us not. Let the galled° jade°
winch;° our withers° are unwrung.

Enter Lucianus.

This is one Lucianus, nephew to the king.
Ophelia: You are as good as a chorus,° my lord.   230
Hamlet: I could interpret between you and your love, if I could
see the puppets° dallying.
Ophelia: You are keen, my lord, you are keen.
Hamlet: It would cost you a groaning to take off my edge.
Ophelia: Still better, and worse.   235
Hamlet: So you must take your husbands. — Begin, murderer.
Leave thy damnable faces and begin. Come, the croaking
raven doth bellow for revenge.
Lucianus: Thoughts black, hands apt, drugs fit, and time agreeing,
Confederate season,° else no creature seeing,   240
Thou mixture rank, of midnight weeds collected,
With Hecate's° ban° thrice blasted, thrice infected,
Thy natural magic and dire property
On wholesome life usurps immediately.

---

219 *argument*: Plot summary.   223 *Tropically*: In the way of a trope or figure (with a play on
"trapically").   227 *free*: Guiltless; *galled*: Sore-backed; *jade*: Horse.   228 *winch*: Wince;
withers: Shoulders.   230 *chorus*: One in a play who explains the action.   232 *puppets*: I.e.,
you and your lover as in a puppet show.   240 *Confederate season*: The occasion being my ally.
242 *Hecate*: Goddess of witchcraft and black magic; *ban*: Curse.

Pours the poison in his ears.

Hamlet: 'A poisons him i' th' garden for his estate. His name 's 245
Gonzago. The story is extant, and written in very choice Ital-
ian. You shall see anon how the murderer gets the love of
Gonzago's wife.
Ophelia: The king rises.
Hamlet: What, frighted with false fire?° 250
Queen: How fares my lord?
Polonius: Give o'er the play.
King: Give me some light. Away!
Polonius: Lights, lights, lights!

Exeunt all but Hamlet and Horatio.

Hamlet: Why, let the strucken deer go weep, 255
  The hart ungallèd play.
For some must watch, while some must sleep;
  Thus runs the world away.
Would not this, sir, and a forest of feathers° — if the rest of
my fortunes turn Turk° with me — with two Provincial roses° 260
on my razed° shoes, get me a fellowship in a cry° of players,
sir?
Horatio: Half a share.
Hamlet: A whole one, I.
For thou dost know, O Damon dear, 265
  This realm dismantled was
Of Jove himself; and now reigns here
  A very, very — peacock.
Horatio: You might have rhymed.
Hamlet: O good Horatio, I'll take the ghost's word for a thousand 270
pound. Didst perceive?
Horatio: Very well, my lord.
Hamlet: Upon the talk of the poisoning?
Horatio: I did very well note him.
Hamlet: Aha! Come, some music! Come, the recorders!° 275
  For if the king like not the comedy,
    Why then, belike he likes it not, perdy.°
Come, some music!

---

250 *false fire*: A firing of a gun charged with powder but no shot, a blank discharge.   259 *feathers*: Plumes for actors' costumes.   260 *turn Turk*: Turn renegade, like a Christian turning
Mohammedan; *Provincial roses*: Ribbon rosettes.   261 *razed*: Decorated with cut patterns; *cry*:
Pack.   275 *recorders*: Musical instruments of the flute class.   277 *perdy*: By God ("*par
dieu*").

Enter Rosencrantz and Guildenstern.

Guildenstern: Good my lord, vouchsafe me a word with you.

Hamlet: Sir, a whole history.   280

Guildenstern: The king, sir —

Hamlet: Ay, sir, what of him?

Guildenstern: Is in his retirement marvellous distempered.°

Hamlet: With drink, sir?

Guildenstern: No, my lord, with choler.°   285

Hamlet: Your wisdom should show itself more richer to signify this to the doctor, for for me to put him to his purgation would perhaps plunge him into more choler.

Guildenstern: Good my lord, put your discourse into some frame,° and start not so wildly from my affair.   290

Hamlet: I am tame, sir; pronounce.

Guildenstern: The queen, your mother, in most great affliction of spirit hath sent me to you.

Hamlet: You are welcome.

Guildenstern: Nay, good my lord, this courtesy is not of the right   295
breed. If it shall please you to make me a wholesome answer, I will do your mother's commandment. If not, your pardon and my return shall be the end of my business.

Hamlet: Sir, I cannot.

Rosencrantz: What, my lord?   300

Hamlet: Make you a wholesome answer; my wit 's diseased. But, sir, such answer as I can make, you shall command, or rather, as you say, my mother. Therefore no more, but to the matter. My mother, you say —

Rosencrantz: Then thus she says: your behavior hath struck her   305
into amazement and admiration.°

Hamlet: O wonderful son, that can so stonish a mother! But is there no sequel at the heels of this mother's admiration? Impart.

Rosencrantz: She desires to speak with you in her closet° ere you   310
go to bed.

Hamlet: We shall obey, were she ten times our mother. Have you any further trade with us?

Rosencrantz: My lord, you once did love me.

Hamlet: And do still, by these pickers and stealers.°   315

---

283 *distempered*: Out of temper, vexed (twisted by Hamlet into "deranged").   285 *choler*:
Anger (twisted by Hamlet into "biliousness").   290 *frame*: Logical order.   306 *admiration*:
Wonder.   310 *closet*: Private room.   315 *pickers and stealers*: I.e., hands.

Rosencrantz: Good my lord, what is your cause of distemper? You
    do surely bar the door upon your own liberty, if you deny
    your griefs to your friend.
Hamlet: Sir, I lack advancement.
Rosencrantz: How can that be, when you have the voice of the king   320
    himself for your succession in Denmark?
Hamlet: Ay, sir, but "while the grass grows"° — the proverb is
    something musty.

Enter the Players with recorders.

    O, the recorders.° Let me see one. To withdraw° with you —
    why do you go about to recover the wind° of me, as if you   325
    would drive me into a toil?°
Guildenstern: O my lord, if my duty be too bold, my love is too
    unmannerly.°
Hamlet: I do not well understand that. Will you play upon this
    pipe?   330
Guildenstern: My lord, I cannot.
Hamlet: I pray you.
Guildenstern: Believe me, I cannot.
Hamlet: I do beseech you.
Guildenstern: I know no touch of it, my lord.   335
Hamlet: It is as easy as lying. Govern these ventages° with your
    fingers and thumb, give it breath with your mouth, and it will
    discourse most eloquent music. Look you, these are the stops.
Guildenstern: But these cannot I command to any utt'rance of
    harmony. I have not the skill.   340
Hamlet: Why, look you now, how unworthy a thing you make of
    me! You would play upon me, you would seem to know my
    stops, you would pluck out the heart of my mystery, you
    would sound me from my lowest note to the top of my
    compass; and there is much music, excellent voice, in this   345
    little organ, yet cannot you make it speak. 'Sblood, do you
    think I am easier to be played on than a pipe? Call me what
    instrument you will, though you can fret° me, you cannot
    play upon me.

Enter Polonius.

322 *while the grass grows:* (A proverb, ending: "the horse starves").   324 *recorders:* See
III.ii.275n.; *withdraw:* Step aside.   325 *recover the wind:* Come up to windward like a hunter.
326 *toil:* Snare.   327–328 *is too unmannerly:* Leads me beyond the restraint of good manners.
336 *ventages:* Holes, vents.   348 *fret:* Irritate (with a play on the fret-fingering of certain
stringed musical instruments).

God bless you, sir!   350
Polonius: My lord, the queen would speak with you, and pres-
    ently.°
Hamlet: Do you see yonder cloud that's almost in shape of a
    camel?
Polonius: By th' mass and 'tis, like a camel indeed.   355
Hamlet: Methinks it is like a weasel.
Polonius: It is backed like a weasel.
Hamlet: Or like a whale.
Polonius: Very like a whale.
Hamlet: Then I will come to my mother by and by.° (*Aside.*) They   360
    fool me to the top of my bent.° — I will come by and by.
Polonius: I will say so.   *Exit.*
Hamlet: "By and by" is easily said. Leave me, friends.

                                 Exeunt all but Hamlet.

'Tis now the very witching time of night,
When churchyards yawn, and hell itself breathes out   365
Contagion to this world. Now could I drink hot blood
And do such bitter business as the day
Would quake to look on. Soft, now to my mother.
O heart, lose not thy nature; let not ever
The soul of Nero° enter this firm bosom.   370
Let me be cruel, not unnatural;
I will speak daggers to her, but use none.
My tongue and soul in this be hypocrites:
How in my words somever she be shent,°
To give them seals° never, my soul, consent!   *Exit.* 375

SCENE III. *A chamber in the castle.*

Enter King, Rosencrantz, and Guildenstern.

King: I like him not, nor stands it safe with us
    To let his madness range. Therefore prepare you.
    I your commission will forthwith dispatch,
    And he to England shall along with you.
    The terms° of our estate° may not endure   5
    Hazard so near 's as doth hourly grow
    Out of his brows.°

352 *presently:* At once.   360 *by and by:* Immediately.   361 *bent:* See II.ii.30n.   370 *Nero:*
Murderer of his mother.   374 *shent:* Reproved.   375 *seals:* Authentications in actions.
SCENE III. 5 *terms:* Circumstances; *estate:* Royal position.   7 *brows:* Effronteries (apparently
with an implication of knitted brows).

Guildenstern: We will ourselves provide.
 Most holy and religious fear it is
 To keep those many many bodies safe
 That live and feed upon your majesty.   10
Rosencrantz: The single and peculiar° life is bound
 With all the strength and armor of the mind
 To keep itself from noyance,° but much more
 That spirit upon whose weal depends and rests
 The lives of many. The cess° of majesty   15
 Dies not alone, but like a gulf° doth draw
 What's near it with it; or 'tis a massy wheel
 Fixed on the summit of the highest mount,
 To whose huge spokes ten thousand lesser things
 Are mortised and adjoined, which when it falls, 20
 Each small annexment, petty consequence,
 Attends° the boist'rous ruin. Never alone
 Did the king sigh, but with a general groan.
King: Arm° you, I pray you, to this speedy voyage,
 For we will fetters put upon this fear,   25
 Which now goes too free-footed.
Rosencrantz: We will haste us.   *Exeunt Gentlemen.*

Enter Polonius.

Polonius: My lord, he's going to his mother's closet.
 Behind the arras I'll convey myself
 To hear the process.° I'll warrant she'll tax him home,°
 And, as you said, and wisely was it said,   30
 'Tis meet that some more audience than a mother,
 Since nature makes them partial, should o'erhear
 The speech, of vantage.° Fare you well, my liege.
 I'll call upon you ere you go to bed
 And tell you what I know.
King: Thanks, dear my lord. *Exit Polonius.* 35
 O, my offense is rank, it smells to heaven;
 It hath the primal eldest curse° upon't,
 A brother's murder. Pray can I not,
 Though inclination be as sharp as will.
 My stronger guilt defeats my strong intent,   40

---

11 *peculiar*: Individual. 13 *noyance*: Harm. 15 *cess*: Cessation, decease. 16 *gulf*: Whirl-pool. 22 *Attends*: Joins in (like a royal attendant). 24 *Arm*: Prepare. 29 *process*: Proceedings; *tax him home*: Thrust home in reprimanding him. 33 *of vantage*: From an advantageous position. 37 *primal eldest curse*: That of Cain, who also murdered a brother.

And like a man to double business bound
I stand in pause where I shall first begin,
And both neglect. What if this cursèd hand
Were thicker than itself with brother's blood,
Is there not rain enough in the sweet heavens   45
To wash it white as snow? Whereto serves mercy
But to confront the visage of offense?°
And what's in prayer but this twofold force,
To be forestallèd ere we come to fall,
Or pardoned being down? Then I'll look up.   50
My fault is past. But, O, what form of prayer
Can serve my turn? "Forgive me my foul murder"?
That cannot be, since I am still possessed
Of those effects° for which I did the murder,
My crown, mine own ambition, and my queen.   55
May one be pardoned and retain th' offense?
In the corrupted currents of this world
Offense's gilded° hand may shove by justice,
And oft 'tis seen the wicked prize itself
Buys out the law. But 'tis not so above.   60
There is no shuffling;° there the action° lies
In his true nature, and we ourselves compelled,
Even to the teeth and forehead° of our faults,
To give in evidence. What then? What rests?
Try what repentance can. What can it not?   65
Yet what can it when one cannot repent?
O wretched state! O bosom black as death!
O limèd° soul, that struggling to be free
Art more engaged!° Help, angels! Make assay.°
Bow, stubborn knees, and, heart with strings of steel,   70
Be soft as sinews of the new-born babe.
All may be well.

He kneels.

Enter Hamlet.

Hamlet: Now might I do it pat,° now 'a is a-praying,
And now I'll do't. And so 'a goes to heaven,
And so am I revenged. That would be scanned.   75

47 *offense*: Sin.   54 *effects*: Things acquired.   58 *gilded*: Gold-laden.   61 *shuffling*: Sharp
practice, double-dealing; *action*: Legal proceeding (in heaven's court).   63 *teeth and forehead*:
Face-to-face recognition.   68 *limèd*: Caught in birdlime, a gluey material spread as a bird-
snare.   69 *engaged*: Embedded; *assay*: An attempt.   73 *pat*: Opportunely.

A villain kills my father, and for that
I, his sole son, do this same villain send
To heaven.
Why, this is hire and salary, not revenge.
'A took my father grossly,° full of bread,°   80
With all his crimes broad blown,° as flush° as May;
And how his audit° stands, who knows save heaven?
But in our circumstance and course of thought,
'Tis heavy with him; and am I then revenged,
To take him in the purging of his soul,   85
When he is fit and seasoned for his passage?
No.
Up, sword, and know thou a more horrid hent.°
When he is drunk asleep, or in his rage,
Or in th' incestuous pleasure of his bed,   90
At game a-swearing, or about some act
That has no relish° of salvation in't —
Then trip him, that his heels may kick at heaven,
And that his soul may be as damned and black
As hell, whereto it goes. My mother stays.   95
This physic but prolongs thy sickly days.   *Exit.*
King (rises): My words fly up, my thoughts remain below.
     Words without thoughts never to heaven go.   *Exit.*

SCENE IV. *The private chamber of the Queen.*

Enter Queen Gertrude and Polonius.

Polonius: 'A will come straight. Look you lay° home to him.
     Tell him his pranks have been too broad° to bear with,
     And that your grace hath screened and stood between
     Much heat and him. I'll silence me even here.
     Pray you be round° with him.   5
Hamlet (within): Mother, mother, mother!
Queen: I'll warrant you; fear me not. Withdraw; I hear him coming.

Polonius hides behind the arras.

Enter Hamlet.

Hamlet: Now, mother, what's the matter?

80 *grossly*: In a state of gross unpreparedness; *bread*: I.e., worldly sense gratification.   81 *broad blown*: Fully blossomed; *flush*: Vigorous.   82 *audit*: Account.   88 *more horrid hent*: Grasping by me on a more horrid occasion.   93 *relish*: Flavor.   SCENE IV. 1 *lay*: Thrust.   2 *broad*: Unrestrained.   5 *round*: Plain-spoken.

Queen: Hamlet, thou hast thy father much offended.
Hamlet: Mother, you have my father much offended.   10
Queen: Come, come, you answer with an idle° tongue.
Hamlet: Go, go, you question with a wicked tongue.
Queen: Why, how now, Hamlet?
Hamlet: What's the matter now?
Queen: Have you forgot me?
Hamlet: No, by the rood,° not so!
    You are the queen, your husband's brother's wife,   15
    And (would it were not so) you are my mother.
Queen: Nay, then I'll set those to you that can speak.
Hamlet: Come, come, and sit you down. You shall not budge.
    You go not till I set you up a glass
    Where you may see the inmost part of you.   20
Queen: What wilt thou do? Thou wilt not murder me?
    Help, ho!
Polonius (behind): What, ho! help!
Hamlet (draws): How now? a rat? Dead for a ducat, dead!

Makes a pass through the arras and kills Polonius.

Polonius (behind): O, I am slain!
Queen: O me, what has thou done?   25
Hamlet: Nay, I know not. Is it the king?
Queen: O, what a rash and bloody deed is this!
Hamlet: A bloody deed — almost as bad, good mother,
    As kill a king, and marry with his brother.
Queen: As kill a king?
Hamlet: Ay, lady, it was my word.   30

Lifts up the arras and sees Polonius.

    Thou wretched, rash, intruding fool, farewell!
    I took thee for thy better. Take thy fortune.
    Thou find'st to be too busy is some danger. —
    Leave wringing of your hands. Peace, sit you down
    And let me wring your heart, for so I shall   35
    If it be made of penetrable stuff,
    If damnèd custom° have not brazed° it so
    That it is proof° and bulwark against sense.°
Queen: What have I done that thou dar'st wag thy tongue
    In noise so rude against me?

---

11 *idle*: Foolish.   14 *rood*: Cross.   37 *custom*: Habit; *brazed*: Hardened like brass.   38 *proof*:
Armor; *sense*: Feeling.

Hamlet: Such an act   40
  That blurs the grace and blush of modesty,
  Calls virtue hypocrite, takes off the rose
  From the fair forehead of an innocent love,
  And sets a blister° there, makes marriage vows
  As false as dicers' oaths. O, such a deed   45
  As from the body of contraction° plucks
  The very soul, and sweet religion° makes
  A rhapsody of words! Heaven's face does glow,
  And this solidity and compound mass,°
  With heated visage, as against° the doom,°   50
  Is thought-sick at the act.
Queen: Ay me, what act,
  That roars so loud and thunders in the index?°
Hamlet: Look here upon this picture, and on this,
  The counterfeit presentment° of two brothers.
  See what a grace was seated on this brow: 55
  Hyperion's° curls, the front° of Jove himself,
  An eye like Mars, to threaten and command,
  A station° like the herald Mercury
  New lighted on a heaven-kissing hill —
  A combination and a form indeed   60
  Where every god did seem to set his seal
  To give the world assurance of a man.
  This was your husband. Look you now what follows.
  Here is your husband, like a mildewed ear
  Blasting his wholesome brother. Have you eyes?   65
  Could you on this fair mountain leave to feed,
  And batten° on this moor? Ha! have you eyes?
  You cannot call it love, for at your age
  The heyday° in the blood is tame, it's humble,
  And waits upon° the judgment, and what judgment   70
  Would step from this to this? Sense° sure you have,
  Else could you not have motion,° but sure that sense
  Is apoplexed,° for madness would not err,
  Nor sense to ecstasy° was ne'er so thralled

---

44 *blister*: Brand (of degradation).   46 *contraction*: The marriage contract.   47 *religion*: I.e.,
sacred marriage vows.   49 *compound mass*: The earth as compounded of the four elements.
50 *against*: In expectation of; *doom*: Day of Judgment.   52 *index*: Table of contents preceding
the body of a book.   54 *counterfeit presentment*: Portrayed representation.   56 *Hyperion*:
The sun god; *front*: Forehead.   58 *station*: Attitude in standing.   67 *batten*: Feed greedily.
69 *heyday*: Excitement of passion.   70 *waits upon*: Yields to.   71 *Sense*: Feeling.   72 *motion*: Desire, impulse.   73 *apoplexed*: Paralyzed.   74 *ecstasy*: Madness.

But it reserved some quantity of choice   75
To serve in such a difference. What devil was't
That thus hath cozened° you at hoodman-blind?°
Eyes without feeling, feeling without sight,
Ears without hands or eyes, smelling sans° all,
Or but a sickly part of one true sense   80
Could not so mope.°
O shame, where is thy blush? Rebellious hell,
If thou canst mutine° in a matron's bones,
To flaming youth let virtue be as wax
And melt in her own fire. Proclaim no shame   85
When the compulsive° ardor gives the charge,°
Since frost itself as actively doth burn,
And reason panders will.°
Queen: O Hamlet, speak no more.
Thou turn'st mine eyes into my very soul,
And there I see such black and grainèd° spots   90
As will not leave their tinct.°
Hamlet: Nay, but to live
In the rank sweat of an enseamèd° bed,
Stewed in corruption, honeying and making love
Over the nasty sty —
Queen: O, speak to me no more.
These words like daggers enter in mine ears.   95
No more, sweet Hamlet.
Hamlet: A murderer and a villain,
A slave that is not twentieth part the tithe°
Of your precedent lord, a vice° of kings,
A cutpurse° of the empire and the rule,
That from a shelf the precious diadem stole   100
And put it in his pocket —
Queen: No more.

Enter the Ghost in his nightgown.°

Hamlet: A king of shreds and patches —
Save me and hover o'er me with your wings,
You heavenly guards? What would your gracious figure?

---

77 *cozened*: Cheated; *hoodman-blind*: Blindman's buff.   79 *sans*: Without.   81 *mope*: Be stupid.   83 *mutine*: Mutiny.   86 *compulsive*: Compelling; *gives the charge*: Delivers the attack.   88 *panders will*: Acts as procurer for desire.   90 *grainèd*: Dyed in grain.   91 *tinct*: Color.   92 *enseamèd*: Grease-laden.   97 *tithe*: Tenth part.   98 *vice*: Clownish rogue (like the Vice of the morality plays).   99 *cutpurse*: Skulking thief.   101 *nightgown*: Dressing gown.

Queen: Alas, he's mad.   105
Hamlet: Do you not come your tardy son to chide,
    That, lapsed in time and passion,° lets go by
    Th' important acting of your dread command?
    O, say!
Ghost: Do not forget. This visitation   110
    Is but to whet thy almost blunted purpose.
    But look, amazement on thy mother sits.
    O, step between her and her fighting soul!
    Conceit° in weakest bodies strongest works.
    Speak to her, Hamlet.
Hamlet: How is it with you, lady?   115
Queen: Alas, how is't with you,
    That you do bend your eye on vacancy,
    And with th' incorporal° air do hold discourse?
    Forth at your eyes your spirits wildly peep,
    And as the sleeping soldiers in th' alarm   120
    Your bedded hairs like life in excrements°
    Start up and stand an° end. O gentle son,
    Upon the heat and flame of thy distemper°
    Sprinkle cool patience. Whereon do you look?
Hamlet: On him, on him! Look you, how pale he glares!   125
    His form and cause conjoined, preaching to stones,
    Would make them capable.° — Do not look upon me,
    Lest with this piteous action you convert
    My stern effects.° Then what I have to do
    Will want true color — tears perchance for blood.   130
Queen: To whom do you speak this?
Hamlet: Do you see nothing there?
Queen: Nothing at all; yet all that is I see.
Hamlet: Nor did you nothing hear?
Queen: No, nothing but ourselves.
Hamlet: Why, look you there! Look how it steals away!
    My father, in his habit as he lived!   135
    Look where he goes even now out at the portal!
                              Exit Ghost.

Queen: This is the very coinage of your brain.
    This bodiless creation ecstasy°
    Is very cunning in.

107 *lapsed . . . passion*: Having let the moment slip and passion cool. 114 *Conceit*: Imagination. 118 *incorporal*: Bodiless. 121 *excrements*: Outgrowths. 122 *an*: On. 123 *distemper*: Mental disorder. 127 *capable*: Susceptible. 129 *effects*: Manifestations of emotion
and purpose. 138 *ecstasy*: Madness.

Hamlet: Ecstasy?
My pulse as yours doth temperately keep time   140
And makes as healthful music. It is not madness
That I have uttered. Bring me to the test,
And I the matter will reword, which madness
Would gambol° from. Mother, for love of grace,
Lay not that flattering unction° to your soul,   145
That not your trespass but my madness speaks.
It will but skin and film the ulcerous place
Whiles rank corruption, mining° all within,
Infects unseen. Confess yourself to heaven,
Repent what's past, avoid what is to come,   150
And do not spread the compost° on the weeds
To make them ranker. Forgive me this my virtue.
For in the fatness° of these pursy° times
Virtue itself of vice must pardon beg,
Yea, curb° and woo for leave to do him good.   155
Queen: O Hamlet, thou hast cleft my heart in twain.
Hamlet: O, throw away the worser part of it,
And live the purer with the other half.
Good night — but go not to my uncle's bed.
Assume a virtue, if you have it not.   160
That monster custom, who all sense doth eat,°
Of habits devil,° is angel yet in this,
That to the use of actions fair and good
He likewise gives a frock or livery°
That aptly is put on. Refrain to-night,   165
And that shall lend a kind of easiness

---

144 *gambol*: Shy (like a startled horse).   145 *unction*: Ointment.   148 *mining*: Undermining.   151 *compost*: Fertilizing mixture.   153 *fatness*: Gross slackness; *pursy*: Corpulent. 155 *curb*: Bow to.   161 *all sense doth eat*: Absorbs and lives upon all human sense, not only that made up of the bodily faculties but also the contrasting "inward" sense made up of the faculties of the mind and soul — all sense, whether low or high and whether bad or good in use (looking forward to completion of the image of custom as a monster of double form, part devil and part angel; see the *Oxford English Dictionary* under "Sense," I, 3 and 7). The crux of which these words make a part has also produced frequent emendation. See the note following.   162 *Of habits devil*: Being a devil in, or in respect of, habits (with a play on "habits," as meaning both settled practices and garments, which by looking forward to "actions fair and good" and to "frock or livery" is subtly involved in the opposition and monstrous combination within the passage of devil and angel, and which contributes to an essential poetic image that tends to be destroyed by a finding of need to emend the phrase, especially when "devil" is changed to "evil"; see the *Oxford English Dictionary* under "Of," XI, 37, for a showing of the use of the preposition in the sense here given, as in the example, dated 1535, "he y^t is a blabbe of his tonge").   164 *livery*: Characteristic dress (accompanying the suggestion of "garb" in *habits*).

To the next abstinence; the next more easy;
For use° almost can change the stamp° of nature,
And either . . . the devil, or throw him out°
With wondrous potency. Once more, good night,   170
And when you are desirous to be blest,
I'll blessing beg of you. — For this same lord,
I do repent; but heaven hath pleased it so,
To punish me with this, and this with me,
That I must be their scourge and minister.   175
I will bestow° him and will answer well
The death I gave him. So again, good night.
I must be cruel only to be kind.
Thus bad begins, and worse remains behind.°
One word more, good lady.
Queen: What shall I do?   180
Hamlet: Not this, by no means, that I bid you do:
Let the bloat° king tempt you again to bed,
Pinch wanton on your cheek, call you his mouse,
And let him, for a pair of reechy° kisses,
Or paddling in your neck with his damned fingers,   185
Make you to ravel all this matter out,°
That I essentially am not in madness,
But mad in craft. 'Twere good you let him know,
For who that's but a queen, fair, sober, wise,
Would from a paddock,° from a bat, a gib,°   190
Such dear concernings° hide? Who would do so?
No, in despite of sense and secrecy,
Unpeg the basket on the house's top,
Let the birds fly, and like the famous ape,°
To try conclusions,° in the basket creep   195
And break your own neck down.
Queen: Be thou assured, if words be made of breath,
And breath of life, I have no life to breathe
What thou hast said to me.
Hamlet: I must to England; you know that?
Queen: Alack,   200
I had forgot. 'Tis so concluded on.

---

168 *use:* Habit; *stamp:* Impression, form.   169 *And . . . out:* This line is usually taken to suffer
from an omission after "either" of some such word as "master," "curb," or "quell."   176 *be-*
stow: Stow, hide.   179 *behind:* To come.   182 *bloat:* Bloated with sense gratification.
184 *reechy:* Filthy.   186 *ravel . . . out:* Disentangle.   190 *paddock:* Toad; *gib:* Tomcat.
191 *dear concernings:* Matters of great personal significance.   194 *famous ape:* One in a story
now unknown.   195 *conclusions:* Experiments.

Hamlet: There's letters sealed, and my two schoolfellows,
 Whom I will trust as I will adders fanged,
 They bear the mandate;° they must sweep my way
 And marshal me to knavery. Let it work.   205
 For 'tis the sport to have the enginer°
 Hoist° with his own petar,° and 't shall go hard
 But I will delve one yard below their mines
 And blow them at the moon. O, 'tis most sweet
 When in one line two crafts directly meet.   210
 This man shall set me packing.°
 I'll lug the guts into the neighbor room.
 Mother, good night. Indeed, this counsellor
 Is now most still, most secret, and most grave,
 Who was in life a foolish prating knave.   215
 Come, sir, to draw toward an end with you.
 Good night, mother.

        Exit the Queen. Then exit Hamlet,
             tugging in Polonius.

ACT IV

SCENE I. *A chamber in the castle.*

Enter King and Queen, with Rosencrantz and Guildenstern.

King: There's matter in these sighs. These profound heaves
 You must translate; 'tis fit we understand them.
 Where is your son?
Queen: Bestow this place on us a little while.

      Exeunt Rosencrantz and Guildenstern.

 Ah, mine own lord, what have I seen to-night!   5
King: What, Gertrude? How does Hamlet?
Queen: Mad as the sea and wind when both contend
 Which is the mightier. In his lawless fit,
 Behind the arras hearing something stir,
 Whips out his rapier, cries, "A rat, a rat!"   10

204 *mandate*: Order. 206 *enginer*: Engineer, constructor of military engines or works. 207 *Hoist*: Blown up; *petar*: Petard, bomb or mine. 211 *packing*: Travelling in a hurry (with a play upon his "packing" or shouldering of Polonius' body and also upon his "packing" in the sense of "plotting" or "contriving").

And in this brainish apprehension° kills
The unseen good old man.
King: O heavy deed!
It had been so with us, had we been there.
His liberty is full of threats to all,
To you yourself, to us, to every one.   15
Alas, how shall this bloody deed be answered?
It will be laid to us, whose providence°
Should have kept short, restrained, and out of haunt°
This mad young man. But so much was our love
We would not understand what was most fit,   20
But, like the owner of a foul disease,
To keep it from divulging,° let it feed
Even on the pith of life. Where is he gone?
Queen: To draw apart the body he hath killed;
O'er whom his very madness, like some ore°   25
Among a mineral° of metals base,
Shows itself pure. 'A weeps for what is done.
King: O Gertrude, come away!
The sun no sooner shall the mountains touch
But we will ship him hence, and this vile deed   30
We must with all our majesty and skill
Both countenance and excuse. Ho, Guildenstern!

Enter Rosencrantz and Guildenstern.

Friends both, go join you with some further aid.
Hamlet in madness hath Polonius slain,
And from his mother's closet hath he dragged him.   35
Go seek him out; speak fair, and bring the body
Into the chapel. I pray you haste in this.

                                   Exeunt Rosencrantz and Guildenstern.

Come, Gertrude, we'll call up our wisest friends
And let them know both what we mean to do
And what's untimely done° . . .   40
Whose whisper o'er the world's diameter,
As level° as the cannon to his blank°

ACT IV, SCENE I. 11 *brainish apprehension*: Headstrong conception.   17 *providence*: Foresight.
18 *haunt*: Association with others.   22 *divulging*: Becoming known.   25 *ore*: Vein of gold.
26 *mineral*: Mine.   40 *And . . . done*: It would seem that after this fragmentary line there is an
omission. Capell's insertion of "So, haply, slander," a purely conjectural completion of the
line, has often been accepted as providing desired clarification of thought.   42 *As level*:
With as direct aim; *blank*: Mark, central white spot on a target.

Transports his poisoned shot, may miss our name
And hit the woundless air. O, come away!
My soul is full of discord and dismay.   *Exeunt.* 45

SCENE II. *A passage in the castle.*

Enter Hamlet.

Hamlet: Safely stowed.
Gentlemen (within): Hamlet! Lord Hamlet!
Hamlet: But soft, what noise? Who calls on Hamlet? O, here they
    come.

Enter Rosencrantz, Guildenstern, and others.

Rosencrantz: What have you done, my lord, with the dead body?   5
Hamlet: Compounded it with dust, whereto 'tis kin.
Rosencrantz: Tell us where 'tis, that we may take it thence
    And bear it to the chapel.
Hamlet: Do not believe it.
Rosencrantz: Believe what?   10
Hamlet: That I can keep your counsel and not mine own. Besides,
    to be demanded of a sponge, what replication° should be
    made by the son of a king?
Rosencrantz: Take you me for a sponge, my lord?
Hamlet: Ay, sir, that soaks up the king's countenance,° his re- 15
    wards, his authorities. But such officers do the king best ser-
    vice in the end. He keeps them, like an ape, in the corner of
    his jaw, first mouthed, to be last swallowed. When he needs
    what you have gleaned, it is but squeezing you and, sponge,
    you shall be dry again.   20
Rosencrantz: I understand you not, my lord.
Hamlet: I am glad of it. A knavish speech sleeps in° a foolish ear.
Rosencrantz: My lord, you must tell us where the body is and go
    with us to the king.
Hamlet: The body is with the king, but the king is not with the 25
    body. The king is a thing —
Guildenstern: A thing, my lord?
Hamlet: Of nothing.° Bring me to him. Hide fox, and all after.°

                                                          Exeunt.

SCENE II. 12 *replication*: Reply.   15 *countenance*: Favor.   22 *sleeps in*: Means nothing to.   28 *Of nothing*: Cf. Prayer Book, Psalm 144:4, "Man is like a thing of naught: his time passeth away like a shadow"; *Hide . . . after*: Apparently well-known words from some game of hide-and-seek.

SCENE III. *A chamber in the castle.*

Enter King, and two or three.

King: I have sent to seek him and to find the body.
How dangerous is it that this man goes loose!
Yet must not we put the strong law on him;
He's loved of the distracted° multitude,
Who like not in their judgment, but their eyes,   5
And where 'tis so, th' offender's scourge° is weighed,
But never the offense. To bear all smooth and even,
This sudden sending him away must seem
Deliberate pause.° Diseases desperate grown
By desperate appliance are relieved,   10
Or not at all.

Enter Rosencrantz, Guildenstern, and all the rest.

               How now? What hath befallen?
Rosencrantz: Where the dead body is bestowed, my lord,
   We cannot get from him.
King: But where is he?
Rosencrantz: Without, my lord; guarded, to know your pleasure.
King: Bring him before us.
Rosencrantz: Ho! Bring in the lord.   15

They enter with Hamlet.

King: Now, Hamlet, where's Polonius?
Hamlet: At supper.
King: At supper? Where?
Hamlet: Not where he eats, but where 'a is eaten. A certain convocation of politic worms° are e'en at him. Your worm is your   20
only emperor for diet.° We fat all creatures else to fat us, and
we fat ourselves for maggots. Your fat king and your lean
beggar is but variable service° — two dishes, but to one
table. That's the end.
King: Alas, alas!   25
Hamlet: A man may fish with the worm that hath eat of a king,
and eat of the fish that hath fed of that worm.

SCENE III. 4 *distracted:* Confused.   6 *scourge:* Punishment.   9 *Deliberate pause:* Something
done with much deliberation.   20 *politic worms:* Political and craftily scheming worms (such
as Polonius might well attract).   21 *diet:* Food and drink (perhaps with a play upon a
famous "convocation," the Diet of Worms opened by the Emperor Charles V on January 28,
1521, before which Luther appeared).   23 *variable service:* Different servings of one food.

King: What dost thou mean by this?

Hamlet: Nothing but to show you how a king may go a progress°
through the guts of a beggar.   30

King: Where is Polonius?

Hamlet: In heaven. Send thither to see. If your messenger find
him not there, seek him i' th' other place yourself. But if
indeed you find him not within this month, you shall nose
him as you go up the stairs into the lobby.   35

King (to Attendants): Go seek him there.

Hamlet: 'A will stay till you come.   *Exeunt Attendants.*

King: Hamlet, this deed, for thine especial safety,
Which we do tender° as we dearly° grieve
For that which thou hast done, must send thee hence   40
With fiery quickness. Therefore prepare thyself.
The bark is ready and the wind at help,
Th' associates tend,° and everything is bent°
For England.

Hamlet: For England?

King: Ay, Hamlet.

Hamlet: Good.

King: So is it, if thou knew'st our purposes.   45

Hamlet: I see a cherub° that sees them. But come, for England!
Farewell, dear mother.

King: Thy loving father, Hamlet.

Hamlet: My mother — father and mother is man and wife, man
and wife is one flesh, and so, my mother. Come, for England!   50

                                               Exit.

King: Follow him at foot;° tempt him with speed aboard.
Delay it not; I'll have him hence to-night.
Away! for everything is sealed and done
That else leans on° th' affair. Pray you make haste.

                              Exeunt all but the King.

And, England,° if my love thou hold'st at aught —   55
As my great power thereof may give thee sense,
Since yet thy cicatrice looks raw and red
After the Danish sword, and thy free awe°

---

29 *progress*: Royal journey of state.   39 *tender*: Hold dear; *dearly*: Intensely.   43 *tend*: Wait;
bent: Set in readiness (like a bent bow).   46 *cherub*: One of the cherubim (angels with a
distinctive quality of knowledge).   51 *at foot*: At heel, close.   54 *leans on*: Is connected
with.   55 *England*: King of England.   58 *free awe*: Voluntary show of respect.

Pays homage to us — thou mayst not coldly set°
Our sovereign process,° which imports at full   60
By letters congruing° to that effect
The present° death of Hamlet. Do it, England,
For like the hectic° in my blood he rages,
And thou must cure me. Till I know 'tis done,
Howe'er my haps,° my joys were ne'er begun.   *Exit.* 65

SCENE IV. *A coastal highway.*

Enter Fortinbras with his Army over the stage.

Fortinbras: Go, captain, from me greet the Danish king.
  Tell him that by his license Fortinbras
  Craves the conveyance° of a promised march
  Over his kingdom. You know the rendezvous.
  If that his majesty would aught with us,   5
  We shall express our duty in his eye;°
  And let him know so.
Captain: I will do't, my lord.
Fortinbras: Go softly° on.   *Exeunt all but the Captain.*

Enter Hamlet, Rosencrantz, Guildenstern, and others.

Hamlet: Good sir, whose powers° are these?
Captain: They are of Norway, sir.   10
Hamlet: How purposed, sir, I pray you?
Captain: Against some part of Poland.
Hamlet: Who commands them, sir?
Captain: The nephew to old Norway, Fortinbras.
Hamlet: Goes it against the main° of Poland, sir,   15
  Or for some frontier?
Captain: Truly to speak, and with no addition,°
  We go to gain a little patch of ground
  That hath in it no profit but the name.
  To pay° five ducats, five, I would not farm it,   20
  Nor will it yield to Norway or the Pole
  A ranker° rate, should it be sold in fee.°
Hamlet: Why, then the Polack never will defend it.
Captain: Yes, it is already garrisoned.

---

59 *set*: Esteem.   60 *process*: Formal command.   61 *congruing*: Agreeing.   62 *present*: Instant.   63 *hectic*: A continuous fever.   65 *haps*: Fortunes.   SCENE IV. 3 *conveyance*: Escort.
6 *eye*: Presence.   8 *softly*: Slowly.   9 *powers*: Forces.   15 *main*: Main body.   17 *addition*:
Exaggeration.   20 *To pay*: I.e., for a yearly rental of.   22 *ranker*: More abundant; *in fee*:
Outright.

Hamlet: Two thousand souls and twenty thousand ducats   25
    Will not debate the question of this straw.
    This is th' imposthume° of much wealth and peace,
    That inward breaks, and shows no cause without
    Why the man dies. I humbly thank you, sir.
Captain: God bye you, sir.   *Exit.*
Rosencrantz: Will't please you go, my lord?   30
Hamlet: I'll be with you straight. Go a little before.

                                        Exeunt all but Hamlet.

    How all occasions do inform° against me
    And spur my dull revenge! What is a man,
    If his chief good and market of° his time
    Be but to sleep and feed? A beast, no more.   35
    Sure he that made us with such large discourse,°
    Looking before and after, gave us not
    That capability and godlike reason
    To fust° in us unused. Now, whether it be
    Bestial oblivion,° or some craven scruple   40
    Of thinking too precisely on th' event° —
    A thought which, quartered, hath but one part wisdom
    And ever three parts coward — I do not know
    Why yet I live to say, "This thing's to do,"
    Sith I have cause, and will, and strength, and means   45
    To do't. Examples gross° as earth exhort me.
    Witness this army of such mass and charge,°
    Led by a delicate and tender prince,
    Whose spirit, with divine ambition puffed,
    Makes mouths° at the invisible event,   50
    Exposing what is mortal and unsure
    To all that fortune, death, and danger dare,
    Even for an eggshell. Rightly to be great
    Is not to stir without great argument,
    But greatly to find quarrel in a straw°   55
    When honor's at the stake. How stand I then,
    That have a father killed, a mother stained,
    Excitements of my reason and my blood,
    And let all sleep, while to my shame I see

---

27 *imposthume*: Abscess.   32 *inform*: Take shape.   34 *market of*: Compensation for.   36 *discourse*: Power of thought.   39 *fust*: Grow mouldy.   40 *oblivion*: Forgetfulness.   41 *event*: Outcome (as also in line 50).   46 *gross*: Large and evident.   47 *charge*: Expense.   50 *Makes mouths*: Makes faces scornfully.   55 *greatly . . . straw*: To recognize the great argument even in some small matter.

The imminent death of twenty thousand men   60
That for a fantasy° and trick° of fame
Go to their graves like beds, fight for a plot
Whereon the numbers cannot try the cause,°
Which is not tomb enough and continent°
To hide the slain? O, from this time forth,   65
My thoughts be bloody, or be nothing worth!   *Exit.*

SCENE V. *A chamber in the castle.*

Enter Horatio, Queen Gertrude, and a Gentleman.

Queen: I will not speak with her.
Gentleman: She is importunate, indeed distract.°
    Her mood will needs be pitied.
Queen: What would she have?
Gentleman: She speaks much of her father, says she hears
    There's tricks° i' th' world, and hems, and beats her heart,   5
    Spurns enviously° at straws,° speaks things in doubt
    That carry but half sense. Her speech is nothing,
    Yet the unshapèd use° of it doth move
    The hearers to collection;° they aim° at it,
    And botch° the words up fit to their own thoughts,   10
    Which, as her winks and nods and gestures yield them,
    Indeed would make one think there might be thought,
    Though nothing sure, yet much unhappily.
Horatio: 'Twere good she were spoken with, for she may strew
    Dangerous conjectures in ill-breeding minds.   15
Queen: Let her come in.   *Exit Gentleman.*

Aside.

    To my sick soul (as sin's true nature is)
    Each toy° seems prologue to some great amiss.°
    So full of artless° jealousy° is guilt
    It spills° itself in fearing to be spilt.   20

---

61 *fantasy*: Fanciful image; *trick*: Toy.   63 *try the cause*: Find space in which to settle the
issue by battle.   64 *continent*: Receptacle.   SCENE V. 2 *distract*: Insane.   5 *tricks*: Deceits.
6 *Spurns enviously*: Kicks spitefully, takes offense; *straws*: Trifles.   8 *unshapèd use*: Disordered
manner.   9 *collection*: Attempts at shaping meaning; *aim*: Guess.   10 *botch*: Patch.
18 *toy*: Trifle; *amiss*: Calamity.   19 *artless*: Unskillfully managed; *jealousy*: Suspicion.
20 *spills*: Destroys.

Enter Ophelia (distracted).

Ophelia: Where is the beauteous majesty of Denmark?
Queen: How now, Ophelia?
Ophelia:

She sings.

> How should I your true-love know
>> From another one?
> By his cockle hat° and staff   25
>> And his sandal shoon.°

Queen: Alas, sweet lady, what imports this song?
Ophelia: Say you? Nay, pray you mark.

> *Song.*

> He is dead and gone, lady,
>> He is dead and gone;   30
> At his head a grass-green turf,
>> At his heels a stone.

O, ho!
Queen: Nay, but Ophelia —
Ophelia: Pray you mark.   35
(Sings.) White his shroud as the mountain snow —

Enter King.

Queen: Alas, look here, my lord.
Ophelia:

> *Song.*

> Larded° all with sweet flowers;
> Which bewept to the grave did not go
>> With true-love showers.   40

King: How do you, pretty lady?
Ophelia: Well, God dild° you! They say the owl° was a baker's
   daughter. Lord, we know what we are, but know not what we
   may be. God be at your table!
King: Conceit° upon her father.   45

---

25 *cockle hat*: Hat bearing a cockle shell, worn by a pilgrim who had been to the shrine of St.
James of Compostela.   26 *shoon*: Shoes.   38 *Larded*: Garnished.   42 *dild*: Yield, repay;
the owl: An owl into which, according to a folk-tale, a baker's daughter was transformed
because of her failure to show whole-hearted generosity when Christ asked for bread in the
baker's shop.   45 *Conceit*: Thought.

Ophelia: Pray let's have no words of this, but when they ask you what it means, say you this:

Song.

To-morrow is Saint Valentine's day.
  All in the morning betime,°
And I a maid at your window,   50
  To be your Valentine.
Then up he rose and donned his clo'es
  And dupped° the chamber door,
Let in the maid, that out a maid
  Never departed more.   55

King: Pretty Ophelia!
Ophelia: Indeed, la, without an oath, I'll make an end on't:
(Sings.)   By Gis° and by Saint Charity,
              Alack, and fie for shame!
          Young men will do't if they come to't.   60
              By Cock,° they are to blame.
          Quoth she, "Before you tumbled me,
              You promised me to wed."

    He answers:
          "So would I 'a' done, by yonder sun,   65
              And thou hadst not come to my bed."

King: How long hath she been thus?
Ophelia: I hope all will be well. We must be patient, but I cannot choose but weep to think they would lay him i' th' cold ground. My brother shall know of it; and so I thank you for   70 your good counsel. Come, my coach! Good night, ladies, good night. Sweet ladies, good night, good night.   *Exit.*
King: Follow her close; give her good watch, I pray you.

                                                   Exit Horatio.

O, this is the poison of deep grief; it springs
All from her father's death — and now behold!   75
O Gertrude, Gertrude,
When sorrows come, they come not single spies,
But in battalions: first, her father slain;
Next, your son gone, and he most violent author
Of his own just remove; the people muddied,°   80
  Thick and unwholesome in their thoughts and whispers

---

49 *betime*: Early.   53 *dupped*: Opened.   58 *Gis*: Jesus.   61 *Cock*: God (with a perversion of the name not uncommon in oaths).   80 *muddied*: Stirred up and confused.

For good Polonius' death, and we have done but greenly°
In hugger-mugger° to inter him; poor Ophelia
Divided from herself and her fair judgment,
Without the which we are pictures or mere beasts;   85
Last, and as much containing as all these,
Her brother is in secret come from France,
Feeds on his wonder, keeps himself in clouds,°
And wants° not buzzers° to infect his ear
With pestilent speeches of his father's death,   90
Wherein necessity, of matter beggared,°
Will nothing stick° our person to arraign°
In ear and ear. O my dear Gertrude, this,
Like to a murd'ring piece,° in many places
Gives me superfluous death.

A noise within.

Enter a Messenger.

Queen: Alack, what noise is this?   95
King: Attend, where are my Switzers?° Let them guard the door.
    What is the matter?
Messenger: Save yourself, my lord.
    The ocean, overpeering of° his list,°
    Eats not the flats with more impiteous° haste
    Than young Laertes, in a riotous head,°   100
    O'erbears your officers. The rabble call him lord,
    And, as the world were now but to begin,
    Antiquity forgot, custom not known,
    The ratifiers and props of every word,°
    They cry, "Choose we! Laertes shall be king!"   105
    Caps, hands, and tongues applaud it to the clouds,
    "Laertes shall be king! Laertes king!"

A noise within.

Queen: How cheerfully on the false trail they cry!
    O, this is counter,° you false Danish dogs!
King: The doors are broke.   110

---

82 *greenly:* Foolishly.   83 *hugger-mugger:* Secrecy and disorder.   88 *clouds:* Obscurity.
89 *wants:* Lacks; *buzzers:* Whispering tale-bearers.   91 *of matter beggared:* Unprovided with
facts.   92 *nothing stick:* In no way hesitate; *arraign:* Accuse.   94 *murd'ring piece:* Cannon
loaded with shot meant to scatter.   96 *Switzers:* Hired Swiss guards.   98 *overpeering of:*
Rising to look over and pass beyond; *list:* Boundary.   99 *impiteous:* Pitiless.   100 *head:*
Armed force.   104 *word:* Promise.   109 *counter:* Hunting backward on the trail.

Enter Laertes with others.

Laertes: Where is this king? — Sirs, stand you all without.
All: No, let's come in.
Laertes: I pray you give me leave.
All: We will, we will.
Laertes: I thank you. Keep the door.   *Exeunt his Followers.*
                                 O thou vile king,
   Give me my father.
Queen: Calmly, good Laertes.   115
Laertes: That drop of blood that's calm proclaims me bastard,
   Cries cuckold to my father, brands the harlot
   Even here between the chaste unsmirchèd brows
   Of my true mother.
King: What is the cause, Laertes,
   That thy rebellion looks so giant-like?   120
   Let him go, Gertrude. Do not fear° our person.
   There's such divinity doth hedge a king
   That treason can but peep to° what it would,
   Acts little of his will. Tell me, Laertes,
   Why thou art thus incensed. Let him go, Gertrude.   125
   Speak, man.
Laertes: Where is my father?
King: Dead.
Queen: But not by him.
King: Let him demand his fill.
Laertes: How came he dead? I'll not be juggled with.
   To hell allegiance, vows to the blackest devil,   130
   Conscience and grace to the profoundest pit!
   I dare damnation. To this point I stand,
   That both the worlds° I give to negligence,°
   Let come what comes, only I'll be revenged
   Most throughly° for my father.
King: Who shall stay you?   135
Laertes: My will, not all the world's.
   And for my means, I'll husband them so well
   They shall go far with little.
King: Good Laertes,
   If you desire to know the certainty
   Of your dear father, is't writ in your revenge   140

---

121 *fear*: Fear for.   123 *peep to*: I.e., through the barrier.   133 *both the worlds*: Whatever may
result in this world or the next; *give to negligence*: Disregard.   135 *throughly*: Thoroughly.

That swoopstake° you will draw both friend and foe,
Winner and loser?
Laertes: None but his enemies.
King: Will you know them then?
Laertes: To his good friends thus wide I'll ope my arms
    And like the kind life-rend'ring° pelican   145
    Repast them with my blood.
King: Why, now you speak
    Like a good child and a true gentleman.
    That I am guiltless of your father's death,
    And am most sensibly° in grief for it,
    It shall as level° to your judgment 'pear   150
    As day does to your eye.

A noise within: "Let her come in."

Laertes: How now? What noise is that?

Enter Ophelia.

O heat, dry up my brains; tears seven times salt
Burn out the sense and virtue of mine eye!
By heaven, thy madness shall be paid by weight   155
Till our scale turn the beam.° O rose of May,
Dear maid, kind sister, sweet Ophelia!
O heavens, is't possible a young maid's wits
Should be as mortal as an old man's life?
Nature is fine° in love, and where 'tis fine,   160
It sends some precious instance° of itself
After the thing it loves.

Ophelia: *Song.*

    They bore him barefaced on the bier
      Hey non nony, nony, hey nony
    And in his grave rained many a tear —
                           165
Fare you well, my dove!
Laertes: Hadst thou thy wits, and didst persuade revenge,
    It could not move thus.
Ophelia: You must sing "A-down a-down, and you call him

---

141 *swoopstake*: Sweepstake, taking all stakes on the gambling table.   145 *life-rend'ring*: Life-yielding (because the mother pelican supposedly took blood from her breast with her bill to feed her young).   149 *sensibly*: Feelingly.   150 *level*: Plain.   156 *beam*: Bar of a balance. 160 *fine*: Refined to purity.   161 *instance*: Token.

a-down-a." O, how the wheel° becomes it! It is the false stew-   170
ard, that stole his master's daughter.
Laertes: This nothing's more than matter.°
Ophelia: There's rosemary, that's for remembrance. Pray you,
love, remember. And there is pansies, that's for thoughts.
Laertes: A document° in madness, thoughts and remembrance   175
fitted.
Ophelia: There's fennel° for you, and columbines.° There's rue°
for you, and here's some for me. We may call it herb of grace
o' Sundays. O, you must wear your rue with a difference.
There's a daisy.° I would give you some violets,° but they   180
withered all when my father died. They say 'a made a good
end.
(*Sings.*) For bonny sweet Robin is all my joy.
Laertes: Thought and affliction, passion, hell itself,
She turns to favor° and to prettiness.   185

Ophelia: *Song.*

    And will 'a not come again?
    And will 'a not come again?
      No, no, he is dead;
      Go to thy deathbed;
    He never will come again.   190
    His beard was as white as snow,
    All flaxen was his poll.°
      He is gone, he is gone,
      And we cast away moan.
    God 'a' mercy on his soul!   195

And of° all Christian souls, I pray God. God bye you.   *Exit.*
Laertes: Do you see this, O God?
King: Laertes, I must commune with your grief,
Or you deny me right. Go but apart,
Make choice of whom your wisest friends you will,   200
And they shall hear and judge 'twixt you and me.
If by direct or by collateral° hand
They find us touched,° we will our kingdom give,
Our crown, our life, and all that we call ours,
To you in satisfaction; but if not,   205

---

170 *wheel*: Burden, refrain.   172 *more than matter*: More meaningful than sane speech.
175 *document*: Lesson.   177 *fennel*: Symbol of flattery; *columbines*: Symbol of thanklessness (?);
rue: Symbol of repentance.   180 *daisy*: Symbol of dissembling; *violets*: Symbol of faithfulness.   185 *favor*: Charm.   192 *poll*: Head.   196 *of*: On.   202 *collateral*: Indirect.
203 *touched*: I.e., with the crime.

Be you content to lend your patience to us,
And we shall jointly labor with your soul
To give it due content.
Laertes: Let this be so.
His means of death, his obscure funeral —
No trophy,° sword, nor hatchment° o'er his bones,   210
No noble rite nor formal ostentation° —
Cry to be heard, as 'twere from heaven to earth,
That° I must call't in question.
King: So you shall;
And where th' offense is, let the great axe fall.
I pray you go with me.   *Exeunt.* 215

SCENE VI. *A chamber in the castle.*

Enter Horatio and others.

Horatio: What are they that would speak with me?
Gentleman: Seafaring men, sir. They say they have letters for you.
Horatio: Let them come in.   *Exit Attendant.*
     I do not know from what part of the world
     I should be greeted, if not from Lord Hamlet.   5

Enter Sailors.

Sailor: God bless you, sir.
Horatio: Let him bless thee too.
Sailor: 'A shall, sir, an't please him. There's a letter for you, sir —
     it came from th' ambassador that was bound for England —
     if your name be Horatio, as I am let to know it is.   10
Horatio (reads the letter): "Horatio, when thou shalt have over
     looked° this, give these fellows some means° to the king.
     They have letters for him. Ere we were two days old at sea, a
     pirate of very warlike appointment° gave us chase. Finding
     ourselves too slow of sail, we put on a compelled valor, and 15
     in the grapple I boarded them. On the instant they got clear
     of our ship; so I alone became their prisoner. They have dealt
     with me like thieves of mercy,° but they knew what they did: I
     am to do a good turn for them. Let the king have the letters I
     have sent, and repair thou to me with as much speed as thou 20
     wouldest fly death. I have words to speak in thine ear will

---

210 *trophy:* Memorial; *hatchment:* Coat of arms.   211 *ostentation:* Ceremony.   213 *That:* So
that.   SCENE VI. 12 *overlooked:* Surveyed, scanned; *means:* I.e., of access.   14 *appointment:*
Equipment.   18 *thieves of mercy:* Merciful thieves.

make thee dumb; yet are they much too light for the bore° of
the matter. These good fellows will bring thee where I am.
Rosencrantz and Guildenstern hold their course for En-
gland. Of them I have much to tell thee. Farewell.   25
                    "He that thou knowest thine, Hamlet."
Come, I will give you way for these your letters,
And do't the speedier that you may direct me
To him from whom you brought them.   *Exeunt.*

SCENE VII. *A chamber in the castle.*

Enter King and Laertes.

King: Now must your conscience my acquittance seal,
        And you must put me in your heart for friend,
        Sith you have heard, and with a knowing ear,
        That he which hath your noble father slain
        Pursued my life.
Laertes: It well appears. But tell me   5
        Why you proceeded not against these feats°
        So crimeful and so capital° in nature,
        As by your safety, wisdom, all things else,
        You mainly° were stirred up.
King: O, for two special reasons,
        Which may to you perhaps seem much unsinewed,   10
        But yet to me they're strong. The queen his mother
        Lives almost by his looks, and for myself —
        My virtue or my plague, be it either which —
        She is so conjunctive° to my life and soul
        That, as the star moves not but in his sphere,   15
        I could not but by her. The other motive
        Why to a public count° I might not go
        Is the great love the general gender° bear him,
        Who, dipping all his faults in their affection,
        Would, like the spring that turneth wood to stone,   20
        Convert his gyves° to graces; so that my arrows,
        Too slightly timbered for so loud a wind,
        Would have reverted to my bow again,
        And not where I had aimed them.
Laertes: And so have I a noble father lost,   25

---

22 *bore*: Caliber (as of a gun).   SCENE VII. 6 *feats*: Deeds.   7 *capital*: Punishable by death.
9 *mainly*: Powerfully.   14 *conjunctive*: Closely united.   17 *count*: Trial, accounting.   18 *general gender*: Common people.   21 *gyves*: Fetters.

A sister driven into desp'rate terms,°
Whose worth, if praises may go back again,°
Stood challenger on mount° of all the age
For her perfections. But my revenge will come.
King: Break not your sleeps for that. You must not think   30
That we are made of stuff so flat and dull
That we can let our beard be shook with danger,
And think it pastime. You shortly shall hear more.
I loved your father, and we love ourself,
And that, I hope, will teach you to imagine —   35

Enter a Messenger with letters.

How now? What news?
Messenger: Letters, my lord, from Hamlet:
These to your majesty, this to the queen.
King: From Hamlet? Who brought them?
Messenger: Sailors, my lord, they say; I saw them not.
They were given me by Claudio; he received them   40
Of him that brought them.
King: Laertes, you shall hear them. —
Leave us.   *Exit Messenger.*
(*Reads.*) "High and mighty, you shall know I am set naked° on
your kingdom. To morrow shall I beg leave to see your kingly
eyes; when I shall (first asking your pardon thereunto) re-   45
count the occasion of my sudden and more strange return.
               "Hamlet."
What should this mean? Are all the rest come back?
Or is it some abuse,° and no such thing?
Laertes: Know you the hand?
King: 'Tis Hamlet's character.° "Naked"!   50
And in a postscript here, he says "alone."
Can you devise° me?
Laertes: I am lost in it, my lord. But let him come.
It warms the very sickness in my heart
That I shall live and tell him to his teeth,   55
"Thus diddest thou."
King: If it be so, Laertes,
(As how should it be so? how otherwise?)
Will you be ruled by me?

---

26 *terms*: Circumstances.   27 *back again*: I.e., to her better circumstances.   28 *on mount*:
On a height.   43 *naked*: Destitute.   49 *abuse*: Imposture.   50 *character*: Handwriting.
52 *devise*: Explain to.

Laertes: Ay, my lord,
   So you will not o'errule me to a peace.
King: To thine own peace. If he be now returned,   60
   As checking at° his voyage, and that he means
   No more to undertake it, I will work him
   To an exploit now ripe in my device,
   Under the which he shall not choose but fall;
   And for his death no wind of blame shall breathe,   65
   But even his mother shall uncharge the practice°
   And call it accident.
Laertes: My lord, I will be ruled;
   The rather if you could devise it so
   That I might be the organ.°
King: It falls right.
   You have been talked of since your travel much,   70
   And that in Hamlet's hearing, for a quality
   Wherein they say you shine. Your sum of parts
   Did not together pluck such envy from him
   As did that one, and that, in my regard,
   Of the unworthiest siege.°
Laertes: What part is that, my lord?   75
King: A very riband° in the cap of youth,
   Yet needful too, for youth no less becomes
   The light and careless livery° that it wears
   Than settled age his sables° and his weeds,°
   Importing health° and graveness. Two months since   80
   Here was a gentleman of Normandy.
   I have seen myself, and served against, the French,
   And they can well° on horseback, but this gallant
   Had witchcraft in't. He grew unto his seat,
   And to such wondrous doing brought his horse   85
   As had he been incorpsed° and demi-natured°
   With the brave beast. So far he topped° my thought°
   That I, in forgery° of shapes and tricks,
   Come short of what he did.
Laertes: A Norman was't?

---

61 *checking at*: Turning aside from (like a falcon turning from its quarry for other prey).   66 *uncharge the practice*: Acquit the stratagem of being a plot.   69 *organ*: Instrument.   75 *siege*: Seat, rank.   76 *riband*: Decoration.   78 *livery*: Distinctive attire.   79 *sables*: Dignified robes richly furred with sable; *weeds*: Distinctive garments.   80 *health*: Welfare, prosperity. 83 *can well*: Can perform well.   86 *incorpsed*: Made one body; *demi-natured*: Made sharer of nature half and half (as man shares with horse in the centaur).   87 *topped*: Excelled; *thought*: Imagination of possibilities.   88 *forgery*: Invention.

King: A Norman.   90
Laertes: Upon my life, Lamord.
King: The very same.
Laertes: I know him well. He is the brooch° indeed
    And gem of all the nation.
King: He made confession° of you,
    And gave you such a masterly report   95
    For art and exercise in your defense,
    And for your rapier most especial,
    That he cried out 'twould be a sight indeed
    If one could match you. The scrimers° of their nation
    He swore had neither motion, guard, nor eye,   100
    If you opposed them. Sir, this report of his
    Did Hamlet so envenom with his envy
    That he could nothing do but wish and beg
    Your sudden coming o'er to play with you.
    Now, out of this —
Laertes: What out of this, my lord?   105
King: Laertes, was your father dear to you?
    Or are you like the painting of a sorrow,
    A face without a heart?
Laertes: Why ask you this?
King: Not that I think you did not love your father,
    But that I know love is begun by time,   110
    And that I see, in passages of proof,°
    Time qualifies° the spark and fire of it.
    There lives within the very flame of love
    A kind of wick or snuff° that will abate it,
    And nothing is at a like goodness still,°   115
    For goodness, growing to a plurisy,°
    Dies in his own too-much. That we would do
    We should do when we would, for this "would" changes,
    And hath abatements and delays as many
    As there are tongues, are hands, are accidents,   120
    And then this "should" is like a spendthrift sigh,
    That hurts° by easing. But to the quick° o' th' ulcer —
    Hamlet comes back; what would you undertake

---

92 *brooch*: Ornament.   94 *made confession*: Admitted the rival accomplishments.   99 *scrimers*: Fencers.   111 *passages of proof*: Incidents of experience.   112 *qualifies*: Weakens.
114 *snuff*: Unconsumed portion of the burned wick.   115 *still*: Always.   116 *plurisy*:
Excess.   122 *hurts*: I.e., shortens life by drawing blood from the heart (as was believed);
quick: Sensitive flesh.

To show yourself your father's son in deed
More than in words?
Laertes: To cut his throat i' th' church!   125
King: No place indeed should murder sanctuarize;°
Revenge should have no bounds. But, good Laertes,
Will you do this? Keep close within your chamber.
Hamlet returned shall know you are come home.
We'll put on° those shall praise your exellence   130
And set a double varnish on the fame
The Frenchman gave you, bring you in fine° together
And wager on your heads. He, being remiss,°
Most generous, and free from all contriving,
Will not peruse° the foils, so that with ease,   135
Or with a little shuffling, you may choose
A sword unbated,° and, in a pass of practice,°
Requite him for your father.
Laertes: I will do't,
And for that purpose I'll anoint my sword.
I bought an unction° of a mountebank,°   140
So mortal that, but dip a knife in it,
Where it draws blood no cataplasm° so rare,
Collected from all simples° that have virtue
Under the moon, can save the thing from death
That is but scratched withal.° I'll touch my point   145
With this contagion, that, if I gall° him slightly,
It may be death.
King: Let's further think of this,
Weigh what convenience both of time and means
May fit us to our shape.° If this should fail,
And that our drift° look° through our bad performance,   150
'Twere better not assayed. Therefore this project
Should have a back or second, that might hold
If this did blast in proof.° Soft, let me see.
We'll make a solemn wager on your cunnings —
I ha't!   155
When in your motion you are hot and dry —
As make your bouts more violent to that end —

---

126 *sanctuarize*: Protect from punishment, give sanctuary to.   130 *put on*: Instigate.   132 *in fine*: Finally.   133 *remiss*: Negligent.   135 *peruse*: Scan.   137 *unbated*: Not blunted; *pass of practice*: Thrust made effective by trickery.   140 *unction*: Ointment; *mountebank*: Quack-doctor.   142 *cataplasm*: Poultice.   143 *simples*: Herbs.   145 *withal*: With it.   146 *gall*: Scratch.   149 *shape*: Plan.   150 *drift*: Intention; *look*: Show.   153 *blast in proof*: Burst during trial (like a faulty cannon).

And that he calls for drink, I'll have preferred° him
A chalice for the nonce,° whereon but sipping,
If he by chance escape your venomed stuck,°   160
Our purpose may hold there. — But stay, what noise?

Enter Queen.

Queen: One woe doth tread upon another's heel,
  So fast they follow. Your sister's drowned, Laertes.
Laertes: Drowned! O, where?
Queen: There is a willow grows askant° the brook,   165
  That shows his hoar° leaves in the glassy stream.
  Therewith fantastic garlands did she make
  Of crowflowers, nettles, daisies, and long purples,
  That liberal° shepherds give a grosser name,
  But our cold maids do dead men's fingers call them.   170
  There on the pendent boughs her crownet° weeds
  Clamb'ring to hang, an envious sliver broke,
  When down her weedy trophies and herself
  Fell in the weeping brook. Her clothes spread wide,
  And mermaid-like awhile they bore her up,   175
  Which time she chanted snatches of old lauds,°
  As one incapable of° her own distress,
  Or like a creature native and indued°
  Unto that element. But long it could not be
  Till that her garments, heavy with their drink,   180
  Pulled the poor wretch from her melodious lay
  To muddy death.
Laertes: Alas, then she is drowned?
Queen: Drowned, drowned.
Laertes: Too much of water hast thou, poor Ophelia,
  And therefore I forbid my tears; but yet   185
  It is our trick;° nature her custom holds,
  Let shame say what it will. When these are gone,
  The woman° will be out. Adieu, my lord.
  I have a speech o' fire, that fain would blaze
  But that this folly drowns it.   *Exit.*
King: Let's follow, Gertrude.   190
  How much I had to do to calm his rage!

---

158 *preferred*: Offered.   159 *nonce*: Occasion.   160 *stuck*: Thrust.   165 *askant*: Alongside.
166 *hoar*: Grey.   169 *liberal*: Free-spoken, licentious.   171 *crownet*: Coronet.   *176 lauds*:
Hymns.   177 *incapable of*: Insensible to.   178 *indued*: Endowed.   186 *trick*: Way (i.e., to
shed tears when sorrowful).   188 *woman*: Unmanly part of nature.

> Now fear I this will give it start again;
> Therefore let's follow.　　　　　　　　　　　*Exeunt.*

ACT V

SCENE I. *A churchyard.*

Enter two Clowns.°

Clown: Is she to be buried in Christian burial° when she willfully
seeks her own salvation?

Other: I tell thee she is. Therefore make her grave straight.° The
crowner° hath sate on her, and finds it Christian burial.

Clown: How can that be, unless she drowned herself in her own　5
defense?

Other: Why, 'tis found so.

Clown: It must be *se offendendo*;° it cannot be else. For here lies the
point: if I drown myself wittingly, it argues an act, and an act
hath three branches — it is to act, to do, and to perform.　10
Argal,° she drowned herself wittingly.

Other: Nay, but hear you, Goodman Delver.°

Clown: Give me leave. Here lies the water — good. Here stands
the man — good. If the man go to this water and drown
himself, it is, will he nill he,° he goes, mark you that. But if　15
the water come to him and drown him, he drowns not himself. Argal, he that is not guilty of his own death shortens not
his own life.

Other: But is this law?

Clown: Ay marry, is't — crowner's quest° law.　　　　　　　20

Other: Will you ha' the truth on't? If this had not been a gentlewoman, she should have been buried out o' Christian burial.

Clown: Why, there thou say'st.° And the more pity that great folk
should have count'nance° in this world to drown or hang
themselves more than their even-Christen.° Come, my spade.　25
There is no ancient gentlemen but gard'ners, ditchers, and
grave-makers. They hold up Adam's profession.

Other: Was he a gentleman?

ACT V, SCENE I. *Clowns:* Rustics.　1 *in Christian burial*: In consecrated ground with the
prescribed service of the Church (a burial denied to suicides).　3 *straight*: Straightway, at
once.　4 *crowner*: Coroner.　8 *se offendendo*: A clownish transformation of "*se defendendo*,"
"in self-defense."　11 *Argal*: For "*ergo*," "therefore."　12 *Delver*: Digger.　15 *will he nill
he*: Willy-nilly.　20 *quest*: Inquest.　23 *thou say'st*: You have it right.　24 *count'nance*:
Privilege.　25 *even-Christen*: Fellow Christian.

Clown: 'A was the first that ever bore arms.

Other: Why, he had none.° 30

Clown: What, art a heathen? How dost thou understand the Scripture? The Scripture says Adam digged. Could he dig without arms? I'll put another question to thee. If thou answerest me not to the purpose, confess thyself —

Other: Go to. 35

Clown: What is he that builds stronger than either the mason, the shipwright, or the carpenter?

Other: The gallows-maker, for that frame outlives a thousand tenants.

Clown: I like thy wit well, in good faith. The gallows does well. 40 But how does it well? It does well to those that do ill. Now thou dost ill to say the gallows is built stronger than the church. Argal, the gallows may do well to thee. To't again, come.

Other: Who builds stronger than a mason, a shipwright, or a 45 carpenter?

Clown: Ay, tell me that, and unyoke.°

Other: Marry, now I can tell.

Clown: To't.

Other: Mass,° I cannot tell. 50

Clown: Cudgel thy brains no more about it, for your dull ass will not mend his pace with beating. And when you are asked this question next, say "a grave-maker." The houses he makes last till doomsday. Go, get thee in, and fetch me a stoup° of liquor. *Exit Other Clown.* 55

Enter Hamlet and Horatio as Clown digs and sings.

Song.

In youth when I did love, did love,
　　Methought it was very sweet
To contract — O — the time for — a — my
　　behove,°
　　O, methought there — a — was nothing — a —
　　meet.

Hamlet: Has this fellow no feeling of his business, that 'a sings at 60 grave-making?

Horatio: Custom hath made it in him a property° of easiness.°

30 *had none*: I.e., had no gentleman's coat of arms.　47 *unyoke*: I.e., unharness your powers of thought after a good day's work.　50 *Mass*: By the Mass.　54 *stoup*: Large mug.　58 *behove*: Behoof, benefit.　62 *property*: Peculiarity; *easiness*: Easy acceptability.

Hamlet: 'Tis e'en so. The hand of little employment hath the daintier° sense.

Clown: *Song.*

But age with his stealing steps   65
    Hath clawed me in his clutch,
And hath shipped me intil° the land,
    As if I had never been such.

Throws up a skull.

Hamlet: That skull had a tongue in it, and could sing once. How
    the knave jowls° it to the ground, as if 'twere Cain's jawbone,   70
    that did the first murder! This might be the pate of a politi-
    cian,° which this ass now o'erreaches;° one that would cir-
    cumvent God, might it not?
Horatio: It might, my lord.
Hamlet: Or of a courtier, which could say "Good morrow, sweet   75
    lord! How dost thou, sweet lord?" This might be my Lord
    Such-a-one, that praised my Lord Such-a-one's horse when 'a
    meant to beg it, might it not?
Horatio: Ay, my lord.
Hamlet: Why, e'en so, and now my Lady Worm's, chapless,° and   80
    knocked about the mazzard° with a sexton's spade. Here's
    fine revolution, an we had the trick to see't. Did these bones
    cost no more the breeding but to play at loggets° with 'em?
    Mine ache to think on't.

Clown: *Song.*

A pickaxe and a spade, a spade,   85
    For and° a shrouding sheet;
O, a pit of clay for to be made
    For such a guest is meet.

Throws up another skull.

Hamlet: There's another. Why may not that be the skull of a law-
    yer? Where be his quiddities° now, his quillities,° his cases,   90

---

64 *daintier sense*: More delicate feeling (because the hand is less calloused).   67 *intil*: Into.
70 *jowls*: Hurls.   71–72 *politician*: Crafty schemer.   72 *o'erreaches*: Gets the better of (with a
play upon the literal meaning).   80 *chapless*: Lacking the lower chap or jaw.   81 *mazzard*:
Head.   83 *loggets*: Small pieces of wood thrown in a game.   86 *For and*: And.   90 *quid-
dities*: Subtleties (from scholastic "*quidditas*," meaning the distinctive nature of anything); *quil-
lities*: Nice distinctions.

his tenures,° and his tricks? Why does he suffer this mad
knave now to knock him about the sconce° with a dirty
shovel, and will not tell him of his action of battery? Hum!
This fellow might be in's time a great buyer of land, with his
statutes, his recognizances,° his fines, his double vouchers,° 95
his recoveries.° Is this the fine° of his fines, and the recovery
of his recoveries, to have his fine pate full of fine dirt? Will
his vouchers vouch him no more of his purchases, and double
ones too, than the length and breadth of a pair of indentures?° The very conveyances° of his lands will scarcely lie in 100
this box, and must th' inheritor himself have no more, ha?
Horatio: Not a jot more, my lord.
Hamlet: Is not parchment made of sheepskins?
Horatio: Ay, my lord, and of calveskins too.
Hamlet: They are sheep and calves which seek out assurance in 105
    that. I will speak to this fellow. Whose grave's this, sirrah?
Clown: Mine, sir.
    (*Sings.*)   O, a pit of clay for to be made
                For such a guest is meet.
Hamlet: I think it be thine indeed, for thou liest in't. 110
Clown: You lie out on't, sir, and therefore 'tis not yours. For my
    part, I do not lie in't, yet it is mine.
Hamlet: Thou dost lie in't, to be in't and say it is thine. 'Tis for the
    dead, not for the quick;° therefore thou liest.
Clown: 'Tis a quick lie, sir; 'twill away again from me to you. 115
Hamlet: What man dost thou dig it for?
Clown: For no man, sir.
Hamlet: What woman then?
Clown: For none neither.
Hamlet: Who is to be buried in't? 120
Clown: One that was a woman, sir; but, rest her soul, she's dead.
Hamlet: How absolute° the knave is! We must speak by the card,°
    or equivocation° will undo us. By the Lord, Horatio, this
    three years I have taken note of it, the age is grown so
    picked° that the toe of the peasant comes so near the heel of 125

---

91 *tenures*: Holdings of property.   92 *sconce*: Head.   95 *statutes, recognizances*: Legal documents or bonds acknowledging debt.   95–96 *fines, recoveries*: Modes of converting estate tail
into fee simple; *vouchers*: Persons vouched or called on to warrant a title.   96 *fine*: End (introducing a word play involving four meanings of "fine").   99–100 *pair of indentures*: Deed
or legal agreement in duplicate.   100 *conveyances*: Deeds.   114 *quick*: Living.   122 *absolute*: Positive; *by the card*: By the card on which the points of the mariner's compass are
marked, absolutely to the point.   123 *equivocation*: Ambiguity.   125 *picked*: Refined,
spruce.

the courtier he galls° his kibe.° — How long hast thou been
a grave-maker?

Clown: Of all the days i' th' year, I came to't that day that our last
king Hamlet overcame Fortinbras.

Hamlet: How long is that since?   130

Clown: Cannot you tell that? Every fool can tell that. It was the
very day that young Hamlet was born — he that is mad, and
sent into England.

Hamlet: Ay, marry, why was he sent into England?

Clown: Why, because 'a was mad. 'A shall recover his wits there;   135
or, if 'a do not, 'tis no great matter there.

Hamlet: Why?

Clown: 'Twill not be seen in him there. There the men are as mad
as he.

Hamlet: How came he mad?   140

Clown: Very strangely, they say.

Hamlet: How strangely?

Clown: Faith, e'en with losing his wits.

Hamlet: Upon what ground?

Clown: Why, here in Denmark. I have been sexton here, man and   145
boy, thirty years.

Hamlet: How long will a man lie i' th' earth ere he rot?

Clown: Faith, if 'a be not rotten before 'a die (as we have many
pocky° corses now-a-days that will scarce hold the laying in),
'a will last you some eight year or nine year. A tanner will last   150
you nine year.

Hamlet: Why he more than another?

Clown: Why, sir, his hide is so tanned with his trade that 'a will
keep out water a great while, and your water is a sore decayer
of your whoreson dead body. Here's a skull now hath lien you   155
i' th' earth three-and-twenty years.

Hamlet: Whose was it?

Clown: A whoreson mad fellow's it was. Whose do you think it
was?

Hamlet: Nay, I know not.   160

Clown: A pestilence on him for a mad rogue! 'A poured a flagon
of Rhenish° on my head once. This same skull, sir, was —
sir — Yorick's skull, the king's jester.

Hamlet: This?

Clown: E'en that.   165

---

126 *galls:* Chafes; *kibe:* Chilblain.   149 *pocky:* Rotten (literally, corrupted by pox, or syphilis).
162 *Rhenish:* Rhine wine.

Hamlet: Let me see. (*Takes the skull.*) Alas, poor Yorick! I knew
  him, Horatio, a fellow of infinite jest, of most excellent fancy.
  He hath borne me on his back a thousand times. And now
  how abhorred in my imagination it is! My gorge rises at it.
  Here hung those lips that I have kissed I know not how oft. 170
  Where be your gibes now? Your gambols, your songs, your
  flashes of merriment that were wont to set the table on a
  roar? Not one now to mock your own grinning? Quite chapfall'n?° Now get you to my lady's chamber, and tell her, let
  her paint an inch thick, to this favor° she must come. Make 175
  her laugh at that. Prithee, Horatio, tell me one thing.
Horatio: What's that, my lord?
Hamlet: Dost thou think Alexander looked o' this fashion i' th'
  earth?
Horatio: E'en so. 180
Hamlet: And smelt so? Pah!

Puts down the skull.

Horatio: E'en so, my lord.
Hamlet: To what base uses we may return, Horatio! Why may not
  imagination trace the noble dust of Alexander till 'a find it
  stopping a bunghole? 185
Horatio: 'Twere to consider too curiously,° to consider so.
Hamlet: No, faith, not a jot, but to follow him thither with mod-
  esty° enough, and likelihood to lead it; as thus: Alexander
  died, Alexander was buried, Alexander returneth to dust;
  the dust is earth; of earth we make loam; and why of that 190
  loam whereto he was converted might they not stop a beer
  barrel?
  Imperious° Caesar, dead and turned to clay,
  Might stop a hole to keep the wind away.
  O, that the earth which kept the world in awe 195
  Should patch a wall t' expel the winter's flaw!°
  But soft, but soft awhile! Here comes the king —

*Enter King, Queen, Laertes, and the Corse with Lords attendant and a Doctor of
Divinity as Priest.*

  The queen, the courtiers. Who is this they follow?
  And with such maimèd rites? This doth betoken

173–74 *chapfall'n*: Lacking the lower chap, or jaw (with a play on the sense "down in the mouth,"
"dejected").   175 *favor*: Countenance, aspect.   186 *curiously*: Minutely.   187–188 *modesty*:
Moderation.   193 *Imperious*: Imperial.   196 *flaw*: Gust of wind.

The corse they follow did with desp'rate hand   200
Fordo° it° own life. 'Twas of some estate.°
Couch° we awhile, and mark.

Retires with Horatio.

Laertes: What ceremony else?
Hamlet: That is Laertes,
     A very noble youth. Mark.
Laertes: What ceremony else?   205
Doctor: Her obsequies have been as far enlarged
     As we have warranty. Her death was doubtful,
     And, but that great command o'ersways the order,
     She should in ground unsanctified have lodged
     Till the last trumpet. For charitable prayers,   210
     Shards,° flints, and pebbles should be thrown on her.
     Yet here she is allowed her virgin crants,°
     Her maiden strewments,° and the bringing home°
     Of bell and burial.
Laertes: Must there no more be done?
Doctor: No more be done.   215
     We should profane the service of the dead
     To sing a requiem and such rest to her
     As to peace-parted souls.
Laertes: Lay her i' th' earth,
     And from her fair and unpolluted flesh
     May violets spring! I tell thee, churlish priest,   220
     A minist'ring angel shall my sister be
     When thou liest howling.
Hamlet: What, the fair Ophelia?
Queen: Sweets to the sweet! Farewell.

Scatters flowers.

     I hoped thou shouldst have been my Hamlet's wife.
     I thought thy bride-bed to have decked, sweet maid, 225
     And not have strewed thy grave.
Laertes: O, treble woe
     Fall ten times treble on that cursèd head
     Whose wicked deed thy most ingenious° sense

---

201 *Fordo*: Destroy; *it*: Its; *estate*: Rank.   202 *Couch*: Hide.   211 *Shards*: Broken pieces of pottery.   212 *crants*: Garland.   213 *strewments*: Strewings of the grave with flowers; *bringing home*: Laying to rest.   228 *most ingenious*: Of quickest apprehension.

Deprived thee of! Hold off the earth awhile,
Till I have caught her once more in mine arms.   230

Leaps in the grave.

Now pile your dust upon the quick and dead
Till of this flat a mountain you have made
T' o'ertop old Pelion° or the skyish head
Of blue Olympus.
Hamlet (coming forward): What is he whose grief
   Bears such an emphasis? whose phrase of sorrow   235
   Conjures° the wand'ring stars,° and makes them stand
   Like wonder-wounded hearers? This is I,
   Hamlet the Dane.

Leaps in after Laertes.

Laertes: The devil take thy soul!

Grapples with him.

Hamlet: Thou pray'st not well.
   I prithee take thy fingers from my throat,   240
   For, though I am not splenitive° and rash,
   Yet have I in me something dangerous,
   Which let thy wisdom fear. Hold off thy hand.
King: Pluck them asunder.
Queen: Hamlet, Hamlet!
All: Gentlemen!
Horatio: Good my lord, be quiet.   245

Attendants part them, and they come out of the grave.

Hamlet: Why, I will fight with him upon this theme
   Until my eyelids will no longer wag.
Queen: O my son, what theme?
Hamlet: I loved Ophelia. Forty thousand brothers
   Could not with all their quantity of love   250
   Make up my sum. What wilt thou do for her?
King: O, he is mad, Laertes.
Queen: For love of God, forbear him.

---

233 *Pelion:* A mountain in Thessaly, like Olympus and also Ossa (the allusion being to the war in which the Titans fought the gods and attempted to heap Ossa and Olympus on Pelion, or Pelion and Ossa on Olympus, in order to scale heaven).   236 *Conjures:* Charms, puts a spell upon; *wand'ring stars:* Planets.   241 *splenitive:* Of fiery temper (the spleen being considered the seat of anger).

Hamlet: 'Swounds, show me what thou't do.
Woo't° weep? woo't fight? woo't fast? woo't tear thyself?   255
Woo't drink up esill?° eat a crocodile?
I'll do't. Dost thou come here to whine?
To outface me with leaping in her grave?
Be buried quick° with her, and so will I.
And if thou prate of mountains, let them throw   260
Millions of acres on us, till our ground,
Singeing his pate against the burning zone,
Make Ossa like a wart! Nay, an thou'lt mouth,
I'll rant as well as thou.
Queen: This is mere° madness;
And thus a while the fit will work on him.   265
Anon, as patient as the female dove
When that her golden couplets° are disclosed,°
His silence will sit drooping.
Hamlet: Hear you, sir.
What is the reason that you use me thus?
I loved you ever. But it is no matter.   270
Let Hercules himself do what he may,
The cat will mew, and dog will have his day.
King: I pray thee, good Horatio, wait upon him.

Exit Hamlet and Horatio.

To Laertes.

Strengthen your patience in° our last night's speech.
We'll put the matter to the present push.° —   275
Good Gertrude, set some watch over your son. —
This grave shall have a living monument.
An hour of quiet shortly shall we see;
Till then in patience our proceeding be.   *Exeunt.*

SCENE II. *The hall of the castle.*

Enter Hamlet and Horatio.

Hamlet: So much for this, sir; now shall you see the other.
You do remember all the circumstance?
Horatio: Remember it, my lord!

---

255 *Woo't:* Wilt (thou).   256 *esill:* Vinegar.   259 *quick:* Alive.   264 *mere:* Absolute.
267 *couplets:* Pair of fledglings; *disclosed:* Hatched.   274 *in:* By calling to mind.   275 *present*
push: Immediate trial.

Hamlet: Sir, in my heart there was a kind of fighting
That would not let me sleep. Methought I lay   5
Worse than the mutines° in the bilboes.° Rashly,
And praised be rashness for it — let us know,
Our indiscretion sometime serves us well
When our deep plots do pall,° and that should learn us
There's a divinity that shapes our ends,   10
Rough-hew° them how we will —
Horatio: That is most certain.
Hamlet: Up from my cabin,
My sea-gown scarfed about me, in the dark
Groped I to find out them, had my desire,
Fingered° their packet, and in fine° withdrew   15
To mine own room again, making so bold,
My fears forgetting manners, to unseal
Their grand commission; where I found, Horatio —
Ah, royal knavery! — an exact command,
Larded° with many several sorts of reasons,   20
Importing° Denmark's health, and England's too,
With, ho! such bugs° and goblins in my life,°
That on the supervise,° no leisure bated,°
No, not to stay the grinding of the axe,
My head should be struck off.
Horatio: Is't possible?   25
Hamlet: Here's the commission; read it at more leisure.
But wilt thou hear me how I did proceed?
Horatio: I beseech you.
Hamlet: Being thus benetted round with villainies,
Or° I could make a prologue to my brains,   30
They had begun the play. I sat me down,
Devised a new commission, wrote it fair.
I once did hold it, as our statists° do,
A baseness to write fair,° and labored much
How to forget that learning, but, sir, now   35
It did me yeoman's service.° Wilt thou know
Th' effect° of what I wrote?

Scene II. 6 *mutines*: Mutineers; *bilboes*: Fetters.   9 *pall*: Fail.   11 *Rough-hew*: Shape roughly in trial form.   15 *Fingered*: Filched; *in fine*: Finally.   20 *Larded*: Enriched.   21 *Importing*: Relating to.   22 *bugs*: Bugbears; *in my life*: To be encountered as dangers if I should be allowed to live.   23 *supervise*: Perusal; *bated*: Deducted, allowed.   30 *Or*: Ere.   33 *statists*: Statesmen.   34 *fair*: With professional clarity (like a clerk or a scrivener, not like a gentleman).   36 *yeoman's service*: Stout service such as yeomen footsoldiers gave as archers.   37 *effect*: Purport.

Horatio: Ay, good my lord.
Hamlet: An earnest conjuration from the king,
    As England was his faithful tributary,
    As love between them like the palm might flourish,   40
    As peace should still her wheaten garland° wear
    And stand a comma° 'tween their amities,
    And many such-like as's of great charge,°
    That on the view and knowing of these contents,
    Without debatement further, more or less,   45
    He should the bearers put to sudden death,
    Not shriving time° allowed.
Horatio: How was this sealed?
Hamlet: Why, even in that was heaven ordinant.°
    I had my father's signet in my purse,
    Which was the model° of that Danish seal,   50
    Folded the writ up in the form of th' other,
    Subscribed it, gave't th' impression,° placed it safely,
    The changeling never known. Now, the next day
    Was our sea-fight, and what to this was sequent°
    Thou know'st already.   55
Horatio: So Guildenstern and Rosencrantz go to't.
Hamlet: Why, man, they did make love to this employment.
    They are not near my conscience; their defeat
    Does by their own insinuation° grow.
    'Tis dangerous when the baser nature comes   60
    Between the pass° and fell° incensèd points
    Of mighty opposites.
Horatio: Why, what a king is this!
Hamlet: Does it not, think thee, stand° me now upon —
    He that hath killed my king, and whored my mother,
    Popped in between th' election° and my hopes,   65
    Thrown out his angle° for my proper° life,
    And with such coz'nage° — is't not perfect conscience
    To quit° him with this arm? And is't not to be damned
    To let this canker° of our nature come
    In further evil?   70

---

41 *wheaten garland*: Adornment of fruitful agriculture.   42 *comma*: Connective (because it indicates continuity of thought in a sentence).   43 *charge*: Burden (with a double meaning to fit a play that makes *as's* into "asses").   47 *shriving time*: Time for confession and absolution.   48 *ordinant*: Controlling.   50 *model*: Counterpart.   52 *impression*: I.e., of the signet.   54 *sequent*: Subsequent.   59 *insinuation*: Intrusion.   61 *pass*: Thrust; *fell*: Fierce.   63 *stand*: Rest incumbent.   65 *election*: I.e., to the kingship (the Danish kingship being elective).   66 *angle*: Fishing line; *proper*: Own.   67 *coz'nage*: Cozenage, trickery.   68 *quit*: Repay.   69 *canker*: Cancer, ulcer.

Horatio: It must be shortly known to him from England
   What is the issue of the business there.
Hamlet: It will be short; the interim is mine,
   And a man's life's no more than to say "one."
   But I am very sorry, good Horatio,   75
   That to Laertes I forgot myself,
   For by the image of my cause I see
   The portraiture of his. I'll court his favors.
   But sure the bravery° of his grief did put me
   Into a tow'ring passion.
Horatio: Peace, who comes here?   80

Enter Osric, a courtier.

Osric: Your lordship is right welcome back to Denmark.
Hamlet: I humbly thank you, sir. (*Aside to Horatio.*) Dost know this
   waterfly?
Horatio (aside to Hamlet): No, my good lord.
Hamlet (aside to Horatio): Thy state is the more gracious, for 'tis a   85
   vice to know him. He hath much land, and fertile. Let a beast
   be lord of beasts, and his crib shall stand at the king's mess.°
   'Tis a chough,° but, as I say, spacious in the possession of
   dirt.
Osric: Sweet lord, if your lordship were at leisure, I should im·   90
   part a thing to you from his majesty.
Hamlet: I will receive it, sir, with all diligence of spirit. Put your
   bonnet to his right use. 'Tis for the head.
Osric: I thank your lordship, it is very hot.
Hamlet: No, believe me, 'tis very cold; the wind is northerly.   95
Osric: It is indifferent° cold, my lord, indeed.
Hamlet: But yet methinks it is very sultry and hot for my com·
   plexion.°
Osric: Exceedingly, my lord; it is very sultry, as 'twere — I cannot
   tell how. But, my lord, his majesty bade me signify to you   100
   that 'a has laid a great wager on your head. Sir, this is the
   matter —
Hamlet: I beseech you remember.°

Hamlet moves him to put on his hat.

Osric: Nay, good my lord; for mine ease,° in good faith. Sir, here

---

79 *bravery*: Ostentatious display.   87 *mess*: Table.   88 *chough*: Jackdaw, chatterer.   96 *indifferent*: Somewhat.   98 *complexion*: Temperament.   103 *remember*: I.e., remember you
have done all that courtesy demands.   104 *for mine ease*: I.e., I keep my hat off just for
comfort (a conventional polite phrase).

is newly come to court Laertes — believe me, an absolute 105
gentleman, full of most excellent differences,° of very soft
society° and great showing.° Indeed, to speak feelingly° of
him, he is the card° or calendar° of gentry;° for you shall
find in him the continent° of what part a gentleman would
see.   110

Hamlet: Sir, his definement° suffers no perdition° in you, though,
I know, to divide him inventorially would dozy° th' arithmetic of memory, and yet but yaw° neither° in respect of° his
quick sail. But, in the verity of extolment, I take him to be a
soul of great article,° and his infusion° of such dearth° and 115
rareness as, to make true diction of him, his semblable° is
his mirror, and who else would trace° him, his umbrage,°
nothing more.

Osric: Your lordship speaks most infallibly of him.

Hamlet: The concernancy,° sir? Why do we wrap the gentleman 120
in our more rawer breath?°

Osric: Sir?

Horatio: Is't not possible to understand in another tongue? You
will to't,° sir, really.

Hamlet: What imports the nomination° of this gentleman?   125

Osric: Of Laertes?

Horatio (aside to Hamlet): His purse is empty already. All's golden
words are spent.

Hamlet: Of him, sir.

Osric: I know you are not ignorant —   130

Hamlet: I would you did, sir; yet, in faith, if you did, it would not
much approve me.° Well, sir?

Osric: You are not ignorant of what excellence Laertes is —

Hamlet: I dare not confess that, lest I should compare° with him
in excellence; but to know a man well were to know himself.   135

Osric: I mean, sir, for his weapon; but in the imputation laid on
him by them, in his meed° he's unfellowed.

Hamlet: What's his weapon?

---

106 *differences*: Differentiating characteristics, special qualities.   106–107 *soft society*: Gentle
manners.   107 *great showing*: Noble appearance; *feelingly*: Appropriately.   108 *card*: Map;
calendar: Guide; *gentry*: Gentlemanliness.   109 *continent*: All-containing embodiment (with
an implication of geographical continent to go with *card*).   111 *definement*: Definition;
perdition: Loss.   112 *dozy*: Dizzy, stagger.   113 *yaw*: Hold to a course unsteadily like a ship
that steers wild; *neither*: For all that; *in respect of*: In comparison with.   115 *article*: Scope,
importance; *infusion*: Essence; *dearth*: Scarcity.   116 *semblable*: Likeness (i.e., only true likeness).   117 *trace*: Follow; *unbrage*: Shadow.   120 *concernancy*: Relevance.   121 *rawer
breath*: Cruder speech.   124 *to't*: I.e., get to an understanding.   125 *nomination*: Mention.
132 *approve me*: Be to my credit.   134 *compare*: Compete.   137 *meed*: Worth.

Osric: Rapier and dagger.

Hamlet: That's two of his weapons — but well. 140

Osric: The king, sir, hath wagered with him six Barbary horses, against the which he has impawned,° as I take it, six French rapiers and poniards, with their assigns,° as girdle, hangers,° and so. Three of the carriages, in faith, are very dear to fancy,° very responsive° to the hilts, most delicate carriages, 145 and of very liberal conceit.°

Hamlet: What call you the carriages?

Horatio (aside to Hamlet): I knew you must be edified by the margent° ere you had done.

Osric: The carriages, sir, are the hangers. 150

Hamlet: The phrase would be more germane to the matter if we could carry a cannon by our sides. I would it might be hangers till then. But on! Six Barbary horses against six French swords, their assigns, and three liberal-conceited carriages — that's the French bet against the Danish. Why is this all 155 impawned, as you call it?

Osric: The king, sir, hath laid, sir, that in a dozen passes between yourself and him he shall not exceed you three hits; he hath laid on twelve for nine, and it would come to immediate trial if your lordship would vouchsafe the answer. 160

Hamlet: How if I answer no?

Osric: I mean, my lord, the opposition of your person in trial.

Hamlet: Sir, I will walk here in the hall. If it please his majesty, it is the breathing time° of day with me. Let the foils be brought, the gentleman willing, and the king hold his pur- 165 pose, I will win for him an° I can; if not, I will gain nothing but my shame and the odd hits.

Osric: Shall I redeliver you e'en so?

Hamlet: To this effect, sir, after what flourish your nature will.

Osric: I commend my duty to your lordship. 170

Hamlet: Yours, yours. (*Exit Osric.*) He does well to commend it himself; there are no tongues else for's turn.

Horatio: This lapwing° runs away with the shell on his head.

Hamlet: 'A did comply,° sir, with his dug° before 'a sucked it. Thus has he, and many more of the same bevy° that I know 175

142: Impawned: Staked.   143 *assigns*: Appurtenances.   143–144 *hangers*: Straps by which the sword hangs from the belt.   144–145 *dear to fancy*: Finely designed.   145 *responsive*: Corresponding closely.   146 *liberal conceit*: Tasteful design, refined conception. 148–149 *margent*: Margin (i.e., explanatory notes there printed).   164 *breathing time*: Exercise hour.   166 *an*: If.   173 *lapwing*: A bird reputed to be so precocious as to run as soon as hatched.   174 *comply*: Observe formalities of courtesy; *dug*: Mother's nipple.   175 *bevy*: Company.

the drossy° age dotes on, only got the tune of the time and, out of an habit of encounter, a kind of yeasty collection, which carries them through and through the most fanned and winnowed° opinions; and do but blow them to their trial, the bubbles are out.　　　　180

Enter a Lord.

Lord: My lord, his majesty commended him to you by young Osric, who brings back to him that you attend him in the hall. He sends to know if your pleasure hold to play with Laertes, or that you will take longer time.

Hamlet: I am constant to my purposes; they follow the king's 185 pleasure. If his fitness speaks, mine is ready; now or whensoever, provided I be so able as now.

Lord: The king and queen and all are coming down.

Hamlet: In happy time.°

Lord: The queen desires you to use some gentle entertainment° 190 to Laertes before you fall to play.

Hamlet: She well instructs me.　　　　　　　*Exit Lord.*

Horatio: You will lose this wager, my lord.

Hamlet: I do not think so. Since he went into France I have been in continual practice. I shall win at the odds. But thou 195 wouldst not think how ill all's here about my heart. But it is no matter.

Horatio: Nay, good my lord —

Hamlet: It is but foolery, but it is such a kind of gaingiving° as would perhaps trouble a woman.　　　　　　200

Horatio: If your mind dislike anything, obey it. I will forestall their repair hither and say you are not fit.

Hamlet: Not a whit, we defy augury. There is special providence in the fall of a sparrow. If it be now, 'tis not to come; if it be not to come, it will be now; if it be not now, yet it will come. 205 The readiness is all.° Since no man of aught he leaves knows, what is't to leave betimes? Let be.

A table prepared. Enter Trumpets, Drums, and Officers with cushions; King, Queen, Osric, and all the State, with foils, daggers, and stoups of wine borne in; and Laertes.

King: Come, Hamlet, come, and take this hand from me.

176 *drossy*: Frivolous.　179 *fanned and winnowed*: Select and refined.　189 *In happy time*: I am happy (a polite response).　190 *entertainment*: Words of reception or greeting.　199 *gaingiving*: Misgiving.　206 *all*: All that matters.

The King puts Laertes' hand into Hamlet's.

Hamlet: Give me your pardon, sir. I have done you wrong,
But pardon't, as you are a gentleman. 210
This presence° knows, and you must needs have heard,
How I am punished with a sore distraction.
What I have done
That might your nature, honor, and exception°
Roughly awake, I here proclaim was madness. 215
Was't Hamlet wronged Laertes? Never Hamlet.
If Hamlet from himself be ta'en away,
And when he's not himself does wrong Laertes,
Then Hamlet does it not, Hamlet denies it.
Who does it then? His madness. If't be so, 220
Hamlet is of the faction° that is wronged;
His madness is poor Hamlet's enemy.
Sir, in this audience,
Let my disclaiming from a purposed evil
Free me so far in your most generous thoughts 225
That I have shot my arrow o'er the house
And hurt my brother.
Laertes: I am satisfied in nature,°
Whose motive in this case should stir me most
To my revenge. But in my terms of honor°
I stand aloof, and will no reconcilement 230
Till by some elder masters of known honor
I have a voice° and precedent of peace
To keep my name ungored.° But till that time
I do receive your offered love like love,
And will not wrong it.
Hamlet: I embrace it freely, 235
And will this brother's wager frankly play.
Give us the foils. Come on.
Laertes: Come, one for me.
Hamlet: I'll be your foil,° Laertes. In mine ignorance
Your skill shall, like a star i' th' darkest night,
Stick fiery off° indeed.
Laertes: You mock me, sir. 240

---

211 *presence*: Assembly.   214 *exception*: Disapproval.   221 *faction*: Body of persons taking
a side in a contention.   227 *nature*: Natural feeling as a person.   229 *terms of honor*: Position as a man of honor.   232 *voice*: Authoritative statement.   233 *ungored*: Uninjured.
238 *foil*: Setting that displays a jewel advantageously (with a play upon the meaning
"weapon").   240 *Stick fiery off*: Show in brilliant relief.

Hamlet: No, by this hand.
King: Give them the foils, young Osric. Cousin Hamlet,
    You know the wager?
Hamlet: Very well, my lord.
    Your grace has laid the odds o' th' weaker side.
King: I do not fear it, I have seen you both;   245
    But since he is bettered, we have therefore odds.
Laertes: This is too heavy; let me see another.
Hamlet: This likes me well. These foils have all a length?

Prepare to play.

Osric: Ay, my good lord.
King: Set me the stoups of wine upon that table.   250
    If Hamlet give the first or second hit,
    Or quit° in answer of the third exchange,
    Let all the battlements their ordnance fire.
    The king shall drink to Hamlet's better breath,
    And in the cup an union° shall he throw   255
    Richer than that which four successive kings
    In Denmark's crown have worn. Give me the cups,
    And let the kettle° to the trumpet speak,
    The trumpet to the cannoneer without,
    The cannons to the heavens, the heaven to earth,   260
    "Now the king drinks to Hamlet." Come, begin.

Trumpets the while.

    And you, the judges, bear a wary eye.
Hamlet: Come on, sir.
Laertes: Come, my lord.

They play.

Hamlet: One.
Laertes: No.
Hamlet: Judgment?
Osric: A hit, a very palpable hit.

Drum, trumpets, and shot. Flourish; a piece goes off.

Laertes: Well, again.
King: Stay, give me drink. Hamlet, this pearl is thine.   265
    Here's to thy health. Give him the cup.

---

252 *quit:* Repay by a hit.   255 *union:* Pearl.   258 *kettle:* Kettledrum.

Hamlet: I'll play this bout first; set it by awhile.
    Come. (*They play.*) Another hit. What say you?
Laertes: A touch, a touch; I do confess't.
King: Our son shall win.
Queen: He's fat,° and scant of breath.   270
    Here, Hamlet, take my napkin,° rub thy brows.
    The queen carouses° to thy fortune, Hamlet.
Hamlet: Good madam!
King: Gertrude, do not drink.
Queen: I will, my lord; I pray you pardon me.

Drinks.

King (aside): It is the poisoned cup; it is too late.   275
Hamlet: I dare not drink yet, madam — by and by.
Queen: Come, let me wipe thy face.
Laertes: My lord, I'll hit him now.
King: I do not think't.
Laertes (aside): And yet it is almost against my conscience.
Hamlet: Come for the third, Laertes. You but dally.   280
    I pray you pass with your best violence;
    I am afeard you make a wanton° of me.
Laertes: Say you so? Come on.

They play.

Osric: Nothing neither way.
Laertes: Have at you now!

In scuffling they change rapiers, and both are wounded with the poisoned weapon.

King: Part them. They are incensed.   285
Hamlet: Nay, come — again!

The Queen falls.

Osric: Look to the queen there, ho!
Horatio: They bleed on both sides. How is it, my lord?
Osric: How is't, Laertes?
Laertes: Why, as a woodcock° to mine own springe,° Osric.
    I am justly killed with mine own treachery.   290
Hamlet: How does the queen?

---

270 *fat*: Not physically fit, out of training.   271 *napkin*: Handkerchief.   272 *carouses*:
Drinks a toast.   282 *wanton*: Pampered child.   289 *woodcock*: A bird reputed to be stupid
and easily trapped; *springe*: Trap.

King: She sounds° to see them bleed.
Queen: No, no, the drink, the drink! O my dear Hamlet!
      The drink, the drink! I am poisoned.

Dies.

Hamlet: O villainy! Ho! let the door be locked.
      Treachery! Seek it out.   295

Laertes falls.

Laertes: It is here, Hamlet. Hamlet, thou art slain;
      No med'cine in the world can do thee good.
      In thee there is not half an hour's life.
      The treacherous instrument is in thy hand,
      Unbated° and envenomed. The foul practice°   300
      Hath turned itself on me. Lo, here I lie,
      Never to rise again. Thy mother's poisoned.
      I can no more. The king, the king's to blame.
Hamlet: The point envenomed too?
      Then venom, to thy work.   305

Hurts the King.

All: Treason! treason!
King: O, yet defend me, friends. I am but hurt.
Hamlet: Here, thou incestuous, murd'rous, damnèd Dane,
      Drink off this potion. Is thy union here?
      Follow my mother.

King dies.

Laertes: He is justly served.   310
      It is a poison tempered° by himself.
      Exchange forgiveness with me, noble Hamlet.
      Mine and my father's death come not upon thee,
      Nor thine on me!

Dies.

Hamlet: Heaven make thee free of it! I follow thee.   315
      I am dead, Horatio. Wretched queen, adieu!
      You that look pale and tremble at this chance,
      That are but mutes° or audience to this act,

---

291 *sounds*: Swoons.   300 *Unbated*: Unblunted; *practice*: Stratagem.   311 *tempered*: Mixed.
318 *mutes*: Actors in a play who speak no lines.

Had I but time — as this fell sergeant,° Death,
Is strict in his arrest — O, I could tell you —   320
But let it be. Horatio, I am dead;
Thou livest; report me and my cause aright
To the unsatisfied.
Horatio: Never believe it.
I am more an antique Roman than a Dane.
Here's yet some liquor left.
Hamlet: As th' art a man,   325
Give me the cup. Let go. By heaven, I'll ha't!
O God, Horatio, what a wounded name,
Things standing thus unknown, shall live behind me!
If thou didst ever hold me in thy heart,
Absent thee from felicity awhile,   330
And in this harsh world draw thy breath in pain,
To tell my story.

A march afar off.

What warlike noise is this?
Osric: Young Fortinbras, with conquest come from Poland,
To the ambassadors of England gives
This warlike volley.
Hamlet: O, I die, Horatio!   335
The potent poison quite o'ercrows° my spirit.
I cannot live to hear the news from England,
But I do prophesy th' election° lights
On Fortinbras. He has my dying voice.°
So tell him, with th' occurrents,° more and less,   340
Which have solicited° — the rest is silence.

Dies.

Horatio: Now cracks a noble heart. Good night, sweet prince,
And flights of angels sing thee to thy rest!

March within.

Why does the drum come hither?

Enter Fortinbras, with the Ambassadors and with his train of Drum, Colors, and Attendants.

319 *sergeant*: Sheriff's officer.   336 *o'ercrows*: Triumphs over (like a victor in a cockfight).
338 *election*: I.e., to the throne.   339 *voice*: Vote.   340 *occurrents*: Occurrences.   341 *solicited*: Incited, provoked.

Fortinbras: Where is this sight?
Horatio: What is it you would see?   345
   If aught of woe or wonder, cease your search.
Fortinbras: This quarry° cries on° havoc.° O proud Death,
   What feast is toward° in thine eternal cell
   That thou so many princes at a shot
   So bloodily hast struck?
Ambassador: The sight is dismal;   350
   And our affairs from England come too late.
   The ears are senseless that should give us hearing
   To tell him his commandment is fulfilled,
   That Rosencrantz and Guildenstern are dead.
   Where should we have our thanks?
Horatio: Not from his mouth,   355
   Had it th' ability of life to thank you.
   He never gave commandment for their death.
   But since, so jump° upon this bloody question,
   You from the Polack wars, and you from England,
   Are here arrived, give order that these bodies   360
   High on a stage° be placèd to the view,
   And let me speak to th' yet unknowing world
   How these things came about. So shall you hear
   Of carnal, bloody, and unnatural acts,
   Of accidental judgments,° casual° slaughters,   365
   Of deaths put on° by cunning and forced cause,
   And, in this upshot, purposes mistook
   Fall'n on th' inventors' heads. All this can I
   Truly deliver.
Fortinbras: Let us haste to hear it,   370
   And call the noblest to the audience.
   For me, with sorrow I embrace my fortune.
   I have some rights of memory° in this kingdom,
   Which now to claim my vantage° doth invite me.
Horatio: Of that I shall have also cause to speak,   375
   And from his mouth whose voice will draw on more.°
   But let this same be presently° performed,

---

347 *quarry*: Pile of dead (literally, of dead deer gathered after the hunt); *cries on*: Proclaims loudly; *havoc*: Indiscriminate killing and destruction such as would follow the order "havoc," or "pillage," given to an army.   348 *toward*: Forthcoming.   358 *jump*: Precisely.
361 *stage*: Platform.   365 *judgments*: Retributions; *casual*: Not humanly planned (reinforcing *accidental*).   366 *put on*: Instigated.   373 *of memory*: Traditional and kept in mind.
374 *vantage*: Advantageous opportunity.   376 *more*: I.e., more voices, or votes, for the kingship.   377 *presently*: Immediately.

Even while men's minds are wild, lest more mischance
On° plots and errors happen.
Fortinbras: Let four captains
Bear Hamlet like a soldier to the stage,   380
For he was likely, had he been put on,°
To have proved most royal; and for his passage°
The soldiers' music and the rites of war
Speak loudly for him.
Take up the bodies. Such a sight as this   385
Becomes the field, but here shows much amiss.
Go, bid the soldiers shoot.

Exeunt marching; after the which
a peal of ordinance are shot off.

---

379 *On*: On the basis of.   381 *put on*: Set to perform in office.   382 *passage*: Death.

3

Observing Change

We have been imagining feelings and characters. Very often in poems, stories, and plays our focus as active readers is upon change within a character — a change of feeling or of attitude. Responding to change is the subject of this chapter.

Bringing to life change in a character means, first of all, being able to *describe* the change in our own words as an event involving lived inner experience. What was going on in the person before the change occurred? What's going on in the person now? Bringing change to life also means drawing close to the origins and causes of the change, understanding its logic from inside. Poems, stories, and plays often develop as sequences of actions or reflections culminating in a moment of moral and emotional intensity. Writers interest themselves in the process by which human beings shift their inner gears at such crises — move from reticence to forthcomingness, or from personal anxiety to impersonal calm, or from wild fantasy to critically objective self-assessment, or from numberless other starting points to numberless other destinations. As summoning, active readers, we bring to life the conditions of feeling at the starting point and at the destination. And, in addition, we probe the processes of change itself — the forces inducing the change, the reasonableness (or lack of reasonableness) of the change, the circumstances that render the change inevitable.

The primary questions, to repeat, are What change occurs, and why? And our initial approach to answering these questions tends to be analytical, as it usually is in life when we try to explain to ourselves behavior that seems puzzling. We aim at detachment, considering various possible influences and forces conditioning the outer behavior; we lean hard on reason. But no text can be brought fully to life solely through detached inquiry. We have to move from detachment to sympathy, entering into the change of feeling as though it was occurring within ourselves, seeing it finally not as a matter of separable components but as a living experience.

JAMES WRIGHT   (1927–1980)

A Blessing

Just off the highway to Rochester, Minnesota,
Twilight bounds softly forth on the grass.
And the eyes of those two Indian ponies
Darken with kindness.
They have come gladly out of the willows   5
To welcome my friend and me.
We step over the barbed wire into the pasture
Where they have been grazing all day, alone.
They ripple tensely, they can hardly contain their happiness
That we have come.   10
They bow shyly as wet swans. They love each other.
There is no loneliness like theirs.
At home once more,
They begin munching the young tufts of spring in the darkness.
I would like to hold the slenderer one in my arms,   15
For she has walked over to me
And nuzzled my left hand.
She is black and white,
Her mane falls wild on her forehead,
And the light breeze moves me to caress her long ear   20
That is delicate as the skin over a girl's wrist.
Suddenly I realize
That if I stepped out of my body I would break
Into blossom.

In the final three lines of this poem the speaker becomes someone to whom the possibility of stepping "out of my body" seems perfectly real. The change that takes place can be described neutrally as a sudden, strong awakening to an unsuspected power. The focus is on the transformation that seems to be worked in the person, turning a human being into a blossoming flower.

But why and how is this change occurring? The experience begins, in a setting of natural beauty, as a moment of welcome, happy trust, eager affection. Two human visitors and two Indian ponies are all at once in easy communication with each other; the gap between human beings and nature narrows; we half sense a shared realization of the essential similar needs — food, companionship — of all animate creatures. For the speaker that feeling of oneness leads straight to a shedding of merely personal intentions. The movement of his hand in a gesture of loving care seems to him directed not by his own will but by "the light breeze" (line 20). Conceivably it's that feeling of being freed from self, tuned to larger, different forces, that opens a path to understanding that it is possible to step out of the body and into a wholly different existence.

APPROACHING THE INNER EXPERIENCE OF CHANGE

Dwelling in this way on the change itself and what lies behind it helps us to approach the inner experience. It concentrates attention, allows us to summon up the various forces that clearly are important to what's happening — the sharp feeling for the beauty of the animals, the happiness of imagining that the creatures who delight us also delight *in* us, the discovery of the difference between personal and impersonal impulses of love. But to step inside this experience, as the speaker imagines stepping outside of himself, asks still more of us. We have to move from objectively recorded descriptions and reasons to subjectively felt realities. We need to make the speaker's sense of surprise and wonder our own, giving ourselves over to that moment of inner newness.

GEORGE HERBERT (1593–1633)

The Collar

I struck the board, and cried, "No more.
        I will abroad.
    What, shall I ever sigh and pine?

My lines and life are free; free as the road,
    Loose as the wind, as large as store.   5
      Shall I be still in suit?°   *in service or attendance*
    Have I no harvest but a thorn
    To let me blood, and not restore
What I have lost with cordial° fruit?   *restorative*
      Sure there was wine   10
    Before my sighs did dry it; there was corn
      Before my tears did drown it.
    Is the year only lost to me?
      Have I no bays to crown it?
No flowers, no garlands gay? all blasted?   15
      All wasted?
    Not so, my heart; but there is fruit,
      And thou hast hands.
      Recover all thy sigh-blown age
On double pleasures; leave thy cold dispute   20
Of what is fit, and not. Forsake thy cage,
      Thy rope of sands,
Which petty thoughts have made, and made to thee
    Good cable, to enforce and draw,
      And be thy law,   25
    While thou didst wink and wouldst not see.
      Away; take heed;
      I will abroad.
Call in thy death's head there; tie up thy fears.
      He that forbears   30
    To suit and serve his need,
    Deserves his load."
But as I raved and grew more fierce and wild
      At every word,
Methought I heard one calling, *Child!*   35
    And I replied, *My Lord.*

    In the closing lines of this poem, rebellious self-regard and bravado undergo swift transformation as the speaker hears a voice calling "*Child!*" In place of furious protest we hear submissive devotion. The change is clear, and several basic Christian themes could be brought forward to explain it. (Among those themes: the universe as the creation of God, the disastrous impact in human history of the original sin of disobedience, the dependency of all human hope on God's forgiving grace.)

Once again, though, the evocation of the poem demands more than an impersonal citing of Christian doctrines. We must penetrate the experience as a whole, imagining the content of feeling — the shame, the sense of personal absurdity — during the transformation. The reasons for a change are always important; when we know why a change has occurred, it's easier to imagine how it feels to undergo the change. That certainly is the case with, for example, Mistress Damon in Hardy's "The Slow Nature" (p. 33). By reasoning out the logic of the change occurring in her when she takes in the fact that Kit Twink is not joking, we moved closer to her feelings. But it's essential that we take the step, in our imagination, from explaining what happens to *feeling* what happens, never cutting ourselves off from a sense of what it would be like to be in the situation we're bringing to life.

ASKING QUESTIONS ABOUT CHANGE

Again we begin with three examples, three instances of change — two occurring in poems, one in a short story. Our goal is to live into the logic of these changes in such a way that we can make the human experience at stake thoroughly expressible in our own language. As always, answering our large questions — What change occurs here, and why? — becomes easier when we scale the questions down into more particular queries. What were the character's attitudes and feelings before the change? How are they different now? What events or forces influenced the change? What is the source of their power over the character? How conscious is the person that a change is occurring? What would it feel like to undergo such a change? What specific words and phrases give us most strongly a sense of the nature of the change?

JAMES JOYCE   (1882–1941)
Araby

North Richmond Street, being blind, was a quiet street except at the hour when the Christian Brothers' School set the boys free. An uninhabited house of two stories stood at the blind end, detached from its neighbors in a square ground. The other houses of the street, conscious of decent lives within them, gazed at one another with brown imperturbable faces.

The former tenant of our house, a priest, had died in the back drawing-room. Air, musty from having long been enclosed, hung in all the rooms, and the waste room behind the kitchen was littered with old useless papers. Among these I found a few paper-covered books, the pages of which were curled and damp: *The Abbot*, by Walter Scott, *The Devout Communicant* and *The Memoirs of Vidocq*. I liked the last best because its leaves were yellow. The wild garden behind the house contained a central apple-tree and a few straggling bushes under one of which I found the late tenant's rusty bicycle-pump. He had been a very charitable priest; in his will he had left all his money to institutions and the furniture of his house to his sister.

When the short days of winter came dusk fell before we had well eaten our dinners. When we met in the street the houses had grown somber. The space of sky above us was the color of ever-changing violet and towards it the lamps of the street lifted their feeble lanterns. The cold air stung us and we played till our bodies glowed. Our shouts echoed in the silent street. The career of our play brought us through the dark muddy lanes behind the houses where we ran the gantlet of the rough tribes from the cottages, to the back doors of the dark dripping gardens where odors arose from the ashpits, to the dark odorous stables where a coachman smoothed and combed the horse or shook music from the buckled harness. When we returned to the street light from the kitchen windows had filled the areas. If my uncle was seen turning the corner we hid in the shadow until we had seen him safely housed. Or if Mangan's sister came out on the doorstep to call her brother in to his tea we watched her from our shadow peer up and down the street. We waited to see whether she would remain or go in and, if she remained, we left our shadow and walked up to Mangan's steps resignedly. She was waiting for us, her figure defined by the light from the half-opened door. Her brother always teased her before he obeyed and I stood by the railings looking at her. Her dress swung as she moved her body and the soft rope of her hair tossed from side to side.

Every morning I lay on the floor in the front parlor watching her door. The blind was pulled down within an inch of the sash so that I could not be seen. When she came out on the doorstep my heart leaped. I ran to the hall, seized my books, and followed her. I kept her brown figure always in my eye and, when we came near the point at which our ways diverged, I quickened my pace and passed her. This happened morning after morning. I had never spoken to her, except for a few casual words, and yet her name was like a summons to all my foolish blood.

Her image accompanied me even in places the most hostile to romance. On Saturday evenings when my aunt went market-ing I had to go to carry some of the parcels. We walked through the flaring streets, jostled by drunken men and bargaining women, amid the curses of laborers, the shrill litanies of shop-boys who stood on guard by the barrels of pigs' cheeks, the nasal chanting of street-singers, who sang a *come-all-you* about O'Dono-van Rossa, or a ballad about the troubles in our native land. These noises converged in a single sensation of life for me: I imagined that I bore my chalice safely through the throng of foes. Her name sprang to my lips at moments in strange prayers and praises which I myself did not understand. My eyes were often full of tears (I could not tell why) and at times a flood from my heart seemed to pour itself out into my bosom. I thought little of the future. I did not know whether I would ever speak to her or not or, if I spoke to her, how I could tell her of my confused adoration. But my body was like a harp and her words and gestures were like fingers running upon the wires.

One evening I went into the back drawing-room in which the priest had died. It was a dark rainy evening and there was no sound in the house. Through one of the broken panes I heard the rain impinge upon the earth, the fine incessant needles of water playing in the sodden beds. Some distant lamp or lighted win-dow gleamed below me. I was thankful that I could see so little. All my senses seemed to desire to veil themselves and, feeling that I was about to slip from them, I pressed the palms of my hands together until they trembled, murmuring: *O love! O love!* many times.

At last she spoke to me. When she addressed the first words to me I was so confused that I did not know what to answer. She asked me was I going to *Araby.* I forget whether I answered yes or no. It would be a splendid bazaar, she said; she would love to go.

— And why can't you? I asked.

While she spoke she turned a silver bracelet round and round her wrist. She could not go, she said, because there would be a retreat that week in her convent. Her brother and two other boys were fighting for their caps and I was alone at the railings. She held one of the spikes, bowing her head towards me. The light from the lamp opposite our door caught the white curve of her neck, lit up her hair that rested there, and, falling, lit up the hand upon the railing. It fell over one side of her dress and caught the white border of a petticoat, just visible as she stood at ease.

    — It's well for you, she said.   10

    — If I go, I said, I will bring you something.

What innumerable follies laid waste my waking and sleeping thoughts after that evening! I wished to annihilate the tedious intervening days. I chafed against the work of school. At night in my bedroom and by day in the classroom her image came between me and the page I strove to read. The syllables of the word *Araby* were called to me through the silence in which my soul luxuriated and cast an Eastern enchantment over me. I asked for leave to go to the bazaar on Saturday night. My aunt was surprised and hoped it was not some Freemason affair. I answered few questions in class. I watched my master's face pass from amiability to sternness; he hoped I was not beginning to idle. I could not call my wandering thoughts together. I had hardly any patience with the serious work of life which, now that it stood between me and my desire, seemed to me child's play, ugly monotonous child's play.

On Saturday morning I reminded my uncle that I wished to go to the bazaar in the evening. He was fussing at the hall-stand, looking for the hat-brush, and answered me curtly:

    — Yes, boy, I know.

As he was in the hall I could not go into the front parlor and   15 lie at the window. I left the house in bad humor and walked slowly towards the school. The air was pitilessly raw and already my heart misgave me.

When I came home to dinner my uncle had not yet been home. Still it was early. I sat staring at the clock for some time and, when its ticking began to irritate me, I left the room. I mounted the staircase and gained the upper part of the house. The high cold empty gloomy rooms liberated me and I went from room to room singing. From the front window I saw my companions playing below in the street. Their cries reached me weakened and indistinct and, leaning my forehead against the cool glass, I looked over at the dark house where she lived. I may have stood there for an hour, seeing nothing but the brown-clad figure cast by my imagination, touched discreetly by the lamplight at the curved neck, at the hand upon the railings, and at the border below the dress.

When I came downstairs again I found Mrs. Mercer sitting at the fire. She was an old garrulous woman, a pawnbroker's widow, who collected used stamps for some pious purpose. I had to endure the gossip of the tea-table. The meal was prolonged beyond an hour and still my uncle did not come. Mrs. Mercer stood up to go: she was sorry she couldn't wait any longer, but it was after eight o'clock and she did not like to be out late, as the night air was bad for her. When she had gone I began to walk up and down the room, clenching my fists. My aunt said:

— I'm afraid you may put off your bazaar for this night of Our Lord.

At nine o'clock I heard my uncle's latchkey in the halldoor. I heard him talking to himself and heard the hall-stand rocking when it had received the weight of his overcoat. I could interpret these signs. When he was midway through his dinner I asked him to give me the money to go to the bazaar. He had forgotten.

— The people are in bed and after their first sleep now, he   20 said.

I did not smile. My aunt said to him energetically:

— Can't you give him the money and let him go? You've kept him late enough as it is.

My uncle said he was very sorry he had forgotten. He said he believed in the old saying: *All work and no play makes Jack a dull boy.* He asked me where I was going and, when I had told him a second time he asked me did I know *The Arab's Farewell to His Steed.* When I left the kitchen he was about to recite the opening lines of the piece to my aunt.

I held a florin tightly in my hand as I strode down Buckingham Street towards the station. The sight of the streets thronged with buyers and glaring with gas recalled to me the purpose of my journey. I took my seat in a third-class carriage of a deserted train. After an intolerable delay the train moved out of the station slowly. It crept onward among ruinous houses and over the twinkling river. At Westland Row Station a crowd of people pressed to the carriage doors; but the porters moved them back, saying that it was a special train for the bazaar. I remained alone in the bare carriage. In a few minutes the train drew up beside an improvised wooden platform. I passed out on to the road and saw by the lighted dial of a clock that it was ten minutes to ten. In front of me was a large building which displayed the magical name.

I could not find any sixpenny entrance and, fearing that the   25 bazaar would be closed, I passed in quickly through a turnstile, handing a shilling to a weary-looking man. I found myself in a big hall girdled at half its height by a gallery. Nearly all the stalls were closed and the greater part of the hall was in darkness. I recognized a silence like that which pervades a church after a service. I walked into the center of the bazaar timidly. A few people were gathered about the stalls which were still open. Before a curtain, over which the words *Café Chantant* were written in colored lamps, two men were counting money on a salver. I listened to the fall of the coins.

Remembering with difficulty why I had come I went over to one of the stalls and examined porcelain vases and flowered tea-sets. At the door of the stall a young lady was talking and laughing with two young gentlemen. I remarked their English accents and listened vaguely to their conversation.

— O, I never said such a thing!

— O, but you did!

— O, but I didn't!

— Didn't she say that? 30

— Yes. I heard her.

— O, there's a . . . fib!

Observing me the young lady came over and asked me did I wish to buy anything. The tone of her voice was not encouraging; she seemed to have spoken to me out of a sense of duty. I looked humbly at the great jars that stood like eastern guards at either side of the dark entrance to the stall and murmured:

— No, thank you.

The young lady changed the position of one of the vases and 35 went back to the two young men. They began to talk of the same subject. Once or twice the young lady glanced at me over her shoulder.

I lingered before her stall, though I knew my stay was useless, to make my interest in her wares seem the more real. Then I turned away slowly and walked down the middle of the bazaar. I allowed the two pennies to fall against the sixpence in my pocket. I heard a voice call from one end of the gallery that the light was out. The upper part of the hall was now completely dark.

Gazing up into the darkness I saw myself as a creature driven and derided by vanity; and my eyes burned with anguish and anger.

Questions

What change occurs here?

Gazing up into the darkness I saw myself as a creature driven and derided by vanity; and my eyes burned with anguish and anger. (para. 37)

Why does the change occur? What would it feel like to undergo such a change? After writing your response, compare it with those that follow.

Responses

COLLEGE FRESHMAN: When he gets to Araby, the narrator realizes that any gift is too expensive for him to buy: "I looked humbly at the great jars that stood like eastern guards at either side of the dark entrance" (para. 33). In the last sentence he comes to understand that Mangan's sister has tried to use his devotion for gain. She must have noticed this young boy following her every morning and gazing at her every night. Now the narrator sees why she has spoken to him only once. This disillusionment brings about the narrator's anguish.

But the situation is more complex than that. The narrator feels ashamed because he has been unfaithful to his ideal. The reader is prepared for this as the narrator approaches the fair, "remembering with difficulty why I had come" (26). We can also guess that the narrator's religious devotion to Mangan's sister is fading when he "recognizes a silence like that which pervades a church after a service" (25). The event that these subtleties point to is the narrator's attraction to the English salesgirl. "I lingered before her stall, though I knew my stay was useless, to make my interest in her wares seem the more real" (36). Why must he feign an interest in her wares? He knows he can't buy anything, but his interest has drifted from Mangan's sister to this new and appealing girl.

Both these realizations make the narrator feel ashamed and foolish. Perhaps his thoughts turn to his private acts of devotion, which now seem meaningless. He might be thinking of when "the high cold empty gloomy rooms liberated me and I went from room to room singing" (16) or how "every morning I lay on the floor in the front parlor watching her door" (4). These acts make the narrator feel immature. He sees his blind devotion as a waste of time. He also carries a burden of guilt because he was not able to remain faithful. Ordinarily, being attracted to someone else while being in love is not a terrible thing, but to this inexperienced and deeply religious mind it is a grievous offense.

Why does this moment of realization occur while the narrator is "gazing up into the darkness"? It may seem strange for Joyce to continue his allusions to blindness in a moment of enlighten-ment. But the narrator does not see that his feelings of foolish-ness and guilt are not so terrible. His is only a perfectly normal infatuation with the opposite sex. It is a positive and healthy thing that most boys experience. The narrator's youth and the overflow of emotion he feels prevent him from seeing this. There is also a loss of happiness at this moment. The narrator's disillu-sionment will most likely keep him from feeling this strongly again. The darkness emphasizes this loss and makes us sad that this boy will probably not like a book again "because its leaves were yellow" (2).

COLLEGE FRESHMAN: "Araby," on the narrative level, is the story of a young boy who becomes infatuated with a girl in his neighbor-hood. The boy's love for the girl, admiration from afar, is com-plicated by his lack of experience in dealing with love, which is intertwined with the strong religious feelings he has acquired from his association with the house of a deceased priest. Thus, the boy battles with these strong passions and comes to a new perspective on himself at the conclusion of the story.

In all likelihood this boy is experiencing his first love; al-though he has barely spoken to the girl, he possesses intense feelings of love and desire for her. His attraction to her is so great that he achieves a certain amount of fulfillment by merely fol-lowing and passing by her. The boy, because of his insecurity, keeps his feelings entirely inside himself. He states, "I had never spoken to her . . . and yet her name was like a summons to all my foolish blood" (para. 4). However, the "musty," enclosed old house of the priest, where he has read books such as *The Memoirs of Vidocq*, has instilled in him equally powerful feelings of love and desire — the love of God and the desire for purity. Thus he views the girl through the clouded lenses of his quasi-religious ideals.

The young boy guards the image of his beloved in much the same way a priest guards the sanctity of the Virgin Mary. After walking through the streets, passing drunken men and cursing laborers, he feels as if he has defended his virtuous goddess. He exclaims victoriously: "I imagined that I bore my chalice safely through the throng of foes" (5). At one point, when he is sitting in the priest's house, the coupling of his religious and emotional desires arouses a struggle within his psyche and he must literally force himself not to let his feelings of love for the girl slip away. Thus the instability of his emotional state sets the stage for the transformation he will undergo by the end of the story.

When the girl speaks to the boy and asks him if he is going to Araby, her action strongly reinforces his desire for her and diminishes his prior guilt. She has now become part of his religion; he idealizes and worships her uncontrollably. The boy declares, "I had hardly any patience with the serious work of life which, now that it stood between me and my desire, seemed to me child's play, ugly monotonous child's play " (12).

The boy envisions the girl's calling to go to Araby as a priest would God's calling to spread the word of the Bible. The moment the boy arrives at the bazaar, however, his idyllic religious feelings begin to collapse. Even though Araby possesses the same silence as an empty church, it has become to the boy a desecrated structure. After stepping off the train onto a shabby wooden platform, he proceeds into the hall and encounters a girl shamelessly flirting with two men. The boy now recognizes the cheapness of his "church"; he associates the frivolous, vulgar flirting of the girl and his own mental flirting with his beloved girl. The boy realizes the emptiness and the unreality of his lovely virginal figure. The temporary blindness that he feels is symbolized by the lights going off in the hall. The boy, alone, is free to repent and chastise himself for his sins.

Through this experience the boy has been confronted with the inherent impurity of love and desire. He is unable to reconcile his natural feelings toward the girl with his perception of the "beauty of love" ingrained in his mind from the priest's house. When he is forced to face his dueling emotions, he becomes ashamed and withdrawn. He sees his love for the girl as something that has "driven and derided" him. In this moment of complete defeat, he feels nothing but "anguish and anger." He has witnessed reality, and it has destroyed the optimistic hopes and ambitions he nurtured for himself and his lovely idol. His "religion" has endured, but his love for the girl has been forever suppressed.

EDITOR: The change that matters most is from hope, dedication, and a conviction of exalted personal worth to defeat, frustration, and self-scorn. The ascent to the summit of self-exaltation begins very early in the story, as the youngster — the "I" who is recalling this episode in his boyish past — remembers the beginning of his infatuation with "Mangan's sister":

> When she came out on the doorstep my heart leaped. I ran to the hall, seized my books, and followed her. I kept her brown figure always in my eye and, when we came near the point at which our ways diverged, I quickened my pace and passed her. This happened morning after morning. I had never spoken to her, except for a few casual words, and yet her name was like a summons to all my foolish blood. (para. 4)

The nature of this infatuation owes a little to the works of fiction that the "I" has been reading — romances offering visions of heroes rising to meet demanding moral challenges in the face of great danger. It owes something too to the imagery of devotion soaked up, perhaps, in church school, confirmation class, choir practice. The combination of heroic self-conception and moral and religious idealism surfaces before the hero ever exchanges a word with Mangan's sister. "I imagined that I bore my chalice safely through the throng of foes. Her name sprang to my lips at moments in strange prayers" (5). And once he does speak with her, his commitment to a mission both holy and romantic, undertaken on her behalf, is complete.

The romance side of the vision is fed, for the hero, by the word *Araby*, with its suggestion of magical Eastern enchantment. It's also fed by the infatuation itself — the sense of Mangan's sister's perfection and purity. The holy side of the vision is nourished by the hero's notion that, by bringing "something" back from the faraway place to a beloved pitiably unable to make the journey for herself, he will have performed an ennobling, selfless act. The sequel to such an exploit can hardly be less than a union of souls, lover and beloved, on a plateau of elevated spirituality.

As already noted, however, change occurs. The hero, who at the midpoint perceives himself as somehow akin to a knight on a white charger striving to bring off a noble deed that will win his lady's hand and raise his moral status, sees himself at the end as a fool — a person victimized by his own vanity. The discovery of the absurdity of his self-spawned fantasies overwhelms him with self-contempt and fury.

The reasons for this change are clear. To begin with, a genuinely heroic mission requires the existence of real dangers —

major obstacles to be overcome, powerful enemies to be slain, pitfalls to be narrowly escaped. But although this young man's trip to Araby is beset by obstacles, they are hardly of a proper scale. One obstacle to the hero's departure is that his uncle comes home late to supper, having tarried too long in a pub. Another obstacle — just barely overcome — is the threatened recital of a sentimental ballad about an Arab in love with his horse. Still another obstacle amounts to nothing more than a ticket taker at a turnstile — not a challenging foe, just a "weary-looking man" (25).

The bazaar itself lacks aura and excitement. It's late, and the place is closing. The hoped-for world of mystery turns out to be as drab as a common store — people counting money, a salesgirl and two customers mindlessly flirting, and no object for sale within the hero's means that contains as much as a hint of the glamour he's after. As for the new identity the hero set off to achieve, it materializes all right, but it's rather ignoble. The countergirl sees in him something closer to a shoplifter than to Galahad.

A severe letdown, in short, more than enough to bring about the humiliating change in question. There's a suggestion early in the story of the probable turn of events — the descent in the second paragraph from the dead priest's romantic novels, which the lad undoubtedly found elevating, to the priest's "rusty bicycle-pump," a rather homelier instrument of uplift. And there are echoes, to the very end of the story, of the religious overtones of the boy's vision. The two men adding up receipts count the money on a salver — and that word in his mind brings the hero back to the church and to the trays used in the service of Holy Communion.

But these echoes only intensify the disappointment. The change that takes place in the hero's feelings is among the most familiar in human life: a change from perceiving things — including ourselves and our surroundings — as we might wish them to be to perceiving things as, alas, they more or less unromantically are. The "I" of "Araby" is, at the close of the story, suffused with shame, but obviously that will pass, and its passing — the development of a sharper sense of realism — surely must not be thought of solely as a loss. How exactly it should be thought of — whether we as readers conclude that this disillusionment is regrettable, necessary, excessive, or something else — depends at least partly on our view of life meanings. Here once again, in short, there's room for difference of opinion. But perhaps there's less room for debate about how this kind of change feels. People who have experienced such disappointment find it difficult, even after many years, to forget the mixture of sadness and raging self-contempt that comes with it.

Continuing the Discussion

1. Reader 1 says that one change occurring in the narrator of "Araby" is that "he comes to understand that Mangan's sister has tried to use his devotion for gain." How do you explain this reading of the change? Can a basis for it be found in the story itself? Where?

2. Reader 2 says that the change occurring in the narrator is that he "recognizes the cheapness of his 'church.'" How do you explain this reading of the change? Can a basis for it be found in the story itself? Where?

3. What is the essential difference between the ways in which Readers 1 and 2 read the story as a whole? How do you account for this difference?

ANONYMOUS   (traditional Scottish ballad)

Edward

"Why dois your brand° sae° drap wi' bluid,   *sword; so*
   Edward, Edward?
Why dois your brand sae drap wi' bluid?
  And why sae sad gang° yee, O?"   *go*
"O, I hae killed my hauke sae guid,   5
   Mither, mither,
O, I hae killed my hauke sae guid,
  And I had nae mair bot° hee, O."   *but*

"Your haukis bluid was nevir sae reid,
   Edward, Edward,   10
Your haukis bluid was nevir sae reid,
  My deir son I tell thee, O."
"O, I hae killed my reid-roan steid,
   Mither, mither,

O, I hae killed my reid-roan steid,   15
    That erst° was sa fair and frie,° O."   *once; free*

"Your steid was auld, and ye hae gat mair,
    Edward, Edward,
Your steid was auld, and ye hae gat mair,
    Sum other dule° ye drie,° O."   *sorrow; suffer*   20
"O, I hae killed my fadir deir,
    Mither, mither,
O, I hae killed my fadir deir,
    Alas, and wae° is mee, O!"   *woe*

"And whatten penance wul ye drie for that,   25
    Edward, Edward?
And whatten penance will ye drie for that?
    My deir son, now tell me, O."
"Ile set my feit in younder boat,
    Mither, mither,   30
Ile set my feit in yonder boat,
    And Ile fare ovir the sea, O."

"And what wul ye doe wi' your towirs and your ha',°   *hall*
    Edward, Edward,
And what wul ye doe wi' your towirs and your ha',   35
    That were sae fair to see, O?"
"Ile let thame stand tul they doun fa',
    Mither, mither,
Ile let thame stand tul they doun fa',
    For here nevir mair maun° I bee, O."   *must*   40

"And what wul ye leive to your bairns and your wife,
    Edward, Edward?
And what wul ye leive to your bairns and your wife,
    When ye gang ovir the sea, O?"
"The warldis° room, late° them beg thrae° life,   *world's; let; through*   45
    Mither, mither,
The warldis room, late them beg thrae life,
    For thame nevir mair wul I see, O."

"And what wul ye leive to your ain° mither deir,   *own*
    Edward, Edward?   50
And what wul ye leive to your ain mither deir?
    My deir son, now tell me, O."
"The curse of hell frae me sall ye beir,
    Mither, mither,
The curse of hell frae me sall ye beir,   55
    Sic° counseils ye gave to me, O."   *such*

Questions

What change occurs in lines 53–56?

> "The curse of hell frae me sall ye beir,
>   Mither, mither,
> The curse of hell frae me sall ye beir,
>   Sic counseils ye gave to me, O."

Why does this change occur? What would it feel like to undergo such a change? Write your response and compare it with the ones that follow.

Responses

COLLEGE FRESHMAN: A gradual intensifying of emotions often triggers what appears to be an immediate change in a character. One views this situation in the ballad "Edward." At first glance, it seems as though Edward undergoes a tremendous change in the last four lines. Upon closer inspection, however, the reader understands that this change is, in fact, a reaction to his mounting feelings of guilt evoked by his mother. He is eventually unable to handle the emotions associated with his murder of his father and thus blames his mother, who is guilty of inciting Edward's guilt, for the crime.

At the start of the ballad, it becomes obvious that Edward feels some regret about committing the crime. By not admitting the truth, Edward shows the reader that he realizes the wrongness of his deed. He tries to diminish the importance of the murder through his progressive lies. He first tells his mother that the victim was a hawk and then claims it was a horse. She knows that he is lying, and he finally admits to killing "my fadir deir" (line 21). Although he knows the murder was wrong, Edward does not truly express his guilt.

Additionally, before his mother's questioning, Edward is blind to the many ramifications of the murder. It is not until his mother begins to interrogate him that Edward fully experiences his feelings toward and views the implications of his crime. Immediately after admitting the truth, Edward expresses his contrition: "I hae killed my fadir deir, / Alas, and wae is mee, O!" (23–24). As a result of his mother's prodding, Edward soon recognizes the necessity that he leave the town, his estate, and his family. The reader views Edward's struggle with family members.

Edward tells his mother how "the warldis room, late them [his wife and children] beg thrae life" (45). The insensitivity here may be a reaction to his penitence for the murder of his father. At this point, all of Edward's emotions are intensified as they are brought to the surface by his mother.

Edward cannot deal with the guilt and the emotional intensity he is feeling, so he transfers the guilt of the murder onto his mother. Because his mother is responsible for bringing out and nurturing his guilty feelings, Edward feels justified in placing the responsibility for the actual murder on her. Edward's cursing his mother is more an inevitable reaction than a sign of a distinct change in character. This reaction is caused by Edward's inability to cope with his guilt.

Another source of Edward's resentment toward his mother and, thus, another justification for placing the blame on her is her apparent indifference to an exploitation of the awful situation in which Edward is embroiled. By asking "what wul ye leive to your ain mither deir?" (49), the mother is, in a sense, stabbing her son in the back. First, she causes him to confess the murder of his father, and then she tries to capitalize on his heinous crime. It is in the last four lines that a moment of self-realization occurs in Edward. He sees that his action was unjustified and, for the previously mentioned reasons, resorts to cursing his mother as he grasps for a means of clearing his conscience.

Although I have never experienced anything even remotely comparable to what Edward goes through here, I can try to empathize with him. I can understand how a person, unable to handle the consequences of an action, would put the blame on another person. He is drained by the realization and mad at himself for being unable to realize the futility of the situation that led to this change.

EDITOR: The most immediately noticeable change here is in the feeling expressed toward the mother. Throughout more than fifty lines of questions and answers, Edward, the son, has uttered no word that at first hearing could be construed to contain any hint of bitterness, resentment, or anger at his mother. His responses carry anguished grief at some moments ("Alas, and wae is mee, O!" line 24), at other moments black, despairing resignation ("For thame nevir mair wul I see, O," 48), and at still other moments stony impassivity toward the helplessness of his wife and children ("late them beg thrae life," 45). But at *this* moment Edward's response to his mother flames out into attack; the dutiful son's mannerly deference (or even love) gives way abruptly to something different — a man laying hell's curse upon his parent, speaking in a voice of iron hate and rage.

One way of uncovering the logic of this change might be to propose that it is more apparent than real, and that hatred and rage have been there from the start, masked but intense, and recognizable every step of the way by mother and son alike. Edward moves from pointlessly disguised expression of his true feeling to direct utterance of it merely because the pointlessness of the disguise becomes clearer to him as the exchange goes on. But to accept this line of reasoning is to assume that the mother proceeds from question to question for no purpose except that of exacerbating the rage — an implausible motive.

To arrive at a more satisfying comprehension of the movements of mind and feeling here, it's necessary to construct the situation more fully, making explicit what is left unsaid, or is said obliquely, and testing out the possibility that the obliquity itself may be the force that drives Edward at length to call down "the curse of hell" upon his mother. What exactly is the situation? A son, asked by his mother why his sword is bloody, twice answers falsely, but in tones of powerful lament, that he's killed a hawk and a horse that were dear to him; twice doubted by his mother, he then admits that he's committed parricide. From the end of stanza 3 we learn that Edward suffers profound guilt and grief over his crime, and from the closing stanza we learn both that among those blood relations closest to Edward the person toward whom he feels most violently is his mother and that the cause of this violent rage lies in some advice she's given him.

Two assumptions seem reasonable at this juncture. The first is that the obnoxious counsel that Edward received from his mother led him toward his murderous crime; the second is that the counsel was indirect. Edward's mother did not say, in so many words, Go and kill your father; she employed suggestion, hint, allusion. Why make this assumption? Because the line of interrogation advanced by Edward's mother in the poem seems itself evasive and circuitous — determined to press for explicit answers but reluctant to frame explicit questions. These are the manners not of candor but of slyness, wariness, furtiveness.

And we can imagine Edward's renewed encounter with these

manners as having a cumulative impact upon him, moment by moment. When the idea of getting rid of his father (for unnamed reasons) was first broached, Edward allowed it to take hold of him partly because the meaning of the crime was obscured by euphemism, uncompleted sentences, and the like. Now that he has passed through the deed, experienced his own violence and subsequent racking guilt, he knows the difference between murder as evasively uttered "counsel" and murder as a reality.

His mother's questions subtly insinuate that she knows little about the crime, that she bears no responsibility, that she deserves kindness and charity; but, listening to her, Edward hears a repetition of the original sly obliquity that urged him to the edge of his crime. Amid his grief, guilt, and self-disgust, he's drawn back to the time when the thought of the crime was planted. He sees himself as cynically manipulated, enticed into damnation by the same voice of indirection that's still trying to work its will on him. And as the voice goes on, its tone never changing, its affectation of innocence and neutrality seemingly undisturbed, the rage and despair within him mount, find their focus outside, and at length he gives vent, in tight-lipped fury, to the curse.

To follow the logic of this change we have to construct an order of events, a pattern of probabilities; we have to reason our way to clarity about motives and responses, ourselves operating on hints, observing the guilefulness of the questioner, sensing the movement of Edward's feelings from grief and horror to rage at the counsel that he failed to resist. But the detached logic that lays out the pattern of probabilities here cannot in itself bring this poem to life; we need to track simultaneously the steadily mounting emotional intensity that breathes at the poem's core.

ANTHONY HECHT   (b. 1923)
Lizards and Snakes

On the summer road that ran by our front porch
   Lizards and snakes came out to sun.
It was hot as a stove out there, enough to scorch
   A buzzard's foot. Still, it was fun
To lie in the dust and spy on them. Near but remote,   5
   They snoozed in the carriage ruts, a smile
In the set of the jaw, a fierce pulse in the throat
Working away like Jack Doyle's after he'd run the mile.

Aunt Martha had an unfair prejudice
   Against them (as well as being cold   10
Toward bats). She was pretty inflexible in this,
   Being a spinster and all, and old.
So we used to slip them into her knitting box.
   In the evening she'd bring in things to mend
And a nice surprise would slide out from under the socks.   15
It broadened her life, as Joe said. Joe was my friend.

But we never did it again after the day
   Of the big wind when you could hear the trees
Creak like rockingchairs. She was looking away
   Off, and kept saying, "Sweet Jesus, please   20
Don't let him near me. He's as like as twins.
   He can crack us like lice with his fingernail.
I can see him plain as a pikestaff. Look how he grins
And swings the scaly horror of his folded tail."

Questions

Two changes take place in this poem. How do you describe them, and why do they occur? Tell what it would feel like to undergo the change occurring in the speaker. Write your response and compare it with those that follow.

Responses

COLLEGE FRESHMAN: As the reader of Hecht's "Lizards and Snakes," I noticed many small changes throughout the poem that help accentuate the significant overall changes in the two major characters, Aunt Martha and the boy. In the first stanza there is a sense of restless curiosity. Hecht's words made me feel like a young carefree girl spending the summer exploring nature and God's beautiful creations in the fields and woods. The boys in the poem are doing the same type of thing. They are acting like the typical adventuresome boys that they are, continually playing their hours away in a benign but mischievous manner.

As the poem moves into the second stanza, the theme of carelessness and relaxation continues. Aunt Martha is introduced as the exemplary kindhearted spinster who spends her time mending and knitting and who looks with disgust and offense at the creepy crawly things boys like to play with.

Everything that Hecht has written up to this point is light

and airy, with a touch of humor thrown in here and there. And then all of a sudden, in the third stanza, Hecht hits us with a heap of seriousness. The first indicator of this change comes in the atmosphere. There is no longer the laid-back feeling of a hot day. That has been replaced by a "big wind" and a seeming unrest in nature. The snakes and lizards are no longer objects of boyhood curiosity. They have become evil entities that should not be fooled with. Even more specifically, they have become serpents that represent the Devil.

Hecht uses much harsher words to project the fear that has overtaken Aunt Martha. Her prior "unfair prejudice" is now a terror of a "scaly horror." I am unsure as to why this change actually takes place in Aunt Martha. Perhaps, nearing death, she feels that the snakes are a forewarning of her possible destiny in hell and therefore cries out to Jesus for help. Or perhaps she views the snakes as the causes of some unrest and misfortune in her life that is also pointed out by the big wind that makes the trees creak. I don't know exactly what has made her change, but I know that by the end of the poem she has definitely been overcome by fear.

The change in the boy appears somewhat clearer to me. He was carefree and happy, but his aunt's words startle and scare him. He does not understand, much as I do not, what has caused this reaction in Aunt Martha. As a result of this lack of understanding, he goes away frightened and confused, but he can sense the seriousness of the situation. It strikes him so that he no longer wants to play with the snakes and lizards.

What it would feel like to undergo the change occurring in the speaker is a question that I don't feel I can sufficiently answer. I could not really understand it. Instead, I simply tried to describe what I took away from the poem.

COLLEGE FRESHMAN: Two changes occur in the poem "Lizards and Snakes." One takes place in the speaker's Aunt Martha. This change is marked by the statement "But we never did it again after the day / Of the big wind" (lines 17–18). Aunt Martha senses the presence of something evil and begs Jesus to keep the evil away from her. She seems to be speaking about the Devil or perhaps death. Maybe the big wind brings to her mind the thought that the end of the world is coming, and with the end comes the Devil to take all the souls Jesus leaves behind. When Aunt Martha begs Jesus to keep the Devil away from her, she is asking him to take her to heaven.

To undergo a change from being a more or less happy woman to one who is sure someone is coming after her would be terrifying. Aunt Martha speaks of being "crack[ed] like lice with his fingernail," as well as the "scaly horror of his folded tail" (22, 24). She seems truly afraid that someone is coming after her.

A change also occurs in the speaker. It too is marked by the words "But we never did it again after . . . the big wind." The speaker and his friend stop teasing Aunt Martha with the lizards and snakes. The lizards were once fun to play with — "they snoozed . . . a smile / In the set of the jaw" (6–7); he describes them as though they are harmless little creatures. But they take on a different form the day of the big wind. The speaker senses Aunt Martha's fright and stops playing such tricks on her when he realizes that her image of the Devil is lizardlike.

It would feel awful to experience the change the speaker goes through. He may feel ashamed that his lizards remind Aunt Martha of the Devil. He may also feel frightened. Aunt Martha is afraid of someone evil; he may feel scared because she is afraid. To him, she may seem to know something worth being afraid about, and he may take on this knowledge. To him, the lizards are no longer fun. They now represent something evil.

FOR FURTHER STUDY

COUNTEE CULLEN   (1903–1946)
Incident

Once riding in old Baltimore,
   Heart-filled, head-filled with glee,
I saw a Baltimorean
   Keep looking straight at me.

Now I was eight and very small,   5
   And he was no whit bigger,
And so I smiled, but he poked out
   His tongue, and called me, "Nigger."

I saw the whole of Baltimore
    From May until December;   10
Of all the things that happened there
    That's all that I remember.

D. H. LAWRENCE   (1885–1930)
Snake

A snake came to my water trough
On a hot, hot day, and I in pajamas for the heat,
To drink there.

In the deep, strange-scented shade of the great dark carob tree
I came down the steps with my pitcher   5
And must wait, must stand and wait, for there he was at the
      trough before me.
He reached down from a fissure in the earth-wall in the gloom
And trailed his yellow-brown slackness soft-bellied down, over
      the edge of the stone trough
And rested his throat upon the stone bottom,
And where the water had dripped from the tap, in a small clear-
      ness,   10
He sipped with his straight mouth,
Softly drank through his straight gums, into his slack long body,
Silently.

Someone was before me at my water trough,
And I, like a second-comer, waiting.   15

He lifted his head from his drinking, as cattle do,
And looked at me vaguely, as drinking cattle do,
And flickered his two-forked tongue from his lips, and mused a
      moment,
And stooped and drank a little more,
Being earth-brown, earth-golden from the burning bowls of the
      earth   20
On the day of Sicilian July, with Etna smoking.

The voice of my education said to me
He must be killed,
For in Sicily the black black snakes are innocent, the gold are ven-
      omous.

And voices in me said, If you were a man   25
You would take a stick and break him now, and finish him off.

But must I confess how I liked him,
How glad I was he had come like a guest in quiet, to drink at my
    water trough
And depart peaceful, pacified, and thankless
Into the burning bowels of this earth?   30

Was it cowardice, that I dared not kill him?
Was it perversity, that I longed to talk to him?
Was it humility, to feel so honored?
I felt so honored.

And yet those voices: 35
If you were not afraid, you would kill him!

And truly I was afraid, I was most afraid,
But even so, honored still more
That he should seek my hospitality
From out the dark door of the secret earth.   40

He drank enough
And lifted his head, dreamily, as one who has drunken,
And flickered his tongue like a forked night on the air, so black,
Seeming to lick his lips,
And looked around like a god, unseeing, into the air,   45
And slowly turned his head,
And slowly, very slowly, as if thrice adream
Proceeded to draw his slow length curving round
And climb the broken bank of my wall-face.

And as he put his head into that dreadful hole,   50
And as he slowly drew up, snake-easing his shoulders, and en-
    tered further,
A sort of horror, a sort of protest against his withdrawing into
    that horrid black hole,
Deliberately going into the blackness, and slowly drawing him-
    self after,
Overcame me now his back was turned.

I looked round, I put down my pitcher,   55
I picked up a clumsy log
And threw it at the water trough with a clatter.

I think it did not hit him;
But suddenly that part of him that was left behind convulsed in
    undignified haste,
Writhed like lightning, and was gone   60
Into the black hole, the earth-lipped fissure in the wall-front
At which, in the intense still noon, I stared with fascination.

And immediately I regretted it.
I thought how paltry, how vulgar, what a mean act!
I despised myself and the voices of my accursed human educa-
    tion.   65

And I thought of the albatross,°
And I wished he would come back, my snake.

For he seemed to me again like a king,
Like a king in exile, uncrowned in the underworld,
Now due to be crowned again.   70

And so, I missed my chance with one of the lords
Of life.
And I have something to expiate:
A pettiness.

66 *albatross*: The bird shot by the narrator in Coleridge's "The Rime of the Ancient Mariner."

FLANNERY O'CONNOR   (1925–1964)
The Artificial Nigger

Mr. Head awakened to discover that the room was full of
moonlight. He sat up and stared at the floor boards — the color
of silver — and then at the ticking on his pillow, which might
have been brocade, and after a second, he saw half of the moon
five feet away in his shaving mirror, paused as if it were waiting
for his permission to enter. It rolled forward and cast a digni-
fying light on everything. The straight chair against the wall
looked stiff and attentive as if it were awaiting an order and Mr.
Head's trousers, hanging to the back of it, had an almost noble
air, like the garment some great man had just flung to his servant; but the face on the moon was a grave one. It gazed across
the room and out the window where it floated over the horsestall
and appeared to contemplate itself with the look of a young man
who sees his old age before him.

Mr. Head could have said to it that age was a choice blessing
and that only with years does a man enter into that calm understanding of life that makes him a suitable guide for the young.
This, at least, had been his own experience.

He sat up and grasped the iron posts at the foot of his bed
and raised himself until he could see the face on the alarm clock
which sat on an overturned bucket beside the chair. The hour
was two in the morning. The alarm on the clock did not work but

he was not dependent on any mechanical means to awaken him. Sixty years had not dulled his responses; his physical reactions, like his moral ones, were guided by his will and strong character, and these could be seen plainly in his features. He had a long tube-like face with a long rounded open jaw and a long depressed nose. His eyes were alert but quiet, and in the miraculous moonlight they had a look of composure and of ancient wisdom as if they belonged to one of the great guides of men. He might have been Vergil summoned in the middle of the night to go to Dante, or better, Raphael, awakened by a blast of God's light to fly to the side of Tobias.° The only dark spot in the room was Nelson's pallet, underneath the shadow of the window.

Nelson was hunched over on his side, his knees under his chin and his heels under his bottom. His new suit and hat were in the boxes that they had been sent in and these were on the floor at the foot of the pallet where he could get his hands on them as soon as he woke up. The slop jar, out of the shadow and made snow-white in the moonlight, appeared to stand guard over him like a small personal angel. Mr. Head lay back down, feeling entirely confident that he could carry out the moral mission of the coming day. He meant to be up before Nelson and to have the breakfast cooking by the time he awakened. The boy was always irked when Mr. Head was the first up. They would have to leave the house at four to get to the railroad junction by five-thirty. The train was to stop for them at five forty-five and they had to be there on time for this train was stopping merely to accommodate them.

This would be the boy's first trip to the city though he 5 claimed it would be his second because he had been born there. Mr. Head had tried to point out to him that when he was born he didn't have the intelligence to determine his whereabouts but this had made no impression on the child at all and he continued to insist that this was to be his second trip. It would be Mr. Head's third trip. Nelson had said, "I will've already been there twice and I ain't but ten."

Mr. Head had contradicted him.

"If you ain't been there in fifteen years, how you know you'll be able to find your way about?" Nelson had asked. "How you know it hasn't changed some?"

"Have you ever," Mr. Head had asked, "seen me lost?"

Raphael . . . Tobias: Raphael, an important angel, guided Tobias to travel to Media, marry, ward off an evil spirit, and cure his father's blindness (see the Book of Tobit in the Apocrypha).

Nelson certainly had not but he was a child who was never satisfied until he had given an impudent answer and he replied, "It's nowhere around here to get lost at."

"The day is going to come," Mr. Head prophesied, "when   10 you'll find you ain't as smart as you think you are." He had been thinking about this trip for several months but it was for the most part in moral terms that he conceived it. It was to be a lesson that the boy would never forget. He was to find out from it that he had no cause for pride merely because he had been born in a city. He was to find out that the city is not a great place. Mr. Head meant him to see everything there is to see in a city so that he would be content to stay at home for the rest of his life. He fell asleep thinking how the boy would at last find out that he was not as smart as he thought he was.

He was awakened at three-thirty by the smell of fatback frying and he leaped off his cot. The pallet was empty and the clothes boxes had been thrown open. He put on his trousers and ran into the other room. The boy had a corn pone on cooking and had fried the meat. He was sitting in the half-dark at the table, drinking cold coffee out of a can. He had on his new suit and his new gray hat pulled low over his eyes. It was too big for him but they had ordered it a size large because they expected his head to grow. He didn't say anything but his entire figure suggested satisfaction at having arisen before Mr. Head.

Mr. Head went to the stove and brought the meat to the table in the skillet. "It's no hurry," he said. "You'll get there soon enough and it's no guarantee you'll like it when you do neither," and he sat down across from the boy whose hat teetered back slowly to reveal a fiercely expressionless face, very much the same shape as the old man's. They were grandfather and grandson but they looked enough alike to be brothers and brothers not too far apart in age, for Mr. Head had a youthful expression by daylight, while the boy's look was ancient, as if he knew everything already and would be pleased to forget it.

Mr. Head had once had a wife and daughter and when the wife died, the daughter ran away and returned after an interval with Nelson. Then one morning, without getting out of bed, she died and left Mr. Head with sole care of the year-old child. He had made the mistake of telling Nelson that he had been born in Atlanta. If he hadn't told him that, Nelson couldn't have insisted that this was going to be his second trip.

"You may not like it a bit," Mr. Head continued. "It'll be full of niggers."

The boy made a face as if he could handle a nigger. 15
"All right," Mr. Head said. "You ain't ever seen a nigger."
"You wasn't up very early," Nelson said.
"You ain't ever seen a nigger," Mr. Head repeated. "There hasn't been a nigger in this county since we run that one out twelve years ago and that was before you were born." He looked at the boy as if he were daring him to say he had ever seen a Negro.
"How you know I never saw a nigger when I lived there before?" Nelson asked. "I probably saw a lot of niggers."
"If you seen one you didn't know what he was," Mr. Head 20 said, completely exasperated. "A six-month-old child don't know a nigger from anybody else."
"I reckon I'll know a nigger if I see one," the boy said and got up and straightened his slick sharply creased gray hat and went outside to the privy.

They reached the junction some time before the train was due to arrive and stood about two feet from the first set of tracks. Mr. Head carried a paper sack with some biscuits and a can of sardines in it for their lunch. A coarse-looking orange-colored sun coming up behind the east range of mountains was making the sky a dull red behind them, but in front of them it was still gray and they faced a gray transparent moon, hardly stronger than a thumbprint and completely without light. A small tin switch box and a black fuel tank were all there was to mark the place as a junction; the tracks were double and did not converge again until they were hidden behind the bends at either end of the clearing. Trains passing appeared to emerge from a tunnel of trees and, hit for a second by the cold sky, vanish terrified into the woods again. Mr. Head had had to make special arrangements with the ticket agent to have this train stop and he was secretly afraid it would not, in which case, he knew Nelson would say, "I never thought no train was going to stop for you." Under the useless morning moon the tracks looked white and fragile. Both the old man and the child stared ahead as if they were awaiting an apparition.
Then suddenly, before Mr. Head could make up his mind to turn back, there was a deep warning bleat and the train appeared, gliding very slowly, almost silently around the bend of trees about two hundred yards down the track, with one yellow front light shining. Mr. Head was still not certain it would stop and he felt it would make an even bigger idiot of him if it went by

slowly. Both he and Nelson, however, were prepared to ignore the train if it passed them.

The engine charged by, filling their noses with the smell of hot metal and then the second coach came to a stop exactly where they were standing. A conductor with the face of an ancient bloated bulldog was on the step as if he expected them, though he did not look as if it mattered one way or the other to him if they got on or not. "To the right," he said.

Their entry took only a fraction of a second and the train was already speeding on as they entered the quiet car. Most of the travelers were still sleeping, some with their heads hanging off the chair arms, some stretched across two seats, and some sprawled out with their feet in the aisle. Mr. Head saw two unoccupied seats and pushed Nelson toward them. "Get in there by the winder," he said in his normal voice which was very loud at this hour of the morning. "Nobody cares if you sit there because it's nobody in it. Sit right there."

"I heard you," the boy muttered. "It's no use in you yelling," and he sat down and turned his head to the glass. There he saw a pale ghost-like face scowling at him beneath the brim of a pale ghost-like hat. His grandfather, looking quickly too, saw a different ghost, pale but grinning, under a black hat.

Mr. Head sat down and settled himself and took out his ticket and started reading aloud everything that was printed on it. People began to stir. Several woke up and stared at him. "Take off your hat," he said to Nelson and took off his own and put it on his knee. He had a small amount of white hair that had turned tobacco-colored over the years and this lay flat across the back of his head. The front of his head was bald and creased. Nelson took off his hat and put it on his knee and they waited for the conductor to come ask for their tickets.

The man across the aisle from them was spread out over two seats, his feet propped on the window and his head jutting into the aisle. He had on a light blue suit and a yellow shirt unbuttoned at the neck. His eyes had just opened and Mr. Head was ready to introduce himself when the conductor came up from behind and growled, "Tickets."

When the conductor had gone, Mr. Head gave Nelson the return half of his ticket and said, "Now put that in your pocket and don't lose it or you'll have to stay in the city."

"Maybe I will," Nelson said as if this were a reasonable suggestion.

Mr. Head ignored him. "First time this boy has ever been on

a train," he explained to the man across the aisle, who was sitting up now on the edge of his seat with both feet on the floor.

Nelson jerked his hat on again and turned angrily to the window.

"He's never seen anything before," Mr. Head continued. "Ignorant as the day he was born, but I mean for him to get his fill once and for all."

The boy leaned forward, across his grandfather and toward the stranger. "I was born in the city," he said. "I was born there. This is my second trip." He said it in a high positive voice but the man across the aisle didn't look as if he understood. There were heavy purple circles under his eyes.

Mr. Head reached across the aisle and tapped him on the arm. "The thing to do with a boy," he said sagely, "is to show him all it is to show. Don't hold nothing back." 35

"Yeah," the man said. He gazed down at his swollen feet and lifted the left one about ten inches from the floor. After a minute he put it down and lifted the other. All through the car people began to get up and move about and yawn and stretch. Separate voices could be heard here and there and then a general hum. Suddenly Mr. Head's serene expression changed. His mouth almost closed and a light, fierce and cautious both, came into his eyes. He was looking down the length of the car. Without turning, he caught Nelson by the arm and pulled him forward. "Look," he said.

A huge coffee-colored man was coming slowly forward. He had on a light suit and a yellow satin tie with a ruby pin in it. One of his hands rested on his stomach which rode majestically under his buttoned coat, and in the other he held the head of a black walking stick that he picked up and set down with a deliberate outward motion each time he took a step. He was proceeding very slowly, his large brown eyes gazing over the heads of the passengers. He had a small white mustache and white crinkly hair. Behind him there were two young women, both coffee-colored, one in a yellow dress and one in a green. Their progress was kept at the rate of his and they chatted in low throaty voices as they followed him.

Mr. Head's grip was tightening insistently on Nelson's arm. As the procession passed them, the light from a sapphire ring on the brown hand that picked up the cane reflected in Mr. Head's eye, but he did not look up nor did the tremendous man look at him. The group proceeded up the rest of the aisle and out of the car. Mr. Head's grip on Nelson's arm loosened. "What was that?" he asked.

"A man," the boy said and gave him an indignant look as if he were tired of having his intelligence insulted.

"What kind of a man?" Mr. Head persisted, his voice expres- 40 sionless.

"A fat man," Nelson said. He was beginning to feel that he had better be cautious.

"You don't know what kind?" Mr. Head said in a final tone.

"An old man," the boy said and had a sudden foreboding that he was not going to enjoy the day.

"That was a nigger," Mr. Head said and sat back.

Nelson jumped up on the seat and stood looking backward 45 to the end of the car but the Negro had gone.

"I'd of thought you'd know a nigger since you seen so many when you was in the city on your first visit," Mr. Head continued. "That's his first nigger," he said to the man across the aisle.

The boy slid down into the seat. "You said they were black," he said in an angry voice. "You never said they were tan. How do you expect me to know anything when you don't tell me right?"

"You're just ignorant is all," Mr. Head said and he got up and moved over in the vacant seat by the man across the aisle.

Nelson turned backward again and looked where the Negro had disappeared. He felt that the Negro had deliberately walked down the aisle in order to make a fool of him and he hated him with a fierce raw fresh hate; and also, he understood now why his grandfather disliked them. He looked toward the window and the face there seemed to suggest that he might be inadequate to the day's exactions. He wondered if he would even recognize the city when they came to it.

After he had told several stories, Mr. Head realized that the 50 man he was talking to was asleep and he got up and suggested to Nelson that they walk over the train and see the parts of it. He particularly wanted the boy to see the toilet so they went first to the men's room and examined the plumbing. Mr. Head demon-strated the ice-water cooler as if he had invented it and showed Nelson the bowl with the single spigot where the travelers brushed their teeth. They went through several cars and came to the diner.

This was the most elegant car in the train. It was painted a rich egg-yellow and had a wine-colored carpet on the floor. There were wide windows over the tables and great spaces of the rolling view were caught in miniature in the sides of the coffee pots and in the glasses. Three very black Negroes in white suits and aprons were running up and down the aisle, swinging trays and bowing and bending over the travelers eating breakfast. One of them rushed up to Mr. Head and Nelson and said, holding up two fingers, "Space for two!" but Mr. Head replied in a loud voice, "We eaten before we left!"

The waiter wore large brown spectacles that increased the size of his eye whites. "Stan' aside then please," he said with an airy wave of the arm as if he were brushing aside flies.

Neither Nelson nor Mr. Head moved a fraction of an inch. "Look," Mr. Head said.

The near corner of the diner, containing two tables, was set off from the rest by a saffron-colored curtain. One table was set but empty but at the other, facing them, his back to the drape, sat the tremendous Negro. He was speaking in a soft voice to the two women while he buttered a muffin. He had a heavy sad face and his neck bulged over his white collar on either side. "They rope them off," Mr. Head explained. Then he said, "Let's go see the kitchen," and they walked the length of the diner but the black waiter was coming fast behind them.

"Passengers are not allowed in the kitchen!" he said in a 55 haughty voice. "Passengers are NOT allowed in the kitchen!"

Mr. Head stopped where he was and turned. "And there's good reason for that," he shouted into the Negro's chest, "because the cockroaches would run the passengers out!"

All the travelers laughed and Mr. Head and Nelson walked out, grinning. Mr. Head was known at home for his quick wit and Nelson felt a sudden keen pride in him. He realized the old man would be his only support in the strange place they were approaching. He would be entirely alone in the world if he were ever lost from his grandfather. A terrible excitement shook him and he wanted to take hold of Mr. Head's coat and hold on like a child.

As they went back to their seats they could see through the passing windows that the countryside was becoming speckled with small houses and shacks and that a highway ran alongside the train. Cars sped by on it, very small and fast. Nelson felt that there was less breath in the air than there had been thirty minutes ago. The man across the aisle had left and there was no one near for Mr. Head to hold a conversation with so he looked out the window, through his own reflection, and read aloud the names of the buildings they were passing. "The Dixie Chemical Corp!" he announced. "Southern Maid Flour! Dixie Doors! Southern Belle Cotton Products! Patty's Peanut Butter! Southern Mammy Cane Syrup!"

"Hush up!" Nelson hissed.

All over the car people were beginning to get up and take 60 their luggage off the overhead racks. Women were putting on their coats and hats. The conductor stuck his head in the car and snarled, "Firstopppppmry," and Nelson lunged out of his sitting position, trembling. Mr. Head pushed him down by the shoulder.

"Keep your seat," he said in dignified tones. "The first stop is on the edge of town. The second stop is at the main railroad station." He had come by this knowledge on his first trip when he had got off at the first stop and had had to pay a man fifteen cents to take him into the heart of town. Nelson sat back down, very pale. For the first time in his life, he understood that his grandfather was indispensable to him.

The train stopped and let off a few passengers and glided on as if it had never ceased moving. Outside, behind rows of brown rickety houses, a line of blue buildings stood up, and beyond them a pale rose-gray sky faded away to nothing. The train moved into the railroad yard. Looking down, Nelson saw lines and lines of silver tracks multiplying and criss-crossing. Then before he could start counting them, the face in the window started out at him, gray but distinct, and he looked the other way. The train was in the station. Both he and Mr. Head jumped up and ran to the door. Neither noticed that they had left the paper sack with the lunch in it on the seat.

They walked stiffly through the small station and came out of a heavy door into the squall of traffic. Crowds were hurrying to work. Nelson didn't know where to look. Mr. Head leaned against the side of the building and glared in front of him.

Finally Nelson said, "Well, how do you see what all it is to see?"

Mr. Head didn't answer. Then as if the sight of people pass- 65
ing had given him the clue, he said, "You walk," and started off down the street. Nelson followed, steadying his hat. So many sights and sounds were flooding in on him that for the first block he hardly knew what he was seeing. At the second corner, Mr. Head turned and looked behind him at the station they had left, a putty-colored terminal with a concrete dome on top. He thought that if he could keep the dome always in sight, he would be able to get back in the afternoon to catch the train again.

As they walked along Nelson began to distinguish details and take note of the store windows, jammed with every kind of equipment — hardware, drygoods, chicken feed, liquor. They passed one that Mr. Head called his particular attention to where you walked in and sat on a chair with your feet upon two rests and let a Negro polish your shoes. They walked slowly and stopped and stood at the entrances so he could see what went on in each place but they did not go into any of them. Mr. Head was determined not to go into any city store because on his first trip here, he had got lost in a large one and had found his way out only after many people had insulted him.

They came in the middle of the next block to a store that had a weighing machine in front of it and they both in turn stepped up on it and put in a penny and received a ticket. Mr. Head's ticket said, "You weigh 120 pounds. You are upright and brave and all your friends admire you." He put the ticket in his pocket, surprised that the machine should have got his character correct but his weight wrong, for he had weighed on a grain scale not long before and knew he weighed 110. Nelson's ticket said, "You weigh 98 pounds. You have a great destiny ahead of you but beware of dark women." Nelson did not know any women and he weighed only 68 pounds but Mr. Head pointed out that the machine had probably printed the number upside-down, meaning the 9 for a 6.

They walked on and at the end of five blocks the dome of the terminal sank out of sight and Mr. Head turned to the left. Nelson could have stood in front of every store window for an hour if there had not been another more interesting one next to it. Suddenly he said, "I was born here!" Mr. Head turned and looked at him with horror. There was a sweaty brightness about his face. "This is where I come from!" he said.

Mr. Head was appalled. He saw the moment had come for drastic action. "Lemme show you one thing you ain't seen yet," he said and took him to the corner where there was a sewer entrance. "Squat down," he said, "and stick you head in there," and he held the back of the boy's coat while he got down and put his head in the sewer. He drew it back quickly, hearing a gurgling in the depths under the sidewalk. Then Mr. Head explained the sewer system, how the entire city was underlined with it, how it contained all the drainage and was full of rats and how a man could slide into it and be sucked along down endless pitchblack tunnels. At any minute any man in the city might be sucked into the sewer and never heard from again. He described it so well that Nelson was for some seconds shaken. He connected the sewer passages with the entrance to hell and understood for the first time how the world was put together in its lower parts. He drew away from the curb.

Then he said, "Yes, but you can stay away from the holes," and his face took on that stubborn look that was so exasperating to his grandfather. "This is where I come from!" he said.

Mr. Head was dismayed but he only muttered, "You'll get

70

your fill," and they walked on. At the end of two more blocks he turned to the left, feeling that he was circling the dome; and he was correct for in a half-hour they passed in front of the railroad station again. At first Nelson did not notice that he was seeing the same stores twice but when they passed the one where you put your feet on the rests while the Negro polished your shoes, he perceived that they were walking in a circle.

"We done been here!" he shouted. "I don't believe you know where you're at!"

"The direction just slipped my mind for a minute," Mr. Head said and they turned down a different street. He still did not intend to let the dome get too far away and after two blocks in their new direction, he turned to the left. This street contained two- and three-story wooden dwellings. Anyone passing on the sidewalk could see into the rooms and Mr. Head, glancing through one window, saw a woman lying on an iron bed, looking out, with a sheet pulled over her. Her knowing expression shook him. A fierce-looking boy on a bicycle came driving down out of nowhere and he had to jump to the side to keep from being hit. "It's nothing to them if they knock you down," he said. "You better keep closer to me."

They walked on for some time on streets like this before he remembered to turn again. The houses they were passing now were all unpainted and the wood in them looked rotten; the street between was narrower. Nelson saw a colored man. Then another. Then another. "Niggers live in these houses," he observed.

"Well come on and we'll go somewheres else," Mr. Head said. 75 "We didn't come to look at niggers," and they turned down another street but they continued to see Negroes everywhere. Nelson's skin began to prickle and they stepped along at a faster pace in order to leave the neighborhood as soon as possible. There were colored men in their undershirts standing in the doors and colored women rocking on the sagging porches. Colored children played in the gutters and stopped what they were doing to look at them. Before long they began to pass rows of stores with colored customers in them but they didn't pause at the entrances of these. Black eyes in black faces were watching them from every direction. "Yes," Mr. Head said, "this is where you were born — right here with all these niggers."

Nelson scowled. "I think you done got us lost," he said.

Mr. Head swung around sharply and looked for the dome. It was nowhere in sight. "I ain't got us lost either," he said. "You're just tired of walking."

"I ain't tired, I'm hungry," Nelson said. "Give me a biscuit."

They discovered then that they had lost the lunch.

"You were the one holding the sack," Nelson said. "I would have kepaholt of it."   80

"If you want to direct this trip, I'll go on by myself and leave you right here," Mr. Head said and was pleased to see the boy turn white. However, he realized they were lost and drifting farther every minute from the station. He was hungry himself and beginning to be thirsty and since they had been in the colored neighborhood, they had both begun to sweat. Nelson had on his shoes and he was unaccustomed to them. The concrete sidewalks were very hard. They both wanted to find a place to sit down but this was impossible and they kept on walking, the boy muttering under his breath, "First you lost the sack and then you lost the way," and Mr. Head growling from time to time, "Anybody wants to be from this nigger heaven can be from it!"

By now the sun was well forward in the sky. The odor of dinners cooking drifted out to them. The Negroes were all at their doors to see them pass. "Whyn't you ast one of these niggers the way?" Nelson said. "You got us lost."

"This is where you were born," Mr. Head said. "You can ast one yourself if you want to."

Nelson was afraid of the colored men and he didn't want to be laughed at by the colored children. Up ahead he saw a large colored woman leaning in a doorway that opened onto the sidewalk. Her hair stood straight out from her head for about four inches all around and she was resting on bare brown feet that turned pink at the sides. She had on a pink dress that showed her exact shape. As they came abreast of her, she lazily lifted one hand to her head and her fingers disappeared into her hair.

Nelson stopped. He felt his breath drawn up by the woman's   85
dark eyes. "How do you get back to town?" he said in a voice that did not sound like his own.

After a minute she said, "You in town now," in a rich low tone that made Nelson feel as if a cool spray had been turned on him.

"How do you get back to the train?" he said in the same reed-like voice.

"You can catch you a car," she said.

He understood she was making fun of him but he was too paralyzed even to scowl. He stood drinking in every detail of her. His eyes traveled up from her great knees to her forehead and then made a triangular path from the glistening sweat on her neck down and across her tremendous bosom and over her bare

arm back to where her fingers lay hidden in her hair. He suddenly wanted her to reach down and pick him up and draw him
against her and then he wanted to feel her breath on his face. He
wanted to look down and down into her eyes while she held him
tighter and tighter. He had never had such a feeling before. He
felt as if he were reeling down through a pitchblack tunnel.

"You can go a block down yonder and catch you a car take   90
you to the railroad station, Sugarpie," she said.

Nelson would have collapsed at her feet if Mr. Head had not
pulled him roughly away. "You act like you don't have any sense!"
the old man growled.

They hurried down the street and Nelson did not look back
at the woman. He pushed his hat sharply forward over his face
which was already burning with shame. The sneering ghost he
had seen in the train window and all the foreboding feelings he
had on the way returned to him and he remembered that his
ticket from the scale had said to beware of dark women and that
his grandfather's had said he was upright and brave. He took
hold of the old man's hand, a sign of dependence that he seldom
showed.

They headed down the street toward the car tracks where a
long yellow rattling trolley was coming. Mr. Head had never
boarded a strectcar and he let that one pass. Nelson was silent.
From time to time his mouth trembled slightly but his grandfather, occupied with his own problems, paid him no attention.
They stood on the corner and neither looked at the Negroes who
were passing, going about their business just as if they had been
white, except that most of them stopped and eyed Mr. Head and
Nelson. It occurred to Mr. Head that since the streetcar ran on
tracks, they could simply follow the tracks. He gave Nelson a
slight push and explained that they would follow the tracks on
into the railroad station, walking, and they set off.

Presently to their great relief they began to see white people
again and Nelson sat down on the sidewalk against the wall of a
building. "I got to rest myself some," he said. "You lost the sack
and the direction. You can just wait on me to rest myself."

"There's the tracks in front of us," Mr. Head said. "All we got   95
to do is keep them in sight and you could have remembered the
sack as good as me. This is where you were born. This is your old
home town. This is your second trip. You ought to know how to
do," and he squatted down and continued in this vein but the
boy, easing his burning feet out of his shoes, did not answer.

"And standing there grinning like a chim-pan-zee while a
nigger woman gives you directions. Great Gawd!" Mr. Head said.

"I never said I was nothing but born here," the boy said in a shaky voice. "I never said I would or wouldn't like it. I never said I wanted to come. I only said I was born here and I never had nothing to do with that. I want to go home. I never wanted to come in the first place. It was all your big idea. How you know you ain't following the tracks in the wrong direction?"

This last had occurred to Mr. Head too. "All these people are white," he said.

"We ain't passed here before," Nelson said. This was a neighborhood of brick buildings that might have been lived in or might not. A few empty automobiles were parked along the curb and there was an occasional passerby. The heat of the pavement came up through Nelson's thin suit. His eyelids began to droop, and after a few minutes his head tilted forward. His shoulders twitched once or twice and then he fell over on his side and lay sprawled in an exhausted fit of sleep.

Mr. Head watched him silently. He was very tired himself but they could not both sleep at the same time and he could not have slept anyway because he did not know where he was. In a few minutes Nelson would wake up, refreshed by his sleep and very cocky, and would begin complaining that he had lost the sack and the way. You'd have a mighty sorry time if I wasn't here, Mr. Head thought; and then another idea occurred to him. He looked at the sprawled figure for several minutes; presently he stood up. He justified what he was going to do on the grounds that it is sometimes necessary to teach a child a lesson he won't forget, particularly when the child is always reasserting his position with some new impudence. He walked without a sound to the corner about twenty feet away and sat down on a covered garbage can in the alley where he could look out and watch Nelson wake up alone.

The boy was dozing fitfully, half conscious of vague noises and black forms moving up from some dark part of him into the light. His face worked in his sleep and he had pulled his knees up under his chin. The sun shed a dull dry light on the narrow street; everything looked like exactly what it was. After a while Mr. Head, hunched like an old monkey on the garbage can lid, decided that if Nelson didn't wake up soon, he would make a loud noise by bamming his foot against the can. He looked at his watch and discovered that it was two o'clock. Their train left at six and the possibility of missing it was too awful for him to think of. He kicked his foot backwards on the can and a hollow boom reverberated in the alley.

Nelson shot up onto his feet with a shout. He looked where

his grandfather should have been and stared. He seemed to whirl several times and then, picking up his feet and throwing his head back, he dashed down the street like a wild maddened pony. Mr. Head jumped off the can and galloped after but the child was almost out of sight. He saw a streak of gray disappearing diagonally a block ahead. He ran as fast as he could, looking both ways down every intersection, but without sight of him again. Then as he passed the third intersection, completely winded, he saw about half a block down the street a scene that stopped him altogether. He crouched behind a trash box to watch and get his bearings.

Nelson was sitting with both legs spread out and by his side lay an elderly woman, screaming. Groceries were scattered about the sidewalk. A crowd of women had already gathered to see justice done and Mr. Head distinctly heard the old woman on the pavement shout, "You've broken my ankle and your daddy'll pay for it! Every nickel! Police! Police!" Several of the women were plucking at Nelson's shoulder but the boy seemed too dazed to get up.

Something forced Mr. Head from behind the trash box and forward, but only at a creeping pace. He had never in his life been accosted by a policeman. The women were milling around Nelson as if they might suddenly all dive on him at once and tear him to pieces, and the old woman continued to scream that her ankle was broken and to call for an officer. Mr. Head came on so slowly that he could have been taking a backward step after each forward one, but when he was about ten feet away, Nelson saw him and sprang. The child caught him around the hips and clung panting against him.

The women all turned on Mr. Head. The injured one sat up   105 and shouted, "You sir! You'll pay every penny of my doctor's bill that your boy has caused. He's a juve-nile delinquent! Where is an officer? Somebody take this man's name and address!"

Mr. Head was trying to detach Nelson's fingers from the flesh in the back of his legs. The old man's head had lowered itself into his collar like a turtle's; his eyes were glazed with fear and caution.

"Your boy has broken my ankle!" the old woman shouted. "Police!"

Mr. Head sensed the approach of the policeman from behind. He stared straight ahead at the women who were massed in their fury like a solid wall to block his escape. "This is not my boy," he said. "I never seen him before."

He felt Nelson's fingers fall out of his flesh.

The women dropped back, staring at him with horror, as if 110
they were so repulsed by a man who would deny his own image
and likeness that they could not bear to lay hands on him. Mr.
Head walked on, through a space they silently cleared, and left
Nelson behind. Ahead of him he saw nothing but a hollow tunnel
that had once been the street.

The boy remained standing where he was, his neck craned
forward and his hands hanging by his sides. His hat was jammed
on his head so that there were no longer any creases in it. The
injured woman got up and shook her fist at him and the others
gave him pitying looks, but he didn't notice any of them. There
was no policeman in sight.

In a minute he began to move mechanically, making no
effort to catch up with his grandfather but merely following at
about twenty paces. They walked on for five blocks in this way.
Mr. Head's shoulders were sagging and his neck hung forward at
such an angle that it was not visible from behind. He was afraid
to turn his head. Finally he cut a short hopeful glance over his
shoulder. Twenty feet behind him, he saw two small eyes piercing
into his back like pitchfork prongs.

The boy was not of a forgiving nature but this was the first
time he had ever had anything to forgive. Mr. Head had never
disgraced himself before. After two more blocks, he turned and
called over his shoulder in a high desperately gay voice, "Let's us
go get us a Co' Cola somewheres!"

Nelson, with a dignity he had never shown before, turned
and stood with his back to his grandfather.

Mr. Head began to feel the depth of his denial. His face as 115
they walked on became all hollows and bare ridges. He saw
nothing they were passing but he perceived that they had lost the
car tracks. There was no dome to be seen anywhere and the
afternoon was advancing. He knew that if dark overtook them in
the city, they would be beaten and robbed. The speed of God's
justice was only what he expected for himself, but he could not
stand to think that his sins would be visited upon Nelson and that
even now, he was leading the boy to his doom.

They continued to walk on block after block through an
endless section of small brick houses until Mr. Head almost fell
over a water spigot sticking up about six inches off the edge of a
grass plot. He had not had a drink of water since early morning
but he felt he did not deserve it now. Then he thought that Nelson
would be thirsty and they would both drink and be brought

together. He squatted down and put his mouth to the nozzle and turned a cold stream of water into his throat. Then he called out in the high desperate voice, "Come on and getcher some water!"

This time the child stared through him for nearly sixty seconds. Mr. Head got up and walked on as if he had drunk poison. Nelson, though he had not had water since some he had drunk out of a paper cup on the train, passed by the spigot, disdaining to drink where his grandfather had. When Mr. Head realized this, he lost all hope. His face in the waning afternoon light looked ravaged and abandoned. He could feel the boy's steady hate, traveling at an even pace behind him and he knew that (if by some miracle they escaped being murdered in the city) it would continue just that way for the rest of his life. He knew that now he was wandering into a black strange place where nothing was like it had ever been before, a long old age without respect and an end that would be welcome because it would be the end.

As for Nelson, his mind had frozen around his grandfather's treachery as if he were trying to preserve it intact to present at the final judgment. He walked without looking to one side or the other, but every now and then his mouth would twitch and this was when he felt, from some remote place inside himself, a black mysterious form reach up as if it would melt his frozen vision in one hot grasp.

The sun dropped down behind a row of houses and hardly noticing, they passed into an elegant suburban section where mansions were set back from the road by lawns with birdbaths on them. Here everything was entirely deserted. For blocks they didn't pass even a dog. The big white houses were like partially submerged icebergs in the distance. There were no sidewalks, only drives, and these wound around and around in endless ridiculous circles. Nelson made no move to come nearer to Mr. Head. The old man felt that if he saw a sewer entrance he would drop down into it and let himself be carried away; and he could imagine the boy standing by, watching with only a slight interest, while he disappeared.

A loud bark jarred him to attention and he looked up to see   120
a fat man approaching with two bulldogs. He waved both arms like someone shipwrecked on a desert island. "I'm lost!" he called. "I'm lost and can't find my way and me and this boy have got to catch this train and I can't find the station. Oh Gawd I'm lost! Oh help me Gawd I'm lost!"

The man, who was bald-headed and had on golf knickers, asked him what train he was trying to catch and Mr. Head began to get out his tickets, trembling so violently he could hardly hold them. Nelson had come up to within fifteen feet and stood watching.

"Well," the fat man said, giving him back the tickets, "you won't have time to get back to town to make this but you can catch it at the suburb stop. That's three blocks from here," and he began explaining how to get there.

Mr. Head stared as if he were slowly returning from the dead and when the man had finished and gone off with the dogs jumping at his heels, he turned to Nelson and said breathlessly, "We're going to get home!"

The child was standing about ten feet away, his face bloodless under the gray hat. His eyes were triumphantly cold. There was no light in them, no feeling, no interest. He was merely there, a small figure, waiting. Home was nothing to him.

Mr. Head turned slowly. He felt he knew now what time   125
would be like without seasons and what heat would be like without light and what man would be like without salvation. He didn't care if he never made the train and if it had not been for what suddenly caught his attention, like a cry out of the gathering dusk, he might have forgotten there was a station to go to.

He had not walked five hundred yards down the road when he saw, within reach of him, the plaster figure of a Negro sitting bent over on a low yellow brick fence that curved around a wide lawn. The Negro was about Nelson's size and he was pitched forward at an unsteady angle because the putty that held him to the wall had cracked. One of his eyes was entirely white and he held a piece of brown watermelon.

Mr. Head stood looking at him silently until Nelson stopped at a little distance. Then as the two of them stood there, Mr. Head breathed, "An artificial nigger!"

It was not possible to tell if the artificial Negro were meant to be young or old; he looked too miserable to be either. He was meant to look happy because his mouth was stretched up at the corners but the chipped eye and the angle he was cocked at gave him a wild look of misery instead.

"An artificial nigger!" Nelson repeated in Mr. Head's exact tone.

The two of them stood there with their necks forward at   130
almost the same angle and their shoulders curved in almost exactly the same way and their hands trembling identically in their pockets. Mr. Head looked like an ancient child and Nelson like a miniature old man. They stood gazing at the artificial

Negro as if they were faced with some great mystery, some monument to another's victory that brought them together in their
common defeat. They could both feel it dissolving their differences like an action of mercy. Mr. Head had never known
before what mercy felt like because he had been too good to
deserve any, but he felt he knew now. He looked at Nelson and
understood that he must say something to the child to show that
he was still wise and in the look the boy returned he saw a hungry
need for that assurance. Nelson's eyes seemed to implore him to
explain once and for all the mystery of existence.

Mr. Head opened his lips to make a lofty statement and
heard himself say, "They ain't got enough real ones here. They
got to have an artificial one."

After a second, the boy nodded with a strange shivering
about his mouth, and said, "Let's go home before we get ourselves
lost again."

Their train glided into the suburb stop just as they reached
the station and they boarded it together, and ten minutes before
it was due to arrive at the junction, they went to the door and
stood ready to jump off it if it did not stop; but it did, just as the
moon, restored to its full splendor, sprang from a cloud and
flooded the clearing with light. As they stepped off, the sage
grass was shivering gently in shades of silver and the clinkers
under their feet glittered with a fresh black light. The treetops,
fencing the junction like the protecting walls of a garden, were
darker than the sky which was hung with gigantic white clouds
illuminated like lanterns.

Mr. Head stood very still and felt the action of mercy touch
him again but this time he knew that there were no words in the
world that could name it. He understood that it grew out of
agony, which is not denied to any man and which is given in
strange ways to children. He understood it was all a man could
carry into death to give his Maker and he suddenly burned with
shame that he had so little of it to take with him. He stood
appalled, judging himself with the thoroughness of God, while
the action of mercy covered his pride like a flame and consumed
it. He had never thought himself a great sinner before but he saw
now that his true depravity had been hidden from him lest it
cause him despair. He realized that he was forgiven for sins from
the beginning of time, when he had conceived in his own heart
the sin of Adam, until the present, when he had denied poor
Nelson. He saw that no sin was too monstrous for him to claim as
his own, and since God loved in proportion as He forgave, he felt
ready at that instant to enter Paradise.

Nelson, composing his expression under the shadow of his 135
hat brim, watched him with a mixture of fatigue and suspicion,
but as the train glided past them and disappeared like a frightened serpent into the woods, even his face lightened and he
muttered, "I'm glad I've went once, but I'll never go back again!"

SAMUEL BECKETT   (b. 1906)

Krapp's Last Tape

A Play in One Act

SCENE: *A late evening in the future.*

*Krapp's den. Front center a small table, the two drawers of which open towards
audience. Sitting at the table, facing front, i.e. across from the drawers, a wearish
old man: Krapp.*

*Rusty black narrow trousers too short for him. Rusty black sleeveless waist-
coat, four capacious pockets. Heavy silver watch and chain. Grimy white shirt
open at neck, no collar. Surprising pair of dirty white boots, size ten at least, very
narrow and pointed.*

White face. Purple nose. Disordered gray hair. Unshaven.

Very near-sighted (but unspectacled). Hard of hearing.

Cracked voice. Distinctive intonation.

Laborious walk.

*On the table a tape-recorder with microphone and a number of cardboard
boxes containing reels of recorded tapes.*

*Table and immediately adjacent area in strong white light. Rest of stage in
darkness.*

*Krapp remains a moment motionless, heaves a great sigh, looks at his watch,
fumbles in his pockets, takes out an envelope, puts it back, fumbles, takes out a
small bunch of keys, raises it to his eyes, chooses a key, gets up and moves to front of
table. He stoops, unlocks first drawer, peers into it, feels about inside it, takes out a
reel of tape, peers at it, puts it back, locks drawer, unlocks second drawer, peers
into it, feels about inside it, takes out a large banana, peers at it, locks drawer,
puts keys back in his pocket. He turns, advances to edge of stage, halts, strokes
banana, peels it, drops skin at his feet, puts end of banana in his mouth and
remains motionless, staring vacuously before him. Finally he bites off the end,
turns aside, and begins pacing to and fro at edge of stage, in the light, i.e. not more
than four or five paces either way, meditatively eating banana. He treads on skin,
slips, nearly falls, recovers himself, stoops and peers at skin and finally pushes it,
still stooping, with his foot over the edge of stage into pit. He resumes his pacing,
finishes banana, returns to table, sits down, remains a moment motionless, heaves
a great sigh, takes keys from his pockets, raises them to his eyes, chooses key, gets up
and moves to front of table, unlocks second drawer, takes out a second large
banana, peers at it, locks drawer, puts back keys in his pocket, turns, advances to
edge of stage, halts, strokes banana, peels it, tosses skin into pit, puts end of
banana in his mouth, and remains motionless, staring vacuously before him.*

Finally he has an idea, puts banana in his waistcoat pocket, the end emerging, and goes with all the speed he can muster backstage into darkness. Ten seconds. Loud pop of cork. Fifteen seconds. He comes back into light carrying an old ledger and sits down at table. He lays ledger on table, wipes his mouth, wipes his hands on the front of his waistcoat, brings them smartly together and rubs them.

Krapp *(briskly):* Ah! (*He bends over ledger, turns the pages, finds the entry he wants, reads.*) Box . . . thrree . . . spool . . . five. (*He raises his head and stares front. With relish.*) Spool! (*Pause.*) Spooool! (*Happy smile. Pause. He bends over table, starts peering and poking at the boxes.*) Box . . . thrree . . . thrree . . . four . . . two . . . (*with surprise*) nine! good God! . . . seven . . . ah! the little rascal! (*He takes up box, peers at it.*) Box thrree. (*He lays it on table, opens it, and peers at spools inside.*) Spool . . . (*he peers at ledger*) . . . five (*he peers at spools*) . . . five . . . five! . . . ah! the little scoundrel! (*He takes out a spool, peers at it.*) Spool five. (*He lays it on table, closes box three, puts it back with the others, takes up the spool.*) Box thrree, spool five. (*He bends, over the machine, looks up. With relish.*) Spooool! (*Happy smile. He bends, loads spool on machine, rubs his hands.*) Ah! (*He peers at ledger, reads entry at foot of page.*) Mother at rest at last . . . Hm . . . The black ball . . . (*He raises his head, stares blankly front. Puzzled.*) Black ball? . . . (*He peers again at ledger, reads.*) The dark nurse . . . (*He raises his head, broods, peers again at ledger, reads.*) Slight improvement in bowel condition . . . Hm . . . Memorable . . . what? (*He peers closer.*) Equinox, memorable equinox. (*He raises his head, stares blankly front. Puzzled.*) Memorable Equinox? . . . (*Pause. He shrugs his shoulders, peers again at ledger, reads.*) Farewell to — (*he turns the page*) — love.

He raises his head, broods, bends over machine, switches on, and assumes listening posture; i.e. leaning forward, elbows on table, hand cupping ear towards machine, face front.

Tape *(strong voice, rather pompous, clearly Krapp's at a much earlier time):* Thirty-nine today, sound as a — (*Settling himself more comfortably he knocks one of the boxes off the table, curses, switches off, sweeps boxes and ledger violently to the ground, winds tape back to beginning, switches on, resumes posture.*) Thirty-nine today, sound as a bell, apart from my old weakness, and intellectually I have now every reason to suspect at the . . . (*hesitates*) . . . crest of the wave — or thereabouts. Celebrated the awful occasion, as in recent years, quietly at the Winehouse. Not a soul. Sat before the fire with closed eyes, separating the grain from the husks. Jotted down a few notes, on the back of an envelope. Good to be back in my den, in my old rags. Have just eaten I regret to say three bananas and only with difficulty refrained from a fourth. Fatal things for a man with my condition. (*Vehemently.*) Cut 'em out! (*Pause.*) The new light above my table is a great improvement. With all this darkness round me I feel less alone. (*Pause.*) In a way. (*Pause.*) I love to get up and move about in it, then back here to . . . (*hesitates*) . . . me. (*Pause.*) Krapp.

Pause.

The grain, now what I wonder do I mean by that, I mean . . . (*hesitates*) . . . I suppose I mean those things worth having when all the dust has — when all *my* dust has settled. I close my eyes and try and imagine them.

Pause. Krapp closes his eyes briefly.

Extraordinary silence this evening, I strain my ears and do not hear a sound. Old Miss McGlome always sings at this hour. But not tonight. Songs of her girlhood, she says. Hard to think of her as a girl. Wonderful woman though. Connaught, I fancy. (*Pause.*) Shall I sing when I am her age, if I ever am? No. (*Pause.*) Did I sing as a boy? No. (*Pause.*) Did I ever sing? No.

Pause.

Just been listening to an old year, passages at random. I did not check in the book, but it must be at least ten or twelve years ago. At that time I think I was still living on and off with Bianca in Kedar Street. Well out of that, Jesus yes! Hopeless business. (*Pause.*) Not much about her, apart from a tribute to her eyes. Very warm. I suddenly saw them again. (*Pause.*) Incomparable! (*Pause.*) Ah well . . . (*Pause.*) These old P.M.s are gruesome, but I often find them — (*Krapp switches off, broods, switches on*) — a help before embarking on a new . . . (*hesitates*) . . . retrospect. Hard to believe I was ever that young whelp. The voice! Jesus! And the aspirations! (*Brief laugh in which Krapp joins.*) And the resolutions! (*Brief laugh in which Krapp joins.*) To drink less, in particular. (*Brief laugh of Krapp alone.*) Statistics. Seventeen hundred hours, out of the preceding eight thousand odd, consumed on licensed premises alone. More than 20%, say 40% of his waking life. (*Pause.*) Plans for a less . . . (*hesitates*) . . . engrossing sexual life. Last illness of his father. Flagging pursuit of happiness.

Unattainable laxation. Sneers at what he calls his youth and thanks to God that it's over. (*Pause.*) False ring there. (*Pause.*) Shadows of the opus . . . magnum. Closing with a — (*brief laugh*) — yelp to Providence. (*Prolonged laugh in which Krapp joins.*) What remains of all that misery? A girl in a shabby green coat, on a railway-station platform? No?

Pause.

When I look —

Krapp switches off, broods, looks at his watch, gets up, goes backstage into darkness. Ten seconds. Pop of cork. Ten seconds. Second cork. Ten seconds. Third cork. Ten seconds. Brief burst of quavering song.

Krapp (sings): Now the day is over,
Night is drawing nigh-igh,
Shadows —°

Fit of coughing. He comes back into light, sits down, wipes his mouth, switches on, resumes his listening posture.

Tape: — back on the year that is gone, with what I hope is perhaps a glint of the old eye to come, there is of course the house on the canal where mother lay a-dying, in the late autumn, after her long viduity (*Krapp gives a start*), and the — (*Krapp switches off, winds back tape a little, bends his ear closer to machine, switches on*) — a — dying, after her long viduity, and the —

Krapp switches off, raises his head, stares blankly before him. His lips move in the syllables of "viduity." No sound. He gets up, goes backstage into darkness, comes back with an enormous dictionary, lays it on table, sits down and looks up the word.

Krapp (reading from dictionary): State — or condition of being — or remaining — a widow — or widower. (*Looks up. Puzzled.*) Being — or remaining? . . . (*Pause. He peers again at dictionary. Reading.*) "Deep weeds of viduity" . . . Also of an animal, especially a bird . . . the vidua or weaver-bird . . . Black plumage of male . . . (*He looks up. With relish.*) The vidua-bird!

Pause. He closes dictionary, switches on, resumes listening posture.

Now . . . Shadows: From the hymn "Now the Day Is Over" by Sabine Baring-Gould (1834–1924), who also wrote "Onward, Christian Soldiers."

Tape: — bench by the weir from where I could see her window. There I sat, in the biting wind, wishing she were gone. (*Pause.*) Hardly a soul, just a few regulars, nursemaids, infants, old men, dogs. I got to know them quite well — oh by appearance of course I mean! One dark young beauty I recollect particularly, all white and starch, incomparable bosom, with a big black hooded perambulator, most funereal thing. Whenever I looked in her direction she had her eyes on me. And yet when I was bold enough to speak to her — not having been introduced — she threatened to call a policeman. As if I had designs on her virtue! (*Laugh. Pause.*) The face she had! The eyes! Like . . . (*hesitates*) . . . chrysolite! (*Pause.*) Ah well . . . (*Pause.*) I was there when — (*Krapp switches off, broods, switches on again*) — the blind went down, one of those dirty brown roller affairs, throwing a ball for a little white dog, as chance would have it. I happened to look up and there it was. All over and done with, at last. I sat on for a few moments with the ball in my hand and the dog yelping and pawing at me. (*Pause.*) Moments. Her moments, my moments. (*Pause.*) The dog's moments. (*Pause.*) In the end I held it out to him and he took it in his mouth, gently, gently. A small, old, black, hard, solid rubber ball. (*Pause.*) I shall feel it, in my hand, until my dying day. (*Pause.*) I might have kept it. (*Pause.*) But I gave it to the dog.

Pause.

Ah well . . .

Pause.

Spiritually a year of profound gloom and indigence until that memorable night in March, at the end of the jetty, in the howling wind, never to be forgotten, when suddenly I saw the whole thing. The vision, at last. This I fancy is what I have chiefly to record this evening, against the day when my work will be done and perhaps no place left in my memory, warm or cold, for the miracle that . . . (*hesitates*) . . . for the fire that set it alight. What I suddenly saw then was this, that the belief I had been going on all my life, namely — (*Krapp switches off impatiently, winds tape forward, switches on again*) — great granite rocks the foam flying up in the light of the lighthouse and the wind-gauge spinning like a propellor, clear to me at last that the dark I have always struggled to keep under is in reality my most — (*Krapp curses, switches off, winds tape forward, switches on again*) — unshatterable association until my dissolution of storm and night with the light of the understanding and the fire — (*Krapp curses louder, switches off, winds tape forward, switches on again*) — my face in her breasts and my hand on her. We lay there without moving. But under us all moved, and moved us, gently, up and down, and from side to side.

Pause.

Past midnight. Never knew such silence. The earth might be uninhabited.

Pause.

Here I end —

Krapp switches off, winds tape back, switches on again.

— upper lake, with the punt, bathed off the bank, then pushed out into the stream and drifted. She lay stretched out on the floorboards with her hands under her head and her eyes closed. Sun blazing down, bit of a breeze, water nice and lively. I noticed a scratch on her thigh and asked her how she came by it. Picking gooseberries, she said. I said again I thought it was hopeless and no good going on, and she agreed, without opening her eyes. (*Pause.*) I asked her to look at me and after a few moments — (*Pause*) — after a few moments she did, but the eyes just slits, because of the glare. I bent over her to get them in the shadow and they opened. (*Pause. Low.*) Let me in. (*Pause.*) We drifted in among the flags and stuck. The way they went down, sighing, before the stem! (*Pause.*) I lay down across her with my face in her breasts and my hand on her. We lay there without moving. But under us all moved, and moved us, gently, up and down, and from side to side.

Pause.

Past midnight. Never knew such silence. The earth might be uninhabited.

Pause.

Here I end —

Krapp switches off, winds tape back, switches on again.

— upper lake, with the punt, bathed off the bank, then pushed out into the stream and drifted. She lay stretched out on the floorboards with her hands under her head and her eyes closed. Sun blazing down, bit of a breeze, water nice and lively. I noticed a scratch on her thigh and asked her how she came by it. Picking gooseberries, she said. I said again I thought it was hopeless and no good going on, and she agreed; without opening her eyes. (*Pause.*) I asked her to look at me and after a few moments — (*Pause*) — after a few moments she did, but the eyes just slits, because of the glare. I bent over her to get them in the shadow and they opened. (*Pause. Low.*) Let me in. (*Pause.*) We drifted in among the flags and stuck. The way they went down, sighing, before the stem! (*Pause.*) I lay down across her with my face in her breasts and my hand on her. We lay there without moving. But under us all moved, and moved us, gently, up and down, and from side to side.

Pause.

Past midnight. Never knew —

Krapp switches off, broods. Finally he fumbles in his pockets, encounters the banana, takes it out, peers at it, puts it back, fumbles, brings out the envelope, fumbles, puts back envelope, looks at his watch, gets up and goes backstage into darkness. Ten seconds. Sound of bottle against glass, then brief siphon. Ten seconds. Bottle against glass alone. Ten seconds. He comes back a little unsteadily into light, goes to front of table, takes out keys, raises them to his eyes, chooses key, unlocks first drawer, peers into it, feels about inside, takes out reel, peers at it, locks drawer, puts keys back in his pocket, goes and sits down, takes reel off machine, lays it on dictionary, loads virgin reel on machine, takes envelope from his pocket, consults back of it, lays it on table, switches on, clears his throat, and begins to record.

Krapp: Just been listening to that stupid bastard I took myself for thirty years ago, hard to believe I was ever as bad as that. Thank God that's all done with anyway. (*Pause.*) The eyes she had! (*Broods, realizes he is recording silence, switches off, broods. Finally.*) Everything there, everything, all the — (*Realizes this is not being recorded, switches on.*) Everything there, everything on this old muckball, all the light and dark and famine and feasting of . . . (*hesitates*) . . . the ages! (*In a shout.*) Yes! (*Pause.*) Let that go! Jesus! Take his mind off his homework! Jesus! (*Pause. Weary.*) Ah well, maybe he was right. (*Pause.*) Maybe he was right. (*Broods. Realizes. Switches off. Consults envelope.*) Pah! (*Crumples it and throws it away. Broods. Switches on.*) Nothing to

say, not a squeak. What's a year now? The sour cud and the
iron stool. (*Pause.*) Revelled in the word spool. (*With relish.*)
Spooool! Happiest moment of the past half million. (*Pause.*)
Seventeen copies sold, of which eleven at trade price to free
circulating libraries beyond the seas. Getting known. (*Pause.*)
One pound six and something, eight I have little doubt.
(*Pause.*) Crawled out once or twice, before the summer was
cold. Sat shivering in the park, drowned in dreams and burn-
ing to be gone. Not a soul (*Pause.*) Last fancies. (*Vehemently.*)
Keep 'em under! (*Pause.*) Scalded the eyes out of me reading
Effie again, a page a day, with tears again. Effie . . . (*Pause.*)
Could have been happy with her, up there on the Baltic, and
the pines, and the dunes. (*Pause.*) Could I? (*Pause.*) And she?
(*Pause.*) Pah! (*Pause.*) Fanny came in a couple of times. Bony
old ghost of a whore. Couldn't do much, but I suppose better
than a kick in the crutch. The last time wasn't so bad. How do
you manage it, she said, at your age? I told her I'd been
saving up for her all my life. (*Pause.*) Went to Vespers once,
like when I was in short trousers. (*Pause. Sings.*)

Now the day is over.
Night is drawing nigh-igh,
Shadows — (*coughing, then almost inaudible*) — of the evening
Steal across the sky.

(*Gasping.*) Went to sleep and fell off the pew. (*Pause.*) Sometimes
wondered in the night if a last effort mightn't — (*Pause.*) Ah
finish your booze now and get to your bed. Go on with this
drivel in the morning. Or leave it at that. (*Pause.*) Leave it at
that. (*Pause.*) Lie propped up in the dark — and wander. Be
again in the dingle on a Christmas Eve, gathering holly, the
red-berried. (*Pause.*) Be again on Croghan on a Sunday morning, in the haze, with the bitch, stop and listen to the bells.
(*Pause.*) And so on. (*Pause.*) Be again, be again. (*Pause.*) All that
old misery. (*Pause.*) Once wasn't enough for you. (*Pause.*) Lie
down across her.

*Long pause. He suddenly bends over machine, switches off, wrenches off tape,
throws it away, puts on the other, winds it forward to the passage he wants,
switches on, listens staring front.*

Tape: — gooseberries, she said. I said again I thought it was
        hopeless and no good going on, and she agreed, without
        opening her eyes. (*Pause.*) I asked her to look at me and after

a few moments — (*pause*) — after a few moments she did, but the eyes just slits, because of the glare. I bent over her to get them in the shadow and they opened. (*Pause. Low.*) Let me in. (*Pause.*) We drifted in among the flags and stuck. The way they went down, sighing, before the stem! (*Pause.*) I lay down across her with my face in her breasts and my hand on her. We lay there without moving. But under us all moved, and moved us, gently, up and down, and from side to side.

Pause. Krapp's lips move. No sound.

Past midnight. Never knew such silence. The earth might be uninhabited.

Pause.

Here I end this reel. Box — (*pause*) — three, spool — (*pause*) — five. (*Pause.*) Perhaps my best years are gone. When there was a chance of happiness. But I wouldn't want them back. Not with the fire in me now. No, I wouldn't want them back.

Krapp motionless staring before him. The tape runs on in silence.

Curtain

4

Ideas: Evoking a Challenge

Feeling, character, change, growth: These are major elements of imaginative literature. And the importance of each is matched only by that of ideas — ideas that, in infinitely various ways, are stirred in readers as they engage with feelings, characters, change, and growth. A central idea stimulated by Joyce's "Araby" (p. 294) is that daily life in twentieth-century Dublin offers nothing to sustain and nourish an obsessively idealizing nature. That idea nowhere receives explicit statement in the story; we generate it, as readers, from details of feeling.

How exactly does this happen? Early in the story we see that Dublin's young are taught to be suspicious of — hostile toward — people different from themselves (see the aunt's attitude toward Freemasons). This is certainly not a liberating experience for anybody, young or old. We see, further, that Dublin's culture — street singers to pop poetry recitals — seems to express repugnance for things as they are. Performers and their audiences turn away from daily life to a pseudoromantic past (ancient Ireland or Arabia). We see youngsters being packed into religious retreats to be taught shame at an age when vital physical energies and appetites are burgeoning. Gestures, behavior, even colors accent the sense of darkness and repression. It's not a huge jump when we move, as readers, from awareness of the nature of this atmosphere to the reflection that Dublin, as we see it here, stifles idealism in the young. We may express that idea to ourselves in the form of a general proposition, but it emerges first as a developing response to a body of feeling within living characters.

Our obligation is to bring this idea to life. Just as we bring feelings to life, and characters, and changes of feeling and attitude, so we bring ideas to life — evoke their content, connect them with our own experience and knowledge, make them matter to us personally. Practice at summoning and animating ideas is our focus in this chapter.

STEPS IN DEFINING IDEAS

When we bring to life the content of feeling at a particular moment in a work of literature, we begin with a tentative organizing framework — a series of locating questions. What's going on here? Where are we? What kinds of events are taking place? What kinds of people are involved? Who *is* Mistress Damon? Who is Kit Twink? (See Hardy's "The Slow Nature," p. 33.)

When we bring to life the content of an idea, we again start with a tentative organizing framework, attempting now to connect the poem, story, or play with knowledge we already possess. We ask: How do we classify these opinions or concepts? Do they involve politics? science? history? biology? Where are we, intellectually speaking? What is the general area, subject, field? What do we already know that's pertinent to the opinions or concepts that we recognize here? Inevitably our first answers are rough, and we use them only as a jumping-off place — a sketch of possibilities that will be refined as we move along.

The process of refinement often involves a decision — again open to change — about whether the poem, story, or play works to challenge or to confirm our present understandings and beliefs. Obviously such decisions must be personal, based on what each of us knows and believes. What some of us perceive as a challenge to our thinking, others will perceive as confirming or substantiating understandings already in place.

This point about the personal nature of decisions concerning challenge and confirmation bears special emphasis. To shed light on the differences between experiences of challenge and confirmation, we will treat them separately. (In this chapter the emphasis falls on experiences of intellectual challenge; in Chapter 5 the emphasis is on experiences of intellectual confirmation.) Would every reader agree that the works treated in this chapter are, in fact, experiences of challenge? No, and the same possibility of argument exists in Chapter 5. Our purpose isn't to lay down some kind of law branding one text as a challenge and another as a confirmation; it is, instead, to make plain a few of the steps readers take in bringing challenges *or* confirmations to life for themselves.

PERCEIVING A CHALLENGE

Some questions we ask in clarifying the nature of an intellectual challenge are the following: What previously held belief seems here to be opened up for fresh scrutiny? Why is this belief challenged? What justifies the challenge? What ground for replacing the older notion can we discern? Should the idea be replaced? What could replace it?

As we pursue such questions it's important to keep alive our sense of the literary work as an experience that we live through, moment by moment, emotionally as well as intellectually. Even as we address ourselves to ideas, we're evoking feelings, drawing close to the insides of a person as well as to the full ramifications of an intellectual or critical perspective. Through the use of our own terms, and for the purposes of clarification, we can momentarily focus our attention solely on intellectual dimensions of our encounter with the text. But ideas, feelings, and character remain interdependent, shaping each other.

Evoking Joyce's "Araby" as an intellectual experience might mean initially exploring the causes of the boy's absurd romantic fantasies. Conventional thinking might insist that he's simply an exceptionally silly youngster — but isn't a challenge to that notion worked into the story almost from the start? (Before the first two paragraphs are over, after all, we learn that the boy is curious, something of a reader, and aware of the difference between charitable and uncharitable priests; we know too that there's nothing really silly about his low estimate of his boozy uncle.) Could it be the special quality — or lack of quality — of this culture that raises such impossible hopes? But that idea must be brought back into touch with our experience of the person, tested against our feeling for the boy's individual nature. Do we bring him alive as an essentially sound mind in an essentially unhealthy society — or as something else?

Three steps are worth particular notice as we bring ideas to life. Initially we locate ourselves on recognizable (to us) intellectual terrain. Later we work at making that location more precise, by establishing whether the ideas in question are best perceived as challenges or confirmations. And thereafter we clarify the relation between our emotional and intellectual engagement with the text, so that we're bringing alive, together with the content of an idea, an understanding of how and why a particular character — or particular author — embraces it.

CREATING THE INTELLECTUAL EXPERIENCE

GALWAY KINNELL   (b. 1927)
Cells Breathe in the Emptiness

1

When the flowers turn to husks
And the great trees suddenly die
And rocks and old weasel bones lose
The little life they suddenly had
And the air quells and goes so still   5
It gives the ears something like the bends,
It is an eerie thing then to keep vigil,
The senses racing in the emptiness.

2

From the compost heap
Now arises the sound of the teeth   10
Of one of those sloppy green cabbageworms
Eating his route through a cabbage,
Now snarling like a petite chainsaw, now droning on . . .

A butterfly blooms on a buttercup,
From the junkpile flames up a junco.   15

3

How many plants are really very quiet animals?
How many inert molecules are ready to break into life?

What sorts of ideas do we need to have in mind as we engage this poem? The general questions with which it ends have to do with classification in the natural world: plants versus animals, molecules versus cells. We might therefore try on, as a tentative framework for organizing our intellectual experience of the poem, "knowledge of nature." "Trying on" simply means probing the text to see which parts of it can be grouped together as belonging to the subject area we've provisionally staked out as relevant.

The four opening lines can be seen to speak of natural process. The next four lines can be seen — with a bit more difficulty — to speak about observation of nature, an observer using "the senses" to "keep vigil." We can read the second section as a series of natural observations, and then come those questions about natural classification.

Where are we, intellectually speaking? Well, we're certainly not in a conventional laboratory with a conventional scientist as our guide. In a lab people don't usually observe so intensely that "it gives the ears . . . the bends" (line 6) or becomes a "vigil" (7). Nor do people talk about butterflies that "bloom" (14) or cabbageworms that resemble chain saws. On the other hand, much of the poem's language does focus on nature, the natural world, botany-biology, amateur scientific observation. Our provisional framework — "knowledge of nature" — seems reasonably plausible. What happens when we work in closer?

Closer to what? Always the answer to this question is *Closer to our own experience of the poem.* But it's one thing to say this and another to decide how to focus that experience as an experience of ideas. A helpful step, as already mentioned, involves deciding whether the ideas work to challenge or confirm some previous assumption. Those final questions in "Cells Breathe in the Emptiness" raise possibilities that are likely to strike many of us as odd. And many details of the poem flesh out those questions into a genuinely unfamiliar version of the world. Familiar lines of demarcation within the natural world are blurred. So too are distinctions between that world and the world of human culture.

A butterfly blooms like a flower, a worm resembles a chain saw, a junco bird flames, perhaps like burning refuse on a junk pile. Is the speaker reaching for a perspective on the whole of existence that discovers unities obscured by standard classifications? Is the speaker imagining energy itself — ceaselessly throbbing everywhere, even where our senses detect only silence or emptiness — as the basic life-substance?

That's certainly possible — but, if we listen hard to the speaker's voice, we realize that the manner in which this vision is being put forward isn't dogmatic or commanding. Phrases such as "something like the bends" (6) and "one of those sloppy green cabbageworms" (11) tell us that we're being spoken to fairly casually. There's amusement in the notion of a *petite* chain saw (13) and some verbal fooling around in "butterfly . . . buttercup" (14) and "junkpile . . . junco" (15). This speaker approaches his own intuition almost as diffidently as we came at the problem of placing his poem's subject in relation to our knowledge. But if we feel with him, we sense that there's more than a witty game in progress; when we bring the ideas to life, we draw close to a mind rediscovering for itself the measureless, unregulated, unregistered, uninterruptible energies breathing in the world just beyond our ears.

ASKING QUESTIONS ABOUT CHALLENGES

We begin practicing bringing ideas to life with a short story and go on to a short poem and a play. With each text it's best to start with questions that set up a framework for the first approach, move on to clarify the nature of the intellectual challenge, and then evoke relations between the pertinent ideas and character and feeling. The right questions to ask are those that bring to life the challenge as an experience that can actually be felt. What idea here is surprising or confusing or mysterious at first sight? Why exactly *is* it surprising? What ordinary assumptions have to be turned upside down in order for this idea to make sense? What truth or useful new perspective becomes available as a result of the challenge? How does it feel to think in these new terms?

D. H. LAWRENCE   (1885–1930)
Odour of Chrysanthemums

I

The small locomotive engine, Number 4, came clanking, stumbling down from Selston with seven full wagons. It appeared round the corner with loud threats of speed, but the colt that it startled from among the gorse, which still flickered indistinctly in the raw afternoon, out-distanced it at a canter. A woman, walking up the railway line to Underwood, drew back into the hedge, held her basket aside, and watched the footplate of the engine advancing. The trucks thumped heavily past, one by one, with slow inevitable movement, as she stood insignificantly trapped between the jolting black wagons and the hedge; then they curved away towards the coppice where the withered oak leaves dropped noiselessly, while the birds, pulling at the scarlet hips beside the track, made off into the dusk that had already crept into the spinney. In the open, the smoke from the engine sank and cleaved to the rough grass. The fields were dreary and forsaken, and in the marshy strip that led to the whimsey, a reedy pit-pond, the fowls had already abandoned their run among the alders, to roost in the tarred fowl-house. The pit-bank loomed up beyond the pond, flames like red sores licking its ashy sides, in the afternoon's stagnant light. Just beyond rose the tapering chimneys and the clumsy black headstocks of Brinsley Colliery. The two wheels were spinning fast up against the sky, and the winding engine rapped out its little spasms. The miners were being turned up.

The engine whistled as it came into the wide bay of railway lines beside the colliery, where rows of trucks stood in harbour.

Miners, single, trailing and in groups, passed like shadows diverging home. At the edge of the ribbed level of sidings squat a low cottage, three steps down from the cinder track. A large bony vine clutched at the house, as if to claw down the tiled roof. Round the bricked yard grew a few wintry primroses. Beyond, the long garden sloped down to a bush-covered brook course. There were some twiggy apple trees, winter-crack trees, and ragged cabbages. Beside the path hung dishevelled pink chrysanthemums, like pink cloths hung on bushes. A woman came stooping out of the felt-covered fowl-house, half-way down the garden. She closed and padlocked the door, then drew herself erect, having brushed some bits from her white apron.

She was a tall woman of imperious mien, handsome, with

definite black eyebrows. Her smooth black hair was parted exactly. For a few moments she stood steadily watching the miners
as they passed along the railway: then she turned towards the
brook course. Her face was calm and set, her mouth was closed
with disillusionment. After a moment she called:

"John!" There was no answer. She waited, and then said 5
distinctly:

"Where are you?"

"Here!" replied a child's sulky voice from among the bushes.
The woman looked piercingly through the dusk.

"Are you at that brook?" she asked sternly.

For answer the child showed himself before the raspberry-
canes that rose like whips. He was a small, sturdy boy of five. He
stood quite still, defiantly.

"Oh!" said the mother, conciliated. "I thought you were down 10
at that wet brook — and you remember what I told you ——"

The boy did not move or answer.

"Come, come on in," she said more gently, "it's getting dark.
There's your grandfather's engine coming down the line!"

The lad advanced slowly, with resentful, taciturn movement.
He was dressed in trousers and waistcoat of cloth that was too
thick and hard for the size of the garments. They were evidently
cut down from a man's clothes.

As they went slowly towards the house he tore at the ragged
wisps of chrysanthemums and dropped the petals in handfuls
among the path.

"Don't do that — it does look nasty," said his mother. He re- 15
frained, and she, suddenly pitiful, broke off a twig with three or
four wan flowers and held them against her face. When mother
and son reached the yard her hand hesitated, and instead of
laying the flower aside, she pushed it in her apron-band. The
mother and son stood at the foot of the three steps looking across
the bay of lines at the passing home of the miners. The trundle of
the small train was imminent. Suddenly the engine loomed past
the house and came to a stop opposite the gate.

The engine-driver, a short man with round grey beard,
leaned out of the cab high above the woman.

"Have you got a cup of tea?" he said in a cheery, hearty
fashion.

It was her father. She went in, saying she would mash. Directly, she returned.

"I didn't come to see you on Sunday," began the little grey-
bearded man.

"I didn't expect you," said his daughter.   20

The engine-driver winced; then, reassuming his cheery, airy manner, he said:

"Oh, have you heard then? Well, and what do you think —— ?"

"I think it is soon enough," she replied.

At her brief censure the little man made an impatient gesture, and said coaxingly, yet with dangerous coldness:

"Well, what's a man to do? It's no sort of life for a man of my   25 years, to sit at my own hearth like a stranger. And if I'm going to marry again it may as well be soon as late — what does it matter to anybody?"

The woman did not reply, but turned and went into the house. The man in the engine-cab stood assertive, till she returned with a cup of tea and a piece of bread and butter on a plate. She went up the steps and stood near the footplate of the hissing engine.

"You needn't 'a' brought me bread an' butter," said her father. "But a cup of tea" — he sipped appreciatively — "it's very nice." He sipped for a moment or two, then: "I hear as Walter's got another bout on," he said.

"When hasn't he?" said the woman bitterly.

"I heerd tell of him in the 'Lord Nelson' braggin' as he was going to spend that b—— afore he went: half a sovereign that was."

"When?" asked the woman.   30

"A' Sat'day night — I know that's true."

"Very likely," she laughed bitterly. "He gives me twenty-three shillings."

"Aye, it's a nice thing, when a man can do nothing with his money but make a beast of himself!" said the grey-whiskered man. The woman turned her head away. Her father swallowed the last of his tea and handed her the cup.

"Aye," he sighed, wiping his mouth. "It's a settler, it is ——"

He put his hand on the lever. The little engine strained   35 and groaned, and the train rumbled towards the crossing. The woman again looked across the metals. Darkness was settling over the spaces of the railway and trucks: the miners, in grey sombre groups, were still passing home. The winding engine pulsed hurriedly, with brief pauses. Elizabeth Bates looked at the dreary flow of men, then she went indoors. Her husband did not come.

The kitchen was small and full of firelight; red coals piled glowing up the chimney mouth. All the life of the room seemed in the white, warm hearth and the steel fender reflecting the red fire. The cloth was laid for tea; cups glinted in the shadows. At the back, where the lowest stairs protruded into the room, the boy sat struggling with a knife and a piece of white wood. He was almost hidden in the shadow. It was half-past four. They had but to await the father's coming to begin tea. As the mother watched her son's sullen little struggle with the wood, she saw herself in his silence and pertinacity; she saw the father in her child's indifference to all but himself. She seemed to be occupied by her husband. He had probably gone past his home, slunk past his own door, to drink before he came in, while his dinner spoiled and wasted in waiting. She glanced at the clock, then took the potatoes to strain them in the yard. The garden and fields beyond the brook were closed in uncertain darkness. When she rose with the saucepan, leaving the drain steaming into the night behind her, she saw the yellow lamps were lit along the high road that went up the hill away beyond the space of the railway lines and the field.

Then again she watched the men trooping home, fewer now and fewer.

Indoors the fire was sinking and the room was dark red. The woman put her saucepan on the hob, and set a batter-pudding near the mouth of the oven. Then she stood unmoving. Directly, gratefully, came quick young steps to the door. Someone hung on the latch a moment, then a little girl entered and began pulling off her outdoor things, dragging a mass of curls, just ripening from gold to brown, over her eyes with her hat.

Her mother chid her for coming late from school, and said she would have to keep her at home the dark winter days.

"Why, mother, it's hardly a bit dark yet. The lamp's not 40 lighted, and my father's not home."

"No, he isn't. But it's a quarter to five! Did you see anything of him?"

The child became serious. She looked at her mother with large, wistful blue eyes.

"No, mother, I've never seen him. Why? Has he come up an' gone past, to Old Brinsley? He hasn't, mother, 'cos I never saw him."

"He'd watch that," said the mother bitterly, "he'd take care as you didn't see him. But you may depend upon it, he's seated in the 'Prince o' Wales.' He wouldn't be this late."

The girl looked at her mother piteously. 45

"Let's have our teas, mother, should we?" said she.

The mother called John to table. She opened the door once more and looked out across the darkness of the lines. All was deserted: she could not hear the winding-engines.

"Perhaps," she said to herself, "he's stopped to get some ripping done."

They sat down to tea. John, at the end of the table near the door, was almost lost in the darkness. Their faces were hidden from each other. The girl crouched against the fender slowly moving a thick piece of bread before the fire. The lad, his face a dusky mark on the shadow, sat watching her who was transfigured in the red glow.

"I do think it's beautiful to look in the fire," said the child.   50

"Do you?" said her mother. "Why?"

"It's so red, and full of little caves — and it feels so nice, and you can fair smell it."

"It'll want mending directly," replied her mother, "and then if your father comes he'll carry on and say there never is a fire when a man comes home sweating from the pit. A public-house is always warm enough."

There was silence till the boy said complainingly: "Make haste, our Annie."

"Well, I am doing! I can't make the fire do it no faster, can I?"   55

"She keeps wafflin' it about so's to make 'er slow," grumbled the boy.

"Don't have such an evil imagination, child," replied the mother.

Soon the room was busy in the darkness with the crisp sound of crunching. The mother ate very little. She drank her tea determinedly, and sat thinking. When she rose her anger was evident in the stern unbending of her head. She looked at the pudding in the fender, and broke out:

"It is a scandalous thing as a man can't even come home to his dinner! If it's crozzled up to a cinder I don't see why I should care. Past his very door he goes to get to a public-house, and here I sit with his dinner waiting for him ——"

She went out. As she dropped piece after piece of coal on the   60
red fire, the shadows fell on the walls, till the room was almost in total darkness.

"I canna see," grumbled the invisible John. In spite of herself, the mother laughed.

"You know the way to your mouth," she said. She set the dust-pan outside the door. When she came again like a shadow on the hearth, the lad repeated, complaining sulkily:

"I canna see."

"Good gracious!" cried the mother irritably, "you're as bad as your father if it's a bit dusk!"

Nevertheless, she took a paper spill from a sheaf on the man- 65
telpiece and proceeded to light the lamp that hung from the ceiling in the middle of the room. As she reached up, her figure displayed itself just rounding with maternity.

"Oh, mother —— !" exclaimed the girl.

"What?" said the woman, suspended in the act of putting the lamp-glass over the flame. The copper reflector shone handsomely on her, as she stood with uplifted arm, turning to face her daughter.

"You've got a flower in your apron!" said the child, in a little rapture at this unusual event.

"Goodness me!" exclaimed the woman, relieved. "One would think the house was afire." She replaced the glass and waited a moment before turning up the wick. A pale shadow was seen floating vaguely on the floor.

"Let me smell!" said the child, still rapturously, coming for- 70
ward and putting her face to her mother's waist.

"Go along, silly!" said the mother, turning up the lamp. The light revealed their suspense so that the woman felt it almost unbearable. Annie was still bending at her waist. Irritably, the mother took the flowers out from her apron-band.

"Oh, mother — don't take them out!" Annie cried, catching her hand and trying to replace the sprig.

"Such nonsense!" said the mother, turning away. The child put the pale chrysanthemums to her lips, murmuring:

"Don't they smell beautiful!"

Her mother gave a short laugh. 75

"No," she said, "not to me. It was chrysanthemums when I married him, and chrysanthemums when you were born, and the first time they ever brought him home drunk, he'd got brown chrysanthemums in his button-hole."

She looked at the children. Their eyes and their parted lips were wondering. The mother sat rocking in silence for some time. Then she looked at the clock.

"Twenty minutes to six!" In a tone of fine bitter carelessness she continued: "Eh, he'll not come now till they bring him. There he'll stick! But he needn't come rolling in here in his pit-dirt, for *I* won't wash him. He can lie on the floor —— Eh, what a fool I've been, what a fool! And this is what I came here for, to this dirty hole, rats and all, for him to slink past his very door. Twice last week — he's begun now ——"

She silenced herself, and rose to clear the table.

While for an hour or more the children played, subduedly   80
intent, fertile of imagination, united in fear of the mother's
wrath, and in dread of their father's home-coming, Mrs. Bates sat
in her rocking-chair making a "singlet" of thick cream-coloured
flannel, which gave a dull wounded sound as she tore off the grey
edge. She worked at her sewing with energy, listening to the
children, and her anger wearied itself, lay down to rest, opening
its eyes from time to time and steadily watching, its ears raised to
listen. Sometimes even her anger quailed and shrank, and the
mother suspended her sewing, tracing the footsteps that thudded
along the sleepers outside; she would lift her head sharply to bid
the children "hush," but she recovered herself in time, and the
footsteps went past the gate, and the children were not flung out
of their play-world.

But at last Annie sighed, and gave in. She glanced at her
wagon of slippers, and loathed the game. She turned plaintively
to her mother.

"Mother!" — but she was inarticulate.

John crept out like a frog from under the sofa. His mother
glanced up.

"Yes," she said, "just look at those shirt-sleeves!"

The boy held them out to survey them, saying nothing. Then   85
somebody called in a hoarse voice away down the line, and
suspense bristled in the room, till two people had gone by outside, talking.

"It is time for bed," said the mother.

"My father hasn't come," wailed Annie plaintively. But her
mother was primed with courage.

"Never mind. They'll bring him when he does come — like a
log." She meant there would be no scene. "And he may sleep on
the floor till he wakes himself. I know he'll not go to work tomorrow after this!"

The children had their hands and faces wiped with a flannel.
They were very quiet. When they had put on their night-dresses,
they said their prayers, the boy mumbling. The mother looked
down at them, at the brown silken bush of interwining curls in
the nape of the girl's neck, at the little black head of the lad, and
her heart burst with anger at their father, who caused all three
such distress. The children hid their faces in her skirts for comfort.

When Mrs. Bates came down, the room was strangely empty,   90
with a tension of expectancy. She took up her sewing and
stitched for some time without raising her head. Meantime her
anger was tinged with fear.

II

The clock struck eight and she rose suddenly, dropping her sewing on her chair. She went to the stair-foot door, opened it, listening. Then she went out, locking the door behind her.

Something scuffled in the yard, and she started, though she knew it was only the rats with which the place was over-run. The night was very dark. In the great bay of railway lines, bulked with trucks, there was no trace of light, only away back she could see a few yellow lamps at the pit-top, and the red smear of the burning pit-bank on the night. She hurried along the edge of the track, then, crossing the converging lines, came to the stile by the white gates, whence she emerged on the road. Then the fear which had led her shrank. People were walking up to New Brinsley; she saw the lights in the houses; twenty yards farther on were the broad windows of the "Prince of Wales," very warm and bright, and the loud voices of men could be heard distinctly. What a fool she had been to imagine that anything had happened to him! He was merely drinking over there at the "Prince of Wales." She faltered. She had never yet been to fetch him, and she never would go. So she continued her walk towards the long straggling line of houses, standing back on the highway. She entered a passage between the dwellings.

"Mr. Rigley — Yes! Did you want him? No, he's not in at this minute."

The raw-boned woman leaned forward from her dark scullery and peered at the other, upon whom fell a dim light through the blind of the kitchen window.

"Is it Mrs. Bates?" she asked in a tone tinged with respect.   95

"Yes. I wondered if your Master was at home. Mine hasn't come yet."

"Asn't 'e! Oh, Jack's been 'ome an' 'ad 'is dinner an' gone out. 'E's just gone for 'alf an hour afore bed-time. Did you call at the 'Prince of Wales'?"

"No ——"

"No, you didn't like ——! It's not very nice." The other woman was indulgent. There was an awkward pause. "Jack never said nothink about — about your Master," she said.

"No — I expect he's stuck in there!"   100

Elizabeth Bates said this bitterly, and with recklessness. She knew that the woman across the yard was standing at her door listening, but she did not care. As she turned:

"Stop a minute! I'll just go an' ask Jack if 'e knows anythink," said Mrs. Rigley.

"Oh no — I wouldn't like to put ——!"

"Yes, I will, if you'll just step inside an' see as th' childer doesn't come downstairs and set theirselves afire."

Elizabeth Bates, murmuring a remonstrance, stepped inside. 105 The other woman apologised for the state of the room.

The kitchen needed apology. There were little frocks and trousers and childish undergarments on the squab and on the floor, and a litter of playthings everywhere. On the black American cloth of the table were pieces of bread and cake, crusts, slops, and a teapot with cold tea.

"Eh, ours is just as bad," said Elizabeth Bates, looking at the woman, not at the house. Mrs. Rigley put a shawl over her head and hurried out, saying:

"I shanna be a minute."

The other sat, noting with faint disapproval the general untidiness of the room. Then she fell to counting the shoes of various sizes scattered over the floor. There were twelve. She sighed and said to herself: "No wonder!" — glancing at the litter. There came the scratching of two pairs of feet on the yard, and the Rigleys entered. Elizabeth Bates rose. Rigley was a big man, with very large bones. His head looked particularly bony. Across his temple was a blue scar, caused by a wound got in the pit, a wound in which the coal-dust remained blue like tattooing.

"'Asna 'e come whoam yit?" asked the man, without any form 110 of greeting, but with deference and sympathy. "I couldna say wheer he is — 'e's non ower theer!" — he jerked his head to signify the "Prince of Wales."

"'E's 'appen gone up to th' 'Yew,'" said Mrs. Rigley.

There was another pause. Rigley had evidently something to get off his mind:

"Ah left 'im finishin' a stint," he began. "Loose-all 'ad bin gone about ten minutes when we com'n away, an' I shouted: 'Are ter comin', Walt?' an' 'e said: 'Go on, Ah shanna be but a'ef a minnit,' so we com'n ter th' bottom, me an' Bowers, thinkin' as 'e wor just behint, an' 'ud come up i' th' next bantle ——"

He stood perplexed, as if answering a charge of deserting his mate. Elizabeth Bates, now again certain of disaster, hastened to reassure him:

"I expect 'e's gone up to th' 'Yew Tree,' as you say. It's not the 115 first time. I've fretted myself into a fever before now. He'll come home when they carry him."

"Ay, isn't it too bad!" deplored the other woman.

"I'll just step up to Dick's an' see if 'e *is* there," offered the man, afraid of appearing alarmed, afraid of taking liberties.

"Oh, I wouldn't think of bothering you that far," said Elizabeth Bates, with emphasis, but he knew she was glad of his offer.

As they stumbled up the entry, Elizabeth Bates heard Rigley's wife run across the yard and open her neighbour's door. At this, suddenly all the blood in her body seemed to switch away from her heart.

"Mind!" warned Rigley. "Ah've said many a time as Ah'd fill up them ruts in this entry, sumb'dy 'll be breakin' their legs yit." 120

She recovered herself and walked quickly along with the miner.

"I don't like leaving the children in bed, and nobody in the house," she said.

"No, you dunna!" he replied courteously. They were soon at the gate of the cottage.

"Well, I shanna be many minnits. Dunna you be frettin' now, 'e'll be all right," said the butty.

"Thank you very much, Mr. Rigley," she replied. 125

"You're welcome!" he stammered, moving away. "I shanna be many minnits."

The house was quiet. Elizabeth Bates took off her hat and shawl, and rolled back the rug. When she had finished, she sat down. It was a few minutes past nine. She was startled by the rapid chuff of the winding-engine at the pit, and the sharp whirr of the brakes on the rope as it descended. Again she felt the painful sweep of her blood, and she put her hand to her side, saying aloud: "Good gracious! — it's only the nine o'clock deputy going down," rebuking herself.

She sat still, listening. Half an hour of this, and she was wearied out.

"What am I working myself up like this for?" she said pitiably to herself, "I s'll only be doing myself some damage."

She took out her sewing again. 130

At a quarter to ten there were footsteps. One person! She watched for the door to open. It was an elderly woman, in a black bonnet and a black woollen shawl — his mother. She was about sixty years old, pale, with blue eyes, and her face all wrinkled and lamentable. She shut the door and turned to her daughter-in-law peevishly.

"Eh, Lizzie, whatever shall we do, whatever shall we do!" she cried.

Elizabeth drew back a little, sharply.

"What is it, mother?" she said.

The elder woman seated herself on the sofa. 135

"I don't know, child, I can't tell you!" — she shook her head slowly. Elizabeth sat watching her, anxious and vexed.

"I don't know," replied the grandmother, sighing very deeply. "There's no end to my troubles, there isn't. The things I've gone through, I'm sure it's enough —— !" She wept without wiping her eyes, the tears running.

"But, mother," interrupted Elizabeth, "what do you mean? What is it?"

The grandmother slowly wiped her eyes. The fountains of her tears were stopped by Elizabeth's directness. She wiped her eyes slowly.

"Poor child! Eh, you poor thing!" she moaned. "I don't know 140 what we're going to do, I don't — and you as you are — it's a thing, it is indeed!"

Elizabeth waited.

"Is he dead?" she asked, and at the words her heart swung violently, though she felt a slight flush of shame at the ultimate extravagance of the question. Her words sufficiently frightened the old lady, almost brought her to herself.

"Don't say so, Elizabeth! We'll hope it's not as bad as that; no, may the Lord spare us that, Elizabeth. Jack Rigley came just as I was sittin' down to a glass afore going to bed, an' 'e said: ''Appen you'll go down th' line, Mrs. Bates. Walt's had an accident. 'Appen you'll go an' sit wi' 'er till we can get him home.' I hadn't time to ask him a word afore he was gone. An' I put my bonnet on an' come straight down, Lizzie. I thought to myself: 'Eh, that poor blessed child, if anybody should come an' tell her of a sudden, there's no knowin' what'll 'appen to 'er.' You mustn't let it upset you, Lizzie — or you know what to expect. How long is it, six months — or is it five, Lizzie? Ay!" — the old woman shook her head — "time slips on, it slips on! Ay!"

Elizabeth's thoughts were busy elsewhere. If he was killed — would she be able to manage on the little pension and what she could earn? — she counted up rapidly. If he was hurt — they wouldn't take him to the hospital — how tiresome he would be to nurse! — but perhaps she'd be able to get him away from the drink and his hateful ways. She would — while he was ill. The tears offered to come to her eyes at the picture. But what sentimental luxury was this she was beginning? She turned to consider the children. At any rate she was absolutely necessary for them. They were her business.

"Ay!" repeated the old woman, "it seems but a week or two 145 since he brought me his first wages. Ay — he was a good lad,

Elizabeth, he was, in his way. I don't know why he got to be such a trouble, I don't. He was a happy lad at home, only full of spirits. But there's no mistake he's been a handful of trouble, he has! I hope the Lord'll spare him to mend his ways. I hope so, I hope so. You've had a sight o' trouble with him, Elizabeth, you have indeed. But he was a jolly enough lad wi' me, he was, I can assure you. I don't know how it is . . ."

The old woman continued to muse aloud, a monotonous irritating sound, while Elizabeth thought concentratedly, startled once, when she heard the winding-engine chuff quickly, and the brakes skirr with a shriek. Then she heard the engine more slowly, and the brakes made no sound. The old woman did not notice. Elizabeth waited in suspense. The mother-in-law talked, with lapses into silence.

"But he wasn't your son, Lizzie, an' it makes a difference. Whatever he was, I remember him when he was little, an' I learned to understand him and to make allowances. You've got to make allowances for them ——"

It was half-past ten, and the old woman was saying: "But it's trouble from beginning to end; you're never too old for trouble, never too old for that ——" when the gate banged back, and there were heavy feet on the steps.

"I'll go, Lizzie, let me go," cried the old woman, rising. But Elizabeth was at the door. It was a man in pit-clothes.

"They're bringin' 'im, Missis," he said. Elizabeth's heart halted a moment. Then it surged on again, almost suffocating her.   150

"Is he — is it bad?" she asked.

The man turned away, looking at the darkness:

"The doctor says 'e'd been dead hours. 'E saw 'im i' th' lamp-cabin."

The old woman, who stood just behind Elizabeth, dropped into a chair, and folded her hands, crying: "Oh, my boy, my boy!"

"Hush!" said Elizabeth, with a sharp twitch of a frown. "Be still, mother, don't waken th' children: I wouldn't have them down for anything!"   155

The old woman moaned softly, rocking herself. The man was drawing away. Elizabeth took a step forward.

"How was it?" she asked.

"Well, I couldn't say for sure," the man replied, very ill at ease. "'E wor finishin' a stint an' th' butties 'ad gone, an' a lot o' stuff come down atop 'n 'im."

"And crushed him?" cried the widow, with a shudder.

"No," said the man, "it fell at th' back of 'im. 'E wor under th'   160
face, an' it niver touched 'im. It seems 'e wor smothered."

Elizabeth shrank back. She heard the old woman behind her
cry:

"What? — what did 'e say it was?"

The man replied, more loudly: "'E wor smothered!"

Then the old woman wailed aloud, and this relieved Elizabeth.

"Oh, mother," she said, putting her hand on the old woman,   165
"don't waken th' children, don't waken th' children."

She wept a little, unknowing, while the old mother rocked
herself and moaned. Elizabeth remembered that they were bringing him home, and she must be ready. "They'll lay him in the
parlour," she said to herself, standing a moment pale and perplexed.

Then she lighted a candle and went into the tiny room. The
air was cold and damp, but she could not make a fire, there was
no fireplace. She set down the candle and looked round. The
candlelight glittered on the lustre-glasses, on the two vases that
held some of the pink chrysanthemums, and on the dark mahogany. There was a cold, deathly smell of chrysanthemums in
the room. Elizabeth stood looking at the flowers. She turned
away, and calculated whether there would be room to lay him on
the floor, between the couch and the chiffonier. She pushed the
chairs aside. There would be room to lay him down and to step
round him. Then she fetched the old red tablecloth, and another
old cloth, spreading them down to save her bit of carpet. She
shivered on leaving the parlour; so, from the dresser drawer she
took a clean shirt and put it at the fire to air. All the time her
mother-in-law was rocking herself in the chair and moaning.

"You'll have to move from there, mother," said Elizabeth.
"They'll be bringing him in. Come in the rocker."

The old mother rose mechanically, and seated herself by the
fire, continuing to lament. Elizabeth went into the pantry for
another candle, and there, in the little pent-house under the
naked tiles, she heard them coming. She stood still in the pantry
doorway, listening. She heard them pass the end of the house,
and come awkwardly down the three steps, a jumble of shuffling
footsteps and muttering voices. The old woman was silent. The
men were in the yard.

Then Elizabeth heard Matthews, the manager of the pit, say: 170
"You go in first, Jim. Mind!"

The door came open, and the two women saw a collier backing into the room, holding one end of a stretcher, on which they

could see the nailed pit-boots of the dead man. The two carriers halted, the man at the head stooping to the lintel of the door.

"Wheer will you have him?" asked the manager, a short, white-bearded man.

Elizabeth roused herself and came from the pantry carrying the unlighted candle.

"In the parlour," she said.

"In there, Jim!" pointed the manager, and the carriers 175 backed round into the tiny room. The coat with which they had covered the body fell off as they awkwardly turned through the two doorways, and the women saw their man, naked to the waist, lying stripped for work. The old woman began to moan in a low voice of horror.

"Lay th' stretcher at th' side," snapped the manager, "an' put 'im on th' cloths. Mind now, mind! Look you now —— !"

One of the men had knocked off a vase of chrysanthemums. He stared awkwardly, then they set down the stretcher. Elizabeth did not look at her husband. As soon as she could get in the room, she went and picked up the broken vase and the flowers.

"Wait a minute!" she said.

The three men waited in silence while she mopped up the water with a duster.

"Eh, what a job, what a job, to be sure!" the manager was say- 180 ing, rubbing his brow with trouble and perplexity. "Never knew such a thing in my life, never! He'd no business to ha' been left. I never knew such a thing in my life! Fell over him clean as a whistle, an' shut him in. Not four foot of space, there wasn't — yet it scarce bruised him."

He looked down at the dead man, lying prone, half naked, all grimed with coal-dust.

"'Sphyxiated,' the doctor said. It *is* the most terrible job I've ever known. Seems as if it was done o' purpose. Clean over him, an' shut 'im in, like a mouse-trap" — he made a sharp, descending gesture with his hand.

The colliers standing by jerked aside their heads in hopeless comment.

The horror of the thing bristled upon them all.

Then they heard the girl's voice upstairs calling shrilly: 185 "Mother, mother — who is it? Mother, who is it?"

Elizabeth hurried to the foot of the stairs and opened the door:

"Go to sleep!" she commanded sharply. "What are you shout-ing about? Go to sleep at once — there's nothing ——"

Then she began to mount the stairs. They could hear her on

the boards, and on the plaster floor of the little bedroom. They
could hear her distinctly:

"What's the matter now? — what's the matter with you, silly
thing?" — her voice was much agitated, with an unreal gentleness.

"I thought it was some men come," said the plaintive voice of   190
the child. "Has he come?"

"Yes, they've brought him. There's nothing to make a fuss
about. Go to sleep now, like a good child."

They could hear her voice in the bedroom, they waited whilst
she covered the children under the bedclothes.

"Is he drunk?" asked the girl, timidly, faintly.

"No! No — he's not! He — he's asleep."

"Is he asleep downstairs?"   195

"Yes — and don't make a noise."

There was silence for a moment, then the men heard the
frightened child again:

"What's that noise?"

"It's nothing, I tell you, what are you bothering for?"

The noise was the grandmother moaning. She was oblivious   200
of everything, sitting on her chair rocking and moaning. The
manager put his hand on her arm and bade her "Sh — sh!!"

The old woman opened her eyes and looked at him. She was
shocked by this interruption, and seemed to wonder.

"What time is it?" the plaintive thin voice of the child, sinking back unhappily into sleep, asked this last question.

"Ten o'clock," answered the mother more softly. Then she
must have bent down and kissed the children.

Matthews beckoned to the men to come away. They put on
their caps and took up the stretcher. Stepping over the body, they
tiptoed out of the house. None of them spoke till they were far
from the wakeful children.

When Elizabeth came down she found her mother alone on   205
the parlour floor, leaning over the dead man, the tears dropping
on him.

"We must lay him out," the wife said. She put on the kettle,
then returning knelt at the feet, and began to unfasten the
knotted leather laces. The room was clammy and dim with only
one candle, so that she had to bend her face almost to the floor.
At last she got off the heavy boots and put them away.

"You must help me now," she whispered to the old woman.
Together they stripped the man.

When they arose, saw him lying in the naïve dignity of death, the women stood arrested in fear and respect. For a few moments they remained still, looking down, the old mother whimpering. Elizabeth felt countermanded. She saw him, how utterly inviolable he lay in himself. She had nothing to do with him. She could not accept it. Stooping, she laid her hand on him, in claim. He was still warm, for the mine was hot where he had died. His mother had his face between her hands, and was murmuring incoherently. The old tears fell in succession as drops from wet leaves; the mother was not weeping, merely her tears flowed. Elizabeth embraced the body of her husband, with cheek and lips. She seemed to be listening, inquiring, trying to get some connection. But she could not. She was driven away. He was impregnable.

She rose, went into the kitchen, where she poured warm water into a bowl, brought soap and flannel and a soft towel.

"I must wash him," she said.   210

Then the old mother rose stiffly, and watched Elizabeth as she carefully washed his face, carefully brushing the big blond moustache from his mouth with the flannel. She was afraid with a bottomless fear, so she ministered to him. The old woman, jealous, said:

"Let me wipe him!" — and she kneeled on the other side drying slowly as Elizabeth washed, her big black bonnet sometimes brushing the dark head of her daughter-in-law. They worked thus in silence for a long time. They never forgot it was death, and the touch of the man's dead body gave them strange emotions, different in each of the women; a great dread possessed them both, the mother felt the lie was given to her womb, she was denied; the wife felt the utter isolation of the human soul, the child within her was a weight apart from her.

At last it was finished. He was a man of handsome body, and his face showed no traces of drink. He was blond, full-fleshed, with fine limbs. But he was dead.

"Bless him," whispered his mother, looking always at his face, and speaking out of sheer terror. "Dear lad — bless him!" She spoke in a faint, sibilant ecstasy of fear and mother love.

Elizabeth sank down again to the floor, and put her face 215 against his neck, and trembled and shuddered. But she had to draw away again. He was dead, and her living flesh had no place against his. A great dread and weariness held her: she was so unavailing. Her life was gone like this.

"White as milk he is, clear as a twelve-month baby, bless him, the darling!" the old mother murmured to herself. "Not a mark on him, clear and clean and white, beautiful as ever a child was made," she murmured with pride. Elizabeth kept her face hidden.

"He went peaceful, Lizzie — peaceful as sleep. Isn't he beautiful, the lamb? Ay — he must ha' made his peace, Lizzie. 'Appen he made it all right, Lizzie, shut in there. He'd have time. He wouldn't look like this if he hadn't made his peace. The lamb, the dear lamb. Eh, but he had a hearty laugh. I loved to hear it. He had the heartiest laugh, Lizzie, as a lad ——"

Elizabeth looked up. The man's mouth was fallen back, slightly open under the cover of the moustache. The eyes, half shut, did not show glazed in the obscurity. Life with its smoky burning gone from him, had left him apart and utterly alien to her. And she knew what a stranger he was to her. In her womb was ice of fear, because of this separate stranger with whom she had been living as one flesh. Was this what it all meant — utter, intact separateness, obscured by heat of living? In dread she turned her face away. The fact was too deadly. There had been nothing between them, and yet they had come together, exchanging their nakedness repeatedly. Each time he had taken her, they had been two isolated beings, far apart as now. He was no more responsible than she. The child was like ice in her womb. For as she looked at the dead man, her mind, cold and detached, said clearly: "Who am I? What have I been doing? I have been fighting a husband who did not exist. *He* existed all the time. What wrong have I done? What was that I have been living with? There lies the reality, this man." And her soul died in her for fear: she knew she had never seen him, he had never seen her, they had met in the dark and had fought in the dark, not knowing whom they met nor whom they fought. And now she saw, and turned silent in seeing. For she had been wrong. She had said he was something he was not; she had felt familiar with him. Whereas he was apart all the while, living as she never lived, feeling as she never felt.

In fear and shame she looked at his naked body, that she had known falsely. And he was the father of her children. Her soul was torn from her body and stood apart. She looked at his naked body and was ashamed, as if she had denied it. After all, it was itself. It seemed awful to her. She looked at his face, and she turned her own face to the wall. For his look was other than hers, his way was not her way. She had denied him what he was — she saw it now. She had refused him as himself. And this had been her life, and his life. She was grateful to death, which restored the truth. And she knew she was not dead.

And all the while her heart was bursting with grief and pity 220 for him. What had he suffered? What stretch of horror for this helpless man! She was rigid with agony. She had not been able to help him. He had been cruelly injured, this naked man, this other being, and she could make no reparation. There were the children — but the children belonged to life. This dead man had nothing to do with them. He and she were only channels through which life had flowed to issue in the children. She was a mother — but how awful she knew it now to have been a wife. And he, dead now, how awful he must have felt it to be a husband. She felt that in the next world he would be a stranger to her. If they met there, in the beyond, they would only be ashamed of what had been before. The children had come, for some mysterious reason, out of both of them. But the children did not unite them. Now he was dead, she knew how eternally he was apart from her, how eternally he had nothing more to do with her. She saw this episode of her life closed. They had denied each other in life. Now he had withdrawn. An anguish came over her. It was finished then: it had become hopeless between them long before he died. Yet he had been her husband. But how little!

"Have you got his shirt, 'Lizabeth?"

Elizabeth turned without answering, though she strove to weep and behave as her mother-in-law expected. But she could not, she was silenced. She went into the kitchen and returned with the garment.

"It is aired," she said, grasping the cotton shirt here and there to try. She was almost ashamed to handle him; what right had she or anyone to lay hands on him; but her touch was humble on his body. It was hard work to clothe him. He was so heavy and inert. A terrible dread gripped her all the while: that he could be so heavy and utterly inert, unresponsive, apart. The horror of the distance between them was almost too much for her — it was so infinite a gap she must look across.

At last it was finished. They covered him with a sheet and left him lying, with his face bound. And she fastened the door of the little parlour, lest the children should see what was lying there. Then, with peace sunk heavy on her heart, she went about making tidy the kitchen. She knew she submitted to life, which was her immediate master. But from death, her ultimate master, she winced with fear and shame.

Questions

Reread the closing pages of "Odour of Chrysanthemums" (from paragraph 218 through the final paragraph of the story). What familiar idea or belief undergoes challenge here? How can we make sense of the challenge? Write a response and then compare it to those that follow.

Responses

COLLEGE FRESHMAN: What does one do when one is expected to feel an emotion that one cannot seem to feel? The natural response is to act accordingly anyway. So often in life we are expected to "put on airs," to assume a certain appearance or mood we cannot or do not want to feel in order to seem acceptable to both our peers and our superiors. It is exactly this situation that Elizabeth Bates finds herself in in the short story "Odour of Chrysanthemums." She is not overcome with the hysteria and deep grief that is expected of recent widows in our society. She instead feels both relieved and grieved. Perhaps her emotions are so deeply impressed within her that she cannot possibly show outward signs of them. This, I believe, is a problem in our culture. We are so quick to judge a person on outward signs, completely forgetting the inner self. Perhaps discovering the inner self is a much more time-consuming process, but the reward reaped is a glimpse of the true person, certainly a worthwhile goal.

It is this goal that we should keep in mind when considering the character of Elizabeth Bates. If we do, we can quickly dispel the notion that she did not love her husband. I believe, in fact, that she loved him very deeply. She did not love his actions or how those actions affected their lives, but his person was very dear to her. She would not degrade him or their relationship by acting out an emotion that did not exist. If she had faked her reaction to his death, she would have, in a sense, been rendering their relationship artificial as well. But she was honest about her reaction, thereby confirming her commitment to him, however strained it may have been.

Her response exemplifies her strong character. She is a woman of steadfastly honest nature who is loyal, but only to the extent that she believes it is right to be so. She is not unwilling to show disgust when she feels it, as in the discussion with her father. She is true to herself. And, most important, she will not conform her beliefs and her reactions to those beliefs to society's expectations of her.

This is not to say that she knew exactly what she felt. It was a very tense and trying evening. In fact the whole day, as well as the way her husband had been living his life, seemed to foreshadow the tragedy of the night, so she was inwardly prepared for his death and somehow possessed a peace about it before it ever occurred. Still, the "peace sunk heavy on her heart" (para. 224). She felt pain but did not burden herself with acting out unfelt emotions, certainly a burden our culture could use a lot less of.

COLLEGE FRESHMAN: Elizabeth Bates becomes devastated when confronted with the death of her husband, a man who she realistically loves very little, because his death causes her to realize the tragic way in which she has lived with her husband. Together they existed in an environment of darkness and total emotional solitude; this environment instilled anger and wrath within Elizabeth and indifference within Walt. Life without spiritual interaction stifles any feelings of tenderness and love and ultimately dooms a marriage to unhappiness.

Elizabeth and Walter Bates lived in a simple cottage in a small mining town; however, the atmosphere of this home is anything but warm and cozy. The words *dark* and *darkness* are used innumerable times in describing not only the physical condition of the house but also the emotional state of its occupants. The only light in the house is the faint red glow of the fire, which is always fading. In this coldness and darkness the emotional tension between the couple was nourished. The two young children truly dread their father's coming home from work. They clearly sense the disillusionment between their parents.

One of the major causes of the lack of spiritual love between the Bateses is Elizabeth's exclusive engagement with the physical aspects of love during their marriage. When her husband's body is brought into her house, the intense sexual desire within her forces her to embrace the naked corpse; she longs for the physical contact which has been the only bond between herself and Walt. She admires his "handsome body" and notices his blond hair and "fine limbs" (para. 213). She initially regrets the loss of such a fine partner for sex. Elizabeth even perceives a certain beauty in his death because it has not distorted any of his fine physical attributes. She sees him lying in the "dignity of death" and considers "how utterly inviolable he lay in himself" (208). This physical obsession, however, comes to a crushing halt when she touches his body.

"He was impregnable" (208), she says to herself as she first touches him. "The touch of the man's dead body gave them [Elizabeth and her mother-in-law] strange emotions . . . the wife felt the utter isolation of the human soul" (212). Elizabeth has come to the shocking realization that there has been an immense spiritual void in her marriage with Walt. The part of her that nurtures these feelings, her soul, has been destroyed, "torn from her body" (219) because of its deprivation. She now understands that they lived a life of "utter, intact separateness, obscured by heat of living" (218). She feels defeat in acknowledging the fact that physical contact was the only thing she shared with Walt. "In fear and shame she looked at his naked body" (219). She is fearful and apologetic when she questions herself: "Who am I? What have I been doing? . . . What wrong have I done?" (218).

As the guilt within her begins to overflow, she reexamines herself and her morals. Walt is no longer a "man" to her but a "being." She realizes that she cannot make any "reparations" (220) to Walt. Their children, the only things they shared in that still exist, belong to a different world than Walt does now, the world of the living. The unborn child she carries is especially painful, "a weight apart" (212), "ice in her womb" (218). She is frightened by the thought that the infant was not conceived out of the warmth and comfort of spiritual love: "He and she were only channels through which life had flowed to issue in the children" (220). She feels regretful and ashamed that she must be grateful that death, her "ultimate master" (224), has restored this truth.

EDITOR: The familiar idea called into question is that the partners in a marriage — who have lived together for years, raising children together, becoming ever more closely acquainted with their shared (and unshared) habits and tastes — must necessarily know each other as well as any two human beings can. Elizabeth

Bates is aroused to doubt all this as she prepares her dead husband's body for burial. She finds herself suddenly thinking of him
not as "Walter" or as "my husband" but rather as "the man," as "a
stranger." She tells herself that, although she "had felt familiar
with him" (para. 218), that feeling was somehow improper —
bore little relation to the facts. The facts were that "she had never
seen him" (218), that "they had been two isolated beings, far
apart as now" (218), that "she had denied him what he was" (219)
and "had said he was something he was not" (218). Neither the
long years of marriage nor their children had brought husband
and wife close; "they had denied each other in life" (220).

One reason these thoughts come to Elizabeth is that she's
driven into consciousness — in that room, at that precise instant
of time — of the vast difference between a life that's ongoing
(her own) and a life that has ended (her husband's). A second
reason is that she is painfully aware that in the very hours Walter
was suffering in the mine, she believed him to be roistering in a
pub — proof in itself of how terribly mistaken she could be
about him. But clearly Elizabeth's sense of the gulf separating her
from her husband has deeper roots than these; ultimately her
new view of the marriage and the state of their understanding of
each other rests on a different foundation. It has to do, prin
cipally, with what they were and were not to each other long
before Walter Bates's fatal accident. To make sense of the idea
that a long-married husband and wife may not know each other
at all, we need to consider the barriers between people in any
relationship.

The chief barrier that's brought into sight in this story is the
tendency to assume (1) that our own explanations of our mate's
behavior — our account of him or her as a person — must necessarily be seen as correct, and (2) that our explanations of our
own behavior — our account of ourselves as persons — must
necessarily be seen as correct by our mate. Elizabeth Bates's
understanding of her husband is that he's irresponsible, sullen,
indifferent "to all but himself" (36), and inadequately conscious
of the debt he owes his wife for her willingness to descend from
her rightful place in the social scale in order to make her life
with him. Elizabeth's sense of herself is that she is a person
struggling to maintain high standards — someone concerned to
teach habits of cleanliness and mannerliness to her children,

someone whose house isn't in the condition of squalor that she sees during her call on Mrs. Rigley, someone who tries to hold all her family, including her elders, to a mark of orderly, decent behavior. (Elizabeth doesn't hesitate, for instance, to indicate disapproval of her widowed father's haste in plunging into a second marriage: "I think it is soon enough," [23] she says with acerbity.) And she perceives herself further as a fool and a victim— someone who had other possibilities yet chose "this dirty hole, rats and all" (78), and a husband who night after night comes slinking "past his very door" (59).

We have no direct account of Walter Bates's assessment either of himself or of his wife, but it's not difficult to speculate about it, given the indirect evidence at hand. From Walter's mother we learn that he was, as a child, intensely lovable and prized for his quick responsiveness ("He had the heartiest laugh, Lizzie, as a lad," 217). Elizabeth's own eyes record for us that, even as a corpse, Walter is a handsome, well-made man with fine limbs and blond hair.

There's ground here for suggesting that Elizabeth Bates's sense of herself as someone who came to "this dirty hole" purely on a selfless mission of mercy is less than the whole truth. She married beneath herself perhaps, but for reasons that had much to do with the vitality, looks, and good humor of her suitor. Presumably Walter Bates as a young man had fair justification for thinking of himself not as a hopeless inferior but as a person of significant qualities — a man who would give to his marriage as well as receive from it. And one can imagine that his shift, during his marriage — from the quick, hearty responsiveness of which his mother speaks to the sullen indifference known to Elizabeth — may have been connected first of all with his feelings about that marriage.

It's likely, indeed, that Elizabeth is swept up into her profound conviction of the truth of their separateness by the reminder, from her mother-in-law, of the difference between Walter "as a lad," and Walter the drunken, irresponsible father. Elizabeth doesn't spell out the particulars of her sudden imagination of Walter as someone whose true feelings were wholly different from those she ascribed to him. She doesn't tell herself, for example, that a man of lively good looks treated as though he's in some respect a social inferior, subjected to a current of criticism, may dispute in his own mind his wife's claims to superiority.

She doesn't tell herself either that her concern for her own son's cleanliness and her general presentation of herself as someone "above" the situation in which she finds herself might come to be regarded by her husband as needlessly finicky, lofty, and emasculating. She doesn't tell herself that her husband might have seen her as cruelly unappreciative of — possibly even contemptuous of — the hard labor in a dangerous place that, regardless of where it situated the couple in the social scale, did keep them fed and housed. She doesn't tell herself that, although she would not have married a man who lacked either personal pride or justification for that pride, she could herself have been the cause of its collapse.

Nor does she tell herself that the very viciousness of her husband's — his boasting in a tavern that he'd spend all his pay rather than bring it home to his wife and children — could have been an attempt, desperate, ignorant, but not finally incomprehensible, to win back some measure of respect, if for nothing else but wild recklessness, from his fellows.

But putting all or any of this into words would be pointless for Elizabeth. She has been brought up short by a variety of forces, including her own imaginative sensitivity and the voice of someone with a wholly positive sense of her husband. For a moment she holds within her an awareness that her husband was, in a sense, a figure she "made up" in accordance solely with her interests, her values, her views of self and the world. Was it not true that he too had interests, values, views of self and the world? Had she ever for a minute sought to penetrate those views, to make them vivid to herself? "As she looked at the dead man, her mind, cold and detached, said clearly: 'Who am I? What have I been doing? I have been fighting a husband who did not exist. *He* existed all the time. What wrong have I done? What was that I have been living with? There lies the reality, this man.' And her soul died in her for fear: she knew she had never seen him, he had never seen her" (218).

A good measure of the power of "Odour of Chrysanthemums" resides in D. H. Lawrence's ability to live into the shock endured by Elizabeth Bates as she confronts her discovery: "She had said he was something he was not" (para. 218). Lawrence asks his reader to feel the emptying force of this surprise, the manner in which it hugely deepens her grief and pity even as it makes her understand "how awful he [Walter Bates] must have felt it to be a husband" (220). And as we feel this, we also feel the force of the challenge to the conventional wisdom about marriage, intimacy, knowledge of the other. In prolonged closeness with another human being, opportunities exist for growth toward knowledge, true inwardness with and understanding of a separate human being. But there are no guarantees: it is perfectly possible for the familiar conception of marriage to have, in any particular case, no relevance whatever.

Continuing the Discussion

Reader 1 says that Elizabeth Bates "loved [her husband] very deeply." Reader 2 says that Walter Bates is "a man who [Elizabeth] realistically loves very little." How might this difference in readings be explained? What personal or other facts could account for such a difference?

DAVE SMITH   (b. 1942)
The Spring Poem

Everyone should write a Spring poem.
— *Louise Glück*

Yes, but we must be sure of verities
such as proper heat and adequate form.
That's what poets are for, is my theory.
This then is a Spring poem. A car warms
its rusting hulk in a meadow; weeds slog   5
up its flanks in martial weather. April
or late March is our month. There is a fog
of spunky mildew and sweaty tufts spill
from the damp rump of a back seat. A spring
thrusts one gleaming tip out, a brilliant tooth   10
uncoiling from Winter's tension, a ring
of insects along, working out the Truth.
Each year this car, melting around that spring,
hears nails trench from boards and every squeak sing.

Questions

What familiar ideas or beliefs undergo challenge in this poem? How can we make sense of the challenge? Write a response and then compare it with the one below.

Response

EDITOR: Among the familiar ideas and beliefs challenged are these: (1) Spring cannot be imagined except as an occasion for exhilaration; (2) the sights and sounds of spring are uniquely nourishing to the sense of beauty; (3) the special vocation of poets is to give utterance to the universal human impulse to salute the season of rebirth.

To whom are these "familiar" ideas? Not to everybody, that's true — but certainly to many readers of poetry. For centuries poets have been producing "spring poems," songs in which the season is hailed as a unique combination of sights and sounds with special significance to poetry. And several poetic gestures have been repeated (with variations) often enough for them to be thought of as *conventions*. One convention, for instance, is mimicry by the poet of birdsong, as in "Spring's Welcome."

JOHN LYLY   (1553–1606)
Spring's Welcome

What bird so sings, yet so does wail?
O 'tis the ravish'd nightingale.
Jug, jug, jug, tereu! she cries!
And still her woes at midnight rise,
Brave prick-song! Who is't now we hear?   5
None but the lark so shrill and clear;
Now at heaven's gate she claps her wings,
The morn not waking till she sings.
Hark, hark, with what a pretty throat
Poor robin redbreast tunes his note!   10
Hark how the jolly cuckoos sing
Cuckoo! to welcome in the spring!
Cuckoo! to welcome in the spring!

Another convention of spring poems is that they consider spring to hold special meaning for lovers. Shakespeare follows this convention in "A Lover and His Lass."

WILLIAM SHAKESPEARE   (1564–1616)

A Lover and His Lass

It was a lover and his lass
 With a hey and a ho, and a hey-nonino!
That o'er the green corn-field did pass
In the spring time, the only pretty ring time,
When birds do sing hey ding a ding: 5
 Sweet lovers love the Spring.

Between the acres of the rye
These pretty country folks would lie:
This carol they began that hour,
How that life was but a flower: 10

And therefore take the present time
 With a hey and a ho, and a hey-nonino!
For love is crownèd with the prime
In the spring time, the only pretty ring time,
When birds do sing hey ding a ding: 15
 Sweet lovers love the Spring.

Still another convention transforms spring into an hour of perfection not merely for birds and lovers but for streets and fields, old and young, animals and human beings alike, as in this poem by Thomas Nashe.

THOMAS NASHE   (1567–1601)

Spring

Spring, the sweet Spring, is the year's pleasant king;
Then blooms each thing, then maids dance in a ring,
Cold doth not sting, the pretty birds do sing,
 Cuckoo, jug-jug, pu-we, to-witta-woo!

The palm and may make country houses gay,   5
Lambs frisk and play, the shepherds pipe all day,
And we hear aye birds tune this merry lay,
 Cuckoo, jug-jug, pu-we, to-witta-woo!

The fields breathe sweet, the daisies kiss our feet,
Young lovers meet, old wives a-sunning sit,   10
In every street these tunes our ears do greet,
   Cuckoo, jug-jug, pu-we, to-witta-woo!
    Spring! the sweet Spring!

The events and experience evoked by all these conventions are pleasant, happy, revivifying; the effect is to characterize the coming of spring as among the most splendid occurrences human creatures can know. We may or may not have all the pertinent poetic conventions about spring in mind when we read Smith's spring poem, but even if we're aware of them only in the vaguest kind of way, we can feel that standard views are under challenge.

One way to make sense of the challenge in "The Spring Poem" to the three familiar ideas just mentioned is to think about the ranges of truth that the ideas omit. The melting of winter that brings up daffodils also uncovers the uglier hulks that merciful snowbanks have hidden for a season. The loosening and easing rejuvenation of the world that brings on birdsong also produces "spunky mildew" (line 8), a fresh start for the processes of decomposition in numberless millions of junk heaps, and new enterprises for the more rancid levels of insect life. And the poets who celebrate spring as though poetry were necessarily or properly a purely upbeat enterprise are obviously betraying their own medium, which at its best has no room for mindless uplift.

We need to go further than this, though, if we're to grasp the interest of Smith's challenge to these notions. Implicit in the careful account of what happens to a rusty car upon the coming of spring is a reminder that the softened landscape so often hailed in art is, in an industrial civilization, defaced, and that nothing in the natural processes of growth and rebirth touches this world of nonbiodegradable stuffs that all of us now inhabit. Smith's wry poem is hardly a sermon against spring and for beat-up car springs (Smith's pun mocks both his own title and the remark by the poet Louise Glück that he uses as an epigraph.)

But the poem does assert, lightly yet firmly, that longing for the good news of nature tends to seduce us into somewhat reductive views of our situation. To claim that our spring has much in common with spring in pastoral cultures as they existed in yesteryear is only to delude ourselves.

CARYL CHURCHILL   (b. 1938)
Light Shining in Buckinghamshire

> You great Curmudgeons, you hang a man for stealing, when
> you yourselves have stolen from your brethren all land and crea-
> tures. *More Light Shining in Buckinghamshire*, a Digger pamphlet, 1649

A revolutionary belief in the millennium went through the
middle ages and broke out strongly in England at the time of the
civil war. Soldiers fought the king in the belief that Christ would
come and establish heaven on earth. What was established instead was an authoritarian parliament, the massacre of the Irish,
the development of capitalism.

For a short time when the king had been defeated anything
seemed possible, and the play shows the amazed excitement of
people taking hold of their own lives, and their gradual betrayal
as those who led them realised that freedom could not be had
without property being destroyed. At the Putney debates Cromwell and Ireton argued for property; Gerrard Winstanley led
Diggers to take over the common land: "There can be no universal liberty till this universal community be established." The Levellers and Diggers were crushed by the Army, and many turned
in desperation to the remaining belief in the millennium, that
Christ would come to do what they had failed in. The last long
scene of the play is a meeting of Ranters, whose ecstatic and
anarchic belief in economic and sexual freedom was the last
desperate burst of revolutionary feeling before the restoration.

The simple "Cavaliers and Roundheads" history taught at
school hides the complexity of the aims and conflicts of those to
the left of Parliament. We are told of a step forward to today's
democracy but not of a revolution that didn't happen; we are
told of Charles and Cromwell but not of the thousands of men
and women who tried to change their lives. Though nobody now
expects Christ to make heaven on earth, their voices are surprisingly close to us.

A NOTE ON THE PRODUCTION

First of all, Max Stafford-Clark and I read and talked till we
had found a subject in the millennial movement in the civil war.
There was then a three-week workshop with the actors in which,

through talk, reading, games, and improvisation, we tried to get closer to the issues and the people. During the next six weeks I wrote a script, and went on working on it with the company during the five-week rehearsal period.

It is hard to explain exactly the relationship between the workshop and the text. The play is not improvised: it is a written text and the actors did not make up its lines. But many of the characters and scenes were based on ideas that came from improvisation at the workshop and during rehearsal. I could give endless examples of how something said or done by one of the actors is directly connected to something in the text. Just as important, though harder to define, was the effect on the writing of the way the actors worked, their accuracy and commitment. I worked very closely with Max, and though I wrote the text the play is something we both imagined.

The characters Claxton and Cobbe are loosely based on Laurence Clarkson, or Claxton, and Abiezer Coppe, or Cobbe, two Ranters whose writings have survived; the others are fictional, except for those in the Putney debates, which is a much-condensed transcript of three days of debate among Army officers and soldiers' delegates which took place in 1647.

The characters are not played by the same actors each time they appear. The audience should not have to worry exactly which character they are seeing. Each scene can be taken as a separate event rather than part of a story. This seems to reflect better the reality of large events like war and revolution where many people share the same kind of experience. I recommend other productions to distribute parts in the same way, since the play was constructed with this in mind; and there would be difficulties if each character was played by one actor — for instance, Briggs's friend in the recruiting scene is by implication Claxton, from the reference to the baby, yet in the last scene Briggs and Claxton meet as strangers. When different actors play the parts what comes over is a large event involving many people, whose characters resonate in a way they wouldn't if they were more clearly defined.

The play was performed with a table and six chairs, which were used as needed in each scene. When any chairs were not used they were put on either side of the stage, and actors who were not in a scene sat at the side and watched the action. They moved the furniture themselves. Props were carefully chosen and minimal.

SCENES

Cobbe Prays	Diggers
The Vicar Talks to His Servant	Claxton Explains
Margaret Brotherton Is Tried	Briggs Writes a Letter
Star Recruits	The War in Ireland
Brotherton Meets the Man	The Vicar Welcomes the New Land-
Briggs Joins Up	lord
Hoskins Interrupts the Preacher	A Woman Leaves Her Baby
Claxton Brings Hoskins Home	A Butcher Talks to His Customers
Cobbe's Vision	Lockyer's Funeral
Two Women Look in a Mirror	The Meeting
Briggs Recalls a Battle	After
The Putney Debates	

DOCUMENTARY MATERIAL

Fear, and the pit . . . Isaiah 24, xvii–xx
A Fiery Flying Roll, Abiezer Coppe 1649[1]
All Seems Beautiful . . . Song of Myself, Walt Whitman
The Putney Debates, 1647
The True Levellers Standard Advanced, Gerrard Winstanley, 1649
The English Soldier's Standard to Repair to, 1649
The Moderate, a Leveller newspaper, 1649
The sleep of the labouring man . . . Ecclesiastes 5

LIST OF CHARACTERS

Cobbe	Claxton's Wife
Vicar	1st Woman
Servant	2nd Woman
1st JP	Colonel Thomas Rainborough
2nd JP	Edward Sexby
Margaret Brotherton	Colonel Nathaniel Rich
Star	John Wildman
Briggs	Oliver Cromwell
Friend	General Ireton
Man	Winstanley
Preacher	Butcher
Hoskins	Drunk
Claxton	

ACT I

All (sing Isaiah 24, xvii–xx): Fear, and the pit, and the snare are
upon thee, O inhabitant of the earth.

[1] The correct date is 1649 though the date 1647 is given in the text as this seemed
the best place for the scene. It seemed unnecessarily confusing for the audience
to go forward to 1649 then back to 1647 for the Putney debates.

And it shall come to pass that he who fleeth from the noise of the fear shall fall into the pit; and he that cometh out of the midst of the pit shall be taken in the snare; for the windows from on high are open, and the foundations of the earth do shake.

The earth is utterly broken down, the earth is clean dissolved, the earth is moved exceedingly.

The earth shall reel to and fro like a drunkard, and shall be removed like a cottage; and the transgression thereof shall be heavy upon it; and it shall fall and not rise again.

Scene. *Cobbe Prays*

Cobbe: Forgive my sins of the night and already this new day. Oh prevent me today from all the sins I will note — action, word, thought, or faint motion less than any of these — or commit unknowing despite my strict guard set. Sloth not rising when mother called, the air so cold, lay five minutes of sin till she called again. Break me, God, to welcome your cold. Lust when the girl gave meat last night, not keeping my eyes on my plate but followed her hand. Repented last night with groans to you, O God, and still dreamt. Guard me today. Let me not go to hell, hot nor cold hell, let me be one of your elect. What is worst, I am not praying to you about the worst sin. I sin in my fear of praying about that sin, I sin in denying my fear. But you cut through that mesh, knowing. Why is it not enough to use your name in prayer, oh God, oh Lord Jesus Christ, amen, this is prayer, oh God, no swearing. Rich men of Antichrist on horses swear, king's officers say "dammee" laughing. The beggar swore when they whipped him through the street and my heart leapt at each curse, a curse for each lash. Is he damned? Would I be? At table last night when father said grace I wanted to seize the table and turn it over so the white cloth slid, silver, glass, capon, claret, comfits overturned. I wanted to shout your name and damn my family and myself eating so quietly when what is going on outside our gate? Words come out of my mouth like toads, I swear toads, toads will sit on me in hell. And what light on my father, still no light? Not to honour my father is sin, and sin to honour a greedy, cruel, hypocritical —— Is it sin to kneel here till he leave the house? I cannot go down to him. It is sin to go down. I will wait till I hear the door. To avoid his blessing.

SCENE. *The Vicar Talks to His Servant (Claxton)*

The Vicar sits at table, with wine and oranges.

Vicar: How's the baby today? Any better?
Servant: No, sir.
Vicar: You saw who were missing again from morning service.
Servant: Sir.
Vicar: No better — no worse, I hope?
Servant: Yes, sir.
Vicar: Good, good. The sermon would have done them good. It wasn't my own, you could probably tell. The Bishop's naturally more gifted. But it's no good having it read in every parish if nobody compels the tenants to hear it. It's the ones who weren't there that I was talking to. "From whence come wars and fightings among you?" From their lusts, from greed and envy and pride, which are from the devil, that's where the wars come from. When you said yes, you meant no worse?
Servant: No sir.
Vicar: Worse.
Servant: Sir.
Vicar: God tries you severely in your children. It must have been a comfort this morning to have the Bishop himself encourage you to suffer. "Be afflicted and mourn and weep." That is the way to heaven.
Servant: Sir.

He pours more wine.

Vicar: Why we have this war is because men want heaven now. If God meant us to have heaven on earth, why did he throw us out of paradise? They're fighting God himself, do they know that? They must be brought before the magistrates and forced to come next Sunday, and I'll tell them in my own words. Thank you, a little. This is a godly estate and they will be evicted if they don't submit.

He gives Servant an orange.

Still we must pray your baby is spared this time. Take it orange.

He drinks and takes an orange.

Servant: Thank you, sir.
Vicar: And if it is not spared, we must submit. We all have to suffer in this life.

He drinks.

SCENE. *Margaret Brotherton Is Tried*

She is barely audible.

1st JP: Is this the last?
2nd JP: One more.
1st JP: It's a long list.
2nd JP: Hard times.
1st JP: Soft hearts. Yours.
2nd JP: Step forward please.
1st JP: I still say he should have been hanged.
2nd JP: He'll die in jail. Name?
Brotherton: Margaret Brotherton.
1st JP: That's no example, nobody sees it.
2nd JP: Margaret Brotherton. Begging. Guilty or not guilty?
Brotherton: I don't know what you mean . . .
1st JP: You're not of this parish?
2nd JP: Where do you come from?
Brotherton: Last week I was at Aston Clinton, and before that from Northampton.
1st JP: I don't want to be told every place you've ever been. Where were you born?
Brotherton: Long Buckby.
1st JP: If you belong fifty miles away, what are you doing here?
2nd JP: Have you relations here? Friends you could stay with?
1st JP: Tell us about your third cousin's wife's brother who has work for you. No? Or have you been told you get something for nothing here?
2nd JP: It's only our own poor who get help from this parish.
1st JP: And we don't give money. So you can't drink it. It's your system of poor relief that brings them — they hear there's free bread and cheese, free fuel, there's no parish for miles that does that.
2nd JP: We can't help every vagrant in the country.
1st JP: You must go back to where you were born.
2nd JP: If her parents didn't come from there they won't take her.
1st JP: Her father's parish.
2nd JP: She's never been there.
1st JP: The parish she last lived in.
2nd JP: They turned her out for begging.
1st JP: Exactly, and so do we.
2nd JP: Why aren't you married?
Brotherton : . . .

1st JP: Can we please agree on a sentence.

2nd JP: First offence. Let's be lenient.

1st JP: It's only fair to warn you in advance that the next council meeting may reconsider the whole question of poor relief.

2nd JP: Margaret Brotherton, we find you guilty of vagrancy and sentence you to be stripped to the waist and beaten to the bounds of this parish and returned parish by parish to . . .

1st JP: Where she was born.

2nd JP: To the parish where you were born. Next please.

Scene. *Star Recruits*

A prayer meeting.

Star: Christ watch over this meeting and grant that your kingdom will come, amen.

All: Amen.

Star: Life is hard, brothers, and how will it get better? I tell you, life in Babylon is hard and Babylon must be destroyed. In Babylon you are slaves. Babylon is the kingdom of Antichrist. The kingdom of popery. The kingdom of the king. And it must be destroyed. Because then will come the kingdom of Jerusalem. And in Jerusalem you will be free. That is why you will join as soldiers. To destroy Antichrist. To fight with parliament for Jerusalem. To fight with Christ's saints for Christ's kingdom. Because when parliament has defeated Antichrist then Christ will come. Christ will come in person, God and man, and will rule over England for one thousand years. And the saints will reign with him. And who are the saints? You are. The poor people of this country. When Christ came, did he come to the rich? No. He came to the poor. He is coming to you again. If you prepare for him by defeating Antichrist which is the royalists. If you join the army now you will be one of the saints. You will rule with Jesus a thousand years. We have just had another bad harvest.* But, it is written, when Jesus comes "the floors shall be full of wheat and the vats overflow with wine." Why did Jesus Christ purchase the earth with his blood? He purchased it for the saints. For you. It will all be yours. You are poor now. You are despised now. But the gentlemen who look down on you will soon find out that the inhabitants of Jerusalem are commonwealth men. Now is the moment. It will be too late when Christ comes to say you want to be saved. Some will be

---

*Dialogue simultaneous with † to † on p. 385.

cast into the pit, into the burning lake, into the unquench-able fire. And some will be clothed in white linen and ride white horses and rule with King Jesus in Jerusalem shinning with jasper and chrysolite. So give now, give what you can to Christ now to pay his soldiers. Christ will pay you back in diamonds. Join now for a soldier of Christ and you will march out of this town to Jerusalem. Who are you? What are you? I know you all and you know me. You are nobody here. You have nothing. But the moment you join the army you will have everything. You will be as important as anybody in England. You will be Christ's Saints.*

†*Briggs:* Going for a soldier?

Friend: What soldier? What side?

Briggs: Parliament, inne, Mr. Star?

Friend: He's a gentleman, inne, Mr. Star?

Briggs: Parliament's gentlemen. But parliament's for us.

Friend: What's the pay?

Briggs: More than I'm getting now. And they give you a musket.

Friend: For yourself?

Briggs: To use it. Heard about the baby.

Friend: Ah.

Briggs: Wife all right? Thinking of going.

Friend: What about . . .

Briggs: Send them money. And where I am now, I'll be out again in the winter like last year. I'm not having that. You keep an eye on them. Won't be long.

Friend: Christ's coming anyway.

Briggs: You reckon?

Friend: Something's going on.†

1st Friend: And when will Christ come?

Star: When will Christ come? "From the abomination that maketh desolate, there shall be one thousand, two hundred and ninety days." Now a day is taken for a year. And that brings us to sixteen hundred and fifty. Yes, sixteen hundred and fifty. So we haven't much time. Jerusalem in England in sixteen fifty. Don't leave it too late. Join the army today and be sure of your place in Jerusalem.

Now I've a list here of names that have joined already. Twenty-three saints that live in this town. Whose name is next on the list of saints?

Briggs: What's the pay?

Star: The pay is eightpence a day. Better than labouring. And it's every day. Not day labour. Not just the days you fight. Every day.

Briggs: And keep?

Star: Keep is taken out. But you're given a musket. Shall I take your name?

Three Listeners speak out.

1st: I won't go to fight. But there's three of us could pay for a musket among the three.

2nd: I've got four silver spoons. They'd pay for something.

3rd: You can have a buckle I was given.

Briggs: I'll give my name. Briggs. Thomas Briggs.

SCENE. *Brotherton Meets the Man*

She has several bags. He has a bottle.

Brotherton: Went up the road about a mile then I come back. There's a dog not tied up. So I started back where I slept last night. But that was into the wind. So I'm stopping here. It's not my shoes. I've got better shoes for walking in my bag. My sister's shoes that's dead. They wouldn't fit you. How much you got?

Man: Drunk it all.

Brotherton: I'm not asking.

He gives her the bottle.

Man: It doesn't matter not eating if you can drink. Doesn't matter not drinking if you can sleep. But you can't sleep in this wind.

He takes the bottle back.

Brotherton: What you got there?

Man: I thought my hands were cold but they're warm to yours.

Brotherton: What you got?

Man: Look, here, that's my Bible. That's my father's name, that's my name. Two and a half acres. I had to sell my knife. I sold my knife.

Brotherton: How much you got now then?

Man: Tenpence.

Brotherton: That's a long time till you got nothing. Then you can sell the Bible.

Man: No, I need that.

Brotherton: What I've got, look. The shoes. A bottle, that's a good bottle. I had another one that was no good. I don't often throw something out but I won't carry anything I don't like. A piece of cloth. You can wrap it round. It's got lots of uses. I could sell you that. You can't see what's in here. That's more of my sister's things that's dead. There's a piece of rope. You could have that for a halfpenny.

Man: Your face is cold. Your neck's cold. Your back's no warmer. The wind goes right through.

Brotherton: You can have the rope and the cloth both for a half-penny.

Man: Come and lie down. Out of the wind. I'll give you a half-penny after.

Brotherton: No. With tenpence, we can get indoors for that.

Man: Wouldn't last long.

Brotherton: Last more than one day. Even one day's good.

Man: If only I knew when Christ was coming.

Brotherton: You think he's coming?

Man: He must. If only the money would last till the world ends then it would be all right. It's warm in heaven.

Brotherton: If he comes tomorrow and you've not drunk your money. Sitting here with tenpence in the cold. Christ laugh at you for that.

Scene. *Briggs Joins Up*

Star eats.

Star: You keep your hat on. New style catching on.

Briggs: Yes sir. I mean, yes, I do.

Star: As a sign you're as good as me?

Briggs: Yes. Nothing personal Mr. Star. Before God only.

Star: Parson seen you like that?

Briggs: He said I was a scorpion, sir. Mr. Star. I mean, he said I was a scorpion.

Star: A hat's all right for a soldier. It shows courage.

Pause, while Star eats.

You know what I'm eating?

Briggs: Your dinner?

Star: What it is.

Briggs: Meat?

Star: The name of it.

Briggs: Beef? Mutton? I can't tell from here.

Star: Sheep. Or, if it was, cow, but it's sheep. Now what language is that, beef, mutton?

Briggs: It's not language —

Star: Beef and mutton is Norman words. The Saxon raised the animal. Sheep. Cow. The Norman ate the meat. Boeuf, mouton. Even the laws of this country aren't written in English.

Briggs: So I've come.

Star: You haven't got a horse, so I can't put you in the horse, though there's more thinking men there with hats on and writing their grievances down on paper. But you'll find plenty to talk about in the foot. Eightpence a day and we deduct food and clothing. Cheese and hard biscuit. Anything else?

Briggs: You don't know how long it's going to be?

Star: Till we win.

Briggs: That's what I mean. How long till we win?

Star: What we're fighting for . . . We've known each other all our lives. Our paths never cross. But you know me as an honest dealer. I've been leant on many times to keep up the price of corn when it could be down. And I'd be a richer man. The hunger now is no fault of mine. You're a Saxon. I'm a Saxon. Our fathers were conquered six hundred years ago by William the Norman. His colonels are our lords. His cavalry are our knights. His common foot soldiers are our squires. When you join this army you are fighting a foreign enemy. You are fighting an invasion of your own soil. Parliament is Saxon. The Army is Saxon. Jesus Christ is Saxon. The Royalists are Normans and the Normans are Antichrist. We are fighting to be free men and own our own land. So we fight as long as it takes. In the meantime there's no looting. No raping. No driving off of cattle or firing ricks. We're not antichristian royalties. We're Christ's saints. It's an army that values godliness. There's no swearing. The men don't like swearing. They like reading their Bibles. They like singing hymns. They like talk. We don't discourage talk. Your officers are not all gentlemen, they're men like you.

Briggs: Bacon. Is bacon Norman?

Star: Pork, Briggs. Pig. Very good.

Briggs: And Jacob the younger brother is the Saxon herds the pigs. And Esau the older brother is the Norman eats the pork.

Star: Very good, Briggs. Excellent. Now one thing. You wear your hat. Will you take orders?

Briggs: If they're not against God.

Star: They can't be against God in God's army.

SCENE. *Hoskins Interrupts the Preacher*

Preacher: My text today is from Psalm one hundred and forty-nine.

"Sing unto the Lord a new song and his praise in the congregation of saints.

Let the high praises of God be in their mouth and a two-edged sword in their hand.

To bind their kings with chains and their nobles with fetters of iron."

All and Hoskins: Amen, amen.

Preacher: It is no sin to take up arms against the king. It is no sin if we fight singing praises to God, if we fight to bind an unjust king with chains.

All: Amen.

Preacher: For it is written: "The saints of the most High shall take the kingdom and possess the kingdom forever, even forever and ever."

Hoskins: Forever and ever, amen.

All: Amen.

Preacher: The saints will take the kingdom. And who are the saints?

Hoskins: We all are.

Preacher: The saints are those whom God has chosen from all eternity to be his people. For he has chosen a certain number of particular men to be his elect. None can be added to them and none can be taken away. And others he has chosen to be eternally damned. As John tells us in Revelation: "Whosoever was not written in the book of life was cast into the lake of fire." So it is God's saints, chosen before their birth, written in the book of life, who will bind the king and the nobles and take the kingdom which will last forever.

All: Amen.

Hoskins: But no one is damned. We can all bind the king.

Preacher: Who are the saints? They are not the same people who rule in this world.

Hoskins: Amen to that.

All: Amen.

Preacher: When Christ first came to earth he came to the poor. And it is to the poor, to you, to tailors, cobblers, chapmen, ploughmen, that he is coming again. He will not set up a kingdom like we have now, a kingdom of Antichrist, a kingdom of a king, nobles, and gentry. In Christ's kingdom no worldly honour counts. A noble can be damned and a beggar saved.

All: Amen.

Preacher: All that counts is whether God has chosen you. Look into your hearts and see whether God has chosen you or ——

Hoskins: He's chosen me. He's chosen everyone.

Preacher: Or whether you are given over to the devil. For those that are not saved will be cast into the pit. "And he that cometh out of the midst of the pit shall be taken in the snare."

Hoskins: There is no pit, there is no snare.

Preacher: For now is the time spoken of in Isaiah, "the earth is utterly broken down, the earth is clean dissolved."

Hoskins: God would not send us into the pit. Christ saves us from that.

Preacher: "And it shall come to pass in that day, that the Lord shall punish the host of the high ones that are on high, and the kings of the earth upon the earth."

Hoskins: Yes he will cast them down but he will not damn them eternally.

Preacher: Why are you speaking? I let it pass but you are too loud. Women can't speak in church.

Hoskins: God speaks in me.

Preacher: For St. Paul says, "I suffer not a woman to teach, nor to usurp authority over the man, but to be in silence."

Hoskins: A text? a text is it? do you want a text?

Preacher: "For Adam was first formed then Eve. And Adam was not deceived but the woman being deceived was in the transgression."

Hoskins: Joel. Chapter two. Verse twenty-eight. "And it shall come to pass that I will pour out my spirit upon all flesh; and your sons and your daughters shall prophesy, and your old men shall dream dreams and your young men shall see visions. And also upon the servants and upon the handmaids in those days will I pour out my spirit."

Preacher: It has got about that I allow answers to my sermons. But this is taking the freedom to speak too far. If anyone can call out whenever they like it will be complete confusion. I allow answers to my sermon if they are sober and godly and if the speaker has the courtesy to wait ——

Hoskins: You say most of us are damned. You say we are chosen to be damned before we are born.

Preacher: I said to wait till the end of the sermon, and I do not allow women to speak at all since it is forbidden.

Hoskins: How can God choose us from all eternity to be saved or damned when there's nothing we've done?

Preacher: I will answer this question because it is a common one and others, who have the grace to wait, may be asking it within themselves. But I am not answering you. How can some people be damned before they are born? Sin is the cause of damnation, but the reason God does not choose to save some people from sin and damnation is his free will and pleasure, not our own.

All: Amen.

Hoskins: God's pleasure? that we burn? what sort of God takes pleasure in pain?

Preacher: And those few that are saved are saved not by their own virtue though if they are the elect they will by their very nature try to live virtuously, but by God's grace and mercy ——

Hoskins: No, it's not just a few. Not just a few elect go to heaven. He thinks most people are bad. The king thinks most people are bad. He's against the king but he's saying the same.

Preacher: Get her out.

Two of the congregation throw Hoskins out.

Hoskins: In his kingdom of heaven there's going to be a few in bliss and the rest of us in hell. What's the difference from what we've got now? You are all saved. Yes, you are all saved. Not one of you is damned ——

Preacher: Woman, you are certainly damned.

SCENE. *Claxton Brings Hoskins Home*

Wife is bathing Hoskins's bruised head.

Wife: What you go there for?

Claxton: When they beat her, you know . . . I couldn't . . .

Wife: But who did it?

Claxton: They chased her down the hill from the church and when she fell over . . . I couldn't stop them. I came up after.

Wife: But what you go there for?

Claxton: Just to see.

Wife: It's not proper church.

Claxton: Just to see.

Wife: Parson won't like it.

Claxton: Parson needn't.

Wife: I'm not going there if they beat women.

Claxton: No but they let you speak.

Wife: No but they beat her.

Claxton: No but men. They let men speak.

Wife: Did you speak?
Claxton: Don't want to work for parson.
Wife: What then?
Claxton: I don't know, I don't know.

Wife finishes bathing Hoskins's head.

Hoskins: Thank you.
Wife: Better?
Hoskins: Yes thank you.
Wife: Where you from?
Hoskins: Near Leicester.
Wife: What are you doing here then?
Hoskins: Travelling.
Wife: Are you married? Or are you on your own?
Hoskins: No, I'm never on my own.
Claxton: Who are you with then?
Hoskins: Different men sometimes. But it's not like you think.
    Well it is like you think. But then nothing's like you think.
    Who I'm with is Jesus Christ.
Claxton: How do you live?
Hoskins: Sometimes people give me money. They give me for
    preaching. I'm not a beggar.
Claxton: Didn't say that.
Hoskins: Steal though if I can. It's only the rich go to hell. Did you
    know that?
Claxton: I think they do.
Hoskins: And we don't, did you know that?
Wife: You don't live anywhere?
Hoskins: I'm not the only one.
Wife: No one look after you?
Hoskins: Jesus God.
Wife: Are your parents living?
Hoskins: You know how Jesus says forsake your parents. Anyone
    who hath forsaken houses, or brethren, or sisters, or father,
    or mother or wife . . . or children, or lands, for my sake. See.
Claxton: No need to go that far.
Hoskins: Well, it's the times. Christ will be here soon so what's it
    matter.
Claxton: Do you believe that?
Hoskins: I do.
Wife: But women can't preach. We bear children in pain, that's
    why. And they die. For our sin, Eve's sin. That's why we have
    pain. We're not clean. We have to obey. The man, whatever

he's like. If he beat us that's why. We have blood, we're shameful, our bodies are worse than a man's. All bodies are evil but ours is worst. That's why we can't speak.

Hoskins: Well I can.

Wife: You haven't had children.

Hoskins: That's all wrong what you said. We're not ——

Wife: Have you had a child?

Hoskins: No but ——

Wife: Then you don't know. We wouldn't be punished if it wasn't for something.

Hoskins: We're not ——

Wife: And then they die. You don't know.

Hoskins: They die because how we live. My brothers did. Died of hunger more than fever. My mother kept boiling up the same bones.

Wife: Go home. Go home.

Hoskins: No, I'm out with God. You want to get out too.

Wife: No. No we don't.

Claxton: Sometimes I read in Revelation. Because people say now is the last days. "And I saw a new heaven and a new earth: for the first heaven and the first earth were passed away. And there was no more sea." Why no more sea? I never seen the sea. But England's got a fine navy and we trade by sea and go to new countries, so why no more sea? Now I think this is why, I can explain this. I see into it. I have something from God. The sea is water. And salt water, not like a stream or a well, you can't drink it. And you can't breathe it. Because it's water. But fish can breathe it. But men can't live in it.

Wife: What are you talking about?

Claxton: What it's saying, seems to me. Fish can live in it. Men can't. Now men can't live here either. How we live is like the sea. We can't breathe. Our squire, he's like a fish. Looks like a fish too, if you saw him. And parson. Parson can breathe. He swims about, waggles his tail. Bitter water and he lives in it. Bailiff. Justices. Hangman. Lawyer. Mayor. All the gentry. Swimming about. We can't live in it. We drown. I'm a drowned man.

Wife: Stop it, you can't do it, you're making a fool ——

Hoskins: No, it's good.

Claxton: Octopus is a kind of fish with lots of arms grasping and full of black stink. Sharks eat you. Whales, you're lost inside them, they're so big, they swallow you up and never notice. They live in it.

Wife: Stop it.

Claxton: We can't live. We are dead. Bitter water. There shall be a
new heaven. And a new earth. And no more sea.
Wife: No, don't start. Don't speak. I can't.

SCENE. *Cobbe's Vision*

One of the Actors (announces a pamphlet by Abiezer Coppe): A fiery flying roll: being a word from the Lord to all the great ones of
the earth, whom this may concern: being the last warning
piece at the dreadful day of Judgment. For now the Lord is
come to first, warn, second, advise and warn, third, charge,
fourth, judge and sentence the great ones. As also most com-
passionately informing, and most lovingly and pathetically
advising and warning London. And all by his most excellent
majesty, dwelling in and shining through Auxilium Patris,
alias Coppe. Imprinted in London, at the beginning of that
notable day, wherein the secrets of all hearts are laid open.
Sixteen hundred and forty-seven.
Cobbe: All my strength, my forces, were utterly routed, my house
I dwelt in fired, my father and mother forsook me, and the
wife of my bosom loathed me, and I was utterly plagued and
sunk into nothing, into the bowels of the still Eternity (my
mother's womb) out of which I came naked, and whereto I
returned again naked. And lying a while there, rapt up in
silence, at length (the body's outward form being all this
while awake) I heard with my outward ear (to my apprehension) a most terrible thunderclap, and after that a second.
And upon the second, which was exceeding terrible, I saw a
great body of light like the light of the sun, and red as fire, in
the form (as it were) of a drum, whereupon with exceeding
trembling and amazement on the flesh, and with joy unspeakable in the spirit, I clapped my hands, and cried out,
Amen, Halelujah, Halelujah, Amen. And so lay trembling
sweating and smoking (for the space of half an hour). At
length with a loud voice I (inwardly) cried out, Lord what wilt
thou do with me? My most excellent majesty and eternal
glory in me answered and said, fear not. I will take thee up
into my everlasting kingdom. But first you must drink a bitter cup, a bitter cup, a bitter cup. Whereupon I was thrown
into the belly of hell (and take what you can of it in these
expressions, though the matter is beyond expression) I was
among all the devils in hell, even in their most hideous crew.

And under all this terror and amazement, a tiny spark of transcendent, unspeakable glory, survived, and sustained itself, triumphing, exulting, and exalting itself above all the fiends. And I heard a voice saying, "Go to London, to London, that great city, and tell them I am coming."

SCENE. *Two Women Look in a Mirror*

1st Woman comes in with a broken mirror. 2nd Woman is mending.

1st Woman: Look, look, you must come quick.
2nd Woman: What you got there?
1st Woman: Look. Who's that? That's you. That's you and me.
2nd Woman: Is that me? Where you get it?
1st Woman: Up the house.
2nd Woman: What? with him away? It's all locked up.
1st Woman: I went in the front door.
2nd Woman: The front door?
1st Woman: Nothing happened to me. You can take things ——
2nd Woman: That's his things. That's stealing. You'll be killed for that.
1st Woman: No, not any more, it's all ours now, so we won't burn the corn because that's our corn now and we're not going to let the cattle out because they're ours too.
2nd Woman: You been in his rooms?
1st Woman: I been upstairs. In the bedrooms.
2nd Woman: I been in the kitchen.
1st Woman: I lay on the bed. White linen sheets. Three wool blankets.
2nd Woman: Did you take one?
1st Woman: I didn't know what to take, there's so much.
2nd Woman: Oh if everyone's taking something I want a blanket. But what when he comes back?
1st Woman: He'll never come back. We're burning his papers, that's the Norman papers that give him his lands. That's like him burnt. There's no one over us. There's pictures of him and his grandfather and his great great — a long row of pictures and we pulled them down.
2nd Woman: But he won't miss a blanket.
1st Woman: There's an even bigger mirror that we didn't break. I'll show you where. You see your whole body at once. You see yourself standing in that room. They must know what they look like all the time. And now we do.

SCENE. *Briggs Recalls a Battle*

Briggs: The noise was very loud, the shouting and the cannon behind us, and it was dark from the clouds of smoke blowing over so you couldn't see more than a few yards, so that when I hit this boy across the face with my musket I was suddenly frightened as he went under that he was on my own side; but another man was on me and I hit at him and I didn't know who I was fighting till the smoke cleared and I saw men I knew and a tree I'd stood under before the shooting began. But after I was wounded, lying with my head downhill, watching men take bodies off the field, I didn't know which was our side and which was them, but then I saw it didn't matter because what we were fighting was not each other but Antichrist and even the soldiers on the other side would be made free and be glad when they saw the paradise we'd won, so that the dead on both sides died for that, to free us of that darkness and confusion we'd lived in and bring us all into the quiet and sunlight. And even when they moved me the pain was less than the joy.

All sing from "Song of the Open Road" by Walt Whitman.

All: All seems beautiful to me.
I can repeat over to men and women, You have done such good to me,
I would do the same to you,
I will recruit for myself and you as I go,
I will scatter myself among men and women as I go,
I will toss a new gladness and roughness among them.
Whoever denies me it shall not trouble me,
Whoever accepts me he or she shall be blessed and shall bless me.

SCENE. *The Putney Debates*

Rainborough: The Putney debates, October the twenty-eighth, sixteen forty-seven. I am Colonel Thomas Rainborough, a Leveller.
Sexby: Edward Sexby, private soldier, elected representative or agitator from Fairfax's regiment of horse.
Rich: Colonel Nathaniel Rich.
Wildman: John Wildman, civilian, writer of Leveller pamphlets who has assisted the agitators in drawing up their proposals.

Cromwell: Oliver Cromwell.

Ireton: Commissary General Henry Ireton.

Cromwell: If anyone has anything to say concerning the public business, he has liberty to speak.

Sexby: Lieutenant General Cromwell, Commissary General Ireton, we have been by providence put upon strange things, such as the ancientest here doth scarce remember. And yet we have found little fruit of our endeavours. Truly our miseries and our fellow soldiers' cry out for present help. We, the agents of the common soldiers, have drawn up an Agreement of the People. We declare:

First: That the people of England being very unequally distributed for the election of their deputies in parliament ought to be proportioned according to the number of inhabitants.

Second: That this present parliament be dissolved.

Third: That the people choose a parliament once in two years.

Fourth: That the power of representatives of this nation is inferior only to theirs who choose them, and the people make the following reservations:

First: That matters of religion are not at all entrusted by us to any human power.

Second: That impressing us to serve in wars is against our freedom.

Third: That no person be at any time questioned for anything said or done in the late wars.

These things we declare to be our native rights and are resolved to maintain them with our utmost possibilities.

Cromwell: These things you have offered, they are new to us. This is the first time we have had a view of them. Truly this paper does contain very great alterations of the very government of the kingdom. If we could leap out of one condition into another, I suppose there would not be much dispute. But how do we know another company of men shall not put out a paper as plausible as this? And not only another, and another, but many of this kind. And what do you think the consequence of that would be? Would it not be confusion? Would it not be utter confusion? As well as the consequences we must consider the ways and means: whether the people are prepared to go along with it and whether the great difficulties in our way are likely to be overcome. But I shall speak to nothing but that that tends to uniting us in one. And I am confident you do not bring this paper in peremptoriness of mind, but to receive amendments. First there is the question what commitments lie upon us. We have in time of danger issued several declarations; we have been required by parliament to declare particularly what we meant, and have done so in proposals drawn up by Commissary General Ireton. So before we consider this paper we must consider how far we are free.

Wildman: I was yesterday at a meeting with divers country gentlemen and soldiers and the agitators of the regiments and I declared my agreement with them. They believe that if an obligation is not just, then it is an act of honesty not to keep it.

Ireton: If anyone is free to break any obligation he has entered into, this is a principle that would take away all government. Men would think themselves not obliged by any law they thought not a good law. They would not think themselves obliged to stand by the authority of your paper. There are plausible things in the paper and things very good in it. If we were free from all other commitments I should concur with it further than I can.

Rainborough: Every honest man is bound in duty to God to decline an obligation when he sees it to be evil: he is obliged to discharge his duty to God. There are two other objections: one is division: I think we are utterly undone if we divide. Another thing is difficulties. Truly I think parliament were very indiscreet to contest with the king if they did not consider first that they should go through difficulties; and I think there was no man that entered into this war that did not engage to go through difficulties. Truly I think let the difficulties be round about you, death before you, the sea behind you, and you are convinced the thing is just, you are bound in conscience to carry it on, and I think at the last day it can never be answered to God that you did not do it.

Cromwell: Truly I am very glad that this gentleman is here. We shall enjoy his company longer than I thought we should have done ——

Rainborough: If I should not be kicked out.

Cromwell: —— And it shall not be long enough. We are almost all soldiers. All considerations of not fearing difficulties do wonderfully please us. I do not think any man here wants courage to do that which becomes an honest man and an Englishman to do. And I do not think it was offered by anyone that though a commitment were never so unrighteous it ought to be kept. But perhaps we are upon commitments here that we cannot with honesty break.

Wildman: There is a principle much spreading and much to my trouble: that though a commitment appear to be unjust, yet a person must sit down and suffer under it. To me this is very dangerous, and I see it spreading in the army again. The chief thing in the agreement is to secure the rights and freedoms of the people, which was declared by the army to be absolutely insisted on.

Ireton: I am far from holding that if a man have committed himself to a thing that is evil, that he is bound to perform what he hath promised. But covenants freely made must be kept. Take away that, I do not know what ground there is of anything you call any man's right. I would know what you gentlemen account the right to anything you have in England; anything of estate, land, or goods, what right you have to it. If you resort only to the Law of Nature, I have as much right to take hold of anything I desire as you. Therefore when I hear men speak of laying aside all commitments I tremble at the boundless and endless consequences of it.

Wildman: You take away the substance of the question. Our sense was that an unjust commitment is rather to be broken than kept.

Ireton: But this leads to the end of all government: if you think something is unjust you are not to obey; and if it tend to your loss it is no doubt unjust and you are to oppose it!

Rainborough: One word, here is the consideration now: do we not engage for the parliament and for the liberties of the people of England? That which is dear to me is my freedom, it is that I would enjoy and I will enjoy it if I can.

Ireton: These gentlemen think their own agreement is so infallibly just and right, that anyone who doesn't agree to it is about a thing unlawful.

Rich: If we do not set upon the work presently we are undone. Since the agreement is ready to our hands, I desire that you would read it and debate it.

Ireton: I think because it is so much insisted on we should read the paper.

Wildman: Twenty-ninth of October.

Ireton: Let us hear the first article again.

Sexby: That the people of England being very unequally distributed for the election of their deputies ——

Ireton: "The people of England." This makes me think that the meaning is that every man that is an inhabitant is to have an equal vote in the election. But if it only means the people that had the election before, I have nothing to say against it.

Do those that brought it know whether they mean all that had a former right, or those that had no right before are to come in?

Rainborough: All inhabitants that have not lost their birthright should have an equal vote in elections. For really I think that the poorest he in England hath a life to live as the greatest he; therefore truly sir, I think it's clear, that every man that is to live under a government ought first by his own consent to put himself under it.

Ireton: I think no person hath a right to an interest in the dispos-ing of the affairs of this kingdom that hath not a permanent fixed interest in this kingdom. We talk of birthright. Men may justly have by their birthright, by their being born in England, that we should not seclude them out of England, that we should not refuse to give them air and place and ground and the freedom of the highways. That I think is due to a man by birth. But that by a man's being born here he shall have a share in that power that shall dispose of the lands here, I do not think it sufficient ground.

Rainborough: Truly sir, I am of the same opinion I was. I do not find anything in the law of God that a lord shall choose twenty members, and a gentleman but two, or a poor man shall choose none. I find no such thing in the law of nature or the law of nations. But I do find that all Englishmen must be subject to English law, and the foundation of the law lies in the people. Every man in England ought not to be ex-empted from the choice of those who are to make laws for him to live under, and for him, for aught I know, to lose his life by.

Ireton: All the main thing that I speak for is because I would have an eye to property. Let every man consider that he do not go that way to take away all property. Now I wish we may con-sider of what right you will claim that all the people should have a right to elections. Is it by right of nature? Then I think you must deny all property too. If you say one man hath an equal right with another to the choosing of him that will govern him, by the same right of nature he hath the same right in any goods he sees — he hath a freedom to the land, to take the ground, to till it. I would fain have any man show me their bounds, where you will end.

Rainborough: Sir, to say that because a man pleads that every man hath a voice, that it destroys all property — this is to forget the law of God. That there's property, the law of God says it, else why hath God made that law, Thou shalt not steal? I am a poor man, therefore I must be oppressed: if I have no interest in the kingdom, I must suffer all their laws be they right or wrong. Nay thus: a gentleman lives in a country and hath three or four lordships, as some men have (God knows how they got them); and when a parliament is called he must be a parliament man; and it may be he sees some poor men, they live near this man, he can crush them — I have known an invasion to turn poor men out of doors; and I would know whether rich men do not do this, and keep them under the greatest tyranny that was ever thought of in the world. And I wish you would not make the world believe we are for anarchy.

Cromwell: Really, sir, this is not right. No man says you have a mind to anarchy, but that the consequence of this rule tends to anarchy. I am confident on 't, we should not be so hot with one another.

Rainborough: I know that some particular men we debate with believe we are for anarchy.

Ireton: I must clear myself as to that point. I cannot allow myself to lay the least scandal upon anyone. And I don't know why the gentleman should take so much offence. We speak to the paper not to persons. Now the main answer against my objection was that there was a divine law, Thou shalt not steal. But we cannot prove property in a thing by divine law any more than prove we have an interest in choosing members for parliament by divine law. Our right of sending members to parliament descends from other things and so does our right to property.

Rainborough: I would fain know what we have fought for. For our laws and liberties? And this is the old law of England — and that which enslaves the people of England — that they should be bound by laws in which they have no voice! And for my part, I look upon the people of England so, that wherein they have not voices in the choosing of their governors they are not bound to obey them.

Ireton: I did not say we should not have any enlargement at all of those who are to be the electors. But if you admit any man that hath breath and being, it may come to destroy property thus: you may have such men chosen as have no local or permanent interest. Why may not those men vote against all property? Show me what you will stop at.

Rich: There is weight in the objection, for you have five to one in

this kingdom that have no permanent interest. Some men
have ten, some twenty servants. If the master and servant be
equal electors, the majority may by law destroy property. But
certainly there may be some other way thought of, that there
may be a representative of the poor as well as the rich.

Rainborough: I think it is a fine gilded pill.

Wildman: Our case is that we have been under slavery. That's
acknowledged by all. Our very laws were made by our con-
querors. We are now engaged for our freedom. The question
is: Whether any person can justly be bound by law, who doth
not give his consent?

Ireton: Yes, and I will make it clear. If a foreigner will have liberty
to dwell here, he may very well be content to submit to the
law of the land. If any man will receive protection from this
people, he ought to be subject to those laws. If this man do
think himself unsatisfied to be subject to this law, he may go
into another kingdom.

Wildman: The gentleman here said five parts of the nation are
now excluded and would then have a voice in elections. At
present one part makes hewers of wood and drawers of water
of the other five, so the greater part of the nation is enslaved.
I do not hear any justification given but that it is the present
law of the kingdom.

Rainborough: What shall become of those men that have laid
themselves out for the parliament in this present war, that
have ruined themselves by fighting? They are Englishmen.
They have now no voice in elections.

Rich: All I urged was that I think it worthy consideration whether
they should have an equal voice. However, I think we have
been a great while upon this point. If we stay but three days
until you satisfy one another the king will come and decide
who will be hanged first.

Sexby: October the thirtieth.

Rainborough: If we can agree where the liberty of the people lies,
that will do all.

Ireton: I cannot consent so far. When I see the hand of God destroying king, and lords, and commons too, when I see God
hath done it, I shall, I hope, comfortably acquiesce in it. But
before that, I cannot give my consent to it because it is not
good. The law of God doth not give me property, nor the law
of nature, but property is of human constitution. I have a
property and this I shall enjoy.

Sexby: I see that though liberty was our end, there is a degenera-
tion from it. We have ventured our lives and it was all for this:
to recover our birthrights as Englishmen; and by the arguments urged there is none. There are many thousands of us
soldiers that have ventured our lives; we have had little property in the kingdom, yet we have had a birthright. But it
seems now, except a man hath a fixed estate in the kingdom,
he hath no right in this kingdom. I wonder we were so much
deceived. If we had not a right to the kingdom, we were mere
mercenary soldiers. I shall tell you in a word my resolution. I
am resolved to give my birthright to none. If this thing be
denied the poor, that with so much pressing after they have
sought, it will be the greatest scandal. It was said that if those
in low condition were given their birthright it would be the
destruction of this kingdom. I think the poor and meaner of
this kingdom have been the means of preservation of this
kingdom. Their lives have not been held dear for purchasing
the good of the kingdom. And now they demand the birthright for which they fought. They are as free from anarchy
and confusion as any, and they have the law of God and the
law of their conscience with them. When men come to understand these things, they will not lose that which they have
contended for.
Ireton: I am very sorry we are come to this point, that from reasoning one to another we should come to express our resolutions. Now let us consider where our difference lies. We all
agree you should be governed by elected representatives. But
I think we ought to keep to that constitution which we have
now, because there is so much justice and reason and prudence in it. And if you merely on pretence of your birthright
pretend that this constitution shall not stand in your way, it is
the same principle to me, say I, as if for your better satisfaction you shall take hold of anything that another man calls
his own.
Rainborough: Sir, I see it is impossible to have liberty without all
property being taken away. If you will say it, it must be so.
But I would fain know what the soldier hath fought for all
this while.
Ireton: I will tell you ——
Rainborough: He hath fought to enslave himself, to give power to
men of riches, men of estates, to make himself a perpetual
slave. We find none must be pressed for the army that have
property. When these gentlemen fall out among themselves,

they shall press the poor scrubs to come and kill one another for them.

Ireton: I will tell you what the soldier of this kingdom hath fought for. The danger that we stood in was that one man's will must be a law. The people have this right, that they should not be governed but by the representative of those that have the interest of the kingdom. In this way liberty may be had and property not be destroyed.

Rich: I hope it is not denied that any wise discreet man that hath preserved England is worthy of a voice in the government of it. The electorate should be amended in that sense and I think they will desire no more liberty.

Cromwell: I confess I was most dissatisfied with that I heard Mr. Sexby speak of any man here, because it did savour so much of will. But let us not spend so much time in debates. Everyone here would be willing that the representation be made better than it is. If we may but resolve on a committee, things may be done.

Wildman: I wonder that should be thought willfulness in one man that is reason in another. I have not heard anything that doth satisfy me. I am not at all against a committee's meeting. But I think it is no fault in any man to refuse to sell his birthright.

Sexby: I am sorry that my zeal to what I apprehend is good should be so ill resented. Do you think it were a sad and miserable condition that we have fought all this time for nothing? All here, both great and small, do think that we fought for something. Many of us fought for those ends which, we since saw, were not those which caused us to venture all in the ship with you. It had been good in you to have advertised us of it, and I believe you would have had fewer under your command to have commanded. Concerning my making rents and divisions in this way. As an individual I could lie down and be trodden there; but truly I am sent by a regiment, and if I should not speak, guilt shall lie upon me. I shall be loath to make a rent and division, but unless I see this put to a vote, I despair of an issue.

Rich: I see you have a long dispute. I see both parties at a stand; and if we dispute here, both are lost.

Cromwell: If you put this paper to the vote without any qualifications it will not pass freely. If we would have no difference when we vote on the paper, it must be put with due qualifications. I have not heard Commissary General Ireton answered, not in a title. To bring this paper nearer a general satisfaction and bring us all to an understanding, I move for a committee.

Interval

ACT II

SCENE. *Diggers*

One of the Actors (announces): Information of Henry Sanders, Walton-upon-Thames, April the sixteenth, sixteen hundred and forty-nine.

One Everard, Gerrard Winstanley, and three more, all living at Cobham, came to St. George's Hill in Surrey and began to dig, and sowed the ground with parsnips and carrots and beans. By Friday last they were increased in number to twenty or thirty. They invite all to come in and help them, and promise them meat, drink, and clothes.

Winstanley (announces): The true Levellers' standard advanced, sixteen hundred and forty-nine:

A declaration to the powers of England and to all the powers of the world, showing the cause why the common people of England have begun to dig up, manure, and sow corn upon George Hill in Surrey. Take notice that England is not a free people till the poor that have no land have a free allowance to dig and labour the commons. It is the sword that brought in property and holds it up, and everyone upon recovery of the conquest ought to return into freedom again, or what benefit have the common people got by the victory over the king?

All men have stood for freedom; and now the common enemy has gone you are all like men in a mist, seeking for freedom, and know not where it is: and those of the richer sort of you that see it are afraid to own it. For freedom is the man that will turn the world upside down, therefore no wonder he hath enemies.

True freedom lies where a man receives his nourishment and that is in the use of the earth. A man had better have no body than have no food for it. True freedom lies in the true enjoyment of the earth. True religion and undefiled is to let every one quietly have earth to manure. There can be no universal liberty till this universal community be established.

1st Actor (announces): A Bill of Account of the most remarkable sufferings that the Diggers have met with since they began to dig the commons for the poor on George Hill in Surrey.

2nd Actor: We were fetched by above a hundred people who took away our spades, and some of them we never had again, and taken to prison at Walton.

3rd Actor: The dragonly enemy pulled down a house we had built and cut our spades to pieces.

4th Actor: One of us had his head sore wounded, and a boy beaten. Some of us were beaten by the gentlemen, the sheriff looking on, and afterwards five were taken to White Lion prison and kept there about five weeks.

5th Actor: We had all our corn spoilt, for the enemy was so mad that they tumbled the earth up and down and would suffer no corn to grow.

6th Actor: Next day two soldiers and two or three men sent by the parson pulled down another house and turned an old man and his wife out of doors to lie in the field on a cold night.

1st Actor: It is understood the General gave his consent that the soldiers should come to help beat off the Diggers, and it is true the soldiers came with the gentlemen and caused others to pull down our houses; but I think the soldiers were sorry to see what was done.

SCENE. *Claxton Explains*

Claxton: Wherever I go I leave men behind surprised I no longer agree with them. But I can't stop. Ever since the day I walked over the hill to Wendover to hear the new preacher for the first time. And though I'd thought of going for weeks, the day I went I didn't think at all, I just put on my coat and started walking. I felt quite calm, as if nothing was happening, as if it was an easy thing to do, not something I'd laid awake over all night, so that I wondered if it even mattered to me. But as I walked I found my heart was pounding and my breath got short going up the hill. My body knew I was doing something amazing. I knew I was in the midst of something, I was doing it, not standing still worrying about it, I was simply walking over the hill to another preacher. I'd found everything in my life hard. But now it seemed everything must be this simple. I felt alone. I felt certain. I felt myself moving faster and faster, more and more certainly towards God. And I am alone, because my wife can't follow me. I send her money when I can. But my body is given to other women now for I have come to see that there is no sin but what man thinks is sin. So we can't be free from sin till we can commit it purely, as if it were no sin. Sometimes I lie or steal to show myself there is no lie or theft but in the mind, and I find it all so easy that I am called the Captain of the Rant, and still my heart pounds and my mouth is dry and I rush on towards the infinite nothing that is God.

SCENE. *Briggs Writes a Letter*

Star: Writing more letters? Our children grow up without us. Is there still no news of your wife? Do you think of leaving the army to look for her? Because if you don't go to Ireland, there's not much to do in the army now.

Briggs: Enough.

Star: You make a mistake about Ireland. I understood two years ago, when the men didn't have their back pay, I was with you then. But now it's different. You were agitator of the regiment then and you still ——

Briggs: I still am agitator of the regiment.

Star: —— Still think you're agitator of the regiment. I know that was a remarkable time for you. To be chosen out of so many. To stand up before the greatest in the country and be heard out. It's a council of officers now, you know that. You know an agitator means nothing. But you won't let it go. You keep on and on. The other men don't admire you for it.

Briggs: We're demanding the council be set up like before. You know that. With two agitators from each regiment.

Star: I know you won't get it. Everyone knows. The other men laugh. You'd far better go home. Or if you still want to serve the cause of the saints, sign for Ireland. Cromwell himself is going, that says something. It's the same war we fought here. We'll be united again. We'll crush the papists just as we did in England. Antichrist will be exterminated.

Briggs: But don't you see, the Irish ——

Star: What, Briggs?

Briggs: The Irish are fighting the same ——

Star: The Irish are traitors. What?

Briggs: Nothing.

Star: Show me the letter.

Briggs: What?

Star: Show me the letter.

Briggs: Can't we even write a letter now without an officer looking it over?

Star: It's not to your family.

Briggs: No. What then?

Star: It's a plot.

Briggs: It's a list of proposals.

Star: It's mutiny.

Briggs: It's a list of proposals. I've made them often enough.

Star: You have, yes, and nobody reads them now. You draw up a third agreement of the people, and a fourth, and a tenth. It's a waste of time.

Briggs: I waste a few hours then. A few days. If I don't get what I fought for, the whole seven years has been wasted. What's a few weeks.

Star: Show me the letter.

Briggs: No.

Star: It wasn't an order. You have not refused to obey my order. But I won't be able to save you from mutiny if that's what you're set on.

Briggs: So we can't write now. We can't speak.

Star: There's officers above me. Some of them think free talk doesn't go with discipline. I've always liked talk. I'd be sad to see us lose that privilege.

Briggs: It's not a privilege. It's a right.

Star: If it's a right, Briggs, why was Arnold shot at Ware? Why were five troopers cashiered for petitioning the council of officers?

Briggs: Shall I tell you why?

Star: It's not because I knew you before. The whole company is my friends. My rank leaves us equal before God. And yet my orders have been obeyed, because they have been seen for what they are, good orders. But lately I am talked of by my superiors ——

Briggs: Shall I tell you why the Levellers have been shot? Because now the officers have all the power, the army is as great a tyrant as the king was.

Star: I can choose to act as if no one is below me. I hope I do. But I can't pretend no one is above me. I have superior officers and I must obey. I don't think you want me removed.

Briggs: You should join us against them.

Star: If everyone says and does what he likes, what army is it? What discipline is there? In army or government. There must be some obedience. With consent, I would say, yes, but then you must consent, or — what? If every man is his own commander? There was a time when we all wanted the same. The army was united. I gave orders from God and you all heard the same orders from God in you. We fought as one man. But now we begin to be thousands of separate men.

Briggs: God is not with this army.

Star: It is the army of saints.

Briggs: And God's saints shot Robert Lockyer for mutiny. By martial law. In time of peace. For demanding what God demanded we fight for.

Star: If the army splits up ——

Briggs: It has done.

Star: If you Levellers split off into conspiracies away from the main army ——

Briggs: It's you who've split off.

Star: You risk the King's party getting back again.

Briggs: Would that be worse?

Star: Briggs. We can still be a united army. Remember how we marched on London, singing the fall of Babylon?

Briggs: It's you who mutiny. Against God. Against the people.

Star: Briggs.

Briggs: It's Cromwell mutinies.

Star: Briggs.

Briggs: If I was Irish I'd be your enemy. And I am.

Star: Briggs.

Briggs: Sir.

SCENE. *The War in Ireland*

One of the Actors (announces): Soldier's standard to repair to, addressed to the army, April sixteen hundred and forty-nine.

Whatever they may tell you or however they may flatter you, there's danger lies at the bottom of this business for Ireland. Consider to what end you should hazard your lives against the Irish: have you not been fighting in England these seven years for rights and liberties you are yet deluded of? and will you go on to kill, slay, and murder men, to make your officers as absolute lords and masters over Ireland as you have made them over England? If you intend not this, it concerns you in the first place to see that evil reformed here. Sending forces into Ireland is for nothing else but to make way by the blood of the army to extending their territories of power and tyranny. For the cause of the Irish natives in seeking their just freedoms, immunities, and liberties is exactly the same with our cause here.

SCENE: *The Vicar Welcomes the New Landlord*

Vicar: Mr. Star. I wonder if I am the first to welcome you as the new squire.

Star: And the last I hope. I'm no squire.

Vicar: You've bought the land, that's all I meant.

Star: I have bought the land, yes. Parliament is selling the confiscated land to parliament men. That does not make me the squire. Just as the country is better run by parliament than by the King, so estates will be better managed by parliament men than by royalists. You don't agree.

Vicar: It's not for a parson to say about running an estate.

Star: No, but you bury the tenants when they starve. You'll have fewer to bury. This country can grow enough to feed every single person. Instead of importing corn we could grow enough to export it if all the land was efficiently made profitable. The price of corn will come down in a few years. Agricultural writers recommend growing clover on barren land. I will have the common ploughed and planted with clover.

Vicar: An excellent idea.

Star: Nettles and thistles cleared, and a great crop.

Vicar: And the little huts cleared, the squatters' huts.

Star: Squatters?

Vicar: On the common. These last two years. Everyone hopes that now the estate is properly managed again they will be moved on. They are not local people.

Star: I haven't been down to the common. Well I'll speak to them. All over England waste land is being reclaimed. Even the fens. Many years ago before the war, Oliver Cromwell himself led tenants in protest against enclosing the fens. But now he sees, now we all see, that it is more important to provide corn for the nation than for a few tenants to fish and trap waterbirds.

Vicar: Yes indeed. Yes indeed.

Star: When I say enclose the commons, I don't mean in the old sense, as the old squire did. I mean to grow corn. To make efficient use of the land. To bring down the price of corn. I'm sure the tenants will understand when I explain it to them.

Vicar: They will do as they're told. I'm sure you'll have no trouble collecting the arrears of rent.

Star: I know one of the reasons they haven't paid is because they've had soldiers billetted in every cottage. So of course

I'll give them time to pay. There is some talk of landlords reducing rents by as much as the tenants have paid out on the soldiers.

Vicar: I have heard talk of that.

Star: I hope very much they're not counting on it. It would make me responsible for the keep for six years of twenty men and would beggar the estate.

Vicar: I told them that. I told them the new squire wouldn't hear of it.

Star: In their own interests. I couldn't afford seed corn. I need two new ploughs.

Vicar: I'm sure they know their own interest. They'll pay.

Star: I don' want to evict anyone.

Vicar: No, indeed, give them time. Three months would be ample.

Star: I thought six.

Vicar: That's very generous. The tenants will certainly bless you.

Star: I thought I would send for them all to drink my health and I'll drink theirs.

Vicar: That is the custom with a new squire. It is what they expect.

Star: Is it? It's what I thought I would do.

Vicar: Well, I can only say I welcome all the changes you are making. And I hope you won't make a change so unwelcome to the whole parish as to turn me away after so many years. I know the tenants here are as good and peace-loving as any in England, and I know they'll join me in supporting you in your plans to make this estate prosperous. It's been an unhappy time but the war is over. We are all glad to be at peace and back to normal.

Star: It will be hard work. For the tenants and for me. I don't shrink from that. It is to God's glory that this land will make a profit.

Vicar: I'm sure it will.

Star: Don't misunderstand me, Parson. Times have changed.

Vicar: I'm not against change, Mr. Star. So long as there's no harm done.

SCENE. *A Woman Leaves Her Baby*

Two women. 1st Woman is carrying a baby.

1st Woman: You'll laugh.

2nd Woman: No?

1st Woman: Now I'm here I can't do it.
2nd Woman: Waiting for that.
1st Woman: Don't. Don't go. Don't be angry.
2nd Woman: We come all this way.
1st Woman: We go back.
2nd Woman: Why we bother?
1st Woman: We go back, quick, never mind.
2nd Woman: We come so they look after her.
1st Woman: I can't.
2nd Woman: I know but just put her down.
1st Woman: Too soon.
2nd Woman: Put her down. Just . . .

Silence.

2nd Woman: She die if you keep her.
1st Woman: I can't.

Silence.

2nd Woman: What you do then? You got no milk. She not even crying now, see. That's not good. You en had one, I'm telling you, she dying.

Silence.

1st Woman: If I drunk more water. Make more milk.
2nd Woman: Not without food. Not how ill you are.

Silence.

1st Women: What if nobody . . . ?
2nd Woman: They will. It's a special house. It's a good town. The mayor himself. Picture inside on the wall with his chain. Mayor himself see her all right.
1st Woman: Another day.
2nd Woman: She'll be dead.
1st Woman: If she was bigger.
2nd Woman: You're not doing it for you. Do it for her. Wouldn't you die to have her live happy? Won't even put her down. It's for her.
1st Woman: Could die. Can't put her down.
2nd Woman: Don't talk. Do it. Do it.
1st Woman: If she was still inside me.

SCENE. *A Butcher Talks to His Customers*

Butcher: Two rabbits, madam, is two shillings, thank you. And sir? A capon? Was yesterday's veal good? Was it? Good. Tender was it? Juicy? Plenty of it? Fill your belly did it? Fill your belly? It can't have done, can it, or you wouldn't want a capon today. Nice capon here, make a fine dinner for half a dozen people. Giving your friends dinner tonight, sir? And another night they give you dinner. You're very generous and christian to each other. There's never a night you don't have dinner. Or do you eat it all yourself, sir? No? You look as if you do. You don't look hungry. You don't look as if you need a dinner. You look less like a man needing a dinner than anyone I've ever seen. What do you need it for? No, tell me. To stuff yourself, that's what for. To make fat. And shit. When it could put a little good flesh on children's bones. It could be the food of life. If it goes into you, it's stink and death. So you can't have it. No, I said you can't have it, take your money back. You're not having meat again this week. You had your meat yesterday. Bacon on Monday. Beef on Sunday. Mutton chops on Saturday. There's no more meat for you. Porridge. Bread. Turnips. No meat for you this week. Not this year. You've had your lifetime's meat. All of you. All of you that can buy meat. You've had your meat. You've had their meat. You've had their meat that can't buy any meat. You've stolen their meat. Are you going to give it back? Are you going to put your hand in your pocket and give them back the price of their meat? I said give them back their meat. You cram yourselves with their children's meat. You cram yourselves with their dead children.

SCENE. *Lockyer's Funeral*

One of the Actors: From *The Moderate*, a Leveller newspaper, April the twenty-ninth, sixteen forty-nine.

Mr. Robert Lockyer, a Leveller leader, that was shot Friday last was this day brought through the heart of the city. The manner of his funeral was most remarkable, considering the person to be in no higher quality than a private trooper. The body was accompanied with many thousand citizens, who seemed much dejected. The trooper's horse was clothed all over with mourning and led by a footman (a funeral honour equal to a chief commander). The corpse was adorned with bundles of rosemary stained in blood, and the sword of the deceased with them. Most of this great number that attended the corpse had sea-green and black ribbons in their hats. By the time the corpse came to the new church-yard, some thousands of the higher sort, that said they would not endanger themselves to be publicly seen marching through the city, were there ready to attend it with the same colours of sea-green and black. Some people derided them with the name of Levellers. Others said that King Charles had not had half so many mourners to attend his corpse when interred, as this trooper. A few weeks later at Burford, the Levellers were finally crushed.

SCENE. *The Meeting*

A drinking place. The Drunk sits apart from the rest.

Hoskins (to Briggs): Come on, plenty to drink. Can't you smile? He wasn't like this last night.

Brotherton: What do I do?

Cobbe: Anything you like. I worship you, more than the Virgin Mary.

Hoskins: She was no virgin.

Claxton: Christ was a bastard.

Hoskins: Still is a bastard.

Brotherton: I thought you said this was a prayer meeting.

Claxton: This is it. This is my one flesh.

Cobbe (to the Drunk): Drinking by yourself? Move in with us, come on. Yes, we need you. Get over there when I tell you or I'll break your arm. That was God telling you.

Claxton: God's a great bully, I've noticed that. Do this. Do that. Shalt not. Drop you in the burning lake.

Hoskins: Give us a sip. He won't give us a sip.

Claxton: He's not very godly. He needs praying.

Hoskins: Let us pray. Or whatever.

Silence.

Brotherton: When's he coming?

Cobbe: Who?

Brotherton: The preacher.

Cobbe: You're the preacher.

Brotherton: What? No. I can't.

Hoskins: Don't frighten her.

Claxton: Anyone has anything to say from God, just say it.

Silence.

Hoskins: There was a preacher. But his head fell off.

Silence.

Claxton: It's a fine shining day. Whatever troubles we have, the sky's not touched. A clear day. Let us not lose it. Let us remember the Levellers shot. Those at Burford. Will Thompson and his brother. Private Arnold shot at Ware.

Hoskins: And the four prisoners in the tower just for writing . . .

Briggs: Avenge Robert Lockyer.

Cobbe: Lockyer's blood. Robert Lockyer's blood. Lockyer's wounds.

Brotherton: I don't know these gentlemen. If they have money. Well if you haven't and you're in the common jail, you're lucky if you don't die. But if they have money for the jailor he gives you a room. With a bed and a window. I was told by a man who'd spent all his money. If you've got money . . .

Cobbe: Damn. Damn. Damn. Damn. Damn.

There's angels swear, angels with flowing hair, you'd think they were men, I've seen them. They say damn the churches, the bloody black clergy with their fat guts, damn their white hands. Damn the hellfire presbyterian hypocrites that call a thief a sinner, rot them in hell's jail. They say Christ's wounds, wounds, wounds, wounds. Stick your fingers in. Christ's arsehole. He had an arsehole. Christ shits on you rich. Christ shits. Shitting pissing spewing puking fucking Jesus Christ. Jesus fucking ——

Brotherton: Is that from God?

Cobbe. What did you say?

Brotherton: Is that from God?

Cobbe: It is, yes. What does he say to you? Does he speak to you? What do you answer? He'll come and speak to you soon enough. The day he comes he'll speak to all of us. He'll come right up to you like this. He wants an answer. What do you say? Nothing? He'll damn and ram you down in the black pit. Is there nothing in you? What are you? Nothing? (*To Briggs.*) Is it nothing but a lifetime of false words, little games, devil's tricks, ways to get by in the world and keep safe? You're plastered over, thick shit mucky lies all over, and what's underneath? Where's your true word? Is there anyone left inside or are you shrivelled away to nothing? (*To each.*) What will you say? Speak up. What do you answer God? What do you answer? Answer. What do you answer?

Hoskins: I love you.
Cobbe: There. There.

He sits down. Brotherton laughs. Silence.

Claxton: I tell you justice. If every judge was hanged.
Hoskins: I steal all I can. Rich steal from us. Everything they got's stolen. What's it mean "Thou shalt not steal"? Not steal stolen goods?
Cobbe: Riches is the cause of all wickedness. From the blood of Abel to those last Levellers shot. But God is coming, the mighty Leveller, Christ the chief of Levellers is at the door, and then we'll see levelling. Not sword levelling. Not man levelling. And they feared that. Now God is coming to level the hills and the valleys. Christ break the mountains.

Silence. Hoskins holds out an apple.

Hoskins: This is something stolen by a farmer. Then by a stall-holder. Then by me. It come to me God's in it. If a man could be so perfect. Look at it.

She gives it to Briggs, who looks at it, then passes it back to her. She gives it to Brotherton.

Brotherton: I always like an apple if I can get it. I haven't been to church for a long time. I don't know if this is a church. It's a drinking place. I always hide on Sunday. They notice you in the street if everyone's in church so I go in the woods on Sunday. I can't see God in this. If God was in it, he'd have us whipped.
Claxton: It wouldn't have you whipped, it would bless you. It does bless you. Touch it again. It blesses you. And my hand. Touch my hand. What's the matter?
Brotherton: Nobody touches me.
Claxton: Why not?
Brotherton: They don't touch, I don't know why, nobody touches. I don't count hitting. Nobody's touched me since . . .
Claxton: Since what?
Brotherton: You don't want to touch me. Don't bother. Pass it on. Pass it on.
Hoskins: Nobody's touched you since what?
Brotherton: It's not right.
Claxton: What's not right? Touching or not touching?
Brotherton: Both are not right. Pass it on.

Claxton: They are, they're both, whichever you want, when you want, is right. Do you want me to touch your hand?

Brotherton: No.

Claxton: That's right. God's in that too. God's in us. This form that I am is the representative of the whole creation. You are the representative of the whole creation. God's in this apple. He's nowhere else but in the creation. This is where he is.

He gives it to Cobbe.

Cobbe: I charge at coaches in the street. I shout at the great ones with my hat on. I proclaim the day of the Lord throughout Southwark. And what do they hear? If they could see God in this apple as I do now, God in the bread that they will not give to the poor who cry out day and night, Bread, bread, bread for the Lord's sake, if they could see it they would rush to the prisons, and they would bow to the poor wretches that are their own flesh, and say, "Your humble servants, we set you free."

Cobbe gives it to the Drunk, who eats it.

Hoskins: There's a man eats God. There's a communion.

Brotherton: You don't often see someone eat. They eat when you're not looking.

Briggs: Friends. I have nothing from God. I'm sitting here. Nothing. If anyone can speak to my condition.

Claxton: You're a soldier?

Briggs: I was.

Cobbe: A Leveller?

Briggs: I was.

Claxton: And now?

Hoskins: Well, a drink would be best.

Claxton: You'll find something. I've been different things. When I was first a Seeker, everything shone. I thought the third age was coming, age of the spirit, age of the lily, everything shining, raindrops on the hedges shining in the sun, worlds of light. Well, we know how parliament betrayed us. Then how the army betrayed us. It was all a cheat.

Hoskins: Preaching itself is a cheat.

Claxton: And then I saw even the Seekers were wrong. Because while I was waiting for God, he was here already. So God was first in the king. Then in parliament. Then in the army. And now he has left all government. And shows himself naked. In us.

Briggs: We were the army of saints.

Claxton: Let it go. Move on. God moves so fast now.

Hoskins: I try to be sad with you but I can't. King Jesus is coming in clouds of glory in a garment dyed red with blood, and the saints in white linen riding on white horses. It's for next year. Now is just a strange time between Antichrist going and Christ coming, so what do you expect in a time like this? There's been nothing like it before and there never will be again. So what's it matter now if we've no work and no food or can't get parliament like we want? It's only till next year. Then Christ will be here in his body like a man and he'll be like a king only you can talk to him. And he's a spirit too and that's in us and it's getting stronger and stronger. And that's why you see men and women shining now, everything sparkles because God's not far above us like he used to be when preachers stood in the way, he's started some great happening and we're in it now.

Claxton: St. Paul to Timothy, "Let the woman learn in silence."

Hoskins: Jone Hoskins to St. Paul, fuck off you silly old bugger.

They laugh and start getting food out.
Claxton holds out food.

Claxton: Christ's body.

Brotherton: I'm afraid I haven't anything.

Claxton: There's plenty.

Hoskins holds out wine.

Hoskins: This is Christ's blood.

Claxton (to Brotherton): When did you last eat? Eat slowly now.

Briggs: Christ will not come. I don't believe it. Everything I've learnt these seven years. He will not come in some bloody red robe and you all put on white frocks, that will not happen. All I've learnt, how to get things done, that wasn't for nothing. I don't believe this is the last days. England will still be here in hundreds of years. And people working so hard they can't grasp how it happens and can't take hold of their own lives, like us till we had this chance, and we're losing it now, as we sit here, every minute. Jesus Christ isn't going to change it.

Claxton: He may not be coming in red.

Briggs: He's not coming at all.

Claxton: But in us ——

Briggs: No, not at all.

Hoskins: He's coming in clouds of glory and the saints ——
Briggs: No, no, no.
Cobbe: Do you think God would do all this for nothing? Think of
the dead. For nothing? Why did he call me to warn London?
What sort of God would he be if he didn't come now?
Briggs: No God at all.
Claxton: But in us. In us. I know there's no heaven or hell, not
places to go, but in us. I know the Bible was written by man
and most of it to trick us. I know there's no God or devil out-
side what's in creation. But in us. I know we can be perfect.
Briggs: Then we must do it.

Cobbe takes off his coat and throws it at Briggs's feet.

Cobbe: My coat's yours. And I hope yours is mine. We'll all live
together, one family, one marriage, one flesh in God. That's
what we do.
Hoskins: Yes, everything in common.
Cobbe: All things common. Or the plague of God will consume
whatever you have.
Claxton: All goods in common, yes, and our bodies in common ——
Briggs: No.
Hoskins: Yes, we'll have no property in the flesh. My wife, that's
property. My husband, that's property. All men are one flesh
and I can lie with any man as my husband and that's no sin
because all men are one man, all my husband's one flesh.
Cobbe: I, the Lord, say once more, deliver deliver my money
which you have to cripples, thieves, whores, or I will torment
you day and night, saith the Lord.
Claxton: We'll take the land, all the land, and Christ will come,
wait, I have something from God, Christ will come in this
sense. He will come in everyone becoming perfect so the
landlords all repent stealing the land. Sin is only the dark
side of God. So when his light blazes everywhere, their greed
will vanish — and that's how evil will go into the pit. Nobody
damned, nobody lost, nobody cast out. But Antichrist cast
out of us so that we become perfect Christ.
Hoskins: Perfect men, perfect Christ in the street, I've seen them.
Claxton: The rich will be broken out of the hell they are, however
they howl to stay there, and when they're out in the light
they'll be glad. They'll join us pulling down the hedges.
Briggs: The landlords where they were digging at Cobham called
the army in. And the soldiers stood by while the diggers'

houses were pulled down, their tools destroyed, the corn trampled so it won't grow, men beaten and dragged off to prison. The landlords gave the soldiers ten shillings for drink. Does that sound like the landlords joining us? Does that sound like heaven on earth? I've a friend wounded in Ireland and nearly mad. When they burned the church at Drogheda he heard a man inside crying out, "God damn me, I burn, I burn." Is that heaven on earth? Or is it hell?

Brotherton: It's hell, life is hell, my life is hell. I can't get out but I'll pull them all in with me.

Hoskins: No, wait, just wait, you'll see when Christ comes ——

Briggs: He's never coming, damn him.

Cobbe: How we know for certain that God is coming is because of the strange work he has set us on. Who can live through one day the way he used to? I've seen poor men all my life. Last week I met a poor man, the ugliest man I've ever seen, he had two little holes where his nose should be. I said to him, "Are you poor?" And he said, "Yes sir, very poor." I began to shake and I said to him again, "Are you poor?" "Yes, very poor." And a voice spoke inside me and said, "It's a poor wretch, give him twopence." But that was the voice of the whore of Babylon and I would not listen. And again, "It's a poor wretch, give him sixpence, and that's enough for a knight to give one poor man and you a preacher without tithes and never know when you'll get a penny; think of your children; true love begins at home." So I put my hand in my pocket and took out a shilling, and said, "Give me sixpence and here's a shilling for you." He said, "I can't, I haven't a penny." And I said, "I'm sorry to hear that. I would have given you something if you could have changed my money." And he said, "God bless you." So I was riding on when the voice spoke in me again, so that I rode back and told him I would leave sixpence for him in the next town at a house I thought he might know. But then, suddenly, the plague of God fell into my pocket and the rust of my silver rose against me, and I was cast into the lake of fire and brimstone. And all the money I had, every penny, I took out of my pocket and thrust into his hands. I hadn't eaten all day, I had nine more miles to ride, it was raining, the horse was lame, I was sure to need money before the night. And I rode away full of trembling joy, feeling the sparkles of a great glory round me. And then God made me turn my horse's head and I saw the poor wretch staring after me, and I was made to take off my hat and bow to him seven times. And I rode back to him again and said, "Because I am a king I have done this, but you need not tell anyone."

Hoskins:⎱
Claxton:⎰ Amen.

Briggs: That man will die without his birthright. I've done all I can and it's not enough.

Claxton: It's not over, there's more, God hasn't finished.

Briggs: I'll tell you who's with God.

He nods at the Drunk. Hoskins laughs, kisses him, gives him drink.

Brotherton: No I can't. I'm not one of you, I try, you're very kind, I'm not one of you, I'm not one flesh. I'm damned, I know it.

Cobbe: You're in hell now but you can come out. Suddenly, suddenly you are out.

Brotherton: I mustn't come in a place where God is. It's your fault bringing me here, I'm no good here, I can't be here ——

Cobbe: We don't want any filthy plague holiness. We want base things. And the baseness confounds the false holiness into nothing. And then, only then, you're like a new-born child in the hands of eternity, picked up, put down, not knowing if you're clean or dirty, good or evil.

Brotherton: No, I'm wicked, all women are wicked, and I'm ——

Hoskins: It's a man wrote the Bible.

Claxton: All damnation is, listen, all it is. Sin is not cast out but cast in, cast deep into God.

Brotherton: No I don't want to.

Claxton: As cloth is dyed in a vat to a new colour, the sin is changed in God's light into light itself.

Brotherton: No.

Claxton: That's all damnation is.

Brotherton: Let me go.

Claxton: It's only God.

Brotherton: I must be punished.

Hoskins: What have you done?

Brotherton: Let me go.

Cobbe: No, what did you do? God is in me, asking you, God is asking, I am perfect Christ asking why you damn yourself, why you hold yourself back from me?

Brotherton: Don't touch me. I'm evil.

Briggs: There's nothing you can have done.

Claxton: There's no sin except what you think is sin.

Hoskins: God makes it all, he makes us do it all, he can't make us sin. The men that crucified Christ, Christ made them do it.

Brotherton: The devil, the devil's got me.

Cobbe: A fart for the devil.

Hoskins: Don't be frightened. We've got you.

Claxton: Sin again, do the same sin as if it were no sin ——

Hoskins: Sin to God's glory.

Claxton: Then you'll be free from sin.

Cobbe: You're in heaven, look, you're shining.

Brotherton: No, how can I do it again? I did it then when I did it. It was a sin. I knew it was. I killed my baby. The same day it was born. I had a bag. I put it in the ditch. There wasn't any noise. The bag moved. I never went back that way.

Briggs: That's not your sin. It's one more of theirs. Damn them.

Cobbe: God bows to you. God worships you. Who did he come to earth for? For you. That's everyone's grief, we take it.

Brotherton: He wasn't baptised. He's lost. I lost him.

Claxton: Baptism is over.

Hoskins: No, wait, sit down, listen ——

Claxton: A baby doesn't need baptism to make him God, he is God. He's not born evil of water poured back in the ocean. He's lost to himself but all the water's God.

Cobbe: Believe us.

Hoskins: He's our fellow creature, and you're our fellow creature.

Claxton: You're God, you, you're God, no one's more God than you if you could know it yourself, you're lovely, you're perfect ——

Brotherton: No, I'm nobody's fellow creature.

Hoskins: God now.

Cobbe: Behold, I come quickly, saith the Lord.

Claxton: God's going through everything.

Briggs: Christ, don't waste those seven years we fought.

Claxton: Everything's changing. Everything's moving. God's going right through everything.

Cobbe: And God for your sin confounds you into unspeakable glory, your life, your self.

Hoskins: God has you now.

Claxton: Nothing we know will be the same.

Briggs: Christ, help her.

Claxton: We won't know our own faces. We won't know the words we speak. New words ——

Cobbe: Believe us.

Briggs: Be safe.

Hoskins: God has you now.

Claxton: Everything new, everything for the first time, everything starting ——

Brotherton: Yes.

Briggs: Be safe.

Brotherton: Yes.

Briggs: So it's over.

Brotherton: Yes.

Hoskins: There.

Briggs: You can be touched. It's not so terrible. I'll tell you what I'll do. Avenge your baby and Robert Lockyer. I'll make Cromwell set England free. And how? Easy. Kill him. Killing's no murder. He wanted to free England. That's how he'll do it. Dead.

Cobbe: God won't be stopped.

Drunk: I'm God. I'm God.

Briggs: Yes, amen, look who's God now.

Drunk: I'm God. And I'm the devil. I'm the serpent. I'm in heaven now and I'm in hell.

Claxton: Amen.

Cobbe: You are God. Every poor man.

Drunk: I'm in hell, I'm not afraid. I seen worse things. If the devil come at me I kick him up the arse.

Claxton: And that's the devil gone.

Hoskins: Amen, no devil.

Drunk: I'm in heaven. And I go up to God. And I say, You great tosspot, I'm as good a man as you, as good a God as you.

Claxton: And so are we all.

Hoskins: And so is everyone in England.

Drunk: Plenty of beer in heaven. Angels all drunk. Devils drunk. Devils and angels all fornicating.

Cobbe: You are God, I am God, and I love you, God loves God.

Claxton: Oh God, let me be God, be clear in me ——

Hoskins: All the light now ——

Cobbe: Sparks of glory under these ashes ——

Hoskins: Light shining from us ——

Drunk: And I say to God, get down below on to earth. Live in my cottage. Pay my rent. Look after my children, mind, they're hungry. And don't ever beat my wife or I'll strike you down.

Brotherton gets out some food.

Brotherton: I didn't give you — I kept it back — let me give you ——

Claxton: Yes, yes, God's here, look, God now ——

Drunk: And I say to God, Wait here in my house. You can have a drink while you're waiting. But wait. Wait. Wait till I come.

All (sing Ecclesiastes 5, viii–x, xii): If thou seest the oppression of the poor, and violent perverting of judgement and justice in a province, marvel not at the matter: for he that is higher than the highest regardeth; and there be higher than they.

Moreover the profit of the earth is for all: the king himself is served by the field.

He that loveth silver shan't be satisfied with silver; nor he that loveth abundance with increase: this is also vanity.

The sleep of the labouring man is sweet, whether he eat little or much: but the abundance of the rich will not suffer him to sleep.

SCENE. *After*

Hoskins: I think what happened was, Jesus Christ did come and nobody noticed. It was the time but we somehow missed it. I don't see how.

Cobbe: It was for me, to stop me, they passed the Blasphemy Act. I was never God in the sense they asked me at my trial did I claim to be God. I could have answered no quite truthfully but I threw apples and pears round the council chamber, that seemed a good answer. Dr. Higham. I changed my name after the restoration.

Brotherton: Stole two loaves yesterday. They caught another woman. They thought she did it, took her away. Bastards won't catch me.

Drunk: The day the king came back there was bread and cheese and beer given free. I went twice. Nobody noticed. Everyone was drunk the day the king came back.

Briggs: I worked all right in a shop for a while. The mercer had been in the army, he put up with me. Then I started giving things away. If a boy stole, I couldn't say anything. So when I left I thought I must do something practical. I decided to bring the price of corn down. A few people eat far too much. So if a few people ate far too little that might balance. Then there would be enough corn and the price would come down. I gave up meat first, then cheese and eggs. I lived on a little porridge and vegetables, then I gave up the porridge and stopped cooking the vegetables. It was easier because I was living out. I ate what I could find but not berries and nuts because so many people want those and I do well with sorrel leaves and dandelion. But grass. It was hard to get my body to take grass. It got very ill. It wouldn't give in to grass. But I forced it on. And now it will. There's many kinds, rye grass, meadow grass, fescue. These two years I've been able to eat grass. Very sweet. People come to watch. They can, I can't stop them. I'm living in a field that belongs to a gentleman that comes sometimes, and sometimes he brings a friend to show. He's not unkind but I don't like to see him. I stand where I am stock still and wait till he's gone.

Claxton: There's an end of outward preaching now. An end of perfection. There may be a time. I went to the Barbados. I sometimes hear from the world that I have forsaken. I see it fraught with tidings of the same clamour, strife, and contention that abounded when I left it. I gave it the hearing and that's all. My great desire is to see and say nothing.

Questions

Reread "Two Women Look in a Mirror" (p. 395) and Hoskins's speeches on stealing in "Claxton Brings Hoskins Home" and "The Meeting" (pp. 391, 414). What familiar idea or belief undergoes challenge in these scenes? How can we make sense of the challenge? Write a response and then compare it with the one that follows.

Response

EDITOR: One familiar idea or belief under challenge in *Light Shining in Buckinghamshire* is that stealing is invariably sinful, never an act of moral regeneration. It's true that much in the play affirms, directly or indirectly, the biblical commandment: Thou shalt not steal. "God made that law," says the Leveller Colonel Rainborough, confirming that although he leads a protest against Generals Cromwell and Ireton, he's in perfect agreement with them about the sanctity of property. What's more, those who disagree seem at first glance a disreputable lot. Cobbe, who consorts with thieves, and Hoskins, who "steal[s] all [she] can," are both blasphemers. Briggs, who tolerated thievery in a shop, advocates murder and at length goes mad. Hoskins's scornful rejection of "thou shalt not steal" has no stated basis except the

conviction that whatever the poor steal from the rich was originally stolen from them. And throughout the so-called prayer
meeting that these three hold with Claxton, the drunk, and the
wretched infanticide Brotherton, the talk often resembles that of
mere sots:

> *Drunk:* Plenty of beer in heaven. Angels all drunk. Devils
> drunk. Devils and angels all fornicating.
> *Cobbe:* You are God, I am God, and I love you, God loves God.
> *Claxton:* Oh God, let me be God, be clear in me ——

Yet despite all this the play's challenge to the biblical commandment is by no means negligible. One reason is the range of
evidence in scene after scene suggesting, first, the absolute lack
of continuity between the lives of the poor and the lives of the
property-holding classes and, second, the obnoxious certainty of
the well-off that poverty itself is a kind of crime. In the scene
called "Two Women Look in a Mirror" we grasp that pleasures
such as seeing oneself are restricted, in this historical period, to
the gentry alone ("They must know what they look like all the
time"). In "A Woman Leaves Her Baby" we grasp that, for the
poor, the choice is often that between abandoning one's child or
watching it die. In both "Margaret Brotherton Is Tried" and
"Diggers" we're shown that fearful punishment is meted out to
those who dare to imagine better lives for the poor. And it's
evident that the religious leaders who presumably should work
to alleviate misery are in fact lazy and complacent, disposed to
assume that misery serves a spiritual purpose. In "The Vicar
Talks to His Servant," the vicar simultaneously eats, pours wine
abundantly for himself, and tells the servant, whose baby is ill, to
rejoice in his suffering, because "that is the way to heaven."

If the thieves and despoilers of property in *Light Shining in
Buckinghamshire* were bent on self-aggrandizement, it would be
easier to indict them as criminals or sinners. But both "Diggers"
and "The Meeting" establish that these thieves aren't driven by
personal rapacity. Large themes of commonality, mutuality, and
sharing resound in their speeches and behavior throughout
much of the play.

The challenge to "thou shalt not steal" arises, in short, from
the dramatization of stealing as a *justified* response to a particular
historical context. (History is the intellectual terrain on which we
locate ourselves in bringing the relevant ideas to life.) The play
asks us to imagine a time when, after centuries of oppression,

people were promised a new life by their former oppressors if they took up arms against their king. The invitation to a crusade was extended with religious fervor. Those who heeded it came to believe in hitherto undreamed-of possibilities of free, fraternal, and communal existence.

But after seven years of bloody struggle, the leaders of the revolution, having achieved the one victory they truly cared about — defeat of the king — called off the crusade, bringing on immense frustration and depression. The would-be free man discovered that, as Rainborough puts it, "he hath fought to enslave himself, to give power to men of riches, men of estates, to make himself a perpetual slave." Or as Sexby puts it, "we have fought all this time for nothing." The idealism, the hope, the solidarities, the dreams of individual spiritual self-realization that had come alive during the struggle were all at once choked off. The minor thefts of those who had been thus cynically deceived and misused were often conceived as attempts to keep faith with former hopes; it is hard therefore to regard them as criminal or sinful.

The history of the seventeenth-century English wars of the Cavaliers and Roundheads is complex, as Churchill declares in the preface to her play. Her version of this history would not satisfy historians of every school. But the feelings that are critical in her scenes — "the amazed excitement of people taking hold of their own lives," the subsequent sense of betrayal, the longing to stay in touch somehow with the murdered dream — are powerfully evoked. Implicit in those feelings — whenever and wherever they exist — is strong ground for more than one challenge to moral and political orthodoxy.

FOR FURTHER STUDY

EMILY DICKINSON   (1830–1886)
I heard a Fly buzz — when I died

I heard a Fly buzz — when I died —
The Stillness in the Room
Was like the Stillness in the Air —
Between the Heaves of Storm —

The Eyes around — had wrung them dry —   5
And Breaths were gathering firm
For that last Onset — when the King
Be witnessed — in the Room —

I willed my Keepsakes — Signed away
What portion of me be   10
Assignable — and then it was
There interposed a Fly —

With Blue — uncertain stumbling Buzz —
Between the light — and me —
And then the Windows failed — and then   15
I could not see to see —

A. R. AMMONS   (b. 1926)
Cascadilla Falls

I went down by Cascadilla
Falls this
evening, the
stream below the falls,
and picked up a   5
handsized stone
kidney-shaped, testicular, and

thought all its motions into it,
the 800 mph earth spin,
the 190-million-mile yearly   10
displacement around the sun,
the overriding
grand
haul

of the galaxy with the 30,000   15
mph of where
the sun's going:
thought all the interweaving
motions
into myself: dropped   20

the stone to dead rest:
the stream from other motions

broke
rushing over it:
shelterless,   25
I turned

to the sky and stood still:
oh
I do
not know where I am going   30
that I can live my life
by this single creek.

MARIANNE MOORE   (1887–1972)
The Pangolin

Another armored animal — scale
    lapping scale with spruce-cone regularity until they
form the uninterrupted central
    tail-row! This near artichoke with head and legs and grit-
      equipped gizzard,
    the night miniature artist engineer is,   5
      yes, Leonardo da Vinci's replica —
      impressive animal and toiler of whom we seldom hear.
    Armor seems extra. But for him,
      the closing ear-ridge —
        or bare ear lacking even this small   10
        eminence and similarly safe

contracting nose and eye apertures
    impenetrably closable, are not; — a true ant-eater,
not cockroach-eater, who endures
    exhausting solitary trips through unfamiliar ground at
      night,   15
    returning before sunrise; stepping in the moonlight,
      on the moonlight peculiarly, that the outside
        edges of his hands may bear the weight and save the
          claws
      for digging. Serpentined about
      the tree, he draws   20
        away from danger unpugnaciously,
        with no sound but a harmless hiss; keeping

the fragile grace of the Thomas
    of-Leighton Buzzard Westminister Abbey wrought-iron
        vine, or
rolls himself into a ball that has   25
    power to defy all effort to unroll it; strongly intailed, neat
    head for core, on neck not breaking off, with curled-in feet.
        Nevertheless he has sting-proof scales; and nest
            of rocks closed with earth from inside, which he can
                thus darken.
        Sun and moon and day and night and man and beast   30
            each with a splendor
                which man in all his vileness cannot
                set aside; each with an excellence!

"Fearful yet to be feared," the armored
    ant-eater met by the driver-ant does not turn back, but   35
engulfs what he can, the flattened sword-
    edged leafpoints on the tail and artichoke set leg- and body-
        plates
    quivering violently when it retaliates
        and swarms on him. Compact like the furled fringed frill
            on the hat-brim of Gargallo's hollow iron head of a   40
        matador, he will drop and will
            then walk away
                unhurt, although if unintruded on,
                he cautiously works down the tree, helped

by his tail. The giant-pangolin-   45
    tail, graceful tool, as prop or hand or broom or ax, tipped
        like
an elephant's trunk with special skin,
    is not lost on this ant- and stone-swallowing uninjurable
    artichoke which simpletons thought a living fable
        whom the stones had nourished, whereas ants had done   50
            so. Pangolins are not aggressive animals; between
                dusk and day they have the not unchain-like machine-like
                    form and frictionless creep of a thing
                    made graceful by adversities, con-

versities. To explain grace requires   55
    a curious hand. If that which is at all were not forever,
why would those who graced the spires
    with animals and gathered there to rest, on cold luxurious
    low stone seats — a monk and monk and monk — between

the thus
ingenious roof-supports, have slaved to confuse   60
   grace with a kindly manner, time in which to pay a debt,
the cure for sins, a graceful use
    of what are yet
       approved stone mullions branching out across
       the perpendiculars? A sailboat   65

was the first machine. Pangolins, made
   for moving quietly also, are models of exactness,
on four legs; on hind feet plantigrade,
  with certain postures of a man. Beneath sun and moon, man
    slaving
  to make his life more sweet, leaves half the flowers worth
    having,   70
      needing to choose wisely how to use his strength;
       a paper-maker like the wasp; a tractor of foodstuffs,
     like the ant; spidering a length
      of web from bluffs
        above a stream; in fighting, mechanicked   75
       like the pangolin; capsizing in

disheartenment. Bedizened or stark
   naked, man, the self, the being we call human, writing-
master to this world, griffons a dark
  "Like does not like like that is obnoxious"; and writes error
    with four   80
  r's. Among animals, *one* has a sense of humor.
    Humor saves a few steps, it saves years. Unignorant,
     modest and unemotional, and all emotion,
    he has everlasting vigor,
      power to grow,   85
       though there are few creatures who can make one
       breathe faster and make one erecter.

Not afraid of anything is he,
   and then goes cowering forth, tread paced to meet an
    obstacle
at every step. Consistent with the   90
  formula — warm blood, no gills, two pairs of hands and a few
    hairs — that
  is a mammal; there he sits in his own habitat,
    serge-clad, strong-shod. The prey of fear, he, always
      curtailed, extinguished, thwarted by the dusk, work
        partly done,

says to the alternating blaze,   95
  "Again the sun!
    anew each day; and new and new and new,
    that comes into and steadies my soul."

ALICE MUNRO   (b. 1931)
Miles City, Montana

My father came across the field carrying the body of the boy who had been drowned. There were several men together, returning from the search, but he was the one carrying the body. The men were muddy and exhausted, and walked with their heads down, as if they were ashamed. Even the dogs were dispirited, dripping from the cold river. When they all set out, hours before, the dogs were nervy and yelping, the men tense and determined, and there was a constrained, unspeakable excitement about the whole scene. It was understood that they might find something horrible.

The boy's name was Steve Gauley. He was eight years old. His hair and clothes were mud-colored now and carried some bits of dead leaves, twigs, and grass. He was like a heap of refuse that had been left out all winter. His face was turned in to my father's chest, but I could see a nostril, an ear, plugged up with greenish mud.

I don't think so. I don't think I really saw all this. Perhaps I saw my father carrying him, and the other men following along, and the dogs, but I would not have been allowed to get close enough to see something like mud in his nostril. I must have heard someone talking about that and imagined that I saw it. I see his face unaltered except for the mud — Steve Gauley's familiar, sharp-honed, sneaky-looking face — and it wouldn't have been like that; it would have been bloated and changed and perhaps muddied all over after so many hours in the water.

To have to bring back such news, such evidence, to a waiting family, particularly a mother, would have made searchers move heavily, but what was happening here was worse. It seemed a worse shame (to hear people talk) that there was no mother, no woman at all — no grandmother or aunt, or even a sister — to receive Steve Gauley and give him his due of grief. His father was a hired man, a drinker but not a drunk, an erratic man without being entertaining, not friendly but not exactly a troublemaker.

His fatherhood seemed accidental, and the fact that the child had been left with him when the mother went away, and that they continued living together, seemed accidental. They lived in a steep-roofed, gray-shingled hillbilly sort of house that was just a bit better than a shack — the father fixed the roof and put sup-ports under the porch, just enough and just in time — and their life was held together in a similar manner; that is, just well enough to keep the Children's Aid at bay. They didn't eat meals together or cook for each other, but there was food. Sometimes the father would give Steve money to buy food at the store, and Steve was seen to buy quite sensible things, such as pancake mix and macaroni dinner.

I had known Steve Gauley fairly well. I had not liked him 5 more often than I had liked him. He was two years older than I was. He would hang around our place on Saturdays, scornful of whatever I was doing but unable to leave me alone. I couldn't be on the swing without him wanting to try it, and if I wouldn't give it up he came and pushed me so that I went crooked. He teased the dog. He got me into trouble — deliberately and maliciously, it seemed to me afterward — by daring me to do things I wouldn't have thought of on my own: digging up the potatoes to see how big they were when they were still only the size of marbles, and pushing over the stacked firewood to make a pile we could jump off. At school, we never spoke to each other. He was solitary, though not tormented. But on Saturday mornings, when I saw his thin, self-possessed figure sliding through the cedar hedge, I knew I was in for something and he would decide what. Sometimes it was all right. We pretended we were cowboys who had to tame wild horses. We played in the pasture by the river, not far from the place where Steve drowned. We were horses and riders both, screaming and neighing and bucking and waving whips of tree branches beside a little nameless river that flows into the Saugeen in southern Ontario.

The funeral was held in our house. There was not enough room at Steve's father's place for the large crowd that was ex-pected because of the circumstances. I have a memory of the crowded room but no picture of Steve in his coffin, or of the minister, or of wreaths of flowers. I remember that I was holding one flower, a white narcissus, which must have come from a pot somebody forced indoors, because it was too early for even the forsythia bush or the trilliums and marsh marigolds in the woods. I stood in a row of children, each of us holding a nar-cissus. We sang a children's hymn, which somebody played on our piano: "When He Cometh, When He Cometh, to Make Up

His Jewels." I was wearing white ribbed stockings, which were disgustingly itchy, and wrinkled at the knees and ankles. The feeling of these stockings on my legs is mixed up with another feeling in my memory. It is hard to describe. It had to do with my parents. Adults in general but my parents in particular. My father, who had carried Steve's body from the river, and my mother, who must have done most of the arranging of this funeral. My father in his dark-blue suit and my mother in her brown velvet dress with the creamy satin collar. They stood side by side opening and closing their mouths for the hymn, and I stood removed from them, in the row of children, watching. I felt a furious and sickening disgust. Children sometimes have an access of disgust concerning adults. The size, the lumpy shapes, the bloated power. The breath, the coarseness, the hairiness, the horrid secretions. But this was more. And the accompanying anger had nothing sharp and self-respecting about it. There was no release, as when I would finally bend and pick up a stone and throw it at Steve Gauley. It could not be understood or expressed, though it died down after a while into a heaviness, then just a taste, an occasional taste — a thin, familiar misgiving.

Twenty years or so later, in 1961, my husband, Andrew, and I got a brand-new car, our first — that is, our first brand-new. It was a Morris Oxford, oyster-colored (the dealer had some fancier name for the color) — a big small car, with plenty of room for us and our two children. Cynthia was six and Meg three and a half.

Andrew took a picture of me standing beside the car. I was wearing white pants, a black turtleneck, and sunglasses. I lounged against the car door, canting my hips to make myself look slim.

"Wonderful," Andrew said. "Great. You look like Jackie Kennedy." All over this continent probably, dark-haired, reasonably slender young women were told, when they were stylishly dressed or getting their pictures taken, that they looked like Jackie Kennedy.

Andrew took a lot of pictures of me, and of the children, our 10 house, our garden, our excursions and possessions. He got copies made, labelled them carefully, and sent them back to his mother and his aunt and uncle in Ontario. He got copies for me to send to my father, who also lived in Ontario, and I did so, but less regularly than he sent his. When he saw pictures he thought I had already sent lying around the house, Andrew was perplexed and annoyed. He liked to have this record go forth.

That summer, we were presenting ourselves, not pictures. We were driving back from Vancouver, where we lived, to Ontario, which we still called "home," in our new car. Five days to get there, ten days there, five days back. For the first time, Andrew had three weeks' holiday. He worked in the legal department at B. C. Hydro.

On a Saturday morning, we loaded suitcases, two thermos bottles — one filled with coffee and one with lemonade — some fruit and sandwiches, picture books and coloring books, crayons, drawing pads, insect repellent, sweaters (in case it got cold in the mountains), and our two children into the car. Andrew locked the house, and Cynthia said ceremoniously, "Goodbye, house."

Meg said, "Goodbye, house." Then she said, "Where will we live now?"

"It's not goodbye forever," said Cynthia. "We're coming back. Mother! Meg thought we weren't ever coming back!"

"I did not," said Meg, kicking the back of my seat.   15

Andrew and I put on our sunglasses, and we drove away, over the Lions Gate Bridge and through the main part of Vancouver. We shed our house, the neighborhod, the city, and — at the crossing point between Washington and British Columbia — our country. We were driving east across the United States, taking the most northerly route, and would cross into Canada again at Sarnia, Ontario. I don't know if we chose this route because the Trans-Canada Highway was not completely finished at the time or if we just wanted the feeling of driving through a foreign, a very slightly foreign, country — that extra bit of interest and adventure.

We were both in high spirits. Andrew congratulated the car several times. He said he felt so much better driving it than our old car, a 1951 Austin that slowed down dismally on the hills and had a fussy-old-lady image. So Andrew said now.

"What kind of image does this one have?" said Cynthia. She listened to us carefully and liked to try out new words such as "image." Usually she got them right.

"Lively," I said. "Slightly sporty. It's not show-off."

"It's sensible, but it has class," Andrew said. "Like my image."   20

Cynthia thought that over and said with a cautious pride, "That means like you think you want to be, Daddy?"

As for me, I was happy because of the shedding. I loved taking off. In my own house, I seemed to be often looking for a place to hide — sometimes from the children but more often from the jobs to be done and the phone ringing and the sociability of the neighborhood. I wanted to hide so that I could get busy at my real work, which was a sort of wooing of distant parts of myself. I lived in a state of siege, always losing just what I wanted to hold on to. But on trips there was no difficulty. I could be talking to Andrew, talking to the children and looking at whatever they wanted me to look at — a pig on a sign, a pony in a field, a Volkswagen on a revolving stand — and pouring lemonade into plastic cups, and all the time those bits and pieces would be flying together inside me. The essential composition would be achieved. This made me hopeful and lighthearted. It was being a watcher that did it. A watcher, not a keeper.

We turned east at Everett and climbed into the Cascades. I showed Cynthia our route on the map. First I showed her the map of the whole United States, which showed also the bottom part of Canada. Then I turned to the separate maps of each of the states we were going to pass through. Washington, Idaho, Montana, North Dakota, Minnesota, Wisconsin. I showed her the dotted line across Lake Michigan, which was the route of the ferry we would take. Then we would drive across Michigan to the bridge that linked the United States and Canada at Sarnia, Ontario. Home.

Meg wanted to see, too.

"You won't understand," said Cynthia. But she took the road 25 atlas into the back seat.

"Sit back," she said to Meg. "Sit still. I'll show you."

I could hear her tracing the route for Meg, very accurately, just as I had done it for her. She looked up all the states' maps, knowing how to find them in alphabetical order.

"You know what that line is?" she said. "It's the road. That line is the road we're driving on. We're going right along this line."

Meg did not say anything.

"Mother, show me where we are right this minute," said Cyn- 30 thia.

I took the atlas and pointed out the road through the mountains, and she took it back and showed it to Meg. "See where the road is all wiggly?" she said. "It's wiggly because there are so many turns in it. The wiggles are the turns." She flipped some pages and waited a moment. "Now," she said, "show me where we are." Then she called to me, "Mother, she understands! She pointed to it! Meg understands maps!"

It seems to me now that we invented characters for our children. We had them firmly set to play their parts. Cynthia was bright and diligent, sensitive, courteous, watchful. Sometimes we teased her for being too conscientious, too eager to be what we in fact depended on her to be. Any reproach or failure, any rebuff, went terribly deep with her. She was fair-haired, fair-skinned, easily showing the effects of the sun, raw winds, pride, or humiliation. Meg was more solidly built, more reticent — not rebellious but stubborn sometimes, mysterious. Her silences seemed to us to show her strength of character, and her negatives were taken as signs of an imperturbable independence. Her hair was brown, and we cut it in straight bangs. Her eyes were a light hazel, clear and dazzling.

We were entirely pleased with these characters, enjoying the contradictions as well as the confirmations of them. We disliked the heavy, the uninventive, approach to being parents. I had a dread of turning into a certain kind of mother — the kind whose body sagged, who moved in a woolly-smelling, milky-smelling fog, solemn with trivial burdens. I believed that all the attention these mothers paid, their need to be burdened, was the cause of colic, bed-wetting, asthma. I favored another approach — the mock desperation, the inflated irony of the professional mothers who wrote for magazines. In those magazine pieces, the children were splendidly self-willed, hard-edged, perverse, indomitable. So were the mothers, through their wit, indomitable. The real-life mothers I warmed to were the sort who would phone up and say, "Is my embryo Hitler by any chance over at your house?" They cackled clear above the milky fog.

We saw a dead deer strapped across the front of a pickup truck.

"Somebody shot it," Cynthia said. "Hunters shoot the deer." 35

"It's not hunting season yet," Andrew said. "They may have hit it on the road. See the sign for deer crossing?"

"I would cry if we hit one," Cynthia said sternly.

I had made peanut-butter-and-marmalade sandwiches for the children and salmon-and-mayonnaise for us. But I had not put any lettuce in, and Andrew was disappointed.

"I didn't have any," I said.

"Couldn't you have got some?" 40

"I'd have had to buy a whole head of lettuce just to get enough for sandwiches, and I decided it wasn't woth it."

This was a lie. I had forgotten.

"They're a lot better with lettuce."

"I didn't think it made that much difference." After a silence, I said, "Don't be mad."

"I'm not mad. I like lettuce on sandwiches." 45
"I just didn't think it mattered that much."
"How would it be if I didn't bother to fill up the gas tank?"
"That's not the same thing."
"Sing a song," said Cynthia. She started to sing:

"Five little ducks went out one day,
Over the hills and far away.
One little duck went
'Quack-quack-quack.'
Four little ducks came swimming back."

Andrew squeezed my hand and said, "Let's not fight."
"You're right. I should have got lettuce." 50
"It doesn't matter that much."

I wished that I could get my feelings about Andrew to come together into a serviceable and dependable feeling. I had even tried writing two lists, one of things I liked about him, one of things I disliked — in the cauldron of intimate life, things I loved and things I hated — as if I hoped by this to prove something, to come to a conclusion one way or the other. But I gave it up when I saw that all it proved was what I already knew — that I had violent contradictions. Sometimes the very sound of his footsteps seemed to me tyrannical, the set of his mouth smug and mean, his hard, straight body a barrier interposed — quite consciously, even dutifully, and with a nasty pleasure in its masculine authority — between me and whatever joy or lightness I could get in life. Then, with not much warning, he became my good friend and most essential companion. I felt the sweetness of his light bones and serious ideas, the vulnerability of his love, which I imagined to be much purer and more straightforward than my own. I could be greatly moved by an inflexibility, a harsh propriety, that at other times I scorned. I would think how humble he was, really, taking on such a ready-made role of husband, father, breadwinner, and how I myself in comparison was really a secret monster of egotism. Not so secret, either — not from him.

At the bottom of our fights, we served up what we thought were the ugliest truths. "I know there is something basically selfish and basically untrustworthy about you," Andrew once said. "I've always known it. I also know that that is why I fell in love with you."

"Yes," I said, feeling sorrowful but complacent.
"I know that I'd be better off without you." 55
"Yes. You would."

"You'd be happier without me."

"Yes."

And finally — finally — racked and purged, we clasped hands and laughed, laughed at those two benighted people, ourselves. Their grudges, their grievances, their self-justification. We leap-frogged over them. We declared them liars. We would have wine with dinner, or decide to give a party.

I haven't seen Andrew for years, don't know if he is still thin, 60 has gone completely gray, insists on lettuce, tells the truth, or is hearty and disappointed.

We stayed the night in Wenatchee, Washington, where it hadn't rained for weeks. We ate dinner in a restaurant built about a tree — not a sapling in a tub but a tall, sturdy cottonwood. In the early-morning light, we climbed out of the irrigated valley, up dry, rocky, very steep hillsides that would seem to lead to more hills, and there on the top was a wide plateau, cut by the great Spokane and Columbia rivers. Grainland and grassland, mile after mile. There were straight roads here, and little farming towns with grain elevators. In fact, there was a sign announcing that this county we were going through, Douglas County, had the second-highest wheat yield of any county in the United States. The towns had planted shade trees. At least, I thought they had been planted, because there were no such big trees in the countryside.

All this was marvellously welcome to me. "Why do I love it so much?" I said to Andrew. "Is it because it isn't scenery?"

"It reminds you of home," said Andrew. "A bout of severe nostalgia." But he said this kindly.

When we said "home" and meant Ontario, we had very different places in mind. My home was a turkey farm, where my father lived as a widower, and though it was the same house my mother had lived in, had papered, painted, cleaned, furnished, it showed the effects now of neglect and of some wild sociability. A life went on in it that my mother could not have predicted or condoned. There were parties for the turkey crew, the gutters and pluckers, and sometimes one or two of the young men would be living there temporarily, inviting their own friends and having their own impromptu parties. This life, I thought, was better for my father than being lonely, and I did not disapprove, had certainly no right to disapprove. Andrew did not like to go there, naturally enough, because he was not the sort who could sit around the kitchen table with the turkey crew, telling jokes. They were intimidated by him and contemptuous of him, and it seemed to me that my father, when they were around, had to be on their side. And it wasn't only Andrew who had trouble. I could manage those jokes, but it was an effort.

I wished for the days when I was little, before we had the turkeys. We had cows, and sold the milk to the cheese factory. A turkey farm is nothing like as pretty as a dairy farm or a sheep farm. You can see that the turkeys are on a straight path to becoming frozen carcasses and table meat. They don't have the pretense of a life of their own, a browsing idyll, that cattle have, or pigs in the dappled orchard. Turkey barns are long, efficient buildings — tin sheds. No beams or hay or warm stables. Even the smell of guano seems thinner and more offensive than the usual smell of stable manure. No hints there of hay coils and rail fences and songbirds and the flowering hawthorn. The turkeys were all let out into one long field, which they picked clean. They didn't look like great birds there but like fluttering laundry.

Once, shortly after my mother died, and after I was married — in fact, I was packing to join Andrew in Vancouver — I was at home alone for a couple of days with my father. There was a freakishly heavy rain all night. In the early light, we saw that the turkey field was flooded. At least, the low-lying parts of it were flooded — it was like a lake with many islands. The turkeys were huddled on these islands. Turkeys are very stupid. (My father would say, "You know a chicken? You know how stupid a chicken is? Well, a chicken is an Einstein compared with a turkey.") But they had managed to crowd to higher ground and avoid drowning. Now they might push each other off, suffocate each other, get cold and die. We couldn't wait for the water to go down. We went out in an old rowboat we had. I rowed and my father pulled the heavy, wet turkeys into the boat and we took them to the barn. It was still raining a little. The job was difficult and absurd and very uncomfortable. We were laughing. I was happy to be working with my father. I felt close to all hard, repetitive, appalling work, in which the body is finally worn out, the mind sunk (though sometimes the spirit can stay marvellously light), and I was homesick in advance for this life and this place. I thought that if Andrew could see me there in the rain, red-handed, muddy, trying to hold on to turkey legs and row the boat at the same time, he would only want to get me out of there and make me forget about it. This raw life angered him. My attachment to it angered him. I thought that I shouldn't have married him. But who else? One of the turkey crew?

And I didn't want to stay there. I might feel bad about leaving, but I would feel worse if somebody made me stay.

Andrew's mother lived in Toronto, in an apartment building looking out on Muir Park. When Andrew and his sister were both at home, his mother slept in the living room. Her husband, a doctor, had died when the children were still too young to go to school. She took a secretarial course and sold her house at Depression prices, moved to this apartment, managed to raise her children, with some help from relatives — her sister Caroline, her brother-in-law Roger. Andrew and his sister went to private schools and to camp in the summer.

"I suppose that was courtesy of the Fresh Air fund?" I said once, scornful of his claim that he had been poor. To my mind, Andrew's urban life had been sheltered and fussy. His mother came home with a headache from working all day in the noise, the harsh light of a department-store office, but it did not occur to me that hers was a hard or admirable life. I don't think she herself believed that she was admirable — only unlucky. She worried about her work in the office, her clothes, her cooking, her children. She worried most of all about what Roger and Caroline would think.

Caroline and Roger lived on the east side of the park, in a handsome stone house. Roger was a tall man with a bald, freckled head, a fat, firm stomach. Some operation on his throat had deprived him of his voice — he spoke in a rough whisper. But everybody paid attention. At dinner once in the stone house — where all the dining-room furniture was enormous, darkly glowing, palatial — I asked him a question. I think it had to do with Whittaker Chambers, whose story was then appearing in the *Saturday Evening Post*. The question was mild in tone, but he guessed its subversive intent and took to calling me Mrs. Gromyko, referring to what he alleged to be my "sympathies." Perhaps he really craved an adversary, and could not find one. At that dinner, I saw Andrew's hand tremble as he lit his mother's cigarette. His Uncle Roger had paid for Andrew's education, and was on the board of directors of several companies.

"He is just an opinionated old man," Andrew said to me later. "What is the point of arguing with him?"

Before we left Vancouver, Andrew's mother had written, "Roger seems quite intrigued by the idea of your buying a small car!" Her exclamation mark showed apprehension. At that time, particularly in Ontario, the choice of a small European car over a large American car could be seen as some sort of declaration —

a declaration of tendencies Roger had been sniffing after all long.

"It isn't that small a car," said Andrew huffily.

"That's not the point," I said. "The point is, it isn't any of his business!"

We spent the second night in Missoula. We had been told in   75
Spokane, at a gas station, that there was a lot of repair work going on along Highway 2, and that we were in for a very hot, dusty drive, with long waits, so we turned onto the interstate and drove through Coeur d'Alene and Kellogg into Montana. After Missoula, we turned south toward Butte, but detoured to see Helena, the state capital. In the car, we played Who Am I?

Cynthia was somebody dead, and an American, and a girl. Possibly a lady. She was not in a story. She had not been seen on television. Cynthia had not read about her in a book. She was not anybody who had come to the kindergarten, or a relative of any of Cynthia's friends.

"Is she human?" said Andrew, with a sudden shrewdness.

"No! That's what you forgot to ask!"

"An animal," I said reflectively.

"Is that a question? Sixteen questions!"   80

"No, it is not a question. I'm thinking. A dead animal."

"It's the deer," said Meg, who hadn't been playing.

"That's not fair!" said Cynthia. "She's not playing!"

"What deer?" said Andrew.

I said, "Yesterday."   85

"The day before," said Cynthia. "Meg wasn't playing. Nobody got it."

"The deer on the truck," said Andrew.

"It was a lady deer, because it didn't have antlers, and it was an American and it was dead," Cynthia said.

Andrew said, "I think it's kind of morbid, being a dead deer."

"I got it," said Meg.   90

Cynthia said, "I think I know what morbid is. It's depressing."

Helena, an old silver-mining town, looked forlorn to us even in the morning sunlight. Then Bozeman and Billings, not forlorn in the slightest — energetic, strung-out towns, with miles of blinding tinsel fluttering over used-car lots. We got too tired and hot even to play Who Am I? These busy, prosaic cities reminded me of similar places in Ontario, and I thought about what was really waiting there — the great tombstone furniture of Roger and Caroline's dining room, the dinners for which I must iron the children's dresses and warn them about forks, and then the

other table a hundred miles away, the jokes of my father's crew.
The pleasures I had been thinking of — looking at the countryside or drinking a Coke in an old-fashioned drugstore with
fans and a high, pressed-tin ceiling — would have to be snatched
in between.

"Meg's asleep," Cynthia said. "She's so hot. She makes me hot
in the same seat with her."

"I hope she isn't feverish," I said, not turning around.

What are we doing this for, I thought, and the answer came 95
— to show off. To give Andrew's mother and my father the
pleasure of seeing their grandchildren. That was our duty. But
beyond that we wanted to show them something. What strenuous
children we were, Andrew and I, what relentless seekers of approbation. It was as if at some point we had received an unforgettable, indigestible message — that we were far from satisfactory, and that the most commonplace success in life was
probably beyond us. Roger dealt out such messages, of course —
that was his style — but Andrew's mother, my own mother and
father couldn't have meant to do so. All they meant to tell us was
"Watch out. Get along." My father, when I was in high school,
teased me that I was getting to think I was so smart I would never
find a boyfriend. He would have forgotten that in a week. I never
forgot it. Andrew and I didn't forget things. We took umbrage.

"I wish there was a beach," said Cynthia.

"There probably is one," Andrew said. "Right around the
next curve."

"There isn't any curve," she said, sounding insulted.

"That's what I mean."

"I wish there was some more lemonade." 100

"I will just wave my magic wand and produce some," I said.
"Okay, Cynthia? Would you rather have grape juice? Will I do a
beach while I'm at it?"

She was silent, and soon I felt repentant. "Maybe in the next
town there might be a pool," I said. I looked at the map. "In Miles
City. Anyway, there'll be something cool to drink."

"How far is it?" Andrew said.

"Not so far," I said. "Thirty miles, about."

"In Miles City," said Cynthia, in the tones of an incantation, 105
"there is a beautiful blue swimming pool for children, and a park
with lovely trees."

Andrew said to me, "You could have started something."

But there was a pool. There was a park, too, though not quite
the oasis of Cynthia's fantasy. Priarie trees with thin leaves —

cottonwoods and poplars — worn grass, and a high wire fence around the pool. Within this fence, a wall, not yet completed, of cement blocks. There were no shouts or splashes; over the entrance I saw a sign that said the pool was closed every day from noon until two o'clock. It was then twenty-five after twelve.

Nevertheless I called out, "Is anybody there?" I thought somebody must be around, because there was a small truck parked near the entrance. On the side of the truck were these words: "We have Brains, to fix your Drains. (We have Roto-Rooter too.)"

A girl came out, wearing a red lifeguard's shirt over her bathing suit. "Sorry, we're closed."

"We were just driving through," I said. 110

"We close every day from twelve until two. It's on the sign." She was eating a sandwich.

"I saw the sign," I said. "But this is the first water we've seen for so long, and the children are awfully hot, and I wondered if they could just dip in and out — just five minutes. We'd watch them."

A boy came into sight behind her. He was wearing jeans and a T-shirt with the words "Roto-Rooter" on it.

I was going to say that we were driving from British Columbia to Ontario, but I remembered that Canadian place names usually meant nothing to Americans. "We're driving right across the country," I said. "We haven't time to wait for the pool to open. We were just hoping the children could get cooled off."

Cynthia came running up barefoot behind me. "Mother, 115 Mother, where is my bathing suit?" Then she stopped, sensing the serious adult negotiations. Meg was climbing out of the car — just wakened, with her top pulled up and her shorts pulled down, showing her pink stomach.

"Is it just those two?" the girl said.

"Just the two. We'll watch them."

"I can't let any adults in. If it's just the two, I guess I could watch them. I'm having my lunch." She said to Cynthia, "Do you want to come in the pool?"

"Yes, please," said Cynthia firmly.

Meg looked at the ground. 120

"Just a short time, because the pool is really closed," I said. "We appreciate this very much," I said to the girl.

"Well, I can eat my lunch out there, if it's just the two of them." She looked toward the car as if she thought I might try to spring some more children on her.

When I found Cynthia's bathing suit, she took it into the

changing room. She would not permit anybody, even Meg, to see her naked. I changed Meg, who stood on the front seat of the car. She had a pink cotton bathing suit with straps that crossed and buttoned. There were ruffles across the bottom.

"She *is* hot," I said. "But I don't think she's feverish."

I loved helping Meg to dress or undress, because her body still had the solid unself-consciousness, the sweet indifference, something of the milky smell, of a baby's body. Cynthia's body had long ago been pared down, shaped and altered, into Cynthia. We all liked to hug Meg, press and nuzzle her. Sometimes she would scowl and beat us off, and this forthright independence, this ferocious bashfulness, simply made her more appealing, more apt to be tormented and tickled in the way of family love. 125

Andrew and I sat in the car with the windows open. I could hear a radio playing, and thought it must belong to the girl or her boyfriend. I was thirsty, and got out of the car to look for a concession stand, or perhaps a soft-drink machine, somewhere in the park. I was wearing shorts, and the backs of my legs were slick with sweat. I saw a drinking fountain at the other side of the park and was walking toward it in a roundabout way, keeping to the shade of the trees. No place became real till you got out of the car. Dazed with the heat, with the sun on the blistered houses, the pavement, the burned grass, I walked slowly. I paid attention to a squashed leaf, ground a Popsicle stick under the heel of my sandal, squinted at a trash can strapped to a tree. This is the way you look at the poorest details of the world resurfaced, after you've been driving for a long time — you feel their singleness and precise location and the forlorn coincidence of your being there to see them.

Where are the children?

I turned around and moved quickly, not quite running, to a part of the fence beyond which the cement wall was not completed. I could see some of the pool. I saw Cynthia, standing about waist-deep in the water, fluttering her hands on the surface and discreetly watching something at the end of the pool, which I could not see. I thought by her pose, her discretion, the look on her face, that she must be watching some byplay between the lifeguard and her boyfriend. I couldn't see Meg. But I thought she must be playing in the shallow — both the shallow and deep ends of the pool were out of my sight.

"Cynthia!" I had to call twice before she knew where my voice was coming from. "Cynthia! Where's Meg?"

It always seems to me, when I recall this scene, that Cynthia 130 turns very gracefully toward me, then turns all around in the water — making me think of a ballerina on point — and spreads her arms in a gesture of the stage. "Dis-ap-peared!"

Cynthia was naturally graceful, and she did take dancing lessons, so these movements may have been as I have described. She did say "Disappeared" after looking all around the pool, but the strangely artificial style of speech and gesture, the lack of urgency, is more likely my invention. The fear I felt instantly when I couldn't see Meg — even while I was telling myself she must be in the shallower water — must have made Cynthia's movements seem unbearably slow and inappropriate to me, and the tone in which she could say "Disappeared" before the implications struck her (or was she covering, at once, some ever-ready guilt?) was heard by me as quite exquisitely, monstrously self-possessed.

I cried out for Andrew, and the lifeguard came into view. She was pointing toward the deep end of the pool, saying, "What's that?"

There, just within my view, a cluster of pink ruffles appeared, a bouquet, beneath the surface of the water. Why would a lifeguard stop and point, why would she ask what that was, why didn't she just dive into the water and swim to it? She didn't swim; she ran all the way around the edge of the pool. But by that time Andrew was over the fence. So many things seemed not quite plausible — Cynthia's behavior, then the lifeguard's — and now I had the impression that Andrew jumped with one bound over this fence, which seemed about seven feet high. He must have climbed it very quickly, getting a grip on the wire.

I could not jump or climb it, so I ran to the entrance, where there was a sort of lattice gate, locked. It was not very high, and I did pull myself over it. I ran through the cement corridors, through the disinfectant pool for your feet, and came out on the edge of the pool.

The drama was over.

Andrew had got to Meg first, and had pulled her out of the water. He just had to reach over and grab her, because she was swimming somehow, with her head underwater — she was moving toward the edge of the pool. He was carrying her now, and the lifeguard was trotting along behind. Cynthia had climbed out of the water and was running to meet them. The only person aloof from the situation was the boyfriend, who had stayed on the bench at the shallow end, drinking a milkshake. He smiled at me,

135

and I thought that unfeeling of him, even though the danger was past. He may have meant it kindly. I noticed that he had not turned the radio off, just down.

Meg had not swallowed any water. She hadn't even scared herself. Her hair was plastered to her head and her eyes were wide open, golden with amazement.

"I was getting the comb," she said. "I didn't know it was deep."

Andrew said, "She was swimming! She was swimming by herself. I saw her bathing suit in the water and then I saw her swimming."

"She nearly drowned," Cynthia said. "Didn't she? Meg nearly   140
drowned."

"I don't know how it could have happened," said the life-guard. "One moment she was there, and the next she wasn't."

What had happened was that Meg had climbed out of the water at the shallow end and run along the edge of the pool toward the deep end. She saw a comb that somebody had dropped lying on the bottom. She crouched down and reached in to pick it up, quite deceived about the depth of the water. She went over the edge and slipped into the pool, making such a light splash that nobody heard — not the lifeguard, who was kissing her boyfriend, or Cynthia, who was watching them. That must have been the moment under the trees when I thought, Where are the children? It must have been the same moment. At that moment, Meg was slipping, surprised, into the treacherously clear blue water.

"It's okay," I said to the lifeguard, who was nearly crying. "She can move pretty fast." (Though that wasn't what we usually said about Meg at all. We said she thought everything over and took her time.)

"You swam, Meg," said Cynthia, in a congratulatory way. (She told us about the kissing later.)

"I didn't know it was deep," Meg said. "I didn't drown."   145

We had lunch at a take-out place, eating hamburgers and fries at a picnic table not far from the highway. In my excitement, I forgot to get Meg a plain hamburger, and had to scrape off the relish and mustard with plastic spoons, then wipe the meat with a paper napkin, before she would eat it. I took advantage of the trash can there to clean out the car. Then we resumed driving east, with the car windows open in front. Cynthia and Meg fell asleep in the back seat.

Andrew and I talked quietly about what had happened. Suppose I hadn't had the impulse just at that moment to check on the children? Suppose we had gone uptown to get drinks, as we had thought of doing? How had Andrew got over the fence? Did he jump or climb? (He couldn't remember.) How had he reached Meg so quickly? And think of the lifeguard not watching. And Cynthia, taken up with the kissing. Not seeing anything else. Not seeing Meg drop over the edge.

Disappeared.

But she swam. She held her breath and came up swimming.

What a chain of lucky links.   150

That was all we spoke about — luck. But I was compelled to picture the opposite. At this moment, we could have been filling out forms. Meg removed from us, Meg's body being prepared for shipment. To Vancouver — where we had never noticed such a thing as a graveyard — or to Ontario? The scribbled drawings she had made this morning would still be in the back seat of the car. How could this be borne all at once, how did people bear it? The plump, sweet shoulders and hands and feet, the fine brown hair, the rather satisfied, secretive expression — all exactly the same as when she had been alive. The most ordinary tragedy. A child drowned in a swimming pool at noon on a sunny day. Things tidied up quickly. The pool opens as usual at two o'clock. The lifeguard is a bit shaken up and gets the afternoon off. She drives away with her boyfriend in the Roto-Rooter truck. The body sealed away in some kind of shipping coffin. Sedatives, phone calls, arrangements. Such a sudden vacancy, a blind sinking and shifting. Waking up groggy from the pills, thinking for a moment it wasn't true. Thinking if only we hadn't stopped, if only we hadn't taken this route, if only they hadn't let us use the pool. Probably no one would ever have known about the comb.

There's something trashy about this kind of imagining, isn't there? Something shameful. Laying your finger on the wire to get the safe shock, feeling a bit of what it's like, then pulling back. I believed that Andrew was more scrupulous than I about such things, and that at this moment he was really trying to think about something else.

When I stood apart from my parents at Steve Gauley's funeral and watched them, and had this new, unpleasant feeling about them, I thought that I was understanding something about them for the first time. It was a deadly serious thing. I was understanding that they were implicated. Their big, stiff, dressed-up bodies did not stand between me and sudden death, or any kind

of death. They gave consent. So it seemed. They gave consent to
the death of children and to my death not by anything they said
or thought but by the very fact that they had made children —
they had made me. They had made me, and for that reason my
death — however grieved they were, however they carried on —
would seem to them anything but impossible or unnatural. This
was a fact, and even then I knew they were not to blame.

But I did blame them. I charged them with effrontery, hypocrisy. On Steve Gauley's behalf, and on behalf of all children, who
knew that by rights they should have sprung up free, to live a
new, superior kind of life, not to be caught in the snares of
vanquished grownups, with their sex and funerals.

Steve Gauley drowned, people said, because he was next   155
thing to an orphan and was let run free. If he had been warned
enough and given chores to do and kept in check, he wouldn't
have fallen from an untrustworthy tree branch into a spring
pond, a full gravel pit near the river — he wouldn't have
drowned. He was neglected, he was free, so he drowned. And his
father took it as an accident, such as might happen to a dog. He
didn't have a good suit for the funeral, and he didn't bow his
head for the prayers. But he was the only grownup that I let off
the hook. He was the only one I didn't see giving consent. He
couldn't prevent anything, but he wasn't implicated in anything,
either — not like the others, saying the Lord's Prayer in their
unnaturally weighted voices, oozing religion and dishonor.

At Glendive, not far from the North Dakota border, we had a
choice — either to continue on the interstate or head northeast,
toward Williston, taking Route 16, then some secondary roads
that would get us back to Highway 2.

We agreed that the interstate would be faster, and that it was
important for us not to spend too much time — that is,
money — on the road. Nevertheless we decided to cut back to
Highway 2.

"I just like the idea of it better," I said.

Andrew said, "That's because it's what we planned to do in
the beginning."

"We missed seeing Kalispell and Havre. And Wolf Point. I   160
like the name."

"We'll see them on the way back."

Andrew's saying "on the way back" was a surprising pleasure
to me. Of course, I had believed that we would be coming back,
with our car and our lives and our family intact, having covered

all that distance, having dealt somehow with those loyalties and problems, held ourselves up for inspection in such a foolhardy way. But it was a relief to hear him say it.

"What I can't get over," said Andrew, "is how you got the signal. It's got to be some kind of extra sense that mothers have."

Partly I wanted to believe that, to bask in my extra sense. Partly I wanted to warn him — to warn everybody — never to count on it.

"What I can't understand," I said, "is how you got over the fence." 165

"Neither can I."

So we went on, with the two in the back seat trusting us, because of no choice, and we ourselves trusting to be forgiven, in time, for everything that had first to be seen and condemned by those children: whatever was flippant, arbitrary, careless, callous — all our natural, and particular, mistakes.

5

Ideas: Experiencing Confirmation

Bringing to life experiences of intellectual challenge was our focus in the previous chapter. Still concerned with engaging ideas, we turn now to experiences of confirmation.

Our activities here have much in common with those we perform in evoking experiences of challenge. What sort of ideas do we need to have in mind? Deciding where we are, intellectually speaking, is once again the essential first step. We move on from here to consider whether the text confirms rather than challenges a familiar assumption. And those reflections can help us begin to define the subject in language of our own. Always we're engaged in evoking feelings as well as ideas, staying in touch with the whole of the experience that we're living through.

LANGSTON HUGHES (1902–1967)
Ballad of the Landlord

Landlord, landlord,
My roof has sprung a leak.
Don't you 'member I told you about it
Way last week?

Landlord, landlord,   5
These steps is broken down.
When you come up yourself
It's a wonder you don't fall down.

Ten Bucks you say I owe you?
Ten Bucks you say is due?   10
Well, that's Ten Bucks more'n I'll pay you
Till you fix this house up new.

What? You gonna get eviction orders?
You gonna cut off my heat?
You gonna take my furniture and   15
Throw it in the street?

Um-huh! You talking high and mighty.
Talk on — till you get through.
You ain't gonna be able to say a word
If I land my fist on you.   20

Police! Police!
Come and get this man!
He's trying to ruin the government
And overturn the land!

Copper's whistle!   25
Patrol bell!
Arrest.

Precinct Station.
Iron cell.
Headlines in press: 30

MAN THREATENS LANDLORD

TENANT HELD NO BAIL

JUDGE GIVES NEGRO 90 DAYS IN COUNTY JAIL

Where are we in this poem? We're observing a series of
events that seem to corroborate many familiar sayings: Can't
fight the system. White is right, blacks get back. The rich get
richer, the poor get poorer. A person without status tries to stand
up for his rights, is provoked to anger by bullying threats, and
learns the hard way that the "justice system" isn't on his side.

If there's nothing here that can be thought of as a challenge
to the notion that might makes right, it still remains true that
"Ballad of the Landlord" doesn't merely restate that notion. As
we bring the poem to life, we draw close to realities of feeling
that standard political speeches about oppression and injustice
seldom succeed in evoking.

One example of vivid reality is the tenant's obvious sense of
the *preposterousness* of the landlord's response to a justified complaint. Regardless of how often one has heard that powerful
people don't brook protest against their ways, an encounter at
first hand with the unshakable arrogance of an oppressor often

rouses incredulity. Can this man be *serious*? Doesn't he realize that anybody with an ounce of brains would see him as outrageously unfair? Reading this poem we enter the consciousness of a tenant who is so staggered by his landlord's infuriating position that he can't imagine any response to it except that of violent physical dismissal. We also experience the swift stilling of that voice of protest, the abrupt, brutal termination of his consciousness — swallowed up by The System in impersonal phrases and headlines. Together with the flat confirmation that might makes right comes knowledge that an individual confrontation with the actualities can be shocking, stupefying, utterly destructive — beyond any normal person's ability to assimilate. When viewed at a distance, "might" in the act of "making right" seldom has the power to horrify; felt and seen at close range, its character and habits are harder to shrug off.

CONFIRMATION AS A PROCESS

The processes of confirmation involved in imaginative literature are subtle and indirect. One literary form — the fable — deals directly in confirmable general propositions. Most of us can remember an Aesop's fable or two — such as "The Shepherd's Boy and the Wolf"

> Every day the shepherd boy was sent with his father's sheep into the mountain pasture to guard the flock. It was, indeed, a lonely spot at the edge of a dark forest, and there were no companions with whom he could pass the long, weary hours of the day.
>
> One day, just to stir up some excitement, he rushed down from the pasture, crying, "Wolf! Wolf!" The villagers heard the alarm and came running with clubs and guns to help chase the marauder away, only to find the sheep grazing peacefully and no wolf in sight.
>
> So well had the trick worked that the foolish boy tried it again and again, and each time the villagers came running, only to be laughed at for their pains.
>
> But there came a day when a wolf really came. The shepherd screamed and called for help. But all in vain! The neighbors, supposing him to be up to his old tricks, paid no heed to his cries, and the wolf devoured the sheep.
>
> *Application*: Liars are not believed even when they tell the truth.

The fable illustrates, or confirms, the "application," or general proposition — and that's that.

Fables, though, are different from the principal body of imaginative literature. Most poems, stories, and plays aren't concerned with laying out a sequence of events that can be seen as an application of a general rule. And we as active readers aren't engaged in reducing works of literature to quickie messages.

Often, however, we do test a general proposition against an experience of a work as a way of penetrating the work's insides. What happens as we read is something like this: We realize gradually — perhaps midway through the poem, story, or play — that one or another notion we're already familiar with has a bearing on the text. (In the case of "Ballad of the Landlord," the notion is, of course, that in contests with the power structure, oppressed blacks seldom win.) Reflecting on the poem, story, or play, we sense that it is deepening our understanding of that familiar notion — making us grasp elements of its meaning not visible before. (The oppressors win — but with an ease and absoluteness that is astounding.) It's as though the notion was hitherto too distant, too abstract. Even as it confirms the general truth, the literary work renders it as a fresh perception.

ABSTRACT TRUTH vs. LIVED TRUTH

Why is this possible? The answer lies in the distinction between abstract truth and lived truth — between ideas that we "know" in nonpractical, theoretical ways, and ideas that have been drawn directly into our own day-to-day reality. Everybody concedes the difference between reflecting on events or conditions — war, poverty, mortality, passionate love, and so on — at a comfortable distance and experiencing them as actuality. Immediacy has immense power. Yesterday's "idea" is transformed into lived life, a configuration of intense feelings.

The job is, at bottom, that of penetrating the specifics. Doing the job means functioning in unusual ways — sometimes like a lens converging light rays. Our alertness, intelligence, and sensitivity register and focus the process by which this or that formerly abstract truth is individually taken in, made new in some respects, deepened, and ultimately confirmed. Often it's the insight into this very process that constitutes a primary reward of literature. We realize vividly, all at once, that ideas come to life —

are transformed from impersonal truisms to personal understanding — in each of us in separate, highly individual ways. And that realization can have a powerful impact on our whole concept of learning and living.

ASKING QUESTIONS
ABOUT CONFIRMATION

It is time once again for practice. An idea that emerges as pertinent to the texts assembled in this chapter is that of the human life cycle. In some sense these works — a poem, a story, and a play — all confirm that nothing is more central to the human condition than the fact of our mortality. But the key to bringing these texts to life lies in moving beyond terms such as *mortality* and *life cycle* into the processes by which individuals learn and experience the meanings of such terms. As readers we aren't functioning now as discoverers of challenges to standard or conventional notions; neither are we being offered "material" to be compressed into capsule messages. What we're doing is drawing close to characters confronting the processes of living and dying — minds discovering truths about the human condition that had no real meaning for them until now. Our purpose is to find language for the lived realities that are confirming and extending and deepening knowledge that might otherwise remain abstract. In pursuing that language we ask, What special aspect of the general truth that's being confirmed seems least familiar? Why is it that, in life as opposed to this particular text, that special aspect seems neglected or difficult to notice? Would we be better off if we were more alert to it from day to day? How might awareness of this dimension of things help us? Is it conceivable that such awareness would be dangerous? How so?

THOMAS, LORD VAUX (1510–1556)
I loathe that I did love

I loathe that I did love,
  In youth that I thought sweet;
As time requires, for my behove,
  Methinks they are not meet.

My lusts they do me leave,   5
  My fancies all be fled,
And tract of time begins to weave
  Grey hairs upon my head.

For age with stealing steps
  Hath clawed me with his crutch,   10
And lusty life away she leaps,
  As there had been none such.

My Muse doth not delight
  Me as she did before;
My hand and pen are not in plight,   15
  As they have been of yore.

For reason me denies
  This youthly idle rhyme;
And day by day to me she cries,
  "Leave off these toys in time."   20

The wrinkles in my brow,
  The furrows in my face,
Say, limping age will lodge him now
  Where youth must give him place.

The harbinger of death,   25
  To me I see him ride;
The cough, the cold, the gasping breath
  Doth bid me to provide

A pickaxe and a spade,
  And eke a shrouding sheet,   30
A house of clay for to be made
  For such a guest most meet.

Methinks I hear the clerk
  That knolls the careful knell,
And bids me leave my woeful work,   35
  Ere nature me compel.

My keepers knit the knot
  That youth did laugh to scorn,
Of me that clean shall be forgot,
  As I had not been born.   40

Thus must I youth give up,
  Whose badge I long did wear;
To them I yield the wanton cup,
  That better may it bear.

Lo, here the bared skull,   45
  By whose bald sign I know
That stooping age away shall pull
  That youthful years did sow.

For beauty with her band
  These crooked cares hath wrought,   50
And shipped me into the land
  From whence I first was brought.

And ye that bide behind,
  Have ye none other trust;
As ye of clay were cast by kind,   55
  So shall ye waste to dust.

Questions

Human creatures are mutable, subject to the natural cycle of
growth and decline, incapable whether great or humble of overcoming the limits of mortality. Nothing in "I loathe that I did
love" could be said to call into question these general propositions. But the propositions *are* general, whereas, except in the
final stanza, the observations in the poem are particular. The
speaker isn't discussing the idea of mortality, he is, seemingly,
showing it forth as an emotional reality — showing us how mortality "happens," at the level of personal awareness and perception, to one human creature, how inner change takes place, what
feelings it inspires. Focus on one of the feelings here that strikes
you as worth thinking about and describe it in a paragraph.
Where in the poem does the feeling run strong? Cite specific
passages and describe the feeling as fully as you can. How does
the creation of that feeling in the poem simultaneously confirm
and deepen knowledge of the meanings of human mortality?
Compare your response to the one that follows.

Response

EDITOR: The speaker in this poem asserts that his tastes and appetites have changed, that his step has lost its strength, that he's
become wrinkled and grey haired, and that his thoughts dwell
increasingly on death and the grave. Everybody recognizes these

symptoms of advancing years, looking at them from outside. Growing awareness of some sign that a family member is aging may surprise us momentarily, but not for long. We understand that people "get older"; we regret the inevitability of the process; we think of it as gradual, continuous.

But that's not the way mortality "happens" in "I loathe that I did love." The stress falls not on slow modifications of attitude and physicality but rather upon abrupt shifts, headlong change, unlooked-for extremes. One of the more striking feelings in the poem is a kind of exasperation at the aging process — resentment at its capriciousness, its seeming aberrance. Life leaps away as though it had never been present (stanza 3). Youth is summarily kicked out in stanza 6, and there's a suggestion in stanza 13 that the "band" of beauties that's set on the speaker over the years in fact kidnapped and shanghaied him. The very process of balding, usually perceived as the gentlest, most passive mode of decline, is dramatized in stanza 12 as a violent ripping away by the roots. In stanza 10 the focus is on a series of radical discontinuities: Not only do youth and age vanish but the very memory of the speaker precipitately and absolutely disappears:

> . . . me that clean shall be forgot,
>   As I had not been born.

That same radical discontinuity figures in the poem's opening lines and title. The speaker isn't talking about a little-by-little loss of interest; loving becomes loathing in the space of a quick phrase. Here and there we come upon an acknowledgment that some changes occur at a slower pace ("tract of time begins to weave / Grey hairs," lines 7–8), but it's plain that the speaker is far from saying that aging was for him a smooth, peaceful alteration. Change skulked in from behind, striking suddenly ("clawed me with his crutch," 10), and the contest was over in a second. And so it will be with you, the speaker warns — "ye that bide behind" (53). You won't believe that it can happen, you'll think there has to be adequate warning, opportunity for preparation — but you're wrong. Old age is all slyness, secretiveness; you may not have time enough even to be surprised.

It's the resentment and indignation at old age as an unfair trick played on unwitting dupes that stops us from experiencing this poem as one of those "discussions" of life, mutability, and mortality that add up to only easy mouthings of big words. Listening to the speaker we grasp that this could well be how it is — how we ourselves will one day wake up to the "facts of life." But is that really possible? we ask. Is it possible that instead of getting help from various early warning systems we'll be thrust unceremoniously into decrepitude? How could such a thing happen? *Why* would it happen?

This last question is the true stopper — the query that points us toward neglected dimensions of mortality. The reason mortality could strike without notice is that we think of it as a condition belonging to a future date, irrelevant to our present. But of course it's not irrelevant to today; mortality is the name of the daily human game, quite as appropriate a theme for reflection today as tomorrow, just as deserving of our attention now, in youth, as in midlife or later. Ceaselessly freshening our knowledge of mortality means allowing it to influence our behavior from moment to moment — our attitudes toward others, our joy in our pleasures, our feelings about our place in the whole order of things. We can let the knowledge go dead in us, hide out from it as the speaker did, but we're only tricking ourselves, setting ourselves up — absurdly — for an abrupt, fearful attack that we'd be less vulnerable to if we were more heedful.

Admittedly there's no news in any of this. Classical as well as Judeo-Christian writers and thinkers have taken up these themes; they are among the most familiar in Western civilization. No single reflection triggered by "I loathe that I did love," when considered separately from the poem, could possibly qualify as much more novel than those embodied in the oldest maxims and mottoes (for instance, Live every day as though it were your last). But the directness with which we're put in touch with the speaker's surprise and initial sense of outrage — this tells us as no abstract counsel could what it's like to discover, much more suddenly than one wants to, that the makers of those old maxims weren't kidding. Once we summon its insides, the poem heightens consciousness of all our styles of evasion, our postponements of understanding — helps us grasp that the compulsion to postpone is, in fact, pretty close to the essence of humanness. In the measure that it does this, "I loathe that I did love" deepens as well as confirms our existing knowledge.

ANTON CHEKHOV   (1860–1904)
The Bishop

TRANSLATED BY RONALD HINGLEY

I

It was on the eve of Palm Sunday; vespers were being sung in the Staro-Petrovski Convent. The hour was nearly ten when the palm leaves were distributed, and the little shrine lamps were growing dim; their wicks had burnt low, and a soft haze hung in the chapel. As the worshippers surged forward in the twilight like the waves of the sea, it seemed to his Reverence Peter, who had been feeling ill for three days, that the people who came to him for palm leaves all looked alike, and, men or women, old or young, all had the same expression in their eyes. He could not see the doors through the haze; the endless procession rolled toward him, and seemed as if it must go on rolling for ever. A choir of women's voices was singing and a nun was reading the canon.

How hot and close the air was, and how long the prayers! His Reverence was tired. His dry, parching breath was coming quickly and painfully, his shoulders were aching, and his legs were trembling. The occasional cries of an idiot in the gallery annoyed him. And now, as a climax, his Reverence saw, as in a delirium, his own mother whom he had not seen for nine years coming toward him in the crowd. She, or an old woman exactly like her, took a palm leaf from his hands, and moved away looking at him all the while with a glad, sweet smile, until she was lost in the crowd. And for some reason the tears began to course down his cheeks. His heart was happy and peaceful, but his eyes were fixed on a distant part of the chapel where the prayers were being read, and where no human being could be distinguished among the shadows. The tears glistened on his cheeks and beard. Then some one who was standing near him began to weep, too, and then another, and then another, until little by little the chapel was filled with a low sound of weeping. Then the convent choir began to sing, the weeping stopped, and everything went on as before.

Soon afterward the service ended. The fine, jubilant notes of the heavy chapel-bells were throbbing through the moonlit garden as the bishop stepped into his coach and drove away. The white walls, the crosses on the graves, the silvery birches, and the far-away moon hanging directly over the monastery, all seemed to be living a life of their own, incomprehensible, but very near to mankind. It was early in April, and a chilly night had suc-ceeded a warm spring day. A light frost was falling, but the breath of spring could be felt in the soft, cool air. The road from the monastery was sandy, the horses were obliged to proceed at a walk, and, bathed in the bright, tranquil moonlight, a stream of pilgrims was crawling along on either side of the coach. All were thoughtful, no one spoke. Everything around them, the trees, the sky, and even the moon, looked so young and intimate and friendly that they were reluctant to break the spell which they hoped might last for ever.

Finally the coach entered the city, and rolled down the main street. All the stores were closed but that of Erakin, the mil-lionaire merchant. He was trying his electric lights for the first time, and they were flashing so violently that a crowd had col-lected in front of the store. Then came wide, dark streets in endless succession, and then the highway, and fields, and the smell of pines. Suddenly a white crenelated wall loomed before him, and beyond it rose a tall belfry flanked by five flashing golden cupolas, all bathed in moonlight. This was the Pan-kratievski Monastery where his Reverence Peter lived. Here, too, the calm, brooding moon was floating directly above the monas-tery. The coach drove through the gate, its wheels crunching on the sand. Here and there the dark forms of monks started out into the moonlight and footsteps rang along the flagstone paths.

"Your mother has been here while you were away, your Rev- 5 erence," a lay brother told the bishop as he entered his room.

"My mother? When did she come?"

"Before vespers. She first found out where you were, and then drove to the convent."

"Then it was she whom I saw just now in the chapel! Oh, Father in heaven!"

And his Reverence laughed for joy.

"She told me to tell you, your Reverence," the lay brother 10 continued, "that she would come back tomorrow. She had a little girl with her, a grandchild, I think. She is stopping at Ovsiani-koff's inn."

"What time is it now?"

"It is after eleven."

"What a nuisance!"

His Reverence sat down irresolutely in his sitting-room, un-willing to believe that it was already so late. His arms and legs were racked with pain, the back of his neck was aching, and he felt uncomfortable and hot. When he had rested a few moments he went into his bedroom and there, too, he sat down, and dreamed of his mother. He heard the lay brother walking away and Father Sisoi the priest coughing in the next room. The mon-astery clock struck the quarter.

His Reverence undressed and began his prayers. He spoke   15 the old, familiar words with scrupulous attention, and at the same time he thought of his mother. She had nine children, and about forty grandchildren. She had lived from the age of seven-teen to the age of sixty with her husband the deacon in a little village. His Reverence remembered her from the days of his earliest childhood, and, ah, how he had loved her! Oh, that dear, precious, unforgettable childhood of his! Why did those years that had vanished for ever seem so much brighter and richer and gayer than they really had been? How tender and kind his mother had been when he was ill in his childhood and youth! His prayers mingled with the memories that burned ever brighter and brighter in his heart like a flame, but they did not hinder his thoughts of his mother.

When he had prayed he lay down, and as soon as he found himself in the dark there rose before his eyes the vision of his dead father, his mother, and Lyesopolye, his native village. The creaking of wagon wheels, the bleating of sheep, the sound of church-bells on a clear summer morning, ah, how pleasant it was to think of these things! He remembered Father Simeon, the old priest at Lyesopolye, a kind, gentle, good-natured old man. He himself had been small, and the priest's son had been a huge strapping novice with a terrible bass voice. He remembered how this young priest had scolded the cook once, and had shouted: "Ah, you she-ass of Jehovah!" And Father Simeon had said nothing, and had only been mortified because he could not for the life of him remember reading of an ass of that name in the Bible!

Father Simeon had been succeeded by Father Demian, a hard drinker who sometimes even went so far as to see green snakes. He had actually borne the nickname of "Demian the Snake-Seer" in the village. Marvei Nikolaitch had been the schoolmaster, a kind, intelligent man, but a hard drinker too. He never thrashed his scholars, but for some reason he kept a little bundle of birch twigs hanging on his wall, under which was a tablet bearing the absolutely unintelligible inscription: "Betula Kinderbalsamica Secuta." He had had a woolly black dog whom he called "Syntax."

The bishop laughed. Eight miles from Lyesopolye lay the village of Obnino possessing a miraculous icon. A procession started from Obnino every summer bearing the wonder-working icon and making the round of all the neighbouring villages. The church-bells would ring all day long first in one village, then in another, and to Little Paul (his Reverence was called Little Paul then) the air itself seemed tremulous with rapture. Barefoot, hatless, and infinitely happy, he followed the icon with a naive smile on his lips and naive faith in his heart.

Until the age of fifteen Little Paul had been so slow at his lessons that his parents had even thought of taking him out of the ecclesiastical school and putting him to work in the village store.

The bishop turned over so as to break the train of his thoughts, and tried to go to sleep.   20

"My mother has come!" he remembered, and laughed.

The moon was shining in through the window, and the floor was lit by its rays while he lay in shadow. A cricket was chirping. Father Sisoi was snoring in the next room, and there was a forlorn, friendless, even a vagrant note in the old man's cadences.

Sisoi had once been the steward of a diocesan bishop and was known as "Father Former Steward." He was seventy years old, and lived sometimes in a monastery sixteen miles away, sometimes in the city, sometimes wherever he happened to be. Three days ago he had turned up at the Pankratievski Monastery, and the bishop had kept him here in order to discuss with him at his leisure the affairs of the monastery.

The bell for matins rang at half past one. Father Sisoi coughed, growled something, and got up.

"Father Sisoi!" called the bishop.   25

Sisoi came in dressed in a white cassock, carrying a candle in his hand.

"I can't go to sleep," his Reverence said. "I must be ill. I don't know what the matter is; I have fever."

"You have caught cold, your Lordship. I must rub you with tallow."

Father Sisoi stood looking at him for a while and yawned: "Ah-h — the Lord have mercy on us!"

"Erakin has electricity in his store now — I hate it!" he continued.   30

Father Sisoi was aged, and round-shouldered, and gaunt. He

was always displeased with something or other, and his eyes, which protruded like those of a crab, always wore an angry expression.

"I don't like it at all," he repeated — "I hate it."

II

Next day, on Palm Sunday, his Reverence officiated at the cathedral in the city. Then he went to the diocesan bishop's, then to see a general's wife who was very ill, and at last he drove home. At two o'clock two beloved guests were having dinner with him, his aged mother, and his little niece Kitty, a child of eight. The spring sun was peeping cheerily in through the windows as they sat at their meal, and was shining merrily on the white tablecloth, and on Kitty's red hair. Through the double panes they heard the rooks cawing, and the magpies chattering in the garden.

"It is nine years since I saw you last," said the old mother, "and yet when I caught sight of you in the convent chapel yesterday I thought to myself: God bless me, he has not changed a bit! Only perhaps you are a little thinner than you were, and your beard has grown longer. Oh, holy Mother, Queen of Heaven! Everybody was crying yesterday. As soon as I saw you, I began to cry myself, I don't know why. His holy will be done!"

In spite of the tenderness with which she said this, it was 35 clear that she was not at her ease. It was as if she did not know whether to address the bishop by the familiar "thee" or the formal "you," and whether she ought to laugh or not. She seemed to feel herself more of a poor deacon's wife than a mother in his presence. Meanwhile Kitty was sitting with her eyes glued to the face of her uncle the bishop as if she were trying to make out what manner of man this was. Her hair had escaped from her comb and her bow of velvet ribbon, and was standing straight up around her head like a halo. Her eyes were foxy and bright. She had broken a glass before sitting down, and now, as she talked, her grandmother kept moving first a glass, and then a wine glass out of her reach. As the bishop sat listening to his mother, he remembered how, many, many years ago, she had sometimes taken him and his brothers and sisters to visit relatives whom they considered rich. She had been busy with her own children in those days, and now she was busy with her grandchildren, and had come to visit him with Kitty here.

"Your sister Varenka has four children" — she was telling

him — "Kitty is the oldest. God knows why, her father fell ill and died three days before Assumption. So my Varenka has been thrown out into the cold world."

"And how is my brother Nikanor?" the bishop asked.

"He is well, thank the Lord. He is pretty well, praise be to God. But his son Nikolasha wouldn't go into the church, and is at college instead learning to be a doctor. He thinks it is best, but who knows? However, God's will be done!"

"Nikolasha cuts up dead people!" said Kitty, spilling some water into her lap.

"Sit still child!" her grandmother said, quietly taking the 40 glass out of her hands.

"How long it is since we have seen one another!" exclaimed his Reverence, tenderly stroking his mother's shoulder and hand. "I missed you when I was abroad, I missed you dreadfully."

"Thank you very much!"

"I used to sit by my window in the evening listening to the band playing, and feeling lonely and forlorn. Sometimes I would suddenly grow so homesick that I used to think I would gladly give everything I had in the world for a glimpse of you and home."

His mother smiled and beamed, and then immediately drew a long face and said stiffly:

"Thank you very much!" 45

The Bishop's mood changed. He looked at his mother, and could not understand where she had acquired that deferential, humble expression of face and voice, and what the meaning of it might be. He hardly recognised her, and felt sorrowful and vexed. Besides, his head was still aching, and his legs were racked with pain. The fish he was eating tasted insipid and he was very thirsty.

After dinner two wealthy lady landowners visited him, and sat for an hour and a half with faces a mile long, never uttering a word. Then an archimandrite, a gloomy, taciturn man, came on business. Then the bells rang for vespers, the sun set behind the woods, and the day was done. As soon as he got back from church the bishop said his prayers, and went to bed, drawing the covers up closely about his ears. The moonlight troubled him, and soon the sound of voices came to his ears. Father Sisoi was talking politics with his mother in the next room.

"There is a war in Japan now," he was saying. "The Japanese belong to the same race as the Montenegrins. They fell under the Turkish yoke at the same time."

And then the bishop heard his mother's voice say:

"And so, you see, when we had said our prayers, and had our tea, we went to Father Yegor ——" 50

She kept saying over and over again that they "had tea," as if all she knew of life was tea-drinking.

The memory of his seminary and college life slowly and mistily took shape in the bishop's mind. He had been a teacher of Greek for three years, until he could no longer read without glasses, and then he had taken the vows, and had been made an inspector. When he was thirty-two he had been made the rector of a seminary, and then an archimandrite. At that time his life had been so easy and pleasant, and had seemed to stretch so far, far into the future that he could see absolutely no end to it. But his health had failed, and he had nearly lost his eyesight. His doctors had advised him to give up his work and go abroad.

"And what did you do next?" asked Father Sisoi in the adjoining room.

"And then we had tea," answered his mother.

"Why, Father, your beard is green!" exclaimed Kitty sud- 55 denly. And she burst out laughing.

The bishop remembered that the colour of Father Sisoi's beard really did verge on green, and he, too, laughed.

"My goodness! What a plague that child is!" cried Father Sisoi in a loud voice, for he was growing angry. "You're a spoiled baby you are! Sit still!"

The bishop recalled the new white church in which he had officiated when he was abroad, and the sound of a warm sea. Eight years had slipped by while he was there; then he had been recalled to Russia, and now he was already a bishop, and the past had faded away into mist as if it had been but a dream.

Father Sisoi came into his room with a candle in his hand.

"Well, well!" he exclaimed, surprised. "Asleep already, your 60 Reverence?"

"Why not?"

"It's early yet, only ten o'clock! I bought a candle this evening and wanted to rub you with tallow."

"I have a fever," the bishop said, sitting up. "I suppose something ought to be done. My head feels so queer."

Sisoi began to rub the bishop's chest and back with tallow.

"There — there —" he said. "Oh, Lord God Almighty! There! 65 I went to town to-day, and saw that — what do you call him? — that archpresbyter Sidonski. I had tea with him. I hate him! Oh, Lord God Almighty! There! I hate him!"

III

The diocesan bishop was very old and very fat, and had been ill in bed with gout for a month. So his Reverence Peter had been visiting him almost every day, and had received his suppliants for him. And now that he was ill he was appalled to think of the futilities and trifles they asked for and wept over. He felt annoyed at their ignorance and cowardice. The very number of all those useless trivialities oppressed him, and he felt as if he could understand the diocesan bishop who had written "Lessons in Free Will" when he was young, and now seemed so absorbed in details that the memory of everything else, even of God, had forsaken him. Peter must have grown out of touch with Russian life while he was abroad, for it was hard for him to grow used to it now. The people seemed rough, the women stupid and tiresome, the novices and their teachers uneducated and often disorderly. And then the documents that passed through his hands by the hundreds of thousands! The provosts gave all the priests in the diocese, young and old, and their wives and children marks for good behaviour, and he was obliged to talk about all this, and read about it, and write serious articles on it. His Reverence never had a moment which he could call his own; all day his nerves were on edge, and he only grew calm when he found himself in church.

He could not grow accustomed to the terror which he involuntarily inspired in every breast in spite of his quiet and modest ways. Every one in the district seemed to shrivel and quake and apologise as soon as he looked at them. Every one trembled in his presence; even the old archpresbyters fell down at his feet, and not long ago one suppliant, the old wife of a village priest, had been prevented by terror from uttering a word, and had gone away without asking for anything. And he, who had never been able to say a harsh word in his sermons, and who never blamed people because he pitied them so, would grow exasperated with these suppliants, and hurl their petitions to the ground. Not a soul had spoken sincerely and naturally to him since he had been here; even his old mother had changed, yes, she had changed very much! Why did she talk so freely to Sisoi when all the while she was so serious and ill at ease with him, her own son? It was not like her at all! The only person who behaved naturally in his presence, and who said whatever came into his head was old man Sisoi, who had lived with bishops all his life, and had outlasted eleven of them. And therefore his Reverence felt at ease with

Sisoi, even though he was, without doubt, a rough and quarrelsome person.

After morning prayers on Tuesday the bishop received his suppliants, and lost his temper with them. He felt ill, as usual, and longed to go to bed, but he had hardly entered his room before he was told that the young merchant Erakin, a benefactor of the monastery, had called on very important business. The bishop was obliged to receive him. Erakin stayed about an hour talking in a very loud voice, and it was hard to understand what he was trying to say.

After he had gone there came an abbess from a distant convent, and by the time she had gone the bells were tolling for vespers; it was time for the bishop to go to church.

The monks sang melodiously and rapturously that evening; a 70
young, black-bearded priest officiated. His Reverence listened as they sang of the Bridegroom and of the chamber swept and garnished, and felt neither repentance nor sorrow, but only a deep peace of mind. He sat by the altar where the shadows were deepest, and was swept in imagination back into the days of his childhood and youth, when he had first heard these words sung. The tears trickled down his cheeks, and he meditated on how he had attained everything in life that it was possible for a man in his position to attain; his faith was unsullied, and yet all was not clear to him; something was lacking, and he did not want to die. It still seemed to him that he was leaving unfound the most important thing of all. Something of which he had dimly dreamed in the past, hopes that had thrilled his heart as a child, a schoolboy, and a traveller in foreign lands, troubled him still.

"How beautifully they are singing to-day!" he thought. "Oh, how beautifully!"

IV

On Thursday he held a service in the cathedral. It was the festival of the Washing of Feet. When the service was over, and the people had gone to their several homes, the sun was shining brightly and cheerily, and the air was warm. The gutters were streaming with bubbling water, and the tender songs of larks came floating in from the fields beyond the city, bringing peace to his heart. The trees were already awake, and over them brooded the blue, unfathomable sky.

His Reverence went to bed as soon as he reached home, and told the lay brother to close his shutters. The room grew dark. Oh, how tired he was!

As on the day before, the sound of voices and the tinkling of glasses came to him from the next room. His mother was gaily recounting some tale to Father Sisoi, with many a quaint word and saying, and the old man was listening gloomily, and answering in a gruff voice:

"Well, I never! Did they, indeed? What do you think of that!" 75

And once more the bishop felt annoyed, and then hurt that the old lady should be so natural and simple with strangers, and so silent and awkward with her own son. It even seemed to him that she always tried to find some pretext for standing in his presence, as if she felt uneasy sitting down. And his father? If he had been alive, he would probably not have been able to utter a word when the bishop was there.

Something in the next room fell to the floor with a crash. Kitty had evidently broken a cup or a saucer, for Father Sisoi suddenly snorted, and cried angrily:

"What a terrible plague this child is! Merciful heavens! No one could keep her supplied with china!"

Then silence fell. When he opened his eyes again, the bishop saw Kitty standing by his bedside staring at him, her red hair standing up around her head like a halo, as usual.

"Is that you, Kitty?" he asked. "Who is that opening and 80 shutting doors down there?"

"I don't hear anything."

He stroked her head.

"So your cousin Nikolasha cuts up dead people, does he?" he asked, after a pause.

"Yes, he is learning to."

"Is he nice?" 85

"Yes, very, only he drinks a lot."

"What did your father die of?"

"Papa grew weaker and weaker, and thinner and thinner, and then came his sore throat. And I was ill, too, and so was my brother Fedia. We all had sore throats. Papa died, Uncle, but we got well."

Her chin quivered, her eyes filled with tears.

"Oh, your Reverence!" she cried in a shrill voice, beginning 90 to weep bitterly. "Dear Uncle, mother and all of us are so unhappy! Do give us a little money! Help us, Uncle darling!"

He also shed tears, and for a moment could not speak for

emotion. He stroked her hair, and touched her shoulder; and said:

"All right, all right, little child. Wait until Easter comes, then we will talk about it. I'll help you."

His mother came quietly and timidly into the room, and said a prayer before the icon. When she saw that he was awake, she asked:

"Would you like a little soup?"

"No thanks," he answered. "I'm not hungry."   95

"I don't believe you are well — I can see that you are not well. You really mustn't fall ill! You have to be on your feet all day long. My goodness, it makes one tired to see you! Never mind, Easter is no longer over the hills and far away. When Easter comes you will rest. God will give us time for a little talk then, but now I'm not going to worry you any more with my silly chatter. Come, Kitty, let his Lordship have another forty winks ——"

And the bishop remembered that, when he was a boy, she had used exactly the same half playful, half respectful tone to all high dignitaries of the church. Only by her strangely tender eyes, and by the anxious look which she gave him as she left the room could any one have guessed that she was his mother. He shut his eyes, and seemed to be asleep, but he heard the clock strike twice, and Father Sisoi coughing next door. His mother came in again, and looked shyly at him. Suddenly there came a bang, and a door slammed; a vehicle of some kind drove up to the front steps. The lay brother came into the bishop's room, and called:

"Your Reverence!"

"What is it?"

"Here is the coach! It is time to go to our Lord's Passion ——"   100

"What time is it?"

"Quarter to eight."

The bishop dressed, and drove to the cathedral. He had to stand motionless in the centre of the church while the twelve gospels were being read, and the first and longest and most beautiful of them all he read himself. A strong, valiant mood took hold of him. He knew this gospel, beginning "The Son of Man is risen to-day — ," by heart, and as he repeated it, he raised his eyes, and saw a sea of little lights about him. He heard the sputtering of candles, but the people had disappeared. He felt surrounded by those whom he had known in his youth; he felt that they would always be here until — God knew when!

His father had been a deacon, his grandfather had been a priest, and his great grandfather a deacon. He sprang from a race that had belonged to the church since Christianity first came to

Russia, and his love for the ritual of the church, the clergy, and the sound of church-bells was inborn in him, deeply, irradicably implanted in his heart. When he was in church, especially when he was taking part in the service himself, he felt active and valorous and happy. And so it was with him now. Only, after the eighth gospel had been read, he felt that his voice was becoming so feeble that even his cough was inaudible; his head was aching, and he began to fear that he might collapse. His legs were growing numb; in a little while he ceased to have any sensation in them at all, and could not imagine what he was standing on, and why he did not fall down.

It was quarter to twelve when the service ended. The bishop   105 went to bed as soon as he reached home, without even saying his prayers. As he pulled his blanket up over him, he suddenly wished that he were abroad; he passionately wished it. He would give his life, he thought, to cease from seeing these cheap, wooden walls and that low ceiling, to cease from smelling the stale scent of the monastery.

If there were only some one with whom he could talk, some one to whom he could unburden his heart!

He heard steps in the adjoining room, and tried to recall who it might be. At last the door opened, and Father Sisoi came in with a candle in one hand, and a teacup in the other.

"In bed already, your Reverence?" he asked. "I have come to rub your chest with vinegar and vodka. It is a fine thing, if rubbed in good and hard. Oh, Lord God Almighty! There — I have just come from our monastery. I hate it. I am going away from here to-morrow, my Lord. Oh, Lord, God Almighty — there —"

Sisoi never could stay long in one place, and he now felt as if he had been in this monastery for a year. It was hard to tell from what he said where his home was, whether there was any one or anything in the world that he loved, and whether he believed in God or not. He himself never could make out why he had become a monk, but then, he never gave it any thought, and the time when he had taken the vows had long since faded from his memory. He thought he must have been born a monk.

"Yes, I am going away to-morrow. Bother this place!"   110

"I want to have a talk with you — I never seem to have the time —" whispered the bishop, making a great effort to speak. "You see, I don't know any one — or anything — here — "

"Very well then, I shall stay until Sunday, but no longer! Bother this place!"

"What sort of a bishop am I?" his Reverence went on, in a

faint voice. "I ought to have been a village priest, or a deacon, or a plain monk. All this is choking me — it is choking me ——"

"What's that? Oh, Lord God Almighty! There — go to sleep now, your Reverence. What do you mean? What's all this you are saying? Good night!"

All night long the bishop lay awake, and in the morning he 115 grew very ill. The lay brother took fright and ran first to the archimandrite, and then for the monastery doctor who lived in the city. The doctor, a stout, elderly man, with a long, grey beard, looked intently at his Reverence, shook his head, knit his brows, and finally said:

"I'll tell you what, your Reverence; you have typhoid."

The bishop grew very thin and pale in the next hour, his eyes grew larger, his face became covered with wrinkles, and he looked quite small and old. He felt as if he were the thinnest, weakest, puniest man in the whole world, and as if everything that had occurred before this had been left far, far behind, and would never happen again.

"How glad I am of that!" he thought. "Oh, how glad!"

His aged mother came into the room. When she saw his wrinkled face and his great eyes, she was seized with fear, and, falling down on her knees by his bedside, she began kissing his face, his shoulders, and his hands. He seemed to her to be the thinnest, weakest, puniest man in the world, and she forgot that he was a bishop, and kissed him as if he had been a little child whom she dearly, dearly loved.

"Little Paul, my dearie!" she cried. "My little son, why do you 120 look like this? Little Paul, oh, answer me!"

Kitty, pale and severe, stood near them, and could not understand what was the matter with her uncle, and why Granny wore such a look of suffering on her face, and spoke such heartrending words. And he, he was speechless, and knew nothing of what was going on around him. He was dreaming that he was an ordinary man once more, striding swiftly and merrily through the open country, a staff in his hand, bathed in sunshine, with the wide sky above him, as free as a bird to go wherever his fancy led him.

"My little son! My little Paul! Answer me!" begged his mother.

"Don't bother his Lordship," said Sisoi. "Let him sleep. What's the matter?"

Three doctors came, consulted together, and drove away. The day seemed long, incredibly long, and then came the long, long night. Just before dawn on Saturday morning the lay brother went to the old mother who was lying on a sofa in the sitting-

room, and asked her to come into the bedroom; his Reverence
had gone to eternal peace.

Next day was Easter. There were forty-two churches in the 125
city, and two monasteries, and the deep, joyous notes of their
bells pealed out over the town from morning until night. The
birds were carolling, the bright sun was shining. The big market
place was full of noise; barrel organs were droning, concertinas
were squealing, and drunken voices were ringing through the air.
Trotting races were held in the main street that afternoon; in a
word, all was merry and gay, as had been the year before and as,
doubtless, it would be the year to come.

A month later a new bishop was appointed, and every one
forgot his Reverence Peter. Only the dead man's mother, who is
living now in a little country town with her son the deacon, when
she goes out at sunset to meet her cow, and joins the other
women on the way, tells them about her children and grandchildren, and her boy who became a bishop.

And when she mentions him she looks at them shyly, for she
is afraid they will not believe her.

And, as a matter of fact, not all of them do.

Questions

What we began by saying about Lord Vaux's poem could also
be said of Chekhov's story. Human creatures are mutable, subject
to the natural cycle of growth and decline, incapable whether
great or humble of overcoming the limits of mortality. Nothing in
"The Bishop" could be said to call into question these general
propositions. But — once again — these are general propositions, and "The Bishop" is particular throughout. The author
isn't discussing the idea of mortality; he's showing it forth as
emotional reality — showing us how mortality "happens," at the
level of personal awareness and perception, to one human creature, how inner change takes place, what feelings it inspires. Focus on one of the feelings here that strikes you as worth thinking about. Where in the story does the feeling run strong? Cite
specific passages and describe the feeling in writing as precisely
as you can. How does the creation of that feeling in the story
simultaneously confirm and deepen knowledge of the meanings
of human mortality? Compare your response to the one that
follows.

Response

EDITOR:

> "Oh, your Reverence!" she cried in a shrill voice, beginning to
> weep bitterly. "Dear Uncle, mother and all of us are so unhappy! Do
> give us a little money! Help us, Uncle darling!" (para. 90)

Tears are shed more than once in this story, but no moment is
more intense than this one as the bishop's niece Kitty pleads for
his help. For many years a man of power deferred to (albeit not at
his own insistence) by nearly everyone, the bishop is now ill and
"tired," in need of a comforting voice — someone who sees him
as an ordinary person rather than as a prestigious churchman
and who cares about him as a human being. The Palm Sunday
worshipers who "surge forward" toward him for palm leaves (1),
the "old archpresbyters who [fall] down at his feet" (67), the
people of the district — none of them see him that way. The
prominent who visit him or exact his attendance upon them —
"two wealthy lady landowners" who sit "never uttering a word"
(47), the merchant Erakin, the general's wife — hardly qualify as
comforters. And although the bishop feels at ease with "Father"
Sisoi, the steward, because he at least behaves naturally, Sisoi has
several defects as a companion. Even as he gives the bishop a
rubdown, he seems only marginally aware of him, preoccupied
with his own bitterness and hate. Nowhere are his addresses to
the bishop marked by affection or understanding.

And, worse by far, the bishop's own mother disappoints him.
"Why did she talk so freely to Sisoi when all the while she was so
serious and ill at ease with him, her own son?" (67). He tries to
show his need, tries to make her see him as he is — as he was
when separated at a young age from home and family — and for
an instant she seems almost to hear him, but quickly stiffness and
deference take over:

> "How long it is since we have seen one another!" exclaimed his
> Reverence, tenderly stroking his mother's shoulder and hand. "I
> missed you when I was abroad, I missed you dreadfully."
> "Thank you very much!"
> "I used to sit by my window in the evening listening to the
> band playing, and feeling lonely and forlorn. Sometimes I would
> suddenly grow so homesick that I used to think I would gladly give
> everything I had in the world for a glimpse of you and home."

His mother smiled and beamed, and then immediately drew a long face and said stiffly:

"Thank you very much!" (41–45)

His frustration, resentment, and exasperation mount to a point at which he actually starts hurling the petitions of supplicants to the ground. "Not a soul had spoken sincerely and naturally to him since he had been here" (67).

The moment of extreme poignance, though, occurs in the exchanges with Kitty — because as we listen we summon the full truth of mortality that will be experienced by this particular man. The core of that truth — namely that each human being faces the end alone — is familiar, but the circumstances under which it's shown forth to the bishop lend it extraordinary force. The bishop has been silently begging the world to see him as he is and to speak to him from the heart. I am what I always was — "Little Paul" (18), vulnerable and lonely. I am a creature in need of plain, straightforward human contact. This is exactly what Kitty gives him, at one level, through her sudden outburst and tears. She calls him "your Reverence," true, but she opens her heart to him; she isn't hiding like the rest of them; her unhappiness and her conviction that "your Reverence" can make everything right in an instant cause her to speak with childish candor.

The bishop hears the direct, unguarded feeling in her voice, and we have to imagine it as a welcome sound. Kitty is saying precisely what she means. But what is most moving — and most frustrating — is that those true words announce to the bishop, with appalling clarity, that his longing to be seen as he is is hopeless. Kitty can't see him any better than anyone else can; like the rest of them, she is locked into her own perception. When she speaks to him with absolute sincerity, she speaks to the figure of power. Kitty is incapable of taking in the defenselessness, the felt forlornness of Little Paul; she cannot know the person he is to and for himself, the person he desperately wants others to recognize. His inner truth is as invisible to her as it is to everyone else.

Mortality is emerging here as an invisibility of heart, a fateful aloneness. The bishop is a large-souled man, and the pity inside him isn't merely pity for himself. He understands that his aloneness is matched by the child's; in time she too will face the hard knowledge that her sudden candor has made him face. "He also

shed tears, and could not speak for emotion" (91); the feeling we
must summon in this passage is compassion for the inevitable
moment when what we want most to tell is untellable.

    In Lord Vaux's poem mortality is felt as a too-sudden
change — an onset of powerlessness that fills a human creature
with resentment at the erratic treachery of the world. In Chekhov's story mortality is felt as the impossibility of making one's
powerlessness known — confessing it to others, pressing others
to shed their view of you as omnipotent and accept the truth of
your helplessness. The bishop weeps because he grasps that his
self-enclosure is finally much like Kitty's; life won't let him out,
won't allow him to be known for what he feels himself to be—
until his time is gone.

    And that is how it happens in the sequel. The moment comes
when the puniness he feels in himself is felt at last by his mother,
"and she forgot that he was a bishop, and kissed him as if he had
been a little child whom she dearly, dearly loved," crying, "Little
Paul, my dearie! . . . My little son" (119–120). But that moment of
self-forgetfulness comes too late. Here again we can step back
from the experience of the story to an abstract summary of its
conclusion, telling ourselves that there's nothing novel or astonishing in the word that people on their deathbed feel weak.
That word only corroborates what we already know. But with
corroboration comes something else; we not only see and feel
with someone who is debilitated, we experience the utter incom-
municability of debilitation. At the crisis of this story mortality,
that most familiar of concepts, becomes inexpressible; with that
transformation the concept is made new.

SOPHOCLES   (496?–406 B.C.)
Antigone

TRANSLATED BY ROBERT FAGLES

CHARACTERS
Antigone, *daughter of Oedipus and
    Jocasta*
Ismene, *sister of Antigone*
A Chorus *of old Theban citizens and
    their* Leader
Creon, *king of Thebes, uncle of
    Antigone and Ismene*

A Sentry
Haemon, *son of Creon and Eurydice*
Tiresias, *a blind prophet*
A Messenger
Eurydice, *wife of Creon*
Guards, attendants, and a boy

TIME AND SCENE. *The royal house of Thebes. It is still night, and the invading armies of Argos have just been driven from the city. Fighting on opposite sides, the sons of Oedipus, Eteocles and Polynices, have killed each other in combat. Their uncle, Creon, is now king of Thebes.*

Enter Antigone, slipping through the central doors of the palace. She motions to her sister, Ismene, who follows her cautiously toward an altar at the center of the stage.

Antigone: My own flesh and blood — dear sister, dear Ismene,
how many griefs our father Oedipus handed down!
Do you know one, I ask you, one grief
that Zeus will not perfect for the two of us
while we still live and breathe? There's nothing,   5
no pain — our lives are pain — no private shame,
no public disgrace, nothing I haven't seen
in your griefs and mine. And now this:
an emergency decree, they say, the Commander
has just declared for all of Thebes.   10
What, haven't you heard? Don't you see?
The doom reserved for enemies
marches on the ones we love the most.
Ismene: Not I, I haven't heard a word, Antigone.
Nothing of loved ones,   15
no joy or pain has come my way, not since
the two of us were robbed of our two brothers,
both gone in a day, a double blow —
not since the armies of Argos vanished,
just this very night. I know nothing more,   20
whether our luck's improved or ruin's still to come.
Antigone: I thought so. That's why I brought you out here,
past the gates, so you could hear in private.
Ismene: What's the matter? Trouble, clearly . . .   .
you sound so dark, so grim.   25
Antigone: Why not? Our own brothers' burial!
Hasn't Creon graced one with all the rites,
disgraced the other? Eteocles, they say,
has been given full military honors,
rightly so — Creon's laid him in the earth.   30
and he goes with glory down among the dead.
But the body of Polynices, who died miserably —
why, a city-wide proclamation, rumor has it,
forbids anyone to bury him, even mourn him.
He's to be left unwept, unburied, a lovely treasure   35
for birds that scan the field and feast to their heart's content.

Such, I hear, is the martial law our good Creon
lays down for you and me — yes, me, I tell you —
and he's coming here to alert the uninformed
in no uncertain terms,   40
and he won't treat the matter lightly. Whoever
disobeys in the least will die, his doom is sealed:
stoning to death inside the city walls!

There you have it. You'll soon show what you are,
worth your breeding, Ismene, or a coward —   45
for all your royal blood.
Ismene: My poor sister, if things have come to this,
who am I to make or mend them, tell me,
what good am I to you?
Antigone: Decide.
Will you share the labor, share the work?   50
Ismene: What work, what's the risk? What do you mean?
Antigone (raising her hands): Will you lift up his body with these
    bare hands and lower it with me?
Ismene: What? You'd bury him —
when a law forbids the city?
Antigone: Yes!
He is my brother and — deny it as you will —   55
your brother too.
No one will ever convict me for a traitor.
Ismene: So desperate, and Creon has expressly —
Antogone: No,
he has no right to keep me from my own.
Ismene: Oh my sister, think —   60
think how our own father died, hated,
his reputation in ruins, driven on
by the crimes he brought to light himself
to gouge out his eyes with his own hands —
then mother . . . his mother and wife, both in one,   65
mutilating her life in the twisted noose —°
and last, our two brothers dead in a single day,
both shedding their own blood, poor suffering boys,
battling out their common destiny hand-to-hand.

60–66 *think . . . noose*: Although he tried to avoid his fate, Oedipus unknowingly killed his father and married his mother, Jocasta. When they learned of his crime, Oedipus blinded himself and Jocasta committed suicide. (This story is told in Sophocles' *Oedipus Rex*.)

Now look at the two of us, left so alone . . .   70
think what a death we'll die, the worst of all
if we violate the laws and override
the fixed decree of the throne, its power —
we must be sensible. Remember we are women,
we're not born to contend with men. Then too,   75
we're underlings, ruled by much stronger hands,
so we must submit in this, and things still worse.

I, for one, I'll beg the dead to forgive me —
I'm forced, I have no choice — I must obey
the ones who stand in power. Why rush to extremes?   80
It's madness, madness.
Antigone: I won't insist,
no, even if you should have a change of heart,
I'd never welcome you in the labor, not with me.
So, do as you like, whatever suits you best —
I'll bury him myself.   85
And even if I die in the act, that death will be a glory.
I'll lie with the one I love and loved by him —
an outrage sacred to the gods! I have longer
to please the dead than please the living here:
in the kingdom down below I'll lie forever.   90
Do as you like, dishonor the laws
the gods hold in honor.
Ismene: I'd do them no dishonor . . .
but defy the city? I have no strength for that.
Antigone: You have your excuses. I am on my way,
I'll raise a mound for him, for my dear brother.   95
Ismene: Oh Antigone, you're so rash   I'm so afraid for you!
Antigone: Don't fear for me. Set your own life in order.
Ismene: Then don't, at least, blurt this out to anyone.
Keep it a secret. I'll join you in that, I promise.
Antigone: Dear god, shout it from the rooftops. I'll hate you   100
all the more for silence — tell the world!
Ismene: So fiery — and it ought to chill your heart.
Antigone: I know I please where I must please the most.
Ismene: Yes, if you can, but you're in love with impossibility.
Antigone: Very well then, once my strength gives out   105
I will be done at last.
Ismene: You're wrong from the start,
you're off on a hopeless quest.
Antigone: If you say so, you will make me hate you,
and the hatred of the dead, by all rights,

will haunt you night and day.   110
But leave me to my own absurdity, leave me
to suffer this — dreadful thing. I'll suffer
nothing as great as death without glory.

Exit to the side.

Ismene: Then go if you must, but rest assured,
wild, irrational as you are, my sister,   115
you are truly dear to the ones who love you.

*Withdrawing to the palace. Enter a Chorus, the old citizens of Thebes, chanting as
the sun begins to rise.*

Chorus: Glory! — great beam of sun, brightest of all
that ever rose on the seven gates of Thebes,
you burn through night at last!
                    Great eye of the golden day,   120
mounting the Dirce's banks you throw him back —
the enemy out of Argos, the white shield, the man of bronze —
he's flying headlong now
            the bridle of fate stampeding him with pain!

And he had driven against our borders,   125
launched by the warring claims of Polynices —
like an eagle screaming, winging havoc
over the land, wings of armor
shielded white as snow,
a huge army massing,   130
crested helmets bristling for assault.

He hovered above our roofs, his vast maw gaping
closing down around our seven gates,
his spears thirsting for the kill
                    but now he's gone, look,   135
before he could glut his jaws with Theban blood
or the god of fire put our crown of towers to the torch.
He grappled the Dragon none can master — Thebes —
            the clang of our arms like thunder at his back!

Zeus hates with a vengeance all bravado,   140
the mighty boasts of men. He watched them
coming on in a rising flood, the pride
of their golden armor ringing shrill —
and brandishing his lightning
blasted the fighter just at the goal,   145
rushing to shout his triumph from our walls.

Down from the heights he crashed, pounding down on the
    earth!
And a moment ago, blazing torch in hand —
        mad for attack, ecstatic
he breathed his rage, the storm   150
    of his fury hurling at our heads!
But now his high hopes have laid him low
and down the enemy ranks the iron god of war
        deals his rewards, his stunning blows — Ares
        rapture of battle, our right arm in the crisis.   155
        Seven captains marshaled at seven gates
        seven against their equals, gave
        their brazen trophies up to Zeus,
        god of the breaking rout of battle,
        all but two: those blood brothers,   160
        one father, one mother — matched in rage,
        spears matched for the twin conquest —
        clashed and won the common prize of death.

But now for Victory! Glorious in the morning,
joy in her eyes to meet our joy   165
        she is winging down to Thebes,
our fleets of chariots wheeling in her wake —
        Now let us win oblivion from the wars,
thronging the temples of the gods
in singing, dancing choirs through the night!   170
        Lord Dionysus, god of the dance
        that shakes the land of Thebes, now lead the way!

Enter Creon from the palace, attended by his guard.

        But look, the king of the realm is coming,
        Creon, the new man for the new day,
        whatever the gods are sending now . . .   175
        what new plan will he launch?
        Why this, this special session?
        Why this sudden call to the old men
        summoned at one command?
Creon: My countrymen,
the ship of state is safe. The gods who rocked her,   180
after a long, merciless pounding in the storm,
have righted her once more.
                      Out of the whole city
I have called you here alone. Well I know,
first, your undeviating respect

for the throne and royal power of King Laius.° 185
Next, while Oedipus steered the land of Thebes,
and even after he died, your loyalty was unshakable,
you still stood by their children. Now then,
since the two sons are dead — two blows of fate
in the same day, cut down by each other's hands, 190
both killers, both brothers stained with blood —
as I am next in kin to the dead,
I now possess the throne and all its powers.

Of course you cannot know a man completely,
his character, his principles, sense of judgment, 195
not till he's shown his colors, ruling the people,
making laws. Experience, there's the test.
As I see it, whoever assumes the task,
the awesome task of setting the city's course,
and refuses to adopt the soundest policies 200
but fearing someone, keeps his lips locked tight,
he's utterly worthless. So I rate him now,
I always have. And whoever places a friend
above the good of his own country, he is nothing:
I have no use for him. Zeus my witness, 205
Zeus who sees all things, always —
I could never stand by silent, watching destruction
march against our city, putting safety to rout,
nor could I ever make that man a friend of mine
who menaces our country. Remember this: 210
our country *is* our safety.
Only while she voyages true on course
can we establish friendships, truer than blood itself.
Such are my standards. They make our city great.

Closely akin to them I have proclaimed, 215
just now, the following decree to our people
concerning the two sons of Oedipus.
Eteocles, who died fighting for Thebes,
excelling all in arms: he shall be buried,
crowned with a hero's honors, the cups we pour 220
to soak the earth and reach the famous dead.

But as for his blood brother, Polynices,
who returned from exile, home to his father-city
and the gods of his race, consumed with one desire —

185 *Laius:* The father of Oedipus.

to burn them roof to roots — who thirsted to drink   225
his kinsmen's blood and sell the rest to slavery:
that man — a proclamation has forbidden the city
to dignify him with burial, mourn him at all.
No, he must be left unburied, his corpse
carrion for the birds and dogs to tear,   230
an obscenity for the citizens to behold!

These are my principles. Never at my hands
will the traitor be honored above the patriot.
But whoever proves his loyalty to the state:
I'll prize that man in death as well as life.   235
Leader: If this is your pleasure, Creon, treating
our city's enemy and our friend this way . . .
The power is yours, I suppose, to enforce it
with the laws, both for the dead and all of us,
the living.
Creon: Follow my orders closely then,   240
be on your guard.
Leader: We're too old.
Lay that burden on younger shoulders.
Creon: No, no,
I don't mean the body — I've posted guards already.
Leader: What commands for us then? What other service?
Creon: See that you never side with those who break my orders. 245
Leader: Never. Only a fool could be in love with death.
Creon: Death is the price — you're right. But all too often
the mere hope of money has ruined many men.

A Sentry enters from the side.

Sentry: My lord,
I can't say I'm winded from running, or set out
with any spring in my legs either — no sir,   250
I was lost in thought, and it made me stop, often,
dead in my tracks, wheeling, turning back,
and all the time a voice inside me muttering,
"Idiot, why? You're going straight to your death."
Then muttering, "Stopped again, poor fool?   255
If somebody gets the news to Creon first,
what's to save your neck?"
                          And so,
mulling it over, on I trudged, dragging my feet,
you can make a short road take forever . . .
but at last, look, common sense won out,   260

I'm here, and I'm all yours,
and even though I come empty-handed
I'll tell my story just the same, because
I've come with a good grip on one hope,
what will come will come, whatever fate —   265

Creon: Come to the point!
What's wrong — why so afraid?

Sentry: First, myself, I've got to tell you,
I didn't do it, didn't see who did —
Be fair, don't take it out on me.   270

Creon: You're playing it safe, soldier,
barricading yourself from any trouble.
It's obvious, you've something strange to tell.

Sentry: Dangerous too, and danger makes you delay
for all you're worth   275

Creon: Out with it — then dismiss!

Sentry: All right, here it comes. The body —
someone's just buried it, then run off . . .
sprinkled some dry dust on the flesh,
given it proper rites.

Creon: What?   280
What man alive would dare —

Sentry: I've no idea, I swear it.
There was no mark of a spade, no pickaxe there,
no earth turned up, the ground packed hard and dry,
unbroken, no tracks, no wheelruts, nothing,
the workman left no trace. Just at sunup   285
the first watch of the day points it out —
it was a wonder! We were stunned . . .
a terrific burden too, for all of us, listen:
you can't see the corpse, not that it's buried,
really, just a light cover of road-dust on it,   290
as if someone meant to lay the dead to rest
and keep from getting cursed.
Not a sign in sight that dogs or wild beasts
had worried the body, even torn the skin.

But what came next! Rough talk flew thick and fast,   295
guard grilling guard — we'd have come to blows
at last, nothing to stop it; each man for himself
and each the culprit, no one caught red-handed,
all of us pleading ignorance, dodging the charges,
ready to take up red-hot iron in our fists,   300
go through fire, swear oaths to the gods —

"I didn't do it, I had no hand in it either,
not in the plotting, not in the work itself!"

Finally, after all this wrangling came to nothing,
one man spoke out and made us stare at the ground,   305
hanging our heads in fear. No way to counter him,
no way to take his advice and come through
safe and sound. Here's what he said:
"Look, we've got to report the facts to Creon,
we can't keep this hidden." Well, that won out,   310
and the lot fell on me, condemned me,
unlucky as ever, I got the prize. So here I am,
against my will and yours too, well I know —
no one wants the man who brings bad news.

Leader: My king,
ever since he began I've been debating in my mind,   315
could this possibly be the work of the gods?

Creon: Stop —
before you make me choke with anger — the gods!
You, you're senile, must you be insane?
You say — why it's intolerable — say the gods
could have the slightest concern for that corpse?   320
Tell me, was it for meritorious service
they proceeded to bury him, prized him so? The hero
who came to burn their temples ringed with pillars,
their golden treasures — scorch their hallowed earth
and fling their laws to the winds.   325
Exactly when did you last see the gods
celebrating traitors? Inconceivable!

No, from the first there were certain citizens
who could hardly stand the spirit of my regime,
grumbling against me in the dark, heads together,   330
tossing wildly, never keeping their necks beneath
the yoke, loyally submitting to their king.
These are the instigators, I'm convinced —
they've perverted my own guard, bribed them
to do their work.

                       Money! Nothing worse   335
in our lives, so current, rampant, so corrupting.
Money — you demolish cities, root men from their homes,
you train and twist good minds and set them on
to the most atrocious schemes. No limit,
you make them adept at every kind of outrage,   340
every godless crime — money!

Everyone —
the whole crew bribed to commit this crime,
they've made one thing sure at least:
sooner or later they will pay the price.

Wheeling on the Sentry.

You —
I swear to Zeus as I still believe in Zeus,   345
if you don't find the man who buried that corpse,
the very man, and produce him before my eyes,
simple death won't be enough for you,
not till we string you up alive
and wring the immorality out of you.   350
Then you can steal the rest of your days,
better informed about where to make a killing.
You'll have learned, at last, it doesn't pay
to itch for rewards from every hand that beckons.
Filthy profits wreck most men, you'll see —   355
they'll never save your life.
Sentry: Please,
may I say a word or two, or just turn and go?
Creon: Can't you tell? Everything you say offends me.
Sentry: Where does it hurt you, in the ears or in the heart?
Creon: And who are you to pinpoint my displeasure?   360
Sentry: The culprit grates on your feelings,
I just annoy your ears.
Creon: Still talking?
You talk too much! A born nuisance —
Sentry: Maybe so,
but I never did this thing, so help me!
Creon: Yes you did —
what's more, you squandered your life for silver!   365
Sentry: Oh it's terrible when the one who does the judging
judges things all wrong.
Creon: Well now,
you just be clever about your judgments —
if you fail to produce the criminals for me,
you'll swear your dirty money brought you pain.   370

Turning sharply, reentering the palace.

Sentry: I hope he's found. Best thing by far.
But caught or not, that's in the lap of fortune;
I'll never come back, you've seen the last of me.

I'm saved, even now, and I never thought,
I never hopcd — 375
dear gods, I owe you all my thanks!

Rushing out.

Chorus: Numberless wonders
terrible wonders walk the world but none the match for man —
that great wonder crossing the heaving gray sea,
                    driven on by the blasts of winter
on through breakers crashing left and right, 380
          holds his steady course
and the oldest of the gods he wears away —
the Earth, the immortal, the inexhaustible —
as his plows go back and forth, year in, year out
          with the breed of stallions turning up the furrows. 385

And the blithe, lightheaded race of birds he snares,
the tribes of savage beasts, the life that swarms the depths —
                    with one fling of his nets
woven and coiled tight, he takes them all,
          man the skilled, the brilliant! 390
He conquers all, taming with his techniques
the prey that roams the cliffs and wild lairs,
training the stallion, clamping the yoke across
          his shaggy neck, and the tireless mountain bull.

And speech and thought, quick as the wind 395
and the mood and mind for law that rules the city —
          all these he has taught himself
and shelter from the arrows of the frost
when there's rough lodging under the cold clear sky
and the shafts of lashing rain — 400
          ready, resourceful man!
                    Never without resources
never an impasse as he marches on the future —
only Death, from Death alone he will find no rescue
but from desperate plagues he has plotted his escapes. 405

Man the master, ingenious past all measure
past all dreams, the skills within his grasp —
          he forges on, now to destruction
now again to greatness. When he weaves in
the laws of the land, and the justice of the gods 410
that binds his oaths together
          he and his city rise high —

> but the city casts out
that man who weds himself to inhumanity
thanks to reckless daring. Never share my hearth   415
never think my thoughts, whoever does such things.

Enter Antigone from the side, accompanied by the Sentry.

> Here is a dark sign from the gods —
what to make of this? I know her,
how can I deny it? That young girl's Antigone!
Wretched, child of a wretched father,   420
Oedipus. Look, is it possible?
They bring you in like a prisoner —
why? did you break the king's laws?
Did they take you in some act of mad defiance?

Sentry: She's the one, she did it single-handed —   425
we caught her burying the body. Where's Creon?

Enter Creon from the palace.

Leader: Back again, just in time when you need him.
Creon: In time for what? What is it?
Sentry: My king,
there's nothing you can swear you'll never do —
second thoughts make liars of us all.   430
I could have sworn I wouldn't hurry back
(what with your threats, the buffeting I just took),
but a stroke of luck beyond our wildest hopes,
what a joy, there's nothing like it. So,
back I've come, breaking my oath, who cares?   435
I'm bringing in our prisoner — this young girl —
we took her giving the dead the last rites.
But no casting lots this time; this is *my* luck,
my prize, no one else's.
                              Now, my lord,
here she is. Take her, question her,   440
cross-examine her to your heart's content.
But set me free, it's only right —
I'm rid of this dreadful business once for all.
Creon: Prisoner! Her? You took her — where, doing what?
Sentry: Burying the man. That's the whole story.
Creon: What?   445
You mean what you say, you're telling me the truth?
Sentry: She's the one. With my own eyes I saw her
bury the body, just what you've forbidden.

There. Is that plain and clear?
Creon: What did you see? Did you catch her in the act?   450
Sentry: Here's what happened. We went back to our post,
    those threats of yours breathing down our necks —
    we brushed the corpse clean of the dust that covered it,
    stripped it bare . . . it was slimy, going soft,
    and we took to high ground, backs to the wind   455
    so the stink of him couldn't hit us;
    jostling, baiting each other to keep awake,
    shouting back and forth — no napping on the job,
    not this time. And so the hours dragged by
    until the sun stood dead above our heads,   460
    a huge white ball in the noon sky, beating,
    blazing down, and then it happened —
    suddenly, a whirlwind!
    Twisting a great dust-storm up from the earth,
    a black plague of the heavens, filling the plain,   465
    ripping the leaves off every tree in sight,
    choking the air and sky. We squinted hard
    and took our whipping from the gods.

    And after the storm passed — it seemed endless —
    there, we saw the girl!   470
    And she cried out a sharp, piercing cry,
    like a bird come back to an empty nest,
    peering into its bed, and all the babies gone . . .
    Just so, when she sees the corpse bare
    she bursts into a long, shattering wail   475
    and calls down withering curses on the heads
    of all who did the work. And she scoops up dry dust,
    handfuls, quickly, and lifting a fine bronze urn,
    lifting it high and pouring, she crowns the dead
    with three full libations.

                Soon as we saw   480
    we rushed her, closed on the kill like hunters,
    and she, she didn't flinch. We interrogated her,
    charging her with offenses past and present —
    she stood up to it all, denied nothing. I tell you,
    it made me ache and laugh in the same breath.   485
    It's pure joy to escape the worst yourself,
    it hurts a man to bring down his friends.
    But all that, I'm afraid, means less to me
    than my own skin. That's the way I'm made.

Creon (wheeling on Antigone):   You,
    with your eyes fixed on the ground — speak up.   490
    Do you deny you did this, yes or no?
Antigone: I did it. I don't deny a thing.
Creon (to the sentry): You, get out, wherever you please —
    you're clear of a very heavy charge.

He leaves; Creon turns back to Antigone.

    You, tell me briefly, no long speeches —   495
    were you aware a decree had forbidden this?
Antigone: Well aware. How could I avoid it? It was public.
Creon: And still you had the gall to break this law?
Antigone: Of course I did. It wasn't Zeus, not in the least,
    who made this proclamation — not to me.   500
    Nor did that Justice, dwelling with the gods
    beneath the earth, ordain such laws for men.
    Nor did I think your edict had such force
    that you, a mere mortal, could override the gods,
    the great unwritten, unshakable traditions.   505
    They are alive, not just today or yesterday:
    they live forever, from the first of time,
    and no one knows when they first saw the light.

    These laws — I was not about to break them,
    not out of fear of some man's wounded pride,   510
    and face the retribution of the gods.
    Die I must, I've known it all my life —
    how could I keep from knowing? — even without
    your death-sentence ringing in my ears.
    And if I am to die before my time   515
    I consider that a gain. Who on earth,
    alive in the midst of so much grief as I,
    could fail to find his death a rich reward?
    So for me, at least, to meet this doom of yours
    is precious little pain. But if I had allowed   520
    my own mother's son to rot, an unburied corpse —
    that would have been an agony! This is nothing.
    And if my present actions strike you as foolish,
    let's just say I've been accused of folly
    by a fool.
Leader: Like father like daughter,   525
    passionate, wild . . .
    she hasn't learned to bend before adversity.
Creon: No? Believe me, the stiffest stubborn wills

fall the hardest; the toughest iron,
tempered strong in the white-hot fire,   530
you'll see it crack and shatter first of all.
And I've known spirited horses you can break
with a light bit — proud, rebellious horses.
There's no room for pride, not in a slave,
not with the lord and master standing by.   535

This girl was an old hand at insolence
when she overrode the edicts we made public.
But once she'd done it — the insolence,
twice over — to glory in it, laughing,
mocking us to our face with what she'd done.   540
I'm not the man, not now: she is the man
if this victory goes to her and she goes free.

Never! Sister's child or closer in blood
than all my family clustered at my altar
worshiping Guardian Zeus — she'll never escape,   545
she and her blood sister, the most barbaric death.
Yes, I accuse her sister of an equal part
in scheming this, this burial.

To his attendants.

                              Bring her here!
I just saw her inside, hysterical, gone to pieces.
It never fails: the mind convicts itself   550
in advance, when scoundrels are up to no good,
plotting in the dark. Oh but I hate it more
when a traitor, caught red-handed,
tries to glorify his crimes.
Antigone: Creon, what more do you want   555
        than my arrest and execution?
Creon: Nothing. Then I have it all.
Antigone: Then why delay? Your moralizing repels me,
        every word you say — pray god it always will.
        So naturally all I say repels you too.
                              Enough.   560
Give me glory! What greater glory could I win
than to give my own brother decent burial?
These citizens here would all agree,

To the Chorus.

        they'd praise me too
        if their lips weren't locked in fear.   565

Pointing to Creon.

      Lucky tyrants — the perquisites of power!
      Ruthless power to do and say whatever pleases *them*.
Creon: You alone, of all the people in Thebes,
      see things that way.
Antigone: They see it just that way
      but defer to you and keep their tongues in leash.   570
Creon: And you, aren't you ashamed to differ so from them?
      So disloyal!
Antigone: Not ashamed for a moment,
      not to honor my brother, my own flesh and blood.
Creon: Wasn't Eteocles a brother too — cut down, facing him?
Antigone: Brother, yes, by the same mother, the same father.   575
Creon: Then how can you render his enemy such honors,
      such impieties in his eyes?
Antigone: He'll never testify to that,
      Eteocles dead and buried.
Creon: He will —
      if you honor the traitor just as much as him.   580
Antigone: But it was his brother, not some slave that died —
Creon: Ravaging our country! —
      but Eteocles died fighting in our behalf.
Antigone: No matter — Death longs for the same rites for all.
Creon: Never the same for the patriot and the traitor.   585
Antigone: Who, Creon, who on earth can say the ones below
      don't find this pure and uncorrupt?
Creon: Never. Once an enemy, never a friend,
      not even after death.
Antigone: I was born to join in love, not hate —   590
      that is my nature.
Creon: Go down below and love,
      if love you must — love the dead! While I'm alive,
      no woman is going to lord it over me.

Enter Ismene from the palace, under guard.

Chorus: Look,
      Ismene's coming, weeping a sister's tears,
      loving sister, under a cloud . . .   595
      her face is flushed, her cheeks streaming.
      Sorrow puts her lovely radiance in the dark.
Creon: You —
      in my house, you viper, slinking undetected,
      sucking my life-blood! I never knew

I was breeding twin disasters, the two of you   600
rising up against my throne. Come, tell me,
will you confess your part in the crime or not?
Answer me. Swear to me.
Ismene: I did it, yes —
if only she consents — I share the guilt,
the consequences too.
Antigone: No,   605
Justice will never suffer that — not you,
you were unwilling. I never brought you in.
Ismene: But now you face such dangers . . . I'm not ashamed
to sail through trouble with you,
make your troubles mine.
Antigone: Who did the work?   610
Let the dead and the god of death bear witness!
I've no love for a friend who loves in words alone.
Ismene: Oh no, my sister, don't reject me, please,
let me die beside you, consecrating
the dead together.
Antigone: Never share my dying,   615
don't lay claim to what you never touched.
My death will be enough.
Ismene: What do I care for life, cut off from you?
Antigone: Ask Creon. Your concern is all for him.
Ismene: Why abuse me so? It doesn't help you now.
Antigone: You're right —   620
if I mock you, I get no pleasure from it,
only pain.
Ismene: Tell me, dear one,
what can I do to help you, even now?
Antigone: Save yourself. I don't grudge you your survival.
Ismene: Oh no, no, denied my portion in your death?   625
Antigone: You chose to live, I chose to die.
Ismene: Not, at least,
without every kind of caution I could voice.
Antigone: Your wisdom appealed to one world — mine, another.
Ismene: But look, we're both guilty, both condemned to death.
Antigone: Courage! Live your life. I gave myself to death,   630
long ago, so I might serve the dead.
Creon: They're both mad, I tell you, the two of them.
One's just shown it, the other's been that way
since she was born.
Ismene: True, my king,
the sense we were born with cannot last forever . . .   635

      commit cruelty on a person long enough
      and the mind begins to go.
Creon: Yours did,
      when you chose to commit your crimes with her.
Ismene: How can I live alone, without her?
Creon: Her?
      Don't even mention her — she no longer exists.   640
Ismene: What? You'd kill your own son's bride?
Creon: Absolutely:
      there are other fields for him to plow.
Ismene: Perhaps,
      but never as true, as close a bond as theirs.
Creon: A worthless woman for my son? It repels me.
Ismene: Dearest Haemon, your father wrongs you so!   645
Creon: Enough, enough — you and your talk of marriage!
Ismene: Creon — you're really going to rob your son of Antigone?
Creon: Death will do it for me — break their marriage off.
Leader: So, it's settled then? Antigone must die?
Creon: Settled, yes — we both know that.   650

To the guards.

      Stop wasting time. Take them in.
      From now on they'll act like women.
      Tie them up, no more running loose;
      even the bravest will cut and run,
      once they see Death coming for their lives.   655

The guards escort Antigone and Ismene into the palace. Creon remains while the old citizens form their chorus.

Chorus: Blest, they are the truly blest who all their lives
      have never tasted devastation. For others, once
      the gods have rocked a house to its foundations
          the ruin will never cease, cresting on and on
      from one generation on throughout the race —   660
      like a great mounting tide
      driven on by savage northern gales,
          surging over the dead black depths
      roiling up from the bottom dark heaves of sand
      and the headlands, taking the storm's onslaught full-force,   665
      roar, and the low moaning
                    echoes on and on
                       and now
      as in ancient times I see the sorrows of the house,

the living heirs of the old ancestral kings,
piling on the sorrows of the dead
      and one generation cannot free the next —   670
some god will bring them crashing down,
the race finds no release.
And now the light, the hope
      springing up from the late last root
in the house of Oedipus, that hope's cut down in turn   675
by the long, bloody knife swung by the gods of death
by a senseless word
                  by fury at the heart.

                            Zeus,
yours is the power, Zeus, what man on earth
can override it, who can hold it back?
Power that neither Sleep, the all-ensnaring   680
      no, nor the tireless months of heaven
can ever overmaster — young through all time,
mighty lord of power, you hold fast
      the dazzling crystal mansions of Olympus.
And throughout the future, late and soon   685
as through the past, your law prevails:
no towering form of greatness
      enters into the lives of mortals
                  free and clear of ruin.

                            True,
our dreams, our high hopes voyaging far and wide   690
bring sheer delight to many, to many others
      delusion, blithe, mindless lusts
and the fraud steals on one slowly . . . unaware
till he trips and puts his foot into the fire.
      He was a wise old man who coined   695
the famous saying: "Sooner or later
foul is fair, fair is foul
to the man the gods will ruin" —
      He goes his way for a moment only
               free of blinding ruin.   700

Enter Haemon from the palace.

      Here's Haemon now, the last of all your sons.
      Does he come in tears for his bride,
      his doomed bride, Antigone —
      bitter at being cheated of their marriage?
Creon: We'll soon know, better than seers could tell us.   705

Turning to Haemon.

Son, you've heard the final verdict on your bride?
Are you coming now, raving against your father?
Or do you love me, no matter what I do?
Haemon: Father, I'm your *son* . . . you in your wisdom
    set my bearings for me — I obey you.   710
No marriage could ever mean more to me than you,
whatever good direction you may offer.
Creon: Fine, Haemon.
That's how you ought to feel within your heart,
subordinate to your father's will in every way.
That's what a man prays for: to produce good sons —   715
households full of them, dutiful and attentive,
so they can pay his enemy back with interest
and match the respect their father shows his friend.
But the man who rears a brood of useless children,
what has he brought into the world, I ask you?   720
Nothing but trouble for himself, and mockery
from his enemies laughing in his face.
                  Oh Haemon,
never lose your sense of judgment over a woman.
The warmth, the rush of pleasure, it all goes cold
in your arms, I warn you . . . a worthless woman   725
in your house, a misery in your bed.
What wound cuts deeper than a loved one
turned against you? Spit her out,
like a mortal enemy — let the girl go.
Let her find a husband down among the dead.   730

Imagine it: I caught her in naked rebellion,
the traitor, the only one in the whole city.
I'm not about to prove myself a liar,
not to my people, no, I'm going to kill her!
That's right — so let her cry for mercy, sing her hymns   735
to Zeus who defends all bonds of kindred blood.
Why, if I bring up my own kin to be rebels,
think what I'd suffer from the world at large.
Show me the man who rules his household well:
I'll show you someone fit to rule the state.   740
That good man, my son,
I have every confidence he and he alone
can give commands and take them too. Staunch
in the storm of spears he'll stand his ground,
a loyal, unflinching comrade at your side.   745

But whoever steps out of line, violates the laws
or presumes to hand out orders to his superiors,
he'll win no praise from me. But that man
the city places in authority, his orders
must be obeyed, large and small,   750
right and wrong.

                Anarchy —
show me a greater crime in all the earth!
She, she destroys cities, rips up houses,
breaks the ranks of spearmen into headlong rout.
But the ones who last it out, the great mass of them   755
owe their lives to discipline. Therefore
we must defend the men who live by law,
never let some woman triumph over us.
Better to fall from power, if fall we must,
at the hands of a man — never be rated   760
inferior to a woman, never.
Leader: To us,
unless old age has robbed us our wits,
you seem to say what you have to say with sense.
Haemon: Father, only the gods endow a man with reason,
the finest of all their gifts, a treasure.   765
Far be it from me — I haven't the skill,
and certainly no desire, to tell you when,
if ever, you make a slip speech . . . though
someone else might have a good suggestion.

Of course it's not for you,   770
in the normal run of things, to watch
whatever men say or do, or find to criticize.
The man in the street, you know, dreads your glance,
he'd never say anything displeasing to your face.
But it's for me to catch the murmurs in the dark,   775
the way the city mourns for this young girl.
"No woman," they say, "ever deserved death less,
and such a brutal death for such a glorious action.
She, with her own dear brother lying in his blood —
she couldn't bear to leave him dead, unburied,   780
food for the wild dogs or wheeling vultures.
Death? She deserves a glowing crown of gold!"
So they say, and the rumor spreads in secret,
darkly . . .

            I rejoice in your success, father —
nothing more precious to me in the world.   785
What medal of honor brighter to his children

than a father's growing glory? Or a child's
to his proud father? Now don't, please,
be quite so single-minded, self-involved,
or assume the world is wrong and you are right.   790
Whoever thinks that he alone possesses intelligence,
the gift of eloquence, he and no one else,
and character too . . . such men, I tell you,
spread them open — you will find them empty.

                           No,
it's no disgrace for a man, even a wise man,   795
to learn many things and not to be too rigid.
You've seen trees by a raging winter torrent,
how many sway with the flood and salvage every twig,
but not the stubborn — they're ripped out, roots and all.
Bend or break. The same when a man is sailing: 800
haul your sheets too taut, never give an inch,
you'll capsize, go the rest of the voyage
keel up and the rowing-benches under.
Oh give way. Relax your anger — change!
I'm young, I know, but let me offer this: 805
it would be best by far, I admit,
if a man were born infallible, right by nature.
If not — and things don't often go that way,
it's best to learn from those with good advice.

Leader: You'd do well, my lord, if he's speaking to the point,   810
to learn from him,

Turning to Haemon.

                and you, my boy, from him.
You both are talking sense.
Creon: So,
men our age, we're to be lectured, are we? —
schooled by a boy his age?
Haemon: Only in what is right. But if I seem young,   815
look less to my years and more to what I do.
Creon: Do? Is admiring rebels an achievement?
Haemon: I'd never suggest that you admire treason.
Creon: Oh? —
isn't that just the sickness that's attacked her?
Haemon: The whole city of Thebes denies it, to a man.   820
Creon: And is Thebes about to tell me how to rule?
Haemon: Now, you see? Who's talking like a child?
Creon: Am I to rule this land for others — or myself?

Haemon: It's no city at all, owned by one man alone.

Creon: What? The city *is* the king's — that's the law!   825

Haemon: What a splendid king you'd make of a desert island —
    you and you alone.

Creon (to the Chorus):   This boy, I do believe,
    is fighting on her side, the woman's side.

Haemon: If you are a woman, yes;
    my concern is all for you.   830

Creon: Why, you degenerate — bandying accusations,
    threatening me with justice, your own father!

Haemon: I see my father offending justice — wrong.

Creon: Wrong?
    To protect my royal rights?

Haemon: Protect your rights?
    When you trample down the honors of the gods?   835

Creon: You, you soul of corruption, rotten through —
    woman's accomplice!

Haemon: That may be,
    but you'll never find me accomplice to a criminal.

Creon: That's what *she* is,
    and every word you say is a blatant appeal for her —   840

Haemon: And you, and me, and the gods beneath the earth.

Creon: You'll never marry her, not while she's alive.

Haemon: Then she'll die . . . but her death will kill another.

Creon: What, brazen threats? You go too far!

Haemon: What threat?
    Combating your empty, mindless judgments with a word?   845

Creon: You'll suffer for your sermons, you and your empty wisdom!

Haemon: If you weren't my father, I'd say you were insane.

Creon: Don't flatter me with Father — you woman's slave!

Haemon: You really expect to fling abuse at me
    and not receive the same?

Creon: Is that so!   850
    Now, by heaven, I promise you, you'll pay —
    taunting, insulting me! Bring her out,
    that hateful — she'll die now, here,
    in front of his eyes, beside her groom!

Haemon: No, no, she will never die beside me —   855
    don't delude yourself. And you will never
    see me, never set eyes on my face again.
    Rage your heart out, rage with friends
    who can stand the sight of you.

Rushing out.

Leader: Gone, my king, in a burst of anger.   860
    A temper young as his . . . hurt him once,
    he may do something violent.
Creon: Let him do —
    dream up something desperate, past all human limit!
    Good riddance. Rest assured,
    he'll never save those two young girls from death.   865
Leader: Both of them, you really intend to kill them both?
Creon: No, not her, the one whose hands are clean;
    you're quite right.
Leader: But Antigone —
    what sort of death do you have in mind for her?
Creon: I'll take her down some wild, desolate path   870
    never trod by men, and wall her up alive
    in a rocky vault, and set out short rations,
    just a gesture of piety
    to keep the entire city free of defilement.
    There let her pray to the one god she worships: 875
    Death — who knows? — may just reprieve her from death.
    Or she may learn at last, better late than never,
    what a waste of breath it is to worship Death.

Exit to the palace.

Chorus: Love, never conquered in battle
    Love the plunderer laying waste the rich!   880
    Love standing the night-watch
                            guarding a girl's soft cheek,
    you range the seas, the shepherds' steadings off in the wilds —
    not even the deathless gods can flee your onset,
    nothing human born for a day —   885
    whoever feels your grip is driven mad.
                                            Love
    you wrench the minds of the righteous into outrage,
    swerve them to their ruin — you have ignited this,
    this kindred strife, father and son at war
                            and Love alone the victor —   890
    warm glance of the bride triumphant, burning with desire!
    Throned in power, side-by-side with the mighty laws!
    Irresistible Aphrodite, never conquered —
    Love, you mock us for your sport.

Antigone is brought from the palace under guard.

    But now, even I'd rebel against the king,   895
    I'd break all bounds when I see this —

I fill with tears, can't hold them back,
not any more . . . I see Antigone make her way
to the bridal vault where all are laid to rest.

Antigone: Look at me, men of my fatherland,   900
    setting out on the last road
looking into the last light of day
the last I'll ever see . . .
the god of death who puts us all to bed
takes me down to the banks of Acheron alive —   905
    denied my part in the wedding-songs,
no wedding-song in the dusk has crowned my marriage —
I go to wed the lord of the dark waters.

Chorus: Not crowned with glory, crowned with a dirge,
you leave for the deep pit of the dead.   910
No withering illness laid you low,
no strokes of the sword — a law to yourself,
alone, no mortal like you, ever, you go down
to the halls of Death alive and breathing.

Antigone: But think of Niobe — well I know her story —   915
    think what a living death she died,
Tantalus' daughter, stranger queen from the east:
there on the mountain heights, growing stone
binding as ivy, slowly walled her round
and the rains will never cease, the legends say   920
the snows will never leave her . . .
        wasting away, under her brows the tears
showering down her breasting ridge and slopes –
a rocky death like hers puts me to sleep.°

Chorus: But she was a god, born of gods,   925
and we are only mortals born to die.
And yet, of course, it's a great thing
for a dying girl to hear, just hear
she shares a destiny equal to the gods,
during life and later, once she's dead.

Antigone: O you mock me!   930
Why, in the name of all my fathers' gods
why can't you wait till I am gone —
    must you abuse me to my face?
O my city, all your fine rich sons!
And you, you springs of the Dirce,   935
holy grove of Thebes where the chariots gather,

915–924 *Niobe . . . sleep*: Because of her pride, the gods killed Niobe's children and turned
Niobe into a rock on Mount Sipylus, where she wept continuously.

         you at least, you'll bear me witness, look,
unmourned by friends and forced by such crude laws
I go to my rockbound prison, strange new tomb —
      always a stranger, O dear god,   940
      I have no home on earth and none below,
         not with the living, not with the breathless dead.
Chorus: You went too far, the last limits of daring —
    smashing against the high throne of Justice!
        Your life's in ruins, child — I wonder . . .   945
do you pay for your father's terrible ordeal?
Antigone: There — at last you've touched it, the worst pain
    the worst anguish! Raking up the grief for father
        three times over, for all the doom
    that's struck us down, the brilliant house of Laius.   950
    O mother, your marriage-bed
    the coiling horrors, the coupling there —
        you with your own son, my father — doomstruck mother!
Such, such were my parents, and I their wretched child.
I go to them now, cursed, unwed, to share their home —   955
      I am a stranger! O dear brother, doomed
      in your marriage — your marriage murders mine,
        your dying drags me down to death alive!

Enter Creon.

Chorus: Reverence asks some reverence in return —
    but attacks on power never go unchecked,   960
        not by the man who holds the reins of power.
    Your own blind will, your passion has destroyed you.
Antigone: No one to weep for me, my friends,
    no wedding-song — they take me away
    in all my pain . . . the road lies open, waiting.   965
    Never again, the law forbids me to see
    the sacred eye of day. I am agony!
    No tears for the destiny that's mine,
    no loved one mourns my death.
Chorus: Can't you see?
    If a man could wail his own dirge *before* he dies,   970
    he'd never finish.

To the guards.

           Take her away, quickly!
Wall her up in the tomb, you have your orders.
Abandon her there, alone, and let her choose —

death or a buried life with a good roof for shelter.
As for myself, my hands are clean. This young girl — 975
dead or alive, she will be stripped of her rights,
her stranger's rights, here in the world above.

Antigone: O tomb, my bridal-bed — my house, my prison
cut in the hollow rock, my everlasting watch!
I'll soon be there, soon embrace my own, 980
the great growing family of our dead
Persephone has received among her ghosts.

        I,
the last of them all, the most reviled by far,
go down before my destined time's run out.
But still I go, cherishing one good hope: 985
my arrival may be dear to father,
dear to you, my mother,
dear to you, my loving brother, Eteocles —
When you died I washed you with my hands,
I dressed you all, I poured the cups 990
across your tombs. But now, Polynices,
because I laid your body out as well,
this, this is my reward. Nevertheless
I honored you — the decent will admit it —
well and wisely too.

      Never, I tell you, 995
if I had been the mother of children
or if my husband died, exposed and rotting —
I'd never have taken this ordeal upon myself,
never defied our people's will. What law,
you ask, do I satisfy with what I say? 1000
A husband dead, there might have been another.
A child by another too, if I had lost the first.
But mother and father both lost in the halls of Death,
no brother could ever spring to light again.

For this law alone I held you first in honor. 1005
For this, Creon, the king, judges me a criminal
guilty of dreadful outrage, my dear brother!
And now he leads me off, a captive in his hands,
with no part in the bridal-song, the bridal-bed,
denied all joy of marriage, raising children — 1010
deserted so by loved ones, struck by fate,
I descend alive to the caverns of the dead.

What law of the mighty gods have I transgressed?
Why look to the heavens any more, tormented as I am?

Whom to call, what comrades now? Just think,   1015
my reverence only brands me for irreverence!
Very well: if this is the pleasure of the gods,
once I suffer I will know that I was wrong.
But if these men are wrong, let them suffer
nothing worse than they mete out to me —   1020
these masters of injustice!
Leader: Still the same rough winds, the wild passion
raging through the girl.
Creon (to the guards):   Take her away.
You're wasting time — you'll pay for it too.
Antigone: Oh god, the voice of death. It's come, it's here. 1025
Creon: True. Not a word of hope — your doom is sealed.
Antigone: Land of Thebes, city of all my fathers —
O you gods, the first gods of the race!
They drag me away, now, no more delay.
Look on me, you noble sons of Thebes —   1030
the last of a great line of kings,
I alone, see what I suffer now
at the hands of what breed of men —
all for reverence, my reverence for the gods!

She leaves under guard; the Chorus gathers.

Chorus: Danaë, Danaë —   1035
even she endured a fate like yours,
    in all her lovely strength she traded
the light of day for the bolted brazen vault —
buried within her tomb, her bridal-chamber,
wed to the yoke and broken.   1040
    But she was of glorious birth
                my child, my child
and treasured the seed of Zeus within her womb,
the cloudburst streaming gold!°
    The power of fate is a wonder,   1045
    dark, terrible wonder —
    neither wealth nor armies
    towered walls nor ships
    black hulls lashed by the salt
    can save us from that force.   1050

1035–44 *Danaë . . . gold:* Her father imprisoned Danaë in an underground house of bronze
when he learned that she would have a son who would kill him. But Zeus came to her in a
shower of gold and she gave birth to Perseus.

The yoke tamed him too
    young Lycurgus flaming in anger
king of Edonia, all for his mad taunts
Dionysus clamped him down, encased
in the chain-mail of rock   1055
    and there his rage
                his terrible flowering rage burst —
sobbing, dying away . . . at last that madman
came to know his god —
    the power he mocked, the power   1060
    he taunted in all his frenzy
    trying to stamp out
    the women strong with the god —
    the torch, the raving sacred cries —
    enraging the Muses who adore the flute.°   1065

And far north where the Black Rocks
    cut the sea in half
and murderous straits
split the coast of Thrace
    a forbidding city stands   1070
where once, hard by the walls
the savage Ares thrilled to watch
a king's new queen, a Fury rearing in rage
    against his two royal sons —
        her bloody hands, her dagger-shuttle   1075
stabbing out their eyes   cursed, blinding wounds —
their eyes blind sockets screaming for revenge!°

They wailed in agony, cries echoing cries
    the princes doomed at birth . . .
and their mother doomed to chains,   1080
walled off in a tomb of stone —
    but she traced her own birth back
to a proud Athenian line and the high gods
and off in caverns half the world away,
born of the wild North Wind   1085
    she sprang on her father's gales,
        racing stallions up the leaping cliffs —
child of the heavens. But even on her the Fates

1051–65 *The yoke . . . the flute*: According to various legends Lycurgus was imprisoned in the stone cell or driven mad by the gods for insulting Dionysus and the Muses.   1066–77 *And far north . . . screaming for revenge*: Eidothea, second wife of King Phineas, blinded her stepsons after the king had imprisoned their mother in a cave. Ares is the god of war.

the gray everlasting Fates rode hard
my child, my child.

Enter Tiresias, the blind prophet, led by a boy.

Tiresias: Lords of Thebes,   1090
    I and the boy have come together,
    hand in hand. Two see with the eyes of one . . .
    so the blind must go, with a guide to lead the way.
Creon: What is it, old Tiresias? What news now?
Tiresias: I will teach you. And you obey the seer.
Creon: I will,   1095
    I've never wavered from your advice before.
Tiresias: And so you kept the city straight on course.
Creon: I owe you a great deal, I swear to that.
Tiresias: Then reflect, my son: you are poised,
    once more on the razor-edge of fate.   1100
Creon: What is it? I shudder to hear you.
Tiresias: You will learn
    when you listen to the warnings of my craft.
    As I sat on the ancient seat of augury,
    in the sanctuary where every bird I know
    will hover at my hands — suddenly I heard it,   1105
    a strange voice in the wingbeats, unintelligible,
    barbaric, a mad scream! Talons flashing, ripping,
    they were killing each other — that much I knew —
    the murderous fury whirring in those wings
    made that much clear!
                              I was afraid,   1110
    I turned quickly, tested the burnt-sacrifice,
    ignited the altar at all points — but no fire,
    the god in the fire never blazed.
    Not from those offerings . . . over the embers
    slid a heavy ooze from the long thighbones,   1115
    smoking, sputtering out, and the bladder
    puffed and burst — spraying gall into the air —
    and the fat wrapping the bones slithered off
    and left them glistening white. No fire!
    The rites failed that might have blazed the future   1120
    with a sign. So I learned from the boy here;
    he is my guide, as I am guide to others.
                              And it's you —
    your high resolve that sets this plague on Thebes.
    The public altars and sacred hearths are fouled,

one and all, by the birds and dogs with carrion   1125
torn from the corpse, the doomstruck son of Oedipus!
And so the gods are deaf to our prayers, they spurn
the offerings in our hands, the flame of holy flesh.
No birds cry out an omen clear and true —
they're gorged with the murdered victim's blood and fat.   1130
Take these things to heart, my son, I warn you.
All men make mistakes, it is only human.
But once the wrong is done, a man
can turn his back on folly, misfortune too,
if he tries to make amends, however low he's fallen,   1135
and stops his bullnecked ways. Stubbornness
brands you for stupidity — pride is a crime.
No, yield to the dead!
Never stab the fighter when he's down.
Where's the glory, killing the dead twice over?   1140

I mean you well. I give you sound advice.
It's best to learn from a good adviser
when he speaks for your own good:
it's pure gain.
Creon: Old man — all of you! So,
you shoot your arrows at my head like archers at the target —   1145
I even have *him* loosed on me, this fortune-teller.
Oh his ilk has tried to sell me short
and ship me off for years. Well,
drive your bargains, traffic — much as you like —
in the gold of India, silver-gold of Sardis.   1150
You'll never bury that body in the grave,
not even if Zeus's eagles rip the corpse
and wing their rotten pickings off to the throne of god!
Never, not even in fear of such defilement
will I tolerate his burial, that traitor.   1155
Well I know, we can't defile the gods —
no mortal has the power.
                         No,
reverend old Tiresias, all men fall,
it's only human, but the wisest fall obscenely
when they glorify obscene advice with rhetoric —   1160
all for their own gain.
Tiresias: Oh god, is there a man alive
who knows, who actually believes . . .
Creon: What now?
What earth-shattering truth are you about to utter?

Tiresias: . . . just how much a sense of judgment, wisdom   1165
  is the greatest gift we have?
Creon: Just as much, I'd say,
  as a twisted mind is the worst affliction going.
Tiresias: You are the one who's sick, Creon, sick to death.
Creon: I am in no mood to trade insults with a seer.
Tiresias: You have already, calling my prophecies a lie.
Creon: Why not?   1170
  You and the whole breed of seers are mad for money!
Tiresias: And the whole race of tyrants lusts to rake it in.
Creon: This slander of yours —
  are you aware you're speaking to the king?
Tiresias: Well aware. Who helped you save the city?
Creon: You —   1175
  you have your skills, old seer, but you lust for injustice!
Tiresias: You will drive me to utter the dreadful secret in my heart.
Creon: Spit it out! Just don't speak it out for profit.
Tiresias: Profit? No, not a bit of profit, not for you.
Creon: Know full well, you'll never buy off my resolve.   1180
Tiresias: Then know this too, learn this by heart!
  The chariot of the sun will not race through
  so many circuits more, before you have surrendered
  one born of your own loins, your own flesh and blood,
  a corpse for corpses given in return, since you have thrust   1185
  to the world below a child sprung for the world above,
  ruthlessly lodged a living soul within the grave —
  then you've robbed the gods below the earth,
  keeping a dead body here in the bright air,
  unburied, unsung, unhallowed by the rites.   1190

  You, you have no business with the dead,
  nor do the gods above — this is violence
  you have forced upon the heavens.
  And so the avengers, the dark destroyers late
  but true to the mark, now lie in wait for you,   1195
  the Furies sent by the gods and the god of death
  to strike you down with the pains that you perfected!

  There. Reflect on that, tell me I've been bribed.
  The day comes soon, no long test of time, not now,
  that wakes the wails for men and women in your halls.   1200
  Great hatred rises against you —
  cities in tumult, all whose mutilated sons
  the dogs have graced with burial, or the wild beasts,

some wheeling crow that wings the ungodly stench of carrion
back to each city, each warrior's hearth and home.   1205

These arrows for your heart! Since you've raked me
I loose them like an archer in my anger,
arrows deadly true. You'll never escape
their burning, searing force.

Motioning to his escort.

Come, boy, take me home.   1210
So he can vent his rage on younger men,
and learn to keep a gentler tongue in his head
and better sense than what he carries now.

Exit to the side.

Leader: The old man's gone, my king —
    terrible prophecies. Well I know,   1215
    since the hair on this old head went gray,
    he's never lied to Thebes.
Creon: I know it myself — I'm shaken, torn.
    It's a dreadful thing to yield . . . but resist now?
    Lay my pride bare to the blows of ruin?   1220
    That's dreadful too.
Leader: But good advice,
    Creon, take it now, you must
Creon: What should I do? Tell me . . . I'll obey.
Leader: Go! Free the girl from the rocky vault
    and raise a mound for the body you exposed.   1225
Creon: That's your advice? You think I should give in?
Leader: Yes, my king, quickly. Disasters sent by the gods
    cut short our follies in a flash.
Creon: Oh it's hard,
    giving up the heart's desire . . . but I will do it —
    no more fighting a losing battle with necessity.   1230
Leader: Do it now, go, don't leave it to others.
Creon: Now — I'm on my way! Come, each of you,
    take up axes, make for the high ground,
    over there, quickly! I and my better judgment
    have come round to this — I shackled her,   1235
    I'll set her free myself. I am afraid . . .
    it's best to keep the established laws
    to the very day we die.

Rushing out, followed by his entourage. The Chorus clusters around the altar.

Chorus: God of a hundred names!
        Great Dionysus —
    Son and glory of Semele! Pride of Thebes —   1240
Child of Zeus whose thunder rocks the clouds —
Lord of the famous lands of evening —
King of the Mysteries!
        King of Eleusis, Demeter's plain
her breasting hills that welcome in the world —
Great Dionysus!
       Bacchus, living in Thebes   1245
the mother-city of all your frenzied women —
            Bacchus
  living along the Ismenus' rippling waters
standing over the field sown with the Dragon's teeth!°

You — we have seen you through the flaring smoky fires,
    your torches blazing over the twin peaks   1250
where nymphs of the hallowed cave climb onward
        fired with you, your sacred rage —
we have seen you at Castalia's running spring
and down from the heights of Nysa crowned with ivy
the greening shore rioting vines and grapes   1255
  down you come in your storm of wild women
      ecstatic, mystic cries —
          Dionysus —
down to watch and ward the roads of Thebes!

First of all cities, Thebes you honor first
you and your mother, bride of the lightning —   1260
come, Dionysus! now your people lie
in the iron grip of plague,
come in your racing, healing stride
      down Parnassus' slopes
or across the moaning straits.
        Lord of the dancing —   1265
dance, dance the constellations breathing fire!
Great master of the voices of the night!
Child of Zeus, God's offspring, come, come forth!
Lord, king, dance with your nymphs, swirling, raving
arm-in-arm in frenzy through the night   1270

1247–48 *Ismenus . . . Dragon's teeth:* Cadmus killed a dragon here and sowed the field with its
teeth, from which the builders of Thebes arose.

        they dance you, Iacchus° —
                             Dance, Dionysus
  giver of all good things!

Enter a Messenger from the side.

Messenger: Neighbors,
    friends of the house of Cadmus°and the kings,
    there's not a thing in this life of ours
    I'd praise or blame as settled once for all.   1275
    Fortune lifts and Fortune fells the lucky
    and unlucky every day. No prophet on earth
    can tell a man his fate. Take Creon:
    there was a man to rouse your envy once,
    as I see it. He saved the realm from enemies;   1280
    taking power, he alone, the lord of the fatherland,
    he set us true on course — flourished like a tree
    with the noble line of sons he bred and reared . . .
    and now it's lost, all gone.
                        Believe me,
    when a man has squandered his true joys,   1285
    he's good as dead, I tell you, a living corpse.
    Pile up riches in your house, as much as you like
    —live like a king with a huge show of pomp,
    but if real delight is missing from the lot,
    I wouldn't give you a wisp of smoke for it,   1290
    not compared with joy.
Leader: What now?
    What new grief do you bring the house of kings?
Messenger: Dead, dead — and the living are guilty of their death!
Leader: Who's the murderer? Who is dead? Tell us.
Messenger: Haemon's gone, his blood spilled by the very hand — 1295
Leader: His father's or his own?
Messenger: His own . . .
    raging mad with his father for the death —
Leader: Oh great seer,
    you saw it all, you brought your word to birth!
Messenger: Those are the facts. Deal with them as you will.

As he turns to go, Eurydice enters from the palace.

1271 *Iacchus:* Another name for Dionysus.   1273 *Cadmus:* The legendary founder of Thebes
(see also 1247–48n.).

Leader: Look, Eurydice. Poor woman, Creon's wife,   1300
   so close at hand. By chance perhaps,
   unless she's heard the news about her son.
Eurydice: My countrymen,
   all of you — I caught the sound of your words
   as I was leaving to do my part,
   to appeal to queen Athena with my prayers.   1305
   I was just loosing the bolts, opening the doors,
   when a voice filled with sorrow, family sorrow,
   struck my ears, and I fell back, terrified,
   into the women's arms — everything went black.
   Tell me the news, again, whatever it is . . .   1310
   sorrow and I are hardly strangers;
   I can bear the worst.
Messenger: I — dear lady,
   I'll speak as an eye-witness. I was there.
   And I won't pass over one word of the truth.
   Why should I try to soothe you with a story,   1315
   only to prove a liar in a moment?
   Truth is always best.
                      So,
   I escorted your lord, I guided him
   to the edge of the plain where the body lay,
   Polynices, torn by the dogs and still unmourned.   1320
   And saying a prayer to Hecate of the Crossroads,
   Pluto too, to hold their anger and be kind,
   we washed the dead in a bath of holy water
   and plucking some fresh branches, gathering . . .
   what was left of him, we burned them all together   1325
   and raised a high mound of native earth, and then
   we turned and made for that rocky vault of hers,
   the hollow, empty bed of the bride of Death.
   And far off, one of us heard a voice,
   a long wail rising, echoing   1330
   out of that unhallowed wedding-chamber;
   he ran to alert the master and Creon pressed on,
   closer — the strange, inscrutable cry came sharper,
   throbbing around him now, and he let loose
   a cry of his own, enough to wrench the heart,   1335
   "Oh god, am I the prophet now? going down
   the darkest road I've ever gone? My son —
   it's *his* dear voice, he greets me! Go, men,
   closer, quickly! Go through the gap,

the rocks are dragged back —   1340
right to the tomb's very mouth — and look,
see if it's Haemon's voice I think I hear,
or the gods have robbed me of my senses."

The king was shattered. We took his orders,
went and searched, and there in the deepest,   1345
dark recesses of the tomb we found her . . .
hanged by the neck in a fine linen noose,
strangled in her veils — and the boy,
his arms flung around her waist,
clinging to her, wailing for his bride,   1350
dead and down below, for his father's crimes
and the bed of his marriage blighted by misfortune.
When Creon saw him, he gave a deep sob,
he ran in, shouting, crying out to him,
"Oh my child — what have you done? what seized you,   1355
what insanity? what disaster drove you mad?
Come out, my son! I beg you on my knees!"
But the boy gave him a wild burning glance,
spat in his face, not a word in reply,
he drew his sword — his father rushed out,   1360
running as Haemon lunged and missed! —
and then, doomed, desperate with himself,
suddenly leaning his full weight on the blade,
he buried it in his body, halfway to the hilt.
And still in his senses, pouring his arms around her, 1365
he embraced the girl and breathing hard,
released a quick rush of blood,
bright red on her cheek glistening white.
And there he lies, body enfolding body . . .
he has won his bride at last, poor boy,   1370
not here but in the houses of the dead.

Creon shows the world that of all the ills
afflicting men the worst is lack of judgment.

Eurydice turns and reenters the palace.

Leader: What do you make of that? The lady's gone,
     without a word, good or bad.
Messenger: I'm alarmed too   1375
     but here's my hope — faced with her son's death,
     she finds it unbecoming to mourn in public.
     Inside, under her roof, she'll set her women

to the task and wail the sorrow of the house.
  She's too discreet. She won't do something rash.   1380
Leader: I'm not so sure. To me, at least,
  a long heavy silence promises danger,
  just as much as a lot of empty outcries.
Messenger: We'll see if she's holding something back,
  hiding some passion in her heart.   1385
  I'm going in. You may be right — who knows?
  Even too much silence has its dangers.

Exit to the palace. Enter Creon from the side, escorted by attendants carrying Haemon's body on a bier.

Leader: The king himself! Coming toward us,
  look, holding the boy's head in his hands.
  Clear, damning proof, if it's right to say so —   1390
  proof of his own madness, no one else's,
        no, his own blind wrongs.
Creon: Ohhh,
  so senseless, so insane . . . my crimes,
  my stubborn, deadly —
  Look at us, the killer, the killed,   1395
  father and son, the same blood — the misery!
  My plans, my mad fanatic heart,
  my son, cut off so young!
  Ai, dead, lost to the world,
  not through your stupidity, no, my own.
Leader: Too late,   1400
  too late, you see what justice means.
Creon: Oh I've learned
  through blood and tears! Then, it was then,
  when the god came down and struck me — a great weight
  shattering, driving me down that wild savage path,
  ruining, trampling down my joy. Oh the agony,   1405
        the heartbreaking agonies of our lives.

Enter the Messenger from the palace.

Messenger: Master,
  what a hoard of grief you have, and you'll have more.
  The grief that lies to hand you've brought yourself —

Pointing to Haemon's body.

  the rest, in the house, you'll see it all too soon.
Creon: What now? What's worse than this?

Messenger: The queen is dead.   1410
   The mother of this dead body . . . mother to the end —
   poor thing, her wounds are fresh.
Creon: No, no,
   harbor of Death, so choked, so hard to cleanse! —
   why me? why are you killing me?
   Herald of pain, more words, more grief?   1415
   I died once, you kill me again and again!
   What's the report, boy . . . some news for me?
   My wife dead? O dear god!
   Slaughter heaped on slaughter?

The doors open; the body of Eurydice is brought out on her bier.

Messenger: See for yourself:
   now they bring her body from the palace.
Creon: Oh, no,   1420
   another, a second loss to break the heart.
   What next, what fate still waits for me?
   I just held my son in my arms and now,
   look, a new corpse rising before my eyes —
   wretched, helpless mother — O my son!   1425
Messenger: She stabbed herself at the altar,
   then her eyes went dark, after she'd raised
   a cry for the noble fate of Megareus,°the hero
   killed in the first assault, then for Haemon,
   then with her dying breath she called down   1430
   torments on your head — you killed her sons.
Creon: Oh the dread,
   I shudder with dread! Why not kill me too? —
   run me through with a good sharp sword?
   Oh god, the misery, anguish —
   I, I'm churning with it, going under.   1435
Messenger: Yes, and the dead, the woman lying there,
   piles the guilt of all their deaths on you.
Creon: How did she end her life, what bloody stroke?
Messenger: She drove home to the heart with her own hand,
   once she learned her son was dead . . . that agony.   1440
Creon: And the guilt is all mine —
   can never be fixed on another man,
   no escape for me. I killed you,
   I, god help me, I admit it all!

1428 *Megareus*: One of Creon and Eurydice's sons, slain when Thebes was attacked.

To his attendants.

Take me away, quickly, out of sight.   1445
I don't even exist — I'm no one. Nothing.
Leader: Good advice, if there's any good in suffering.
Quickest is best when troubles block the way.
Creon (kneeling in prayer):
Come, let it come — that best of fates for me
that brings the final day, best fate of all.   1450
Oh quickly, now —
so I never have to see another sunrise.
Leader: That will come when it comes;
we must deal with all that lies before us.
The future rests with the ones who tend the future.   1455
Creon: That prayer — I poured my heart into that prayer!
Leader: No more prayers now. For mortal men
there is no escape from the doom we must endure.
Creon: Take me away, I beg you, out of sight.
A rash, indiscriminate fool!   1460
I murdered you, my son, against my will —
you too, my wife . . .
                         Wailing wreck of a man,
whom to look to? where to lean for support?

Desperately turning from Haemon to Eurydice on their biers.

Whatever I touch goes wrong — once more
a crushing fate's come down upon my head.   1465

The Messenger and attendants lead Creon into the palace.

Chorus: Wisdom is by far the greatest part of joy,
and reverence toward the gods must be safeguarded.
The mighty words of the proud are paid in full
with mighty blows of fate, and at long last
those blows will teach us wisdom.   1470

The old citizens exit to the side.

Questions

Sometimes in works of literary art it's the absence of a feeling, not its presence, that shapes our understanding. Instead of
watching a concept achieving powerful, personal immediacy
within a single consciousness, we focus on a closed mind and an

unresponsive heart — a person who refuses to learn, who denies the meaning of the experience he or she is passing through. We live into *in*capacity; we speculate about its causes and track its emotional bearings. And by following the pattern of denials and negations, we arrive at comprehension of familiar truths that is unattainable any other way.

Several great themes in Sophocles' *Antigone* are anchored in the title character — loyalty, heroic commitment versus prudence, family versus state. The experience in the play that draws us into the freshest reflection upon human mortality, however, is that of Creon. One can imagine him assenting, in a casual fashion, to the proposition that human creatures are mutable, subject to the natural cycle of growth and decline, incapable whether great or humble of overcoming the limits of mortality. Nothing in the action of the play — including the action that Creon himself precipitates — could be said to call into question these general propositions. But although Creon stands face to face with the propositions, throughout the play he never penetrates them, never discovers the specifics that would bring them vitally alive in his consciousness. To the very end Creon remains impervious to just the feelings that, in his situation, experience of the meaning of human mortality ought to inspire. And all through the play we, as summoning readers, press closer to understanding this imperviousness and are instructed by Creon's blindness and unresponsiveness.

In the following four passages we can sense the nature of the internal obstacles that block Creon from achieving the kind of awareness he most urgently needs. After reading and rereading the play, choose one or more of the passages quoted and write a page telling what Creon feels as he speaks and why that feeling might be seen as inappropriate. How does the reader's developing awareness of appropriate and inappropriate feelings in this play confirm knowledge of the meanings of human mortality?

> Never the same for the patriot and the traitor. (line 585)
> Once an enemy, never a friend, not even after death. (588–89)
> Are you aware you're speaking to the king? (1174)
> Know full well, you'll never buy off my resolve. (1180)

Compare your response with those that follow.

Responses

EDITOR: Creon's dimness derives partly from excessive self-satisfaction — egoism, imperiousness, pomposity. Tiresias tells him he's a tyrant — "Stubbornness / brands you for stupidity" (lines 1136–37) — but Creon can't hear because his ear isn't tuned to substance. He listens for the sounds of subordination or insubordination, and when he hears insubordination, he shuts off every other message — "Are you aware you're speaking to the king?" (1174). (Antigone herself makes this point earlier.) Another root of dimness in Creon is moral vanity: his delusion that he possesses a higher order of virtue than others do, that he's surrounded by money grubbers prepared to sell out country and faith — "Know full well, you'll never buy off my resolve" (1180).

The center of Creon's problem, however, lies in his inability to grasp that human mortality presents us with a reality that transcends designs, agendas, and preoccupations, whether personal or social, political or national. Humankind is powerful and ingenious; we make the earth our servant by cultivating it; we subject beasts to our will; we defend ourselves with invented weapons, we cure maladies, we think, write, compose laws. But, as the Chorus adds, "from Death alone [we] will find no rescue" (404). (The Chorus isn't an infallible or for that matter always comprehensible commentator on the action, but the good sense of its observations on the limits of human power can't be challenged.)

Because the fact of mortality stands separate from local interests and obsessions, intelligent human beings understand that it demands unique respect — or awe. Opposed factions are united in this overwhelming respect: All are subjects in the kingdom of death, all have to acknowledge that they are alike in their endings. In recognition of this circumstance, nation-states caught up in the most intense hostility lay hatred aside at least briefly at the death of each other's leaders. The decrees and rules of mortality are its own; death is natural, we say, but in its timing and circumstances, as in numberless other aspects, it is mysterious.

Creon can't fathom this mystery. He wishes to turn mortality to his own personal and political ends. He will honor the corpse of the loyal brother, humiliate the corpse of the disloyal one. He refuses to acknowledge the interruptive powers of death — not merely its power to put an end to life and to sweep the living into grief but its power to move all humanity into a confrontation, however momentary, with the unknowable nature of human existence. When Tiresias tells Creon that "you've robbed the gods below the earth, / [by] keeping a dead body here" (1188–89) and that "you have no business with the dead" (1191), he is saying what everyone is presumed to know; namely, that thinking of death as a mere adjunct to one's own policies and affinities is criminally ignorant.

As we listen and watch, we see dimensions of mortality altogether different from those dramatized in the poem by Lord Vaux and the story by Chekhov. For nearly the entire length of this play a ruler behaves as though the processes of decay and putrefaction could somehow be made to serve the special interests of a contemporary administration, as though it's acceptable to set aside the long moral tradition that teaches each new generation the appropriateness of solemn and fearful regard for those processes. We see in this behavior the absence of appropriate feeling as well as small-mindedness and overregard for earthly power. In the end, connecting what is missing with what is present, we see that awareness of the universal vulnerability of humankind is all that can save us from becoming victims of our own ambitions and obsessions, from being stupefied by immoderate attachment to personal interest.

Here, as with the preceding poem and story, it's possible to reduce the knowledge gained to an abstract formula, a familiar comment on the evanescence of things. But as we live into Creon's blindness, realizing the consequences of his particular unresponsiveness to a universal truth, our knowledge of the dimensions of mortality feels less conjectural, less distant; it becomes as close to us as our own hands.

WALLACE GRAY: Sophocles is careful to point out that Polynices has been buried by Antigone the first time, before she was caught. Sophocles has the Guard tell Creon that the "burial is accomplished," that the dust on the flesh makes the "ritual complete." To drive home his point, Sophocles continues with the Guard saying that the dust Antigone hastily sprinkled on the body was "enough to turn the curse," as no wild beast or dog had been near and the body had thus been buried untorn [lines 277–294].

And so Creon gives the desperate order that the dust be removed from the body and that it remain in the open to be mutilated by wild animals. Does this mean the body is returned to an unburied state? Do the gods of the underworld wait around for Creon's permission before they accept the soul, or do they claim what is theirs the moment Antigone "accomplishes" the burial? Sophocles certainly believes the latter to be the case. The "ritual is complete," he writes. Then what is Creon doing? At this point the outrageous [tyrant] is insulting the body of Polynices; he can no longer touch the soul. . . .

If the burial is now complete, then why does Antigone make her dangerous return when the body is even more closely guarded? It cannot be to protect the body from wild beasts: no specks of dust or drops of wine are going to accomplish that. Antigone returns to be apprehended. To be tried. To be stoned to death. She grasps at straws when she says, in the syntactically mangled speech that betrays her inner turmoil, that she buried him only because he was a brother and thus irreplaceable. No, Antigone buries her brother so that she can join him and Eteocles and Oedipus and Jocasta in death. Truly, for Antigone, her life ended long ago when she was a child and discovered that her father was also her dishonored brother. . . .

Sophocles believes that man cannot make himself the center of the universe. Antigone . . . does put herself at the center of the universe . . . Sophocles, a deeply religious and patriotic man, is presenting a secular view of man as the center of the universe to which Sophocles is not committed.

But death will claim everyone, and pride and stubbornness will show their destructive power in this play about a man and a woman who refuse to honor both god and state. Antigone dies; Creon becomes a "living corpse." One must, Sophocles is saying, accept the human condition and not try to become a god. Antigone is wrong; Creon is wrong. The action of the play pits wrong against wrong.

Homer to Joyce: Interpretations of the Classic Works of Western Literature (Macmillan, Collier Books, 1985), pp. 65–67.

Continuing the Discussion

The editor speaks mainly about Creon's blindness; Wallace Gray, a literary critic, insists that Antigone and Creon are equally wrong. How is this kind of difference in reading best explained? Which reading do you prefer? Where in the play do you find further support for your preference?

FOR FURTHER STUDY

GERARD MANLEY HOPKINS   (1844–1889)
Felix Randal

Felix Randal the farrier, O is he dead then? my duty all ended,
Who have watched his mould of man, big-boned and hardy-
        handsome
Pining, pining, till time when reason rambled in it and some
Fatal four disorders, fleshed there, all contended?

Sickness broke him. Impatient, he cursed at first, but
        mended   5
Being anointed and all; though a heavenlier heart began
        some
Months earlier, since I had our sweet reprieve and ransom°
Tendered to him. Ah well, God rest him all road ever he
        offended!

This seeing the sick endears them to us, us too it endears.
My tongue had taught thee comfort, touch had quenched thy
        tears,   10
Thy tears that touched my heart, child, Felix, poor Felix Randal;

How far from then forethought of, all thy more boisterous years,
When thou at the random grim forge, powerful amidst peers,
Didst fettle for the great grey drayhorse his bright and battering
        sandal!

7 *sweet reprieve and ransom*: Holy Communion.

RALPH WALDO EMERSON   (1803–1882)
Hamatreya

Bulkeley, Hunt, Willard, Hosmer, Meriam, Flint,
Possessed the land which rendered to their toil
Hay, corn, roots, hemp, flax, apples, wool, and wood.

Each of these landlords walked amidst his farm,
Saying, " 'Tis mine, my children's and my name's.   5
How sweet the west wind sounds in my own trees!
How graceful climb those shadows on my hill!
I fancy these pure waters and the flags
Know me, as does my dog: we sympathize;
And, I affirm, my actions smack of the soil."   10

Where are these men? Asleep beneath their grounds:
And strangers, fond as they, their furrows plough.
Earth laughs in flowers, to see her boastful boys
Earth-proud, proud of the earth which is not theirs;
Who steer the plough, but cannot steer their feet   15
Clear of the grave.
They added ridge to valley, brook to pond,
And sighed for all that bounded their domain;
"This suits me for a pasture; that's my park;
We must have clay, lime, gravel, granite-ledge,   20
And misty lowland, where to go for peat.
The land is well — lies fairly to the south.
'Tis good, when you have crossed the sea and back,
To find the sitfast acres where you left them."
Ah! the hot owner sees not Death, who adds   25
Him to his land, a lump of mold the more.
Hear what the Earth says:

Earth-song

"Mine and yours;
Mine, not yours.
Earth endures;   30
Stars abide —
Shine down in the old sea;
Old are the shores;
But where are old men?
I who have seen much,   35
Such have I never seen.

"The lawyer's deed
Ran sure,
In tail,
To them, and to their heirs   40

Who shall succeed,
Without fail,
Forevermore.

"Here is the land,
Shaggy with wood,   45
With its old valley,
Mound and flood.
But the heritors?
Fled like the flood's foam.
The lawyer, and the laws,   50
And the kingdom,
Clean swept herefrom.

"They called me theirs,
Who so controlled me;
Yet every one   55
Wished to stay, and is gone,
How am I theirs,
If they cannot hold me,
But I hold them?"

When I heard the Earth-song,   60
I was no longer brave;
My avarice cooled
Like lust in the chill of the grave.

JORIE GRAHAM   (b. 1951)
Over and Over Stitch

Late in the season the world digs in, the fat blossoms
hold still for just a moment longer.
Nothing looks satisfied,
but there is no real reason to move on much further:
this isn't a bad place;   5
why not pretend

we wished for it?
The bushes have learned to live with their haunches.
The hydrangea is resigned
to its pale and inconclusive utterances.   10
Towards the end of the season
it is not bad

to have the body. To have experienced joy
as the mere lifting of hunger
is not to have known it   15
less. The tobacco leaves
don't mind being removed
to the long racks — all uses are astounding

to the used.
There are moments in our lives which, threaded, give us
    heaven —   20
noon, for instance, or all the single victories
of gravity, or the kudzu vine,
most delicate of manias,
which has pressed its luck

this far this season.   25
It shines a gloating green.
Its edges darken with impatience, a kind of wind.

Nothing again will ever be this easy, lives
being snatched up like dropped stitches, the dry stalks of
    daylilies
marking a stillness we can't keep.   30

IVAN TURGENEV   (1818–1883)
Meeting

TRANSLATED BY RICHARD FREEBORN

    I was sitting in a birch wood one autumn, about the middle
of September. From early morning there had been occasional
drizzle, succeeded from time to time by periods of warm sunny
radiance; a season of changeable weather. The sky was either
covered with crumbling white clouds or suddenly clear for an
instant in a few places, and then, from behind the parted clouds,
blue sky would appear, lucid and smiling, like a beautiful eye. I
sat and looked around me and listened. The leaves scarcely rus-
tled above my head; by their very noise one could know what
time of year it was. It was not the happy, laughing *tremolo* of
spring, not the soft murmuration and long-winded talkativeness
of summer, not the shy and chill babblings of late autumn, but a
hardly audible dreamy chattering. A faint wind ever so slightly
moved through the treetops. The interior of the wood, damp

from the rain, was continually changing, depending on whether
the sun was shining or whether it was covered by cloud; the
interior was either flooded with light, just as if everything in it
had suddenly smiled: the delicate trunks of the not-too-numerous
birches would suddenly acquire the soft sheen of white silk, the
wafer-thin leaves which lay on the ground would suddenly grow
multi-coloured and burn with crimson and gold, while the
beautiful stems of tall curly bracken, already embellished with
their autumn colouring which resembles the colour of overripe
grapes, would stand there shot through with light, endlessly
entangling and criss-crossing before one's eyes; or suddenly one
would again be surrounded by a bluish dusk: the bright colours
would instantly be extinguished and the birches would all stand
there white, without a gleam on them, white as snow that has only
just fallen and has not yet been touched by the chilly sparkling
rays of the winter sun; and secretively, slyly, thinly drizzling rain
would begin to filter and whisper through the wood.

The foliage on the birches was still almost completely green,
although it had noticeably faded; only here and there stood a
young tree all decked out in red or gold, and one could not help
watching how brightly it flared up when the sun's rays broke,
gliding and scintillating, through the myriad network of fine
branches only just washed by glittering rain. There was not a
single bird to be heard: all had taken cover and fallen silent; only
the mocking little voice of the tom-tit tinkled occasionally like a
little steel bell.

Before I had stopped in this little birch wood, I had gone
with my dog through a grove of tall aspens. I confess that I am not
particularly fond of that tree — the aspen — with its pale-mauve
trunk and grey-green, metallic foliage which it raises as high as
possible and spreads out in the air like a quivering fan; nor do I
like the continual flutterings of its round untidy leaves which are
so awkwardly attached to their long stalks. It acquires beauty only
on certain summer evenings when, rising on high in isolation
among low bushy undergrowth, it meets the challenge of the
ebbing rays of the sunset and gleams and trembles, suffused from
its topmost branches to its roots by a uniform yellow and purple
light; or when, on a clear windy day, it is all noisily streaming and
babbling against the blue sky, and every leaf, seized by the wind's
ardour, appears to want to tear itself free, fly away and hurry off
into the distance. But in general I dislike this tree and therefore,
without stopping to rest in the aspen grove, I made my way to the
little birch wood, settled myself under a tree whose branches

began close to the ground and were able, in consequence, to shelter me from the rain, and, having gazed admiringly at the surrounding view, fell into the kind of untroubled and mild sleep familiar only to hunters.

I cannot say how long I was asleep, but when I opened my eyes the entire interior of the wood was filled with sunlight and in all directions through the jubilantly rustling foliage a bright blue sky peered and seemed to sparkle; the clouds had vanished, dispersed by the wind that had sprung up; the weather had cleared, and in the air could be felt that special dry freshness which, imbuing the heart with a feeling of elation, almost always means a peaceful and clear evening after a rainy day.

I was on the point of rising and again trying my luck, when 5 suddenly my eyes lighted on a motionless human form. I looked closely and saw that it was a young peasant girl. She was sitting twenty paces from me, her head lowered in thought and both hands dropped on her knees; in the half-open palm of one of them lay a thick bunch of wild flowers and at each breath she took the bunch slipped quietly down on to her checked skirt. A clean white blouse, buttoned at the neck and at the wrists, gathered in short soft folds about her waist; two rows of large yellow beads fell from her neck on to her bosom. She was very pretty in her own way. Her thick fair hair of a beautiful ash colour was parted into two carefully styled semicircles below a narrow crimson ribbon drawn almost down to her temples, which were white as ivory; the rest of her face was faintly sun-burned to that golden hue which is only acquired by a delicate skin. I could not see her eyes because she did not raise them; but I clearly saw her fine, high eyebrows and long eyelashes, which were damp, and on one of her cheeks I saw the dried traces of a tear that had come to rest at the edge of her slightly pale lips and glittered in the sunlight. The whole appearance of her head was very charming; even the slightly thick and rounded nose did nothing to spoil it. I particularly liked the expression on her face for the way in which it was so artless and gentle, so melancholy and full of childish bewilderment at her own grief.

She was evidently waiting for someone. Something crackled faintly in the wood and she at once raised her head and looked round; in the transparent shade her large eyes, bright and fright-ened, flashed quickly before me like the eyes of a doe. She lis-tened for a few moments without taking her wide-open eyes from the place where the faint sound had been made, then heaved a sigh, turned her head calmly back, bent still farther down and began slowly to finger the flowers. Her eyelids reddened, her lips gave a quiver of bitterness and another tear slipped from beneath her thick lashes, coming to rest on her cheek where it glittered radiantly. Some time passed in this way, and the poor girl did not move save to make a few regretful gestures with her hands and to go on listening and listening. Again something made a noise in the wood and she was instantly alerted. The noise continued, grew louder as it approached, and finally could be heard the noise of rapid, decisive footsteps. She straightened herself and appeared to be overcome with shyness; her attentive features began to quiver and burn with expectation. The figure of a man could be glimpsed through the thicket. She peered in that direction, blushed suddenly, gave a joyful and happy smile, got ready to stand up and once again suddenly lowered her head, growing pale and confused — and she only raised her faltering, almost imploring gaze to the newcomer when he had stopped beside her.

I examined him with curiosity from my hiding-place. I confess that he produced an unpleasant impression on me. To all appearances he was the pampered valet of some rich young master. His clothes displayed pretensions to good taste and dandified casualness: they consisted of a short, bronze-coloured topcoat buttoned up to the neck and inherited, more than likely, from his master; a little rose-tinted necktie with mauve tips, and a black velvet cap with gold lace edging worn pulled down over the eyebrows. The rounded collar of his white shirt pressed unmercifully up against his ears and bit into his cheek, while his starched cuffs covered his hands right down to the red and crooked fingers which were embellished with gold and silver rings containing turquoise forget-me-nots. His face — ruddy, fresh-complexioned, and impudent — belonged to the category of faces which, so far as I have been able to judge, almost invariably annoy men and, unfortunately, are very often pleasing to women. He clearly made an effort to endow his rather coarse features with an expression of superciliousness and boredom; he endlessly screwed up his already tiny milk-grey eyes, frowned, let his mouth droop at the edges, gave forced yawns, and with a casual, though not entirely skilled, air of abandon either patted the reddish, artfully coiled hair on his temples or twiddled the little yellow hairs that stuck out on his fat upper lip — in a word, he showed off insufferably. He began to show off as soon as he saw the young peasant girl waiting for him; he slowly approached her at a lounging pace, came to a stop, shrugged his shoulders, stuck both hands into the pockets of his topcoat and, with hardly more than a fleeting and indifferent glance at the poor girl, lowered himself to the ground.

"Well," he began, still looking away to one side, swinging his leg and yawning, "have you been here long?"

The girl was unable to answer him immediately.

"A long time, sir, Victor Alexandrych," she said eventually in   10
a scarcely audible voice.

"Ah!" He removed his cap, grandly drew his hand through his thick, tightly coiled hair, which began almost at his eyebrows, and, glancing round with dignity, once more carefully covered his priceless head. "And I'd almost completely forgotten. After all, look how it rained!" He yawned once more. "There's a mass of things to be done, what with everything to be got ready and the master swearing as well. Tomorrow we'll be off . . ."

"Tomorrow?" the girl said and directed at him a look of fright.

"That's right — tomorrow. Now, now, now, please," he added hastily and with annoyance, seeing that she had begun to tremble all over and was quietly lowering her head, "please, Akulina, no crying. You know I can't stand crying." And he puckered up his snub nose. "If you start, I'll leave at once. What silliness — blubbering!"

"No, I won't, I won't," Akulina uttered hurriedly, making herself swallow her tears. "So you're leaving tomorrow?" she added after a brief pause. "When will God bring you back to see me again, Victor Alexandrych?"

"We'll meet again, we'll meet again. If not next year, then   15
later. It seems the master wants to enter government service in St. Petersburg," he continued, speaking the words casually and slightly through the nose, "and maybe we'll go abroad."

"You'll forget me, Victor Alexandrych," Akulina said sadly.

"No, why should I? I won't forget you. Only you've got to be sensible, not start playing up, obey your father . . . I'll not forget you — no-o-o." And he calmly stretched himself and again yawned.

"You mustn't forget me, Victor Alexandrych," she continued in an imploring voice. "I've loved you so much, it seems, and it seems I've done everything for you. . . . You tell me to listen to my father, Victor Alexandrych. . . . There's no point in listening to my father . . ."

"Why not?" He uttered these words as it were from his stomach, lying on his back with his arms behind his head.

"There's no point, Victor Alexandrych. You know that your- 20
self . . ."

She said nothing. Victor played with the steel chain of his
watch.

"You're not a fool, Akulina," he started saying at last, "so
don't talk nonsense. I want what's best for you, do you understand me? Of course, you're not stupid, you're not a complete
peasant girl, so to speak; and your mother also wasn't always a
peasant girl. But you're without any education, so you've got to
listen when people tell you things."

"I'm frightened, Victor Alexandrych."

"Hey, there, that's a lot of nonsense, my dear. What's there to
be frightened of! What's that you've got there," he added, turning
to her, "flowers?"

"Flowers," answered Akulina despondently. "They're some 25
field tansies I've picked," she continued, brightening slightly,
"and they're good for calves. And these are marigolds, they help
against scrofula. Just look what a lovely little flower it is! I've
never seen such a lovely little flower before in all my born days.
Then there are some forget-me-nots, here are some violets. But
these I got for you," she added, taking out from beneath the
yellow tansies a small bunch of blue cornflowers tied together
with a fine skein of grass, "would you like them?"

Victor languidly stretched out his hand, took the bunch,
casually sniffed the flowers and began to twiddle them in his
fingers, gazing up in the air from time to time with thoughtful
self-importance. Akulina looked at him and her sad gaze contained such tender devotion, such worshipful humility and love.
Yet she was also afraid of him, and fearful of crying; and taking
her own leave of him and doting on him for the last time; but he
lay there in the lounging pose of a sultan and endured her
worship of him with magnanimous patience and condescension.
I confess that his red face vexed me with its pretentiously dis-
dainful indifference through which could be discerned a replete
and self-satisfied vanity. Akulina was so fine at that moment, for
her whole heart was trustfully and passionately laid open before
him, craving him and yearning to be loved, but he . . . he simply
let the cornflowers drop on the grass, took a round glass in a
bronze frame out of the side pocket of his topcoat and started
trying to fix it in place over his eye; but no matter how hard he
tried to keep it in place with a puckered brow, a raised cheek and
even with his nose, the little eyeglass kept on falling out and
dropping into his hand.

"What's that?" Akulina asked finally in astonishment.

"A lorgnette," he answered self-importantly.

"What's it for?"

"So as to see better."   30

"Show it me."

Victor frowned, but he gave her the eyeglass.

"Don't break it, mind."

"You needn't worry, I won't." She raised it timidly to her eye.
"I don't see anything," she said artlessly.

"It's your eye, you've got to screw up your eye," he retorted in   35
the voice of a dissatisfied mentor. She screwed up the eye before
which she was holding the little glass. "Not that one, not that
one, idiot! The other one!" exclaimed Victor and, giving her no
chance to correct her mistake, took the lorgnette from her.

Akulina reddened, gave a nervous laugh, and turned away.

"It's obviously not for the likes of me," she murmured.

"That's for sure!"

The poor girl was silent and let fall a deep sigh.

"Oh, Victor Alexandrych, what'll I do without you?" she sud-   40
denly said.

Victor wiped the lorgnette with the edge of his coat and put
it back in his pocket.

"Yes, yes," he said eventually, "it sure will be hard for you to
start with." He gave her several condescending pats on the shoulder; she ever so quietly lifted his hand from her shoulder and
timidly kissed it. "Well, all right, all right, you're a good kid," he
went on, giving a self-satisfied smile, "but what can I do about it?
Judge for yourself! The master and I can't stay here; it'll be winter
soon now and to spend the winter in the country — you know
this yourself — is just horrible. But it's another matter in St.
Petersburg! There are simply such wonderful things there, such
as you, stupid, wouldn't be able to imagine even in your wildest
dreams! What houses and streets, and the so*ch*iety, the culture —
it's simply stupendous!" Akulina listened to him with greedy
interest, her lips slightly parted like a child's. "Anyhow," he
added, turning over, "why am I telling you all this? You won't be
able to understand it."

"Why say that, Victor Alexandrych? I've understood it, I've
understood everything."

"What a bright one you are!"

Akulina lowered her head.   45

"You never used to talk to me like that before, Victor Alexandrych," she said without raising her eyes.

"Didn't I before? Before! You're a one! Before indeed!" he commented, pretending to be indignant.

Both were silent for a while.

"However, it's time for me to be going," said Victor, and was on the point of raising himself on one elbow.

"Stay a bit longer," Akulina declared in an imploring voice. 50

"What's there to wait for? I've already said good-bye to you."

"Stay a bit," Akulina repeated.

Victor again lay back and started whistling. Akulina never took her eyes off him. I could tell that she was slowly working herself into a state of agitation: her lips were working and her pale cheeks were faintly crimsoning.

"Victor Alexandrych," she said at last in a breaking voice, "it's sinful of you . . . sinful of you, Victor Alexandrych, in God's name it is!"

"What's sinful?" he asked, knitting his brows, and he raised 55 himself slightly and turned his head towards her.

"It's sinful, Victor Alexandrych. If you'd only say one kind word to me now you're leaving, just say one word to me, wretched little orphan that I am . . ."

"But what should I say to you?"

"I don't know. You should know that better than me, Victor Alexandrych. Now you're going away, and if only you'd say a word . . . Why should I deserve this?"

"What a strange girl you are! What can I say?"

"Just say one word . . ." 60

"Well, you've certainly gone on and on about the same thing," he said in disgruntlement and stood up.

"Don't be angry, Victor Alexandrych," she added quickly, hardly restraining her tears.

"I'm not angry, it's only that you're stupid . . . What do you want? You know I can't marry you, don't you? Surely you know I can't? So what's it you want? What is it?" He stuck his face forward in expectation of her answer and opened wide his fingers.

"I don't want anything . . . anything," she answered, stammering and scarcely daring to stretch her trembling hands out towards him, "only if you'd just say one word in farewell . . ."

And tears streamed from her eyes. 65

"Well, so there it is, you've started crying," Victor said callously, tipping his cap forward over his eyes.

"I don't want anything," she went on, swallowing her tears and covering her face with both hands, "but what'll it be like for me in the family, what'll there be for me? And what's going to happen to me, what's going to become of me, wretch that I am! They'll give their orphan girl away to someone who doesn't love her . . . O poor me, poor me!"

"Moan away, moan away!" muttered Victor under his breath, shifting from one foot to the other.

"If only he'd say one little word, just one word . . . Such as, Akulina, I . . . I . . ."

Sudden heart-rending sobs prevented her from finishing what she was saying. She flopped on her face in the grass and burst into bitter, bitter tears. Her whole body shook convulsively, the nape of her neck rising and falling. Her long-restrained grief finally poured forth in torrents. Victor stood for a moment or so above her, shrugged his shoulders, turned, and walked away with big strides. 70

Several moments passed. She grew quiet, raised her head, jumped up, looked about her, and wrung her hands; she was on the point of rushing after him, but her legs collapsed under her and she fell on her knees. I could not hold myself back and rushed towards her, but she had hardly had time to look at me before she found the strength from somewhere to raise herself with a faint cry and vanish through the trees, leaving her flowers scattered on the ground.

I stopped there a moment, picked up the bunch of cornflowers, and walked out of the wood into a field. The sun was low in the pale clear sky and its rays had, as it were, lost their colour and grown cold; they did not shine so much as flow out in an even, almost watery, light. No more than half an hour remained until evening, but the sunset was only just beginning to crimson the sky. A flurrying wind raced towards me across the dry, yellow stubble; hastily spinning before it, little shrivelled leaves streamed past me across the track and along the edge of the wood; the side which faced on to the field like a wall shuddered all over and glistened with a faint sparkling, distinctly though not brightly; on the red-tinted grass, on separate blades of grass, on pieces of straw, everywhere innumerable strands of autumn cobwebs glittered and rippled. I stopped, and a feeling of melancholy stole over me, for it seemed to me that the sombre terror associated with the approaching winter was breaking through the cheerless, though fresh, smile of nature at this time of withering. High above me, ponderously and sharply sundering the air with its wings, a vigilant raven flew by, turned its head, looked sidewards at me, took wing, and disappeared beyond the wood with strident cawings; a large flock of pigeons rose smartly from a place where there had been threshing and after suddenly making a huge wheeling turn in the air settled busily on to the field — a sure sign of autumn! Someone rode by on the other side of a bare hillock, his empty cart clattering noisily . . .

I returned home; but the image of the poor Akulina took a long time to fade from my mind, and her cornflowers, which have long since withered, remain with me to this day . . .

PART TWO

The Experience *of* Language

In the preceding five chapters we attended directly to our own activities and experience as readers engaged in imagining feelings, characters, change, and the causes and meanings of events and behavior. We were guided about what and how to imagine by the poet's, storyteller's, and playwright's language, but we were constantly looking through that language, treating it as a window, using it as a pointer. Seldom did we focus on patterns within the language itself. The Introduction to this book speaks of the need to separate certain activities that are actually performed simultaneously in order to facilitate practice. The major separation thus far has been that between imagining feeling, character, and the rest, and bringing to life patterns in literary language.

The artificial nature of this separation becomes evident when we look back at any of the texts discussed in Part One, attending now to features of their language. In Chapter 1 we worked at constructing the feeling at a particular moment in Thomas Hardy's "The Slow Nature" (see p. 33):

> She laid a hand on the dresser-ledge,
>   And scanned far Egdon-side;
> And stood; and you heard the wind-swept sedge
>   And the rippling Froom; till she cried: (lines 17–20)

We imagined this moment, for Mistress Damon, as a space of time different in intensity and weight from everything preceding it in the poem. One student reader whose paper about the poem was quoted saw Mistress Damon laying her hand on the dresser-ledge "for support." The student was sensing that time had abruptly stopped for Mistress Damon; it was impossible to go forward.

This held-up sense that the student brought to life was a response not only to character, situation, and feeling but also to the lay of the words on the page. The pace of this poem — the movement of the words and phrases that we respond to — changes sharply in the middle. After three and a half loosely punctuated stanzas (Hardy uses dashes and exclamation marks), we're slowed down by a succession of semicolons that ask for more sustained pauses. The phrase *And stood* at the beginning of the poem's nineteenth line stops us short, changing the tempo. These changes interact with — work to sustain — our imagining of a particular kind of emotional stress. They guide us toward a sense of a mind interrupted, struggling, seeking and momentarily not finding a way to advance.

THE UNIQUENESS
OF LITERARY LANGUAGE

When we read a newspaper or a tax form or instructions about how to hook up speakers to the stereo, we don't focus on the way things are said — the sentence rhythms, molding of phrases, figures of speech. But in literary language the way things are said asks for careful attention. Verbal patterns, often intricate and subtle, not only enrich and complicate our imagining of character and feeling but offer musical satisfactions as well. Developing a sensitive ear and eye for patternings of language is in some respects the most demanding challenge faced by active readers. And it's this challenge that we'll now be confronting.

In separate sections we'll examine particular verbal elements of poetry, fiction, and drama to clarify their interaction with the other resources on which we, as close imaginers, draw. Our aim is to sharpen alertness to literary artistry not as a thing in itself but as a charged wire connecting writers and readers in their broad imaginative collaboration.

Once again to facilitate practice we'll partition our activities somewhat artificially. We'll separate responses to patterned language from our other responses as constructive imaginers. As we do this, we need to keep firmly in mind the ultimate interdependency of all the elements. Good readers live simultaneously in the art of the poem, story, or play and in the feelings they themselves construct, in the figures of speech and in the intellectual and emotional needs that those figures meet, in the movements of imagined characters' minds, and in the beat and change of beat of verbal rhythms.

TECHNICAL TERMS AS TOOLS

Throughout Part Two, technical terms will be introduced, usually one at a time. Among the terms are tone, metaphor, irony, point of view, conflict, and resolution. (The Glossary contains definitions and explanations of these and other much-used literary terms.) These terms are helpful to readers working to heighten their responses to patterned language. But they are only tools — means to an end. Only if we stay in touch with the whole of our imaginative experience can we avoid turning poems, stories, and plays into clumps of technical devices. There's a temptation to allow discussion of a figure of speech or feature of sound to displace our experience of the text as a whole, and that temptation has to be resisted.

POETRY

The primary elements of poetry treated in the next six chapters are sound and rhythm, tone, imagery, metaphor and simile, symbol, and irony. One or more of these elements played key roles in shaping our experience of each of the poems in the earlier chapters of *Close Imagining*. Look back, for example, at Dave Smith's "The Spring Poem" (p. 374). In Chapter 4 we considered this poem as a way to challenge familiar ideas of spring, the season of beautiful rebirths; we focused on its rejection of the conventions observed by earlier poets in their spring poems. We might well have gone on to consider the ways in which that rejection involves sound and rhythm as well as sense and meaning. Other poets' spring poems have a peppy tunefulness, the lilt and movement of song, as in Shakespeare's "A Lover and His Lass" (p. 376):

> With a hey and a ho, and a hey-nonino!
> . . . . .
> When birds do sing hey ding a ding:
> Sweet lovers love the Spring.

But the rhythm of Smith's poem is flat and nondanceable:

> A car warms
> its rusting hulk in a meadow . . .

The *sound* of the line comments critically on older poetic versions of spring wherein skipping and frolicking were the rule. In bringing to life our experience of a poem we almost invariably respond directly to sound and rhythm — the subjects taken up in Chapter 6.

But always in poetry everything happens at once. The *image* seems inseparable from the swing (or lack of swing) in the *rhythm*,

538

and neither is easily detached from our sense of the nature of the person speaking. For a reminder of our need to be attentive concurrently to sound, image, feeling, character, and challenge — a wide variety of elements — consider the following poem.

THOMAS HARDY (1840–1928)
The Man He Killed

Had he and I but met
By some old ancient inn,
We should have sat us down to wet
Right many a nipperkin!

But ranged as infantry, 5
And staring face to face,
I shot at him as he at me,
And killed him in his place.

I shot him dead because —
Because he was my foe. 10
Just so: my foe of course he was;
That's clear enough; although

He thought he'd list, perhaps,
Off-hand like — just as I —
Was out of work — had sold his traps — 15
No other reason why.

Yes; quaint and curious war is!
You shoot a fellow down
You'd treat, if met where any bar is,
Or help to half-a-crown. 20

As we engage with this poem, we imagine a single man's experience of fathoming for himself the relation between bits of his own behavior and feelings and the grand concerns of the larger society beyond him. We could approach the poem by thinking a little about how we place ourselves in relation to the state or nation. When do we have a "citizen feeling"? seeing our flag or the Capitol? seeing the Statue of Liberty? the Lincoln Memorial at night? watching an inauguration on television?

What is it like to be a loyal citizen? What are the elements of this
experience? Have we ever been puzzled about where we are in
relation to an official policy or a public decision or even the
country itself? "This is my country" — how much ownership do
we feel in the *my*?

We're building up for ourselves now, as we did often in Part
One, an idea of the circumstances and feelings of an imagined
human being — in this case an ex-soldier talking out loud about
how he makes sense of the relation between himself and the
public weal, public choices, issues, wars. Part of our attitude has
to focus on the confidence with which he answers the questions
that crop up in his mind. *Is* he confident? He seems to speak with
a sort of faintly overacted concentration, frowning, bemused, as
though he were saying, "I'm taking your question seriously, because I happen to be (within my limits — and don't think I'm
without pride, I've got as much of that as the next man!) a serious,
independent, thoughtful person." We *hear* that concentration in
the strained turning of the lines as they follow hesitations and
pauses on to the release of a wry, hand-lifted shrug. The movement of the words matches the movement of a mind, that of a
simple man seeming to think it through, seeming to work something out for himself.

An important activity for us in bringing this poem to life is
deciding how the man "solves" his problem. Here, after all, is
somebody trying to grasp a public mystery: Why do I shoot and
kill another man under the sponsorship of the state? What does it
mean that I do this? The answer amounts to only a gesture and a
tag phrase: War is paradoxical, "quaint and curious" (line 17).
The man meets his need by acting in a certain way, doing a sort
of philosophical turn, lifting a shoulder in a manner that says,
"We're not so dumb, you know. We at least know that we don't
know much, and when we admit that, we at least know a lot more
than your supereducated types — people who think they know
everything." When we live along his nerves we feel a bit more
clearly how most of us face our puzzles, bridge the gap between
our slim certainties and the complicated rationale of events: We
do so by accepting our socially imposed obligation to behave as
though everything does finally add up.

Our power to live inside this mind depends heavily on the
patterning of the poet's language. The speech rhythms give

formed substance to a human effort to comprehend what is beyond comprehension. The triviality the mind offers in such efforts is carried in the silly patness of the sounds — *foe, so, foe, although*. The small, messy cluster of rhymes introduces words as words into the equation at just the instant the man is discovering a word as a word — *foe* is "just a word," somebody's taught word. Just a foe, just so. *Foe*'s the right word. It is "right" because there is no way to move out of the suspension of thought in cliché, empty sound, or half-smiling gestures of reconciliation.

The poem comes to life in the mingling of our experience with its character, its rhythms of speech, and our imagining of the inner feelings that such rhythms must embody. As we've said often before, we practice our activities one at a time; when the poem is fully imagined, it comes together as a unity in which each part relates to every other part.

6

Sound and Rhythm

In the closing lines of James Wright's "A Blessing" (p. 291), as the speaker pets a black-and-white pony in a pasture, he sees himself as someone who could leave his body and become a flower:

And the light breeze moves me to caress her long ear
That is delicate as the skin over a girl's wrist.
Suddenly I realize
That if I stepped out of my body I would break
Into blossom.

One reason it's easy to bring these lines to life is that, as active readers, we have been responding, almost from the beginning of the poem, to the speaker's movement from his own consciousness into the feelings of the ponies ("They bow shyly. . . . They love each other," line 11). Another reason is that the meanings and associations we generate as we live into the words fill out our intuition of what it would be like to pass through such a moment. And still another reason is that our experience of the poem's sound helps us to enter the speaker's experience of momentary fragility, softness, lightness.

SOUND AND SENSE

The idea that the sound of a particular set of words, in combination with associations and meanings, can suggest a particular condition of feeling isn't unique to James Wright. Most poets are engrossed by the relationships between sound and meaning. Down through the years many have amused themselves with demonstrations of the ways in which, by subtle, dexterous management of sounds, a group of words can be transformed into almost physical equivalents for the action they describe. In a poetic "Essay on Criticism" the eighteenth-century English poet Alexander Pope showed how the use of a series of short, one-syllable words in an unpunctuated line of verse can slow the movement and create an impression of muscular strain:

> When Ajax strives some rock's vast weight to throw,
> The line too labours, and the words move slow.

In the same poem Pope produced line after line illustrating the impact of subtle alterations of rhythm and sound. Readers of poetry in English are accustomed to a basic dah-DUM rhythm — an unaccented syllable followed closely by an accented syllable in a way that creates a more or less regular meter. This metrical pattern is called the iamb; most of Hardy's "The Slow Nature" is written in iambics: "While Kit soon lost his mournful mood." But Pope's verbal pyrotechnics demonstrated that by altering this pattern in a manner that mutes the accented beats, a poet can create an impression of even-flowing speed:

> Soft is the strain when Zephyr gently blows,
> And the smooth stream in smoother numbers flows.

He also demonstrated that a different kind of alteration — one that emphasizes accented beats — can create an entirely opposite impression:

> But when loud surges lash the sounding shore,
> The hoarse, rough verse should like the torrent roar.

Sound and rhythm in relation to sense is an intriguing subject — and one of its more fascinating aspects is the linkage often felt between certain combinations of consonants and certain sensations. The consonant combination *sl*, as in *slick, slide, slush*, and so on, is held to suggest smoothness and wetness. Certain combinations of sounds are held to suggest darkness and sadness (for example, the double *o* in *doom, gloom, moody*, and so on). Scientists working in the field of phonetics have developed subtle analytical classifications of the sounds of human speech, and rigorous descriptions of sound patterns in poetry make frequent use of these classifications. (A thoroughgoing comparison of the sound patterns in the two passages just quoted from Alexander Pope would emphasize that the silken, swift-flowing texture of the first and the rough, broken texture of the second are directly traceable to specific differences in the kinds of speech sounds predominant in each.)

There is a technical term — onomatopoeia — to describe the use of words that are presumed to sound like what they mean: words such as *bowwow* and *hiss*. And most students of poetry can quote passages notable for sustained onomatopoeic effects. For instance, there's this from Edgar Allan Poe's "The Bells":

> Hear the sledges with the bells —
> Silver bells!
> What a world of merriment their melody foretells!
> How they tinkle, tinkle, tinkle,
> In the icy air of night!
> While the stars that oversprinkle
> All the heavens, seem to twinkle
> With a crystalline delight;
> Keeping time, time, time,
> In a sort of Runic rhyme,
> To the tintinnabulation that so musically wells
> From the bells, bells, bells, bells,
> Bells, bells, bells —
> From the jingling and the tinkling of the bells.

And an almost equally famous passage occurs in Alfred, Lord Tennyson's "Come down, O maid":

> Myriads of rivulets hurrying through the lawn,
> The moan of doves in immemorial elms,
> And murmuring of innumerable bees.

Onomatopoeia calls attention to itself and is hard to miss. But many less obvious arrangements of sound can play pivotal roles in shaping our experience as readers. In the third line of the third stanza of Thomas Hardy's "The Man He Killed" (p. 539), for example, we have a sense of the speaker pausing, turning back on himself, discovering on the spot some implications of his own thinking that he had missed. And a change of rhythm alerts us to that moment as a discovery. "Júst śo" sharply alters the pattern of stresses — unaccented syllable followed by accented syllable — that has been consistently maintained from the first line of the poem.

Or, for another example, in James Wright's "A Blessing" (p. 291), we sense a change in the speaker — toward a gentler, more yielding physicality — partly because the repeated sounds become notably light and soft. Here once again are the lines in question:

And the *l*ight breeze moves me to care*ss* her *l*ong ear
That i*s* de*l*icate a*s* the *s*kin over a gir*l's* wrist.
Sudden*ly* I rea*l*ize
That if Ĭ stepped ōut ōf m̆y bŏdў Í wōuld br̆eak
Ĭntō b*l*o̅ssom.

The stillness of the verbal music and the repeated *l* and *s* sounds alert us to the speaker's inner tremulousness. The grouping of lightly stressed syllables also creates a floating effect in the lines — "That if Ĭ stepped ōut ōf m̆y bŏdў Í wōuld br̆eak." Furthermore, the placing of the final verb *break* at the end of the line encourages a pause in which there is time for associated meanings of the word to nudge each other in our minds. Through association and anticipation a wide range of phrases and possible meanings come alive: break into tears, into pieces, into song, and so on. Each of those associations works to enrich the ultimate meanings of the change of feeling we evoke in the poem.

DESCRIBING EXPERIENCES OF SOUND

The experience of sound is, in short, a subtle blend of many kinds of responsiveness, and each kind can be refined and deepened through practice that concentrates on bringing poems to life. Technical terms are of real assistance in such practice. They help us to articulate our experience of sound. They function as pointers, enabling us to locate with precision significant moments or places where sound and sense echo and reinforce each other. They make it easier for us to grasp how our responses to verbal patterns interact with our responses to feeling, character, and ideas. As we develop familiarity with that interaction, we increase our capacity to live poems through as experiences of art.

The following are some technical terms useful in probing the interaction of feeling and verbal pattern in "A Blessing."

Stressed and unstressed syllables. These terms are used to describe gradations of heaviness and lightness, loudness and softness of accents on words and syllables. When we scan poems for their rhythmic patterns, we mark relatively unstressed syllables with a curved symbol, ˘ ; strongly stressed syllables are marked thus, ´ ; lightly stressed syllables are marked so, ˋ .

And the light breeze moves me to caress her long ear.

Alliteration. This term describes the repetition, usually within the same line or two, of initial consonant sounds in stressed syllables (*l*ight and *l*ong in the line just quoted).

Assonance. This term is used to describe the repetition, usually within the same line or two, of vowel sounds (br*ee*ze, m*e*, and *ea*r in line quoted).

End-stopped and run-on lines. In an end-stopped line both sense and punctuation seem to dictate a pause at the final word. In a run-on line both sense and absence of punctuation dictate uninterrupted progress to the beginning of the next line:

> That is delicate as the skin over a girl's wrist. (end-stopped)
> Suddenly I realize (run-on)

Sometimes we read a line simultaneously — and momentarily — as run-on *and* end-stopped. One possible meaning dictates a pause; another pushes us forward without pause. We have already looked at an example of such a line in "A Blessing":

> That if I stepped out of my body I would break
> Into blossom.

Liquid and explosive consonants. The liquid consonants are *l, m, n, r, th*, and *wh*, and often *v, f*, and the unvoiced *s* as well. The explosives are *b, d, g, k, p*, and *t*. Liquid consonants and the unvoiced *s* (wri*s*t, *s*kin) are dominant in all but the last six words of "A Blessing."

The array of technical terms used for the discussion of the music of poetry is indeed impressive and can be intimidating. In addition to terms describing patterns of stress, of repeated consonant and vowel sounds, and of line endings, there are terms describing a half-dozen or more different kinds of rhyme and an equal number of standard poetic meters (arrangements, that is, of stressed and unstressed syllables kept up fairly regularly for the whole length of a poem). A variety of fixed poetic forms exists — such as the sonnet, haiku, and limerick — in which the number of lines, the meter, and the pattern of the rhymes are precisely specified.

In the Glossary at the back of this book is a fuller account of some of the more frequently used technical terms concerning meter and sound. Each has its function, which is to help us relate verbal patterns to what we see and feel when we are looking out through language at the worlds it constructs. Apart from that function, none of the terms can give us much of a clue to any individual text as a potential poetic experience. We can light on this or that interesting feature of sound in a poem, and we can talk about it as though it were separable from everything else — but such talk is always misleading. It's not the liquid consonants and the unstressed syllables that matter in Wright's "A Blessing." What matters is that our activity as readers fuses these features of sound with our sense of how it would feel to be the speaker as he passes through this moment of change. To put it another way: Bringing a poem to life as an experience of sound means living through the ways in which all elements of the poem relate to and enrich each other.

ASKING QUESTIONS ABOUT SOUND AND RHYTHM

In the three poems that follow in this section, particular organizations of sound help to shape our understanding, first, of how we should say a line or a phrase and, second, of the nature of the human attitude and feeling in the passage. The purpose of these exercises is to clarify how organizations of sound actually work. The questions we'll concentrate on are: Which features of sound help shape our understanding of the attitudes and feelings in the poem? How exactly does sound interact with other elements to show us what to imagine and how to read?

The best way to use the reflections and queries that follow the three texts is as suggestions about how to begin probing your own experience of the poems' sounds. You need to be patient with yourself as you probe; the experience you are trying to describe can't really be packaged as a set of quick answers to somebody else's tentative questions. What you are aiming at is a thought-out response, putting into words the interactions of sound and sense that matter to you as you bring to life the language of the poem.

SYLVIA PLATH   (1932–1963)

Mushrooms

Overnight, very
Whitely, discreetly,
Very quietly

Our toes, our noses
Take hold on the loam,   5
Acquire the air.

Nobody sees us,
Stops us, betrays us;
The small grains make room.

Soft fists insist on   10
Heaving the needles,
The leafy bedding,

Even the paving.
Our hammers, our rams,
Earless and eyeless,   15

Perfectly voiceless,
Widen the crannies,
Shoulder through holes. We

Diet on water,
On crumbs of shadow,   20
Bland-mannered, asking

Little or nothing.
So many of us!
So many of us!

We are shelves, we are   25
Tables, we are meek,
We are edible,

Nudgers and shovers
In spite of ourselves.
Our kind multiplies: 30

We shall by morning
Inherit the earth.
Our foot's in the door.

Questions

1. In the first stanza of "Mushrooms," the sound of each of the words contains an echo of the sound of one of the other words in the stanza. And the echoes and repetitions continue thereafter. Make a list of the echoes and repetitions heard in the poem.
2. Subtly and indirectly these repetitions and echoes tell us things about the speaker — the collective "we" of mush-roomness. What things do they tell us? How in this poem do sounds come to resemble qualities and characteristics? How does all this repetition help to characterize the imagined behavior and nature of mushrooms? Write your response and then compare it with the one that follows.

Response

EDITOR: Sometimes the repetitions in the poem are just that ("So many of us! / So many of us!" lines 23–24). Sometimes they are internal rhymes or half-rhymes (overnight/whitely, 1–2; whitely/quietly, 2–3; toes/noses, 4; sees us/stops us, 7–8; fists/insist, 10; earless/eyeless, 15). Sometimes they are repeated phrasal pat-terns ("We are shelves, we are / Tables," 25–26). Everywhere the ear notices this irregular but dogged duplication, not flashy or witty or noisy, neither exciting nor surprising, only — every-where — unremitting. The sound becomes a sign of a special kind of indefatigability, a ceaseless, unflagging return to — to what?

Well, a return to the speaker's project, which is simply to push and push, throb and throb, upward ever upward, patiently, tenaciously, until there's a nose through a cranny, a soft fist into needles, a foot in the door. The "speaker" is, of course, not a person, not a single individual of any sort, but rather a collective body of nudgers and shovers which, when it appears above ground, will be called, by human creatures, a patch of mush-rooms. The sound — the unflagging, almost boring repeti-tions — links up with a mindless, stick-to-it ramming and bam-ming that's imagined as the core of mushroomness. Poking and pounding, helpless in their enforced drivenness, these soft fists are absolutely choiceless, imprisoned in the dull imperatives of natural process. Their sound is the beat of a level of existence that human creatures are heedless of — the level of existence that the poem invites us to bring to life. When we imagine this meek, edible "we," speakers who unstoppably push, repeat, push some more, we are edging inside the processes of nature, life maintenance itself. We sense the continuities that link infinitudes of oscillating hammers and rams all through the universe with the bumping redundancies of our own dogged hearts.

JOHN DONNE   (1572–1631)
Batter my heart

Batter my heart, three-personed God; for You
As yet but knock, breathe, shine, and seek to mend;
That I may rise and stand, o'erthrow me, and bend
Your force to break, blow, burn, and make me new.
I, like an usurped town, to another due,   5
Labor to admit You, but O, to no end;
Reason, Your viceroy in me, me should defend,
But is captived, and proves weak or untrue.
Yet dearly I love You, and would be loved fain,
But am betrothed unto Your enemy.   10
Divorce me, untie or break that knot again;
Take me to You, imprison me, for I,
Except You enthrall me, never shall be free,
Nor ever chaste, except You ravish me.

Questions

1. Make notes on the relation between the sound of *batter* at the start of the poem and the attitude of the speaker. What kind of person *is* the speaker? How do his sounds — his use of *batter, break,* and *burn,* his way of addressing his God — help to characterize him?

2. The sound of "break, blow, burn, and make me new" (line 4) differs considerably from that of "Yet dearly I love you . . ." (9). How is this difference best described? What movements of feeling — *changes* of feeling — does the difference in sound help to express?

EMILY DICKINSON   (1830–1886)

I like to see it lap the Miles

I like to see it lap the Miles —
And lick the Valleys up —
And stop to feed itself at Tanks —
And then — prodigious step

Around a Pile of Mountains —   5
And supercilious peer
In Shanties — by the sides of Roads —
And then a Quarry pare

To fit its Ribs
And crawl between   10
Complaining all the while
In horrid — hooting stanza —
Then chase itself down Hill —

And neigh like Boanerges —°
Then — punctual as a Star   15
Stop — docile and omnipotent
At its own stable door —

14 *Boanerges*: A name that Christ gave to his disciples James and John meaning "Sons of thunder" or "Sons of tumult." (See Mark 3:17.)

Questions

1.   Although its pace changes once or twice, this poem from start almost to finish keeps to a constant rocking rhythm — dah-DUM, dah-DUM, dah-DUM. But all at once, in the next to last line, comes an abrupt reversal. Instead of another line beginning dah-DUM, we're surprised by DUM.

      punctual as a Star
     Stop — docile and omnipotent

     What is the effect of this unanticipated change of rhythmic pattern?

2.   In the third stanza the speaker sees a resemblance between the hooting whistle of an engine and a stanza itself. Implicit is the notion that a whistle stands in the same relation to the engine that a poet stands in relation to her poem. How can

this be? What resemblances can you see between the relation of a whistle to an engine and that of a poet to a poem?

3. By making such a comparison — between herself and an engine whistle — the poet-speaker tells us things both about her own nature and about the experience of being a master of sound and movement. What things does she tell us?

FOR FURTHER STUDY

JOHN MILTON   (1608–1674)
On the Late Massacre in Piedmont °

Avenge, O Lord, thy slaughtered saints, whose bones
   Lie scattered on the Alpine mountains cold,
   Even them who kept thy truth so pure of old
   When all our fathers worshiped stocks and stones,
Forget not: in thy book record their groans   5
   Who were thy sheep and in their ancient fold
   Slain by the bloody Piedmontese that rolled
   Mother with infant down the rocks. Their moans
The vales redoubled to the hills, and they
   To Heaven. Their martyred blood and ashes sow   10
   O'er all th' Italian fields where still doth sway
The triple tyrant:° that from these may grow   *the Pope*
   A hundredfold, who having learnt thy way
   Early may fly the Babylonian woe.°

On the Late Massacre . . . : Milton is protesting the killing of over 1,000 Waldensians, members of a Puritan sect, in 1655.   14 *Babylonian woe:* The wicked city of Babylon, whose destruction is foretold in Revelation 17–18, was equated by Protestants with the Catholic church.

WILLIAM BUTLER YEATS   (1865–1939)
Leda and the Swan °

A sudden blow: the great wings beating still
Above the staggering girl, her thighs caressed

Leda and the Swan: In the form of a swan, the Greek god Zeus came to Leda, fathering Helen (over whom the Trojan War was fought) and Clytemnestra (murderer of her husband, Agamemnon).

By the dark webs, her nape caught in his bill,
He holds her helpless breast upon his breast.

How can those terrified vague fingers push   5
The feathered glory from her loosening thighs?
And how can body, laid in that white rush,
But feel the strange heart beating where it lies?

A shudder in the loins engenders there
The broken wall, the burning roof and tower   10
And Agamemnon dead.

                  Being so caught up,
So mastered by the brute blood of the air,
Did she put on his knowledge with his power
Before the indifferent beak could let her drop?

WILLIAM CARLOS WILLIAMS   (1883–1963)
The Dance

In Breughel's great picture, The Kermess,
the dancers go round, they go round and
around, the squeal and the blare and the
tweedle of bagpipes, a bugle and fiddles
tipping their bellies (round as the thick-   5
sided glasses whose wash they impound)
their hips and bellies off balance
to turn them. Kicking and rolling about
the Fair Grounds, swinging their butts, those
shanks must be sound to bear up under such   10
rollicking measures, prance as they dance
in Breughel's great picture, The Kermess.

7

Tone

In bringing to life the language of poems, stories, and plays, we often focus on words that reveal the writer's attitudes. Attitudes are important matters in every poem — poets' attitudes toward the persons, subjects, or situations their poems confront, poets' attitudes toward their readers and toward themselves. Close imagining means, in part, stepping inside these attitudes, understanding them from within. And we do this by focusing intensely on the precise way things are said — upon choices of words.

"The Death of a Soldier," by Wallace Stevens, expresses attitudes toward both the cycle of human existence and conventional efforts to find meaning in the cycle. The initial focus is on the difference between memorialized and unmemorialized deaths.

WALLACE STEVENS   (1879–1955)
The Death of a Soldier

Life contracts and death is expected,
As in a season of autumn.
The soldier falls.

He does not become a three-days personage,
Imposing his separation,   5
Calling for pomp.

Death is absolute and without memorial,
As in a season of autumn,
When the wind stops,

When the wind stops and, over the heavens,   10
The clouds go, nevertheless,
In their direction.

Living into the phrase "three-days personage" (line 4) helps
bring to life the poet's attitude in this poem. For a second or two
we may be uncertain about the meaning of the words. What *is* a
"three-days personage"? One part of the answer has to be that
the phrase is the poet's label for military bigwigs — "personages" whose names everybody knows and whose deaths become
great public events that stretch over days. (First come the newspaper headlines and television reports telling us about the place
and causes of death; next we hear about the preparations for the
funeral and the departures of world leaders for the funeral site;
next comes the media report on the funeral and burial themselves.)

But we haven't brought the attitude to life simply by explaining to ourselves that "three-day personages" is the poet's name
for military celebrities. We have to hear the phrase as an expression of attitude toward the celebrity and the ritual, and that
means hearing its tone.

We hear tone all the time in daily life. When we say to someone, "Don't take that tone with me," we're telling that person
we're onto the attitude toward us as expressed in words, and we
don't like it. We're asserting our ability to penetrate the surface
(the spoken word) and dig out the underlying attitude. And we're
also implicitly saying that we care less about the words than
about the snottiness at their source. In reading, though, we don't
race to the attitude, ignoring the word. We savor the word or
phrase because its tone not only defines the attitude but also
helps us imagine a particular speaker — and even guess at the
subject that is about to emerge.

It's that way with "three-days personage." The poet is drawing a contrast between a death that is obscure and unmarked and
a death that occasions public commotion. Plain, predictable,
unmelodramatized, an ordinary soldier's death possesses the
dignity of natural process itself. It doesn't lead anyone into
extravagant notions of human importance or permanence. It
calls for nothing, imposes nothing, except recognition of the
absoluteness of our human end.

The death of a "three-days personage" is another story altogether, and we bring that story to life by calling up the politely expressed but nevertheless genuine distaste that we hear in the poet's tone. When we focus on that distaste, we feel the words physically, as a way of holding the mouth while the words are uttered. We hear an extension of the sound that suggests an edge of mockery.

Responding fully to tone, living into an attitude, requires considerable care. In the case of "The Death of a Soldier" we have to clarify for ourselves whether the distaste we're responding to is personal or impersonal, whether we hear it as hostile to military hierarchy, as antimilitary, antihype, or anti- something else altogether. (In my opinion the distaste is impersonal, not really concerned with military hierarchy, and directed less at hype than at sentimental ceremonies exaggerating the significance of any single human life.) To clarify such matters we have to engage all the language of the poem, determining for ourselves how the context of the phrase — the surrounding words — gives definition to the attitude in (the tone of) "three-days personage." Everywhere, in collaboration with the writer, our attention is sharply directed at the words themselves.

To repeat, the word *tone* is a tool. We use it as a means of focusing those moments in a poem at which the imagined sound of a voice seems to become a key to the content of the poet's attitude. The voice we hear need not be that of the poet; it can be that of a created character who is entirely separate from the poet. If we turn back, for example, to the fifth stanza of Robert Browning's "Soliloquy of the Spanish Cloister" (p. 167), we find an example of such a character:

> When he finishes refection,
>   Knife and fork he never lays
> Cross-wise, to my recollection,
>   As I do, in Jesu's praise.

As active readers of this stanza we hear the monk's pride in his pious placing of his knife and fork in the shape of a cross, and we sense, through the tone, that the poet considers this pride absurd, smug, prissy. We are not explicitly told this. The speaker himself certainly doesn't know that he sounds smug. But his words betray his smugness, and we grasp that the poet sees him as a fussy, self-satisfied, arrogant man utterly incapable of distinguishing true faith from empty religiosity. We take the smug-ness of "As I do" as a sign of the poet's firmly critical attitude toward the character. Through tone we discover exactly what kind of man the poet Browning's monk is and exactly what Browning thinks of him. In "The Death of a Soldier" — again through tone — we learn exactly how Stevens regards the pomp of public mourning and how that attitude fits into a broader philosophy of life. In both works reader and writer together have created tone as a significant element of the total imaginative experience.

TONE IN RELATION TO CHARACTER

Reading for tone means, then, becoming alert to the ways in which we hear particular words, phrases, or lines in a poem. It means focusing hard on our experience of language.

Often as we listen we're simultaneously shaping an idea of a person — an individual speaker whom we imagine saying the words we're reading, taking up the positions and attitudes im-plicit in the tones we hear. Sometimes, in fact, before we can explain to ourselves what we seem to be hearing, we have to summon up a certain kind of human being — the person to whom the attitude or look or gesture that fits the tone would be appropriate. The words that are helpful in describing the tone of a phrase — neutral or patronizing or friendly or pleading or scornful or commanding or amused or meditative or apologetic or exuberant or smug or a hundred others — turn out to be use-ful in characterizing the person who is speaking.

Always, though, our starting point is with language itself — a sound of voice in the words that triggers our imagination as listeners. As we hold that sound alive in our minds, it functions like a magnet, drawing other verbal details to it. And out of these materials we construct our understanding of the poet's attitudes.

ASKING QUESTIONS ABOUT TONE

In the first of the three poems that follow in this section, the speaker is issuing an invitation to a friend. In the second the speaker, a soldier in a rifle class, is talking to himself and reflecting on the voice of his instructor. In the third the speaker is saying farewell to a beloved. The tone of each of these speakers is highly individual and does much to shape our experience of the respective poems. The questions after the texts ask you to focus on specific language as you bring to life the tone and the speaker's attitudes.

BEN JONSON (1572?–1637)
Inviting a Friend to Supper

Tonight, grave sir, both my poor house and I
Do equally desire your company;
Not that we think us worthy such a guest,
But that your worth will dignify our feast,
With those that come, whose grace may make that seem   5
Something, which else could hope for no esteem.
It is the fair acceptance, sir, creates
The entertainment perfect, not the cates.
Yet shall you have, to rectify your palate,
An olive, capers, or some better salad   10
Ushering the mutton; with a short-legged hen,
If we can get her, full of eggs; and then,
Lemons, and wine for sauce: to these, a cony
Is not to be despaired of for our money;
And though fowl now be scarce, yet there are clerks,   15
The sky not falling, think we may have larks.
I'll tell you of more, and lie, so you will come:
Of partridge, pheasant, woodcock, of which some
May yet be there; and godwit if we can:
Gnat, rail, and ruff, too. Howsoe'er, my man   20
Shall read a piece of Virgil, Tacitus,
Livy, or of some better book to us,
Of which we'll speak our minds, amidst our meat;
And I'll profess no verses to repeat:
To this, if aught appear, which I not know of,   25
That will the pastry, not my paper, show of.
Digestive cheese, and fruit there sure will be;
But that which most doth take my muse and me,
Is a pure cup of rich Canary wine,
Which is the Mermaid's now, but shall be mine: 30
Of which had Horace, or Anacreon tasted,

Their lives, as do their lines, till now had lasted.
Tobacco, nectar, or the Thespian spring,
Are all but Luther's beer, to this I sing.
Of this we will sup free, but moderately,   35
And we will have no Pooly or Parrot by;
Nor shall our cups make any guilty men,
But at our parting, we will be as when
We innocently met. No simple word
That shall be uttered at our mirthful board   40
Shall make us sad next morning, or affright
The liberty that we'll enjoy tonight.

Question

How would you describe the speaker's attitude toward his audience in this poem? Point to words and phrases in which you hear the tone vividly and tell what you hear. Compare your description to those that follow.

Responses

COLLEGE SENIOR: The voice first heard by the reader of "Inviting a Friend to Supper" is that of an apparently mild, unassuming host inviting and trying to persuade a hesitant, wished-for guest to come to an informal dinner party. "It is the fair acceptance, sir, creates / The entertainment perfect" (lines 7–8). Here one listens to a self-abasing, humble man of "poor house" (1) and (according to himself) of little objectively visible worth. He is trying to squeeze out the acceptance of this grave or, more specifically, skeptical man. And the "fair acceptance" is obviously not forthcoming. When the reader catches wind of the slightly too highly piled humility of Mr. Host and compares it with the not slight skepticism of Mr. Grave, the poem becomes more than the situation of a simple invitation from a friend to a friend. Perhaps "Inviting a Friend to Supper" might better be called "Inviting a Professor-Colleague to Supper." The audience witnesses a lot of pushing and pulling — jockeying for position.

First the audience hears the note of respect — but the tone does begin to change. The host moves from seeing himself perceived as simply of humble taste to realizing that in this grave man's eyes he may be completely contemptible. He ups his offer. He moves from tempting his guest with a simple salad to tempting him with game aplenty. And there will be more than game. Instead of pheasant there will be some light good-time larking around ("And though fowl now be scarce, yet there are clerks, / The sky not falling, think we may have larks," 15–16). The host is continually changing his tactics and tone. He moves from humility to the grand manner but always with a playful reserve for larking around. If the suggestion of a full table provokes no response, what will? Virgil, Tacitus, Livy? The listener hears: "You want lofty discourse, you got it." A little Virgil or Livy over steak? A little Greek theater and beer?

But no, only at the end does the host seem to find the root of the grave man's hesitation. The host is a fundamental believer in what he describes as "no simple word" (39) that neither "make[s] us sad next morning, or affright[s] / The liberty that we'll enjoy tonight" (41–42). There won't be any bemoaning of man's fate or moralizing about his nature at my party — so concludes our host. And the audience hears finally neither the voice of an artificially genuflecting man nor the voice of a stodgy pedant but the voice of someone hoping that all his friends and acquaintances, whatever their particular tastes, will enjoy an unrestrained, unrestricted moment of fraternity. Accept or don't accept, as you wish. That is the tone. The abasement is gone.

EDITOR: The poet is addressing a friend, inviting him to supper, and at first it seems that his attitude is that of extreme deference. Calling somebody "grave sir" (line 1) implies distance if not reverence, and that implication is reinforced by the host speaking of himself as unworthy of "such a guest" (3).

Soon enough we realize, though, that the speaker's tone is playful, and that his lowly attitude at the start is a genial joke — a way of expressing witty affection. The speaker isn't seriously prostrating himself but instead amusing himself and his friend by improvising on two themes: his own pretended inferiority to his friend and his need to produce an extravaganza if he's to deserve his friend's company. What a party he imagines! A wildly inventive menu from gnats to larks, and pastry that's better than poetry. He even has a man standing by to read excerpts from the classics when conversation slows.

How do we know what lies behind all this fancifulness? That becomes clearer as the invitation develops. Professions of inequality disappear; the speaker imagines himself and his friend speaking their minds straightforwardly to each other as they relish their meal (23), and in the closing lines he evokes a sort of moral model for a night of drink and talk: no malicious gossip, no meanness toward others, companionable merriment absolutely clean of spite. By turns joshing and complimentary, teasing and earnest, always good-natured, outgoing, and welcoming, the tone of "Inviting a Friend to Supper" is perhaps best described as unsentimentally warm and affectionate — in short, as civilized.

HENRY REED   (b. 1914)
Naming of Parts

Today we have naming of parts. Yesterday,
We had daily cleaning. And tomorrow morning,
We shall have what to do after firing. But today,
Today we have naming of parts. Japonica
Glistens like coral in all of the neighboring gardens,   5
       And today we have naming of parts.

This is the lower sling swivel. And this
Is the upper sling swivel, whose use you will see,
When you are given your slings. And this is the piling swivel,
Which in your case you have not got. The branches   10
Hold in the gardens their silent, eloquent gestures,
       Which in our case we have not got.

This is the safety-catch, which is always released
With an easy flick of the thumb. And please do not let me
See anyone using his finger. You can do it quite easy   15
If you have any strength in your thumb. The blossoms
Are fragile and motionless, never letting anyone see
       Any of them using their finger.

And this you can see is the bolt. The purpose of this
Is to open the breech, as you see. We can slide it   20
Rapidly backwards and forwards: we call this
Easing the spring. And rapidly backwards and forwards
The early bees are assaulting and fumbling the flowers:
       They call it easing the Spring.

They call it easing the Spring: it is perfectly easy   25
If you have any strength in your thumb: like the bolt,
And the breech, and the cocking-piece, and the point of balance,
Which in our case we have not got; and the almond-blossom
Silent in all of the gardens and the bees going backwards and
    forwards,
           For today we have naming of parts.   30

Questions

1. How many voices do you hear in this poem? What differences between these voices are you aware of?
2. Which voice seems to you likely to be that of the poet? What are his attitudes?
3. Describe the overall tone of the poem.

MICHAEL DRAYTON   (1563–1631)

Since there's no help,
come let us kiss and part

Since there's no help, come let us kiss and part;
Nay, I have done, you get no more of me;
And I am glad, yea, glad with all my heart,
That thus so cleanly I myself can free.
Shake hands for ever, cancel all our vows,   5
And when we meet at any time again,
Be it not seen in either of our brows
That we one jot of former love retain.
Now at the last gasp of love's latest breath,
When, his pulse failing, passion speechless lies,   10
When faith is kneeling by his bed of death,
And innocence is closing up his eyes,
Now if thou wouldst, when all have given him over,
From death to life thou might'st him yet recover.

Questions

1. Describe how you hear the speaker's voice in line 2 ("Nay, I have done . . .").
2. Characterize both the speaker's tone and his attitude to the person addressed.

3. Some readers of "Since there's no help" bring to life a change of tone beginning at line 9. Do you hear a change at this point, and if so, how would you describe it?

FOR FURTHER STUDY

ROBERT BROWNING   (1812–1889)

The Bishop Orders His Tomb
at Saint Praxed's Church

Rome, 15 —

Vanity, saith the preacher, vanity!°
Draw round my bed: is Anselm keeping back?
Nephews — sons mine . . . ah God, I know not! Well —
She, men would have to be your mother once,
Old Gandolf envied me, so fair she was!   5
What's done is done, and she is dead beside,
Dead long ago, and I am Bishop since,
And as she died so must we die ourselves,
And thence ye may perceive the world's a dream.
Life, how and what is it? As here I lie   10
In this state-chamber, dying by degrees,
Hours and long hours in the dead night, I ask
"Do I live, am I dead?" Peace, peace seems all.
Saint Praxed's ever was the church for peace;
And so, about this tomb of mine. I fought   15
With tooth and nail to save my niche, ye know:
— Old Gandolf cozened me, despite my care;
Shrewd was that snatch from out the corner south
He graced his carrion with, God curse the same!
Yet still my niche is not so cramped but thence   20
One sees the pulpit o' the epistle-side,
And somewhat of the choir, those silent seats,
And up into the aery dome where live
The angels, and a sunbeam's sure to lurk:
And I shall fill my slab of basalt there,   25
And 'neath my tabernacle take my rest,
With those nine columns round me, two and two,

---

1 *Vanity . . . vanity:* An echo of Ecclesiastes 1:2, which reads, "Vanity of vanities, says the Preacher, vanity of vanities! All is vanity."

The odd one at my feet where Anselm stands:
Peach-blossom marble all, the rare, the ripe
As fresh-poured red wine of a mighty pulse.   30
— Old Gandolf with his paltry onion-stone,
Put me where I may look at him! True peach,
Rosy and flawless: how I earned the prize!
Draw close: that conflagration of my church
— What then? So much was saved if aught were missed!   35
My sons, ye would not be my death? Go dig
The white-grape vineyard where the oil-press stood,
Drop water gently till the surface sink,
And if ye find . . . Ah God, I know not, I! . . .
Bedded in store of rotten fig-leaves soft,   40
And corded up in a tight olive-frail,
Some lump, ah God, of *lapis lazuli*,
Big as a Jew's head cut off at the nape,
Blue as a vein o'er the Madonna's breast . . .
Sons, all have I bequeathed you, villas, all,   45
That brave Frascati villa with its bath,
So, let the blue lump poise between my knees,
Like God the Father's globe on both his hands
Ye worship in the Jesu Church° so gay,
For Gandolf shall not choose but see and burst!   50
Swift as a weaver's shuttle fleet our years:°
Man goeth to the grave, and where is he?
Did I say basalt for my slab, sons? Black —
'Twas ever antique-black I meant! How else
Shall ye contrast my frieze to come beneath?   55
The bas-relief in bronze ye promised me,
Those Pans and Nymphs ye wot of, and perchance
Some tripod, thyrsus, with a vase or so,
The Saviour at his sermon on the mount,
Saint Praxed in a glory, and one Pan   60
Ready to twitch the Nymph's last garment off,
And Moses with the tables . . . but I know
Ye mark me not! What do they whisper thee,
Child of my bowels, Anselm? Ah, ye hope
To revel down my villas while I gasp   65

48–49 *Like God the Father's . . . Jesu Church*: The figure of God the Father in the sculpture group of the Trinity in the Jesuit baroque church Il Gesù holds a large globe carved from a single piece of lapis lazuli.   51 *Swift . . . our years*: An echo of Job 7:6, which reads, "My days are swifter than a weaver's shuttle, and come to their end without hope."

Bricked o'er with beggar's moldy travertine
Which Gandolf from his tomb-top chuckles at!
Nay, boys, ye love me — all of jasper, then!
'T is jasper ye stand pledged to, lest I grieve
My bath must needs be left behind, alas!   70
One block, pure green as a pistachio-nut,
There's plenty jasper somewhere in the world —
And have I not Saint Praxed's ear to pray
Horses for ye, and brown Greek manuscripts,
And mistresses with great smooth marbly limbs?   75
— That's if ye carve my epitaph aright,
Choice Latin, picked phrase, Tully's every word,
No gaudy ware like Gandolf's second line —
Tully, my masters? Ulpian° serves his need!
And then how I shall lie through centuries,   80
And hear the blessed mutter of the mass,
And see God made and eaten all day long,°
And feel the steady candle-flame, and taste
Good strong thick stupefying incense-smoke!
For as I lie here, hours of the dead night,   85
Dying in state and by such slow degrees,
I fold my arms as if they clasped a crook,
And stretch my feet forth straight as stone can point,
And let the bedclothes, for a mortcloth, drop
Into great laps and folds of sculptor's-work: 90
And as yon tapers dwindle, and strange thoughts
Grow, with a certain humming in my ears,
About the life before I lived this life,
And this life too, popes, cardinals and priests,
Saint Praxed at his sermon on the mount,   95
Your tall pale mother with her talking eyes,
And new-found agate urns as fresh as day,
And marble's language, Latin pure, discreet,
— Aha, ELUCESCEBAT quoth our friend?
No Tully, said I, Ulpian at the best!   100
Evil and brief hath been my pilgrimage.°
All *lapis*, all, son! Else I give the Pope

77–79 *Tully's . . . Ulpian*: Tully (the Roman author and statesman Cicero) wrote in a style considered superior to that of his later compatriot Ulpian.   82 *God . . . long*: The transubstantiation of the bread and wine during celebration of the mass.   101 *Evil . . . pilgrimage*: An echo of Genesis 47:9, in which Jacob says, "Few and evil have been the days of the years of my life."

My villas! Will ye ever eat my heart?
Ever your eyes were as a lizard's quick,
They glitter like your mother's for my soul,   105
Or ye would heighten my impoverished frieze,
Piece out its starved design, and fill my vase
With grapes, and add a vizor and a Term,
And to the tripod ye would tie a lynx
That in his struggle throws the thyrsus down,   110
To comfort me on my entablature
Whereon I am to lie till I must ask
"Do I live, am I dead?" There, leave me, there!
For ye have stabbed me with ingratitude
To death — ye wish it — God, ye wish it! Stone —   115
Gritstone, a-crumble! Clammy squares which sweat
As if the corpse they keep were oozing through —
And no more *lapis* to delight the world!
Well, go! I bless ye. Fewer tapers there,
But in a row: and, going, turn your backs   120
— Ay, like departing altar-ministrants,
And leave me in my church, the church for peace,
That I may watch at leisure if he leers —
Old Gandolf, at me, from his onion-stone,
As still he envied me, so fair she was!   125

JOHN CLARE   (1793–1864)
Badger

When midnight comes a host of dogs and men
Go out and track the badger to his den,
And put a sack within the hole, and lie
Till the old grunting badger passes by.
He comes and hears — they let the strongest loose.   5
The old fox hears the noise and drops the goose.
The poacher shoots and hurries from the cry,
And the old hare half wounded buzzes by.
They get a forked stick to bear him down
And clap the dogs and take him to the town,   10
And bait him all the day with many dogs,
And laugh and shout and fright the scampering hogs.
He runs along and bites at all he meets:
They shout and hollo down the noisy streets.

He turns about to face the loud uproar 15
And drives the rebels to their very door.
The frequent stone is hurled where'er they go;
When badgers fight, then everyone's a foe.
The dogs are clapped and urged to join the fray;
The badger turns and drives them all away. 20
Though scarcely half as big, demure and small,
He fights with dogs for hours and beats them all.
The heavy mastiff, savage in the fray,
Lies down and licks his feet and turns away.
The bulldog knows his match and waxes cold, 25
The badger grins and never leaves his hold.
He drives the crowd and follows at their heels
And bites them through — the drunkard swears and reels.

The frighted women take the boys away,
The blackguard laughs and hurries on the fray. 30
He tries to reach the woods, an awkward race,
But sticks and cudgels quickly stop the chase.
He turns again and drives the noisy crowd
And beats the many dogs in noises loud.
He drives away and beats them every one, 35
And then they loose them all and set them on.
He falls as dead and kicked by dogs and men,
Then starts and grins and drives the crowd again;
Till kicked and torn and beaten out he lies
And leaves his hold and cackles, groans, and dies. 40

ELIZABETH BISHOP   (1911–1979)
Filling Station

Oh, but it is dirty!
— this little filling station,
oil-soaked, oil-permeated
to a disturbing, over-all
black translucency. 5
Be careful with that match!

Father wears a dirty,
oil-soaked monkey suit
that cuts him under the arms,
and several quick and saucy 10
and greasy sons assist him

(it's a family filling station),
all quite thoroughly dirty.

Do they live in the station?
It has a cement porch   15
behind the pumps, and on it
a set of crushed and grease-
impregnated wickerwork;
on the wicker sofa
a dirty dog, quite comfy.   20

Some comic books provide
the only note of color—
of certain color. They lie
upon a big dim doily
draping a taboret   25
(part of the set), beside
a big hirsute begonia.

Why the extraneous plant?
Why the taboret?
Why, oh why, the doily?   30
(Embroidered in daisy stitch
with marguerites, I think,
and heavy with gray crochet.)

Somebody embroidered the doily.
Somebody waters the plant,   35
or oils it, maybe. Somebody
arranges the rows of cans
so that they softly say:
ESSO — SO — SO — SO —
to high-strung automobiles.   40
Somebody loves us all.

8

Imagery

Sight, sound, taste, touch, smell — these are our means of sensing the physicality of the world. For some of us awareness of physicality is nearly always vivid. For others that awareness comes only in unusual circumstances — when we're taking in a majestic view or an exotic new taste or when we're surprised momentarily by, say, the weight of a small object made of solid gold. The language of poetry functions much of the time as a kind of wake-up call to the senses, alerting us to the presence and interest of the physical world. It's predominantly a language of images — clear, concrete words representing objects that are taken in through the senses. As active readers we engage these images by evoking the sense experience associated with them.

Just as sense experience varies from person to person, differences exist in people's power to communicate the nature of their physical experience to others. As readers of poems our goal isn't to arrive at consensus about the effect of any single image. It is instead to engage the images as we read, working to evoke for ourselves the physical experience we feel that the images represent.

WILLIAM CARLOS WILLIAMS   (1883–1963)
This Is Just to Say

I have eaten
the plums
that were in
the icebox

and which   5
you were probably
saving
for breakfast

Forgive me
they were delicious   10
so sweet
and so cold

   We can tell ourselves that this little poem uses imagery of
fruit. But the only way to bring the poem to life is to summon to
our own imagination the plumminess of those plums — their
coolness and slipperiness on the palm; the shiny-dark streak on
their skin where fingers slide condensation away; their mouth-
filling textures: chewiness, juice, meat. We begin as readers by
making certain what kind of images are central in a poem. We
move on by using our direct knowledge of the pertinent objects
and actions to create them as sense experiences.

SUMMONING SENSE EXPERIENCE

   On occasion a poet will offer us indirectly a kind of model of
the sort of activity readers engage in when they call up sense
experience from images. In her poem "Balms," Amy Clampitt
does just that. She writes about the impact of seeing a particular
illustration in a nineteenth-century book on color. The book was
displayed in a glass case in a rare book room — the kind of place
that's carefully sanitized to lessen wear and tear on old paper
and bindings. The illustration, presumably of bars of color, was
based on "garden nasturtium hues." And the sight of the colors,
together with her personal memories of nasturtiums, took instant hold of the poet's imagination:

        Sudden as
   on hands and knees
   I felt the smell of them
   suffuse the catacomb
   so much of us lives in —
   horned, pungent, velvet-
   eared succulence, a perfume
   without hokum, the intimate
   of trudging earthworms

and everyone's last end's
unnumbered, milling tenants.

All at once here a particular corner of the physical world
becomes extraordinarily vivid to the speaker *as physical sensation.*
The combination of an image, personal associations, and remembered sense experiences has the effect of an awakening. The
speaker becomes sharply conscious of the difference between a
relatively blank, unphysical sense of surroundings and heightened awareness of the reality that lives most powerfully in sight,
smell, taste, touch, and sound. Through the encounter

> pure hue set loose
unearthly gusts of odor
from earthbound nasturtiums.

This poem wasn't written, of course, as a case study on how
to bring an image to life. It's not trying to teach us how to respond to images. But we can learn things from it. It shows us,
from inside, a mind responding to an image, hooking it up with
memory, living close to it, calling it forth as felt sensation. What
the poet does with that bar of color — moving from it to flowers,
fragrance, texture of earth — is much like what a reader does in
bringing to life the plums in Williams's "This Is Just to Say." It's a
job of evocation that involves vivifying simultaneously the associations we bring to words and to things and actions.

ASKING QUESTIONS ABOUT IMAGERY

Each of the three poems in this section is remarkable partly
for the power of its images. The questions following the poems
focus on the sensations that we bring to life through those
images. Your purpose is to name the sensations as evocatively as
possible in your own language.

ELIZABETH BISHOP   (1911–1979)
The Armadillo

For Robert Lowell

This is the time of year
when almost every night

the frail, illegal fire balloons appear.
Climbing the mountain height,

rising toward a saint   5
still honored in these parts,
the paper chambers flush and fill with light
that comes and goes, like hearts.

Once up against the sky it's hard
to tell them from the stars —   10
planets, that is — the tinted ones:
Venus going down, or Mars,

or the pale green one. With a wind,
they flare and falter, wobble and toss;
but if it's still they steer between   15
the kite sticks of the Southern Cross,

receding, dwindling, solemnly
and steadily forsaking us,
or, in the downdraft from a peak,
suddenly turning dangerous.   20

Last night another big one fell.
It splattered like an egg of fire
against the cliff behind the house.
The flame ran down. We saw the pair

of owls who nest there flying up   25
and up, their whirling black-and-white
stained bright pink underneath, until
they shrieked up out of sight.

The ancient owls' nest must have burned.
Hastily, all alone,   30
a glistening armadillo left the scene,
rose-flecked, head down, tail down,

and then a baby rabbit jumped out,
short-eared, to our surprise.
So soft! — a handful of intangible ash   35
with fixed, ignited eyes.

Too pretty, dreamlike mimicry!
O falling fire and piercing cry
and panic, and a weak mailed fist
clenched ignorant against the sky!   40

Questions

1. What experiences and happenings figure in the imagery in these selected lines?

> they shrieked up out of sight. (line 28)
>
> Hastily, all alone,
> a glistening armadillo left the scene,
> rose-flecked, head down, tail down, (30–32)
>
> So soft! — a handful of intangible ash (35)

2. How do the sensations associated with these images help us to evoke the experiences they describe? Write your response and then compare it with the one that follows.

Response

EDITOR: Carnival-time fire balloons, swept to earth by a down-draft, pour flames on animal habitats; the burning creatures flee. In rendering their panic the poet appeals directly to our senses — sight, hearing, touch. Answering that appeal as readers means entering imaginatively, via our senses, into the creatures' experience. It means making real to ourselves the inner transformation undergone as the owls, ordinarily placid and rooted, whirl up ward "shriek[ing]." It means living into the similar transformation in the armadillo, seeing its hasty scrambling movement as total change. (Bombarded out of its customary brave unshrinkingness, the creature dares not even a pause of inquiry — "head down, tail down.") And it means taking in, through the sense of touch, the transformation from "soft" to "intangible" of a cremated baby rabbit.

   Bringing dread and horror to life requires that we draw events close to ourselves, penetrating their actualities as sense experiences. As we do this, we're not merely understanding abstractly the "environmental impact" — the effect on animal habitats, for example, of human recreations. We're feeling the fragility and vulnerability of life — the terrible "ignorant" "clench[ing]" (line 40) within as a creature's entire world is destroyed and its skin and eyes commence to burn. The fire in "The Armadillo" is beautiful as well as terrible, and the beauty reminds us of how often we distance ourselves from horror by adopting an aesthetic view. But by living into the poem's images as sensations, we move with the poet beyond mere "pretty, dreamlike mimicry" (37). We feel within ourselves what it might be like to utter the piercing cry in answer to searing pain.

JOHN KEATS (1795–1821)

To Autumn

1

Season of mists and mellow fruitfulness,
  Close bosom-friend of the maturing sun;
Conspiring with him how to load and bless
  With fruit the vines that round the thatch-eves run;
To bend with apples the moss'd cottage-trees,   5
  And fill all fruit with ripeness to the core;
    To swell the gourd, and plump the hazel shells
With a sweet kernel; to set budding more,
  And still more, later flowers for the bees,
    Until they think warm days will never cease,   10
    For Summer has o'er-brimm'd their clammy cells.

2

Who hath not seen thee oft amid thy store?
  Sometimes whoever seeks abroad may find
Thee sitting careless on a granary floor,
  Thy hair soft-lifted by the winnowing wind;   15
Or on a half-reap'd furrow sound asleep,
  Drows'd with the fume of poppies, while thy hook
    Spares the next swath and all its twined flowers:
And sometimes like a gleaner thou dost keep
  Steady thy laden head across a brook;
  Or by a cyder-press, with patient look,   20
    Thou watchest the last oozings hours by hours.

3

Where are the songs of Spring? Ay, where are they?
  Think not of them, thou hast thy music too, —

While barred clouds bloom the soft-dying day,   25
   And touch the stubble-plains with rosy hue;
Then in a wailful choir the small gnats mourn
    Among the river sallows, borne aloft
      Or sinking as the light wind lives or dies;
And full-grown lambs loud bleat from hilly bourn;   30

   Hedge-crickets sing; and now with treble soft
The red-breast whistles from a garden-croft;
   And gathering swallows twitter in the skies.

Questions

1.   What objects and happenings figure in the imagery here?

    For Summer has o'er-brimm'd their clammy cells. (line 11)

    Can the sensations associated with these images be evoked by imagining the bees' visual experience? What else needs to be called up?

2.   What objects and happenings figure in the imagery here?

    Drows'd with the fume of poppies. (17)

    Name some sensations associated with these images that help evoke this physical experience.

WALT WHITMAN   (1818–1892)
The Dalliance of the Eagles

Skirting the river road, (my forenoon walk, my rest)
Skyward in air a sudden muffled sound, the dalliance of the
    eagles,
The rushing amorous contact high in space together,
The clinching interlocking claws, a living, fierce, gyrating wheel,
Four beating wings, two beaks, a swirling mass tight grappling,   5
In tumbling turning clustering loops, straight downward falling,
Till o'er the river poised, the twain yet one, a moment's lull,
A motionless still balance in the air, then parting, talons loosing,
Upward again on slow-firm pinions slanting, their separate
    diverse flight,
She hers, he his, pursuing.   10

Question

What objects and happenings figure in the imagery here?

A motionless still balance in the air, then parting, talons loosing.
(line 8)

Name some sensations associated with these images that help evoke this physical experience.

FOR FURTHER STUDY

WILLIAM SHAKESPEARE (1564–1616)
That time of year thou mayst in me behold

That time of year thou mayst in me behold
When yellow leaves, or none, or few, do hang
Upon those boughs which shake against the cold,
Bare ruined choirs where late the sweet birds sang.
In me thou see'st the twilight of such day   5
As after sunset fadeth in the west,
Which by-and-by black night doth take away,
Death's second self that seals up all in rest.
In me thou see'st the glowing of such fire
That on the ashes of his youth doth lie,   10
As the deathbed whereon it must expire,
Consumed with that which it was nourished by.
    This thou perceiv'st, which makes thy love more strong,
    To love that well which thou must leave ere long.

JONATHAN SWIFT (1667–1745)
A Description of the Morning

Now hardly here and there an hackney coach
Appearing, showed the ruddy morn's approach.
Now Betty from her master's bed had flown,
And softly stole to discompose her own;
The slipshod 'prentice from his master's door   5
Had pared the dirt, and sprinkled round the floor.
Now Moll had whirled her mop with dextrous airs,
Prepared to scrub the entry and the stairs
The youth with broomy stumps began to trace

The kennel's edge, where wheels had worn the place.   10
The small-coal man was heard with cadence deep,
Till drowned in shriller notes of chimney sweep:
Duns at his lordship's gate began to meet;
And brickdust Moll had screamed through half the street.
The turnkey now his flock returning sees,   15
Duly let out a-nights to steal for fees:
The watchful bailiffs take their silent stands,
And schoolboys lag with satchels in their hands.

ADRIENNE RICH   (b. 1929)
The Middle-Aged

Their faces, safe as an interior
Of Holland tiles and Oriental carpet,
Where the fruit-bowl, always filled, stood in a light
Of placid afternoon — their voices' measure,
Their figures moving in the Sunday garden   5
To lay the tea outdoors or trim the borders,
Afflicted, haunted us. For to be young
Was always to live in other peoples' houses
Whose peace, if we sought it, had been made by others,
Was ours at second-hand and not for long.   10
The custom of the house, not ours, the sun
Fading the silver-blue Fortuny curtains,
The reminiscence of a Christmas party
Of fourteen years ago — all memory,
Signs of possession and of being possessed,   15
We tasted, tense with envy. They were so kind,
Would have given us anything; the bowl of fruit
Was filled for us, there was a room upstairs
We must call ours: but twenty years of living
They could not give. Nor did they ever speak   20
Of the coarse stain on that polished balustrade,
The crack in the study window, or the letters
Locked in a drawer and the key destroyed.
All to be understood by us returning
Late, in our own time — how that peace was made,   25
Upon what terms, with how much left unsaid.

9

Figures of Speech: Metaphor and Simile

In bringing images to life, we heighten our alertness to the physical sensations associated with the pertinent words and things. In bringing metaphors and similes to life, our starting point is often the same, for comparisons in poems are usually worked up from concrete images.

MARY OLIVER   (b. 1935)
Milkweed

The milkweed now with their many pods are standing
like a country of dry women.
The wind lifts their flat leaves and drops them.
This is not kind, but they retain a certain crisp glamour;
moreover, it's easy to believe   5
each one was once young and delicate, also
frightened; also capable
of a certain amount of rough joy.
I wish you could walk with me out into the world.
I wish you could see what has to happen, how   10
each one crackles like a blessing
over its thin children as they rush away.

If we know the look and feel of milkweed, that knowledge provides associations through which the images in this poem can be evoked as sense experiences. But focusing the images as sensations is only the beginning. As active readers evoking the substance of a comparison, we need to think the comparison through in all its dimensions. This means reflecting on the nature of the new connection that the comparison puts before us. We ask about the logic of the comparison and the kinds of feelings it brings to life. We look into whether, when we ourselves compare the objects that are freshly connected by the figure, we discover new qualities in them. And we come to decisions about both the strengths and the limits of the comparison. What dimensions of mature life and motherhood are illuminated by Oliver's simile linking milkweed with "dry women"? What feelings and assumptions about old age do we find built into this comparison? Do we — should we — share them?

Always we begin by clarifying to ourselves what is being compared to what, and how. In a simile the act of comparison is explicitly acknowledged, by the use of a word such as *like* or *as* or *seems*.

> The milkweed now with their many pods are standing
> like a country of dry women. (lines 1–2)

In a metaphor the act of comparison is not explicitly acknowledged by any term.

> I like to see it lap the Miles —
> And lick the Valleys up —

Emily Dickinson's poem (p. 551) links train and kitten metaphorically, without any specific connective. In another common poetic comparison, personification, a concept or inanimate object is treated as possessing human qualities. John Keats speaks of autumn as a woman: "Who hath not seen thee oft amid thy store?" (see "To Autumn," p. 574).

BRINGING COMPARISONS TO LIFE

Bringing a comparison to life, however, entails much more than merely recognizing a figure as a simile or metaphor or personification. When we say that John Donne's "Batter my heart" (p. 550) offers a metaphor comparing a sinful, imperfectly faithful human being to a walled town that's been unlawfully seized by a usurping conqueror, we've only started the process of thinking the comparison through. We have to work *with* the comparison — *think* with it — in order to summon its meanings. Probed carefully, Donne's figure of speech becomes a means of clarifying a psychology of moral and spiritual self-alibi. It shows us how human beings attempt to locate the causes of their weakness outside themselves — in this instance, in the imagined failure of a divinity to demand absolute faith. It can help us grasp the way fear and guilt, self-defense and self-condemnation are inter-woven in a certain kind of person. Each element of the comparison of a human being to a conquered town casts further light on the nature of the speaker, enabling us to grasp more fully the complexities of his impatient pride: his feelings of entrapment and commitment, power and powerlessness, torment and longing.

Poetic thinking constantly assembles seemingly unrelated images of the world that turn out — as we explore them — to have astonishing points of connection. In a Shakespeare sonnet we explore resemblances between a burned-down church and human physicality in late middle age (See "That time of year thou mayst in me behold," p. 576). In a Richard Wilbur lyric we connect the experience of observing a beloved's smile with waiting at a raised drawbridge for a vessel to pass by (see "A Simile for Her Smile," p. 583). As we live into poetic comparisons, we grasp that each part of life is capable of showing us something interesting — and often hitherto hidden — about every other part.

Through spelling out the links and connections implied in a comparison, we become more alert to the dimensions of metaphor making. We look into metaphors and similes to find the light they cast on a state of mind and feeling within a speaker. We take into account the power of these verbal figures to encompass complexities that slip out of the mind's grasp when it tries, in its customary oversimplifying way, to take one thing at a time. Through metaphor and simile human mysteries, problems, joys, frustrations, and needs that can't finally be understood — as, for example, the urge to express one's overpowering awareness of the richness of a season (see Keats's "To Autumn") — are often brought under the partial mastery of clear definition. Our final step as readers engaged in bringing metaphors to life is in fact that of imagining and describing the *need* that generated the original drive for clarifying comparison.

ASKING QUESTIONS
ABOUT COMPARISONS

In the three poems in this section, a writer compares his pen to a gun and then to a spade, a lover compares his beloved's smile to the "pause and ease" he experiences when he's stopped by a highway bridgegate, and a worshiper compares the voice of his Lord to a collar that subdues a wild creature. The questions that follow focus on the speakers' state of mind and on the needs that their acts of comparison enable them to meet. Your purpose is to evoke those states of mind and needs as fully as you can in your own words.

SEAMUS HEANEY   (b. 1939)
Digging

Between my finger and my thumb
The squat pen rests; snug as a gun.

Under my window, a clean rasping sound
When the spade sinks into gravelly ground.
My father, digging. I look down   5

Till his straining rump among the flowerbeds
Bends low, comes up twenty years away
Stooping in rhythm through potato drills
Where he was digging.

The coarse boot nestled on the lug, the shaft   10
Against the inside knee was levered firmly.
He rooted out tall tops, buried the bright edge deep
To scatter new potatoes that we picked
Loving their cool hardness in our hands.

By God, the old man could handle a spade.   15
Just like his old man.

My grandfather cut more turf in a day
Than any other man on Toner's bog.
Once I carried him milk in a bottle
Corked sloppily with paper. He straightened up   20
To drink it, then fell to right away

Nicking and slicing neatly, heaving sods
Over his shoulder, going down and down
For the good turf. Digging.

The cold smell of potato mould, the squelch and slap   25
Of soggy peat, the curt cuts of an edge
Through living roots awaken in my head.
But I've no spade to follow men like them.

Between my finger and my thumb
The squat pen rests.   30
I'll dig with it.

Questions

1. What elements of the speaker's state of mind and feeling does the comparison between pen and spade illuminate?
2. What emotional, intellectual, or psychological needs, large or small, grave or mild, does the act of comparison help to meet here? Write your response and then compare it with the one that follows.

Response

EDITOR: In the opening lines of this poem the speaker compares his pen to a gun, but at the end that comparison is withdrawn in favor of another. The speaker explicitly compares the work he does as a writer to the work done by his father and grandfather with their spades, whether as potato diggers or peat cutters. The comparison helps to meet the speaker's need for a means of overcoming the self-dismissive sense of poetry writing as an effete, abstract activity removed from the lives of ordinary working men and women — people who sell their hard labor. Partly as a result of the family past that he's thinking of as he sits down to his stint of writing, the speaker is aware that for numberless human beings work means physical engagement — the use of hands, arms, shoulders and backs. He's aware, further, that such expenditures of energy cost something in bodily strain, and, still further, he knows that such work can be well or poorly done and can occasion genuine pride in the worker and genuine admiration in others.

There's a gap, obviously, between writing poetry, at ease, at a desk, and sweating it out as a peat miner in a bog. Not just differences in physical positioning but a social and educational gap separates the occupations. The speaker's need to bridge that gap arises from many sources: family loyalty, desire not to see himself or be seen by others as someone who's lost touch with his roots, belief in the worth of physical labor, conviction that elements of craftsmanship can enter into all occupations, a fundamentally democratic sense of fellowship and solidarity.

The pen in the speaker's hand is, clearly, nothing like a spade. But thinking of it as a tool with which hard labor can be performed enables the speaker to connect himself with other tool users. By restating to himself the codes and values implicit in their work, the poet-speaker sets fresh standards for his own. As we bring to life the metaphor in this poem, we draw closer both to the need and to the way the comparison helps meet the need. We sense that the metaphor moderates the potential feeling of isolation — of setting out on a morning's work in the presence of others who have worked all their lives in wholly different ways and of setting out on a life course remote from that followed by one's closest blood relations. We grasp that the metaphor also meets the need for a standard of excellence derived from immediate experience rather than solely from books.

RICHARD WILBUR   (b. 1921)
A Simile for Her Smile

Your smiling, or the hope, the thought of it,
Makes in my mind such pause and abrupt ease
As when the highway bridgegates fall,
Balking the hasty traffic, which must sit
On each side massed and staring, while   5
Deliberately the drawbridge starts to rise:

Then horns are hushed, the oilsmoke rarifies,
Above the idling motors one can tell
The packet's smooth approach, the slip,
Slip of the silken river past the sides,   10
The ringing of clear bells, the dip
And slow cascading of the paddle wheel.

Questions

1. What is compared to what in this poem's simile?
2. What elements of the speaker's state of mind and feeling does the comparison illuminate?
3. What needs does this act of comparison help to meet?

GEORGE HERBERT   (1593–1633)
The Collar

I struck the board and cried, "No more;
         I will abroad!
   What? shall I ever sigh and pine?
My lines and life are free, free as the road,
  Loose as the wind, as large as store.   5
    Shall I be still in suit?°   *in service or attendance*
  Have I no harvest but a thorn
  To let me blood, and not restore
What I have lost with cordial° fruit?   *restorative*
    Sure there was wine   10
  Before my sighs did dry it; there was corn
   Before my tears did drown it.
  Is the year only lost to me?
   Have I no bays to crown it,
No flowers, no garlands gay? All blasted?   15
    All wasted?
  Not so, my heart; but there is fruit,
    And thou hast hands.
    Recover all thy sigh-blown age
On double pleasures; leave thy cold dispute   20
Of what is fit and not. Forsake thy cage,
    Thy rope of sands,
Which petty thoughts have made, and made to thee
  Good cable, to enforce and draw,
    And be thy law,   25
  While thou didst wink and wouldst not see.
    Away! take heed;
    I will abroad.
Call in thy death's-head there; tie up thy fears.
    He that forbears   30
  To suit and serve his need,
    Deserves his load."

But as I raved and grew more fierce and wild
    At every word,
Methought I heard one calling, *Child!*   35
    And I replied, *My Lord.*

Questions

1. A wide variety of comparisons figure in "The Collar." Spell them out carefully and show how you relate them to each other.
2. What needs within the speaker do these acts of comparison help to meet?

FOR FURTHER STUDY

SIR WALTER RALEIGH   (1552–1618)
The Author's Epitaph, Made by Himself

Even such is time, which takes in trust
Our youth, our joys, and all we have,
And pays us but with age and dust,
Who in the dark and silent grave
When we have wandered all our ways   5
Shuts up the story of our days,
And from which earth, and grave, and dust
The Lord shall raise me up, I trust.

WILLIAM SHAKESPEARE   (1564–1616)
Poor soul, the center of my sinful earth

Poor soul, the center of my sinful earth,
Lord of these rebel powers that thee array,
Why dost thou pine within and suffer death,
Painting thy outward walls so costly gay?
Why so large cost, having so short a lease,   5
Dost thou upon thy fading mansion spend?
Shall worms, inheritors of this excess,
Eat up thy charge? Is this thy body's end?
Then, soul, live thou upon thy servant's loss,

And let that pine to aggravate thy store;   10
Buy terms divine in selling hours of dross;
Within be fed, without be rich no more.
  So shalt thou feed on death, that feeds on men,
  And death once dead, there's no more dying then.

MARIANNE MOORE   (1887–1972)
Nevertheless

you've seen a strawberry
        that's had a struggle; yet
        was, where the fragments met,

a hedgehog or a star-
        fish for the multitude   5
        of seeds. What better food

than apple-seeds — the fruit
        within the fruit — locked in
        like counter-curved twin

hazel-nuts? Frost that kills   10
        the little rubber-plant-
        leaves of *kok-saghyz*-stalks, can't

harm the roots; they still grow
        in frozen ground. Once where
        there was a prickly-pear-   15

leaf clinging to barbed wire,
        a root shot down to grow
        in earth two feet below;

as carrots form mandrakes
        or a ram's-horn root some-   20
        times. Victory won't come

to me unless I go
        to it; a grape-tendril
        ties a knot in knots till

knotted thirty times, — so   25
        the bound twig that's under-
        gone and over-gone, can't stir.

The weak overcomes its
    menace, the strong over-
    comes itself. What is there   30

like fortitude! What sap
    went through that little thread
    to make the cherry red!

10

Symbol

As active readers bringing a metaphor to life, we think through a given comparison, exploring its appropriateness, logic, limits, and emotional bearings. Our focus is the specific new connection mapped out in the poem between objects or experiences or concepts. Sometimes perceiving the resemblance between the elements requires an imaginative leap. Usually our ordinary, realistic awareness of the differences between the elements in question stays with us as we read. As active readers probing the symbolic dimensions of a poem, we are in a more complicated situation and our experience is more fluid. In bringing symbols to life we're dealing once again with terms describing objects, experiences, or concepts generally regarded as different from each other. But now we aren't evoking likenesses, we're evoking identities.

How is this possible? How can we create identities out of differences? No fully satisfying answer to that question can be given; our power to respond to different items as though their differences didn't exist remains mysterious. All that's clear is that, whether we speak of reading or of life, our power to respond to symbols varies according to the intensity of our emotional commitment.

An example: The college at which I teach lowers the flag over the chapel for some days after the death of a member of the college community. The conventional way of describing such an act is to say that the flag at half-mast is a "sign of mourning." When we say this, we're clear in our minds about the difference between a lowered flag and a death. A piece of cloth flapping in the breeze isn't the deceased. Yet more than once when a colleague and friend has died, the flag at half-mast that I've caught sight of as I walked home in the evening has seemed to me to *be* the death itself. Grief, anger, pity flood to life within me at the sight — the entire range of thoughts and feelings associated with loss. You could say, of course, that the sight simply reminds me of the death. But that's not how it feels. For an instant the identity of flag and death that common sense necessarily denies becomes, under pressure of strong feeling, overpoweringly real.

The human power to live into theoretically impossible experiences of identity is our chief resource when we explore the symbolic dimensions of a poem. And we engage in that exploration whenever the combination of our own emotional experience and suggestions in the language of the poem lead us to believe that certain words or phrases carry their ordinary meanings and something more as well (as the flag at half-staff simultaneously carries public news of a death and summons personal grief and memory).

BRINGING SYMBOLS TO LIFE

The speaker in "The Collar-Bone of a Hare," by William Butler Yeats, imagines a journey toward delight that would link him with kings and their daughters. The focus at the start is upon freedom, beauty, and merriment.

WILLIAM BUTLER YEATS   (1865–1939)
The Collar-Bone of a Hare

Would I could cast a sail on the water
Where many a king has gone
And many a king's daughter,
And alight at the comely trees and the lawn,
The playing upon pipes and the dancing,   5
And learn that the best thing is
To change my loves while dancing
And pay but a kiss for a kiss.

I would find by the edge of that water
The collar-bone of a hare   10
Worn thin by the lapping of water,

And pierce it through with a gimlet, and stare
At the old bitter world where they marry in churches,
And laugh over the untroubled water
At all who marry in churches,   15
Through the white thin bone of a hare.

The two stanzas of this poem contrast two worlds of love —
one that happily approves carefree changes of attachments and
the absence of obligations ("pay but a kiss for a kiss," line 8) and
the other that solemnly observes the restrictions imposed by
religious vows. Preferring the carefree world but living in the restricted one, the speaker imagines escape — and he goes on to
insist that "the old bitter world where they marry in churches"
(13) deserves to be mocked. Once free he'd stare back at that
world through a frame carved out of animal bone and laugh at
those unlucky enough to be stuck in it.

In reading this poem we sense that the phrases about the
animal bone mean what they ordinarily mean as well as something beyond. And that sense leads us to explore the symbolic
dimensions of the poem. For this speaker ranges of meaning
usually thought of as separate become identical. The suggestions
of expanded identity come from various directions but center
always on the "collar-bone of a hare." The repetitions of this
phrase ask us to examine it with special care. And the word *collar-
bone*, because it carries a reminder of common physical structures
in animal and human worlds, opens a door through which we
glimpse the possibility that a single word may draw together
different meanings.

We interpret the speaker's use of the bone to be his way of
saying that human beings who make a great fuss about the terms
of their lives and loves ought to bear in mind what's in store for
them. In the end we're no different from animals whose remains
become beach junk, weathering away into inconsequence. We
share animal desires and mortality with the whole of creation, so
why shouldn't we relax these lofty, self-deceiving spiritual pretensions a bit, accept the temporary nature of every action taken,
every pledge made on earth? When fully evoked, the "collar-
bone of a hare" is simultaneously a bone *and* the truth of the
inescapable mutability of all living creatures. In the act of sensing how hitherto diverse elements are drawn together into identity by the speaker, we bring the collarbone to life as a symbol.

ASKING QUESTIONS ABOUT SYMBOLS

The poems opening this section focus on a human embrace, a job (apple-picking), and a flower, and in addition, upon diverse elements of experience not usually associated with hugs, jobs, or flowers. The questions concentrate on the details of the poems that draw together those diverse elements. Your purpose is to show how you bring those details to life as symbols.

TESS GALLAGHER   (b. 1943)
The Hug

A woman is reading a poem on the street
and another woman stops to listen. We stop too,
with our arms around each other. The poem
is being read and listened to out here
in the open. Behind us   5
no one is entering or leaving the houses.

Suddenly a hug comes over me and I'm
giving it to you, like a variable star shooting light
off to make itself comfortable, then
subsiding. I finish but keep on holding   10
you. A man walks up to us and we know he hasn't
come out of nowhere, but if he could, he
would have. He looks homeless because of how
he needs. "Can I have one of those?" he asks you,
and I feel you nod. I'm surprised,   15
surprised you don't tell him how
it is — that I'm yours, only
yours, etc., exclusive as a nose to
its face. Love — that's what we're talking about, love
that nabs you with "for me   20
only" and holds on.

So I walk over to him and put my
arms around him and try to
hug him like I mean it. He's got an overcoat on
so thick I can't feel   25
him past it. I'm starting the hug
and thinking, "How big a hug is this supposed to be?
How long shall I hold this hug?" Already
we could be eternal, his arms falling over my

shoulders, my hands not   30
meeting behind his back, he is so big!

I put my head into his chest and snuggle
in. I lean into him. I lean my blood and my wishes
into him. He stands for it. This is his
and he's starting to give it back so well I know he's   35
getting it. This hug. So truly, so tenderly
we stop having arms and I don't know if
my lover has walked away or what, or
if the woman is still reading the poem, or the houses —
what about them? — the houses.   40

Clearly, a little permission is a dangerous thing.
But when you hug someone you want it
to be a masterpiece of connection, the way the button
on his coat will leave the imprint of
a planet in my cheek   45
when I walk away. When I try to find some place
to go back to.

Questions

1. What details of this poem lead us as readers to probe for
   symbolic dimensions?
2. What words in the poem can be brought to life as symbols —
   as terms drawing together into identity ranges of meaning
   ordinarily considered different? Write your response and
   then compare it with the one that follows.

Response

EDITOR: The story told in "The Hug" seems perfectly simple at
first glance. A pair of lovers pauses in the street to listen to a
poem being read aloud. On an impulse that arises perhaps in
happy awareness that both had shared the desire to stop and
listen, one of the lovers hugs the other. A third party, observing
this spontaneous embrace, seeks and is given permission to
"have one" like it. Following this new embrace, which is both
tender and extended, the two part, and the lover whose spontaneous feeling initiated the sequence of actions walks away (try-

ing "to find some place to go back to," lines 46–47), as her lover one minute before had walked away from her.

One detail that leads us to probe for symbolic dimensions here is the oddly parallel action that links up an attached and an unattached couple: the action of first drawing close to each other, then walking away from each other, connecting and disconnecting. Another detail is the character of the embrace between the lover and the "homeless" stranger: "I lean into him. I lean my blood and my wishes / into him. . . . So truly, so tenderly / we stop having arms" (33–37). No dictionary-style definition of the noun *hug* quite reaches the intensity of this embrace. Yet another detail is the repeated contrast between the open, free mingling of human beings out of doors and the stiff, aloof containment of the houses, from which "no one is entering or leaving" (6). The details work together to suggest that wider than usual ranges of meaning can be explored through the incident the speaker describes.

It is the word *hug* in particular that draws those ranges of meaning together. For the speaker the word begins as an expression of momentary delight — easy happiness in sharing an experience with a beloved. But thereafter its focus changes. The speaker experiences the "surprise" of discovering that her beloved refuses to claim "exclusive" rights. She makes a passionate effort to duplicate that lack of possessiveness through a physical gesture of her own and ends in a kind of disorientation, no longer as certain of her place as she was at the start. As we bring the hug to life as a symbol, we sense that it is a means of speaking simultaneously about the happiness and the frustration of human connection — about the way in which the profound need for and joy in giving ourselves to a carefully chosen other person coexists with darker realities. No embrace, however intense, ends for long our separateness; the imprint of the button on the cheek is infinitely more transitory than the planet it resembles.

Further, the attempt to shift from a purely possessive attachment to a more universal sympathy leads away from delight. In place of spontaneity stands something a shade closer (despite the tenderness) to desperate clutching, and what comes after that *is* disorientation.

In the context of "alternative life-styles," "The Hug" inquires into the meanings of one of the simplest human gestures. As we search out those meanings, framing them in our own language, we bring the hug to life as a symbol and experience the human embrace as the closing of one gap and the opening of others.

ROBERT FROST   (1874–1963)

After Apple-Picking

My long two-pointed ladder's sticking through a tree
Toward heaven still,
And there's a barrel that I didn't fill
Beside it, and there may be two or three
Apples I didn't pick upon some bough.   5
But I am done with apple-picking now.
Essence of winter sleep is on the night.
The scent of apples: I am drowsing off.
I cannot rub the strangeness from my sight
I got from looking through a pane of glass   10
I skimmed this morning from the drinking trough
And held against the world of hoary grass.
It melted, and I let it fall and break.
But I was well
Upon my way to sleep before it fell.   15
And I could tell
What form my dreaming was about to take.
Magnified apples appear and disappear,
Stem end and blossom end,
And every fleck of russet showing clear.   20
My instep arch not only keeps the ache,
It keeps the pressure of a ladder-round.
I feel the ladder sway as the boughs bend.
And I keep hearing from the cellar bin
The rumbling sound   25
Of load on load of apples coming in.
For I have had too much
Of apple-picking: I am overtired
Of the great harvest I myself desired.
There were ten thousand thousand fruit to touch.   30
Cherish in hand, lift down, and not let fall.
For all
That struck the earth,
No matter if not bruised or spiked with stubble,

Went surely to the cider-apple heap   35
As of no worth.
One can see what will trouble
This sleep of mine, whatever sleep it is.
Were he not gone,
The woodchuck could say whether it's like his   40
Long sleep, as I describe its coming on,
Or just some human sleep.

Questions

1. What details of this poem lead us as readers to probe for
    symbolic dimensions?
2. What words in the poem can be brought to life as symbols —
    as terms drawing together into identity ranges of meaning
    ordinarily considered different?
3. The poet Richard Wilbur writes that this poem is "concerned
    with spiritual activity. . . . " What details of the poem might
    lead a reader to probe for symbols of "spiritual activity"?

WILLIAM BLAKE   (1757–1827)

The Sick Rose

O rose, thou art sick:
The invisible worm
That flies in the night.
In the howling storm,
Has found out thy bed
Of crimson joy;
And his dark secret love
Does thy life destroy.

Questions

1. What details of this poem lead us as readers to probe for symbolic dimensions?
2. Both *rose* and *worm* can be brought to life as symbols. What different ranges of meaning are drawn together into identity when we evoke these words as symbols? (Blake's own illustration of the poem suggests several answers to this question.)

FOR FURTHER STUDY

ROBERT HERRICK   (1591–1674)
To the Virgins, to Make Much of Time

Gather ye rosebuds while ye may,
   Old time is still a-flying;
And this same flower that smiles today
   Tomorrow will be dying.

The glorious lamp of heaven, the sun,   5
   The higher he's a-getting,
The sooner will his race be run,
   And nearer he's to setting.

That age is best which is the first,
   When youth and blood are warmer;   10
But being spent, the worse, and worst
   Times still succeed the former.

Then be not coy, but use your time;
   And while ye may, go marry;
For having lost but once your prime,   15
   You may forever tarry.

GEORGE HERBERT   (1593–1633)
Peace

Sweet Peace, where dost thou dwell, I humbly crave?
        Let me once know.

I sought thee in a secret cave,
    And ask'd if Peace were there.
A hollow winde did seem to answer, "No;   5
    Go seek elsewhere."

I did; and going did a rainbow note:
    Surely, thought I,
This is the lace of Peace's coat:
    I will search out the matter.   10
But while I lookt, the clouds immediately
    Did break and scatter.

Then went I to a garden, and did spy
    A gallant flower,
The Crown Imperiall. Sure, said I,   15
    Peace at the root must dwell.
But when I digg'd, I saw a worme devoure
    What show'd so well.

At length I met a rev'rend good old man,
    Whom when for Peace   20
I did demand, he thus began:
    "There was a Prince of old
At Salem dwelt, Who liv'd with good increase
    Of flock and fold.

He sweetly liv'd; yet sweetnesse did not save   25
    His life from foes.
But after death out of His grave
    There sprang twelve stalks of wheat;
Which many wond'ring at, got some of those
    To plant and set.   30

It prosper'd strangely, and did soon disperse
    Through all the earth;
For they that taste it do rehearse
    That vertue lies therein;
A secret vertue, bringing peace and mirth   35
    By flight of sinne.

Take of this grain, which in my garden grows,
    And grows for you;
Make bread of it; and that repose
    And peace, which ev'ry where   40
With so much earnestnesse you do pursue,
    Is onely there."

SAMUEL TAYLOR COLERIDGE (1772–1834)

Kubla Khan

Or, A Vision in a Dream. A Fragment.°

In Xanadu did Kubla Khan
A stately pleasure-dome decree:
Where Alph, the sacred river, ran
Through caverns measureless to man
   Down to a sunless sea.   5
So twice five miles of fertile ground
With walls and towers were girdled round:
And there were gardens bright with sinuous rills,
Where blossomed many an incense-bearing tree;
And here were forests ancient as the hills,   10
Enfolding sunny spots of greenery.

But oh! that deep romantic chasm which slanted
Down the green hill athwart a cedarn cover!
A savage place! as holy and enchanted
As e'er beneath a waning moon was haunted   15
By woman wailing for her demon-lover!
And from this chasm, with ceaseless turmoil seething,
As if this earth in fast thick pants were breathing,
A mighty fountain momently was forced:
Amid whose swift half-intermitted burst   20
Huge fragments vaulted like rebounding hail,
Or chaffy grain beneath the thresher's flail:
And 'mid these dancing rocks at once and ever
It flung up momently the sacred river.
Five miles meandering with a mazy motion   25
Through wood and dale the sacred river ran,
Then reached the caverns measureless to man,
And sank in tumult to a lifeless ocean:
And 'mid this tumult Kubla heard from far
Ancestral voices prophesying war!   30
   The shadow of the dome of pleasure
   Floated midway on the waves;
   Where was heard the mingled measure
   From the fountain and the caves.

A Vision . . . Fragment: This poem recounts a dream Coleridge had under the influence of opium; interrupted while recording it, he was unable to remember the rest of the vision. There are historic sources for Kubla Khan (Kublai Khan, founder of the Mongol dynasty in thirteenth-century China) and Xanadu (the Chinese city of Xamdu).

It was a miracle of rare device, 35
A sunny pleasure-dome with caves of ice!

   A damsel with a dulcimer
   In a vision once I saw:
   It was an Abyssinian maid,
   And on her dulcimer she played, 40
   Singing of Mount Abora.
   Could I revive within me
   Her symphony and song,
   To such a deep delight 'twould win me,
That with music loud and long, 45
I would build that dome in air,
That sunny dome! those caves of ice!
And all who heard should see them there,
And all should cry, Beware! Beware!
His flashing eyes, his floating hair! 50
Weave a circle round him thrice,
And close your eyes with holy dread,
For he on honey-dew hath fed,
And drunk the milk of Paradise.

11

Irony

President Kennedy once held a dinner at the White House for American Nobel laureates, Pulitzer Prize winners, and other high achievers. At the end of the meal, rising to welcome his distinguished guests, he remarked that the White House had not seen so much wit, intelligence, and creativity gathered together in one room "since Jefferson dined alone." The president's words communicated, at the literal level, enthusiasm for the triumph of bringing so much genius to the White House for recognition. But the irony in his words invited the audience to contemplate simultaneously a variety of somewhat deflating perspectives on themselves: Nobody nowadays, no matter how gifted, excels in both the arts and sciences — as Thomas Jefferson did. The much-vaunted progress of the human intellect from the early nineteenth century to the mid-twentieth century may not really be progress at all (since, if we think of Jefferson's example, it would appear that the gifted people who have come after him know more and more about less and less).

The president spelled out none of this for his audience; he assumed, flatteringly to the accomplished people who were listening, that they knew what to do with irony — how to connect one line of thought with another without explicit directives, how to "see through" his literal enthusiasm to the wry, pride-puncturing observation implicit within it.

Kennedy was not, however, implying that this assemblage of noted minds was meaningless. Maybe the knowledge in the noted minds when added together would amount to less than what Thomas Jefferson knew — but part of the president's meaning was positive. He was drawing attention, after all, to the truth that the White House hadn't recently been, except in his presidency, the scene of gatherings of significant American scientists, philosophers, artists, and intellectuals. And he was saying, Let's not be *too* self-congratulatory either about our own achievements or about my concern, as president, with culture and the arts. Through ironic speech, in other words, he was simultaneously staking out a claim for himself and for his listeners *and* criticizing and evaluating that claim in such a way as to shape a new, surprising perspective on the moment at hand.

There is always some loss when the layers of meaning in ironic utterance are taken apart (as I have just been doing) — when they are examined, mechanically translated into a series of competing messages. And this is especially true in the case of ironic utterance in poetry. As we respond to irony rereading a poem, clusters of ideas seem to come to life all at once. We not only take in assertion and counterassertion, claim and criticism of claim, but we also move in our minds to grasp the new slant on things brought into existence by the swift assembling of more familiar perspectives. That's the delight of the experience overall: the opportunity to rise to intellectual speed and agility.

BRINGING IRONY TO LIFE

Rising to the demands of irony takes practice, though, and the key to effective practice lies in careful sorting out of the attitudes at play in a poem. Glance back at the discussions of tone and attitude in Chapter 7 and then reconsider the Henry Reed poem "Naming of Parts" (p. 561).

> Today we have naming of parts. Yesterday,
> We had daily cleaning. And tomorrow morning,
> We shall have what to do after firing. But today,
> Today we have naming of parts. Japonica
> Glistens like coral in all of the neighboring gardens,
>   And today we have naming of parts. (lines 1–6)

In evoking irony we start by asking these questions: What attitudes or perspectives figure in the text? Where and how do we become aware that one or another of these attitudes is being criticized and evaluated? What new attitude or perspective emerges as we engage with this criticism?

The attitude in the opening lines of "Naming of Parts" could be termed businesslike, and the appropriateness to the situation of this crisp, methodically tabulating voice would seem unquestionable. For a soldier facing combat, care of his personal weapon is a matter of life and death consequence. Whatever can be done to put the essentials across with absolute directness, clarity, and precision certainly should be done. In the prenuclear age — Reed's poem belongs to the period of the Battle of Britain, around 1940 — battles were often decided by the quality of training and discipline of infantry. And the stakes were high: Nationhood, freedom, inherited values hung in the balance.

Yet as much as we sense the rightness, in this situation, of an attitude that is to-the-point, impersonal, and nonfrivolous, we know — the poem *makes* us know — that that attitude can't do justice to the situation in its fullness. Military urgencies — military reality — exist in a world in which other realities inevitably impinge. There's the reality experienced by an intelligent member of this class who finds offensive the condescending manner of the instructor ("And please do not let me / See anyone using his finger," lines 14–15). What's more, there surely are other topics of concern to men soon to be sent out to kill and be killed besides the mechanics of the springs and firing action of a rifle. At the very moment that all this controlled, systematic, mechanical instruction in the technology of killing is going on, the free and unregulated freshening of growth from a different spring — spring as enacted in the natural world — is in progress. Shouldn't that count for something?

> And rapidly backwards and forwards
> The early bees are assaulting and fumbling the flowers:
> They call it easing the Spring. (22–24)

When we say that "Naming of Parts" is an ironic poem, we mean that its opening lines, expressing satisfaction in the neat, orderly schedule of teaching, offer a piece of the truth about the situation in view — but no more than a piece. We can take the words literally, telling ourselves that the seeming satisfaction they express constitutes the whole story as known by those caught up in this actual moment either as participants or readers. If we do so, though, we miss the complexity that the whole poem evokes. Its compressed language opens up a field for reflection in which we weigh sharply contrasting perspectives on military training and war itself. We understand the demands of "national security" — including the demand that personal feelings be obliterated. But we reflect on those demands in light of further facts. One is that personal feeling always refuses to be obliterated. Another is that nature itself poses challenges to the tyranny of mechanical systematizers. The poem doesn't settle the claims of these competing realities; no force on earth can do that. But readers who bring to life its ironic play of voice and counter-voice, its oppositions of frivolity and obligation, may be drawn closer to the dimensions of the great issues — War, Peace, Survival, Surrender — than they can come either as listeners to reports about arms reduction negotiations or as soldiers in training.

The important point is that the reader must get into the act — must raise questions about the adequacy of the literal statement and must reflect on the nature of the complexity that this passage of irony invites us to bring to life. Nobody ever listens to irony and simply "gets" it. What happens is that we engage with irony as a way of speaking long enough for us to make up, seemingly almost *for* ourselves, almost *by* ourselves, the range of critical meanings that it assembles before us.

ASKING QUESTIONS ABOUT IRONY

In the three poems that follow, questions need to be raised about the adequacy of the speakers' literal statements. (Those statements concern a child's dream, an uncooperative mistress, and a shipwreck.) The questions to be asked focus on the kinds of criticism that each speaker's expressed attitudes appear to warrant. Your purpose is to spell out the appropriate criticism in a way that brings each poem's ironies to life.

WILLIAM BLAKE   (1757–1827)
The Chimney Sweeper

When my mother died I was very young,
And my father sold me while yet my tongue
Could scarcely cry " 'weep! 'weep! 'weep! 'weep!"
So your chimneys I sweep, and in soot I sleep.

There's little Tom Dacre, who cried when his head,   5
That curled like a lamb's back, was shaved; so I said,
"Hush, Tom! never mind it, for, when your head's bare,
You know that the soot cannot spoil your white hair."

And so he was quiet, and that very night,
As Tom was asleeping, he had such a sight!   10
That thousands of sweepers, Dick, Joe, Ned, and Jack,
Were all of them locked up in coffins of black.

And by came an Angel who had a bright key,
And he opened the coffins and set them all free;
Then down a green plain leaping, laughing, they run,   15
And wash in a river, and shine in the sun.

Then naked and white, all their bags left behind,
They rise upon clouds and sport in the wind;
And the Angel told Tom, if he'd be a good boy,
He'd have God for his father, and never want joy.   20

And so Tom awoke, and we rose in the dark,
And got with our bags and our brushes to work.
Though the morning was cold, Tom was happy and warm;
So if all do their duty they need not fear harm.

Questions

1. Describe the attitude of the speaker in this poem. What value resides in such an attitude? Where and how in this poem is the attitude criticized? What value resides in the criticism?
2. What fresh perspective on the situation and feelings of the speaker — and on the larger issues implicit in the poem — emerges as irony is brought to life here? Write your response and then compare it with the one that follows.

Response

EDITOR: The speaker in this poem, a child, reports another child's dream of being released by an angel into an existence filled with happiness, beauty, and promise. The speaker's voice is filled with gratitude: The speaker believes that the dream is a great gift, warming little Tom Dacre and offering comfort to all chimney sweepers who might otherwise feel sorry for themselves. The dream proves to the speaker the existence of a benign, paternal deity and of a fair system of justice throughout the world (". . . if all do their duty they need not fear harm," line 24).

The value of this perspective lies in its faithfulness to several truths often neglected. Even the most wretchedly situated and pitiably injured often succeed in the struggle to find grounds for hope. Even under the most hopeless circumstances, the impulse survives in the older or stronger of us not only to protect and care for the weak but also to attempt to offer example and guidance. Even in surroundings testifying to the pervasiveness of greed and corruption, innocence manages to breathe. In touch with these truths, guided by this perspective, we achieve insight into the means by which the unendurable is rendered endurable on this earth.

At the same time that we hear virtue in this voice, though, we hear other qualities that, however estimable, are more open to criticism. The speaker is clearly innocent, but he sounds a bit *too* obedient to Sunday school platitudes, too patronizing to poor Tom Dacre. And his acceptance of things as they are provokes our vexation. Is not this compliant acquiescence in the face of brutal injustice outrageous? Listening to the message that, because a miserably exploited child one night had a "happy" dream, everyone should assume that God's in his heaven and all's right with the world, we're roused to reflect on certain fundamentals of the situation that are obscured by the speaker's naive voice. What we're looking at, after all, is an obscene child labor system in which the young are stripped from — or sold by — their families into slavery, deformed or maddened by "work" long before their adolescence is even begun. The speaker says none of this directly, but behind his sunny voice we sense a darker presence, aware of the limits of the child's perspective, aware of the child's inability to understand the gross meanness of the grown-up world, which not only permits such exploitation but shamelessly salutes acquiescence without complaint as "proper" for the poor.

Is it not ironic, this dark presence seems to ask, that the human being with the least reason for satisfaction with the arrangements of God's world should feel obliged to express the greatest faith that those arrangements are just and good? Subtly but powerfully this question shifts the focus of criticism from the guileless, overobedient speaker to the system that entraps both him and Tom Dacre. And the value of the criticism lies just here, in the shift it causes us to make from a momentary sense of adult-to-child superiority to a grasp of a profound truth: All over the world the follies and cruelty of allegedly mature human beings punish children who have no defense, no comfort, except the empty pieties and illusions drilled into them by their theoretically virtuous elders.

To speak of a "fresh perspective on the situation and feelings of the speaker" and on the "larger issues" is simply to acknowledge that the ironies of this poem allow us to think about cruelty from two points of view. We are brought indirectly into touch with the facts of fearful exploitation — the kind of exploitation that well-intentioned, often well-heeled outsiders are forever lecturing us to care about — and at the same time we hear the wretched as they improvise their own consolation, seeking to make some kind of order out of vast pain. Pulled closer to the reality of oppression, seeing and feeling it both from outside and from within, we sense the speaker's gratitude for the dream not as naive foolishness but as an enormity in itself: something almost worse than persecution and slavery. Helpless in subjection, a child is led, in the name of obedience, to mistake evil for good, to accept cruelty as God's way. Through the poem's ironies we come to grasp that the initial gratitude is a gross perversion of innocent idealism — a more shocking, more hateful consequence of "the system" than any hitherto known. To be kidnapped, misused, beaten is monstrous, but to be led on to believe that such a fate is proof of the goodness of one's deity — what is this but an atrocity beyond reckoning?

ANDREW MARVELL   (1621–1678)

To His Coy Mistress

Had we but world enough, and time,
This coyness, lady, were no crime.
We would sit down and think which way
To walk, and pass our long love's day.
Thou by the Indian Ganges' side°   *river in India*   5
Should'st rubies find; I by the tide
Of Humber would complain. I would
Love you ten years before the Flood,
And you should, if you please, refuse

Till the conversion of the Jews.°   10
My vegetable love should grow
Vaster than empires, and more slow.
An hundred years should go to praise
Thine eyes, and on thy forehead gaze,
Two hundred to adore each breast,   15
But thirty thousand to the rest.
An age at least to every part,
And the last age should show your heart.
For, lady, you deserve this state,
Nor would I love at lower rate.   20
    But at my back I always hear
Time's winged chariot hurrying near;
And yonder all before us lie
Deserts of vast eternity.
Thy beauty shall no more be found,   25
Nor in thy marble vault shall sound
My echoing song; then worms shall try
That long preserved virginity,
And your quaint honor turn to dust,
And into ashes all my lust.   30
The grave's a fine and private place,
But none, I think, do there embrace.
    Now therefore, while the youthful hue
Sits on thy skin like morning glew,°   *glow*
And while thy willing soul transpires   35
At every pore with instant fires,
Now let us sport us while we may;
And now, like am'rous birds of prey,
Rather at once our time devour,
Than languish in his slow-chapped power,   40
Let us roll all our strength, and all
Our sweetness, up into one ball;
And tear our pleasures with rough strife
Thorough° the iron gates of life.   *through*
Thus, though we cannot make our sun   45
Stand still, yet we will make him run.

10 *conversion of the Jews*: One of the events that will occur just before the end of the world.

Questions

1. Describe the attitudes of both the speaker and his mistress in
    this poem.

2. What attitude is criticized through the words *coy* and *coyness*? What value resides in that attitude? What value resides in the criticism?
3. Where and how is this criticism developed elsewhere in the poem?
4. What fresh perspective on the situation and feelings of the speaker — and on the larger issues implicit in his arguments — emerges as irony is brought to life here?

THOMAS HARDY   (1840–1928)
The Convergence of the Twain
Lines on the Loss of the Titanic

I

In a solitude of the sea
Deep from human vanity,
And the Pride of Life that planned her, stilly couches she.

II

Steel chambers, late the pyres
Of her salamandrine fires,   5
Cold currents thrid,° and turn to rhythmic tidal lyres.   *thread*

III

Over the mirrors meant
To glass the opulent
The sea-worm crawls — grotesque, slimed, dumb, indifferent.

IV

Jewels in joy designed   10
To ravish the sensuous mind
Lie lightless, all their sparkles bleared and black and blind.

V

        Dim moon-eyed fishes near
        Gaze at the gilded gear
And query: "What does this vaingloriousness down here?"   15

VI

        Well: while was fashioning
        This creature of cleaving wing,
The Immanent Will that stirs and urges everything

VII

        Prepared a sinister mate
        For her — so gaily great —   20
A Shape of Ice, for the time far and dissociate.

VIII

        And as the smart ship grew
        In stature, grace, and hue,
In shadowy silent distance grew the Iceberg too.

IX

        Alien they seemed to be: 25
        No mortal eye could see
The intimate welding of their later history,

X

        Or sign that they were bent
        By paths coincident
On being anon twin halves of one august event,   30

XI

> Till the Spinner of the Years
> Said "Now!" And each one hears,
> And consummation comes, and jars two hemispheres.

Questions

1. In stanzas VI and VII the speaker claims that the sinking of the Titanic was no accident. "Immanent Will" planned it. Describe the attitudes toward life implicit in such a view. What values reside in them?
2. How are these attitudes criticized elsewhere in the poem — for example, in stanzas IX and X?
3. What fresh perspective on the larger issues implicit in the poem emerges as irony is brought to life here?

FOR FURTHER STUDY

D. H. LAWRENCE   (1885–1930)
Tortoise Gallantry

Making his advances
He does not look at her, nor sniff at her,
No, not even sniff at her, his nose is blank.

Only he senses the vulnerable folds of skin
That work beneath her while she sprawls along   5
In her ungainly pace,
Her folds of skin that work and row
Beneath the earth-soiled hovel in which she moves.

And so he strains beneath her housey walls
And catches her trouser-legs in his beak   10
Suddenly, or her skinny limb,
And strange and grimly drags at her
Like a dog,
Only agelessly silent, with a reptile's awful persistency.

Grim, gruesome gallantry, to which he is doomed.   15
Dragged out of an eternity of silent isolation
And doomed to partiality, partial being,

Ache, and want of being,
Want,
Self-exposure, hard humiliation, need to add himself on to her. 20

Born to walk alone,
Fore-runner,
Now suddenly distracted into this mazy side-track,
This awkward, harrowing pursuit,
This grim necessity from within.   25

Does she know
As she moves eternally slowly away?
Or is he driven against her with a bang, like a bird flying in the
       dark against a window,
All knowledgeless?

The awful concussion,   30
And the still more awful need to persist, to follow, follow,
       continue,

Driven, after aeons of pristine, fore-god-like singleness and
       oneness,
At the end of some mysterious, red-hot iron,
Driven away from himself into her tracks,
Forced to crash against her.   35

Stiff, gallant, irascible, crook-legged reptile,
Little gentleman,
Sorry plight,
We ought to look the other way.

Save that, having come with you so far,   40
We will go on to the end.

GWENDOLYN BROOKS   (b. 1917)
The Lovers of the Poor

                        arrive. The Ladies from the Ladies'
       Betterment League
Arrive in the afternoon, the late light slanting
In diluted gold bars across the boulevard brag
Of proud, seamed faces with mercy and murder hinting   5
Here, there, interrupting, all deep and debonair,
The pink paint on the innocence of fear;
Walk in a gingerly manner up the hall.

Cutting with knives served by their softest care,
Served by their love, so barbarously fair. 10
Whose mothers taught: You'd better not be cruel!
You had better not throw stones upon the wrens!
Herein they kiss and coddle and assault
Anew and dearly in the innocence
With which they baffle nature. Who are full, 15
Sleek, tender-clad, fit, fiftyish, a-glow, all
Sweetly abortive, hinting at fat fruit,
Judge it high time that fiftyish fingers felt
Beneath the lovelier planes of enterprise.
To resurrect. To moisten with milky chill. 20
To be a random hitching-post or plush.
To be, for wet eyes, random and handy hem.
     Their guild is giving money to the poor.
The worthy poor. The very very worthy
And beautiful poor. Perhaps just not too swarthy? 25
Perhaps just not too dirty nor too dim
Nor — passionate. In truth, what they could wish
Is — something less than derelict or dull.
Not staunch enough to stab, though, gaze for gaze!
God shield them sharply from the beggar-bold! 30
The noxious needy ones whose battle's bald
Nonetheless for being voiceless, hits one down.
     But it's all so bad! and entirely too much for
  them.
The stench; the urine, cabbage, and dead beans,
Dead porridges of assorted dusty grains, 35
The old smoke, *heavy* diapers, and, they're told,
Something called chitterlings. The darkness. Drawn
Darkness, or dirty light. The soil that stirs.
The soil that looks the soil of centuries.
And for that matter the *general* oldness. Old 40
Wood. Old marble. Old tile. Old old old.
Not homekind Oldness! Not Lake Forest, Glencoe.
Nothing is sturdy, nothing is majestic,
There is no quiet drama, no rubbed glaze, no
Unkillable infirmity of such 45
A tasteful turn as lately they have left,
Glencoe, Lake Forest, and to which their cars
Must presently restore them. When they're done
With dullards and distortions of this fistic
Patience of the poor and put-upon. 50
    They've never seen such a make-do-ness as

Newspaper rugs before! In this, this "flat,"
Their hostess is gathering up the oozed, the rich
Rugs of the morning (tattered! the bespattered. . . .)
Readies to spread clean rugs for afternoon.   55
Here is a scene for you. The Ladies look,
In horror, behind a substantial citizeness
Whose trains clank out across her swollen heart.
Who, arms akimbo, almost fills a door.
All tumbling children, quilts dragged to the floor   60
And tortured thereover, potato peelings, soft-
Eyed kitten, hunched-up, haggard, to-be-hurt.
          Their League is allotting largesse to the Lost.
But to put their clean, their pretty money, to put
Their money collected from delicate rose-fingers   65
Tipped with their hundred flawless rose-nails seems . . .
          They own Spode, Lowestoft, candelabra,
Mantels, and hostess gowns, and sunburst clocks,
Turtle soup, Chippendale, red satin "hangings,"
Aubussons and Hattie Carnegie. They Winter   70
In Palm Beach; cross the Water in June; attend,
When suitable, the nice Art Institute;
Buy the right books in the best bindings; saunter
On Michigan, Easter mornings, in sun or wind.
Oh Squalor! This sick four story hulk, this fibre   75
With fissures everywhere! Why, what are bringings
Of loathe-love largesse? What shall peril hungers
So old old, what shall flatter the desolate?
Tin can, blocked fire escape and chitterling
And swaggering seeking youth and the puzzled wreckage   80
Of the middle passage, and urine and stale shames
And, again, the porridges of the underslung
And children children children. Heavens! That
Was a rat, surely, off there, in the shadows? Long
And long-tailed? Gray? The Ladies from the Ladies'   85
Betterment League agree it will be better
To achieve the outer air that rights and steadies,
To hie to a house that does not holler, to ring
Bells elsetime, better presently to cater
To no more Possibilities, to get   90
Away. Perhaps the money can be posted.
Perhaps they two may choose another Slum!
Some serious sooty half-unhappy home! —
Where loathe-love likelier may be invested.
          Keeping their scented bodies in the center   95

Of the hall as they walk down the hysterical hall,
They allow their lovely skirts to graze no wall,
Are off at what they manage of a canter,
And, resuming all the clues of what they were,
Try to avoid inhaling the laden air.   100

ROBERT LOWELL   (1917–1977)
For the Union Dead

"*Relinquunt Omnia Servare Rem Publicam.*"°

The old South Boston Aquarium stands
in a Sahara of snow now. Its broken windows are boarded.
The bronze weathervane cod has lost half its scales.
The airy tanks are dry.

Once my nose crawled like a snail on the glass;   5
my hand tingled
to burst the bubbles
drifting from the noses of the cowed, compliant fish.

My hand draws back. I often sigh still
for the dark downward and vegetating kingdom   10
of the fish and reptile. On a morning last March,
I pressed against the new barbed and galvanized

fence on the Boston Common. Behind their cage,
yellow dinosaur steamshovels were grunting
as they cropped up tons of mush and grass   15
to gouge their underworld garage.

Parking spaces luxuriate like civic
sandpiles in the heart of Boston.
A girdle of orange, Puritan-pumpkin colored girders
braces the tingling Statehouse,   20

shaking over the excavations, as it faces Colonel Shaw
and his bell-checked Negro infantry
on St. Gaudens' shaking Civil War relief,
propped by a plank splint against the garage's earthquake.

Two months after marching through Boston,   25
half the regiment was dead;
at the dedication,
William James could almost hear the bronze Negroes breathe.

"*Relinquunt . . . Publicam*: "They gave up everything to serve the State.""

Their monument sticks like a fishbone
in the city's throat.   30
Its Colonel is as lean
as a compass-needle.

He has an angry wrenlike vigilance,
a greyhound's gentle tautness;
he seems to wince at pleasure,   35
and suffocate for privacy.

He is out of bounds now. He rejoices in man's lovely,
peculiar power to choose life and die —
when he leads his black soldiers to death,
he cannot bend his back.   40

On a thousand small town New England greens,
the old white churches hold their air
of sparse, sincere rebellion; frayed flags
quilt the graveyards of the Grand Army of the Republic.

The stone statues of the abstract Union Soldier   45
grow slimmer and younger each year —
wasp-waisted, they doze over muskets
and muse through their sideburns . . .

Shaw's father wanted no monument
except the ditch,   50
when his son's body was thrown
and lost with his "niggers."

The ditch is nearer.
There are no statues for the last war here;
on Boylston Street, a commercial photograph   55
shows Hiroshima boiling

over a Mosler Safe, the "Rock of Ages"
that survived the blast. Space is nearer.
When I crouch to my television set,
the drained faces of Negro school-children rise like balloons. 60

Colonel Shaw
is riding on his bubble,
he waits
for the blesséd break.

The Aquarium is gone. Everywhere,   65
giant finned cars nose forward like fish;
a savage servility
slides by on grease.

12

Poems for Further Study

ANONYMOUS   (thirteenth-century English lyric)
The Cuckoo Song°

Sing, cuccu, nu. Sing, cuccu.
Sing, cuccu. Sing, cuccu, nu.

Summer is i-cumen in —
   Lhude sing, cuccu!
Groweth sed and bloweth med   5
   And springth the wude nu.
      Sing, cuccu!

Awe bleteth after lomb,
   Lhouth after calve cu,
Bulluc sterteth, bucke verteth —   10
   Murie sing, cuccu!
      Cuccu, cuccu.
   Wel singes thu, cuccu.
   Ne swik thu naver nu!

Translation: Sing, cuckoo, now. Sing, cuckoo. / Sing, cuckoo. Sing, cuckoo, now. / Summer is a-coming in — / Loud sing, cuckoo! / Groweth seed and bloweth mead / And springeth the wood new. / Sing, cuckoo! / Ewe bleateth after lamb, / Loweth after calf [the] cow, / Bullock starteth, buck farteth — / Merry sing, cuckoo! / Cuckoo, cuckoo. / Well singest thou, cuckoo. / Cease thou never now.

ANONYMOUS   (traditional Scottish ballad)
The Twa Corbies

As I was walking all alane,
I heard twa corbies° making a mane;°   *two ravens; lament*

The tane° unto the t'other say, *one*
"Where sall we gang° and dine today?" *go*

"In behint yon auld fail° dyke *turf* 5
I wot there lies a new slain knight;
And naebody kens that he lies there,
But his hawk, his hound, and lady fair.

"His hound is to the hunting gane,
His hawk to fetch the wild-fowl hame, 10
His lady's ta'en another mate,
So we may mak our dinner sweet.

"Ye'll sit on his white hause-bane,° *neck bone*
And I'll pike out his bonny blue een;
Wi' ae° lock o' his gowden hair *one* 15
We'll theek° our nest when it grows bare. *thatch*

"Mony a one for him makes mane,
But nane sall ken where he is gane;
O'er his white banes, when they are bare,
The wind sall blaw for evermair." 20

ANONYMOUS (English lyric)
Western Wind

Western wind, when wilt thou blow,
The small rain down can rain?
Christ, if my love were in my arms,
And I in my bed again!

SIR THOMAS WYATT (1503–1542)
They flee from me that sometime did me sekë

They flee from me that sometime did me sekë
  With naked fotë stalking in my chamber.
I have seen them gentle, tame and mekë
    That now are wild, and do not remember
    That sometime they put themself in danger 5
To take bread at my hand; and now they range
Busily seeking with a continual change.

Thankèd be fortune, it hath been otherwise
  Twenty times better; but once in speciàll,

In thin array, after a pleasant guise,   10
  When her loose gown from her shoulders did fall,
  And she me caught in her armës long and small,
Therëwith all sweetly did me kiss,
And softly said, *Dear heart, how like you this?*

It was no dremë: I lay broadë waking.   15
  But all is turned thorough° my gentleness   *through*
Into a strangë fashion of forsaking;
  And I have leave to go of her goodness,
  And she also to use newfangleness.°   *to pursue novelty*
But since that I so kindëly am served   20
I would fain knowë what she hath deserved.

SIR THOMAS WYATT   (1503–1542)

Whoso list to hunt

Whoso list° to hunt, I know where is an hind,   *wishes*
But as for me, alas, I may no more
The vain travail hath wearied me so sore
I am of them that farthest cometh behind.
Yet may I, by no means, my wearied mind   5
Draw from the deer, but as she fleeth afore,
Fainting I follow. I leave off therefore,
Since in a net I seek to hold the wind.
Who list her hunt, I put him out of doubt,
As well as I, may spend his time in vain.   10
And graven with diamonds in letters plain
There is written, her fair neck round about,
"*Noli me tangere*° for Caesar's I am,
And wild for to hold, though I seem tame."

13 *Noli me tangere*: "Do not touch me" (Latin), said to have been written on the collars of
Caesar's deer so that others would not kill them.

EDMUND SPENSER   (1552?–1599)

Fresh spring the herald of loves mighty king

Fresh spring the herald of loves mighty king,
In whose cote armour° richly are displayd   *coat of arms*

All sorts of flowers the which on earth do spring
In goodly colours gloriously arrayd.
Goe to my love, where she is carelesse layd,   5
Yet in her winters bowre not well awake:
Tell her the joyous time wil not be staid
Unless she doe him by the forelock take.
Bid her therefore her selfe soone ready make,
To wayt on love amongst his lovely crew: 10
Where every one that misseth then her make,°   *mate*
Shall be by him amearst° with penance dew.   *chastised*
Make hast therefore sweet love, whilest it is prime,
For none can call againe the passed time.

SIR PHILIP SIDNEY   (1554–1586)

Leave me, O Love

Leave me, O Love which reachest but to dust,
And thou my mind aspire to higher things;
Grow rich in that which never taketh rust;
Whatever fades but fading pleasure brings.

Draw in thy beams, and humble all thy might   5
To that sweet yoke where lasting freedoms be;
Which breaks the clouds and opens forth the light,
That doth both shine and give us sight to see.

O take fast hold; let that light be thy guide
In this small course which birth draws out to death,   10
And think how evil becometh him to slide,
Who seeketh heav'n, and comes of heav'nly breath.
    Then farewell world; thy uttermost I see;
    Eternal Love, maintain thy life in me.

SIR PHILIP SIDNEY   (1554–1586)

With how sad steps, O Moon,
thou climb'st the skies

With how sad steps, O Moon, thou climb'st the skies,
    How silently, and with how wan a face!
    What, may it be that even in heavenly place

That busy archer his sharp arrows tries?
Sure, if that long-with-love-acquainted eyes   5
   Can judge of Love, thou feel'st a Lover's case;
   I read it in thy looks: thy languished grace,
To me that feel the like, thy state descries.
   Then even of fellowship, O Moon, tell me
Is constant *love* deemed there but want of wit?   10
Are beauties there as proud as here they be?
Do they above love to be loved, and yet
   Those lovers scorn whom that *love* doth possess?
   Do they call *virtue* there ungratefulness?

CHRISTOPHER MARLOWE (1564–1593)
The Passionate Shepherd to His Love

Come live with me and be my love,
And we will all the pleasures prove
That valleys, groves, hills, and fields,
Woods, or steepy mountain yields.

And we will sit upon the rocks,   5
Seeing the shepherds feed their flocks
By shallow rivers, to whose falls
Melodious birds sing madrigals.

And I will make thee beds of roses
And a thousand fragrant posies,   10
A cap of flowers and a kirtle
Embroidered all with leaves of myrtle;

A gown made of the finest wool
Which from our pretty lambs we pull;
Fair-lined slippers for the cold,   15
With buckles of the purest gold;

A belt of straw and ivy buds,
With coral clasps and amber studs.
And if these pleasures may thee move,
Come live with me and be my love.   20

The shepherds' swains shall dance and sing
For thy delight each May morning:
If these delights thy mind may move,
Then live with me and be my love.

SIR WALTER RALEIGH   (1552–1618)
The Nymph's Reply to the Shepherd

If all the world and love were young,
And truth in every shepherd's tongue,
These pretty pleasures might me move
To live with thee and be thy love.

Time drives the flocks from field to fold   5
When rivers rage and rocks grow cold,
And Philomel becometh dumb;
The rest complains of cares to come.

The flowers do fade, and wanton fields
To wayward winter reckoning yields;   10
A honey tongue, a heart of gall,
Is fancy's spring, but sorrow's fall.

Thy gowns, thy shoes, thy beds of roses,
Thy cap, thy kirtle, and thy posies
Soon break, soon wither, soon forgotten —   15
In folly ripe, in reason rotten.

Thy belt of straw and ivy buds,
Thy coral clasps and amber studs,
All these in me no means can move
To come to thee and be thy love.   20

But could youth last and love still breed,
Had joys no date nor age no need,
Then these delights my mind might move
To live with thee and be thy love.

WILLIAM SHAKESPEARE   (1564–1616)
Devouring Time, blunt thou the lion's paws

Devouring Time, blunt thou the lion's paws,
And make the earth devour her own sweet brood;
Pluck the keen teeth from the fierce tiger's jaws,
And burn the long-lived phoenix in her blood;
Make glad and sorry seasons as thou fleet'st,   5
And do what e'er thou wilt, swift-footed Time,
To the wide world and all her fading sweets:

But I forbid thee one most heinous crime,
O carve not with thy hours my love's fair brow,
Nor draw no lines there with thine antique pen; 10
Him in thy course untainted do allow,
For beauty's pattern to succeeding men.
   Yet do thy worst, old Time: despite thy wrong,
    My love shall in my verse ever live young.

WILLIAM SHAKESPEARE   (1564–1616)

Not marble, nor the gilded monuments

Not marble, nor the gilded monuments
Of princes, shall outlive this powerful rhyme;
But you shall shine more bright in these contents
Than unswept stone, besmeared with sluttish time.
When wasteful war shall statues overturn, 5
And broils root out the work of masonry,
Nor Mars his sword nor war's quick fire shall burn
The living record of your memory.
'Gainst death and all-oblivious enmity
Shall you pace forth; your praise shall still find room 10
Even in the eyes of all posterity
That wear this world out to the ending doom.
   So, till the judgment that yourself arise,
    You live in this, and dwell in lovers' eyes.

WILLIAM SHAKESPEARE   (1564–1616)

Shall I compare thee to a summer's day?

Shall I compare thee to a summer's day?
Thou art more lovely and more temperate.
Rough winds do shake the darling buds of May,
And summer's lease hath all too short a date.
Sometime too hot the eye of heaven shines, 5
And often is his gold complexion dimmed;
And every fair from fair sometime declines,
By chance, or nature's changing course, untrimmed.
But thy eternal summer shall not fade,
Nor lose possession of that fair thou ow'st;° *possess* 10
Nor shall death brag thou wand'rest in his shade,
When in eternal lines to time thou grow'st.

So long as men can breathe or eyes can see,
So long lives this, and this gives life to thee.

WILLIAM SHAKESPEARE   (1564–1616)
Winter °

When icicles hang by the wall
    And Dick the shepherd blows his nail,°
And Tom bears logs into the hall,
    And milk comes frozen home in pail.
When blood is nipped and ways be foul,   5
Then nightly sings the staring owl,
                Tu-who;
Tu-whit, tu-who: a merry note,
While greasy Joan doth keel the pot.°

When all aloud the wind doth blow,   10
    And coughing drowns the parson's saw,
And birds sit brooding in the snow,
    And Marian's nose looks red and raw,
When roasted crabs° hiss in the bowl,   *crab apples*
Then nightly sings the staring owl,   15
                Tu-who;
Tu-whit, tu-who: a merry note
While greasy Joan doth keel the pot.

Winter Song from *Love's Labour's Lost*, V.ii.   2 *blows his nail*: Blows on his hands to warm them.   9 *keel the pot*: Cool the contents of the pot by stirring.

JOHN DONNE   (1572–1631)
At the round earth's imagined corners, blow

At the round earth's imagined corners, blow
Your trumpets, angels; and arise, arise
From death, you numberless infinities
Of souls, and to your scattered bodies go:
All whom the flood did, and fire shall, o'erthrow,   5
All whom war, dearth, age, agues, tyrannies,
Despair, law, chance hath slain, and you whose eyes
Shall behold God, and never taste death's woe.
But let them sleep, Lord, and me mourn a space;
For, if above all these, my sins abound,   10

'Tis late to ask abundance of thy grace
When we are there. Here on this lowly ground,
Teach me how to repent; for that's as good
As if thou hadst sealed my pardon with thy blood.

JOHN DONNE   (1572–1631)

The Canonization

For God's sake hold your tongue, and let me love,
   Or chide my palsy, or my gout,
My five gray hairs, or ruined fortune, flout,
   With wealth your state, your mind with arts improve,
      Take you a course, get you a place,   5
      Observe His Honor, or His Grace,
Or the King's real, or his stampéd face°   *coins*
      Contemplate; what you will, approve,°   *test by experience*
      So you will let me love.

Alas, alas, who's injured by my love?   10
   What merchant's ships have my sighs drowned?
Who says my tears have overflowed his ground?
   When did my colds a forward spring remove?
      When did the heats which my veins fill
      Add one man to the plaguy bill?°   15
Soldiers find wars, and lawyers find out still
   Litigious men, which quarrels move,
   Though she and I do love.

Call us what you will, we are made such by love,
   Call her one, me another fly,   20
We're tapers too, and at our own cost die,
   And we in us find the eagle and the dove.
      The phoenix riddle hath more wit
      By us: we two being one, are it.
So, to one neutral thing both sexes fit.   25
   We die and rise the same, and prove
   Mysterious by this love.

We can die by it, if not live by love,
   And if unfit for tombs and hearse
Our legend be, it will be fit for verse;   30
   And if no piece of chronicle we prove,

15 *plaguy bill*: Weekly record of deaths from the plague.

We'll build in sonnets pretty rooms;
   As well a well-wrought urn becomes
The greatest ashes, as half-acre tombs,
   And by these hymns, all shall approve   35
   Us canonized for love:

And thus invoke us: You whom reverend love
   Made one another's hermitage;
You, to whom love was peace, that now is rage;
   Who did the whole world's soul contract, and drove   40
      Into the glasses of your eyes
      (So made such mirrors, and such spies,
That they did all to you epitomize)
      Countries, towns, courts: Beg from above
      A pattern of your love!   45

JOHN DONNE   (1572–1631)
Death, be not proud

Death, be not proud, though some have callèd thee
Mighty and dreadful, for thou art not so;
For those whom thou think'st thou dost overthrow
Die not, poor Death, nor yet canst thou kill me.
From rest and sleep, which but thy pictures be,   5
Much pleasure; then from thee much more must flow,
And soonest our best men with thee do go,
Rest of their bones, and soul's delivery.
Thou art slave to fate, chance, kings, and desperate men,
And dost with poison, war, and sickness dwell,   10
And poppy or charms can make us sleep as well
And better than thy stroke; why swell'st thou then?
One short sleep past, we wake eternally
And death shall be no more; Death, thou shalt die.

JOHN DONNE   (1572–1631)
The Sun Rising

   Busy old fool, unruly sun,
     Why dost thou thus,
Through windows and through curtains call on us?
Must to thy motions lovers' seasons run?
     Saucy pedantic wretch, go chide   5

Late schoolboys and sour prentices,
Go tell court huntsmen that the King will ride,
Call country ants° to harvest offices;   *farm workers*
Love, all alike, no season knows nor clime,
Nor hours, days, months, which are the rags of time.   10

Thy beams, so reverend and strong
Why shouldst thou think?
I could eclipse and cloud them with a wink,
But that I would not lose her sight so long;
If her eyes have not blinded thine,   15
Look, and tomorrow late, tell me.
Whether both th' Indias of spice and mine°   *East and West Indies*
Be where thou leftst them, or lie here with me.
Ask for those kings whom thou saw'st yesterday,
And thou shalt hear, "All here in one bed lay."   20

She is all states, and all princes I,
Nothing else is.
Princes do but play us; compared to this,
All honor's mimic, all wealth alchemy.
Thou, sun, art half as happy as we,   25
In that the world's contracted thus;
Thine age asks ease, and since thy duties be
To warm the world, that's done in warming us.
Shine here to us, and thou art everywhere;
This bed thy center° is, these walls thy sphere.   *of the sun's orbit*   30

GEORGE HERBERT   (1593–1633)

Love

Love bade me welcome: yet my soul drew back,
        Guilty of dust and sin.
But quick-eyed Love, observing me grow slack
        From my first entrance in,
Drew nearer to me, sweetly questioning   5
        If I lack'd anything.

A guest, I answer'd, worthy to be here:
        Love said, You shall be he.
I, the unkind, ungrateful? Ah, my dear,
        I cannot look on thee.   10
Love took my hand, and smiling did reply,
        Who made the eyes but I?

Truth, Lord, but I have marr'd them: let my shame
  Go where it doth deserve.
And know you not, says Love, who bore the blame?   15
  My dear, then I will serve.
You must sit down, says Love, and taste my meat:
  So I did sit and eat.

GEORGE HERBERT (1593–1633)

Virtue

Sweet day, so cool, so calm, so bright,
The bridal of the earth and sky:
The dew shall weep thy fall tonight;
  For thou must die.

Sweet rose, whose hue, angry and brave,   5
Bids the rash gazer wipe his eye:
Thy root is ever in its grave,
  And thou must die.

Sweet spring, full of sweet days and roses,
A box where sweets° compacted lie;   *perfumes* 10
My music shows ye have your closes,°
  And all must die.

Only a sweet and virtuous soul,
Like seasoned timber, never gives;
But though the whole world turn to coal,   15
  Then chiefly lives.

11 *closes*: Ending cadences in a piece of music.

GEORGE HERBERT (1593–1633)

The Windows

Lord, how can man preach thy eternal word?
  He is a brittle, crazy° glass,   *flawed*
Yet in thy temple thou dost him afford
  This glorious and transcendent place,
  To be a window through thy grace.   5

But when thou dost anneal in glass thy story,
  Making thy life to shine within

The holy preachers, then the light and glory
　　More reverend grows, and more doth win,
　　Which else shows wat'rish, bleak, and thin.　　　　　　10

Doctrine and life, colors and light, in one
　　When they combine and mingle, bring
A strong regard and awe; but speech alone
　　Doth vanish like a flaring thing,
　　And in the ear, not conscience, ring.　　　　　　　　15

JOHN MILTON　　(1608–1674)

Lycidas °

In this monody the author bewails a learned friend,° unfortunately drowned in
his passage from Chester on the Irish seas, 1637. And by occasion foretells the
ruin of our corrupted clergy, then in their height.

　　Yet once more, O ye laurels, and once more
Ye myrtles brown, with ivy° never sere,
I come to pluck your berries harsh and crude,°　　　　　*unripened*
And with forced fingers rude,
Shatter your leaves before the mellowing year.　　　　　　5
Bitter constraint, and sad occasion dear,
Compels me to disturb your season due;
For Lycidas is dead, dead ere his prime,
Young Lycidas, and hath not left his peer
Who would not sing for Lycidas? He knew　　　　　　　10
Himself to sing, and build the lofty rhyme.
He must not float upon his watery bier
Unwept, and welter to the parching wind,
Without the meed of some melodious tear.
　　Begin then, sisters of the sacred well°　　　　　*the Muses*　15
That from beneath the seat of Jove doth spring,
Begin, and somewhat loudly sweep the string.
Hence with denial vain, and coy excuse;
So may some gentle Muse
With lucky words favor my destined urn,　　　　　　　20
And as he passes turn,
And bid fair peace be to my sable shroud.
For we were nursed upon the selfsame hill,

Lycidas: Conventional shepherd's name in pastoral poetry.　　*learned friend*: Edward King, a
poet, scholar, candidate for the ministry, and classmate of Milton at Cambridge University.
1–2 laurels, . . . myrtles, . . . ivy: Plants traditionally used to make poets' garlands.

Fed the same flock, by fountain, shade, and rill.
   Together both, ere the high lawns appeared   25
Under the opening eyelids of the morn,
We drove afield, and both together heard
What time the grayfly winds her sultry horn.
Battening our flocks with the fresh dews of night,
Oft till the star that rose at evening bright   30
Toward Heaven's descent had sloped his westering wheel.
Meanwhile the rural ditties were not mute,
Tempered to th' oaten flute,
Rough satyrs danced, and fauns with cloven heel
From the glad sound would not be absent long,   35
And old Damoetas° loved to hear our song.
   But O the heavy change, now thou art gone,
Now thou art gone, and never must return!
Thee, shepherd, thee the woods and desert caves,
With wild thyme and the gadding vine o'ergrown,   40
And all their echoes mourn.
The willows and the hazel copses green
Shall now no more be seen,
Fanning their joyous leaves to thy soft lays.
As killing as the canker to the rose,   45
Or taint-worm to the weanling herds that graze,
Or frost to flowers that their gay wardrobe wear,
When first the white thorn blows,
Such, Lycidas, thy loss to shepherd's ear.
   Where were ye, nymphs, when the remorseless deep   50
Closed o'er the head of your loved Lycidas?
For neither were ye playing on the steep,
Where your old Bards, the famous Druids lie,
Nor on the shaggy top of Mona° high,
Nor yet where Deva° spreads her wizard stream: 55
Ay me! I fondly dream —
Had ye been there — for what could that have done?
What could the Muse herself that Orpheus bore,
The Muse herself, for her inchanting son
Whom universal Nature did lament,   60
When by the rout that made the hideous roar,

---

36 *Damoetas*: Another conventional pastoral name, possibly referring to a tutor at Cambridge.
54 *Mona*: Anglesey, an island off the Welsh coast, believed to be the home of the Druids.
55 *Deva*: The River Dee, flowing between Wales and England, whose changes were believed to presage shifts in the fortunes of the two countries.

His gory visage down the stream was sent,
Down the swift Hebrus to the Lesbian shore?°
    Alas! What boots it with incessant care
To tend the homely slighted shepherd's trade,   65
And strictly meditate the thankless Muse?
Were it not better done as others use,
To sport with Amaryllis in the shade,
Or with the tangles of Neaera's° hair?
Fame is the spur that the clear spirit doth raise   70
(That last infirmity of noble mind)
To scorn delights, and live laborious days;
But the fair guerdon when we hope to find,
And think to burst out into sudden blaze,
Comes the blind Fury with th' abhorréd shears,   75
And slits the thin spun life.° "But not the praise,"
Phoebus replied, and touched my trembling ears;°
"Fame is no plant that grows on mortal soil,
Not in the glistering foil°
Set off to th' world, nor in broad rumor° lies,   *reputation*   80
But lives and spreads aloft by those pure eyes,
And perfect witness of all-judging Jove;
As he pronounces lastly on each deed,
Of so much fame in Heaven expect thy meed."
    O fountain Arethuse,° and thou honored flood,   85
Smooth-sliding Mincius,° crowned with vocal reeds,
That strain I heard was of a higher mood.
But now my oat° proceeds,
And listens to the herald of the sea°
That came in Neptune's plea.   90
He asked the waves, and asked the felon winds,
"What hard mishap hath doomed this gentle swain?"
And questioned every gust of rugged wings
That blows from off each beakéd promontory;

58–63 *the Muse . . . shore*: Orpheus, son of Apollo and Calliope and a consummate musician, was torn to pieces by jealous Thracian women, who threw his head and his lyre into the Hebrus River.   68–69 *Amaryllis . . . Neaera*: Conventional names for shepherdesses in pastoral poetry.   75–76 *blind Fury . . . life*: A conflation of the Furies, avenging deities, and the Fates, who spun and then cut the thread of each person's life.   77 *Phoebus . . . ears*: Apollo, god of both the sun and poetry, bids the poet to remember.   79 *glistering foil*: A thin piece of silver or gold placed behind a gem to enhance its appearance.   85 *fountain Arethuse*: Near the birthplace in Sicily of the pastoral poet Theocritus; named for the nymph Arethusa, who turned into a fountain while being pursued by Alpheus.   86 *Mincius*: River near the birthplace in Lombardy of Virgil.   88 *oat*: Oaten flute or panpipe, thus its song.   89 *herald of the sea*: Triton, a demigod.

They knew not of his story,   95
And sage Hippotades° their answer brings,
That not a blast was from his dungeon strayed,
The air was calm, and on the level brine,
Sleek Panope° with all her sisters played.
It was that fatal and perfidious bark   100
Built in th' eclipse, and rigged with curses dark,
That sunk so low that sacred head of thine.
   Next Camus,° reverend sire, went footing slow,
His mantle hairy, and his bonnet sedge,
Inwrought with figures dim, and on the edge   105
Like to that sanguine flower inscribed with woe.°
"Ah! who hath reft," quoth he, "my dearest pledge?"
Last came and last did go
The pilot of the Galilean lake;
Two massy keys he bore of metals twain   110
(The golden opes, the iron shuts amain).°
He shook his mitered locks,° and stern bespake:
"How well could I have spared for thee, young swain,
Enow of such as for their bellies' sake
Creep and intrude and climb into the fold!   115
Of other care they little reckoning make,
Than how to scramble at the shearers' feast,
And shove away the worthy bidden guest.
Blind mouths! that scarce themselves know how to hold
A sheep-hook,° or have learned aught else the least   120
That to the faithful herdsman's art belongs!
What recks it them? What need they? They are sped;°   *prosperous*
And when they list,° their lean and flashy songs   *desire*
Grate on their scrannel pipes of wretched straw.
The hungry sheep look up, and are not fed,   125
But swoln with wind, and the rank mist they draw,
Rot inwardly, and foul contagion spread,
Besides what the grim wolf° with privy paw
Daily devours apace, and nothing said.

---

96 *Hippotades*: God of the winds.   99 *Panope*: One of the sea nymphs.   103 *Camus*: Spirit of
the Cam River, standing for Cambridge University.   106 *Sanguine flower . . . woe*: The
hyacinth, which Apollo created from the blood of Hyacinthus and marked *AIAI* ("alas, alas")
to express his remorse at having accidentally killed the youth.   109–111 *pilot . . . amain*: St.
Peter, originally a fisherman in Galilee, was told he would be given the keys to heaven
(Matthew 16:19).   112 *mitered locks*: As the first head of the church, Peter wears the bishop's
headdress.   120 *sheep-hook*: Refers to a bishop's staff, which resembles it.   128 *grim wolf*:
Anti-Protestantism.

But that two-handed engine° at the door   130
Stands ready to smite once, and smite no more."
   Return, Alpheus,° the dread voice is past,
That shrunk thy streams; return, Sicilian muse,°
And call the vales, and bid them hither cast
Their bells and flowerets of a thousand hues.   135
Ye valleys low where the mild whispers use,
Of shades and wanton winds, and gushing brooks,
On whose fresh lap the swart star° sparely looks,
Throw hither all your quaint enameled eyes,
That on the green turf suck the honeyed showers,   140
And purple all the ground with vernal flowers.
Bring the rathe primrose that forsaken dies,
The tufted crow-toe, and pale jessamine,
The white pink, and the pansy freaked with jet,
The glowing violet,   145
The musk-rose, and the well-attired woodbine,
With cowslips wan that hang the pensive head,
And every flower that sad embroidery wears:
Bid amaranthus all his beauty shed,
And daffadillies fill their cups with tears,   150
To strew the laureate hearse where Lycid lies.
For so to interpose a little ease,
Let our frail thoughts dally with false surmise.°
Ay me! whilst thee the shores and sounding seas
Wash far away, where'er thy bones are hurled,   155
Whether beyond the stormy Hebrides,
Where thou perhaps under the whelming tide
Visit'st the bottom of the monstrous world;
Or whether thou, to our moist vows° denied,   *prayers*
Sleep'st by the fable of Bellerus° old,   160
Where the great vision of the guarded mount°
Looks toward Namancos and Bayona's hold;°

130 *two-handed engine*: May be either the sword of the Archangel Michael or the Word of God,
Seen as a swordlike thunderbolt or some other instrument of judgment.   132 *Alpheus*: A
river god who dove under the sea and resurfaced on Sicily while chasing the nymph
Arethusa.   133 *Sicilian muse*: The inspirer of Theocritus.   138 *swart star*: Sirius, which was
thought to turn plants black when at its zenith, but which here shines gently.   153 *false
surmise*: The possibility that Lycidas's body had been recovered.   160 *Bellerus*: A legendary
giant believed to have been buried at Land's End in Cornwall.   161 *guarded mount*: Michael's Mount, at the tip of Land's End, protected by the Archangel Michael.   162 *Namancos,
Bayona's hold*: In northwestern Spain.

Look homeward angel now, and melt with ruth:
And, O ye dolphins,° waft the hapless youth.
    Weep no more, woeful shepherds, weep no more,   165
For Lycidas your sorrow is not dead,
Sunk though he be beneath the wat'ry floor;
So sinks the day-star in the ocean bed,
And yet anon repairs his drooping head,
And tricks his beams, and with new-spangled ore   170
Flames in the forehead of the morning sky:
So Lycidas sunk low, but mounted high,
Through the dear might of him that walked the waves,
Where, other groves and other streams along,
With nectar pure his oozy locks he laves,   175
And hears the unexpressive nuptial song,°
In the blest kingdoms meek of joy and love.
There entertain him all the saints above,
In solemn troops and sweet societies
That sing, and singing in their glory move,   180
And wipe the tears forever from his eyes.
Now, Lycidas, the shepherds weep no more;
Henceforth thou art the genius of the shore,
In thy large recompense, and shalt be good
To all that wander in that perilous flood.   185
    Thus sang the uncouth swain to th' oaks and rills,
While the still morn went out with sandals gray;
He touched the tender stops of various quills,
With eager thought warbling his Doric lay.°   *pastoral poem*
And now the sun had stretched out all the hills,   190
And now was dropped into the western bay;
At last he rose, and twitched° his mantle blue: *put on*
Tomorrow to fresh woods, and pastures new.

164 *dolphins*: Carriers of the spirits of the dead to Elysium, beyond the Atlantic Ocean.
176 *nuptial song*: Possibly the hymn sung at "the marriage supper of the Lamb" (see Revelation 19:9).   188 *stops of . . . quills*: Parts of a panpipe.

JOHN MILTON   (1608–1674)
Methought I Saw

Methought I saw my late espoused saint
    Brought to me like Alcestis from the grave,

Whom Jove's great son to her glad husband gave,°
Rescued from Death by force, though pale and faint.
Mine, as whom washed from spot of child-bed taint   5
Purification in the Old Law did save,°
And such, as yet once more I trust to have
Full sight of her in heaven without restraint,
Came vested all in white, pure as her mind.
Her face was veiled; yet to my fancied sight   10
Love, sweetness, goodness, in her person shined
So clear as in no face with more delight.
But O, as to embrace me she inclined,
I waked, she fled, and day brought back my night.

2–3 *Alcestis . . . gave*: Alcestis volunteered to die so that her husband could live longer, but Hercules brought her back from Death.   5–6 *washed . . . save*: One of the Old Testament laws required that women who had given birth be considered unclean until a specified number of days had passed and a cleansing ritual had been performed (see Leviticus 12).

ANDREW MARVELL   (1621–1678)

The Picture of Little T.C. in a Prospect of Flowers

See with what simplicity
This nymph begins her golden days!
In the green grass she loves to lie,
And there with her fair aspect tames
The wilder flowers and gives them names,   5
But only with the roses plays,
    And them does tell
What color best becomes them and what smell.

Who can foretell for what high cause
This darling of the gods was born?   10
Yet this is she whose chaster laws
The wanton Love shall one day fear,
And under her command severe
See his bow broke and ensigns torn.
    Happy who can   15
Appease this virtuous enemy of man!

O then let me in time compound
And parley with those conquering eyes

Ere they have tried their force to wound,
Ere with their glancing wheels they drive
In triumph over hearts that strive
And them that yield but more despise:
    Let me be laid
Where I may see thy glories from some shade.

Meantime, whilst every verdant thing
Itself does at thy beauty charm,
Reform the errors of the spring;
Make that the tulips may have share
Of sweetness, seeing they are fair,
And roses of their thorns disarm:
    But most procure
That violets may a longer age endure.

But O, young beauty of the woods,
Whom Nature courts with fruit and flowers,
Gather the flowers but spare the buds,
Lest Flora, angry at thy crime
To kill her infants in their prime,
Do quickly make th' example yours;
    And ere we see,
Nip in the blossom all our hopes and thee.

JONATHAN SWIFT (1667–1745)

*A Satirical Elegy on the Death
of a Late Famous General*

His Grace! impossible! what dead!
Of old Age too, and in his Bed!
And could that Mighty Warrior fall?
And so inglorious, after all!
Well, since he's gone, no matter how,
The last loud Trump must wake him now:
And, trust me, as the Noise grows stronger,
He'd wish to sleep a little longer.
And could he be indeed so old
As by the News-papers we're told?
Threescore, I think, is pretty high;
'Twas time in Conscience he should die.

This World he cumber'd long enough;
He burnt his Candle to the Snuff;
And that's the Reason, some Folks think,   15
He left behind *so great a Stink.*
Behold his Funeral appears,
Nor Widow's Sighs, nor Orphan's Tears,
Wont at such Times each Heart to pierce,
Attend the Progress of his Herse.   20
But what of that, his Friends may say,
He had those Honours in his Day.
True to his Profit and his Pride,
He made them weep before he dy'd.
   Come hither, all ye empty Things,   25
Ye Bubbles rais'd by Breath of Kings;
Who float upon the Tide of State,
Come hither, and behold your Fate.
Let Pride be taught by this Rebuke,
How very mean a Thing's a Duke;   30
From all his ill-got Honours flung,
Turned to that Dirt from whence he sprung.

ALEXANDER POPE   (1688–1744)

From *An Essay on Man*

From *Epistle 2. Of the Nature and State of Man with Respect to Himself, as an Individual*

   1. Know then thyself, presume not God to scan;
The proper study of mankind is Man.
Placed on this isthmus of a middle state,
A being darkly wise, and rudely great:
With too much knowledge for the skeptic side,   5
With too much weakness for the stoic's pride,
He hangs between; in doubt to act, or rest,
In doubt to deem himself a god, or beast;
In doubt his mind or body to prefer,
Born but to die, and reasoning but to err;   10
Alike in ignorance, his reason such,
Whether he thinks too little, or too much:
Chaos of thought and passion, all confused;
Still by himself abused, or disabused;

Created half to rise, and half to fall;   15
Great lord of all things, yet a prey to all;
Sole judge of truth, in endless error hurled:
The glory, jest, and riddle of the world!

WILLIAM COLLINS   (1721–1759)
Ode
Written in the Beginning of the Year 1746

How sleep the brave, who sink to rest,
By all their country's wishes blest!
When Spring, with dewy fingers cold,
Returns to deck their hallow'd mould,
She there shall dress a sweeter sod   5
Than Fancy's feet have ever trod.

By fairy hands their knell is rung;
By forms unseen their dirge is sung;
There Honour comes, a pilgrim gray,
To bless the turf that wraps their clay;   10
And Freedom shall awhile repair,
To dwell a weeping hermit there!

WILLIAM BLAKE   (1757–1827)
The Ecchoing Green

The Sun does arise,
And make happy the skies.
The merry bells ring
To welcome the Spring.
The sky-lark and thrush,   5
The birds of the bush,
Sing louder around,
To the bells chearful sound.
While our sports shall be seen
On the Ecchoing Green.   10

Old John with white hair
Does laugh away care,

Sitting under the oak,
Among the old folk,
They laugh at our play,   15
And soon they all say.
Such such were the joys.
When we all girls & boys,
In our youth-time were seen,
On the Ecchoing Green.   20

Till the little ones weary
No more can be merry
The sun does descend,
And our sports have an end:
Round the laps of their mothers,   25
Many sisters and brothers,
Like birds in their nest,
Are ready for rest;
And sport no more seen,
On the darkening Green.   30

WILLIAM BLAKE   (1757–1827)
London

I wander thro' each charter'd street,
Near where the charter'd Thames does flow,
And mark in every face I meet
Marks of weakness, marks of woe.

In every cry of every Man,   5
In every Infant's cry of fear,
In every voice, in every ban,
The mind-forg'd manacles I hear.

How the Chimney-sweeper's cry
Every black'ning Church appalls;   10
And the hapless Soldier's sigh
Runs in blood down Palace walls.

But most thro' midnight streets I hear
How the youthful Harlot's curse
Blasts the new-born Infant's tear,   15
And blights with plagues the Marriage hearse.

WILLIAM BLAKE (1757–1827)
A Poison Tree

I was angry with my friend:
I told my wrath, my wrath did end.
I was angry with my foe:
I told it not, my wrath did grow.

And I water'd it in fears,   5
Night & morning with my tears;
And I sunnéd it with smiles,
And with soft deceitful wiles.

And it grew both day and night,
Till it bore an apple bright.   10
And my foe beheld it shine,
And he knew that it was mine,

And into my garden stole,
When the night had veil'd the pole;
In the morning glad I see   15
My foe outstretch'd beneath the tree.

WILLIAM BLAKE (1757–1827)
The Tyger

Tyger! Tyger! burning bright
In the forests of the night,
What immortal hand or eye
Could frame thy fearful symmetry?

In what distant deeps or skies   5
Burnt the fire of thine eyes?
On what wings dare he aspire?
What the hand dare seize the fire?

And what shoulder, & what art,
Could twist the sinews of thy heart?   10
And when thy heart began to beat,
What dread hand? & what dread feet?

What the hammer? what the chain?
In what furnace was thy brain?

What the anvil? what dread grasp   15
Dare its deadly terrors clasp?

When the stars threw down their spears
And water'd heaven with their tears,
Did he smile his work to see?
Did he who made the Lamb make thee?   20

Tyger! Tyger! burning bright
In the forests of the night,
What immortal hand or eye
Dare frame thy fearful symmetry?

WILLIAM WORDSWORTH   (1770–1850)
The Solitary Reaper

Behold her, single in the field,
Yon solitary Highland Lass!
Reaping and singing by herself;
Stop here, or gently pass!
Alone she cuts and binds the grain,   5
And sings a melancholy strain;
O listen! for the Vale profound
Is overflowing with the sound.

No Nightingale did ever chaunt
More welcome notes to weary bands   10
Of travellers in some shady haunt,
Among Arabian sands:
A voice so thrilling ne'er was heard
In spring-time from the Cuckoo-bird,
Breaking the silence of the seas   15
Among the farthest Hebrides.

Will no one tell me what she sings? —
Perhaps the plaintive numbers flow
For old, unhappy, far-off things,
And battles long ago: 20
Or is it some more humble lay,
Familiar matter of to-day?
Some natural sorrow, loss, or pain,
That has been, and may be again?

Whate'er the theme, the Maiden sang   25
As if her song could have no ending;

I saw her singing at her work,
And o'er the sickle bending: —
I listened, motionless and still;
And, as I mounted up the hill,   30
The music in my heart I bore,
Long after it was heard no more.

WILLIAM WORDSWORTH   (1770–1850)

The world is too much with us

The world is too much with us; late and soon,
Getting and spending, we lay waste our powers;
Little we see in Nature that is ours;
We have given our hearts away, a sordid boon!
This Sea that bares her bosom to the moon,   5
The winds that will be howling at all hours,
And are up-gathered now like sleeping flowers,
For this, for everything, we are out of tune;
It moves us not. — Great God! I'd rather be
A Pagan suckled in a creed outworn;   10
So might I, standing on this pleasant lea,
Have glimpses that would make me less forlorn;
Have sight of Proteus rising from the sea;
Or hear old Triton blow his wreathéd horn.

GEORGE GORDON, LORD BYRON   (1788–1824)

So we'll go no more a-roving

1

So we'll go no more a-roving
   So late into the night,
Though the heart be still as loving,
   And the moon be still as bright.

2

For the sword outwears its sheath,   5
   And the soul wears out the breast,

And the heart must pause to breathe,
    And Love itself have rest.

3

Though the night was made for loving,
    And the day returns too soon,   10
Yet we'll go no more a-roving
    By the light of the moon.

PERCY BYSSHE SHELLEY   (1792-1822)
Ode to the West Wind

I

O wild West Wind, thou breath of Autumn's being,
Thou, from whose unseen presence the leaves dead
Are driven, like ghosts from an enchanter fleeing,

Yellow, and black, and pale, and hectic red,
Pestilence-stricken multitudes: O thou,   5
Who chariotest to their dark wintry bed

The wingéd seeds, where they lie cold and low,
Each like a corpse within its grave, until
Thine azure sister of the Spring shall blow

Her clarion o'er the dreaming earth, and fill   10
(Driving sweet buds like flocks to feed in air)
With living hues and odors plain and hill:

Wild Spirit, which art moving everywhere;
Destroyer and preserver; hear, oh, hear!

II

Thou on whose stream, mid the steep sky's commotion,   15
Loose clouds like earth's decaying leaves are shed,
Shook from the tangled boughs of Heaven and Ocean,

Angels° of rain and lightning: there are spread   *messengers*
On the blue surface of thine airy surge,
Like the bright hair uplifted from the head   20

Of some fierce Maenad,° even from the dim verge
Of the horizon to the zenith's height,
The locks of the approaching storm. Thou dirge

Of the dying year, to which this closing night
Will be the dome of a vast sepulcher,   25
Vaulted with all thy congregated might

Of vapors, from whose solid atmosphere
Black rain, and fire, and hail will burst: oh, hear!

III

Thou who didst waken from his summer dreams
The blue Mediterranean, where he lay,   30
Lulled by the coil of his crystálline streams,

Beside a pumice isle in Baiae's bay,
And saw in sleep old palaces and towers
Quivering within the wave's intenser day,

All overgrown with azure moss and flowers   35
So sweet, the sense faints picturing them! Thou
For whose path the Atlantic's level powers

Cleave themselves into chasms, while far below
The sea-blooms and the oozy woods which wear
The sapless foliage of the ocean, know   40

Thy voice, and suddenly grow gray with fear,
And tremble and despoil themselves: oh, hear!

IV

If I were a dead leaf thou mightest bear;
If I were a swift cloud to fly with thee;
A wave to pant beneath thy power, and share   45

The impulse of thy strength, only less free
Than thou, O uncontrollable! If even
I were as in my boyhood, and could be

---

21 *Maenad*: In Greek mythology, a frenzied worshiper of Dionysus.

The comrade by thy wanderings over Heaven,
As then, when to outstrip thy skyey speed   50
Scarce seemed a vision; I would ne'er have striven

As thus with thee in prayer in my sore need.
Oh, lift me as a wave, a leaf, a cloud!
I fall upon the thorns of life! I bleed!

A heavy weight of hours has chained and bowed   55
One too like thee: tameless, and swift, and proud.

V

Make me thy lyre,° even as the forest is:
What if my leaves are falling like its own!
The tumult of thy mighty harmonies

Will take from both a deep, autumnal tone,   60
Sweet though in sadness. Be thou, Spirit fierce,
My spirit! Be thou me, impetuous one!

Drive my dead thoughts over the universe
Like withered leaves to quicken a new birth!
And, by the incantation of this verse,   65

Scatter, as from an unextinguished hearth
Ashes and sparks, my words among mankind!
Be through my lips to unawakened earth

The trumpet of a prophecy! O Wind,
If Winter comes, can Spring be far behind?   70

57 *lyre*: An Aeolian lyre, or wind harp, makes its sound when wind blows across the strings.

PERCY BYSSHE SHELLEY   (1792–1822)
Ozymandias°

I met a traveler from an antique land
Who said: Two vast and trunkless legs of stone
Stand in the desert. Near them, on the sand,
Half sunk, a shattered visage lies, whose frown,
And wrinkled lip, and sneer of cold command,   5

Ozymandias: Ramses II, pharaoh of Egypt in the thirteenth century B.C. The inscription on his statue, which lies in ruins in Luxor, was said to read, "I am Ozymandias, King of Kings; if anyone wishes to know what I am and where I lie, let him surpass me in some of my exploits."

Tell that its sculptor well those passions read
Which yet survive, stamped on these lifeless things,
The hand that mocked them and the heart that fed;
And on the pedestal these words appear:
"My name is Ozymandias, king of kings: 10
Look on my works, ye Mighty, and despair!"
Nothing beside remains. Round the decay
Of that colossal wreck, boundless and bare
The lone and level sands stretch far away.

JOHN KEATS   (1795–1821)
La Belle Dame sans Merci °

O what can ail thee, knight-at-arms,
    Alone and palely loitering?
The sedge has withered from the lake,
    And no birds sing.

O what can ail thee, knight-at-arms,   5
    So haggard and so woe-begone?
The squirrel's granary is full,
    And the harvest's done.

I see a lily on thy brow,
    With anguish moist and fever dew,   10
And on thy cheeks a fading rose
    Fast withereth too.

I met a lady in the meads,
    Full beautiful   – a faery's child,
Her hair was long, her foot was light,   15
    And her eyes were wild.

I made a garland for her head,
    And bracelets too, and fragrant zone;
She looked at me as she did love,
    And made sweet moan.   20

I set her on my pacing steed,
    And nothing else saw all day long,
For sidelong would she bend, and sing
    A faery's song.

La Belle Dame sans Merci: "The Beautiful Lady without Mercy" (French), borrowed from a
medieval poem.

She found me roots of relish sweet,   25
   And honey wild, and manna dew,
And sure in language strange she said,
   "I love thee true."

She took me to her elfin grot,
   And there she wept, and sighed full sore,   30
And there I shut her wild wild eyes
   With kisses four.

And there she lulléd me asleep,
   And there I dreamed — Ah! woe betide!
The latest° dream I ever dreamed   *last*   35
   On the cold hill side.

I saw pale kings and princes too,
   Pale warriors, death-pale were they all;
They cried — "La Belle Dame sans Merci
   Hath thee in thrall!"   40

I saw their starved lips in the gloam,
   With horrid warning gapéd wide,
And I awoke and found me here,
   On the cold hill's side.

And this is why I sojourn here,   45
   Alone and palely loitering,
Though the sedge has withered from the lake,
   And no birds sing.

JOHN KEATS   (1795–1821)

Ode on a Grecian Urn

Thou still unravished bride of quietness,
   Thou foster-child of silence and slow time,
Sylvan historian, who canst thus express
   A flowery tale more sweetly than our rhyme:
What leaf-fringed legend haunts about thy shape   5
   Of deities or mortals, or of both,
     In Tempe or the dales of Arcady?

   What men or gods are these? What maidens loth?
What mad pursuit? What struggle to escape?
     What pipes and timbrels? What wild ecstasy?   10

Heard melodies are sweet, but those unheard
   Are sweeter; therefore, ye soft pipes, play on;
Not to the sensual ear, but, more endeared
   Pipe to the spirit ditties of no tone:
Fair youth, beneath the trees, thou canst not leave   15
   Thy song, nor ever can those trees be bare;
      Bold Lover, never, never canst thou kiss,
Though winning near the goal — yet, do not grieve,
    She cannot fade, though thou hast not thy bliss,
   For ever wilt thou love, and she be fair!   20

Ah, happy, happy boughs! that cannot shed
   Your leaves, nor ever bid the Spring adieu;
And, happy melodist, unweariéd,
   For ever piping songs for ever new;
More happy love! more happy, happy love!   25
   For ever warm and still to be enjoyed,
      For ever panting, and for ever young;
All breathing human passion far above,
    That leaves a heart high-sorrowful and cloyed,
    A burning forehead, and a parching tongue.   30

Who are these coming to the sacrifice?
   To what green altar, O mysterious priest,
Lead'st thou that heifer lowing at the skies,
   And all her silken flanks with garlands drest?
What little town by river or sea shore,   35
   Or mountain-built with peaceful citadel,
      Is emptied of this folk, this pious morn?
And, little town, thy streets for evermore
   Will silent be; and not a soul to tell
    Why thou art desolate, can e'er return.   40

O Attic shape! Fair attitude! with brede
   Of marble men and maidens overwrought,
With forest branches and the trodden weed;
   Thou, silent form, dost tease us out of thought
As doth Eternity: Cold Pastoral!   45
   When old age shall this generation waste,
    Thou shalt remain, in midst of other woe
   Than ours, a friend to man to whom thou say'st,
Beauty is truth, truth beauty, — that is all
    Ye know on earth, and all ye need to know.   50

JOHN KEATS   (1795–1821)
Ode to a Nightingale

I

My heart aches, and a drowsy numbness pains
   My sense, as though of hemlock I had drunk,
Or emptied some dull opiate to the drain
   One minute past, and Lethe-wards° had sunk:
'Tis not through envy of thy happy lot,   5
   But being too happy in thine happiness, —
      That thou, light-winged Dryad of the trees,
         In some melodious plot
Of beechen green and shadows numberless,
      Singest of summer in full-throated ease.   10

II

O, for a draught of vintage! that hath been
   Cool'd a long age in the deep-delved earth,
Tasting of Flora and the country green,
   Dance, and Provençal song, and sunburnt mirth!
O for a beaker full of the warm South,   15
   Full of the true, the blushful Hippocrene,°
      With beaded bubbles winking at the brim,
         And purple-stained mouth;
That I might drink, and leave the world unseen,
      And with thee fade away into the forest dim: 20

III

Fade far away, dissolve, and quite forget
   What thou among the leaves hast never known,
The weariness, the fever, and the fret
   Here, where men sit and hear each other groan;
Where palsy shakes a few, sad, last gray hairs,   25
      Where youth grows pale, and spectre-thin, and dies;
         Where but to think is to be full of sorrow

4 *Lethe-wards*: Toward Lethe, the river of forgetfulness, which marks the border of the under-world.   16 *Hippocrene*: The fountain of the Muses, and thus the source of poetic inspiration.

     And leaden-eyed despairs,
Where Beauty cannot keep her lustrous eyes,
    Or new Love pine at them beyond to-morrow.   30

IV

Away! away! for I will fly to thee,
    Not charioted by Bacchus and his pards,°   *leopards*
But on the viewless wings of Poesy,
    Though the dull brain perplexes and retards:
Already with thee! tender is the night,   35
    And haply the Queen-Moon is on her throne,
      Cluster'd around by all her starry Fays;
      But here there is no light,
Save what from heaven is with the breezes blown
    Through verdurous glooms and winding mossy ways.   40

V

I cannot see what flowers are at my feet,
    Nor what soft incense hangs upon the boughs,
But, in embalmed darkness, guess each sweet
    Wherewith the seasonable month endows
The grass, the thicket, and the fruit-tree wild;   45
    White hawthorn, and the pastoral eglantine;
      Fast fading violets cover'd up in leaves;
      And mid-May's eldest child,
The coming musk-rose, full of dewy wine,
    The murmurous haunt of flies on summer eves.   50

VI

Darkling° I listen; and, for many a time   *in the dark*
    I have been half in love with easeful Death,
Call'd him soft names in many a mused rhyme,
    To take into the air my quiet breath;
Now more than ever seems it rich to die,   55
    To cease upon the midnight with no pain,
      While thou art pouring forth thy soul abroad
      In such an ecstasy!

Still wouldst thou sing, and I have ears in vain —
    To thy high requiem become a sod.   60

VII

Thou wast not born for death, immortal Bird!
    No hungry generations tread thee down;
The voice I hear this passing night was heard
    In ancient days by emperor and clown:
Perhaps the self-same song that found a path   65
    Through the sad heart of Ruth, when, sick for home,
        She stood in tears amid the alien corn;°
            The same that oft-times hath
    Charm'd magic casements, opening on the foam
        Of perilous seas, in faery lands forlorn.   70

VIII

Forlorn! the very word is like a bell
    To toll me back from thee to my sole self!
Adieu! the fancy cannot cheat so well
    As she is fam'd to do, deceiving elf.
Adieu! adieu! thy plaintive anthem fades   75
    Past the near meadows, over the still stream,
        Up the hill-side; and now 'tis buried deep
            In the next valley-glades:
    Was it a vision or a waking dream?
        Fled is that music — Do I wake or sleep?   80

66–67 *Ruth . . . corn*: A young widow who left her homeland to return with her mother-in-law
to Judah (see the Book of Ruth).

JOHN KEATS   (1795–1821)
On First Looking into Chapman's Homer °

Much have I traveled in the realms of gold,
    And many goodly states and kingdoms seen;
    Round many western islands have I been

Chapman's Homer: Translations of the *Iliad* and the *Odyssey* by George Chapman (1559?–1634).

Which bards in fealty to Apollo hold.
Oft of one wide expanse had I been told   5
    That deep-browed Homer ruled as his demesne;
    Yet did I never breathe its pure serene°   *atmosphere*
Till I heard Chapman speak out loud and bold:
Then felt I like some watcher of the skies
    When a new planet swims into his ken;   10
Or like stout Cortez when with eagle eyes
    He stared at the Pacific — and all his men
Looked at each other with a wild surmise —
    Silent, upon a peak in Darien.°

11–14 *Cortez . . . Darien*: Keats confused Hemando Cortés, the Spaniard who conquered Mexico, with Vasco Nuñez de Balboa, the Spaniard who first sighted the Pacific from Panama.

ALFRED, LORD TENNYSON   (1809–1892)
The Eagle
A Fragment

He clasps the crag with crooked hands;
Close to the sun in lonely lands,
Ringed with the azure world, he stands.

The wrinkled sea beneath him crawls:
He watches from his mountain walls,
And like a thunderbolt he falls.

ALFRED, LORD TENNYSON   (1809–1892)
Ulysses°

It little profits that an idle king
By this still hearth, among these barren crags,
Matched with an agéd wife, I mete and dole
Unequal laws unto a savage race
That hoard, and sleep, and feed, and know not me.   5
I cannot rest from travel; I will drink
Life to the lees. All times I have enjoyed
Greatly, have suffered greatly, both with those

Ulysses: Hero of Homer's *Odyssey*, who led the Greeks in the Trojan War, then traveled for ten years. In *The Inferno* Dante portrays him as restless after his return to Ithaca (see canto 26).

That loved me, and alone: on shore, and when
Through scudding drifts the rainy Hyades   10
Vexed the dim sea. I am become a name;
For always roaming with a hungry heart
Much have I seen and known — cities of men
And manners, climates, councils, governments,
Myself not least, but honored of them all —   15
And drunk delight of battle with my peers,
Far on the ringing plains of windy Troy.
I am a part of all that I have met;
Yet all experience is an arch wherethrough
Gleams that untraveled world whose margin fades   20
Forever and forever when I move.
How dull it is to pause, to make an end,
To rust unburnished, not to shine in use!
As though to breathe were life! Life piled on life
Were all too little, and of one to me   25
Little remains; but every hour is saved
From that eternal silence, something more,
A bringer of new things; and vile it were
For some three suns to store and hoard myself,
And this grey spirit yearning in desire   30
To follow knowledge like a sinking star,
Beyond the utmost bound of human thought.
    This is my son, mine own Telemachus,
To whom I leave the scepter and the isle —
Well-loved of me, discerning to fulfill   35
This labor, by slow prudence to make mild
A rugged people, and through soft degrees
Subdue them to the useful and the good.
Most blameless is he, centered in the sphere
Of common duties, decent not to fail   40
In offices of tenderness, and pay
Meet adoration to my household gods,
When I am gone. He works his work, I mine.
    There lies the port; the vessel puffs her sail;
There gloom the dark, broad seas. My mariners,   45
Souls that have toiled, and wrought, and thought with me —
That ever with a frolic welcome took
The thunder and the sunshine, and opposed
Free hearts, free foreheads — you and I are old;
Old age hath yet his honor and his toil.   50
Death closes all; but something ere the end,
Some work of noble note, may yet be done,

Not unbecoming men that strove with Gods.
The lights begin to twinkle from the rocks;
The long day wanes; the slow moon climbs; the deep   55
Moans round with many voices. Come, my friends,
'Tis not too late to seek a newer world.
Push off, and sitting well in order smite
The sounding furrows; for my purpose holds
To sail beyond the sunset, and the baths   60
Of all the western stars, until I die.
It may be that the gulfs will wash us down;
It may be we shall touch the Happy Isles,°
And see the great Achilles, whom we knew.
Though much is taken, much abides; and though   65
We are not now that strength which in old days
Moved earth and heaven, that which we are, we are —
One equal temper of heroic hearts,
Made weak by time and fate, but strong in will
To strive, to seek, to find, and not to yield.   70

63 *Happy Isles*: Elysium, Paradise for heroes and those the gods favored, believed to lie beyond
the sunset.

ROBERT BROWNING   (1812–1889)
My Last Duchess

That's my last Duchess painted on the wall,
Looking as if she were alive. I call
That piece a wonder, now: Frà Pandolf's° hands
Worked busily a day, and there she stands.
Will't please you sit and look at her? I said   5
"Frà Pandolf" by design, for never read
Strangers like you that pictured countenance.
The depth and passion of its earnest glance,
But to myself they turned (since none puts by
The curtain I have drawn for you, but I)   10
And seemed as they would ask me, if they durst,
How such a glance came there; so, not the first
Are you to turn as ask thus. Sir, 't was not
Her husband's presence only, called that spot
Of joy into the Duchess' cheek: perhaps   15
Frà Pandolf chanced to say "Her mantle laps

3 *Frà Pandolf*: A fictitious artist.

Over my lady's wrist too much," or "Paint
Must never hope to reproduce the faint
Half-flush that dies along her throat": such stuff
Was courtesy, she thought, and cause enough   20
For calling up that spot of joy. She had
A heart — how shall I say? — too soon made glad,
Too easily impressed; she liked whate'er
She looked on, and her looks went everywhere.
Sir, 't was all one! My favour at her breast,   25
The dropping of the daylight in the West,
The bough of cherries some officious fool
Broke in the orchard for her, the white mule
She rode with round the terrace — all and each
Would draw from her alike the approving speech,   30
Or blush, at least. She thanked men, — good! but thanked
Somehow — I know not how — as if she ranked
My gift of a nine-hundred-years-old name
With anybody's gift. Who'd stoop to blame
This sort of trifling? Even had you skill   35
In speech — (which I have not) — to make your will
Quite clear to such an one, and say, "Just this
Or that in you disgusts me; here you miss,
Or there exceed the mark" — and if she let
Herself be lessoned so, nor plainly set   40
Her wits to yours, forsooth, and made excuse,
— E'en then would be some stooping; and I choose
Never to stoop. Oh sir, she smiled, no doubt,
Whene'er I passed her; but who passed without
Much the same smile? This grew; I gave commands;   45
Then all smiles stopped together. There she stands
As if alive. Will 't please you rise? We'll meet
The company below, then I repeat,
The Court your master's known munificence
Is ample warrant that no just pretence   50
Of mine for dowry will be disallowed;
Though his fair daughter's self, as I avowed
At starting, is my object. Nay, we'll go
Together down, sir! Notice Neptune, though,
Taming a sea-horse, thought a rarity,   55
Which Claus of Innsbruck° cast in bronze for me!

56 *Claus of Innsbruck*: Also a fictitious artist.

WALT WHITMAN   (1819–1892)
A noiseless patient spider

A noiseless patient spider,
I mark'd where on a little promontory it stood isolated,
Mark'd how to explore the vacant vast surrounding,
It launch'd forth filament, filament, filament, out of itself,
Ever unreeling them, ever tirelessly speeding them.   5

And you O my soul where you stand,
Surrounded, detached, in measureless oceans of space,
Ceaselessly musing, venturing, throwing, seeking the spheres to
      connect them,
Till the bridge you will need be form'd, till the ductile anchor
      hold,
Till the gossamer thread you fling catch somewhere, O my
      soul.   10

WALT WHITMAN   (1819–1892)
Out of the cradle endlessly rocking

Out of the cradle endlessly rocking,
Out of the mocking-bird's throat, the musical shuttle,
Out of the Ninth-month midnight,
Over the sterile sands and the fields beyond, where the child
      leaving his bed wander'd alone, bareheaded, barefoot,
Down from the shower'd halo,   5
Up from the mystic play of shadows twining and twisting as if
      they were alive,
Out from the patches of briers and blackberries,
From the memories of the bird that chanted to me,
From your memories sad brother, from the fitful risings and
      fallings I heard,
From under that yellow half-moon late-risen and swollen as if
      with tears,   10
From those beginning notes of yearning and love there in the
      mist,
From the thousand responses of my heart never to cease,
From the myriad thence-arous'd words,
From the word stronger and more delicious than any,

From such as now they start the scene revisiting,   15
As a flock, twittering, rising, or overhead passing,
Borne hither, ere all eludes me, hurriedly,
A man, yet by these tears a little boy again,
Throwing myself on the sand, confronting the waves,
I, chanter of pains and joys, uniter of here and hereafter,   20
Taking all hints to use them, but swiftly leaping beyond them,
A reminiscence sing.

Once Paumanok,°   *Long Island*
When the lilac-scent was in the air and Fifth-month grass was
        growing,
Up this seashore in some briers,   25
Two feather'd guests from Alabama, two together,
And their nest, and four light-green eggs spotted with brown,
And every day the he-bird to and fro near at hand,
And every day the she-bird crouch'd on her nest, silent, with
        bright eyes,
And every day I, a curious boy, never too close, never disturbing
        them,   30
Cautiously peering, absorbing, translating.

Shine! shine! shine!
Pour down your warmth, great sun!
While we bask, we two together.

Two together!   35
Winds blow south, or winds blow north,
Day come white, or night come black,
Home, or rivers and mountains from home,
Singing all time, minding no time,
While we two keep together.   40

Till of a sudden,
May-be kill'd, unknown to her mate,
One forenoon the she-bird crouch'd not on the nest,
Nor return'd that afternoon, nor the next,
Nor ever appear'd again.   45

And thenceforward all summer in the sound of the sea,
And at night under the full of the moon in calmer weather,
Over the hoarse surging of the sea,
Or flitting from brier to brier by day,
I saw, I heard at intervals the remaining one, the he-bird,   50
The solitary guest from Alabama.

Blow! blow! blow!
Blow up sea-winds along Paumanok's shore;
I wait and I wait till you blow my mate to me.

Yes, when the stars glisten'd,   55
All night long on the prong of a moss-scallop'd stake,
Down almost amid the slapping waves,
Sat the lone singer wonderful causing tears.

He call'd on his mate,
He pour'd forth the meanings which I of all men know.   60

Yes, my brother, I know,
The rest might not, but I have treasur'd every note,
For more than once dimly down to the beach gliding,
Silent, avoiding the moonbeams, blending myself with the
    shadows,
Recalling now the obscure shapes, the echoes, the sounds and
    sights after their sorts,   65
The white arms out in the breakers tirelessly tossing,
I, with bare feet, a child, the wind wafting my hair,
Listen'd long and long.

Listen'd to keep, to sing, now translating the notes,
Following you, my brother.   70

Soothe! soothe! soothe!
Close on its wave soothes the wave behind,
And again another behind embracing and lapping, every one close,
But my love soothes not me, not me.

Low hangs the moon, it rose late,   75
It is lagging — O I think it is heavy with love, with love.

O madly the sea pushes upon the land,
With love, with love.

O night! do I not see my love fluttering out among the breakers?
What is that little black thing I see there in the white?   80

Loud! loud! loud!
Loud I call to you, my love!

High and clear I shoot my voice over the waves,
Surely you must know who is here, is here,
You must know who I am, my love.   85

Low-hanging moon!
What is that dusky spot in your brown yellow?

O it is the shape, the shape of my mate!
O moon do not keep her from me any longer.

Land! land! O land!   90
Whichever way I turn, O I think you could give me my mate back again if
*   you only would,*
For I am almost sure I see her dimly whichever way I look.

O rising stars!
Perhaps the one I want so much will rise, will rise with some of you.

O throat! O trembling throat!   95
Sound clearer through the atmosphere!
Pierce the woods, the earth,
Somewhere listening to catch you must be the one I want.

Shake out carols!
Solitary here, the night's carols!   100
Carols of lonesome love! death's carols!
Carols under that lagging, yellow, waning moon!
O under that moon where she droops almost down into the sea!
O reckless despairing carols.

But soft! sink low!   105
Soft! let me just murmur,
And do you wait a moment, you husky-nois'd sea,
For somewhere I believe I heard my mate responding to me,
So faint, I must be still, be still to listen,
But not altogether still, for then she might not come immediately
*   to me.*   110

Hither my love!
Here I am! here!
With this just-sustain'd note I announce myself to you,
This gentle call is for you my love, for you.

Do not be decoy'd elsewhere,   115
That is the whistle of the wind, it is not my voice,
That is the fluttering, the fluttering of the spray,
Those are the shadows of leaves.

O darkness! O in vain!
O I am very sick and sorrowful.   120

O brown halo in the sky near the moon, drooping upon the sea!
O troubled reflection in the sea!
O throat! O throbbing heart!
And I singing uselessly, uselessly all the night.

O past! O happy life! O songs of joy!   125
In the air, in the woods, over fields.
Loved! loved! loved! loved!
But my mate no more, no more with me!
We two together no more.

The aria sinking,   130
All else continuing, the stars shining,
The winds blowing, the notes of the bird continuous echoing,
With angry moans the fierce old mother incessantly moaning,
On the sands of Paumanok's shore gray and rustling,
The yellow half-moon enlarged, sagging down, drooping, the face
    of the sea almost touching,   135
The boy ecstatic, with his bare feet the waves, with his hair the
    atmosphere dallying,
The love in the heart long pent, now loose, now at last
    tumultuously bursting,
The aria's meaning, the ears, the soul, swiftly depositing,
The strange tears down the cheeks coursing,
The colloquy there, the trio, each uttering,   140
The undertone, the savage old mother incessantly crying,
To the boy's soul's questions sullenly timing, some drown'd secret
    hissing,
To the outsetting bard.

Demon or bird! (said the boy's soul,)
Is it indeed toward your mate you sing? or is it really to me?   145
For I, that was a child, my tongue's use sleeping, now I have heard
    you,
Now in a moment I know what I am for, I awake,
And already a thousand singers, a thousand songs, clearer, louder
    and more sorrowful than yours,
A thousand warbling echoes have started to life within me, never
    to die.

O you singer solitary, singing by yourself, projecting me,   150
O solitary me listening, never more shall I cease perpetuating
    you,
Never more shall I escape, never more the reverberations,
Never more the cries of unsatisfied love be absent from me,
Never again leave me to be the peaceful child I was before what
    there in the night,
By the sea under the yellow and sagging moon,   155
The messenger there arous'd, the fire, the sweet hell within,
The unknown want, the destiny of me.

O give me the clew! (it lurks in the night here somewhere)
O if I am to have so much, let me have more!

A word then, (for I will conquer it)   160
The word final, superior to all,
Subtle, sent up — what is it? — I listen;
Are you whispering it, and have been all the time, you sea-waves?
Is that it from your liquid rims and wet sands?

Whereto answering, the sea,   165
Delaying not, hurrying not,
Whisper'd me through the night, and very plainly before daybreak,
Lisp'd to me the low and delicious word death,
And again death, death, death, death,
Hissing melodious, neither like the bird nor like my arous'd
        child's heart,   170
But edging near as privately for me rustling at my feet,
Creeping thence steadily up to my ears and laving me softly all
        over,
Death, death, death, death, death.

Which I do not forget,
But fuse the song of my dusky demon and brother,   175
That he sang to me in the moonlight on Paumanok's gray beach,
With the thousand responsive songs at random,
My own songs awaked from that hour,
And with them the key, the word up from the waves,
The word of the sweetest song and all songs,   180
That strong and delicious word which, creeping to my feet,
(Or like some old crone rocking the cradle, swathed in sweet
        garment bending aside)
The sea whisper'd me.

MATTHEW ARNOLD   (1822–1888)
Dover Beach

The sea is calm to-night.
The tide is full, the moon lies fair
Upon the straits — on the French coast, the light
Gleams and is gone; the cliffs of England stand,
Glimmering and vast, out in the tranquil bay.   5
Come to the window, sweet is the night air!
Only, from the long line of spray
Where the ebb meets the moon-blanched land,
Listen! you hear the grating roar

Of pebbles which the waves draw back, and fling,   10
At their return, up the high strand,
Begin, and cease, and then again begin,
With tremulous cadence slow, and bring
The eternal note of sadness in.

Sophocles long ago   15
Heard it on the Aegean, and it brought
Into his mind the turbid ebb and flow
Of human misery; we
Find also in the sound a thought,
Hearing it by this distant northern sea.   20

The Sea of Faith
Was once, too, at the full, and round earth's shore
Lay like the folds of a bright girdle furled.
But now I only hear
Its melancholy, long, withdrawing roar,   25
Retreating, to the breath
Of the night wind, down the vast edges drear
And naked shingles of the world.

Ah, love, let us be true
To one another! for the world, which seems   30
To lie before us like a land of dreams,
So various, so beautiful, so new,
Hath really neither joy, nor love, nor light,
Nor certitude, nor peace, nor help for pain;
And we are here as on a darkling plain   35
Swept with confused alarms of struggle and flight,
Where ignorant armies clash by night.

EMILY DICKINSON (1830–1886)
After great pain, a formal feeling comes

After great pain, a formal feeling comes —
The Nerves sit ceremonious, like Tombs —
The stiff Heart questions was it He, that bore,
And Yesterday, or Centuries before?

The Feet, mechanical, go round —   5
Of Ground, or Air, or Ought —
A Wooden way
Regardless grown,
A Quartz contentment, like a stone —

This is the Hour of Lead — 10
Remembered, if outlived,
As Freezing persons, recollect the Snow —
First — Chill — then Stupor — then the letting go —

EMILY DICKINSON (1830–1886)

Because I could not stop for Death

Because I could not stop for Death —
He kindly stopped for me —
The Carriage held but just Ourselves —
And Immortality.

We slowly drove — He knew no haste 5
And I had put away
My labor and my leisure too,
For His Civility —

We passed the School, where Children strove
At Recess — in the Ring — 10
We passed the Fields of Gazing Grain —
We passed the Setting Sun —

Or rather — He passed Us —
The Dews drew quivering and chill —
For only Gossamer, my Gown — 15
My Tippet — only Tulle —

We paused before a House that seemed
A Swelling of the Ground —
The Roof was scarcely visible —
The Cornice — in the Ground — 20

Since then — 'tis Centuries — and yet
Feels shorter than the Day
I first surmised the Horses' Heads
Were toward Eternity —

EMILY DICKINSON (1830–1886)

A Bird came down the Walk

A Bird came down the Walk —
He did not know I saw —

He bit an Angleworm in halves
And ate the fellow, raw,

And then he drank a Dew   5
From a convenient Grass —
And then hopped sidewise to the Wall
To let a Beetle pass —

He glanced with rapid eyes
That hurried all around —   10
They looked like frightened Beads, I thought —
He stirred his Velvet Head

Like one in danger, Cautious,
I offered him a Crumb
And he unrolled his feathers   15
And rowed him softer home —

Than Oars divide the Ocean,
Too silver for a seam —
Or Butterflies, off Banks of Noon
Leap, plashless as they swim.   20

EMILY DICKINSON   (1830–1886)

There's a certain Slant of light

There's a certain Slant of light,
Winter Afternoons —
That oppresses, like the Heft
Of Cathedral Tunes —

Heavenly Hurt, it gives us —   5
We can find no scar,
But internal difference,
Where the Meanings, are —

None may teach it —Any —
'Tis the Seal Despair —   10
An imperial affliction
Sent us of the Air —

When it comes, the Landscape listens —
Shadows — hold their breath —
When it goes, 'tis like the Distance   15
On the look of Death —

EMILY DICKINSON (1830–1886)

'Twas warm — at first — like Us

'Twas warm — at first — like Us —
Until there crept upon
A Chill — like frost upon a Glass —
Till all the scene — be gone.

The Forehead copied Stone —   5
The Fingers grew too cold
To ache — and like a Skater's Brook —
The busy eyes — congealed —

It straightened — that was all —
It crowded Cold to Cold —   10
It multiplied indifference —
As Pride were all it could —

And even when with Cords —
'Twas lowered, like a Weight —
It made no Signal, nor demurred, —   15
But dropped like Adamant.

THOMAS HARDY (1840–1928)

After a Journey

Hereto I come to view a voiceless ghost;
    Whither, O whither will its whim now draw me?
Up the cliff, down, till I'm lonely, lost,
    And the unseen waters' ejaculations awe me.
Where you will next be there's no knowing,   5
    Facing round about me everywhere,
        With your nut-coloured hair,
And gray eyes, and rose-flush coming and going.

Yes: I have re-entered your olden haunts at last;
    Through the years, through the dead scenes I have tracked
        you;   10
What have you now found to say of our past —
    Scanned across the dark space wherein I have lacked you?
Summer gave us sweets, but autumn wrought division?
    Things were not lastly as firstly well
        With us twain, you tell?   15
But all's closed now, despite Time's derision.

I see what you are doing: you are leading me on
   To the spots we knew when we haunted here together,
The waterfall, above which the mist-bow shone
   At the then fair hour in the then fair weather,   20
And the cave just under, with a voice still so hollow
    That it seems to call out to me from forty years ago,
        When you were all aglow,
And not the thin ghost that I now frailly follow!

Ignorant of what there is flitting here to see,   25
    The waked birds preen and the seals flop lazily,
Soon you will have, Dear, to vanish from me,
    For the stars close their shutters and the dawn whitens hazily.
Trust me, I mind not, though Life lours,
    The bringing me here; nay, bring me here again!   30
        I am just the same as when
Our days were a joy, and our paths through flowers.

THOMAS HARDY   (1840–1928)

The Darkling Thrush

I leant upon a coppice gate
    When Frost was spectre-gray,
And Winter's dregs made desolate
    The weakening eye of day.
The tangled bine-stems scored the sky   5
    Like strings of broken lyres,
And all mankind that haunted nigh
    Had sought their household fires.

The land's sharp features seemed to be
    The Century's corpse outleant,   10
His crypt the cloudy canopy,
    The wind his death-lament.
The ancient pulse of germ and birth
    Was shrunken hard and dry,
And every spirit upon earth   15
    Seemed fervorless as I.

At once a voice arose among
    The bleak twigs overhead
In a full-hearted evensong
    Of joy illimited;   20

An aged thrush, frail, gaunt, and small,
    In blast-beruffled plume,
Had chosen thus to fling his soul
    Upon the growing gloom.

So little cause for carolings   25
    Of such ecstatic sound
Was written on terrestrial things
    Afar or nigh around,
That I could think there trembled through
    His happy good-night air   30
Some blessed Hope, whereof he knew
    And I was unaware.

THOMAS HARDY   (1840–1928)
Neutral Tones

We stood by a pond that winter day,
And the sun was white, as though chidden of God,
And a few leaves lay on the starving sod;
    — They had fallen from an ash, and were gray.

Your eyes on me were as eyes that rove   5
Over tedious riddles of years ago;
And some words played between us to and fro
    On which lost the more by our love.

The smile on your mouth was the deadest thing
Alive enough to have strength to die;   10
And a grin of bitterness swept thereby
    Like an ominous bird a-wing. . . .

Since then, keen lessons that love deceives,
And wrings with wrong, have shaped to me
Your face, and the God-curst sun, and a tree,   15
    And a pond edged with grayish leaves.

THOMAS HARDY   (1840–1928)
The Oxen

Christmas Eve, and twelve of the clock.
    "Now they are all on their knees,"

An elder said as we sat in a flock
  By the embers in hearthside ease.

We pictured the meek mild creatures where   5
  They dwelt in their strawy pen,
Nor did it occur to one of us there
  To doubt they were kneeling then.

So fair a fancy few would weave
  In these years! Yet, I feel,   10
If someone said on Christmas Eve,
  "Come; see the oxen kneel

"In the lonely barton° by yonder coomb°   *farmyard; ravine*
  Our childhood used to know,"
I should go with him in the gloom,   15
  Hoping it might be so.

GERARD MANLEY HOPKINS   (1844–1889)

Binsey Poplars

Felled 1879

My aspens dear, whose airy cages quelled,
Quelled or quenched in leaves the leaping sun,
All felled, felled, are all felled;
    Of a fresh and following folded rank
        Not spared, not one   5
        That dandled a sandalled
      Shadow that swam or sank
On meadow and river and wind-wandering
    weed-wandering bank.

O if we but knew what we do   10
    When we delve or hew —
  Hack and rack the growing green!
      Since country is so tender
  To touch, her being só slender,
  That, like this sleek and seeing ball   15
  But a prick will make no eye at all,

  Where we, even where we mean
      To mend her we end her,
    When we hew or delve:
After-comers cannot guess the beauty been.   20
    Ten or twelve, only ten or twelve

Strokes of havoc únselve
     The sweet especial scene,
Rural scene, a rural scene,
Sweet especial rural scene.   25

GERARD MANLEY HOPKINS   (1844–1889)
Pied Beauty

Glory be to God for dappled things —
     For skies of couple-colour as a brinded cow;
          For rose-moles all in stipple upon trout that swim;
Fresh-firecoal chestnut-falls; finches' wings;
     Landscape plotted and pieced — fold, fallow, and plough;   5
          And áll trádes, their gear and tackle and trim.

All things counter, original, spare, strange;
     Whatever is fickle, freckled (who knows how?)
          With swift, slow; sweet, sour; adazzle, dim;
He fathers-forth whose beauty is past change: 10
               Praise him.

GERARD MANLEY HOPKINS   (1844–1889)
Thou art indeed just, Lord

*Justus quidem tu es, Domine, si disputem tecum: verumtamen justa loquar ad te: Quare via
impiorum prosperatur? &c.°*

Thou art indeed just, Lord, if I contend
With thee; but, sir, so what I plead is just.
Why do sinners' ways prosper? and why must
Disappointment all I endeavor end?
     Wert thou my enemy, O thou my friend,   5
How wouldst thou worse, I wonder, than thou dost
Defeat, thwart me? Oh, the sots and thralls of lust
Do in spare hours more thrive than I that spend,
Sir, life upon thy cause. See, banks and brakes
Now, leavèd how thick! lacèd they are again   10
With fretty chervil, look, and fresh wind shakes
Them; birds build — but not I build; no, but strain,
Time's eunuch, and not breed one work that wakes.
Mine, O thou lord of life, send my roots rain.

Justus quidem . . . : Latin version of the biblical quotation in lines 1–4 (Jeremiah 12:1).

GERARD MANLEY HOPKINS   (1844–1889)
The Windhover °
To Christ Our Lord

I caught this morning morning's minion, king-
  dom of daylight's dauphin, dapple-dawn-drawn Falcon, in his
    riding
Of the rolling level underneath him steady air, and striding
High there, how he rung upon the rein of a wimpling wing
In his ecstasy! then off, off forth on swing,   5
  As a skate's heel sweeps smooth on a bow-bend: the hurl and
    gliding
Rebuffed the big wind. My heart in hiding
Stirred for a bird — the achieve of, the mastery of the thing!

Brute beauty and valor and act, oh, air, pride, plume, here
  Buckle! AND the fire that breaks from thee then, a billion   10
Times told lovelier, more dangerous, O my chevalier!

  No wonder of it: shéer plód makes plough down sillion°   *furrow*
Shine, and blue-bleak embers, ah my dear,
  Fall, gall themselves, and gash gold-vermilion.

Windhover: Another name for a kestrel, describing how it can hang on the air currents.

A. E. HOUSMAN   (1859–1936)
Eight O'Clock

He stood, and heard the steeple
  Sprinkle the quarters on the morning town.
One, two, three, four, to market place and people
  It tossed them down.

Strapped, noosed, nighing his hour,
  He stood and counted them and cursed his luck;
And then the clock collected in the tower
  Its strength, and struck.

WILLIAM BUTLER YEATS   (1865–1939)
Crazy Jane Talks with the Bishop

I met the Bishop on the road
And much said he and I.

"Those breasts are flat and fallen now,
Those veins must soon be dry;
Live in a heavenly mansion,   5
Not in some foul sty."

"Fair and foul are near of kin,
And fair needs foul," I cried.
"My friends are gone, but that's a truth
Nor grave nor bed denied,   10
Learned in bodily lowliness
And in the heart's pride.

"A woman can be proud and stiff
When on love intent;
But Love has pitched his mansion in   15
The place of excrement;
For nothing can be sole or whole
That has not been rent."

WILLIAM BUTLER YEATS   (1865–1939)

A Prayer for My Daughter

Once more the storm is howling, and half hid
Under this cradle-hood and coverlid
My child sleeps on. There is no obstacle
But Gregory's wood and one bare hill
Whereby the haystack- and roof-levelling wind,   5
Bred on the Atlantic, can be stayed;
And for an hour I have walked and prayed
Because of the great gloom that is in my mind.

I have walked and prayed for this young child an hour
And heard the sea-wind scream upon the tower,   10
And under the arches of the bridge, and scream
In the elms above the flooded stream;
Imagining in excited reverie
That the future years had come,
Dancing to a frenzied drum,   15
Out of the murderous innocence of the sea.

May she be granted beauty and yet not
Beauty to make a stranger's eye distraught,
Or hers before a looking-glass, for such,
Being made beautiful overmuch,   20

Consider beauty a sufficient end,
Lose natural kindness and maybe
The heart-revealing intimacy
That chooses right, and never find a friend.

Helen being chosen found life flat and dull   25
And later had much trouble from a fool,°
While that great Queen, that rose out of the spray,
Being fatherless could have her way
Yet chose a bandy-leggèd smith for man.°
It's certain that fine women eat   30
A crazy salad with their meat,
Whereby the Horn of Plenty is undone.

In courtesy I'd have her chiefly learned;
Hearts are not had as a gift but hearts are earned
By those that are not entirely beautiful;   35
Yet many, that have played the fool
For beauty's very self, has charm made wise,
And many a poor man that has roved,
Loved and thought himself beloved,
From a glad kindness cannot take his eyes.   40

May she become a flourishing hidden tree
That all her thoughts may like the linnet be,
And have no business but dispensing round
Their magnanimities of sound,
Nor but in merriment begin a chase,   45
Nor but in merriment a quarrel.
Oh, may she live like some green laurel
Rooted in one dear perpetual place.

My mind, because the minds that I have loved,
The sort of beauty that I have approved,   50
Prosper but little, has dried up of late,
Yet knows that to be choked with hate
May well be of all evil chances chief.
If there's no hatred in a mind
Assault and battery of the wind   55
Can never tear the linnet from the leaf.

25-26 *Helen . . . fool*: Helen of Troy, the most beautiful woman in the world, was married to
Menelaus, king of Sparta, but ran away with Paris, (the "fool"), thus causing the Trojan War.
27-29 *great Queen . . . man*: Aphrodite, goddess of love and beauty, was born out of the sea
foam. She married Hephaestus, the only lame and ugly god, the blacksmith of Olympus.

An intellectual hatred is the worst,
So let her think opinions are accursed.
Have I not seen the loveliest woman born
Out of the mouth of Plenty's horn,   60
Because of her opinionated mind
Barter that horn and every good
By quiet natures understood
For an old bellows full of angry wind?

Considering that, all hatred driven hence,   65
The soul recovers radical innocence
And learns at last that it is self-delighting,
Self-appeasing, self-affrighting,
And that its own sweet will is Heaven's will;
She can, though every face should scowl   70
And every windy quarter howl
Or every bellows burst, be happy still.

And may her bridegroom bring her to a house
Where all's accustomed, ceremonious;
For arrogance and hatred are the wares   75
Peddled in the thoroughfares.
How but in custom and in ceremony
Are innocence and beauty born?
Ceremony's a name for the rich horn,
And custom for the spreading laurel tree.   80

WILLIAM BUTLER YEATS   (1865–1939)
Sailing to Byzantium °

That° is no country for old men. The young   *Ireland*
In one another's arms, birds in the trees
— Those dying generations — at their song,
The salmon-falls, the mackerel-crowded seas,
Fish, flesh, or fowl, commend all summer long   5
Whatever is begotten, born, and dies.
Caught in that sensual music all neglect
Monuments of unaging intellect.

An aged man is but a paltry thing,
A tattered coat upon a stick, unless   10

Byzantium: The capital and intellectual and artistic center of the Eastern Roman Empire, symbolizing immortal art.

Soul clap its hands and sing, and louder sing
For every tatter in its mortal dress,
Nor is there singing school but studying
Monuments of its own magnificence;
And therefore I have sailed the seas and come   15
To the holy city of Byzantium.

O sages standing in God's holy fire
As in the gold mosaic of a wall,
Come from the holy fire, perne° in a gyre,   *bobbin*
And be the singing-masters of my soul.   20
Consume my heart away; sick with desire
And fastened to a dying animal
It knows not what it is; and gather me
Into the artifice of eternity.

Once out of nature I shall never take   25
My bodily form from any natural thing,
But such a form as Grecian goldsmiths make
Of hammered gold and gold enamelling
To keep a drowsy emperor awake;
Or set upon a golden bough to sing   30
To lords and ladies of Byzantium
Of what is past, or passing, or to come.

WILLIAM BUTLER YEATS (1865–1939)
The Second Coming °

Turning and turning in the widening gyre
The falcon cannot hear the falconer;
Things fall apart; the centre cannot hold;
Mere anarchy is loosed upon the world,
The blood-dimmed tide is loosed, and everywhere   5
The ceremony of innocence is drowned;
The best lack all conviction, while the worst
Are full of passionate intensity.

Surely some revelation is at hand;
Surely the Second Coming is at hand.   10
The Second Coming! Hardly are those words out

The Second Coming: Christ's return to establish heaven on earth (see Matthew 24:29–44) would
follow a period of turbulence and, in Yeats's view of history, mark the start of a new cycle.

When a vast image out of *Spiritus Mundi*°
Troubles my sight: somewhere in sands of the desert
A shape with lion body and the head of a man,
A gaze blank and pitiless as the sun,   15
Is moving its slow thighs, while all about it
Reel shadows of the indignant desert birds.
The darkness drops again; but now I know
That twenty centuries of stony sleep
Were vexed to nightmare by a rocking cradle,   20
And what rough beast, its hour come round at last,
Slouches towards Bethlehem to be born?

12 *Spiritus Mundi*: Soul of the world (Latin), and for Yeats the collective unconscious.

EDWIN ARLINGTON ROBINSON   (1869–1935)
For a Dead Lady

No more with overflowing light
Shall fill the eyes that now are faded,
Nor shall another's fringe with night
Their woman-hidden world as they did,
No more shall quiver down the days   5
The flowing wonder of her ways,
Whereof no language may requite
The shifting and the many-shaded.

The grace, divine, definitive,
Clings only as a faint forestalling;   10
The laugh that love could not forgive
Is hushed, and answers to no calling;
The forehead and the little ears
Have gone where Saturn keeps the years;
The breast where roses could not live   15
Has done with rising and with falling.

The beauty, shattered by the laws
That have creation in their keeping,
No longer trembles at applause,
Or over children that are sleeping;   20
And we who delve in beauty's lore
Know all that we have known before
Of what inexorable cause
Makes Time so vicious in his reaping.

EDWIN ARLINGTON ROBINSON   (1869–1935)
Richard Cory

Whenever Richard Cory went down town,
We people on the pavement looked at him:
He was a gentleman from sole to crown,
Clean favored, and imperially slim.

And he was always quietly arrayed,   5
And he was always human when he talked;
But still he fluttered pulses when he said,
"Good-morning," and he glittered when he walked.

And he was rich — yes, richer than a king —
And admirably schooled in every grace: 10
In fine, we thought that he was everything
To make us wish that we were in his place.

So on we worked, and waited for the light,
And went without the meat, and cursed the bread,
And Richard Cory, one calm summer night,   15
Went home and put a bullet through his head.

ROBERT FROST   (1874–1963)
Design

I found a dimpled spider, fat and white,
On a white heal-all,° holding up a moth
Like a white piece of rigid satin cloth —
Assorted characters of death and blight
Mixed ready to begin the morning right,   5
Like the ingredients of a witch's broth —
A snow-drop spider, a flower like froth,
And dead wings carried like a paper kite.

What had that flower to do with being white,
The wayside blue and innocent heal-all?   10
What brought the kindred spider to that height,
Then steered the white moth thither in the night?
What but design of darkness to appall? —
If design govern in a thing so small.

---

2 *heal-all*: A common wildflower, usually blue, with medical properties.

ROBERT FROST   (1874–1963)
Once by the Pacific

The shattered water made a misty din.
Great waves looked over others coming in,
And thought of doing something to the shore
That water never did to land before.
The clouds were low and hairy in the skies,   5
Like locks blown forward in the gleam of eyes.
You could not tell, and yet it looked as if
The shore was lucky in being backed by cliff,
The cliff in being backed by continent;
It looked as if a night of dark intent   10
Was coming, and not only a night, an age.
Someone had better be prepared for rage.
There would be more than ocean-water broken
Before God's last *Put out the Light* was spoken.

ROBERT FROST   (1874–1963)
The Oven Bird

There is a singer everyone has heard,
Loud, a mid-summer and a mid-wood bird,
Who makes the solid tree trunks sound again.
He says that leaves are old and that for flowers
Mid-summer is to spring as one to ten.   5
He says the early petal-fall is past
When pear and cherry bloom went down in showers
On sunny days a moment overcast;
And comes that other fall we name the fall.
He says the highway dust is over all.   10
The bird would cease and be as other birds
But that he knows in singing not to sing.
The question that he frames in all but words
Is what to make of a diminished thing.

ROBERT FROST   (1874–1963)
The Silken Tent

She is as in a field a silken tent
At midday when a sunny summer breeze

Has dried the dew and all its ropes relent,
So that in guys it gently sways at ease,
And its supporting central cedar pole,   5
That is its pinnacle to heavenward
And signifies the sureness of the soul,
Seems to owe naught to any single cord,
But strictly held by none, is loosely bound
By countless silken ties of love and thought   10
To everything on earth the compass round,
And only by one's going slightly taut
In the capriciousness of summer air
Is of the slightest bondage made aware.

ROBERT FROST   (1874–1963)

Spring Pools

These pools that, though in forest, still reflect
The total sky almost without defect,
And like the flowers beside them, chill and shiver,
Will like the flowers beside them soon be gone,
And yet not out by any brook or river,   5
But up by roots to bring dark foliage on.

The trees that have it in their pent-up buds
To darken nature and be summer woods –
Let them think twice before they use their powers
To blot out and drink up and sweep away   10
These flowery waters and these watery flowers
From snow that melted only yesterday.

WALLACE STEVENS   (1879–1955)

Peter Quince° at the Clavier

I

Just as my fingers on these keys
Make music, so the selfsame sounds
On my spirit make a music, too.

Peter Quince: An allusion to the comic carpenter who stage-manages "Pyramus and Thisbe,"
the play within a play in Shakespeare's *Midsummer Night's Dream*.

Music is feeling, then, not sound;
And thus it is that what I feel, 5
Here in this room, desiring you,

Thinking of your blue-shadowed silk,
Is music. It is like the strain
Waked in the elders by Susanna.°

Of a green evening, clear and warm, 10
She bathed in her still garden, while
The red-eyed elders watching, felt

The basses of their beings throb
In witching chords, and their thin blood
Pulse pizzicati of Hosanna. 15

II

In the green water, clear and warm,
Susanna lay.
She searched
The touch of springs,
And found 20
Concealed imaginings.
She sighed,
For so much melody.

Upon the bank, she stood
In the cool 25
Of spent emotions.
She felt, among the leaves,
The dew
Of old devotions.

She walked upon the grass, 30
Still quavering.
The winds were like her maids,
On timid feet,
Fetching her woven scarves,
Yet wavering. 35

9 *Susanna*: Susanna was falsely accused of adultery by two elders who had hidden in her
garden to watch her bathe and attempted to seduce her. She was saved for the moment when
her servants came in answer to her cry and ultimately vindicated by Daniel, the Old
Testament prophet, who proved that the elders were lying. (See the Book of Susanna in the
Apocrypha.)

A breath upon her hand
Muted the night.
She turned —
A cymbal crashed,
And roaring horns.   40

III

Soon, with a noise like tambourines,
Came her attendant Byzantines.

They wondered why Susanna cried
Against the elders by her side;

And as they whispered, the refrain   45
Was like a willow swept by rain.

Anon, their lamps' uplifted flame
Revealed Susanna and her shame.

And then, the simpering Byzantines
Fled, with a noise like tambourines.   50

IV

Beauty is momentary in the mind —
The fitful tracing of a portal;
But in the flesh it is immortal.

The body dies; the body's beauty lives.
So evenings die, in their green going,   55
A wave, interminably flowing.
So gardens die, their meek breath scenting
The cowl of winter, done repenting.
So maidens die, to the auroral
Celebration of a maiden's choral.   60

Susanna's music touched the bawdy strings
Of those white elders; but, escaping,
Left only Death's ironic scraping.
Now, in its immortality, it plays
On the clear viol of her memory,   65
And makes a constant sacrament of praise.

WALLACE STEVENS   (1879–1955)
The Snow Man

One must have a mind of winter
To regard the frost and the boughs
Of the pine-trees crusted with snow:

And have been cold a long time
To behold the junipers shagged with ice,   5
The spruces rough in the distant glitter

Of the January sun; and not to think
Of any misery in the sound of the wind,
In the sound of a few leaves,

Which is the sound of the land   10
Full of the same wind
That is blowing in the same bare place

For the listener, who listens in the snow,
And, nothing himself, beholds
Nothing that is not there and the nothing that is.   15

WALLACE STEVENS   (1879–1955)
Sunday Morning

I

Complacencies of the peignoir, and late
Coffee and oranges in a sunny chair,
And the green freedom of a cockatoo
Upon a rug mingle to dissipate
The holy hush of ancient sacrifice.   5
She dreams a little, and she feels the dark
Encroachment of that old catastrophe,°   *the Crucifixion*
As a calm darkens among water-lights.
The pungent oranges and bright, green wings
Seem things in some procession of the dead,   10
Winding across wide water, without sound.
The day is like wide water, without sound,
Stilled for the passing of her dreaming feet
Over the seas, to silent Palestine,
Dominion of the blood and sepulcher.   15

II

Why should she give her bounty to the dead?
What is divinity if it can come
Only in silent shadows and in dreams?
Shall she not find in comforts of the sun,
In pungent fruit and bright, green wings, or else   20
In any balm or beauty of the earth,
Things to be cherished like the thought of heaven?
Divinity must live within herself:
Passions of rain, or moods in falling snow;
Grievings in loneliness, or unsubdued   25
Elations when the forest blooms; gusty
Emotions on wet roads on autumn nights;
All pleasures and all pains, remembering
The bough of summer and the winter branch.
These are the measures destined for her soul.   30

III

Jove in the clouds had his inhuman birth.
No mother suckled him, no sweet land gave
Large-mannered motions to his mythy mind.
He moved among us, as a muttering king,
Magnificent, would move among his hinds,°   *peasant subjects*   35
Until our blood, commingling, virginal,
With heaven, brought such requital to desire
The very hinds discerned it, in a star.°   *of Bethlehem*
Shall our blood fail? Or shall it come to be
The blood of paradise? And shall the earth   40
Seem all of paradise that we shall know?
The sky will be much friendlier then than now,
A part of labor and a part of pain,
And next in glory to enduring love,
Not this dividing and indifferent blue.   45

IV

She says, "I am content when wakened birds,
Before they fly, test the reality

Of misty fields, by their sweet questionings;
But when the birds are gone, and their warm fields
Return no more, where, then, is paradise?"   50
There is not any haunt of prophecy,
Nor any old chimera of the grave,
Neither the golden underground, nor isle
Melodious, where spirits gat them home,
Nor visionary south, nor cloudy palm   55
Remote on heaven's hill, that has endured
As April's green endures, or will endure
Like her remembrance of awakened birds,
Or her desire for June and evening, tipped
By the consummation of the swallow's wings.   60

V

She says, "But in contentment I still feel
The need of some imperishable bliss."
Death is the mother of beauty; hence from her,
Alone, shall come fulfillment to our dreams
And our desires. Although she strews the leaves   65
Of sure obliteration on our paths,
The path sick sorrow took, the many paths
Where triumph rang its brassy phrase, or love
Whispered a little out of tenderness,
She makes the willow shiver in the sun   70
For maidens who were wont to sit and gaze
Upon the grass, relinquished to their feet.
She causes boys to pile new plums and pears
On disregarded plate. The maidens taste
And stray impassioned in the littering leaves.   75

VI

Is there no change of death in paradise?
Does ripe fruit never fall? Or do the boughs
Hang always heavy in that perfect sky,
Unchanging, yet so like our perishing earth,
With rivers like our own that seek for seas   80

They never find, the same receding shores
That never touch with inarticulate pang?
Why set the pear upon those river-banks
Or spice the shores with odors of the plum?
Alas, that they should wear our colors there,   85
The silken weavings of our afternoons,
And pick the strings of our insipid lutes!
Death is the mother of beauty, mystical,
Within whose burning bosom we devise
Our earthly mothers waiting, sleeplessly.   90

VII

Supple and turbulent, a ring of men
Shall chant in orgy on a summer morn
Their boisterous devotion to the sun,
Not as a god, but as a god might be,
Naked among them, like a savage source.   95
Their chant shall be a chant of paradise,
Out of their blood, returning to the sky;
And in their chant shall enter, voice by voice,
The windy lake wherein their lord delights,
The trees, like serafin,° and echoing hills,   *seraphim*   100
That choir among themselves long afterward.
They shall know well the heavenly fellowship
Of men that perish and of summer morn.
And whence they came and whither they shall go
The dew upon their feet shall manifest.   105

VIII

She hears, upon that water without sound,
A voice that cries, "The tomb in Palestine
Is not the porch of spirits lingering.
It is the grave of Jesus, where he lay."
We live in an old chaos of the sun,   110
Or old dependency of day and night,
Or island solitude, unsponsored, free,
Of that wide water, inescapable.

Deer walk upon our mountains, and the quail
Whistle about us their spontaneous cries;   115
Sweet berries ripen in the wilderness;
And, in the isolation of the sky,
At evening, casual flocks of pigeons make
Ambiguous undulations as they sink,
Downward to darkness, on extended wings.   120

WILLIAM CARLOS WILLIAMS   (1883–1963)

Spring and All

By the road to the contagious hospital
under the surge of the blue
mottled clouds driven from the
northeast — a cold wind. Beyond, the
waste of broad, muddy fields   5
brown with dried weeds, standing and fallen

patches of standing water
and scattering of tall trees

All along the road the reddish
purplish, forked, upstanding, twiggy   10
stuff of bushes and small trees
with dead, brown leaves under them
leafless vines —

Lifeless in appearance, sluggish
dazed spring approaches —   15

They enter the new world naked,
cold, uncertain of all
save that they enter. All about them
the cold, familiar wind —

Now the grass, tomorrow   20
the stiff curl of wildcarrot leaf
One by one objects are defined —
It quickens: clarity, outline of leaf

But now the stark dignity of
entrance — Still, the profound change   25
has come upon them: rooted, they
grip down and begin to awaken

D. H. LAWRENCE   (1885–1930)
Humming-bird

I can imagine, in some otherworld
Primeval-dumb, far back
In that most awful stillness, that only gasped and hummed,
Humming-birds raced down the avenues.

Before anything had a soul,   5
While life was a heave of Matter, half inanimate,
This little bit chipped off in brilliance
And went whizzing through the slow, vast, succulent stems.

I believe there were no flowers then,
In the world where the humming-bird flashed ahead of
     creation.   10
I believe he pierced the slow vegetable veins with his long beak.

Probably he was big
As mosses, and little lizards, they say, were once big.
Probably he was a jabbing, terrifying monster.

We look at him through the wrong end of the telescope of
     Time,   15
Luckily for us.

D. H. LAWRENCE   (1885–1930)
Piano

Softly, in the dusk, a woman is singing to me;
Taking me back down the vista of years, till I see
A child sitting under the piano, in the boom of the tingling
     strings
And pressing the small, poised feet of a mother who smiles as she
     sings.

In spite of myself, the insidious mastery of song   5
Betrays me back, till the heart of me weeps to belong
To the old Sunday evenings at home, with winter outside
And hymns in the cozy parlour, the tinkling piano our guide.

So now it is vain for the singer to burst into clamour
With the great black piano appassionato. The glamour   10

Of childish days is upon me, my manhood is cast
Down in the flood of remembrance, I weep like a child for the
        past.

ERZA POUND   (1885–1972)
The River Merchant's Wife: A Letter
By Rihaku°

While my hair was still cut straight across my forehead
I played about the front gate, pulling flowers.
You came by on bamboo stilts, playing horse,
You walked about my seat, playing with blue plums.
And we went on living in the village of Chokan: 5
Two small people, without dislike or suspicion.

At fourteen I married My Lord you.
I never laughed, being bashful.
Lowering my head, I looked at the wall.
Called to, a thousand times, I never looked back.   10

At fifteen I stopped scowling,
I desired my dust to be mingled with yours
Forever and forever and forever.
Why should I climb the lookout?

At sixteen you departed,   15
You went into far Ku-to-yen, by the river of swirling eddies,
And you have been gone five months.
The monkeys make sorrowful noise overhead.

You dragged your feet when you went out.
By the gate now, the moss is grown, the different mosses,   20
Too deep to clear them away!
The leaves fall early this autumn, in wind.
The paired butterflies are already yellow with August
Over the grass in the West garden;
They hurt me. I grow older.   25
If you are coming down through the narrows of the river Kiang,
Please let me know beforehand,
And I will come out to meet you
              As far as Cho-fu-Sa.

Rihaku: The Japanese name for Li Po, an eighth-century Chinese poet; Pound's poem is a
loose translation.

MARIANNE MOORE   (1887–1972)
The Fish

wade
through black jade.
  Of the crow-blue mussel-shells, one keeps
  adjusting the ash-heaps;
    opening and shutting itself like   5

an
injured fan.
  The barnacles which encrust the side
  of the wave, cannot hide
    there for the submerged shafts of the   10

sun,
split like spun
  glass, move themselves with spotlight swiftness
  into the crevices —
    in and out, illuminating   15

the
turquoise sea
  of bodies. The water drives a wedge
  of iron through the iron edge
    of the cliff; whereupon the stars,   20

pink
rice-grains, ink
  bespattered jelly-fish, crabs like green
  lilies, and submarine
    toadstools, slide each on the other.   25

All
external
  marks of abuse are present on this
  defiant edifice —
    all the physical features of   30

ac-
cident — lack
  of cornice, dynamite grooves, burns, and
  hatchet strokes, these things stand
    out on it; the chasm-side is   35

dead.
Repeated
   evidence has proved that it can live
   on what cannot revive
      its youth. The sea grows old in it.   40

T. S. ELIOT   (1888–1965)
Gerontion°

    Thou hast nor youth nor age
But as it were an after dinner sleep
Dreaming of both.°

Here I am, an old man in a dry month,
Being read to by a boy, waiting for rain.
I was neither at the hot gates
Nor fought in the warm rain
Nor knee deep in the salt marsh, heaving a cutlass,   5
Bitten by flies, fought.
My house is a decayed house,
And the jew squats on the window sill, the owner,
Spawned in some estaminet of Antwerp,
Blistered in Brussels, patched and peeled in London.   10
The goat coughs at night in the field overhead;
Rocks, moss, stonecrop, iron, merds.°   *excrement*
The woman keeps the kitchen, makes tea,
Sneezes at evening, poking the peevish gutter.°   *drain*
               I an old man,   15
A dull head among windy spaces.

   Signs are taken for wonders. "We would see a sign."
The word within a word, unable to speak a word,°
Swaddled with darkness. In the juvescence° of the   *youth, thus spring*
   year
Came Christ the tiger   20

In depraved May, dogwood and chestnut, flowering judas,
To be eaten, to be divided, to be drunk
Among whispers; by Mr. Silvero°

Gerontion: "Little old man" (Greek).   *Thou . . . both*: Words addressed by the duke of Vienna to Claudio in Shakespeare's *Measure for Measure* (III.i.32–34).   *17–18 Signs . . . word*: Echoes from the Christmas Day 1618 sermon of Bishop Lancelot Andrewes.   *23 Mr. Silvero*: This and the personal names through line 28 are fictitious.

With caressing hands, at Limoges
Who walked all night in the next room;   25

By Hakagawa, bowing among the Titians;
By Madame de Tornquist, in the dark room
Shifting the candles; Fräulein von Kulp
Who turned in the hall, one hand on the door. Vacant shuttles
Weave the wind. I have no ghosts,   30
An old man in a draughty house
Under a windy knob.

    After such knowledge, what forgiveness? Think now
History has many cunning passages, contrived corridors
And issues, deceives with whispering ambitions,   35
Guides us by vanities. Think now
She gives when our attention is distracted
And what she gives, gives with such supple confusions
That the giving famishes the craving. Gives too late
What's not believed in, or if still believed,   40
In memory only, reconsidered passion. Gives too soon
Into weak hands, what's thought can be dispensed with
Till the refusal propagates a fear. Think
Neither fear nor courage saves us. Unnatural vices
Are fathered by our heroism. Virtues   45
Are forced upon us by our impudent crimes.
These tears are shaken from the wrath-bearing tree.

    The tiger springs in the new year. Us he devours. Think at last
We have not reached conclusion, when I
Stiffen in a rented house. Think at last   50
I have not made this show purposelessly
And it is not by any concitation°   *stirring*
Of the backward devils.
I would meet you upon this honestly.
I that was near your heart was removed therefrom   55
To lose beauty in terror, terror in inquisition.
I have lost my passion; why should I need to keep it
Since what is kept must be adulterated?
I have lost my sight, smell, hearing, taste and touch:
How should I use them for your closer contact?   60

    These with a thousand small deliberations
Protract the profit of their chilled delirium,
Excite the membrane, when the sense has cooled,
With pungent sauces, multiply variety

In a wilderness of mirrors. What will the spider do, 65
Suspend its operations, will the weevil
Delay? De Bailhache, Fresca, Mrs. Cammel,° whirled
Beyond the circuit of the shuddering Bear°
In fractured atoms. Gull against the wind, in the windy straits
Of Belle Isle, or running on the Horn. 70
White feathers in the snow, the Gulf claims,
And an old man driven by the Trades
To a sleepy corner.

                      Tenants of the house,
Thoughts of a dry brain in a dry season. 75

67 *De Bailhache . . . Mrs. Cammel*: Also fictitious names.   68 *shuddering Bear*: A constellation
visible in the Northern Hemisphere.

T. S. ELIOT   (1888–1965)
Journey of the Magi°

"A cold coming we had of it,
Just the worst time of the year
For a journey, and such a long journey:
The ways deep and the weather sharp,
The very dead of winter."° 5
And the camels galled, sore-footed, refractory,
Lying down in the melting snow.
There were times we regretted
The summer palaces on slopes, the terraces,
And the silken girls bringing sherbet. 10
Then the camel men cursing and grumbling
And running away, and wanting their liquor and women,
And the night-fires going out, and the lack of shelters,
And the cities hostile and the towns unfriendly
And the villages dirty and charging high prices: 15
A hard time we had of it.
At the end we preferred to travel all night,
Sleeping in snatches,
With the voices singing in our ears, saying
That this was all folly. 20

Magi: The three wise men who followed the star to see the newborn Christ (see Matthew 2:1–
12).   1–5 "*A cold . . . winter*": Borrowed from the Christmas Day 1622 sermon of Bishop
Lancelot Andrewes.

Then at dawn we came down to a temperate valley,
Wet, below the snow line, smelling of vegetation;
With a running stream and a water-mill beating the darkness,
And three trees° on the low sky,
And an old white horse galloped away in the meadow.   25
Then we came to a tavern with vine-leaves over the lintel,
Six hands at an open door dicing for pieces of silver,°
And feet kicking the empty wine-skins.
But there was no information, and so we continued
And arrived at evening, not a moment too soon   30
Finding the place; it was (you may say) satisfactory.

All this was a long time ago, I remember,
And I would do it again, but set down
This set down
This: were we led all that way for   35
Birth or Death? There was a Birth, certainly,
We had evidence and no doubt. I had seen birth and death,
But had thought they were different; this Birth was
Hard and bitter agony for us, like Death, our death.
We returned to our places, these Kingdoms,   40
But no longer at ease here, in the old dispensation,
With an alien people clutching their gods.
I should be glad of another death.

---

24 *three trees*: Suggests the crosses on which Christ and the two thieves were crucified (see Luke 23:32–33).   27 *Six hands . . . silver*: Suggests two events in Christ's life: the soldiers casting lots for Christ's robes at the Crucifixion (see Matthew 27:35) and Judas betraying Christ for thirty pieces of silver (see Matthew 26:14–16).

JOHN CROWE RANSOM   (1888–1974)
Bells for John Whiteside's Daughter

There was such speed in her little body,
And such lightness in her footfall,
It is no wonder her brown study
Astonishes us all.

Her wars were bruited in our high window.   5
We looked among orchard trees and beyond
Where she took arms against her shadow,
Or harried unto the pond

The lazy geese, like a snow cloud
Dripping their snow on the green grass,   10
Tricking and stopping, sleepy and proud,
Who cried in goose, Alas,

For the tireless heart within the little
Lady with rod that made them rise
From their noon apple-dreams and scuttle   15
Goose-fashion under the skies!

But now go the bells, and we are ready,
In one house we are sternly stopped
To say we are vexed at her brown study,
Lying so primly propped.   20

LANGSTON HUGHES   (1902–1967)
Dream Boogie

Good morning, daddy!
Ain't you heard
The boogie-woogie rumble
Of a dream deferred?

Listen closely: 5
You'll hear their feet
Beating out and beating out a —

    You think
    It's a happy beat?

Listen to it closely: 10
Ain't you heard
Something underneath
like a —

    What did I say?

Sure,   15
I'm happy!
Take it away!

    Hey, pop!
    Re-bop!
    Mop!   20

        Y-e-a-h!

LANGSTON HUGHES   (1902–1967)
Harlem (A Dream Deferred)

What happens to a dream deferred?
   Does it dry up
   like a raisin in the sun?
   Or fester like a sore —
   And then run?   5
   Does it stink like rotten meat?
   Or crust and sugar over —
   like a syrupy sweet?

   Maybe it just sags
   like a heavy load   10

   Or does it explode?

C. DAY-LEWIS   (1904–1972)
Sheepdog Trials in Hyde Park

A shepherd stands at one end of the arena.
Five sheep are unpenned at the other. His dog runs out
In a curve to behind them, fetches them straight to the shepherd,
Then drives the flock round a triangular course
Through a couple of gates and back to his master: two   5
Must be sorted there from the flock, then all five penned.
Gathering, driving away, shedding and penning
Are the plain words for the miraculous game.

An abstract game. What can the sheepdog make of such
Simplified terrain? — no hills, dales, bogs, walls, tracks,   10
Only a quarter-mile plain of grass, dumb crowds
Like crowds on hoardings around it, and behind them
Traffic or mounds of lovers and children playing.
Well, the dog is no landscape-fancier: his whole concern
Is with his master's whistle and of course   15
With the flock — sheep are sheep anywhere for him.

The sheep are the chanciest element. Why, for instance,
Go through this gate when there's on either side of it
No wall or hedge but huge and viable space?
Why not eat the grass instead of being pushed around it?   20
Like a blob of quicksilver on a tilting board
The flock erratically runs, dithers, breaks up,

Is reassembled: their ruling idea is the dog;
And behind the dog, though they know it not yet, is a shepherd.

The shepherd knows that time is of the essence   25
But haste calamitous. Between dog and sheep
There is always an ideal distance, a perfect angle;
But these are constantly varying, so the man
Should anticipate each move through the dog, his medium.
The shepherd is the brain behind the dog's brain,   30
But his control of dog, like dog's of sheep,
Is never absolute — that's the beauty of it.

For beautiful it is. The guided missiles,
The black-and-white angels follow each quirk and jink of
The evasive sheep, play grandmother's-steps behind them,   35
Freeze to the ground, or leap to head off a straggler
Almost before it knows that it wants to stray,
As if radar-controlled. But they are not machines —
You can feel them feeling mastery, doubt, chagrin:
Machines don't frolic when their job is done.   40

What's needfully done in the solitude of sheep-runs —
Those rough, real tasks become this stylized game,
A demonstration of intuitive wit
Kept natural by the saving grace of error.
To lift, to fetch, to drive, to shed, to pen   45
Are acts I recognize, with all they mean
Of shepherding the unruly, for a kind of
Controlled woolgathering is my work too.

W. H. AUDEN   (1907–1973)
Musée des Beaux Arts

About suffering they were never wrong,
The Old Masters: how well they understood
Its human position; how it takes place
While someone else is eating or opening a window or just
        walking dully along;
How, when the aged are reverently, passionately waiting   5
For the miraculous birth, there always must be
Children who did not specially want it to happen, skating
On a pond at the edge of the wood:
They never forgot
That even the dreadful martyrdom must run its course   10

Anyhow in a corner, some untidy spot
Where the dogs go on with their doggy life and the torturer's
    horse
Scratches its innocent behind on a tree.

In Breughel's *Icarus°* for instance: how everything turns away
Quite leisurely from the disaster; the ploughman may   15
Have heard the splash, the forsaken cry,
But for him it was not an important failure; the sun shone
As it had to on the white legs disappearing into the green
Water; and the expensive delicate ship that must have seen
Something amazing, a boy falling out of the sky,   20
Had somewhere to get to and sailed calmly on.

14 *Breughel's* Icarus: Depiction of the fall of Icarus, who flew too close to the sun with the war
wings his father had made and fell into the sea when they melted. Pieter Breughel was a sixteenth-century Flemish painter.

W. H. AUDEN (1907–1973)
Petition

Sir, no man's enemy, forgiving all
But will its negative inversion, be prodigal:
Send to us power and light, a sovereign touch
Curing the intolerable neural itch,
The exhaustion of weaning, the liar's quinsy,   5
And the distortions of ingrown virginity.
Prohibit sharply the rehearsed response
And gradually correct the coward's stance;
Cover in time with beams those in retreat
That, spotted, they turn though the reverse were great;   10
Publish each healer that in city lives
Or country houses at the end of drives;
Harrow the house of the dead; look shining at
New styles of architecture, a change of heart.

THEODORE ROETHKE (1908–1963)
Cuttings

Sticks-in-a-drowse droop over sugary loam,
Their intricate stem-fur dries;

But still the delicate slips keep coaxing up water;
The small cells bulge;

One nub of growth   5
Nudges a sand-crumb loose,
Pokes through a musty sheath
Its pale tendrilous horn.

THEODORE ROETHKE   (1908–1963)
Cuttings
(Later)

This urge, wrestle, resurrection of dry sticks,
Cut stems struggling to put down feet,
What saint strained so much,
Rose on such lopped limbs to a new life?

I can hear, underground, that sucking and sobbing,   5
In my veins, in my bones I feel it, —
The small waters seeping upward,
The tight grains parting at last.
When sprouts break out,
Slippery as fish,
I quail, lean to beginnings, sheath-wet.   10

THEODORE ROETHKE   (1908–1963)
Elegy for Jane
My Student, Thrown by a Horse

I remember the neckcurls, limp and damp as tendrils;
And her quick look, a sidelong pickerel smile:
And how, once startled into talk, the light syllables leaped for
    her,
And she balanced in the delight of her thought,
A wren, happy tail into the wind,   5
Her song trembling the twigs and small branches.
The shade sang with her;
The leaves, their whispers turned to kissing;
And the mold sang in the bleached valleys under the rose.

Oh, when she was sad, she cast herself down into such a pure
    depth,   10

Even a father could not find her:
Scraping her cheek against straw:
Stirring the clearest water.

My sparrow, you are not here,
Waiting like a fern, making a spiny shadow.   15
The sides of wet stones cannot console me,
Nor the moss, wound with the last light.

If only I could nudge you from this sleep,
My maimed darling, my skittery pigeon.
Over this damp grave I speak the words of my love: 20
I, with no rights in this matter,
Neither father nor lover.

THEODORE ROETHKE   (1908–1963)
The Minimal

I study the lives on a leaf: the little
Sleepers, numb nudgers in cold dimensions,
Beetles in caves, newts, stone-deaf fishes,
Lice tethered to long limp subterranean weeds,
Squirmers in bogs,   5
And bacterial creepers
Wriggling through wounds
Like elvers in ponds,
Their wan mouths kissing the warm sutures,
Cleaning and caressing,   10
Creeping and healing.

ELIZABETH BISHOP   (1911–1979)
At the Fishhouses

Although it is a cold evening,
down by one of the fishhouses
an old man sits netting,
his net, in the gloaming almost invisible
a dark purple-brown,   5
and his shuttle worn and polished.
The air smells so strong of codfish
it makes one's nose run and one's eyes water.
The five fishhouses have steeply peaked roofs

and narrow, cleated gangplanks slant up   10
to storerooms in the gables
for the wheelbarrows to be pushed up and down on.
All is silver: the heavy surface of the sea,
swelling slowly as if considering spilling over,
is opaque, but the silver of the benches,   15
the lobster pots, and masts, scattered
among the wild jagged rocks,
is of an apparent translucence
like the small old buildings with an emerald moss
growing on their shoreward walls.   20
The big fish tubs are completely lined
with layers of beautiful herring scales
and the wheelbarrows are similarly plastered
with creamy iridescent coats of mail,
with small iridescent flies crawling on them.   25
Up on the little slope behind the houses,
set in the sparse bright sprinkle of grass,
is an ancient wooden capstan,
cracked, with two long bleached handles
and some melancholy stains, like dried blood,   30
where the ironwork has rusted.
The old man accepts a Lucky Strike.
He was a friend of my grandfather.
We talk of the decline in the population
and of codfish and herring   35
while he waits for a herring boat to come in.
There are sequins on his vest and on his thumb.
He has scraped the scales, the principal beauty,
from unnumbered fish with that black old knife,
the blade of which is almost worn away.   40

Down at the water's edge, at the place
where they haul up the boats, up the long ramp
descending into the water, thin silver
tree trunks are laid horizontally
across the gray stones, down and down   45
at intervals of four or five feet.

Cold dark deep and absolutely clear,
element bearable to no mortal,
to fish and to seals . . . One seal particularly
I have seen here evening after evening.   50
He was curious about me. He was interested in music;
like me a believer in total immersion,

so I used to sing him Baptist hymns.
I also sang "A Mighty Fortress Is Our God."
He stood up in the water and regarded me   55
steadily, moving his head a little.
Then he would disappear, then suddenly emerge
almost in the same spot, with a sort of shrug
as if it were against his better judgment.
Cold dark deep and absolutely clear,   60
the clear gray icy water . . . Back, behind us,
the dignified tall firs begin.
Bluish, associating with their shadows,
a million Christmas trees stand
waiting for Christmas. The water seems suspended   65
above the rounded gray and blue-gray stones.
I have seen it over and over, the same sea, the same,
slightly, indifferently swinging above the stones,
icily free above the stones,
above the stones and then the world.   70
If you should dip your hand in,
your wrist would ache immediately,
your bones would begin to ache and your hand would burn
as if the water were a transmutation of fire
that feeds on stones and burns with a dark gray flame.   75
If you tasted it, it would first taste bitter,
then briny, then surely burn your tongue.
It is like what we imagine knowledge to be:
dark, salt, clear, moving, utterly free,
drawn from the cold hard mouth   80
of the world, derived from the rocky breasts
forever, flowing and drawn, and since
our knowledge is historical, flowing, and flown.

ELIZABETH BISHOP   (1911–1979)
Questions of Travel

There are too many waterfalls here; the crowded streams
hurry too rapidly down to the sea,
and the pressure of so many clouds on the mountaintops
makes them spill over the sides in soft slow-motion,
turning to waterfalls under our very eyes.   5
— For if those streaks, those mile-long, shiny, tearstains,
aren't waterfalls yet,
in a quick age or so, as ages go here,

they probably will be.
But if the streams and clouds keep travelling, travelling,   10
the mountains look like the hulls of capsized ships,
slime-hung and barnacled.

Think of the long trip home.
Should we have stayed at home and thought of here?
Where should we be today?   15
Is it right to be watching strangers in a play
in this strangest of theatres?
What childishness is it that while there's a breath of life
in our bodies, we are determined to rush
to see the sun the other way around?   20
The tiniest green hummingbird in the world?
To stare at some inexplicable old stonework,
inexplicable and impenetrable,
at any view,
instantly seen and always, always delightful?   25
Oh, must we dream our dreams
and have them, too?
And have we room
for one more folded sunset, still quite warm?

But surely it would have been a pity   30
not to have seen the trees along this road,
really exaggerated in their beauty,
not to have seen them gesturing
like noble pantomimists, robed in pink.
— Not to have had to stop for gas and heard   35
the sad, two-noted, wooden tune
of disparate wooden clogs
carelessly clacking over
a grease-stained filling-station floor.
(In another country the clogs would all be tested.   40
Each pair there would have identical pitch.)
— A pity not to have heard
the other, less primitive music of the fat brown bird
who sings above the broken gasoline pump
in a bamboo church of Jesuit baroque: 45
three towers, five silver crosses.
— Yes, a pity not to have pondered,
blurr'dly and inconclusively,
on what connection can exist for centuries
between the crudest wooden footwear   50
and, careful and finicky,

the whittled fantasies of wooden cages.
— Never to have studied history in
the weak calligraphy of songbirds' cages.
— And never to have had to listen to rain   55
so much like politicians' speeches:
two hours of unrelenting oratory
and then a sudden golden silence
in which the traveller takes a notebook, writes:

"Is it lack of imagination that makes us come   60
to imagined places, not just stay at home?
Or could Pascal have been not entirely right
about just sitting quietly in one's room?

Continent, city, country, society:
the choice is never wide and never free.   65
And here, or there . . . No. Should we have stayed at home,
wherever that may be?"

RANDALL JARRELL   (1914–1965)
Well Water

What a girl called "the dailiness of life"
(Adding an errand to your errand. Saying,
"Since you're up . . ." Making you a means to
A means to a means to) is well water
Pumped from an old well at the bottom of the world.   5
The pump you pump the water from is rusty
And hard to move and absurd, a squirrel-wheel
A sick squirrel turns slowly, through the sunny
Inexorable hours. And yet sometimes
The wheel turns of its own weight, the rusty   10
Pump pumps over your sweating face the clear
Water, cold, so cold! you cup your hands
And gulp from them the dailiness of life.

RANDALL JARRELL   (1914–1965)
The Woman at the Washington Zoo

The saris go by me from the embassies.

Cloth from the moon. Cloth from another planet.
They look back at the leopard like the leopard.

And I. . . .
    this print of mine, that has kept its color   5
Alive through so many cleanings; this dull null
Navy I wear to work, and wear from work, and so
To my bed, so to my grave, with no
Complaints, no comment: neither from my chief,
The Deputy Chief Assistant, nor his chief —   10
Only I complain. . . . this serviceable
Body that no sunlight dyes, no hand suffuses
But, dome-shadowed, withering among columns,
Wavy beneath fountains — small, far-off, shining
In the eyes of animals, these beings trapped   15
As I am trapped but not, themselves, the trap,
Aging, but without knowledge of their age,
Kept safe here, knowing not of death, for death —
Oh, bars of my own body, open, open!
The world goes by my cage and never sees me.   20
And there come not to me, as come to these,
The wild beast, sparrows pecking the llamas' grain,
Pigeons settling on the bears' bread, buzzards
Tearing the meat the flies have clouded. . . .
    Vulture,   25
When you come for the white rat that the foxes left,
Take off the red helmet of your head, the black
Wings that have shadowed me, and step to me as man:
The wild brother at whose feet the white wolves fawn,
To whose hand of power the great lioness   30
Stalks, purring. . . .
    You know what I was,
You see what I am: change me, change me!

DYLAN THOMAS   (1914–1953)

Do not go gentle into that good night

Do not go gentle into that good night,
Old age should burn and rave at close of day;
Rage, rage against the dying of the light.

Though wise men at their end know dark is right,
Because their words had forked no lightning they   5
Do not go gentle into that good night.

Good men, the last wave by, crying how bright

Their frail deeds might have danced in a green bay,
Rage, rage against the dying of the light.

Wild men who caught and sang the sun in flight,   10
And learn, too late, they grieved it on its way,
Do not go gentle into that good night.

Grave men, near death, who see with blinding sight
Blind eyes could blaze like meteors and be gay,
Rage, rage against the dying of the light.   15

And you, my father, there on the sad height,
Curse, bless, me now with your fierce tears, I pray.
Do not go gentle into that good night.
Rage, rage against the dying of the light.

DYLAN THOMAS   (1914–1953)
Fern Hill

Now as I was young and easy under the apple boughs
About the lilting house and happy as the grass was green,
    The night above the dingle starry,
        Time let me hail and climb
        Golden in the heydays of his eyes,   5
And honored among wagons I was prince of the apple towns
And once below a time I lordly had the trees and leaves
        Trail with daisies and barley
    Down the rivers of the windfall light.

And as I was green and carefree, famous among the barns   10
About the happy yard and singing as the farm was home,
    In the sun that is young once only,
        Time let me play and be
        Golden in the mercy of his means,
And green and golden I was huntsman and herdsman, the
    calves   15
Sang to my horn, the foxes on the hills barked clear and cold,
        And the sabbath rang slowly
    In the pebbles of the holy streams.

All the sun long it was running, it was lovely, the hay
Fields high as the house, the tunes from the chimneys, it was
    air   20
        And playing, lovely and watery

And fire green as grass.
And nightly under the simple stars
As I rode to sleep the owls were bearing the farm away,
All the moon long I heard, blessed among stables, the nightjars 25
Flying with the ricks, and the horses
Flashing into the dark.

And then to awake, and the farm, like a wanderer white
With the dew, come back, the cock on his shoulder: it was all
Shining, it was Adam and maiden, 30
The sky gathered again
And the sun grew round that very day.
So it must have been after the birth of the simple light
In the first, spinning place, the spellbound horses walking warm
Out of the whinnying green stable 35
On to the fields of praise.

And honored among foxes and pheasants by the gay house
Under the new made clouds and happy as the heart was long,
In the sun born over and over,
I ran my heedless ways, 40
My wishes raced through the house high hay
And nothing I cared, at my sky blue trades, that time allows
In all his tuneful turning so few and such morning songs
Before the children green and golden
Follow him out of grace, 45

Nothing I cared, in the lamb white days, that time would take me
Up to the swallow thronged loft by the shadow of my hand,
In the moon that is always rising,
Nor that riding to sleep
I should hear him fly with the high fields 50
And wake to the farm forever fled from the childless land.
Oh as I was young and easy in the mercy of his means,
Time held me green and dying
Though I sang in my chains like the sea.

GWENDOLYN BROOKS (b. 1917)

We Real Cool

The Pool Players.
Seven at the Golden Shovel.

We real cool. We
Left school. We

Lurk late. We
Strike straight. We

Sing sin. We
Thin gin. We

Jazz June. We
Die soon.   10

5

ROBERT LOWELL   (1917–1977)
Skunk Hour

For Elizabeth Bishop

Nautilus Island's hermit
heiress still lives through winter in her Spartan cottage;
her sheep still graze above the sea.
Her son's a bishop. Her farmer
is first selectman in our village;   5
she's in her dotage.

Thirsting for
the hierarchic privacy
of Queen Victoria's century,
she buys up all   10
the eyesores facing her shore,
and lets them fall.

The season's ill —
we've lost our summer millionaire,
who seemed to leap from an L. L. Bean   15
catalogue. His nine-knot yawl
was auctioned off to lobstermen.
A red fox stain covers Blue Hill.

And now our fairy
decorator brightens his shop for fall;   20
his fishnet's filled with orange cork,
orange, his cobbler's bench and awl;
there is no money in his work,
he'd rather marry.

One dark night,   25
my Tudor Ford climbed the hill's skull;
I watched for love-cars. Lights turned down,
they lay together, hull to hull,

where the graveyard shelves on the town. . . .
My mind's not right.   30

A car radio bleats,
"Love, O careless Love. . . ." I hear
my ill-spirit sob in each blood cell,
as if my hand were at its throat. . . .
I myself am hell;   35
nobody's here —

only skunks, that search
in the moonlight for a bite to eat.
They march on their soles up Main Street:
white stripes, moonstruck eyes' red fire   40
under the chalk-dry and spar spire
of the Trinitarian Church.

I stand on top
of our back steps and breathe the rich air —
a mother skunk with her column of kittens swills the garbage
    pail.   45
She jabs her wedge-head in a cup
of sour cream, drops her ostrich tail,
and will not scare.

RICHARD WILBUR   (b. 1921)

The Writer

In her room at the prow of the house
Where light breaks, and the windows are tossed with linden,
My daughter is writing a story.

I pause in the stairwell, hearing
From her shut door a commotion of typewriter-keys   5
Like a chain hauled over a gunwale.

Young as she is, the stuff
Of her life is a great cargo, and some of it heavy:
I wish her a lucky passage.

But now it is she who pauses,   10
As if to reject my thought and its easy figure.
A stillness greatens, in which

The whole house seems to be thinking,
And then she is at it again with a bunched clamor
Of strokes, and again is silent.   15

I remember the dazed starling
Which was trapped in that very room, two years ago;
How we stole in, lifted a sash

And retreated, not to affright it;
And how for a helpless hour, through the crack of the door,   20
We watched the sleek, wild, dark

And iridescent creature
Batter against the brilliance, drop like a glove
To the hard floor, or the desk-top,

And wait then, humped and bloody,   25
For the wits to try it again; and how our spirits
Rose when, suddenly sure,

It lifted off from a chair-back,
Beating a smooth course for the right window
And clearing the sill of the world.   30

It is always a matter, my darling,
Of life or death, as I had forgotten. I wish
What I wished you before, but harder.

PHILIP LARKIN   (1922–1985)
Church Going

Once I am sure there's nothing going on
I step inside, letting the door thud shut.
Another church: matting, seats, and stone,
And little books; sprawlings of flowers, cut
For Sunday, brownish now; some brass and stuff   5
Up at the holy end; the small neat organ;
And a tense, musty, unignorable silence,
Brewed God knows how long. Hatless, I take off
My cycle-clips in awkward reverence,

Move forward, run my hand around the font.   10
From where I stand, the roof looks almost new —
Cleaned, or restored? Someone would know: I don't.
Mounting the lectern, I peruse a few
Hectoring large-scale verses, and pronounce
"Here endeth" much more loudly than I'd meant.   15
The echoes snigger briefly. Back at the door
I sign the book, donate an Irish sixpence,
Reflect the place was not worth stopping for.

Yet stop I did: in fact I often do,
And always end much at a loss like this,   20
Wondering what to look for; wondering, too,
When churches fall completely out of use
What we shall turn them into, if we shall keep
A few cathedrals chronically on show,
Their parchment, plate and pyx in locked cases,   25
And let the rest rent-free to rain and sheep.
Shall we avoid them as unlucky places?

Or, after dark, will dubious women come
To make their children touch a particular stone;
Pick simples° for a cancer; or on some   *herbs*   30
Advised night see walking a dead one?
Power of some sort or other will go on
In games, in riddles, seemingly at random;
But superstition, like belief, must die,
And what remains when disbelief has gone?   35
Grass, weedy pavement, brambles, buttress, sky,

A shape less recognisable each week,
A purpose more obscure. I wonder who
Will be the last, the very last, to seek
This place for what it was; one of the crew   40
That tap and jot and know what rood-lofts were?
Some ruin-bibber, randy for antique,
Or Christmas-addict, counting on a whiff
Of gown-and-bands and organ-pipes and myrrh?
Or will he be my representative,   45

Bored, uninformed, knowing the ghostly silt
Dispersed, yet tending to this cross of ground
Through suburb scrub because it held unspilt
So long and equably what since is found
Only in separation — marriage, and birth,   50
And death, and thoughts of these — for which was built
This special shell? For, though I've no idea
What this accoutred frowsty barn is worth,
It pleases me to stand in silence here;

A serious house on serious earth it is,   55
In whose blent air all our compulsions meet,
Are recognised, and robed as destinies.
And that much never can be obsolete,
Since someone will forever be surprising
A hunger in himself to be more serious,   60

And gravitating with it to this ground,
Which, he once heard, was proper to grow wise in,
If only that so many dead lie round.

PHILIP LARKIN (1922–1985)
The Whitsun° Weddings

That Whitsun, I was late getting away:
   Not till about
One-twenty on the sunlit Saturday
Did my three-quarters-empty train pull out,
All windows down, all cushions hot, all sense   5
Of being in a hurry gone. We ran
Behind the backs of houses, crossed a street
Of blinding windscreens, smelt the fish-dock; thence
The river's level drifting breadth began,
Where sky and Lincolnshire and water meet.   10

All afternoon, through the tall heat that slept
   For miles inland,
A slow and stopping curve southwards we kept.
Wide farms went by, short-shadowed cattle, and
Canals with floatings of industrial froth;   15
A hothouse flashed uniquely: hedges dipped
And rose: and now and then a smell of grass
Displaced the reek of buttoned carriage-cloth
Until the next town, new and nondescript,
Approached with acres of dismantled cars.   20

At first, I didn't notice what a noise
   The weddings made
Each station that we stopped at: sun destroys
The interest of what's happening in the shade,
And down the long cool platforms whoops and skirls   25
I took for porters larking with the mails,
And went on reading. Once we started, though,
We passed them, grinning and pomaded, girls
In parodies of fashion, heels and veils,
All posed irresolutely, watching us go,   30

As if out on the end of an event
   Waving goodbye

Whitsun: Whitsunday, the seventh Sunday after Easter and a legal holiday and long weekend
in England.

To something that survived it. Struck, I leant
More promptly out next time, more curiously,
And saw it all again in different terms: 35
The fathers with broad belts under their suits
And seamy foreheads; mothers loud and fat;
An uncle shouting smut; and then the perms,
The nylon gloves and jewellery-substitutes,
The lemons, mauves, and olive-ochres that   40

Marked off the girls unreally from the rest.
    Yes, from cafés
And banquet-halls up yards, and bunting-dressed
Coach-party annexes, the wedding-days
Were coming to an end. All down the line   45
Fresh couples climbed aboard: the rest stood round;
The last confetti and advice were thrown,
And, as we moved, each face seemed to define
Just what it saw departing: children frowned
At something dull; fathers had never known   50

Success so huge and wholly farcical;
    The women shared
The secret like a happy funeral;
While girls, gripping their handbags tighter, stared
At a religious wounding. Free at last,   55
And loaded with the sum of all they saw,
We hurried towards London, shuffling gouts of steam.
Now fields were building-plots, and poplars cast
Long shadows over major roads, and for
Some fifty minutes, that in time would seem   60

Just long enough to settle hats and say
    I nearly died,
A dozen marriages got under way.
They watched the landscape, sitting side by side
— An Odeon went past, a cooling tower,   65
And someone running up to bowl — and none
Thought of the others they would never meet
Or how their lives would all contain this hour.
I thought of London spread out in the sun,
Its postal districts packed like squares of wheat: 70

There we were aimed. And as we raced across
    Bright knots of rail
Past standing Pullmans, walls of blackened moss

Came close, and it was nearly done, this frail
Travelling coincidence; and what it held   75
Stood ready to be loosed with all the power
That being changed can give. We slowed again,
And as the tightened brakes took hold, there swelled
A sense of falling, like an arrow-shower
Sent out of sight, somewhere becoming rain.   80

A. R. AMMONS   (b. 1926)
I went out to the sun

I went out to the sun
where it burned over a desert willow
and getting under the shade of the willow
I said
   It's very hot in this country   5
The sun said nothing so I said
   The moon has been talking about you
and he said
   Well what is it this time

   She says it's her own light   10
He threw his flames out so far
they almost scorched the top of the willow
   Well I said of course I don't know

The sun went on and the willow was glad
I found an arroyo and dug for water   15
which I got muddy and then clear
so I drank a lot
and washed the salt from my eyes
and taking off my shirt
hung it on the willow to dry and said   20
   This land where whirlwinds
walking at noon in tall columns of dust
   take stately turns about the desert
   is a very dry land
So I went to sleep under the willow tree   25

When the moon came up it was cold
and reaching to the willow for my shirt
I said to the moon
   You make it a pretty night
so she smiled   30

A night-lizard rattled stems behind me
and the moon said
   I see over the mountain
   the sun is angry
Not able to see him I called and said   35
   Why are you angry with the moon
   since all at last must be lost
   to the great vacuity

JAMES MERRILL   (b. 1926)

An Urban Convalescence

Out for a walk, after a week in bed,
I find them tearing up part of my block
And, chilled through, dazed and lonely, join the dozen
In meek attitudes, watching a huge crane
Fumble luxuriously in the filth of years.   5
Her jaws dribble rubble. An old man
Laughs and curses in her brain,
Bringing to mind the close of *The White Goddess.*°

As usual in New York, everything is torn down
Before you have had time to care for it.   10
Head bowed, at the shrine of noise, let me try to recall
What building stood here. Was there a building at all?
I have lived on this same street for a decade.

Wait. Yes. Vaguely a presence rises
Some five floors high, of shabby stone   15
— Or am I confusing it with another one
In another part of town, or of the world? —
And over its lintel into focus vaguely
Misted with blood (my eyes are shut)
A single garland sways, stone fruit, stone leaves,   20
Which years of grit had etched until it thrust
Roots down, even into the poor soil of my seeing.
When did the garland become part of me?
I ask myself, amused almost,
Then shiver once from head to toe,   25

8 *The White Goddess*: Robert Graves's study of the female principle concludes with the conviction that the return of reverence for the Goddess, which is necessary to social and natural
balance, will be accompanied by her destruction of the logical, patriarchal, and predominantly urban products of modern Western civilization.

Transfixed by a particular cheap engraving of garlands
Bought for a few francs long ago,
All calligraphic tendril and cross-hatched rondure,
Ten years ago, and crumpled up to stanch
Boughs dripping, whose white gestures filled a cab, 30
And thought of neither then nor since.
Also, to clasp them, the small, red-nailed hand
Of no one I can place. Wait. No. Her name, her features
Lie toppled underneath that year's fashions.
The words she must have spoken, setting her face 35
To fluttering like a veil, I cannot hear now,
Let alone understand.

So that I am already on the stair,
As it were, of where I lived,
When the whole structure shudders at my tread 40
And soundlessly collapses, filling
The air with motes of stone.
Onto the still erect building next door
Are pressed levels and hues —
Pocked rose, streaked greens, brown whites. 45
Who drained the pousse-café?
Wires and pipes, snapped off at the roots, quiver.

Well, that is what life does. I stare
A moment longer, so. And presently
The massive volume of the world 50
Closes again.

Upon that book I swear
To abide by what it teaches:
Gospels of ugliness and waste,
Of towering voids, of soiled gusts, 55
Of a shrieking to be faced
Full into, eyes astream with cold —

With cold?
All right then. With self-knowledge.

Indoors at last, the pages of *Time* are apt 60
To open, and the illustrated mayor of New York,
Given a glimpse of how and where I work,
To note yet one more house that can be scrapped.

Unwillingly I picture
My walls weathering in the general view. 65

It is not even as though the new
Buildings did very much for architecture.

Suppose they did. The sickness of our time requires
That these as well be blasted in their prime.
You would think the simple fact of having lasted   70
Threatened our cities like mysterious fires.

There are certain phrases which to use in a poem
Is like rubbing silver with quicksilver. Bright
But facile, the glamour deadens overnight.
For instance, how "the sickness of our time"   75

Enhances, then debases, what I feel.
At my desk I swallow in a glass of water
No longer cordial, scarcely wet, a pill
They had told me not to take until much later.

With the result that back into my imagination   80
The city glides, like cities seen from the air,
Mere smoke and sparkle to the passenger
Having in mind another destination

Which now is not that honey-slow descent
Of the Champs-Elysées, her hand in his,   85
But the dull need to make some kind of house
Out of the life lived, out of the love spent.

JOHN ASHBERY   (b. 1927)
The Instruction Manual

As I sit looking out of a window of the building
I wish I did not have to write the instruction manual on the uses
     of a new metal.
I look down into the street and see people, each walking with an
     inner peace,
And envy them — they are so far away from me!
Not one of them has to worry about getting out this manual on
     schedule.   5
And, as my way is, I begin to dream, resting my elbows on the
     desk and leaning out of the window a little,
Of dim Guadalajara! City of rose-colored flowers!
City I wanted most to see, and most did not see, in Mexico!
But I fancy I see, under the press of having to write the
     instruction manual,

Your public square, city, with its elaborate little bandstand! 10
The band is playing *Scheherazade* by Rimsky-Korsakov.
Around stand the flower girls, handing out rose- and lemon-
    colored flowers,
Each attractive in her rose-and-blue striped dress (Oh! such
    shades of rose and blue),
And nearby is the little white booth where women in green serve
    you green and yellow fruit.
The couples are parading; everyone is in a holiday mood. 15
First, leading the parade, is a dapper fellow
Clothed in deep blue. On his head sits a white hat
And he wears a mustache, which has been trimmed for the
    occasion.
His dear one, his wife, is young and pretty; her shawl is rose,
    pink, and white.
Her slippers are patent leather, in the American fashion, 20
And she carries a fan, for she is modest, and does not want the
    crowd to see her face too often.
But everybody is so busy with his wife or loved one
I doubt they would notice the mustachioed man's wife.
Here come the boys! They are skipping and throwing little things
    on the sidewalk
Which is made of gray tile. One of them, a little older, has a
    toothpick in his teeth, 25
He is silenter than the rest, and affects not to notice the pretty
    young girls in white.
But his friends notice them, and shout their jeers at the laughing
    girls.
Yet soon all this will cease, with the deepening of their years,
And love bring each to the parade grounds for another reason.
But I have lost sight of the young fellow with the toothpick. 30
Wait — there he is — on the other side of the bandstand,
Secluded from his friends, in earnest talk with a young girl
Of fourteen or fifteen. I try to hear what they are saying
But it seems they are just mumbling something — shy words of
    love, probably.
She is slightly taller than he, and looks quietly down into his
    sincere eyes. 35
She is wearing white. The breeze ruffles her long fine black hair
    against her olive cheek.
Obviously she is in love. The boy, the young boy with the
    toothpick, he is in love too;
His eyes show it. Turning from this couple,
I see there is an intermission in the concert.

The paraders are resting and sipping drinks through straws   40
(The drinks are dispensed from a large glass crock by a lady in
    dark blue),
And the musicians mingle among them, in their creamy white
    uniforms, and talk
About the weather, perhaps, or how their kids are doing at
    school.
Let us take this opportunity to tiptoe into one of the side streets.
Here you may see one of those white houses with green trim   45
That are so popular here. Look — I told you!
It is cool and dim inside, but the patio is sunny.
An old woman in gray sits there, fanning herself with a palm leaf
    fan.
She welcomes us to her patio, and offers us a cooling drink.
"My son is in Mexico City," she says. "He would welcome you
    too   50
If he were here. But his job is with a bank there.
Look, here is a photograph of him."
And a dark-skinned lad with pearly teeth grins out at us from the
    worn leather frame.
We thank her for her hospitality, for it is getting late
And we must catch a view of the city, before we leave, from a
    good high place.   55
That church tower will do — the faded pink one, there against
    the fierce blue of the sky. Slowly we enter.
The caretaker, an old man dressed in brown and gray, asks us
    how long we have been in the city, and how we like it here.
His daughter is scrubbing the steps — she nods to us as we pass
    into the tower.
Soon we have reached the top, and the whole network of the city
    extends before us.
There is the rich quarter, with its houses of pink and white, and
    its crumbling, leafy terraces.   60
There is the poorer quarter, its homes a deep blue.
There is the market, where men are selling hats and swatting
    flies
And there is the public library, painted several shades of pale
    green and beige.
Look! There is the square we just came from, with the
    promenaders.
There are fewer of them, now that the heat of the day has
    increased,   65
But the young boy and girl still lurk in the shadows of the
    bandstand.

And there is the home of the little old lady —
She is still sitting in the patio, fanning herself.
How limited, but how complete withal, has been our experience
    of Guadalajara!
We have seen young love, married love, and the love of an aged
    mother for her son.   70
We have heard the music, tasted the drinks, and looked at
    colored houses.
What more is there to do, except stay? And that we cannot do.
And as a last breeze freshens the top of the weathered old tower, I
    turn my gaze
Back to the instruction manual which has made me dream of
    Guadalajara.

PHILIP LEVINE   (b. 1928)

They Feed They Lion

Out of burlap sacks, out of bearing butter,
Out of black bean and wet slate bread,
Out of the acids of rage, the candor of tar,
Out of creosote, gasoline, drive shafts, wooden dollies,
They Lion grow.   5

          Out of the grey hills
Of industrial barns, out of rain, out of bus ride,
West Virginia to Kiss My Ass, out of buried aunties,
Mothers hardening like pounded stumps, out of stumps,
Out of the bones' need to sharpen and the muscles' to stretch,   10
They lion grow.

          Earth is eating trees, fence posts,
Gutted cars, earth is calling her little ones,
"Come home, Come home!" From pig balls,
From the ferocity of pig driven to holiness,   15
From the furred ear and the full jowl come
The repose of the hung belly, from the purpose
They Lion grow.

          From the sweet glues of the trotters
Come the sweet kinks of the fist, from the full flower   20
Of the hams the thorax of caves,
From "Bow Down" come "Rise Up,"
Come they Lion from the reeds of shovels,

The grained arm that pulls the hands,
They Lion grow.   25

       From my five arms and all my hands,
From all my white sins forgiven, they feed,
From my car passing under the stars,
They Lion, from my children inherit,
From the oak turned to a wall, they Lion,   30
From they sack and they belly opened
And all that was hidden burning on the oil-stained earth
They feed they Lion and he comes.

ANNE SEXTON   (1928–1974)
For My Lover, Returning to His Wife

She is all there.
She was melted carefully down for you
and cast up from your childhood,
cast up from your one hundred favorite aggies.

She has always been there, my darling.   5
She is, in fact, exquisite.
Fireworks in the dull middle of February
and as real as a cast-iron pot.

Let's face it, I have been momentary.
A luxury. A bright red sloop in the harbor.   10
My hair rising like smoke from the car window.
Littleneck clams out of season.

She is more than that. She is your have to have,
has grown you your practical your tropical growth.
This is not an experiment. She is all harmony.   15
She sees to oars and oarlocks for the dinghy,

has placed wild flowers at the window at breakfast,
sat by the potter's wheel at midday,
set forth three children under the moon,
three cherubs drawn by Michelangelo,   20

done this with her legs spread out
in the terrible months in the chapel.
If you glance up, the children are there
like delicate balloons resting on the ceiling.

She has also carried each one down the hall   25
after supper, their heads privately bent,

two legs protesting, person to person,
her face flushed with a song and their little sleep.

I give you back your heart.
I give you permission —   30

for the fuse inside her, throbbing
angrily in the dirt, for the bitch in her
and the burying of her wound —
for the burying of her small red wound alive —

for the pale flickering flare under her ribs,   35
for the drunken sailor who waits in her left pulse,
for the mother's knee, for the stockings,
for the garter belt, for the call —

the curious call
when you will burrow in arms and breasts   40
and tug at the orange ribbon in her hair
and answer the call, the curious call.

She is so naked and singular.
She is the sum of yourself and your dream.
Climb her like a monument, step after step.   45
She is solid.

As for me, I am a watercolor.
I wash off.

ADRIENNE RICH   (b. 1929)

Diving into the Wreck

First having read the book of myths,
and loaded the camera,
and checked the edge of the knife-blade,
I put on
the body-armor of black rubber   5
the absurd flippers
the grave and awkward mask.
I am having to do this
not like Cousteau with his
assiduous team   10
aboard the sun-flooded schooner
but here alone.

There is a ladder.
The ladder is always there

hanging innocently   15
close to the side of the schooner.
We know what it is for,
we who have used it.
Otherwise
it's a piece of maritime floss   20
some sundry equipment.

I go down.
Rung after rung and still
the oxygen immerses me
the blue light   25
the clear atoms
of our human air.
I go down.
My flippers cripple me,
I crawl like an insect down the ladder   30
and there is no one
to tell me when the ocean
will begin.

First the air is blue and then
it is bluer and then green and then   35
black I am blacking out and yet
my mask is powerful
it pumps my blood with power
the sea is another story
the sea is not a question of power   40
I have to learn alone
to turn my body without force
in the deep element.

And now: it is easy to forget
what I came for   45
among so many who have always
lived here
swaying their crenellated fans
between the reefs
and besides   50
you breathe differently down here.

I came to explore the wreck.
The words are purposes.
The words are maps.

I came to see the damage that was done   55
and the treasures that prevail.
I stroke the beam of my lamp
slowly along the flank
of something more permanent
than fish or weed   60

the thing I came for:
the wreck and not the story of the wreck
the thing itself and not the myth
the drowned face always staring
toward the sun   65
the evidence of damage
worn by salt and sway into this threadbare beauty
the ribs of the disaster
curving their assertion
among the tentative haunters.   70

This is the place.
And I am here, the mermaid whose dark hair
streams black, the merman in his armored body
We circle silently
about the wreck   75
we dive into the hold.
I am she: I am he

whose drowned face sleeps with open eyes
whose breasts still bear the stress
whose silver, copper, vermeil cargo lies   80
obscurely inside barrels
half-wedged and left to rot
we are the half-destroyed instruments
that once held to a course
the water-eaten log   85
the fouled compass

We are, I am, you are
by cowardice or courage
the one who find our way
back to this scene   90
carrying a knife, a camera
a book of myths
in which
our names do not appear.

ADRIENNE RICH   (b. 1929)
Living in Sin

She had thought the studio would keep itself;
no dust upon the furniture of love.
Half heresy, to wish the taps less vocal,
the panes relieved of grime. A plate of pears,
a piano with a Persian shawl, a cat   5
stalking the picturesque amusing mouse
had risen at his urging.
Not that at five each separate stair would writhe
under the milkman's tramp; that morning light
so coldly would delineate the scraps   10
of last night's cheese and three sepulchral bottles;
that on the kitchen shelf among the saucers
a pair of beetle-eyes would fix her own —
Envoy from some village in the moldings . . .
Meanwhile, he, with a yawn,   15
sounded a dozen notes upon the keyboard,
declared it out of tune, shrugged at the mirror,
rubbed at his beard, went out for cigarettes;
while she, jeered by the minor demons,
pulled back the sheets and made the bed and found   20
a towel to dust the table-top,
and let the coffee-pot boil over on the stove.
By evening she was back in love again,
though not so wholly but throughout the night
she woke sometimes to feel the daylight coming   25
like a relentless milkman up the stairs.

TED HUGHES   (b. 1930)
View of a Pig

The pig lay on a barrow dead.
It weighed, they said, as much as three men.
Its eyes closed, pink white eyelashes.
Its trotters stuck straight out.

Such weight and thick pink bulk   5
Set in death seemed not just dead.
It was less than lifeless, further off.
It was like a sack of wheat.

I thumped it without feeling remorse.
One feels guilty insulting the dead,   10
Walking on graves. But this pig
Did not seem able to accuse.

It was too dead. Just so much
A poundage of lard and pork.
Its last dignity had entirely gone.   15
It was not a figure of fun.

Too dead now to pity.
To remember its life, din, stronghold
Of earthly pleasure as it had been,
Seemed a false effort, and off the point.   20

Too deadly factual. Its weight
Oppressed me — how could it be moved?
And the trouble of cutting it up!
The gash in its throat was shocking, but not pathetic.

Once I ran at a fair in the noise   25
To catch a greased piglet
That was faster and nimbler than a cat,
Its squeal was the rending of metal.

Pigs must have hot blood, they feel like ovens.
Their bite is worse than a horse's —   30
They chop a half-moon clean out
They eat cinders, dead cats.

Distinctions and admirations such
As this one was long finished with.
I stared at it a long time. They were going to scald it,   35
Scald it and scour it like a doorstep.

SYLVIA PLATH   (1932–1963)

The Arrival of the Bee Box

I ordered this, this clean wood box
Square as a chair and almost too heavy to lift.
I would say it was the coffin of a midget
Or a square baby
Were there not such a din in it.   5

The box is locked, it is dangerous.
I have to live with it overnight

And I can't keep away from it.
There are no windows, so I can't see what is in there.
There is only a little grid, no exit.   10

I put my eye to the grid.
It is dark, dark,
With the swarmy feeling of African hands
Minute and shrunk for export,
Black on black, angrily clambering.   15

How can I let them out?
It is the noise that appals me most of all,
The unintelligible syllables.
It is like a Roman mob,
Small, taken one by one, but my god, together!   20

I lay my ear to furious Latin.
I am not a Caesar.
I have simply ordered a box of maniacs.
They can be sent back.
They can die, I need feed them nothing, I am the owner.   25

I wonder how hungry they are.
I wonder if they would forget me
If I just undid the locks and stood back and turned into a tree.
There is the laburnum, its blond colonnades,
And the petticoats of the cherry.   30

They might ignore me immediately
In my moon suit and funeral veil.
I am no source of honey
So why should they turn on me?
Tomorrow I will be sweet God, I will set them free.   35

The box is only temporary.

SYLVIA PLATH   (1932–1963)
Lady Lazarus°

I have done it again.
One year in every ten
I manage it —

Lazarus: Raised from the dead by Jesus (see John 11:38–44).

A sort of walking miracle, my skin
Bright as a Nazi lampshade,   5
My right foot

A paperweight,
My face a featureless, fine
Jew linen.

Peel off the napkin   10
O my enemy.
Do I terrify? —

The nose, the eye pits, the full set of teeth?
The sour breath
Will vanish in a day.   15

Soon, soon the flesh
The grave cave ate will be
At home on me

And I a smiling woman.
I am only thirty.   20
And like the cat I have nine times to die.

This is Number Three.
What a trash
To annihilate each decade.

What a million filaments.   25
The peanut-crunching crowd
Shoves in to see

Them unwrap me hand and foot —
The big strip tease.
Gentleman, ladies,   30

These are my hands,
My knees.
I may be skin and bone,

Nevertheless, I am the same, identical woman.
The first time it happened I was ten.   35
It was an accident.

The second time I meant
To last it out and not come back at all.
I rocked shut

As a seashell. 40
They had to call and call
And pick the worms off me like sticky pearls.

Dying
Is an art, like everything else.
I do it exceptionally well. 45

I do it so it feels like hell.
I do it so it feels real.
I guess you could say I've a call.

It's easy enough to do it in a cell.
It's easy enough to do it and stay put. 50
It's the theatrical

Comeback in broad day
To the same place, the same face, the same brute
Amused shout:

"A miracle!" 55
That knocks me out.
There is a charge

For the eyeing of my scars, there is a charge
For the hearing of my heart —
It really goes. 60

And there is a charge, a very large charge
For a word or a touch
Or a bit of blood

Or a piece of my hair or my clothes.
So, so, Herr Doktor. 65
So, Herr Enemy.

I am your opus,
I am your valuable,
The pure gold baby

That melts to a shriek. 70
I turn and burn.
Do not think I underestimate your great concern.

Ash, ash —
You poke and stir.
Flesh, bone, there is nothing there — 75

A cake of soap,
A wedding ring,
A gold filling.

Herr God, Herr Lucifer,
Beware   80
Beware.

Out of the ash
I rise with my red hair
And I eat men like air.

AUDRE LORDE   (b. 1934)
Hanging Fire

I am fourteen
and my skin has betrayed me
the boy I cannot live without
still sucks his thumb
in secret   5
how come my knees are
always so ashy
what if I die
before morning
and momma's in the bedroom   10
with the door closed.

I have to learn how to dance
in time for the next party
my room is too small for me
suppose I die before graduation   15
they will sing sad melodies
but finally
tell the truth about me
There is nothing I want to do
and too much   20
that has to be done
and momma's in the bedroom
with the door closed.

Nobody even stops to think
about my side of it   25
I should have been on Math Team

my marks were better than his
why do I have to be
the one
wearing braces   30
I have nothing to wear tomorrow
will I live long enough
to grow up
and momma's in the bedroom
with the door closed.   35

WOLE SOYINKA   (b. 1934)
Telephone Conversation

The price seemed reasonable, location
Indifferent. The landlady swore she lived
Off premises. Nothing remained
But self-confession. "Madam," I warned,
"I hate a wasted journey — I am African."   5
Silence. Silenced transmission of
Pressurized good-breeding. Voice, when it came,
Lipstick-coated, long gold-rolled
Cigarette-holder tipped. Caught I was, foully.
"HOW DARK?" . . . I had not misheard . . . "ARE YOU LIGHT   10
OR VERY DARK?" Button B. Button A.° Stench
Of rancid breath of public hide-and-speak.
Red booth. Red pillar box.° Red double-tiered   *mailbox*
Omnibus squelching tar. It *was* real! Shamed
By ill-mannered silence, surrender   15
Pushed dumbfounded to beg simplification.
Considerate she was, varying the emphasis —
"ARE YOU DARK? OR VERY LIGHT?" Revelation came.
"You mean — like plain or milk chocolate?"
Her assent was clinical, crushing in its light   20
Impersonality. Rapidly, wave-length adjusted,
I chose. "West African sepia" — and as afterthought,
"Down in my passport." Silence for spectroscopic
Flight of fancy, till truthfulness clanged her accent
Hard on the mouthpiece. "WHAT'S THAT?" conceding   25
"DON'T KNOW WHAT THAT IS." "Like brunette."

---

11 *Button B. Button A.*: Buttons on the public telephone that had to be pushed when depositing coins.

"THAT'S DARK, ISN'T IT?" "Not altogether."
Facially, I am brunette, but madam, you should see
The rest of me. Palm of my hand, soles of my feet
Are a peroxide blonde. Friction, caused —   30
Foolishly madam — by sitting down, has turned
My bottom raven black — One moment, madam! — sensing
Her receiver rearing on the thunderclap
About my ears — "Madam," I pleaded, "wouldn't you rather
See for yourself?"   35

MARY OLIVER   (b. 1935)
The Truro Bear

There's a bear in the Truro woods.
People have seen it — three or four,
or two, or one. I think
of the thickness of the serious woods
around the dark bowls of the Truro ponds;   5
I think of the blueberry fields, the blackberry tangles,
the cranberry bogs. And the sky
with its new moon, its familiar star-trails,
burns down like a brand-new heaven,
while everywhere I look on the scratchy hillsides   10
shadows seem to grow shoulders. Surely
a beast might be clever, be lucky, move quietly
through the woods for years, learning to stay away
from roads and houses. Common sense mutters:
it can't be true, it must be somebody's   15
runaway dog. But the seed
has been planted, and when has happiness ever
required much evidence to begin
its leaf-green breathing?

MICHAEL HARPER   (b. 1938)
Martin's Blues

He came apart in the open,
the slow motion cameras
falling quickly
neither alive nor kicking;
stone blind dead   5

on the balcony
that old melody
etched his black lips
in a pruned echo:
We shall overcome   10
some day —
Yes we did!
Yes we did!

MARGARET ATWOOD   (b. 1939)

Landcrab

A lie, that we come from water.
The truth is we were born
from stones, dragons, the sea's
teeth, as you testify,
with your crust and jagged scissors.   5

Hermit, hard socket
for a timid eye,
you're a soft gut scuttling
sideways, a blue skull,
round bone on the prowl.   10
Wolf of treeroots and gravelly holes,
a mouth on stilts,
the husk of a small demon.

Attack, voracious
eating, and flight: 15
it's a sound routine
for staying alive on edges.
Then there's the tide, and that dance
you do for the moon
on wet sand, claws raised   20
to fend off your mate,
your coupling a quick
dry clatter of rocks.
For mammals
with their lobes and bulbs,   25
scruples and warm milk,
you've nothing but contempt.

Here you are, a frozen scowl
targeted in flashlight,

then gone: a piece of what

30

we are, not all,
my stunted child, my momentary
face in the mirror,
my tiny nightmare.

FICTION

We turn now to fiction — made-up stories written in prose — but let's pause first to remind ourselves of where we are and what we're practicing. In Part One we concentrated on our activity in bringing to life feelings, characters, change, and ideas; our texts were poems, plays, and stories. In the Poetry section of Part Two — the last seven chapters — we concentrated on our activity in bringing language to life. We noted that all the elements of a reading experience are interdependent and that it's only for purposes of practice that we separate the evocation of language from the evocation of the events and behavior that the language describes. And then we went on to practice. Instead of looking through the words of a text, attentive mainly to what the words point at, we focused on verbal patterns — sound, rhythm, tone, imagery, metaphor and simile, symbol, and irony.

We'll be continuing that kind of practice as we consider here the language of fiction and later, in the next segment, the language of plays. And there will be many opportunities, now and later, for sharpening responsiveness to tone, attitude, imagery, and complex verbal patterns. Stories have tone, for example; storytellers take up attitudes toward the people and places they create. (James Joyce's tone in "Araby," p. 294, is mordantly objective; the attitudes toward Dublin life are clearly unenthusiastic.) And the patterns of language in both stories and plays are shaped through imagery, metaphor, and symbol. When we evoke the bazaar in "Araby" as a symbol, we link it with many of the story's earlier images of exotic escape. In short, our activity when we evoke the language of poetry has much in common with what we do when we evoke the language of fiction.

Obviously, however, some broad differences exist between the language of fiction and poetry — differences that aren't merely a matter of the way words are laid out on a printed page. And several terms specific to fiction are used to define special characteristics of its language. *Plot* is probably the most familiar of these terms. It is usually defined as a series of events or actions possessing cause-and-effect relations with each other. But our activity as readers is indispensable to the creation of these relations — vital to the construction of plot.

To construct the plot of John Updike's "Snowing in Greenwich Village" (p. 19), we focus on the arrangement of the events of the story: the arrival of Rebecca at the Maples' apartment, the conversation between hosts and guest, the passing of the mounted police in the snow, Dick Maple's and Rebecca's walk home to her apartment, their arrival, and Dick's departure. We see that a key element in the organization of these events — significant in creating a cohesive pattern — is the pairing of moments of arrival (Rebecca's arrival at the beginning and Dick's arrival at the end of the story). And we connect that pattern in the bare bones of the narrative with other patterns in the story's language. There's the business with the coat at the beginning and end, for example. And there's the significant repetition of the word *close* in the opening and closing sentences.

Plot design, like every other aspect of verbal patterning in imaginative writing, possesses real interest in itself. But we bother with such details primarily because they clue us to the interaction of verbal patterns with our sense of character and feeling, ultimately helping us move closer to the complications of human responses and behavior. The plot pairings and word repetitions that we bring to life at the end of "Snowing in Greenwich Village" clarify the limits of Dick Maple's understanding. For him Rebecca's perfectly safe and normal arrival at the start of the story is altogether different from his own dangerous arrival at Rebecca's apartment close to the end. But the subtle verbal patterns contest that understanding. They remind us that neither event led to anything truly momentous and hint that Dick's supercharged view of things — "we were close" — could be the result of adolescent fantasy.

Some other frequently used terms in discussions of narrative form in fiction are *exposition, complication, conflict*, and *denouement*.

The material in a story giving us the background and present situation of the characters is spoken of as *exposition*. The moment at which Dick Maple senses himself as capable of making a pass at Rebecca introduces *complication* or *conflict* — in this case conflict *within* Maple. (Other kinds of conflict in fiction pit characters against other characters or against natural forces.) Dick's departure from Rebecca's apartment, virtue intact, serves as the story's resolution or *denouement*.

In a *scene* events are presented to us as though we were there, observing for ourselves on the spot, listening to the characters, watching them interact from moment to moment in real time. (The last few paragraphs of "Snowing in Greenwich Village" constitute a scene.) When storytellers appear to observe for us, recording events without putting us in position to observe for ourselves, the method of narrative is called *summary*. (The first paragraph of the Updike story constitutes an example of summary narration.)

Our most intense activity, as evokers of the language of fiction, is that which occurs from moment to moment throughout the whole length of the story. Few of us fret much about which part of a story is exposition, which part is complication, and so on. But we are preoccupied, as we read, with what happens next and with the problem of deciding how to take — whether to accept as plausible — the events being described. We work to decide for ourselves, on the basis of the words on the page, how far we should go in believing what's said. And we work with equal intensity to come to terms with the doubt and uncertainty stirred in us about how the story will "come out." Putting the same point in different words: We're concerned with the *point of view* of the storyteller and with the development of *suspense*. The following chapters center on these and other pivotally important aspects of our experience of the language of fiction.

13

Eyewitnesses and Others

Some years ago a terrible helicopter accident occurred at a heliport atop the Pan Am Building in midtown Manhattan. (I was nearby at the time.) The chopper's rotor flew off during a landing; people on the roof were killed; a piece of the rotor tore into windows on the building's west side.

It was a Saturday afternoon. Ambulances, fire engines, and police cars raced past. Pedestrians on the streets knew only that whatever had happened was somewhere close by. A small crowd gathered at one point — they were gathered around a boy, a ten- or eleven-year-old who was talking excitedly, pointing up at an office building. "What is it?" people in the crowd asked each other, not catching his words, asking him to repeat, then interrupting him. "What happened?" "A plane hit the building," the boy said. "A plane smacked it; it came right into it; you can see the wing. See the wing? That's a wing in the window, see it?"

The crowd looked up and saw — in disbelief — what did indeed look like part of an airplane wing. But where was the plane? "The plane's in the building," the boy said. "It went right into the building."

A dozen or so passersby stood there asking more questions, looking up at the wing wedged into the side of the building, everyone engaged in pretty much the same operation: deciding how good a witness this eyewitness was. As grown-ups, the people on the sidewalk knew that kids enjoy being the center of attention, that sometimes they exaggerate, that they may not be able to articulate clearly what they see. But without this boy's version of events, nobody would have thought to look up. And plainly that piece of whatever it was — Was it *really* a wing? Could it really be part of an airplane? — held a key to the wild sirens screaming past. With no police officer, newspaper reporter, or other authority at hand, people on this corner were stuck with a single source, trying to piece out the facts from his words, using the "evidence" far up the side of the building, weighing probabilities, testing the words of the immensely agitated observer who claimed to have seen "it" happen.

A street encounter of this kind is clearly different from proceedings in a court of law, where contesting attorneys work through complex systems of interrogation to clarify the strengths and weaknesses of particular bits of testimony. Each person standing with this youngster had opinions, prejudices, knowledge that shaped his or her way of interpreting and evaluating the boy's words; few went at the problem of evaluation systematically. Still, everybody was concentrating, at least momentarily, on a single task: trying to grasp the level of understanding and of imagination that The Source brought to the events he was recounting.

EVOKING A LEVEL OF UNDERSTANDING

That mode of concentration is shared by readers of stories as they bring individual narrators to life. The fundamental job is assessing the kind, quantity, and quality of knowledge possessed by the source of the story. Sometimes the avowed source is a speaker who, like the boy on Forty-fourth Street and Madison Avenue, speaks as *I* — I saw it happen. (In fiction that kind of storyteller is called a *first-person narrator*.) Invariably, though, the source is a creation of the author; the writer imagines a certain specific level of understanding and finds language with which to tell the story from that perspective. The pleasure and instruction offered by a story often flow directly from the precision with which a level of human understanding is characterized and evoked. The writer shows us an individual mind in operation; we see that mind in the process of organizing reality for itself, deciding what's going on around it, arriving at hypotheses or conclusions about the meaning of a set of events. We see strengths and weaknesses alike; we catch glimpses of the causes of mistakes as well as of the aptitudes that produce right answers. On occasion a writer even arranges to shape a storytelling source in such a way as to force us to examine our own levels of understanding.

None of this can happen, though, unless we ourselves once again get into the act. It's up to us as readers to work up, in partnership with the author, a sense of how a particular mind is functioning at any given moment — what it's taking in, what it's missing, and why. We're being shown somebody else's point of view as a whole condition of knowledge, a way of understanding the world that's rooted in the person's age, education, class, sex, religion, and a variety of other circumstances. And as we take in this perspective, we learn how reality is made intelligible by individual human beings. We also learn about what's involved for any one of us in the struggle to grasp "the whole story," and, finally, we learn about how the enterprise of responding actively to a given set of words, spoken by another and set down on a page, can help us come to know our own minds.

ASKING QUESTIONS
ABOUT POINT OF VIEW

Three points of view — three levels of understanding — are considered in this section. First we see with a five-year-old boy attempting to understand why his mother seems to care less about him than about her husband just home from a war. Next we see with a young mother the fear, exhaustion, and isolation of an encroaching mental breakdown. Then we see with a pair of lovers trying to imagine a happy future for themselves.

As in Poetry, questions follow each story, and, for the first text, a sample answer is supplied. That response, as you will notice, does not consist of a point-by-point, one-two-three answer to the questions. Instead, it uses the questions as jumping-off places — helpful ways of starting the process of formulating a personal response. That is how the questions should function for you. Your purpose in writing isn't to hit on some magical "right answer" but rather to enable you to think out your response — to put it into words, clarify it for yourself, assess its meanings.

A NOTE ON TECHNICAL TERMS

A first-person narrator, as already noted, speaks as "I" and as an eyewitness of the events recounted. (See Deborah Eisenberg's "What It Was Like, Seeing Chris," p. 41.) A *third-person narrator* speaks of characters by their proper names and as "he" and "she" and often tells a story from a single character's point of view. (John Updike's "Snowing in Greenwich Village," p. 19, is an example of a third-person narrative told from one character's — Dick Maple's — point of view.) An *omniscient narrator* writes in the third person but enters at will into any character's point of view, instead of being restricted to a single perspective or event. (See William Faulkner's "Barn Burning," p. 143.) Still another method of storytelling is called *stream of consciousness*: This kind of narrative focuses on the mess of miscellaneous, jumbled-up mental activity that's imagined to constitute a character's ongoing inner consciousness. As readers we pick our way among the debris, seeking a story-path to follow. *Any* level of understanding may turn out to be flawed or limited; narrators who deceive themselves or the reader, or are of markedly limited intelligence or mentally deranged are spoken of as *unreliable narrators*.

FRANK O'CONNOR   (1903–1966)
My Oedipus Complex

Father was in the army all through the war — the first war, I mean — so, up to the age of five, I never saw much of him, and what I saw did not worry me. Sometimes I woke and there was a big figure in khaki peering down at me in the candlelight. Sometimes in the early morning I heard the slamming of the front door and the clatter of nailed boots down the cobbles of the lane. These were Father's entrances and exits. Like Santa Claus he came and went mysteriously.

In fact, I rather liked his visits, though it was an uncomfortable squeeze between Mother and him when I got into the big bed in the early morning. He smoked, which gave him a pleasant musty smell, and shaved, an operation of astounding interest. Each time he left a trail of souvenirs — model tanks and Gurkha knives with handles made of bullet cases, and German helmets and cap badges and button-sticks, and all sorts of military equipment — carefully stowed away in a long box on top of the wardrobe, in case they ever came in handy. There was a bit of the magpie about Father; he expected everything to come in handy. When his back was turned, Mother let me get a chair and rummage through his treasures. She didn't seem to think so highly of them as he did.

The war was the most peaceful period of my life. The window of my attic faced southeast. My mother had curtained it, but that had small effect. I always woke with the first light and, with all the responsibilities of the previous day melted, feeling myself rather like the sun, ready to illumine and rejoice. Life never seemed so simple and clear and full of possibilities as then. I put my feet out from under the clothes — I called them Mrs. Left and Mrs. Right — and invented dramatic situations for them in which they discussed the problems of the day. At least Mrs. Right did; she was very demonstrative, but I hadn't the same control of Mrs. Left, so she mostly contented herself with nodding agreement.

They discussed what Mother and I should do during the day, what Santa Claus should give a fellow for Christmas, and what steps should be taken to brighten the home. There was that little matter of the baby, for instance. Mother and I could never agree about that. Ours was the only house in the terrace without a new baby, and Mother said we couldn't afford one till Father came back from the war because they cost seventeen and six. That showed how simple she was. The Geneys up the road had a baby, and everyone knew they couldn't afford seventeen and six. It was probably a cheap baby, and Mother wanted something really good, but I felt she was too exclusive. The Geneys' baby would have done us fine.

Having settled my plans for the day, I got up, put a chair 5 under the attic window, and lifted the frame high enough to stick out my head. The window overlooked the front gardens of the terrace behind ours, and beyond these it looked over a deep valley to the tall, red-brick houses terraced up the opposite hillside, which were all still in shadow, while those at our side of the valley were all lit up, though with long strange shadows that made them seem unfamiliar; rigid and painted.

After that I went into Mother's room and climbed into the big bed. She woke and I began to tell her of my schemes. By this time, though I never seem to have noticed it, I was petrified in my nightshirt, and I thawed as I talked until, the last frost melted, I fell asleep beside her and woke again only when I heard her below in the kitchen, making the breakfast.

After breakfast we went into town; heard Mass at St. Augustine's and said a prayer for Father, and did the shopping. If the afternoon was fine we either went for a walk in the country or a visit to Mother's great friend in the convent, Mother St. Dominic. Mother had them all praying for Father, and every night, going to bed, I asked God to send him back safe from the war to us. Little, indeed, did I know what I was praying for!

One morning, I got into the big bed, and there, sure enough, was Father in his usual Santa Claus manner, but later, instead of uniform, he put on his best blue suit, and Mother was as pleased as anything. I saw nothing to be pleased about, because, out of uniform, Father was altogether less interesting, but she only beamed, and explained that our prayers had been answered, and off we went to Mass to thank God for having brought Father safely home.

The irony of it! That very day when he came in to dinner he took off his boots and put on his slippers, donned the dirty old cap he wore about the house to save him from colds, crossed his legs, and began to talk gravely to Mother, who looked anxious. Naturally, I disliked her looking anxious, because it destroyed her good looks, so I interrupted him.

"Just a moment, Larry!" she said gently.   10

This was only what she said when we had boring visitors, so I attached no importance to it and went on talking.

"Do be quiet, Larry!" she said impatiently. "Don't you hear me talking to Daddy?"

This was the first time I had heard those ominous words, "talking to Daddy," and I couldn't help feeling that if this was how God answered prayers, he couldn't listen to them very attentively.

"Why are you talking to Daddy?" I asked with as great a show of indifference as I could muster.

"Because Daddy and I have business to discuss. Now, don't   15 interrupt again!"

In the afternoon, at Mother's request, Father took me for a walk. This time we went into town instead of out the country, and I thought at first, in my usual optimistic way, that it might be an improvement. It was nothing of the sort. Father and I had quite different notions of a walk in town. He had no proper interest in trams, ships, and horses, and the only thing that seemed to divert him was talking to fellows as old as himself. When I wanted to stop he simply went on, dragging me behind him by the hand; when he wanted to stop I had no alternative but to do the same. I noticed that it seemed to be a sign that he wanted to stop for a long time whenever he leaned against a wall. The second time I saw him do it I got wild. He seemed to be settling himself forever. I pulled him by the coat and trousers, but, unlike Mother who, if you were too persistent, got into a wax and said: "Larry, if you don't behave yourself, I'll give you a good slap," Father had an extraordinary capacity for amiable inattention. I sized him up and wondered would I cry, but he seemed to be too remote to be annoyed even by that. Really, it was like going for a walk with a mountain! He either ignored the wrenching and pummelling entirely, or else glanced down with a grin of amusement from his peak. I had never met anyone so absorbed in himself as he seemed.

At teatime, "talking to Daddy" began again, complicated this time by the fact that he had an evening paper, and every few minutes he put it down and told Mother something new out of it. I felt this was foul play. Man for man, I was prepared to compete with him any time for Mother's attention, but when he had it all made up for him by other people it left me no chance. Several times I tried to change the subject without success.

"You must be quiet while Daddy is reading, Larry," Mother said impatiently.

It was clear that she either genuinely liked talking to Father better than talking to me, or else that he had some terrible hold on her which made her afraid to admit the truth.

"Mummy," I said that night when she was tucking me up, "do 20 you think if I prayed hard God would send Daddy back to the war?"

She seemed to think about that for a moment.

"No, dear," she said with a smile. "I don't think he would."

"Why wouldn't he, Mummy?"

"Because there isn't a war any longer, dear."

"But, Mummy, couldn't God make another war, if He liked?" 25

"He wouldn't like to, dear. It's not God who makes wars, but bad people."

"Oh!" I said.

I was disappointed about that. I began to think that God wasn't quite what he was cracked up to be.

Next morning I woke at my usual hour, feeling like a bottle of champagne. I put out my feet and invented a long conversation in which Mrs. Right talked of the trouble she had with her own father till she put him in the Home. I didn't quite know what the Home was but it sounded the right place for Father. Then I got my chair and stuck my head out of the attic window. Dawn was just breaking, with a guilty air that made me feel I had caught it in the act. My head bursting with stories and schemes, I stumbled in next door, and in the half-darkness scrambled into the big bed. There was no room at Mother's side so I had to get between her and Father. For the time being I had forgotten about him, and for several minutes I sat bolt upright, racking my brains to know what I could do with him. He was taking up more than his fair share of the bed, and I couldn't get comfortable, so I gave him several kicks that made him grunt and stretch. He made room all right, though. Mother waked and felt for me. I settled back comfortably in the warmth of the bed with my thumb in my mouth.

"Mummy!" I hummed, loudly and contentedly.   30

"Sssh! dear," she whispered. "Don't wake Daddy!"

This was a new development, which threatened to be even more serious than "talking to Daddy." Life without my early-morning conferences was unthinkable.

"Why?" I asked severely.

"Because poor Daddy is tired."

This seemed to me a quite inadequate reason, and I was sick-   35
ened by the sentimentality of her "poor Daddy." I never liked that sort of gush; it always struck me as insincere.

"Oh!" I said lightly. Then in my most winning tone: "Do you know where I want to go with you today, Mummy?"

"No dear," she sighed.

"I want to go down the Glen and fish for thornybacks with my new net, and then I want to go out to the Fox and Hounds, and — "

"Don't-wake-Daddy!" she hissed angrily, clapping her hand across my mouth.

But it was too late. He was awake, or nearly so. He grunted   40
and reached for the matches. Then he stared incredulously at his watch.

"Like a cup of tea, dear?" asked Mother in a meek, hushed voice I had never heard her use before. It sounded almost as though she were afraid.

"Tea?" he exclaimed indignantly. "Do you know what the time is?"

"And after that I want to go up the Rathcooney Road," I said loudly, afraid I'd forget something in all those interruptions.

"Go to sleep at once, Larry!" she said sharply.

I began to snivel. I couldn't concentrate, the way that pair   45
went on, and smothering my early-morning schemes was like burying a family from the cradle.

Father said nothing, but lit his pipe and sucked it, looking out into the shadows without minding Mother or me. I knew he

was mad. Every time I made a remark Mother hushed me irritably. I was mortified. I felt it wasn't fair; there was even something
sinister in it. Every time I had pointed out to her the waste of
making two beds when we could both sleep in one, she had told
me it was healthier like that, and now here was this man, this
stranger, sleeping with her without the least regard for her
health!

He got up early and made tea, but though he brought Mother
a cup he brought none for me.

"Mummy," I shouted, "I want a cup of tea, too."

"Yes, dear," she said patiently. "You can drink from Mummy's
saucer."

That settled it. Either Father or I would have to leave the 50
house. I didn't want to drink from Mother's saucer; I wanted to be
treated as an equal in my own home, so, just to spite her, I drank
it all and left none for her. She took that quietly, too.

But that night when she was putting me to bed she said
gently:

"Larry, I want you to promise me something."

"What is it?" I asked.

"Not to come in and disturb poor Daddy in the morning.
Promise?"

"Poor Daddy" again! I was becoming suspicious of every- 55
thing involving that quite impossible man.

"Why?" I asked.

"Because poor Daddy is worried and tired and he doesn't
sleep well."

"Why doesn't he, Mummy?"

"Well, you know, don't you, that while he was at the war
Mummy got the pennies from the Post Office?"

"From Miss MacCarthy?" 60

"That's right. But now, you see, Miss MacCarthy hasn't any
more pennies, so Daddy must go out and find us some. You know
what would happen if he couldn't?"

"No," I said, "tell us."

"Well, I think we might have to go out and beg for them like
the poor old woman on Fridays. We wouldn't like that, would
we?"

"No," I agreed. "We wouldn't."

"So you'll promise not to come in and wake him?" 65

"Promise."

Mind you, I meant that. I knew pennies were a serious matter, and I was all against having to go out and beg like the old
woman on Fridays. Mother laid out all my toys in a complete ring

round the bed so that, whatever way I got out, I was bound to fall over one of them.

When I woke I remembered my promise all right. I got up and sat on the floor and played — for hours, it seemed to me. Then I got my chair and looked out the attic window for more hours. I wished it was time for Father to wake; I wished someone would make me a cup of tea. I didn't feel in the least like the sun; instead, I was bored and so very, very cold! I simply longed for the warmth and depth of the big featherbed.

At last I could stand it no longer. I went into the next room. As there was still no room at Mother's side I climbed over her and she woke with a start.

"Larry," she whispered, gripping my arm very tightly, "what 70 did you promise?"

"But I did, Mummy," I wailed, caught in the very act. "I was quiet for ever so long."

"Oh, dear, and you're perished!" she said sadly, feeling me all over. "Now, if I let you stay will you promise not to talk?"

"But I want to talk, Mummy," I wailed.

"That has nothing to do with it," she said with a firmness that was new to me. "Daddy wants to sleep. Now, do you understand that?"

I understood it only too well. I wanted to talk, he wanted to 75 sleep — whose house was it, anyway?

"Mummy," I said with equal firmness, "I think it would be healthier for Daddy to sleep in his own bed."

That seemed to stagger her, because she said nothing for a while.

"Now, once for all," she went on, "you're to be perfectly quiet or go back to your own bed. Which is it to be?"

The injustice of it got me down. I had convicted her out of her own mouth of inconsistency and unreasonableness, and she hadn't even attempted to reply. Full of spite, I gave Father a kick, which she didn't notice but which made him grunt and open his eyes in alarm.

"What time is it?" he asked in a panic-stricken voice, not 80 looking at Mother but at the door, as if he saw someone there.

"It's early yet," she replied soothingly. "It's only the child. Go to sleep again. . . . Now, Larry," she added, getting out of bed, "you've wakened Daddy and you must go back."

This time, for all her quiet air, I knew she meant it, and knew that my principal rights and privileges were as good as lost unless I asserted them at once. As she lifted me, I gave a screech, enough to wake the dead, not to mind Father. He groaned.

"That damn child! Doesn't he ever sleep?"

"It's only a habit, dear," she said quietly, though I could see she was vexed.

"Well, it's time he got out of it," shouted Father, beginning to 85 heave in the bed. He suddenly gathered all the bedclothes about him, turned to the wall, and then looked back over his shoulder with nothing showing only two small, spiteful, dark eyes. The man looked very wicked.

To open the bedroom door, Mother had to let me down, and I broke free and dashed for the farthest corner, screeching. Father sat bolt upright in bed.

"Shut up, you little puppy!" he said in a choking voice.

I was so astonished that I stopped screeching. Never, never had anyone spoken to me in that tone before. I looked at him incredulously and saw his face convulsed with rage. It was only then that I fully realized how God had codded me, listening to my prayers for the safe return of this monster.

"Shut up, you!" I bawled, beside myself.

"What's that you said?" shouted Father, making a wild leap 90 out of the bed.

"Mick, Mick!" cried Mother. "Don't you see the child isn't used to you?"

"I see he's better fed than taught," snarled Father, waving his arms wildly. "He wants his bottom smacked."

All his previous shouting was as nothing to these obscene words referring to my person. They really made my blood boil.

"Smack your own!" I screamed hysterically. "Smack your own! Shut up! Shut up!"

At this he lost his patience and let fly at me. He did it with 95 the lack of conviction you'd expect of a man under Mother's horrified eyes, and it ended up as a mere tap, but the sheer indignity of being struck at all by a stranger, a total stranger who had cajoled his way back from the war into our big bed as a result of my innocent intercession, made me completely dotty. I shrieked and shrieked, and danced in my bare feet, and Father, looking awkward and hairy in nothing but a short gray army shirt, glared down at me like a mountain out for murder. I think it must have been then that I realized he was jealous too. And there stood Mother in her nightdress, looking as if her heart was broken between us. I hoped she felt as she looked. It seemed to me that she deserved it all.

From that morning out my life was a hell. Father and I were enemies, open and avowed. We conducted a series of skirmishes against one another, he trying to steal my time with Mother and I his. When she was sitting on my bed, telling me a story, he took to looking for some pair of old boots which he alleged he had left behind him at the beginning of the war. While he talked to Mother I played loudly with my toys to show my total lack of concern. He created a terrible scene one evening when he came in from work and found me at his box, playing with his regimental badges, Gurkha knives, and button-sticks. Mother got up and took the box from me.

"You mustn't play with Daddy's toys unless he lets you, Larry," she said severely. "Daddy doesn't play with yours."

For some reason Father looked at her as if she had struck him and then turned away with a scowl.

"Those are not toys," he growled, taking down the box again to see had I lifted anything. "Some of those curios are very rare and valuable."

But as time went on I saw more and more how he managed to   100 alienate Mother and me. What made it worse was that I couldn't grasp his method or see what attraction he had for Mother. In every possible way he was less winning than I. He had a common accent and made noises at his tea. I thought for a while that it might be the newspapers she was interested in, so I made up bits of news of my own to read to her. Then I thought it might be the smoking, which I personally thought attractive, and took his pipes and went round the house dribbling into them till he caught me. I even made noises at my tea, but Mother only told me I was disgusting. It all seemed to hinge round that unhealthy habit of sleeping together, so I made a point of dropping into their bedroom and nosing round, talking to myself, so that they wouldn't know I was watching them, but they were never up to anything that I could see. In the end it beat me. It seemed to depend on being grown-up and giving people rings, and I realized I'd have to wait.

But at the same time I wanted him to see that I was only waiting, not giving up the fight. One evening when he was being particularly obnoxious, chattering away well above my head, I let him have it.

"Mummy," I said, "do you know what I'm going to do when I grow up?"

"No, dear," she replied. "What?"

"I'm going to marry you," I said quietly.

Father gave a great guffaw out of him, but he didn't take me   105 in. I knew it must only be pretense. And Mother, in spite of everything, was pleased. I felt she was probably relieved to know that one day Father's hold on her would be broken.

"Won't that be nice?" she said with a smile.

"It'll be very nice," I said confidently. "Because we're going to have lots and lots of babies."

"That's right, dear," she said placidly. "I think we'll have one soon, and then you'll have plenty of company."

I was no end pleased about that because it showed that in spite of the way she gave in to Father she still considered my wishes. Besides, it would put the Geneys in their place.

It didn't turn out like that, though. To begin with, she was 110 very preoccupied — I supposed about where she would get the seventeen and six — and though Father took to staying out late in the evenings it did me no particular good. She stopped taking me for walks, became as touchy as blazes, and smacked me for nothing at all. Sometimes I wished I'd never mentioned the confounded baby — I seemed to have a genius for bringing calamity on myself.

And calamity it was! Sonny arrived in the most appalling hullabaloo — even that much he couldn't do without a fuss — and from the first moment I disliked him. He was a difficult child — so far as I was concerned he was always difficult — and demanded far too much attention. Mother was simply silly about him, and couldn't see when he was only showing off. As company he was worse than useless. He slept all day, and I had to go round the house on tiptoe to avoid waking him. It wasn't any longer a question of not waking Father. The slogan now was "Don't-wake-Sonny!" I couldn't understand why the child wouldn't sleep at the proper time, so whenever Mother's back was turned I woke him. Sometimes to keep him awake I pinched him as well. Mother caught me at it one day and gave me a most unmerciful flaking.

One evening, when Father was coming in from work, I was playing trains in the front garden. I let on not to notice him; instead, I pretended to be talking to myself, and said in a loud voice: "If another bloody baby comes into this house, I'm going out."

Father stopped dead and looked at me over his shoulder.

"What's that you said?" he asked sternly.

"I was only talking to myself," I replied, trying to conceal my 115 panic. "It's private."

He turned and went in without a word. Mind you, I intended it as a solemn warning, but its effect was quite different. Father started being quite nice to me. I could understand that, of course. Mother was quite sickening about Sonny. Even at mealtimes she'd get up and gawk at him in the cradle with an idiotic smile, and tell Father to do the same. He was always polite about it, but he looked so puzzled you could see he didn't know what she was talking about. He complained of the way Sonny cried at night, but she only got cross and said that Sonny never cried except when there was something up with him — which was a flaming lie, because Sonny never had anything up with him, and only cried for attention. It was really painful to see how simple-minded she was. Father wasn't attractive, but he had a fine intelligence. He saw through Sonny, and now he knew that I saw through him as well.

One night I woke with a start. There was someone beside me in the bed. For one wild moment I felt sure it must be Mother, having come to her senses and left Father for good, but then I heard Sonny in convulsions in the next room, and Mother saying: "There! There! There!" and I knew it wasn't she. It was Father. He was lying beside me, wide awake, breathing hard and apparently as mad as hell.

After a while it came to me what he was mad about. It was his turn now. After turning me out of the big bed, he had been turned out himself. Mother had no consideration now for anyone but that poisonous pup, Sonny. I couldn't help feeling sorry for Father. I had been through it all myself, and even at that age I was magnanimous. I began to stroke him down and say: "There! There!" He wasn't exactly responsive.

"Aren't you asleep either?" he snarled.

"Ah, come on and put your arm around us, can't you?" I said, 120 and he did, in a sort of way. Gingerly, I suppose, is how you'd describe it. He was very bony but better than nothing.

At Christmas he went out of his way to buy me a really nice model railway.

Questions

Using the language of this passage as a starting point, bring to life Larry's level of understanding — his point of view — as fully as you can.

> What made it worse was that I couldn't grasp his method or see what attraction he had for Mother. . . . It all seemed to hinge round that unhealthy habit of sleeping together, so I made a point of dropping into their bedroom and nosing around, talking to myself, so that they wouldn't know I was watching them, but they were never up to anything that I could see. (para. 100)

1. How does Larry arrive at the conclusion that sleeping to-gether is an "unhealthy habit"?

2. What assumptions lie behind the boy's belief that he can fool his parents into not noticing he's watching them?

3. If Larry doesn't completely understand his situation, neither does he completely *mis*understand it. Name his chief strengths and weaknesses as an interpreter of what he sees and what he does. Then compare your response with the one that follows.

Response

EDITOR: Larry's defects of understanding stem, obviously, from ignorance of sex: aged five at the start of the story, perhaps a year or so older at the end, this youngster isn't acquainted with the physical facts of life, and his innocence would mark him as a child even if we didn't know his age.

But what a child! Larry is mighty precocious, and his precocity can be variously explained. His mother's need for adult companionship during his father's war service would have encouraged her to treat him, at some moments in his infant life, as an adult. His quick intelligence — that grown-up vocabulary! — could easily have made it seem improper to treat him any other way. He emerges as a wonderfully funny mixture of shrewdness, naiveté, pomposity, possessiveness, and guilefulness. And he has extraordinary intuitive alertness to grown-up feelings the precise nature of which lies far beyond his conscious understanding.

Larry doesn't know that his belief in the power of a child's prayers to bring a soldier safely home from the war isn't widely shared in the adult world. He doesn't know that a whole raft of his remarks — and his responses to his parents — would strike most grown-ups as absurdly old for his years. Normal five- and six-year-olds don't say "Having settled my plans for the day, I got up" (para. 5) or "Never, never had anyone spoken to me in that tone before" (88). Neither do they refer to a parent as "this man, this stranger" (46) or condescend to him ("There was a bit of the magpie about Father," 2). Nor are pity and impatience ("that quite impossible man," 55) standard responses of young children to their parents. It's fair to say that a great deal of what most children know about correct relationships between parents and offspring — about the need for deference, obedience, and the like — simply hasn't penetrated Larry's coddled skull.

On the other hand, this boy is more than a mere too-big-for-his-britches busybody. If he lacks knowledge, he has antennae; he noses out parental feelings and attitudes that are clearly meant to be hidden from him, and there's more than one occasion in this story when he's simultaneously naive *and* uncommonly knowing, ignorant and yet mysteriously, instinctively sophisticated.

One such moment occurs in the passage in which Larry undertakes to check out the special attractions of his parents' "unhealthy habit" of sleeping together. Larry's assurance that he can put one over on his parents by "talking to myself, so that they wouldn't know I was watching them," displays the same naiveté that's apparent in his notion that babies can be bought in a market for "seventeen and six" (4). But the language in which Larry dramatizes his style of bedroom surveillance is far less easy to patronize. The boy somehow intuits that, for his parents, the world of the bedroom is a scene of concealments, a place in which a child could fall into the role of moral superior because of sensing a furtive, secretive impulse, even perhaps a tinge of guilt, in his elders. The notion of Larry as cop, nosing around for criminal activity, seems again — on its face — absurd. But the notion that parents in bed, visited unexpectedly by a child, may in fact experience feelings of guilt is one by which few grown-ups will be surprised.

Larry is an innocent, but like many innocents he knows more than he understands, feels truths that he can't express. And it's this half-conscious knowledge that needs to be brought to life as we work to grasp Larry's level of understanding, his point of view. At its conclusion, the story shows us Larry and his father drawn together in a common situation of exclusion and jealousy. And Larry is given a grown-up role, becoming the voice of reconciliation after a quarrel ("Ah, come on and put your arm around us, can't you?" 120). Implicit in this momentary unity is a clue to the meaning and interest of Larry's point of view. His perspective, once we make it vivid to ourselves, isn't merely "outrageous" or "too old for his years." It's a challenge to the standard humorless assumption that a huge gulf separates a child's knowledge from a grown-up's. And the fascination of this point of view lies in its subtle, half-joking, half-serious way of putting that challenge — of suggesting that people who draw absolute lines between a child's knowledge and a grown-up's may themselves be childish.

But are we really to believe that such a level of understanding as Larry's could exist? Well, believing at any point in Larry as
a five-year-old isn't altogether easy. "Never, never had anyone
spoken to me in that tone before" — as we noted, this isn't five-
year-old talk. No child at that age would tell this tale in quite
these words. Clearly there's a grown-up in here somewhere, imagining or remembering incidents from his childhood while being
careful not to corrupt Larry's version of events with interpretations the child himself couldn't have made at the time. One part
of the grown-up author's fun comes, perhaps, from recreating
himself as a knowing kid; another part comes from teasing the
theory of the "Oedipal stage," which holds that youngsters are in
the grip of an unconscious desire to eliminate the parent whose
sex is the same as theirs. The active reader's fun lies in the game
itself — participation in the playful interaction of naive and
knowing readings of the world. And participation depends on
careful, moment-to-moment engagement with — evocation of —
the precise language in which Larry phrases his understanding.

CHARLOTTE PERKINS GILMAN   (1860–1935)
The Yellow Wallpaper

It is very seldom that mere ordinary people like John and
myself secure ancestral halls for the summer.

A colonial mansion, a hereditary estate, I would say a
haunted house and reach the height of romantic felicity — but
that would be asking too much of fate!

Still I will proudly declare that there is something queer
about it.

Else, why should it be let so cheaply? And why have stood so
long untenanted?

John laughs at me, of course, but one expects that.   5

John is practical in the extreme. He has no patience with
faith, an intense horror of superstition, and he scoffs openly at
any talk of things not to be felt and seen and put down in figures.

John is a physician, and *perhaps* — (I would not say it to a
living soul, of course, but this is dead paper and a great relief to
my mind) — *perhaps* that is one reason I do not get well faster.

You see, he does not believe I am sick! And what can one do?

If a physician of high standing, and one's own husband,
assures friends and relatives that there is really nothing the

matter with one but temporary nervous depression — a slight
hysterical tendency — what is one to do?

My brother is also a physician, and also of high standing, and 10
he says the same thing.

So I take phosphates or phosphites — whichever it is — and
tonics, and air and exercise, and journeys, and am absolutely
forbidden to "work" until I am well again.

Personally, I disagree with their ideas.

Personally, I believe that congenial work, with excitement
and change, would do me good.

But what is one to do?

I did write for a while in spite of them; but it *does* exhaust me 15
a good deal — having to be so sly about it, or else meet with
heavy opposition.

I sometimes fancy that in my condition, if I had less opposition and more society and stimulus — but John says the very
worst thing I can do is to think about my condition, and I confess
it always makes me feel bad.

So I will let it alone and talk about the house.

The most beautiful place! It is quite alone, standing well back
from the road, quite three miles from the village. It makes me
think of English places that you read about, for there are hedges
and walls and gates that lock, and lots of separate little houses for
the gardeners and people.

There is a *delicious* garden! I never saw such a garden — large
and shady, full of box-bordered paths, and lined with long grape-
covered arbors with seats under them.

There were greenhouses, but they are all broken now. 20

There was some legal trouble, I believe, something about the
heirs and co-heirs; anyhow, the place has been empty for years.

That spoils my ghostliness, I am afraid, but I don't care —
there is something strange about the house — I can feel it.

I even said so to John one moonlight evening, but he said
what I felt was a draught, and shut the window.

I get unreasonably angry with John sometimes. I'm sure I
never used to be so sensitive. I think it is due to this nervous
condition.

But John says if I feel so I shall neglect proper self-control; so 25
I take pains to control myself — before him, at least, and that
makes me very tired.

I don't like our room a bit. I wanted one downstairs that
opened onto the piazza and had roses all over the window, and
such pretty old-fashioned chintz hangings! But John would not
hear of it.

He said there was only one window and not room for two beds, and no near room for him if he took another.

He is very careful and loving, and hardly lets me stir without special direction.

I have a schedule prescription for each hour in the day; he takes all care from me, and so I feel basely ungrateful not to value it more.

He said he came here solely on my account, that I was to have 30 perfect rest and all the air I could get. "Your exercise depends on your strength, my dear," said he, "and your food somewhat on your appetite; but air you can absorb all the time." So we took the nursery at the top of the house.

It is a big, airy room, the whole floor nearly, with windows that look all ways, and air and sunshine galore. It was nursery first, and then playroom and gymnasium, I should judge, for the windows are barred for little children, and there are rings and things in the walls.

The paint and paper look as if a boys' school had used it. It is stripped off — the paper — in great patches all around the head of my bed, about as far as I can reach, and in a great place on the other side of the room low down. I never saw a worse paper in my life. One of those sprawling, flamboyant patterns committing every artistic sin.

It is dull enough to confuse the eye in following, pronounced enough constantly to irritate and provoke study, and when you follow the lame uncertain curves for a little distance they suddenly commit suicide — plunge off at outrageous angles, destroy themselves in unheard-of contradictions.

The color is repellent, almost revolting: a smouldering unclean yellow, strangely faded by the slow-turning sunlight. It is a dull yet lurid orange in some places, a sickly sulphur tint in others.

No wonder the children hated it! I should hate it myself if I 35 had to live in this room long.

There comes John, and I must put this away — he hates to have me write a word.

We have been here two weeks, and I haven't felt like writing before, since that first day.

I am sitting by the window now, up in this atrocious nursery, and there is nothing to hinder my writing as much as I please, save lack of strength.

John is away all day, and even some nights when his cases are serious.

I am glad my case is not serious! 40

But these nervous troubles are dreadfully depressing.

John does not know how much I really suffer. He knows there is no reason to suffer, and that satisfies him.

Of course it is only nervousness. It does weigh on me so not to do my duty in any way!

I meant to be such a help to John, such a real rest and comfort, and here I am a comparative burden already!

Nobody would believe what an effort it is to do what little I 45 am able — to dress and entertain, and order things.

It is fortunate Mary is so good with the baby. Such a dear baby!

And yet I *cannot* be with him, it makes me so nervous.

I suppose John never was nervous in his life. He laughs at me so about this wallpaper!

At first he meant to repaper the room, but afterward he said that I was letting it get the better of me, and that nothing was worse for a nervous patient than to give way to such fancies.

He said that after the wallpaper was changed it would be the 50 heavy bedstead, and then the barred windows, and then that gate at the head of the stairs, and so on.

"You know the place is doing you good," he said, "and really, dear, I don't care to renovate the house just for a three months' rental."

"Then do let us go downstairs," I said. "There are such pretty rooms there."

Then he took me in his arms and called me a blessed little goose, and said he would go down cellar, if I wished, and have it whitewashed into the bargain.

But he is right enough about the beds and windows and things.

It is as airy and comfortable a room as anyone need wish, 55 and, of course, I would not be so silly as to make him uncomfortable just for a whim.

I'm really getting quite fond of the big room, all but that horrid paper.

Out of one window I can see the garden — those mysterious deep-shaded arbors, the riotous old-fashioned flowers, and bushes and gnarly trees.

Out of another I get a lovely view of the bay and a little private wharf belonging to the estate. There is a beautiful shaded lane that runs down there from the house. I always fancy I see people walking in these numerous paths and arbors, but John has cautioned me not to give way to fancy in the least. He says that with my imaginative power and habit of story-making, a nervous weakness like mine is sure to lead to all manner of excited fancies, and that I ought to use my will and good sense to check the tendency. So I try.

I think sometimes that if I were only well enough to write a little it would relieve the press of ideas and rest me.

But I find I get pretty tired when I try. 60

It is so discouraging not to have any advice and companionship about my work. When I get really well, John says we will ask Cousin Henry and Julia down for a long visit; but he says he would as soon put fireworks in my pillow-case as to let me have those stimulating people about now.

I wish I could get well faster.

But I must not think about that. This paper looks to me as if it *knew* what a vicious influence it had!

There is a recurrent spot where the pattern lolls like a broken neck and two bulbous eyes stare at you upside down.

I get positively angry with the impertinence of it and the 65 everlastingness. Up and down and sideways they crawl, and those absurd unblinking eyes are everywhere. There is one place where two breadths didn't match, and the eyes go all up and down the line, one a little higher than the other.

I never saw so much expression in an inanimate thing before, and we all know how much expression they have! I used to lie awake as a child and get more entertainment and terror out of blank walls and plain furniture than most children could find in a toy-store.

I remember what a kindly wink the knobs of our big old bureau used to have, and there was one chair that always seemed like a strong friend.

I used to feel that if any of the other things looked too fierce I could always hop into that chair and be safe.

The furniture in this room is no worse than inharmonious, however, for we had to bring it all from downstairs. I suppose when this was used as a playroom they had to take the nursery things out, and no wonder! I never saw such ravages as the children have made here.

The wallpaper, as I said before, is torn off in spots, and it 70 sticketh closer than a brother — they must have had perseverance as well as hatred.

Then the floor is scratched and gouged and splintered, the plaster itself is dug out here and there, and this great heavy bed, which is all we found in the room, looks as if it had been through the wars.

But I don't mind it a bit — only the paper.

There comes John's sister. Such a dear girl as she is, and so careful of me! I must not let her find me writing.

She is a perfect and enthusiastic housekeeper, and hopes for no better profession. I verily believe she thinks it is the writing which made me sick!

But I can write when she is out, and see her a long way off 75 from these windows.

There is one that commands the road, a lovely shaded winding road, and one that just looks off over the country. A lovely country, too, full of great elms and velvet meadows.

This wallpaper has a kind of subpattern in a different shade, a particularly irritating one, for you can only see it in certain lights, and not clearly then.

But in the places where it isn't faded and where the sun is just so — I can see a strange, provoking, formless sort of figure that seems to skulk about behind that silly and conspicuous front design.

There's sister on the stairs!

Well, the Fourth of July is over! The people are all gone, and I 80 am tired out. John thought it might do me good to see a little company, so we just had Mother and Nellie and the children down for a week.

Of course I didn't do a thing. Jennie sees to everything now.

But it tired me all the same.

John says if I don't pick up faster he shall send me to Weir Mitchell° in the fall.

But I don't want to go there at all. I had a friend who was in his hands once, and she says he is just like John and my brother, only more so!

Besides, it is such an undertaking to go so far. 85

I don't feel as if it was worthwhile to turn my hand over for anything, and I'm getting dreadfully fretful and querulous.

I cry at nothing, and cry most of the time.

Of course I don't when John is here, or anybody else, but when I am alone.

And I am alone a good deal just now. John is kept in town very often by serious cases, and Jennie is good and lets me alone when I want her to.

So I walk a little in the garden or down that lovely lane, sit on 90 the porch under the roses, and lie down up here a good deal.

Weir Mitchell (1829–1914): Eminent Philadelphia neurologist who advocated "rest cures" for nervous disorders.

I'm getting really fond of the room in spite of the wallpaper. Perhaps *because* of the wallpaper.

It dwells in my mind so!

I lie here on this great immovable bed — it is nailed down, I believe — and follow that pattern about by the hour. It is as good as gymnastics, I assure you. I start, we'll say, at the bottom, down in the corner over there where it has not been touched, and I determine for the thousandth time that I *will* follow that pointless pattern to some sort of a conclusion.

I know a little of the principle of design, and I know this thing was not arranged on any laws of radiation, or alternation, or repetition, or symmetry, or anything else that I ever heard of.

It is repeated, of course, by the breadths, but not otherwise. 95

Looked at in one way, each breadth stands alone; the bloated curves and flourishes — a kind of "debased Romanesque" with dilirium tremens — go waddling up and down in isolated columns of fatuity.

But, on the other hand, they connect diagonally, and the sprawling outlines run off in great slanting waves of optic horror, like a lot of wallowing sea-weeds in full chase.

The whole thing goes horizontally, too, at least it seems so, and I exhaust myself trying to distinguish the order of its going in that direction.

They have used a horizontal breadth for a frieze, and that adds wonderfully to the confusion.

There is one end of the room where it is almost intact, and 100 there, when the crosslights fade and the low sun shines directly upon it, I can almost fancy radiation after all — the interminable grotesque seems to form around a common center and rush off in headlong plunges of equal distraction.

It makes me tired to follow it. I will take a nap, I guess.

I don't know why I should write this.

I don't want to.

I don't feel able.

And I know John would think it absurd. But I *must* say what I 105 feel and think in some way — it is such a relief!

But the effort is getting to be greater than the relief.

Half the time now I am awfully lazy, and lie down ever so much. John says I mustn't lose my strength, and has me take cod liver oil and lots of tonics and things, to say nothing of ale and wines and rare meat.

Dear John! He loves me very dearly, and hates to have me sick. I tried to have a real earnest reasonable talk with him the other day, and tell him how I wish he would let me go and make a visit to Cousin Henry and Julia.

But he said I wasn't able to go, nor able to stand it after I got there; and I did not make out a very good case for myself, for I was crying before I had finished.

It is getting to be a great effort for me to think straight. Just 110 this nervous weakness, I suppose.

And dear John gathered me up in his arms, and just carried me upstairs and laid me on the bed, and sat by me and read to me till it tired my head.

He said I was his darling and his comfort and all he had, and that I must take care of myself for his sake, and keep well.

He says no one but myself can help me out of it, that I must use my will and self-control and not let any silly fancies run away with me.

There's one comfort — the baby is well and happy, and does not have to occupy this nursery with the horrid wallpaper.

If we had not used it, that blessed child would have! What a 115 fortunate escape! Why, I wouldn't have a child of mine, an impressionable little thing, live in such a room for worlds.

I never thought of it before, but it is lucky that John kept me here after all; I can stand it so much easier than a baby, you see.

Of course I never mention it to them any more — I am too wise — but I keep watch for it all the same.

There are things in the wallpaper that nobody knows about but me, or ever will.

Behind that outside pattern the dim shapes get clearer every day.

It is always the same shape, only very numerous. 120

And it is like a woman stooping down and creeping about behind that pattern. I don't like it a bit. I wonder — I begin to think — I wish John would take me away from here!

It is so hard to talk with John about my case, because he is so wise, and because he loves me so.

But I tried it last night.

It was moonlight. The moon shines in all around just as the sun does.

I hate to see it sometimes, it creeps so slowly, and always 125 comes in by one window or another.

John was asleep and I hated to waken him, so I kept still and watched the moonlight on that undulating wallpaper till I felt creepy.

The faint figure behind seemed to shake the pattern, just as if she wanted to get out.

I got up softly and went to feel and see if the paper *did* move, and when I came back John was awake.

"What is it, little girl?" he said. "Don't go walking about like that — you'll get cold."

I thought it was a good time to talk, so I told him that I really 130 was not gaining here, and that I wished he would take me away.

"Why, darling!" said he. "Our lease will be up in three weeks, and I can't see how to leave before.

"The repairs are not done at home, and I cannot possibly leave town just now. Of course, if you were in any danger, I could and would, but you really are better, dear, whether you can see it or not. I am a doctor, dear, and I know. You are gaining flesh and color, your appetite is better, I feel really much easier about you."

"I don't weigh a bit more," said I, "nor as much; and my appetite may be better in the evening when you are here but it is worse in the morning when you are away!"

"Bless her little heart!" said he with a big hug. "She shall be as sick as she pleases! But now let's improve the shining hours by going to sleep, and talk about it in the morning!"

"And you won't go away?" I asked gloomily. 135

"Why, how can I, dear? It is only three weeks more and then we will take a nice little trip for a few days while Jennie is getting the house ready. Really, dear, you are better!"

"Better in body perhaps — " I began, and stopped short, for he sat up straight and looked at me with such a stern, reproachful look that I could not say another word.

"My darling," said he, "I beg you, for my sake and for our child's sake, as well as for your own, that you will never for one instant let that idea enter your mind! There is nothing so dangerous, so fascinating, to a temperament like yours. It is a false and foolish fancy. Can you trust me as a physician when I tell you so?"

So of course I said no more on that score, and we went to sleep before long. He thought I was asleep first, but I wasn't, and lay there for hours trying to decide whether that front pattern and the back pattern really did move together or separately.

On a pattern like this, by daylight, there is a lack of sequence, 140 a defiance of law, that is a constant irritant to a normal mind.

The color is hideous enough, and unreliable enough, and infuriating enough, but the pattern is torturing.

You think you have mastered it, but just as you get well under way in following, it turns a back-somersault and there you are. It slaps you in the face, knocks you down, and tramples upon you. It is like a bad dream.

The outside pattern is a florid arabesque, reminding one of a fungus. If you can imagine a toadstool in joints, an interminable string of toadstools, budding and sprouting in endless convolutions — why, that is something like it.

That is, sometimes!

There is one marked peculiarity about this paper, a thing   145 nobody seems to notice but myself, and that is that it changes as the light changes.

When the sun shoots in through the east window — I always watch for that first long, straight ray — it changes so quickly that I never can quite believe it.

That is why I watch it always.

By moonlight — the moon shines in all night when there is a moon — I wouldn't know it was the same paper.

At night in any kind of light, in twilight, candlelight, lamplight, and worst of all by moonlight, it becomes bars! The outside pattern, I mean, and the woman behind it is as plain as can be.

I didn't realize for a long time what the thing was that   150 showed behind, that dim subpattern, but now I am quite sure it is a woman.

By daylight she is subdued, quiet. I fancy it is the pattern that keeps her so still. It is so puzzling. It keeps me quiet by the hour.

I lie down ever so much now. John says it is good for me, and to sleep all I can.

Indeed he started the habit by making me lie down for an hour after each meal.

It is a very bad habit, I am convinced, for you see, I don't sleep.

And that cultivates deceit, for I don't tell them I'm awake —   155 oh, no!

The fact is I am getting a little afraid of John.

He seems very queer sometimes, and even Jennie has an inexplicable look.

It strikes me occasionally, just as a scientific hypothesis, that perhaps it is the paper!

I have watched John when he did not know I was looking, and come into the room suddenly on the most innocent excuses, and I've caught him several times *looking at the paper!* And Jennie too. I caught Jennie with her hand on it once.

She didn't know I was in the room, and when I asked her in a   160 quiet, a very quiet voice, with the most restrained manner possible, what she was doing with the paper, she turned around as if she had been caught stealing, and looked quite angry — asked me why I should frighten her so!

Then she said that the paper stained everything it touched, that she had found yellow smooches on all my clothes and John's and she wished we would be more careful!

Did not that sound innocent? But I know she was studying that pattern, and I am determined that nobody shall find it out but myself!

Life is very much more exciting now than it used to be. You see, I have something more to expect, to look forward to, to watch. I really do eat better, and am more quiet than I was.

John is so pleased to see me improve! He laughed a little the other day, and said I seemed to be flourishing in spite of my wallpaper.

I turned it off with a laugh. I had no intention of telling him   165
it was *because* of the wallpaper — he would make fun of me. He might even want to take me away.

I don't want to leave now until I have found it out. There is a week more, and I think that will be enough.

I'm feeling so much better!

I don't sleep much at night, for it is so interesting to watch developments; but I sleep a good deal during the daytime.

In the daytime it is tiresome and perplexing.

There are always new shoots on the fungus, and new shades   170
of yellow all over it. I cannot keep count of them, though I have tried conscientiously.

It is the strangest yellow, that wallpaper! It makes me think of all the yellow things I ever saw — not beautiful ones like butter-cups, but old, foul, bad yellow things.

But there is something else about that paper — the smell! I noticed it the moment we came into the room, but with so much air and sun it was not bad. Now we have had a week of fog and rain, and whether the windows are open or not, the smell is here.

It creeps all over the house.

I find it hovering in the dining-room, skulking in the parlor, hiding in the hall, lying in wait for me on the stairs.

It gets into my hair.   175

Even when I go to ride, if I turn my head suddenly and surprise it — there is that smell!

Such a peculiar odor, too! I have spent hours in trying to analyze it, to find what it smelled like.

It is not bad — at first — and very gentle, but quite the subtlest, most enduring odor I ever met.

In this damp weather it is awful. I wake up in the night and find it hanging over me.

It used to disturb me at first. I thought seriously of burning 180 the house — to reach the smell.

But now I am used to it. The only thing I can think of that it is like is the *color* of the paper! A yellow smell.

There a very funny mark on this wall, low down, near the mopboard. A streak that runs round the room. It goes behind every piece of furniture, except the bed, a long, straight, even *smooch*, as if it had been rubbed over and over.

I wonder how it was done and who did it, and what they did it for. Round and round and round — round and round and round — it makes me dizzy!

I really have discovered something at last.

Through watching so much at night, when it changes so, I 185 have finally found out.

The front pattern *does* move — and no wonder! The woman behind shakes it!

Sometimes I think there are a great many women behind, and sometimes only one, and she crawls around fast, and her crawling shakes it all over.

Then in the very bright spots she keeps still, and in the very shady spots she just takes hold of the bars and shakes them hard.

And she is all the time trying to climb through. But nobody could climb through that pattern — it strangles so; I think that is why it has so many heads.

They get through and then the pattern strangles them off 190 and turns them upside down, and makes their eyes white!

If those heads were covered or taken off it would not be half so bad.

I think that woman gets out in the daytime!

And I'll tell you why — privately — I've seen her!

I can see her out of every one of my windows!

It is the same woman, I know, for she is always creeping, and 195 most women do not creep by daylight.

I see her in that long shaded lane, creeping up and down. I see her in those dark grape arbors, creeping all round the garden.

I see her on that long road under the trees, creeping along, and when a carriage comes she hides under the blackberry vines.

I don't blame her a bit. It must be very humiliating to be caught creeping by daylight!

I always lock the door when I creep by daylight. I can't do it at night, for I know John would suspect something at once.

And John is so queer now that I don't want to irritate him. I 200
wish he would take another room! Besides, I don't want anybody
to get that woman out at night but myself.

I often wonder if I could see her out of all the windows at
once.

But, turn as fast as I can, I can only see out of one at one time.

And though I always see her, she *may* be able to creep faster
than I can turn! I have watched her sometimes away off in the
open country, creeping as fast as a cloud shadow in a wind.

If only that top pattern could be gotten off from the under
one! I mean to try it, little by little.

I have found out another funny thing, but I shan't tell it this 205
time! It does not do to trust people too much.

There are only two more days to get this paper off, and I
believe John is beginning to notice. I don't like the look in his
eyes.

And I heard him ask Jennie a lot of professional questions
about me. She had a very good report to give.

She said I slept a good deal in the daytime.

John knows I don't sleep very well at night, for all I'm so
quiet!

He asked me all sorts of questions too, and pretended to be 210
very loving and kind.

As if I couldn't see through him!

Still, I don't wonder he acts so, sleeping under this paper for
three months.

It only interests me, but I feel sure John and Jennie are
affected by it.

Hurrah! This is the last day, but it is enough. John is to stay in
town over night, and won't be out until this evening.

Jennie wanted to sleep with me — the sly thing; but I told 215
her I should undoubtedly rest better for a night all alone.

That was clever, for really I wasn't alone a bit! As soon as it
was moonlight and that poor thing began to crawl and shake the
pattern, I got up and ran to help her.

I pulled and she shook. I shook and she pulled, and before
morning we had peeled off yards of that paper.

A strip about as high as my head and half around the room.

And then when the sun came and that awful pattern began to
laugh at me, I declared I would finish it today!

We go away tomorrow, and they are moving all my furniture 220
down again to leave things as they were before.

Jennie looked at the wall in amazement, but I told her merrily that I did it out of pure spite at the vicious thing.

She laughed and said she wouldn't mind doing it herself, but I must not get tired.

How she betrayed herself that time!

But I am here, and no person touches this paper but Me — not *alive!*

She tried to get me out of the room — it was too patent! But I 225 said it was so quiet and empty and clean now that I believed I would lie down again and sleep all I could, and not to wake me even for dinner — I would call when I woke.

So now she is gone, and the servants are gone, and the things are gone, and there is nothing left but that great bedstead nailed down, with the canvas mattress we found on it.

We shall sleep downstairs tonight, and take the boat home tomorrow.

I quite enjoy the room, now it is bare again.

How those children did tear about here!

This bedstead is fairly gnawed! 230

But I must get to work.

I have locked the door and thrown the key down into the front path.

I don't want to go out, and I don't want to have anybody come in, till John comes.

I want to astonish him.

I've got a rope up here that even Jennie did not find. If that 235 woman does get out, and tries to get away, I can tie her!

But I forgot I could not reach far without anything to stand on!

This bed will *not* move!

I tried to lift and push it until I was lame, and then I got so angry I bit off a little piece at one corner — but it hurt my teeth.

Then I peeled off all the paper I could reach standing on the floor. It sticks horribly and the pattern just enjoys it! All those strangled heads and bulbous eyes and waddling fungus growths just shriek with derision!

I am getting angry enough to do something desperate. To 240 jump out of the window would be admirable exercise, but the bars are too strong even to try.

Besides I wouldn't do it. Of course not. I know well enough that a step like that is improper and might be misconstrued.

I don't like to *look* out of the windows even — there are so many of those creeping women, and they creep so fast.

I wonder if they all come out of that wallpaper as I did!

But I am securely fastened now by my well-hidden rope — you don't get *me* out in the road there!

I suppose I shall have to get back behind the pattern when it 245 comes night, and that is hard!

It is so pleasant to be out in this great room and creep around as I please.

I don't want to go outside. I won't, even if Jennie asks me to.

For outside you have to creep on the ground, and everything is green instead of yellow.

But here I can creep smoothly on the floor, and my shoulder just fits in that long smooch around the wall, so I cannot lose my way.

Why, there's John at the door! 250

It is no use, young man, you can't open it!

How he does call and pound!

Now he's crying to Jennie for an axe.

It would be a shame to break down that beautiful door!

"John, dear!" said I in the gentlest voice. "The key is down by 255 the front steps, under a plantain leaf!"

That silenced him for a few moments.

Then he said, very quietly indeed, "Open the door, my darling!"

"I can't," said I. "The key is down by the front door under a plantain leaf!" And then I said it again, several times, very gently and slowly, and said it so often that he had to go and see, and he got it of course, and came in. He stopped short by the door.

"What is the matter?" he cried. "For God's sake, what are you doing!"

I kept on creeping just the same, but I looked at him over my 260 shoulder.

"I've got out at last," said I, "in spite of you and Jane. And I've pulled off most of the paper, so you can't put me back!"

Now why should that man have fainted? But he did, and right across my path by the wall, so that I had to creep over him every time!

Questions

1. Focusing on the language of these paragraphs, bring to life the narrator's level of understanding at this moment in the story.

> John is a physician, and perhaps — (I would not say it to a living soul, of course, but this is dead paper and a great relief to my mind) — perhaps that is one reason I do not get well faster

> You see, he does not believe I am sick! And what can one do?
> If a physician of high standing, and one's own husband, assures friends and relatives that there is really nothing the matter with one but temporary nervous depression — a slight hysterical tendency — what is one to do? (paras. 7–9)

When she says that one reason she doesn't get well faster is perhaps that her husband is a physician, she emphasizes the "perhaps." In what respects is this notion of hers sound? In what respects is it unsound?

2.   Focusing on the language of these paragraphs, bring to life the narrator's level of understanding at this moment.

> I am glad my case is not serious!
> But these nervous troubles are dreadfully depressing.
> John does not know how much I really suffer. He knows there is no reason to suffer, and that satisfies him.
> Of course it is only nervousness. It does weigh on me so not to do my duty in any way! (40–43)

What judgments of hers seem sound? What judgments seem unsound? Explain your answer.

3.   On the basis of your reading of the whole story, name the narrator's chief strengths and weaknesses as an interpreter of her own observations, feelings, and actions.

ANTON CHEKHOV   (1860–1904)
The Lady with the Pet Dog

TRANSLATED BY AVRAHM YARMOLINSKY

I

A new person, it was said, had appeared on the esplanade: a lady with a pet dog. Dmitry Dmitrich Gurov, who had spent a fortnight at Yalta and had got used to the place, had also begun to take an interest in new arrivals. As he sat in Vernet's confectionery shop, he saw, walking on the esplanade, a fair-haired young woman of medium height, wearing a beret; a white Pomeranian was trotting behind her.

And afterwards he met her in the public garden and in the square several times a day. She walked alone, always wearing the same beret and always with the white dog; no one knew who she was and everyone called her simply "the lady with the pet dog."

"If she is here alone without husband or friends," Gurov reflected, "it wouldn't be a bad thing to make her acquaintance."

He was under forty, but he already had a daughter twelve years old, and two sons at school. They had found a wife for him when he was very young, a student in his second year, and by now she seemed half as old again as he. She was a tall, erect woman with dark eyebrows, stately and dignified and, as she said of herself, intellectual. She read a great deal, used simplified spelling in her letters, called her husband, not Dmitry, but Dimitry, while he privately considered her of limited intelligence, narrow-minded, dowdy, was afraid of her, and did not like to be at home. He had begun being unfaithful to her long ago — had been unfaithful to her often and, probably for that reason, almost always spoke ill of women, and when they were talked of in his presence used to call them "the inferior race."

It seemed to him that he had been sufficiently tutored by 5 bitter experience to call them what he pleased, and yet he could not have lived without "the inferior race" for two days together. In the company of men he was bored and ill at ease, he was chilly and uncommunicative with them; but when he was among women he felt free, and knew what to speak to them about and how to comport himself; and even to be silent with them was no strain on him. In his appearance, in his character, in his whole make-up there was something attractive and elusive that disposed women in his favor and allured them. He knew that, and some force seemed to draw him to them, too.

Oft-repeated and really bitter experience had taught him long ago that with decent people — particularly Moscow people — who are irresolute and slow to move, every affair which at first seems a light and charming adventure inevitably grows into a whole problem of extreme complexity, and in the end a painful situation is created. But at every new meeting with an interesting woman this lesson of experience seemed to slip from his memory, and he was eager for life, and everything seemed so simple and diverting.

One evening while he was dining in the public garden the lady in the beret walked up without haste to take the next table. Her expression, her gait, her dress, and the way she did her hair told him that she belonged to the upper class, that she was married, that she was in Yalta for the first time and alone, and that she was bored there. The stories told of the immorality in Yalta are to a great extent untrue; he despised them, and knew that such stories were made up for the most part by persons who would have been glad to sin themselves if they had had the chance; but when the lady sat down at the next table three paces from him, he recalled these stories of easy conquests, of trips to the mountains, and the tempting thought of a swift, fleeting liaison, a romance with an unknown woman of whose very name he was ignorant suddenly took hold of him.

He beckoned invitingly to the Pomeranian, and when the dog approached him, shook his finger at it. The Pomeranian growled; Gurov threatened it again.

The lady glanced at him and at once dropped her eyes.

"He doesn't bite," she said and blushed. 10

"May I give him a bone?" he asked; and when she nodded he inquired affably, "Have you been in Yalta long?"

"About five days."

"And I am dragging out the second week here."

There was a short silence.

"Time passes quickly, and yet it is so dull here!" she said, not 15 looking at him.

"It's only the fashion to say it's dull here. A provincial will live in Belyov or Zhizdra and not be bored, but when he comes here it's 'Oh, the dullness! Oh, the dust!' One would think he came from Granada."

She laughed. Then both continued eating in silence, like strangers, but after dinner they walked together and there sprang up between them the light banter of people who are free and contented, to whom it does not matter where they go or what they talk about. They walked and talked of the strange light on the sea: the water was a soft, warm, lilac color, and there was a golden band of moonlight upon it. They talked of how sultry it was after a hot day. Gurov told her that he was a native of Moscow, that he had studied languages and literature at the university, but had a post in a bank; that at one time he had trained to become an opera singer but had given it up, that he owned two houses in Moscow. And he learned from her that she had grown up in Petersburg, but had lived in S—— since her marriage two years previously, that she was going to stay in Yalta for about another month, and that her husband, who needed a rest, too, might perhaps come to fetch her. She was not certain whether her husband was a member of a Government Board or served on a Zemstvo Council,° and this amused her. And Gurov learned too that her name was Anna Sergeyevna.

Zemstvo Council: At the time, a newly established district or provincial assembly.

Afterwards in his room at the hotel he thought about her — and was certain that he would meet her the next day. It was bound to happen. Getting into bed he recalled that she had been a schoolgirl only recently, doing lessons like his own daughter; he thought how much timidity and angularity there was still in her laugh and her manner of talking with a stranger. It must have been the first time in her life that she was alone in a setting in which she was followed, looked at, and spoken to for one secret purpose alone, which she could hardly fail to guess. He thought of her slim, delicate throat, her lovely gray eyes.

"There's something pathetic about her, though," he thought, and dropped off.

II

A week had passed since they had struck up an acquaintance. 20 It was a holiday. It was close indoors, while in the street the wind whirled the dust about and blew people's hats off. One was thirsty all day, and Gurov often went into the restaurant and offered Anna Sergeyevna a soft drink or ice cream. One did not know what to do with oneself.

In the evening when the wind had abated they went out on the pier to watch the steamer come in. There were a great many people walking about the dock; they had come to welcome someone and they were carrying bunches of flowers. And two peculiarities of a festive Yalta crowd stood out: the elderly ladies were dressed like young ones and there were many generals.

Owing to the choppy sea, the steamer arrived late, after sunset, and it was a long time tacking about before it put in at the pier. Anna Sergeyevna peered at the steamer and the passengers through her lorgnette as though looking for acquaintances, and whenever she turned to Gurov her eyes were shining. She talked a great deal and asked questions jerkily, forgetting the next moment what she had asked; then she lost her lorgnette in the crush.

The festive crowd began to disperse; it was now too dark to see people's faces; there was no wind any more, but Gurov and Anna Sergeyevna still stood as though waiting to see someone else come off the steamer. Anna Sergeyevna was silent now, and sniffed her flowers without looking at Gurov.

"The weather has improved this evening," he said. "Where shall we go now? Shall we drive somewhere?"

She did not reply.   25
Then he looked at her intently, and suddenly embraced her
and kissed her on the lips, and the moist fragrance of her flowers
enveloped him; and at once he looked round him anxiously,
wondering if anyone had seen them.
"Let us go to your place," he said softly. And they walked off
together rapidly.
The air in her room was close and there was the smell of the
perfume she had bought at the Japanese shop. Looking at her,
Gurov thought: "What encounters life offers!" From the past he
preserved the memory of carefree, good-natured women whom
love made gay and who were grateful to him for the happiness he
gave them, however brief it might be; and of women like his wife
who loved without sincerity, with too many words, affectedly,
hysterically, with an expression that it was not love or passion
that engaged them but something more significant; and of two or
three others, very beautiful, frigid women, across whose faces
would suddenly flit a rapacious expression — an obstinate desire to take from life more than it could give, and these were
women no longer young, capricious, unreflecting, domineering,
unintelligent, and when Gurov grew cold to them their beauty
aroused his hatred, and the lace on their lingerie seemed to him
to resemble scales.
But here there was the timidity, the angularity of inexperienced youth, a feeling of awkwardness; and there was a sense
of embarrassment, as though someone had suddenly knocked at
the door. Anna Sergeyevna, "the lady with the pet dog," treated
what had happened in a peculiar way, very seriously, as though it
were her fall — so it seemed, and this was odd and inappropriate. Her features drooped and faded, and her long hair hung
down sadly on either side of her face; she grew pensive and her
dejected pose was that of a Magdalene in a picture by an old
master.
"It's not right," she said. "You don't respect me now, you first 30
of all."
There was a watermelon on the table. Gurov cut himself a
slice and began eating it without haste. They were silent for at
least half an hour.
There was something touching about Anna Sergeyevna; she
had the purity of a well-bred, naive woman who has seen little of
life. The single candle burning on the table barely illumined her
face, yet it was clear that she was unhappy.
"Why should I stop respecting you, darling?" asked Gurov.
"You don't know what you're saying."

"God forgive me," she said, and her eyes filled with tears. "It's terrible."

"It's as though you were trying to exonerate yourself." 35

"How can I exonerate myself? No. I am a bad, low woman; I despise myself and I have no thought of exonerating myself. It's not my husband but myself I have deceived. And not only just now; I have been deceiving myself for a long time. My husband may be a good, honest man, but he is a flunkey! I don't know what he does, what his work is, but I know he is a flunkey! I was twenty when I married him. I was tormented by curiosity; I wanted something better. 'There must be a different sort of life,' I said to myself. I wanted to live! To live, to live! Curiosity kept eating at me — you don't understand it, but I swear to God I could no longer control myself; something was going on in me; I could not be held back. I told my husband I was ill, and came here. And here I have been walking about as though in a daze, as though I were mad; and now I have become a vulgar, vile woman whom anyone may despise."

Gurov was already bored with her; he was irritated by her naive tone, by her repentance, so unexpected and so out of place; but for the tears in her eyes he might have thought she was joking or play-acting.

"I don't understand, my dear," he said softly. "What do you want?"

She hid her face on his breast and pressed close to him.

"Believe me, believe me, I beg you," she said, "I love honesty 40 and purity, and sin is loathsome to me; I don't know what I'm doing. Simple people say, 'The Evil One has led me astray.' And I may say of myself now that the Evil One has led me astray."

"Quiet, quiet," he murmured.

He looked into her fixed, frightened eyes, kissed her, spoke to her softly and affectionately, and by degrees she calmed down, and her gaiety returned; both began laughing.

Afterwards when they went out there was not a soul on the esplanade. The town with its cypresses looked quite dead, but the sea was still sounding as it broke upon the beach; a single launch was rocking on the waves and on it a lantern was blinking sleepily.

They found a cab and drove to Oreanda.

"I found out your surname in the hall just now: it was written 45 on the board — von Dideritz," said Gurov. "Is your husband German?"

"No; I believe his grandfather was German, but he is Greek Orthodox himself."

At Oreanda they sat on a bench not far from the church, looked down at the sea, and were silent. Yalta was barely visible through the morning mist; white clouds rested motionlessly on the mountaintops. The leaves did not stir on the trees, cicadas twanged, and the monotonous muffled sound of the sea that rose from below spoke of the peace, the eternal sleep awaiting us. So it rumbled below when there was no Yalta, no Oreanda here; so it rumbles now, and it will rumble as indifferently and as hollowly when we are no more. And in this constancy, in this complete indifference to the life and death of each of us, there lies, perhaps, a pledge of our eternal salvation, of the unceasing advance of life upon earth, of unceasing movement towards perfection. Sitting beside a young woman who in the dawn seemed so lovely, Gurov, soothed and spellbound by these magical surroundings — the sea, the mountains, the clouds, the wide sky — thought how everything is really beautiful in this world when one reflects: everything except what we think or do ourselves when we forget the higher aims of life and our own human dignity.

A man strolled up to them — probably a guard — looked at them and walked away. And this detail, too, seemed so mysterious and beautiful. They saw a steamer arrive from Feodosia, its lights extinguished in the glow of dawn.

"There is dew on the grass," said Anna Sergeyevna, after a silence.

"Yes, it's time to go home."   50

They returned to the city.

Then they met every day at twelve o'clock on the esplanade, lunched and dined together, took walks, admired the sea. She complained that she slept badly, that she had palpitations, asked the same questions, troubled now by jealousy and now by the fear that he did not respect her sufficiently. And often in the square or the public garden, when there was no one near them, he suddenly drew her to him and kissed her passionately. Complete idleness, these kisses in broad daylight exchanged furtively in dread of someone's seeing them, the heat, the smell of the sea, and the continual flitting before his eyes of idle, well-dressed, well-fed people, worked a complete change in him; he kept telling Anna Sergeyevna how beautiful she was, how seductive, was urgently passionate; he would not move a step away from her, while she was often pensive and continually pressed him to confess that he did not respect her, did not love her in the least, and saw in her nothing but a common woman. Almost every evening rather late they drove somewhere out of town, to Oreanda or to the waterfall; and the excursion was always a success, the scenery invariably impressed them as beautiful and magnificent.

They were expecting her husband, but a letter came from him saying that he had eye-trouble, and begging his wife to return home as soon as possible. Anna Sergeyevna made haste to go.

"It's a good thing I am leaving," she said to Gurov. "It's the hand of Fate!"

She took a carriage to the railway station, and he went with   55
her. They were driving the whole day. When she had taken her place in the express, and when the second bell had rung, she said, "Let me look at you once more — let me look at you again. Like this."

She was not crying but was so sad that she seemed ill and her face was quivering.

"I shall be thinking of you — remembering you," she said. "God bless you; be happy. Don't remember evil against me. We are parting forever — it has to be, for we ought never to have met. Well, God bless you."

The train moved off rapidly, its lights soon vanished, and a minute later there was no sound of it, as though everything had conspired to end as quickly as possible that sweet trance, that madness. Left alone on the platform, and gazing into the dark distance, Gurov listened to the twang of the grasshoppers and the hum of the telegraph wires, feeling as though he had just waked up. And he reflected, musing, that there had now been another episode or adventure in his life, and it, too, was at an end, and nothing was left of it but a memory. He was moved, sad, and slightly remorseful: this young woman whom he would never meet again had not been happy with him; he had been warm and affectionate with her, but yet in his manner, his tone, and his caresses there had been a shade of light irony, the slightly coarse arrogance of a happy male who was, besides, almost twice her age. She had constantly called him kind, exceptional, high-minded; obviously he had seemed to her different from what he really was, so he had involuntarily deceived her.

Here at the station there was already a scent of autumn in the air; it was a chilly evening.

"It is time for me to go north, too," thought Gurov as he left   60
the platform. "High time!"

III

At home in Moscow the winter routine was already established; the stoves were heated, and in the morning it was still dark when the children were having breakfast and getting ready for school, and the nurse would light the lamp for a short time. There were frosts already. When the first snow falls, on the first day the sleighs are out, it is pleasant to see the white earth, the white roofs; one draws easy, delicious breaths, and the season brings back the days of one's youth. The old limes and birches, white with hoar-frost, have a good-natured look; they are closer to one's heart than cypresses and palms, and near them one no longer wants to think of mountains and the sea.

Gurov, a native of Moscow, arrived there on a fine frosty day, and when he put on his fur coat and warm gloves and took a walk along Petrovka, and when on Saturday night he heard the bells ringing, his recent trip and the places he had visited lost all charm for him. Little by little he became immersed in Moscow life, greedily read three newspapers a day, and declared that he did not read the Moscow papers on principle. He already felt a longing for restaurants, clubs, formal dinners, anniversary celebrations, and it flattered him to entertain distinguished lawyers and actors, and to play cards with a professor at the physicians' club. He could eat a whole portion of meat stewed with pickled cabbage and served in a pan, Moscow style.

A month or so would pass and the image of Anna Sergeyevna, it seemed to him, would become misty in his memory, and only from time to time he would dream of her with her touching smile as he dreamed of others. But more than a month went by, winter came into its own, and everything was still clear in his memory as though he had parted from Anna Sergeyevna only yesterday. And his memories glowed more and more vividly. When in the evening stillness the voices of his children preparing their lessons reached his study, or when he listened to a song or to an organ playing in a restaurant, or when the storm howled in the chimney, suddenly everything would rise up in his memory; what had happened on the pier and the early morning with the mist on the mountains, and the steamer coming from Feodosia, and the kisses. He would pace about his room a long time, remembering and smiling; then his memories passed into reveries, and in his imagination the past would mingle with what was to come. He did not dream of Anna Sergeyevna, but she followed him about everywhere and watched him. When he shut his eyes he saw her before him as though she were there in the flesh, and she seemed to him lovelier, younger, tenderer than she had been, and he imagined himself a finer man than he had been in Yalta. Of evenings she peered out at him from the bookcase, from the fireplace, from the corner — he heard her breathing, the caressing rustle of her clothes. In the street he followed the women with his eyes, looking for someone who resembled her.

Already he was tormented by a strong desire to share his memories with someone. But in his home it was impossible to talk of his love, and he had no one to talk to outside; certainly he could not confide in his tenants or in anyone at the bank. And what was there to talk about? He hadn't loved her then, had he? Had there been anything beautiful, poetical, edifying, or simply interesting in his relations with Anna Sergeyevna? And he was forced to talk vaguely of love, of women, and no one guessed what he meant; only his wife would twitch her black eyebrows and say, "The part of a philanderer does not suit you at all, Dimitry."

One evening, coming out of the physicians' club with an 65 official with whom he had been playing cards, he could not resist saying:

"If you only knew what a fascinating woman I became acquainted with at Yalta!"

The official got into his sledge and was driving away, but turned suddenly and shouted:

"Dmitry Dmitrich!"

"What is it?"

"You were right this evening: the sturgeon was a bit high."   70

These words, so commonplace, for some reason moved Gurov to indignation, and struck him as degrading and unclean. What savage manners, what mugs! What stupid nights, what dull, humdrum days! Frenzied gambling, gluttony, drunkenness, continual talk always about the same thing! Futile pursuits and conversations always about the same topics take up the better part of one's time, the better part of one's strength, and in the end there is left a life clipped and wingless, an absurd mess, and there is no escaping or getting away from it — just as though one were in a madhouse or a prison.

Gurov, boiling with indignation, did not sleep all night. And he had a headache all the next day. And the following nights too he slept badly; he sat up in bed, thinking, or paced up and down his room. He was fed up with his children, fed up with the bank; he had no desire to go anywhere or to talk of anything.

In December during the holidays he prepared to take a trip

and told his wife he was going to Petersburg to do what he could for a young friend — and he set off for S——. What for? He did not know, himself. He wanted to see Anna Sergeyevna and talk with her, to arrange a rendezvous if possible.

He arrived at S—— in the morning, and at the hotel took the best room, in which the floor was covered with gray army cloth, and on the table there was an inkstand, gray with dust and topped by a figure on horseback, its hat in its raised hand and its head broken off. The porter gave him the necessary information: von Dideritz lived in a house of his own on Staro-Goncharnaya Street, not far from the hotel: he was rich and lived well and kept his own horses; everyone in the town knew him. The porter pronounced the name: "Dridiritz."

Without haste Gurov made his way to Staro-Goncharnaya 75 Street and found the house. Directly opposite the house stretched a long gray fence studded with nails.

"A fence like that would make one run away," thought Gurov, looking now at the fence, now at the windows of the house.

He reflected: this was a holiday, and the husband was apt to be at home. And in any case, it would be tactless to go into the house and disturb her. If he were to send her a note, it might fall into her husband's hands, and that might spoil everything. The best thing was to rely on chance. And he kept walking up and down the street and along the fence, waiting for the chance. He saw a beggar go in at the gate and heard the dogs attack him; then an hour later he heard a piano, and the sound came to him faintly and indistinctly. Probably it was Anna Sergeyevna playing. The front door opened suddenly, and an old woman came out, followed by the familiar white Pomeranian. Gurov was on the point of calling to the dog, but his heart began beating violently, and in his excitement he could not remember the Pomeranian's name.

He kept walking up and down, and hated the gray fence more and more, and by now he thought irritably that Anna Sergeyevna had forgotten him, and was perhaps already diverting herself with another man, and that that was very natural in a young woman who from morning till night had to look at that damn fence. He went back to his hotel room and sat on the couch for a long while, not knowing what to do, then he had dinner and a long nap.

"How stupid and annoying all this is!" he thought when he woke and looked at the dark windows: it was already evening. "Here I've had a good sleep for some reason. What am I going to do at night?"

He sat on the bed, which was covered with a cheap gray 80
blanket of the kind seen in hospitals, and he twitted himself in
his vexation:

"So there's your lady with the pet dog. There's your adventure. A nice place to cool your heels in."

That morning at the station a playbill in large letters had
caught his eye. *The Geisha* was to be given for the first time. He
thought of this and drove to the theater.

"It's quite possible that she goes to first nights," he thought.

The theater was full. As in all provincial theaters, there was a
haze above the chandelier, the gallery was noisy and restless; in
the front row, before the beginning of the performance the local
dandies were standing with their hands clasped behind their
backs; in the Governor's box the Governor's daughter, wearing a
boa, occupied the front seat, while the Governor himself hid
modestly behind the portiere and only his hands were visible; the
curtain swayed; the orchestra was a long time tuning up. While
the audience was coming in and taking their seats, Gurov
scanned the faces eagerly.

Anna Sergeyevna, too, came in. She sat down in the third 85
row, and when Gurov looked at her his heart contracted, and he
understood clearly that in the whole world there was no human
being so near, so precious, and so important to him; she, this
little, undistinguished woman, lost in a provincial crowd, with a
vulgar lorgnette in her hand, filled his whole life now, was his
sorrow and his joy, the only happiness that he now desired for
himself, and to the sounds of the bad orchestra, of the miserable
local violins, he thought how lovely she was. He thought and
dreamed.

A young man with small side-whiskers, very tall and stooped,
came in with Anna Sergeyevna and sat down beside her; he
nodded his head at every step and seemed to be bowing continually. Probably this was the husband whom at Yalta, in an
access of bitter feeling, she had called a flunkey. And there really
was in his lanky figure, his side-whiskers, his small bald patch,
something of a flunkey's retiring manner; his smile was mawkish,
and in his buttonhole there was an academic badge like a waiter's
number.

During the first intermission the husband went out to have a
smoke; she remained in her seat. Gurov, who was also sitting in
the orchestra, went up to her and said in a shaky voice, with a
forced smile:

"Good evening!"

She glanced at him and turned pale, then looked at him

again in horror, unable to believe her eyes, and gripped the fan
and the lorgnette tightly together in her hands, evidently trying
to keep herself from fainting. Both were silent. She was sitting, he
was standing, frightened by her distress and not daring to take a
seat beside her. The violins and the flute that were being tuned
up sang out. He suddenly felt frightened: it seemed as if all the
people in the boxes were looking at them. She got up and went
hurriedly to the exit; he followed her, and both of them walked
blindly along the corridors and up and down stairs, and figures
in the uniforms prescribed for magistrates, teachers, and offi-
cials of the Department of Crown Lands, all wearing badges,
flitted before their eyes, as did also ladies, and fur coats on
hangers; they were conscious of drafts and the smell of stale
tobacco. And Gurov, whose heart was beating violently, thought:

"Oh, Lord! Why are these people here and this orchestra!"   90

And at that instant he suddenly recalled how when he had
seen Anna Sergeyevna off at the station he had said to himself
that all was over between them and that they would never meet
again. But how distant the end still was!

On the narrow, gloomy staircase over which it said "To the
Amphitheatre," she stopped.

"How you frightened me!" she said, breathing hard, still pale
and stunned. "Oh, how you frightened me! I am barely alive.
Why did you come? Why?"

"But do understand, Anna, do understand — " he said hurriedly, under his breath. "I implore you, do understand — "

She looked at him with fear, with entreaty, with love; she   95
looked at him intently, to keep his features more distinctly in her
memory.

"I suffer so," she went on, not listening to him. "All this time
I have been thinking of nothing but you; I live only by the
thought of you. And I wanted to forget, to forget; but why, oh,
why have you come?"

On the landing above them two high school boys were looking down and smoking, but it was all the same to Gurov; he drew
Anna Sergeyevna to him and began kissing her face and hands.

"What are you doing, what are you doing!" she was saying in
horror, pushing him away. "We have lost our senses. Go away
today; go away at once — I conjure you by all that is sacred, I
implore you — People are coming this way!"

Someone was walking up the stairs.

"You must leave," Anna Sergeyevna went on in a whisper.   100
"Do you hear, Dmitry Dmitrich? I will come and see you in
Moscow. I have never been happy; I am unhappy now, and I

never, never shall be happy, never! So don't make me suffer still more! I swear I'll come to Moscow. But now let us part. My dear, good, precious one, let us part!"

She pressed his hand and walked rapidly downstairs, turning to look round at him, and from her eyes he could see that she really was unhappy. Gurov stood for a while, listening, then when all grew quiet, he found his coat and left the theater.

IV

And Anna Sergeyevna began coming to see him in Moscow. Once every two or three months she left S—— telling her husband that she was going to consult a doctor about a woman's ailment from which she was suffering — and her husband did and did not believe her. When she arrived in Moscow she would stop at the Slavyansky Bazar Hotel, and at once send a man in a red cap to Gurov. Gurov came to see her, and no one in Moscow knew of it.

Once he was going to see her in this way on a winter morning (the messenger had come the evening before and not found him in). With him walked his daughter, whom he wanted to take to school; it was on the way. Snow was coming down in big wet flakes.

"It's three degrees above zero,° and yet it's snowing," Gurov was saying to his daughter. "But this temperature prevails only on the surface of the earth; in the upper layers of the atmosphere there is quite a different temperature."

"And why doesn't it thunder in winter, papa?"

He explained that, too. He talked, thinking all the while that he was on his way to a rendezvous, and no living soul knew of it, and probably no one would ever know. He had two lives, an open one, seen and known by all who needed to know it, full of conventional truth and conventional falsehood, exactly like the lives of his friends and acquaintances; and another life that went on in secret. And through some strange, perhaps accidental, combination of circumstances, everything that was of interest and importance to him, everything that was essential to him, everything about which he felt sincerely and did not deceive himself, everything that constituted the core of his life, was going on concealed from others; while all that was false, the shell in which

105

---

three degrees above zero: Temperatures in the story are given in centigrade.

he hid to cover the truth — his work at the bank, for instance, his discussions at the club, his references to the "inferior race," his appearances at anniversary celebrations with his wife — all that went on in the open. Judging others by himself, he did not believe what he saw, and always fancied that every man led his real, most interesting life under cover of secrecy as under cover of night. The personal life of every individual is based on se-crecy, and perhaps it is partly for that reason that civilized man is so nervously anxious that personal privacy should be respected.

Having taken his daughter to school, Gurov went on to the Slavyansky Bazar Hotel. He took off his fur coat in the lobby, went upstairs, and knocked gently at the door. Anna Sergeyevna, wearing his favorite gray dress, exhausted by the journey and by waiting, had been expecting him since the previous evening. She was pale, and looked at him without a smile, and he had hardly entered when she flung herself on his breast. That kiss was a long, lingering one, as though they had not seen one another for two years.

"Well, darling, how are you getting on there?" he asked. "What news?"

"Wait; I'll tell you in a moment — I can't speak."

She could not speak; she was crying. She turned away from   110
him, and pressed her handkerchief to her eyes.

"Let her have her cry; meanwhile I'll sit down," he thought, and he seated himself in an armchair.

Then he rang and ordered tea, and while he was having his tea she remained standing at the window with her back to him. She was crying out of sheer agitation, in the sorrowful conscious-ness that their life was so sad; that they could only see each other in secret and had to hide from people like thieves! Was it not a broken life?

"Come, stop now, dear!" he said.

It was plain to him that this love of theirs would not be over soon, that the end of it was not in sight. Anna Sergeyevna was growing more and more attached to him. She adored him, and it was unthinkable to tell her that their love was bound to come to an end some day; besides, she would not have believed it!

He went up to her and took her by the shoulders, to fondle   115
her and say something diverting, and at that moment he caught sight of himself in the mirror.

His hair was already beginning to turn gray. And it seemed odd to him that he had grown so much older in the last few years, and lost his looks. The shoulders on which his hands rested were warm and heaving. He felt compassion for this life, still so warm and lovely, but probably already about to begin to fade and wither like his own. Why did she love him so much? He always seemed to women different from what he was, and they loved in him not himself, but the man whom their imagination created and whom they had been eagerly seeking all their lives; and afterwards, when they saw their mistake, they loved him nevertheless. And not one of them had been happy with him. In the past he had met women, come together with them, parted from them, but he had never once loved; it was anything you please, but not love. And only now when his head was gray he had fallen in love, really, truly — for the first time in his life.

Anna Sergeyevna and he loved each other as people do who are very close and intimate, like man and wife, like tender friends; it seemed to them that Fate itself had meant them for one another, and they could not understand why he had a wife and she a husband; and it was as though they were a pair of migratory birds, male and female, caught and forced to live in different cages. They forgave each other what they were ashamed of in their past, they forgave everything in the present, and felt that this love of theirs had altered them both.

Formerly in moments of sadness he had soothed himself with whatever logical arguments came into his head, but now he no longer cared for logic; he felt profound compassion, he wanted to be sincere and tender.

"Give it up now, my darling," he said. "You've had your cry; that's enough. Let us have a talk now, we'll think up something."

Then they spent a long time taking counsel together, they 120 talked of how to avoid the necessity for secrecy, for deception, for living in different cities, and not seeing one another for long stretches of time. How could they free themselves from these intolerable fetters?

"How? How?" he asked, clutching his head. "How?"

And it seemed as though in a little while the solution would be found, and then a new and glorious life would begin; and it was clear to both of them that the end was still far off, and that what was to be most complicated and difficult for them was only just beginning.

Questions

Using the language of this passage as a starting point, bring to life Gurov's and Anna's level of understanding — their point of view — as fully as you can.

And it seemed as though in a little while the solution would be
found, and then a new and glorious life would begin; and it was
clear to both of them that the end was still far off, and that what was
to be most complicated and difficult for them was only just beginning. (para. 122)

1. At earlier moments in the story Anna and Gurov do not
share a single point of view; they see things quite differently.
How, for example, does Anna's attitude toward "sin" differ
from Gurov's?
2. Obviously a change comes over Gurov, causing him to wish
"to be sincere and tender" (118). How is this change best
explained?
3. Are the lovers correct or incorrect in believing that a "solution" will be found, leading to a "new and glorious life"?
Explain.
4. Name Anna's and Gurov's chief strengths and weaknesses as
assessors and interpreters of their situation.

14

Suspense

As we've just seen, story readers in action ask questions about the point of view from which events are being recounted. Whose perception are we relying on as we follow the development of a human situation? What kind of perception is it? Trustworthy? alert? comprehensive? skewed? how badly skewed?

But story readers also formulate questions about the events themselves — the occurrences the perceivers are interpreting. Our questions come thick and fast as we read; we move through a ceaselessly changing series of uncertainties generating partial answers that in turn produce new questions — straight on to the end. Our simplest question, in every kind of fiction that holds us, is, of course, *What will happen next?* And in certain forms of writing the questions we ask *don't* change a lot as we proceed. In much crime fiction, *Whodunit?* remains the pressing problem from start to finish. In stories in which the protagonists are in danger, we concentrate from page to page on whether they will escape; if the protagonists are engaged in a struggle or contest, we ask from page to page whether they'll win.

More often than not, however, there's great variety both in the uncertainties we experience in the course of reading a single story and in the questions we generate to ease those uncertainties. And a major element in our performance is that of animating and defining our own uncertainty — discovering and naming the specific perplexities that rivet us from moment to moment, observing the development of our own irresolutions and doubts.

The familiar, all-encompassing name for a reader's doubt is *suspense*. We say the author kept us in suspense from beginning to end. But the term *suspense* tends to hide from us both the role of the author's language and the roles we ourselves play in creating, sustaining, continually redefining, and reinvigorating our curiosities and anxieties. Bringing stories to life means in part bringing closer to consciousness our own activity in framing questions, locating mysteries. When we know, at any moment, what we're keeping ourselves in suspense about, we know something significant about the kind of experience our collaboration with the author is shaping. And in order to know what we're keeping ourselves in suspense about we need to know the general nature of the conflict figuring in the story and the broad relation between the events of the story and that conflict. We need something further, too: knowledge of the particulars of feeling and action that show us the conflict continuously developing — gathering new meanings — under the pressure of moment-to-moment happenings.

TRACKING THE PATH OF SUSPENSE

Look again at paragraphs 96–105 of William Faulkner's "Barn Burning" (p. 157).

> "I'll hold him," his mother whispered.
> "See you do then." Then his father was gone, the stiff foot heavy and measured upon the boards, ceasing at last.
> Then he began to struggle. His mother caught him in both arms, he jerking and wrenching at them. He would be stronger in the end, he knew that. But he had no time to wait for it. "Lemme go!" he cried. "I don't want to have to hit you!"
> "Let him go!" the aunt said. "If he don't go, before God, I am going up there myself!"
> "Don't you see I can't?" his mother cried. "Sarty! Sarty! No! No! Help me, Lizzie!"
> Then he was free. His aunt grasped at him but it was too late. He whirled, running, his mother stumbled forward on to her knees behind him, crying to the nearer sister: "Catch him, Net! Catch him!" But that was too late too, the sister (the sisters were twins, born at the same time, yet either of them now gave the impression of being, encompassing as much living meat and volume and weight as any other two of the family) not yet having begun to rise from the chair, her head, face, alone merely turned, presenting to him in the flying instant an astonishing expanse of young female features untroubled by any surprise even, wearing only an expression of

bovine interest. Then he was out of the room, out of the house, in the mild dust of the starlit road and the heavy rifeness of honey-suckle, the pale ribbon unspooling with terrific slowness under his running feet, reaching the gate at last and turning in, running, his heart and lungs drumming, on up the drive toward the lighted house, the lighted door. He did not knock, he burst in, sobbing for breath, incapable for the moment of speech; he saw the astonished face of the Negro in the linen jacket without knowing when the Negro had appeared.

"De Spain!" he cried, panted. "Where's . . ." then he saw the white man too emerging from a white door down the hall. "Barn!" he cried. "Barn!"

"What?" the white man said. "Barn?"

"Yes!" the boy cried. "Barn!"

"Catch him!" the white man shouted.

Ab Snopes orders his wife to hold young Sarty tight, not to allow him to escape the house. We know that the conflict between father and son arises from Ab's destructive hatred of Major de Spain, which Sarty doesn't share. We're also entirely clear about the connection between the conflict and the plot action involving restraining the boy. The suspense-filled question that we're about to generate involves the race between father and son. (Who will get to the de Spain place first?)

Before that race begins, though, we generate different questions — see the conflict in a different light — because of the moment-to-moment happenings. Sarty's mother struggles to hold him; Sarty's aunt commands her to let him go. Our questions center not only on whether the boy will break free but also on the feelings of the mother and the aunt. They're torn between fear of Ab Snopes and awareness of the madness of Ab's behavior. Are they in fact victims of the same kind of divided loyalty that grips the boy himself? Will their habit of obedience make it impossible for them to free *themselves*?

Suddenly Sarty is out the door, tearing down the starlit road — and we have a fresh set of questions. (Will the butler at the door grasp Sarty's warning fast enough? Will the major act?) But now, as before, the questions we generate flow not just from our grasp of the broad conflict between father and son and its relation to the physical action but from our response to the ways in which the pressure of events keeps modifying the meaning of that basic conflict. We ask, with Sarty, *who* "the white man" is who emerges from the "white door down the hall." And the question opens yet

another view of the conflict. In revolting against his father, Sarty
Snopes joins up with total strangers, people utterly uncommitted
to him. Will this not spell ultimate disaster for him, regardless of
whether he wins the race?

As we frame our successive questions, the language of the
story is our pivotal resource. (Change the three words *the white
man* to a proper name and our question disappears.) Suspense
has its origin in sympathy — our capacity to care about the fates
of others, to imagine ourselves facing dilemmas and conflicts
altogether different from those familiar to us in our real life. But
the quality of suspense differs from narrative to narrative and is
a direct function of word choices by individual writers —
choices controlling the flow of information. It is the encounter
between tightly organized language on the page and our specific
capacities for involvement and concern with perils and problems
not our own that produces the tension-building questions that
grip us.

ASKING QUESTIONS ABOUT SUSPENSE

The three stories that follow focus on, respectively, an act of
violence that a whole community commits on a single individual,
a struggle for survival by the victims of a shipwreck, and a quarrel between a man and woman about an abortion. The exercises
following the stories center on changes in the questions we ask as
we read a passage in each story. The purpose is to sharpen
alertness to the progress of our own curiosity as we bring to life
narrative tension. For further practice, choose passages different
from those selected in the exercises and track the questions that
your reading generates.

SHIRLEY JACKSON   (1919–1965)
The Lottery

The morning of June 27th was clear and sunny, with the fresh
warmth of a full-summer day; the flowers were blossoming pro-
fusely and the grass was richly green. The people of the village
began to gather in the square, between the post office and the
bank, around ten o'clock; in some towns there were so many

people that the lottery took two days and had to be started on June 26th, but in this village, where there were only about three hundred people, the whole lottery took less than two hours, so it could begin at ten o'clock in the morning and still be through in time to allow the villagers to get home for noon dinner.

The children assembled first, of course. School was recently over for the summer, and the feeling of liberty sat uneasily on most of them; they tended to gather together quietly for a while before they broke into boisterous play, and their talk was still of the classroom and the teacher, of books and reprimands. Bobby Martin had already stuffed his pockets full of stones, and the other boys soon followed his example, selecting the smoothest and roundest stones; Bobby and Harry Jones and Dickie Delacroix — the villagers pronounced this name "Dellacroy" — eventually made a great pile of stones in one corner of the square and guarded it against the raids of the other boys. The girls stood aside, talking among themselves, looking over their shoulders at the boys, and the very small children rolled in the dust or clung to the hands of their older brothers or sisters.

Soon the men began to gather, surveying their own children, speaking of planting and rain, tractors and taxes. They stood together, away from the pile of stones in the corner, and their jokes were quiet and they smiled rather than laughed. The women, wearing faded house dresses and sweaters, came shortly after their menfolk. They greeted one another and exchanged bits of gossip as they went to join their husbands. Soon the women, standing by their husbands, began to call to their children, and the children came reluctantly, having to be called four or five times. Bobby Martin ducked under his mother's grasping hand and ran, laughing, back to the pile of stones. His father spoke up sharply, and Bobby came quickly and took his place between his father and his oldest brother.

The lottery was conducted — as were the square dances, the teen-age club, the Halloween program — by Mr. Summers, who had time and energy to devote to civic activities. He was a round-faced, jovial man and he ran the coal business, and people were sorry for him, because he had no children and his wife was a scold. When he arrived in the square, carrying the black wooden box, there was a murmur of conversation among the villagers, and he waved and called, "Little late today, folks." The postmaster, Mr. Graves, followed him, carrying a three-legged stool, and the stool was put in the center of the square and Mr. Summers set the black box down on it. The villagers kept their distance, leaving a space between themselves and the stool, and when Mr.

Summers said, "Some of you fellows want to give me a hand?" there was a hesitation before two men, Mr. Martin and his oldest son, Baxter, came forward to hold the box steady on the stool while Mr. Summers stirred up the papers inside it.

The original paraphernalia for the lottery had been lost long 5 ago, and the black box now resting on the stool had been put into use even before Old Man Warner, the oldest man in town, was born. Mr. Summers spoke frequently to the villagers about making a new box, but no one liked to upset even as much tradition as was represented by the black box. There was a story that the present box had been made with some pieces of the box that had preceded it, the one that had been constructed when the first people settled down to make a village here. Every year, after the lottery, Mr. Summers began talking again about a new box, but every year the subject was allowed to fade off without anything's being done. The black box grew shabbier each year; by now it was no longer completely black but splintered badly along one side to show the original wood color, and in some places faded or stained.

Mr. Martin and his oldest son, Baxter, held the black box securely on the stool until Mr. Summers had stirred the papers thoroughly with his hand. Because so much of the ritual had been forgotten or discarded, Mr. Summers had been successful in having slips of paper substituted for the chips of wood that had been used for generations. Chips of wood, Mr. Summers had argued, had been all very well when the village was tiny, but now that the population was more than three hundred and likely to keep on growing, it was necessary to use something that would fit more easily into the black box. The night before the lottery, Mr. Summers and Mr. Graves made up the slips of paper and put them in the box, and it was then taken to the safe of Mr. Summers' coal company and locked up until Mr. Summers was ready to take it to the square next morning. The rest of the year, the box was put away, sometimes one place, sometimes another; it had spent one year in Mr. Graves's barn and another year underfoot in the post office, and sometimes it was set on a shelf in the Martin grocery and left there.

There was a great deal of fussing to be done before Mr. Summers declared the lottery open. There were the lists to make up — of heads of families, heads of households in each family, members of each household in each family. There was the proper swearing-in of Mr. Summers by the postmaster, as the official of the lottery; at one time, some people remembered, there had been a recital of some sort, performed by the official of the lottery, a perfunctory, tuneless chant that had been rattled off duly each year; some people believed that the official of the lottery used to stand just so when he said or sang it, others believed that he was supposed to walk among the people, but years and years ago this part of the ritual had been allowed to lapse. There had been, also, a ritual salute, which the official of the lottery had had to use in addressing each person who came up to draw from the box, but this also had changed with time, until now it was felt necessary only for the official to speak to each person approaching. Mr. Summers was very good at all this; in his clean white shirt and blue jeans, with one hand resting carelessly on the black box, he seemed very proper and impor- tant as he talked interminably to Mr. Graves and the Martins.

Just as Mr. Summers finally left off talking and turned to the assembled villagers, Mrs. Hutchinson came hurriedly along the path to the square, her sweater thrown over her shoulders, and slid into place in the back of the crowd. "Clean forgot what day it was," she said to Mrs. Delacroix, who stood next to her, and they both laughed softly. "Thought my old man was out back stacking wood," Mrs. Hutchinson went on, "and then I looked out the window and the kids were gone, and then I remembered it was the twenty-seventh and came a-running." She dried her hands on her apron, and Mrs. Delacroix said, "You're in time, though. They're still talking away up there."

Mrs. Hutchinson craned her neck to see through the crowd and found her husband and children standing near the front. She tapped Mrs. Delacroix on the arm as a farewell and began to make her way through the crowd. The people separated good- humoredly to let her through; two or three people said, in voices just loud enough to be heard across the crowd, "Here comes your Missus, Hutchinson," and "Bill, she made it after all." Mrs. Hutchinson reached her husband, and Mr. Summers, who had been waiting, said cheerfully, "Thought we were going to have to get on without you, Tessie." Mrs. Hutchinson said, grinning, "Wouldn't have me leave m'dishes in the sink, now, would you, Joe?" and soft laughter ran through the crowd as the people stirred back into position after Mrs. Hutchinson's arrival.

"Well, now," Mr. Summers said soberly, "guess we better get 10 started, get this over with, so's we can go back to work. Anybody ain't here?"

"Dunbar," several people said. "Dunbar, Dunbar."

Mr. Summers consulted his list. "Clyde Dunbar," he said. "That's right. He's broke his leg, hasn't he? Who's drawing for him?"

"Me, I guess," a woman said, and Mr. Summers turned to look at her. "Wife draws for her husband," Mr. Summers said. "Don't you have a grown boy to do it for you, Janey?" Although Mr. Summers and everyone else in the village knew the answer perfectly well, it was the business of the official of the lottery to ask such questions formally. Mr. Summers waited with an expression of polite interest while Mrs. Dunbar answered.

"Horace's not but sixteen yet," Mrs. Dunbar said regretfully. "Guess I gotta fill in for the old man this year."

"Right," Mr. Summers said. He made a note on the list he was holding. Then he asked, "Watson boy drawing this year?" 15

A tall boy in the crowd raised his hand. "Here," he said. "I'm drawing for m'mother and me." He blinked his eyes nervously and ducked his head as several voices in the crowd said things like "Good fellow, Jack," and "Glad to see your mother's got a man to do it."

"Well," Mr. Summers said, "guess that's everyone. Old Man Warner make it?"

"Here," a voice said, and Mr. Summers nodded.

A sudden hush fell on the crowd as Mr. Summers cleared his throat and looked at the list. "All ready?" he called. "Now, I'll read the names — heads of families first — and the men come up and take a paper out of the box. Keep the paper folded in your hand without looking at it until everyone has had a turn. Everything clear?"

The people had done it so many times that they only half 20 listened to the directions; most of them were quiet, wetting their lips, not looking around. Then Mr. Summers raised one hand high and said, "Adams." A man disengaged himself from the crowd and came forward. "Hi, Steve," Mr. Summers said, and Mr. Adams said, "Hi, Joe." They grinned at one another humorlessly and nervously. Then Mr. Adams reached into the black box and took out a folded paper. He held it firmly by one corner as he turned and went hastily back to his place in the crowd, where he stood a little apart from his family, not looking down at his hand.

"Allen," Mr. Summers said. "Anderson . . . Bentham."

"Seems like there's no time at all between lotteries any more," Mrs. Delacroix said to Mrs. Graves in the back row. "Seems like we got through with the last one only last week."

"Time sure goes fast," Mrs. Graves said.

"Clark . . . Delacroix."

"There goes my old man," Mrs. Delacroix said. She held her 25 breath while her husband went forward.

"Dunbar," Mr. Summers said, and Mrs. Dunbar went steadily

to the box while one of the women said, "Go on, Janey," and another said, "There she goes."

"We're next," Mrs. Graves said. She watched while Mr. Graves came around from the side of the box, greeted Mr. Summers gravely, and selected a slip of paper from the box. By now, all through the crowd there were men holding the small folded papers in their large hands, turning them over and over nervously. Mrs. Dunbar and her two sons stood together, Mrs. Dunbar holding the slip of paper.

"Harburt . . . Hutchinson."

"Get up there, Bill," Mrs. Hutchinson said, and the people near her laughed.

"Jones."   30

"They do say," Mr. Adams said to Old Man Warner, who stood next to him, "that over in the north village they're talking of giving up the lottery."

Old Man Warner snorted. "Pack of crazy fools," he said. "Listening to the young folks, nothing's good enough for *them.* Next thing you know, they'll be wanting to go back to living in caves, nobody work any more, live *that* way for a while. Used to be a saying about 'Lottery in June, corn be heavy soon.' First thing you know, we'd all be eating stewed chickweed and acorns. There's *always* been a lottery," he added petulantly. "Bad enough to see young Joe Summers up there joking with everybody."

"Some places have already quit lotteries," Mrs. Adams said.

"Nothing but trouble in *that,*" Old Man Warner said stoutly. "Pack of young fools."

"Martin." And Bobby Martin watched his father go forward. 35
"Overdyke . . . Percy."

"I wish they'd hurry," Mrs. Dunbar said to her older son. "I wish they'd hurry."

"They're almost through," her son said.

"You get ready to run tell Dad," Mrs. Dunbar said.

Mr. Summers called his own name and then stepped forward precisely and selected a slip from the box. Then he called, "Warner."

"Seventy-seventh year I been in the lottery," Old Man War- 40
ner said as he went through the crowd. "Seventy-seventh time."

"Watson." The tall boy came awkwardly through the crowd. Someone said, "Don't be nervous, Jack," and Mr. Summers said, "Take your time, son."

"Zanini."

After that, there was a long pause, a breathless pause, until

Mr. Summers, holding his slip of paper in the air, said, "All right, fellows." For a minute, no one moved, and then all the slips of paper were opened. Suddenly, all the women began to speak at once, saying, "Who is it?" "Who's got it?" "Is it the Dunbars?" "Is it the Watsons?" Then the voices began to say, "It's Hutchinson. It's Bill," "Bill Hutchinson's got it."

"Go tell your father," Mrs. Dunbar said to her older son.

People began to look around to see the Hutchinsons. Bill 45
Hutchinson was standing quiet, staring down at the paper in his hand. Suddenly, Tessie Hutchinson shouted to Mr. Summers, "You didn't give him time enough to take any paper he wanted. I saw you. It wasn't fair."

"Be a good sport, Tessie," Mrs. Delacroix called, and Mrs. Graves said, "All of us took the same chance."

"Shut up, Tessie," Bill Hutchinson said.

"Well, everyone," Mr. Summers said, "that was done pretty fast, and now we've got to be hurrying a little more to get done in time." He consulted his next list. "Bill," he said, "you draw for the Hutchinson family. You got any other households in the Hutchinsons?"

"There's Don and Eva," Mrs. Hutchinson yelled. "Make *them* take their chance!"

"Daughters draw with their husbands' families, Tessie," Mr. 50
Summers said gently. "You know that as well as anyone else."

"It wasn't *fair*," Tessie said.

"I guess not, Joe," Bill Hutchinson said regretfully. "My daughter draws with her husband's family, that's only fair. And I've got no other family except the kids."

"Then, as far as drawing for families is concerned, it's you," Mr. Summers said in explanation, "and as far as drawing for households is concerned, that's you, too. Right?"

"Right," Bill Hutchinson said.

"How many kids, Bill?" Mr. Summers asked formally. 55

"Three," Bill Hutchinson said. "There's Bill, Jr., and Nancy, and little Dave. And Tessie and me."

"All right, then," Mr. Summers said. "Harry, you got their tickets back?"

Mr. Graves nodded and held up the slips of paper. "Put them in the box, then," Mr. Summers directed. "Take Bill's and put it in."

"I think we ought to start over," Mrs. Hutchinson said, as quietly as she could. "I tell you it wasn't *fair*. You didn't give him time enough to choose. *Every*body saw that."

Mr. Graves had selected the five slips and put them in the 60 box, and he dropped all the papers but those onto the ground, where the breeze caught them and lifted them off.

"Listen, everybody," Mrs. Hutchinson was saying to the people around her.

"Ready, Bill?" Mr. Summers asked, and Bill Hutchinson, with one quick glance around at his wife and children, nodded.

"Remember," Mr. Summers said, "take the slips and keep them folded until each person has taken one. Harry, you help little Dave." Mr. Graves took the hand of the little boy, who came willingly with him up to the box. "Take a paper out of the box, Davy," Mr. Summers said. Davy put his hand into the box and laughed. "Take just *one* paper," Mr. Summers said. "Harry, you hold it for him." Mr. Graves took the child's hand and removed the folded paper from the tight fist and held it while little Dave stood next to him and looked up at him wonderingly.

"Nancy next," Mr. Summers said. Nancy was twelve, and her school friends breathed heavily as she went forward, switching her skirt, and took a slip daintily from the box. "Bill, Jr.," Mr. Summers said, and Billy, his face red and his feet over-large, nearly knocked the box over as he got a paper out. "Tessie," Mr. Summers said. She hesitated for a minute, looking around defiantly, and then set her lips and went up to the box. She snatched a paper out and held it behind her.

"Bill," Mr. Summers said, and Bill Hutchinson reached into   65
the box and felt around, bringing his hand out at last with the slip of paper in it.

The crowd was quiet. A girl whispered, "I hope it's not Nancy," and the sound of the whisper reached the edges of the crowd.

"It's not the way it used to be," Old Man Warner said clearly. "People ain't the way they used to be."

"All right," Mr. Summers said. "Open the papers. Harry, you open little Dave's."

Mr. Graves opened the slip of paper and there was a general sigh through the crowd as he held it up and everyone could see that it was blank. Nancy and Bill, Jr., opened theirs at the same time, and both beamed and laughed, turning around to the crowd and holding their slips of paper above their heads.

"Tessie," Mr. Summers said. There was a pause, and then Mr.   70
Summers looked at Bill Hutchinson, and Bill unfolded his paper and showed it. It was blank.

"It's Tessie," Mr. Summers said, and his voice was hushed. "Show us her paper, Bill."

Bill Hutchinson went over to his wife and forced the slip of paper out of her hand. It had a black spot on it, the black spot Mr. Summers had made the night before with the heavy pencil in the coal-company office. Bill Hutchinson held it up, and there was a stir in the crowd.

"All right, folks," Mr. Summers said. "Let's finish quickly."

Although the villagers had forgotten the ritual and lost the original black box, they still remembered to use stones. The pile of stones the boys had made earlier was ready; there were stones on the ground with the blowing scraps of paper that had come out of the box. Mrs. Delacroix selected a stone so large she had to pick it up with both hands and turned to Mrs. Dunbar. "Come on," she said. "Hurry up."

Mrs. Dunbar had small stones in both hands, and she said, gasping for breath, "I can't run at all. You'll have to go ahead and I'll catch up with you." 75

The children had stones already, and someone gave little Davy Hutchinson a few pebbles.

Tessie Hutchinson was in the center of a cleared space by now, and she held her hands out desperately as the villagers moved in on her. "It isn't fair," she said. A stone hit her on the side of the head.

Old Man Warner was saying, "Come on, come on, everyone." Steve Adams was in the front of the crowd of villagers, with Mrs. Graves beside him.

"It isn't fair, it isn't right," Mrs. Hutchinson screamed, and then they were upon her.

Questions

For the active reader of "The Lottery," the focus of uncertainty or suspense shifts repeatedly in this sequence of sentences.

> (1) Bill Hutchinson was standing quiet, staring down at the paper in his hand. (2) Suddenly, Tessie Hutchinson shouted to Mr. Summers, "You didn't give him time enough to take any paper he wanted. (3) I saw you. (4) It wasn't fair."
>
> (5) "Be a good sport, Tessie," Mrs. Delacroix called, and Mrs. Graves said, "All of us took the same chance." (paras. 45–46)

For example, the most obvious question we ask at the end of sentence 1 — What's *on* that paper in Bill Hutchinson's hand? — isn't answered by sentence 2. And the questions we ask at the end of sentence 2 aren't answered in sentences 3, 4, and 5.

One way of grasping how our questions change as we move

through the passage is by considering how different word choices would affect those questions.

1. "Bill Hutchinson was *staring in horror* at the paper in his hand." What effect does this revision have on the questions we ask?
2. "Suddenly, Tessie Hutchinson shouted *desperately* to Mr. Summers, "You didn't give him time enough to take any paper he wanted."" What effect does this revision have on the questions we ask?

After thinking through the effects of such revisions, write a short paper showing how your questions shift and develop as you move through this passage. Then go on to the final sentence of the story. What question do you ask here? Is the suspense fully over? Write your response and then compare it with the one that follows.

Response

EDITOR: Are the events in progress in this section of "The Lottery" harmless? ominous? pleasant? malevolent? This is a significant uncertainty before the moment at hand (other early mysteries concern where and when the events are taking place). The mounding up of stones by the children in the second paragraph of the story, the contrast between the children's boisterousness and the "quiet" jokes (3) and smiles of the elders, the hint of an argument about whether the town should continue on its present way when "some places have already quit lotteries" (33) — these and other signs suggest that the events, whatever they are, may not be entirely harmless. On the other hand, the gathered elders do smile, the master of ceremonies is "jovial" (4), and the word *fussing* (7) downplays any tension, as does the description of the crowd separating "good-humoredly" (9) for a latecomer whose joke about unfinished dishes makes people laugh.

As we read about Bill Hutchinson "standing quiet, staring down" at the paper in his hand, however, and as we connect that behavior with the word that "Bill Hutchinson's got it" (43), we move to a new stage of understanding: This sober reaction on the part of the person whom the proceedings have most intensely spotlighted thus far has to mean that *he* doesn't find the goings-on pleasant or amusing.

And that realization brings to birth a new question: Just how unpleasant will things prove to be? (If the writer had written "staring in horror" the question would be different.) We've grown accustomed by now to uncertainty about the precise nature of the events in progress; we've moved through a whole series of questions involving whether the events are or are not harmless. Now we ask: How worrisome, how harmful *is* this lottery anyway?

We ask that question as readers of sentence 1. Sentence 2 partly answers the question: What is in progress is worrisome enough to disturb Hutchinson's wife, to cause her to protest against the way the proceedings have thus far been conducted. But now we're asking a different question. We remember that earlier in the story there were suggestions — did they also come from women? — that not everybody was completely happy with the continuance of this ritual. *Can an effective protest be mounted, perhaps by this speaker joining with others? Is Mrs. Hutchinson a lone voice of complaint, or will others join in, creating a resistance that will bring these worrisome/harmful proceedings to an end?* That's one focus of our questions as we finish sentence 2. (The addition of "desperately" would imply the impossibility of protest, thereby changing our questions.)

Sentence 5 partly answers these questions: Two other voices in the crowd chide Mrs. Hutchinson for complaining and thereby discourage — at least for the moment — hope that some kind of resistance can be mounted. But almost instantly we move to a fresh uncertainty: Why is it that some people in this crowd seem so utterly unruffled, as though nothing more than a minor defeat in an innocent children's game were taking place ("Be a good sport"), while others seem gripped by real anger and fear (Mr. Hutchinson staring at the paper in his hand, Mrs. Hutchinson shouting her complaint at the jovial man in charge)? How can we possibly explain this wide a gap between reactions to the ritual? Why does one voice take lightly matters that rouse another almost to hysteria?

Continuously from here to the end of the story our questions — our uncertainties — are in constant flux, and in truth they don't really end. By the close of the story we know that some kind of relatively contemporary (the post office, bank, and talk of tractors confirm that much) scapegoat ritual is being enacted — punishing one innocent to atone for the guilt of a group — and all doubt about whether rage and terror are appropriate has vanished. But the question we began to pose earlier, in our reading of Mrs. Hutchinson's first protest, has deepened: How can such a gap exist between human reactions to the same event? This question, too, has shifted a little since we framed it. We know that a piece of the answer lies in the difference between suffering that's personally experienced and suffering observed from outside. Yet that answer can't satisfy us. Even granted the difficulty of fully imagining what it would be like to be the victim of such a proceeding, is it conceivable that an entire crowd would actually shut its eyes to the human disaster, rendering itself totally indifferent? Who ever heard of comparable obliviousness and cruelty?

This last question is *not* unanswerable, but after we've answered it, our state of mind remains one of doubt. The focus of mystery here is the human condition itself: Who *are* we as human creatures? What are the limits of our altruism, our concern for others, our capacity for selflessness? "Suspense" involves more, in short, than uncertainty about what will happen next; it involves conflicts in our very nature — the endless war of good and evil fought in the human heart.

STEPHEN CRANE   (1871–1900)
The Open Boat
A Tale Intended to be after the Fact.
Being the Experience of Four Men from the Sunk Steamer *Commodore*

I

None of them knew the color of the sky. Their eyes glanced level, and were fastened upon the waves that swept toward them. These waves were of the hue of slate, save for the tops, which were of foaming white, and all of the men knew the colors of the sea. The horizon narrowed and widened, and dipped and rose, and at all times its edge was jagged with waves that seemed thrust up in points like rocks.

Many a man ought to have a bathtub larger than the boat which here rode upon the sea. These waves were most wrongfully and barbarously abrupt and tall, and each frothtop was a problem in small-boat navigation.

The cook squatted in the bottom, and looked with both eyes at the six inches of gunwale which separated him from the ocean. His sleeves were rolled over his fat forearms, and the two flaps of his unbuttoned vest dangled as he bent to bail out the boat. Often he said, "Gawd! that was a narrow clip." As he remarked it he invariably gazed eastward over the broken sea.

The oiler, steering with one of the two oars in the boat, sometimes raised himself suddenly to keep clear of water that swirled in over the stern. It was a thin little oar, and it seemed often ready to snap.

The correspondent, pulling at the other oar, watched the waves and wondered why he was there. 5

The injured captain, lying in the bow, was at this time buried in that profound dejection and indifference which comes, temporarily at least, to even the bravest and most enduring when, willy-nilly, the firm fails, the army loses, the ship goes down. The mind of the master of a vessel is rooted deep in the timbers of her, though he command for a day or a decade; and this captain had on him the stern impression of a scene in the greys of dawn of seven turned faces, and later a stump of a topmast with a white ball on it, that slashed to and fro at the waves, went low and lower, and down. Thereafter there was something strange in his voice. Although steady, it was deep with mourning, and of a quality beyond oration or tears.

"Keep 'er a little more south, Billie," said he.

"A little more south, sir," said the oiler in the stern.

A seat in this boat was not unlike a seat upon a bucking broncho, and by the same token a broncho is not much smaller. The craft pranced and reared and plunged like an animal. As each wave came, and she rose for it, she seemed like a horse making at a fence outrageously high. The manner of her scramble over these walls of water is a mystic thing, and, moreover, at the top of them were ordinarily these problems in white water, the foam racing down from the summit of each wave requiring a new leap, and a leap from the air. Then, after scornfully bumping a crest, she would slide and race and splash down a long incline, and arrive bobbing and nodding in front of the next menace.

A singular disadvantage of the sea lies in the fact that after successfully surmounting one wave you discover that there is another behind it just as important and just as nervously anxious to do something effective in the way of swamping boats. In a ten-foot dinghy one can get an idea of the resources of the sea in the line of waves that is not probable to the average experience which is never at sea in a dinghy. As each slaty wall of water approached, it shut all else from the view of the men in the boat, and it was not difficult to imagine that this particular wave was 10 the final outburst of the ocean, the last effort of the grim water. There was a terrible grace in the move of the waves, and they came in silence, save for the snarling of the crests.

In the wan light the faces of the men must have been grey. Their eyes must have glinted in strange ways as they gazed steadily astern. Viewed from a balcony, the whole thing would doubtless have been weirdly picturesque. But the men in the boat had no time to see it, and if they had had leisure, there were other things to occupy their minds. The sun swung steadily up the sky, and they knew it was broad day because the colour of the sea changed from slate to emerald green streaked with amber lights, and the foam was like tumbling snow. The process of the breaking day was unknown to them. They were aware only of this effect upon the colour of the waves that rolled toward them.

In disjointed sentences the cook and the correspondent argued as to the difference between a life-saving station and a house of refuge. The cook had said: "There's a house of refuge just north of the Mosquito Inlet Light, and as soon as they see us they'll come off in their boat and pick us up."

"As soon as who see us?" said the correspondent.

"The crew," said the cook.

"Houses of refuge don't have crews," said the correspondent. 15 "As I understand them, they are only places where clothes and grub are stored for the benefit of shipwrecked people. They don't carry crews."

"Oh, yes, they do," said the cook.

"No, they don't," said the correspondent.

"Well, we're not there yet, anyhow," said the oiler, in the stern.

"Well," said the cook, "perhaps it's not a house of refuge that I'm thinking of as being near Mosquito Inlet Light; perhaps it's a life-saving station."

"We're not there yet," said the oiler in the stern. 20

II

As the boat bounced from the top of each wave the wind tore through the hair of the hatless men, and as the craft plopped her stern down again the spray slashed past them. The crest of each of these waves was a hill, from the top of which the men surveyed for a moment a broad tumultuous expanse, shining and wind-riven. It was probably splendid, it was probably glorious, this play of the free sea, wild with lights of emerald and white and amber.

"Bully good thing it's an on-shore wind," said the cook. "If not, where would we be? Wouldn't have a show."

"That's right," said the correspondent.

The busy oiler nodded his assent.

Then the captain, in the bow, chuckled in a way that ex- 25 pressed humor, contempt, tragedy, all in one. "Do you think we've got much of a show now, boys?" said he.

Whereupon the three were silent, save for a trifle of hemming and hawing. To express any particular optimism at this time they felt to be childish and stupid, but they all doubtless possessed this sense of the situation in their minds. A young man thinks doggedly at such times. On the other hand, the ethics of their condition was decidely against any open suggestion of hopelessness. So they were silent.

"Oh, well," said the captain, soothing his children, "we'll get ashore all right."

But there was that in his tone which made them think; so the oiler quoth, "Yes! if this wind holds."

The cook was bailing. "Yes! if we don't catch hell in the surf."

Canton-flannel gulls flew near and far. Sometimes they sat 30 down on the sea, near patches of brown seaweed that rolled over the waves with a movement like carpets on a line in a gale. The birds sat comfortably in groups, and they were envied by some in the dinghy, for the wrath of the sea was no more to them than it was to a covey of prairie chickens a thousand miles inland. Often they came very close and stared at the men with black bead-like eyes. At these times they were uncanny and sinister in their unblinking scrutiny, and the men hooted angrily at them, telling them to be gone. One came, and evidently decided to alight on the top of the captain's head. The bird flew parallel to the boat and did not circle, but made short sidelong jumps in the air in chicken-fashion. His black eyes were wistfully fixed upon the captain's head. "Ugly brute," said the oiler to the bird. "You look as if you were made with a jackknife." The cook and the correspondent swore darkly at the creature. The captain naturally wished to knock it away with the end of the heavy painter, but he did not dare do it, because anything resembling an emphatic gesture would have capsized this freighted boat; and so, with his open hand, the captain gently and carefully waved the gull away. After it had been discouraged from the pursuit the captain breathed easier on account of his hair, and others breathed easier

because the bird struck their minds at this time as being somehow gruesome and ominous.

In the meantime the oiler and the correspondent rowed. And
also they rowed. They sat together in the same seat, and each
rowed an oar. Then the oiler took both oars; then the correspondent took both oars; then the oiler; then the correspondent. They
rowed and they rowed. The very ticklish part of the business was
when the time came for the reclining one in the stern to take his
turn at the oars. By the very last star of truth, it is easier to steal
eggs from under a hen than it was to change seats in the dinghy.
First the man in the stern slid his hand along the thwart and
moved with care, as if he were of Sèvres. Then the man in the
rowing-seat slid his hand along the other thwart. It was all done
with the most extraordinary care. As the two sidled past each
other, the whole party kept watchful eyes on the coming wave,
and the captain cried: "Look out, now! Steady, there!"

The brown mats of seaweed that appeared from time to time
were like islands, bits of earth. They were travelling, apparently,
neither one way nor the other. They were, to all intents, station-
ary. They informed the men in the boat that it was making
progress slowly toward the land.

The captain, rearing cautiously in the bow after the dinghy
soared on a great swell, said that he had seen the lighthouse at
Mosquito Inlet. Presently the cook remarked that he had seen it.
The correspondent was at the oars then, and for some reason he
too wished to look at the lighthouse; but his back was toward the
far shore, and the waves were important, and for some time he
could not seize an opportunity to turn his head. But at last there
came a wave more gentle than the others, and when at the crest of
it he swiftly scoured the western horizon.

"See it?" said the captain.

"No," said the correspondent, slowly; "I didn't see anything." 35

"Look again," said the captain. He pointed. "It's exactly in
that direction."

At the top of another wave the correspondent did as he was
bid, and this time his eyes chanced on a small, still thing on the
edge of the swaying horizon. It was precisely like the point of a
pin. It took an anxious eye to find a lighthouse so tiny.

"Think we'll make it, Captain?"

"If this wind holds and the boat don't swamp, we can't do
much else," said the captain.

The little boat, lifted by each towering sea and splashed vi- 40
ciously by the crests, made progress that in the absence of seaweed

was not apparent to those in her. She seemed just a wee thing wallowing, miraculously top up, at the mercy of five oceans. Occasionally a great spread of water, like white flames, swarmed into her.

"Bail her, cook," said the captain, serenely.

"All right, Captain," said the cheerful cook.

III

It would be difficult to describe the subtle brotherhood of men that was here established on the seas. No one said that it was so. No one mentioned it. But it dwelt in the boat, and each man felt it warm him. They were a captain, an oiler, a cook, and a correspondent, and they were friends — friends in a more curiously iron-bound degree than may be common. The hurt captain, lying against the water-jar in the bow, spoke always in a low voice and calmly; but he could never command a more ready and swiftly obedient crew than the motley three of the dinghy. It was more than a mere recognition of what was best for the common safety. There was surely in it a quality that was personal and heart-felt. And after this devotion to the commander of the boat, there was this comradeship, that the correspondent, for instance, who had been taught to be cynical of men, knew even at the time was the best experience of his life. But no one said that it was so. No one mentioned it.

"I wish we had a sail," remarked the captain. "We might try my overcoat on the end of an oar, and give you two boys a chance to rest." So the cook and the correspondent held the mast and spread wide the overcoat; the oiler steered; and the little boat made good way with her new rig. Sometimes the oiler had to scull sharply to keep a sea from breaking into the boat, but otherwise sailing was a success.

Meanwhile the lighthouse had been growing slowly larger. It 45 had now almost assumed color, and appeared like a little gray shadow on the sky. The man at the oars could not be prevented from turning his head rather often to try for a glimpse of this little gray shadow.

At last, from the top of each wave, the men in the tossing boat could see land. Even as the lighthouse was an upright shadow on the sky, this land seemed but a long black shadow on the sea. It certainly was thinner than paper. "We must be about opposite New Smyrna," said the cook, who had coasted this shore often in schooners. "Captain, by the way, I believe they abandoned that life-saving station there about a year ago."

"Did they?" said the captain.

The wind slowly died away. The cook and the correspondent were not now obliged to slave in order to hold high the oar. But the waves continued their old impetuous swooping at the dinghy, and the little craft, no longer under way, struggled woundily over them. The oiler or the correspondent took the oars again.

Shipwrecks are apropos of nothing. If men could only train for them and have them occur when the men had reached pink condition, there would be less drowning at sea. Of the four in the dinghy none had slept any time worth mentioning for two days and two nights previous to embarking in the dinghy, and in the excitement of clambering about the deck of a foundering ship they had also forgotten to eat heartily.

For these reasons, and for others, neither the oiler nor the 50 correspondent was fond of rowing at this time. The correspondent wondered ingenuously how in the name of all that was sane could there be people who thought it amusing to row a boat. It was not an amusement; it was a diabolical punishment, and even a genius of mental aberrations could never conclude that it was anything but a horror to the muscles and a crime against the back. He mentioned to the boat in general how the amusement of rowing struck him, and the weary-faced oiler smiled in full sympathy. Previously to the foundering, by the way, the oiler had worked double watch in the engine-room of the ship.

"Take her easy now, boys," said the captain. "Don't spend yourselves. If we have to run a surf you'll need all your strength, because we'll sure have to swim for it. Take your time."

Slowly the land arose from the sea. From a black line it became a line of black and a line of white — trees and sand. Finally the captain said that he could make out a house on the shore. "That's the house of refuge, sure," said the cook. "They'll see us before long, and come out after us."

The distant lighthouse reared high. "The keeper ought to be able to make us out now, if he's looking through a glass," said the captain. "He'll notify the life-saving people."

"None of those other boats could have got ashore to give word of the wreck," said the oiler, in a low voice, "else the life-boat would be out hunting us."

Slowly and beautifully the land loomed out of the sea. The 55 wind came again. It had veered from the north-east to the south-east. Finally a new sound struck the ears of the men in the boat. It was the low thunder of the surf on the shore. "We'll never be able to make the lighthouse now," said the captain. "Swing her head a little more north, Billie."

"A little more north, sir," said the oiler.

Whereupon the little boat turned her nose once more down the wind, and all but the oarsman watched the shore grow. Under the influence of this expansion doubt and direful apprehension were leaving the minds of the men. The management of the boat was still most absorbing, but it could not prevent a quiet cheerfulness. In an hour, perhaps, they would be ashore.

Their backbones had become thoroughly used to balancing in the boat, and they now rode this wild colt of a dinghy like circus men. The correspondent thought that he had been drenched to the skin, but happening to feel in the top pocket of his coat, he found therein eight cigars. Four of them were soaked with seawater; four were perfectly scatheless. After a search, somebody produced three dry matches; and thereupon the four waifs rode impudently in their little boat and, with an assurance of an impending rescue shining in their eyes, puffed at the big cigars, and judged well and ill of all men. Everybody took a drink of water.

IV

"Cook," remarked the captain, "there don't seem to be any signs of life about your house of refuge."

"No," replied the cook. "Funny they don't see us!"   60

A broad stretch of lowly coast lay before the eyes of the men. It was of low dunes topped with dark vegetation. The roar of the surf was plain, and sometimes they could see the white lip of a wave as it spun up the beach. A tiny house was blocked out black upon the sky. Southward, the slim lighthouse lifted its little gray length.

Tide, wind, and waves were swinging the dinghy northward. "Funny they don't see us," said the men.

The surf's roar was here dulled, but its tone was nevertheless thunderous and mighty. As the boat swam over the great rollers the men sat listening to this roar. "We'll swamp sure," said everybody.

It is fair to say here that there was not a life-saving station within twenty miles in either direction; but the men did not know this fact, and in consequence they made dark and opprobrious remarks concerning the eyesight of the nation's life-savers. Four scowling men sat in the dinghy and surpassed records in the invention of epithets.

"Funny they don't see us."   65

The light-heartedness of a former time had completely faded. To their sharpened minds it was easy to conjure pictures of all kinds of incompetency and blindness and, indeed, coward-ice. There was the shore of the populous land, and it was bitter and bitter to them that from it came no sign.

"Well," said the captain, ultimately, "I suppose we'll have to make a try for ourselves. If we stay out here too long, we'll none of us have strength left to swim after the boat swamps."

And so the oiler, who was at the oars, turned the boat straight for the shore. There was a sudden tightening of muscles. There was some thinking.

"If we don't all get ashore," said the captain — "if we don't all get ashore, I suppose you fellows know where to send news of my finish?"

They then briefly exchanged some addresses and admoni- 70 tions. As for the reflections of the men, there was a great deal of rage in them. Perchance they might be formulated thus: "If I am going to be drowned — if I am going to be drowned — if I am going to be drowned, why, in the name of the seven mad gods who rule the sea, was I allowed to come thus far and contemplate sand and trees? Was I brought here merely to have my nose dragged away as I was about to nibble the sacred cheese of life? It is preposterous. If this old ninny-woman, Fate, cannot do better than this, she should be deprived of the management of men's fortunes. She is an old hen who knows not her intention. If she has decided to drown me, why did she not do it in the beginning and save me all this trouble? The whole affair is absurd. — But no; she cannot mean to drown me. She dare not drown me. She cannot drown me. Not after all this work." Afterward the man might have had an impulse to shake his fist at the clouds. "Just you drown me, now, and then hear what I call you!"

The billows that came at this time were more formidable. They seemed always just about to break and roll over the little boat in a turmoil of foam. There was a preparatory and long growl in the speech of them. No mind unused to the sea would have concluded that the dinghy could ascend these sheer heights in time. The shore was still afar. The oiler was a wily surfman. "Boys," he said swiftly, "she won't live three minutes more, and we're too far out to swim. Shall I take her to sea again, Captain?"

"Yes; go ahead!" said the captain.

This oiler, by a series of quick miracles and fast and steady

oarsmanship, turned the boat in the middle of the surf and took
her safely to sea again.

There was a considerable silence as the boat bumped over
the furrowed sea to deeper water. Then somebody in gloom
spoke: "Well, anyhow, they must have seen us from the shore by
now."

The gulls went in slanting flight up the wind toward the gray, 75
desolate east. A squall, marked by dingy clouds and clouds brick-
red like smoke from a burning building, appeared from the
south-east.

"What do you think of those life-saving people? Ain't they
peaches?"

"Funny they haven't seen us."

"Maybe they think we're out here for sport! Maybe they think
we're fishin'. Maybe they think we're damned fools."

It was a long afternoon. A changed tide tried to force them
southward, but wind and wave said northward. Far ahead, where
coast-line, sea, and sky formed their mighty angle, there were
little dots which seemed to indicate a city on the shore.

"St. Augustine?" 80

The captain shook his head. "Too near Mosquito Inlet."

And the oiler rowed, and then the correspondent rowed;
then the oiler rowed. It was a weary business. The human back
can become the seat of more aches and pains than are registered
in books for the composite anatomy of a regiment. It is a limited
area, but it can become the theatre of innumerable muscular conflicts, tangles, wrenches, knots, and other comforts.

"Did you ever like to row, Billie?" asked the correspondent.

"No," said the oiler; "hang it!"

When one exchanged the rowing-seat for a place in the bot- 85
tom of the boat, he suffered a bodily depression that caused him
to be careless of everything save an obligation to wiggle one
finger. There was cold sea-water swashing to and fro in the boat,
and he lay in it. His head, pillowed on a thwart, was within an
inch of the swirl of a wave-crest, and sometimes a particularly
obstreperous sea came inboard and drenched him once more.
But these matters did not annoy him. It is almost certain that if
the boat had capsized he would have tumbled comfortably upon
the ocean as if he felt sure that it was a great soft mattress.

"Look! There's a man on the shore!"

"Where?"

"There! See 'im?"

"Yes, sure! He's walking along."

"Now he's stopped. Look! He's facing us!" 90

"He's waving at us!"

"So he is! By thunder!"

"Ah, now we're all right! Now we're all right! There'll be a
boat out here for us in half an hour."

"He's going on. He's running. He's going up to that house
there."

The remote beach seemed lower than the sea, and it required   95
a searching glance to discern the little black figure. The captain
saw a floating stick, and they rowed to it. A bath towel was by
some weird chance in the boat, and, tying this on the stick, the
captain waved it. The oarsman did not dare turn his head, so he
was obliged to ask questions.

"What's he doing now?"

"He's standing still again. He's looking, I think. — There he
goes again — toward the house. — Now he's stopped again."

"Is he waving at us?"

"No, not now; he was, though."

"Look! There comes another man!"   100

"He's running."

"Look at him go, would you!"

"Why, he's on a bicycle. Now he's met the other man. They're
both waving at us. Look!"

"There comes something up the beach."

"What the devil is that thing?"   105

"Why, it looks like a boat."

"Why, certainly, it's a boat."

"No; it's on wheels."

"Yes, so it is. Well, that must be the life-boat. They drag them
along shore on a wagon."

"That's the life-boat, sure."   110

"No, by God, it's — it's an omnibus."

"I tell you it's a life-boat."

"It is not! It's an omnibus. I can see it plain. See? One of these
big hotel omnibuses."

"By thunder, you're right. It's an omnibus, sure as fate. What
do you suppose they are doing with an omnibus? Maybe they are
going around collecting the life-crew, hey?"

"That's it, likely. Look! There's a fellow waving a little black   115
flag. He's standing on the steps of the omnibus. There come
those other two fellows. Now they're all talking together. Look at
the fellow with the flag. Maybe he ain't waving it!"

"That ain't a flag, is it? That's his coat. Why, certainly, that's
his coat."

"So it is; it's his coat. He's taken it off and is waving it around
his head. But would you look at him swing it!"

"Oh, say, there isn't any life-saving station there. That's just a

winter-resort hotel omnibus that has brought over some of the
boarders to see us drown."

"What's that idiot with the coat mean? What's he signalling,
anyhow?"

"It looks as if he were trying to tell us to go north. There   120
must be a life-saving station up there."

"No; he thinks we're fishing. Just giving us a merry hand.
See? Ah, there, Willie!"

"Well, I wish I could make something out of those signals.
What do you suppose he means?"

"He don't mean anything; he's just playing."

"Well, if he'd just signal us to try the surf again, or to go to
sea and wait, or go north, or go south, or go to hell, there would
be some reason in it. But look at him! He just stands there and
keeps his coat revolving like a wheel. The ass!"

"There come more people."   125

"Now there's quite a mob. Look! Isn't that a boat?"

"Where? Oh, I see where you mean. No, that's no boat."

"That fellow is still waving his coat."

"He must think we like to see him do that. Why don't he quit
it? It don't mean anything."

"I don't know. I think he is trying to make us go north. It   130
must be that there's a life-saving station there somewhere."

"Say, he ain't tired yet. Look at 'im wave!"

"Wonder how long he can keep that up. He's been revolving
his coat ever since he caught sight of us. He's an idiot. Why aren't
they getting men to bring a boat out? A fishing boat — one of
those big yawls — could come out here all right. Why don't he do
something?"

"Oh, it's all right now."

"They'll have a boat out here for us in less than no time, now
that they've seen us."

A faint yellow tone came into the sky over the low land. The   135
shadows on the sea slowly deepened. The wind bore coldness
with it, and the men began to shiver.

"Holy smoke!" said one, allowing his voice to express his
impious mood, "if we keep on monkeying out here! If we've got to
flounder out here all night!"

"Oh, we'll never have to stay here all night! Don't you worry.
They've seen us now, and it won't be long before they'll come
chasing out after us."

The shore grew dusky. The man waving a coat blended gradually into this gloom, and it swallowed in the same manner the
omnibus and the group of people. The spray, when it dashed

uproariously over the side, made the voyagers shrink and swear like men who were being branded.

"I'd like to catch the chump who waved the coat. I feel like socking him one, just for luck."

"Why? What did he do?" 140

"Oh, nothing, but then he seemed so damned cheerful."

In the meantime the oiler rowed, and then the correspondent rowed, and then the oiler rowed. Gray-faced and bowed forward, they mechanically, turn by turn, plied the leaden oars. The form of the lighthouse had vanished from the southern horizon, but finally a pale star appeared, just lifting from the sea. The streaked saffron in the west passed before the all-merging darkness, and the sea to the east was black. The land had vanished, and was expressed only by the low and drear thunder of the surf.

"If I am going to be drowned — if I am going to be drowned — if I am going to be drowned, why, in the name of the seven gods who rule the sea, was I allowed to come thus far and contemplate sand and trees? Was I brought here merely to have my nose dragged away as I was about to nibble the sacred cheese of life?"

The patient captain, drooped over the water-jar, was sometimes obliged to speak to the oarsman.

"Keep her head up! Keep her head up!" 145

"Keep her head up, sir." The voices were weary and low.

This was surely a quiet evening. All save the oarsman lay heavily and listlessly in the boat's bottom. As for him, his eyes were just capable of noting the tall black waves that swept forward in a most sinister silence, save for an occasional subdued growl of a crest.

The cook's head was on a thwart, and he looked without interest at the water under his nose. He was deep in other scenes. Finally he spoke. "Billie," he murmured, dreamfully, "what kind of pie do you like best?"

V

"Pie!" said the oiler and the correspondent, agitatedly. "Don't talk about those things, blast you!"

"Well," said the cook, "I was just thinking about ham sand- 150
wiches, and — "

A night on the sea in an open boat is a long night. As dark-ness settled finally, the shine of the light, lifting from the sea in the south, changed to full gold. On the northern horizon a new light appeared, a small bluish gleam on the edge of the waters. These two lights were the furniture of the world. Otherwise there was nothing but waves.

Two men huddled in the stern, and distances were so magnif-icent in the dinghy that the rower was enabled to keep his feet partly warm by thrusting them under his companions. Their legs indeed extended far under the rowing seat until they touched the feet of the captain forward. Sometimes, despite the efforts of the tired oarsman, a wave came piling into the boat, an icy wave of the night, and the chilling water soaked them anew. They would twist their bodies for a moment and groan, and sleep the dead sleep once more, while the water in the boat gurgled about them as the craft rocked.

The plan of the oiler and the correspondent was for one to row until he lost the ability, and then arouse the other from his sea-water couch in the bottom of the boat.

The oiler plied the oars until his head drooped forward and the overpowering sleep blinded him; and he rowed yet afterward. Then he touched a man in the bottom of the boat, and called his name. "Will you spell me for a little while?" he said meekly.

"Sure, Billie," said the correspondent, awaking and dragging himself to a sitting position. They exchanged places carefully, and the oiler, cuddling down in the sea-water at the cook's side, seemed to go to sleep instantly. 155

The particular violence of the sea had ceased. The waves came without snarling. The obligation of the man at the oars was to keep the boat headed so that the tilt of the rollers would not capsize her, and to preserve her from filling when the crests rushed past. The black waves were silent and hard to be seen in the darkness. Often one was almost upon the boat before the oarsman was aware.

In a low voice the correspondent addressed the captain. He was not sure that the captain was awake, although this iron man seemed to be always awake. "Captain, shall I keep her making for that light north, sir?"

The same steady voice answered him. "Yes. Keep it about two points off the port bow."

The cook had tied a life-belt around himself in order to get even the warmth which this clumsy cork contrivance could do-nate, and he seemed almost stove-like when a rower, whose teeth invariably chattered wildly as soon as he ceased his labor, dropped down to sleep.

The correspondent, as he rowed, looked down at the two 160 men sleeping underfoot. The cook's arm was around the oiler's shoulders, and, with their fragmentary clothing and haggard faces, they were the babes of the sea — a grotesque rendering of the old babes in the wood.

Later he must have grown stupid at his work, for suddenly there was a growling of water, and a crest came with a roar and a swash into the boat, and it was a wonder that it did not set the cook afloat in his life-belt. The cook continued to sleep, but the oiler sat up, blinking his eyes and shaking with the new cold.

"Oh, I'm awful sorry, Billie," said the correspondent, con- tritely.

"That's all right, old boy," said the oiler, and lay down again and was asleep.

Presently it seemed that even the captain dozed, and the correspondent thought that he was the one man afloat on all the oceans. The wind had a voice as it came over the waves, and it was sadder than the end.

There was a long, loud swishing astern of the boat, and a 165 gleaming trail of phosphorescence, like blue flame, was furrowed on the black waters. It might have been made by a monstrous knife.

Then there came a stillness, while the correspondent breathed with open mouth and looked at the sea.

Suddenly there was another swish and another long flash of bluish light, and this time it was alongside the boat, and might almost have been reached with an oar. The correspondent saw an enormous fin speed like a shadow through the water, hurling the crystalline spray and leaving the long glowing trail.

The correspondent looked over his shoulder at the captain. His face was hidden, and he seemed to be asleep. He looked at the babes of the sea. They certainly were asleep. So, being bereft of sympathy, he leaned a little way to one side and swore softly into the sea.

But the thing did not then leave the vicinity of the boat. Ahead or astern, on one side or the other, at intervals long or short, fled the long sparkling streak, and there was to be heard the *whirroo* of the dark fin. The speed and power of the thing was greatly to be admired. It cut the water like a gigantic and keen projectile.

The presence of this biding thing did not affect the man with 170 the same horror that it would if he had been a picnicker. He simply looked at the sea dully and swore in an undertone.

Nevertheless, it is true that he did not wish to be alone with the thing. He wished one of his companions to awake by chance and keep him company with it. But the captain hung motionless over the water-jar, and the oiler and the cook in the bottom of the boat were plunged in slumber.

VI

"If I am going to be drowned — if I am going to be drowned — if I am going to be drowned, why, in the name of the seven mad gods who rule the sea, was I allowed to come thus far and contemplate sand and trees?"

During this dismal night, it may be remarked that a man would conclude that it was really the intention of the seven mad gods to drown him, despite the abominable injustice of it. For it was certainly an abominable injustice to drown a man who had worked so hard, so hard. The man felt it would be a crime most unnatural. Other people had drowned at sea since galleys swarmed with painted sails, but still —

When it occurs to a man that nature does not regard him as important, and that she feels she would not maim the universe by disposing of him, he at first wishes to throw bricks at the temple, and he hates deeply the fact that there are no bricks and no temples. Any visible expression of nature would surely be pelleted with his jeers.

Then, if there be no tangible thing to hoot, he feels, perhaps, 175 the desire to confront a personification and indulge in pleas, bowed to one knee, and with hands supplicant, saying, "Yes, but I love myself."

A high cold star on a winter's night is the word he feels that she says to him. Thereafter he knows the pathos of his situation.

The men in the dinghy had not discussed these matters, but each had, no doubt, reflected upon them in silence and according to his mind. There was seldom any expression upon their faces save the general one of complete weariness. Speech was devoted to the business of the boat.

To chime the notes of his emotion, a verse mysteriously entered the correspondent's head. He had even forgotten that he had forgotten this verse, but it suddenly was in his mind.

A soldier of the Legion lay dying in Algiers;

There was lack of woman's nursing, there was dearth of woman's
   tears;
But a comrade stood beside him, and he took that comrade's hand,
And he said, "I never more shall see my own, my native land."

In his childhood the correspondent had been made acquainted with the fact that a soldier of the Legion lay dying in
Algiers, but he had never regarded the fact as important. Myriads
of his school-fellows had informed him of the soldier's plight, but
the dinning had naturally ended by making him perfectly indifferent. He had never considered it his affair that a soldier of the
Legion lay dying in Algiers, nor had it appeared to him as a matter for sorrow. It was less to him than the breaking of a pencil's
point.

Now, however, it quaintly came to him as a human, living   180
thing. It was no longer merely a picture of a few throes in the
breast of a poet, meanwhile drinking tea and warming his feet at
the grate; it was an actuality — stern, mournful, and fine.

The correspondent plainly saw the soldier. He lay on the
sand with his feet out straight and still. While his pale left hand
was upon his chest in an attempt to thwart the going of his life,
the blood came between his fingers. In the far Algerian distance,
a city of low square forms was set against a sky that was faint with
the last sunset hues. The correspondent, plying the oars and
dreaming of the slow and slower movements of the lips of the
soldier, was moved by a profound and perfectly impersonal comprehension. He was sorry for the soldier of the Legion who lay
dying in Algiers.

The thing which had followed the boat and waited had
evidently grown bored at the delay. There was no longer to be
heard the slash of the cutwater, and there was no longer the
flame of the long trail. The light in the north still glimmered, but
it was apparently no nearer to the boat. Sometimes the boom of
the surf rang in the correspondent's ears, and he turned the craft
seaward then and rowed harder. Southward, some one had evidently built a watch-fire on the beach. It was too low and too far
to be seen, but it made a shimmering, roseate reflection upon the
bluff in back of it, and this could be discerned from the boat. The
wind came stronger, and sometimes a wave suddenly raged out
like a mountain cat, and there was to be seen the sheen and
sparkle of a broken crest.

The captain, in the bow, moved on his water-jar and sat erect.
"Pretty long night," he observed to the correspondent. He looked
at the shore. "Those life-saving people take their time."

"Did you see that shark playing around?"

"Yes, I saw him. He was a big fellow, all right."   185
"Wish I had known you were awake."
Later the correspondent spoke into the bottom of the boat.
"Billie!" There was a slow and gradual disentanglement.
"Billie, will you spell me?"
"Sure," said the oiler.   190
As soon as the correspondent touched the cold, comfortable
sea-water in the bottom of the boat and had huddled close to the
cook's life-belt he was deep in sleep, despite the fact that his teeth
played all the popular airs. This sleep was so good to him that it
was but a moment before he heard a voice call his name in a tone
that demonstrated the last stages of exhaustion. "Will you spell
me?"
"Sure, Billie."
The light in the north had mysteriously vanished, but the
correspondent took his course from the wide-awake captain.
Later in the night they took the boat farther out to sea, and
the captain directed the cook to take one oar at the stern and
keep the boat facing the seas. He was to call out if he should hear
the thunder of the surf. This plan enabled the oiler and the
correspondent to get respite together. "We'll give those boys a
chance to get into shape again," said the captain. They curled
down and, after a few preliminary chatterings and trembles,
slept once more the dead sleep. Neither knew they had bequeathed to the cook the company of another shark, or perhaps
the same shark.
As the boat caroused on the waves, spray occasionally   195
bumped over the side and gave them a fresh soaking, but this had
no power to break their repose. The ominous slash of the wind
and the water affected them as it would have affected mummies.
"Boys," said the cook, with the notes of every reluctance in
his voice, "she's drifted in pretty close. I guess one of you had
better take her to sea again." The correspondent, aroused, heard
the crash of the toppled crests.
As he was rowing, the captain gave him some whisky-and-
water, and this steadied the chills out of him. "If I ever get ashore
and anybody shows me even a photograph of an oar ——"
At last there was a short conversation.
"Billie — Billie, will you spell me?"
"Sure," said the oiler.   200

VII

When the correspondent again opened his eyes, the sea and
the sky were each of the gray hue of the dawning. Later, carmine

and gold was painted upon the waters. The morning appeared finally, in its splendor, with a sky of pure blue, and the sunlight flamed on the tips of the waves.

On the distant dunes were set many little black cottages, and a tall white windmill reared above them. No man, nor dog, nor bicycle appeared on the beach. The cottages might have formed a deserted village.

The voyagers scanned the shore. A conference was held in the boat. "Well," said the captain, "if no help is coming, we might better try a run through the surf right away. If we stay out here much longer we will be too weak to do anything for ourselves at all." The others silently acquiesced in this reasoning. The boat was headed for the beach. The correspondent wondered if none ever ascended the tall wind-tower, and if then they never looked seaward. This tower was a giant, standing with its back to the plight of the ants. It represented in a degree, to the correspondent, the serenity of nature amid the struggles of the individual — nature in the wind, and nature in the vision of men. She did not seem cruel to him then, nor beneficent, nor treacherous, nor wise. But she was indifferent, flatly indifferent. It is, perhaps, plausible that a man in this situation, impressed with the unconcern of the universe, should see the innumerable flaws of his life, and have them taste wickedly in his mind, and wish for another chance. A distinction between right and wrong seems absurdly clear to him, then, in this new ignorance of the grave-edge, and he understands that if he were given another opportunity he would mend his conduct and his words, and be better and brighter during an introduction or at a tea.

"Now, boys," said the captain, "she is going to swamp sure. All we can do is to work her in as far as possible, and then when she swamps, pile out and scramble for the beach. Keep cool now, and don't jump until she swamps sure."

The oiler took the oars. Over his shoulders he scanned the 205 surf. "Captain," he said, "I think I'd better bring her about and keep her head-on to the seas and back her in."

"All right, Billie," said the captain. "Back her in." The oiler swung the boat then, and, seated in the stern, the cook and the correspondent were obliged to look over their shoulders to contemplate the lonely and indifferent shore.

The monstrous inshore rollers heaved the boat high until the men were again enabled to see the white sheets of water scudding up the slanted beach. "We won't get in very close," said the captain. Each time a man could wrest his attention from the rollers, he turned his glance toward the shore, and in the expression of

the eyes during this contemplation there was a singular quality.
The correspondent, observing the others, knew that they were
not afraid, but the full meaning of their glances was shrouded.

As for himself, he was too tired to grapple fundamentally
with the fact. He tried to coerce his mind into thinking of it, but
the mind was dominated at this time by the muscles, and the
muscles said they did not care. It merely occurred to him that if
he should drown it would be a shame.

There were no hurried words, no pallor, no plain agitation.
The men simply looked at the shore. "Now, remember to get well
clear of the boat when you jump," said the captain.

Seaward the crest of a roller suddenly fell with a thunderous   210
crash, and the long white comber came roaring down upon the
boat.

"Steady now," said the captain. The men were silent. They
turned their eyes from the shore to the comber and waited. The
boat slid up the incline, leaped at the furious top, bounced over
it, and swung down the long back of the wave. Some water had
been shipped, and the cook bailed it out.

But the next crest crashed also. The tumbling, boiling flood
of white water caught the boat and whirled it almost perpendicu-
lar. Water swarmed in from all sides. The correspondent had his
hands on the gunwale at this time, and when the water entered at
that place he swiftly withdrew his fingers, as if he objected to
wetting them.

The little boat, drunken with this weight of water, reeled and
snuggled deeper into the sea.

"Bail her out, cook! Bail her out!" said the captain

"All right, Captain," said the cook.   215

"Now, boys, the next one will do for us sure," said the oiler.
"Mind to jump clear of the boat."

The third wave moved forward, huge, furious, implacable. It
fairly swallowed the dinghy, and almost simultaneously the men
tumbled into the sea. A piece of life-belt had lain in the bottom
of the boat, and as the correspondent went overboard he held
this to his chest with his left hand.

The January water was icy, and he reflected immediately that
it was colder than he had expected to find it off the coast of
Florida. This appeared to his dazed mind as a fact important
enough to be noted at the time. The coldness of the water was
sad; it was tragic. This fact was somehow mixed and confused
with his opinion of his own situation, so that it seemed almost a
proper reason for tears. The water was cold.

When he came to the surface he was conscious of little but

the noisy water. Afterward he saw his companions in the sea. The oiler was ahead in the race. He was swimming strongly and rapidly. Off to the correspondent's left, the cook's great white and corked back bulged out of the water; and in the rear the captain was hanging with his one good hand to the keel of the overturned dinghy.

There is a certain immovable quality to a shore, and the cor- 220 respondent wondered at it amid the confusion of the sea.

It seemed also very attractive; but the correspondent knew that it was a long journey, and he paddled leisurely. The piece of life-preserver lay under him, and sometimes he whirled down the incline of a wave as if he were on a hand-sled.

But finally he arrived at a place in the sea where travel was beset with difficulty. He did not pause swimming to inquire what manner of current had caught him, but there his progress ceased. The shore was set before him like a bit of scenery on a stage, and he looked at it and understood with his eyes each detail of it.

As the cook passed, much farther to the left, the captain was calling to him, "Turn over on your back, cook! Turn over on your back and use the oar."

"All right, sir." The cook turned on his back, and, paddling with an oar, went ahead as if he were a canoe.

Presently the boat also passed to the left of the correspon- 225 dent, with the captain clinging with one hand to the keel. He would have appeared like a man raising himself to look over a board fence if it were not for the extraordinary gymnastics of the boat. The correspondent marvelled that the captain could still hold to it.

They passed on nearer to shore — the oiler, the cook, the captain — and following them went the water-jar, bouncing gaily over the seas.

The correspondent remained in the grip of this strange new enemy — a current. The shore, with its white slope of sand and its green bluff topped with little silent cottages, was spread like a picture before him. It was very near to him then, but he was impressed as one who, in a gallery, looks at a scene from Brittany or Algiers.

He thought: "I am going to drown? Can it be possible? Can it be possible? Can it be possible?" Perhaps an individual must consider his own death to be the final phenomenon of nature.

But later a wave perhaps whirled him out of this small deadly current, for he found suddenly that he could again make progress toward the shore. Later still he was aware that the captain, clinging with one hand to the keel of the dinghy, had his face turned away from the shore and toward him, and was calling his name. "Come to the boat! Come to the boat!"

In his struggle to reach the captain and the boat, he reflected 230 that when one gets properly wearied drowning must really be a comfortable arrangement — a cessation of hostilities accompanied by a large degree of relief; and he was glad of it, for the main thing in his mind for some moments had been horror of the temporary agony. He did not wish to be hurt.

Presently he saw a man running along the shore. He was undressing with most remarkable speed. Coat, trousers, shirt, everything flew magically off him.

"Come to the boat!" called the captain.

"All right, Captain." As the correspondent paddled, he saw the captain let himself down to bottom and leave the boat. Then the correspondent performed his one little marvel of the voyage. A large wave caught him and flung him with ease and supreme speed completely over the boat and far beyond it. It struck him even then as an event in gymnastics and a true miracle of the sea. An overturned boat in the surf is not a plaything to a swimming man.

The correspondent arrived in water that reached only to his waist, but his condition did not enable him to stand for more than a moment. Each wave knocked him into a heap, and the undertow pulled at him.

Then he saw the man who had been running and undressing, 235 and undressing and running, come bounding into the water. He dragged ashore the cook, and then waded toward the captain; but the captain waved him away and sent him to the correspondent. He was naked — naked as a tree in winter; but a halo was about his head, and he shone like a saint. He gave a strong pull, and a long drag, and a bully heave at the correspondent's hand. The correspondent, schooled in the minor formulae, said, "Thanks, old man." But suddenly the man cried, "What's that?" He pointed a swift finger. The correspondent said, "Go."

In the shallows, face downward, lay the oiler. His forehead touched sand that was periodically, between each wave, clear of the sea.

The correspondent did not know all that transpired afterward. When he achieved safe ground he fell, striking the sand with each particular part of his body. It was as if he had dropped from a roof, but the thud was grateful to him.

It seems that instantly the beach was populated with men with blankets, clothes, and flasks, and women with coffee-pots and all the remedies sacred to their minds. The welcome of the land to the men from the sea was warm and generous; but a still and dripping shape was carried slowly up the beach, and the land's welcome for it could only be the different and sinister hospitality of the grave.

When it came night, the white waves paced to and fro in the moonlight, and the wind brought the sound of the great sea's voice to the men on the shore, and they felt that they could then be interpreters.

Questions

Consider these five paragraphs.

(1) . . . Later still he was aware that the captain, clinging with one hand to the keel of the dinghy, had his face turned away from the shore and toward him, and was calling his name. "Come to the boat! Come to the boat!"

(2) In his struggle to reach the captain and the boat, he reflected that when one gets properly wearied drowning must really be a comfortable arrangement — a cessation of hostilities accompanied by a large degree of relief; and he was glad of it, for the main thing in his mind for some moments had been horror of the temporary agony. He did not wish to be hurt.

(3) Presently he saw a man running along the shore. He was undressing with most remarkable speed. Coat, trousers, shirt, everything flew magically off him.

(4) "Come to the boat!" called the captain.

(5) "All right, Captain." (paras. 229–233)

1. One of our questions at the end of paragraph 1 concerns whether the correspondent understands why the captain is telling him to come to the boat. What else are we unsure about here?

2. A question at the end of paragraph 2 concerns whether this is, for the correspondent, the moment of surrender. What other uncertainties do we bring to life here?

3. At the end of paragraph 3 we ask whether the runner on shore is or isn't a phantasm. What other uncertainties do we bring to life here?

4. Is uncertainty ended at last when we read the final sentence of the story? What question might we ask here?

ERNEST HEMINGWAY   (1899–1961)
Hills Like White Elephants

The hills across the valley of the Ebro were long and white. On this side there was no shade and no trees and the station was between two lines of rails in the sun. Close against the side of the station there was the warm shadow of the building and a curtain, made of strings of bamboo beads, hung across the open door into the bar, to keep out flies. The American and the girl with him sat at a table in the shade, outside the building. It was very hot and the express from Barcelona would come in forty minutes. It stopped at this junction for two minutes and went on to Madrid.

"What should we drink?" the girl asked. She had taken off her hat and put it on the table.

"It's pretty hot," the man said.

"Let's drink beer."

"Dos cervezas," the man said into the curtain.   5

"Big ones?" a woman asked from the doorway.

"Yes. Two big ones."

The woman brought two glasses of beer and two felt pads. She put the felt pads and the beer glasses on the table and looked at the man and the girl. The girl was looking off at the line of hills. They were white in the sun and the country was brown and dry.

"They look like white elephants," she said.

"I've never seen one," the man drank his beer.   10

"No, you wouldn't have."

"I might have," the man said. "Just because you say I wouldn't have doesn't prove anything."

The girl looked at the bead curtain. "They've painted something on it," she said. "What does it say?"

"Anis del Toro. It's a drink."

"Could we try it?"   15

The man called "Listen" through the curtain. The woman came out from the bar.

"Four reales."

"We want two Anis del Toro."

"With water?"

"Do you want it with water?"   20

"I don't know," the girl said. "Is it good with water?"

"It's all right."

"You want them with water?" asked the woman.

"Yes, with water."

"It tastes like licorice," the girl said and put the glass down.   25
"That's the way with everything."

"Yes," said the girl. "Everything tastes of licorice. Especially
all the things you've waited so long for, like absinthe."

"Oh, cut it out."

"You started it," the girl said. "I was being amused. I was
having a fine time."

"Well, let's try and have a fine time."   30

"All right. I was trying. I said the mountains looked like
white elephants. Wasn't that bright?"

"That was bright."

"I wanted to try this new drink. That's all we do, isn't it —
look at things and try new drinks?"

"I guess so."

The girl looked across at the hills.   35

"They're lovely hills," she said. "They don't really look like
white elephants. I just meant the coloring of their skin through
the trees."

"Should we have another drink?"

"All right."

The warm wind blew the bead curtain against the table.

"The beer's nice and cool," the man said.   40

"It's lovely," the girl said.

"It's really an awfully simple operation, Jig," the man said.
"It's not really an operation at all."

The girl looked at the ground the table legs rested on.

"I know you wouldn't mind it, Jig. It's really not anything. It's
just to let the air in."

The girl did not say anything.   45

"I'll go with you and I'll stay with you all the time. They just
let the air in and then it's all perfectly natural."

"Then what will we do afterward?"

"We'll be fine afterward. Just like we were before."

"What makes you think so?"

"That's the only thing that bothers us. It's the only thing that's   50
made us unhappy."

The girl looked at the bead curtain, put her hand out and
took hold of two of the strings of beads.

"And you think then we'll be all right and be happy."

"I know we will. You don't have to be afraid. I've known lots
of people that have done it."

"So have I," said the girl. "And afterward they were all so
happy."

"Well," the man said, "if you don't want to you don't have to.   55

I wouldn't have you do it if you didn't want to. But I know it's perfectly simple."

"And you really want to?"

"I think it's the best thing to do. But I don't want you to do it if you don't really want to."

"And if I do it you'll be happy and things will be like they were and you'll love me?"

"I love you now. You know I love you."

"I know. But if I do it, then it will be nice again if I say things are like white elephants, and you'll like it?" 60

"I'll love it. I love it now but I just can't think about it. You know how I get when I worry."

"If I do it you won't ever worry?"

"I won't worry about that because it's perfectly simple."

"Then I'll do it. Because I don't care about me."

"What do you mean?" 65

"I don't care about me."

"Well, I care about you."

"Oh, yes. But I don't care about me. And I'll do it and then everything will be fine."

"I don't want you to do it if you feel that way."

The girl stood up and walked to the end of the station. 70 Across, on the other side, were fields of grain and trees along the banks of the Ebro. Far away, beyond the river, were mountains. The shadow of a cloud moved across the field of grain and she saw the river through the trees.

"And we could have all this," she said. "And we could have everything and every day we make it more impossible."

"What did you say?"

"I said we could have everything."

"We can have everything."

"No, we can't." 75

"We can have the whole world."

"No, we can't."

"We can go everywhere."

"No, we can't. It isn't ours any more."

"It's ours." 80

"No, it isn't. And once they take it away, you never get it back."

"But they haven't taken it away."

"We'll wait and see."

"Come on back in the shade," he said. "You mustn't feel that way."

"I don't feel any way," the girl said. "I just know things." 85

"I don't want you to do anything that you don't want to do ——"

"Nor that isn't good for me," she said. "I know. Could we have another beer?"

"All right. But you've got to realize ——"

"I realize," the girl said. "Can't we maybe stop talking?"

They sat down at the table and the girl looked across at the hills on the dry side of the valley and the man looked at her and at the table.

"You've got to realize," he said, "that I don't want you to do it if you don't want to. I'm perfectly willing to go through with it if it means anything to you."

"Doesn't it mean anything to you? We could get along."

"Of course it does. But I don't want anybody but you. I don't want any one else. And I know it's perfectly simple."

"Yes, you know it's perfectly simple."

"It's all right for you to say that, but I do know it."

"Would you do something for me now?"

"I'd do anything for you."

"Would you please please please please please please please stop talking?"

He did not say anything but looked at the bags against the wall of the station. There were labels on them from all the hotels where they had spent nights.

"But I don't want you to," he said, "I don't care anything about it."

"I'll scream," the girl said.

The woman came out through the curtains with two glasses of beer and put them down on the damp felt pads. "The train comes in five minutes," she said.

"What did she say?" asked the girl.

"That the train is coming in five minutes."

The girl smiled brightly at the woman, to thank her.

"I'd better take the bags over to the other side of the station," the man said. She smiled at him.

"All right. Then come back and we'll finish the beer."

He picked up the two heavy bags and carried them around the station to the other tracks. He looked up the tracks but could not see the train. Coming back, he walked through the barroom, where people waiting for the train were drinking. He drank an Anis at the bar and looked at the people. They were all waiting reasonably for the train. He went out through the bead curtain. She was sitting at the table and smiled at him. "Do you feel better?" he asked.

"I feel fine," she said. "There's nothing wrong with me. I feel 110
fine."

Questions

1. What is the focus of our uncertainty here? What questions do
    we ask?

    "No, you wouldn't have."
    "I might have," the man said. "Just because you say I wouldn't
    have doesn't prove anything." (paras. 11–12)

2. What is the focus of our uncertainty here? What questions
    are we now asking?

    "I won't worry about that because it's perfectly simple."
    "Then I'll do it. Because I don't care about me." (63–64)

3. What is the focus of uncertainty here? What questions are we
    asking?

    "But I don't want you to," he said, "I don't care anything
    about it."
    "I'll scream," the girl said. (100–101)

4. Where are we at the end of this story?

    "Do you feel better?" he asked.
    "I feel fine," she said. "There's nothing wrong with me. I feel
    fine." (109–110)

    What uncertainties — new questions — are generated by
    Jig's final comment ("I feel fine")?

15

Key Passages

A story sets forth a series of events — physical, emotional, intellectual. Its pace is usually steady, seemingly uninterruptible; seldom does a narrator come to center stage with explicit interpretive comment. Yet out of our continuing, close, silent collaboration with writers, we as readers manage to define comprehensive order and meaning and spell it out in our own terms. We often do this by organizing our perceptions — after we have read the entire story — into an extended commentary on a single section of the story. The section — a few sentences, a paragraph, sometimes a bit of conversation — is one that we ourselves believe, on the basis of our reading, casts direct light upon every other part of the story. To center our understandings of the story as a whole, we bring the section to life as a *key passage*.

CHOOSING KEY PASSAGES

The choice of a key passage is, obviously, a creative act. Writers don't compose by inserting key passages into their narratives like clues in a treasure hunt. We, as readers, arrive *on our own* at decisions about what should be treated as a key passage. We settle on a definition of the subject of the story — our own definition expressed in our own terms. In addition, we reorganize the story's time frame, singling out a few sentences to be considered at a quite different pace from that at which we originally read them. And we commit ourselves to an especially intensive engagement with the words in question — because what first drew us to the passage was the sense that these particular words, if set under concentrated examination, would have the power to illuminate practically every other moment in the text.

Look back, for a moment, at Stephen Crane's "The Open Boat" (p. 797). It's plain that the entire course of events that story describes has been governed by accident. Our suspense questions continually shifted the focus of our uncertainty, but, to the very end, the answers to those questions provided no basis whatever for logical interpretation of what happened. Why, for example, were the correspondent and captain saved but not their comrade, the oiler? What solid reasons could possibly be given to justify either the death or the survival? What else but accident ruled this episode from beginning to end?

As we look back over the story, the absence of any principle that could serve as a reasonable explanation of the happenings becomes indisputable. And that absence suggests a possible subject for the story — *the irrationality of life in this world* — that's large enough to encompass both the adventure and the philosophy. We "try on" that subject in a manner paralleling the way we tried on a field of knowledge when bringing ideas to life in a poem, play, or story (see Chapters 4 and 5). And in trying it on we alert ourselves to passages that seem to speak directly to the subject we ourselves are generating.

DEVELOPING A KEY PASSAGE

A key passage from "The Open Boat" emerges in the sentences describing the event that saved the correspondent:

> Then the correspondent performed his one little marvel of the voyage. A large wave caught him and flung him with ease and supreme speed completely over the boat and far beyond it. It struck him even then as an event in gymnastics and a true miracle of the sea. An overturned boat in the surf is not a plaything to a swimming man. (para. 233)

The language of these sentences, when considered in relation to "irrationality," seems charged with implications. Clearly the assertion that the correspondent "performed his one little marvel" is ironic. He may have had an odd sense that somehow he had saved himself, but it's plain that that feeling had no basis in fact. There had been for him, as for the others, an immense and terrible struggle — yet at the last moment safety arrived with total ease, in utter contradiction of the desperation preceding it. What is more, release, through the capricious "large wave," could perfectly easily have come not as an escape onto the sand but as a life-ending collision with the overturned boat. The correspondent thinks of the event as a "marvel," an "event in gymnastics," and a "true miracle." But we as readers see through these attempts to find an explanatory label for this rescue. We see that the behavior of the world doesn't accord with our categories — unless we're prepared to say that the death of the oiler is just as much a miracle and marvel and gymnastic event as is the correspondent's survival. At the same time, we also see that, for the survivor, the temptation is strong to find rationality — the blessed rationality of a "true miracle" — in events in which rationality is in fact not discernible.

In bringing to life these sentences as a key passage, we read them as a comment on the whole action of the story, not only on the feelings of the individual survivors. We perceive the correspondent's natural gratitude for the "miracle" as at once an understandable response and a mistake. We move from the highly immediate, precise details of dangerous hours at sea to the largest questions human beings can ask: questions about the presence or absence of order in the universe. Why is this creature drowned and that one saved? Why is nature seemingly as oblivious to marvels as to disasters? Why do we give ourselves so passionately to the belief that we know the difference between the two?

As it happens, our chosen key passage here coincides with the climax or turning point of the story. But that need not be true. We might have chosen the opening paragraph of the story as our key passage — or we might have chosen the mysterious paragraph about the running man on shore. Certainly both these moments could be evoked as suggestive of a fundamental irrationality at the core of life in this world. Readers can create key passages from a wide variety of materials. They may choose a moment when central characters discover an aspect of themselves hitherto unrecognized and resolve to change their nature or behavior. Such a passage occurs in the final half-dozen paragraphs of Anton Chekhov's "The Lady with the Pet Dog" (p. 766). Or readers may choose a moment at which an entire situation undergoes significant reversal in the mind of a character. Such a reversal takes place in Frank O'Connor's "My Oedipus Complex" (p. 738) when the narrator's feeling for his father changes from anger to pity.

The point that can't be overemphasized is that we ourselves *are* the creators. Key passages may consist of a moment of silence or of a striking gesture or of a swift change of mood. We may find our key early in a story or late or in the middle. Always, though, our aim in choosing is to place ourselves in position to make an attentive, organized survey of the text as a whole. We want to be able to think, talk, and write about a story without collapsing into unsupported generalizations. The ultimate goal is to achieve the kind of retrospective look that opens up relations among a wide variety of details both of language and of feeling.

ASKING QUESTIONS
ABOUT KEY PASSAGES

You can practice choosing key passages and justifying your choices with any story (and with many poems) in *Close Imagining*. A good first step, as already indicated, is to come to a decision about what seems to be the most interesting subject engaged. Next comes a survey of the text for short passages that bring that subject, or theme, into sharp focus. In order for you to develop the passage you choose as a key passage, you will need to ask questions about how its specific details link up with the life of the work as a whole. The final step is to answer those questions in a way that evokes the full experience of the story.

KATHERINE MANSFIELD   (1888–1923)
A Dill Pickle

And then, after six years, she saw him again. He was seated at one of those little bamboo tables decorated with a Japanese vase of paper daffodils. There was a tall plate of fruit in front of him, and very carefully, in a way she recognized immediately as his "special" way, he was peeling an orange.

He must have felt that shock of recognition in her for he looked up and met her eyes. Incredible! He didn't know her! She smiled; he frowned. She came towards him. He closed his eyes an instant, but opening them his face lit up as though he had struck a match in a dark room. He laid down the orange and pushed back his chair, and she took her little warm hand out of her muff and gave it to him.

"Vera!" he exclaimed. "How strange. Really, for a moment I didn't know you. Won't you sit down? You've had lunch? Won't you have some coffee?"

She hesitated, but of course she meant to.

"Yes, I'd like some coffee." And she sat down opposite him.   5

"You've changed. You've changed very much," he said, staring at her with that eager, lighted look. "You look so well. I've never seen you look so well before."

"Really?" She raised her veil and unbuttoned her high fur collar. "I don't feel very well. I can't bear this weather, you know."

"Ah, no. You hate the cold. . . ."

"Loathe it." She shuddered. "And the worst of it is that the older one grows . . ."

He interrupted her. "Excuse me," and tapped on the table   10 for the waitress. "Please bring some coffee and cream." To her: "You are sure you won't eat anything? Some fruit, perhaps. The fruit here is very good."

"No, thanks. Nothing."

"Then that's settled." And smiling just a hint too broadly he took up the orange again. "You were saying — the older one grows — "

"The colder," she laughed. But she was thinking how well she remembered that trick of his — the trick of interrupting her — and of how it used to exasperate her six years ago. She used to feel then as though he, quite suddenly, in the middle of what she was saying, put his hand over her lips, turned from her, attended to something different, and then took his hand away, and with just the same slightly too broad smile, gave her his attention again. . . . Now we are ready. That is settled.

"The colder!" He echoed her words, laughing too. "Ah, ah. You still say the same things. And there is another thing about you that is not changed at all — your beautiful voice — your beautiful way of speaking." Now he was very grave; he leaned towards her, and she smelled the warm, stinging scent of the orange peel. "You have only to say one word and I would know your voice among all other voices. I don't know what it is — I've often wondered — that makes your voice such a — haunting memory. . . . Do you remember that first afternoon we spent together at Kew Gardens? You were so surprised because I did not know the names of any flowers. I am still just as ignorant for all your telling me. But whenever it is very fine and warm, and I see some bright colors — it's awfully strange — I hear your voice saying: 'Geranium, marigold, and verbena.' And I feel those three words are all I recall of some forgotten, heavenly language. . . . You remember that afternoon?"

"Oh, yes, very well." She drew a long, soft breath, as though 15 the paper daffodils between them were almost too sweet to bear. Yet, what had remained in her mind of that particular afternoon was an absurd scene over the tea table. A great many people taking tea in a Chinese pagoda, and he behaving like a maniac about the wasps — waving them away, flapping at them with his straw hat, serious and infuriated out of all proportion to the occasion. How delighted the sniggering tea drinkers had been. And how she had suffered.

But now, as he spoke, that memory faded. His was the truer. Yes, it had been a wonderful afternoon, full of geranium and marigold and verbena, and — warm sunshine. Her thoughts lingered over the last two words as though she sang them.

In the warmth, as it were, another memory unfolded. She saw herself sitting on a lawn. He lay beside her, and suddenly, after a long silence, he rolled over and put his head in her lap.

"I wish," he said, in a low, troubled voice, "I wish that I had taken poison and were about to die — here now!"

At that moment a little girl in a white dress, holding a long, dripping water lily, dodged from behind a bush, stared at them, and dodged back again. But he did not see. She leaned over him.

"Ah, why do you say that? I could not say that." 20

But he gave a kind of soft moan, and taking her hand he held it to his cheek.

"Because I know I am going to love you too much — far too much. And I shall suffer so terribly, Vera, because you never, never will love me."

He was certainly far better looking now than he had been then. He had lost all that dreamy vagueness and indecision. Now he had the air of a man who has found his place in life, and fills it with a confidence and an assurance which was, to say the least, impressive. He must have made money, too. His clothes were admirable, and at that moment he pulled a Russian cigarette case out of his pocket.

"Won't you smoke?"

"Yes, I will." She hovered over them. "They look very good." 25

"I think they are. I get them made for me by a little man in St. James's Street. I don't smoke very much. I'm not like you — but when I do, they must be delicious, very fresh cigarettes. Smoking isn't a habit with me; it's a luxury — like perfume. Are you still so fond of perfumes? Ah, when I was in Russia . . ."

She broke in: "You've really been to Russia?"

"Oh, yes. I was there for over a year. Have you forgotten how we used to talk of going there?"

"No, I've not forgotten."

He gave a strange half laugh and leaned back in his chair. 30 "Isn't it curious, I have really carried out all those journeys that we planned. Yes, I have been to all those places that we talked of, and stayed in them long enough to — as you used to say, 'air oneself' in them. In fact, I have spent the last three years of my life travelling all the time. Spain, Corsica, Siberia, Russia, Egypt. The only country left is China, and I mean to go there, too, when the war is over."

As he spoke, so lightly, tapping the end of his cigarette against the ashtray, she felt the strange beast that had slumbered so long within her bosom stir, stretch itself, yawn, prick up its ears, and suddenly bound to its feet, and fix its longing, hungry stare upon those far away places. But all she said was, smiling gently: "How I envy you."

He accepted that. "It has been," he said, "very wonderful — especially Russia. Russia was all that we had imagined, and far, far more. I even spent some days on a river boat on the Volga. Do you remember that boatman's song that you used to play?"

"Yes." It began to play in her mind as she spoke.

"Do you ever play it now?"

"No, I've no piano." 35

He was amazed at that. "But what has become of your beautiful piano?"

She made a little grimace. "Sold. Ages ago."

"But you were so fond of music," he wondered.

"I've no time for it now," said she.

He let it go at that. "That river life," he went on, "is some- 40 thing quite special. After a day or two you cannot realize that you have ever known another. And it is not necessary to know the language — the life of the boat creates a bond between you and the people that's more than sufficient. You eat with them, pass the day with them, and in the evening there is that endless singing."

She shivered, hearing the boatman's song break out again loud and tragic, and seeing the boat floating on the darkening river with melancholy trees on either side. . . . "Yes, I should like that," said she, stroking her muff.

"You'd like almost everything about Russian life," he said warmly. "It's so informal, so impulsive, so free without question. And then the peasants are so splendid. They are such human beings — yes, that is it. Even the man who drives your carriage has — has some real part in what is happening. I remember the evening a party of us, two friends of mine and the wife of one of them, went for a picnic by the Black Sea. We took supper and champagne and ate and drank on the grass. And while we were eating the coachman came up. 'Have a dill pickle,' he said. He wanted to share with us. That seemed to me so right, so — you know what I mean?"

And she seemed at that moment to be sitting on the grass beside the mysteriously Black Sea, black as velvet, and rippling against the banks in silent, velvet waves. She saw the carriage drawn up to one side of the road, and the little group on the grass, their faces and hands white in the moonlight. She saw the pale dress of the woman outspread and her folded parasol, lying on the grass like a huge pearl crochet hook. Apart from them, with his supper in a cloth on his knees, sat the coachman. "Have a dill pickle," said he, and although she was not certain what a dill pickle was, she saw the greenish glass jar with a red chili like a parrot's beak glimmering through. She sucked in her cheeks; the dill pickle was terribly sour. . . .

"Yes, I know perfectly what you mean," she said.

In the pause that followed they looked at each other. In the 45 past when they had looked at each other like that they had felt such a boundless understanding between them that their souls had, as it were, put their arms round each other and dropped into the same sea, content to be drowned, like mournful lovers. But now, the surprising thing was that it was he who held back. He who said:

"What a marvellous listener you are. When you look at me with those wild eyes I feel that I could tell you things that I would never breathe to another human being."

Was there just a hint of mockery in his voice or was it her fancy? She could not be sure.

"Before I met you," he said, "I had never spoken of myself to anybody. How well I remember one night, the night that I brought you the little Christmas tree, telling you all about my childhood. And of how I was so miserable that I ran away and lived under a cart in our yard for two days without being discovered. And you listened, and your eyes shone, and I felt that you had even made the little Christmas tree listen too, as in a fairy story."

But of that evening she had remembered a little pot of caviar. It had cost seven and sixpence. He could not get over it. Think of it — a tiny jar like that costing seven and sixpence. While she ate it he watched her, delighted and shocked.

"No, really, that is eating money. You could not get seven shillings into a little pot that size. Only think of the profit they must make...." And he had begun some immensely complicated calculations.... But now good-bye to the caviar. The Christmas tree was on the table, and the little boy lay under the cart with his head pillowed on the yard dog. 50

"The dog was called Bosun," she cried delightedly.

But he did not follow. "Which dog? Had you a dog? I don't remember a dog at all."

"No, no. I mean the yard dog when you were a little boy." He laughed and snapped the cigarette case to.

"Was he? Do you know I had forgotten that. It seems such ages ago. I cannot believe that it is only six years. After I had recognized you to-day — I had to take such a leap — I had to take a leap over my whole life to get back to that time. I was such a kid then." He drummed on the table. "I've often thought how I must have bored you. And now I understand so perfectly why you wrote to me as you did — although at the time that letter nearly finished my life. I found it again the other day, and I couldn't help laughing as I read it. It was so clever — such a true picture of me." He glanced up. "You're not going?"

She had buttoned her collar again and drawn down her veil. 55

"Yes, I am afraid I must," she said, and managed a smile. Now she knew that he had been mocking.

"Ah, no, please," he pleaded. "Don't go just for a moment," and he caught up one of her gloves from the table and clutched at it as if that would hold her. "I see so few people to talk to nowadays, that I have turned into a sort of barbarian," he said. "Have I said something to hurt you?"

"Not a bit," she lied. But as she watched him draw her glove through his fingers, gently, gently, her anger really did die down, and besides, at the moment he looked more like himself of six years ago....

"What I really wanted then," he said softly, "was to be a sort of carpet — to make myself into a sort of carpet for you to walk on so that you need not be hurt by the sharp stones and the mud that you hated so. It was nothing more positive than that — nothing more selfish. Only I did desire, eventually, to turn into a magic carpet and carry you away to all those lands you longed to see."

As he spoke she lifted her head as though she drank some- 60
thing; the strange beast in her bosom began to purr. . . .

"I felt that you were more lonely than anybody else in the
world," he went on, "and yet, perhaps, that you were the only
person in the world who was really, truly alive. Born out of your
time," he murmured, stroking the glove, "fated."

Ah, God! What had she done! How had she dared to throw
away her happiness like this. This was the only man who had ever
understood her. Was it too late? Could it be too late? *She* was that
glove that he held in his fingers. . . .

"And then the fact that you had no friends and never had
made friends with people. How I understood that, for neither
had I. Is it just the same now"

"Yes," she breathed. "Just the same. I am as alone as ever."

"So am I," he laughed gently, "just the same."   65

Suddenly with a quick gesture he handed her back the glove
and scraped his chair on the floor. "But what seemed to me so
mysterious then is perfectly plain to me now. And to you, too, of
course. . . . It simply was that we were such egoists, so self-
engrossed, so wrapped up in ourselves that we hadn't a corner in
our hearts for anybody else. Do you know," he cried, naive and
hearty, and dreadfully like another side of that old self again,
"I began studying a Mind System when I was in Russia, and I
found that we were not peculiar at all. It's quite a well known
form of . . ."

She had gone. He sat there, thunder-struck, astounded beyond words. . . . And then he asked the waitress for his bill.

"But the cream has not been touched," he said. "Please do
not charge me for it."

Questions

1. What subject or subjects do you find at the center of "A Dill
    Pickle"?
2. What passages in the story seem to you to focus that subject
    or subjects most directly?
3. Choose one of these passages and develop it as a key passage.
    Show how your reading of specific language in it draws to-
    gether the story's details and illuminates the work as a whole.
4. Compare the key passage you have developed with the key
    passage developed in the response that follows.

Response

> "But the cream has not been touched," he said. "Please do not
> charge me for it." (para. 68)

EDITOR: "A Dill Pickle" is about egotism, self-misrepresentation,
and irresponsible trifling with feelings. And the passage in which
we see most clearly into the heart of the fraud is, arguably, the
story's very last sentence. Earlier we've been obliged, for several
reasons, to pull back at least slightly from condemnation of the
man. Here, though, he seems to lay himself bare — shows that
both his professed sensitivity to his former beloved and his
dismay at her departure ("He sat there, thunder-struck, astounded," 67) are phony. This self-lover can't be fazed, can't be
discommoded or shaken for longer than a second by anybody
else's behavior. He is the original hard nose, unremittingly concerned about his own advantage: a basic bottom-line man, anxious — in the middle of a fake emotional crisis — about not
being charged for the cream. His last order to the waitress is, like
his first, a gesture of control, a prop for ego. Life as he lives it is a
never-ending game of putting others down.

   The man's friend Vera is by no means blind to his defects.
She remembers his exasperating trick of cutting her off in mid-
sentence, putting her on hold, as we would now say, as though
nothing mattered save his following through on whatever impulse momentarily seized his head. (Such as the impulse to order
coffee and cream.) She may miss — during this brief meeting —
a few of his gestures of superiority, as for example his preening
about nonaddiction ("I'm not like you. . . . Smoking isn't a habit
with me," 26). But she was once clear enough about him to write
an analysis, accurate yet probably more loving than scathing, of
his character, *and* to break off with him. And she's freshly alerted
to his capacity for cruelty by his tactless insistence that both her
letter and their breakup now seem comic to him ("I couldn't help
laughing," 54).

   But still, despite all her knowledge, he's able to cast a spell.
His stories — the anecdote about the Russian coachman who
offers the pickle — are provocative and filled with apparent
relish of life. And his flattery is immensely guileful ("you were
the only person in the world who was really, truly alive," 61). The
minute he turns on the intensity, turns up his confessional mode

("you had no friends. . . . neither had I," 63), he makes himself irresistible to her all over again. He plays viciously with her, though, extracting acknowledgments of her helplessness ("I am as alone as ever," 64), cynically insinuating — for the pleasure of observing his own manipulative power — that he might like to resume their interrupted affair.

And then, the moment he sees her vulnerability, he abruptly humiliates her — as he doubtless often did in the past. This time, to be sure, Vera belatedly wakes up. Her response to humiliation is a gesture that cuts *him* off: She walks out.

That quick moment of turnabout-revenge helps us to see the half-comic, half-infuriating vanity on both sides — the unsatis- fied hunger in Vera for confirmation that she is the only "really, truly alive" person on earth, the heartless hunger in the man for proof of his capacity to enslave others with a few words. And there's exceptional subtlety in the basic rhythm of the story — the repeated movement from bewitchment to repulsion, cap- tivation to disenchantment.

It is the final sentence, however, that allows us the fullest glimpse of Mansfield's theme. One second before, at Vera's abrupt, awakened departure, the man is depicted as — by his standards — "thunder-struck, astounded beyond words." But, as we saw, no response by this fellow to another human being can last longer than a second. Swiftly he's back in control, dumping that contrived gentle laugh and revealing his stony nature — to a waitress. Mansfield has her eye on both sides of the coin of "charm." In "A Dill Pickle" she reminds us that people who go far out of their way to seem winning are often characters with no commitment on earth except to win. She reminds us, too, that such characters have a taste *only* for victory itself — not for the prizes, whether beautiful women . . . or ounces of cream.

BERNARD MALAMUD   (1914–1986)
The Magic Barrel

Not long ago there lived in uptown New York, in a small, almost meager room, though crowded with books, Leo Finkle, a rabbinical student at the Yeshiva University. Finkle, after six years of study, was to be ordained in June and had been advised by an acquaintance that he might find it easier to win himself a

congregation if he were married. Since he had no present prospects of marriage, after two tormented days of turning it over in
his mind, he called in Pinye Salzman, a marriage broker whose
two-line advertisement he had read in the *Forward*.

The matchmaker appeared one night out of the dark fourth-
floor hallway of the graystone rooming house where Finkle lived,
grasping a black, strapped portfolio that had been worn thin
with use. Salzman, who had been long in the business, was of
slight but dignified build, wearing an old hat, and an overcoat
too short and tight for him. He smelled frankly of fish, which he
loved to eat, and although he was missing a few teeth, his presence was not displeasing, because of an amiable manner curiously contrasted with mournful eyes. His voice, his lips, his wisp
of beard, his bony fingers were animated, but give him a moment
of repose and his mild blue eyes revealed a depth of sadness, a
characteristic that put Leo a little at ease although the situation,
for him, was inherently tense.

He at once informed Salzman why he had asked him to
come, explaining that but for his parents, who had married comparatively late in life, he was alone in the world. He had for six
years devoted himself almost entirely to his studies, as a result of
which, understandably, he had found himself without time for
social life and the company of young women. Therefore he
thought it the better part of trial and error — of embarrassing
fumbling — to call in an experienced person to advise him on
these matters. He remarked in passing that the function of the
marriage broker was ancient and honorable, highly approved in
the Jewish community, because it made practical the necessary
without hindering joy. Moreover, his own parents had been
brought together by a matchmaker. They had made, if not a fi-
nancially profitable marriage — since neither had possessed any
worldly goods to speak of — at least a successful one in the sense
of their everlasting devotion to each other. Salzman listened in
embarrassed surprise, sensing a sort of apology. Later, however,
he experienced a glow of pride in his work, an emotion that had
left him years ago, and he heartily approved of Finkle.

The two went to their business. Leo had led Salzman to the
only clear place in the room, a table near a window that overlooked the lamp-lit city. He seated himself at the matchmaker's
side but facing him, attempting by an act of will to suppress the
unpleasant tickle in his throat. Salzman eagerly unstrapped his
portfolio and removed a loose rubber band from a thin packet of
much-handled cards. As he flipped through them, a gesture and
sound that physically hurt Leo, the student pretended not to see

and gazed steadfastly out the window. Although it was still February, winter was on its last legs, signs of which he had for the first time in years begun to notice. He now observed the round white moon, moving high in the sky through a cloud menagerie, and watched with half-open mouth as it penetrated a huge hen, and dropped out of her like an egg laying itself. Salzman, though pretending through eyeglasses he had just slipped on to be engaged in scanning the writing on the cards, stole occasional glances at the young man's distinguished face, noting with pleasure the long, severe scholar's nose, brown eyes heavy with learning, sensitive yet ascetic lips, and a certain almost hollow quality of the dark cheeks. He gazed around at shelves upon shelves of books and let out a soft, contented sigh.

When Leo's eyes fell upon the cards, he counted six spread 5 out in Salzman's hand.

"So few?" he asked in disappointment.

"You wouldn't believe me how much cards I got in my office," Salzman replied. "The drawers are already filled to the top, so I keep them now in a barrel, but is every girl good for a new rabbi?"

Leo blushed at this, regretting all he had revealed of himself in a curriculum vitae he had sent to Salzman. He had thought it best to acquaint him with his strict standards and specifications, but in having done so, felt he had told the marriage broker more than was absolutely necessary.

He hesitantly inquired, "Do you keep photographs of your clients on file?"

"First comes family, amount of dowry, also what kind prom- 10 ises," Salzman replied, unbuttoning his tight coat and settling himself in the chair. "After comes pictures, rabbi."

"Call me Mr. Finkle. I'm not yet a rabbi."

Salzman said he would, but instead called him doctor, which he changed to rabbi when Leo was not listening too attentively.

Salzman adjusted his horn-rimmed spectacles, gently cleared his throat, and read in an eager voice the contents of the top card:

"Sophie P. Twenty-four years. Widow one year. No children. Educated high school and two years college. Father promises eight thousand dollars. Has wonderful wholesale business. Also real estate. On the mother's side comes teachers, also one actor. Well known on Second Avenue."

Leo gazed up in surprise. "Did you say a widow?"   15

"A widow don't mean spoiled, rabbi. She lived with her husband maybe four months. He was a sick boy she made a mistake to marry him."

"Marrying a widow has never entered my mind."

"This is because you have no experience. A widow, especially if she is young and healthy like this girl, is a wonderful person to marry. She will be thankful to you the rest of her life. Believe me, if I was looking now for a bride, I would marry a widow."

Leo reflected, then shook his head.

Salzman hunched his shoulders in an almost imperceptible   20 gesture of disappointment. He placed the card down on the wooden table and began to read another:

"Lily H. High school teacher. Regular. Not a substitute. Has savings and new Dodge car. Lived in Paris one year. Father is successful dentist thirty-five years. Interested in professional man. Well-Americanized family. Wonderful opportunity.

"I know her personally," said Salzman. "I wish you could see this girl. She is a doll. Also very intelligent. All day you could talk to her about books and theyater and what not. She also knows current events."

"I don't believe you mentioned her age?"

"Her age?" Salzman said, raising his brows. "Her age is thirty-two years."

Leo said after a while, "I'm afraid that seems a little too old."   25

Salzman let out a laugh. "So how old are you, rabbi?"

"Twenty-seven."

"So what is the difference, tell me, between twenty-seven and thirty-two? My own wife is seven years older than me. So what did I suffer? — Nothing. If Rothschild's a daughter wants to marry you, would you say on account her age, no?"

"Yes," Leo said dryly.

Salzman shook off the no in the yes. "Five years don't mean a   30 thing. I give you my word that when you will live with her for one week you will forget her age. What does it mean five years — that she lived more and knows more than somebody who is younger? On this girl, God bless her, years are not wasted. Each one that it comes makes better the bargain."

"What subject does she teach in high school?"

"Languages. If you heard the way she speaks French, you will think it is music. I am in the business twenty-five years, and I recommend her with my whole heart. Believe me, I know what I'm talking, rabbi."

"What's on the next card?" Leo said abruptly.

Salzman reluctantly turned up the third card:

"Ruth K. Nineteen years. Honor student. Father offers thir- 35
teen thousand cash to the right bridegroom. He is a medical
doctor. Stomach specialist with marvelous practice. Brother-in-
law owns own garment business. Particular people."

Salzman looked as if he had read his trump card.

"Did you say nineteen?" Leo asked with interest.

"On the dot."

"Is she attractive?" He blushed. "Pretty?"

Salzman kissed his fingertips. "A little doll. On this I give 40
you my word. Let me call the father tonight and you will see what
means pretty."

But Leo was troubled. "You're sure she's that young?"

"This I am positive. The father will show you the birth certificate."

"Are you positive there isn't something wrong with her?" Leo
insisted.

"Who says there is wrong?"

"I don't understand why an American girl her age should go 45
to a marriage broker."

A smile spread over Salzman's face.

"So for the same reason you went, she comes."

Leo flushed. "I am pressed for time."

Salzman, realizing he had been tactless, quickly explained.
"The father came, not her. He wants she should have the best, so
he looks around himself. When we will locate the right boy he
will introduce him and encourage. This makes a better marriage
than if a young girl without experience takes for herself. I don't
have to tell you this."

"But don't you think this young girl believes in love?" Leo 50
spoke uneasily.

Salzman was about to guffaw but caught himself and said
soberly, "Love comes with the right person, not before."

Leo parted dry lips but did not speak. Noticing that Salzman
had snatched a glance at the next card, he cleverly asked, "How is
her health?"

"Perfect," Salzman said, breathing with difficulty. "Of
course, she is a little lame on her right foot from an auto accident
that it happened to her when she was twelve years, but nobody
notices on account she is so brilliant and also beautiful."

Leo got up heavily and went to the window. He felt curiously
bitter and upbraided himself for having called in the marriage
broker. Finally, he shook his head.

"Why not?" Salzman persisted, the pitch of his voice rising. 55

"Because I detest stomach specialists."

"So what do you care what is his business? After you marry her do you need him? Who says he must come every Friday night in your house?"

Ashamed of the way the talk was going, Leo dismissed Salzman, who went home with heavy, melancholy eyes.

Though he had felt only relief at the marriage broker's departure, Leo was in low spirits the next day. He explained it as arising from Salzman's failure to produce a suitable bride for him. He did not care for his type of clientele. But when Leo found himself hesitating whether to seek out another matchmaker, one more polished than Pinye, he wondered if it could be — his protestations to the contrary, and although he honored his father and mother — that he did not, in essence, care for the matchmaking institution? This thought he quickly put out of mind yet found himself still upset. All day he ran around in the woods — missed an important appointment, forgot to give out his laundry, walked out of a Broadway cafeteria without paying and had to run back with the ticket in his hand; had even not recognized his landlady in the street when she passed with a friend and courteously called out, "A good evening to you, Doctor Finkle." By nightfall, however, he had regained sufficient calm to sink his nose into a book and there found peace from his thoughts.

Almost at once there came a knock on the door. Before Leo could say enter, Salzman, commercial cupid, was standing in the room. His face was gray and meager, his expression hungry, and he looked as if he would expire on his feet. Yet the marriage broker managed, by some trick of the muscles, to display a broad smile.

"So good evening. I am invited?"

Leo nodded, disturbed to see him again, yet unwilling to ask the man to leave.

Beaming still, Salzman laid his portfolio on the table. "Rabbi, I got for you tonight good news."

"I've asked you not to call me rabbi. I'm still a student."

"Your worries are finished. I have for you a first-class bride."

"Leave me in peace concerning this subject." Leo pretended lack of interest.

"The world will dance at your wedding."

"Please, Mr. Salzman, no more."

"But first must come back my strength," Salzman said weakly. He fumbled with the portfolio straps and took out of the leather case an oily paper bag, from which he extracted a hard, seeded roll and a small smoked whitefish. With a quick motion

of his hand he stripped the fish out of its skin and began
ravenously to chew. "All day in a rush," he muttered.

Leo watched him eat.   70

"A sliced tomato you have maybe?" Salzman hesitantly inquired.

"No."

The marriage broker shut his eyes and ate. When he had
finished he carefully cleaned up the crumbs and rolled up the
remains of the fish, in the paper bag. His spectacled eyes roamed
the room until he discovered, amid some piles of books, a one-
burner gas stove. Lifting his hat he humbly asked, "A glass tea
you got, rabbi?"

Conscience-stricken, Leo rose and brewed the tea. He served
it with a chunk of lemon and two cubes of lump sugar, delighting
Salzman.

After he had drunk his tea, Salzman's strength and good   75
spirits were restored.

"So tell me, rabbi," he said amiably, "you considered some
more the three clients I mentioned yesterday?"

"There was no need to consider."

"Why not?"

"None of them suits me."

"What then suits you?"   80

Leo let it pass because he could give only a confused answer.

Without waiting for a reply, Salzman asked, "You remember
this girl I talked to you — the high school teacher?"

"Age thirty-two?"

But, surprisingly, Salzman's face lit in a smile. "Age twenty-
nine."

Leo shot him a look. "Reduced from thirty-two?"   85

"A mistake," Salzman avowed. "I talked today with the dentist. He took me to his safety deposit box and showed me the
birth certificate. She was twenty-nine years last August. They
made her a party in the mountains where she went for her vacation. When her father spoke to me the first time I forgot to write
the age and I told you thirty-two, but now I remember this was a
different client, a widow."

"The same one you told me about, I thought she was twenty-
four?"

"A different. Am I responsible that the world is filled with
widows?"

"No, but I'm not interested in them, nor, for that matter, in
schoolteachers."

Salzman pulled his clasped hands to his breast. Looking at   90 the ceiling he devoutly exclaimed, "Yiddishe kinder, what can I say to somebody that he is not interested in high school teachers? So what then you are interested?"

Leo flushed but controlled himself.

"In what else will you be interested," Salzman went on, "if you not interested in this fine girl that she speaks four languages and has personally in the bank ten thousand dollars? Also her father guarantees further twelve thousand. Also she has a new car, wonderful clothes, talks on all subjects, and she will give you a first-class home and children. How near do we come in our life to paradise?"

"If she's so wonderful, why wasn't she married ten years ago?"

"Why?" said Salzman with a heavy laugh. " — Why? Because she is *partikiler*. This is why. She wants the *best*."

Leo was silent, amused at how he had entangled himself. But 95 Salzman had aroused his interest in Lily H., and he began seriously to consider calling on her. When the marriage broker observed how intently Leo's mind was at work on the facts he had supplied, he felt certain they would soon come to an agreement.

Late Saturday afternoon, conscious of Salzman, Leo Finkle walked with Lily Hirschorn along Riverside Drive. He walked briskly and erectly, wearing with distinction the black fedora he had that morning taken with trepidation out of the dusty hat box on his closet shelf, and the heavy black Saturday coat he had thoroughly whisked clean. Leo also owned a walking stick, a present from a distant relative, but quickly put temptation aside and did not use it. Lily, petite and not unpretty, had on something signifying the approach of spring. She was au courant, animatedly, with all sorts of subjects, and he weighed her words and found her surprisingly sound — score another for Salzman, whom he uneasily sensed to be somewhere around, hiding perhaps high in a tree along the street, flashing the lady signals with a pocket mirror; or perhaps a cloven-hoofed Pan, piping nuptial ditties as he danced his invisible way before them, strewing wild buds on the walk and purple grapes in their path, symbolizing fruit of a union, though there was of course still none.

Lily startled Leo by remarking, "I was thinking of Mr. Salzman, a curious figure, wouldn't you say?"

Not certain what to answer, he nodded.

She bravely went on, blushing, "I for one am grateful for his introducing us. Aren't you?"

He courteously replied, "I am." 100

"I mean," she said with a little laugh — and it was all in good taste, or at least gave the effect of being not in bad — "do you mind that we came together so?"

He was not displeased with her honesty, recognizing that she meant to set the relationship aright, and understanding that it took a certain amount of experience in life, and courage, to want to do it quite that way. One had to have some sort of past to make that kind of beginning.

He said that he did not mind. Salzman's function was traditional and honorable — valuable for what it might achieve, which, he pointed out, was frequently nothing.

Lily agreed with a sigh. They walked on for a while and she said after a long silence, again with a nervous laugh, "Would you mind if I asked you something a little bit personal? Frankly, I find the subject fascinating." Although Leo shrugged, she went on half embarrassedly, "How was it that you came to your calling? I mean, was it a sudden passionate inspiration?"

Leo, after a time, slowly replied, "I was always interested in   105
the Law."

"You saw revealed in it the presence of the Highest?"

He nodded and changed the subject. "I understand that you spent a little time in Paris, Miss Hirschorn?"

"Oh, did Mr. Salzman tell you, Rabbi Finkle?" Leo winced but she went on, "It was ages ago and almost forgotten. I remember I had to return for my sister's wedding."

And Lily would not be put off. "When," she asked in a slightly trembly voice, "did you become enamored of God?"

He stared at her. Then it came to him that she was talking not   110
about Leo Finkle but a total stranger, some mystical figure, perhaps even passionate prophet that Salzman had dreamed up for her — no relation to the living or dead. Leo trembled with rage and weakness. The trickster had obviously sold her a bill of goods, just as he had him, who'd expected to become acquainted with a young lady of twenty-nine, only to behold, the moment he had laid eyes upon her strained and anxious face, a woman past thirty-five and aging rapidly. Only his self-control had kept him this long in her presence.

"I am not," he said gravely, "a talented religious person," and in seeking words to go on, found himself possessed by shame and fear. "I think," he said in a strained manner, "that I came to God not because I loved Him but because I did not."

This confession he spoke harshly because its unexpectedness shook him.

Lily wilted. Leo saw a profusion of loaves of bread go flying like ducks high over his head, not unlike the winged loaves by which he had counted himself to sleep last night. Mercifully, then, it snowed, which he would not put past Salzman's machinations.

He was infuriated with the marriage broker and swore he would throw him out of the room the moment he reappeared. But Salzman did not come that night, and when Leo's anger had subsided, an unaccountable despair grew in its place. At first he thought this was caused by his disappointment in Lily, but before long it became evident that he had involved himself with Salzman without a true knowledge of his own intent. He gradually realized — with an emptiness that seized him with six hands — that he had called in the broker to find him a bride because he was incapable of doing it himself. This terrifying insight he had derived as a result of his meeting and conversation with Lily Hirschorn. Her probing questions had somehow irritated him into revealing — to himself more than her — the true nature of his relationship to God, and from that it had come upon him, with shocking force, that apart from his parents, he had never loved anyone. Or perhaps it went the other way, that he did not love God so well as he might, because he had not loved man. It seemed to Leo that his whole life stood starkly revealed and he saw himself for the first time as he truly was — unloved and loveless. This bitter but somehow not fully unexpected revelation brought him to a point of panic, controlled only by extraordinary effort. He covered his face with his hands and cried.

The week that followed was the worst of his life. He did not eat and lost weight. His beard darkened and grew ragged. He stopped attending seminars and almost never opened a book. He seriously considered leaving the Yeshiva, although he was deeply troubled at the thought of the loss of all his years of study — saw them like pages torn from a book, strewn over the city — and at the devastating effect of this decision upon his parents. But he had lived without knowledge of himself, and never in the Five Books and all the Commentaries — mea culpa — had the truth been revealed to him. He did not know where to turn, and in all this desolating loneliness there was no *to whom*, although he often thought of Lily but not once could bring himself to go downstairs and make the call. He became touchy and irritable, especially with his landlady, who asked him all manner of personal questions; on the other hand, sensing his own disagreeableness, he

¹¹⁵

waylaid her on the stairs and apologized abjectly, until, mortified, she ran from him. Out of this, however, he drew the consolation that he was a Jew and that a Jew suffered. But gradually, as the long and terrible week drew to a close, he regained his composure and some idea of purpose in life: to go on as planned. Although he was imperfect, the ideal was not. As for his quest of a bride, the thought of continuing afflicted him with anxiety and heartburn, yet perhaps with this new knowledge of himself he would be more successful than in the past. Perhaps love would now come to him and a bride to that love. And for this sanctified seeking who needed a Salzman?

The marriage broker, a skeleton with haunted eyes, returned that very night. He looked, withal, the picture of frustrated expectancy — as if he had steadfastly waited the week at Miss Lily Hirschorn's side for a telephone call that never came.

Casually coughing, Salzman came immediately to the point: "So how did you like her?"

Leo's anger rose and he could not refrain from chiding the matchmaker: "Why did you lie to me, Salzman?"

Salzman's pale face went dead white, the world had snowed on him.

"Did you not state that she was twenty-nine?" Leo insisted.   120

"I give you my word — "

"She was thirty-five, if a day. At *least* thirty-five."

"Of this don't be too sure. Her father told me — "

"Never mind. The worst of it is that you lied to her."

"How did I lie to her, tell me?"   125

"You told her things about me that weren't true. You made me out to be more, consequently less than I am. She had in mind a totally different person, a sort of semi-mystical Wonder Rabbi."

"All I said, you was a religious man."

"I can imagine."

Salzman sighed. "This is my weakness that I have," he confessed. "My wife says to me I shouldn't be a salesman, but when I have two fine people that they would be wonderful to be married, I am so happy that I talk too much." He smiled wanly. "This is why Salzman is a poor man."

Leo's anger left him. "Well, Salzman, I'm afraid that's all."   130

The marriage broker fastened hungry eyes on him.

"You don't want any more a bride?"

"I do," said Leo, "but I have decided to seek her in another way. I am no longer interested in an arranged marriage. To be frank, I now admit the necessity of premarital love. That is, I want to be in love with the one I marry."

"Love?" said Salzman, astounded. After a moment he re-marked, "For us, our love is our life, not for the ladies. In the ghetto they — "

"I know, I know," said Leo. "I've thought of it often. Love, I 135 have said to myself, should be a product of living and worship rather than its own end. Yet for myself I find it necessary to establish the level of my need and fulfill it."

Salzman shrugged but answered, "Listen, rabbi, if you want love, this I can find for you also. I have such beautiful clients that you will love them the minute your eyes will see them."

Leo smiled unhappily. "I'm afraid you don't understand."

But Salzman hastily unstrapped his portfolio and withdrew a manila packet from it.

"Pictures," he said, quickly laying the envelope on the table.

Leo called after him to take the pictures away, but as if on the 140 wings of the wind, Salzman had disappeared.

March came. Leo had returned to his regular routine. Although he felt not quite himself yet — lacked energy — he was making plans for a more active social life. Of course it would cost something, but he was an expert in cutting corners; and when there were no corners left he would make circles rounder. All the while Salzman's pictures had lain on the table, gathering dust. Occasionally as Leo sat studying, or enjoying a cup of tea, his eyes fell on the manila envelope, but he never opened it.

The days went by and no social life to speak of developed with a member of the opposite sex — it was difficult, given the circumstances of his situation. One morning Leo toiled up the stairs to his room and stared out the window at the city. Although the day was bright his view of it was dark. For some time he watched the people in the street below hurrying along and then turned with a heavy heart to his little room. On the table was the packet. With a sudden relentless gesture he tore it open. For a half hour he stood by the table in a state of excitement, examining the photographs of the ladies Salzman had included. Finally, with a deep sigh he put them down. There were six, of varying degrees of attractiveness, but look at them long enough and they all became Lily Hirschorn: all past their prime, all starved behind bright smiles, not a true personality in the lot. Life, despite their frantic yoohooings, had passed them by; they were pictures in a briefcase that stank of fish. After a while, however, as Leo attempted to return the photographs into the envelope, he found in it another, a snapshot of the type taken by a machine for a quarter. He gazed at it a moment and let out a low cry.

Her face deeply moved him. Why, he could at first not say. It gave him the impression of youth — spring flowers, yet age — a sense of having been used to the bone, wasted: this came from the eyes, which were hauntingly familiar, yet absolutely strange. He had a vivid impression that he had met her before, but try as he might he could not place her although he could almost recall her name, as if he had read it in her own handwriting. No, this couldn't be; he would have remembered her. It was not, he affirmed, that she had an extraordinary beauty — no, though her face was attractive enough; it was that *something* about her moved him. Feature for feature, even some of the ladies of the photographs could do better; but she leaped forth to his heart — had *lived*, or wanted to — more than just wanted, perhaps regretted how she had lived — had somehow deeply suffered: it could be seen in the depths of those reluctant eyes, and from the way the light enclosed and shone from her, and within her, opening realms of possibility: this was her own. Her he desired. His head ached and eyes narrowed with the intensity of his gazing, then as if an obscure fog had blown up in the mind, he experienced fear of her and was aware that he had received an impression, somehow, of evil. He shuddered, saying softly, it is thus with us all. Leo brewed some tea in a small pot and sat sipping it without sugar, to calm himself. But before he had finished drinking, again with excitement he examined the face and found it good: good for Leo Finkle. Only such a one could understand him and help him seek whatever he was seeking. She might, perhaps, love him. How she had happened to be among the discards in Salzman's barrel he could never guess, but he knew he must urgently go find her.

Leo rushed downstairs, grabbed up the Bronx telephone book, and searched for Salzman's home address. He was not listed, nor was his office. Neither was he in the Manhattan book. But Leo remembered having written down the address on a slip of paper after he had read Salzman's advertisement in the "personals" column of the *Forward*. He ran up to his room and tore through his papers, without luck. It was exasperating. Just when he needed the matchmaker he was nowhere to be found. Fortunately Leo remembered to look in his wallet. There on a card he found his name written and a Bronx address. No phone number was listed, the reason — Leo now recalled — he had originally communicated with Salzman by letter. He got on his coat, put a hat on over his skullcap and hurried to the subway station. All the way to the far end of the Bronx he sat on the edge of his seat. He was more than once tempted to take out the picture and see if the girl's face was as he remembered, but he refrained, allowing the snapshot to remain in his inside coat pocket, content to have her so close. When the train pulled into the station he was waiting at the door and bolted out. He quickly located the street Salzman had advertised.

The building he sought was less than a block from the subway, but it was not an office building, nor even a loft, nor a store in which one could rent office space. It was a very old tenement house. Leo found Salzman's name in pencil on a soiled tag under the bell and climbed three dark flights to his apartment. When he knocked, the door was opened by a thin, asthmatic, gray-haired woman, in felt slippers.

"Yes?" she said, expecting nothing. She listened without listening. He could have sworn he had seen her, too, before but knew it was an illusion.

"Salzman — does he live here? Pinye Salzman," he said, "the matchmaker?"

She stared at him a long minute. "Of course."

He felt embarrassed. "Is he in?"

"No." Her mouth, though left open, offered nothing more.

"The matter is urgent. Can you tell me where his office is?"

"In the air." She pointed upward.

"You mean he has no office?" Leo asked.

"In his socks."

He peered into the apartment. It was sunless and dingy, one large room divided by a half open curtain, beyond which he could see a sagging metal bed. The near side of the room was crowded with rickety chairs, old bureaus, a three-legged table, racks of cooking utensils, and all the apparatus of a kitchen. But there was no sign of Salzman or his magic barrel, probably also a figment of the imagination. An odor of frying fish made Leo weak to the knees.

"Where is he?" he insisted. "I've got to see your husband."

At length she answered, "So who knows where he is? Every time he thinks a new thought he runs to a different place. Go home, he will find you."

"Tell him Leo Finkle."

She gave no sign she had heard.

He walked downstairs, depressed.

But Salzman, breathless, stood waiting at his door.

Leo was astounded and overjoyed. "How did you get here before me?"

"I rushed."

"Come inside."

They entered. Leo fixed tea, and a sardine sandwich for Salz-   165
man. As they were drinking he reached behind him for the
packet of pictures and handed them to the marriage broker.

Salzman put down his glass and said expectantly, "You found
somebody you like?"

"Not among these."

The marriage broker turned away.

"Here is the one I want." Leo held forth the snapshot.

Salzman slipped on his glasses and took the picture into his   170
trembling hand. He turned ghastly and let out a groan.

"What's the matter?" cried Leo.

"Excuse me. Was an accident this picture. She isn't for you."

Salzman frantically shoved the manila packet into his portfolio. He thrust the snapshot into his pocket and fled down the
stairs.

Leo, after momentary paralysis, gave chase and cornered the
marriage broker in the vestibule. The landlady made hysterical
outcries but neither of them listened.

"Give me back the picture, Salzman."   175

"No." The pain in his eyes was terrible.

"Tell me who she is then."

"This I can't tell you. Excuse me."

He made to depart, but Leo, forgetting himself, seized the
matchmaker by his tight coat and shook him frenziedly.

"Please," sighed Salzman. "*Please*."   180

Leo ashamedly let him go. "Tell me who she is," he begged.
"It's very important for me to know."

"She is not for you. She is a wild one — wild, without shame.
This is not a bride for a rabbi."

"What do you mean wild?"

"Like an animal. Like a dog. For her to be poor was a sin.
This is why to me she is dead now."

"In God's name, what do you mean?"   185

"Her I can't introduce to you," Salzman cried.

"Why are you so excited?"

"Why, he asks," Salzman said, bursting into tears. "This is my
baby, my Stella, she should burn in hell."

Leo hurried up to bed and hid under the covers. Under the
covers he thought his life through. Although he soon fell asleep
he could not sleep her out of his mind. He woke, beating his
breast. Though he prayed to be rid of her, his prayers went un-
answered. Through days of torment he endlessly struggled not to
love her; fearing success, he escaped it. He then concluded to

convert her to goodness, himself to God. The idea alternately nauseated and exalted him.

He perhaps did not know that he had come to a final deci- 190 sion until he encountered Salzman in a Broadway cafeteria. He was sitting alone at a rear table, sucking the bony remains of a fish. The marriage broker appeared haggard, and transparent to the point of vanishing.

Salzman looked up at first without recognizing him. Leo had grown a pointed beard and his eyes were weighted with wisdom.

"Salzman," he said, "love has at last come to my heart."

"Who can love from a picture?" mocked the marriage broker.

"It is not impossible."

"If you can love her, then you can love anybody. Let me show 195 you some new clients that they just sent me their photographs. One is a little doll."

"Just her I want," Leo murmured.

"Don't be a fool, doctor. Don't bother with her."

"Put me in touch with her, Salzman," Leo said humbly. "Perhaps I can be of service."

Salzman had stopped eating and Leo understood with emotion that it was now arranged.

Leaving the cafeteria, he was, however, afflicted by a tor- 200 menting suspicion that Salzman had planned it all to happen this way.

Leo was informed by letter that she would meet him on a certain corner, and she was there one spring night, waiting under a street lamp. He appeared, carrying a small bouquet of violets and rosebuds. Stella stood by the lamppost, smoking. She wore white with red shoes, which fitted his expectations, although in a troubled moment he had imagined the dress red, and only the shoes white. She waited uneasily and shyly. From afar he saw that her eyes — clearly her father's — were filled with desperate innocence. He pictured, in her, his own redemption. Violins and lit candles revolved in the sky. Leo ran forward with flowers outthrust.

Around the corner, Salzman, leaning against a wall, chanted prayers for the dead.

Questions

1. What subject or subjects do you find at the center of "The Magic Barrel"?

2. What passages in the story seem to you to focus that subject
    or subjects most directly?
3. Choose one of these passages and show how your reading of
    specific language in it draws together the story's details and
    illuminates the work as a whole.

RENATA ADLER   (b. 1938)

Brownstone

The camel, I had noticed, was passing, with great difficulty,
through the eye of the needle. The Apollo flight, the four-minute
mile, Venus in Scorpio, human records on land and at sea —
these had been events of enormous importance. But the camel,
practicing in near obscurity for almost two thousand years, was
passing through. First the velvety nose then the rest. Not many
were aware. But if the lead camel and then perhaps the entire
caravan could make it, the thread, the living thread of camels,
would exist, could not be lost. No one could lose the thread. The
prospects of the rich would be enhanced. "Ortega tells us that the
business of philosophy," the professor was telling his class of
indifferent freshmen, "is to crack open metaphors which are
dead."

"I shouldn't have come," the Englishman said, waving his
drink and breathing so heavily at me that I could feel my bangs
shift. "I have a terrible cold."

"He would probably have married her," a voice across the
room said, "with the exception that he died."

"Well, I am a personality that prefers not be annoyed."

"We should all prepare ourselves for this eventuality."   5

A six-year-old was passing the hors d'oeuvres. The baby, not
quite steady on his feet, was hurtling about the room.

"He's following me," the six-year-old said, in despair.

"Then lock yourself in the bathroom, dear," Inez replied.

"He always waits outside the door."

"He loves you, dear."   10

"Well, I don't like it."

"How I envy you," the minister's wife was saying to a courteous, bearded boy, "reading *Magic Mountain* for the first time."

The homosexual across the hall from me always takes Valium
and walks his beagle. I borrow Valium from him from time to
time, and when he takes a holiday the dog is left with me. On our

floor of this brownstone, we are friends. Our landlord, Roger Somerset, was murdered last July. He was a kind and absent-minded man, and on the night when he was stabbed there was a sort of requiem for him in the heating system. There is a lot of music in this building anyway. The newlyweds on the third floor play Bartók on their stereo. The couple on the second floor play clarinet quintets; their kids play rock. The girl on the fourth floor, who has been pining for two months, plays Judy Collins' "Maid of Constant Sorrow" all day long. We have a kind of orchestra in here. The ground floor is a shop. The owner of the shop speaks of our landlord's murder still. Shaking his head, he says that he suspects "foul play." We all agree with him. We changed our locks. But "foul play" seems a weird expression for the case.

It is all weird. I am not always well. One block away (I often think of this), there was ten months ago an immense crash. Water mains broke. There were small rivers in the streets. In a great skyscraper that was being built, something had failed. The news-papers reported the next day that by some miracle only two people had been "slightly injured" by ten tons of falling steel. The steel fell from the eighteenth floor. The question that preoc-cupies me now is how, under the circumstances, slight injuries could occur. Perhaps the two people were grazed in passing by. Perhaps some fragments of the sidewalk ricocheted. I knew a deliverer of flowers who, at Sixty-ninth and Lexington, was hit by a flying suicide. Situations simply do not yield to the most likely structures of the mind. A "self-addressed envelope," if you are inclined to brood, raises deep questions of identity. Such an envelope, immutably itself, is always precisely where it belongs. "Self-pity" is just sadness, I think, in the pejorative. But "joking with nurses" fascinates me in the press. Whenever someone has been quite struck down, lost faculties, members of his family, he is said to have "joked with his nurses" quite a lot. What a mine of humor every nurse's life must be.

I have a job, of course. I have had several jobs. I've had our 15 paper's gossip column since last month. It is egalitarian. I look for people who are quite obscure, and report who is breaking up with whom and where they go and what they wear. The person who invented this new form for us is on antidepressants now. He lives in Illinois. He says there are people in southern Illinois who have not yet been covered by the press. I often write about families in Queens. Last week, I went to a dinner party on Park

Avenue. After 1 A.M. something called the Alive or Dead Game was being played. Someone would mention an old character from Tammany or Hollywood. "Dead," "Dead," "Dead," everyone would guess. "No, no. Alive. I saw him walking down the street just yesterday," or "Yes. Dead. I read a little obituary notice about him last year." One of the little truths people can subtly enrage or reassure each other with is who — when you have looked away a month, a year — is still around.

The St. Bernard at the pound on Ninety-second Street was named Bonnie and would have cost five dollars. The attendant held her tightly on a leash of rope. "Hello, Bonnie," I said. Bonnie growled. "I wouldn't talk to her if I was you," the attendant said. I leaned forward to pat her ear. Bonnie snarled. "I wouldn't touch her if I was you," the attendant said. I held out my hand under Bonnie's jowls. She strained against the leash, and choked and coughed. "Now cut that out, Bonnie," the attendant said. "Could I just take her for a walk around the block," I said, "before I decide?" "Are you out of your mind?" the attendant said. Aldo patted Bonnie, and we left.

Dear Tenant:

We have reason to believe that there are impostors posing as Con Ed repairmen and inspectors circulating in this area.

Do not permit any Con Ed man to enter your premises or the building, if possible.

The Precinct

The New York Chinese cabdriver lingered at every corner and at every traffic light, to read his paper. I wondered what the news was. I looked over his shoulder. The illustrations and the type were clear enough: newspaper print, pornographic fiction. I leaned back in my seat. A taxi-driver who happened to be Oriental with a sadomasochistic cast of mind was not my business. I lit a cigarette, looked at my bracelet. I caught the driver's eyes a moment in the rearview mirror. He picked up his paper. "I don't think you ought to read," I said, "while you are driving." Traffic was slow. I saw his mirrored eyes again. He stopped his reading. When we reached my address, I did not tip him. Racism and prudishness, I thought, and reading over people's shoulders.

But there are moments in this place when everything becomes a show of force. He can read what he likes at home. Tipping is still my option. Another newspaper event, in our brownstone. It was a holiday. The superintendent normally hauls the garbage down and sends the paper up, by dumbwaiter, each morning. On holidays, the garbage stays upstairs, the paper on the sidewalk. At 8 A.M., I went downstairs. A ragged man was lying across the little space that separates the inner door, which locks, from the outer door, which doesn't. I am not a news addict. I could have stepped over the sleeping man, picked up my *Times*, and gone upstairs to read it. Instead, I knocked absurdly from inside the door, and said, "Wake up. You'll have to leave now." He got up, lifted the flattened cardboard he had been sleeping on, and walked away, mumbling and reeking. It would have been kinder, certainly, to let the driver read, the wino sleep. One simply cannot bear down so hard on all these choices.

What is the point. That is what must be borne in mind. Some-times the point is really who wants what. Sometimes the point is what is right or kind. Sometimes the point is a momentum, a fact, a quality, a voice, an intimation, a thing said or unsaid. Some-times it's who's at fault, or what will happen if you do not move at once. The point changes and goes out. You cannot be forever watching for the point, or you lose the simplest thing: being a major character in your own life. But if you are, for any length of time, custodian of the point — in art, in court, in politics, in lives, in rooms — it turns out there are rear-guard actions every-where. To see a thing clearly, and when your vision of it dims, or when it goes to someone else, if you have a gentle nature, keep your silence, that is lovely. Otherwise, now and then, a small foray is worthwhile. Just so that being always, complacently, thoroughly wrong does not become the safest position of them all. The point has never quite been entrusted to me.

My cousin, who was born on February 29th, became a vet- 20 erinarian. Some years ago, when he was twenty-eight (seven, by our childhood birthday count), he was drafted, and sent to Ma-laysia. He spent most of his military service there, assigned to the zoo. He operated on one tiger, which, in the course of abdominal surgery, began to wake up and wag its tail. The anesthetist grabbed the tail, and injected more sodium pentothal. That tiger survived. But two flamingos, sent by the city of Miami to Kuala Lumpur as a token of good will, could not bear the trip or the climate and in spite of my cousin's efforts, died. There was also a cobra — the largest anyone in Kuala Lumpur could remember having seen. An old man had brought it, in an immense sack, from somewhere in the countryside. The zoo director called my cousin at once, around dinnertime, to say that an unprecedented cobra had arrived. Something quite drastic, however, seemed wrong with its neck. My cousin, whom I have always admired — for his leap-year birthday, for his pilot's license, for his presence of mind — said that he would certainly examine the cobra in the morning but that the best thing for it after its long journey must be a good night's rest. By morning, the cobra was dead.

My cousin is well. The problem is this. Hardly anyone about whom I deeply care at all resembles anyone else I have ever met, or heard of, or read about in the literature. I know an Israeli general who, in 1967, retook the Mitla Pass but who, since his mandatory retirement from military service at fifty-five, has been trying to repopulate the Ark. He asked me, over breakfast at the Drake, whether I knew any owners of oryxes. Most of the vegetarian species he has collected have already multiplied enough, since he has found and cared for them, to be permitted to run wild. The carnivorous animals, though, must still be kept behind barbed wire — to keep them from stalking the rarer vegetarians. I know a group that studies Proust one Sunday afternoon a month, and an analyst, with that Exeter laugh (embittered mooing noises, and mirthless heaving of the shoulder blades), who has the most remarkable terrorist connections in the Middle East.

The conversation of *The Magic Mountain* and the unrequited love of six-year-olds occurred on Saturday, at brunch. "Bring someone new," Inez had said. "Not queer. Not married, maybe separated. John and I are breaking up." The invitation was not of a kind that I had heard before. Aldo, who lives with me between the times when he prefers to be alone, refused to come. He despises brunch. He detests Inez. I went, instead, with an editor who has been a distant, steady friend but who, ten years ago, when we first came to New York, had once put three condoms on the night table beside the phone. We both had strange ideas about New York. Aldo is a gentle, orderly, soft-spoken man, slow to conclude. I try to be tidy when he is here, but I have often made his cigarettes, and once his manuscript, into the bed. Our paper's publisher is an intellectual from Baltimore. He has read Wittgenstein; he's always making unimpeachable remarks. Our music critic throws a tantrum every day, in print. Our book reviewer is looking for another job. He found that the packages in which all books are mailed could not, simply could not, be opened without doing considerable damage — through staples, tape, wire, fluttering gray stuff, recalcitrance — to the reviewer's hands. He felt it was a symptom of some kind — one of those cases where incompetence at every stage, across the board, acquired a certain independent force. Nothing to do with books, he thought, worked out at all. We also do the news. For horoscopes, there are the ladies' magazines, which tell you — earnestly — auspicious times to shave your legs. We just cannot compete.

"All babies are natural swimmers," John said, lowering his two-year-old son gently over the side of the rowboat, and smiling. The child thrashed and sank. Aldo dived in and grabbed him. The baby came up coughing, not crying, and looked with pure fear at his father. John looked with dismay at his son. "He would have come up in a minute," John said to Aldo, who was dripping and rowing. "You have to give nature a chance."

My late landlord was from Scarsdale. The Maid of Constant Sorrow is from Texas. Aldo is from St. Louis. Inez's versions vary about where she's from. I grew up in a New England mill town, where, in the early thirties, all the insured factories burned down. It has been difficult to get fire insurance in that region ever since. The owner of a hardware store, whose property adjoined an insured factory at the time, lost everything. Afterward, he walked all day along the railroad track, waiting for a train to run him down. Railroad service has never been very good up there. No trains came. His children own the town these days, for what it's worth. The two cobbled streets where black people always lived have been torn up and turned into a public park since a flood that occurred some years ago. Unprecedented rains came. Retailers had to destroy their sodden products, for fear of contamination. The black section was torn up and seeded over in the town's rezoning project. No one knows where the blacks live now. But there are Negroes in the stores and schools, and on the football team. It is assumed that the park integrated the town. Those black families must be living somewhere. It is a mystery.

At the women's college where I went, we had distinguished faculty in everything, digs at Nuoro and Mycenae. We had a quality of obsession in our studies. For professors who had quarrelled with their wives at breakfast, those years of bright-eyed young women, never getting any older, must have been a trial. The head of the history department once sneezed into his best student's honors thesis. He slammed it shut. It was ultimately published. When I was there, a girl called Cindy Melchior was immensely fat. She wore silk trousers and gilt mules. One day, in the overheated classroom, she laid aside her knitting and lumbered to the window, which she opened. Then she lumbered back. "Do you think," the professor asked, "you are so graceful?" 25

He somehow meant it kindly. Cindy wept. That year, Cindy's
brother Melvin phoned me. "I would have called you sooner," he
said, "but I had the most terrible eczema." All the service staff on
campus in those days were black. Many of them were followers of
Father Divine. They took new names in the church. I remember
the year when a maid called Serious Heartbreak married a jani-
tor called Universal Dictionary. At a meeting of the faculty last
fall, the college president, who is new and male, spoke of raising
money. A female professor of Greek was knitting — and working
on Linear B, with an abacus before her. In our time, there was a
vogue for madrigals. Some of us listened, constantly, to a single
record. There was a phrase we could not decipher. A professor of
symbolic logic, a French Canadian, had sounds that matched but
a meaning that seemed unlikely: Sheep are no angels; come
upstairs. A countertenor explained it, after a local concert: She'd
for no angel's comfort stay. Correct, but not so likely either.

> Paul: "Two diamonds."
> Inez: "Two hearts."
> Mary: "Three clubs."
> John: "Four kings."
> Inez: "Darling, you know you can't just bid four kings."   30
> John: "I don't see why. I might have been bluffing."
> Inez: "No, darling. That's poker. This is bridge. And even in
> poker you can't just bid four kings."
> John: "No. Well, I guess we'd better deal another hand."

The host, for some reason, was taking Instamatic pictures of
his guests. It was not clear whether he was doing this in order to
be able to show, at some future time, that there had been this
gathering in his house. Or whether he thought of pictures in
some voodoo sense. Or whether he found it difficult to talk. Or
whether he was bored. Two underground celebrities — one of
whom had become a sensation by never generating or exhibiting
a flicker of interest in anything, the other of whom was known
mainly for hanging around the first — were taking pictures too.
I was there with an actor I've known for years. He had already
been received in an enormous embrace by an Eastern European
poet, whose hair was cut too short but who was neither as awkwardly spontaneous nor as drunk as he cared to seem. The party
was in honor of the poet, who celebrated the occasion by insulting everyone and being fawned upon, by distinguished and undistinguished writers alike. "This group looks as though someone had torn up a few guest lists and floated the pieces on the

air," the actor said. The friend of the underground sensation walked up to us and said hello. Then, in a verbal seizure of some sort, he began muttering obscenities. The actor said a few calming things that didn't work. He finally put his finger on the mutterer's lips. The mutterer bit that finger extremely hard, and walked away. The actor wrapped his finger in a paper napkin, and got himself another drink. We stayed till twelve.

When I worked, for a time, in the infirmary of a branch of an 35 upstate university, it was becoming more difficult with each passing semester, except in the most severe cases, to determine which students had mental or medical problems. At the clinic, young men with straggly beards and stained bluejeans wept alongside girls in jeans and frayed sweaters — all being fitted with contact lenses, over which they then wore granny glasses. There was no demand for prescription granny glasses at all. For the severely depressed, the paranoids, and the hallucinators, our young psychiatrists prescribed "mood elevators," pills that were neither uppers nor downers but which affected the bloodstream in such a way that within three to five weeks many sad outpatients became very cheerful, and several saints and historical figures became again Midwestern graduate students under tolerable stress. On one, not unusual, morning, the clinic had a call from an instructor in political science. "I am in the dean's office," he said. "My health is quite perfect. They want me to have a checkup."

"Oh?" said the doctor on duty. "Perhaps you could come in on Friday."

"The problem is," the voice on the phone said, "I have always thought myself, and been thought by others, a Negro. Now, through research, I have found that my family on both sides have always been white."

"Oh," the doctor on duty said. "Perhaps you could just take a cab and come over."

Within twenty minutes, the political-science instructor appeared at the clinic. He was black. The doctor said nothing, and began a physical examination. By the time his blood pressure was taken, the patient confided that his white ancestors were, in fact, royal. The mood elevators restored him. He and the doctor became close friends besides. A few months later, the instructor took a job with the government in Washington. Two weeks after that, he was calling the clinic again. "I have found new documentation," he said. "All eight of my great-grandparents were pureblooded Germans — seven from Prussia, one from Alsace. I thought I should tell you, dear friend." The doctor suggested he come for the weekend. By Sunday afternoon, a higher dose of the pill had had its effect. The problem has not since recurred.

The Maid of Constant Sorrow said our landlord's murder 40 marked a turning point in her analysis. "I don't feel guilty. I feel hated," she said. It is true, for a time, we all wanted to feel somehow part — if only because violence offset the ineluctable in our lives. My grandfather said that some people have such extreme insomnia that they look at their watches every hour after midnight, to see how sorry they ought to be feeling for themselves. Aldo says he does not care what my grandfather said. My grandmother refused to concede that any member of the family died of natural causes. An uncle's cancer in middle age occurred because all the suitcases fell off the luggage rack onto him when he was in his teens, and so forth. Death was an acquired characteristic. My grandmother, too, used to put other people's ailments into the diminutive: strokelets were what her friends had. Aldo said he was bored to tearsies by my grandmother's diminutives.

The weather last Friday was terrible. The flight to Martha's Vineyard was "decisional."

"What does 'decisional' mean?" a small boy asked. "It means we might have to land in Hyannis," his mother said. It is hard to understand how anyone learns anything.

Scattered through the two cars of the Brewster–New York train last week were adults with what seemed to be a clandestine understanding. They did not look at each other. They stared out the windows. They read. "Um," sang a lady at our fourth stop on the way to Grand Central. She appeared to be reading the paper. She kept singing her "Um," as one who is getting the pitch. A young man had already been whistling "Frère Jacques" for three stops. When the "Um" lady found her pitch and began to sing the national anthem, he looked at her with rage. The conductor passed through, punching tickets in his usual fashion, not in the aisle but directly over people's laps. Every single passenger was obliged to flick the tiny punched part of the ticket from his lap onto the floor. Conductors have this process as their own little show of force. The whistler and the singer were in a dead heat when we reached the city. The people with the clandestine understanding turned out to be inmates from somewhere upstate, now on leave with their families, who met them in New York.

I don't think much of writers in whom nothing is at risk. It is possible, though, to be too literal-minded about this question. In a magazine, under the heading "$3,000 for First-Person Articles," for example: "An article for this series must be a true, hitherto unpublished narrative of an unusual personal experience. It may be dramatic, inspirational, or humorous, but it must have, in the opinion of the editors, a quality of narrative interest comparable to 'How I Lost My Eye' (June '72) and 'Attacked by a Killer Shark' (April '72). Contributions must be typewritten, preferably *double-spaced* . . ." I particularly like where the stress, the italics, goes.

When the nanny drowned in the swimming pool, the 45 parents reacted sensibly. They had not been there for the event. They had left the nanny at poolside with their youngest child, a girl of five, and the neighbor's twins, a boy and a girl of five, and the neighbor's baby-sitter, an *au pair*, who had become the nanny's dearest friend. When they returned from their morning round of golf, they found a fire truck in the yard, the drowned body of the nanny on the tiles, the three children playing, apparently calmly, under a tree, and two disconsolate firemen trying to deal with the neighbor's baby-sitter, who was hysterical. As an ambulance pulled into the driveway, the mother was already telephoning a doctor; her husband was giving the baby-sitter a glass of water and a sedative. When her hysterics had subsided, the baby-sitter explained what she could. Neither she nor the nanny, it turned out, could really swim. They could both manage a few strokes of the breaststroke, but they had a great fear of water over their heads. All three of what she called the "little ones" were strong and intrepid dog-paddlers. She and the nanny had always confined themselves to admonitions, and their own few stroking motions, from the shallow end. It was on account of these stroking motions that their inability really to swim had never come to anyone's attention or, for that matter, to their own. That morning, the nanny had, unaccountably, stroked a few feet out of her depth, in the direction of her charge. Then, according to the baby-sitter, who may have confused the sequence, things happened very rapidly, in the following order. Nanny's face turned blue. *Then* she swallowed water. Coughing and struggling, she reached her charge and clung to her. They both went under. Long seconds later, the little girl came up, crying and sputtering. In clear view, a few feet beyond the shallow end and beyond the grasp of the baby-sitter, who was trying to maintain her feet and her depth as she held out her hands, the nanny surfaced briefly once more, sank, and drowned.

I once met a polo-playing Argentine existential psychiatrist, who had lived for months in a London commune. He said that on days when the ordinary neurotics in the commune were getting on each other's nerves the few psychopaths and schizophrenics in their midst retired to their rooms and went their version of berserk, alone. On days when the neurotics got along, the psychopaths calmed down, tried to make contact, cooked. It was, he said, as though the sun came out for them. I hope that's true. Although altogether too much of life is mood. Aldo has a married friend who was in love for years with someone, also married. Her husband found out. He insisted that there be no more calls or letters. Aldo's friend called several times, reaching the husband. The girl herself would never answer. In the end, Aldo's friend — in what we regard as not his noblest gesture — sent all the girl's letters, addressed in a packet, to her husband. There was nothing more. I wonder whether the husband read those letters. If he did, I suppose he may have been a writer. In some sense. If not, he was a gentleman. There are also, on the bus, quite often ritual dancers, near-spastics who release the strap and begin a weird sequence of movements, always punctual, always the same. There are some days when everyone I see is lunatic.

I love the laconic. Clearly, I am not of their number. When animated conversations are going on, even with people interrupting one another, I have to curb an impulse to field every remark, by everybody, as though it were addressed to me. I have noticed this impulse in other people. It electrifies the room. It is resolved, sometimes, by conversations in a foreign language. One thinks, it is my turn to try to say something, to make an effort. One polishes a case, a tense, a comment. The subject passes. Just as well. There are, however, people who just sit there, silent. A question is addressed to them. They do not answer. Another question. Silence. It is a position of great power. Talkative people running toward those silences are jarred, time after time, by a straight arm rebuff. A quizzical look, a beautiful face perhaps, but silence. Everyone is exhausted, drinks too much, snarls later at home, wonders about the need for aspirin. It has been that stubborn wall.

I receive communications almost every day from an institution called the Center for Short-Lived Phenomena. Reporting
sources all over the world, and an extensive correspondence.
Under the title "Type of Event: Biological," I have received
postcards about the progress of the Dormouse Invasion of For-
mentera: "Apart from population density, the dormouse of For-
mentera had a peak of reproduction in 1970. All females
checked were pregnant, and perhaps this fact could have been
the source of the idea of an 'invasion.'" And the Northwest
Atlantic Puffin Decline. I have followed the Tanzanian Army
Worm Outbreak. The San Fernando Earthquake. The Green
Pond Fish Kill ("Eighty percent of the numbers involved," the
Center's postcard reports, "were mummichogs.") The Samar
Spontaneous Oil Burn. The Hawaiian Monk Seal Disappearance.
And also, the Naini Tal Sudden Sky Brightening.

Those are accounts of things that did not last long, but if you
become famous for a single thing in the country, and just endure,
it is certain you will recur, enlarged. Of the eighteen men who
were indicted for conspiracy to murder Schwerner, Goodman,
and Chaney, seven were convicted by a Mississippi jury — a
surprising thing. But then a year later, a man was wounded and a
woman killed in a shootout while trying to bomb the house of
some Mississippi Jews. It turned out that the informer, the man
who had helped the bombers, and led the F.B.I. to them, was one
of the convicted seven -- the one, in fact, who was alleged to
have killed two of the three boys who were found in that Mississippi dam. And what's more, and what's more, the convicted
conspirator, alleged double killer, was paid thirty-six thousand
dollars by the F.B.I. for bringing the bombers in. Yet the wave of
anti-Semitic bombings in Mississippi stopped after the shootout.
I don't know what it means. I am in this brownstone.

Last year, Aldo moved out and went to Los Angeles on a 50
story. I called him to ask whether I could come. He said, "Are you
going to stay this time?" I said I wasn't sure. I flew out quite early
in the morning. On the plane, there was the most banal, unendurable pickup, lasting the whole flight. A young man and a
young woman — he was Italian, I think; she was German — had
just met, and settled on French as their common language. They
asked each other where they were from, and where they were
going. They posed each other riddles. He took out a pencil and
paper and sketched her portrait. She giggled. He asked her
whether she had ever considered a career as a model. She said
she had considered it, but she feared that all men in the field

were after the same thing. He agreed. He began to tell off-color stories. She laughed and reproached him. It was like that. I wondered whether these things were always, to captive eaves-droppers, so dreary. When I arrived at Aldo's door, he met me with a smile that seemed surprised, a little sheepish. We talked awhile. Sometimes he took, sometimes I held, my suitcase. I tried, I thought, a joke. I asked whether there was already a girl there. He said there was. He met me in an hour at the corner drugstore for a cup of coffee. We talked. We returned to the apartment. We had Scotch. That afternoon, quite late, I flew home. I called him from time to time. He had his telephone removed a few days later. Now, for a while, he's here again. He's doing a political essay. It begins, "Some things cannot be said too often; and some can." That's all he's got so far.

We had people in for drinks one night last week. The cork in the wine bottle broke. Somebody pounded it into the bottle with a chisel and a hammer. We went to a bar. I have never under-stood the feeling men seem to have for bars they frequent. A single-story drunk told his single story. A fine musician who was with us played Mozart, Chopin, and Beethoven on the piano. It seemed a great, impromptu occasion. Then he said, we thought, "I am now going to play some Yatz." From what he played, it turned out he meant jazz. He played it badly.

We had driven in from another weekend in the country while it was still daylight. Lots of cars had their headlights on. We weren't sure whether it was for or against peace, or just for highway safety. Milly, a secretary in a brokerage office, was married in our ground-floor shop that evening. She cried hys-terically. Her mother and several people from her home town and John, whose girl she had been before he married Inez, thought it was from sentiment or shyness, or for some conven-tional reason. Milly explained it to Aldo later. She and her husband had really married two years before — the week they met, in fact — in a chapel in Las Vegas. They hadn't wanted to tell their parents, or anybody, until he finished college. They had torn up their Las Vegas license. She had been crying out of some legal fear of being married twice, it turned out. Their best man, a Puerto Rican doctor, said his aunt had been mugged in a ceme-tery in San Juan by a man on horseback. She thought it was her husband, returned from the dead. She had required sedation. We laughed. My friend across the hall, who owns the beagle, looked very sad all evening. He said, abruptly, that he was cracking up, and no one would believe him. There were sirens in the street.

Inez said she knew exactly what he meant: she was cracking up also. Her escort, a pale Italian jeweler said, "I too. I too have it. The most terrible anguishes, anguishes all in the night."

Inez said she knew the most wonderful man for the problem. "He may strike you at first as a phony," she said, "but then, when you're with him, you find yourself naturally screaming. It's such a relief. And he teaches you how you can practice at home." Milly said she was not much of a screamer — had never, in fact, screamed in her life. "High time you did, then," Inez said. Our sportswriter said he had recently met a girl whose problem was stealing all the suede garments of house guests, and another, in her thirties, who cried all the time because she had not been accepted at Smith. We heard many more sirens in the streets. We all went home.

At 4 A.M., the phone rang about fifty times. I did not answer it. Aldo suggested that we remove it. I took three Valium. The whole night was sirens, then silence. The phone rang again. It is still ringing. The paper goes to press tomorrow. It is possible that I know who killed our landlord. So many things point in one direction. But too strong a case, I find, is often lost. It incurs doubts, suspicions. Perhaps I do not know. Perhaps it doesn't matter. I think it does, though. When I wonder what it is that we are doing — in this brownstone, on this block, with this paper — the truth is probably that we are fighting for our lives.

Questions

1. What subject or subjects do you find at the center of "Brownstone"?
2. What passages in the story seem to you to focus that subject or subjects most directly?
3. Choose one of these passages and show how your reading of specific language in it draws together the story's details and illuminates the work as a whole. Compare your response to the one that follows.

Response

COLLEGE FRESHMAN: The key subject which Renata Adler is trying to convey to us as readers in the story "Brownstone" is that of human relationships and experiences. For Adler, two levels of human relations and interaction exist. On one level, there are relations which can be described as occurrences taking place in the outside, "real world." For example, "the Apollo flight, the four-minute mile, . . . human records on land and at sea" are described by Adler as "events of enormous importance" (para. 1). They are not, however, the type of human interactions Adler wants to focus on. In "Brownstone," Adler turns away from the "newspaper events" because in reality they are related to only a very small percentage of individuals. They don't represent the everyday struggles that go on in the unobserved person's life. It is these struggles which are the kind of human relationships and experiences Adler is concentrating on.

"Practicing in near obscurity" and "not many were aware" (1) is the language used by Adler to begin her focus on the trials of the average person's life. She is focusing on the isolation of the individual, for example, "the newlyweds on the third floor . . . the couple on the second floor [with] . . . their kids . . . [and] the girl on the fourth floor, who has been pining for two months" (13). Alone each one represents a unique, small, and somewhat self-centered world, each of which has its own story to tell, but together they make up the "orchestra" and the "friends" on "our floor of this brownstone" (13), which Adler writes of. There are many other characters which could also be cited as examples: the Englishman at the cocktail party, the Chinese cabdriver, the wino in the doorway, the "people in southern Illinois who have not yet been covered by the press" (15). Each one is worthy of a news-paper story and no one should be overlooked, but it is not possible to cover all the stories. Who is it that decides who should be passed over? Perhaps it is best not to think about it too much and just pick the outstanding stories. After all, "one simply cannot bear down so hard on all these choices" (18).

So people get passed by, but what does it do to them? Per-haps the result can be explained by the "sirens in the streets" (53). The sirens are actually individuals crying out, trying to tell their untold story, hoping someone will listen. They are fighting to make it from day to day in search of some relief. Perhaps if they could just learn to scream as Inez did, they would find deliverance. Perhaps also, if each story was let out it would make the individual's struggle to survive just a bit easier. The knowl-edge that the individual's life was important, that it did make a difference, could make "fighting for our lives" (54) a little less of a fight.

16

Allegory

Think back for a moment to the story by Katherine Mansfield in the last chapter, "A Dill Pickle." Its title spotlights the anecdote about the coachman at the Russian picnic, suggesting that this anecdote might be seen as the nub of the story as a whole. A dill pickle bears a certain resemblance — distant but undeniable — to the manipulative male character. Perfectly smooth, pleasant, unintimidating on the outside, it has an interior with a tart, sharp bite. Furthermore, the repeated movement of the story — from harmony to discord, sweet to sour — bears a certain resemblance (again, distant but undeniable) to the intermittent stab of the taste buds, during a bland meal, by a pickle.

We could go a fanciful step further and actually think about the general phenomenon of dill pickleness in relation to the particular human situation which in this story is flavored by its presence. If there's a place in human diets for a taste as prickly as that of a dill pickle, why not a place for prickliness in our other appetites? Is a person like Vera, so hungry for comforting assurances of her uniqueness, perhaps in need of an interruptive nudge? Mean and self-involved as this male charmer is, is it not possible that he — and people like him — have a function in the world?

Traveling down these speculative roads needn't mean losing our humor — or missing the denigration implicit in comparing a man to a pickle. Neither should it mean losing touch with the normal, ordinary, homely dill pickle that we began with — the object familiar to anybody who's ever shopped in a deli. It does, however, entail working some changes on pickles, making them into vehicles for thought (in this case, half-serious thought), imagining some new dimensions and meanings for picklehood. In doing this we're accepting a witty invitation issued by the author — an invitation to go into action as imaginative transformers and see identities between a certain kind of tart table relish and a certain kind of self-confident male. Mansfield asks us to use our intellectual resources, in collaboration with hers, in the shaping of a not-too-solemn symbol.

In our earlier discussion (Chapter 10), the activity of bringing symbols to life was described as that of evoking identities between objects, concepts, or experiences generally regarded as different. Implicit in some of the poetic examples was the idea that when we evoke a symbol we often draw together a relatively concrete object and a relatively abstract concept. The collarbone of a hare, in William Butler Yeats's poem (p. 589), is simultaneously a bone *and* the truth of the inescapable mortality of all living creatures. The relevance to "A Dill Pickle" is clear: We understand the pickle simultaneously as a bit of food and as a reminder of the human preference for small as opposed to large doses of disagreeable reality.

The earlier discussion also emphasized that in evoking symbols we often come close to the inexpressible — to levels where fear, taboos, and religious as well as sexual feelings have vital existence. And this, too, is illustrated by the Mansfield story. It's possible to bring the pickle to life as a sexual symbol and to imagine Vera as someone simultaneously evading and arousing her own sexuality. As these examples should suggest, we bring symbols to life in stories in much the same way that we bring them to life in poems.

OPENING THE ALLEGORICAL DOOR

The reason for reviewing symbols in poetry and stories at this point is that our new subject — allegory — connects with the subject of symbols in several ways. An *allegory* is an extended narrative that calls for sustained, continuous activity in bringing a series of interrelated symbols to life. Narratives of this sort were once common in poetry (the most famous example in English is Edmund Spenser's sixteenth-century poem *The Faerie*

Queene), and they have continued to appear in prose down to the present. Such stories are haunted through their whole lengths by correspondences and equivalents. In a realistic story such as "A Dill Pickle," we may feel — once or twice — that it's right for us to speculate on possible symbolic dimensions of familiar objects. In an allegory we're engaged in translative activity from start to finish. We connect one symbol with another, ultimately bringing to life a structure of symbolic meaning extending throughout the narrative. Never entirely departing from the familiar definitions of the words composing the text, always attempting to connect those definitions with meanings that are broader and deeper, we find ourselves fusing many strands of significance.

The unfolding narrative in an allegory involves a character or characters in a developing life situation, and this narrative structure links allegory with every other kind of fiction. But as we follow the events we are obliged to interpret them in large moral, psychological, or historical contexts. We're dealing, to repeat, not with a single symbol but with a system of symbols. We sense that each element of the story has not only a simple existence as part of a what-happens-next narrative but also a complex existence in which it is intermingled with a succession of speculative concepts. At no point can we pull back and say, Oh, *I* see: The hero of this story is really an abstraction, such as Courage or Virtue or Christianity, and then proceed to deal with the character *as* an abstraction, forgetting the human reality. Instead, we have to think along two or more tracks simultaneously, making sense of the interpenetration of concept and person, idea and situation, building an interpretation for ourselves that does justice to the full variety of the perspectives.

Why bother? The answer to that question has to be philosophical. Without difficulty we can usually see an individual life as an ongoing personal narrative, shaped by familiar, relatively visible forces and influences — ambition, love, fecklessness, sense of duty; age, health, income, and so on. But we can also see that same life as reflective of much that's relatively hidden: buried psychic drives, class, cultural and historical conditioning, religious belief or unbelief. Writing that asks a reader to be alert to the whole configuration of forces embodied in our humanity

can be extremely demanding, even frustrating. Who can deal
with all the world at once! How can any life be, simultaneously, a
story *and* a philosophy?

Lives do, though, continuously combine events and ideas,
speculative thought and daily reality. In bringing allegory to life,
writers and readers work to perceive that complex whole, and
their collaboration often creates experiences of extraordinary
richness — and strangeness. In Franz Kafka's "The Metamorphosis" — one of the stories in this chapter — a man wakes up in
the morning to discover he's a bug. *Very* strange. In beginning to
make sense of this event, we have to ask a wide variety of
questions. At the simplest level: How can a human being "be" a
bug? When are human beings called insects? What might it mean
that this human being calls *himself* a bug?

As we consider these questions, we're deciding how to name,
in our own terms, the kinds of attitudes that figure in the story.
We are also working out for ourselves a provisional concept of
the levels of thought and experience that are being connected.
Since we start with a man becoming a bug, we might assume that
the story should be evoked as simultaneously about human life
and insect life. But we notice that other important levels of
experience figure in "The Metamorphosis," including family life
and work life. Why is Gregor the only bug in this household?
What does it mean that his father, mother, sister, and employers
have escaped his fate?

After coming to decisions about the ranges of meaning embraced in an allegory, we move on to explore the effect of their
combination on each other. A son and employee is envisaged as a
bug. How does this perception alter our sense of all three identities? What new light is cast on each level of being by this particular attempt to draw them into an identity?

ASKING QUESTIONS ABOUT ALLEGORY

Because evoking allegory is an especially complex activity,
it's best to concentrate initially on one or two key passages. Questions about passages in two allegorical stories, followed by sample responses, are provided in this section. A third story is followed by questions for further practice.

NATHANIEL HAWTHORNE (1804–1864)
Young Goodman Brown

Young Goodman Brown came forth, at sunset, into the street of Salem village, but put his head back, after crossing the threshold, to exchange a parting kiss with his young wife. And Faith, as the wife was aptly named, thrust her own pretty head into the street, letting the wind play with the pink ribbons of her cap, while she called to Goodman Brown.

"Dearest heart," whispered she, softly and rather sadly, when her lips were close to his ear, "pr'y thee, put off your journey until sunrise, and sleep in your own bed to-night. A lone woman is troubled with such dreams and such thoughts, that she's afeard of herself, sometimes. Pray, tarry with me this night, dear husband, of all nights in the year!"

"My love and my Faith," replied young Goodman Brown, "of all nights in the year, this one night must I tarry away from thee. My journey, as thou callest it, forth and back again, must needs be done 'twixt now and sunrise. What, my sweet, pretty wife, dost thou doubt me already, and we but three months married!"

"Then, God bless you!" said Faith, with the pink ribbons, "and may you find all well, when you come back."

"Amen!" cried Goodman Brown. "Say thy prayers, dear 5 Faith, and go to bed at dusk, and no harm will come to thee."

So they parted; and the young man pursued his way, until, being about to turn the corner by the meeting-house, he looked back, and saw the head of Faith still peeping after him, with a melancholy air, in spite of her pink ribbons.

"Poor little Faith!" thought he, for his heart smote him. "What a wretch am I, to leave her on such an errand! She talks of dreams, too. Methought, as she spoke, there was trouble in her face, as if a dream had warned her what work is to be done tonight. But, no, no! 'twould kill her to think it. Well; she's a blessed angel on earth; and after this one night, I'll cling to her skirts and follow her to Heaven."

With this excellent resolve for the future, Goodman Brown felt himself justified in making more haste on his present evil purpose. He had taken a dreary road, darkened by all the gloomiest trees of the forest, which barely stood aside to let the narrow path creep through, and closed immediately behind. It was all as lonely as could be; and there is this peculiarity in such a solitude, that the traveller knows not who may be concealed by the innumerable trunks and the thick boughs overhead; so that, with

lonely footsteps, he may yet be passing through an unseen multitude.

"There may be a devilish Indian behind every tree," said
Goodman Brown, to himself; and he glanced fearfully behind
him, as he added, "What if the devil himself should be at my very
elbow!"

His head being turned back, he passed a crook of the road, 10
and looking forward again, beheld the figure of a man, in grave
and decent attire, seated at the foot of an old tree. He arose, at
Goodman Brown's approach, and walked onward, side by side
with him.

"You are late, Goodman Brown," said he. "The clock of the
Old South was striking as I came through Boston; and that is full
fifteen minutes agone."

"Faith kept me back awhile," replied the young man, with a
tremor in his voice, caused by the sudden appearance of his
companion, though not wholly unexpected.

It was now deep dusk in the forest, and deepest in that part
of it where these two were journeying. As nearly as could be
discerned, the second traveller was about fifty years old, apparently in the same rank of life as Goodman Brown, and bearing a
considerable resemblance to him, though perhaps more in expression than features. Still, they might have been taken for
father and son. And yet, though the elder person was as simply
clad as the younger, and as simple in manner too, he had an
indescribable air of one who knew the world, and would not have
felt abashed at the governor's dinner-table, or in King William's
court, were it possible that his affairs should call him thither. But
the only thing about him, that could be fixed upon as remarkable, was his staff, which bore the likeness of a great black snake,
so curiously wrought, that it might almost be seen to twist and
wriggle itself, like a living serpent. This, of course, must have
been an ocular deception, assisted by the uncertain light.

"Come, Goodman Brown!" cried his fellow-traveller, "this is
a dull pace for the beginning of a journey. Take my staff, if you
are so soon weary."

"Friend," said the other, exchanging his slow pace for a full 15
stop, "having kept covenant by meeting thee here, it is my purpose now to return whence I came. I have scruples, touching the
matter thou wot'st of."

"Sayest thou so?" replied he of the serpent, smiling apart.
"Let us walk on, nevertheless, reasoning as we go, and if I convince thee not, thou shalt turn back. We are but a little way in the
forest, yet."

"Too far, too far!" exclaimed the goodman, unconsciously resuming his walk. "My father never went into the woods on such
an errand, nor his father before him. We have been a race of
honest men and good Christians, since the days of the martyrs.
And shall I be the first of the name of Brown, that ever took this
path, and kept — "

"Such company, thou wouldst say," observed the elder person, interpreting his pause. "Well said, Goodman Brown! I have
been as well acquainted with your family as with ever a one
among the Puritans; and that's no trifle to say. I helped your
grandfather, the constable, when he lashed the Quaker woman so
smartly through the streets of Salem. And it was I that brought
your father a pitch-pine knot, kindled at my own hearth, to set
fire to an Indian village, in King Philip's war. They were my good
friends, both; and many a pleasant walk have we had along this
path, and returned merrily after midnight. I would fain be
friends with you, for their sake."

"If it be as thou sayest," replied Goodman Brown, "I marvel
they never spoke of these matters. Or, verily, I marvel not, seeing
that the least rumor of the sort would have driven them from
New-England. We are a people of prayer, and good works, to
boot, and abide no such wickedness."

"Wickedness or not," said the traveller with the twisted staff. 20
"I have a very general acquaintance here in New-England. The
deacons of many a church have drunk the communion wine with
me; the selectmen, of divers towns, make me their chairman; and
a majority of the Great and General Court are firm supporters
of my interest. The governor and I, too — but these are state-
secrets."

"Can this be so!" cried Goodman Brown, with a stare of
amazement at his undisturbed companion. "Howbeit, I have
nothing to do with the governor and council; they have their own
ways, and are no rule for a simple husbandman, like me. But,
were I to go on with thee, how should I meet the eye of that good
old man, our minister, at Salem village? Oh, his voice would
make me tremble, both Sabbath-day and lecture-day!"

Thus far, the elder traveller had listened with due gravity,
but now burst into a fit of irrepressible mirth, shaking himself so
violently, that his snake-like staff actually seemed to wriggle in
sympathy.

"Ha! ha! ha!" shouted he, again and again; then composing
himself, "Well, go on, Goodman Brown, go on; but pr'y thee,
don't kill me with laughing!"

"Well, then, to end the matter at once," said Goodman

Brown, considerably nettled, "there is my wife, Faith. It would break her dear little heart; and I'd rather break my own!"

"Nay, if that be the case," answered the other, "e'en go thy 25 ways, Goodman Brown. I would not, for twenty old women like the one hobbling before us, that Faith should come to any harm."

As he spoke, he pointed his staff at a female figure on the path, in whom Goodman Brown recognized a very pious and exemplary dame, who had taught him his catechism, in youth, and was still his moral and spiritual adviser, jointly with the minister and Deacon Gookin.

"A marvel, truly, that Goody Cloyse should be so far in the wilderness, at night-fall!" said he. "But, with your leave, friend, I shall take a cut through the woods, until we have left this Christian woman behind. Being a stranger to you, she might ask whom I was consorting with, and whither I was going."

"Be it so," said his fellow-traveller. "Betake you to the woods, and let me keep the path."

Accordingly, the young man turned aside, but took care to watch his companion, who advanced softly along the road, until he had come within a staff's length of the old dame. She, meanwhile, was making the best of her way, with singular speed for so aged a woman, and mumbling some indistinct words, a prayer, doubtless, as she went. The traveller put forth his staff, and touched her withered neck with what seemed the serpent's tail.

"The devil!" screamed the pious old lady.   30

"Then Goody Cloyse knows her old friend?" observed the traveller, confronting her, and leaning on his writhing stick.

"Ah, forsooth, and is it your worship, indeed?" cried the good dame. "Yea, truly is it, and in the very image of my old gossip, Goodman Brown, the grandfather of the silly fellow that now is. But — would your worship believe it? — my broomstick hath strangely disappeared, stolen, as I suspect, by that unhanged witch, Goody Cory, and that, too, when I was all anointed with the juice of smallage and cinque-foil and wolf's-bane — "

"Mingled with fine wheat and the fat of a new-born babe," said the shape of old Goodman Brown.

"Ah, your worship knows the receipt," cried the old lady, cackling aloud. "So, as I was saying, being all ready for the meeting, and no horse to ride on, I made up my mind to foot it; for they tell me, there is a nice young man to be taken into communion to-night. But now your good worship will lend me your arm, and we shall be there in a twinkling."

"That can hardly be," answered her friend. "I may not spare 35 you my arm, Goody Cloyse, but here is my staff, if you will."

So saying, he threw it down at her feet, where, perhaps, it assumed life, being one of the rods which its owner had formerly lent to the Egyptian Magi. Of this fact, however, Goodman Brown could not take cognizance. He had cast up his eyes in astonishment, and looking down again, beheld neither Goody Cloyse nor the serpentine staff, but his fellow-traveller alone, who waited for him as calmly as if nothing had happened.

"That old woman taught me my catechism!" said the young man; and there was a world of meaning in this simple comment.

They continued to walk onward, while the elder traveller exhorted his companion to make speed and persevere in the path, discoursing so aptly, that his arguments seemed rather to spring up in the bosom of his auditor, than to be suggested by himself. As they went, he plucked a branch of maple, to serve for a walking-stick, and began to strip it of the twigs and little boughs, which were wet with evening dew. The moment his fingers touched them, they became strangely withered and dried up, as with a week's sunshine. Thus the pair proceeded, at a good free pace, until suddenly, in a gloomy hollow of the road, Goodman Brown sat himself down on the stump of a tree, and refused to go any farther.

"Friend," said he, stubbornly, "my mind is made up. Not another step will I budge on this errand. What if a wretched old woman do choose to go to the devil, when I thought she was going to Heaven! Is that any reason why I should quit my dear Faith, and go after her?"

"You will think better of this, by-and-by," said his acquaintance, composedly. "Sit here and rest yourself awhile; and when you feel like moving again, there is my staff to help you along." 40

Without more words, he threw his companion the maple stick, and was as speedily out of sight, as if he had vanished into the deepening gloom. The young man sat a few moments, by the road-side, applauding himself greatly, and thinking with how clear a conscience he should meet the minister, in his morning-walk, nor shrink from the eye of good old Deacon Gookin. And what calm sleep would be his, that very night, which was to have been spent so wickedly, but purely and sweetly now, in the arms of Faith! Amidst these pleasant and praiseworthy meditations, Goodman Brown heard the tramp of horses along the road, and deemed it advisable to conceal himself within the verge of the forest, conscious of the guilty purpose that had brought him thither, though now so happily turned from it.

On came the hoof-tramps and the voices of the riders, two grave old voices, conversing soberly as they drew near. These mingled sounds appeared to pass along the road, within a few yards of the young man's hiding-place; but owing, doubtless, to the depth of the gloom, at that particular spot, neither the travellers nor their steeds were visible. Though their figures brushed the small boughs by the way-side, it could not be seen that they intercepted, even for a moment, the faint gleam from the strip of bright sky, athwart which they must have passed. Goodman Brown alternately crouched and stood on tip-toe, pulling aside the branches, and thrusting forth his head as far as he durst, without discerning so much as a shadow. It vexed him the more, because he could have sworn, were such a thing possible, that he recognized the voices of the minister and Deacon Gookin, jogging along quietly, as they were wont to do, when bound to some ordination or ecclesiastical council. While yet within hearing, one of the riders stopped to pluck a switch.

"Of the two, reverend Sir," said the voice like the deacon's, "I had rather miss an ordination-dinner than to-night's meeting. They tell me that some of our community are to be here from Falmouth and beyond, and others from Connecticut and Rhode-Island; besides several of the Indian powows, who, after their fashion, know almost as much deviltry as the best of us. Moreover, there is a goodly young woman to be taken into communion."

"Mighty well, Deacon Gookin!" replied the solemn old tones of the minister. "Spur up, or we shall be late. Nothing can be done, you know, until I get on the ground."

The hoofs clattered again, and the voices, talking so strangely 45 in the empty air, passed on through the forest, where no church had ever been gathered, nor solitary Christian prayed. Whither, then, could these holy men be journeying, so deep into the heathen wilderness? Young Goodman Brown caught hold of a tree, for support, being ready to sink down on the ground, faint and overburdened with the heavy sickness of his heart. He looked up to the sky, doubting whether there really was a Heaven above him. Yet, there was the blue arch, and the stars brightening in it.

"With Heaven above, and Faith below, I will yet stand firm against the devil!" cried Goodman Brown.

While he still gazed upward, into the deep arch of the firmament, and had lifted his hands to pray, a cloud, though no wind was stirring, hurried across the zenith, and hid the brightening stars. The blue sky was still visible, except directly overhead, where this black mass of cloud was sweeping swiftly northward. Aloft in the air, as if from the depths of the cloud, came a confused and doubtful sound of voices. Once, the listener fancied that he could distinguish the accents of town's-people of his own, men and women, both pious and ungodly, many of whom he had met at the communion-table, and had seen others rioting at the tavern. The next moment, so indistinct were the sounds, he doubted whether he had heard aught but the murmur of the old forest, whispering without a wind. Then came a stronger swell of those familiar tones, heard daily in the sunshine, at Salem village, but never, until now, from a cloud of night. There was one voice, of a young woman, uttering lamentations, yet with an uncertain sorrow, and entreating for some favor, which, perhaps, it would grieve her to obtain. And all the unseen multitude, both saints and sinners, seemed to encourage her onward.

"Faith!" shouted Goodman Brown, in a voice of agony and desperation; and the echoes of the forest mocked him, crying — "Faith! Faith!" as if bewildered wretches were seeking her, all through the wilderness.

The cry of grief, rage, and terror, was yet piercing the night, when the unhappy husband held his breath for a response. There was a scream, drowned immediately in a louder murmur of voices, fading into far-off laughter, as the dark cloud swept away, leaving the clear and silent sky above Goodman Brown. But something fluttered lightly down through the air, and caught on the branch of a tree. The young man seized it, and beheld a pink ribbon.

"My Faith is gone!" cried he, after one stupefied moment. 50 "There is no good on earth; and sin is but a name. Come, devil! for to thee is this world given."

And maddened with despair, so that he laughed loud and long, did Goodman Brown grasp his staff and set forth again, at such a rate, that he seemed to fly along the forest-path, rather than to walk or run. The road grew wilder and drearier, and more faintly traced, and vanished at length, leaving him in the heart of the dark wilderness, still rushing onward, with the instinct that guides mortal man to evil. The whole forest was peopled with frightful sounds; the creaking of the trees, the howling of wild beasts, and the yell of Indians; while, sometimes, the wind tolled like a distant church-bell, and sometimes gave a broad roar around the traveller, as if all Nature were laughing him to scorn. But he was himself the chief horror of the scene, and shrank not from its other horrors.

"Ha! ha! ha!" roared Goodman Brown, when the wind laughed at him. "Let us hear which will laugh loudest! Think not to frighten me with your deviltry! Come witch, come wizard, come Indian powow, come devil himself! and here comes Goodman Brown. You may as well fear him as he fear you!"

In truth, all through the haunted forest, there could be nothing more frightful than the figure of Goodman Brown. On he flew, among the black pines, brandishing his staff with frenzied gestures, now giving vent to an inspiration of horrid blasphemy, and now shouting forth such laughter, as set all the echoes of the forest laughing like demons around him. The fiend in his own shape is less hideous, than when he rages in the breast of man. Thus sped the demoniac on his course, until, quivering among the trees, he saw a red light before him, as when the felled trunks and branches of a clearing have been set on fire, and throw up their lurid blaze against the sky, at the hour of midnight. He paused, in a lull of the tempest that had driven him onward, and heard the swell of what seemed a hymn, rolling solemnly from a distance, with the weight of many voices. He knew the tune; it was a familiar one in the choir of the village meeting-house. The verse died heavily away, and was lengthened by a chorus, not of human voices, but of all the sounds of the benighted wilderness, pealing in awful harmony together. Goodman Brown cried out; and his cry was lost to his own ear, by its unison with the cry of the desert.

In the interval of silence, he stole forward, until the light glared full upon his eyes. At one extremity of an open space, hemmed in by the dark wall of the forest, arose a rock, bearing some rude, natural resemblance either to an altar or a pulpit, and surrounded by four blazing pines, their tops aflame, their stems untouched, like candles at an evening meeting. The mass of foliage, that had overgrown the summit of the rock, was all on fire, blazing high into the night, and fitfully illuminating the whole field. Each pendent twig and leafy festoon was in a blaze. As the red light arose and fell, a numerous congregation alternately shone forth, then disappeared in shadow, and again grew, as it were, out of the darkness, peopling the heart of the solitary woods at once.

"A grave and dark-clad company!" quoth Goodman Brown.   55

In truth, they were such. Among them, quivering to-and-fro, between gloom and splendor, appeared faces that would be seen, next day, at the council-board of the province, and others which, Sabbath after Sabbath, looked devoutly heavenward, and benignantly over the crowded pews, from the holiest pulpits in the land. Some affirm, that the lady of the governor was there. At least, there were high dames well known to her, and wives of honored husbands, and widows, a great multitude, and ancient maidens, all of excellent repute, and fair young girls, who trembled, lest their mothers should espy them. Either the sudden gleams of light, flashing over the obscure field, bedazzled Goodman Brown, or he recognized a score of the church-members of Salem village, famous for their especial sanctity. Good old Deacon Gookin had arrived, and waited at the skirts of that venerable saint, his revered pastor. But, irreverently consorting with these grave, reputable, and pious people, these elders of the church, these chaste dames and dewy virgins, there were men of dissolute lives and women of spotted fame, wretches given over to all mean and filthy vice, and suspected even of horrid crimes. It was strange to see, that the good shrank not from the wicked, nor were the sinners abashed by the saints. Scattered, also, among their pale-faced enemies, were the Indian priests, or powows, who had often scared their native forest with more hideous incantations than any known to English witchcraft.

"But, where is Faith?" thought Goodman Brown; and, as hope came into his heart, he trembled.

Another verse of the hymn arose, a slow and mournful strain, such as the pious love, but joined to words which expressed all that our nature can conceive of sin, and darkly hinted at far more. Unfathomable to mere mortals is the lore of fiends. Verse after verse was sung, and still the chorus of the desert swelled between, like the deepest tone of a mighty organ. And, with the final peal of that dreadful anthem, there came a sound, as if the roaring wind, the rushing streams, the howling beasts, and every other voice of the unconverted wilderness, were mingling and according with the voice of guilty man, in homage to the prince of all. The four blazing pines threw up a loftier flame, and obscurely discovered shapes and visages of horror on the smoke-wreaths, above the impious assembly. At the same moment, the fire on the rock shot redly forth, and formed a glowing arch above its base, where now appeared a figure. With reverence be it spoken, the figure bore no slight similitude, both in garb and manner, to some grave divine of the New-England churches.

"Bring forth the converts!" cried a voice, that echoed through the field and rolled into the forest.

At the word, Goodman Brown stept forth from the shadow of the trees, and approached the congregation, with whom he felt a loathful brotherhood, by the sympathy of all that was wicked in his heart. He could have well nigh sworn, that the shape of his own dead father beckoned him to advance, looking downward from a smoke-wreath, while a woman, with dim features of despair, threw out her hand to warn him back. Was it his mother? But he had no power to retreat one step, nor to resist, even in thought, when the minister and good old Deacon Gookin seized his arms, and led him to the blazing rock. Thither came also the slender form of a veiled female, led between Goody Cloyse, that pious teacher of the catechism, and Martha Carrier, who had received the devil's promise to be queen of hell. A rampant hag was she! And there stood the proselytes, beneath the canopy of fire.

"Welcome, my children," said the dark figure, "to the communion of your race! Ye have found, thus young, your nature and your destiny. My children, look behind you!"

They turned; and flashing forth, as it were, in a sheet of flame, the fiend-worshippers were seen; the smile of welcome gleamed darkly on every visage.

"There," resumed the sable form, "are all whom ye have reverenced from youth. Ye deemed them holier than yourselves, and shrank from your own sin, contrasting it with their lives of righteousness, and prayerful aspirations heavenward. Yet, here are they all, in my worshipping assembly! This night it shall be granted you to know their secret deeds; how hoary-bearded elders of the church have whispered wanton words to the young maids of their households; how many a woman, eager for widow's weeds, has given her husband a drink at bed-time, and let him sleep his last sleep in her bosom; how beardless youths have made haste to inherit their fathers' wealth; and how fair damsels — blush not, sweet ones! — have dug little graves in the garden, and bidden me, the sole guest, to an infant's funeral. By the sympathy of your human hearts for sin, ye shall scent out all the places — whether in church, bed-chamber, street, field, or forest — where crime has been committed, and shall exult to behold the whole earth one stain of guilt, one mighty blood-spot. Far more than this! It shall be yours to penetrate, in every bosom, the deep mystery of sin, the fountain of all wicked arts, and which inexhaustibly supplies more evil impulses than human power — than my power, at its utmost! — can make manifest in deeds. And now, my children, look upon each other."

They did so; and, by the blaze of the hell-kindled torches, the wretched man beheld his Faith, and the wife her husband, trembling before that unhallowed altar.

"Lo! there ye stand, my children," said the figure, in a deep 65 and solemn tone, almost sad, with its despairing awfulness, as if his once angelic nature could yet mourn for our miserable race. "Depending upon one another's hearts, ye had still hoped, that virtue were not all a dream. Now are ye undeceived! Evil is the nature of mankind. Evil must be your only happiness. Welcome, again, my children, to the communion of your race!"

"Welcome!" repeated the fiend-worshippers, in one cry of despair and triumph.

And there they stood, the only pair, as it seemed, who were yet hesitating on the verge of wickedness, in this dark world. A basin was hollowed, naturally, in the rock. Did it contain water, reddened by the lurid light? or was it blood? or, perchance, a liquid flame? Herein did the Shape of Evil dip his hand, and prepare to lay the mark of baptism upon their foreheads, that they might be partakers of the mystery of sin, more conscious of the secret guilt of others, both in deed and thought, than they could now be of their own. The husband cast one look at his pale wife, and Faith at him. What polluted wretches would the next glance shew them to each other, shuddering alike at what they disclosed and what they saw!

"Faith! Faith!" cried the husband. "Look up to Heaven, and resist the Wicked One!"

Whether Faith obeyed, he knew not. Hardly had he spoken, when he found himself amid calm night and solitude, listening to a roar of the wind, which died heavily away through the forest. He staggered against the rock and felt it chill and damp, while a hanging twig, that had been all on fire, besprinkled his cheek with the coldest dew.

The next morning, young Goodman Brown came slowly into 70 the street of Salem village, staring around him like a bewildered man. The good old minister was taking a walk along the grave-yard, to get an appetite for breakfast and meditate his sermon, and bestowed a blessing, as he passed, on Goodman Brown. He shrank from the venerable saint, as if to avoid an anathema. Old Deacon Gookin was at domestic worship, and the holy words of his prayer were heard through the open window. "What God doth the wizard pray to?" quoth Goodman Brown. Goody Cloyse, that excellent old Christian, stood in the early sunshine, at her own lattice, catechising a little girl, who had brought her a pint of morning's milk. Goodman Brown snatched away the child, as from the grasp of the fiend himself. Turning the corner by the meeting-house, he spied the head of Faith, with the pink ribbons, gazing anxiously forth, and bursting into such joy at sight of him, that she skipt along the street, and almost kissed her husband before the whole village. But, Goodman Brown looked sternly and sadly into her face, and passed on without a greeting.

Had Goodman Brown fallen asleep in the forest, and only dreamed a wild dream of a witch-meeting?

Be it so, if you will. But, alas! it was a dream of evil omen for young Goodman Brown. A stern, a sad, a darkly meditative, a distrustful, if not a desperate man, did he become, from the night of that fearful dream. On the Sabbath-day, when the congregation were singing a holy psalm, he could not listen, because an anthem of sin rushed loudly upon his ear, and drowned all the blessed strain. When the minister spoke from the pulpit, with power and fervid eloquence, and, with his hand on the open Bible, of the sacred truths of our religion, and of saint-like lives and triumphant deaths, and of future bliss or misery unutterable, then did Goodman Brown turn pale, dreading, lest the roof should thunder down upon the gray blasphemer and his hearers. Often, awakening suddenly at midnight, he shrank from the bosom of Faith, and at morning or eventide, when the family knelt down at prayer, he scowled, and muttered to himself, and gazed sternly at his wife, and turned away. And when he had lived long, and was borne to his grave, a hoary corpse, followed by Faith, an aged woman, and children and grand-children, a goodly procession, besides neighbors, not a few, they carved no hopeful verse upon his tomb-stone; for his dying hour was gloom.

Questions

"Young Goodman Brown" follows a young man's separation from his wife, Faith, and from his religious faith, and while reading it we bring to life both separations simultaneously. We do this by exploring parallels, within the character of Young Goodman Brown, between attitudes or feelings concerning marital relationships and attitudes or feelings concerning religious belief. Read over the following passage with an eye to evoking some of these parallels:

> "Poor little Faith!" thought he, for his heart smote him. "What a wretch am I, to leave her on such an errand! She talks of dreams, too. Methought, as she spoke, there was trouble in her face, as if a dream had warned her what work is to be done to-night. But, no, no! 'twould kill her to think it. Well; she's a blessed angel on earth; and after this one night, I'll cling to her skirts and follow her to Heaven." (para. 7)

1. What is Goodman Brown's attitude toward his wife as characterized in this passage?
2. What parallel can you draw between this attitude and
   Brown's attitude toward his religious belief? In what respects
   could these attitudes be described as identical?
3. How does your understanding of the tight interrelatedness
   of these attitudes affect your perception of Brown's religious
   faith? How does it affect your perception of the relationship
   between Brown and his wife?
4. Reread the final paragraph of the story, probing parallels
   and identities that you see in its language. What effect does
   your movement between allegorical levels have on your perception of religious faith and relationships between the
   sexes?
5. Write a response based on the first four questions and then
   compare it with the response that follows.

Response

EDITOR: In the opening paragraph of "Young Goodman Brown,"
Faith has only a single significance: It's the name of the hero's
young wife — a not uncommon name in late seventeenth-
century Puritan New England. Well before the end of the story,
though, we're aware of a relationship between Faith understood
as a person and Faith understood as a religious belief. At some
time prior to his involvement with the devil and the evil congregation, Goodman Brown was a believing Christian, but at the
end of the story he scowls and mutters at prayers; at the start of
the story he is close to his wife, at the end he shrinks from her.
The parallel is intensified because at every moment in the story's
course, except in the opening paragraph, it is possible to read
the word *Faith* as an allusion both to a person and to a condition
of religious belief.

When we read in this manner, tracking the doubleness, both
Faith, the young bride, and religious faith are freshly seen. Neither loses its original identity in the world of social reality or on
the plane of the abstract and ineffable. Faith the young woman is
and remains a wife, a helpmeet, a companion, a person who has
given and received vows of permanent commitment. Religious
belief is and remains what it was: acceptance of the reality of God

and of our obligations of prayer and worship. But our understanding of both sides of the equation is altered as we shuttle
between levels of meaning. And the terms of the transformation
are set in sharp relief by paragraph 7.

Evident in Young Goodman Brown's tone toward his wife are
a feeling and attitude which prove fatal both to their commitment to each other and to their commitment to God. The attitude is that of superiority. This is not, to be sure, the only attitude expressed in Goodman Brown's exclamation ("Poor little
Faith! . . . she's a blessed angel on earth"). He truly feels pity for
her and regret at their separation; his assertion that "after this
one night" he will "cling to her skirts" is doubtless sincere.

But the pity is from above to below; Goodman Brown's sense
of his Faith is that there's something childlike about her; she must
be protected from knowing the worst about him; she must be lied
to. Faith is made into something separate from real life at a time
of crisis; Faith is virtue and innocence that cannot be put to a
test, cannot possibly be strong enough to face serious challenge.

Implicit in this sense of things is Goodman Brown's conception of himself: He's free to break his vows, less dependent upon
Faith than she upon him, better placed without her as an encumbrance when dealing with the forces of darkness. In a word,
Goodman Brown's inconstancy is a sign of inner pride. And
that pride is deadly to both partners' commitment to each other
and ultimately to Goodman Brown's belief in God.

What exactly does it mean to say this? One must answer on
two levels, and the answers define the subtle transformations of
Faith that occur as this allegory is brought to life. In the opening
paragraph Faith is fearful, troubled at the prospect of being left
alone — and Goodman Brown treats her feelings as a mark of
childlike femininity ("Poor little Faith!"). The "pretty head," the
"pink ribbons" (1), the plea that he stay bespeak, to his mind,
both frailty and dependence. And because he sees them that way,
he turns condescending, imagines himself as self-sufficient and
*in*dependent, commences to patronize his own ideal. Putting it
more flatly, he misreads Faith as weak and timid and himself as
strong and daring — and that misreading is the root of the self-
inflation that leads to his ruin.

How should Goodman Brown have perceived Faith? As a
resource with which to meet the moral and spiritual challenges
of existence; as a peer in every respect whose understanding of

separation as perilous is a strength, not a weakness. Faith the young bride is not a mere pretty head and a set of girlish ribbons to be paid perfunctory compliments. Under the vows this couple has exchanged, Faith is an equal in their joint life; her contribu- tions differ from her husband's but are as deserving of honor — as essential to their well-being — as his. In defining her as less than himself — as "poor" and "little" — Goodman Brown be- trays both Faith and his own pledge. At intervals in the allegory he seems almost to grasp, freshly, their interdependency. Cer- tainly this is true when he cries out his wife's name "in a voice of agony and desperation" (48), and again as the two stand together finally at "that unhallowed altar" (64). But by then the damage has been done. Pride has separated them; the refusal to trust Faith's intuition, to believe in the courage and wisdom of her intitial protectiveness, has led them both to ruin. As we move back and forth between the significations of Faith, we come to see the young woman as strength and intelligence unvalued, as truth and wisdom belittled. And by the same token we see re- ligious faith as crippled by the perception that *it* lacks strength, is not equal to the harsh reality of the world, can't be counted on in a storm.

The effect of bringing this allegory to life isn't to substitute one abstraction for another. What happens instead is that the original terms and characters come to exist in a unique config- uration that opens up new perspectives on the loss of religious faith, on infidelity in marriage, and on relationships between the sexes. We see how pride figures both in unbelief and in incon- stancy. We see that human beings *cannot* see, do not grasp even after suffering tragic losses how the losses occurred, how they might have been avoided. Marriage and religion are the central concerns here; active readers of "Young Goodman Brown" col- laborate with Hawthorne in transforming understandings of both.

JOHN BARTH   (b. 1930)
Lost in the Funhouse

For whom is the funhouse fun? Perhaps for lovers. For Am- brose it is *a place of fear and confusion.* He has come to the seashore with his family for the holiday, *the occasion of their visit is Indepen-*

dence Day, the most important secular holiday of the United States of *America.* A single straight underline is the manuscript mark for italic type, *which in turn* is the printed equivalent to oral emphasis of words and phrases as well as the customary type for titles of complete works, not to mention. Italics are also employed, in fiction stories especially, for "outside," intrusive, or artificial voices, such as radio announcements, the texts of telegrams and newspaper articles, et cetera. They should be used *sparingly.* If passages originally in roman type are italicized by someone repeating them, it's customary to acknowledge the fact. *Italics mine.*

Ambrose was "at that awkward age." His voice came out high-pitched as a child's if he let himself get carried away; to be on the safe side, therefore, he moved and spoke with *deliberate calm* and *adult gravity.* Talking soberly of unimportant or irrelevant matters and listening consciously to the sound of your own voice are useful habits for maintaining control in this difficult interval. *En route* to Ocean City he sat in the back seat of the family car with his brother Peter, age fifteen, and Magda G——, age fourteen, a pretty girl an exquisite young lady, who lived not far from them on B—— Street in the town of D——, Maryland. Initials, blanks, or both were often substituted for proper names in nineteenth-century fiction to enhance the illusion of reality. It is as if the author felt it necessary to delete the names for reasons of tact or legal liability. Interestingly, as with other aspects of realism, it is an *illusion* that is being enhanced, by purely artificial means. It is likely, does it violate the principle of verisimilitude, that a thirteen-year-old boy could make such a sophisticated observation? A girl of fourteen is *the psychological coeval* of a boy of fifteen or sixteen; a thirteen-year-old boy, therefore, even one precocious in some other respects, might be three years *her emotional junior.*

Thrice a year — on Memorial, Independence, and Labor Days — the family visits Ocean City for the afternoon and evening. When Ambrose and Peter's father was their age, the excursion was made by train, as mentioned in the novel *The 42nd Parallel* by John Dos Passos. Many families from the same neighborhood used to travel together, with dependent relatives and often with Negro servants; schoolfuls of children swarmed through the railway cars; everyone shared everyone else's Maryland fried chicken, Virginia ham, deviled eggs, potato salad, beaten biscuits, iced tea. Nowadays (that is, in 19—, the year of our story) the journey is made by automobile — more comfortably and quickly though without the extra fun though without the

camaraderie of a general excursion. It's all part of the deterioration of American life, their father declares; Uncle Karl supposes
that when the boys take *their* families to Ocean City for the
holidays they'll fly in Autogiros. Their mother, sitting in the
middle of the front seat like Magda in the second, only with her
arms on the seat-back behind the men's shoulders, wouldn't want
the good old days back again, the steaming trains and stuffy long
dresses; on the other hand she can do without Autogiros, too, if
she has to become a grandmother to fly in them.

Description of physical appearance and mannerisms is one
of several standard methods of characterization used by writers
of fiction. It is also important to "keep the senses operating";
when a detail from one of the five senses, say visual, is "crossed"
with a detail from another, say auditory, the reader's imagination
is oriented to the scene, perhaps unconsciously. This procedure
may be compared to the way surveyors and navigators determine
their positions by two or more compass bearings, a process
known as triangulation. The brown hair on Ambrose's mother's
forearms gleamed in the sun like. Though right-handed, she took
her left arm from the seat-back to press the dashboard cigar
lighter for Uncle Karl. When the glass bead in its handle glowed
red, the lighter was ready for use. The smell of Uncle Karl's cigar
smoke reminded one of. The fragrance of the ocean came strong
to the picnic ground where they always stopped for lunch, two
miles inland from Ocean City. Having to pause for a full hour
almost within sound of the breakers was difficult for Peter and
Ambrose when they were younger; even at their present age it
was not easy to keep their anticipation, *stimulated by the briny
spume,* from turning into short temper. The Irish author James
Joyce, in his unusual novel entitled *Ulysses,* now available in this
country, uses the adjectives *snot-green* and *scrotum-tightening* to
describe the sea. Visual, auditory, tactile, olfactory, gustatory.
Peter and Ambrose's father, while steering their black 1936
LaSalle sedan with one hand, could with the other remove the
first cigarette from a white pack of Lucky Strikes and, more
remarkably, light it with a match forefingered from its book and
thumbed against the flint paper without being detached. The
matchbook cover merely advertised U.S. War Bonds and Stamps.
A fine metaphor, simile, or other figure of speech, in addition to
its obvious "first-order" relevance to the thing it describes, will
be seen upon reflection to have a second order of significance: it
may be drawn from the *milieu* of the action, for example, or be
particularly appropriate to the sensibility of the narrator, even
hinting to the reader things of which the narrator is unaware; or

it may cast further and subtler lights upon the thing it describes, sometimes ironically qualifying the more evident sense of the comparison.

To say that Ambrose's and Peter's mother was *pretty* is to 5 accomplish nothing; the reader may acknowledge the proposition, but his imagination is not engaged. Besides, Magda was also pretty, yet in an altogether different way. Although she lived on B—— Street she had very good manners and did better than average in school. Her figure was very well developed for her age. Her right hand lay casually on the plush upholstery of the seat, very near Ambrose's left leg, on which his own hand rested. The space between their legs, between her right and his left leg, was out of the line of sight of anyone sitting on the other side of Magda, as well as anyone glancing into the rear-view mirror. Uncle Karl's face resembled Peter's — rather, vice versa. Both had dark hair and eyes, short husky statures, deep voices. Magda's left hand was probably in a similar position on her left side. The boy's father is difficult to describe; no particular feature of his appearance or manner stood out. He wore glasses and was principal of a T—— County grade school. Uncle Karl was a masonry contractor.

Although Peter must have known as well as Ambrose that the latter, because of his position in the car, would be the first to see the electrical towers of the power plant at V——, the halfway point of their trip, he leaned forward and slightly toward the center of the car and pretended to be looking for them through the flat pinewoods and tuckahoe creeks along the highway. For as long as the boys could remember, "looking for the Towers" had been a feature of the first half of their excursions to Ocean City, "looking for the standpipe" of the second. Though the game was childish, their mother preserved the tradition of rewarding the first to see the Towers with a candy-bar or piece of fruit. She insisted now that Magda play the game; the prize, she said, was "something hard to get nowadays." Ambrose decided not to join in; he sat far back in his seat. Magda, like Peter, leaned forward. Two sets of straps were discernible through the shoulders of her sun dress; the inside right one a brassiere-strap, was fastened or shortened with a small safety pin. The right armpit of her dress, presumably the left as well, was damp with perspiration. The simple strategy for being first to espy the Towers, which Ambrose had understood by the age of four, was to sit on the right-hand side of the car. Whoever sat there, however, had also to put up with the worst of the sun, and so Ambrose, without mentioning the matter, chose sometimes the one and sometimes the other.

Not impossibly Peter had never caught on to the trick, or thought that his brother hadn't simply because Ambrose on occasion preferred shade to a Baby Ruth or tangerine.

The shade-sun situation didn't apply to the front seat, owing to the windshield; if anything the driver got more sun, since the person on the passenger side not only was shaded below by the door and dashboard but might swing down his sunvisor all the way too.

"Is that them?" Magda asked. Ambrose's mother teased the boys for letting Magda win, insinuating that "somebody [had] a girlfriend." Peter and Ambrose's father reached a long thin arm across their mother to butt his cigarette in the dashboard ashtray, under the lighter. The prize this time for seeing the Towers first was a banana. Their mother bestowed it after chiding their father for wasting a half-smoked cigarette when everything was so scarce. Magda, to take the prize, moved her hand from so near Ambrose's that he could have touched it as though accidentally. She offered to share the prize, things like that were so hard to find; but everyone insisted it was hers alone. Ambrose's mother sang an iambic trimeter couplet from a popular song, femininely rhymed:

> "*What's good is in the Army;*
> *What's left will never harm me.*"

Uncle Karl tapped his cigar ash out the ventilator window; some particles were sucked by the slipstream back into the car through the rear window on the passenger side. Magda demonstrated her ability to hold a banana in one hand and peel it with her teeth. She still sat forward; Ambrose pushed his glasses back onto the bridge of his nose with his left hand, which he then negligently let fall to the seat cushion immediately behind her. He even permitted the single hair, gold, on the second joint of his thumb to brush the fabric of her skirt. Should she have sat back at that instant, his hand would have been caught under her.

Plush upholstery prickles uncomfortably through gabardine slacks in the July sun. The function of the *beginning* of a story is to introduce the principal characters, establish their initial relationships, set the scene for the main action, expose the background of the situation if necessary, plant motifs and foreshadowings where appropriate, and initiate the first complication or whatever of the "rising action." Actually, if one imagines a story called "The Funhouse," or "Lost in the Funhouse," the details of the drive to Ocean City don't seem especially relevant. The *begin-*

ning should recount the events between Ambrose's first sight of the funhouse early in the afternoon and his entering it with Magda and Peter in the evening. The *middle* would narrate all relevant events from the time he goes in to the time he loses his way; middles have the double and contradictory function of delaying the climax while at the same time preparing the reader for it and fetching him to it. Then the *ending* would tell what Ambrose does while he's lost, how he finally finds his way out, and what everybody makes of the experience. So far there's been no real dialogue, very little sensory detail, and nothing in the way of a *theme*. And a long time has gone by already without anything happening; it makes a person wonder. We haven't even reached Ocean City yet: we will never get out of the funhouse.

The more closely an author identifies with the narrator, 10 literally or metaphorically, the less advisable it is, as a rule, to use the first-person narrative viewpoint. Once three years previously the young people *aforementioned* played Niggers and Masters in the backyard; when it was Ambrose's turn to be Master and theirs to be Niggers Peter had to go serve his evening papers; Ambrose was afraid to punish Magda alone, but she led him to the white-washed Torture Chamber between the woodshed and the privy in the Slaves Quarters; there she knelt sweating among bamboo rakes and dusty Mason jars, pleadingly embraced his knees, and while bees droned in the lattice as if on an ordinary summer afternoon, purchased clemency at a surprising price set by her-self. Doubtless she remembered nothing of this event; Ambrose on the other hand seemed unable to forget the least detail of his life. He even recalled how, standing beside himself with awed impersonality in the reeky heat, he'd stared the while at an empty cigar box in which Uncle Karl kept stone-cutting chisels: beneath the words *El Producto*, a laureled, loose-toga'd lady regarded the sea from a marble bench; beside her, forgotten or not yet turned to, was a five-stringed lyre. Her chin reposed on the back of her right hand; her left depended negligently from the bench-arm. The lower half of scene and lady was peeled away; the words EXAMINED BY _____ were inked there into the wood. Nowadays cigar boxes are made of pasteboard. Ambrose wondered what Magda would have done, Ambrose wondered what Magda would do when she sat back on his hand as he resolved she should. Be angry. Make a teasing joke of it. Give no sign at all. For a long time she leaned forward, playing cow-poker with Peter against Uncle Karl and Mother and watching for the first sign of Ocean City. At nearly the same instant, picnic ground and Ocean City standpipe hove into view; an Amoco filling station on their side of the road cost Mother and Uncle Karl fifty cows and the game; Magda bounced back, clapping her right hand on Mother's right arm; Ambrose moved clear "in the nick of time."

At this rate our hero, at this rate our protagonist will remain in the funhouse forever. Narrative ordinarily consists of alternating dramatization and summarization. One symptom of nervous tension, paradoxically, is repeated and violent yawning; neither Peter nor Magda nor Uncle Karl nor Mother reacted in this manner. Although they were no longer small children, Peter and Ambrose were each given a dollar to spend on boardwalk amusements in addition to what money of their own they'd brought along. Magda too, though she protested she had ample spending money. The boys' mother made a little scene out of distributing the bills; she pretended that her sons and Magda were small children and cautioned them not to spend the sum too quickly or in one place. Magda promised with a merry laugh and, having both hands free, took the bill with her left. Peter laughed also and pledged in a falsetto to be a good boy. His imitation of a child was not clever. The boys' father was tall and thin, balding, fair-complexioned. Assertions of that sort are not effective; the reader may acknowledge the proposition, but. We should be much farther along than we are; something has gone wrong; not much of this preliminary rambling seems relevant. Yet everyone begins in the same place; how is it that most go along without difficulty but a few lose their way?

"Stay out from under the boardwalk," Uncle Karl growled from the side of his mouth The boys' mother pushed his shoulder *in mock annoyance*. They were all standing before Fat May the Laughing Lady who advertised the funhouse. Larger than life, Fat May mechanically shook, rocked on her heels, slapped her thighs while recorded laughter — uproarious, female — came amplified from a hidden loudspeaker. It chuckled, wheezed, wept; tried in vain to catch its breath; tittered, groaned, exploded raucous and anew. You couldn't hear it without laughing yourself, no matter how you felt. Father came back from talking to a Coast-Guardsman on duty and reported that the surf was spoiled with crude oil from tankers recently torpedoed offshore. Lumps of it, difficult to remove, made tarry tidelines on the beach and stuck on swimmers. Many bathed in the surf nevertheless and came out speckled; others paid to use a municipal pool and only sunbathed on the beach. We would do the latter. We would do the latter. We would do the latter.

Under the boardwalk, matchbook covers, grainy other things. What is the story's theme? Ambrose is ill. He perspires in the dark passages; candied apples-on-a-stick, delicious-looking, disappointing to eat. Funhouses need men's and ladies' rooms at intervals. Others perhaps have also vomited in corners and corridors; may even have had bowel movements liable to be stepped in in the dark. The word *fuck* suggests suction and/or and/or flatulence. Mother and Father; grandmothers and grandfathers on both sides; great-grandmothers and great-grandfathers on four sides, et cetera. Count a generation as thirty years: in approximately the year when Lord Baltimore was granted charter to the province of Maryland by Charles I, five hundred twelve women — English, Welsh, Bavarian, Swiss — of every class and character, received into themselves the penises the intromittent organs of five hundred twelve men, ditto, in every circumstance and posture, to conceive the five hundred twelve ancestors of the two hundred fifty-six ancestors of the et cetera et cetera et cetera et cetera et cetera et cetera et cetera of the author, of the narrator, of this story, *Lost in the Funhouse*. In alleyways, ditches, canopy beds, pinewoods, bridal suites, ship's cabins, coach-and-fours, coaches-and-four, sultry toolsheds; on the cold sand under boardwalks, littered with *El Producto* cigar butts, treasured with Lucky Strike cigarette stubs, Coca-Cola caps, gritty turds, cardboard lollipop sticks, matchbook covers warning that A Slip of the Lip Can Sink a Ship. The shluppish whisper, continuous as seawash round the globe, tidelike falls and rises with the circuit of dawn and dusk.

Magda's teeth. She *was* left-handed. Perspiration. They've gone all the way, through, Magda and Peter, they've been waiting for hours with Mother and Uncle Karl while Father searches for his lost son; they draw french-fried potatoes from a paper cup and shake their heads. They've named the children they'll one day have and bring to Ocean City on holidays. Can spermatozoa properly be thought of as male animalcules when there are no female spermatozoa? They grope through hot, dark windings, past Love's Tunnel's fearsome obstacles. Some perhaps lose their way.

Peter suggested then and there that they do the funhouse; he 15 had been through it before, so had Magda, Ambrose hadn't and suggested, his voice cracking on account of Fat May's laughter, that they swim first. All were chuckling, couldn't help it; Ambrose's father, Ambrose's and Peter's father came up grinning like a lunatic with two boxes of syrup-coated popcorn, one for Mother, one for Magda; the men were to help themselves. Ambrose walked on Magda's right; being by nature left-handed, she

carried the box in her left hand. Up front the situation was re-
versed.

"What are you limping for?" Magda inquired of Ambrose. He
supposed in a husky tone that his foot had gone to sleep in the
car. Her teeth flashed. "Pins and needles?" It was the honeysuckle on the lattice of the former privy that drew the bees.
Imagine being stung there. How long is this going to take?

The adults decided to forgo the pool; but Uncle Karl insisted
they change into swimsuits and do the beach. "He wants to watch
the pretty girls," Peter teased, and ducked behind Magda from
Uncle Karl's pretended wrath. "You've got all the pretty girls you
need right here," Magda declared, and Mother said: "Now that's
the gospel truth." Magda scolded Peter, who reached over her
shoulder to sneak some popcorn. "Your brother and father aren't
getting any." Uncle Karl wondered if they were going to have
fireworks that night, what with the shortages. It wasn't the shortages, Mr. M—— replied; Ocean City had fireworks from pre-war.
But it was too risky on account of the enemy submarines, some
people thought.

"Don't seem like Fourth of July without fireworks," said
Uncle Karl. The inverted tag in dialogue writing is still considered permissible with proper names or epithets, but sounds old-
fashioned with personal pronouns. "We'll have 'em again soon
enough," predicted the boys' father. Their mother declared she
could do without fireworks: they reminded her too much of the
real thing. Their father said all the more reason to shoot off a few
now and again. Uncle Karl asked *rhetorically* who needed reminding, just look at people's hair and skin.

"The oil, yes," said Mrs. M——.

Ambrose had a pain in his stomach and so didn't swim but 20
enjoyed watching the others. He and his father burned red easily.
Magda's figure was exceedingly well developed for her age. She
too declined to swim, and got mad, and became angry when
Peter attempted to drag her into the pool. She always swam, he
insisted; what did she mean not swim? Why did a person come to
Ocean City?

"Maybe I want to lay here with Ambrose," Magda teased.

Nobody likes a pedant.

"Aha," said Mother. Peter grabbed Magda by one ankle and
ordered Ambrose to grab the other. She squealed and rolled over
on the beach blanket. Ambrose pretended to help hold her back.
Her tan was darker than even Mother's and Peter's. "Help out,
Uncle Karl!" Peter cried. Uncle Karl went to seize the other ankle.

Inside the top of her swimsuit, however, you could see the line where the sunburn ended and, when she hunched her shoulders and squealed again, one nipple's auburn edge. Mother made them behave themselves. *"You* should certainly know," she said to Uncle Karl. Archly. "That when a lady says she doesn't feel like swimming, a gentleman doesn't ask questions." Uncle Karl said excuse *him*; Mother winked at Magda; Ambrose blushed; stupid Peter kept saying "Phooey on *feel like!"* and tugging at Magda's ankle; then even he got the point, and cannonballed with a holler into the pool.

"I swear," Magda said, in mock *in feigned* exasperation.

The diving would make a suitable literary symbol. To go off 25 the high board you had to wait in a line along the poolside and up the ladder. Fellows tickled girls and goosed one another and shouted to the ones at the top to hurry up, or razzed them for bellyfloppers. Once on the springboard some took a great while posing or clowning or deciding on a dive or getting up their nerve; others ran right off. Especially among the younger fellows the idea was to strike the funniest pose or do the craziest stunt as you fell, a thing that got harder to do as you kept on and kept on. But whether you hollered *Geronimo!* or *Sieg heil!*, held your nose or "rode a bicycle," pretended to be shot or did a perfect jackknife or changed your mind halfway down and ended up with nothing, it was over in two seconds, after all that wait. Spring, pose, splash. Spring, neat-o, splash. Spring, aw fooey, splash.

The grown-ups had gone on; Ambrose wanted to converse with Magda; she was remarkably well developed for her age; it was said that that came from rubbing with a turkish towel, and there were other theories. Ambrose could think of nothing to say except how good a diver Peter was, who was showing off for her benefit. You could pretty well tell by looking at their bathing suits and arm muscles how far along the different fellows were. Ambrose was glad he hadn't gone in swimming, the cold water shrank you up so. Magda pretended to be uninterested in the diving; she probably weighed as much as he did. If you knew your way around in the funhouse like your own bedroom, you could wait until a girl came along and then slip away without ever getting caught, even if her boyfriend was right with her. She'd think *he* did it! It would be better to be the boyfriend, and act outraged, and tear the funhouse apart.

Not act; *be.*

"He's a master diver," Ambrose said. In feigned admiration. "You really have to slave away at it to get that good." What would

it matter anyhow if he asked her right out whether she remembered, even teased her with it as Peter would have?

There's no point in going farther; this isn't getting anybody
anywhere; they haven't even come to the funhouse yet. Ambrose
is off the track, in some new or old part of the place that's not
supposed to be used; he strayed into it by some one-in-a-million
chance, like the time the roller-coaster car left the tracks in the
nineteen-teens against all the laws of physics and sailed over the
boardwalk in the dark. And they can't locate him because they
don't know where to look. Even the designer and operator have
forgotten this other part, that winds around on itself like a whelk
shell. That winds around the right part like the snakes on Mercury's caduceus. Some people, perhaps, don't "hit their stride"
until their twenties, when the growing-up business is over and
women appreciate other things besides wisecracks and teasing
and strutting. Peter didn't have one-tenth the imagination *he* had,
not one-tenth. Peter did this naming-their-children thing as a
joke, making up names like Aloysius and Murgatroyd, but Ambrose knew *exactly* how it would feel to be married and have
children of your own, and be a loving husband and father, and go
comfortably to work in the mornings and to bed with your wife at
night, and wake up with her there. With a breeze coming through
the sash and birds and mockingbirds singing in the Chinese-cigar
trees. His eyes watered, there aren't enough ways to say that. He
would be quite famous in his line of work. Whether Magda was
his wife or not, one evening when he was wise-lined and gray at
the temples he'd smile gravely, at a fashionable dinner party, and
remind her of his youthful passion. The time they went with his
family to Ocean City; the *erotic fantasies* he used to have about her.
How long ago it seemed, and childish! Yet tender, too, *n'est-ce pas?*
Would she have imagined that the world-famous whatever remembered how many strings were on the lyre on the bench
beside the girl on the label of the cigar box he'd stared at in the
toolshed at age ten while she, age eleven. Even then he had felt
wise beyond his years; he'd stroked her hair and said in his deepest
voice and correctest English, as to a dear child: "I shall never
forget this moment."

But though he had breathed heavily, groaned as if ecstatic,   30
what he'd really felt throughout was an odd detachment, as
though someone else were Master. Strive as he might to be transported, he heard his mind take notes upon the scene: *This is what
they call* passion. *I am experiencing it.* Many of the digger machines
were out of order in the penny arcades and could not be repaired

or replaced for the duration. Moreover the prizes, made now in USA, were less interesting than formerly, pasteboard items for the most part, and some of the machines wouldn't work on white pennies. The gypsy fortune-teller machine might have provided a foreshadowing of the climax of this story if Ambrose had operated it. It was even dilapidateder than most: the silver coating was worn off the brown metal handles, the glass windows around the dummy were cracked and taped, her kerchiefs and silks long-faded. If a man lived by himself, he could take a department-store mannequin with flexible joints and modify her in certain ways. *However:* by the time he was that old he'd have a real woman. There was a machine that stamped your name around a white-metal coin with a star in the middle: *A*——. His son would be the second, and when the lad reached thirteen or so he would put a strong arm around his shoulder and tell him calmly: "It is perfectly normal. We have all been through it. It will not last forever." Nobody knew how to be what they were right. He'd smoke a pipe, teach his son how to fish and softcrab, assure him he needn't worry about himself. Magda would certainly give, Magda would certainly yield a great deal of milk, although guilty of occasional solecisms. It don't taste so bad. Suppose the lights came on now!

The day wore on. You think you're yourself, but there are other persons in you. Ambrose gets hard when Ambrose doesn't want to, *and obversely.* Ambrose watches them disagree; Ambrose watches him watch. In the funhouse mirror-room you can't see yourself go on forever, because no matter how you stand, your head gets in the way. Even if you had a glass periscope, the image of your eye would cover up the thing you really wanted to see. The police will come; there'll be a story in the papers. That must be where it happened. Unless he can find a surprise exit, an unofficial backdoor or escape hatch opening on an alley, say, and then stroll up to the family in front of the funhouse and ask where everybody's been; *he's* been out of the place for ages. That's just where it happened, in that last lighted room: Peter and Magda found the right exit; he found one that you weren't supposed to find and strayed off into the works somewhere. In a perfect funhouse you'd be able to go only one way, like the divers off the highboard; getting lost would be impossible; the doors and halls would work like minnow traps or the valves in veins.

On account of German U-boats, Ocean City was "browned out": streetlights were shaded on the seaward side; shop-windows and boardwalk amusement places were kept dim, not to silhouette tankers and Liberty-ships for torpedoing. In a short story about Ocean City, Maryland, during World War II, the author could make use of the image of sailors on leave in the penny arcades and shooting galleries, sighting through the crosshairs of toy machine guns at swastika'd subs, while out in the black Atlantic a U-boat skipper squints through his periscope at real ships outlined by the glow of penny arcades. After dinner the family strolled back to the amusement end of the boardwalk. The boys' father had burnt red as always and was masked with Noxzema, a minstrel in reverse. The grownups stood at the end of the boardwalk where the Hurricane of '33 had cut an inlet from the ocean to Assawoman Bay.

"Pronounced with a long *o*," Uncle Karl reminded Magda with a wink. His shirt sleeves were rolled up; Mother punched his brown biceps with the arrowed heart on it and said his mind was naughty. Fat May's laugh came suddenly from the funhouse, as if she'd just got the joke; the family laughed too at the coincidence. Ambrose went under the boardwalk to search for out-of-town matchbook covers with the aid of his pocket flashlight; he looked out from the edge of the North American continent and wondered how far their laughter carried over the water. Spies in rubber rafts; survivors in lifeboats. If the joke had been beyond his understanding, he could have said: "*The laughter was over his head.*" And let the reader see the serious wordplay on second reading.

He turned the flashlight on and then off at once even before the woman whooped. He sprang away, heart athud, dropping the light. What had the man grunted? Perspiration drenched and chilled him by the time he scrambled up to the family. "See anything?" his father asked. His voice wouldn't come; he shrugged and violently brushed sand from his pants legs.

"Let's ride the old flying horses!" Magda cried. I'll never be 35 an author. It's been forever already, everybody's gone home, Ocean City's deserted, the ghost-crabs are tickling across the beach and down the littered cold streets. And the empty halls of clapboard hotels and abandoned funhouses. A tidal wave; an enemy air raid; a monster-crab swelling like an island from the sea. *The inhabitants fled in terror.* Magda clung to his trouser leg; he alone knew the maze's secret. "He gave his life that we might live," said Uncle Karl with a scowl of pain, as he. The fellow's hands had been tattooed; the woman's legs, the woman's fat white legs had. *An astonishing coincidence.* He yearned to tell Peter. He wanted to throw up for excitement. They hadn't even chased him. He wished he were dead.

One possible ending would be to have Ambrose come across

another lost person in the dark. They'd match their wits together against the funhouse, struggle like Ulysses past obstacle after obstacle, help and encourage each other. Or a girl. By the time they found the exit they'd be closest friends, sweethearts if it were a girl; they'd know each other's inmost souls, be bound together *by the cement of shared adventure*; then they'd emerge into the light and it would turn out that his friend was a Negro. A blind girl. President Roosevelt's son. Ambrose's former archenemy.

Shortly after the mirror room he'd groped along a musty corridor, his heart already misgiving him at the absence of phosphorescent arrows and other signs. He'd found a crack of light — not a door, it turned out, but a seam between the plyboard wall panels — and squinting up to it, espied a small old man, *in appearance not unlike* the photographs at home of Ambrose's late grandfather, nodding upon a stool beneath a bare, speckled bulb. A crude panel of toggle- and knife-switches hung beside the open fuse box near his head; elsewhere in the little room were wooden levers and ropes belayed to boat cleats. At the time, Ambrose wasn't lost enough to rap or call; later he couldn't find that crack. Now it seemed to him that he'd possibly dozed off for a few minutes somewhere along the way; certainly he was exhausted from the afternoon's sunshine and the evening's problems; he couldn't be sure he hadn't dreamed part or all of the sight. Had an old black wall fan droned like bees and shimmied two flypaper streamers? Had the funhouse operator — gentle, somewhat sad and tired-appearing, in expression not unlike the photographs at home of Ambrose's late Uncle Konrad — murmured in his sleep? Is there really such a person as Ambrose, or is he a figment of the author's imagination? Was it Assawoman Bay or Sinepuxent? Are there other errors of fact in this fiction? Was there another sound besides the little slap slap of thigh on ham, like water sucking at the chine-boards of a skiff?

When you're lost, the smartest thing to do is stay put till you're found, hollering if necessary. But to holler guarantees humiliation as well as rescue; keeping silent permits some saving of face — you can act surprised at the fuss when your rescuers find you and swear you weren't lost, if they do. What's more you might find your own way yet, *however belatedly*.

"Don't tell me your foot's still asleep!" Magda exclaimed as the three young people walked from the inlet to the area set aside for ferris wheels, carrousels, and other carnival rides, they having decided in favor of the vast and ancient merry-go-round instead of the funhouse. What a sentence, everything was wrong from the outset. People don't know what to make of him, he doesn't know what to make of himself, he's only thirteen, *athletically and socially inept*, not astonishingly bright, but there are antennae; he has . . . some sort of receivers in his head; things speak to him, he understands more than he should, the world winks at him through its objects, grabs grinning at his coat. Everybody else is in on some secret he doesn't know; they've forgotten to tell him. Through simple *procrastination* his mother put off his baptism until this year. Everyone else had it done as a baby; he'd assumed the same of himself, as had his mother, so she claimed, until it was time for him to join Grace Methodist–Protestant and the oversight came out. He was mortified, but pitched sleepless through his private catechizing, intimidated by the ancient mysteries, a thirteen year old would never say that, resolved to experience conversion like St. Augustine. When the water touched his brow and Adam's sin left him, he contrived by a strain like defecation to bring tears into his eyes — but felt nothing. There was some simple, radical difference about him; he hoped it was genius, feared it was madness, devoted himself to amiability and inconspicuousness. Alone on the seawall near his house he was seized by the terrifying transports he'd thought to find in toolshed, in Communion-cup. The grass was alive! The town, the river, himself, were not imaginary; time roared in his ears like wind; the world was *going on!* This part ought to be dramatized. The Irish author James Joyce once wrote. Ambrose M—— is going to scream.

There is no *texture of rendered sensory detail*, for one thing. The 40 faded distorting mirrors beside Fat May; the impossibility of choosing a mount when one had but a single ride on the great carrousel; the *vertigo attendant on his recognition* that Ocean City was worn out, the place of fathers and grandfathers, straw-boatered men and parasoled ladies survived by their amusements. Money spent, the three paused at Peter's insistence beside Fat May to watch the girls get their skirts blown up. The object was to tease Magda, who said: "I swear, Peter M——, you've got a one-track mind! Amby and me aren't *interested* in such things." In the tumbling-barrel, too, just inside the Devil's-mouth entrance to the funhouse, the girls were upended and their boyfriends and others could see up their dresses if they cared to. Which was the whole point, Ambrose realized. Of the entire funhouse! If you looked around, you noticed that almost all the people on the boardwalk were paired off into couples except the small children; in a way, that was the whole point of Ocean City! If you had X-ray eyes and could see everything going on at that instant under the boardwalk and in all the hotel rooms and cars and alleyways, you'd realize that all that normally *showed*, like restaurants and dance halls and clothing and test-your-strength machines, was merely preparation and intermission. Fat May screamed.

Because he watched the goings-on from the corner of his eye, it was Ambrose who spied the half-dollar on the boardwalk near the tumbling-barrel. Losers weepers. The first time he'd heard some people moving through a corridor not far away, just after he'd lost sight of the crack of light, he'd decided not to call to them, for fear they'd guess he was scared and poke fun; it sounded like roughnecks; he'd hoped they'd come by and he could follow in the dark without their knowing. Another time he'd heard just one person, unless he imagined it, bumping along as if on the other side of the plywood; perhaps Peter coming back for him, or Father, or Magda lost too. Or the owner and operator of the funhouse. He'd called out once, as though merrily: "Anybody know where the heck we are?" But the query was too stiff, his voice cracked, when the sounds stopped he was terrified: maybe it was a queer who waited for fellows to get lost, or a longhaired filthy monster that lived in some cranny of the funhouse. He stood rigid for hours it seemed like, scarcely respiring. His future was shockingly clear, in outline. He tried holding his breath to the point of unconsciousness. There ought to be a button you could push to end your life absolutely without pain; disappear in a flick, like turning out a light. He would push it instantly! He despised Uncle Karl. But he despised his father too, for not being what he was supposed to be. Perhaps his father hated *his* father, and so on, and his son would hate him, and so on. Instantly!

Naturally he didn't have nerve enough to ask Magda to go through the funhouse with him. With incredible nerve and to everyone's surprise he invited Magda, quietly and politely, to go through the funhouse with him. "I warn you, I've never been through it before," he added, *laughing easily*; "but I reckon we can manage somehow. The important thing to remember, after all, is that it's meant to be a *fun*house; that is, a place of amusement. If people really got lost or injured or too badly frightened in it, the owner'd go out of business. There'd even be lawsuits. No character in a work of fiction can make a speech this long without interruption or acknowledgment from the other characters."

Mother teased Uncle Karl: "Three's a crowd, I always heard." But actually Ambrose was relieved that Peter now had a quarter too. Nothing was what it looked like. Every instant, under the surface of the Atlantic Ocean, millions of living animals devoured one another. Pilots were falling in flames over Europe; women were being forcibly raped in the South Pacific. His father should have taken him aside and said: "There is a simple secret to getting through the funhouse, as simple as being first to see the Towers. Here it is. Peter does not know it; neither does your Uncle Karl. You and I are different. Not surprisingly, you've often wished you weren't. Don't think I haven't noticed how unhappy your childhood has been! But you'll understand, when I tell you, why it had to be kept secret until now. And you won't regret not being like your brother and your uncle. *On the contrary!*" If you knew all the stories behind all the people on the boardwalk, you'd see that *nothing* was what it looked like. Husbands and wives often hated each other; parents didn't necessarily love their children; et cetera. A child took things for granted because he had nothing to compare his life to and everybody acted as if things were as they should be. Therefore each saw himself as the hero of the story, when the truth might turn out to be that he's the villain, or the coward. And there wasn't one thing you could do about it!

Hunchbacks, fat ladies, fools — that no one chose what he was was unbearable. In the movies he'd meet a beautiful young girl in the funhouse; they'd have hairs-breadth escapes from real dangers; he'd do and say the right things; she also; in the end they'd be lovers; their dialogue lines would match up; he'd be perfectly at ease; she'd not only like him well enough, she'd think he was *marvelous*; she'd lie awake thinking about *him*, instead of vice versa — the way *his* face looked in different lights and how he stood and exactly what he'd said — and yet that would be only one small episode in his wonderful life, among many many others. Not a *turning point* at all. What had happened in the toolshed was nothing. He hated, he loathed his parents! One reason for not writing a lost-in-the-funhouse story is that either everybody's felt what Ambrose feels, in which case it goes without saying, or else no normal person feels such things, in which case Ambrose is a freak. "Is anything more tiresome, in fiction, than the problems of sensitive adolescents?" And it's all too long and rambling, as if the author. For all a person knows the first time through, the end could be just around any corner; perhaps, *not impossibly* it's been within reach any number of times. On the other hand he may be scarcely past the start, with everything yet to get through, an intolerable idea.

Fill in: His father's raised eyebrows when he announced his decision to do the funhouse with Magda. Ambrose understands now, but didn't then, that his father was wondering whether he 45 knew what the funhouse was *for* — especially since he didn't object, as he should have, when Peter decided to come along too. The ticket-woman, witchlike, mortifying him when inadvertently he gave her his name-coin instead of the half-dollar, then un-kindly calling Magda's attention to the birthmark on his temple: "Watch out for him, girlie, he's a marked man!" She wasn't even cruel, he understood, only vulgar and insensitive. Somewhere in the world there was a young woman with such splendid under-standing that she'd see him entire, like a poem or story, and find his words so valuable after all that when he confessed his ap-prehensions she would explain why they were in fact the very things that made him precious to her . . . and to Western Civiliza-tion! There was no such girl, the simple truth being. Violent yawns as they approached the mouth. Whispered advice from an old-timer on a bench near the barrel: "Go crabwise and ye'll get an eyeful without upsetting!" Composure vanished at the first pitch: Peter hollered joyously, Magda tumbled, shrieked, clutched her skirt; Ambrose scrambled crabwise, tight-lipped with terror, was soon out, watched his dropped name-coin slide among the couples. Shame-faced he saw that to get through expeditiously was not the point; Peter feigned assistance in order to trip Magda up, shouted "I see Christmas!" when her legs went flying. The old man, his latest betrayer, cackled approval. A dim hall then of black-thread cobwebs and recorded gibber: he took Magda's elbow to steady her against revolving discs set in the slanted floor to throw your feet out from under, and explained to her in a calm, deep voice his theory that each phase of the funhouse was triggered either automatically, by a series of pho-toelectric devices, or else manually by operators stationed at peepholes. But he lost his voice thrice as the discs unbalanced him; Magda was anyhow squealing; but at one point she clutched him about the waist to keep from falling, and her right cheek pressed for a moment against his belt-buckle. Heroically he drew her up, it was his chance to clutch her close as if for support and say: "I love you." He even put an arm lightly about the small of her back before a sailor-and-girl pitched into them from behind, sorely treading his left big toe and knocking Magda asprawl with them. The sailor's girl was a string-haired hussy with a loud laugh and light blue drawers; Ambrose realized that he wouldn't have said "I love you" anyhow, and was smitten with self-contempt. How much better it would be to be that common sailor! A wiry little Seaman 3rd, the fellow squeezed a girl to each side and stumbled hilarious into the mirror room, closer to Magda in thirty seconds than Ambrose had got in thirteen years. She giggled at something the fellow said to Peter; she drew her hair from her eyes with a movement so womanly it struck Ambrose's heart; Peter's smacking her backside then seemed particularly coarse. But Magda made a pleased indignant face and cried, "All right for *you*, mister!" and pursued Peter into the maze without a backward glance. The sailor followed after, leisurely, drawing his girl against his hip; Ambrose understood not only that they were all so relieved to be rid of his burdensome company that they didn't even notice his absence, but that he himself shared their relief. Stepping from the treacherous passage at last into the mirror-maze, he saw once again, more clearly than ever, how readily he deceived himself into supposing he was a person. He even foresaw, wincing at his dreadful self-knowledge, that he would repeat the deception, at ever-rarer intervals, all his wretched life, so fearful were the alternatives. Fame, madness, suicide; perhaps all three. It's not believable that so young a boy could articulate that reflection, and in fiction the merely true must always yield to the plausible. Moreover, the symbolism is in places heavy-footed. Yet Ambrose M—— understood, as few adults do, that the famous loneliness of the great was no popular myth but a general truth — furthermore, that it was as much cause as effect.

All the preceding except the last few sentences is exposition that should've been done earlier or interspersed with the present action instead of lumped together. No reader would put up with so much with such *prolixity*. It's interesting that Ambrose's father, though presumably an intelligent man (as indicated by his role as grade-school principal), neither encouraged nor discouraged his sons at all in any way — as if he either didn't care about them or cared all right but didn't know how to act. If this fact should contribute to one of them's becoming a celebrated but wretchedly unhappy scientist, was it a good thing or not? He too might someday face the question; it would be useful to know whether it had tortured his father for years, for example, or never once crossed his mind.

In the maze two important things happened. First, our hero found a name-coin someone else had lost or discarded: AMBROSE, suggestive of the famous lightship and of his late grandfather's favorite dessert, which his mother used to prepare on special occasions out of coconut, oranges, grapes, and what else. Second, as he wondered at the endless replication of his image in the mirrors, second, as he *lost himself in the reflection* that the necessity for an observer makes perfect observation impossible, better make him eighteen at least, yet that would render other things unlikely, he heard Peter and Magda chuckling somewhere together in the maze. "Here!" "No, here!" they shouted to each other; Peter said, "Where's Amby?" Magda murmured. "Amb?" Peter called. In a pleased, friendly voice. He didn't reply. The truth was, his brother was a *happy-go-lucky youngster* who'd've been better off with a regular brother of his own, but who seldom complained of his lot and was generally cordial. Ambrose's throat ached; there aren't enough different ways to say that. He stood quietly while the two young people giggled and thumped through the glittering maze, hurrah'd their discovery of its exit, cried out in joyful alarm at what next beset them. Then he set his mouth and followed after, as he supposed, took a wrong turn, strayed into the pass *wherein he lingers yet.*

The action of conventional dramatic narrative may be represented by a diagram called Freitag's Triangle:

or more accurately by a variant of that diagram:

in which *AB* represents the exposition, *B* the introduction of conflict, *BC* the "rising action," complication, or development of the conflict, *C* the climax, or turn of the action, *CD* the dénouement, or resolution of the conflict. While there is no reason to regard this pattern as an absolute necessity, like many other conventions it became conventional because great numbers of people over many years learned by trial and error that it was effective; one ought not to forsake it, therefore, unless one wishes to forsake as well the effect of drama or has clear cause to feel that deliberate violation of the "normal" pattern can better can better effect that effect. This can't go on much longer; it can go on forever. He died telling stories to himself in the dark; years later, when that vast unsuspected area of the funhouse came to light, the first expedition found his skeleton in one of its labyrinthine corridors and mistook it for part of the entertainment. He died of starvation telling himself stories in the dark; but unbeknownst to him, an assistant operator of the funhouse, happening to overhear him, crouched just behind the plyboard partition and wrote down his every word. The operator's daughter, an exquisite young woman with a figure unusually well developed for her age, crouched just behind the partition and transcribed his every word. Though she had never laid eyes on him, she recognized that here was one of Western Culture's truly great imaginations, the eloquence of whose suffering would be an inspiration to unnumbered. And her heart was torn between her love for the misfortunate young man (yes, she loved him, though she had never laid though she knew him only — but how well! — through his words, and the deep, calm voice in which he spoke them) between her love et cetera and her womanly intuition that only in suffering and isolation could he give voice et cetera. Lone dark dying. Quietly she kissed the rough plyboard, and a tear fell upon the page. Where she had written in short-hand *Where she had written in shorthand* Where she had written in shorthand *Where she* et cetera. A long time ago we should have passed the apex of Freitag's Triangle and made brief work of the *dénouement*; the plot doesn't rise by meaningful steps but winds upon itself, digresses, retreats, hesitates, sighs, collapses, expires. The climax of the story must be its protagonist's discovery of a way to get through the funhouse. But he has found none, may have ceased to search.

What relevance does the war have to the story? Should there be fireworks outside or not?

Ambrose wandered, languished, dozed Now and then he fell into his habit of rehearsing to himself the unadventurous story of his life, narrated from the third-person point of view, from his earliest memory parenthesis of maple leaves stirring in the summer breath of tidewater Maryland end of parenthesis to the present moment. Its principal events, on this telling, would appear to have been *A, B, C,* and *D.*

He imagined himself years hence, successful, married, at ease in the world, the trials of his adolescence far behind him. He has come to the seashore with his family for the holiday: how Ocean City has changed! But at one seldom at one ill-frequented end of the boardwalk a few derelict amusements survive from times gone by: the great carrousel from the turn of the century, with its monstrous griffins and mechanical concert band; the roller coaster rumored since 1916 to have been condemned; the mechanical shooting gallery in which only the image of our enemies changed. His own son laughs with Fat May and wants to know what a funhouse is; Ambrose hugs the sturdy lad close and smiles around his pipestem at his wife.

The family's going home. Mother sits between Father and Uncle Karl, who teases him good-naturedly who chuckles over the fact that the comrade with whom he'd fought his way shoulder to shoulder through the funhouse had turned out to be a blind Negro girl — to their mutual discomfort, as they'd opened their souls. But such are the walls of custom, which even. Whose arm is where? How must it feel. He dreams of a funhouse vaster by far than any yet constructed; but by then they may be out of fashion, like steamboats and excursion trains. Already quaint and seedy: the draperied ladies on the frieze of the carrousel are his father's father's mooncheeked dreams; if he thinks of it more he will vomit his apple-on-a-stick.

He wonders: will he become a regular person? Something has gone wrong; his vaccination didn't take; at the Boy-Scout initiation campfire he only pretended to be deeply moved, as he pretends to this hour that it is not so bad after all in the funhouse, and that he has a little limp. How long will it last? He envisions a truly astonishing funhouse, incredibly complex yet utterly controlled from a great central switchboard like the console of a pipe organ. Nobody had enough imagination. He could design such a place himself, wiring and all, and he's only thirteen years old. He would be its operator: panel lights would show what was up in every cranny of its cunning of its multifarious vastness; a switch-flick would ease this fellow's way, complicate that's, to balance things out; if anyone seemed lost or frightened, all the operator had to do was.

He wishes he had never entered the funhouse. But he has. Then he wishes he were dead. But he's not. Therefore he will construct funhouses for others and be their secret operator — though he would rather be among the lovers for whom funhouses are designed.

Questions

We move from level to level as we read "Lost in the Funhouse," following events during an amusement park outing and simultaneously seeing those events in relation to the literary conventions governing their depiction and to the impersonal biogenetic forces driving the human beings caught up in the events.

The action of conventional dramatic narrative may be represented by a diagram called Freitag's Triangle:

or more accurately by a variant of that diagram:

in which *AB* represents the exposition, *B* the introduction of conflict, *BC* the "rising action," complication, or development of the
conflict, *C* the climax, or turn of the action, *CD* the dénouement, or
resolution of the conflict. While there is no reason to regard this
pattern as an absolute necessity, like many other conventions it became conventional because great numbers of people over many
years learned by trial and error that it was effective; one ought not
to forsake it, therefore, unless one wishes to forsake as well the
effect of drama or has clear cause to feel that deliberate violation of
the "normal" pattern can better can better effect that effect. This
can't go on much longer; it can go on forever. He died telling stories
to himself in the dark. (para. 48)

How might the events described in paragraph 31 ("Ambrose gets
hard . . .") be related to Freitag's Triangle? How are they related
to impersonal forces? Using the selected passage as your focus,
show how your oscillation between levels comes to shape your
understanding of Ambrose. Compare your response with the one
that follows.

Response

EDITOR: Here and elsewhere in the story we lose sight of young
Ambrose for several sentences; the writer interrupts himself with
theoretical discourse about standard narrative patterns — conflict, "rising action," and so on — and we're obliged to think
simultaneously about the problems of a young male adolescent
with a girl slightly older than himself in a funhouse *and* about the
problems of the writer whose job it is to keep us interested in
what is, after all, a pretty familiar chain of events.

The juxtaposition of these problems leads us toward reflections on the subject of identity. Young Ambrose is, like most
adolescents (and everybody else) highly self-absorbed. There's no

question in his mind but that he exists and is uniquely himself (among his fantasies is that he's "one of Western Culture's truly great imaginations," para. 48). But, as the writer's regular interruptions ceaselessly remind us, Ambrose is — in an immensely significant dimension — *language*, as much a word as a person. Ambrose's being is given to us in signs; we know him only through the rules of English and of print, and those rules do not vary in accordance with the person. The stories of numberless thousands of youths, each convinced of his or her uniqueness, have found their way into print — and always the form of the story takes precedence over the human substance. One of Ambrose's implicit questions about himself is, inevitably, Who am I? One source of his confusion is that, like everybody else, he must answer that question through personal narrative the conventions and shape of which cannot be adjusted significantly to particular cases. As we shuttle between Ambrose as living being and Ambrose as literary/linguistic convention, we see further into the complications of our concept (and his) of personal identity.

And the movement from these levels to another allegorical level of the story — the biogenetic context — further deepens our sense of this complexity. We see Ambrose not only as a *term* but, in an inaccessible past time, as a "male animalcule," as spermatozoa groping "through hot, dark windings, past Love's Tunnel's fearsome obstacles" (14). We see him as driven, as an *x* conditioned as powerfully as narratives themselves by forces totally unknown and uncontrollable by the individual character. Ambrose is one among numberless others in an unknowably large family:

> Mother and Father; grandmothers and grandfathers on both sides; great-grandmothers and great-grandfathers on four sides, et cetera. Count a generation as thirty years: in approximately the year when Lord Baltimore was granted charter to the province of Maryland by Charles I, five hundred twelve women — English, Welsh, Bavarian, Swiss — of every class and character, received into themselves the penises the intromittent organs of five hundred twelve men, ditto, in every circumstance and posture, to conceive the five hundred twelve ancestors of the two hundred fifty-six ancestors of the et cetera . . . of the author, of the narrator, of this story, *Lost in the Funhouse*. In alleyways, ditches, canopy beds, pinewoods, bridal suites, ship's cabins, coach-and-fours, coaches-and-four, sultry toolsheds; on the cold sand under boardwalks, littered with *El Producto* cigar butts, treasured with Lucky Strike cigarette stubs, Coca-Cola caps,

gritty turds, cardboard lollipop sticks, matchbook covers warning that A Slip of the Lip Can Sink a Ship. (13)

The counterpart of the culturally conditioned "rising action" of a story is, we see, the biologically determined penile erection of the sexually awakened adolescent male. We connect story climax with ejaculation; we understand that the fearful humiliation of inexplicable nocturnal emissions and sudden stiffening of the male member must be understood as modes of a universal arbitrariness, universal accidentality. We catch intimations and echoes of this arbitrariness, at the literary level, when this particular narrator announces in one paragraph that Ambrose is dead and brings him back alive in the next.

"You think you're yourself," says the narrator, "but there are other persons in you" (31). The achievement of the collaboration of writer and reader in "Lost in the Funhouse" is the creation of the "other persons" in Ambrose — the numberless legions gone under the hill before his life (and our own) began, whose appetites for connection with others brought us (and Ambrose) to life. And that same appetite for means of linking ourselves with others created the models of "story" that we now bring to life as readers. Shuttling between the levels of this story we discover how little of Ambrose — how little of the selves in which *we* are absorbed — can truly be said to be his/our own. And as we transform Ambrose into the "other persons," we connect his example with our own. Are we, too, made of "other persons"? Is not our conviction of the importance and uniqueness — and freestandingness — of our Almighty Self entirely self-deceiving? Thanks to our allegorical collaboration we grasp the idea that anyone alive can be taken apart, seen as a set of historical components. We begin to imagine disaggregating the heroes of our own lives, namely ourselves.

FRANZ KAFKA   (1883–1924)

The Metamorphosis

TRANSLATED BY WILLA AND EDWIN MUIR

I

As Gregor Samsa awoke one morning from uneasy dreams he found himself transformed in his bed into a gigantic insect. He was lying on his hard, as it were armor-plated, back and when he lifted his head a little he could see his dome-like brown belly divided into stiff arched segments on top of which the bed quilt could hardly keep in position and was about to slide off completely. His numerous legs, which were pitifully thin compared to the rest of his bulk, waved helplessly before his eyes.

What has happened to me? he thought. It was no dream. His room, a regular human bedroom, only rather too small, lay quiet between the four familiar walls. Above the table on which a collection of cloth samples was unpacked and spread out — Samsa was a commercial traveler — hung the picture which he had recently cut out of an illustrated magazine and put into a pretty gilt frame. It showed a lady, with a fur cap on and a fur stole, sitting upright and holding out to the spectator a huge fur muff into which the whole of her forearm had vanished!

Gregor's eyes turned next to the window, and the overcast sky — one could hear rain drops beating on the window gutter — made him quite melancholy. What about sleeping a little longer and forgetting all this nonsense, he thought, but it could not be done, for he was accustomed to sleep on his right side and in his present condition he could not turn himself over. However violently he forced himself towards his right side he always rolled on to his back again. He tried it at least a hundred times, shutting his eyes to keep from seeing his struggling legs, and only desisted when he began to feel in his side a faint dull ache he had never experienced before.

Oh God, he thought, what an exhausting job I've picked on! Traveling about day in, day out. It's much more irritating work than doing the actual business in the office, and on top of that there's the trouble of constant traveling, of worrying about train connections, the bed and irregular meals, casual acquaintances that are always new and never become intimate friends. The devil take it all! He felt a slight itching up on his belly; slowly pushed himself on his back nearer to the top of the bed so that he could lift his head more easily; identified the itching place which was surrounded by many small white spots the nature of which he could not understand and made to touch it with a leg, but drew the leg back immediately, for the contact made a cold shiver run through him.

He slid down again into his former position. This getting up early, he thought, makes one quite stupid. A man needs his sleep. Other commercials live like harem women. For instance, when I come back to the hotel of a morning to write up the orders I've got, these others are only sitting down to breakfast. Let me just try that with my chief; I'd be sacked on the spot. Anyhow, that might be quite a good thing for me, who can tell? If I didn't have to hold my hand because of my parents I'd have given notice long ago, I'd have gone to the chief and told him exactly what I think of him. That would knock him endways from his desk! It's a queer way of doing, too, this sitting on high at a desk and talking down to employees, especially when they have to come quite near because the chief is hard of hearing. Well, there's still hope; once I've saved enough money to pay back my parents' debts to him — that should take another five or six years — I'll do it without fail. I'll cut myself completely loose then. For the moment, though, I'd better get up, since my train goes at five.

He looked at the alarm clock ticking on the chest. Heavenly Father! he thought. It was half-past six o'clock and the hands were quietly moving on, it was even past the half-hour, it was getting on toward a quarter to seven. Had the alarm clock not gone off? From the bed one could see that it had been properly set for four o'clock; of course it must have gone off. Yes, but was it possible to sleep quietly through that ear-splitting noise? Well, he had not slept quietly, yet apparently all the more soundly for that. But what was he to do now? The next train went at seven o'clock; to catch that he would need to hurry like mad and his samples weren't even packed up, and he himself wasn't feeling particularly fresh and active. And even if he did catch the train he wouldn't avoid a row with the chief, since the firm's porter would have been waiting for the five o'clock train and would have long since reported his failure to turn up. The porter was a creature of the chief's, spineless and stupid. Well, supposing he were to say he was sick? But that would be most unpleasant and would look suspicious, since during his five years' employment he had not been ill once. The chief himself would be sure to come with the sick-insurance doctor, would reproach his parents with their son's laziness and would cut all excuses short by referring to the insurance doctor, who of course regarded all mankind as perfectly healthy malingerers. And would he be so far wrong on this occasion? Gregor really felt quite well, apart from a drowsiness that was utterly superfluous after such a long sleep, and he was even unusually hungry.

As all this was running through his mind at top speed without his being able to decide to leave his bed — the alarm clock had just struck a quarter to seven — there came a cautious tap at the door behind the head of his bed. "Gregor," said a voice — it was his mother's — "it's a quarter to seven. Hadn't you a train to catch?" That gentle voice! Gregor had a shock as he heard his own voice answering hers, unmistakably his own voice, it was true, but with a persistent horrible twittering squeak behind it like an undertone, that left the words in their clear shape only for the first moment and then rose up reverberating round them to destroy their sense, so that one could not be sure one had heard them rightly. Gregor wanted to answer at length and explain everything, but in the circumstances he confined himself to saying: "Yes, yes, thank you, Mother, I'm getting up now." The wooden door between them must have kept the change in his voice from being noticeable outside, for his mother contented herself with this statement and shuffled away. Yet this brief exchange of words had made the other members of the family aware that Gregor was still in the house, as they had not expected, and at one of the side doors his father was already knocking, gently, yet with his fist. "Gregor, Gregor," he called, "what's the matter with you?" And after a little while he called again in a deeper voice: "Gregor! Gregor!" At the other side door his sister was saying in a low, plaintive tone: "Gregor? Aren't you well? Are you needing anything?" He answered them both at once: "I'm just ready," and did his best to make his voice sound as normal as possible by enunciating the words very clearly and leaving long pauses between them. So his father went back to his breakfast, but his sister whispered: "Gregor, open the door, do." However, he was not thinking of opening the door, and felt thankful for the prudent habit he had acquired in traveling of locking all doors during the night, even at home.

His immediate intention was to get up quietly without being disturbed, to put on his clothes and above all eat his breakfast, and only then to consider what else was to be done, since in bed, he was well aware, his meditations would come to no sensible conclusion. He remembered that often enough in bed he had felt small aches and pains, probably caused by awkward postures, which had proved purely imaginary once he got up, and he looked forward eagerly to seeing this morning's delusions gradually fall away. That the change in his voice was nothing but the precursor of a severe chill, a standing ailment of commercial travelers, he had not the least possible doubt.

To get rid of the quilt was quite easy; he had only to inflate himself a little and it fell off by itself. But the next move was difficult, especially because he was so uncommonly broad. He would have needed arms and hands to hoist himself up; instead he had only the numerous little legs which never stopped waving in all directions and which he could not control in the least. When he tried to bend one of them it was the first to stretch itself straight; and did he succeed at last in making it do what he wanted, all the other legs meanwhile waved the more wildly in a high degree of unpleasant agitation. "But what's the use of lying idle in bed," said Gregor to himself.

He thought that he might get out of bed with the lower part of his body first, but this lower part, which he had not yet seen and of which he could form no clear conception, proved too difficult to move; it shifted so slowly; and when finally, almost wild with annoyance, he gathered his forces together and thrust out recklessly, he had miscalculated the direction and bumped heavily against the lower end of the bed, and the stinging pain he felt informed him that precisely this lower part of his body was at the moment probably the most sensitive. 10

So he tried to get the top part of himself out first, and cautiously moved his head towards the edge of the bed. That proved easy enough, and despite its breadth and mass the bulk of his body at last slowly followed the movement of his head. Still, when he finally got his head free over the edge of the bed he felt too scared to go on advancing, for after all if he let himself fall in this way it would take a miracle to keep his head from being injured. And at all costs he must not lose consciousness now, precisely now; he would rather stay in bed.

But when after a repetition of the same efforts he lay in his former position again, sighing, and watched his little legs struggling against each other more wildly than ever, if that were possible, and saw no way of bringing any order into this arbitrary confusion, he told himself again that it was impossible to stay in bed and that the most sensible course was to risk everything for the smallest hope of getting away from it. At the same time he did not forget meanwhile to remind himself that cool reflection, the coolest possible, was much better than desperate resolves. In such moments he focused his eyes as sharply as possible on the window, but, unfortunately, the prospect of the morning fog, which muffled even the other side of the narrow street, brought him little encouragement and comfort. "Seven o'clock already," he said to himself when the alarm clock chimed again, "seven o'clock already and still such a thick fog." And for a little while he lay quiet, breathing lightly, as if perhaps expecting such complete repose to restore all things to their real and normal condition.

But then he said to himself: "Before it strikes a quarter past seven I must be quite out of this bed, without fail. Anyhow, by that time someone will have come from the office to ask for me, since it opens before seven." And he set himself to rocking his

whole body at once in a regular rhythm, with the idea of swinging
it out of the bed. If he tipped himself out in that way he could
keep his head from injury by lifting it at an acute angle when he
fell. His back seemed to be hard and was not likely to suffer from
a fall on the carpet. His biggest worry was the loud crash he
would not be able to help making, which would probably cause
anxiety, if not terror, behind all the doors. Still, he must take the
risk.

When he was already half out of the bed — the new method
was more a game than an effort, for he needed only to hitch
himself across by rocking to and fro — it struck him how simple
it would be if he could get help. Two strong people — he thought
of his father and the servant girl — would be amply sufficient;
they would only have to thrust their arms under his convex back,
lever him out of the bed, bend down with their burden and then
be patient enough to let him turn himself right over on to the
floor, where it was to be hoped his legs would then find their
proper function. Well, ignoring the fact that the doors were all
locked, ought he really to call for help? In spite of his misery he
could not suppress a smile at the very idea of it.

He had got so far that he could barely keep his equilibrium 15
when he rocked himself strongly, and he would have to nerve
himself very soon for the final decision since in five minutes'
time it would be a quarter past seven — when the front doorbell
rang. "That's someone from the office," he said to himself, and
grew almost rigid, while his little legs only jigged about all the
faster. For a moment everything stayed quiet. "They're not going
to open the door," said Gregor to himself, catching at some kind
of irrational hope. But then of course the servant girl went as
usual to the door with her heavy tread and opened it. Gregor
needed only to hear the first good morning of the visitor to know
immediately who it was — the chief clerk himself. What a fate, to
be condemned to work for a firm where the smallest omission at
once gave rise to the gravest suspicion! Were all employees in a
body nothing but scoundrels, was there not among them one
single loyal devoted man who, had he wasted only an hour or so
of the firm's time in a morning, was so tormented by conscience
as to be driven out of his mind and actually incapable of leaving
his bed? Wouldn't it really have been sufficient to send an
apprentice to inquire — if any inquiry were necessary at all —
did the chief clerk himself have to come and thus indicate to the
entire family, an innocent family, that this suspicious circumstance could be investigated by no one less versed in affairs than
himself? And more through the agitation caused by these reflec-

tions than through any act of will Gregor swung himself out of bed with all his strength. There was a loud thump, but it was not really a crash. His fall was broken to some extent by the carpet, his back, too, was less stiff than he thought, and so there was merely a dull thud, not so very startling. Only he had not lifted his head carefully enough and had hit it; he turned it and rubbed it on the carpet in pain and irritation.

"That was something falling down in there," said the chief clerk in the next room to the left. Gregor tried to suppose to himself that something like what had happened to him today might some day happen to the chief clerk; one really could not deny that it was possible. But as if in brusque reply to this supposition the chief clerk took a couple of firm steps in the next-door room and his patent leather boots creaked. From the right-hand room his sister was whispering to inform him of the situation: "Gregor, the chief clerk's here." "I know," muttered Gregor to himself; but he didn't dare to make his voice loud enough for his sister to hear it.

"Gregor," said his father now from the left-hand room, "the chief clerk has come and wants to know why you didn't catch the early train. We don't know what to say to him. Besides, he wants to talk to you in person. So open the door, please. He will be good enough to excuse the untidiness of your room." "Good morning, Mr. Samsa," the chief clerk was calling amiably meanwhile. "He's not well," said his mother to the visitor, while his father was still speaking through the door, "he's not well, sir, believe me. What else would make him miss a train! The boy thinks about nothing but his work. It makes me almost cross the way he never goes out in the evenings; he's been here the last eight days and has stayed at home every single evening. He just sits there quietly at the table reading a newspaper or looking through railway timetables. The only amusement he gets is doing fretwork. For instance, he spent two or three evenings cutting out a little picture frame; you would be surprised to see how pretty it is; it's hanging in his room; you'll see it in a minute when Gregor opens the door. I must say I'm glad you've come, sir; we should never have got him to unlock the door by ourselves; he's so obstinate; and I'm sure he's unwell, though he wouldn't have it to be so this morning." "I'm just coming," said Gregor slowly and carefully, not moving an inch for fear of losing one word of the conversation. "I can't think of any other explanation, madam," said the chief clerk, "I hope it's nothing serious. Although on the other hand I must say that we men of business — fortunately or unfortunately — very often simply have to ignore any slight indisposition, since business must be attended to." "Well, can the chief clerk come in now?" asked Gregor's father impatiently, again knocking on the door. "No," said Gregor. In the left-hand room a painful silence followed this refusal, in the right-hand room his sister began to sob.

Why didn't his sister join the others? She was probably newly out of bed and hadn't even begun to put on her clothes yet. Well, why was she crying? Because he wouldn't get up and let the chief clerk in, because he was in danger of losing his job, and because the chief would begin dunning his parents again for the old debts? Surely these were things one didn't need to worry about for the present. Gregor was still at home and not in the least thinking of deserting the family. At the moment, true, he was lying on the carpet and no one who knew the condition he was in could seriously expect him to admit the chief clerk. But for such a small discourtesy, which could plausibly be explained away somehow later on, Gregor could hardly be dismissed on the spot. And it seemed to Gregor that it would be much more sensible to leave him in peace for the present than to trouble him with tears and entreaties. Still, of course, their uncertainty bewildered them all and excused their behavior.

"Mr. Samsa," the chief clerk called now in a louder voice, "what's the matter with you? Here you are, barricading yourself in your room, giving only 'yes' and 'no' for answers, causing your parents a lot of unnecessary trouble and neglecting — I mention this only in passing — neglecting your business duties in an incredible fashion. I am speaking here in the name of your parents and of your chief, and I beg you quite seriously to give me an immediate and precise explanation. You amaze me, you amaze me. I thought you were a quiet, dependable person, and now all at once you seem bent on making a disgraceful exhibition of yourself. The chief did hint to me early this morning a possible explanation for your disappearance — with reference to the cash payments that were entrusted to you recently — but I almost pledged my solemn word of honor that this could not be so. But now that I see how incredibly obstinate you are, I no longer have the slightest desire to take your part at all. And your position in the firm is not so unassailable. I came with the intention of telling you all this in private, but since you are wasting my time so needlessly I don't see why your parents shouldn't hear it too. For some time past your work has been most unsatisfactory; this is not the season of the year for a business boom, of course, we admit that, but a season of the year for doing no business at all, that does not exist, Mr. Samsa, must not exist."

"But, sir," cried Gregor, beside himself and in his agitation 20 forgetting everything else, "I'm just going to open the door this very minute. A slight illness, an attack of giddiness, has kept me from getting up. I'm still lying in bed. But I feel all right again. I'm getting out of bed now. Just give me a moment or two longer! I'm not quite so well as I thought. But I'm all right, really. How a thing like that can suddenly strike one down! Only last night I was quite well, my parents can tell you, or rather I did have a slight presentiment. I must have showed some sign of it. Why didn't I report it at the office! But one always thinks that an indisposition can be got over without staying in the house. Oh sir, do spare my parents! All that you're reproaching me with now has no foundation; no one has ever said a word to me about it. Perhaps you haven't looked at the last orders I sent in. Anyhow, I can still catch the eight o'clock train, I'm much the better for my few hours' rest. Don't let me detain you here, sir; I'll be attending to business very soon, and do be good enough to tell the chief so and to make my excuses to him!"

And while all this was tumbling out pell-mell and Gregor hardly knew what he was saying, he had reached the chest quite easily, perhaps because of the practice he had had in bed, and was now trying to lever himself upright by means of it. He meant actually to open the door, actually to show himself and speak to the chief clerk; he was eager to find out what the others, after all their insistence, would say at the sight of him. If they were horrified then the responsibility was no longer his and he could stay quiet. But if they took it calmly, then he had no reason either to be upset, and could really get to the station for the eight o'clock train if he hurried. At first he slipped down a few times from the polished surface of the chest, but at length with a last heave he stood upright; he paid no more attention to the pains in the lower part of his body, however they smarted. Then he let himself fall against the back of a nearby chair, and clung with his little legs to the edges of it. That brought him into control of himself again and he stopped speaking, for now he could listen to what the chief clerk was saying.

"Did you understand a word of it?" the chief clerk was asking; "surely he can't be trying to make fools of us?" "Oh dear," cried his mother, in tears, "perhaps he's terribly ill and we're tormenting him. Grete! Grete!" she called out then. "Yes Mother?" called his sister from the other side. They were calling to each other across Gregor's room. "You must go this minute for the doctor. Gregor is ill. Go for the doctor, quick. Did you hear how he was speaking?" "That was no human voice," said the chief clerk in a voice noticeably low beside the shrillness of the mother's. "Anna! Anna!" his father was calling through the hall to the kitchen, clapping his hands, "get a locksmith at once!" And the two girls were already running through the hall with a swish of skirts — how could his sister have got dressed so quickly? — and were tearing the front door open. There was no sound of its closing again; they had evidently left it open, as one does in houses where some great misfortune has happened.

But Gregor was now much calmer. The words he uttered were no longer understandable, apparently, although they seemed clear enough to him, even clearer than before, perhaps because his ear had grown accustomed to the sound of them. Yet at any rate people now believed that something was wrong with him, and were ready to help him. The positive certainty with which these first measures had been taken comforted him. He felt himself drawn once more into the human circle and hoped for great and remarkable results from both the doctor and the locksmith, without really distinguishing precisely between them. To make his voice as clear as possible for the decisive conversation that was now imminent he coughed a little, as quietly as he could, of course, since this noise too might not sound like a human cough for all he was able to judge. In the next room meanwhile there was complete silence. Perhaps his parents were sitting at the table with the chief clerk, whispering, perhaps they were all leaning against the door and listening.

Slowly Gregor pushed the chair towards the door, then let go of it, caught hold of the door for support — the soles at the end of his little legs were somewhat sticky — and rested against it for a moment after his efforts. Then he set himself to turning the key in the lock with his mouth. It seemed, unhappily, that he hadn't really any teeth — what could he grip the key with? — but on the other hand his jaws were certainly very strong; with their help he did manage to set the key in motion, heedless of the fact that he was undoubtedly damaging them somewhere, since a brown fluid issued from his mouth, flowed over the key, and dripped on the floor. "Just listen to that," said the chief clerk next door; "he's turning the key." That was a great encouragement to Gregor; but they should all have shouted encouragement to him, his father and mother too: "Go on, Gregor," they should have called out, "keep going, hold on to that key!" And in the belief that they were all following his efforts intently, he clenched his jaws recklessly on the key with all the force at his command. As the turning of the key progressed he circled round the lock, holding on now only with his mouth, pushing on the key, as required, or pulling it down again with all the weight of his body. The louder click of the finally yielding lock literally quickened Gregor. With a deep breath of relief he said to himself: "So I didn't need the locksmith," and laid his head on the handle to open the door wide.

Since he had to pull the door towards him, he was still invisible when it was really wide open. He had to edge himself very slowly round the near half of the double door, and to do it very carefully if he was not to fall plump upon his back just on the threshold. He was still carrying out this difficult manoeuvre, with no time to observe anything else, when he heard the chief clerk utter a loud "Oh!" — it sounded like a gust of wind — and now he could see the man, standing as he was nearest to the door, clapping one hand before his open mouth and slowly backing away as if driven by some invisible steady pressure. His mother — in spite of the chief clerk's being there her hair was still undone and sticking up in all directions — first clasped her hands and looked at his father, then took two steps towards Gregor and fell on the floor among her outspread skirts, her face quite hidden on her breast. His father knotted his fist with a fierce expression on his face as if he meant to knock Gregor back into his room, then looked uncertainly round the living room, covered his eyes with his hands and wept till his great chest heaved.

Gregor did not go now into the living room, but leaned against the inside of the firmly shut wing of the door, so that only half his body was visible and his head above it bending sideways to look at the others. The light had meanwhile strengthened; on the other side of the street one could see clearly a section of the endlessly long, dark gray building opposite — it was a hospital — abruptly punctuated by its row of regular windows; the rain was still falling, but only in large singly discernible and literally singly splashing drops. The breakfast dishes were set out on the table lavishly, for breakfast was the most important meal of the day to Gregor's father, who lingered it out for hours over various newspapers. Right opposite Gregor on the wall hung a photograph of himself on military service, as a lieutenant, hand on sword, a carefree smile on his face, inviting one to respect his uniform and military bearing. The door leading to the hall was open, and one could see that the front door stood open too, showing the landing beyond and the beginning of the stairs going down.

"Well," said Gregor, knowing perfectly that he was the only one who had retained any composure, "I'll put my clothes on at once, pack up my samples, and start off. Will you only let me go? You see, sir, I'm not obstinate, and I'm willing to work; traveling is a hard life, but I couldn't live without it. Where are you going, sir? To the office? Yes? Will you give a true account of all this? One can be temporarily incapacitated, but that's just the moment for remembering former services and bearing in mind that later on, when the incapacity has been got over, one will certainly work with all the more industry and concentration. I'm loyally bound to serve the chief, you know that very well. Besides, I have to provide for my parents and my sister. I'm in great difficulties, but I'll get out of them again. Don't make things any worse for me than they are. Stand up for me in the firm. Travelers are not popular there, I know. People think they earn sacks of money and just have a good time. A prejudice there's no particular reason for revising. But you, sir, have a more comprehensive view of affairs than the rest of the staff, yes, let me tell you in confidence, a more comprehensive view than the chief himself, who, being the owner, lets his judgment easily be swayed against one of his employees. And you know very well that the traveler, who is never seen in the office almost the whole year round, can so easily fall a victim to gossip and ill luck and unfounded complaints, which he mostly knows nothing about, except when he comes back exhausted from his rounds, and only then suffers in person from their evil consequences, which he can no longer trace back to the original causes. Sir, sir, don't go away without a word to me to show that you think me in the right at least to some extent!"

But at Gregor's very first words the chief clerk had already backed away and only stared at him with parted lips over one twitching shoulder. And while Gregor was speaking he did not stand still one moment but stole away towards the door, without taking his eyes off Gregor, yet only an inch at a time, as if obeying some secret injunction to leave the room. He was already at the hall, and the suddenness with which he took his last step out of the living room would have made one believe he had burned the sole of his foot. Once in the hall he stretched his right arm before him towards the staircase, as if some supernatural power were waiting there to deliver him.

Gregor perceived that the chief clerk must on no account be allowed to go away in this frame of mind if his position in the firm were not to be endangered to the utmost. His parents did not understand this so well; they had convinced themselves in the course of years that Gregor was settled for life in this firm, and besides they were so occupied with their immediate troubles that all foresight had forsaken them. Yet Gregor had this foresight. The chief clerk must be detained, soothed, persuaded and finally won over; the whole future of Gregor and his family depended on it! If only his sister had been there! She was intelligent; she had begun to cry while Gregor was still lying quietly on his back. And no doubt the chief clerk, so partial to ladies, would have been guided by her; she would have shut the door of the flat and in the hall talked him out of his horror. But she was not there, and Gregor would have to handle the situation himself. And without remembering that he was still unaware what powers of movement he possessed, without even remembering that his words in all possibility, indeed in all likelihood, would again be unintelligible, he let go the wing of the door, pushed himself through the opening, started to walk towards the chief clerk, who was already ridiculously clinging with both hands to the railing on the landing; but immediately, as he was feeling for a support, he fell down with a little cry upon all his numerous legs. Hardly was he down when he experienced for the first time this morning a sense of physical comfort; his legs had firm ground under them; they were completely obedient, as he noted with joy; they even strove to carry him forward in whatever direction he chose; and he was inclined to believe that a final relief from all his sufferings was at hand. But in the same moment as he found himself on the floor, rocking with suppressed eagerness to move, not far from his mother, indeed just in front of her, she, who had seemed so completely crushed, sprang all at once to her feet, her arms and fingers outspread, cried: "Help, for God's sake, help!" bent her head down as if to see Gregor better, yet on the contrary kept backing senselessly away; had quite forgotten that the laden table stood behind her; sat upon it hastily, as if in absence of mind, when she bumped into it; and seemed altogether unaware that the big coffee pot beside her was upset and pouring coffee in a flood over the carpet.

"Mother, Mother," said Gregor in a low voice, and looked up 30 at her. The chief clerk, for the moment, had quite slipped from his mind; instead he could not resist snapping his jaws together at the sight of the streaming coffee. That made his mother scream again, she fled from the table and fell into the arms of his father, who hastened to catch her. But Gregor had now no time to spare for his parents; the chief clerk was already on the stairs; with his chin on the banisters he was taking one last backward look, Gregor made a spring, to be as sure as possible of overtaking him; the chief clerk must have divined his intention, for he leaped down several steps and vanished; he was still yelling "Ugh!" and it echoed through the whole staircase.

Unfortunately, the flight of the chief clerk seemed completely to upset Gregor's father, who had remained relatively calm until now, for instead of running after the man himself, or at least not hindering Gregor in his pursuit, he seized in his right hand the walking stick which the chief clerk had left behind on a chair, together with a hat and greatcoat, snatched in his left hand a large newspaper from the table, and began stamping his feet and flourishing the stick and the newspaper to drive Gregor back into his room. No entreaty of Gregor's availed, indeed no entreaty was even understood; however humbly he bent his head his father only stamped on the floor the more loudly. Behind his father his mother had torn open a window, despite the cold weather, and was leaning far out of it with her face in her hands. A strong draught set in from the street to the staircase, the window curtain blew in, the newspapers on the table fluttered, stray pages whisked over the floor. Pitilessly Gregor's father drove him back, hissing and crying "Shoo!" like a savage. But Gregor was quite unpracticed in walking backwards, it really was a slow business. If he only had a chance to turn round he could get back to his room at once, but he was afraid of exasperating his father by the slowness of such a rotation and at any moment the stick in his father's hand might hit him a fatal blow on the back or on the head. In the end, however, nothing else was left for him to do since to his horror he observed that in moving backwards he could not even control the direction he took; and so, keeping an anxious eye on his father all the time over his shoulder, he began to turn round as quickly as he could, which was in reality very slowly. Perhaps his father noted his good intentions, for he did not interfere except every now and then to help him in the manoeuvre from a distance with the point of the stick. If only he would have stopped making that unbearable hissing noise! It made Gregor quite lose his head. He had turned almost completely round when the hissing noise so distracted him that he even turned a little the wrong way again. But when at last his head was fortunately right in front of the doorway, it appeared that his body was too broad simply to get through the opening. His father, of course, in his present mood was far from thinking of such a thing as opening the other half of the door, to let Gregor have enough space. He had merely the fixed idea of driving Gregor back into his room as quickly as possible. He would have never suffered Gregor to make the circumstantial preparations for standing up on end and perhaps slipping his way through the door. Maybe he was now making more noise than ever to urge Gregor forward, as if no obstacle impeded him; to Gregor, anyhow, the noise in his rear sounded no longer like the voice of one single father; this was really no joke, and Gregor thrust himself — come what might — into the doorway. One side of his body rose up, he was tilted at an angle in the doorway, his flank was quite bruised, horrid blotches stained the white door, soon he was stuck fast and, left to himself, could not have moved at all, his legs on one side fluttered trembling in the air, those on the other were crushed painfully to the floor — when from behind his father gave him a strong push which was literally a deliverance and he flew far into the room, bleeding freely. The door was slammed behind him with the stick, and then at last there was silence.

II

Not until it was twilight did Gregor awake out of a deep sleep, more like a swoon than a sleep. He would certainly have waked up of his own accord not much later, for he felt himself sufficiently rested and well-slept, but it seemed to him as if a fleeting step and a cautious shutting of the door leading into the hall had aroused him. The electric lights in the street cast a pale sheen here and there on the ceiling and the upper surfaces of the furniture, but down below, where he lay, it was dark. Slowly, awkwardly trying out his feelers, which he now first learned to appreciate, he pushed his way to the door to see what had been happening there. His left side felt like one single long, unpleasantly tense scar, and he had actually to limp on his two rows of legs. One little leg, moreover, had been severely damaged in the course of that morning's events — it was almost a miracle that only one had been damaged — and trailed uselessly behind him.

He had reached the door before he discovered what had really drawn him to it: the smell of food. For there stood a basin filled with fresh milk in which floated little sops of white bread. He could almost have laughed with joy, since he was now still hungrier than in the morning, and dipped his head almost over the eyes straight into the milk. But soon in disappointment he withdrew it again: not only did he find it difficult to feed because of his tender left side — and he could only feed with the palpitating collaboration of his whole body — he did not like the milk either, although milk had been his favorite drink and that was certainly why his sister had set it there for him, indeed it was almost with repulsion that he turned away from the basin and crawled back to the middle of the room.

He could see through the crack of the door that the gas was turned on in the living room, but while usually at this time his father made a habit of reading the afternoon newspaper in a loud voice to his mother and occasionally to his sister as well, not a sound was now to be heard. Well, perhaps his father had recently given up this habit of reading aloud, which his sister had mentioned so often in conversation and in her letters. But there was the same silence all around, although the flat was certainly not empty of occupants. "What a quiet life our family has been leading," said Gregor to himself, and as he sat there motionless staring into the darkness he felt great pride in the fact that he had been able to provide such a life for his parents and sister in such a fine flat. But what if all the quiet, the comfort, the contentment were now to end in horror? To keep himself from being lost in such thoughts Gregor took refuge in movement and crawled up and down the room.

Once during the long evening one of the side doors was 35 opened a little and quickly shut again, later the other side door too; someone had apparently wanted to come in and then thought better of it. Gregor now stationed himself immediately before the living-room door, determined to persuade any hesitating visitor to come in or at least to discover who it might be; but the door was not opened again and he waited in vain. In the early morning, when the doors were locked, they had all wanted to come in, now that he had opened one door and the other had apparently been opened during the day, no one came in and even the keys were on the other side of the doors.

It was late at night before the gas went out in the living room, and Gregor could easily tell that his parents and his sister had all stayed awake until then, for he could clearly hear the three of them stealing away on tiptoe. No one was likely to visit him, not until the morning, that was certain; so he had plenty of time to mediate at his leisure on how he was to arrange his life afresh. But the lofty, empty room in which he had to lie flat on the floor filled him with an apprehension he could not account for, since it had been his very own room for the past five years — and with a half-unconscious action, not without a slight feeling of shame, he scuttled under the sofa, where he felt comfortable at once, although his back was a little cramped and he could not lift his head up, and his only regret was that his body was too broad to get the whole of it under the sofa.

He stayed there all night, spending the time partly in a light slumber, from which his hunger kept waking him up with a start, and partly in worrying and sketching vague hopes, which all led to the same conclusion, that he must lie low for the present and, by exercising patience and the utmost consideration, help the family to bear the inconvenience he was bound to cause them in his present condition.

Very early in the morning, it was still almost night, Gregor had the chance to test the strength of his new resolutions, for his sister, nearly fully dressed, opened the door from the hall and peered in. She did not see him at once, yet when she caught sight of him under the sofa — well, he had to be somewhere, he couldn't have flown away, could he? — she was so startled that without being able to help it she slammed the door shut again. But as if regretting her behavior she opened the door again immediately and came in on tiptoe, as if she were visiting an invalid or even a stranger. Gregor had pushed his head forward to the very edge of the sofa and watched her. Would she notice that he had left the milk standing, and not for lack of hunger, and would she bring in some other kind of food more to his taste? If she did not do it of her own accord, he would rather starve than draw her attention to the fact, although he felt a wild impulse to dart out from under the sofa, throw himself at her feet and beg her for something to eat. But his sister at once noticed, with surprise, that the basin was still full, except for a little milk that had been spilt all around it, she lifted it immediately, not with her bare hands, true, but with a cloth and carried it away. Gregor was wildly curious to know what she would bring instead, and made various speculations about it. Yet what she actually did next, in the goodness of her heart, he could never have guessed at. To find out what he liked she brought him a whole selection of food, all set out on an old newspaper. There were old, half-decayed vegetables, bones from last night's supper covered with a white sauce that had thickened; some raisins and almonds; a piece of cheese that Gregor would have called uneatable two days ago; a dry roll of bread, a buttered roll, and a roll both buttered and salted. Besides all that, she set down again the same basin, into which she had poured some water, and which was apparently to be reserved for his exclusive use. And with fine tact, knowing that Gregor would not eat in her presence, she withdrew quickly and even turned the key, to let him understand that he could take his ease as much as he liked. Gregor's legs all whizzed towards the food. His wounds must have healed completely, moreover, for he felt no disability, which amazed him and made

him reflect how more than a month ago he had cut one finger a
little with a knife and had still suffered pain from the wound
only the day before yesterday. Am I less sensitive now? he
thought, and sucked greedily at the cheese, which above all the
other edibles attracted him at once and strongly. One after another and with tears of satisfaction in his eyes he quickly devoured the cheese, the vegetables and the sauce; the fresh food,
on the other hand, had no charms for him, he could not even
stand the smell of it and actually dragged away to some little
distance the things he could eat. He had long finished his meal
and was only lying lazily on the same spot when his sister turned
the key slowly as a sign for him to retreat. That roused him at
once, although he was nearly asleep, and he hurried under the
sofa again. But it took considerable self-control for him to stay
under the sofa, even for the short time his sister was in the room,
since the large meal had swollen his body somewhat and he was
so cramped he could hardly breathe. Slight attacks of breathless-
ness afflicted him and his eyes were starting a little out of his
head as he watched his unsuspecting sister sweeping together
with a broom not only the remains of what he had eaten but even
the things he had not touched, as if these were now of no use to
anyone, and hastily shoveling it all into a bucket, which she
covered with a wooden lid and carried away. Hardly had she
turned her back when Gregor came from under the sofa and
stretched and puffed himself out.

In this manner Gregor was fed, once in the early morning
while his parents and the servant girl were still asleep, and a
second time after they had all had their midday dinner, for then
his parents took a short nap and the servant girl could be sent
out on some errand or other by his sister. Not that they would
have wanted him to starve, of course, but perhaps they could not
have borne to know more about his feeding than from hearsay,
perhaps too his sister wanted to spare them such little anxieties
wherever possible, since they had quite enough to bear as it was.

Under what pretext the doctor and the locksmith had been 40
got rid of on that first morning Gregor could not discover, for
since what he said was not understood by the others it never
struck any of them, not even his sister, that he could understand
what they said, and so whenever his sister came into his room he
had to content himself with hearing her utter only a sigh now and
then and an occasional appeal to the saints. Later on, when she
had got a little used to the situation — of course she could never
get completely used to it — she sometimes threw out a remark
which was kindly meant or could be so interpreted. "Well, he

liked his dinner today," she would say when Gregor had made a good clearance of his food; and when he had not eaten, which gradually happened more and more often, she would say almost sadly: "Everything's been left standing again."

But although Gregor could get no news directly, he overheard a lot from the neighboring rooms, and as soon as voices were audible, he would run to the door of the room concerned and press his whole body against it. In the first few days especially there was no conversation that did not refer to him somehow, even if only indirectly. For two whole days there were family consultations at every mealtime about what should be done; but also between meals the same subject was discussed, for there were always at least two members of the family at home, since no one wanted to be alone in the flat and to leave it quite empty was unthinkable. And on the very first of these days the household cook — it was not quite clear what and how much she knew of the situation — went down on her knees to his mother and begged leave to go, and when she departed, a quarter of an hour later, gave thanks for her dismissal with tears in her eyes as if for the greatest benefit that could have been conferred on her, and without any prompting swore a solemn oath that she would never say a single word to anyone about what had happened.

Now Gregor's sister had to cook too, helping her mother; true, the cooking did not amount to much, for they ate scarcely anything. Gregor was always hearing one of the family vainly urging another to eat and getting no answer but· "Thanks, I've had all I want," or something similar. Perhaps they drank nothing either. Time and again his sister kept asking his father if he wouldn't like some beer and offered kindly to go and fetch it herself, and when he made no answer suggested that she could ask the concierge to fetch it, so that he need feel no sense of obligation, but then a round "No" came from his father and no more was said about it.

In the course of that very first day Gregor's father explained the family's financial position and prospects to both his mother and his sister. Now and then he rose from the table to get some voucher or memorandum out of the small safe he had rescued from the collapse of his business five years earlier. One could hear him opening the complicated lock and rustling papers out and shutting it again. This statement made by his father was the first cheerful information Gregor had heard since his imprisonment. He had been of the opinion that nothing at all was left over from his father's business, at least his father had never said anything to the contrary, and of course he had not asked him directly. At that time Gregor's sole desire was to do his utmost to help the family to forget as soon as possible the catastrophe which had overwhelmed the business and thrown them all into a state of complete despair. And so he had set to work with unusual ardor and almost overnight had become a commercial traveler instead of a little clerk, with of course much greater chances of earning money, and his success was immediately translated into good round coin which he could lay on the table for his amazed and happy family. These had been fine times, and they had never recurred, at least not with the same sense of glory, although later on Gregor had earned so much money that he was able to meet the expenses of the whole household and did so. They had simply got used to it, both the family and Gregor; the money was gratefully accepted and gladly given, but there was no special uprush of warm feeling. With his sister alone had he remained intimate, and it was a secret plan of his that she, who loved music, unlike himself, and could play movingly on the violin, should be sent next year to study at the Conservatorium, despite the great expense that would entail, which must be made up in some other way. During his brief visits home the Conservatorium was often mentioned in the talks he had with his sister, but always merely as a beautiful dream which could never come true, and his parents discouraged even these innocent references to it; yet Gregor had made up his mind firmly about it and meant to announce the fact with due solemnity on Christmas Day.

Such were the thoughts, completely futile in his present condition, that went through his head as he stood clinging upright to the door and listening. Sometimes out of sheer weariness he had to give up listening and let his head fall negligently against the door, but he always had to pull himself together again at once, for even the slight sound his head made was audible next door and brought all conversation to a stop. "What can he be doing now?" his father would say after a while, obviously turning towards the door, and only then would the interrupted conversation gradually be set going again.

Gregor was now informed as amply as he could wish — for 45 his father tended to repeat himself in his explanations, partly because it was a long time since he had handled such matters and partly because his mother could not always grasp things at once — that a certain amount of investments, a very small amount it was true, had survived the wreck of their fortunes and had even increased a little because the dividends had not been touched meanwhile. And besides that, the money Gregor brought home every month — he had kept only a few dollars for himself — had never been quite used up and now amounted to a small capital sum. Behind the door Gregor nodded his head eagerly, rejoiced at this evidence of unexpected thrift and fore-sight. True, he could really have paid off some more of his father's debts to the chief with his extra money, and so brought much nearer the day on which he could quit his job, but doubt-less it was better the way his father had arranged it.

Yet this capital was by no means sufficient to let the family live on the interest of it; for one year, perhaps, or at the most two, they could live on the principal, that was all. It was simply a sum that ought not to be touched and should be kept for a rainy day; money for living expenses would have to be earned. Now his father was still hale enough but an old man, and he had done no work for the past five years and could not be expected to do much; during these five years, the first years of leisure in his laborious though unsuccessful life, he had grown rather fat and become sluggish. And Gregor's old mother, how was she to earn a living with her asthma, which troubled her even when she walked through the flat and kept her lying on a sofa every other day panting for breath beside an open window? And was his sister to earn her bread, she who was still a child of seventeen and whose life hitherto had been so pleasant, consisting as it did in dressing herself nicely, sleeping long, helping in the housekeeping, going out to a few modest entertainments, and above all playing the violin? At first whenever the need for earning money was men-tioned Gregor let go his hold on the door and threw himself down on the cool leather sofa beside it, he felt so hot with shame and grief.

Often he just lay there the long nights through without sleep-ing at all, scrabbling for hours on the leather. Or he nerved himself to the great effort of pushing an armchair to the window, then crawled up over the window sill and, braced against the chair, leaned against the window panes, obviously in some rec-ollection of the sense of freedom that looking out of a window always used to give him. For in reality day by day things that were even a little way off were growing dimmer to his sight; the hospital across the street, which he used to execrate for being all too often before his eyes, was not quite beyond his range of vision, and if he had not known that he lived in Charlotte Street, a quiet street but still a city street, he might have believed that his window gave on a desert waste where gray sky and gray land blended indistinguishably into each other. His quick-witted sister only needed to observe twice that the armchair stood by the window; after that whenever she had tidied the room she always pushed the chair back to the same place at the window and even left the inner casements open.

If he could have spoken to her and thanked her for all she had to do for him, he could have borne her ministrations better; as it was, they oppressed him. She certainly tried to make as light as possible of whatever was disagreeable in her task, and as time went on she succeeded, of course, more and more, but time brought more enlightenment to Gregor too. The very way she came in distressed him. Hardly was she in the room when she rushed to the window, without even taking time to shut the door, careful as she was usually to shield the sight of Gregor's room from the others, and as if she were almost suffocating tore the casements open with hasty fingers, standing then in the open draught for a while even in the bitterest cold and drawing deep breaths. This noisy scurry of hers upset Gregor twice a day; he would crouch trembling under the sofa all the time, knowing quite well that she would certainly have spared him such a disturbance had she found it at all possible to stay in his presence without opening the window.

On one occasion, about a month after Gregor's metamorphosis, when there was surely no reason for her to be still startled at his appearance, she came a little earlier than usual and found him gazing out of the window, quite motionless, and thus well placed to look like a bogey. Gregor would not have been surprised had she not come in at all, for she could not immediately open the window while he was there, but not only did she retreat, she jumped back as if in alarm and banged the door shut; a stranger might well have thought that he had been lying in wait for her there meaning to bite her. Of course he hid himself under the sofa at once, but he had to wait until midday before she came again, and she seemed more ill at ease than usual. This made him realize how repulsive the sight of him still was to her, and that it was bound to go on being repulsive, and what an effort it must cost her not to run away even from the sight of the small portion of his body that stuck out from under the sofa. In order to spare her that, therefore, one day he carried a sheet on his back to the sofa — it cost him four hours' labor — and arranged it there in such a way as to hide him completely, so that even if she were to bend down she could not see him. Had she considered the sheet unnecessary, she would certainly have stripped it off the sofa again, for it was clear enough that this curtaining and confining of himself was not likely to conduce Gregor's comfort, but she left it where it was, and Gregor even fancied that he caught a thankful glance from her eye when he lifted the sheet carefully a very little with his head to see how she was taking the new arrangement.

For the first fortnight his parents could not bring themselves 50 to the point of entering his room, and he often heard them expressing their appreciation of his sister's activities, whereas formerly they had frequently scolded her for being as they thought a somewhat useless daughter. But now, both of them often waited outside the door, his father and his mother, while his sister tidied his room, and as soon as she came out she had to tell them exactly how things were in the room, what Gregor had eaten, how he had conducted himself this time and whether there was not perhaps some slight improvement in his condition. His mother, moreover, began relatively soon to want to visit him, but his father and sister dissuaded her at first with arguments which Gregor listened to very attentively and altogether approved. Later, however, she had to be held back by main force, and when she cried out: "Do let me in to Gregor, he is my unfortunate son! Can't you understand that I must go to him?" Gregor thought that it might be well to have her come in, not every day, of course, but perhaps once a week; she understood things, after all, much better than his sister, who was only a child despite the efforts she was making and had perhaps taken on so difficult a task merely out of childish thoughtlessness.

Gregor's desire to see his mother was soon fulfilled. During the daytime he did not want to show himself at the window, out of consideration for his parents, but he could not crawl very far around the few square yards of floor space he had, nor could he bear lying quietly at rest all during the night, while he was fast losing any interest he had ever taken in food, so that for mere recreation he had formed the habit of crawling crisscross over the walls and ceiling. He especially enjoyed hanging suspended from the ceiling; it was much better than lying on the floor. One could breathe more freely; one's body swung and rocked lightly; and in the almost blissful absorption induced by this suspension it could happen to his own surprise that he let go and fell plump on the floor. Yet he now had his body much better under control than formerly, and even such a big fall did him no harm. His sister at once remarked the new distraction Gregor had found for himself — he left traces behind him of the sticky stuff on his soles wherever he crawled — and she got the idea in her head of giving him as wide a field as possible to crawl in and of removing the pieces of furniture that hindered him, above all the chest of drawers and the writing desk. But that was more than she could manage all by herself; she did not dare ask her father to help her;

and as for the servant girl, a young creature of sixteen who had had the courage to stay on after the cook's departure, she could not be asked to help, for she had begged as an especial favor that she might keep the kitchen door locked and open it only on a definite summons; so there was nothing left but to apply to her mother at an hour when her father was out. And the old lady did come, with exclamations of joyful eagerness, which, however, died away at the door of Gregor's room. Gregor's sister, of course, went in first, to see that everything was in order before letting his mother enter. In great haste Gregor pulled the sheet lower and tucked it more in folds so that it really looked as if it had been thrown accidentally over the sofa. And this time he did not peer out from under it; he renounced the pleasure of seeing his mother on this occasion and was only glad that she had come at all. "Come in, he's out of sight," said his sister, obviously leading her mother by the hand. Gregor could now hear the two women struggling to shift the heavy old chest from its place, and his sister claiming the greater part of the labor for herself, without listening to the admonitions of her mother who feared she might overstrain herself. It took a long time. After at least a quarter of an hour's tugging his mother objected that the chest had better be left where it was, for in the first place it was too heavy and could never be got out before his father came home, and standing in the middle of the room like that it would only hamper Gregor's movements, while in the second place it was not at all certain that removing the furniture would be doing a service to Gregor. She was inclined to think to the contrary; the sight of the naked walls made her own heart heavy, and why shouldn't Gregor have the same feeling, considering that he had been used to his furniture for so long and might feel forlorn without it. "And doesn't it look," she concluded in a low voice — in fact she had been almost whispering all the time as if to avoid letting Gregor, whose exact whereabouts she did not know, hear even the tones of her voice, for she was convinced that he could not understand her words — "doesn't it look as if we were showing him, by taking away his furniture, that we have given up hope of his ever getting better and are just leaving him coldly to himself? I think it would be best to keep his room exactly as it has always been, so that when he comes back to us he will find everything unchanged and be able all the more easily to forget what has happened in between."

On hearing these words from his mother Gregor realized that the lack of all direct human speech for the past two months together with the monotony of family life must have confused his mind, otherwise he could not account for the fact that he had quite earnestly looked forward to having his room emptied of furnishing. Did he really want his warm room, so comfortably fitted with old family furniture, to be turned into a naked den in which he would certainly be able to crawl unhampered in all directions but at the price of shedding simultaneously all recol-lection of his human background? He had indeed been so near the brink of forgetfulness that only the voice of his mother, which he had not heard for so long, had drawn him back from it. Nothing should be taken out of his room; everything must stay as it was; he could not dispense with the good influence of the furniture on his state of mind; and even if the furniture did hamper him in his senseless crawling round and round, that was no drawback but a great advantage.

Unfortunately his sister was of the contrary opinion; she had grown accustomed, and not without reason, to consider herself an expert in Gregor's affairs as against her parents, and so her mother's advice was now enough to make her determined on the removal not only of the chest and the writing desk, which had been her first intention, but of all the furniture except the indispensable sofa. This determination was not, of course, merely the outcome of childish recalcitrance and of the self-confidence she had recently developed so unexpectedly and at such cost; she had in fact perceived that Gregor needed a lot of space to crawl about in, while on the other hand he never used the furniture at all, so far as could be seen. Another factor might have been also the enthusiastic temperament of an adolescent girl, which seeks to indulge itself on every opportunity and which now tempted Grete to exaggerate the horror of her brother's circumstances in order that she might do all the more for him. In a room where Gregor lorded it all alone over empty walls no one save herself was likely ever to set foot.

And so she was not to be moved from her resolve by her mother who seemed moreover to be ill at ease in Gregor's room and therefore unsure of herself, was soon reduced to silence, and helped her daughter as best she could to push the chest outside. Now, Gregor could do without the chest, if need be, but the writing desk he must retain. As soon as the two women had got the chest out of his room, groaning as they pushed it, Gregor stuck his head out from under the sofa to see how he might intervene as kindly and cautiously as possible. But as bad luck would have it, his mother was the first to return, leaving Grete clasping the chest in the room next door where she was trying to shift it all by herself, without of course moving it from the spot.

His mother however was not accustomed to the sight of him, it might sicken her and so in alarm Gregor backed quickly to the other end of the sofa, yet could not prevent the sheet from swaying a little in front. That was enough to put her on the alert. She paused, stood still for a moment, and then went back to Grete.

Although Gregor kept reassuring himself that nothing out of 55 the way was happening, but only a few bits of furniture were being changed round, he soon had to admit that all this trotting to and fro of the two women, their little ejaculations, and the scraping of furniture along the floor affected him like a vast disturbance coming from all sides at once, and however much he tucked in his head and legs and cowered to the very floor he was bound to confess that he would not be able to stand it for long. They were clearing his room out; taking away everything he loved; the chest in which he kept his fret saw and other tools was already dragged off; they were now loosening the writing desk which had almost sunk into the floor, the desk at which he had done all his homework when he was at the commercial academy, at the grammar school before that, and, yes, even at the primary school — he had no more time to waste in weighing the good intentions of the two women, whose existence he had by now almost forgotten, for they were so exhausted that they were laboring in silence and nothing could be heard but the heavy scuffling of their feet.

And so he rushed out — the women were just leaning against the writing desk in the next room to give themselves a breather — and four times changed his direction, since he really did not know what to rescue first, then on the wall opposite, which was already otherwise cleared, he was struck by the picture of the lady muffled in so much fur and quickly crawled up to it and pressed himself to the glass, which was a good surface to hold on to and comforted his hot belly. This picture at least, which was entirely hidden beneath him, was going to be removed by nobody. He turned his head towards the door of the living room so as to observe the women when they came back.

They had not allowed themselves much of a rest and were already coming; Grete had twined her arm round her mother and was almost supporting her. "Well, what shall we take now?" said Grete, looking round. Her eyes met Gregor's from the wall. She kept her composure, presumably because of her mother, bent her head down to her mother, to keep her from looking up, and said, although in a fluttering, unpremeditated voice: "Come, hadn't we better go back to the living room for a moment?" Her intentions were clear enough to Gregor, she wanted to bestow her mother in safety and then chase him down from the wall. Well, just let her try it! He clung to his picture and would not give it up. He would rather fly in Grete's face.

But Grete's words had succeeded in disquieting her mother, who took a step to one side, caught sight of the huge brown mass on the flowered wallpaper, and before she was really conscious that what she saw was Gregor screamed in a loud, hoarse voice: "Oh God, oh God!" fell with outspread arms over the sofa as if giving up and did not move. "Gregor!" cried his sister, shaking her fist and glaring at him. This was the first time she had directly addressed him since his metamorphosis. She ran into the next room for some aromatic essence with which to rouse her mother from her fainting fit. Gregor wanted to help too — there was still time to rescue the picture — but he was stuck fast to the glass and had to tear himself loose; he then ran after his sister into the next room as if he could advise her, as he used to do; but then had to stand helplessly behind her; she meanwhile searched among various small bottles and when she turned round started in alarm at the sight of him; one bottle fell on the floor and broke; a splinter of glass cut Gregor's face and some kind of corrosive medicine splashed him; without pausing a moment longer Grete gathered up all the bottles she could carry and ran to her mother with them; she banged the door shut with her foot. Gregor was now cut off from his mother, who was perhaps nearly dying because of him; he dared not open the door for fear of frightening away his sister, who had to stay with her mother; there was nothing he could do but wait; and harassed by self-reproach and worry he began now to crawl to and fro, over everything, walls, furniture and ceiling, and finally in his despair, when the whole room seemed to be reeling round him, fell down on to the middle of the big table.

A little while elapsed, Gregor was still lying there feebly and all around was quiet, perhaps that was a good omen. Then the doorbell rang. The servant girl was of course locked in her kitchen, and Grete would have to open the door. It was his father. "What's been happening?" were his first words; Grete's face must have told him everything. Grete answered in a muffled voice, apparently hiding her head on his breast: "Mother has been fainting, but she's better now. Gregor's broken loose." "Just what I expected," said his father, "just what I've been telling you, but you women would never listen." It was clear to Gregor that his father had taken the worst interpretation of Grete's all too brief statement and was assuming that Gregor had been guilty of some violent act. Therefore Gregor must now try to propitiate his father, since he had neither time nor means for an explanation. And so he fled to the door of his own room and crouched against it, to let his father see as soon as he came in from the hall that his son had the good intention of getting back into his room imme- diately and that it was not necessary to drive him there, but that if only the door were opened he would disappear at once.

Yet his father was not in the mood to perceive such fine   60 distinctions. "Ah!" he cried as soon as he appeared, in a tone which sounded at once angry and exultant. Gregor drew his head back from the door and lifted it to look at his father. Truly, this was not the father he had imagined to himself; admittedly he had been too absorbed of late in his new recreation of crawling over the ceiling to take the same interest as before in what was hap- pening elsewhere in the flat, and he ought really to be prepared for some changes. And yet, and yet, could that be his father? The man who used to lie wearily sunk in bed whenever Gregor set out on a business journey; who welcomed him back of an evening lying in a long chair in a dressing gown; who could not really rise to his feet but only lifted his arms in greeting, and on the rare occasions when he did go out with his family, on one or two Sundays a year and on high holidays, walked between Gregor and his mother, who were slow walkers anyhow, even more slowly than they did, muffled in his old greatcoat, shuffling laboriously forward with the help of his crook-handled stick which he set down most cautiously at every step and, whenever he wanted to say anything, nearly always came to a full stop and gathered his escort around him? Now he was standing there in fine shape; dressed in a smart blue uniform with gold buttons, such as bank messengers wear; his strong double chin bulged over the stiff high collar of his jacket; from under his bushy eyebrows his black eyes darted fresh and penetrating glances; his one-time tangled white hair had been combed flat on either side of a shining and carefully exact parting. He pitched his cap, which bore a gold monogram, probably the badge of some bank, in a wide sweep across the whole room on to a sofa and with the tail-ends of his jacket thrown back, his hands in his trouser pockets, advanced with a grim visage towards Gregor. Likely enough he did not himself know what he meant to do; at any rate he lifted his feet uncommonly high, and Gregor was dumbfounded at the enor- mous size of his shoe soles. But Gregor could not risk standing up to him, aware as he had been from the very first day of his new life that his father believed only the severest measures suitable for dealing with him. And so he ran before his father, stopping when he stopped and scuttling forward again when his father made any kind of move. In this way they circled the room several times without anything decisive happening, indeed the whole operation did not even look like a pursuit because it was carried out so slowly. And so Gregor did not leave the floor, for he feared that his father might take as a piece of peculiar wickedness any excursion of his over the walls or the ceiling. All the same, he could not stay this course much longer, for while his father took one step he had to carry out a whole series of movements. He was already beginning to feel breathless, just as in his former life his lungs had not been very dependable. As he was staggering along, trying to concentrate his energy on running, hardly keeping his eyes open; in his dazed state never even thinking of any other escape than simply going forward; and having almost forgotten that the walls were free to him, which in this room were well provided with finely carved pieces of furniture full of knobs and crevices — suddenly something lightly flung landed close behind him and rolled before him. It was an apple; a second apple followed immediately; Gregor came to a stop in alarm; there was no point in running on, for his father was determined to bombard him. He had filled his pockets with fruit from the dish on the sideboard and was now shying apple after apple, without taking particularly good aim for the moment. The small red apples rolled about the floor as if magnetized and cannoned into each other. An apple thrown without much force grazed Gregor's back and glanced off harmlessly. But another following immediately landed right on his back and sank in; Gregor wanted to drag himself forward, as if this startling, incredible pain could be left behind him; but he felt as if nailed to the spot and flattened himself out in a complete derangement of all his senses. With his last conscious look he saw the door of his room being torn open and his mother rushing out ahead of his screaming sister, in her underbodice, for her daughter had loosened her clothing to let her breathe more freely and recover from her swoon, he saw his mother rushing towards his father, leaving one after another behind her on the floor her loosened petticoats, stumbling over her petticoats straight to his father and embracing him, in complete union with him — but here Gregor's sight began to fail — with her hands clasped round his father's neck as she begged for her son's life.

III

The serious injury done to Gregor, which disabled him for more than a month — the apple went on sticking in his body as a visible reminder, since no one ventured to remove it — seemed to have made even his father recollect that Gregor was a member of the family, despite his present unfortunate and repulsive shape, and ought not to be treated as an enemy, that, on the contrary, family duty required the suppression of disgust and the exercise of patience, nothing but patience.

And although his injury had impaired, probably forever, his power of movement, and for the time being it took him long, long minutes to creep across his room like an old invalid — there was no question now of crawling up the wall — yet in his own opinion he was sufficiently compensated for this worsening of his condition by the fact that towards evening the living-room door, which he used to watch intently for an hour or two beforehand, was always thrown open, so that lying in the darkness of his room, invisible to the family, he could see them all at the lamp-lit table and listen to their talk, by general consent as it were, very different from his earlier eavesdropping.

True, their intercourse lacked the lively character of former times, which he had always called to mind with a certain wistfulness in the small hotel bedrooms where he had been wont to throw himself down, tired out, on damp bedding. They were now mostly very silent. Soon after supper his father would fall asleep in his armchair; his mother and sister would admonish each other to be silent; his mother, bending low over the lamp, stitched at fine sewing for an underwear firm; his sister, who had taken a job as a salesgirl, was learning shorthand and French in the evenings on the chance of bettering herself. Sometimes his father woke up, and as if quite unaware that he had been sleeping said to his mother: "What a lot of sewing you're doing today!" and at once fell asleep again, while the two women exchanged a tired smile.

With a kind of mulishness his father persisted in keeping his uniform on even in the house; his dressing gown hung uselessly on its peg and he slept fully dressed where he sat, as if he were ready for service at any moment and even here only at the beck and call of his superior. As a result, his uniform, which was not brand-new to start with, began to look dirty, despite all the loving care of the mother and sister to keep it clean, and Gregor often spent whole evenings gazing at the many greasy spots on the garment, gleaming with gold buttons always in a high state of polish, in which the old man sat sleeping in extreme discomfort and yet quite peacefully.

As soon as the clock struck ten his mother tried to rouse his 65 father with gentle words and to persuade him after that to get into bed, for sitting there he could not have a proper sleep and that was what he needed most, since he had to go to duty at six. But with the mulishness that had obsessed him since he became a bank messenger he always insisted on staying longer at the table, although he regularly fell asleep again and in the end only with the greatest trouble could be got out of his armchair and into his bed. However insistently Gregor's mother and sister kept urging him with gentle reminders, he would go on slowly shaking his head for a quarter of an hour, keeping his eyes shut, and refuse to get to his feet. The mother plucked at his sleeve, whispering endearments in his ear, the sister left her lessons to come to her mother's help, but Gregor's father was not to be caught. He would only sink down deeper in his chair. Not until the two women hoisted him up by the armpits did he open his eyes and look at them both, one after the other, usually with the remark: "This is a life. This is the peace and quiet of my old age." And leaning on the two of them he would heave himself up, with difficulty, as if he were a great burden to himself, suffer them to lead him as far as the door and then wave them off and go on alone, while the mother abandoned her needlework and the sister her pen in order to run after him and help him farther.

Who could find time, in this overworked and tired-out family, to bother about Gregor more than was absolutely needful? The household was reduced more and more; the servant girl was turned off; a gigantic bony charwoman with white hair flying round her head came in morning and evening to do the rough work; everything else was done by Gregor's mother, as well as great piles of sewing. Even various family ornaments, which his mother and sister used to wear with pride at parties and celebrations, had to be sold, as Gregor discovered of an evening from hearing them all discuss the prices obtained. But what they lamented most was the fact that they could not leave the flat which was much too big for their present circumstances, because they could not think of any way to shift Gregor. Yet Gregor saw well enough that consideration for him was not the main difficulty preventing the removal, for they could have easily shifted him in some suitable box with a few air holes in it; what really kept them from moving into another flat was rather their own complete hopelessness and the belief that they had been singled out for a misfortune such as had never happened to any of their relations or acquaintances. They fulfilled to the uttermost all that the world demands of poor people, the father fetched break-fast for the small clerks in the bank, the mother devoted her energy to making underwear for strangers, the sister trotted to and fro behind the counter at the behest of customers, but more than this they had not the strength to do. And the wound in Gregor's back began to nag at him afresh when his mother and sister, after getting his father into bed, came back again, left their work lying, drew close to each other and sat cheek by cheek; when his mother, pointing towards his room, said: "Shut that door now, Grete," and he was left again in darkness, while next door the women mingled their tears or perhaps sat dry-eyed staring at the table.

Gregor hardly slept at all by night or by day. He was often haunted by the idea that next time the door opened he would take the family's affairs in hand again just as he used to do; once more, after this long interval, there appeared in his thoughts the figures of the chief and the chief clerk, the commercial travelers and the apprentices, the porter who was so dull-witted, two or three friends in other firms, a chambermaid in one of the rural hotels, a sweet and fleeting memory, a cashier in a milliner's shop, whom he had wooed earnestly but too slowly — they all appeared, together with strangers or people he had quite forgot-ten, but instead of helping him and his family they were one and all unapproachable and he was glad when they vanished. At other times he would not be in the mood to bother about his family, he was only filled with rage at the way they were neglect-ing him, and although he had no clear idea of what he might care to eat he would make plans for getting into the larder to take the food that was after all his due, even if he were not hungry. His sister no longer took thought to bring him what might especially please him, but in the morning and at noon before she went to business hurriedly pushed into his room with her foot any food that was available, and in the evening cleared it out again with one sweep of the broom, heedless of whether it had been merely tasted, or — as most frequently happened — left untouched. The cleaning of his room, which she now did always in the evenings, could not have been more hastily done. Streaks of dirt stretched along the walls, here and there lay balls of dust and filth. At first Gregor used to station himself in some particularly filthy corner when his sister arrived, in order to reproach her with it, so to speak. But he could have sat there for weeks without getting her to make any improvements; she could see the dirt as well as he did, but she had simply made up her mind to leave it alone. And yet, with a touchiness that was new to her, which seemed anyhow to have infected the whole family, she jealously guarded her claim to be the sole caretaker of Gregor's room. His mother once subjected his room to a thorough cleaning, which was achieved only by means of several buckets of water — all this dampness of course upset Gregor too and he lay widespread, sulky, and motionless on the sofa — but she was well punished for it. Hardly had his sister noticed the changed aspect of his room that evening than she rushed in high dudgeon into the living room and, despite the imploringly raised hands of her mother, burst into a storm of weeping, while her parents — her father had of course been startled out of his chair — looked on at first in helpless amazement; then they too began to go into action; the father reproached the mother on his right for not having left the cleaning of Gregor's room to his sister; shrieked at the sister on his left that never again was she to be allowed to clean Gregor's room, while the mother tried to pull the father into his bedroom, since he was beyond himself with agitation; the sister, shaken with sobs, then beat upon the table with her small fists; and Gregor hissed loudly with rage because not one of them thought of shutting the door to spare him such a spectacle and so much noise.

Still, even if the sister, exhausted by her daily work, had grown tired of looking after Gregor as she did formerly, there was no need for his mother's intervention or for Gregor's being neglected at all. The charwoman was there. This old widow, whose strong bony frame had enabled her to survive the worst a long life could offer, by no means recoiled from Gregor. Without being in the least curious she had once by chance opened the door of his room and at the sight of Gregor, who, taken by surprise, began to rush to and fro although no one was chasing him, merely stood there with her arms folded. From that time she never failed to open his door a little for a moment, morning and evening, to have a look at him. At first she even used to call him to her, with words which apparently she took to be friendly; such as: "Come along, then, you old dung beetle!" or "Look at the old dung beetle, then!" To such allocutions Gregor made no answer, but stayed motionless where he was, as if the door had never been opened. Instead of being allowed to disturb him so senselessly whenever the whim took her, she should rather have been ordered to clean out his room daily, that charwoman! Once, early in the morning — heavy rain was lashing on the windowpanes, perhaps a sign that spring was on the way — Gregor was so exasperated when she began addressing him again that he ran for her, as if to attack her, although slowly and feebly enough. But the charwoman instead of showing fright merely lifted high a chair that happened to be beside the door, and as she stood there with her mouth wide open it was clear that she meant to shut it only when she brought the chair down on Gregor's back. "So you're not coming any nearer?" she asked, as Gregor turned away again, and quietly put the chair back into the corner.

Gregor was now eating hardly anything. Only when he happened to pass the food laid out for him did he take a bit of something in his mouth as a pastime, kept it there for an hour at a time and usually spat it out again. At first he thought it was chagrin over the state of his room that prevented him from eating, yet he soon got used to the various changes in his room. It had become a habit in the family to push into his room things there was no room for elsewhere, and there were plenty of these now, since one of the rooms had been let to three lodgers. These serious gentlemen — all three of them with full beards, as Gregor once observed through a crack in the door — had a passion for order, not only in their own room but, since they were now members of the household, in all its arrangements, especially in the kitchen. Superfluous, not to say dirty, objects they could not bear. Besides, they had brought with them most of the furnishings they needed. For this reason many things could be dispensed with that it was no use trying to sell but that should not be thrown away either. All of them found their way into Gregor's room. The ash can likewise and the kitchen garbage can. Anything that was not needed for the moment was simply flung into Gregor's room by the charwoman, who did everything in a hurry; fortunately Gregor usually saw only the object, whatever it was, and the hand that held it. Perhaps she intended to take the things away again as time and opportunity offered, or to collect them until she could throw them all out in a heap, but in fact they just lay wherever she happened to throw them, except when Gregor pushed his way through the junk heap and shifted it somewhat, at first out of necessity, because he had not room enough to crawl, but later with increasing enjoyment, although after such excursions, being sad and weary to death, he would lie motionless for hours. And since the lodgers often ate their supper at home in the common living room, the living-room door stayed shut many an evening, yet Gregor reconciled himself quite easily to the shutting of the door, for often enough on evenings when it was opened he had disregarded it entirely and lain in the darkest corner of his room, quite unnoticed by the family. But on one occasion the charwoman left the door open a little and it stayed ajar even when the lodgers came in for supper and the lamp was lit. They set themselves at the top end of the table where formerly Gregor and his father and mother had eaten their meals, unfolded their napkins and took knife and fork in hand. At once his mother appeared in the doorway with a dish of meat and close behind her his sister with a dish of potatoes piled high. The food steamed with a thick vapor. The lodgers bent over the food set before them as if to scrutinize it before eating, in fact the man in the middle, who seemed to pass for an authority with the other two, cut a piece of meat as it lay on the dish, obviously to discover if it were tender or should be sent back to the kitchen. He showed satisfaction, and Gregor's mother and sister, who had been watching anxiously, breathed freely and began to smile.

The family itself took its meals in the kitchen. None the less, 70 Gregor's father came into the living room before going into the kitchen and with one prolonged bow, cap in hand, made a round of the table. The lodgers all stood up and murmured something in their beards. When they were alone again they ate their food in almost complete silence. It seemed remarkable to Gregor that among the various noises coming from the table he could always distinguish the sound of their masticating teeth, as if this were a sign to Gregor that one needed teeth in order to eat, and that with toothless jaws even of the finest make one could do nothing. "I'm hungry enough," said Gregor sadly to himself, "but not for that kind of food. How these lodgers are stuffing themselves, and here am I dying of starvation!"

On that very evening — during the whole of his time there Gregor could not remember ever having heard the violin — the sound of violin-playing came from the kitchen. The lodgers had already finished their supper, the one in the middle had brought out a newspaper and given the other two a page apiece, and now they were leaning back at ease reading and smoking. When the violin began to play they pricked up their ears, got to their feet, and went on tiptoe to the hall door where they stood huddled together. Their movements must have been heard in the kitchen, for Gregor's father called out: "Is the violin-playing disturbing you gentlemen? It can be stopped at once." "On the contrary," said the middle lodger, "could not Fräulein Samsa come and play in this room, beside us, where it is much more convenient and comfortable?" "Oh certainly," cried Gregor's father, as if he were the violin-player. The lodgers came back into the living room and waited. Presently Gregor's father arrived with the music stand, his mother carrying the music, and his sister with the violin. His sister quietly made everything ready to start playing; his parents,

who had never let rooms before and so had an exaggerated idea
of the courtesy due to lodgers, did not venture to sit down on
their own chairs; his father leaned against the door, the right
hand thrust between two buttons of his livery coat, which was
formally buttoned up; but his mother was offered a chair by one
of the lodgers and, since she left the chair just where he had
happened to put it, sat down in a corner to one side.

Gregor's sister began to play; the father and mother, from
either side, intently watched the movements of her hands.
Gregor, attracted by the playing, ventured to move forward a
little until his head was actually inside the living room. He felt
hardly any surprise at his growing lack of consideration for the
other; there had been a time when he prided himself on being
considerate. And yet just on this occasion he had more reason
than ever to hide himself, since owing to the amount of dust
which lay thick in his room and rose into the air at the slightest
movement, he too was covered with dust; fluff and hair and
remnants of food trailed with him, caught on his back and along
his sides; his indifference to everything was much too great for
him to turn on his back and scrape himself clean on the carpet,
as once he had done several times a day. And in spite of his
condition, no shame deterred him from advancing a little over
the spotless floor of the living room.

To be sure, no one was aware of him. The family was entirely
absorbed in the violin-playing; the lodgers, however, who first of
all had stationed themselves, hands in pockets, much too close
behind the music stand so that they could all have read the
music, which must have bothered his sister, had soon retreated to
the window, half-whispering with downbent heads, and stayed
there while his father turned an anxious eye on them. Indeed,
they were making it more than obvious that they had been
disappointed in their expectation of hearing good or enjoyable
violin-playing, that they had had more than enough of the performance and only out of courtesy suffered a continued disturbance of their peace. From the way they all kept blowing the
smoke of their cigars high in the air through nose and mouth one
could divine their irritation. And yet Gregor's sister was playing
so beautifully. Her face leaned sideways, intently and sadly her
eyes followed the notes of music. Gregor crawled a little farther
forward and lowered his head to the ground so that it might be
possible for his eyes to meet hers. Was he an animal, that music
had such an effect upon him? He felt as if the way were opening
before him to the unknown nourishment he craved. He was determined to push forward till he reached his sister, to pull at her

skirt and so let her know that she was to come into his room with her violin, for no one here appreciated her playing as he would appreciate it. He would never let her out of his room, at least, not so long as he lived; his frightful appearance would become, for the first time, useful to him; he would watch all the doors of his room at once and spit at intruders; but his sister should need no constraint, she should stay with him of her own free will; she should sit beside him on the sofa, bend down her ear to him, and hear him confide that he had had the firm intention of sending her to the Conservatorium, and that, but for his mishap, last Christmas — surely Christmas was long past? — he would have announced it to everybody without allowing a single objection. After this confession his sister would be so touched that she would burst into tears, and Gregor would then raise himself to her shoulder and kiss her on the neck, which, now that she went to business, she kept free of any ribbon or collar.

"Mr. Samsa!" cried the middle lodger, to Gregor's father, and pointed, without wasting any more words, at Gregor, now working himself slowly forwards. The violin fell silent, the middle lodger first smiled to his friends with a shake of the head and then looked at Gregor again. Instead of driving Gregor out, his father seemed to think it more needful to begin by soothing down the lodgers, although they were not at all agitated and apparently found Gregor more entertaining than the violin-playing. He hurried towards them and, spreading out his arms, tried to urge them back into their own room and at the same time to block their view of Gregor. They now began to be really a little angry, one could not tell whether because of the old man's behavior or because it just dawned on them that all unwittingly they had such a neighbor as Gregor next door. They demanded explanations of his father, they waved their arms like him, tugged uneasily at their beards, and only with reluctance backed towards their room. Meanwhile Gregor's sister, who stood there as if lost when her playing was so abruptly broken off, came to life again, pulled herself together all at once after standing for a while holding violin and bow in nervelessly hanging hands and staring at her music, pushed her violin into the lap of her mother, who was still sitting in her chair fighting asthmatically for breath, and ran into the lodgers' room to which they were now being shepherded by her father rather more quickly than before. One could see the pillows and blankets on the beds flying under her accustomed fingers and being laid in order. Before the lodgers had actually reached their room she had finished making the beds and slipped out.

The old man seemed once more to be so possessed by his 75 mulish self-assertiveness that he was forgetting all the respect he should show to his lodgers. He kept driving them on and driving them on until in the very door of the bedroom the middle lodger stamped his foot loudly on the floor and so brought him to a halt. "I beg to announce," said the lodger, lifting one hand and looking also at Gregor's mother and sister, "that because of the disgusting conditions prevailing in this household and family" — here he spat on the floor with emphatic brevity — "I give you notice on the spot. Naturally I won't pay you a penny for the days I have lived here, on the contrary I shall consider bringing an action for damages against you, based on claims — believe me — that will be easily susceptible of proof." He ceased and stared straight in front of him, as if he expected something. In fact his two friends at once rushed into the breach with these words: "And we too give notice on the spot." On that he seized the door-handle and shut the door with a slam.

Gregor's father, groping with his hands, staggered forward and fell into his chair; it looked as if he were stretching himself there for his ordinary evening nap, but the marked jerkings of his head, which was as if uncontrollable, showed that he was far from asleep. Gregor had simply stayed quietly all the time on the spot where the lodgers had espied him. Disappointment at the failure of his plan, perhaps also the weakness arising from extreme hunger, made it impossible for him to move. He feared, with a fair degree of certainty, that at any moment the general tension would discharge itself in a combined attack upon him, and he lay waiting. He did not react even to the noise made by the violin as it fell off his mother's lap from under her trembling fingers and gave out a resonant note.

"My dear parents," said his sister, slapping her hand on the table by way of introduction, "things can't go on like this. Perhaps you don't realize that, but I do. I won't utter my brother's name in the presence of this creature, and so all I say is: we must try to get rid of it. We've tried to look after it and to put up with it as far as is humanly possible, and I don't think anyone could reproach us in the slightest."

"She is more than right," said Gregor's father to himself. His mother, who was still choking for lack of breath, began to cough hollowly into her hand with a wild look in her eyes.

His sister rushed over to her and held her forehead. His father's thoughts seemed to have lost their vagueness at Grete's words, he sat more upright, fingering his service cap that lay among the plates still lying on the table from the lodgers' supper, and from time to time looked at the still form of Gregor.

"We must try to get rid of it," his sister now said explicitly to 80 her father, since her mother was coughing too much to hear a word, "it will be the death of both of you, I can see that coming. When one has to work as hard as we do, all of us, one can't stand this continual torment at home on top of it. At least I can't stand it any longer." And she burst into such a passion of sobbing that her tears dropped on her mother's face, where she wiped them off mechanically.

"My dear," said the old man sympathetically, and with evident understanding. "but what can we do?"

Gregor's sister merely shrugged her shoulders to indicate the feeling of helplessness that had now overmastered her during her weeping fit, in contrast to her former confidence.

"If he could understand us," said her father, half questioningly; Grete, still sobbing, vehemently waved a hand to show how unthinkable that was.

"If he could understand us," repeated the old man, shutting his eyes to consider his daughter's conviction that understanding was impossible, "then perhaps we might come to some agreement with him. But as it is —"

"He must go," cried Gregor's sister, "that's the only solution, 85 Father. You must just try to get rid of the idea that this is Gregor. The fact that we've believed it for so long is the root of all our trouble. But how can it be Gregor? If this were Gregor, he would have realized long ago that human beings can't live with such a creature, and he'd have gone away on his own accord. Then we wouldn't have any brother, but we'd be able to go on living and keep his memory in honor. As it is, this creature persecutes us, drives away our lodgers, obviously wants the whole apartment to himself, and would have us all sleep in the gutter. Just look, Father," she shrieked all at once, "he's at it again!" And in an access of panic that was quite incomprehensible to Gregor she even quitted her mother, literally thrusting the chair from her as if she would rather sacrifice her mother than stay so near to Gregor, and rushed behind her father, who also rose up, being simply upset by her agitation, and half-spread his arms out as if to protect her.

Yet Gregor had not the slightest intention of frightening anyone, far less his sister. He had only begun to turn round in order to crawl back to his room, but it was certainly a startling operation to watch, since because of his disabled condition he could not execute the difficult turning movements except by lifting his head and then bracing it against the floor over and over again. He paused and looked round. His good intentions seemed to have been recognized; the alarm had only been momentary. Now they were all watching him in melancholy silence. His mother lay in her chair, her legs stiffly outstretched and pressed together, her eyes almost closing for sheer weariness; his father and his sister were sitting beside each other, his sister's arm around the old man's neck.

Perhaps I can go on turning round now, thought Gregor, and began his labors again. He could not stop himself from panting with the effort, and had to pause now and then to take breath. Nor did anyone harass him, he was left entirely to himself. When he had completed the turn-round he began at once to crawl straight back. He was amazed at the distance separating him from his room and could not understand how in his weak state he had managed to accomplish the same journey so recently, almost without remarking it. Intent on crawling as fast as possible, he barely noticed that not a single word, not an ejaculation from his family, interfered with his progress. Only when he was already in the doorway did he turn his head round, not completely, for his neck muscles were getting stiff, but enough to see that nothing had changed behind him except that his sister had risen to her feet. His last glance fell on his mother, who was not quite overcome by sleep.

Hardly was he well inside his room when the door was hastily pushed shut, bolted, and locked. The sudden noise in his rear startled him so much that his little legs gave beneath him. It was his sister who had shown such haste. She had been standing ready waiting and had made a light spring forward. Gregor had not even heard her coming, and she cried "At last!" to her parents as she turned the key in the lock.

"And what now?" said Gregor to himself, looking round in the darkness. Soon he made the discovery that he was now unable to stir a limb. This did not surprise him, rather it seemed unnatural that he should ever actually have been able to move on these feeble little legs. Otherwise he felt relatively comfortable. True, his whole body was aching, but it seemed that the pain was gradually growing less and would finally pass away. The rotting apple in his back and the inflamed area around it, all covered with soft dust, already hardly troubled him. He thought of his family with tenderness and love. The decision that he must disappear was one that he held to even more strongly than his sister, if that were possible. In this state of vacant and peaceful meditation he remained until the tower clock struck three in the morning. The first broadening of light in the world outside the window entered his consciousness once more. Then his head sank to the floor of its own accord and from his nostrils came the last faint flicker of his breath.

When the charwoman arrived early in the morning — what 90 between her strength and her impatience she slammed all the doors so loudly, never mind how often she had been begged not to do so, that no one in the whole apartment could enjoy any quiet sleep after her arrival — she noticed nothing unusual as she took her customary peep into Gregor's room. She thought he was lying motionless on purpose, pretending to be in the sulks; she credited him with every kind of intelligence. Since she happened to have the long-handled broom in her hand she tried to tickle him up with it from the doorway. When that too produced no reaction she felt provoked and poked at him a little harder, and only when she had pushed him along the floor without meeting any resistance was her attention aroused. It did not take her long to establish the truth of the matter, and her eyes widened, she let out a whistle, yet did not waste much time over it but tore open the door of the Samsas' bedroom and yelled into the darkness at the top of her voice: "Just look at this, it's dead; it's lying here dead and done for!"

Mr. and Mrs. Samsa started up in their double bed and before they realized the nature of the charwoman's announcement had some difficulty in overcoming the shock of it. But then they got out of bed quickly, one on either side, Mr. Samsa throwing a blanket over his shoulders, Mrs. Samsa in nothing but her nightgown; in this array they entered Gregor's room. Meanwhile the door of the living room opened, too, where Grete had been sleeping since the advent of the lodgers; she was completely dressed as if she had not been to bed, which seemed to be confirmed also by the paleness of her face. "Dead?" said Mrs. Samsa, looking questioningly at the charwoman, although she could have investigated for herself, and the fact was obvious enough without investigation. "I should say so," said the charwoman, proving her words by pushing Gregor's corpse a long way to one side with her broomstick. Mrs. Samsa made a movement as if to stop her, but checked it. "Well," said Mr. Samsa, "now thanks be to God." He crossed himself, and the three women followed his example. Grete, whose eyes never left the corpse, said: "Just see how thin he was. It's such a long time since he's eaten anything. The food came out again just as it went in." Indeed, Gregor's body was completely flat and dry, as could only now be seen when it was no longer supported by the legs and nothing prevented one from looking closely at it.

"Come in beside us, Grete, for a little while," said Mrs. Samsa with a tremulous smile, and Grete, not without looking back at the corpse, followed her parents into their bedroom. The charwoman shut the door and opened the window wide. Although it was so early in the morning a certain softness was perceptible in the fresh air. After all, it was already the end of March.

The three lodgers emerged from their room and were surprised to see no breakfast; they had been forgotten. "Where's our breakfast?" said the middle lodger peevishly to the charwoman. But she put her finger to her lips and hastily, without a word, indicated by gestures that they should go into Gregor's room. They did so and stood, their hands in the pockets of their somewhat shabby coats, around Gregor's corpse in the room where it was now fully light.

At that the door of the Samsas' bedroom opened and Mr. Samsa appeared in his uniform, his wife on one arm, his daughter on the other. They all looked a little as if they had been crying; from time to time Grete hid her face on her father's arm.

"Leave my house at once!" said Mr. Samsa, and pointed to 95 the door without disengaging himself from the women. "What do you mean by that?" said the middle lodger, taken somewhat aback, with a feeble smile. The two others put their hands behind them and kept rubbing them together, as if in gleeful expectation of a fine set-to in which they were bound to come off the winners. "I mean just what I say," answered Mr. Samsa, and advanced in a straight line with his two companions towards the lodger. He stood his ground at first quietly, looking at the floor as if his thoughts were taking a new pattern in his head. "Then let us go, by all means," he said and looked up at Mr. Samsa as if in a sudden access of humility he were expecting some renewed sanction for this decision. Mr. Samsa merely nodded briefly once or twice with meaning eyes. Upon that the lodger really did go with long strides into the hall; his two friends had been listening and had quite stopped rubbing their hands for some moments and now went scuttling after him as if afraid that Mr. Samsa might get into the hall before them and cut them off from their leader. In the hall they all three took their hats from the rack, their sticks from the umbrella stand, bowed in silence, and quitted the apartment. With a suspiciousness which proved quite unfounded Mr. Samsa and the two women followed them out to the landing; leaning over the banister they watched the three figures slowly but surely going down the long stairs, vanishing from sight at a certain turn of the staircase on every floor and coming into view again after a moment or so; the more they dwindled, the more the Samsa family's interest in them dwindled, and when a butcher's boy met them and passed them on the stairs coming up proudly with a tray on his head, Mr. Samsa and the two women soon left the landing and as if a burden had been lifted from them went back into their apartment.

They decided to spend this day in resting and going for a stroll; they had not only deserved such a respite from work, but absolutely needed it. And so they sat down at the table and wrote three notes of excuse, Mr. Samsa to his board of management, Mrs. Samsa to her employer, and Grete to the head of her firm. While they were writing, the charwoman came in to say that she was going now, since her morning's work was finished. At first they only nodded without looking up, but as she kept hovering there they eyed her irritably. "Well?" said Mr. Samsa. The charwoman stood grinning in the doorway as if she had good news to impart to the family but meant not to say a word unless properly questioned. The small ostrich feather standing upright on her hat, which had annoyed Mr. Samsa ever since she was engaged, was waving gaily in all directions. "Well, what is it then?" asked Mrs. Samsa, who obtained more respect from the charwoman than the others. "Oh," said the charwoman, giggling so amiably that she could not at once continue, "just this, you don't need to bother about how to get rid of the thing next door. It's been seen to already." Mrs. Samsa and Grete bent over their letters again, as if preoccupied; Mr. Samsa, who perceived that she was eager to begin describing it all in detail, stopped her with a decisive hand. But since she was not allowed to tell her story, she remembered the great hurry she was in, being obviously deeply huffed: "Bye, everybody," she said, whirling off violently, and departed with a frightful slamming of doors.

"She'll be given notice tonight," said Mr. Samsa, but neither from his wife nor his daughter did he get any answer, for the charwoman seemed to have shattered again the composure they had barely achieved. They rose, went to the window, and stayed there, clasping each other tight. Mr. Samsa turned in his chair to look at them and quietly observed them for a little. Then he called out: "Come along, now, do. Let bygones be bygones. And you might have some consideration for me." The two of them complied at once, hastened to him, caressed him, and quickly finished their letters.

Then they all three left the apartment together, which was more than they had done for months, and went by tram into the open country outside the town. The tram, in which they were the only passengers, was filled with warm sunshine. Leaning comfortably back in their seats they canvassed their prospects for the future, and it appeared on closer inspection that these were not at all bad, for the jobs they had got, which so far they had never really discussed with each other, were all three admirable and likely to lead to better things later on. The greatest immediate improvement in their condition would of course arise from moving to another house; they wanted to take a smaller and cheaper but also better situated and more easily run apartment than the one they had, which Gregor had selected. While they were thus conversing, it struck both Mr. and Mrs. Samsa, almost at the same moment, as they became aware of their daughter's increasing vivacity, that in spite of all the sorrow of recent times, which had made her cheeks pale, she had bloomed into a pretty girl with a good figure. They grew quieter and half unconsciously exchanged glances of complete agreement, having come to the conclusion that it would soon be time to find a good husband for her. And it was like a confirmation of their new dreams and excellent intentions that at the end of their journey their daughter sprang to her feet first and stretched her young body.

Questions

Gregor Samsa is a man become insect, and in "The Metamorphosis" we bring to life both existences simultaneously. We do this by exploring parallels, within the character, between behavior and attitudes that we see as worthy of human beings and behavior and attitudes that we see as ignominiously insectlike. Read over the following passage with an eye to evoking some of these parallels:

> Gregor could not risk standing up to him, aware as he had been from the very first day of his new life that his father believed only the severest measures suitable for dealing with him. And so he ran before his father, stopping when he stopped and scuttling forward again when his father made any kind of move. (para. 60)

1. What is Gregor's attitude toward his father as characterized in this passage?
2. What parallel can you draw between this attitude and behavior and an insect's response to its environment?
3. How does your understanding of the interrelatedness of

these attitudes affect your perception both of family life and of insecthood?

4. What is Samsa's attitude toward his work and employer as characterized in the following passage?

> If I didn't have to hold my hand because of my parents I'd have given notice long ago, I'd have gone to the chief and told him exactly what I think of him. That would knock him endways from his desk! (5)

5. What parallel can you draw between this attitude and behavior and an insect's response to its environment?

6. How does your understanding of the interrelatedness of these attitudes affect your perception both of economic life and of insecthood?

7. Questions 1–6 probe your oscillation as reader between the allegorical levels of "The Metamorphosis." How exactly does that movement come to shape your understanding of Gregor Samsa?

17

Stories for Further Study

JOSEPH CONRAD (1857–1924)
The Secret Sharer

I

On my right hand there were lines of fishing stakes resembling a mysterious system of half-submerged bamboo fences, incomprehensible in its division of the domain of tropical fishes, and crazy of aspect as if abandoned forever by some nomad tribe of fishermen now gone to the other end of the ocean; for there was no sign of human habitation as far as the eye could reach. To the left a group of barren islets, suggesting ruins of stone walls, towers, and blockhouses, had its foundations set in a blue sea that itself looked solid, so still and stable did it lie below my feet; even the track of light from the westering sun shone smoothly, without that animated glitter which tells of an imperceptible ripple. And when I turned my head to take a parting glance at the tug which had just left us anchored outside the bar, I saw the straight line of the flat shore joined to the stable sea, edge to edge, with a perfect and unmarked closeness, in one leveled floor half brown, half blue under the enormous dome of the sky. Corresponding in their insignificance to the islets of the sea, two small clumps of trees, one on each side of the only fault in the impeccable joint, marked the mouth of the river Meinam we had just left on the first preparatory stage of our homeward journey; and, far back on the inland level, a larger and loftier mass, the grove surrounding the great Paknam pagoda, was the only thing on which the eye could rest from the vain task of exploring the monotonous sweep of the horizon. Here and there gleams as of a few scattered pieces of silver marked the windings of the great river; and on the nearest of them, just within the bar, the tug steaming right into the land became lost to my sight, hull and funnel and masts, as though the impassive earth had swallowed her up without an effort, without a tremor. My eye followed the light cloud of her smoke, now here, now there, above the plain, according to the devious curves of the stream, but always fainter and farther away, till I lost it at last behind the miter-shaped hill of the great pagoda. And then I was left alone with my ship, anchored at the head of the Gulf of Siam.

She floated at the starting point of a long journey, very still in an immense stillness, the shadows of her spars flung far to the eastward by the setting sun. At that moment I was alone on her decks. There was not a sound in her — and around us nothing moved, nothing lived, not a canoe on the water, not a bird in the air, not a cloud in the sky. In this breathless pause at the threshold of a long passage we seemed to be measuring our fitness for a long and arduous enterprise, the appointed task of both our existences to be carried out, far from all human eyes, with only sky and sea for spectators and for judges.

There must have been some glare in the air to interfere with one's sight, because it was only just before the sun left us that my roaming eyes made out beyond the highest ridge of the principal islet of the group something which did away with the solemnity of perfect solitude. The tide of darkness flowed on swiftly; and with tropical suddenness a swarm of stars came out above the shadowy earth, while I lingered yet, my hand resting lightly on my ship's rail as if on the shoulder of a trusted friend. But, with all that multitude of celestial bodies staring down at one, the comfort of quiet communion with her was gone for good. And there were also disturbing sounds by this time — voices, footsteps forward; the steward flitted along the main deck, a busily ministering spirit; a hand bell tinkled urgently under the poop deck. . . .

I found my two officers waiting for me near the supper table, in the lighted cuddy. We sat down at once, and as I helped the chief mate, I said:

"Are you aware that there is a ship anchored inside the 5 islands? I saw her mastheads above the ridge as the sun went down."

He raised sharply his simple face, overcharged by a terrible growth of whisker, and emitted his usual ejaculations: "Bless my soul, sir! You don't say so!"

My second mate was a round-cheeked, silent young man, grave beyond his years, I thought; but as our eyes happened to meet I detected a slight quiver on his lips. I looked down at once. It was not my part to encourage sneering on board my ship. It must be said, too, that I knew very little of my officers. In consequence of certain events of no particular significance, except to myself, I had been appointed to the command only a fortnight before. Neither did I know much of the hands forward. All these people had been together for eighteen months or so, and my position was that of the only stranger on board. I mention this because it has some bearing on what is to follow. But what I felt most was my being a stranger to the ship; and if all the truth must be told, I was somewhat of a stranger to myself. The youngest man on board (barring the second mate), and untried as yet by a position of the fullest responsibility, I was willing to take the adequacy of the others for granted. They had simply to be equal to their tasks; but I wondered how far I should turn out faithful to that ideal conception of one's own personality every man sets up for himself secretly.

Meantime the chief mate, with an almost visible effect of collaboration on the part of his round eyes and frightful whiskers, was trying to evolve a theory of the anchored ship. His dominant trait was to take all things into earnest consideration. He was of a painstaking turn of mind. As he used to say, he "liked to account to himself" for practically everything that came in his way, down to a miserable scorpion he had found in his cabin a week before. The why and the wherefore of that scorpion — how it got on board and came to select his room rather than the pantry (which was a dark place and more what a scorpion would be partial to), and how on earth it managed to drown itself in the inkwell of his writing desk — had exercised him infinitely. The ship within the islands was much more easily accounted for; and just as we were about to rise from the table he made his pronouncement. She was, he doubted not, a ship from home lately arrived. Probably she drew too much water to cross the bar except at the top of spring tides. Therefore she went into that natural harbor to wait for a few days in preference to remaining in an open roadstead.

"That's so," confirmed the second mate, suddenly, in his slightly hoarse voice. "She draws over twenty feet. She's the Liverpool ship *Sephora* with a cargo of coal. Hundred and twenty-three days from Cardiff."

We looked at him in surprise.　　　　　　　　　　　　　　10

"The tugboat skipper told me when he came on board for your letters, sir," explained the young man. "He expects to take her up the river the day after tomorrow."

After thus overwhelming us with the extent of his information he slipped out of the cabin. The mate observed regretfully that he "could not account for that young fellow's whims." What prevented him telling us all about it at once, he wanted to know.

I detained him as he was making a move. For the last two days the crew had had plenty of hard work, and the night before they had very little sleep. I felt painfully that I — a stranger — was doing something unusual when I directed him to let all hands turn in without setting an anchor watch. I proposed to keep on deck myself till one o'clock or thereabouts. I would get the second mate to relieve me at that hour.

"He will turn out the cook and the steward at four," I concluded, "and then give you a call. Of course at the slightest sign of any sort of wind we'll have the hands up and make a start at once."

He concealed his astonishment. "Very well, sir." Outside the cuddy he put his head in the second mate's door to inform him of my unheard-of caprice to take a five hours' anchor watch on myself. I heard the other raise his voice incredulously: "What? The captain himself?" Then a few more murmurs, a door closed, then another. A few moments later I went on deck. 15

My strangeness, which had made me sleepless, had prompted that unconventional arrangement, as if I had expected in those solitary hours of the night to get on terms with the ship of which I knew nothing, manned by men of whom I knew very little more. Fast alongside a wharf, littered like any ship in port with a tangle of unrelated things, invaded by unrelated shore people, I had hardly seen her yet properly. Now, as she lay cleared for sea, the stretch of her main deck seemed to me very fine under the stars. Very fine, very roomy for her size, and very inviting. I descended the poop and paced the waist, my mind picturing to myself the coming passage through the Malay Archipelago, down the Indian Ocean, and up the Atlantic. All its phases were familiar enough to me, every characteristic, all the alternatives which were likely to face me on the high seas — everything! . . . except the novel responsibility of command. But I took heart from the reasonable thought that the ship was like other ships, the men like other men, and that the sea was not likely to keep any special surprises expressly for my discomfiture.

Arrived at that comforting conclusion, I bethought myself of a cigar and went below to get it. All was still down there. Everybody at the after end of the ship was sleeping profoundly. I came out again on the quarterdeck, agreeably at ease in my sleeping suit on that warm breathless night, barefooted, a glowing cigar in my teeth, and, going forward, I was met by the profound silence of the fore end of the ship. Only as I passed the door of the forecastle I heard a deep, quiet, trustful sigh of some sleeper inside. And suddenly I rejoiced in the great security of the sea as compared with the unrest of the land, in my choice of that untempted life presenting no disquieting problems, invested with an elementary moral beauty by the absolute straightfor-wardness of its appeal and by the singleness of its purpose.

The riding light in the fore-rigging burned with a clear, untroubled, as if symbolic, flame, confident and bright in the mysterious shades of the night. Passing on my way aft along the other side of the ship, I observed that the rope side ladder, put over, no doubt, for the master of the tug when he came to fetch away our letters, had not been hauled in as it should have been. I became annoyed at this, for exactitude in small matters is the very soul of discipline. Then I reflected that I had myself pe-remptorily dismissed my officers from duty, and by my own act had prevented the anchor watch being formally set and things properly attended to. I asked myself whether it was wise ever to interfere with the established routine of duties even from the kindest of motives. My action might have made me appear eccen-tric. Goodness only knew how that absurdly whiskered mate would "account" for my conduct, and what the whole ship thought of that informality of their new captain. I was vexed with myself.

Not from compunction certainly, but, as it were mechan-ically, I proceeded to get the ladder in myself. Now a side ladder of that sort is a light affair and comes in easily, yet my vigorous tug, which should have brought it flying on board, merely re-coiled upon my body in a totally unexpected jerk. What the devil! . . . I was so astounded by the immovableness of that ladder that I remained stock-still, trying to account for it to myself like that imbecile mate of mine. In the end, of course, I put my head over the rail.

The side of the ship made an opaque belt of shadow on the 20 darkling glassy shimmer of the sea. But I saw at once something elongated and pale floating very close to the ladder. Before I could form a guess a faint flash of phosphorescent light, which seemed to issue suddenly from the naked body of a man, flicked in the sleeping water with the elusive, silent play of summer lightning in a night sky. With a gasp I saw revealed to my stare a pair of feet, the long legs, a broad livid back immersed right up to the neck in a greenish cadaverous glow. One hand, awash, clutched the bottom rung of the ladder. He was complete but for the head. A headless corpse! The cigar dropped out of my gaping mouth with a tiny plop and a short hiss quite audible in the absolute stillness of all things under heaven. At that I suppose he raised up his face, a dimly pale oval in the shadow of the ship's side. But even I could only barely make out down there the shape of his black-haired head. However, it was enough for the horrid, frost-bound sensation which had gripped me about the chest to pass off. The movement of vain exclamations was past, too. I only climbed on the spare spar and leaned over the rail as far as I could, to bring my eyes nearer to that mystery floating alongside.

As he hung by the ladder, like a resting swimmer, the sea lightning played about his limbs at every stir; and he appeared in it ghastly, silvery, fishlike. He remained as mute as a fish, too. He made no motion to get out of the water, either. It was inconceivable that he should not attempt to come on board, and strangely troubling to suspect that perhaps he did not want to. And my first words were prompted by just that troubled incertitude.

"What's the matter?" I asked in my ordinary tone, speaking down to the face upturned exactly under mine.

"Cramp," it answered, no louder. Then slightly anxious, "I say, no need to call anyone."

"I was not going to," I said.

"Are you alone on deck?" 25

"Yes."

I had somehow the impression that he was on the point of letting go the ladder to swim away beyond my ken — mysterious as he came. But, for the moment, this being appearing as if he had risen from the bottom of the sea (it was certainly the nearest land to the ship) wanted only to know the time. I told him. And he, down there, tentatively:

"I suppose your captain's turned in?"

"I am sure he isn't," I said.

He seemed to struggle with himself, for I heard something 30 like the low, bitter murmur of doubt, "What's the good?" His next words came out with a hesitating effort.

"Look here, my man. Could you call him out quietly?"

I thought the time had come to declare myself.

"*I* am the captain."

I heard a "By Jove!" whispered at the level of the water. The phosphorescence flashed in the swirl of the water all about his limbs, his other hand seized the ladder.

"My name's Leggatt." 35

The voice was calm and resolute. A good voice. The self-possession of that man had somehow induced a corresponding state in myself. It was very quietly that I remarked:

"You must be a good swimmer."

"Yes. I've been in the water practically since nine o'clock. The question for me now is whether I am to let go this ladder and go on swimming till I sink from exhaustion, or — to come on board here."

I felt this was no mere formula of desperate speech, but a real alternative in the view of a strong soul. I should have gathered from this that he was young; indeed, it is only the young who are ever confronted by such clear issues. But at the time it was pure intuition on my part. A mysterious communication was established already between us two — in the face of that silent, darkened tropical sea. I was young, too; young enough to make no comment. The man in the water began suddenly to climb up the ladder, and I hastened away from the rail to fetch some clothes.

Before entering the cabin I stood still, listening in the lobby 40 at the foot of the stairs. A faint snore came through the closed door of the chief mate's room. The second mate's door was on the hook, but the darkness in there was absolutely soundless. He, too, was young and could sleep like a stone. Remained the steward, but he was not likely to wake up before he was called. I got a sleeping suit out of my room and, coming back on deck, saw the naked man from the sea sitting on the main hatch, glimmering white in the darkness, his elbows on his knees and his head in his hands. In a moment he had concealed his damp body in a sleeping suit of the same gray-stripe pattern as the one I was wearing and followed me like my double on the poop. Together we moved right aft, barefooted, silent.

"What is it?" I asked in a deadened voice, taking the lighted lamp out of the binnacle, and raising it to his face.

"An ugly business."

He had rather regular features; a good mouth; light eyes under somewhat heavy, dark eyebrows; a smooth, square forehead; no growth on his cheeks; a small, brown mustache, and a well-shaped, round chin. His expression was concentrated, meditative, under the inspecting light of the lamp I held up to his face; such as a man thinking hard in solitude might wear. My sleeping suit was just right for his size. A well-knit young fellow of twenty-five at most. He caught his lower lip with the edge of white, even teeth.

"Yes," I said, replacing the lamp in the binnacle. The warm, heavy tropical night closed upon his head again.

"There's a ship over there," he murmured.   45

"Yes, I know. The *Sephora*. Did you know of us?"

"Hadn't the slightest idea. I am the mate of her — " He paused and corrected himself. "I should say I *was*."

"Aha! Something wrong?"

"Yes. Very wrong indeed. I've killed a man."

"What do you mean? Just now?"   50

"No, on the passage. Weeks ago. Thirty-nine south. When I say a man — "

"Fit of temper," I suggested, confidently.

The shadowy, dark head, like mine, seemed to nod imperceptibly above the ghostly gray of my sleeping suit. It was, in the night, as though I had been faced by my own reflection in the depths of a somber and immense mirror.

"A pretty thing to have to own up to for a Conway boy," murmured my double, distinctly.

"You're a Conway boy?"   55

"I am," he said, as if startled. Then, slowly . . . "Perhaps you too — "

It was so; but being a couple of years older I had left before he joined. After a quick interchange of dates a silence fell; and I thought suddenly of my absurd mate with his terrific whiskers and the "Bless my soul — you don't say so" type of intellect. My double gave me an inkling of his thoughts by saying:

"My father's a parson in Norfolk. Do you see me before a judge and jury on that charge? For myself I can't see the necessity. There are fellows that an angel from heaven —— And I am not that. He was one of those creatures that are just simmering all the time with a silly sort of wickedness. Miserable devils that have no business to live at all. He wouldn't do his duty and wouldn't let anybody else do theirs. But what's the good of talking! You know well enough the sort of ill-conditioned snarling cur — "

He appealed to me as if our experiences had been as identical as our clothes. And I knew well enough the pestiferous danger of such a character where there are no means of legal repression. And I knew well enough also that my double there was no homicidal ruffian. I did not think of asking him for details, and he told me the story roughly in brusque, disconnected sentences. I needed no more. I saw it all going on as though I were myself inside that other sleeping suit.

"It happened while we were setting a reefed foresail, at dusk.   60

Reefed foresail! You understand the sort of weather. The only sail we had left to keep the ship running; so you may guess what it had been like for days. Anxious sort of job, that. He gave me some of his cursed insolence at the sheet. I tell you I was over-done with this terrific weather that seemed to have no end to it. Terrific, I tell you — and a deep ship. I believe the fellow him-self was half crazed with funk. It was no time for gentlemanly reproof, so I turned round and felled him like an ox. He up and at me. We closed just as an awful sea made for the ship. All hands saw it coming and took to the rigging, but I had him by the throat, and went on shaking him like a rat, the men above us yelling, 'Look out! look out!' Then a crash as if the sky had fallen on my head. They saw that for over ten minutes hardly anything was to be seen of the ship — just the three masts and a bit of the forecastle head and of the poop all awash driving along in a smother of foam. It was a miracle that they found us, jammed together behind the forebits. It's clear that I meant business, because I was holding him by the throat still when they picked us up. He was black in the face. It was too much for them. It seems they rushed us aft together, gripped as we were, screaming 'Murder!' like a lot of lunatics, and broke into the cuddy. And the ship running for her life, touch and go all the time, any minute her last in a sea fit to turn your hair gray only a-looking at it. I understand that the skipper, too, started raving like the rest of them. The man had been deprived of sleep for more than a week, and to have this sprung on him at the height of a furious gale nearly drove him out of his mind. I wonder they didn't fling me overboard after getting the carcass of their precious shipmate out of my fingers. They had rather a job to separate us, I've been told. A sufficiently fierce story to make an old judge and a respectable jury sit up a bit. The first thing I heard when I came to myself was the maddening howling of that endless gale, and on that the voice of the old man. He was hanging on to my bunk, staring into my face out of his sou'wester.

"'Mr. Leggatt, you have killed a man. You can act no longer as chief mate of this ship.'"

His care to subdue his voice made it sound monotonous. He rested a hand on the end of the skylight to steady himself with, and all that time did not stir a limb, so far as I could see. "Nice little tale for a quiet tea party," he concluded in the same tone.

One of my hands, too, rested on the end of the skylight; neither did I stir a limb, so far as I knew. We stood less than a foot from each other. It occurred to me that if old "Bless my soul — you don't say so" were to put his head up the companion and

catch sight of us, he would think he was seeing double, or imagine himself come upon a scene of weird witchcraft; the strange
captain having a quiet confabulation by the wheel with his own
gray ghost. I became very much concerned to prevent anything
of the sort. I heard the other's soothing undertone.

"My father's a parson in Norfolk," it said. Evidently he had
forgotten he had told me this important fact before. Truly a nice
little tale.

"You had better slip down into my stateroom now," I said,   65
moving off stealthily. My double followed my movements; our
bare feet made no sound; I let him in, closed the door with care,
and, after giving a call to the second mate, returned on deck for
my relief.

"Not much sign of any wind yet," I remarked when he approached.

"No, sir. Not much," he assented, sleepily, in his hoarse voice,
with just enough deference, no more, and barely suppressing a
yawn.

"Well, that's all you have to look out for. You have got your
orders."

"Yes, sir."

I paced a turn or two on the poop and saw him take up his   70
position face forward with his elbow in the ratlines of the mizzen
rigging before I went below. The mate's faint snoring was still
going on peacefully. The cuddy lamp was burning over the table
on which stood a vase with flowers, a polite attention from the
ship's provision merchant — the last flowers we should see for
the next three months at the very least. Two bunches of bananas
hung from the beam symmetrically, one on each side of the
rudder casing. Everything was as before in the ship — except
that two of her captain's sleeping suits were simultaneously in
use, one motionless in the cuddy, the other keeping very still in
the captain's stateroom.

It must be explained here that my cabin had the form of the
capital letter L, the door being within the angle and opening into
the short part of the letter. A couch was to the left, the bed-place
to the right; my writing desk and the chronometers' table faced
the door. But anyone opening it, unless he stepped right inside,
had no view of what I call the long (or vertical) part of the letter.
It contained some lockers surmounted by a bookcase; and a few
clothes, a thick jacket or two, caps, oilskin coat, and such like,
hung on hooks. There was at the bottom of that part a door opening into my bathroom, which could be entered also directly from
the saloon. But that way was never used.

The mysterious arrival had discovered the advantage of this particular shape. Entering my room, lighted strongly by a big bulkhead lamp swung on gimbals above my writing desk, I did not see him anywhere till he stepped out quietly from behind the coats hung in the recessed part.

"I heard somebody moving about, and went in there at once," he whispered.

I, too, spoke under my breath.

"Nobody is likely to come in here without knocking and   75 getting permission."

He nodded. His face was thin and the sunburn faded, as though he had been ill. And no wonder. He had been, I heard presently, kept under arrest in his cabin for nearly seven weeks. But there was nothing sickly in his eyes or in his expression. He was not a bit like me, really; yet, as we stood leaning over my bed-place, whispering side by side, with our dark heads together and our backs to the door, anybody bold enough to open it stealthily would have been treated to the uncanny sight of a double captain busy talking in whispers with his other self.

"But all this doesn't tell me how you came to hang on to our side ladder," I inquired, in the hardly audible murmurs we used, after he had told me something more of the proceedings on board the *Sephora* once the bad weather was over.

"When we sighted Java Head I had had time to think all those matters out several times over. I had six weeks of doing nothing else, and with only an hour or so every evening for a tramp on the quarter-deck."

He whispered, his arms folded on the side of my bed-place, staring through the open port. And I could imagine perfectly the manner of this thinking out — a stubborn if not a steadfast operation; something of which I should have been perfectly incapable.

"I reckoned it would be dark before we closed with the land,"   80 he continued, so low that I had to strain my hearing, near as we were to each other, shoulder touching shoulder almost. "So I asked to speak to the old man. He always seemed very sick when he came to see me — as if he could not look me in the face. You know, that foresail saved the ship. She was too deep to have run long under the bare poles. And it was I that managed to set it for him. Anyway, he came. When I had him in my cabin — he stood by the door looking at me as if I had the halter around my neck already — I asked him right away to leave my cabin door unlocked at night while the ship was going through Sunda Straits. There would be the Java coast within two or three miles, off

Angier Point. I wanted nothing more. I've had a prize for swimming my second year in the Conway."

"I can believe it," I breathed out.

"God only knows why they locked me in every night. To see
some of their faces you'd have thought they were afraid I'd go
about at night strangling people. Am I a murdering brute? Do I
look it? By Jove! if I had been he wouldn't have trusted himself
like that into my room. You'll say I might have chucked him aside
and bolted out, there and then — it was dark already. Well, no.
And for the same reason I wouldn't think of trying to smash the
door. There would have been a rush to stop me at the noise, and I
did not mean to get into a confounded scrimmage. Somebody
else might have got killed — for I would not have broken out
only to get chucked back, and I did not want any more of that
work. He refused, looking more sick than ever. He was afraid of
the men, and also of that old second mate of his who had been
sailing with him for years — a gray-headed old humbug; and his
steward, too, had been with him devil knows how long —
seventeen years or more — a dogmatic sort of loafer who hated
me like poison, just because I was the chief mate. No chief mate
ever made more than one voyage in the *Sephora*, you know. Those
two old chaps ran the ship. Devil only knows what the skipper
wasn't afraid of (all his nerve went to pieces altogether in that
hellish spell of bad weather we had) — of what the law would do
to him — of his wife, perhaps. Oh, yes! she's on board. Though I
don't think she would have meddled. She would have been only
too glad to have me out of the ship in any way. The 'brand of
Cain' business, don't you see. That's all right. I was ready enough
to go off wandering on the face of the earth — and that was
price enough to pay for an Abel of that sort. Anyhow, he wouldn't
listen to me. 'This thing must take its course. I represent the law
here.' He was shaking like a leaf. 'So you won't?' 'No!' 'Then I
hope you will be able to sleep on that,' I said, and turned my back
on him. 'I wonder that *you* can,' cries he, and locks the door.

"Well, after that, I couldn't. Not very well. That was three
weeks ago. We have had a slow passage through the Java Sea;
drifted about Carimata for ten days. When we anchored here
they thought, I suppose, it was all right. The nearest land (and
that's five miles) is the ship's destination; the consul would soon
set about catching me; and there would have been no object in
bolting to these islets there. I don't suppose there's a drop of
water on them. I don't know how it was, but tonight that steward,
after bringing me my supper, went out to let me eat it, and left
the door unlocked. And I ate it — all there was, too. After I had

finished I strolled out on the quarter-deck. I don't know that I meant to do anything. A breath of fresh air was all I wanted, I believe. Then a sudden temptation came over me. I kicked off my slippers and was in the water before I had made up my mind fairly. Somebody heard the splash and they raised an awful hullabaloo. 'He's gone! Lower the boats! He's committed suicide! No, he's swimming.' Certainly I was swimming. It's not so easy for a swimmer like me to commit suicide by drowning. I landed on the nearest islet before the boat left the ship's side. I heard them pulling about in the dark, hailing, and so on, but after a bit they gave up. Everything quieted down and the anchorage became as still as death. I sat down on a stone and began to think. I felt certain they would start searching for me at daylight. There was no place to hide on those stony things — and if there had been, what would have been the good? But now I was clear of that ship, I was not going back. So after a while I took off all my clothes, tied them up in a bundle with a stone inside, and dropped them in the deep water on the outer side of that islet. That was suicide enough for me. Let them think what they liked, but I didn't mean to drown myself. I meant to swim till I sank — but that's not the same thing. I struck out for another of these little islands, and it was from that one that I first saw your riding light. Something to swim for. I went on easily, and on the way I came upon a flat rock a foot or two above water. In the daytime, I dare say, you might make it out with a glass from your poop. I scrambled up on it and rested myself for a bit. Then I made another start. That last spell must have been over a mile."

His whisper was getting fainter and fainter, and all the time he stared straight out through the porthole, in which there was not even a star to be seen. I had not interrupted him. There was something that made comment impossible in his narrative, or perhaps in himself; a sort of feeling, a quality, which I can't find a name for. And when he ceased, all I found was a futile whisper: "So you swam for our light?"

"Yes — straight for it. It was something to swim for. I couldn't see any stars low down because the coast was in the way, and I couldn't see the land, either. The water was like glass. One might have been swimming in a confounded thousand-feet deep cistern with no place for scrambling out anywhere; but what I didn't like was the notion of swimming round and round like a crazed bullock before I gave out; and as I didn't mean to go back . . . No. Do you see me being hauled back, stark naked, off one of these little islands by the scruff of the neck and fighting like a 85 wild beast? Somebody would have got killed for certain, and I did not want any of that. So I went on. Then your ladder — "

"Why didn't you hail the ship?" I asked, a little louder.

He touched my shoulder lightly. Lazy footsteps came right over our heads and stopped. The second mate had crossed from the other side of the poop and might have been hanging over the rail, for all we knew.

"He couldn't hear us talking — could he?" My double breathed into my very ear, anxiously.

His anxiety was an answer, a sufficient answer, to the question I had put to him. An answer containing all the difficulty of that situation. I closed the porthole quietly, to make sure. A louder word might have been overheard.

"Who's that?" he whispered then. 90

"My second mate. But I don't know much more of the fellow than you do."

And I told him a little about myself. I had been appointed to take charge while I least expected anything of the sort, not quite a fortnight ago. I didn't know either the ship or the people. Hadn't had the time in port to look about me or size anybody up. And as to the crew, all they knew was that I was appointed to take the ship home. For the rest, I was almost as much of a stranger on board as himself, I said. And at the moment I felt it most acutely. I felt that it would take very little to make me a suspect person in the eyes of the ship's company.

He had turned about meantime; and we, the two strangers in the ship, faced each other in identical attitudes.

"Your ladder — " he murmured, after a silence. "Who'd have thought of finding a ladder hanging over at night in a ship anchored out here! I felt just then a very unpleasant faintness. After the life I've been leading for nine weeks, anybody would have got out of condition. I wasn't capable of swimming round as far as your rudder chains. And, lo and behold! there was a ladder to get hold of. After I gripped it I said to myself, 'What's the good?' When I saw a man's head looking over I thought I would swim away presently and leave him shouting — in whatever language it was. I didn't mind being looked at. I — I liked it. And then you speaking to me so quietly — as if you had expected me — made me hold on a little longer. It had been a confounded lonely time — I don't mean while swimming. I was glad to talk a little to somebody that didn't belong to the *Sephora*. As to asking for the captain, that was a mere impulse. It could have been no use, with all the ship knowing about me and the other people pretty certain to be round here in the morning. I don't know — I wanted to be seen, to talk with somebody, before I went on. I don't know what I would have said. . . . 'Fine night, isn't it?' or something of the sort."

"Do you think they will be round here presently?" I asked 95 with some incredulity.

"Quite likely," he said, faintly.

He looked extremely haggard all of a sudden. His head rolled on his shoulders.

"H'm. We shall see then. Meantime get into that bed," I whispered. "Want help? There."

It was a rather high bed-place with a set of drawers underneath. This amazing swimmer really needed the lift I gave him by seizing his leg. He tumbled in, rolled over on his back, and flung one arm across his eyes. And then, with his face nearly hidden, he must have looked exactly as I used to look in that bed. I gazed upon my other self for a while before drawing across carefully the two green serge curtains which ran on a brass rod. I thought for a moment of pinning them together for greater safety, but I sat down on the couch, and once there I felt unwilling to rise and hunt for a pin. I would do it in a moment. I was extremely tired, in a peculiarly intimate way, by the strain of stealthiness, by the effort of whispering and the general secrecy of this excitement. It was three o'clock by now and I had been on my feet since nine, but I was not sleepy; I could not have gone to sleep. I sat there, fagged out, looking at the curtains, trying to clear my mind of the confused sensation of being in two places at once, and greatly bothered by an exasperating knocking in my head. It was a relief to discover suddenly that it was not in my head at all, but on the outside of the door. Before I could collect myself the words "Come in" were out of my mouth, and the steward entered with a tray, bringing in my morning coffee. I had slept, after all, and I was so frightened that I shouted, "This way! I am here, steward," as though he had been miles away. He put down the tray on the table next the couch and only then said, very quietly, "I can see you are here, sir." I felt him give me a keen look, but I dared not meet his eyes just then. He must have wondered why I had drawn the curtains of my bed before going to sleep on the couch. He went out, hooking the door open as usual.

I heard the crew washing decks above me. I knew I would 100 have been told at once if there had been any wind. Calm, I thought, and I was doubly vexed. Indeed, I felt dual more than ever. The steward reappeared suddenly in the doorway. I jumped up from the couch so quickly that he gave a start.

"What do you want here?"

"Close your port, sir — they are washing decks."

"It is closed," I said, reddening.

"Very well, sir." But he did not move from the doorway and returned my stare in an extraordinary, equivocal manner for a time. Then his eyes wavered, all his expression changed, and in a voice unusually gentle, almost coaxing:

"May I come in to take the empty cup away, sir?" 105

"Of course!" I turned my back on him while he popped in and out. Then I unhooked and closed the door and even pushed the bolt. This sort of thing could not go on very long. The cabin was as hot as an oven, too. I took a peep at my double, and discovered that he had not moved, his arm was still over his eyes; but his chest heaved; his hair was wet; his chin glistened with perspiration. I reached over him and opened the port.

"I must show myself on deck," I reflected.

Of course, theoretically, I could do what I liked, with no one to say nay to me within the whole circle of the horizon; but to lock my cabin door and take the key away I did not dare. Directly I put my head out of the companion I saw the group of my two officers, the second mate barefooted, the chief mate in long india-rubber boots, near the break of the poop, and the steward halfway down the poop ladder talking to them eagerly. He happened to catch sight of me and dived, the second ran down on the main deck shouting some order or other, and the chief mate came to meet me, touching his cap.

There was a sort of curiosity in his eyes that I did not like. I don't know whether the steward had told them that I was "queer" only, or downright drunk, but I know the man meant to have a good look at me. I watched him coming with a smile which, as he got into point-blank range, took effect and froze his very whiskers. I did not give him time to open his lips.

"Square the yards by lifts and braces before the hands go to 110 breakfast."

It was the first particular order I had given on board that ship; and I stayed on deck to see it executed, too. I had felt the need of asserting myself without loss of time. That sneering young cub got taken down a peg or two on that occasion, and I also seized the opportunity of having a good look at the face of every foremast man as they filed past me to go to the after braces. At breakfast time, eating nothing myself, I presided with such frigid dignity that the two mates were only too glad to escape from the cabin as soon as decency permitted; and all the time the dual working of my mind distracted me almost to the point of insanity. I was constantly watching myself, my secret self, as dependent on my actions as my own personality, sleeping in that bed, behind that door which faced me as I sat at the head of the table. It was very much like being mad, only it was worse because one was aware of it.

I had to shake him for a solid minute, but when at last he opened his eyes it was in the full possession of his senses, with an inquiring look.

"All's well so far," I whispered. "Now you must vanish into the bathroom."

He did so, as noiseless as a ghost, and I then rang for the steward, and facing him boldly, directed him to tidy up my stateroom while I was having my bath — "and be quick about it." As my tone admitted of no excuses, he said, "Yes, sir," and ran off to fetch his dustpan and brushes. I took a bath and did most of my dressing, splashing, and whistling softly for the steward's edification, while the secret sharer of my life stood drawn up bolt upright in that little space, his face looking very sunken in daylight, his eyelids lowered under the stern, dark line of his eyebrows drawn together by a slight frown.

When I left him there to go back to my room the steward was 115 finishing dusting. I sent for the mate and engaged him in some insignificant conversation. It was, as it were, trifling with the terrific character of his whiskers; but my object was to give him an opportunity for a good look at my cabin. And then I could at last shut, with a clear conscience, the door of my stateroom and get my double back into the recessed part. There was nothing else for it. He had to sit still on a small folding stool, half smothered by the heavy coats hanging there. We listened to the steward going into the bathroom out of the saloon, filling the water bottles there, scrubbing the bath, setting things to rights, whisk, bang, clatter — out again into the saloon — turn the key — click. Such was my scheme for keeping my second self invisible. Nothing better could be contrived under the circumstances. And there we sat; I at my writing desk ready to appear busy with some papers, he behind me, out of sight of the door. It would not have been prudent to talk in daytime; and I could not have stood the excitement of that queer sense of whispering to myself. Now and then, glancing over my shoulder, I saw him far back there, sitting rigidly on the low stool, his bare feet close together, his arms folded, his head hanging on his breast — and perfectly still. Anybody would have taken him for me.

I was fascinated by it myself. Every moment I had to glance

over my shoulder. I was looking at him when a voice outside the door said:

"Beg pardon, sir."

"Well!" . . . I kept my eyes on him, and so, when the voice outside the door announced, "There's a ship's boat coming our way, sir," I saw him give a start — the first movement he had made for hours. But he did not raise his bowed head.

"All right. Get the ladder over."

I hesitated. Should I whisper something to him? But what? His immobility seemed to have been never disturbed. What could I tell him he did not know already? . . . Finally I went on deck. 120

II

The skipper of the *Sephora* had a thin red whisker all round his face, and the sort of complexion that goes with hair of that color; also the particular, rather smeary shade of blue in the eyes. He was not exactly a showy figure; his shoulders were high, his stature but middling — one leg slightly more bandy than the other. He shook hands, looking vaguely around. A spiritless tenacity was his main characteristic, I judged. I behaved with a politeness which seemed to disconcert him. Perhaps he was shy. He mumbled to me as if he were ashamed of what he was saying; gave his name (it was something like Archbold — but at this distance of years I hardly am sure), his ship's name, and a few other particulars of that sort, in the manner of a criminal making a reluctant and doleful confession. He had had terrible weather on the passage out — terrible — terrible — wife aboard, too.

By this time we were seated in the cabin and the steward brought in a tray with a bottle and glasses. "Thanks! No." Never took liquor. Would have some water, though. He drank two tumblerfuls. Terrible thirsty work. Ever since daylight had been exploring the islands round his ship.

"What was that for — fun?" I asked, with an appearance of polite interest.

"No!" He sighed. "Painful duty."

As he persisted in his mumbling and I wanted my double to hear every word, I hit upon the notion of informing him that I regretted to say I was hard of hearing. 125

"Such a young man, too!" he nodded, keeping his smeary blue, unintelligent eyes fastened upon me. What was the cause of it — some disease? he inquired, without the least sympathy and as if he thought that, if so, I'd got no more than I deserved.

"Yes; disease," I admitted in a cheerful tone which seemed to shock him. But my point was gained, because he had to raise his voice to give me his tale. It is not worth while to record that version. It was just over two months since all this had happened, and he had thought so much about it that he seemed completely muddled as to its bearings, but still immensely impressed.

"What would you think of such a thing happening on board your own ship? I've had the *Sephora* for these fifteen years. I am a well-known shipmaster."

He was densely distressed — and perhaps I should have sympathized with him if I had been able to detach my mental vision from the unsuspected sharer of my cabin as though he were my second self. There he was on the other side of the bulkhead, four or five feet from us, no more, as we sat in the saloon. I looked politely at Captain Archbold (if that was his name), but it was the other I saw, in a gray sleeping suit, seated on a low stool, his bare feet close together, his arms folded, and every word said between us falling into the ears of his dark head bowed on his chest.

"I have been at sea now, man and boy, for seven-and-thirty 130 years, and I've never heard of such a thing happening in an English ship. And that it should be my ship. Wife on board, too."

I was hardly listening to him.

"Don't you think," I said, "that the heavy sea which, you told me, came aboard just then might have killed the man? I have seen the sheer weight of a sea kill a man very neatly, by simply breaking his neck."

"Good God!" he uttered impressively, fixing his smeary blue eyes on me. "The sea! No man killed by the sea ever looked like that." He seemed positively scandalized at my suggestion. And as I gazed at him, certainly not prepared for anything original on his part, he advanced his head close to mine and thrust his tongue out at me so suddenly that I couldn't help starting back.

After scoring over my calmness in this graphic way he nodded wisely. If I had seen the sight, he assured me, I would never forget it as long as I lived. The weather was too bad to give the corpse a proper sea burial. So next day at dawn they took it up on the poop, covering its face with a bit of bunting; he read a short prayer, and then, just as it was, in its oilskins and long boots, they launched it amongst those mountainous seas that seemed ready every moment to swallow up the ship herself and the terrified lives on board of her.

"That reefed foresail saved you," I threw in. 135

"Under God — it did," he exclaimed fervently. "It was by a special mercy, I firmly believe, that it stood some of those hurricane squalls."

"It was the setting of that sail which — " I began.

"God's own hand in it," he interrupted me. "Nothing less could have done it. I don't mind telling you that I hardly dared give the order. It seemed impossible that we could touch anything without losing it, and then our last hope would have been gone."

The terror of that gale was on him yet. I let him go on for a bit, then said, casually — as if returning to a minor subject:

"You were very anxious to give up your mate to the shore 140 people, I believe?"

He was. To the law. His obscure tenacity on that point had in it something incomprehensible and a little awful; something, as it were, mystical, quite apart from his anxiety that he should not be suspected of "countenancing any doings of that sort." Seven-and-thirty virtuous years at sea, of which over twenty of immaculate command, and the last fifteen in the *Sephora*, seemed to have laid him under some pitiless obligation.

"And you know," he went on, groping shamefacedly amongst his feelings, "I did not engage that young fellow. His people had some interest with my owners. I was in a way forced to take him on. He looked very smart, very gentlemanly, and all that. But do you know — I never liked him, somehow. I am a plain man. You see, he wasn't exactly the sort for the chief mate of a ship like the *Sephora*."

I had become so connected in thoughts and impressions with the secret sharer of my cabin that I felt as if I, personally, were being given to understand that I, too, was not the sort that would have done for the chief mate of a ship like the *Sephora*. I had no doubt of it in my mind.

"Not at all the style of man. You understand," he insisted, superfluously, looking hard at me.

I smiled urbanely. He seemed at a loss for a while. 145

"I suppose I must report a suicide."

"Beg pardon?"

"Sui-cide! That's what I'll have to write to my owners directly I get in."

"Unless you manage to recover him before tomorrow," I assented, dispassionately. . . . "I mean, alive."

He mumbled something which I really did not catch, and I 150 turned my ear to him in a puzzled manner. He fairly bawled:

"The land — I say, the mainland is at least seven miles off my anchorage."

"About that."

My lack of excitement, of curiosity, of surprise, of any sort of pronounced interest, began to arouse his distrust. But except for the felicitous pretense of deafness I had not tried to pretend anything. I had felt utterly incapable of playing the part of ignorance properly, and therefore was afraid to try. It is also certain that he had brought some ready-made suspicions with him, and that he viewed my politeness as a strange and unnatural phenomenon. And yet how else could I have received him? Not heartily! That was impossible for psychological reasons, which I need not state here. My only object was to keep off his inquiries. Surlily? Yes, but surliness might have provoked a point-blank question. From its novelty to him and from its nature, punctilious courtesy was the manner best calculated to restrain the man. But there was the danger of his breaking through my defense bluntly. I could not, I think, have met him by a direct lie, also for psychological (not moral) reasons. If he had only known how afraid I was of his putting my feeling of identity with the other to the test! But, strangely enough — (I thought of it only afterward) — I believe that he was not a little disconcerted by the reverse side of that weird situation, by something in me that reminded him of the man he was seeking — suggested a mysterious similitude to the young fellow he had distrusted and disliked from the first.

However that might have been, the silence was not very prolonged. He took another oblique step.

"I reckon I had no more than a two-mile pull to your ship. Not a bit more." 155

"And quite enough, too, in this awful heat," I said.

Another pause full of mistrust followed. Necessity, they say, is mother of invention, but fear, too, is not barren of ingenious suggestions. And I was afraid he would ask me point-blank for news of my other self.

"Nice little saloon, isn't it?" I remarked, as if noticing for the first time the way his eyes roamed from one closed door to the other. "And very well fitted out, too. Here, for instance," I continued, reaching over the back of my seat negligently and flinging the door open, "is my bathroom."

He made an eager movement, but hardly gave it a glance. I got up, shut the door of the bathroom, and invited him to have a look round, as if I were very proud of my accommodation. He had to rise and be shown round, but he went through the business without any raptures whatever.

"And now we'll have a look at my stateroom," I declared, in a   160
voice as loud as I dared to make it, crossing the cabin to the starboard side with purposely heavy steps.

He followed me in and gazed around. My intelligent double had vanished. I played my part.

"Very convenient — isn't it?"

"Very nice. Very comf . . ." He didn't finish, and went out brusquely as if to escape from some unrighteous wiles of mine. But it was not to be. I had been too frightened not to feel vengeful; I felt I had him on the run, and I meant to keep him on the run. My polite insistence must have had something menacing in it, because he gave in suddenly. And I did not let him off a single item; mate's room, pantry, storerooms, the very sail locker which was also under the poop — he had to look into them all. When at last I showed him out on the quarter-deck he drew a long, spiritless sigh, and mumbled dismally that he must really be going back to his ship now. I desired my mate, who had joined us, to see to the captain's boat.

The man of whiskers gave a blast on the whistle which he used to wear hanging round his neck, and yelled, "*Sephora's* away!" My double down there in my cabin must have heard, and certainly could not feel more relieved than I. Four fellows came running out from somewhere forward and went over the side, while my own men, appearing on deck too, lined the rail. I escorted my visitor to the gangway ceremoniously, and nearly overdid it. He was a tenacious beast. On the very ladder he lingered, and in that unique, guiltily conscientious manner of sticking to the point:

"I say . . . you . . . you don't think that — "   165

I covered his voice loudly:

"Certainly not. . . . I am delighted. Good-by."

I had an idea of what he meant to say, and just saved myself by the privilege of defective hearing. He was too shaken generally to insist, but my mate, close witness of that parting, looked mystified and his face took on a thoughtful cast. As I did not want to appear as if I wished to avoid all communication with my officers, he had the opportunity to address me.

"Seems a very nice man. His boat's crew told our chaps a very extraordinary story, if what I am told by the steward is true. I suppose you had it from the captain, sir?"

"Yes. I had a story from the captain."   170

"A very horrible affair — isn't it, sir?"

"It is."

"Beats all these tales we hear about murders in Yankee ships."

"I don't think it beats them. I don't think it resembles them in the least."

"Bless my soul — you don't say so! But of course I've no 175 acquaintance whatever with American ships, not I, so I couldn't go against your knowledge. It's horrible enough for me. . . . But the queerest part is that those fellows seemed to have some idea the man was hidden aboard here. They had really. Did you ever hear of such a thing?"

"Preposterous — isn't it?"

We were walking to and fro athwart the quarter-deck. No one of the crew forward could be seen (the day was Sunday), and the mate pursued:

"There was some little dispute about it. Our chaps took offense. 'As if we would harbor a thing like that,' they said. 'Wouldn't you like to look for him in our coal hole?' Quite a tiff. But they made it up in the end. I suppose he did drown himself. Don't you, sir?"

"I don't suppose anything."

"You have no doubt in the matter, sir?"   180

"None whatever."

I left him suddenly. I felt I was producing a bad impression, but with my double down there it was most trying to be on deck. And it was almost as trying to be below. Altogether a nerve-trying situation. But on the whole I felt less torn in two when I was with him. There was no one in the whole ship whom I dared take into my confidence. Since the hands had got to know his story, it would have been impossible to pass him off for anyone else, and an accidental discovery was to be dreaded now more than ever. . . .

The steward being engaged in laying the table for dinner, we could talk only with our eyes when I first went down. Later in the afternoon we had a cautious try at whispering. The Sunday quietness of the ship was against us; the stillness of air and water around her was against us; the elements, the men were against us — everything was against us in our secret partnership; time itself — for this could not go on forever. The very trust in Providence was, I suppose, denied to his guilt. Shall I confess that this thought cast me down very much? And as to the chapter of accidents which counts for so much in the book of success, I could only hope that it was closed. For what favorable accident could be expected?

"Did you hear everything?" were my first words as soon as we took up our position side by side, leaning over my bed-place.

He had. And the proof of it was his earnest whisper, "The man told you he hardly dared to give the order." 185

I understood the reference to be to that saving foresail.

"Yes. He was afraid of it being lost in the setting."

"I assure you he never gave the order. He may think he did, but he never gave it. He stood there with me on the break of the poop after the maintopsail blew away, and whimpered about our last hope — positively whimpered about it and nothing else — and the night coming on! To hear one's skipper go on like that in such weather was enough to drive any fellow out of his mind. It worked me up into a sort of desperation. I just took it into my own hands and went away from him, boiling, and — . But what's the use telling you? *You* know! . . . Do you think that if I had not been pretty fierce with them I should have got the men to do anything? Not it! The bosun perhaps? Perhaps! It wasn't a heavy sea — it was a sea gone mad! I suppose the end of the world will be something like that; and a man may have the heart to see it coming once and be done with it — but to have to face it day after day — I don't blame anybody. I was precious little better than the rest. Only — I was an officer of that old coal-wagon, anyhow — "

"I quite understand," I conveyed that sincere assurance into his ear. He was out of breath with whispering; I could hear him pant slightly. It was all very simple. The same strung-up force which had given twenty-four men a chance, at least, for their lives, had, in a sort of recoil, crushed an unworthy mutinous existence.

But I had no leisure to weigh the merits of the matter — 190 footsteps in the saloon, a heavy knock. "There's enough wind to get under way with, sir." Here was the call of a new claim upon my thoughts and even upon my feelings.

"Turn the hands up," I cried through the door. "I'll be on deck directly."

I was going out to make the acquaintance of my ship. Before I left the cabin our eyes met — the eyes of the only two strangers on board. I pointed to the recessed part where the little camp-stool awaited him and laid my finger on my lips. He made a gesture — somewhat vague — a little mysterious, accompanied by a faint smile, as if of regret.

This is not the place to enlarge upon the sensations of a man who feels for the first time a ship move under his feet to his own independent word. In my case they were not unalloyed. I was not wholly alone with my command; for there was that stranger in my cabin. Or rather, I was not completely and wholly with her. Part of me was absent. That mental feeling of being in two places at once affected me physically as if the mood of secrecy had penetrated my very soul. Before an hour had elapsed since the ship had begun to move, having occasion to ask the mate (he stood by my side) to take a compass bearing of the Pagoda, I caught myself reaching up to his ear in whispers. I say I caught myself, but enough had escaped to startle the man. I can't describe it otherwise than by saying that he shied. A grave, preoccupied manner, as though he were in possession of some perplexing intelligence, did not leave him henceforth. A little later I moved away from the rail to look at the compass with such a stealthy gait that the helmsman noticed it — and I could not help noticing the unusual roundness of his eyes. These are triflng instances, though it's to no commander's advantage to be suspected of ludicrous eccentricities. But I was also more seriously affected. There are to a seaman certain words, gestures, that should in given conditions come as naturally, as instinctively as the winking of a menaced eye. A certain order should spring on to his lips without thinking; a certain sign should get itself made, so to speak, without reflection. But all unconscious alertness had abandoned me. I had to make an effort of will to recall myself back (from the cabin) to the conditions of the moment. I felt that I was appearing an irresolute commander to those people who were watching me more or less critically.

And, besides, there were the scares. On the second day out, for instance, coming off the deck in the afternoon (I had straw slippers on my bare feet) I stopped at the open pantry door and spoke to the steward. He was doing something there with his back to me. At the sound of my voice he nearly jumped out of his skin, as the saying is, and incidentally broke a cup.

"What on earth's the matter with you?" I asked, astonished.   195

He was extremely confused. "Beg your pardon, sir. I made sure you were in your cabin."

"You see I wasn't."

"No, sir. I could have sworn I had heard you moving in there not a moment ago. It's most extraordinary . . . very sorry, sir."

I passed on with an inward shudder. I was so identified with my secret double that I did not even mention the fact in those scanty, fearful whispers we exchanged. I suppose he had made some slight noise of some kind or other. It would have been miraculous if he hadn't at one time or another. And yet, haggard as he appeared, he looked always perfectly self-controlled, more than calm — almost invulnerable. On my suggestion he remained almost entirely in the bathroom, which, upon the whole, was the safest place. There could be really no shadow of an excuse for anyone ever wanting to go in there, once the steward had done with it. It was a very tiny place. Sometimes he reclined on the floor, his legs bent, his head sustained on one elbow. At others I would find him on the campstool, sitting in his gray sleeping suit and with his cropped dark hair like a patient, unmoved convict. At night I would smuggle him into my bedplace, and we would whisper together, with the regular footfalls of the officer of the watch passing and repassing over our heads. It was an infinitely miserable time. It was lucky that some tins of fine preserves were stowed in a locker in my stateroom; hard bread I could always get hold of; and so he lived on stewed chicken, pâté de foie gras, asparagus, cooked oysters, sardines — on all sorts of abominable sham delicacies out of tins. My early morning coffee he always drank; and it was all I dared do for him in that respect.

Every day there was the horrible maneuvering to go through   200 so that my room and then the bathroom should be done in the usual way. I came to hate the sight of the steward, to abhor the voice of that harmless man. I felt that it was he who would bring on the disaster of discovery. It hung like a sword over our heads.

The fourth day out, I think (we were then working down the east side of the Gulf of Siam, tack for tack, in light winds and smooth water) — the fourth day, I say, of this miserable juggling with the unavoidable, as we sat at our evening meal, that man, whose slightest movement I dreaded, after putting down the dishes ran up on deck busily. This could not be dangerous. Presently he came down again; and then it appeared that he had remembered a coat of mine which I had thrown over a rail to dry after having been wetted in a shower which had passed over the ship in the afternoon. Sitting stolidly at the head of the table I became terrified at the sight of the garment on his arm. Of course he made for my door. There was no time to lose.

"Steward," I thundered. My nerves were so shaken that I could not govern my voice and conceal my agitation. This was the sort of thing that made my terrifically whiskered mate tap his forehead with his forefinger. I had detected him using that ges-

ture while talking on deck with a confidential air to the carpenter. It was too far to hear a word, but I had no doubt that this
pantomime could only refer to the strange new captain.

"Yes, sir," the pale-faced steward turned resignedly to me. It
was this maddening course of being shouted at, checked without
rhyme or reason, arbitrarily chased out of my cabin, suddenly
called into it, sent flying out of his pantry on incomprehensible
errands, that accounted for the growing wretchedness of his
expression.

"Where are you going with that coat?"

"To your room, sir."   205

"Is there another shower coming?"

"I'm sure I don't know, sir. Shall I go up again and see, sir?"

"No! never mind."

My object was attained, as of course my other self in there
would have heard everything that passed. During this interlude
my two officers never raised their eyes off their respective plates;
but the lip of that confounded cub, the second mate, quivered
visibly.

I expected the steward to hook my coat on and come out at   210
once. He was very slow about it; but I dominated my nervousness
sufficiently not to shout after him. Suddenly I became aware (it
could be heard plainly enough) that the fellow for some reason
or other was opening the door of the bathroom. It was the end.
The place was literally not big enough to swing a cat in. My voice
died in my throat and I went stony all over. I expected to hear a
yell of surprise and terror, and made a movement, but had not
the strength to get on my legs. Everything remained still. Had my
second self taken the poor wretch by the throat? I don't know
what I would have done next moment if I had not seen the
steward come out of my room, close the door, and then stand
quietly by the sideboard.

Saved, I thought. But, no! Lost! Gone! He was gone!

I laid my knife and fork down and leaned back in my chair.
My head swam. After a while, when sufficiently recovered to
speak in a steady voice, I instructed my mate to put the ship
round at eight o'clock himself.

"I won't come on deck," I went on. "I think I'll turn in, and
unless the wind shifts I don't want to be disturbed before midnight. I feel a bit seedy."

"You did look middling bad a little while ago," the chief
mate remarked without showing any great concern.

They both went out, and I stared at the steward clearing the   215
table. There was nothing to be read on that wretched man's face.

But why did he avoid my eyes, I asked myself. Then I thought I should like to hear the sound of his voice.

"Steward!"

"Sir!" Startled as usual.

"Where did you hang up that coat?"

"In the bathroom, sir." The usual anxious tone. "It's not quite dry yet, sir."

For some time longer I sat in the cuddy. Had my double 220 vanished as he had come? But of his coming there was an explanation, whereas his disappearance would be inexplicable. . . . I went slowly into my dark room, shut the door, lighted the lamp, and for a time dared not turn round. When at last I did I saw him standing bolt upright in the narrow recessed part. It would not be true to say I had a shock, but an irresistible doubt of his bodily existence flitted through my mind. Can it be, I asked myself, that he is not visible to other eyes than mine? It was like being haunted. Motionless, with a grave face, he raised his hands slightly at me in a gesture which meant clearly, "Heavens! what a narrow escape!" Narrow indeed. I think I had come creeping quietly as near insanity as any man who has not actually gone over the border. That gesture restrained me, so to speak.

The mate with the terrific whiskers was now putting the ship on the other tack. In the moment of profound silence which follows upon the hands going to their stations I heard on the poop his raised voice: "Hard alee!" and the distant shout of the order repeated on the maindeck. The sails, in that light breeze, made but a faint fluttering noise. It ceased. The ship was coming round slowly; I held my breath in the renewed stillness of expectation; one wouldn't have thought that there was a single living soul on her decks. A sudden brisk shout, "Mainsail haul!" broke the spell, and in the noisy cries and rush overhead of the men running away with the main brace we two, down in my cabin, came together in our usual position by the bed-place.

He did not wait for my question. "I heard him fumbling here and just managed to squat myself down in the bath," he whispered to me. "The fellow only opened the door and put his arm in to hang the coat up. All the same — "

"I never thought of that," I whispered back, even more appalled than before at the closeness of the shave, and marveling at that something unyielding in his character which was carrying him through so finely. There was no agitation in his whisper. Whoever was being driven distracted, it was not he. He was sane. And the proof of his sanity was continued when he took up the whispering again.

"It would never do for me to come to life again."

It was something that a ghost might have said. But what he   225
was alluding to was his old captain's reluctant admission of the
theory of suicide. It would obviously serve his turn — if I had
understood at all the view which seemed to govern the unalter-
able purpose of his action.

"You must maroon me as soon as ever you can get amongst
these islands off the Cambodje shore," he went on.

"Maroon you! We are not living in a boy's adventure tale," I
protested. His scornful whispering took me up.

"We aren't indeed! There's nothing of a boy's tale in this. But
there's nothing else for it. I want no more. You don't suppose I am
afraid of what can be done to me? Prison or gallows or whatever
they may please. But you don't see me coming back to explain
such things to an old fellow in a wig and twelve respectable
tradesmen, do you? What can they know whether I am guilty or
not — or of *what* I am guilty, either? That's my affair. What does
the Bible say? 'Driven off the face of the earth.' Very well. I am off
the face of the earth now. As I came at night so I shall go."

"Impossible!" I murmured. "You can't."

"Can't? . . . Not naked like a soul on the Day of Judgment. I   230
shall freeze on to this sleeping suit. The Last Day is not yet —
and . . . you have understood thoroughly. Didn't you?"

I felt suddenly ashamed of myself. I may say truly that I
understood — and my hesitation in letting that man swim away
from my ship's side had been a mere sham sentiment, a sort of
cowardice.

"It can't be done now till next night," I breathed out. "The
ship is on the offshore tack and the wind may fail us."

"As long as I know that you understand," he whispered. "But
of course you do. It's a great satisfaction to have got somebody to
understand. You seem to have been there on purpose." And in
the same whisper, as if we two whenever we talked had to say
things to each other which were not fit for the world to hear, he
added, "It's very wonderful."

We remained side by side talking in our secret way — but
sometimes silent or just exchanging a whispered word or two at
long intervals. And as usual he stared through the port. A breath
of wind came now and again into our faces. The ship might have
been moored in dock, so gently and on an even keel she slipped
through the water, that did not murmur even at our passage,
shadowy and silent like a phantom sea.

At midnight I went on deck, and to my mate's great surprise   235
put the ship round on the other tack. His terrible whiskers flitted

round me in silent criticism. I certainly should not have done it if it had been only a question of getting out of that sleepy gulf as quickly as possible. I believe he told the second mate, who relieved him, that it was a great want of judgment. The other only yawned. That intolerable cub shuffled about so sleepily and lolled against the rails in such a slack, improper fashion that I came down on him sharply.

"Aren't you properly awake yet?"

"Yes, sir! I am awake."

"Well, then, be good enough to hold yourself as if you were. And keep a lookout. If there's any current we'll be closing with some islands before daylight."

The east side of the gulf is fringed with islands, some solitary, others in groups. On the blue background of the high coast they seem to float on silvery patches of calm water, arid and gray, or dark green and rounded like clumps of evergreen bushes, with the larger ones, a mile or two long, showing the outlines of ridges, ribs of gray rock under the dark mantle of matted leafage. Unknown to trade, to travel, almost to geography, the manner of life they harbor is an unsolved secret. There must be villages — settlements of fishermen at least — on the largest of them, and some communication with the world is probably kept up by native craft. But all that forenoon, as we headed for them, fanned along by the faintest of breezes, I saw no sign of man or canoe in the field of the telescope I kept on pointing at the scattered group.

At noon I gave no orders for a change of course, and the mate's whiskers became much concerned and seemed to be offering themselves unduly to my notice. At last I said:

"I am going to stand right in. Quite in — as far as I can take her."

The stare of extreme surprise imparted an air of ferocity also to his eyes, and he looked truly terrific for a moment.

"We're not doing well in the middle of the gulf," I continued, casually. "I am going to look for the land breezes tonight."

"Bless my soul! Do you mean, sir, in the dark amongst the lot of all them islands and reefs and shoals?"

"Well — if there are any regular land breezes at all on this coast one must get close inshore to find them, mustn't one?"

"Bless my soul!" he exclaimed again under his breath. All that afternoon he wore a dreamy, contemplative appearance which in him was a mark of perplexity. After dinner I went into my stateroom as if I meant to take some rest. There we two bent our dark heads over a half-unrolled chart lying on my bed.

"There," I said. "It's got to be Koh-ring. I've been looking at it
ever since sunrise. It has got two hills and a low point. It must be
inhabited. And on the coast opposite there is what looks like the
mouth of a biggish river — with some town, no doubt, not far up.
It's the best chance for you that I can see."

"Anything. Koh-ring let it be."

He looked thoughtfully at the chart as if surveying chances
and distances from a lofty height — and following with his eyes
his own figure wandering on the blank land of Cochin-China,
and then passing off that piece of paper clean out of sight into
uncharted regions. And it was as if the ship had two captains to
plan her course for her. I had been so worried and restless
running up and down that I had not had the patience to dress
that day. I had remained in my sleeping suit, with straw slippers
and a soft floppy hat. The closeness of the heat in the gulf had
been most oppressive, and the crew were used to see me wandering in that airy attire.

"She will clear the south point as she heads now," I whis- 250
pered into his ear. "Goodness only knows when, though, but
certainly after dark. I'll edge her in to half a mile, as far as I may
be able to judge in the dark — "

"Be careful," he murmured, warningly — and I realized suddenly that all my future, the only future for which I was fit, would
perhaps go irretrievably to pieces in any mishap to my first
command.

I could not stop a moment longer in the room. I motioned
him to get out of sight and made my way on the poop. That
unplayful cub had the watch. I walked up and down for a while
thinking things out, then beckoned him over.

"Send a couple of hands to open the two quarter-deck ports,"
I said, mildly.

He actually had the impudence, or else so forgot himself in
his wonder at such an incomprehensible order, as to repeat:

"Open the quarter-deck ports! What for, sir?" 255

"The only reason you need concern yourself about is because
I tell you to do so. Have them open wide and fastened properly."

He reddened and went off, but I believe made some jeering
remark to the carpenter as to the sensible practice of ventilating
a ship's quarter-deck. I know he popped into the mate's cabin to
impart the fact to him because the whiskers came on deck, as it
were by chance, and stole glances at me from below — for signs
of lunacy or drunkenness, I suppose.

A little before supper, feeling more restless than ever, I

rejoined, for a moment, my second self. And to find him sitting so quietly was surprising, like something against nature, inhuman.

I developed my plan in a hurried whisper.

"I shall stand in as close as I dare and then put her round. I 260 shall presently find means to smuggle you out of here into the sail locker, which communicates with the lobby. But there is an opening, a sort of square for hauling the sails out, which gives straight on the quarter-deck and which is never closed in fine weather, so as to give air to the sails. When the ship's way is deadened in stays and all the hands are aft at the main braces you shall have a clear road to slip out and get overboard through the open quarter-deck port. I've had them both fastened up. Use a rope's end to lower yourself into the water so as to avoid a splash — you know. It could be heard and cause some beastly complication."

He kept silent for a while, then whispered, "I understand."

"I won't be there to see you go," I began with an effort. "The rest . . . I only hope I have understood, too."

"You have. From first to last," and for the first time there seemed to be a faltering, something strained in his whisper. He caught hold of my arm, but the ringing of the supper bell made me start. He didn't, though; he only released his grip.

After supper I didn't come below again till well past eight o'clock. The faint, steady breeze was loaded with dew; and the wet, darkened sails held all there was of propelling power in it. The night, clear and starry, sparkled darkly, and the opaque, lightless patches shifting slowly against the low stars were the drifting islets. On the port bow there was a big one more distant and shadowily imposing by the great space of sky it eclipsed.

On opening the door I had a back view of my very own self 265 looking at a chart. He had come out of the recess and was standing near the table.

"Quite dark enough," I whispered.

He stepped back and leaned against my bed with a level, quiet glance. I sat on the couch. We had nothing to say to each other. Over our heads the officer of the watch moved here and there. Then I heard him move quickly. I knew what that meant. He was making for the companion; and presently his voice was outside my door.

"We are drawing in pretty fast, sir. Land looks rather close."

"Very well," I answered. "I am coming on deck directly."

I waited till he was gone out of the cuddy, then rose. My 270 double moved too. The time had come to exchange our last whispers, for neither of us was ever to hear each other's natural voice.

"Look here!" I opened a drawer and took out three sovereigns. "Take this, anyhow. I've got six and I'd give you the lot, only I must keep a little money to buy some fruit and vegetables for the crew from native boats as we go through Sunda Straits."

He shook his head.

"Take it," I urged him, whispering desperately. "No one can tell what — "

He smiled and slapped meaningly the only pocket of the sleeping jacket. It was not safe, certainly. But I produced a large old silk handkerchief of mine, and tying the three pieces of gold in a corner, pressed it on him. He was touched, I suppose, because he took it at last and tied it quickly round his waist under the jacket, on his bare skin.

Our eyes met; several seconds elapsed, till, our glances still 275 mingled, I extended my hand and turned the lamp out. Then I passed through the cuddy, leaving the door of my room wide open. . . . "Steward!"

He was still lingering in the pantry in the greatness of his zeal, giving a rub-up to a plated cruet stand the last thing before going to bed. Being careful not to wake up the mate, whose room was opposite, I spoke in an undertone.

He looked round anxiously. "Sir!"

"Can you get me a little hot water from the galley?"

"I am afraid, sir, the galley fire's been out for some time now."

"Go and see."   280

He fled up the stairs.

"Now," I whispered, loudly, into the saloon — too loudly, perhaps, but I was afraid I couldn't make a sound. He was by my side in an instant — the double captain slipped past the stairs — through the tiny dark passage . . . a sliding door. We were in the sail locker, scrambling on our knees over the sails. A sudden thought struck me. I saw myself wandering barefooted, bareheaded, the sun beating on my dark poll. I snatched off my floppy hat and tried hurriedly in the dark to ram it on my other self. He dodged and fended off silently. I wonder what he thought had come to me before he understood and suddenly desisted. Our hands met gropingly, lingered united in a steady, motionless clasp for a second. . . . No word was breathed by either of us when they separated.

I was standing quietly by the pantry door when the steward returned.

"Sorry, sir. Kettle barely warm. Shall I light the spirit lamp?"

"Never mind." 285

I came out on deck slowly. It was now a matter of conscience to shave the land as close as possible — for now he must go overboard whenever the ship was put in stays. Must! There could be no going back for him. After a moment I walked over to leeward and my heart flew into my mouth at the nearness of the land on the bow. Under any other circumstances I would not have held on a minute longer. The second mate had followed me anxiously.

I looked on till I felt I could command my voice.

"She will weather," I said then in a quiet tone.

"Are you going to try that, sir?" he stammered out incredulously.

I took no notice of him and raised my tone just enough to be 290
heard by the helmsman.

"Keep her good full."

"Good full, sir."

The wind fanned my cheek, the sails slept, the world was silent. The strain of watching the dark loom of the land grow bigger and denser was too much for me. I had shut my eyes — because the ship must go closer. She must! The stillness was intolerable. Were we standing still?

When I opened my eyes the second view started my heart with a thump. The black southern hill of Koh-ring seemed to hang right over the ship like a towering fragment of the everlasting night. On that enormous mass of blackness there was not a gleam to be seen, not a sound to be heard. It was gliding irresistibly toward us and yet seemed already within reach of the hand. I saw the vague figures of the watch grouped in the waist, gazing in awed silence.

"Are you going on, sir?" inquired an unsteady voice at my 295
elbow.

I ignored it. I had to go on.

"Keep her full. Don't check her way. That won't do now," I said warningly.

"I can't see the sails very well," the helmsman answered me, in strange, quavering tones.

Was she close enough? Already she was, I won't say in the shadow of the land, but in the very blackness of it, already swallowed up as it were, gone too close to be recalled, gone from me altogether.

"Give the mate a call," I said to the young man who stood at 300
my elbow as still as death. "And turn all hands up."

My tone had a borrowed loudness reverberated from the
height of the land. Several voices cried out together: "We are all
on deck, sir."

Then stillness again, with the great shadow gliding closer,
towering higher, without a light, without a sound. Such a hush
had fallen on the ship that she might have been a bark of the
dead floating in slowly under the very gate of Erebus.°

"My God! Where are we?"

It was the mate moaning at my elbow. He was thunderstruck,
and as it were deprived of the moral support of his whiskers. He
clapped his hands and absolutely cried out, "Lost!"

"Be quiet," I said sternly.   305

He lowered his tone, but I saw the shadowy gesture of his
despair. "What are we doing here?"

"Looking for the land wind."

He made as if to tear his hair, and addressed me recklessly.
"She will never get out. You have done it, sir. I knew it'd end
in something like this. She will never weather, and you are too
close now to stay. She'll drift ashore before she's round. O my
God!"

I caught his arm as he was raising it to batter his poor 310
devoted head, and shook it violently.

"She's ashore already," he wailed, trying to tear himself away.

"Is she? . . . Keep good full there!"

"Good full, sir," cried the helmsman in a frightened, thin,
childlike voice.

I hadn't let go the mate's arm and went on shaking it. "Ready
about, do you hear? You go forward" — shake — "and stop
there" — shake — "and hold your noise" — shake — "and see
these head sheets properly overhauled" — shake, shake —
shake.

And all the time I dared not look toward the land lest my 315
heart should fail me. I released my grip at last and he ran forward
as if fleeing for dear life.

I wondered what my double there in the sail locker thought
of this commotion. He was able to hear everything — and perhaps he was able to understand why, on my conscience, it had to
be thus close — no less. My first order "Hard alee!" re-echoed
ominously under the towering shadow of Koh-ring as if I had

gate of Erebus: The entrance to the first section of the underworld in Greek mythology.

shouted in a mountain gorge. And then I watched the land intently. In that smooth water and light wind it was impossible to feel the ship coming-to. No! I could not feel her. And my second self was making now ready to slip out and lower himself overboard. Perhaps he was gone already . . . ?

The great black mass brooding over our very mastheads began to pivot away from the ship's side silently. And now I forgot the secret stranger ready to depart, and remembered only that I was a total stranger to the ship. I did not know her. Would she do it? How was she to be handled?

I swung the mainyard and waited helplessly. She was perhaps stopped, and her very fate hung in the balance, with the black mass of Koh-ring like the gate of the everlasting night towering over her taffrail. What would she do now? Had she way on her yet? I stepped to the side swiftly, and on the shadowy water I could see nothing except a faint phosphorescent flash revealing the glassy smoothness of the sleeping surface. It was impossible to tell — and I had not learned yet the feel of my ship. Was she moving? What I needed was something easily seen, a piece of paper, which I could throw overboard and watch. I had nothing on me. To run down for it I didn't dare. There was no time. All at once my strained, yearning stare distinguished a white object floating within a yard of the ship's side. White on the black water. A phosphorescent flash passed under it. What was that thing? . . . I recognized my own floppy hat. It must have fallen off his head . . . and he didn't bother. Now I had what I wanted — the saving mark for my eyes. But I hardly thought of my other self, now gone from the ship, to be hidden forever from all friendly faces, to be a fugitive and a vagabond on the earth, with no brand of the curse on his sane forehead to stay a slaying hand . . . too proud to explain.

And I watched the hat — the expression of my sudden pity for his mere flesh. It had been meant to save his homeless head from the dangers of the sun. And now — behold — it was saving the ship, by serving me for a mark to help out the ignorance of my strangeness. Ha! It was drifting forward, warning me just in time that the ship had gathered sternway.

"Shift the helm," I said in a low voice to the seaman standing 320 still like a statue.

The man's eyes glistened wildly in the binnacle light as he jumped round to the other side and spun round the wheel.

I walked to the break of the poop. On the overshadowed deck all hands stood by the forebraces waiting for my order. The stars ahead seemed to be gliding from right to left. And all was so still in the world that I heard the quiet remark "She's round," passed in a tone of intense relief between two seamen.

"Let go and haul."

The foreyards ran round with a great noise, amidst cheery cries. And now the frightful whiskers made themselves heard giving various orders. Already the ship was drawing ahead. And I was alone with her. Nothing! no one in the world should stand now between us, throwing a shadow on the way of silent knowledge and mute affection, the perfect communion of a seaman with his first command.

Walking to the taffrail, I was in time to make out, on the very 325 edge of a darkness thrown by a towering black mass like the very gateway of Erebus — yes, I was in time to catch an evanescent glimpse of my white hat left behind to mark the spot where the secret sharer of my cabin and of my thoughts, as though he were my second self, had lowered himself into the water to take his punishment; a free man, a proud swimmer striking out for a new destiny.

JAMES BALDWIN (b. 1924)
Sonny's Blues

I read about it in the paper, in the subway, on my way to work. I read it, and I couldn't believe it, and I read it again. Then perhaps I just stared at it, at the newsprint spelling out his name, spelling out the story. I stared at it in the swinging lights of the subway car, and in the faces and bodies of the people, and in my own face, trapped in the darkness which roared outside.

It was not to be believed and I kept telling myself that, as I walked from the subway station to the high school. And at the same time I couldn't doubt it. I was scared, scared for Sonny. He became real to me again. A great block of ice got settled in my belly and kept melting there slowly all day long, while I taught my classes algebra. It was a special kind of ice. It kept melting, sending trickles of ice water all up and down my veins, but it never got less. Sometimes it hardened and seemed to expand until I felt my guts were going to come spilling out or that I was going to choke or scream. This would always be at a moment when I was remembering some specific thing Sonny had once said or done.

When he was about as old as the boys in my classes his face had been bright and open, there was a lot of copper in it; and he'd had wonderfully direct brown eyes, and great gentleness and privacy. I wondered what he looked like now. He had been picked up, the evening before, in a raid on an apartment downtown, for peddling and using heroin.

I couldn't believe it: but what I mean by that is that I couldn't find any room for it anywhere inside me. I had kept it outside me for a long time. I hadn't wanted to know. I had had suspicions, but I didn't name them, I kept putting them away. I told myself that Sonny was wild, but he wasn't crazy. And he'd always been a good boy, he hadn't ever turned hard or evil or disrespectful, the way kids can, so quick, so quick, especially in Harlem. I didn't want to believe that I'd ever see my brother going down, coming to nothing, all that light in his face gone out, in the condition I'd already seen so many others. Yet it had happened and here I was, talking about algebra to a lot of boys who might, every one of them for all I knew, be popping off needles every time they went to the head. Maybe it did more for them than algebra could.

I was sure that the first time Sonny had ever had horse, he 5 couldn't have been much older than these boys were now. These boys, now, were living as we'd been living then, they were growing up with a rush and their heads bumped abruptly against the low ceiling of their actual possibilities. They were filled with rage. All they really knew were two darknesses, the darkness of their lives, which was now closing in on them, and the darkness of the movies, which had blinded them to that other darkness, and in which they now, vindictively, dreamed, at once more together than they were at any other time, and more alone.

When the last bell rang, the last class ended, I let out my breath. It seemed I'd been holding it for all that time. My clothes were wet — I may have looked as though I'd been sitting in a steam bath, all dressed up, all afternoon. I sat alone in the classroom a long time. I listened to the boys outside, downstairs, shouting and cursing and laughing. Their laughter struck me for perhaps the first time. It was not the joyous laughter which — God knows why — one associates with children. It was mocking and insular, its intent to denigrate. It was disenchanted, and in this, also, lay the authority of their curses. Perhaps I was listening to them because I was thinking about my brother and in them I heard my brother. And myself.

One boy was whistling a tune, at once very complicated and very simple, it seemed to be pouring out of him as though he were a bird, and it sounded very cool and moving through all that harsh, bright air, only just holding its own through all those other sounds.

I stood up and walked over to the window and looked down into the courtyard. It was the beginning of the spring and the sap was rising in the boys. A teacher passed through them every now and again, quickly, as though he or she couldn't wait to get out of that courtyard, to get those boys out of their sight and off their minds. I started collecting my stuff. I thought I'd better get home and talk to Isabel.

The courtyard was almost deserted by the time I got downstairs. I saw this boy standing in the shadow of a doorway, looking just like Sonny. I almost called his name. Then I saw that it wasn't Sonny, but somebody we used to know, a boy from around our block. He'd been Sonny's friend. He'd never been mine, having been too young for me, and, anyway, I'd never liked him. And now, even though he was a grown-up man, he still hung around that block, still spent hours on the street corners, was always high and raggy. I used to run into him from time to time and he'd often work around to asking me for a quarter or fifty cents. He always had some real good excuse, too, and I always gave it to him, I don't know why.

But now, abruptly, I hated him. I couldn't stand the way he   10 looked at me, partly like a dog, partly like a cunning child. I wanted to ask him what the hell he was doing in the school courtyard.

He sort of shuffled over to me, and he said, "I see you got the papers. So you already know about it."

"You mean about Sonny? Yes, I already know about it. How come they didn't get you?"

He grinned. It made him repulsive and it also brought to mind what he'd looked like as a kid. "I wasn't there. I stay away from them people."

"Good for you." I offered him a cigarette and I watched him through the smoke. "You come all the way down here just to tell me about Sonny?"

"That's right." He was sort of shaking his head and his eyes   15 looked strange, as though they were about to cross. The bright sun deadened his damp dark brown skin and it made his eyes look yellow and showed up the dirt in his kinked hair. He smelled funky. I moved a little away from him and I said, "Well, thanks. But I already know about it and I got to get home."

"I'll walk you a little ways," he said. We started walking. There were a couple of kids still loitering in the courtyard and one of them said goodnight to me and looked strangely at the boy beside me.

"What're you going to do?" he asked me. "I mean, about Sonny?"

"Look. I haven't seen Sonny for over a year, I'm not sure I'm going to do anything. Anyway, what the hell *can* I do?"

"That's right," he said quickly, "ain't nothing you can do. Can't much help old Sonny no more, I guess."

It was what I was thinking and so it seemed to me he had no   20 right to say it.

"I'm surprised at Sonny, though," he went on — he had a funny way of talking, he looked straight ahead as though he were talking to himself — "I thought Sonny was a smart boy, I thought he was too smart to get hung."

"I guess he thought so too," I said sharply, "and that's how he got hung. And now about you? You're pretty goddamn smart, I bet."

Then he looked directly at me, just for a minute. "I ain't smart," he said. "If I was smart, I'd have reached for a pistol a long time ago."

"Look. Don't tell *me* your sad story; if it was up to me, I'd give you one." Then I felt guilty — guilty, probably, for never having supposed that the poor bastard *had* a story of his own, much less a sad one, and I asked, quickly, "What's going to happen to him now?"

He didn't answer this. He was off by himself some place.   25 "Funny thing," he said, and from his tone we might have been discussing the quickest way to get to Brooklyn, "when I saw the papers this morning, the first thing I asked myself was if I had anything to do with it. I felt sort of responsible."

I began to listen more carefully. The subway station was on the corner, just before us, and I stopped. He stopped, too. We were in front of a bar and he ducked slightly, peering in, but whoever he was looking for didn't seem to be there. The juke box was blasting away with something black and bouncy and I half watched the barmaid as she danced her way from the juke box to her place behind the bar. And I watched her face as she laughingly responded to something someone said to her, still keeping time to the music. When she smiled one saw the little girl, one sensed the doomed, still-struggling woman beneath the battered face of the semi-whore.

"I never *give* Sonny nothing," the boy said finally, "but a long time ago I come to school high and Sonny asked me how it felt." He paused, I couldn't bear to watch him, I watched the barmaid, and I listened to the music which seemed to be causing the pavement to shake. "I told him it felt great." The music stopped, the barmaid paused and watched the juke box until the music began again. "It did."

All this was carrying me some place I didn't want to go. I certainly didn't want to know how it felt. It filled everything, the people, the houses, the music, the dark, quicksilver barmaid, with menace; and this menace was their reality.

"What's going to happen to him now?" I asked again.

"They'll send him away some place and they'll try to cure 30 him." He shook his head. "Maybe he'll even think he's kicked the habit. Then they'll let him loose" — he gestured, throwing his cigarette into the gutter. "That's all."

"What do you mean, that's *all*?"

But I knew what he meant.

"I *mean*, that's *all*." He turned his head and looked at me, pulling down the corners of his mouth. "Don't you know what I mean?" he asked, softly.

"How the hell *would* I know what you mean?" I almost whispered it, I don't know why.

"That's right," he said to the air, "how would *he* know what I 35 mean?" He turned toward me again, patient and calm, and yet I somehow felt him shaking, shaking as though he were going to fall apart. I felt that ice in my guts again, the dread I'd felt all afternoon; and again I watched the barmaid, moving about the bar, washing glasses, and singing. "Listen. They'll let him out and then it'll just start all over again. That's what I mean."

"You mean — they'll let him out. And then he'll just start working his way back in again. You mean he'll never kick the habit. Is that what you mean?"

"That's right," he said, cheerfully. "*You* see what I mean."

"Tell me," I said at last, "why does he want to die? He must want to die, he's killing himself, why does he want to die?"

He looked at me in surprise. He licked his lips. "He don't want to die. He wants to live. Don't nobody want to die, ever."

Then I wanted to ask him — too many things. He could not 40 have answered, or if he had, I could not have borne the answers. I started walking. "Well, I guess it's none of my business."

"It's going to be rough on old Sonny," he said. We reached the subway station. "This is your station?" he asked. I nodded. I took one step down. "Damn!" he said, suddenly. I looked up at him. He grinned again. "Damn it if I didn't leave all my money home. You ain't got a dollar on you, have you? Just for a couple of days, is all."

All at once something inside gave and threatened to come

pouring out of me. I didn't hate him any more. I felt that in another moment I'd start crying like a child.

"Sure," I said. "Don't sweat." I looked in my wallet and didn't have a dollar, I only had a five. "Here," I said. "That hold you?"

He didn't look at it — he didn't want to look at it. A terrible closed look came over his face, as though he were keeping the number on the bill a secret from him and me. "Thanks," he said, and now he was dying to see me go. "Don't worry about Sonny. Maybe I'll write him or something."

"Sure," I said. "You do that. So long."   45

"Be seeing you," he said. I went on down the steps.

And I didn't write Sonny or send him anything for a long time. When I finally did, it was just after my little girl died, he wrote me back a letter which made me feel like a bastard.

Here's what he said:

> Dear brother,
> You don't know how much I needed to hear from you. I wanted to write you many a time but I dug how much I must have hurt you and so I didn't write. But now I feel like a man who's been trying to climb up out of some deep, real deep and funky hole and just saw the sun up there, outside. I got to get outside.
> I can't tell you much about how I got here. I mean I don't know how to tell you. I guess I was afraid of something or I was trying to escape from something and you know I have never been very strong in the head (smile). I'm glad Mama and Daddy are dead and can't see what's happened to their son and I swear if I'd known what I was doing I would never have hurt you so, you and a lot of other fine people who were nice to me and who believed in me.
> I don't want you to think it had anything to do with me being a musician. It's more than that. Or maybe less than that. I can't get anything straight in my head down here and I try not to think about what's going to happen to me when I get outside again. Sometime I think I'm going to flip and *never* get outside and sometime I think I'll come straight back. I tell you one thing, though, I'd rather blow my brains out than go through this again. But that's what they all say, so they tell me. If I tell you when I'm coming to New York and if you could meet me, I sure would appreciate it. Give my love to Isabel and the kids and I was sure sorry to hear about little Gracie. I wish I could be like Mama and say the Lord's will be done, but I don't know it seems to me that trouble is the one thing that never does get stopped and I don't know what good it does to blame it on the Lord. But maybe it does some good if you believe it.
>
> Your brother,
> Sonny

Then I kept in constant touch with him and I sent him whatever I could and I went to meet him when he came back to New York. When I saw him many things I thought I had forgotten came flooding back to me. This was because I had begun, finally, to wonder about Sonny, about the life that Sonny lived inside. This life, whatever it was, had made him older and thinner and it had deepened the distant stillness in which he had always moved. He looked very unlike my baby brother. Yet, when he smiled, when we shook hands, the baby brother I'd never known looked out from the depths of his private life, like an animal waiting to be coaxed into the light.

"How you been keeping?" he asked me.   50

"All right. And you?"

"Just fine." He was smiling all over his face. "It's good to see you again."

"It's good to see you."

The seven years' difference in our ages lay between us like a chasm: I wondered if these years would ever operate between us as a bridge. I was remembering, and it made it hard to catch my breath, that I had been there when he was born; and I had heard the first words he had ever spoken. When he started to walk, he walked from our mother straight to me. I caught him just before he fell when he took the first steps he ever took in this world.

"How's Isabel?"   55

"Just fine. She's dying to see you."

"And the boys?"

"They're fine, too. They're anxious to see their uncle."

"Oh, come on. You know they don't remember me."

"Are you kidding? Of course they remember you."   60

He grinned again. We got into a taxi. We had a lot to say to each other, far too much to know how to begin.

As the taxi began to move, I asked, "You still want to go to India?"

He laughed. "You still remember that. Hell, no. This place is Indian enough for me."

"It used to belong to them," I said.

And he laughed again. "They damn sure knew what they   65
were doing when they got rid of it."

Years ago, when he was around fourteen, he'd been all hipped on the idea of going to India. He read books about people sitting on rocks, naked, in all kinds of weather, but mostly bad, naturally, and walking barefoot through hot coals and arriving at wisdom. I used to say that it sounded to me as though they were getting away from wisdom as fast as they could. I think he sort of looked down on me for that.

"Do you mind," he asked, "if we have the driver drive alongside the park? On the west side — I haven't seen the city in so long."

"Of course not," I said. I was afraid that I might sound as though I were humoring him, but I hoped he wouldn't take it that way.

So we drove along, between the green of the park and the stony, lifeless elegance of hotels and apartment buildings, toward the vivid, killing streets of our childhood. These streets hadn't changed, though housing projects jutted up out of them now like rocks in the middle of a boiling sea. Most of the houses in which we had grown up had vanished, as had the stores from which we had stolen, the basements in which we had first tried sex, the rooftops from which we· had hurled tin cans and bricks. But houses exactly like the houses of our past yet dominated the landscape, boys exactly like the boys we once had been found themselves smothering in these houses, came down into the streets for light and air and found themselves encircled by disaster. Some escaped the trap, most didn't. Those who got out always left something of themselves behind, as some animals amputate a leg and leave it in the trap. It might be said, perhaps, that I had escaped, after all, I was a school teacher; or that Sonny had, he hadn't lived in Harlem for years. Yet, as the cab moved uptown through streets which seemed, with a rush, to darken with dark people, and as I covertly studied Sonny's face, it came to me that what we both were seeking through our separate cab windows was that part of ourselves which had been left behind. It's always at the hour of trouble and confrontation that the missing member aches.

We hit 110th Street and started rolling up Lenox Avenue. 70 And I'd known this avenue all my life, but it seemed to me again, as it had seemed on the day I'd first heard about Sonny's trouble, filled with a hidden menace which was its very breath of life.

"We almost there," said Sonny.

"Almost." We were both too nervous to say anything more.

We live in a housing project. It hasn't been up long. A few days after it was up it seemed uninhabitably new, now, of course, it's already rundown. It looks like a parody of the good, clean, faceless life — God knows the people who live in it do their best to make it a parody. The beat-looking grass lying around isn't enough to make their lives green, the hedges will never hold out the streets, and they know it. The big windows fool no one, they aren't big enough to make space out of no space. They don't bother with the windows, they watch the TV screen instead. The playground is most popular with the children who don't play at jacks, or skip rope, or roller skate, or swing, and they can be found in it after dark. We moved in partly because it's not too far from where I teach, and partly for the kids; but it's really just like the houses in which Sonny and I grew up. The same things happen, they'll have the same things to remember. The moment Sonny and I started into the house I had the feeling that I was simply bringing him back into the danger he had almost died trying to escape.

Sonny has never been talkative. So I don't know why I was sure he'd be dying to talk to me when supper was over the first night. Everything went fine, the oldest boy remembered him, and the youngest boy liked him, and Sonny had remembered to bring something for each of them; and Isabel, who is really much nicer than I am, more open and giving, had gone to a lot of trouble about dinner and was genuinely glad to see him. And she's always been able to tease Sonny in a way that I haven't. It was nice to see her face so vivid again and to hear her laugh and watch her make Sonny laugh. She wasn't, or, anyway, she didn't seem to be, at all uneasy or embarrassed. She chatted as though there were no subject which had to be avoided and she got Sonny past his first, faint stiffness. And thank God she was there, for I was filled with that icy dread again. Everything I did seemed awkward to me, and everything I said sounded freighted with hidden meaning. I was trying to remember everything I'd heard about dope addiction and I couldn't help watching Sonny for signs. I wasn't doing it out of malice. I was trying to find out something about my brother. I was dying to hear him tell me he was safe.

"Safe!" my father grunted, whenever Mama suggested trying 75 to move to a neighborhood which might be safer for children. "Safe, hell! Ain't no place safe for kids, nor nobody."

He always went on like this, but he wasn't, ever, really as bad as he sounded, not even on weekends, when he got drunk. As a matter of fact, he was always on the lookout for "something a little better," but he died before he found it. He died suddenly, during a drunken weekend in the middle of the war, when Sonny was fifteen. He and Sonny hadn't ever got on too well. And this was partly because Sonny was the apple of his father's eye. It was because he loved Sonny so much and was frightened for him, that he was always fighting with him. It doesn't do any good to fight with Sonny. Sonny just moves back, inside himself, where he can't be reached. But the principal reason that they never hit it off is that they were so much alike. Daddy was big and rough and loud-talking, just the opposite of Sonny, but they both had — that same privacy.

Mama tried to tell me something about this, just after Daddy died. I was home on leave from the army.

This was the last time I ever saw my mother alive. Just the same, this picture gets all mixed up in my mind with pictures I had of her when she was younger. The way I always see her is the way she used to be on a Sunday afternoon, say, when the old folks were talking after the big Sunday dinner. I always see her wearing pale blue. She'd be sitting on the sofa. And my father would be sitting in the easy chair, not far from her. And the living room would be full of church folks and relatives. There they sit, in chairs all around the living room, and the night is creeping up outside, but nobody knows it yet. You can see the darkness grow-ing against the windowpanes and you hear the street noises every now and again, or maybe the jangling beat of a tambourine from one of the churches close by, but it's real quiet in the room. For a moment nobody's talking, but every face looks darkening, like the sky outside. And my mother rocks a little from the waist, and my father's eyes are closed. Everyone is looking at something a child can't see. For a minute they've forgotten the children. Maybe a kid is lying on the rug, half asleep. Maybe somebody's got a kid in his lap and is absent-mindedly stroking the kid's head. Maybe there's a kid, quiet and big-eyed, curled up in a big chair in the corner. The silence, the darkness coming, and the darkness in the faces frightens the child obscurely. He hopes that the hand which strokes his forehead will never stop — will never die. He hopes that there will never come a time when the old folks won't be sitting around the living room, talking about where they've come from, and what they've seen, and what's happened to them and their kinfolk.

But something deep and watchful in the child knows that this is bound to end, is already ending. In a moment someone will get up and turn on the light. Then the old folks will remem-ber the children and they won't talk any more that day. And when light fills the room, the child is filled with darkness. He knows that everytime this happens he's moved just a little closer to that darkness outside. The darkness outside is what the old folks have been talking about. It's what they've come from. It's what they endure. The child knows that they won't talk any more because if he knows too much about what's happened to *them*, he'll know too much too soon, about what's going to happen to *him*.

The last time I talked to my mother, I remember I was rest-less. I wanted to get out and see Isabel. We weren't married then and we had a lot to straighten out between us. 80

There Mama sat, in black, by the window. She was humming an old church song, *Lord, you brought me from a long ways off.* Sonny was out somewhere. Mama kept watching the streets.

"I don't know," she said, "if I'll ever see you again, after you go off from here. But I hope you'll remember the things I tried to teach you."

"Don't talk like that," I said, and smiled. "You'll be here a long time yet."

She smiled, too, but she said nothing. She was quiet for a long time. And I said, "Mama, don't you worry about nothing. I'll be writing all the time, and you be getting the checks. . . . ."

"I want to talk to you about your brother," she said, suddenly. 85 "If anything happens to me he ain't going to have nobody to look out for him."

"Mama," I said, "ain't nothing going to happen to you *or* Sonny. Sonny's all right. He's a good boy and he's got good sense."

"It ain't a question of his being a good boy," Mama said, "nor of his having good sense. It ain't only the bad ones, nor yet the dumb ones that gets sucked under." She stopped, looking at me. "Your Daddy once had a brother," she said, and she smiled in a way that made me feel she was in pain. "You didn't never know that, did you?"

"No," I said, "I never knew that," and I watched her face.

"Oh, yes," she said, "your Daddy had a brother." She looked out of the window again. "I know you never saw your Daddy cry. But *I* did — many a time, through all these years."

I asked her, "What happened to his brother? How come no- 90 body's ever talked about him?"

This was the first time I ever saw my mother look old.

"His brother got killed," she said, "when he was just a little younger than you are now. I knew him. He was a fine boy. He was maybe a little full of the devil, but he didn't mean nobody no harm."

Then she stopped and the room was silent, exactly as it had sometimes been on those Sunday afternoons. Mama kept looking out into the streets.

"He used to have a job in the mill," she said, "and, like all young folks, he just liked to perform on Saturday nights. Saturday nights, him and your father would drift around to different places, go to dances and things like that, or just sit around with people they knew, and your father's brother would sing, he had a fine voice, and play along with himself on his guitar. Well, this particular Saturday night, him and your father was coming home from some place, and they were both a little drunk and there was a moon that night, it was bright like day. Your father's brother was feeling kind of good, and he was whistling to himself, and he had his guitar slung over his shoulder. They was coming down a hill and beneath them was a road that turned off from the highway. Well, your father's brother, being always kind of frisky, decided to run down this hill, and he did, with that guitar banging and clanging behind him, and he ran across the road, and he was making water behind a tree. And your father was sort of amused at him and he was still coming down the hill, kind of slow. Then he heard a car motor and that same minute his brother stepped from behind the tree, into the road, in the moonlight. And he started to cross the road. And your father started to run down the hill, he says he don't know why. This car was full of white men. They was all drunk, and when they seen your father's brother they let out a great whoop and holler and they aimed the car straight at him. They was having fun, they just wanted to scare him, the way they do sometimes, you know. But they was drunk. And I guess the boy, being drunk, too, and scared, kind of lost his head. By the time he jumped it was too late. Your father says he heard his brother scream when the car rolled over him, and he heard the wood of that guitar when it give, and he heard them strings go flying, and he heard them white men shouting, and the car kept on a-going and it ain't stopped till this day. And, time your father got down the hill, his brother weren't nothing but blood and pulp."

Tears were gleaming on my mother's face. There wasn't anything I could say. 95

"He never mentioned it," she said, "because I never let him mention it before you children. Your Daddy was like a crazy man that night and for many a night thereafter. He says he never in his life seen anything as dark as that road after the lights of that car had gone away. Weren't nothing, weren't nobody on that road, just your Daddy and his brother and that busted guitar. Oh, yes. Your Daddy never did really get right again. Till the day he died he weren't sure but that every white man he saw was the man that killed his brother."

She stopped and took out her handkerchief and dried her eyes and looked at me.

"I ain't telling you all this," she said, "to make you scared or bitter or to make you hate nobody. I'm telling you this because you got a brother. And the world ain't changed."

I guess I didn't want to believe this. I guess she saw this in my face. She turned away from me, toward the window again, searching those streets.

"But I praise my Redeemer," she said at last, "that He called   100
your Daddy home before me. I ain't saying it to throw no flowers at myself, but, I declare, it keeps me from feeling too cast down to know I helped your father get safely through this world. Your father always acted like he was the roughest, strongest man on earth. And everybody took him to be like that. But if he hadn't had *me* there — to see his tears!"

She was crying again. Still, I couldn't move. I said, "Lord, Lord, Mama, I didn't know it was like that."

"Oh, honey," she said, "there's a lot that you don't know. But you are going to find it out." She stood up from the window and came over to me. "You got to hold on to your brother," she said, "and don't let him fall, no matter what it looks like is happening to him and no matter how evil you gets with him. You going to be evil with him many a time. But don't you forget what I told you, you hear?"

"I won't forget," I said. "Don't you worry, I won't forget. I won't let nothing happen to Sonny."

My mother smiled as though she were amused at something she saw in my face. Then, "You may not be able to stop nothing from happening. But you got to let him know you's *there*."

Two days later I was married, and then I was gone. And I had   105
a lot of things on my mind and I pretty well forgot my promise to Mama until I got shipped home on a special furlough for her funeral.

And, after the funeral, with just Sonny and me alone in the empty kitchen, I tried to find out something about him.

"What do you want to do?" I asked him.

"I'm going to be a musician," he said.

For he had graduated, in the time I had been away, from dancing to the juke box to finding out who was playing what, and what they were doing with it, and he had bought himself a set of drums.

"You mean, you want to be a drummer?" I somehow had the   110
feeling that being a drummer might be all right for other people but not for my brother Sonny.

"I don't think," he said, looking at me very gravely, "that I'll ever be a good drummer. But I think I can play a piano." I frowned. I'd never played the role of the older brother quite so seriously before, had scarcely ever, in fact, *asked* Sonny a damn thing. I sensed myself in the presence of something I didn't really know how to handle, didn't understand. So I made my frown a little deeper as I asked: "What kind of musician do you want to be?"

He grinned. "How many kinds do you think there are?"

"Be *serious*," I said.

He laughed, throwing his head back, and then looked at me. 115 "I *am* serious."

"Well, then, for Christ's sake, stop kidding around and answer a serious question. I mean, do you want to be a concert pianist, you want to play classical music and all that, or — or what?" Long before I finished he was laughing again. "For Christ's *sake*, Sonny!"

He sobered, but with difficulty. "I'm sorry. But you sound so — *scared!*" and he was off again.

"Well, you may think it's funny now, baby, but it's not going to be so funny when you have to make your living at it, let me tell you *that*." I was furious because I knew he was laughing at me and I didn't know why.

"No," he said, very sober now, and afraid, perhaps, that he'd hurt me, "I don't want to be a classical pianist. That isn't what interests me. I mean" — he paused, looking hard at me, as though his eyes would help me to understand, and then gestured helplessly, as though perhaps his hand would help — "I mean, I'll have a lot of studying to do, and I'll have to study *everything*, but, I mean, I want to play *with* — jazz musicians." He stopped. "I want to play jazz," he said.

Well, the word had never before sounded as heavy, as real, 120 as it sounded that afternoon in Sonny's mouth. I just looked at him and I was probably frowning a real frown by this time. I simply couldn't see why on earth he'd want to spend his time hanging around nightclubs, clowning around on bandstands, while people pushed each other around a dance floor. It seemed — beneath him, somehow. I had never thought about it before, had never been forced to, but I suppose I had always put jazz musicians in a class with what Daddy called "good-time people."

"Are you *serious?*"

"Hell, *yes*, I'm serious."

He looked more helpless than ever, and annoyed, and deeply hurt.

1004 STORIES FOR FURTHER STUDY

I suggested, helpfully: "You mean — like Louis Armstrong?"

His face closed as though I'd struck him. "No. I'm not talking 125 about none of that old-time, down home crap."

"Well, look, Sonny, I'm sorry, don't get mad. I just don't altogether get it, that's all. Name somebody — you know, a jazz musician you admire."

"Bird."

"Who?"

"Bird! Charlie Parker! Don't they teach you nothing in the goddamn army?"

I lit a cigarette. I was surprised and then a little amused to 130 discover that I was trembling. "I've been out of touch," I said. "You'll have to be patient with me. Now. Who's this Parker character?"

"He's just one of the greatest jazz musicians alive," said Sonny, sullenly, his hands in his pockets, his back to me. "Maybe *the* greatest," he added, bitterly, "that's probably why *you* never heard of him."

"All right," I said, "I'm ignorant. I'm sorry. I'll go out and buy all the cat's records right away, all right?"

"It don't," said Sonny, with dignity, "make any difference to me. I don't care what you listen to. Don't do me no favors."

I was beginning to realize that I'd never seen him so upset before. With another part of my mind I was thinking that this would probably turn out to be one of those things kids go through and that I shouldn't make it seem important by pushing it too hard. Still, I didn't think it would do any harm to ask: "Doesn't all this take a lot of time? Can you make a living at it?"

He turned back to me and half leaned, half sat, on the 135 kitchen table. "Everything takes time," he said, "and — well, yes, sure, I can make a living at it. But what I don't seem to be able to make you understand is that it's the only thing I want to do."

"Well, Sonny," I said, gently, "you know people can't always do exactly what they *want* to do —"

"*No*, I don't know that," said Sonny, surprising me. "I think people *ought* to do what they want to do, what else are they alive for?"

"You getting to be a big boy," I said desperately, "it's time you started thinking about your future."

"I'm thinking about my future," said Sonny, grimly. "I think about it all the time."

I gave up. I decided, if he didn't change his mind, that we 140 could always talk about it later. "In the meantime," I said, "you got to finish school." We had already decided that he'd have to move in with Isabel and her folks. I knew this wasn't the ideal arrangement because Isabel's folks are inclined to be dicty and they hadn't especially wanted Isabel to marry me. But I didn't know what else to do. "And we have to get you fixed up at Isabel's."

There was a long silence. He moved from the kitchen table to the window. "That's a terrible idea. You know it yourself."

"Do you have a *better* idea?"

He just walked up and down the kitchen for a minute. He was as tall as I was. He had started to shave. I suddenly had the feeling that I didn't know him at all.

He stopped at the kitchen table and picked up my cigarettes. Looking at me with a kind of mocking, amused defiance, he put one between his lips. "You mind?"

"You smoking already?"   145

He lit the cigarette and nodded, watching me through the smoke. "I just wanted to see if I'd have the courage to smoke in front of you." He grinned and blew a great cloud of smoke to the ceiling. "It was easy." He looked at my face. "Come on, now. I bet you was smoking at my age, tell the truth."

I didn't say anything but the truth was on my face, and he laughed. But now there was something very strained in his laugh. "Sure. And I bet that ain't all you was doing."

He was frightening me a little. "Cut the crap," I said. "We already decided that you was going to go and live at Isabel's. Now what's got into you all of a sudden?"

"*You* decided it," he pointed out. "*I* didn't decide nothing." He stopped in front of me, leaning against the stove, arms loosely folded. "Look, brother. I don't want to stay in Harlem no more, I really don't." He was very earnest. He looked at me, then over toward the kitchen window. There was something in his eyes I'd never seen before, some thoughtfulness, some worry all his own. He rubbed the muscle of one arm. "It's time I was getting out of here."

"Where do you want to *go*, Sonny?"   150

"I want to join the army. Or the navy, I don't care. If I say I'm old enough, they'll believe me."

Then I got mad. It was because I was so scared. "You must be crazy. You goddamn fool, what the hell do you want to go and join the *army* for?"

"I just told you. To get out of Harlem."

"Sonny, you haven't even finished *school*. And if you really want to be a musician, how do you expect to study if you're in the *army?*"

He looked at me, trapped, and in anguish. "There's ways. I   155
might be able to work out some kind of deal. Anyway, I'll have
the G.I. Bill when I come out."

"*If* you come out." We stared at each other. "Sonny, please. Be
reasonable. I know the setup is far from perfect. But we got to do
the best we can."

"I ain't learning nothing in school," he said. "Even when I
go." He turned away from me and opened the window and threw
his cigarette out into the narrow alley. I watched his back. "At
least, I ain't learning nothing you'd want me to learn." He
slammed the window so hard I thought the glass would fly out,
and turned back to me. "And I'm sick of the stink of these garbage cans!"

"Sonny," I said, "I know how you feel. But if you don't finish
school now, you're going to be sorry later that you didn't." I
grabbed him by the shoulders. "And you only got another year. It
ain't so bad. And I'll come back and I swear I'll help you do
whatever you want to do. Just try to put up with it till I come back.
Will you please do that? For me?"

He didn't answer and he wouldn't look at me.

"Sonny. You hear me?"   160

He pulled away. "I hear you. But you never hear anything *I*
say."

I didn't know what to say to that. He looked out of the window and then back at me. "OK," he said, and sighed. "I'll try."

Then I said, trying to cheer him up a little, "They got a piano
at Isabel's. You can practice on it."

And as a matter of fact, it did cheer him up for a minute.
"That's right," he said to himself. "I forgot that." His face relaxed
a little. But the worry, the thoughtfulness, played on it still, the
way shadows play on a face which is staring into the fire.

But I thought I'd never hear the end of that piano. At first,   165
Isabel would write me, saying how nice it was that Sonny was so
serious about his music and how, as soon as he came in from
school, or wherever he had been when he was supposed to be at
school, he went straight to that piano and stayed there until
suppertime. And, after supper, he went back to that piano and
stayed there until everybody went to bed. He was at the piano all
day Saturday and all day Sunday. Then he bought a record player
and started playing records. He'd play one record over and over
again, all day long sometimes, and he'd improvise along with it
on the piano. Or he'd play one section of the record, one chord,

one change, one progression, then he'd do it on the piano. Then back to the record. Then back to the piano.

Well, I really don't know how they stood it. Isabel finally confessed that it wasn't like living with a person at all, it was like living with sound. And the sound didn't make any sense to her, didn't make any sense to any of them — naturally. They began, in a way, to be afflicted by this presence that was living in their home. It was as though Sonny were some sort of god, or monster. He moved in an atmosphere which wasn't like theirs at all. They fed him and he ate, he washed himself, he walked in and out of their door; he certainly wasn't nasty or unpleasant or rude, Sonny isn't any of those things; but it was as though he were all wrapped up in some cloud, some fire, some vision all his own; and there wasn't any way to reach him.

At the same time, he wasn't really a man yet, he was still a child, and they had to watch out for him in all kinds of ways. They certainly couldn't throw him out. Neither did they dare to make a great scene about that piano because even they dimly sensed, as I sensed, from so many thousands of miles away, that Sonny was at that piano playing for his life.

But he hadn't been going to school. One day a letter came from the school board and Isabel's mother got it — there had, apparently, been other letters but Sonny had torn them up. This day, when Sonny came in, Isabel's mother showed him the letter and asked where he'd been spending his time. And she finally got it out of him that he'd been down in Greenwich Village, with musicians and other characters, in a white girl's apartment. And this scared her and she started to scream at him and what came up, once she began — though she denies it to this day — was what sacrifices they were making to give Sonny a decent home and how little he appreciated it.

Sonny didn't play the piano that day. By evening, Isabel's mother had calmed down but then there was the old man to deal with, and Isabel herself. Isabel says she did her best to be calm but she broke down and started crying. She says she just watched Sonny's face. She could tell, by watching him, what was happening with him. And what was happening was that they penetrated his cloud, they had reached him. Even if their fingers had been a thousand times more gentle than human fingers ever are, he could hardly help feeling that they had stripped him naked and were spitting on that nakedness. For he also had to see that his presence, that music, which was life or death to him, had been torture for them and that they had endured it, not at all for his sake, but only for mine. And Sonny couldn't take that. He can take it a little better today than he could then but he's still not very good at it and, frankly, I don't know anybody who is.

The silence of the next few days must have been louder than 170 the sound of all the music ever played since time began. One morning, before she went to work, Isabel was in his room for something and she suddenly realized that all of his records were gone. And she knew for certain that he was gone. And he was. He went as far as the navy would carry him. He finally sent me a postcard from some place in Greece and that was the first I knew that Sonny was still alive. I didn't see him any more until we were both back in New York and the war had long been over.

He was a man by then, of course, but I wasn't willing to see it. He came by the house from time to time, but we fought almost every time we met. I didn't like the way he carried himself, loose and dreamlike all the time, and I didn't like his friends, and his music seemed to be merely an excuse for the life he led. It sounded just that weird and disordered.

Then we had a fight, a pretty awful fight, and I didn't see him for months. By and by I looked him up, where he was living, in a furnished room in the Village, and I tried to make it up. But there were lots of people in the room and Sonny just lay on his bed, and he wouldn't come downstairs with me, and he treated these other people as though they were his family and I weren't. So I got mad and then he got mad, and then I told him that he might just as well be dead as live the way he was living. Then he stood up and he told me not to worry about him any more in life, that he *was* dead as far as I was concerned. Then he pushed me to the door and the other people looked on as though nothing were happening, and he slammed the door behind me. I stood in the hallway, staring at the door. I heard somebody laugh in the room and then the tears came to my eyes. I started down the steps, whistling to keep from crying, I kept whistling to myself, *You going to need me, baby, one of these cold, rainy days.*

I read about Sonny's trouble in the spring. Little Grace died in the fall. She was a beautiful little girl. But she only lived a little over two years. She died of polio and she suffered. She had a slight fever for a couple of days, but it didn't seem like anything and we just kept her in bed. And we would certainly have called the doctor, but the fever dropped, she seemed to be all right. So we thought it had just been a cold. Then, one day, she was up, playing, Isabel was in the kitchen fixing lunch for the two boys when they'd come in from school, and she heard Grace fall down in the living room. When you have a lot of children you don't always start running when one of them falls, unless they start screaming or something. And, this time, Grace was quiet. Yet, Isabel says that when she heard that *thump* and then that silence, something happened in her to make her afraid. And she ran to the living room and there was little Grace on the floor, all twisted up, and the reason she hadn't screamed was that she couldn't get her breath. And when she did scream, it was the worst sound, Isabel says, that she'd ever heard in all her life, and she still hears it sometimes in her dreams. Isabel will sometimes wake me up with a low, moaning, strangled sound and I have to be quick to awaken her and hold her to me and where Isabel is weeping against me seems a mortal wound.

I think I may have written Sonny the very day that little Grace was buried. I was sitting in the living room in the dark, by myself, and I suddenly thought of Sonny. My trouble made his real.

One Saturday afternoon, when Sonny had been living with 175 us, or, anyway, been in our house, for nearly two weeks, I found myself wandering aimlessly about the living room, drinking from a can of beer, and trying to work up the courage to search Sonny's room. He was out, he was usually out whenever I was home, and Isabel had taken the children to see their grandparents. Suddenly I was standing still in front of the living room window, watching Seventh Avenue. The idea of searching Sonny's room made me still. I scarcely dared to admit to myself what I'd be searching for. I didn't know what I'd do if I found it. Or if I didn't.

On the sidewalk across from me, near the entrance to a barbecue joint, some people were holding an old-fashioned revival meeting. The barbecue cook, wearing a dirty white apron, his conked hair reddish and metallic in the pale sun, and a cigarette between his lips, stood in the doorway, watching them. Kids and older people paused in their errands and stood there, along with some older men and a couple of very tough-looking women who watched everything that happened on the avenue, as though they owned it, or were maybe owned by it. Well, they were watching this, too. The revival was being carried on by three sisters in black, and a brother. All they had were their voices and their Bibles and a tambourine. The brother was testifying and while he testified two of the sisters stood together, seeming to say, amen, and the third sister walked around with the tambourine outstretched and a couple of people dropped coins into it. Then the brother's testimony ended and the sister who had been taking up the collection dumped the coins into her palm and transferred them to the pocket of her long black robe. Then she raised both hands, striking the tambourine against the air, and then against one hand, and she started to sing. And the two other sisters and the brother joined in.

It was strange, suddenly, to watch, though I had been seeing these street meetings all my life. So, of course, had everybody else down there. Yet, they paused and watched and listened and I stood still at the window. *"Tis the old ship of Zion,"* they sang, and the sister with the tambourine kept a steady, jangling beat, *"it has rescued many a thousand!"* Not a soul under the sound of their voices was hearing this song for the first time, not one of them had been rescued. Nor had they seen much in the way of rescue work being done around them. Neither did they especially believe in the holiness of the three sisters and the brother, they knew too much about them, knew where they lived, and how. The woman with the tambourine, whose voice dominated the air, whose face was bright with joy, was divided by very little from the woman who stood watching her, a cigarette between her heavy, chapped lips, her hair a cuckoo's nest, her face scarred and swollen from many beatings, and her black eyes glittering like coal. Perhaps they both knew this, which was why, when, as rarely, they addressed each other, they addressed each other as Sister. As the singing filled the air the watching, listening faces underwent a change, the eyes focusing on something within; the music seemed to soothe a poison out of them; and time seemed, nearly, to fall away from the sullen, belligerent, battered faces, as though they were fleeing back to their first condition, while dreaming of their last. The barbecue cook half shook his head and smiled, and dropped his cigarette and disappeared into his joint. A man fumbled in his pockets for change and stood holding it in his hand impatiently, as though he had just remembered a pressing appointment further up the avenue. He looked furious. Then I saw Sonny, standing on the edge of the crowd. He was carrying a wide, flat notebook with a green cover, and it made him look, from where I was standing, almost like a schoolboy. The coppery sun brought out the copper in his skin, he was very faintly smiling, standing very still. Then the singing stopped, the tambourine turned into a collection plate again. The furious man dropped in his coins and vanished, so did a couple of the women, and Sonny dropped some change in the plate, looking directly at the woman with a little smile. He started across the avenue, toward the house. He has a slow, loping walk, something like the way Harlem hipsters walk, only he's imposed on this his own half-beat. I had never really noticed it before.

I stayed at the window, both relieved and apprehensive. As Sonny disappeared from my sight, they began singing again. And they were still singing when his key turned in the lock.

"Hey," he said.

"Hey, yourself. You want some beer?"   180

"No. Well, maybe." But he came up to the window and stood beside me, looking out. "What a warm voice," he said.

They were singing *If I could only hear my mother pray again!*

"Yes," I said, "and she can sure beat that tambourine."

"But what a terrible song," he said, and laughed. He dropped his notebook on the sofa and disappeared into the kitchen. "Where's Isabel and the kids?"

"I think they went to see their grandparents. You hungry?"   185

"No." He came back into the living room with his can of beer. "You want to come some place with me tonight?"

I sensed, I don't know how, that I couldn't possibly say no. "Sure. Where?"

He sat down on the sofa and picked up his notebook and started leafing through it. "I'm going to sit in with some fellows in a joint in the Village."

"You mean, you're going to play, tonight?"

"That's right." He took a swallow of his beer and moved back   190
to the window. He gave me a sidelong look. "If you can stand it."

"I'll try," I said.

He smiled to himself and we both watched as the meeting across the way broke up. The three sisters and the brother, heads bowed, were singing *God be with you till we meet again.* The faces around them were very quiet. Then the song ended. The small crowd dispersed. We watched the three women and the lone man walk slowly up the avenue.

"When she was singing before," said Sonny, abruptly, "her voice reminded me for a minute of what heroin feels like some-times — when it's in your veins. It makes you feel sort of warm and cool at the same time. And distant. And — and sure." He sipped his beer, very deliberately not looking at me. I watched his face. "It makes you feel — in control. Sometimes you've got to have that feeling."

"Do you?" I sat down slowly in the easy chair.

"Sometimes." He went to the sofa and picked up his note-   195
book again. "Some people do."

"In order," I asked, "to play?" And my voice was very ugly, full of contempt and anger.

"Well" — he looked at me with great, troubled eyes, as though, in fact, he hoped his eyes would tell me things he could never otherwise say — "they *think* so. And *if* they think so — "

"And what do *you* think?" I asked.

He sat on the sofa and put his can of beer on the floor. "I don't know," he said, and I couldn't be sure if he were answering my question or pursuing his thoughts. His face didn't tell me. "It's not so much to *play*. It's to *stand* it, to be able to make it at all. On any level." He frowned and smiled: "In order to keep from shaking to pieces."

"But these friends of yours," I said, "they seem to shake   200
themselves to pieces pretty goddamn fast."

"Maybe." He played with the notebook. And something told me that I should curb my tongue, that Sonny was doing his best to talk, that I should listen. "But of course you only know the ones that've gone to pieces. Some don't — or at least they haven't *yet* and that's just about all *any* of us can say." He paused. "And then there are some who just live, really, in hell, and they know it and they see what's happening and they go right on. I don't know." He sighed, dropped the notebook, folded his arms. "Some guys, you can tell from the way they play, they on something *all* the time. And you can see that, well, it makes something real for them. But of course," he picked up his beer from the floor and sipped it and put the can down again, "they *want* to, too, you've got to see that. Even some of them that say they don't — *some*, not all."

"And what about you?" I asked — I couldn't help it. "What about you? Do *you* want to?"

He stood up and walked to the window and remained silent for a long time. Then he sighed. "Me," he said. Then: "While I was downstairs before, on my way here, listening to that woman sing, it struck me all of a sudden how much suffering she must have had to go through — to sing like that. It's *repulsive* to think you have to suffer that much."

I said: "But there's no way not to suffer — is there, Sonny?"

"I believe not," he said and smiled, "but that's never stopped   205
anyone from trying." He looked at me. "Has it?" I realized, with this mocking look, that there stood between us, forever, beyond the power of time or forgiveness, the fact that I had held silence — so long — when he had needed human speech to help him. He turned back to the window. "No, there's no way not to suffer. But you try all kinds of ways to keep from drowning in it, to keep on top of it, and to make it seem — well, like *you*. Like you did something, all right, and now you're suffering for it. You

know?" I said nothing. "Well you know," he said, impatiently, "why *do* people suffer? Maybe it's better to do something to give it a reason, *any* reason."

"But we just agreed," I said, "that there's no way not to suffer. Isn't it better, then, just to — take it?"

"But nobody just takes it," Sonny cried, "that's what I'm telling you! *Everybody* tries not to. You're just hung up on the *way* some people try — it's not *your* way!"

The hair on my face began to itch, my face felt wet. "That's not true," I said, "that's not true. I don't give a damn what other people do, I don't even care how they suffer. I just care how *you* suffer." And he looked at me. "Please believe me," I said, "I don't want to see you — die — trying not to suffer."

"I won't," he said, flatly, "die trying not to suffer. At least, not any faster than anybody else."

"But there's no need," I said, trying to laugh, "is there? in killing yourself." 210

I wanted to say more, but I couldn't. I wanted to talk about will power and how life could be — well, beautiful. I wanted to say that it was all within; but was it? or, rather, wasn't that exactly the trouble? And I wanted to promise that I would never fail him again. But it would all have sounded — empty words and lies.

So I made the promise to myself and prayed that I would keep it.

"It's terrible sometimes, inside," he said, "that's what's the trouble. You walk these streets, black and funky and cold, and there's not really a living ass to talk to, and there's nothing shaking, and there's no way of getting it out — that storm inside. You can't talk it and you can't make love with it, and when you finally try to get with it and play it, you realize *nobody's* listening. So *you've* got to listen. You got to find a way to listen."

And then he walked away from the window and sat on the sofa again, as though all the wind had suddenly been knocked out of him. "Sometimes you'll do *anything* to play, even cut your mother's throat." He laughed and looked at me. "Or your brother's." Then he sobered. "Or your own." Then: "Don't worry. I'm all right now and I think I'll *be* all right. But I can't forget — where I've been. I don't mean just the physical place I've been, I mean where I've *been*. And *what* I've been."

"What have you been, Sonny?" I asked. 215

He smiled — but sat sideways on the sofa, his elbow resting on the back, his fingers playing with his mouth and chin, not looking at me. "I've been something I didn't recognize, didn't know I could be. Didn't know anybody could be." He stopped, looking inward, looking helplessly young, looking old. "I'm not talking about it now because I feel *guilty* or anything like that — maybe it would be better if I did, I don't know. Anyway, I can't really talk about it. Not to you, not to anybody," and now he turned and faced me. "Sometimes, you know, and it was actually when I was most *out* of the world, I felt that I was in it, that I was *with* it, really, and I could play or I didn't really have to *play*, it just came out of me, it was there. And I don't know how I played, thinking about it now, but I know I did awful things, those times, sometimes, to people. Or it wasn't that I *did* anything to them — it was that they weren't real." He picked up the beer can; it was empty; he rolled it between his palms: "And other times — well, I needed a fix, I needed to find a place to lean, I needed to clear a space to *listen* — and I couldn't find it, and — went crazy, I did terrible things to *me*, I was terrible *for* me." He began pressing the beer can between his hands, I watched the metal begin to give. It glittered, as he played with it, like a knife, and I was afraid he would cut himself, but I said nothing. "Oh well. I can never tell you. I was all by myself at the bottom of something, stinking and sweating and crying and shaking, and I smelled it, you know? *my* stink, and I thought I'd die if I couldn't get away from it and yet, all the same, I knew that everything I was doing was just locking me in with it. And I didn't know," he paused, still flattening the beer can, "I didn't know, I still *don't* know, something kept telling me that maybe it was good to smell your own stink, but I didn't think that *that* was what I'd been trying to do — and — who can stand it?" and he abruptly dropped the ruined beer can, looking at me with a small, still smile, and then rose, walking to the window as though it were the lodestone rock. I watched his face, he watched the avenue. "I couldn't tell you when Mama died — but the reason I wanted to leave Harlem so bad was to get away from drugs. And then, when I ran away, that's what I was running from — really. When I came back, nothing had changed, *I* hadn't changed, I was just — older." And he stopped, drumming with his fingers on the windowpane. The sun had vanished, soon darkness would fall. I watched his face. "It can come again," he said, almost as though speaking to himself. Then he turned to me. "It can come again," he repeated. "I just want you to know that."

"All right," I said, at last. "So it can come again. All right."

He smiled, but the smile was sorrowful. "I had to try to tell you," he said.

"Yes," I said. "I understand that."

"You're my brother," he said, looking straight at me, and not 220
smiling at all.

"Yes," I repeated, "yes. I understand that."

He turned back to the window, looking out. "All that hatred
down there," he said, "all that hatred and misery and love. It's a
wonder it doesn't blow the avenue apart."

We went to the only nightclub on a short, dark street, downtown. We squeezed through the narrow, chattering, jam-packed
bar to the entrance of the big room, where the bandstand was.
And we stood there for a moment, for the lights were very dim in
this room and we couldn't see. Then, "Hello, boy," said a voice
and an enormous black man, much older than Sonny or myself,
erupted out of all that atmospheric lighting and put an arm
around Sonny's shoulder. "I been sitting right here," he said,
"waiting for you."

He had a big voice, too, and heads in the darkness turned
toward us.

Sonny grinned and pulled a little away, and said, "Creole, 225
this is my brother. I told you about him."

Creole shook my hand. "I'm glad to meet you, son," he said,
and it was clear that he was glad to meet me *there*, for Sonny's
sake. And he smiled, "You got a real musician in *your* family," and
he took his arm from Sonny's shoulder and slapped him, lightly,
affectionately, with the back of his hand.

"Well. Now I've heard it all," said a voice behind us. This was
another musician, and a friend of Sonny's, a coal-black, cheerful-
looking man, built close to the ground. He immediately began
confiding to me, at the top of his lungs, the most terrible things
about Sonny, his teeth gleaming like a lighthouse and his laugh
coming up out of him like the beginning of an earthquake. And
it turned out that everyone at the bar knew Sonny, or almost
everyone; some were musicians, working there, or nearby, or not
working, some were simple hangers-on, and some were there to
hear Sonny play. I was introduced to all of them and they were all
very polite to me. Yet, it was clear that, for them, I was only
Sonny's brother. Here, I was in Sonny's world. Or, rather: his
kingdom. Here, it was not even a question that his veins bore
royal blood.

They were going to play soon and Creole installed me, by
myself, at a table in a dark corner. Then I watched them, Creole,
and the little black man, and Sonny, and the others, while they
horsed around, standing just below the bandstand. The light

from the bandstand spilled just a little short of them and, watching them laughing and gesturing and moving about, I had the feeling that they, nevertheless, were being most careful not to step into that circle of light too suddenly: that if they moved into the light too suddenly, without thinking, they would perish in flame. Then, while I watched, one of them, the small, black man, moved into the light and crossed the bandstand and started fooling around with his drums. Then — being funny and being, also, extremely ceremonious — Creole took Sonny by the arm and led him to the piano. A woman's voice called Sonny's name and a few hands started clapping. And Sonny, also being funny and being ceremonious, and so touched, I think, that he could have cried, but neither hiding it nor showing it, riding it like a man, grinned, and put both hands to his heart and bowed from the waist.

Creole then went to the bass fiddle and a lean, very bright-skinned brown man jumped up on the bandstand and picked up his horn. So there they were, and the atmosphere on the bandstand and in the room began to change and tighten. Someone stepped up to the microphone and announced them. Then there were all kinds of murmurs. Some people at the bar shushed others. The waitress ran around, frantically getting in the last orders, guys and chicks got closer to each other, and the lights on the bandstand, on the quartet, turned to a kind of indigo. Then they all looked different there. Creole looked about him for the last time, as though he were making certain that all his chickens were in the coop, and then he — jumped and struck the fiddle. And there they were.

All I know about music is that not many people ever really 230 hear it. And even then, on the rare occasions when something opens within, and the music enters, what we mainly hear, or hear corroborated, are personal, private, vanishing evocations. But the man who creates the music is hearing something else, is dealing with the roar rising from the void and imposing order on it as it hits the air. What is evoked in him, then, is of another order, more terrible because it has no words, and triumphant, too, for that same reason. And his triumph, when he triumphs, is ours. I just watched Sonny's face. His face was troubled, he was working hard, but he wasn't with it. And I had the feeling that, in a way, everyone on the bandstand was waiting for him, both waiting for him and pushing him along. But as I began to watch Creole, I realized that it was Creole who held them all back. He had them on a short rein. Up there, keeping the beat with his whole body, wailing on the fiddle, with his eyes half closed, he was listening to everything, but he was listening to Sonny. He was having a dialogue with Sonny. He wanted Sonny to leave the shoreline and strike out for the deep water. He was Sonny's witness that deep water and drowning were not the same thing — he had been there, and he knew. And he wanted Sonny to know. He was waiting for Sonny to do the things on the keys which would let Creole know that Sonny was in the water.

And, while Creole listened, Sonny moved, deep within, exactly like someone in torment. I had never before thought of how awful the relationship must be between the musician and his instrument. He has to fill it, this instrument, with the breath of life, his own. He has to make it do what he wants it to do. And a piano is just a piano. It's made out of so much wood and wires and little hammers and big ones, and ivory. While there's only so much you can do with it, the only way to find this out is to try; to try and make it do everything.

And Sonny hadn't been near a piano for over a year. And he wasn't on much better terms with his life, not the life that stretched before him now. He and the piano stammered, started one way, got scared, stopped; started another way, panicked, marked time, started again; then seemed to have found a direction, panicked again, got stuck. And the face I saw on Sonny I'd never seen before. Everything had been burned out of it, and, at the same time, things usually hidden were being burned in, by the fire and fury of the battle which was occurring in him up there.

Yet, watching Creole's face as they neared the end of the first set, I had the feeling that something had happened, something I hadn't heard. Then they finished, there was scattered applause, and then, without an instant's warning, Creole started into something else, it was almost sardonic, it was *Am I Blue*. And, as though he commanded, Sonny began to play. Something began to happen. And Creole let out the reins. The dry, low, black man said something awful on the drums, Creole answered, and the drums talked back. Then the horn insisted, sweet and high, slightly detached perhaps, and Creole listened, commenting now and then, dry, and driving, beautiful and calm and old. Then they all came together again, and Sonny was part of the family again. I could tell this from his face. He seemed to have found, right there beneath his fingers, a damn brand-new piano. It seemed that he couldn't get over it. Then, for a while, just being happy with Sonny, they seemed to be agreeing with him that brand-new pianos certainly were a gas.

Then Creole stepped forward to remind them that what they

were playing was the blues. He hit something in all of them, he hit something in me, myself, and the music tightened and deepened, apprehension began to beat the air. Creole began to tell us what the blues were all about. They were not about anything very new. He and his boys up there were keeping it new, at the risk of ruin, destruction, madness, and death, in order to find new ways to make us listen. For, while the tale of how we suffer, and how we are delighted, and how we may triumph is never new, it always must be heard. There isn't any other tale to tell, it's the only light we've got in all this darkness.

And this tale, according to that face, that body, those strong 235 hands on those strings, has another aspect in every country, and a new depth in every generation. Listen, Creole seemed to be saying, listen. Now these are Sonny's blues. He made the little black man on the drums know it, and the bright brown man on the horn. Creole wasn't trying any longer to get Sonny in the water. He was wishing him Godspeed. Then he stepped back, very slowly, filling the air with the immense suggestion that Sonny speak for himself.

Then they all gathered around Sonny and Sonny played. Every now and again one of them seemed to say, amen. Sonny's fingers filled the air with life, his life. But that life contained so many others. And Sonny went all the way back, he really began with the spare, flat statement of the opening phrase of the song. Then he began to make it his. It was very beautiful because it wasn't hurried and it was no longer a lament. I seemed to hear with what burning he had made it his, with what burning we had yet to make it ours, how we could cease lamenting. Freedom lurked around us and I understood, at last, that he could help us to be free if we would listen, that he would never be free until we did. Yet, there was no battle in his face now. I heard what he had gone through, and would continue to go through until he came to rest in earth. He had made it his: that long line, of which we knew only Mama and Daddy. And he was giving it back, as everything must be given back, so that, passing through death, it can live forever. I saw my mother's face again, and felt, for the first time, how the stones of the road she had walked on must have bruised her feet. I saw the moonlit road where my father's brother died. And it brought something else back to me, and carried me past it. I saw my little girl again and felt Isabel's tears again, and I felt my own tears begin to rise. And I was yet aware that this was only a moment, that the world waited outside, as hungry as a tiger, and that trouble stretched above us, longer than the sky.

Then it was over. Creole and Sonny let out their breath, both soaking wet, and grinning. There was a lot of applause and some of it was real. In the dark, the girl came by and I asked her to take drinks to the bandstand. There was a long pause while they talked up there in the indigo light and after a while I saw the girl put a Scotch and milk on top of the piano for Sonny. He didn't seem to notice it but just before they started playing again, he sipped from it and looked toward me, and nodded. Then he put it back on top of the piano. For me, then, as they began to play again, it glowed and shook above my brother's head like the very cup of trembling.

TONI CADE BAMBARA   (b. 1939)

The Lesson

Back in the days when everyone was old and stupid or young and foolish and me and Sugar were the only ones just right, this lady moved on our block with nappy hair and proper speech and no makeup. And quite naturally we laughed at her, laughed the way we did at the junk man who went about his business like he was some big-time president and his sorry-ass horse his secretary. And we kinda hated her too, hated the way we did the winos who cluttered up our parks and pissed on our handball walls and stank up our hallways and stairs so you couldn't halfway play hide-and-seek without a goddamn gas mask. Miss Moore was her name. The only woman on the block with no first name. And she was black as hell, cept for her feet, which were fish-white and spooky. And she was always planning these boring-ass things for us to do, us being my cousin, mostly, who lived on the block cause we all moved North the same time and to the same apartment then spread out gradual to breathe. And our parents would yank our heads into some kinda shape and crisp up our clothes so we'd be presentable for travel with Miss Moore, who always looked like she was going to church, though she never did. Which is just one of things the grown-ups talked about when they talked behind her back like a dog. But when she came calling with some sachet she'd sewed up or some gingerbread she'd made or some book, why then they'd all be too embarrassed to turn her down and we'd get handed over all spruced up. She'd been to college and said it was only right that she should take responsibility for the young ones' education, and she not even related by marriage or blood. So they'd go for it. Specially Aunt Gretchen. She was the main gofer in the family. You got some ole dumb shit foolishness you want somebody to go for, you send for Aunt Gretchen. She been screwed into the go-along for so long, it's a blood-deep natural thing with her. Which is how she got saddled with me and Sugar and Junior in the first place while our mothers were in a la-de-da apartment up the block having a good ole time.

So this one day Miss Moore rounds us all up at the mailbox and it's puredee hot and she's knockin herself out about arithmetic. And school suppose to let up in summer I heard, but she don't never let up. And the starch in my pinafore scratching the shit outta me and I'm really hating this nappy-head bitch and her goddamn college degree. I'd much rather go to the pool or to the show where it's cool. So me and Sugar leaning on the mailbox being surly, which is a Miss Moore word. And Flyboy checking out what everybody brought for lunch. And Fat Butt already wasting his peanut-butter-and-jelly sandwich like the pig he is. And Junebug punchin on Q.T.'s arm for potato chips. And Rosie Giraffe shifting from one hip to the other waiting for somebody to step on her foot or ask her if she from Georgia so she can kick ass, preferably Mercedes'. And Miss Moore asking us do we know what money is, like we a bunch of retards. I mean real money, she say, like it's only poker chips or monopoly papers we lay on the grocer. So right away I'm tired of this and say so. And would much rather snatch Sugar and go to the Sunset and terrorize the West Indian kids and take their hair ribbons and their money too. And Miss Moore files that remark away for next week's lesson on brotherhood, I can tell. And finally I say we oughta get to the subway cause it's cooler and besides we might meet some cute boys. Sugar done swiped her mama's lipstick, so we ready.

So we heading down the street and she's boring us silly about what things cost and what our parents make and how much goes for rent and how money ain't divided up right in this country. And then she gets to the part about we all poor and live in the slums, which I don't feature. And I'm ready to speak on that, but she steps out in the street and hails two cabs just like that. Then she hustles half the crew in with her and hands me a five-dollar bill and tells me to calculate 10 percent tip for the driver. And we're off. Me and Sugar and Junebug and Flyboy hangin out the window and hollering to everybody, putting lipstick on each other cause Flyboy a faggot anyway, and making farts with our sweaty armpits. But I'm mostly trying to figure how to spend this money. But they all fascinated with the meter ticking and Junebug starts laying bets as to how much it'll read when Flyboy can't hold his breath no more. Then Sugar lays bets as to how much it'll be when we get there. So I'm stuck. Don't nobody want to go for my plan, which is to jump out at the next light and run off to the first bar-b-que we can find. Then the driver tells us to get the hell out cause we there already. And the meter reads eighty-five cents. And I'm stalling to figure out the tip and Sugar say give him a dime. And I decide he don't need it bad as I do, so later for him. But then he tries to take off with Junebug foot still in the door so we talk about his mama something ferocious. Then we check out that we on Fifth Avenue and everybody dressed up in stockings. One lady in a fur coat, hot as it is. White folks crazy.

"This is the place," Miss Moore say, presenting it to us in the voice she uses at the museum. "Let's look in the windows before we go in."

"Can we steal?" Sugar asks very serious like she's getting the 5 ground rules squared away before she plays. "I beg your pardon," say Miss Moore, and we fall out. So she leads us around the windows of the toy store and me and Sugar screamin, "This is mine, that's mine, I gotta have that, that was made for me, I was born for that," till Big Butt drowns us out.

"Hey, I'm goin to buy that there."

"That there? You don't even know what it is, stupid."

"I do so," he say punchin on Rosie Giraffe. "It's a micro-scope."

"Whatcha gonna do with a microscope, fool?"

"Look at things." 10

"Like what, Ronald?" ask Miss Moore. And Big Butt ain't got the first notion. So here go Miss Moore gabbing about the thousands of bacteria in a drop of water and the somethinorother in a speck of blood and the million and one living things in the air around us is invisible to the naked eye. And what she say that for? Junebug go to town on that "naked" and we rolling. Then Miss Moore ask what it cost. So we all jam into the window smudgin it up and the price tag say $300. So then she ask how long'd take for Big Butt and Junebug to save up their allowances. "Too long," I say. "Yeh," adds Sugar, "outgrown it by that time." And Miss Moore say no, you never outgrow learning instruments. "Why, even medical students and interns and," blah, blah, blah. And we ready to choke Big Butt for bringing it up in the first damn place.

"This here costs four hundred eighty dollars," say Rosie Giraffe. So we pile up all over her to see what she pointin out. My eyes tell me it's a chunk of glass cracked with something heavy, and different-color inks dripped into the splits, then the whole thing put into a oven or something. But for $480 it don't make sense.

"That's a paperweight made of semi-precious stones fused together under tremendous pressure," she explains slowly, with her hands doing the mining and all the factory work.

"So what's a paperweight?" asks Rosie Giraffe.

"To weigh paper with, dumbbell," say Flyboy, the wise man from the East.   15

"Not exactly," say Miss Moore, which is what she say when you warm or way off too. "It's to weigh paper down so it won't scatter and make your desk untidy." So right away me and Sugar curtsy to each other and then to Mercedes who is more the tidy type.

"We don't keep paper on top of the desk in my class," say Junebug, figuring Miss Moore crazy or lyin one.

"At home, then," she say. "Don't you have a calendar and a pencil case and a blotter and a letter-opener on your desk at home where you do your homework?" And she know damn well what our homes look like cause she nosys around in them every chance she gets.

"I don't even have a desk," say Junebug. "Do we?"

"No. And I don't get no homework neither," say Big Butt.   20

"And I don't even have a home," say Flyboy like he do at school to keep the white folks off his back and sorry for him. Send this poor kid to camp posters, is his specialty.

"I do," says Mercedes. "I have a box of stationery on my desk and a picture of my cat. My godmother bought the stationery and the desk. There's a big rose on each sheet and the envelopes smell like roses."

"Who wants to know about your smelly-ass stationery," say Rosie Giraffe fore I can get my two cents in.

"It's important to have a work area all your own so that . . ."

"Will you look at this sailboat, please," say Flyboy, cuttin her off and pointin to the thing like it was his. So once again we   25
tumble all over each other to gaze at this magnificent thing in the toy store which is just big enough to maybe sail two kittens across the pond if you strap them to the posts tight. We all start reciting the price tag like we in assembly. "Handcrafted sailboat of fiberglass at one thousand one hundred ninety-five dollars."

"Unbelievable," I hear myself say and am really stunned. I read it again for myself just in case the group recitation put me in a trance. Same thing. For some reason this pisses me off. We look at Miss Moore and she lookin at us, waiting for I dunno what.

"Who'd pay all that when you can buy a sailboat set for a quarter at Pop's, a tube of glue for a dime, and a ball of string for eight cents? It must have a motor and a whole lot else besides," I say. "My sailboat cost me about fifty cents."

"But will it take water?" say Mercedes with her smart ass.

"Took mine to Alley Pond Park once," say Flyboy. "String broke. Lost it. Pity."

"Sailed mine in Central Park and it keeled over and sank. 30 Had to ask my father for another dollar."

"And you got the strap," laugh Big Butt. "The jerk didn't even have a string on it. My old man wailed on his behind."

Little Q.T. was staring hard at the sailboat and you could see he wanted it bad. But he too little and somebody'd just take it from him. So what the hell. "This boat for kids, Miss Moore?"

"Parents silly to buy something like that just to get all broke up," say Rosie Giraffe.

"That much money it should last forever," I figure.

"My father'd buy it for me if I wanted it." 35

"Your father, my ass," say Rosie Giraffe getting a chance to finally push Mercedes.

"Must be rich people shop here," say Q.T.

"You are a very bright boy," say Flyboy. "What was your first clue?" And he rap him on the head with the back of his knuckles, since Q.T. the only one he could get away with. Though Q.T. liable to come up behind you years later and get his licks in when you half expect it.

"What I want to know is," I says to Miss Moore though I never talk to her, I wouldn't give the bitch that satisfaction, "is how much a real boat costs? I figure a thousand'd get you a yacht any day."

"Why don't you check that out," she says, "and report back to 40 the group?" Which really pains my ass. If you gonna mess up a perfectly good swim day least you could do is have some answers. "Let's go in," she say like she got something up her sleeve. Only she don't lead the way. So me and Sugar turn the corner to where the entrance is, but when we get there I kinda hang back. Not that I'm scared, what's there to be afraid of, just a toy store. But I feel funny, shame. But what I got to be shamed about? Got as much right to go in as anybody. But somehow I can't seem to get hold of the door, so I step away for Sugar to lead. But she hangs back too. And I look at her and she looks at me and this is ridiculous. I mean, damn, I have never ever been shy about doing nothing or going nowhere. But then Mercedes steps up and then Rosie

Giraffe and Big Butt crowd in behind and shove, and next thing we all stuffed into the doorway with only Mercedes squeezing past us, smoothing out her jumper and walking right down the aisle. Then the rest of us tumble in like a glued-together jigsaw done all wrong. And people lookin at us. And it's like the time me and Sugar crashed into the Catholic church on a dare. But once we got in there and everything so hushed and holy and the candles and the bowin and the handkerchiefs on all the drooping heads, I just couldn't go through with the plan. Which was for me to run up to the altar and do a tap dance while Sugar played the nose flute and messed around in the holy water. And Sugar kept givin me the elbow. Then later teased me so bad I tied her up in the shower and turned it on and locked her in. And she'd be there till this day if Aunt Gretchen hadn't finally figured I was lyin about the boarder takin a shower.

Same thing in the store. We all walkin on tiptoe and hardly touchin the games and puzzles and things. And I watched Miss Moore who is steady watchin us like she waitin for a sign. Like Mama Drewery watches the sky and sniffs the air and takes note of just how much slant is in the bird formation. Then me and Sugar bump smack into each other, so busy gazing at the toys, 'specially the sailboat. But we don't laugh and go into our fat-lady bump-stomach routine. We just stare at that price tag. Then Sugar run a finger over the whole boat. And I'm jealous and want to hit her. Maybe not her, but I sure want to punch somebody in the mouth.

"Watcha bring us here for, Miss Moore?"

"You sound angry, Sylvia. Are you mad about something?" Givin me one of them grins like she tellin a grown-up joke that never turns out to be funny. And she's lookin very closely at me like maybe she plannin to do my portrait from memory. I'm mad, but I won't give her that satisfaction. So I slouch around the store bein very bored and say, "Let's go."

Me and Sugar at the back of the train watchin the tracks whizzin by large then small then gettin gobbled up in the dark. I'm thinkin about this tricky toy I saw in the store. A clown that somersaults on a bar then does chin-ups just cause you yank lightly at his leg. Cost $35. I could see me askin my mother for a $35 birthday clown. "You wanna who that costs what?" she'd say, cocking her head to the side to get a better view of the hole in my head. Thirty-five dollars could buy new bunk beds for Junior and Gretchen's boy. Thirty-five dollars and the whole household could go visit Granddaddy Nelson in the country. Thirty-five dollars would pay for the rent and the piano bill too. Who are these people that spend that much for performing clowns and $1,000 for toy sailboats? What kinda work they do and how they live and how come we ain't in on it? Where we are is who we are, Miss Moore always pointin out. But it don't necessarily have to be that way, she always adds then waits for somebody to say that poor people have to wake up and demand their share of the pie and don't none of us know what kind of pie she talkin about in the first damn place. But she ain't so smart cause I still got her four dollars from the taxi and she sure ain't gettin it. Messin up my day with this shit. Sugar nudges me in my pocket and winks.

Miss Moore lines up in front of the mailbox where we started 45 from, seem like years ago, and I got a headache for thinkin so hard. And we lean all over each other so we can hold up under the draggy-ass lecture she always finishes us off with at the end before we thank her for borin us to tears. But she just looks at us like she readin tea leaves. Finally she say, "Well, what did you think of F.A.O. Schwartz?"

Rosie Giraffe mumbles, "White folks crazy."

"I'd like to go there again when I get my birthday money," says Mercedes, and we shove her out the pack so she has to lean on the mailbox by herself.

"I'd like a shower. Tiring day," say Flyboy.

Then Sugar surprises me by sayin, "You know, Miss Moore, I don't think all of us here put together eat in a year what that sailboat costs." And Miss Moore lights up like somebody goosed her. "And?" she say, urging Sugar on. Only I'm standin on her foot so she don't continue.

"Imagine for a minute what kind of society it is in which 50 some people can spend on a toy what it would cost to feed a family of six or seven. What do you think?"

"I think," say Sugar pushing me off her feet like she never done before, cause I whip her ass in a minute, "that this is not much of a democracy if you ask me. Equal chance to pursue happiness means an equal crack at the dough, don't it?" Miss Moore is besides herself and I am disgusted with Sugar's treach-ery. So I stand on her foot one more time to see if she'll shove me. She shuts up, and Miss Moore looks at me, sorrowfully I'm thinkin. And somethin weird is goin on, I can feel it in my chest.

"Anybody else learn anything today?" lookin dead at me. I walk away and Sugar has to run to catch up and don't even seem to notice when I shrug her arm off my shoulder.

"Well, we got four dollars anyway," she says.

"Uh hunh."

"We could go to Hascombs and get half a chocolate layer and 55 then go to the Sunset and still have plenty money for potato chips and ice-cream sodas."

"Uh hunh."

"Race you to Hascombs," she say.

We start down the block and she gets ahead which is O.K. by me cause I'm goin to the West End and then over to the Drive to think this day through. She can run if she want to and even run faster. But ain't nobody gonna beat me at nuthin.

JAMAICA KINCAID   (b. 1949)
In the Night

In the night, way into the middle of the night, when the night isn't divided like a sweet drink into little sips, when there is no just before midnight, midnight, or just after midnight, when the night is round in some places, flat in some places, and in some places like a deep hole, blue at the edge, black inside, the night-soil men come.

They come and go, walking on the damp ground in straw shoes. Their feet in the straw shoes make a scratchy sound. They say nothing.

The night-soil men can see a bird walking in trees. It isn't a bird. It is a woman who has removed her skin and is on her way to drink the blood of her secret enemies. It is a woman who has left her skin in a corner of a house made out of wood. It is a woman who is reasonable and admires honeybees in the hibiscus. It is a woman who, as a joke, brays like a donkey when he is thirsty.

There is the sound of a cricket, there is the sound of a church bell, there is the sound of this house creaking, that house creaking, and the other house creaking as they settle into the ground. There is the sound of a radio in the distance — a fisherman listening to merengue music. There is the sound of a man groaning in his sleep; there is the sound of a woman disgusted at the man groaning. There is the sound of the man stabbing the woman, the sound of her blood as it hits the floor, the sound of Mr. Straffee, the undertaker, taking her body away. There is the sound of her spirit back from the dead, looking at the man who used to groan; he is running a fever forever. There is the sound of a woman writing a letter; there is the sound of her pen nib on the white writing paper; there is the sound of the kerosene lamp dimming; there is the sound of her head aching.

The rain falls on the tin roofs, on the leaves in the trees, on 5 the stones in the yard, on sand, on the ground. The night is wet in some places, warm in some places.

There is Mr. Gishard, standing under a cedar tree which is in full bloom, wearing that nice white suit, which is as fresh as the day he was buried in it. The white suit came from England in a brown package: "To: Mr. John Gishard," and so on and so on. Mr. Gishard is standing under the tree, wearing his nice suit and holding a glass full of rum in his hand — the same glass full of rum that he had in his hand shortly before he died — and looking at the house in which he used to live. The people who now live in the house walk through the door backward when they see Mr. Gishard standing under the tree, wearing his nice white suit. Mr. Gishard misses his accordion; you can tell by the way he keeps tapping his foot.

In my dream I can hear a baby being born. I can see its face, a pointy little face — so nice. I can see its hands — so nice, again. Its eyes are closed. It's breathing, the little baby. It's breathing. It's bleating, the little baby. It's bleating. The baby and I are now walking to pasture. The baby is eating green grass with its soft and pink lips. My mother is shaking me by the shoulders. My mother says, "Little Miss, Little Miss." I say to my mother, "But it's still night." My mother says, "Yes, but you have wet your bed again." And my mother, who is still young, and still beautiful, and still has pink lips, removes my wet nightgown, removes my wet sheets from my bed. My mother can change everything. In my dream I am in the night.

"What are the lights in the mountains?"

"The lights in the mountains? Oh, it's a jablesse."

"A jablesse! But why? What's a jablesse?"   10

"It's a person who can turn into anything. But you can tell they aren't real because of their eyes. Their eyes shine like lamps, so bright that you can't look. That's how you can tell it's a jablesse. They like to go up in the mountains and gallivant. Take good care when you see a beautiful woman. A jablesse always tries to look like a beautiful woman."

No one has ever said to me, "My father, a night-soil man, is very nice and very kind. When he passes a dog, he give a pat and not a kick. He likes all the parts of a fish but especially the head. He goes to church quite regularly and is always glad when the minister calls out, 'A Mighty Fortress Is Our God,' his favorite hymn. He would like to wear pink shirts and pink pants but knows that this color isn't very becoming to a man, so instead he wears navy blue and brown, colors he does not like at all. He met my mother on what masquerades as a bus around here, a long time ago, and he still likes to whistle. Once, while running to catch a bus, he fell and broke his ankle and had to spend a week in hospital. This made him miserable, but he cheered up quite a bit when he saw my mother and me, standing over his white cot, holding bunches of yellow roses and smiling down at him. Then he said, 'Oh, my. Oh, my.' What he likes to do most, my father the night-soil man, is to sit on a big stone under a mahogany tree and watch small children playing play-cricket while he eats the intestines of animals stuffed with blood and rice and drinks ginger beer. He has told me this many times: 'My dear, what I like to do most,' and so on. He is always reading botany books and knows a lot about rubber plantations and rubber trees; but this is an interest I can't explain, since the only rubber tree he has ever seen is a specially raised one in the botanic gardens. He sees to it that my school shoes fit comfortably. I love my father the night-soil man. My mother loves my father the night-soil man. Everybody loves him and waves to him whenever they see him. He is very handsome, you know, and I have seen women look at him twice. On special days he wears a brown felt hat, which he orders from England, and brown leather shoes, which he also orders from England. On ordinary days he goes barehead. When he calls me, I say, 'Yes, sir.' On my mother's birthday he always buys her some nice cloth for a new dress as a present. He makes us happy, my father the night-soil man, and has promised that one day he will take us to see something he has read about called the circus."

In the night, the flowers close up and thicken. The hibiscus flowers, the flamboyant flowers, the bachelor's buttons, the irises, the marigolds, the whiteheadbush flowers, the lilies, the flowers on the daggerbush, the flowers on the turtleberry bush, the flowers on the soursop tree, the flowers on the sugar-apple tree, the flowers on the mango tree, the flowers on the guava tree, the flowers on the cedar tree, the flowers on the stinking-toe tree, the flowers on the dumps tree, the flowers on the papaw tree, the flowers everywhere close up and thicken. The flowers are vexed.

Someone is making a basket, someone is making a girl a dress or a boy a shirt, someone is making her husband a soup with cassava so that he can take it to the cane field tomorrow, someone is making his wife a beautiful mahogany chest, someone is sprinkling a colorless powder outside a closed door so that someone else's child will be stillborn, someone is praying that a bad child who is living prosperously abroad will be good and send a package filled with new clothes, someone is sleeping.

Now I am a girl, but one day I will marry a woman — a red- 15 skin woman with black bramblebush hair and brown eyes, who wears skirts that are so big I can easily bury my head in them. I would like to marry this woman and live with her in a mud hut near the sea. In the mud hut will be two chairs and one table, a lamp that burns kerosene, a medicine chest, a pot, one bed, two pillows, two sheets, one looking glass, two cups, two saucers, two dinner plates, two forks, two drinking-water glasses, one china pot, two fishing strings, two straw hats to ward the hot sun off our heads, two trunks for things we have very little use for, one basket, one book of plain paper, one box filled with twelve crayons of different colors, one loaf of bread wrapped in a piece of brown paper, one coal pot, one picture of two women standing on a jetty, one picture of the same two women embracing, one picture of the same two women waving goodbye, one box of matches. Every day this red-skin woman and I will eat bread and milk for breakfast, hide in bushes and throw hardened cow dung at people we don't like, climb coconut trees, pick coconuts, eat and drink the food and water from the coconuts we have picked, throw stones in the sea, put on John Bull° masks and frighten defenseless little children on their way home from school, go fishing and catch only our favorite fishes to roast and have for dinner, steal green figs to eat for dinner with the roast fish. Every day we would do this. Every night I would sing this woman a song; the words I don't know yet, but the tune is in my head. This woman I would like to marry knows many things, but to me she will only tell about things that would never dream of making me cry; and every night, over and over, she will tell me something that begins, "Before you were born." I will marry a woman like this, and every night, every night, I will be completely happy.

John Bull: The personification of a typical Englishman.

DRAMA

Scene: a theater. We're seated chatting with friends, awaiting the start of the performance. The lights dim, crowd noise subsides, the curtain rises — and there in front of us, straight ahead onstage, vivid and concrete, other people are talking and moving, events are in progress. No outside voice instructs us about what's going on; we operate on our own, seemingly, deciding for ourselves how to interpret what we see and hear, arriving independently at decisions about whom we like, trust, detest, and so on. The absence of a narrator or speaker, together with the presence of solid objects and people, creates a sense of reality different from that familiar to readers of poems and stories. In this place we're not judging the credibility of reporters describing events that happened elsewhere, at another time; the events are happening here and now, and we seem ourselves to have become eyewitnesses.

This feeling of independence — of on-the-spot autonomy — is partly an illusion. The players, through their gestures and inflections, their ways of dealing with each other, provide guidance that shapes our reading of the ongoing events. Other help comes from the pacing, the lighting, the look of the sets and costumes. A largish number of unseen figures — director, stage manager, designers, costumers, technicians, producers — have in fact collaborated with the actors in bringing to life the work before us, transforming a script into the immediate dramatic experience we assess according to our understanding of theater and of life.

THE THEATER OF THE MIND

The situation of a reader of a play obviously differs from that of a member of a theater audience. As readers, we are not attending a performance, we are putting on a performance in the theater of our minds. We're making decisions about how lines should be said — the kinds of decisions we make as we read poems or dialogue in certain prose fiction. And we're also making decisions about movement and placing on a stage, about the look of the players and of the stage itself, and about many other matters as well. Sometimes playwrights offer ideas of their own about performance, in the form of stage directions printed in the text of their plays. But more often than not their help is lightly weighed by theater people, who correctly regard the playwright as one voice among many in a collaboration. And for readers, too, the playwright's vision of a performance cannot be the last word.

In putting on performances in our own mental theater, we as readers function in unique ways. We aren't members of a theater audience — but neither are we directors or set designers. Our imagining of a moment onstage may require only a decision about whether the players are in motion or standing still; a director's notes will be technically detailed, often specifying exactly where the players should stand or move or stop. As play readers we make some of our staging decisions unconsciously, and we *sketch* movement as we go, roughing out the appearances of characters and interiors. We sense the appropriateness of a gesture here, an underlining of a parallel or contrast there. We're aware that filling in the particulars requires mastery of crafts we ourselves don't possess — don't need to possess because the imagination that lights and furnishes the theater of the mind can cope adequately even when following fairly shadowy suggestions.

But if that imagination doesn't require detailed blueprints, it does demand some envisioning of a stage translation of the words on the page. When we read a symbolical or allegorical work, we join with the writer to create new levels of meaning for a pickle or a funhouse or a wife named Faith. When we read plays, we join playwrights and production crews in imagining total performances: again, another level of meaning. Play readers reach out constantly toward the physical reality without which there can't be a performance. We imagine the sounds of the words as they're uttered, and simultaneously we imagine the space in which the sound occurs. We ask: How shall I group these people onstage? Are they together or apart? Do I move them closer or farther away from each other as the scene proceeds? Where do I focus this character's glance? Do I have her address the other figure directly? Avoid his gaze? Seek (successfully or unsuccessfully) the other's eye? Out of the answers to these and numberless comparable questions, we, as readers in action, mount our silent productions.

TRAGIC AND COMIC RANGES OF FEELING

The first resource for such work, as with all imaginative writing, is the human power of probing situations from inside, working up the probabilities of immediate feeling on the basis of our understanding of character, history, class, and other forces. A second resource is the clarity that emerges, as we read, about the kind of play we're mounting. Many categories and classifications of dramatic literature exist: tragedy, comedy, tragicomedy, melodrama, farce, burlesque, social drama, to name a few. Especially in the twentieth century, lines between these so-called *genres* are blurred: characters dressed like down-and-out vaudeville comics do a number of funny turns in Samuel Beckett's *Waiting for Godot*, but imagining this play as light, sun filled, and sustainedly hilarious is next to impossible.

Still, our minds — and playwrights' minds as well — take hold of immediate experience by rather crude handles. We guess about the right mood or atmosphere for the players and the action by deciding whether tragic or comic accents and rhythms ought to predominate at any given moment — whether or not we're to make light of the events we're putting on. It's rarely a flat-out choice. Every Shakespearean tragedy has scenes that call for comic effects. Many comedies develop as complex struggles between serious intellectual positions. Readers who base their decisions about how any individual scene should be imagined solely on a descriptive label attached to the play (*A tragedy by*, etc.) are likely to experience only tedium.

Some guidance about how to imagine — how to bring a play to life — can be derived from our gradually developing confidence about which tones and atmosphere should predominate. Awe, wonder, fear, reverence, grief, torment — examples of these can be found in comedy, but not as predominant emotions. That range of feeling is basically tragic. Disparagement, mockery, irreverence, lightheartedness, gaiety — examples of these can be found in tragedy, but not as predominant: this is a comic range.

Because the link between range of feeling and kind or genre of play is tight, separating literary form from emotional substance isn't feasible. As we work for a sense of the norms of feeling in a play, we're simultaneously approaching an understanding of the kind of work we're imagining. And language is always a pivotally important focus. The emotions we think of as dominant in tragedy call for elevated styles of speech — speech that's strongly rhythmic, weighted in its sound, dignified or even solemn in tone. The emotions we think of as dominant in comedy call for lighter, more colloquial styles of speech — speech that's closer to the patterns of ordinary conversation, easygoing, casual.

To repeat, theatergoers and play readers alike savor variety. A considerable measure of the interest of any production depends upon the diversity of emotional experience that's presented. But the parts must cohere. Our reading of any one moment needs to be related to the play as a whole. The overarching concern must always be: If we play the scene this way, how will it fit with what comes before and after? If it's totally discordant, is the contrast purposeful?

The questions after each play in this part focus on a particular scene, asking how it should be imagined. The central problem is always the same: how to present one moment so that it carries the sum of our understanding of every other moment in the work. Plays are built, moment to moment, of particulars as tiny and brief as the raising of an eyebrow; but their effect is cumulative, and it's with overall effect that we are, finally, concerned.

18

Tragedy

DIMENSIONS OF TRAGIC CHARACTERS

The best (and best-known) generalizations about plays called tragedies are those of the Greek philosopher Aristotle. Arising from his examination of Greek drama, Aristotle's generalizations focus on the nature of the action occurring in tragedy, the nature of tragic heroes, and the effect on the audience of watching tragic drama.

The action of tragedy, Aristotle said, consists of a fall or overturn: A distinguished, highly placed hero or protagonist loses place and power partly through his or her own mistake or fault, yet achieves some understanding, at the end, of the causes and meaning of the mistake. The protagonist commands respect for the power wielded before the fall. But he or she matters for other reasons as well: for instance, capacity to suggest possibilities of true grandeur for humankind, ability to learn. Watching the events, the audience experiences both fear and pity: A disaster for greatness underlines the pitiable and frightening vulnerability of all of us who are less than great. The final result of the experience, though, is a movement out of darkness, a purgation of fear and sorrow, an achievement of enlightenment and balance.

Other kinds of tragedy exist besides the sort described by Aristotle — social drama that's focused on protagonists whose fall strikes us as attributable to circumstances well beyond their control. Perceiving these heroes and heroines as prisoners of overpowering social and environmental forces, we place them as victims rather than as shapers of personal destiny. (An example

DIMENSIONS OF TRAGIC CHARACTERS **1035**

of such a tragedy is Arthur Miller's *Death of a Salesman*, p. 1290.) Essential in bringing to life most social drama is the capacity for imagining helplessness and impotence as normal if not inevitable human feelings.

Those feelings aren't absent from tragedies that fit the Aristotelian model. But they are marginal. As readers evoking *Antigone* (see p. 476) or Shakespeare's *Macbeth*, we have to imagine the sense of empowerment as normal. The figures we observe in this world understand themselves to be responsible for their actions and situations. They believe that it is possible for human beings to act on their own behalf, that their actions will have consequences, and that what happens as a result of their actions will be intelligible to them. They make mistakes and commit fearful wrongs; they suffer confusion. Interpretation of *Macbeth* often concentrates on such issues as the fundamental cause and nature of the protagonist's fall and whether the fall leads toward self-knowledge. Making up our minds about these issues is an important step, obviously, in arriving at an overall understanding of the play.

No less important, however, is the need to imagine human will and desire on a truly challenging scale. The speaker in Denise Levertov's "The Dogwood" (p. 127) — the mother whose refrain is "Oh well" — is an entirely familiar person: somebody trying to claim a small bit of space and time to call her own and finding it hard to do so. The figures in tragedy make huge claims — aspire to take direct control of their existence - and they have a conception of personal significance and accountability that is unfamiliar to us. We sense their dimensions — their personal force, moral or amoral distinctiveness, imaginative range — in and through the lofty variousness of their language. The work of bringing them to life asks a certain height of us as readers.

And it demands, as every poem and every story demands, steady engagement with the movement of feeling and action from moment to moment, line to line. Putting *Macbeth* on in the theater of our minds means drawing close to the major people of the play. It means imagining minds that don't see themselves as controlled by "flaws," don't fully grasp the dimensions of their mistakes, indeed, don't know what the next instant will bring. Such minds have no choice, it seems, except to imagine themselves as rulers of themselves. They are open to possibility each step of the way, not locked into obedience to any outside theory about what a tragic hero may or may not do or be. It's this sense of personal empowerment and of openness, of meeting each new instant of life freshly, that we need to strive for in imagining what's going on, and in making notes on the action and feeling to be brought alive scene by scene.

A NOTE ON SHAKESPEARE'S THEATER

When the theather companies of Shakespeare's time weren't on the road, they performed in open-air playhouses within easy walking distance of London. The most famous of these was called the Globe; Shakespeare owned a one-eighth share of it. The building was round or polygonal in shape, about a third the size of a football field, and it consisted of three wooden galleries surrounding a yard in which a raised, forty-foot-wide platform — the stage — jutted out from the rear wall. Actors entered and exited from doors in this rear wall, behind which were their dressing rooms. In alcoves above the exit-entrance doors — the most expensive seats in the house — sat lords and ladies. Sometimes the alcove space was preempted for stage action, for example, when a balcony was required.

The Globe Theater seems to have had large double doors in the middle of the stage wall in addition to the doors through which actors entered. The space behind these center doors could be curtained off for use as an inner stage (it may have been used for the performance of the "play within the play" in *Hamlet*). The stage itself was equipped with a trapdoor (perhaps used, in performances of *Hamlet*, as Ophelia's grave). Costumes were lavish; plays were put on nearly every afternoon. In good weather, when a hit show was scheduled, the tiny amphitheater would be jammed with as many as 3,000 playgoers.

ASKING QUESTIONS ABOUT *MACBETH*

The three assignments in this chapter focus on three different scenes. I walk through the first assignment, providing reading notes and other materials and my own response. The second assignment provides some questions to stimulate your thinking, and the third assignment is followed by sample responses from students.

In working with any individual passage in a play, readers draw on their knowledge of other pertinent scenes as well as on a careful reading of the play as a whole. This means there is much to keep track of and consider, and the problem of how to hold the relevant details in mind needs to be directly addressed.

One way of handling the problem is suggested by the materials accompanying my response to the first assignment. These include, first, rough notes about the players' movements and gestures at this moment in the play and reminders of other moments in the play that seem relevant; and second, a list of key elements for close imagining that I drew up based on the rough reading notes. My response used these materials together with a series of decisions about the play as a whole — decisions about differences between characters and about the moral and other meanings of the differences. The point that counts is that the response began not with thought-out sentences and paragraphs but with quick, fragmentary observations about moment-to-moment events. Most people's early responses don't look like finished essays; they are more like lists of errands to be done — reminders of the variety of separate imaginative sectors that need to be scouted out and explored.

WILLIAM SHAKESPEARE   (1564–1616)
Macbeth

EDITED BY ALFRED HARBAGE

NAMES OF THE ACTORS

Duncan, *King of Scotland*

Malcolm
Donalbain } *his sons*

Macbeth
Banquo
Macduff
Lennox
Ross } *noblemen of Scotland*
Menteith
Angus
Caithness

Fleance, *son to Banquo*
Siward, *Earl of Northumberland*
Young Siward, *his son*
Seyton, *an officer attending on Macbeth*
Boy, *son to Macduff*
A Captain
An English Doctor
A Scottish Doctor
A Porter
An Old Man

Three Murderers	Hecate
Lady Macbeth	The Ghost of Banquo
Lady Macduff	Apparitions
A Gentlewoman, *attending on Lady*	Lords, Officers, Soldiers,
Macbeth	Messengers, Attendants
The Weird Sisters	

SCENE: *Scotland and England*

ACT I

SCENE I. *An open place*

Thunder and lightning. Enter three Witches.

1. Witch: When shall we three meet again
        In thunder, lightning, or in rain?
2. Witch: When the hurlyburly's done,
        When the battle's lost and won.
3. Witch: That will be ere the set of sun.   5
1. Witch: Where the place?
2. Witch: Upon the heath.
3. Witch: There to meet with Macbeth.
1. Witch: I come, Graymalkin!°
2. Witch: Paddock° calls.
3. Witch: Anon!°
All: Fair is foul, and foul is fair.   10
        Hover through the fog and filthy air.   *Exeunt.*

SCENE II. *A field near Forres*

*Alarum within. Enter King Duncan, Malcolm, Donalbain, Lennox, with Atten-
dants, meeting a bleeding Captain.*

King: What bloody man is that? He can report,
        As seemeth by his plight, of the revolt
        The newest state.
Malcolm: This is the sergeant°
        Who like a good and hardy soldier fought
        'Gainst my captivity. Hail, brave friend!   5

ACT I, SCENE I. 8 *Graymalkin:* Her familiar spirit, a gray cat.   9 *Paddock:* A toad; *Anon:* At
once.   SCENE II. 3 *sergeant:* So designated, apparently, as a staff-officer; he ranks as a
captain.

Say to the King the knowledge of the broil
As thou didst leave it.
Captain: Doubtful it stood,
As two spent swimmers that do cling together
And choke their art. The merciless Macdonwald
(Worthy to be a rebel, for to that   10
The multiplying villainies of nature
Do swarm upon him) from the Western Isles°
Of kerns° and gallowglasses° is supplied;
And Fortune, on his damned quarrel smiling,
Showed like a rebel's whore. But all's too weak: 15
For brave Macbeth (well he deserves that name),
Disdaining Fortune, with his brandished steel,
Which smoked with bloody execution,
Like valor's minion° carved out his passage
Till he faced the slave;   20
Which ne'er shook hands nor bade farewell to him
Till he unseamed him from the nave° to th' chops
And fixed his head upon our battlements.
King: O valiant cousin! worthy gentleman!
Captain: As whence the sun 'gins his reflection   25
Shipwracking storms and direful thunders break,
So from that spring whence comfort seemed to come
Discomfort swells. Mark, King of Scotland, mark.
No sooner justice had, with valor armed,
Compelled these skipping kerns to trust their heels   30
But the Norweyan lord, surveying vantage,°
With furbished arms and new supplies of men,
Began a fresh assault.
King: Dismayed not this
Our captains, Macbeth and Banquo?
Captain: Yes,
As sparrows eagles, or the hare the lion.   35
If I say sooth, I must report they were
As cannons overcharged with double cracks,°
So they doubly redoubled strokes upon the foe.
Except they meant to bathe in reeking wounds,
Or memorize another Golgotha,°   40

---

12 *Western Isles:* Hebrides (and Ireland?).   13 *kerns:* Irish bush-fighters; *gallowglasses:* Irish regulars, armored infantrymen.   19 *minion:* Darling.   22 *nave:* Navel.   31 *surveying vantage:* Seeing opportunity.   37 *cracks:* Explosives.   40 *memorize another Golgotha:* Make memorable as another "place of the dead."

   I cannot tell —
   But I am faint; my gashes cry for help.
King: So well thy words become thee as thy wounds,
   They smack of honor both. Go get him surgeons.

             Exit Captain, attended.

Enter Ross and Angus.

   Who comes here?
Malcolm: The worthy Thane° of Ross.   45
Lennox: What a haste looks through his eyes! So should he look
   That seems to° speak things strange.
Ross: God save the King!
King: Whence cam'st thou, worthy Thane?
Ross: From Fife, great King,
   Where the Norweyan banners flout the sky
   And fan our people cold.   50
   Norway himself, with terrible numbers,
   Assisted by that most disloyal traitor
   The Thane of Cawdor, began a dismal° conflict,
   Till that Bellona's° bridegroom, lapped in proof,°
   Confronted him with self-comparisons,°   55
   Point against point rebellious, arm 'gainst arm,
   Curbing his lavish spirit: and to conclude,
   The victory fell on us.
King: Great happiness!
Ross: That now
   Sweno, the Norways' king, craves composition;°
   Nor would we deign him burial of his men   60
   Till he disbursed, at Saint Colme's Inch,°
   Ten thousand dollars° to our general use.
King: No more that Thane of Cawdor shall deceive
   Our bosom interest.° Go pronounce his present death
   And with his former title greet Macbeth.   65
Ross: I'll see it done.
King: What he hath lost noble Macbeth hath won. *Exeunt.*

---

45 *Thane:* A Scottish lord. 47 *seems to:* Seems about to. 53 *dismal:* Ominous. 54 *Bellona:* Goddess of war; *lapped in proof:* Clad in proven armor. 55 *self-comparisons:* Cancelling powers. 59 *composition:* Terms of surrender. 61 *Inch:* Island. 62 *dollars:* Spanish or Dutch coins. 64 *bosom interest:* Heart's trust.

SCENE III. *A heath*

Thunder. Enter the three Witches.

1. Witch: Where hast thou been, sister?
2. Witch: Killing swine.
3. Witch: Sister, where thou?
1. Witch: A sailor's wife had chestnuts in her lap
 And mounched and mounched and mounched. "Give me,"
  quoth I.   5
 "Aroint thee,° witch!" the rump-fed ronyon° cries.
 Her husband's to Aleppo gone, master o' th' Tiger:
 But in a sieve I'll thither sail
 And, like a rat without a tail,
 I'll do, I'll do, and I'll do.   10
2. Witch: I'll give thee a wind.
1. Witch: Th' art kind.
3. Witch: And I another.
1. Witch: I myself have all the other,
 And the very ports they blow,°   15
 All the quarters that they know
 I' th' shipman's card.°
 I'll drain him dry as hay.
 Sleep shall neither night nor day
 Hang upon his penthouse lid.°   20
 He shall live a man forbid.°
 Weary sev' nights, nine times nine,
 Shall he dwindle, peak, and pine.
 Though his bark cannot be lost,
 Yet it shall be tempest-tost.   25
 Look what I have.
2. Witch: Show me, show me.
1. Witch: Here I have a pilot's thumb,
 Wracked as homeward he did come.

Drum within.

3. Witch: A drum, a drum!   30
 Macbeth doth come.
All: The weird° sisters, hand in hand,

SCENE III. 6 *Aroint thee:* Get thee gone; *rump-fed ronyon:* Fat-rumped scab.   15 *very ports they blow:* I.e., their power to blow ships to ports.   17 *card:* Compass card.   20 *penthouse lid:* Eyelid.   21 *forbid:* Accursed.   32 *weird:* Fate-serving.

Posters° of the sea and land,
Thus do go about, about,
Thrice to thine, and thrice to mine,   35
And thrice again, to make up nine.
Peace! The charm's wound up.

Enter Macbeth and Banquo.

Macbeth: So foul and fair a day I have not seen.
Banquo: How far is't called to Forres? What are these,
    So withered and so wild in their attire   40
    That look not like th' inhabitants o' th' earth
    And yet are on't? Live you, or are you aught
    That man may question?° You seem to understand me,
    By each at once her choppy° finger laying
    Upon her skinny lips. You should be women,   45
    And yet your beards forbid me to interpret
    That you are so.
Macbeth: Speak, if you can. What are you?
1. Witch: All hail, Macbeth! Hail to thee, Thane of Glamis!
2. Witch: All hail, Macbeth! Hail to thee, Thane of Cawdor!
3. Witch: All hail, Macbeth, that shalt be King hereafter!   50
Banquo: Good sir, why do you start and seem to fear
    Things that do sound so fair? I' th' name of truth,
    Are ye fantastical,° or that indeed
    Which outwardly ye show? My noble partner
    You greet with present grace° and great prediction   55
    Of noble having and of royal hope,
    That he seems rapt withal.° To me you speak not.
    If you can look into the seeds of time°
    And say which grain will grow and which will not,
    Speak then to me, who neither beg nor fear   60
    Your favors nor your hate.
1. Witch: Hail!
2. Witch: Hail!
3. Witch: Hail!
1. Witch: Lesser than Macbeth, and greater.   65
2. Witch: Not so happy,° yet much happier.
3. Witch: Thou shalt get° kings, though thou be none.
    So all hail, Macbeth and Banquo!

---

33 *Posters:* Swift travellers.   43 *question:* Confer with.   44 *choppy:* Chapped.   53 *fantastical:* Creatures of fantasy.   55 *grace:* Honor.   57 *rapt withal:* Spellbound at the thought.
58 *seeds of time:* Genesis of events.   66 *happy:* Fortunate.   67 *get:* Beget.

1. Witch: Banquo and Macbeth, all hail!
Macbeth: Stay, you imperfect° speakers, tell me more: 70
  By Sinel's° death I know I am Thane of Glamis,
  But how of Cawdor? The Thane of Cawdor lives,
  A prosperous gentleman; and to be King
  Stands not within the prospect of belief,
  No more than to be Cawdor. Say from whence 75
  You owe this strange intelligence, or why
  Upon this blasted heath you stop our way
  With such prophetic greeting. Speak, I charge you.

                                      Witches vanish.

Banquo: The earth hath bubbles as the water has,
  And these are of them. Whither are they vanished? 80
Macbeth: Into the air, and what seemed corporal° melted
  As breath into the wind. Would they had stayed!
Banquo: Were such things here as we do speak about?
  Or have we eaten on the insane° root
  That takes the reason prisoner? 85
Macbeth: Your children shall be kings.
Banquo: You shall be King.
Macbeth: And Thane of Cawdor too. Went it not so?
Banquo: To th' selfsame tune and words. Who's here?

Enter Ross and Angus.

Ross: The King hath happily received, Macbeth,
  The news of thy success; and when he reads°
  Thy personal venture in the rebels' fight, 90
  His wonders and his praises do contend
  Which should be thine or his.° Silenced with that,
  In viewing o'er the rest o' th' selfsame day,
  He finds thee in the stout Norweyan ranks, 95
  Nothing afeard of what thyself didst make,
  Strange images of death. As thick as tale°
  Came post with post,° and every one did bear
  Thy praises in his kingdom's great defense
  And poured them down before him.

---

70 *imperfect:* Incomplete.   71 *Sinel:* I.e., Macbeth's father.   81 *corporal:* Corporeal.   84 *insane:* Madness-inducing.   90 *reads:* Considers.   92–93 *His wonders . . . or his:* I.e., dumbstruck admiration makes him keep your praises to himself.   97 *thick as tale:* I.e., as fast as they can be counted.   98 *post with post:* Messenger after messenger.

Angus: We are sent   100
  To give thee from our royal master thanks;
  Only to herald thee into his sight,
  Not pay thee.
Ross: And for an earnest of a greater honor,
  He bade me, from him, call thee Thane of Cawdor;   105
  In which addition,° hail, most worthy Thane,
  For it is thine.
Banquo: What, can the devil speak true?
Macbeth: The Thane of Cawdor lives. Why do you dress me
  In borrowed robes?
Angus: Who was the Thane lives yet,
  But under heavy judgment bears that life   110
  Which he deserves to lose. Whether he was combined°
  With those of Norway, or did line° the rebel
  With hidden help and vantage,° or that with both
  He labored in his country's wrack, I know not;
  But treasons capital, confessed and proved,   115
  Have overthrown him.
Macbeth (aside):   Glamis, and Thane of Cawdor —
  The greatest is behind!°
  (*To Ross and Angus.*) Thanks for your pains.
  (*Aside to Banquo.*)
  Do you not hope your children shall be kings,
  When those that gave the Thane of Cawdor to me
  Promised no less to them?
Banquo (to Macbeth):   That, trusted home°   120
  Might yet enkindle you unto the crown,
  Besides the Thane of Cawdor. But 'tis strange:
  And oftentimes, to win us to our harm,
  The instruments of darkness tell us truths,
  Win us with honest trifles, to betray's   125
  In deepest consequence° —
  Cousins,° a word, I pray you.
Macbeth (aside):   Two truths are told,
  As happy prologues to the swelling act
  Of the imperial theme° — I thank you, gentlemen. —
  (*Aside.*)
  This supernatural soliciting°   130

---

106 *addition:* Title.   111 *combined:* Leagued.   112 *line:* Support.   113 *vantage:* Assistance.
117 *is behind:* Is to come.   120 *home:* All the way.   126 *deepest consequence:* I.e., in the vital
sequel.   127 *Cousins:* I.e., fellow lords.   128–129 *swelling act . . . imperial theme:* I.e., stately
drama of rise to sovereignty.   130 *soliciting:* Inviting, beckoning.

Cannot be ill, cannot be good. If ill,
Why hath it given me earnest of success,
Commencing in a truth? I am Thane of Cawdor.
If good, why do I yield to that suggestion
Whose horrid image doth unfix my hair   135
And make my seated° heart knock at my ribs
Against the use° of nature? Present fears
Are less than horrible imaginings.
My thought, whose murder yet is but fantastical,°
Shakes so my single° state of man that function°   140
Is smothered in surmise and nothing is
But what is not.
Banquo: Look how our partner's rapt.°
Macbeth (aside): If chance will have me King, why chance may
    crown me
Without my stir.
Banquo: New honors come upon him,
Like our strange° garments, cleave not to their mould   145
But with the aid of use.
Macbeth (aside):   Come what come may,
Time and the hour runs through the roughest day.
Banquo: Worthy Macbeth, we stay upon your leisure.
Macbeth: Give me your favor.° My dull brain was wrought
With things forgotten. Kind gentlemen, your pains   150
Are regist'red where every day I turn
The leaf to read them. Let us toward the King.
(Aside to Banquo.)
Think upon what hath chanced, and at more time,
The interim having weighed it, let us speak
Our free hearts° each to other.
Banquo.   Very gladly.   155
Macbeth: Till then, enough. — Come, friends.   *Exeunt.*

SCENE IV. *A field near Forres as before or a place in the palace itself*

Flourish. Enter King Duncan, Lennox, Malcolm, Donalbain, and Attendants.

King: Is execution done on Cawdor? Are not
    Those in commission° yet returned?

---

136 *seated:* Fixed.   137 *use:* Way.   139 *fantastical:* Imaginary.   140 *single:* Unaided, weak;
function: Normal powers.   142 *rapt:* Bemused.   145 *strange:* New.   149 *favor:* Pardon.
155 *Our free hearts:* Our thoughts freely.   SCENE IV. 2 *in commission:* Commissioned to carry
out the execution.

Malcolm: My liege,
They are not yet come back. But I have spoke
With one that saw him die; who did report
That very frankly he confessed his treasons,   5
Implored your Highness' pardon, and set forth
A deep repentance. Nothing in his life
Became him like the leaving it. He died
As one that had been studied° in his death
To throw away the dearest thing he owed°   10
As 'twere a careless trifle.
King: There's no art
To find the mind's construction in the face.
He was a gentleman on whom I built
An absolute trust.

Enter Macbeth, Banquo, Ross, and Angus.

                                   O worthiest cousin,
The sin of my ingratitude even now   15
Was heavy on me. Thou art so far before°
That swiftest wing of recompense is slow
To overtake thee. Would thou hadst less deserved,
That the proportion° both of thanks and payment
Might have been mine! Only I have left to say,   20
More is thy due than more than all can pay.
Macbeth: The service and the loyalty I owe,
In doing it pays itself. Your Highness' part
Is to receive our duties, and our duties
Are to your throne and state children and servants,   25
Which do but what they should by doing everything
Safe° toward your love and honor.
King: Welcome hither.
I have begun to plant° thee and will labor
To make thee full of growing. Noble Banquo,
That hast no less deserved nor must be known   30
No less to have done so, let me enfold thee
And hold thee to my heart.
Banquo: There if I grow,
The harvest is your own.
King: My plenteous joys,
Wanton° in fullness, seek to hide themselves

---

9 *studied:* Rehearsed.   10 *owed:* Owned.   16 *before:* Ahead in deserving.   19 *proportion:*
Preponderance.   27 *Safe:* Fitting.   28 *plant:* Nurture.   34 *Wanton:* Unrestrained.

In drops of sorrow. Sons, kinsmen, thanes,   35
And you whose places are the nearest, know
We will establish our estate upon
Our eldest, Malcolm, whom we name hereafter
The Prince of Cumberland; which honor must
Not unaccompanied invest him only,   40
But signs of nobleness, like stars, shall shine
On all deservers. From hence to Inverness,
And bind us further to you.
Macbeth: The rest is labor which is not used for you.
I'll be myself the harbinger, and make joyful   45
The hearing of my wife with your approach;
So, humbly take my leave.
King: My worthy Cawdor!
Macbeth (aside): The Prince of Cumberland — that is a step
On which I must fall down or else o'erleap,
For in my way it lies. Stars, hide your fires;   50
Let not light see my black and deep desires.
The eye wink at the hand;° yet let that be
Which the eye fears, when it is done, to see.   *Exit.*
King: True, worthy Banquo: he is full so valiant,
And in his commendations I am fed;   55
It is a banquet to me. Let's after him,
Whose care is gone before to bid us welcome.
It is a peerless kinsman.   *Flourish. Exeunt.*

SCENE V. *Within Macbeth's castle at Inverness*

Enter Macbeth's Wife, alone, with a letter.

Lady (reads): "They met me in the day of success; and I have
learned by the perfect'st report they have more in them than
mortal knowledge. When I burned in desire to question them
further, they made themselves air, into which they vanished.
Whiles I stood rapt in the wonder of it, came missives° from   5
the King, who all-hailed me Thane of Cawdor, by which title,
before, these weird sisters saluted me, and referred me to the
coming on of time with 'Hail, King that shalt be!' This have I
thought good to deliver thee, my dearest partner of greatness, that thou mightst not lose the dues of rejoicing by being   10

---

52 *wink at the hand:* Blind itself to what the hand does.   SCENE V. 5 *missives:* Messengers.

ignorant of what greatness is promised thee. Lay it to thy
heart, and farewell."

Glamis thou art, and Cawdor, and shalt be
What thou art promised. Yet do I fear thy nature.
It is too full o' th' milk of human kindness   15
To catch the nearest way. Thou wouldst be great,
Art not without ambition, but without
The illness° should attend it. What thou wouldst highly,
That wouldst thou holily; wouldst not play false,
And yet wouldst wrongly win. Thou'ldst have, great Glamis,   20
That which cries "Thus thou must do" if thou have it;
And that which rather thou dost fear to do
Than wishest should be undone. Hie thee hither,
That I may pour my spirits in thine ear
And chastise with the valor of my tongue   25
All that impedes thee from the golden round°
Which fate and metaphysical° aid doth seem
To have thee crowned withal.°

Enter Messenger.

                                                    What is your tidings?
Messenger: The King comes here to-night.
Lady: Thou'rt mad to say it!
    Is not thy master with him? who, were't so,   30
    Would have informed for preparation.
Messenger: So please you, it is true. Our Thane is coming.
    One of my fellows had the speed of him,
    Who, almost dead for breath,° had scarcely more
    Than would make up his message.
Lady: Give him tending;   35
    He brings great news.   *Exit Messenger.*
                            The raven himself is hoarse
    That croaks the fatal entrance of Duncan
    Under my battlements. Come, you spirits
    That tend on mortal° thoughts, unsex me here,
    And fill me from the crown to the toe top-full   40
    Of direst cruelty. Make thick my blood;
    Stop us th' access and passage to remorse,°

---

18 *illness:* Ruthlessness.   26 *round:* Crown.   27 *metaphysical:* Supernatural.   28 *withal:*
With.   34 *breath:* Want of breath.   39 *mortal:* Deadly.   42 *remorse:* Pity.

That no compunctious visitings of nature°
Shake my fell° purpose nor keep peace between
Th' effect and it.° Come to my woman's breasts   45
And take my milk for gall,° you murd'ring ministers,°
Wherever in your sightless° substances
You wait on° nature's mischief. Come, thick night,
And pall thee° in the dunnest° smoke of hell,
That my keen knife see not the wound it makes,   50
Nor heaven peep through the blanket of the dark
To cry "Hold, hold!"

Enter Macbeth.

Great Glamis! worthy Cawdor!
Greater than both, by the all-hail hereafter!
Thy letters have transported me beyond   55
This ignorant° present, and I feel now
The future in the instant.
Macbeth: My dearest love,
Duncan comes here to-night.
Lady: And when goes hence?
Macbeth: To-morrow, as he purposes.
Lady: O, never
Shall sun that morrow see!   60
Your face, my Thane, is as a book where men
May read strange matters. To beguile the time,°
Look like the time;° bear welcome in your eye,
Your hand, your tongue; look like th' innocent flower,
But be the serpent under't. He that's coming   65
Must be provided for; and you shall put
This night's great business into my dispatch,°
Which shall to all our nights and days to come
Give solely sovereign sway and masterdom.
Macbeth: We will speak further.
Lady: Only look up clear.°   70
To alter favor° ever is to fear.°
Leave all the rest to me.   *Exeunt.*

---

43 *nature:* Natural feeling.   44 *fell:* Fierce.   44–45 *keep peace . . . and it:* I.e., lull it from
achieving its end.   46 *for gall:* In exchange for gall; *ministers:* Agents.   47 *sightless:* Invisible.   48 *wait on:* Aid.   49 *pall thee:* Shroud thyself; *dunnest:* Darkest.   56 *ignorant:* I.e.,
ordinarily unaware.   62 *beguile the time:* Make sly use of the occasion.   63 *Look like the time:*
Play up to the occasion.   67 *dispatch:* Swift management.   70 *look up clear:* Appear untroubled.   71 *alter favor:* Change countenance; *fear:* Incur risk.

Scene VI. *At the portal of Inverness*

*Hautboys° and torches. Enter King Duncan, Malcolm, Donalbain, Banquo, Len-
nox, Macduff, Ross, Angus, and Attendants.*

King: This castle hath a pleasant seat.° The air
    Nimbly and sweetly recommends itself
    Unto our gentle° senses.
Banquo: This guest of summer,
    The temple-haunting° martlet,° does approve°
    By his loved mansionry° that the heaven's breath   5
    Smells wooingly here. No jutty,° frieze,
    Buttress, nor coign of vantage,° but this bird
    Hath made his pendent bed and procreant° cradle.
    Where they most breed and haunt, I have observed
    The air is delicate.

Enter Lady Macbeth.

King: See, see, our honored hostess!   10
    The love that follows us sometime is our trouble,
    Which still we thank as love.° Herein I teach you
    How you shall bid God 'ield us° for your pains
    And thank us for your trouble.
Lady: All our service
    In every point twice done, and then done double,   15
    Were poor and single business to contend
    Against those honors deep and broad wherewith
    Your Majesty loads our house. For those of old,
    And the late dignities heaped up to them,
    We rest your hermits.°
King: Where's the Thane of Cawdor?   20
    We coursed him at the heels and had a purpose
    To be his purveyor;° but he rides well,
    And his great love, sharp as his spur, hath holp him
    To his home before us. Fair and noble hostess,
    We are your guest to-night.

Scene VI. *Hautboys:* Oboes.   1 *seat:* Site.   3 *gentle:* Soothed.   4 *temple-haunting:* Nesting in
church spires; *martlet:* Martin, swallow; *approve:* Prove.   5 *loved mansionry:* Beloved nests.
6 *jutty:* Projection.   7 *coign of vantage:* Convenient corner.   8 *procreant:* Breeding.
11–12 *The love . . . as love:* The love that sometimes inconveniences us we still hold precious.
13 *God 'ield us:* God reward me.   20 *hermits:* Beadsmen.   22 *purveyor:* Advance agent of
supplies.

Lady: Your servants ever   25
Have theirs,° themselves, and what is theirs,° in compt,°
To make their audit at your Highness' pleasure,
Still° to return your own.
King: Give me your hand.
Conduct me to mine host; we love him highly.
And shall continue our graces towards him.   30
By your leave, hostess.   *Exeunt.*

SCENE VII. *The courtyard of Inverness from which open the chambers of the castle*

*Hautboys. Torches. Enter a Sewer,° and divers Servants with dishes and service
over the stage. Then enter Macbeth.*

Macbeth: If it were done° when 'tis done, then 'twere well
It were done quickly. If th' assassination
Could trammel up the consequence,° and catch
With his surcease° success,° that but this blow
Might be the be-all and the end-all -- ; here,   5
But here upon this bank and shoal of time,
We'ld jump° the life to come. But in these cases
We still have judgment here, that we but teach
Bloody instructions,° which, being taught, return
To plague th' inventor. This even-handed justice   10
Commends th' ingredience of our poisoned chalice
To our own lips. He's here in double trust:
First, as I am his kinsman and his subject,
Strong both against the deed; then, as his host,
Who should against his murderer shut the door,   15
Not bear the knife myself. Besides, this Duncan
Hath borne his faculties° so meek, hath been
So clear° in his great office, that his virtues
Will plead like angels, trumpet-tongued against
The deep damnation of his taking-off;   20
And pity, like a naked new-born babe
Striding the blast, or heaven's cherubin horsed
Upon the sightless couriers° of the air,

26 *Have theirs:* Have their servants; *what is theirs:* Their possessions; *in compt:* In trust.
28 *Still:* Always.   Scene VII. *Sewer:* Chief waiter.   1 *done:* Done with.   3 *trammel up the
consequence:* Enclose the consequences in a net.   4 *his surcease:* Its (the assassination's)
completion; *success:* All that follows.   7 *jump:* Risk.   9 *instructions:* Lessons.   17 *faculties:*
Powers.   18 *clear:* Untainted.   23 *sightless couriers:* Invisible coursers (the winds).

Shall blow the horrid deed in every eye
That tears shall drown the wind. I have no spur   25
To prick the sides of my intent, but only
Vaulting ambition, which o'erleaps itself
And falls on th' other —

Enter Lady Macbeth.

                                   How now? What news?
Lady: He has almost supped. Why have you left the chamber?
Macbeth: Hath he asked for me?
Lady: Know you not he has?   30
Macbeth: We will proceed no further in this business.
He hath honored me of late, and I have bought°
Golden opinions from all sorts of people,
Which would be worn now in their newest gloss,
Not cast aside so soon.
Lady: Was the hope drunk   35
Wherein you dressed yourself? Hath it slept since?
And wakes it now to look so green° and pale
At what it did so freely? From this time
Such I account thy love. Art thou afeard
To be the same in thine own act and valor   40
As thou art in desire? Wouldst thou have that
Which thou esteem'st the ornament of life,
And live a coward in thine own esteem,
Letting "I dare not" wait upon "I would,"
Like the poor cat i' th' adage?°
Macbeth: Prithee peace!   45
I dare do all that may become a man;
Who dares do more is none.
Lady: What beast was't then
That made you break° this enterprise to me?
When you durst do it, then you were a man;
And to be more than what you were, you would   50
Be so much more the man. Nor time nor place
Did then adhere,° and yet you would make both.
They have made themselves, and that their fitness° now
Does unmake you. I have given suck, and know
How tender 'tis to love the babe that milks me: 55

---

32 *bought:* Acquired.   37 *green:* Bilious.   45 *cat i' th' adage:* (Who wants the fish but doesn't
want to get its paws wet).   48 *break:* Broach.   52 *adhere:* Lend themselves to the occasion.
53 *that their fitness:* Their very fitness.

I would, while it was smiling in my face,
Have plucked my nipple from his boneless gums
And dashed the brains out, had I so sworn as you
Have done to this.
Macbeth: If we should fail?
Lady: We fail?
But screw your courage to the sticking place° 60
And we'll not fail. When Duncan is asleep
(Whereto the rather shall his day's hard journey
Soundly invite him), his two chamberlains
Will I with wine and wassail so convince°
That memory, the warder of the brain, 65
Shall be a fume, and the receipt° of reason
A limbeck° only. When in swinish sleep
Their drenchèd natures lies as in a death,
What cannot you and I perform upon
Th' unguarded Duncan? what not put upon 70
His spongy officers, who shall bear the guilt
Of our great quell?°
Macbeth: Bring forth men-children only;
For thy undaunted mettle° should compose
Nothing but males. Will it not be received,
When we have marked with blood those sleepy two 75
Of his own chamber and used their very daggers,
That they have done't?
Lady: Who dares receive it other,°
As we shall make our griefs and clamor roar
Upon his death?
Macbeth: I am settled, and bend up
Each corporal agent to this terrible feat. 80
Away, and mock° the time with fairest show;
False face must hide what the false heart doth know. *Exeunt.*

ACT II

Scene I. *The same*

Enter Banquo, and Fleance, with a torch before him.

---

60 *sticking place:* Notch (holding the string of a crossbow cranked taut for shooting). 64 *convince:* Overcome. 66 *receipt:* Container. 67 *limbeck:* Cap of a still (to which the fumes rise). 72 *quell:* Killing. 73 *mettle:* Vital substance. 77 *other:* Otherwise. 81 *mock:* Delude.

Banquo: How goes the night, boy?
Fleance: The moon is down; I have not heard the clock.
Banquo: And she goes down at twelve.
Fleance: I take't, 'tis later, sir.
Banquo: Hold, take my sword. There's husbandry° in heaven;
    Their candles are all out. Take thee that too.   5
    A heavy summons° lies like lead upon me,
    And yet I would not sleep. Merciful powers,
    Restrain in me the cursèd thoughts that nature
    Gives way to in repose.

Enter Macbeth, and a Servant with a torch.

                                Give me my sword!
    Who's there?   10
Macbeth: A friend.
Banquo: What, sir, not yet at rest? The King's abed.
    He hath been in unusual pleasure and
    Sent forth great largess to your offices.°
    This diamond he greets your wife withal   15
    By the name of most kind hostess, and shut up°
    In measureless content.
Macbeth: Being unprepared,
    Our will° became the servant to defect,°
    Which else should free have wrought.
Banquo: All's well.
    I dreamt last night of the three weird sisters.   20
    To you they have showed some truth.
Macbeth: I think not of them.
    Yet when we can entreat an hour to serve,
    We would spend it in some words upon that business,
    If you would grant the time.
Banquo: At your kind'st leisure.
Macbeth: If you shall cleave to my consent, when 'tis,°   25
    It shall make honor for you.
Banquo: So I lose none
    In seeking to augment it, but still keep
    My bosom franchised° and allegiance clear,
    I shall be counselled.°
Macbeth: Good repose the while.

ACT II, Scene I. 4 *husbandry:* Economy.   6 *summons:* Signal to sleep.   14 *largess to your offices:* Gratuities to your household departments.   16 *shut up:* Concluded.   18 *will:* Good will; *defect:* Deficient means.   25 *cleave . . . when 'tis:* Favor my cause at the proper time.   28 *franchised:* Free from guilt.   29 *counselled:* Open to persuasion.

Banquo: Thanks, sir. The like to you.   30

Exeunt Banquo and Fleance.

Macbeth: Go bid thy mistress, when my drink is ready,
She strike upon the bell. Get thee to bed.   *Exit Servant.*
Is this a dagger which I see before me,
The handle toward my hand? Come, let me clutch thee!
I have thee not, and yet I see thee still.   35
Art thou not, fatal vision, sensible
To feeling as to sight? or art thou but
A dagger of the mind, a false creation
Proceeding from the heat-oppressèd brain?
I see thee yet, in form as palpable   40
As this which now I draw.
Thou marshall'st me the way that I was going,
And such an instrument I was to use.
Mine eyes are made the fools o' th' other senses,
Or else worth all the rest. I see thee still,   45
And on thy blade and dudgeon° gouts° of blood,
Which was not so before. There's no such thing.
It is the bloody business which informs°
Thus to mine eyes. Now o'er the one half-world
Nature seems dead, and wicked dreams abuse°   50
The curtained sleep. Witchcraft celebrates
Pale Hecate's offerings;° and withered murder,
Alarumed° by his sentinel, the wolf,
Whose howl's his watch, thus with his stealthy pace,
With Tarquin's° ravishing strides, towards his design   55
Moves like a ghost. Thou sure and firm set earth,
Hear not my steps which way they walk, for fear
Thy very stones prate of my whereabout
And take the present horror from the time,
Which now suits with it.° Whiles I threat, he lives;   60
Words to the heat of deeds too cold breath gives.

A bell rings.

I go, and it is done. The bell invites me.
Hear it not, Duncan, for it is a knell
That summons thee to heaven, or to hell.   *Exit.*

---

46 *dudgeon:* Wooden hilt; *gouts:* Blobs.   48 *informs:* Creates impressions.   50 *abuse:* Deceive.   52 *Hecate's offerings:* Worship of Hecate (goddess of sorcery).   53 *Alarumed:* Given the signal.   55 *Tarquin:* Roman tyrant, ravisher of Lucrece.   59–60 *take . . . suits with it:* Delay, by prating, the commission of the deed at this suitably horrible moment (?), reduce, by breaking the silence, the suitable horror of this moment (?).

SCENE II

Enter Lady Macbeth.

Lady: That which hath made them drunk hath made me bold;
　　What hath quenched them hath given me fire. Hark! Peace!
　　It was the owl that shrieked, the fatal bellman
　　Which gives the stern'st good-night.° He is about it.
　　The doors are open, and the surfeited grooms　　　　　　　　5
　　Do mock their charge with snores. I have drugged their
　　　　possets,°
　　That death and nature do contend about them
　　Whether they live or die.
Macbeth (within):　　　　　Who's there? What, ho?
Lady: Alack, I am afraid they have awaked,
　　And 'tis not done! Th' attempt, and not the deed,　　　　　10
　　Confounds° us. Hark! I laid their daggers ready —
　　He could not miss 'em. Had he not resembled
　　My father as he slept, I had done't.

Enter Macbeth.

　　　　　　　　　　　　　　　My husband!
Macbeth: I have done the deed. Didst thou not hear a noise?
Lady: I heard the owl scream and the crickets cry.　　　　　15
　　Did not you speak?
Macbeth:　　　　When?
Lady:　　　　　　　Now.
Macbeth:　　　　　　　As I descended?
Lady: Ay.
Macbeth: Hark!
　　Who lies i' th' second chamber?
Lady:　　　　　　　Donalbain.
Macbeth: This is a sorry sight.　　　　　　　　　　　　　　20
Lady: A foolish thought, to say a sorry sight.
Macbeth: There's one did laugh in's sleep, and one cried
　　　"Murder!"
　　That° they did wake each other. I stood and heard them.
　　But they did say their prayers and addressed them
　　Again to sleep.
Lady:　　　　　There are two lodged together.　　　　　　　25

SCENE II. 3–4 *fatal bellman . . . good-night:* I.e., like the night-watch cry to felons scheduled for execution in the morning.　6 *possets:* Bedtime drinks.　11 *Confounds:* Ruins.　23 *That:* So that.

Macbeth: One cried "God bless us!" and "Amen!" the other,
     As they had seen me with these hangman's hands,°
     List'ning their fear. I could not say "Amen!"
     When they did say "God bless us!"
Lady: Consider it not so deeply.
Macbeth: But wherefore could not I pronounce "Amen"?   30
     I had most need of blessing, and "Amen"
     Stuck in my throat.
Lady: These deeds must be thought
     After these ways; so, it will make us mad.
Macbeth: Methought I heard a voice cry "Sleep no more!
     Macbeth does murder sleep" — the innocent sleep,   35
     Sleep that knits up the ravelled sleave° of care,
     The death of each day's life, sore labor's bath,
     Balm of hurt minds, great nature's second course,°
     Chief nourisher in life's feast.
Lady: What do you mean?
Macbeth: Still it cried "Sleep no more!" to all the house;   40
     "Glamis hath murdered sleep, and therefore Cawdor
     Shall sleep no more, Macbeth shall sleep no more."
Lady: Who was it that thus cried? Why, worthy Thane,
     You do unbend° your noble strength to think
     So brainsickly of things. Go get some water   45
     And wash this filthy witness° from your hand.
     Why did you bring these daggers from the place?
     They must lie there: go carry them and smear
     The sleepy grooms with blood.
Macbeth: I'll go no more.
     I am afraid to think what I have done;   50
     Look on't again I dare not.
Lady: Infirm of purpose!
     Give me the daggers. The sleeping and the dead
     Are but as pictures.° 'Tis the eye of childhood
     That fears a painted devil. If he do bleed,
     I'll gild° the faces of the grooms withal,   55
     For it must seem their guilt.   *Exit.*

Knock within.

Macbeth: Whence is that knocking?
     How is't with me when every noise appals me?

27 *hangman's hands:* I.e., bloody, like an executioner's.   36 *knits up . . . sleave:* Smooths out
the tangled skein.   38 *second course:* I.e., sleep, after food.   44 *unbend:* Relax.   46 *witness:*
Evidence.   53 *as pictures:* Like pictures (since without motion).   55 *gild:* Paint.

What hands are here? Ha! they pluck out mine eyes.
Will all great Neptune's ocean wash this blood   60
Clear from my hand? No, this my hand will rather
The multitudinous seas incarnadine,°
Making the green one° red.

Enter Lady Macbeth.

Lady: My hands are of your color, but I shame
To wear a heart so white. (*Knock.*) I hear a knocking   65
At the south entry. Retire we to our chamber.
A little water clears us of this deed.
How easy is it then! Your constancy
Hath left you unattended.°

Knock.

                   Hark! more knocking.
Get on your nightgown,° lest occasion call us   70
And show us to be watchers.° Be not lost
So poorly° in your thoughts.
Macbeth: To know my deed, 'twere best not know myself.

Knock.

Wake Duncan with thy knocking! I would thou couldst.

                          Exeunt.

SCENE III

Enter a Porter. Knocking within.

Porter: Here's a knocking indeed! If a man were porter of hell
gate, he should have old° turning the key. (*Knock.*) Knock,
knock, knock. Who's there, i' th' name of Belzebub? Here's a
farmer° that hanged himself on th' expectation of plenty.°
Come in time! Have napkins enow° about you; here you'll   5
sweat for't. (*Knock.*) Knock, knock. Who's there, in th' other

---

62 *incarnadine:* Redden.   63 *one:* Uniformly.   69 *unattended:* Deserted.   70 *nightgown:*
Dressing gown.   71 *watchers:* I.e., awake.   72 *poorly:* Weakly.   SCENE III. 2 *old:* Much.
4 *farmer:* I.e., one who has hoarded crops.   4 *expectation of plenty:* Prospect of a crop surplus
(which will lower prices).   5 *enow:* Enough.

devil's name? Faith, here's an equivocator,° that could swear in both the scales against either scale; who committed trea-son enough for God's sake, yet could not equivocate to heaven. O come in, equivocator. (*Knock*.) Knock, knock, 10 knock. Who's there? Faith, here's an English tailor come hither for stealing out of a French hose.° Come in, tailor. Here you may roast your goose.° (*Knock*.) Knock, knock. Never at quiet! What are you? — But this place is too cold for hell. I'll devil-porter it no further. I had thought to have let in 15 some of all professions that go the primrose way to th' everlasting bonfire. (*Knock*.) Anon, anon! (*Opens the way*.) I pray you remember the porter.

Enter Macduff and Lennox.

Macduff: Was it so late, friend, ere you went to bed,
That you do lie so late? 20
Porter: Faith, sir, we were carousing till the second cock;° and drink, sir, is a great provoker of three things.
Macduff: What three things does drink especially provoke?
Porter: Marry, sir, nose-painting, sleep, and urine. Lechery, sir, it provokes, and unprovokes: it provokes the desire, but it takes 25 away the performance. Therefore much drink may be said to be an equivocator with lechery: it makes him, and it mars him; it sets him on, and it takes him off; it persuades him, and disheartens him; makes him stand to,° and not stand to; in conclusion, equivocates him in a sleep, and, giving him the 30 lie, leaves him.
Macduff: I believe drink gave thee the lie° last night.
Porter: That it did, sir, i' the very throat on me; but I requited him for his lie; and, I think, being too strong for him, though he took up my legs sometime, yet I made a shift to cast°him. 35
Macduff: Is thy master stirring?

Enter Macbeth.

Our knocking has awaked him: here he comes.
Lennox: Good morrow, noble sir.
Macbeth: Good morrow, both.

---

7 *equivocator:* (Usually considered an allusion to the Jesuits tried for political conspiracy). 12 *French hose:* Close-fitting breeches.   13 *roast your goose:* Heat your pressing-iron.   21 *second cock:* Second cockcrow (3 A.M.).   29 *stand to:* Stand his guard.   32 *gave thee the lie:* Called you a liar (i.e., unable to stand).   35 *cast:* Throw.

Macduff: Is the King stirring, worthy Thane?
Macbeth: Not yet.
Macduff: He did command me to call timely°on him;   40
    I have almost slipped° the hour.
Macbeth: I'll bring you to him.
Macduff: I know this is a joyful trouble to you;
    But yet 'tis one.
Macbeth: The labor we delight in physics pain.°
    This is the door.
Macduff: I'll make so bold to call,   45
    For 'tis my limited° service.   *Exit Macduff.*
Lennox: Goes the King hence to-day?
Macbeth: He does; he did appoint so.
Lennox: The night has been unruly. Where we lay,
    Our chimneys were blown down; and, as they say,
    Lamentings heard i' th' air, strange screams of death,   50
    And prophesying, with accents terrible,
    Of dire combustion° and confused events
    New hatched to th' woeful time. The obscure bird°
    Clamored the livelong night. Some say the earth
    Was feverous and did shake.
Macbeth: 'Twas a rough night.   55
Lennox: My young remembrance cannot parallel
    A fellow to it.

Enter Macduff.

Macduff: O horror, horror, horror! Tongue nor heart
    Cannot conceive nor name thee!
Macbeth and Lennox: What's the matter?
Macduff: Confusion° now hath made his masterpiece: 60
    Most sacrilegious murder hath broke ope
    The Lord's anointed temple and stole thence
    The life o' th' building!
Macbeth: What is't you say? the life?
Lennox: Mean you his Majesty?
Macduff: Approach the chamber and destroy your sight   65
    With a new Gorgon.° Do not bid me speak.
    See, and then speak yourselves.   *Exeunt Macbeth and Lennox.*
                        Awake, awake!

---

40 *timely:* Early.   41 *slipped:* Let slip.   44 *physics pain:* Cures trouble.   46 *limited:* Appointed.   52 *combustion:* Tumult.   53 *obscure bird:* I.e., the owl.   60 *Confusion:* Destruction.   66 *a new Gorgon:* A new Medusa (capable of turning the beholder's eyes to stone).

Ring the alarum bell! Murder and treason!
Banquo and Donalbain! Malcolm, awake!
Shake off this downy sleep, death's counterfeit,   70
And look on death itself. Up, up, and see
The great doom's image.° Malcolm! Banquo!
As from your graves rise up and walk like sprites
To countenance° this horror. Ring the bell!

Bell rings. Enter Lady Macbeth.

Lady: What's the business,   75
That such a hideous trumpet calls to parley
The sleepers of the house? Speak, speak!
Macduff: O gentle lady,
'Tis not for you to hear what I can speak:
The repetition° in a woman's ear
Would murder as it fell.

Enter Banquo.

      O Banquo, Banquo,   80
Our royal master's murdered!
Lady: Woe, alas!
What, in our house?
Banquo: Too cruel anywhere.
Dear Duff, I prithee contradict thyself
And say it is not so.

Enter Macbeth, Lennox, and Ross.

Macbeth: Had I but died an hour before this chance,   85
I had lived a blessed time; for from this instant
There's nothing serious in mortality:°
All is but toys.° Renown and grace is dead,
The wine of life is drawn, and the mere lees°
Is left this vault° to brag of.   90

Enter Malcolm and Donalbain.

Donalbain: What is amiss?
Macbeth: You are, and do not know't.
The spring, the head, the fountain of your blood
Is stopped, the very source of it is stopped.

---

72 *great doom's image:* Resemblance of the day of judgment.   74 *countenance:* Appear in
keeping with.   79 *repetition:* Recital.   87 *serious in mortality:* Worthwhile in human life.
88 *toys:* Trifles.   89 *lees:* Dregs.   90 *vault:* Wine-vault.

Macduff: Your royal father's murdered.
Malcolm: O, by whom?
Lennox: Those of his chamber, as it seemed, had done't.   95
    Their hands and faces were all badged° with blood;
    So were their daggers, which unwiped we found
    Upon their pillows. They stared and were distracted.
    No man's life was to be trusted with them.
Macbeth: O, yet I do repent me of my fury   100
    That I did kill them.
Macduff: Wherefore did you so?
Macbeth: Who can be wise, amazed,° temp'rate and furious,
    Loyal and neutral, in a moment? No man.
    The expedition° of my violent love
    Outrun the pauser, reason. Here lay Duncan,   105
    His silver skin laced with his golden blood;
    And his gashed stabs looked like a breach in nature
    For ruin's wasteful entrance: there, the murderers,
    Steeped in the colors of their trade, their daggers
    Unmannerly breeched with gore.° Who could refrain°   110
    That had a heart to love, and in that heart
    Courage to make 's love known?
Lady: Help me hence, ho!
Macduff: Look to° the lady.
Malcolm (aside to Donalbain): Why do we hold our tongues,
    That most may claim this argument for ours?°   115
Donalbain (to Malcolm): What should be spoken here,
    Where our fate, hid in an auger hole,°
    May rush and seize us? Let's away:
    Our tears are not yet brewed.
Malcolm (to Donalbain): Nor our strong sorrow   120
    Upon the foot of motion.°
Banquo: Look to the lady.

                                        Lady Macbeth is carried out.

And when we have our naked frailties hid,°
That suffer in exposure, let us meet
And question° this most bloody piece of work,
To know it further. Fears and scruples° shake us.   125

96 *badged:* Marked.   102 *amazed:* Confused.   104 *expedition:* Haste.   110 *Unmannerly* . . .
gore: Crudely wearing breeches of blood; *refrain:* Restrain oneself.   113 *Look to:* Look after.
115 *argument for ours:* Topic as chiefly our concern.   117 *auger hole:* I.e., any tiny cranny.
121 *Upon the foot of motion:* Yet in motion.   122 *frailties hid:* Bodies clothed.   124 *question:*
Discuss.   125 *scruples:* Doubts.

In the great hand of God I stand, and thence
Against the undivulged pretense° I fight
Of treasonous malice.
Macduff: And so do I.
All: So all.
Macbeth: Let's briefly put on manly readiness
And meet i' th' hall together.
All: Well contented.   130

> *Exeunt all but Malcolm and Donalbain.*

Malcolm: What will you do? Let's not consort with them.
To show an unfelt sorrow is an office
Which the false man does easy. I'll to England.
Donalbain: To Ireland I. Our separated fortune
Shall keep us both the safer. Where we are   135
There's daggers in men's smiles; the near° in blood,
The nearer bloody.
Malcolm: This murderous shaft that's shot
Hath not yet lighted, and our safest way
Is to avoid the aim. Therefore to horse,   140
And let us not be dainty of leave-taking
But shift away. There's warrant° in that theft
Which steals itself when there's no mercy left.   *Exeunt.*

SCENE IV. *Outside Inverness Castle*

Enter Ross with an Old Man.

Old Man: Threescore and ten I can remember well;
Within the volume of which time I have seen
Hours dreadful and things strange, but this sore night
Hath trifled former knowings.°
Ross: Ha, good father,
Thou seest the heavens, as troubled with man's act,°   5
Threatens his bloody stage. By th' clock 'tis day,
And yet dark night strangles the travelling lamp.°
Is't night's predominance,° or the day's shame,
That darkness does the face of earth entomb
When living light should kiss it?

---

127 *undivulged pretense:* Secret stratagems.   136 *near:* Nearer.   142 *warrant:* Justification.
SCENE IV. 4 *trifled former knowings:* Made former experiences seem trifling.   5 *man's act:* The
human drama.   7 *travelling lamp:* I.e., of Phoebus, the sun.   8 *predominance:* Supernatural
ascendancy.

Old Man: 'Tis unnatural,   10
  Even like the deed that's done. On Tuesday last
  A falcon, tow'ring° in her pride of place,
  Was by a mousing° owl hawked at° and killed.
Ross: And Duncan's horses (a thing most strange and certain°),
  Beauteous and swift, the minions° of their race,   15
  Turned wild in nature, broke their stalls, flung out,°
  Contending 'gainst obedience, as they would make
  War with mankind.
Old Man: 'Tis said they eat° each other.
Ross: They did so, to th' amazement of mine eyes
  That looked upon't.

Enter Macduff.

                                  Here comes the good Macduff.   20
  How goes the world, sir, now?
Macduff: Why, see you not?
Ross: Is't known who did this more than bloody deed?
Macduff: Those that Macbeth hath slain.
Ross: Alas the day,
  What good could they pretend?°
Macduff: They were suborned.°
  Malcolm and Donalbain, the King's two sons,   25
  Are stol'n away and fled, which puts upon them
  Suspicion of the deed.
Ross: 'Gainst nature still.
  Thriftless° ambition, that will ravin° up
  Thine own live's means! Then 'tis most like
  The sovereignty will fall upon Macbeth.   30
Macduff: He is already named, and gone to Scone
  To be invested.°
Ross: Where is Duncan's body?
Macduff: Carried to Colmekill,
  The sacred storehouse of his predecessors
  And guardian of their bones.
Ross: Will you to Scone?   35
Macduff: No, cousin, I'll to Fife.
Ross: Well, I will thither.

---

12 *tow'ring:* Soaring.   13 *mousing:* I.e., ordinarily preying on mice; *hawked at:* Swooped upon.
14 *certain:* Significant.   15 *minions:* Darlings.   16 *flung out:* Lunged about.   18 *eat:* Ate.
24 *pretend:* Expect; *suborned:* Bribed.   28 *Thriftless:* Wasteful; *ravin up:* Bolt, swallow.
32 *invested:* Crowned.

Macduff: Well, may you see things well done there. Adieu,
    Lest our old robes sit easier than our new!
Ross: Farewell, father.
Old Man: God's benison° go with you, and with those   40
    That would make good of bad, and friends of foes.

                                                    Exeunt omnes.

ACT III

Scene I. *Within the royal palace (at Forres)*

Enter Banquo.

Banquo: Thou hast it now — King, Cawdor, Glamis, all,
    As the weird women promised; and I fear
    Thou play'dst most foully° for't. Yet it was said
    It should not stand° in thy posterity,
    But that myself should be the root and father   5
    Of many kings. If there come truth from them
    (As upon thee, Macbeth, their speeches shine°),
    Why, by the verities on thee made good,
    May they not be my oracles as well
    And set me up in hope? But hush, no more!   10

*Sennet° sounded. Enter Macbeth as King, Lady Macbeth, Lennox, Ross, Lords,
and Attendants.*

Macbeth: Here's our chief guest.
Lady: If he had been forgotten,
    It had been as a gap in our great feast,
    And all-thing° unbecoming.
Macbeth: To-night we hold a solemn° supper, sir,
    And I'll request your presence.
Banquo: Let your Highness   15
    Command upon me, to the which my duties
    Are with a most indissoluble tie
    For ever knit.
Macbeth: Ride you this afternoon?
Banquo: Ay, my good lord.
Macbeth: We should have else desired your good advice   20

---

40 *benison:* Blessing.   ACT III, Scene I. 3 *foully:* Cheatingly.   4 *stand:* Continue as a legacy.
7 *shine:* Are brilliantly substantiated.   *Sennet:* Trumpet salute.   13 *all-thing:* Altogether.
14 *solemn:* State.

(Which still° hath been both grave and prosperous°)
In this day's council; but we'll take to-morrow.
Is't far you ride?
Banquo: As far, my lord, as will fill up the time
    'Twixt this and supper. Go not my horse the better,°   25
    I must become a borrower of° the night
    For a dark hour or twain.
Macbeth: Fail not our feast.
Banquo: My lord, I will not.
Macbeth: We hear our bloody cousins are bestowed
    In England and in Ireland, not confessing   30
    Their cruel parricide, filling their hearers
    With strange invention.° But of that to-morrow,
    When therewithal we shall have cause of state
    Craving us jointly.° Hie you to horse. Adieu,
    Till you return at night. Goes Fleance with you?   35
Banquo: Ay, my good lord. Our time does call upon's.
Macbeth: I wish your horses swift and sure of foot,
    And so I do commend you to their backs.
    Farewell.   *Exit Banquo.*
    Let every man be master of his time   40
    Till seven at night. To make society
    The sweeter welcome, we will keep ourself
    Till supper time alone. While° then, God be with you!

                            Exeunt Lords and others.

    Sirrah,° a word with you. Attend° those men
    Our pleasure?   45
Servant: They are, my lord, without the palace gate.
Macbeth: Bring them before us.   *Exit Servant.*
    To be thus is nothing; but° to be safely thus —
    Our fears in Banquo° stick deep,°
    And in his royalty of nature reigns that   50
    Which would be° feared. 'Tis much he dares;
    And to that dauntless temper of his mind
    He hath a wisdom that doth guide his valor
    To act in safety. There is none but he

---

21 *still:* Always; *prosperous:* Profitable.   25 *Go not my horse the better:* I.e., unless my horse goes
faster than anticipated.   26 *borrower of:* I.e., borrower of time from.   32 *invention:* Falsehoods.   33–34 *cause . . . jointly:* State business requiring our joint attention.   43 *While:*
Until.   44 *Sirrah:* Form used in addressing inferiors; *Attend:* Await.   48 *but:* Unless.   49 *in
Banquo:* About Banquo; *stick deep:* Are deeply imbedded in me.   51 *would be:* Deserves to be.

Whose being I do fear; and under him   55
My genius is rebuked,° as it is said
Mark Antony's was by Caesar. He chid the sisters
When first they put the name of King upon me,
And bade them speak to him. Then, prophet-like,
They hailed him father to a line of kings.   60
Upon my head they placed a fruitless crown
And put a barren sceptre in my gripe,°
Thence to be wrenched with an unlineal hand,
No son of mine succeeding. If 't be so,
For Banquo's issue have I filed° my mind;   65
For them the gracious Duncan have I murdered;
Put rancors° in the vessel of my peace
Only for them, and mine eternal jewel°
Given to the common enemy of man°
To make them kings — the seeds of Banquo kings.   70
Rather than so, come, Fate, into the list,°
And champion me to th' utterance!° Who's there?

Enter Servant and two Murderers.

Now go to the door and stay there till we call.   *Exit Servant.*
Was it not yesterday we spoke together?
Murderers: It was, so please your Highness.
Macbeth: Well then, now   75
Have you considered of my speeches? Know
That it was he, in the times past, which held you
So under fortune,° which you thought had been
Our innocent self. This I made good to you
In our last conference, passed in probation° with you   80
How you were borne in hand,° how crossed;° the instruments;°
Who wrought with them; and all things else that might
To half a soul° and to a notion° crazed
Say "Thus did Banquo."
1. Murderer: You made it known to us.
Macbeth: I did so; and went further, which is now   85
Our point of° second meeting. Do you find

---

56 *genius is rebuked:* Controlling spirit is daunted.   62 *gripe:* Grasp.   65 *filed:* Defiled.
67 *rancors:* Bitter enmities.   68 *jewel:* Soul.   69 *common enemy of man:* I.e., Satan.   71 *list:*
Lists, field of combat.   72 *champion . . . utterance:* Engage with me to the death.   78 *under
fortune:* Out of favor with fortune.   80 *passed in probation:* Reviewed the evidence.
81 *borne in hand:* Manipulated; *crossed:* Thwarted; *instruments:* Agents.   83 *half a soul:* A
halfwit; *notion:* Mind.   86 *Our point of:* The point of our.

Your patience so predominant in your nature
That you can let this go? Are you so gospelled°
To pray for this good man and for his issue,
Whose heavy hand hath bowed you to the grave   90
And beggared yours for ever?
1. Murderer: We are men, my liege.
Macbeth: Ay, in the catalogue° ye go for men,
    As hounds and greyhounds, mongrels, spaniels, curs,
    Shoughs,° water-rugs,° and demi-wolves are clept°
    All by the name of dogs. The valued file°   95
    Distinguishes the swift, the slow, the subtle,
    The housekeeper,° the hunter, every one
    According to the gift which bounteous nature
    Hath in him closed,° whereby he does receive
    Particular addition, from the bill°   100
    That writes them all alike; and so of men.
    Now, if you have a station in the file,
    Not i' th' worst rank of manhood, say't;
    And I will put that business in your bosoms°
    Whose execution takes your enemy off,   105
    Grapples you to the heart and love of us,
    Who wear our health but sickly in his life,
    Which in his death were perfect.
2. Murderer: I am one, my liege,
    Whom the vile blows and buffets of the world
    Have so incensed that I am reckless what   110
    I do to spite the world.
1. Murderer: And I another,
    So weary with disasters, tugged with fortune,
    That I would set° my life on any chance
    To mend it or be rid on't.
Macbeth: Both of you
    Know Banquo was your enemy.
Murderers: True, my lord.   115
Macbeth: So is he mine, and in such bloody distance°
    That every minute of his being thrusts
    Against my near'st of life;° and though I could
    With barefaced power sweep him from my sight

---

88 *gospelled:* Tamed by gospel precepts.   92 *catalogue:* Inventory, classification.
94 *Shoughs:* Shaggy pet dogs; *water-rugs:* Long-haired water-dogs; *clept:* Named.   95 *valued file:*
Classification according to valuable traits.   97 *housekeeper:* Watchdog.   99 *closed:* Invested.
100 *addition, from the bill:* Distinction, contrary to the listing.   104 *in your bosoms:* In your
trust.   113 *set:* Risk.   116 *distance:* Enmity.   118 *near'st of life:* Vital parts.

And bid my will avouch° it, yet I must not,　　　　120
For° certain friends that are both his and mine,
Whose loves I may not drop, but wail° his fall
Who I myself struck down. And thence it is
That I to your assistance do make love,
Masking the business from the common eye　　　125
For sundry weighty reasons.
2. Murderer:　　　　　　　　We shall, my lord,
Perform what you command us.
1. Murderer:　　　　　　　Though our lives —
Macbeth: Your spirits shine through you. Within this hour at most
I will advise you where to plant yourselves,
Acquaint you with the perfect spy o' th' time°　　　130
The moment on't, for't must be done to-night
And something from the palace (always thought°
That I require a clearness°); and with him,
To leave no rubs° nor botches in the work,
Fleance his son, that keeps him company,　　　135
Whose absence is no less material to me
Than is his father's, must embrace the fate
Of that dark hour. Resolve yourselves apart;
I'll come to you anon.
Murderers:　　　　　　　We are resolved, my lord.
Macbeth: I'll call upon you straight. Abide within.　　　140
It is concluded. Banquo, thy soul's flight,
If it find heaven, must find it out to-night.　　　*Exeunt.*

SCENE II. *The same*

Enter Macbeth's Lady and a Servant.

Lady: Is Banquo gone from court?
Servant: Ay, madam, but returns again to-night.
Lady: Say to the King I would attend his leisure
For a few words.
Servant:　　　　　　Madam, I will.　　　　　*Exit.*
Lady:　　　　　　　Naught's had, all's spent,
Where our desire is got without content.　　　5
'Tis safer to be that which we destroy
Than by destruction dwell in doubtful joy.

---

120 *avouch:* Justify.　　121 *For:* Because of.　　122 *wail:* I must wail.　　130 *with the perfect spy o'
th' time:* By means of a perfect look-out (?), with precise timing (?).　　132 *thought:* Borne in
mind.　　133 *clearness:* Alibi.　　134 *rubs:* Defects.

Enter Macbeth.

    How now, my lord? Why do you keep alone,
    Of sorriest° fancies your companions making,
    Using those thoughts which should indeed have died   10
    With them they think on? Things without all remedy°
    Should be without regard. What's done is done.
Macbeth: We have scorched° the snake, not killed it.
    She'll close° and be herself, whilst our poor malice°
    Remains in danger of her former tooth.   15
    But let the frame of things disjoint,° both the worlds° suffer,
    Ere we will eat our meal in fear, and sleep
    In the affliction of these terrible dreams
    That shake us nightly. Better be with the dead,
    Whom we, to gain our peace, have sent to peace,   20
    Than on the torture° of the mind to lie
    In restless ecstasy.° Duncan is in his grave;
    After life's fitful fever he sleeps well.
    Treason has done his worst: nor steel nor poison,
    Malice domestic,° foreign levy, nothing,   25
    Can touch him further.
Lady: Come on.
    Gentle my lord, sleek o'er your rugged looks;
    Be bright and jovial among your guests to-night.
Macbeth: So shall I, love; and so, I pray, be you.
    Let your remembrance° apply to Banquo;   30
    Present him eminence° both with eye and tongue:
    Unsafe the while, that we must lave°
    Our honors in these flattering streams
    And make our faces vizards° to our hearts,
    Disguising what they are.
Lady: You must leave this.   35
Macbeth: O, full of scorpions is my mind, dear wife!
    Thou know'st that Banquo, and his Fleance, lives.
Lady: But in them Nature's copy's° not eterne.
Macbeth: There's comfort yet; they are assailable.
    Then be thou jocund. Ere the bat hath flown   40

Scene II. 9 *sorriest:* Most comtemptible.   11 *all remedy:* Any form of remedy.   13 *scorched:*
Slashed.   14 *close:* Heal; *poor malice:* Feeble opposition.   16 *frame of things disjoint:* Structure of the universe collapse; *both the worlds:* I.e., heaven and earth.   21 *torture:* Rack.
22 *ecstasy:* Frenzy.   25 *Malice domestic:* Civil war.   30 *remembrance:* I.e., awareness of the
necessity.   31 *Present him eminence:* Exalt him.   32 *lave:* Dip.   34 *vizards:* Masks.
38 *Nature's copy:* Nature's copyhold, lease on life.

His cloistered flight, ere to black Hecate's summons
The shard-borne° beetle with his drowsy hums
Hath rung night's yawning peal, there shall be done
A deed of dreadful note.
Lady: What's to be done?
Macbeth: Be innocent of the knowledge, dearest chuck,   45
Till thou applaud the deed. Come, seeling° night,
Scarf up° the tender eye of pitiful day,
And with thy bloody and invisible hand
Cancel and tear to pieces that great bond°
Which keeps me pale. Light thickens, and the crow   50
Makes wing to th' rooky° wood.
Good things of day begin to droop and drowse,
Whiles night's black agents to their preys do rouse.
Thou marvell'st at my words, but hold thee still;
Things bad begun make strong themselves by ill.   55
So prithee go with me.   *Exeunt.*

SCENE III. *An approach to the palace*

Enter three Murderers.

1. Murderer: But who did bid thee join with us?
3. Murderer: Macbeth.
2. Murderer: He needs not our mistrust,° since he delivers
Our offices° and what we have to do
To the direction just.
1. Murderer: Then stand with us.
The west yet glimmers with some streaks of day.   5
Now spurs the lated° traveller apace
To gain the timely inn, and near approaches
The subject of our watch.
3. Murderer: Hark, I hear horses.
Banquo (within): Give us a light there, ho!
2. Murderer: Then 'tis he: the rest
That are within the note of expectation°   10
Already are i' th' court.
1. Murderer: His horses go about.

---

42 *shard-borne:* Borne on scaly wings.   46 *seeling:* Sewing together the eyelids (from fal-
conry).   47 *Scarf up:* Blindfold.   49 *great bond:* I.e., Banquo's lease on life (with suggestion
also of the bond of human feeling).   51 *rooky:* Harboring rooks.   SCENE III. 2 *He needs not
our mistrust:* I.e., we need not mistrust this man.   3 *offices:* Duties.   6 *lated:* Belated.
10 *within the note of expectation:* On the list of those expected (invited).

3. Murderer: Almost a mile; but he does usually,
So all men do, from hence to th' palace gate
Make it their walk.

Enter Banquo and Fleance, with a torch.

2. Murderer: A light, a light!
3. Murderer: 'Tis he.
1. Murderer: Stand to 't.   15
Banquo: It will be rain to-night.
1. Murderer: Let it come down!
Banquo: O, treachery! Fly, good Fleance, fly, fly, fly!   *Exit Fleance.*
Thou mayst revenge — O slave!

Banquo slain.

3. Murderer: Who did strike out the light?
1. Murderer: Was 't not the way?°
3. Murderer: There's but one down: the son is fled.   20
2. Murderer: We have lost best half of our affair.
1. Murderer: Well, let's away, and say how much is done.   *Exeunt.*

SCENE IV. *The hall of the palace*

Banquet prepared. Enter Macbeth, Lady Macbeth, Ross, Lennox, Lords, and Attendants.

Macbeth: You know your own degrees° — sit down:
At first and last the hearty welcome.
Lords: Thanks to your Majesty.
Macbeth: Ourself will mingle with society°
And play the humble host.   5
Our hostess keeps her state,° but in best time
We will require her welcome.
Lady: Pronounce it for me, sir, to all our friends,
For my heart speaks they are welcome.

Enter First Murderer.

Macbeth: See, they encounter° thee with their hearts' thanks.   10
Both sides are even. Here I'll sit i' th' midst.
Be large in mirth; anon we'll drink a measure
The table round.

---

19 *Was't not the way:* I.e., was it not the right thing to do.   SCENE IV. 1 *degrees:* Relative rank, order of precedence.   4 *society:* The company.   6 *keeps her state:* Remains seated in her chair of state.   10 *encounter:* Greet.

Goes to Murderer.

> There's blood upon thy face.
> **Murderer:**   'Tis Banquo's then.
> **Macbeth:** 'Tis better thee without than he within.   15
> Is he dispatched?
> **Murderer:**   My lord, his throat is cut:
> That I did for him.
> **Macbeth:**   Thou are the best o' th' cut-throats.
> Yet he's good that did the like for Fleance:
> If thou didst it, thou art the nonpareil.
> **Murderer:** Most royal sir, Fleance is 'scaped.   20
> **Macbeth (aside):** Then comes my fit again. I had else been
>   perfect;°
> Whole as the marble, founded° as the rock,
> As broad and general° as the casing° air.
> But now I am cabined, cribbed,° confined, bound in
> To saucy° doubts and fears. — But Banquo's safe?   25
> **Murderer:** Ay, my good lord. Safe in a ditch he bides,
> With twenty trenchèd° gashes on his head,
> The least a death to nature.
> **Macbeth:**   Thanks for that —

Aside.

> There the grown serpent lies; the worm° that's fled
> Hath nature that in time will venom breed,   30
> No teeth for th' present. — Get thee gone. To-morrow
> We'll hear ourselves° again.   *Exit Murderer.*
> **Lady:**   My royal lord,
> You do not give the cheer.° The feast is sold°
> That is not often vouched,° while 'tis a-making,
> 'Tis given with welcome. To feed were best at home;°   35
> From thence, the sauce to meat° is ceremony:
> Meeting were bare° without it.

Enter the Ghost of Banquo, and sits in Macbeth's place.

> **Macbeth:**   Sweet remembrancer!°

---

21 *perfect:* Sound of health.   22 *founded:* Solidly based.   23 *broad and general:* Unconfined; *casing:* Enveloping.   24 *cribbed:* Boxed in.   25 *saucy:* Insolent.   27 *trenchèd:* Deep, trench-like.   29 *worm:* Serpent.   32 *hear ourselves:* Confer.   33 *cheer:* Tokens of convivial hospitality; *sold:* I.e., not freely given.   34 *vouched:* Sworn.   35 *To feed . . . home:* I.e., mere eating is best done at home.   36 *meat:* Food.   37 *bare:* Barren, pointless; *remembrancer:* Prompter.

Now good digestion wait on appetite,
And health on both!

Lennox: May't please your Highness sit.

Macbeth: Here had we now our country's honor roofed   40
Were the graced person of our Banquo present —
Who may I rather challenge° for unkindness
Than pity for mischance!

Ross: His absence, sir
Lays blame upon his promise. Please't your Highness
To grace us with your royal company?   45

Macbeth: The table's full.

Lennox: Here is a place reserved, sir.

Macbeth: Where?

Lennox: Here, my good lord. What is't that moves your Highness?

Macbeth: Which of you have done this?

Lords: What, my good lord?

Macbeth: Thou canst not say I did it. Never shake   50
Thy gory locks at me.

Ross: Gentlemen, rise. His Highness is not well.

Lady: Sit, worthy friends. My lord is often thus,
And hath been from his youth. Pray you keep seat.
The fit is momentary; upon a thought   55
He will again be well. If much you note him,
You shall offend him and extend his passion.°
Feed, and regard him not. — Are you a man?

Macbeth: Ay, and a bold one, that dare look on that
Which might appal the devil.

Lady: O proper stuff!   60
This is the very painting of your fear.
This is the air-drawn° dagger which you said
Led you to Duncan. O, these flaws° and starts
(Impostors to true fear°) would well become
A woman's story at a winter's fire,   65
Authorized° by her grandam. Shame itself!
Why do you make such faces? When all's done,
You look but on a stool.

Macbeth: Prithee see there!
Behold! Look! Lo! — How say you?

---

42 *Who may . . . challenge:* Whom I hope I may reprove.   57 *extend his passion:* Prolong his seizure.   62 *air-drawn:* Fashioned of air.   63 *flaws:* Outbursts.   64 *Impostors to true fear:* I.e., because they are authentic signs of false or unjustified fear.   66 *Authorized:* Sanctioned.

Why, what care I? If thou canst nod, speak too.   70
If charnel houses and our graves must send
Those that we bury back, our monuments°
Shall be the maws of kites.°   *Exit Ghost.*
Lady: What, quite unmanned in folly?
Macbeth: If I stand here, I saw him.
Lady: Fie, for shame!
Macbeth: Blood hath been shed ere now, i' th' olden time,   75
Ere humane statute purged the gentle weal;°
Ay, and since too, murders have been performed
Too terrible for the ear. The time has been
That, when the brains were out, the man would die,
And there an end. But now they rise again,   80
With twenty mortal murders on their crowns,°
And push us from our stools. This is more strange
Than such a murder is.
Lady: My worthy lord,
Your noble friends do lack you.
Macbeth: I do forget.
Do not muse at me, my most worthy friends: 85
I have a strange infirmity, which is nothing
To those that know me. Come, love and health to all!
Then I'll sit down. Give me some wine, fill full.

Enter Ghost.

I drink to th' general joy o' th' whole table,
And to our dear friend Banquo, whom we miss.   90
Would he were here! To all, and him, we thirst,°
And all to all.°
Lords: Our duties, and the pledge.
Macbeth: Avaunt, and quit my sight! Let the earth hide thee!
Thy bones are marrowless, thy blood is cold;
Thou hast no speculation° in those eyes   95
Which thou dost glare with!
Lady: Think of this, good peers,
But as a thing of custom. 'Tis no other.
Only it spoils the pleasure of the time.
Macbeth: What man dare, I dare.

---

72 *monuments:* I.e., our only tombs.   73 *maws of kites:* Bellies of ravens.   76 *purged the gentle
weal:* I.e., purged the state of savagery.   81 *murders on their crowns:* Murderous gashes on
their heads.   91 *thirst:* Are eager to drink.   92 *all to all:* Let everyone drink to everyone.
95 *speculation:* Intelligence, power of rational observation.

Approach thou like the rugged Russian bear,   100
The armed rhinoceros, or th' Hyrcan° tiger;
Take any shape but that, and my firm nerves
Shall never tremble. Or be alive again
And dare me to the desert° with thy sword.
If trembling I inhabit° then, protest me   105
The baby of a girl.° Hence, horrible shadow
Unreal mock'ry, hence!   *Exit Ghost.*
        Why, so; being gone,
I am a man again. Pray you sit still.
Lady: You have displaced the mirth, broke the good meeting
    With most admired° disorder.
Macbeth: Can such things be,   110
And overcome us° like a summer's cloud
Without our special wonder? You make me strange
Even to the disposition that I owe,°
When now I think you can behold such sights
And keep the natural ruby of your cheeks   115
When mine is blanched° with fear.
Ross: What sights, my lord?
Lady: I pray you speak not: he grows worse and worse;
    Question enrages him. At once, good night.
    Stand not upon the order of your going,
    But go at once.
Lennox: Good night and better health   120
    Attend his Majesty.
Lady: A kind good night to all.   *Exeunt Lords.*
Macbeth: It will have blood, they say: blood will have blood.
    Stones have been known to move and trees to speak;
    Augures° and understood relations° have
    By maggot-pies° and choughs° and rooks brought forth   125
    The secret'st man of blood. What is the night?
Lady: Almost at odds with morning, which is which.
Macbeth: How say'st thou, that Macduff denies his person
    At our great bidding?
Lady: Did you send to him, sir?
Macbeth: I hear it by the way,° but I will send.   130

---

101 *Hyrcan:* From Hyrcania, anciently a region near the Caspian Sea.   104 *the desert:* A
solitary place.   105 *If trembling I inhabit:* If I tremble.   106 *The baby of a girl:* A baby girl.
110 *admired:* Wondered at.   111 *overcome us:* Come over us.   112–113 *You make . . . I owe:*
You oust me from my proper role (as a brave man).   116 *blanched:* Made pale.
124 *Augures:* Auguries; *relations:* Utterances.   125 *maggot-pies:* Magpies; *choughs:* Jackdaws
(capable of "utterances," as are magpies and rooks).   130 *by the way:* Casually.

There's not a one of them but in his house
I keep a servant fee'd.° I will to-morrow
(And betimes° I will) to the weird sisters.
More shall they speak, for now I am bent° to know
By the worst means the worst. For mine own good   135
All causes shall give way. I am in blood
Stepped in so far that, should I wade no more,
Returning were as tedious as go o'er.
Strange things I have in head, that will to hand,
Which must be acted ere they may be scanned.°   140
Lady: You lack the season° of all natures, sleep.
Macbeth: Come, we'll to sleep. My strange and self-abuse°
Is the initiate fear° that wants hard use.°
We are yet but young in deed.   *Exeunt.*

SCENE V.° *An open place*

Thunder. Enter the three Witches, meeting Hecate.

1. Witch: Why, how now, Hecate? You look angerly.
Hecate: Have I not reason, beldams° as you are,
Saucy and overbold? How did you dare
To trade and traffic with Macbeth
In riddles and affairs of death;   5
And I, the mistress of your charms,
The close° contriver of all harms,
Was never called to bear my part
Or show the glory of our art?
And, which is worse, all you have done   10
Hath been but for a wayward son,
Spiteful and wrathful, who, as others do,
Loves for his own ends, not for you.
But make amends now: get you gone
And at the pit of Acheron°   15
Meet me i' th' morning. Thither he
Will come to know his destiny.
Your vessels and your spells provide,
Your charms and everything beside.

132 *fee'd:* Paid to spy.   133 *betimes:* Speedily.   134 *bent:* Inclined, determined.   140 *ere they may be scanned:* I.e., without being closely studied.   141 *season:* Seasoning, preservative.   142 *self-abuse:* Delusion.   143 *initiate fear:* Beginner's fear; *wants hard use:* Lacks toughening practice.   SCENE V. An interpolated scene, by a different author.   2 *beldams:* Old crones.   7 *close:* Secret.   15 *Acheron:* A river of Hades.

I am for th' air. This night I'll spend   20
Unto a dismal and a fatal end.
Great business must be wrought ere noon.
Upon the corner of the moon
There hangs a vap'rous drop profound;°
I'll catch it ere it come to ground: 25
And that, distilled by magic sleights,°
Shall raise such artificial sprites°
As by the strength of their illusion
Shall draw him on to his confusion.
He shall spurn fate, scorn death, and bear   30
His hopes 'bove wisdom, grace, and fear:
And you all know security°
Is mortals' chiefest enemy.

Music, and a song.

Hark! I am called. My little spirit, see,
Sits in a foggy cloud and stays for me.   *Exit.* 35

Sing within, "Come away, come away," &c.

1. Witch: Come, let's make haste: she'll soon be back again. *Exeunt.*

SCENE VI. *Any meeting place in Scotland*

Enter Lennox and another Lord.

Lennox: My former speeches° have but hit° your thoughts,
Which can interpret farther.° Only I say
Things have been strangely borne. The gracious Duncan
Was pitied of Macbeth. Marry, he was dead.
And the right valiant Banquo walked too late;   5
Whom, you may say (if't please you) Fleance killed,
For Fleance fled. Men must not walk too late.
Who cannot want the thought° how monstrous
It was for Malcolm and for Donalbain
To kill their gracious father? Damned fact,°   10
How it did grieve Macbeth! Did he not straight,
In pious rage, the two delinquents tear

24 *profound:* Weighty.   26 *sleights:* Devices.   27 *artificial sprites:* Spirits created by magic
arts.   32 *security:* Over-confidence.   SCENE VI. 1 *My former speeches:* What I have just said;
hit: Matched.   2 *interpret farther:* Draw further conclusions.   8 *cannot want the thought:* Can
avoid thinking.   10 *fact:* Deed.

That were the slaves of drink and thralls° of sleep?
Was not that nobly done? Ay, and wisely too,
For 'twould have angered any heart alive   15
To hear the men deny't. So that I say
He has borne° all things well; and I do think
That, had he Duncan's sons under his key
(As, an't° please heaven, he shall not), they should find
What 'twere to kill a father. So should Fleance.   20
But peace! for from broad words,° and 'cause he failed
His presence at the tyrant's feast, I hear
Macduff lives in disgrace. Sir, can you tell
Where he bestows himself?
Lord: The son of Duncan,
From whom this tyrant holds the due of birth,°   25
Lives in the English court, and is received
Of the most pious Edward with such grace
That the malevolence of fortune nothing
Takes from his high respect.° Thither Macduff
Is gone to pray the holy King upon his aid°   30
To wake° Northumberland° and warlike Siward;
That by the help of these (with Him above
To ratify the work) we may again
Give to our tables meat, sleep to our nights,
Free from our feasts and banquets bloody knives,   35
Do faithful homage and receive free° honors —
All which we pine for now. And this report
Hath so exasperate the King that he
Prepares for some attempt of war.
Lennox: Sent he to Macduff?
Lord: He did; and with an absolute "Sir, not I,"   40
The cloudy° messenger turns me his back
And hums, as who should say, "You'll rue the time
That clogs° me with this answer."
Lennox: And that well might
Advise him to a caution t' hold what distance
His wisdom can provide.° Some holy angel   45
Fly to the court of England and unfold

---

13 *thralls:* Slaves.   17 *borne:* Carried off.   19 *an't:* If it.   21 *from broad words:* Through
plain speaking.   25 *due of birth:* Birthright.   29 *his high respect:* High respect for him.
30 *upon his aid:* Upon Malcolm's behalf.   31 *wake:* Arouse; *Northumberland:* English county
bordering Scotland.   36 *free:* Untainted.   41 *cloudy:* Angry.   43 *clogs:* Encumbers.
44–45 *Advise him . . . can provide:* Warn him to keep at as safe a distance as he can devise.

His message ere he come, that a swift blessing
May soon return to this our suffering country
Under a hand accursed!
Lord: I'll send my prayers with him. *Exeunt.*

ACT IV

Scene I. *A cave* °

Thunder. Enter the three Witches.

1. Witch: Thrice the brinded° cat hath mewed.
2. Witch: Thrice, and once the hedge-pig whined.
3. Witch: Harpier° cries. — 'Tis time, 'tis time!
1. Witch: Round about the cauldron go;
    In the poisoned entrails throw.   5
    Toad, that under cold stone
    Days and nights has thirty-one
    Swelt'red venom, sleeping got,°
    Boil thou first i' th' charmèd pot.
All: Double, double, toil and trouble,   10
    Fire burn and cauldron bubble.
2. Witch: Fillet of a fenny° snake,
    In the cauldron boil and bake;
    Eye of newt, and toe of frog,
    Wool of bat, and tongue of dog,   15
    Adder's fork, and blindworm's° sting,
    Lizard's leg, and howlet's wing —
    For a charm of pow'rful trouble
    Like a hell-broth boil and bubble.
All: Double, double, toil and trouble,   20
    Fire burn and cauldron bubble.
3. Witch: Scale of dragon, tooth of wolf,
    Witch's mummy,° maw and gulf°
    Of the ravined° salt-sea shark,
    Root of hemlock digged i' th' dark,   25
    Liver of blaspheming Jew,
    Gall of goat, and slips of yew

ACT IV, Scene I. Cf. III.v.15. 1 *brinded:* Brindled, striped.   3 *Harpier:* Name of familiar spirit, suggestive of harpy.   8 *Swelt'red venom, sleeping got:* Exuded venom formed while sleeping. 12 *fenny:* Swamp.   16 *blindworm:* A lizard, popularly supposed poisonous. 23 *mummy:* Mummified flesh; *maw and gulf:* Stomach and gullet.   24 *ravined:* Insatiable.

Slivered in the moon's eclipse,
Nose of Turk, and Tartar's lips,
Finger of birth-strangled babe   30
Ditch-delivered by a drab°
Make the gruel thick and slab.°
Add thereto a tiger's chaudron°
Forth' ingredience of our cauldron.
All: Double, double, toil and trouble,   35
Fire burn and cauldron bubble.
2. Witch: Cool it with a baboon's blood,
Then the charm is firm and good.

Enter Hecate and the other three Witches.°

Hecate: O, well done! I commend your pains,
And every one shall share i' th' gains.   40
And now about the cauldron sing
Like elves and fairies in a ring,
Enchanting all that you put in.

Music and a song, "Black spirits," &c.°
                                            Exeunt Hecate and singers.

2. Witch: By° the pricking of my thumbs,
Something wicked this way comes.   45
Open locks,
Whoever knocks!

Enter Macbeth.

Macbeth: How now, you secret, black, and midnight hags,
What is't you do?
All: A deed without a name.
Macbeth: I conjure you by that which you profess,   50
Howe'er you come to know it, answer me.
Though you untie the winds and let them fight
Against the churches, though the yesty° waves
Confound° and swallow navigation up,
Though bladed corn be lodged° and trees blown down,   55
Though castles topple on their warders' heads,
Though palaces and pyramids do slope°

---

31 *drab:* Harlot.   32 *slab:* Sticky.   33 *chaudron:* Guts.   *Enter . . . Witches:* An interpolation.
Music . . . &c.: A. interpolation.   44 *By:* I.e., I know by.   53 *yesty:* Yeasty, foamy.   54 *Confound:* Destroy.   55 *bladed corn be lodged:* Ripe grain be beaten to earth.   57 *slope:* Incline.

Their heads to their foundations, though the treasure
Of Nature's germains° tumble all together
Even till destruction sicken,° answer me   60
To what I ask you.
1. Witch: Speak.
2. Witch: Demand.
3. Witch: We'll answer.
1. Witch: Say if th' hadst rather hear it from our mouths
    Or from our masters.
Macbeth: Call 'em. Let me see 'em.
1. Witch: Pour in sow's blood, that hath eaten
    Her nine farrow;° grease that's sweaten   65
    From the murderer's gibbet throw
    Into the flame.
All: Come, high or low,
    Thyself and office° deftly show!

Thunder. First Apparition, an Armed Head.

Macbeth: Tell me, thou unknown power —
1. Witch: He knows thy thought:
    Hear his speech, but say thou naught.   70
1. Apparition: Macbeth, Macbeth, Macbeth, beware Macduff!
    Beware the Thane of Fife! Dismiss me. — Enough.

                                                He descends.

Macbeth: Whate'er thou art, for thy good caution thanks:
    Thou has harped° my fear aright. But one word more —
1. Witch: He will not be commanded. Here's another,   75
    More potent than the first.

Thunder. Second Apparition, a Bloody Child.

2. Apparition: Macbeth, Macbeth, Macbeth —
Macbeth: Had I three ears, I'ld hear thee.
2. Apparition: Be bloody, bold, and resolute! Laugh to scorn
    The pow'r of man, for none of woman born   80
    Shall harm Macbeth.   *Descends.*
Macbeth: Then live, Macduff, — what need I fear of thee?
    But yet I'll make assurance double sure
    And take a bond of° fate. Thou shalt not live;

---

59 *Nature's germains:* Seeds of creation.   60 *sicken:* Shall surfeit.   65 *nine farrow:* Litter of
nine.   68 *office:* Function.   74 *harped:* Hit the tune of.   84 *take a bond of:* Secure a
guarantee from.

That I may tell pale-hearted fear it lies   85
And sleep in spite of thunder.

Thunder. Third Apparition, a Child Crowned, with a tree in his hand.

                    What is this
That rises like the issue of a king
And wears upon his baby-brow the round°
And top of sovereignty?
All: Listen, but speak not to't.
3. Apparition: Be lion-mettled, proud, and take no care   90
Who chafes, who frets, or where conspirers are!
Macbeth shall never vanquished be until
Great Birnam Wood to high Dunsinane Hill
Shall come against him.   *Descends.*
Macbeth: That will never be.
Who can impress° the forest, bid the tree   95
Unfix his earth-bound root? Sweet bodements,° good!
Rebellious dead rise never till the Wood
Of Birnam rise, and our high-placed Macbeth
Shall live the lease of nature,° pay his breath
To time and mortal custom.° Yet my heart   100
Throbs to know one thing. Tell me, if your art
Can tell so much: Shall Banquo's issue° ever
Reign in this kingdom?
All: Seek to know no more.
Macbeth: I will be satisfied. Deny me this,
And an eternal curse fall on you! Let me know.   105
Why sinks that cauldron? and what noise° is this?

Hautboys.

1. Witch: Show!
2. Witch: Show!
3. Witch: Show!
All: Show his eyes, and grieve his heart!   110
Come like shadows, so depart!

A show of eight Kings and Banquo, last King with a glass in his hand.

Macbeth: Thou art too like the spirit of Banquo. Down!
Thy crown does sear mine eyeballs. And thy hair,

---

88 *round:* Crown.   95 *impress:* Conscript.   96 *bodements:* Prophecies.   99 *lease of nature:*
I.e., the full life-span.   100 *mortal custom:* Normal death.   102 *issue:* Offspring.   106 *noise:*
Music.

Thou other gold-bound brow, is like the first.
A third is like the former. Filthy hags,   115
Why do you show me this? A fourth? Start,° eyes!
What, will the line stretch out to th' crack of doom?
Another yet? A seventh? I'll see no more.
And yet the eighth appears, who bears a glass
Which shows me many more; and some I see   120
That twofold balls and treble sceptres° carry.
Horrible sight! Now I see 'tis true;
For the blood-boltered° Banquo smiles upon me
And points at them for his. What? Is this so?
1. Witch: Ay, sir, all this is so. But why   125
    Stands Macbeth thus amazedly?
    Come, sisters, cheer we up his sprites°
    And show the best of our delights.
    I'll charm the air to give a sound
    While you perform your antic round,°   130
    That this great king may kindly say
    Our duties did his welcome pay.°

              Music. The Witches dance, and vanish.

Macbeth: Where are they? Gone? Let this pernicious hour
    Stand aye accursèd in the calendar!
    Come in, without there!

Enter Lennox.

Lennox: What's your Grace's will?   135
Macbeth: Saw you the weird sisters?
Lennox: No, my lord.
Macbeth: Came they not by you?
Lennox: No indeed, my lord.
Macbeth: Infected be the air whereon they ride,
    And damned all those that trust them! I did hear
    The galloping of horse. Who was't came by?   140
Lennox: 'Tis two or three, my lord, that bring you word
    Macduff is fled to England.
Macbeth: Fled to England?
Lennox: Ay, my good lord.

---

116 *Start:* Bulge.   121 *twofold balls and treble sceptres:* English coronation insignia.
123 *blood-boltered:* Matted with blood.   125–132 *Ay, sir . . . pay:* An interpolation.
127 *sprites:* Spirits.   130 *antic round:* Grotesque circular dance.

Macbeth (aside): Time, thou anticipat'st° my dread exploits.
The flighty° purpose never is o'ertook   145
Unless the deed go with it. From this moment
The very firstlings of my heart shall be
The firstlings of my hand.° And even now,
To crown my thoughts with acts, be it thought and done:
The castle of Macduff I will surprise,   150
Seize upon Fife, give to th' edge o' th' sword
His wife, his babes, and all unfortunate souls
That trace° him in his line.° No boasting like a fool:
This deed I'll do before this purpose cool.
But no more sights! — Where are these gentlemen?   155
Come, bring me where they are.   *Exeunt.*

SCENE II. *Within the castle at Fife*

Enter Macduff's Wife, her Son, and Ross.

Wife: What had he done to make him fly the land?
Ross: You must have patience,° madam.
Wife: He had none.
His flight was madness. When our actions do not,
Our fears do make us traitors.°
Ross: You know not
Whether it was his wisdom or his fear.   5
Wife: Wisdom? To leave his wife, to leave his babes,
His mansion and his titles in a place
From whence himself does fly? He loves us not,
He wants° the natural touch. For the poor wren
(The most diminutive of birds) will fight,   10
Her young ones in her nest, against the owl.
All is the fear and nothing is the love,
As little is the wisdom, where the flight
So runs against all reason.
Ross: My dearest coz,°
I pray you school yourself. But for your husband,   15
He is noble, wise, judicious, and best knows
The fits o' th' season.° I dare not speak much further,
But cruel are the times when we are traitors

---

144 *anticipat'st:* Forestall.   145 *flighty:* Fleeting.   147–148 *firstling . . . my hand:* I.e., I shall
act at the moment I feel the first impulse.   153 *trace:* Follow; *line:* Family line.   Scene II. 2
patience: Self-control.   4 *traitors:* I.e., traitors to ourselves.   9 *wants:* Lacks.   14 *coz:*
Cousin, kinswoman.   17 *fits o' th' season:* Present disorders.

And do not know ourselves;° when we hold rumor
From what we fear,° yet know not what we fear   20
But float upon a wild and violent sea
Each way and none. I take my leave of you.
Shall not be long but I'll be here again.
Things at the worst will cease,° or else climb upward
To what they were before. — My pretty cousin,   25
Blessing upon you!
Wife: Fathered he is, and yet he's fatherless.
Ross: I am so much a fool, should I stay longer
It would be my° disgrace and your discomfort.
I take my leave at once.   *Exit.*
Wife: Sirrah, your father's dead;   30
And what will you do now? How will you live?
Son: As birds do, mother.
Wife: What, with worms and flies?
Son: With what I get, I mean; and so do they.
Wife: Poor bird! thou'dst never fear the net nor lime,°
The pitfall nor the gin.°   35
Son: Why should I, mother? Poor birds they are not set for.
My father is not dead for all your saying.
Wife: Yes, he is dead. How wilt thou do for a father?
Son: Nay, how will you do for a husband?
Wife: Why, I can buy me twenty at any market.   40
Son: Then you'll buy 'em to sell° again.
Wife: Thou speak'st with all thy wit; and yet, i' faith,
With wit enough for thee.°
Son: Was my father a traitor, mother?
Wife: Ay, that he was!   45
Son: What is a traitor?
Wife: Why, one that swears and lies.
Son: And be all traitors that do so?
Wife: Every one that does so is a traitor and must be hanged.
Son: And must they all be hanged that swear and lie?   50
Wife: Every one.
Son: Who must hang them?

---

19 *know ourselves:* Know ourselves to be so.   19–20 *hold rumor . . . we fear:* Are credulous in
accordance with our fears.   24 *will cease:* I.e., must cease descending.   29 *would be my:*
Would be to my (i.e., his weeping).   34 *lime:* Birdlime.   35 *gin:* Trap.   41 *sell:* Betray.
42–43 *Thou speak'st . . . for thee:* I.e., you use all the intelligence you have, and it is quite
enough.

Wife: Why, the honest men.
Son: Then the liars and swearers are fools, for there are liars and
   swearers enow° to beat the honest men and hang up them.   55
Wife: Now God help thee, poor monkey! But how wilt thou do for
   a father?
Son: If he were dead, you'ld weep for him. If you would not, it
   were a good sign that I should quickly have a new father.
Wife: Poor prattler, how thou talk'st!   60

Enter a Messenger.

Messenger: Bless you, fair dame! I am not to you known,
   Though in your state of honor I am perfect.°
   I doubt° some danger does approach you nearly.
   If you will take a homely° man's advice,
   Be not found here. Hence with your little ones!   65
   To fright you thus methinks I am too savage;
   To do worse to you were fell cruelty,
   Which is too nigh your person.° Heaven preserve you!
   I dare abide no longer.   *Exit.*
Wife: Whither should I fly?
   I have done no harm. But I remember now   70
   I am in this earthly world, where to do harm
   Is often laudable, to do good sometime
   Accounted dangerous folly. Why then, alas,
   Do I put up that womanly defense
   To say I have done no harm?

Enter Murderers.

               What are these faces?   75
Murderer: Where is your husband?
Wife: I hope in no place so unsanctified
   Where such as thou mayst find him.
Murderer: He's a traitor.
Son: Thou liest, thou shag-eared° villain!
Murderer: What, you egg!

Stabs him.

---

55 *enow:* Enough.   62 *in your state . . . perfect:* I am informed of your noble identity.   63 *doubt:*
Fear.   64 *homely:* Plain.   67–68 *To do worse . . . your person:* I.e., not to frighten you were to
do worse, expose you to that fierce cruelty which is impending.   79 *shag-eared:* I.e., with
shaggy hair falling about the ears.

Young fry° of treachery!
Son: He has killed me, mother.   80
Run away, I pray you!

Dies.   *Exit Wife, crying "Murder!"*
                                                      pursued by Murderers.

SCENE III. *The grounds of the King's palace in England*

Enter Malcolm and Macduff.

Malcolm: Let us seek out some desolate shade, and there
     Weep our sad bosoms empty.
Macduff: Let us rather
     Hold fast the mortal° sword and, like good men,
     Bestride° our downfall'n birthdom.° Each new morn
     New widows howl, new orphans cry, new sorrows   5
     Strike heaven on the face, that it resounds
     As if it felt with Scotland and yelled out
     Like syllable of dolor.°
Malcolm: What I believe, I'll wail;
     What know, believe; and what I can redress,
     As I shall find the time to friend,° I will.   10
     What you have spoke, it may be so perchance.
     This tyrant, whose sole name° blisters our tongues,
     Was once thought honest; you have loved him well;
     He hath not touched you yet. I am young;° but something
     You may deserve of him through me, and wisdom°   15
     To offer up a weak, poor, innocent lamb
     T' appease an angry god.
Macduff: I am not treacherous.
Malcolm: But Macbeth is.
     A good and virtuous nature may recoil
     In an imperial charge.° But I shall crave your pardon.   20
     That which you are, my thoughts cannot transpose:°
     Angels are bright still though the brightest° fell;
     Though all things foul would wear the brows of grace,
     Yet grace must still look so.

80 *fry:* Spawn.   SCENE III. 3 *mortal:* Deadly.   4 *Bestride:* I.e., stand over protectively; *birth-
dom:* Place of birth.   8 *Like syllable of dolor:* A similar cry of pain.   10 *time to friend:* Time
propitious.   12 *sole name:* Very name.   14 *young:* I.e., young and inexperienced.   15 *wisdom:* I.e., it may be wise.   19–20 *recoil . . . imperial charge:* Reverse itself under royal pressure.
21 *transpose:* Alter.   22 *the brightest:* I.e., Lucifer.

Macduff: I have lost my hopes.
Malcolm: Perchance even there where I did find my doubts.   25
    Why in that rawness° left you wife and child,
    Those precious motives, those strong knots of love,
    Without leave-taking? I pray you,
    Let not my jealousies° be your dishonors,
    But mine own safeties. You may be rightly just   30
    Whatever I shall think.
Macduff: Bleed, bleed, poor country!
    Great tyranny, lay thou thy basis° sure,
    For goodness dare not check thee; wear thou thy wrongs,
    The title is affeered!° Fare thee well, lord.
    I would not be the villain that thou think'st   35
    For the whole space that's in the tyrant's grasp
    And the rich East to boot.
Malcolm: Be not offended.
    I speak not as in absolute° fear of you.
    I think our country sinks beneath the yoke,
    It weeps, it bleeds, and each new day a gash   40
    Is added to her wounds. I think withal°
    There would be hands uplifted in my right;
    And here from gracious England have I offer
    Of goodly thousands. But, for all this,
    When I shall tread upon the tyrant's head   45
    Or wear it on my sword, yet my poor country
    Shall have more vices than it had before,
    More suffer, and more sundry ways than ever,
    By him that shall succeed.
Macduff: What should he be?
Malcolm: It is myself I mean, in whom I know   50
    All the particulars° of vice so grafted.°
    That, when they shall be opened,° black Macbeth
    Will seem as pure as snow, and the poor state
    Esteem him as a lamb, being compared
    With my confineless harms.°
Macduff: Not in the legions   55
    Of horrid hell can come a devil more damned
    In evils to top Macbeth.
Malcolm: I grant him bloody,

---

26 *rawness:* Unprotected state.   29 *jealousies:* Suspicions.   32 *basis:* Foundation.   34 *af-
feered:* Confirmed by law.   38 *absolute:* Complete.   41 *withal:* Furthermore.   51 *particulars:* Varieties; *grafted:* Implanted.   52 *opened:* Revealed.   55 *confineless harms:* Unlimited
vices.

Luxurious,° avaricious, false, deceitful,
Sudden,° malicious, smacking of every sin
That has a name. But there's no bottom, none,   60
In my voluptuousness. Your wives, your daughters,
Your matrons, and your maids could not fill up
The cistern of my lust; and my desire
All continent° impediments would o'erbear
That did oppose my will. Better Macbeth   65
Than such an one to reign.
Macduff: Boundless intemperance
In nature° is a tyranny. It hath been
Th' untimely emptying of the happy throne
And fall of many kings. But fear not yet
To take upon you what is yours. You may   70
Convey° your pleasures in a spacious plenty
And yet seem cold — the time you may so hoodwink.
We have willing dames enough. There cannot be
That vulture in you to devour so many
As will to greatness dedicate themselves,   75
Finding it so inclined.
Malcolm: With this there grows
In my most ill-composed affection° such
A stanchless° avarice that, were I King,
I should cut off the nobles for their lands,
Desire his jewels, and this other's house,   80
And my more-having would be as a sauce
To make me hunger more, that I should forge°
Quarrels unjust against the good and loyal,
Destroying them for wealth.
Macduff: This avarice
Sticks deeper, grows with more pernicious root   85
Than summer-seeming° lust, and it hath been
The sword of our slain° kings. Yet do not fear.
Scotland hath foisons to fill up your will
Of your mere own.° All these are portable,°
With other graces weighed.   90
Malcolm: But I have none. The king-becoming graces,
As justice, verity, temp'rance, stableness,

58 *Luxurious:* Lecherous.   59 *Sudden:* Violent.   64 *continent:* Containing, restraining.
67 *In nature:* In one's nature.   71 *Convey:* Obtain by stealth.   77 *ill-composed affection:*
Disordered disposition.   78 *stanchless:* Insatiable.   82 *forge:* Fabricate.   86 *summer-seem-ing:* I.e., seasonal, transitory.   87 *sword of our slain:* Cause of death of our.   88–89 *foisons . . . mere own:* Riches of your own enough to satisfy you.   89 *portable:* Bearable.

Bounty, perseverance, mercy, lowliness,°
Devotion, patience, courage, fortitude,
I have no relish° of them, but abound   95
In the division° of each several crime,
Acting in many ways. Nay, had I pow'r, I should
Pour the sweet milk of concord into hell,
Uproar° the universal peace, confound
All unity on earth.
Macduff: O Scotland, Scotland!   100
Malcolm: If such a one be fit to govern, speak.
I am as I have spoken.
Macduff: Fit to govern?
No, not to live! O nation miserable,
With an untitled tyrant bloody-sceptred,
When shalt thou see thy wholesome days again,   105
Since that the truest issue of thy throne
By his own interdiction° stands accursed
And does blaspheme his breed? Thy royal father
Was a most sainted king; the queen that bore thee,
Oft'ner upon her knees than on her feet,   110
Died° every day she lived. Fare thee well.
These evils thou repeat'st upon thyself
Hath banished me from Scotland. O my breast,
Thy hope ends here!
Malcolm: Macduff, this noble passion,
Child of integrity, hath from my soul   115
Wiped the black scruples,° reconciled my thoughts
To thy good truth and honor. Devilish Macbeth
By many of these trains° hath sought to win me
Into his power; and modest° wisdom plucks° me
From over-credulous haste; but God above   120
Deal between thee and me, for even now
I put myself to thy direction and
Unspeak mine own detraction, here abjure
The taints and blames I laid upon myself
For° strangers to my nature. I am yet   125
Unknown to woman, never was forsworn,
Scarcely have coveted what was mine own,
At no time broke my faith, would not betray
The devil to his fellow, and delight

---

93 *lowliness:* Humility.   95 *relish:* Trace.   96 *division:* Subdivisions.   99 *Uproar:* Blast.
107 *interdiction:* Curse.   111 *Died:* I.e., turned away from this life.   116 *scruples:* Doubts.
118 *trains:* Plots.   119 *modest:* Cautious; *plucks:* Holds.   125 *For:* As.

No less in truth than life. My first false speaking   130
Was this upon° myself. What I am truly,
Is thine and my poor country's to command;
Whither indeed, before thy here-approach,
Old Siward with ten thousand warlike men
Already at a point° was setting forth;   135
Now we'll together; and the chance of goodness
Be like our warranted quarrel!° Why are you silent?
Macduff: Such welcome and unwelcome things at once
   'Tis hard to reconcile.

Enter a Doctor.

Malcolm: Well, more anon.° Comes the King forth, I pray you?   140
Doctor: Ay, sir. There are a crew of wretched souls
   That stay° his cure. Their malady convinces°
   The great assay of art;° but at his touch,
   Such sanctity hath heaven given his hand,
   They presently amend.
Malcolm: I thank you, doctor.   *Exit Doctor.* 145
Macduff: What's the disease he means?
Malcolm: 'Tis called the evil.°
   A most miraculous work in this good King,
   Which often since my here-remain in England
   I have seen him do: how he solicits heaven
   Himself best knows, but strangely-visited° people,   150
   All swol'n and ulcerous, pitiful to the eye,
   The mere° despair of surgery, he cures,
   Hanging a golden stamp° about their necks,
   Put on with holy prayers; and 'tis spoken,
   To the succeeding royalty he leaves   155
   The healing benediction. With this strange virtue,
   He hath a heavenly gift of prophecy,
   And sundry blessings hang about his throne
   That speak him full of grace.

Enter Ross.

Macduff: See who comes here.

---

131 *upon:* Against.   135 *at a point:* Armed.   136–137 *the chance . . . warranted quarrel:* I.e., let
the chance of success equal the justice of our cause.   140 *anon:* Soon.   142 *stay:* Await;
convinces: Baffles.   143 *assay of art:* Resources of medical science.   146 *evil:* Scrofula
(king's evil).   150 *strangely-visited:* Unusually afflicted.   152 *mere:* Utter.   153 *stamp:*
Coin.

Malcolm: My countryman; but yet I know him not.   160
Macduff: My ever gentle cousin, welcome hither.
Malcolm: I know him now. Good God betimes° remove
    The means that makes us strangers!
Ross: Sir, amen.
Macduff: Stands Scotland where it did?
Ross: Alas, poor country,
    Almost afraid to know itself. It cannot   165
    Be called our mother but our grave, where nothing°
    But who knows nothing is once seen to smile;
    Where signs and groans, and shrieks that rent the air,
    Are made, not marked;° where violent sorrow seems
    A modern ecstasy.° The dead man's knell   170
    Is there scarce asked for who,° and good men's lives
    Expire before the flowers in their caps,
    Dying or ere they sicken.
Macduff: O, relation°
    Too nice,° and yet too true!
Malcolm: What's the newest grief?
Ross: That of an hour's age doth hiss the speaker;°   175
    Each minute teems° a new one.
Macduff: How does my wife?
Ross: Why, well.
Macduff: And all my children?
Ross: Well too.
Macduff: The tyrant has not battered at their peace?
Ross: No, they were well at peace when I did leave 'em.
Macduff: Be not a niggard of your speech. How goes't?   180
Ross: When I came hither to transport the tidings
    Which I have heavily borne,° there ran a rumor
    Of many worthy fellows that were out,°
    Which was to my belief witnessed° the rather
    For that I saw the tyrant's power afoot.   185
    Now is the time of help. Your eye in Scotland
    Would create soldiers, make our women fight
    To doff their dire distresses.
Malcolm: Be't their comfort
    We are coming thither. Gracious England hath
    Lent us good Siward and ten thousand men,   190

162 *betimes:* Quickly.   166 *nothing:* No one.   169 *marked:* Noticed.   170 *modern ecstasy:*
Commonplace emotion.   171 *Is there . . . for who:* Scarcely calls forth an inquiry about
identity.   173 *relation:* Report.   174 *nice:* Precise.   175 *doth hiss the speaker:* Causes the
speaker to be hissed (for stale repetition).   176 *teems:* Brings forth.   182 *heavily borne:*
Sadly carried.   183 *out:* Up in arms.   184 *witnessed:* Attested.

An older and a better soldier none
That Christendom gives out.°
Ross: Would I could answer
This comfort with the like. But I have words
That would be howled out in the desert air,
Where hearing should not latch° them.
Macduff: What concern they,   195
The general cause or is it a fee-grief°
Due° to some single breast?
Ross: No mind that's honest
But in it shares some woe, though the main part
Pertains to you alone.
Macduff: If it be mine,
Keep it not from me; quickly let me have it.   200
Ross: Let not your ears despise my tongue for ever,
Which shall possess them with the heaviest sound
That ever yet they heard.
Macduff: Humh! I guess at it.
Ross: Your castle is surprised,° your wife and babes
Savagely slaughtered. To relate the manner   205
Were, on the quarry° of these murdered deer,
To add the death of you.
Malcolm: Merciful heaven!
What, man! Ne'er pull your hat upon your brows.
Give sorrow words. The grief that does not speak°
Whispers° the o'erfraught heart and bids it break.   210
Macduff: My children too?
Ross: Wife, children, servants, all
That could be found.
Macduff: And I must be from thence?
My wife killed too?
Ross: I have said.
Malcolm: Be comforted.
Let's make us med'cines of our great revenge
To cure this deadly grief.   215
Macduff: He has no children. All my pretty ones?
Did you say all? O hell-kite! All?
What, all my pretty chickens and their dam
At one fell swoop?

---

192 *gives out:* Reports.   195 *latch:* Catch hold of.   196 *fee-grief:* I.e., a grief possessed in
private.   197 *Due:* Belonging.   204 *surprised:* Attacked.   206 *quarry:* Heap of game.
209 *speak:* Speak aloud.   210 *Whispers:* Whispers to.

Malcolm: Dispute° it like a man.
Macduff: I shall do so;   220
But I must also feel it as a man.
I cannot but remember such things were
That were most precious to me. Did heaven look on
And would not take their part? Sinful Macduff,
They were all struck for thee! Naught° that I am,   225
Not for their own demerits but for mine
Fell slaughter on their souls. Heaven rest them now!
Malcolm: Be this the whetstone of your sword. Let grief
Convert to anger; blunt not the heart, enrage it.
Macduff: O, I could play the woman with mine eyes   230
And braggart with my tongue. But, gentle heavens,
Cut short all intermission.° Front to front°
Bring thou this fiend of Scotland and myself.
Within my sword's length set him. If he scape,
Heaven forgive him too!
Malcolm: This tune goes manly.   235
Come, go we to the King. Our power° is ready;
Our lack is nothing but our leave.° Macbeth
Is ripe for shaking, and the pow'rs above
Put on their instruments.° Receive what cheer you may.
The night is long that never finds the day.   *Exeunt.* 240

ACT V

SCENE I. *Within Macbeth's Castle at Dunsinane*

Enter a Doctor of Physic and a Waiting Gentlewoman.

Doctor: I have two nights watched with you, but can perceive no
truth in your report. When was it she last walked?
Gentlewoman: Since his Majesty went into the field I have seen
her rise from her bed, throw her nightgown° upon her,
unlock her closet,° take forth paper, fold it, write upon't,   5
read it, afterwards seal it, and again return to bed; yet all this
while in a most fast sleep.

---

220 *Dispute:* Revenge.   225 *Naught:* Wicked.   232 *intermission:* Interval; *Front to front:* Face
to face.   236 *power:* Army.   237 *Our lack . . . our leave:* I.e., nothing remains but to say
farewell.   239 *Put on their instruments:* Urge on their agents.   ACT V, SCENE I. 4 *nightgown:*
Dressing gown.   5 *closet:* A chest, or desk.

Doctor: A great perturbation in nature, to receive at once the
benefit of sleep and do the effects of watching!° In this
slumb'ry agitation, besides her walking and other actual per-   10
formances, what (at any time) have you heard her say?
Gentlewoman: That, sir, which I will not report after her.
Doctor: You may to me, and 'tis most meet° you should.
Gentlewoman: Neither to you nor any one, having no witness to
confirm my speech.   15

Enter Lady Macbeth, with a taper.

Lo you, here she comes! This is her very guise,° and, upon my
life, fast asleep! Observe her; stand close.°
Doctor: How came she by that light?
Gentlewoman: Why, it stood by her. She has light by her con-
tinually. 'Tis her command.   20
Doctor: You see her eyes are open.
Gentlewoman: Ay, but their sense° are shut.
Doctor: What is it she does now? Look how she rubs her hands.
Gentlewoman: It is an accustomed action with her, to seem thus
washing her hands. I have known her continue in this a   25
quarter of an hour.
Lady: Yet here's a spot.
Doctor: Hark, she speaks. I will set down what comes from her, to
satisfy my remembrance the more strongly.
Lady: Out, damned spot! Out, I say! One — two — why then 'tis   30
time to do't. Hell is murky. Fie, my lord, fie! a soldier and
afeard? What need we fear who knows it, when none can call
our power to accompt?° Yet who would have thought the old
man to have had so much blood in him?
Doctor: Do you mark that?   35
Lady: The Thane of Fife had a wife. Where is she now? What, will
these hands ne'er be clean? No more o' that, my lord, no
more o' that! You mar all with this starting.°
Doctor: Go to, go to! You have known what you should not.
Gentlewoman: She has spoke what she should not, I am sure of   40
that. Heaven knows what she has known.
Lady: Here's the smell of the blood still. All the perfumes of
Arabia will not sweeten this little hand. Oh, oh, oh!

---

9 *do the effects of watching:* Act as if awake.   13 *meet:* Fitting.   16 *guise:* Habit.   17 *close:*
Concealed.   22 *sense:* Powers of sensation.   32–33 *call our power to accompt:* Call to account
anyone so powerful as we.   38 *starting:* Startled movements.

Doctor: What a sigh is there! The heart is sorely charged.°
Gentlewoman: I would not have such a heart in my bosom for the   45
dignity of the whole body.
Doctor: Well, well, well.
Gentlewoman: Pray God it be, sir.
Doctor: This disease is beyond my practice.° Yet I have known
those which have walked in their sleep who have died holily   50
in their beds.
Lady: Wash your hands, put on your nightgown, look not so pale!
I tell you yet again, Banquo 's buried. He cannot come out
on's grave.
Doctor: Even so?   55
Lady: To bed, to bed! There's knocking at the gate. Come, come,
come, come, give me your hand! What's done cannot be
undone. To bed, to bed, to bed!   *Exit.*
Doctor: Will she go now to bed?
Gentlewoman: Directly.   60
Doctor: Foul whisp'rings are abroad. Unnatural deeds
Do breed unnatural troubles. Infected minds
To their deaf pillows will discharge their secrets.
More needs she the divine than the physician.
God, God forgive us all! Look after her;   65
Remove from her the means of all annoyance,°
And still keep eyes upon her. So good night.
My mind she has mated,° and amazed my sight.
I think, but dare not speak.
Gentlewoman: Good night, good doctor.   *Exeunt.*

SCENE II. *Open country near Birnam Wood and Dunsinane*

Drum and Colors. Enter Menteith, Caithness, Angus, Lennox, Soldiers.

Menteith: The English pow'r is near, led on by Malcolm,
His uncle Siward, and the good Macduff.
Revenges burn in them; for their dear causes
Would to the bleeding° and the grim alarm
Excite° the mortified° man.   5
Angus: Near Birnam Wood

---

44 *charged:* Laden.   49 *practice:* Professional competence.   66 *annoyance:* Self-injury.
68 *mated:* Bemused.   SCENE II. 4 *bleeding:* Blood of battle.   5 *Excite:* Incite; *mortified:* Dead.

Shall we well° meet them; that way are they coming.
Caithness: Who knows if Donalbain be with his brother?
Lennox: For certain, sir, he is not. I have a file°
   Of all the gentry. There is Siward's son
   And many unrough° youths that even now   10
   Protest° their first of manhood.
Menteith: What does the tyrant?
Caithness: Great Dunsinane he strongly fortifies.
   Some say he's mad; others, that lesser hate him,
   Do call it valiant fury; but for certain
   He cannot buckle his distempered° cause   15
   Within the belt of rule.°
Angus: Now does he feel
   His secret murders sticking on his hands.
   Now minutely° revolts° upbraid his faith-breach.
   Those he commands move only in command,
   Nothing in love. Now does he feel his title   20
   Hang loose about him, like a giant's robe
   Upon a dwarfish thief.
Menteith: Who then shall blame
   His pestered° senses to recoil and start,
   When all that is within him does condemn
   Itself for being there?
Caithness: Well, march we on   25
   To give obedience where 'tis truly owed.
   Meet we the med'cine° of the sickly weal;°
   And with him pour we in our country's purge
   Each drop of us.
Lennox: Or so much as it needs
   To dew° the sovereign flower and drown the weeds.   30
   Make we our march towards Birnam.   *Exeunt, marching.*

SCENE III. *Within Dunsinane Castle*

Enter Macbeth, Doctor, and Attendants.

Macbeth: Bring me no more reports. Let them fly all!
   Till Birnam Wood remove to Dunsinane,
   I cannot taint° with fear. What's the boy Malcolm?
   Was he not born of woman? The spirits that know

---

6 *well:* Surely.   8 *file:* List.   10 *unrough:* Unbearded.   11 *Protest:* Assert.   15 *distempered:* Disease-swollen.   16 *rule:* Reason.   18 *minutely:* Every minute; *revolts:* Rebellions.   23 *pestered:* Tormented.   27 *med'cine:* Cure (i.e., Malcolm); *weal:* Commonwealth.   30 *dew:* Water. SCENE III. 3 *taint:* Become tainted.

All mortal consequences° have pronounced me thus: 5
"Fear not, Macbeth. No man that's born of woman
Shall e'er have power upon thee." Then fly, false thanes,
And mingle with the English epicures.°
The mind I sway° by and the heart I bear
Shall never sag with doubt nor shake with fear.   10

Enter Servant.

The devil damn thee black, thou cream-faced loon!°
Where got'st thou that goose look?
Servant: There is ten thousand —
Macbeth: Geese, villain?
Servant: Soldiers, sir.
Macbeth: Go prick thy face and over-red thy fear,°
Thou lily-livered boy. What soldiers, patch?°   15
Death of thy soul! those linen cheeks of thine
Are counsellors to fear. What soldiers, whey-face?
Servant: The English force, so please you.
Macbeth: Take thy face hence.   *Exit Servant.*
                          Seyton! — I am sick at heart,
When I behold — Seyton, I say! — This push°   20
Will cheer me ever, or disseat me now.
I have lived long enough. My way of life
Is fall'n into the sear,° the yellow leaf,
And that which should accompany old age,
As honor, love, obedience, troops of friends,   25
I must not look to have; but, in their stead,
Curses not loud but deep, mouth-honor, breath,
Which the poor heart would fain deny, and dare not.
Seyton!

Enter Seyton.

Seyton: What's your gracious pleasure?
Macbeth: What news more?   30
Seyton: All is confirmed, my lord, which was reported.
Macbeth: I'll fight till from my bones my flesh be hacked.
Give me my armor.
Seyton: 'Tis not needed yet.

---

5 *consequences:* Sequence of events.   8 *English epicures:* I.e., as compared with the austerely
living Scots.   9 *sway:* Direct myself.   11 *loon:* Lout.   14 *over-red thy fear:* I.e., paint red
over your fearful pallor.   15 *patch:* Fool.   20 *push:* Struggle.   23 *sear:* Dry, withered.

Macbeth: I'll put it on.
Send out moe° horses, skirr° the country round,   35
Hang those that talk of fear. Give me mine armor.
How does your patient, doctor?
Doctor: Not so sick, my lord,
As she is troubled with thick-coming fancies
That keep her from her rest.
Macbeth: Cure her of that!
Canst thou not minister to a mind diseased,   40
Pluck from the memory a rooted sorrow,
Raze° out the written troubles of the brain,
And with some sweet oblivious antidote°
Cleanse the stuffed° bosom of that perilous stuff
Which weighs upon the heart?
Doctor: Therein the patient   45
Must minister to himself.
Macbeth: Throw physic° to the dogs, I'll none of it!
Come, put mine armor on. Give me my staff.
Seyton, send out. — Doctor, the thanes fly from me. —
Come, sir, dispatch.° — If thou couldst, doctor, cast   50
The water° of my land, find her disease,
And purge it to a sound and pristine health,
I would applaud thee to the very echo,
That should applaud again. — Pull't off, I say. —
What rhubarb, senna, or what purgative drug   55
Would scour these English hence? Hear'st thou of them?
Doctor: Ay, my good lord. Your royal preparation
Makes us hear something.
Macbeth: Bring it° after me!
I will not be afraid of death and bane°
Till Birnam Forest come to Dunsinane.   60

Exeunt all but the Doctor.

Doctor: Were I from Dunsinane away and clear,
Profit again should hardly draw me here.   *Exit.*

SCENE IV. *Birnam Wood*

Drum and Colors. Enter Malcolm, Siward, Macduff, Siward's Son, Mentieth, Caithness, Angus, Lennox, Ross, and Soldiers, marching.

35 *moe:* More; *skirr:* Scour.   42 *Raze:* Erase.   43 *oblivious antidote:* Opiate, medicine of forgetfulness.   44 *stuffed:* Choked up.   47 *physic:* Medicine.   50 *dispatch:* Hasten.   50–51 *cast . . . water:* Analyze the urine.   58 *it:* I.e., the remainder of the armor.   59 *bane:* Destruction.

Malcolm: Cousins, I hope the days are near at hand
   That chambers° will be safe.
Menteith: We doubt it nothing.°
Siward: What wood is this before us?
Menteith: The Wood of Birnam.
Malcolm: Let every soldier hew him down a bough
   And bear't before him. Thereby shall we shadow   5
   The numbers of our host and make discovery°
   Err in report of us.
Soldiers: It shall be done.
Siward: We learn no other but the confident tyrant
   Keeps still in Dunsinane and will endure
   Our setting down before't.
Malcolm: 'Tis his main hope,   10
   For where there is advantage° to be gone
   Both more and less° have given him the revolt,
   And none serve with him but constrained things
   Whose hearts are absent too.
Macduff: Let our just censures°
   Attend° the true event, and put we on°   15
   Industrious soldiership.
Siward: The time approaches
   That will with due decision make us know
   What we shall say we have and what we owe.
   Thoughts speculative their unsure hopes relate,°
   But certain issue° strokes must arbitrate° —   20
   Towards which advance the war.°   *Exeunt, marching.*

SCENE V. *Within Dunsinane Castle*

Enter Macbeth, Seyton, and Soldiers, with Drum and Colors.

Macbeth: Hang out our banners on the outward walls.
   The cry is still,° "They come!" Our castle's strength
   Will laugh a siege to scorn. Here let them lie
   Till famine and the ague eat them up.
   Were they not forced° with those that should be ours,   5
   We might have met them dareful, beard to beard,
   And beat them backward home.

SCENE IV. 2 *That chambers:* When sleeping-chambers; *nothing:* Not at all.   6 *discovery:* I.e.,
reports by scouts.   11 *advantage:* Opportunity.   12 *more and less:* High and low.   14 *just
censures:* Impartial judgment.   15 *Attend:* Await; *put we on:* Let us put on.   19 *relate:*
Convey.   20 *certain issue:* The definite outcome; *arbitrate:* Decide.   21 *war:* Army.   SCENE
V. 2 *still:* Always.   5 *forced:* Reinforced.

A cry within of women.

What is that noise?
Seyton: It is the cry of women, my good lord.   *Exit.*
Macbeth: I have almost forgot the taste of fears.
    The time has been my senses would have cooled   10
    To hear a night-shriek, and my fell° of hair
    Would at a dismal treatise° rouse and stir
    As life were in't. I have supped full with horrors.
    Direness,° familiar to my slaughterous thoughts,
    Cannot once start me.°

Enter Seyton.

Wherefore was that cry?   15
Seyton: The Queen, my lord, is dead.
Macbeth: She should have died hereafter:
    There would have been a time for such a word.
    To-morrow, and to-morrow, and to-morrow
    Creeps in this petty pace from day to day   20
    To the last syllable of recorded time,
    And all our yesterdays have lighted fools
    The way to dusty death. Out, out, brief candle!
    Life's but a walking shadow, a poor player
    That struts and frets his hour upon the stage   25
    And then is heard no more. It is a tale
    Told by an idiot, full of sound and fury,
    Signifying nothing.

Enter a Messenger.

Thou com'st to use thy tongue: thy story quickly!
Messenger: Gracious my lord,   30
    I should report that which I say° I saw,
    But know not how to do't.
Macbeth: Well, say, sir.
Messenger: As I did stand my watch upon the hill,
    I looked toward Birnam, and anon methought
    The wood began to move.
Macbeth: Liar and slave!   35
Messenger: Let me endure your wrath if't be not so.
    Within this three mile may you see it coming.
    I say, a moving grove.

11 *fell:* Pelt.   12 *treatise:* Story.   14 *Direness:* Horror.   15 *start me:* Make me start.   31 *say:*
I.e., affirm.

Macbeth: If thou speak'st false,
   Upon the next tree shalt thou hang alive
   Till famine cling° thee. If thy speech be sooth,°   40
   I care not if thou dost for me as much.
   I pull in° resolution, and begin
   To doubt° th' equivocation° of the fiend,
   That lies like truth. "Fear not, till Birnam Wood
   Do come to Dunsinane!" and now a wood   45
   Comes toward Dunsinane. Arm, arm, and out!
   If this which he avouches° does appear,
   There is nor flying hence nor tarrying here.
   I 'gin to be aweary of the sun,
   And wish th' estate o' th' world were now undone.   50
   Ring the alarum bell! Blow wind, come wrack,
   At least we'll die with harness° on our back.   *Exeunt.*

SCENE VI. *Fields outside Dunsinane Castle*

Drum and Colors. Enter Malcolm, Siward, Macduff, and their Army, with boughs.

Malcolm: Now near enough. Your leavy screens throw down
   And show like those you are. You, worthy uncle,
   Shall with my cousin, your right noble son,
   Lead our first battle.° Worthy Macduff and we
   Shall take upon's what else remains to do,   5
   According to our order.°
Siward: Fare you well.
   Do we but find the tyrant's power° to-night,
   Let us be beaten if we cannot fight.
Macduff: Make all our trumpets speak, give them all breath,
   Those clamorous harbingers of blood and death.   10

                                   Exeunt. Alarums continued.

SCENE VII. *The same*

Enter Macbeth.

Macbeth: They have tied me to a stake. I cannot fly,
   But bear-like I must fight the course.° What's he

---

40 *cling:* Shrivel; *sooth:* Truth.   42 *pull in:* Curb, check.   43 *doubt:* Suspect; *equivocation:*
Double-talk.   47 *avouches:* Affirms.   52 *harness:* Armor.   SCENE VI. 4 *battle:* Battalion.
6 *order:* Battle-plan.   7 *power:* Forces.   SCENE VII. 2 *course:* Attack (like a bear tied to a stake
and baited by dogs or men).

That was not born of woman? Such a one
Am I to fear, or none.

Enter Young Siward.

Young Siward: What is thy name?
Macbeth: Thou'lt be afraid to hear it. 5
Young Siward: No, though thou call'st thyself a hotter name
 Than any is in hell.
Macbeth: My name's Macbeth.

Young Siward: The devil himself could not pronounce a title
 More hateful to mine ear.
Macbeth: No, nor more fearful.
Young Siward: Thou liest, abhorred tyrant! With my sword 10
 I'll prove the lie thou speak'st.

Fight, and Young Siward slain.

         Thou wast born of woman.
But swords I smile at, weapons laugh to scorn,
Brandished by man that's of a woman born.   *Exit.*

Alarums. Enter Macduff.

Macduff: That way the noise is. Tyrant, show thy face!
 If thou beest slain and with no stroke of mine, 15
 My wife and children's ghosts will haunt me still.
 I cannot strike at wretched kerns,° whose arms
 Are hired to bear their staves.° Either thou, Macbeth,
 Or else my sword with an unbattered edge
 I sheathe again undeeded.° There thou shouldst be: 20
 By this great clatter one of greatest note
 Seems bruited.° Let me find him, Fortune,
 And more I beg not!   *Exit. Alarums.*

Enter Malcolm and Siward.

Siward: This way, my lord. The castle's gently rend'red:°
 The tyrant's people on both sides do fight, 25
 The noble thanes do bravely in the war,
 The day almost itself professes° yours
 And little is to do.

---

17 *kerns:* Soldiers of meanest rank. 18 *staves:* Spears. 20 *undeeded:* Not glorified by
deeds. 22 *bruited:* Reported. 24 *rend'red:* Surrendered. 27 *itself professes:* Declares
itself.

Malcolm: We have met with foes
   That strike beside us.°
Siward: Enter, sir, the castle.   *Exeunt. Alarum.*

SCENE VIII

Enter Macbeth.

Macbeth: Why should I play the Roman fool and die
   On mine own sword? Whiles I see lives,° the gashes
   Do better upon them.

Enter Macduff.

Macduff: Turn, hellhound, turn!
Macbeth: Of all men else I have avoided thee.
   But get thee back! My soul is too much charged°   5
   With blood of thine already.
Macduff: I have no words;
   My voice is in my sword, thou bloodier villain
   Than terms can give thee out!

Fight. Alarum.

Macbeth: Thou losest labor.
   As easy mayst thou the intrenchant° air
   With thy keen sword impress° as make me bleed.   10
   Let fall thy blade on vulnerable crests.
   I bear a charmed life, which must not yield
   To one of woman born.
Macduff: Despair° thy charm,
   And let the angel° whom thou still° hast served
   Tell thee, Macduff was from his mother's womb   15
   Untimely ripped.
Macbeth: Accursed be that tongue that tells me so,
   For it hath cowed my better part of man!°
   And be these juggling fiends no more believed,
   That palter° with us in a double sense,   20
   That keep the word of promise to our ear
   And break it to our hope. I'll not fight with thee.

---

29 *beside us:* At our side (?), without trying to hit us (?).   SCENE VIII. 2 *lives:* Living bodies.
5 *charged:* Burdened.   9 *intrenchant:* Incapable of being trenched (gashed).   10 *impress:*
Leave a mark on.   13 *Despair:* Despair of.   14 *angel:* I.e., of the host of Lucifer; *still:*
Always.   18 *better part of man:* Most manly side.   20 *palter:* Quibble.

Macduff: Then yield thee, coward,
    And live to be the show and gaze° o' th' time.
    We'll have thee, as our rarer monsters° are,   25
    Painted upon a pole,° and underwrit
    "Here may you see the tyrant."
Macbeth: I will not yield,
    To kiss the ground before young Malcolm's feet
    And to be baited with the rabble's curse,
    Though Birnam Wood be come to Dunsinane,   30
    And thou opposed, being of no woman born,
    Yet I will try the last. Before my body
    I throw my warlike shield. Lay on, Macduff,
    And damned be him that first cries "Hold, enough!"

Exeunt fighting. Alarums.
Re-enter fighting, and Macbeth slain.°
Exit Macduff.

Retreat and flourish. Enter, with Drum and Colors, Malcolm, Siward, Ross, Thanes, and Soldiers.

Malcolm: I would the friends we miss were safe arrived.   35
Siward: Some must go off;° and yet, by these° I see,
    So great a day as this is cheaply bought.
Malcolm: Macduff is missing, and your noble son.
Ross: Your son, my lord, has paid a soldier's debt.
    He only lived but till he was a man,   40
    The which no sooner had his prowess confirmed
    In the unshrinking station° where he fought
    But like a man he died.
Siward: Then he is dead?
Ross: Ay, and brought off the field. Your cause of sorrow
    Must not be measured by his worth, for then   45
    It hath no end.
Siward: Had he his hurts before?
Ross: Ay, on the front.
Siward: Why then, God's soldier be he.
    Had I as many sons as I have hairs,

---

24 *gaze:* Sight.   25 *monsters:* Freaks.   26 *Painted upon a pole:* Pictured on a showman's banner.   *Exeunt . . . slain:* After this action the scene apparently shifts to within Dunsinane Castle; cf. V.vii.29.   36 *go off:* Perish; *these:* I.e., these here assembled.   42 *unshrinking station:* Place from which he did not retreat.

I would not wish them to a fairer death:
And so his knell is knolled.
Malcolm: He's worth more sorrow,   50
And that I'll spend for him.
Siward: He's worth no more.
They say he parted° well and paid his score,°
And so, God be with him. Here comes newer comfort.

Enter Macduff, with Macbeth's head.

Macduff: Hail, King, for so thou art. Behold where stands
Th' usurper's cursed head. The time is free.°   55
I see thee compassed° with thy kingdom's pearl,
That speak my salutation in their minds,
Whose voices I desire aloud with mine —
Hail, King of Scotland!
All: Hail, King of Scotland!

Flourish.

Malcolm: We shall not spend a large expense of time   60
Before we reckon° with your several loves
And make us even with you.° My Thanes and kinsmen,
Henceforth be Earls, the first that ever Scotland
In such an honor named. What's more to do
Which would be planted newly with the time° —   65
As calling home our exiled friends abroad
That fled the snares of watchful tyranny,
Producing forth the cruel ministers°
Of this dead butcher and his fiend-like queen,
Who (as 'tis thought) by self and violent° hands   70
Took off her life — this, and what needful else
That calls upon us, by the grace of Grace
We will perform in measure,° time, and place.°
So thanks to all at once and to each one,
Whom we invite to see us crowned at Scone.   75

Flourish. Exeunt omnes.

52 *parted:* Departed; *score:* Reckoning.   55 *free:* Released from tyranny.   56 *compassed:*
Surrounded.   61 *reckon:* Come to an accounting.   62 *make us even with you:* Repay you.
65 *would be planted newly with the time:* I.e., should be done at the outset of this new era.   68 *min-*
isters: Agents.   70 *self and violent:* Her own violent.   73 *in measure:* With decorum; *time, and*
place: At the proper time and place.

Questions about Macbeth:
Act I, Scene III, lines 39–47, 51–61

Focus on Act I, Scene III, lines 39–47 and 51–61 — Macbeth and Banquo encountering the witches. What actions, thoughts, and feelings need to be brought alive in this passage? How do Banquo and Macbeth appear to each other during these moments? Make careful notes on your reading, deciding what each speaker is for himself and for the other during these moments; base your decisions on the assessment of each speaker's nature that you have arrived at through knowledge of the play as a whole. Build up the insides of the appropriate tones, gestures, and tonal contrasts by which each character's separateness can be realized from moment to moment. Then write a paper naming the elements (movements, gestures, expressions, motives) that figure crucially in staging the scene and explain why they are all-important.

Note: The following response begins with reading notes and a list of key elements for close imagining. Such a list can help you keep track of the wide range of focal points that need attention when bringing to life any individual scene in a full-length play.

Response

EDITOR'S READING NOTES: Eye movements — Banquo: looks back and forth to witches, to Macbeth, back to witches. Puts first question to Macbeth but no answer, so again to witches: "Live you?" Then back to Macbeth, maybe. Has to come back to M. because he's now talking about them — the witches — in the third person. "By each at once," etc. So he has to be talking at this minute to Macbeth. Starts out talking to them (calls them "you"). Then it's the third person. Then back to witches a third and fourth time. Lots of movement for Banquo. He has to turn toward and away from them repeatedly because no answer to his questions from Macbeth.

Eye movements — Macbeth: no turning. No shifts of gaze. Fixed. Rooted. Hears nothing, says nothing. Banquo probably not even present for him. He gets his voice back after a minute — but loses it again the second the prophecy comes. Back out of Banquo's reach then. Fixed and rooted again.

So it's Banquo trying *to wake Macbeth up*. Gently chiding, maybe almost teasing. "Good sir, why do you . . . fear/Things that do sound so fair?" But no answers: Macbeth is riveted. So when Banquo returns to the witches as he has to do, he now talks to them almost as though they were old friends. He's not wholly serious, almost has a joke with himself. Pretends to complain: Why am *I* left out of this prophecy game?

Pertinent scene for Banquo is the little bit with Duncan (I.vi) because you can feel Banquo's inner ease, natural happiness, appreciation of the good things — the natural world. Agreeable man, polite, pleased with life.

For Macbeth one pertinent scene is II.i.31 ff. — where he sees the dagger, or imagines it and is transfixed. Same capacity in him to be seized by imagined reality when the ghost of Banquo appears (III.iv.50 ff.).

EDITOR'S KEY ELEMENTS:

1. Macbeth's silence, Banquo's quickness of speech
2. Macbeth's motionlessness, Banquo's movement (shifts toward and away from Macbeth, toward and away from the witches)
3. Banquo's characteristic activities of mind (observing, questioning, classifying, sifting evidence, publicly reporting conclusions)
4. Macbeth's heedlessness of Banquo's questions, deductions, explications
5. Banquo's comparative inattention — at first — to his comrade's absorption

EDITOR: The differences between Macbeth and Banquo aren't absolute, but they are real. On the basis of his speech, one can say that Banquo is the kind of man who, when presented with the unknown, is immediately eager to share his puzzlement and curious about the best means of resolving it. For him the unfamiliar *x* presented to the senses becomes quite quickly a problem to be framed into publicly utterable questions:

Banquo: How far is't called to Forres? What are these,
   So withered and so wild in their attire

That look not like th' inhabitants o' th' earth
And yet are on't? Live you, or are you aught
That man may question? You seem to understand me,
By each at once her choppy finger laying
Upon her skinny lips. You should be women,
And yet your beards forbid me to interpret
That you are so.

Can the witches understand human speech? Are they male
or female? The act of asking such questions lends a sense of
manageability to the ongoing experience, fitting it to familiar
rhythms of anticipation and recognition, proposing and dispos-
ing. Banquo is surprised, excited, interested, wary; his surprise
and interest are those of a social, commonsensical human being — a creature relatively unacquainted with doubt about customary explanations and evaluations of events and persons. He
is disinclined to raise to himself the possibility that received
versions of good, evil, God, humanity, authority, and rebellion
are so much rubbish. Time cannot stop for such a sensibility as it
stops for Macbeth. The abyss doesn't open; the briefly tensed
frame of Banquo's body soon enough resumes its normal condition, its habitually relaxed decency, its expectation that life generally will be pleasing. (Moments before he's struck down, later in
the play, by barbarous hit men, Banquo passes a completely civil,
easygoing word concerning the weather.)

Banquo is hardly a fool — but he is a human being who
finds the world comprehensible on the usually given terms. Exceptions prove rules to this mind, and the job of the intelligence
is seeing into the way in which apparent inexplicables — such as
the weird sisters — can be folded understandingly into the system — in this case as creatures who do or don't possess gender,
do or don't understand human speech. (Play readers who know
other works by Shakespeare will remember that the playwright had
a certain condescending relish of minds for whom the standard experience of life is that of confirmation — people who
move with ease from being startled to being in possession of "The
Answers." Horatio, for instance, resumes his self-confidence
after the momentarily disarraying sight of the ghost in *Hamlet*:
"So have I heard and do in part believe it," I.i.165.)

Macbeth's is a different consciousness. The accidental,
strange, and unknown *erupt* and hold him fast. His inner being is

shaken, and his sense of succession — one moment following on from a known *before* to a predictable *after* — is gone. There is the physical stress of concentrated attention — a blotting out of sen- sation — and the moment possesses intensity greater by far for this mind than for Banquo's. Speech, sequence, capacity for anal- ysis — all are graveled, blocked. The moment may be an echo, some kind of recollected intimation. In any event, the content it carries is something like *The world strange, stranger than anyone admits — can't be predicted, doesn't follow logical rules or expectations.* (Later in the play Macbeth asserts that "Stones have been known to move and trees to speak . . . ," III.iv.123.)

Ordinarily Macbeth's consciousness isn't pitched so high. We say about such a consciousness that it's imaginative, meaning that it has the power to bring to life, to make present, what is absent or invisible or out of the question. It has the capacity to accept that what is not believed by others may yet be believable, or at least worthy of consideration. Its excitement is profound because it senses the possibility that vast significance may dwell in the strange and the exceptional.

In a measure this quality of consciousness could be described as an *aptitude*, something like a gift for music — or for sports — or even for faith itself. But while the aptitude is natural, Macbeth has cultivated it. His capacity to be a nondismissive, nonreduc- tive, believing witness of the strange stems in part from his knowledge that the outrageous thoughts and forbidden feelings that visit him visit elsewhere as well. They're familiar to at least one other soul — the soul who happens to be closer to him than anyone on earth. Moreover, to Macbeth's knowledge, forbidden thoughts are not just familiar to Lady Macbeth; she welcomes them unashamedly, as though their strangeness were itself worth but a shrug.

Macbeth and his wife have spoken together about the un- thinkable. They have faced the truth of their mutual ambition with trust that neither would perceive those yearnings as evi- dence of madness, ground for suicide, or so immediately hateful as to shock. The world says that to covet what cannot be won except through an act of hideous brutality is to behave unpar- donably. Yet Macbeth knows that he and his wife have exchanged intimations of their covetousness and have not been struck dead

— have not even been revulsed by each other, have in truth drawn closer through their implicit experiment with the un-thinkable.

Not so Banquo. He has had no occasion to live easily with thoughts against which the whole weight of custom, country, society, church, and history is counterpoised. He has known no companion of years whose readiness to consider the unthinkable works to confirm the suggestion that unthinkableness itself is only a convention of the fainthearted. In Banquo's world, no evidence exists that the common arrangements and hierarchies of value are arbitrary and weightless; in Macbeth's world such evidence is met with every day, in the image of his own ambitions that's reflected in his wife's gaze. The profoundly disordered therefore grips Macbeth as an emblem of what may truly be the substance of the world beyond him, the lesson lying at the heart of things. The "weirdness" perceived by Banquo is, for Macbeth, at once more and less than weird. He cannot then deal with the witches as objects to be classified and thereafter disregarded. They are seizing embodiments of a wild intuition.

What we're imagining at the start of the scene is two military men returning from a successful battle — weary, wishing the journey done, bored, impatient. Between "Forres" and "What" the witches are espied. Both men are surprised. Are these crea-tures mysterious hags, or apparitions? The first movement of Banquo's mind is toward a question: What's that over there? He sees something odd, and it occurs to him right away to ask what it is. Who can he ask? The witches? Macbeth? Or himself? He turns to ask his comrade: Do you see what I see? Banquo deals with the witches immediately in the third person, understanding that they can be talked about. He's not terrified, not so absorbed he can't say, What's that over there?

To bring this scene alive play readers must make vivid to themselves two strikingly dissimilar physical, mental, and emo-tional worlds. The good reader's mind and feelings teem with the pressure of two fully realized beings sealed into their uniquely configured and conflicting assumptions, two men each hearing and reading every sight and sound in accordance only with his individual will. The questions that concern us at this early mo-ment don't lead directly into the depths of moral exhaustion, fear, horror, complexly mingled repugnance and pity that mark later scenes. But Macbeth's behavior here must have premonitory intensity. We need to feel the difference *now* between sane decency and imaginative ferocity.

Questions about Macbeth:
Act III, Scene IV, lines 40–121

In arriving at a sense of how to imagine Act I, Scene III, we move through the lines repeatedly, clarifying relations among them, coming to an awareness of how each phrase, gesture, or turn is connected to what precedes and follows it, and making deductions on this basis about the nature of the characters and their feelings. This process grows richer and more complicated as we go further into the play, because each scene adds to the materials with which we work in creating our vision of the moment-to-moment reality of the scene.

In imagining any particular moment we need always to ask two questions: First, which previous moments are especially alive in the minds of the characters onstage in this scene? Second, where and how do the language and action of the characters in this scene connect with the language and action of earlier scenes? Our goal, in other words, is to bring to life the feeling, action, and language of each particular moment as events growing out of earlier feelings, action, and language.

In the scene in which Lady Macbeth walks in her sleep (V.i), it's clear that two previous moments are fearfully vivid in her memory — Duncan's murder and its aftermath, and the period at the banquet when she had to summon all her resources of will to prevent the assemblage from discovering, on the spot, Macbeth's and her own guilt. We need to have those moments in our minds as we imagine this scene and Lady Macbeth's feelings; we need also to feel the pressure, on this stage action of sleepwalking, of all the previous language in the play that's been focused on ease, rest, and sleep (for example, Macbeth's tortured cry: "Macbeth doth murder sleep," I.i.36). The moment-to-moment life of the play takes into itself an extraordinary variety of elements as we move toward the climax, and our job as imaginers is to bring to life as much of that richness as we can.

In this second assignment on *Macbeth* our focus will be Act III, Scene IV, lines 40–121, the banquet at which the ghost of Banquo appears. The overall task is to produce a paper naming

the elements (movements, gestures, expressions) that figure crucially in staging the scene, and explaining why they are important. Toward that end it's necessary, as before, to decide what
each speaker is for himself during these moments, basing these
decisions on readings of each speaker's nature. We need to build
up the insides of the appropriate tones, gestures, and tonal contrasts by which each character's separateness can be realized
from moment to moment. Key elements for close imagining of
the banquet scene can be derived from answers to the following
questions.

1. What change of tone occurs here?

    Feed, and regard him not. — Are you a man? (line 58)

    What is taking place within Lady Macbeth at this moment of
    change?

2. What changes of feeling occur in Macbeth between the two
    questions in these lines?

    Prithee see there!
    Behold! Look! Lo! — How say you?
    Why, what care I? If thou canst nod, speak too. (68–70)

3. This question from Ross —

    What sights, my lord? (116)

    — tells us that the private talk between Macbeth and his wife
    in this scene has now become public. That is, everyone is now
    assumed to have heard such lines as Macbeth's "When now I
    think you can behold such sights" (114). When exactly in this
    scene did the secrecy break down? What effect does the
    breakdown have on Macbeth's feelings? What effect does it
    have on Lady Macbeth's feelings?

4. What takes place within Lady Macbeth at this moment?

    I pray you, speak not. (117)

5. The murderer's phrase

    The least a death to nature (28)

    connects with much of the language and action of the play,
    including the final action (Birnam Wood coming to Dun-
    sinane). Look back at Act I, Scene VI, lines 1–9, and explain
    how these lines work to connect Banquo with the opposite of
    "a death to nature."

Questions about Macbeth:
Act IV, Scene III, lines 176–227

Focus on Act IV, Scene III, lines 176–227 — Ross delaying the fearful news about Macduff's wife and children, Macduff responding to that news. Make careful notes on the actions, thoughts, and feelings that need to be brought to life in the course of this scene. Decide what each of the three men is for himself and for the others during these moments, basing decisions on readings of each man's nature. What do we learn about Ross through his evasions? What do we learn about Macduff from his phrase "my pretty ones"? What feelings is Macduff struggling with when he asks: "And I must be from thence?" Build up the insides of the appropriate tones, gestures, and tonal contrasts by which each character's separateness can be realized from moment to moment. Then in an essay respond to the following questions about two specific passages in the scene.

Note: At the end of the assignment you'll find excerpts from six student responses to these questions. You may wish to compare the responses with your own.

1. What is taking place within Malcolm here?

Merciful heaven! (207)

2. Why does Macduff speak of Macbeth's childlessness here?

He has no children. (216)

What is the movement of Macduff's feeling?

Responses

Merciful heaven!

COLLEGE SENIOR: Between Ross's speech and this outcry there is anywhere from a second or two to what seem like interminable minutes. This ejaculation of grief and concern takes the place of all that Macduff in his unspeakable horror and disbelief can't get out. Macduff "pull[s] his hat over his brows" (line 208) — maybe metaphorically — so that it will cover his ears, as if he had not heard and refuses to believe. I see the cry "Merciful heaven!" as a verbal blow from Malcolm to drive the terrible news home to Macduff, to wake him out of his stricken stupor or catatonia. He feels it all for Macduff because the loss is not his. Malcolm can "process" it, and he realizes Macduff must react, must be shaken or even slapped, so that unexpressed grief will not break his heart. He, Malcolm, must express the grief for Macduff. There is sympathy here, true concern and identification, full understanding of what Macduff is feeling.

COLLEGE SOPHOMORE: Malcolm is impatient as well as scared. Speak, say something, he says. He cannot wait for Macduff's words and tears and realization to evolve slowly. He must hear his friend's voice *now*. He is prodding Macduff, urging him to respond to the news — as full of his own fear and need for some sort of relief as he is full of sympathy. He is completely on edge and powerless — an onlooker reaching, *straining* to touch Macduff, but so far away, even though he feels Macduff's pain. He knows he cannot approach Macduff's loss. He must hear Macduff's voice, must have something to grasp that will restore reality and fill the awful gap between them. Macduff is completely alone, isolated by the horror of the loss and his friends' impotence. Malcolm can't stand it — impatience and fear push the words out of his mouth: Speak so I can know something. There is no pleading in his voice — it sounds harsh and urgent. His words are too full of urgency and impatience and pity to be pleading.

COLLEGE SENIOR: Malcolm is frightened by the stone man beside him. There they stand — three big strong men, safe in England, while women and children — their own people — are being butchered in their homeland. Malcolm demands that Macduff speak, urges him to vent so he will not self-destruct before their eyes.

He has no children.

COLLEGE SENIOR: Macduff is numb with grief, perhaps crying without knowing or feeling it, explaining to himself that Macbeth could never have done it if he'd had children. He's answering the unspoken question, How? If he were less sick or dumbstruck he might be able to scream out in rage — How could this monstrosity have been committed? How could any man slaughter my babes? "He has no children" is a logical deduction out of numbness, a kind of grim explanation. Everyone, when something bad hits, asks How? or Why — Why me? But this goes so far beyond something bad that Macduff can't even utter Why? The answer "he has no children" — it's the only way this could have happened. It comes across not as an excuse but a step in comprehension.

COLLEGE SENIOR: Here Macduff turns around. The first words house a complete and utter contempt as well as rage — I cannot properly revenge myself. The disbelief here turns *into* rage. The floodwaters of Macduff's rage are now released — he's ignited, on fire with anger.

COLLEGE SOPHOMORE: Macduff's words here are savage and tormented, grating across Malcolm's speech. How can Malcolm say anything, how dare he? Macbeth has no children. Macbeth has done the unthinkable, and no true revenge can ever be won. Macduff denies Macbeth's ability ever to feel the pain that he, Macduff, is feeling. He is damning Macbeth here. "Children" — the word here represents something almost sacred, an intrinsic part of a man, a piece of his being. Macduff's words slice through Malcolm's feeling, withering it, making it meaningless. "Great revenge"? "Let's make . , , great revenge" (line 214)? No, never, Macbeth has no children. Malcolm's attempt to turn Macduff's grief into hunger for revenge is useless. Macbeth is no target. Macbeth is safe. *He* has no children — accent (if any) on the *he*. Macbeth can never have taken away from him what he has taken from me. Macbeth is *immune!*

19

Comedy

DIMENSIONS OF COMIC CHARACTERS

Two kinds of plays, widely divergent in mood and atmosphere, are grouped under the label *comedy*. There's romantic comedy, wherein lovers overcome obstacles in the path of bliss (usually the ending is a joyously celebrated marriage). And there's satiric comedy, wherein mockery and disparagement are norms, the idea of bliss seldom figures, and the aim is to correct human follies. The two kinds of comedy share a commitment to happy endings and a preference for scaled-down ranges of feeling. Both are more concerned with human limits than with human possibilities, and more inclined to be amused than impressed by our habit of inventing ideals. And neither is greatly interested in human complexity.

As a result, characters in comedy tend not to embody contradictions that cause us to speculate ceaselessly about the motives behind their behavior, or about the dynamics of good and evil in their souls. Murderous King Claudius in the tragedy of *Hamlet* has it within him not only to express what appears to be genuine pity for the suffering of others (as, for example, Ophelia) but also to be very nearly overpowered by a sense of guilt as he prays for forgiveness. Macbeth and Lady Macbeth are partners in brutal crime — but in the moments after the carnage in Duncan's bedchamber, we sense that they themselves are totally paralyzed by horror at their own deeds. And for centuries actors, scholars, and critics have debated "the question of Hamlet" — the problem of how to interpret seeming contradictions in Hamlet's nature.

The world of comedy rarely triggers such debate. A character introduced as a miser, or hypocrite, or passionate young lover, or stupid, noisy bully, or unreasonably stern parent is likely to be seen as just that from the first scene to the last. Complexity enters not by way of irreconcilable traits within a person but via the delusions and illusions arising out of social life and convention.

COMIC CONFRONTATIONS
WITH ILLUSION

One illusion that comedy often confronts is that appearance and reality are the same — the belief, say, that someone who looks good is good. Another illusion comedy enjoys confronting is that infatuations are forever — can't be altered by time or circumstances or love potions. Still another is that the rich and powerful are incapable of making fools of themselves. Each of these illusions exists in an intricate web of moral, economic, social, and psychological assumptions, and, in showing us how the assumptions interconnect and reinforce each other, comedy makes intellectual demands fully as rigorous as any imposed by tragedy.

When we put on a comedy in the theater of our minds, however, our initial focus isn't upon such relatively abstract matters as the difference between comedy and tragedy. (The same is true, of course, when we bring to life a tragedy.) Our focus is on the events of feeling and action that must be animated as each scene develops. Like tragedy, a comedy is lived moment by moment; the play reader needs to come to the edge of each moment as it's known by the figures onstage, freshly sensing their way of occupying space, of thinking and responding, each time they speak, move, or listen. The task is always, to repeat, that of *getting into the act*.

ASKING QUESTIONS
ABOUT *TARTUFFE*

The two assignments on *Tartuffe* center on scenes in which changes occur in the perception of one character by the other characters. The changes of perception are individual; they don't occur in the same way or at the same time for each of the

characters who experience them. To bring them to life it's necessary to imagine — separately — each character's movements of
mind, eye, and body, and the assignment questions focus on these
movements. As with *Macbeth*, I walk through the first assignment,
providing reading notes and other materials and my own response.

MOLIÈRE [JEAN-BAPTISTE POQUELIN]   (1622–1673)

Tartuffe

TRANSLATED BY RICHARD WILBUR

CHARACTERS

Madame Pernelle, *Orgon's mother*
Orgon, *Elmire's husband*
Elmire, *Orgon's wife*
Damis, *Orgon's son, Elmire's stepson*
Mariane, *Orgon's daughter, Elmire's*
    stepdaughter, in love with Valère
Valère, *in love with Mariane*

Cléante, *Orgon's brother-in-law*
Tartuffe, *a hypocrite*
Dorine, *Mariane's lady's-maid*
Monsieur Loyal, *a bailiff*
A Police Officer
Flipote, *Madame Pernelle's maid*

THE SCENE THROUGHOUT: *Orgon's house in Paris*

ACT I

SCENE I. *Madame Pernelle and Flipote, her maid, Elmire, Dorine, Cléante,
Mariane, Damis*

Madame Pernelle: Come, come, Flipote; it's time I left this place.
Elmire: I can't keep up, you walk at such a pace.
Madame Pernelle: Don't trouble, child; no need to show me out.
    It's not your manners I'm concerned about.
Elmire: We merely pay you the respect we owe.   5
    But, Mother, why this hurry? Must you go?
Madame Pernelle: I must. This house appalls me. No one in it
    Will pay attention for a single minute.
    Children, I take my leave much vexed in spirit.
    I offer good advice, but you won't hear it.   10
    You all break in and chatter on and on.
    It's like a madhouse with the keeper gone.
Dorine: If . . .
Madame Pernelle: Girl, you talk too much, and I'm afraid

You're far too saucy for a lady's-maid.
You push in everywhere and have your say.   15
Damis: But . . .
Madame Pernelle: You, boy, grow more foolish every day.
To think my grandson should be such a dunce!
I've said a hundred times, if I've said it once,
That if you keep the course on which you've started,
You'll leave your worthy father broken-hearted.   20
Mariane: I think . . .
Madame Pernelle: And you, his sister, seems so pure,
So shy, so innocent, and so demure.
But you know what they say about still waters.
I pity parents with secretive daughters.
Elmire: Now, Mother . . .
Madame Pernelle: And as for you, child, let me add   25
That your behavior is extremely bad,
And a poor example for these children, too.
Their dear, dead mother did far better than you.
You're much too free with money, and I'm distressed
To see you so elaborately dressed.   30
When it's one's husband that one aims to please,
One has no need of costly fripperies.
Cléante: Oh, Madam, really . . .
Madame Pernelle: You are her brother, Sir,
And I respect and love you; yet if I were
My son, this lady's good and pious spouse,   35
I wouldn't make you welcome in my house.
You're full of worldly counsels which, I fear,
Aren't suitable for decent folk to hear.
I've spoken bluntly, Sir; but it behooves us
Not to mince words when righteous fervor moves us.   40
Damis: Your man Tartuffe is full of holy speeches . . .
Madame Pernelle: And practises precisely what he preaches.
He's a fine man, and should be listened to.
I will not hear him mocked by fools like you.
Damis: Good God! Do you expect me to submit   45
To the tyranny of that carping hypocrite?
Must we forgo all joys and satisfactions
Because that bigot censures all our actions?
Dorine: To hear him talk — and he talks all the time —
There's nothing one can do that's not a crime.   50
He rails at everything, your dear Tartuffe.
Madame Pernelle: Whatever he reproves deserves reproof.

He's out to save your souls, and all of you
Must love him, as my son would have you do.
Damis: Ah no, Grandmother, I could never take   55
To such a rascal, even for my father's sake.
That's how I feel, and I shall not dissemble.
His every action makes me seethe and tremble
With helpless anger, and I have no doubt
That he and I will shortly have it out.   60
Dorine: Surely it is a shame and a disgrace
To see this man usurp the master's place —
To see this beggar who, when first he came,
Had not a shoe or shoestring to his name
So far forget himself that he behaves   65
As if the house were his, and we his slaves.
Madame Pernelle: Well, mark my words, your souls would fare far
      better
If you obeyed his precepts to the letter.
Dorine: You see him as a saint. I'm far less awed;
In fact, I see right through him. He's a fraud.   70
Madame Pernelle: Nonsense!
Dorine: His man Laurent's the same, or worse;
I'd not trust either with a penny purse.
Madame Pernelle: I can't say what his servant's morals may be;
His own great goodness I can guarantee.
You all regard him with distaste and fear   75
Because he tells you what you're loath to hear,
Condemns your sins, points out your moral flaws,
And humbly strives to further Heaven's cause.
Dorine: If sin is all that bothers him, why is it
He's so upset when folk drop in to visit?   80
Is Heaven so outraged by a social call
That he must prophesy against us all?
I'll tell you what I think: if you ask me,
He's jealous of my mistress' company.
Madame Pernelle: Rubbish! (*To Elmire.*) He's not alone, child, in
      complaining   85
Of all your promiscuous entertaining.
Why, the whole neighborhood's upset, I know,
By all these carriages that come and go,
With crowds of guests parading in and out
And noisy servants loitering about.   90
In all of this, I'm sure there's nothing vicious;
But why give people cause to be suspicious?

Cléante: They need no cause; they'll talk in any case.
　　Madam, this world would be a joyless place
　　If, fearing what malicious tongues might say,　　　　　　95
　　We locked our doors and turned our friends away.
　　And even if one did so dreary a thing,
　　D'you think those tongues would cease their chattering?
　　One can't fight slander; it's a losing battle;
　　Let us instead ignore their tittle-tattle.　　　　　　　100
　　Let's strive to live by conscience' clear decrees,
　　And let the gossips gossip as they please.
Dorine: If there is talk against us, I know the source:
　　It's Daphne and her little husband, of course.
　　Those who have greatest cause for guilt and shame　　105
　　Are quickest to besmirch a neighbor's name.
　　When there's a chance for libel, they never miss it;
　　When something can be made to seem illicit
　　They're off at once to spread the joyous news,
　　Adding to fact what fantasies they choose.　　　　　　110
　　By talking up their neighbor's indiscretions
　　They seek to camouflage their own transgressions,
　　Hoping that others' innocent affairs
　　Will lend a hue of innocence to theirs,
　　Or that their own black guilt will come to seem　　　115
　　Part of a general shady color-scheme.
Madame Pernelle: All that is quite irrelevant. I doubt
　　That anyone's more virtuous and devout
　　Than dear Orante; and I'm informed that she
　　Condemns your mode of life most vehemently.　　　　120
Dorine: Oh, yes, she's strict, devout, and has no taint
　　Of worldliness; in short, she seems a saint.
　　But it was time which taught her that disguise;
　　She's thus because she can't be otherwise.
　　So long as her attractions could enthrall,　　　　　　125
　　She flounced and flirted and enjoyed it all,
　　But now that they're no longer what they were
　　She quits a world which fast is quitting her,
　　And wears a veil of virtue to conceal
　　Her bankrupt beauty and her lost appeal.　　　　　　130
　　That's what becomes of old coquettes today:
　　Distressed when all their lovers fall away,
　　They see no recourse but to play the prude,
　　And so confer a style on solitude.
　　Thereafter, they're severe with everyone,　　　　　　135

Condemning all our actions, pardoning none,
And claiming to be pure, austere, and zealous
When, if the truth were known, they're merely jealous,
And cannot bear to see another know
The pleasures time has forced them to forgo.   140
Madame Pernelle (initially to Elmire): That sort of talk is what you
      like to hear;
Therefore you'd have us all keep still, my dear,
While Madam rattles on the livelong day.
Nevertheless, I mean to have my say.
I tell you that you're blest to have Tartuffe   145
Dwelling, as my son's guest, beneath this roof;
That Heaven has sent him to forestall its wrath
By leading you, once more, to the true path;
That all he reprehends is reprehensible,
And that you'd better heed him, and be sensible.   150
These visits, balls, and parties in which you revel
Are nothing but inventions of the Devil.
One never hears a word that's edifying:
Nothing but chaff and foolishness and lying,
As well as vicious gossip in which one's neighbor   155
Is cut to bits with epee, foil, and saber.
People of sense are driven half-insane
At such affairs, where noise and folly reign
And reputations perish thick and fast.
As a wise preacher said on Sunday last,   160
Parties are Towers of Babylon, because
The guests all babble on with never a pause;
And then he told a story which, I think . . .
(To Cléante.) I heard that laugh, Sir, and I saw that wink!
Go find your silly friends and laugh some more!   165
Enough; I'm going; don't show me to the door.
I leave this household much dismayed and vexed;
I cannot say when I shall see you next.
(Slapping Flipote.) Wake up, don't stand there gaping into
      space!
I'll slap some sense into that stupid face.   170
Move, move, you slut.

SCENE II. *Cléante, Dorine*

Cléante: I think I'll stay behind;
I want no further pieces of her mind.
How that old lady . . .

Dorine: Oh, what wouldn't she say
    If she could hear you speak of her that way!
    She'd thank you for the *lady*, but I'm sure   5
    She'd find the *old* a little premature.
Cléante: My, what a scene she made, and what a din!
    And how this man Tartuffe has taken her in!
Dorine: Yes, but her son is even worse deceived;
    His folly must be seen to be believed.   10
    In the late troubles, he played an able part
    And served his king with wise and loyal heart,
    But he's quite lost his senses since he fell
    Beneath Tartuffe's infatuating spell.
    He calls him brother, and loves him as his life,   15
    Preferring him to mother, child, or wife.
    In him and him alone will he confide;
    He's made him his confessor and his guide;
    He pets and pampers him with love more tender
    Than any pretty mistress could engender,   20
    Gives him the place of honor when they dine,
    Delights to see him gorging like a swine,
    Stuffs him with dainties till his guts distend,
    And when he belches, cries "God bless you, friend!"
    In short, he's mad; he worships him; he dotes;   25
    His deeds he marvels at, his words he quotes,
    Thinking each act a miracle, each word
    Oracular as those that Moses heard.
    Tartuffe, much pleased to find so easy a victim,
    Has in a hundred ways beguiled and tricked him,   30
    Milked him of money, and with his permission
    Established here a sort of Inquisition.
    Even Laurent, his lackey, dares to give
    Us arrogant advice on how to live;
    He sermonizes us in thundering tones   35
    And confiscates our ribbons and colognes.
    Last week he tore a kerchief into pieces
    Because he found it pressed in a *Life of Jesus*.
    He said it was a sin to juxtapose
    Unholy vanities and holy prose.   40

SCENE III. *Elmire, Damis, Dorine, Mariane, Cléante*

Elmire (to Cléante): You did well not to follow; she stood in the
        door
    And said *verbatim* all she'd said before.

I saw my husband coming. I think I'd best
Go upstairs now, and take a little rest.
Cléante: I'll wait and greet him here; then I must go.   5
I've really only time to say hello.
Damis: Sound him about my sister's wedding, please.
I think Tartuffe's against it, and that he's
Been urging Father to withdraw his blessing.
As you well know, I'd find that most distressing.   10
Unless my sister and Valère can marry,
My hopes to wed *his* sister will miscarry,
And I'm determined . . .
Dorine: He's coming.

Scene IV. *Orgon, Cléante, Dorine*

Orgon: Ah, Brother, good-day.
Cléante: Well, welcome back. I'm sorry I can't stay.
How was the country? Blooming, I trust, and green?
Orgon: Excuse me, Brother; just one moment.
   (*To Dorine.*)   Dorine . . .
   (*To Cléante.*) To put my mind at rest, I always learn   5
The household news the moment I return.
   (*To Dorine.*) Has all been well, these two days I've been gone?
How are the family? What's been going on?
Dorine: Your wife, two days ago, had a bad fever,
And a fierce headache which refused to leave her.   10
Orgon: Ah. And Tartuffe?
Dorine: Tartuffe? Why, he's round and red,
Bursting with health, and excellently fed.
Orgon: Poor fellow!
Dorine: That night, the mistress was unable
To take a single bite at the dinner-table.
Her headache-pains, she said, were simply hellish.   15
Orgon: Ah. And Tartuffe?
Dorine: He ate his meal with relish,
And zealously devoured in her presence
A leg of mutton and a brace of pheasants.
Orgon: Poor fellow!
Dorine: Well, the pains continued strong,
And so she tossed and tossed the whole night long,   20
Now icy-cold, now burning like a flame.
We sat beside her bed till morning came.
Orgon: Ah. And Tartuffe?

Dorine: Why, having eaten, he rose
  And sought his room, already in a doze,
  Got into his warm bed, and snored away   25
  In perfect peace until the break of day.
Orgon: Poor fellow!
Dorine: After much ado, we talked her
  Into dispatching someone for the doctor.
  He bled her, and the fever quickly fell.
Orgon: Ah. And Tartuffe?
Dorine: He bore it very well.   30
  To keep his cheerfulness at any cost,
  And make up for the blood *Madame* had lost,
  He drank, at lunch, four beakers full of port.
Orgon: Poor fellow!
Dorine: Both are doing well, in short.
  I'll go and tell *Madame* that you've expressed   35
  Keen sympathy and anxious interest.

SCENE V. *Orgon, Cléante*

Cléante: That girl was laughing in your face, and though
  I've no wish to offend you, even so
  I'm bound to say that she had some excuse.
  How can you possibly be such a goose?
  Are you so dazed by this man's hocus-pocus   5
  That all the world, save him, is out of focus?
  You've given him clothing, shelter, food, and care;
  Why must you also . . .
Orgon: Brother, stop right there.
  You do not know the man of whom you speak.
Cléante: I grant you that. But my judgment's not so weak   10
  That I can't tell, by his effect on others . . .
Orgon: Ah, when you meet him, you two will be like brothers!
  There's been no loftier soul since time began.
  He is a man who . . . an excellent man.
  To keep his precepts is to be reborn,   15
  And view this dunghill of a world with scorn.
  Yes, thanks to him I'm a changed man indeed.
  Under his tutelage my soul's been freed
  From earthly loves, and every human tie:
  My mother, children, brother, and wife could die,   20
  And I'd not feel a single moment's pain.
Cléante: That's a fine sentiment, Brother; most humane.

Orgon: Oh, had you seen Tartuffe as I first knew him,
  Your heart, like mine, would have surrendered to him.
  He used to come into our church each day   25
  And humbly kneel nearby, and start to pray.
  He'd draw the eyes of everybody there
  By the deep fervor of his heartfelt prayer;
  He'd sigh and weep, and sometimes with a sound
  Of rapture he would bend and kiss the ground;   30
  And when I rose to go, he'd run before
  To offer me holy-water at the door.
  His serving-man, no less devout than he,
  Informed me of his master's poverty;
  I gave him gifts, but in his humbleness   35
  He'd beg me every time to give him less.
  "Oh, that's too much," he'd cry, "too much by twice!
  I don't deserve it. The half, Sir, would suffice."
  And when I wouldn't take it back, he'd share
  Half of it with the poor, right then and there.   40
  At length, Heaven prompted me to take him in
  To dwell with us, and free our souls from sin.
  He guides our lives, and to protect my honor
  Stays by my wife, and keeps an eye upon her;
  He tells me whom she sees, and all she does,   45
  And seems more jealous than I ever was!
  And how austere he is! Why, he can detect
  A mortal sin where you would least suspect;
  In smallest trifles, he's extremely strict.
  Last week, his conscience was severely pricked   50
  Because, while praying, he had caught a flea
  And killed it, so he felt, too wrathfully.
Cléante: Good God, man! Have you lost your common sense —
  Or is this all some joke at my expense?
  How can you stand there and in all sobriety . . .   55
Orgon: Brother, your language savors of impiety.
  Too much free-thinking's made your faith unsteady,
  And as I've warned you many times already,
  'Twill get you into trouble before you're through.
Cléante: So I've been told before by dupes like you: 60
  Being blind, you'd have all others blind as well;
  The clear-eyed man you call an infidel,
  And he who sees through humbug and pretense
  Is charged, by you, with want of reverence.
  Spare me your warnings, Brother; I have no fear   65
  Of speaking out, for you and Heaven to hear,

Against affected zeal and pious knavery.
There's true and false in piety, as in bravery,
And just as those whose courage shines the most
In battle, are the least inclined to boast,   70
So those whose hearts are truly pure and lowly
Don't make a flashy show of being holy.
There's a vast difference, so it seems to me,
Between true piety and hypocrisy:
How do you fail to see it, may I ask?   75
Is not a face quite different from a mask?
Cannot sincerity and cunning art,
Reality and semblance, be told apart?
Are scarecrows just like men, and do you hold
That a false coin is just as good as gold?   80
Ah, Brother, man's a strangely fashioned creature
Who seldom is content to follow Nature,
But recklessly pursues his inclination
Beyond the narrow bounds of moderation,
And often, by transgressing Reason's laws,   85
Perverts a lofty aim or noble cause.
A passing observation, but it applies.
Orgon: I see, dear Brother, that you're profoundly wise;
You harbor all the insight of the age
You are our one clear mind, our only sage,   90
The era's oracle, its Cato too,
And all mankind arc fools compared to you.
Cléante: Brother, I don't pretend to be a sage,
Nor have I all the wisdom of the age.
There's just one insight I would dare to claim: 95
I know that true and false are not the same;
And just as there is nothing I more revere
Than a soul whose faith is steadfast and sincere,
Nothing that I more cherish and admire
Than honest zeal and true religious fire,   100
So there is nothing that I find more base
Than specious piety's dishonest face —
Than these bold mountebanks, these histrios
Whose impious mummeries and hollow shows
Exploit our love of Heaven, and make a jest   105
Of all that men think holiest and best;
These calculating souls who offer prayers
Not to their Maker, but as public wares,
And seek to buy respect and reputation
With lifted eyes and sighs of exaltation;   110

These charlatans, I say, whose pilgrim souls
Proceed, by way of Heaven, toward earthly goals,
Who weep and pray and swindle and extort,
Who preach the monkish life, but haunt the court,
Who make their zeal the partner of their vice —   115
Such men are vengeful, sly, and cold as ice,
And when there is an enemy to defame
They cloak their spite in fair religion's name,
Their private spleen and malice being made
To seem a high and virtuous crusade,   120
Until, to mankind's reverent applause,
They crucify their foe in Heaven's cause.
Such knaves are all too common; yet, for the wise,
True piety isn't hard to recognize,
And, happily, these present times provide us   125
With bright examples to instruct and guide us.
Consider Ariston and Périandre;
Look at Oronte, Alcidamas, Clitandre;°
Their virtue is acknowledged; who could doubt it?
But you won't hear them beat the drum about it.   130
They're never ostentatious, never vain,
And their religion's moderate and humane;
It's not their way to criticize and chide:
They think censoriousness a mark of pride,
And therefore, letting others preach and rave,   135
They show, by deeds, how Christians should behave.
They think no evil of their fellow man,
But judge of him as kindly as they can.
They don't intrigue and wangle and conspire;
To lead a good life is their one desire;   140
The sinner wakes no rancorous hate in them;
It is the sin alone which they condemn;
Nor do they try to show a fiercer zeal
For Heaven's cause than Heaven itself could feel.
These men I honor, these men I advocate   145
As models for us all to emulate.
Your man is not their sort at all, I fear:
And, while your praise of him is quite sincere,
I think that you've been dreadfully deluded.
Orgon: Now then, dear Brother, is your speech concluded?   150
Cléante: Why, yes.

127–128 *Ariston . . . Clitandre:* Classical-sounding but fictitious names.

Orgon:	Your servant, Sir. (*He turns to go.*)
Cléante:	No, Brother; wait.

There's one more matter. You agreed of late
That young Valère might have your daughter's hand.
Orgon: I did.
Cléante: And set the date, I understand.
Orgon: Quite so.
Cléante: You've now postponed it; is that true?   155
Orgon: No doubt.
Cléante: The match no longer pleases you?
Orgon: Who knows?
Cléante: D'you mean to go back on your word?
Orgon: I won't say that.
Cléante: Has anything occurred
Which might entitle you to break your pledge?
Orgon: Perhaps.
Cléante: Why must you hem, and haw, and hedge?   160
The boy asked me to sound you in this affair . . .
Orgon: It's been a pleasure.
Cléante: But what shall I tell Valère?
Orgon: Whatever you like.
Cléante: But what have you decided?
What are your plans?
Orgon: I plan, Sir, to be guided
By Heaven's will.
Cléante: Come, Brother, don't talk rot.   165
You've given Valère your word; will you keep it, or not?
Orgon: Good day.
Cléante: This looks like poor Valère's undoing;
I'll go and warn him that there's trouble brewing.

ACT II

Scene I. *Orgon, Mariane*

Orgon: Mariane.
Mariane: Yes, Father?
Orgon: A word with you; come here.
Mariane: What are you looking for?
Orgon (peering into a small closet): Eavesdroppers, dear.
I'm making sure we shan't be overheard.
Someone in there could catch our every word.
Ah, good, we're safe. Now, Mariane, my child,   5

You're a sweet girl who's tractable and mild,
Whom I hold dear, and think most highly of.
Mariane: I'm deeply grateful, Father, for your love.
Orgon: That's well said, Daughter; and you can repay me
    If, in all things, you'll cheerfully obey me.   10
Mariane: To please you, Sir, is what delights me best
Orgon: Good, good. Now, what d'you think of Tartuffe, our guest?
Mariane: I, Sir?
Orgon: Yes. Weigh your answer; think it through.
Mariane: Oh, dear. I'll say whatever you wish me to.
Orgon: That's wisely said, my Daughter. Say of him, then,   15
    That he's the very worthiest of men,
    And that you're fond of him, and would rejoice
    In being his wife, if that should be my choice.
    Well?
Mariane: What?
Orgon: What's that?
Mariane: I . . .
Orgon: Well?
Mariane: Forgive me, pray.
Orgon: Did you not hear me?
Mariane: Of *whom*, Sir, must I say   20
    That I am fond of him, and would rejoice
    In being his wife, if that should be your choice?
Orgon: Why, of Tartuffe.
Mariane: But, Father, that's false, you know.
    Why would you have me say what isn't so?
Orgon: Because I am resolved it shall be true.   25
    That it's my wish should be enough for you.
Mariane: You can't mean, Father . . .
Orgon: Yes, Tartuffe shall be
    Allied by marriage to this family,
    And he's to be your husband, is that clear?
    It's a father's privilege . . .   30

SCENE II. *Dorine, Orgon, Mariane*

Orgon (to Dorine):   What are you doing in here?
    Is curiosity so fierce a passion
    With you, that you must eavesdrop in this fashion?
Dorine: There's lately been a rumor going about —
    Based on some hunch or chance remark, no doubt —   5
    That you mean Mariane to wed Tartuffe.
    I've laughed it off, of course, as just a spoof.

Orgon: You find it so incredible?
Dorine: Yes, I do.
   I won't accept that story, even from you.
Orgon: Well, you'll believe it when the thing is done.   10
Dorine: Yes, yes, of course. Go on and have your fun.
Orgon: I've never been more serious in my life.
Dorine: Ha!
Orgon: Daughter, I mean it; you're to be his wife.
Dorine: No, don't believe your father; it's all a hoax.
Orgon: See here, young woman . . .
Dorine: Come, Sir, no more jokes;   15
   You can't fool us.
Orgon: How dare you talk that way?
Dorine: All right, then: we believe you, sad to say.
   But how a man like you, who looks so wise
   And wears a moustache of such splendid size,
   Can be so foolish as to . . .
Orgon: Silence, please!   20
   My girl, you take too many liberties.
   I'm master here, as you must not forget.
Dorine: Do let's discuss this calmly; don't be upset.
   You can't be serious, Sir, about this plan.
   What should that bigot want with Marianc?   25
   Praying and fasting ought to keep him busy.
   And then, in terms of wealth and rank, what is he?
   Why should a man of property like you
   Pick out a beggar son-in-law?
Orgon: That will do.
   Speak of his poverty with reverence.   30
   His is a pure and saintly indigence
   Which far transcends all worldly pride and pelf.
   He lost his fortune, as he says himself,
   Because he cared for Heaven alone, and so
   Was careless of his interests here below.   35
   I mean to get him out of his present straits
   And help him to recover his estates —
   Which, in his part of the world, have no small fame.
   Poor though he is, he's a gentleman just the same.
Dorine: Yes, so he tells us; and, Sir, it seems to me   40
   Such pride goes very ill with piety.
   A man whose spirit spurns this dungy earth
   Ought not to brag of lands and noble birth;
   Such worldly arrogance will hardly square
   With meek devotion and the life of prayer.   45

      . . . But this approach, I see, has drawn a blank;
      Let's speak, then, of his person, not his rank.
      Doesn't it seem to you a trifle grim
      To give a girl like her to a man like him?
      When two are so ill-suited, can't you see   50
      What the sad consequence is bound to be?
      A young girl's virtue is imperilled, Sir,
      When such a marriage is imposed on her;
      For if one's bridegroom isn't to one's taste,
      It's hardly an inducement to be chaste,   55
      And many a man with horns upon his brow
      Has made his wife the thing that she is now.
      It's hard to be a faithful wife, in short,
      To certain husbands of a certain sort,
      And he who gives his daughter to a man she hates   60
      Must answer for her sins at Heaven's gates.
      Think, Sir, before you play so risky a role.
Orgon: This servant-girl presumes to save my soul!
Dorine: You would do well to ponder what I've said.
Orgon: Daughter, we'll disregard this dunderhead.   65
      Just trust your father's judgment. Oh, I'm aware
      That I once promised you to young Valère;
      But now I hear he gambles, which greatly shocks me;
      What's more, I've doubts about his orthodoxy.
      His visits to church, I note, are very few.   70
Dorine: Would you have him go at the same hours as you,
      And kneel nearby, to be sure of being seen?
Orgon: I can dispense with such remarks, Dorine.
      (*To Mariane.*) Tartuffe, however, is sure of Heaven's blessing,
      And that's the only treasure worth possessing.   75
      This match will bring you joys beyond all measure;
      Your cup will overflow with every pleasure;
      You two will interchange your faithful loves
      Like two sweet cherubs, or two turtle-doves.
      No harsh word shall be heard, no frown be seen,   80
      And he shall make you happy as a queen.
Dorine: And she'll make him a cuckold, just wait and see.
Orgon: What language!
Dorine: Oh, he's a man of destiny;
      He's *made* for horns, and what the stars demand
      Your daughter's virtue surely can't withstand.   85
Orgon: Don't interrupt me further. Why can't you learn
      That certain things are none of your concern?
Dorine: It's for your own sake that I interfere.

She repeatedly interrupts Orgon just as he is turning to speak to his daughter.

Orgon: Most kind of you. Now, hold your tongue, d'you hear?
Dorine: If I didn't love you . . .
Orgon: Spare me your affection.   90
Dorine: I love you, Sir, in spite of your objection.
Orgon: Blast!
Dorine: I can't bear, Sir, for your honor's sake,
    To let you make this ludicrous mistake.
Orgon: You mean to go on talking?
Dorine: If I didn't protest
    This sinful marriage, my conscience couldn't rest.   95
Orgon: If you don't hold your tongue, you little shrew . . .
Dorine: What, lost your temper? A pious man like you?
Orgon: Yes! Yes! You talk and talk. I'm maddened by it.
    Once and for all, I tell you to be quiet.
Dorine: Well, I'll be quiet. But I'll be thinking hard.   100
Orgon: Think all you like, but you had better guard
    That saucy tongue of yours, or I'll . . .
    (Turning back to Mariane.)   Now, child,
    I've weighed this matter fully.
Dorine (aside):   It drives me wild
    That I can't speak.

Orgon turns his head, and she is silent.

Orgon: Tartuffe is no young dandy,
    But, still, his person . . .
Dorine (aside):   Is as sweet as candy.   105
Orgon: Is such that, even if you shouldn't care
    For his other merits . . .

He turns and stands facing Dorine, arms crossed.

Dorine (aside):   They'll make a lovely pair.
    If I were she, no man would marry me
    Against my inclination, and go scot-free.
    He'd learn, before the wedding-day was over,   110
    How readily a wife can find a lover.
Orgon (to Dorine): It seems you treat my orders as a joke.
Dorine: Why, what's the matter? 'Twas not to you I spoke.
Orgon: What *were* you doing?
Dorine: Talking to myself, that's all.
Orgon: Ah! *(Aside.)* One more bit of impudence and gall,   115
    And I shall give her a good slap in the face.

He puts himself in position to slap her; Dorine, whenever he glances at her, stands immobile and silent.

> Daughter, you shall accept, and with good grace,
> The husband I've selected . . . Your wedding-day . . .
> (*To Dorine.*) Why don't you talk to yourself?
> *Dorine:*   I've nothing to say.
> *Orgon:* Come, just one word.
> *Dorine:*   No thank you, Sir. I pass.   120
> *Orgon:* Come, speak; I'm waiting.
> *Dorine:*   I'd not be such an ass.
> *Orgon (turning to Mariane):* In short, dear Daughter, I mean to be
>   obeyed,
> And you must bow to the sound choice I've made.
> *Dorine (moving away):* I'd not wed such a monster, even in jest.

Orgon attempts to slap her, but misses.

> *Orgon:* Daughter, that maid of yours is a thorough pest;   125
>   She makes me sinfully annoyed and nettled.
>   I can't speak further; my nerves are too unsettled.
>   She's so upset me by her insolent talk,
>   I'll calm myself by going for a walk.

SCENE III. *Dorine, Mariane*

> *Dorine (returning):* Well, have you lost your tongue, girl? Must I
>   play
>   Your part, and say the lines you ought to say?
>   Faced with a fate so hideous and absurd,
>   Can you not utter one dissenting word?
> *Mariane:* What good would it do? A father's power is great.   5
> *Dorine:* Resist him now, or it will be too late.
> *Mariane:* But . . .
> *Dorine:*   Tell him one cannot love at a father's whim;
>   That you shall marry for yourself, not him;
>   That since it's you who are to be the bride,
>   It's you, not he, who must be satisfied;   10
>   And that if his Tartuffe is so sublime,
>   He's free to marry him at any time.
> *Mariane:* I've bowed so long to Father's strict control,
>   I couldn't oppose him now, to save my soul.
> *Dorine:* Come, come, Mariane. Do listen to reason, won't you?   15
>   Valère has asked your hand. Do you love him, or don't you?
> *Mariane:* Oh, how unjust of you! What can you mean

By asking such a question, dear Dorine?
You know the depth of my affection for him;
I've told you a hundred times how I adore him.   20
Dorine: I don't believe in everything I hear;
Who knows if your professions were sincere?
Mariane: They were, Dorine, and you do me wrong to doubt it;
Heaven knows that I've been all too frank about it.
Dorine: You love him, then?
Mariane: Oh, more than I can express.   25
Dorine: And he, I take it, cares for you no less?
Mariane: I think so.
Dorine: And you both, with equal fire,
Burn to be married?
Mariane: That is our one desire.
Dorine: What of Tartuffe, then? What of your father's plan?
Mariane: I'll kill myself, if I'm forced to wed that man.   30
Dorine: I hadn't thought of that recourse. How splendid!
Just die, and all your troubles will be ended!
A fine solution. Oh, it maddens me
To hear you talk in that self-pitying key.
Mariane: Dorine, how harsh you are! It's most unfair.   35
You have no sympathy for my despair.
Dorine: I've none at all for people who talk drivel
And, faced with difficulties, whine and snivel.
Mariane: No doubt I'm timid, but it would be wrong . . .
Dorine: True love requires a heart that's firm and strong. 40
Mariane: I'm strong in my affection for Valère,
But coping with my father is his affair.
Dorine: But if your father's brain has grown so cracked
Over his dear Tartuffe that he can retract
His blessing, though your wedding-day was named,   45
It's surely not Valère who's to be blamed.
Mariane: If I defied my father, as you suggest,
Would it not seem unmaidenly, at best?
Shall I defend my love at the expense
Of brazenness and disobedience?   50
Shall I parade my heart's desires, and flaunt . . .
Dorine: No, I ask nothing of you. Clearly you want
To be Madame Tartuffe, and I feel bound
Not to oppose a wish so very sound.
What right have I to criticize the match?   55
Indeed, my dear, the man's a brilliant catch.
Monsieur Tartuffe! Now, there's a man of weight!
Yes, yes, Monsieur Tartuffe, I'm bound to state,

Is quite a person; that's not to be denied;
'Twill be no little thing to be his bride.   60
The world already rings with his renown;
He's a great noble — in his native town;
His ears are red, he has a pink complexion,
And all in all, he'll suit you to perfection.
Mariane: Dear God!
Dorine: Oh, how triumphant you will feel   65
At having caught a husband so ideal!
Mariane: Oh, do stop teasing, and use your cleverness
To get me out of this appalling mess.
Advise me, and I'll do whatever you say.
Dorine: Ah no, a dutiful daughter must obey   70
Her father, even if he weds her to an ape.
You've a bright future; why struggle to escape?
Tartuffe will take you back where his family lives,
To a small town aswarm with relatives —
Uncles and cousins whom you'll be charmed to meet.   75
You'll be received at once by the elite,
Calling upon the bailiff's wife, no less —
Even, perhaps, upon the mayoress,
Who'll sit you down in the *best* kitchen chair.
Then, once a year, you'll dance at the village fair   80
To the drone of bagpipes — two of them, in fact —
And see a puppet-show, or an animal act.
Your husband . . .
Mariane: Oh, you turn my blood to ice!
Stop torturing me, and give me your advice.
Dorine (threatening to go): Your servant, Madam.
Mariane: Dorine, I beg of you . . .   85
Dorine: No, you deserve it; this marriage must go through.
Mariane: Dorine!
Dorine: No.
Mariane: Not Tartuffe! You know I think him . . .
Dorine: Tartuffe's your cup of tea, and you shall drink him.
Mariane: I've always told you everything, and relied . . .
Dorine: No. You deserve to be tartuffified.   90
Mariane: Well, since you mock me and refuse to care,
I'll henceforth seek my solace in despair:
Despair shall be my counsellor and friend,
And help me bring my sorrows to an end.

She starts to leave.

Dorine: There now, come back; my anger has subsided.   95
  You do deserve some pity, I've decided.
Mariane: Dorine, if Father makes me undergo
  This dreadful martyrdom, I'll die, I know.
Dorine: Don't fret; it won't be difficult to discover
  Some plan of action . . . But here's Valère, your lover.   100

SCENE IV. *Valère, Mariane, Dorine*

Valère: Madam, I've just received some wondrous news
  Regarding which I'd like to hear your views.
Mariane: What news?
Valère: You're marrying Tartuffe.
Mariane: I find
  That Father does have such a match in mind.
Valère: Your father, Madam . . .
Mariane: . . . has just this minute said   5
  That it's Tartuffe he wishes me to wed.
Valère: Can he be serious?
Mariane: Oh, indeed he can;
  He's clearly set his heart upon the plan.
Valère: And what position do you propose to take,
  Madam?
Mariane: Why — I don't know.
Valère: For heaven's sake —   10
  You don't know?
Mariane: No.
Valère: Well, well!
Mariane: Advise me, do.
Valère: Marry the man. That's my advice to you.
Mariane: That's your advice?
Valère: Yes.
Mariane: Truly?
Valère: Oh, absolutely.
  You couldn't choose more wisely, more astutely.
Mariane: Thanks for this counsel; I'll follow it, of course.   15
Valère: Do, do; I'm sure 'twill cost you no remorse.
Mariane: To give it didn't cause your heart to break.
Valère: I gave it, Madam, only for your sake.
Mariane: And it's for your sake that I take it, Sir.
Dorine (withdrawing to the rear of the stage): Let's see which fool will
  prove the stubborner.   20

Valère: So! I am nothing to you, and it was flat
    Deception when you . . .
Mariane: Please, enough of that.
    You've told me plainly that I should agree
    To wed the man my father's chosen for me,
    And since you've designed to counsel me so wisely,   25
    I promise, Sir, to do as you advise me.
Valère: Ah, no, 'twas not by me that you were swayed.
    No, your decision was already made;
    Though now, to save appearances, you protest
    That you're betraying me at my behest.   30
Mariane: Just as you say.
Valère: Quite so. And I now see
    That you were never truly in love with me.
Mariane: Alas, you're free to think so if you choose.
Valère: I choose to think so, and here's a bit of news:
    You've spurned my hand, but I know where to turn   35
    For kinder treatment, as you shall quickly learn.
Mariane: I'm sure you do. Your noble qualities
    Inspire affection . . .
Valère: Forget my qualities, please.
    They don't inspire you overmuch, I find.
    But there's another lady I have in mind   40
    Whose sweet and generous nature will not scorn
    To compensate me for the loss I've borne.
Mariane: I'm no great loss, and I'm sure that you'll transfer
    Your heart quite painlessly from me to her.
Valère: I'll do my best to take it in my stride.   45
    The pain I feel at being cast aside
    Time and forgetfulness may put an end to.
    Or if I can't forget, I shall pretend to.
    No self-respecting person is expected
    To go on loving once he's been rejected.   50
Mariane: Now, that's a fine, high-minded sentiment.
Valère: One to which any sane man would assent.
    Would you prefer it if I pined away
    In hopeless passion till my dying day?
    Am I to yield you to a rival's arm   55
    And not console myself with other charms?
Mariane: Go then: console yourself; don't hesitate.
    I wish you to; indeed, I cannot wait.
Valère: You wish me to?
Mariane: Yes.

Valère: That's the final straw.
        Madam, farewell. Your wish shall be my law.   60

He starts to leave, and then returns: this repeatedly.

Mariane: Splendid.
Valère (coming back again):
                        This breach, remember, is of your making;
        It's you who've driven me to the step I'm taking.
Mariane: Of course.
Valère (coming back again):
                        Remember, too, that I am merely
        Following your example.
Mariane: I see that clearly.
Valère: Enough. I'll go and do your bidding, then.   65
Mariane: Good.
Valère (coming back again):
                        You shall never see my face again.
Mariane: Excellent.
Valère (walking to the door, then turning about):
                        Yes?
Mariane: What?
Valère: What's that? What did you say?
Mariane: Nothing. You're dreaming.
Valère: Ah. Well, I'm on my way.
        Farewell, *Madame.*

He moves slowly away.

Mariane: Farewell.
Dorine (to Mariane):   If you ask me,
        Both of you are as mad as mad can be.   70
        Do stop this nonsense, now. I've only let you
        Squabble so long to see where it would get you.
        Whoa there, Monsieur Valère!

She goes and seizes Valère by the arm; he makes a great show of resistance.

Valère: What's this, Dorine?
Dorine: Come here.
Valère: No, no, my heart's too full of spleen.
        Don't hold me back; her wish must be obeyed.   75
Dorine: Stop!
Valère: It's too late now; my decision's made.
Dorine: Oh, pooh!

Mariane (aside):   He hates the sight of me, that's plain.
   I'll go, and so deliver him from pain.
Dorine (leaving Valère, running after Mariane):
   And now *you* run away! Come back.
Mariane: No, no.
   Nothing you say will keep me here. Let go!   80
Valère (aside): She cannot bear my presence, I perceive.
   To spare her further torment, I shall leave.
Dorine (leaving Mariane, running after Valère): Again! You'll not
      escape, Sir; don't you try it.
   Come here, you two. Stop fussing, and be quiet.

She takes Valère by the hand, then Mariane, and draws them together.

Valère (to Dorine): What do you want of me?
Mariane (to Dorine):   What is the point of this? 85
Dorine: We're going to have a little armistice.
      (*To Valère.*) Now weren't you silly to get so overheated?
Valère: Didn't you see how badly I was treated?
Dorine (to Mariane): Aren't you a simpleton, to have lost your
      head?
Mariane: Didn't you hear the hateful things he said?   90
Dorine (to Valère): You're both great fools. Her sole desire, Valère,
   Is to be yours in marriage. To that I'll swear.
      (*To Mariane.*) He loves you only, and he wants no wife
   But you, Mariane. On that I'll stake my life.
Mariane (to Valère): Then why you advised me so, I cannot see.   95
Valère (to Mariane): On such a question, why ask advice of *me*?
Dorine: Oh, you're impossible. Give me your hands, you two.
      (*To Valère.*)   Yours first.
Valère (giving Dorine his hand): But why?
Dorine (to Mariane):   And now a hand from you.
Mariane (also giving Dorine her hand):
   What are you doing?
Dorine: There: a perfect fit.
   You suit each other better than you'll admit.   100

Valère and Mariane hold hands for some time without looking at each other.

Valère (turning toward Mariane): Ah, come, don't be so haughty.
      Give a man
   A look of kindness, won't you, Mariane?

Mariane turns toward Valère and smiles.

Dorine: I tell you, lovers are completely mad!
Valère (to Mariane): Now come, confess that you were very bad
To hurt my feelings as you did just now.   105
I have a just complaint, you must allow.
Mariane: You must allow that you were most unpleasant . . .
Dorine: Let's table that discussion for the present;
Your father has a plan which must be stopped.
Mariane: Advise us, then; what means must we adopt?   110
Dorine: We'll use all manner of means, and all at once.
   (*To Mariane.*) Your father's addled; he's acting like a dunce.
   Therefore you'd better humor the old fossil.
   Pretend to yield to him, be sweet and docile,
   And then postpone, as often as necessary,   115
   The day on which you have agreed to marry.
   You'll thus gain time, and time will turn the trick.
   Sometimes, for instance, you'll be taken sick,
   And that will seem good reason for delay;
   Or some bad omen will make you change the day —   120
   You'll dream of muddy water, or you'll pass
   A dead man's hearse, or break a looking-glass.
   If all else fails, no man can marry you
   Unless you take his ring and say "I do."
   But now, let's separate. If they should find   125
   Us talking here, our plot might be divined.
   (*To Valère.*) Go to your friends, and tell them what's
       occurred,
   And have them urge her father to keep his word.
   Meanwhile, we'll stir her brother into action,
   And get Elmire, as well, to join our faction.   130
   Good-bye.
Valère (to Mariane):
              Though each of us will do his best,
   It's your true heart on which my hopes shall rest.
Mariane (to Valère): Regardless of what Father may decide,
   None but Valère shall claim me as his bride.
Valère: Oh, how those words content me! Come what will . . .   135
Dorine: Oh, lovers, lovers! Their tongues are never still.
   Be off, now.
Valère (turning to go, then turning back):
              One last word . . .
Dorine: No time to chat:
   You leave by this door; and *you* leave by that.

Dorine pushes them, by the shoulders, toward opposing doors.

ACT III

SCENE I. *Damis, Dorine*

Damis: May lightning strike me even as I speak,
       May all men call me cowardly and weak,
       If any fear or scruple holds me back
       From settling things, at once, with that great quack!
Dorine: Now, don't give way to violent emotion.   5
       Your father's merely talked about this notion,
       And words and deeds are far from being one.
       Much that is talked about is left undone.
Damis: No, I must stop that scoundrel's machinations;
       I'll go and tell him off; I'm out of patience.   10
Dorine: Do calm down and be practical. I had rather
       My mistress dealt with him — and with your father.
       She has some influence with Tartuffe, I've noted.
       He hangs upon her words, seems most devoted,
       And may, indeed, be smitten by her charm.   15
       Pray Heaven it's true! 'Twould do our cause no harm.
       She sent for him, just now, to sound him out
       On this affair you're so incensed about;
       She'll find out where he stands, and tell him, too,
       What dreadful strife and trouble will ensue   20
       If he lends countenance to your father's plan.
       I couldn't get in to see him, but his man
       Says that he's almost finished with his prayers.
       Go, now. I'll catch him when he comes downstairs.
Damis: I want to hear this conference, and I will.   25
Dorine: No, they must be alone.
Damis: Oh, I'll keep still.
Dorine: Not you. I know your temper. You'd start a brawl,
       And shout and stamp your foot and spoil it all.
       Go on.
Damis: I won't; I have a perfect right . . .
Dorine: Lord, you're a nuisance! He's coming; get out of sight.   30

Damis conceals himself in a closet at the rear of the stage.

SCENE II. *Tartuffe, Dorine*

Tartuffe (observing Dorine, and calling to his manservant offstage):
       Hang up my hair-shirt, put my scourge in place,

And pray, Laurent, for Heaven's perpetual grace.
I'm going to the prison now, to share
My last few coins with the poor wretches there.
Dorine (aside): Dear God, what affectation! What a fake!   5
Tartuffe: You wished to see me?
Dorine: Yes . . . .
Tartuffe (taking a handkerchief from his pocket):
                                    For mercy's sake,
Please take this handkerchief, before you speak.
Dorine: What?
Tartuffe: Cover that bosom, girl. The flesh is weak,
And unclean thoughts are difficult to control.
Such sights as that can undermine the soul.   10
Dorine: Your soul, it seems, has very poor defenses,
And flesh makes quite an impact on your senses.
It's strange that you're so easily excited;
My own desires are not so soon ignited,
And if I saw you naked as a beast,   15
Not all your hide would tempt me in the least.
Tartuffe: Girl, speak more modestly; unless you do,
I shall be forced to take my leave of you.
Dorine: Oh, no, it's I who must be on my way;
I've just one little message to convey.   20
Madame is coming down, and begs you, Sir,
To wait and have a word or two with her.
Tartuffe: Gladly.
Dorine (aside):   *That* had a softening effect!
I think my guess about him was correct.
Tartuffe: Will she be long?
Dorine: No: that's her step I hear.   25
Ah, here she is, and I shall disappear.

SCENE III. *Elmire, Tartuffe*

Tartuffe: May Heaven, whose infinite goodness we adore,
Preserve your body and soul forevermore,
And bless your days, and answer thus the plea
Of one who is its humblest votary.
Elmire: I thank you for that pious wish. But please,   5
Do take a chair and let's be more at ease.

They sit down.

Tartuffe: I trust that you are once more well and strong?

Elmire: Oh, yes: the fever didn't last for long.
Tartuffe: My prayers are too unworthy, I am sure,
    To have gained from Heaven this most gracious cure;   10
    But lately, Madam, my every supplication
    Has had for object your recuperation.
Elmire: You shouldn't have troubled so. I don't deserve it.
Tartuffe: Your health is priceless, Madam, and to preserve it
    I'd gladly give my own, in all sincerity.   15
Elmire: Sir, you outdo us all in Christian charity.
    You've been most kind. I count myself your debtor.
Tartuffe: 'Twas nothing, Madam. I long to serve you better.
Elmire: There's a private matter I'm anxious to discuss.
    I'm glad there's no one here to hinder us.   20
Tartuffe: I too am glad; it floods my heart with bliss
    To find myself alone with you like this.
    For just this chance I've prayed with all my power —
    But prayed in vain, until this happy hour.
Elmire: This won't take long, Sir, and I hope you'll be   25
    Entirely frank and unconstrained with me.
Tartuffe: Indeed, there's nothing I had rather do
    Than bare my inmost heart and soul to you.
    First, let me say that what remarks I've made
    About the constant visits you are paid   30
    Were prompted not by any mean emotion,
    But rather by a pure and deep devotion,
    A fervent zeal . . .
Elmire: No need for explanation.
    Your sole concern, I'm sure, was my salvation.
Tartuffe (taking Elmire's hand and pressing her fingertips): Quite so;
    and such great fervor do I feel . . .   35
Elmire: Ooh! Please! You're pinching!
Tartuffe: 'Twas from excess of zeal.
    I never meant to cause you pain, I swear.
    I'd rather . . .

He places his hand on Elmire's knee.

Elmire: What can your hand be doing there?
Tartuffe: Feeling your gown; what soft, fine-woven stuff!
Elmire: Please, I'm extremely ticklish. That's enough.   40

She draws her chair away; Tartuffe pulls his after her.

Tartuffe (fondling the lace collar of her gown): My, my, what lovely
    lacework on your dress!

The workmanship's miraculous, no less.
I've not seen anything to equal it.
Elmire: Yes, quite. But let's talk business for a bit.
They say my husband means to break his word   45
And give his daughter to you, Sir. Had you heard?
Tartuffe: He did once mention it. But I confess
I dream of quite a different happiness.
It's elsewhere, Madam, that my eyes discern
The promise of that bliss for which I yearn.   50
Elmire: I see: you care for nothing here below.
Tartuffe: Ah, well — my heart's not made of stone, you know.
Elmire: All your desires mount heavenward, I'm sure,
In scorn of all that's earthly and impure.
Tartuffe: A love of heavenly beauty does not preclude   55
A proper love for earthly pulchritude;
Our senses are quite rightly captivated
By perfect works our Maker has created.
Some glory clings to all that Heaven has made;
In you, all Heaven's marvels are displayed.   60
On that fair face, such beauties have been lavished,
The eyes are dazzled and the heart is ravished;
How could I look on you, O flawless creature,
And not adore the Author of all Nature,
Feeling a love both passionate and pure   65
For you, his triumph of self-portraiture?
At first, I trembled lest that love should be
A subtle snare that Hell had laid for me;
I vowed to flee the sight of you, eschewing
A rapture that might prove my soul's undoing;   70
But soon, fair being, I became aware
That my deep passion could be made to square
With rectitude, and with my bounden duty.
I thereupon surrendered to your beauty.
It is, I know, presumptuous on my part   75
To bring you this poor offering of my heart,
And it is not my merit, Heaven knows,
But your compassion on which my hopes repose.
You are my peace, my solace, my salvation;
On you depends my bliss — or desolation;   80
I bide your judgment and, as you think best,
I shall be either miserable or blest.
Elmire: Your declaration is most gallant, Sir,
But don't you think it's out of character?
You'd have done better to restrain your passion   85

　　　　And think before you spoke in such a fashion.
　　　　It ill becomes a pious man like you . . .
Tartuffe:　I may be pious, but I'm human too:
　　　　With your celestial charms before his eyes,
　　　　A man has not the power to be wise.　　　　　　　　90
　　　　I know such words sound strangely, coming from me,
　　　　But I'm no angel, nor was meant to be,
　　　　And if you blame my passion, you must needs
　　　　Reproach as well the charms on which it feeds.
　　　　Your loveliness I had no sooner seen　　　　　　95
　　　　Than you became my soul's unrivalled queen;
　　　　Before your seraph glance, divinely sweet,
　　　　My heart's defenses crumbled in defeat,
　　　　And nothing fasting, prayer, or tears might do
　　　　Could stay my spirit from adoring you.　　　　　100
　　　　My eyes, my sighs have told you in the past
　　　　What now my lips make bold to say at last,
　　　　And if, in your great goodness, you will deign
　　　　To look upon your slave, and ease his pain, —
　　　　If, in compassion for my soul's distress,　　　105
　　　　You'll stoop to comfort my unworthiness,
　　　　I'll raise to you, in thanks for that sweet manna,
　　　　An endless hymn, an infinite hosanna.
　　　　With me, of course, there need be no anxiety,
　　　　No fear of scandal or of notoriety.　　　　　　110
　　　　These young court gallants, whom all the ladies fancy,
　　　　Are vain in speech, in action rash and chancy;
　　　　When they succeed in love, the world soon knows it;
　　　　No favor's granted them but they disclose it
　　　　And by the looseness of their tongues profane　　115
　　　　The very altar where their hearts have lain.
　　　　Men of my sort, however, love discreetly,
　　　　And one may trust our reticence completely.
　　　　My keen concern for my good name insures
　　　　The absolute security of yours;　　　　　　　120
　　　　In short, I offer you, my dear Elmire,
　　　　Love without scandal, pleasure without fear.
Elmire:　I've heard your well-turned speeches to the end,
　　　　And what you urge I clearly apprehend.
　　　　Aren't you afraid that I may take a notion　　125
　　　　To tell my husband of your warm devotion,
　　　　And that, supposing he were duly told,
　　　　His feelings toward you might grow rather cold?
Tartuffe:　I know, dear lady, that your exceeding charity

Will lead your heart to pardon my temerity;   130
That you'll excuse my violent affection
As human weakness, human imperfection;
And that — O fairest! — you will bear in mind
That I'm but flesh and blood, and am not blind.

Elmire: Some women might do otherwise, perhaps,   135
But I shall be discreet about your lapse;
I'll tell my husband nothing of what's occurred
If, in return, you'll give your solemn word
To advocate as forcefully as you can
The marriage of Valère and Mariane,   140
Renouncing all desire to dispossess
Another of his rightful happiness,
And . . .

SCENE IV. *Damis, Elmire, Tartuffe*

Damis (emerging from the closet where he has been hiding): No! We'll
    not hush up this vile affair;
I heard it all inside that closet there,
Where Heaven, in order to confound the pride
Of this great rascal, prompted me to hide.
Ah, now I have my long-awaited chance   5
To punish his deceit and arrogance,
And give my father clear and shocking proof
Of the black character of his dear Tartuffe.

Elmire: Ah no, Damis; I'll be content if he
Will study to deserve my leniency.   10
I've promised silence — don't make me break my word;
To make a scandal would be too absurd.
Good wives laugh off such trifles, and forget them;
Why should they tell their husbands, and upset them?

Damis: You have your reasons for taking such a course,   15
And I have reasons, too, of equal force.
To spare him now would be insanely wrong.
I've swallowed my just wrath for far too long
And watched this insolent bigot bringing strife
And bitterness into our family life.   20
Too long he's meddled in my father's affairs,
Thwarting my marriage-hopes, and poor Valère's.
It's high time that my father was undeceived,
And now I've proof that can't be disbelieved —
Proof that was furnished me by Heaven above.   25
It's too good not to take advantage of.

This is my chance, and I deserve to lose it
If, for one moment, I hesitate to use it.
Elmire: Damis . . .
Damis: No, I must do what I think right.
Madam, my heart is bursting with delight,   30
And, say whatever you will, I'll not consent
To lose the sweet revenge on which I'm bent.
I'll settle matters without more ado;
And here, most opportunely, is my cue.

SCENE V. *Orgon, Tartuffe, Damis, Elmire*

Damis: Father, I'm glad you've joined us. Let us advise you
Of some fresh news which doubtless will surprise you.
You've just now been repaid with interest
For all your loving-kindness to our guest.
He's proved his warm and grateful feelings toward you;   5
It's with a pair of horns he would reward you.
Yes, I surprised him with your wife, and heard
His whole adulterous offer, every word.
She, with her all too gentle disposition,
Would not have told you of his proposition;   10
But I shall not make terms with brazen lechery,
And feel that not to tell you would be treachery.
Elmire: And I hold that one's husband's peace of mind
Should not be spoilt by tattle of this kind.
One's honor doesn't require it: to be proficient   15
In keeping men at bay is quite sufficient.
These are my sentiments, and I wish, Damis,
That you had heeded me and held your peace.

SCENE VI. *Orgon, Damis, Tartuffe*

Orgon: Can it be true, this dreadful thing I hear?
Tartuffe: Yes, Brother, I'm a wicked man, I fear:
A wretched sinner, all depraved and twisted,
The greatest villain that has ever existed.
My life's one heap of crimes, which grows each minute;   5
There's naught but foulness and corruption in it;
And I perceive that Heaven, outraged by me,
Has chosen this occasion to mortify me.
Charge me with any deed you wish to name;
I'll not defend myself, but take the blame.   10
Believe what you are told, and drive Tartuffe

    Like some base criminal from beneath your roof;
    Yes, drive me hence, and with a parting curse:
    I shan't protest, for I deserve far worse.
Orgon (to Damis): Ah, you deceitful boy, how dare you try   15
    To stain his purity with so foul a lie?
Damis: What! Are you taken in by such a bluff?
    Did you not hear . . . ?
Orgon: Enough, you rogue, enough!
Tartuffe: Ah, Brother, let him speak; you're being unjust.
    Believe his story; the boy deserves your trust.   20
    Why, after all, should you have faith in me?
    How can you know what I might do, or be?
    Is it on my good actions that you base
    Your favor? Do you trust my pious face?
    Ah, no, don't be deceived by hollow shows;   25
    I'm far, alas, from being what men suppose;
    Though the world takes me for a man of worth,
    I'm truly the most worthless man on earth.
    (To Damis.) Yes, my dear son, speak out now: call me the chief
    Of sinners, a wretch, a murderer, a thief;   30
    Load me with all the names men most abhor;
    I'll not complain; I've earned them all, and more;
    I'll kneel here while you pour them on my head
    As a just punishment for the life I've led.
Orgon (to Tartuffe): This is too much, dear Brother.
    (To Damis.)   Have you no heart? 35
Damis: Are you so hoodwinked by this rascal's art . . . ?
Orgon: Be still, you monster.
    (To Tartuffe.)   Brother, I pray you, rise.
    (To Damis.) Villain!
Damis: But . . .
Orgon: Silence!
Damis: Can't you realize . . . ?
Orgon: Just one word more, and I'll tear you limb from limb.
Tartuffe: In God's name, Brother, don't be harsh with him.   40
    I'd rather far be tortured at the stake
    Than see him bear one scratch for my poor sake.
Orgon (to Damis): Ingrate!
Tartuffe: If I must beg you, on bended knee,
    To pardon him . . .
Orgon (falling to his knees, addressing Tartuffe):
               Such goodness cannot be!
    (To Damis.) Now, *there's* true charity!
Damis: What, you . . . ?

Orgon: Villain, be still! 45
  I know your motives; I know you wish him ill:
  Yes, all of you — wife, children, servants, all —
  Conspire against him and desire his fall,
  Employing every shameful trick you can
  To alienate me from this saintly man.   50
  Ah, but the more you seek to drive him away,
  The more I'll do to keep him. Without delay,
  I'll spite this household and confound its pride
  By giving him my daughter as his bride.
Damis: You're going to force her to accept his hand?   55
Orgon: Yes, and this very night, d'you understand?
  I shall defy you all, and make it clear
  That I'm the one who gives the orders here.
  Come, wretch, kneel down and clasp his blessed feet,
  And ask his pardon for your black deceit.   60
Damis: I ask that swindler's pardon? Why, I'd rather . . .
Orgon: So! You insult him, and defy your father!
  A stick! A stick! (*To Tartuffe.*) No, no — release me, do.
  (*To Damis.*) Out of my house this minute! Be off with you,
  And never dare set foot in it again.   65
Damis: Well, I shall go, but . . .
Orgon: Well, go quickly, then.
  I disinherit you; an empty purse
  Is all you'll get from me — except my curse!

Scene VII. *Orgon, Tartuffe*

Orgon: How he blasphemed your goodness! What a son!
Tartuffe: Forgive him, Lord, as I've already done.
  (*To Orgon.*) You can't know how it hurts when someone tries
  To blacken me in my dear Brother's eyes.
Orgon: Ahh!
Tartuffe: The mere thought of such ingratitude   5
  Plunges my soul into so dark a mood . . .
  Such horror grips my heart . . . I gasp for breath,
  And cannot speak, and feel myself near death.
Orgon (he runs, in tears, to the door through which he has just driven
  his son): You blackguard! Why did I spare you? Why did I not
  Break you in little pieces on the spot?   10
  Compose yourself, and don't be hurt, dear friend.
Tartuffe: These scenes, these dreadful quarrels, have got to end.
  I've much upset your household, and I perceive
  That the best thing will be for me to leave.

Orgon: What are you saying!
Tartuffe: They're all against me here;   15
    They'd have you think me false and insincere.
Orgon: Ah, what of that? Have I ceased believing in you?
Tartuffe: Their adverse talk will certainly continue,
    And charges which you now repudiate
    You may find credible at a later date.   20
Orgon: No, Brother, never.
Tartuffe: Brother, a wife can sway
    Her husband's mind in many a subtle way.
Orgon: No, no.
Tartuffe: To leave at once is the solution;
    Thus only can I end their persecution.
Orgon: No, no, I'll not allow it; you shall remain.   25
Tartuffe: Ah, well; 'twill mean much martyrdom and pain,
    But if you wish it . . .
Orgon: Ah!
Tartuffe: Enough; so be it.
    But one thing must be settled, as I see it.
    For your dear honor, and for our friendship's sake,
    There's one precaution I feel bound to take.   30
    I shall avoid your wife, and keep away . . .
Orgon: No, you shall not, whatever they may say.
    It pleases me to vex them, and for spite
    I'd have them see you with her day and night.
    What's more, I'm going to drive them to despair   35
    By making you my only son and heir;
    This very day, I'll give to you alone
    Clear deed and title to everything I own.
    A dear, good friend and son-in-law-to-be
    Is more than wife, or child, or kin to me.   40
    Will you accept my offer, dearest son?
Tartuffe: In all things, let the will of Heaven be done.
Orgon: Poor fellow! Come, we'll go draw up the deed.
    Then let them burst with disappointed greed!

ACT IV

SCENE I. *Cléante, Tartuffe*

Cléante: Yes, all the town's discussing it, and truly,
    Their comments do not flatter you unduly.

I'm glad we've met, Sir, and I'll give my view
Of this sad matter in a word or two.
As for who's guilty, that I shan't discuss;   5
Let's say it was Damis who caused the fuss;
Assuming, then, that you have been ill-used
By young Damis, and groundlessly accused,
Ought not a Christian to forgive, and ought
He not to stifle every vengeful thought?   10
Should you stand by and watch a father make
His only son an exile for your sake?
Again I tell you frankly, be advised:
The whole town, high and low, is scandalized;
This quarrel must be mended, and my advice is   15
Not to push matters to a further crisis.
No, sacrifice your wrath to God above,
And help Damis regain his father's love.
Tartuffe: Alas, for my part I should take great joy
In doing so. I've nothing against the boy.   20
I pardon all, I harbor no resentment;
To serve him would afford me much contentment.
But Heaven's interest will not have it so:
If he comes back, then I shall have to go.
After his conduct — so extreme, so vicious —   25
Our further intercourse would look suspicious.
God knows what people would think! Why, they'd describe
My goodness to him as a sort of bribe;
They'd say that out of guilt I made pretense
Of loving-kindness and benevolence —   30
That, fearing my accuser's tongue, I strove
To buy his silence with a show of love.
Cléante: Your reasoning is badly warped and stretched,
And these excuses, Sir, are most far-fetched.
Why put yourself in charge of Heaven's cause?   35
Does Heaven need our help to enforce its laws?
Leave vengeance to the Lord, Sir; while we live,
Our duty's not to punish, but forgive;
And what the Lord commands, we should obey
Without regard to what the world may say   40
What! Shall the fear of being misunderstood
Prevent our doing what is right and good?
No, no; let's simply do what Heaven ordains,
And let no other thoughts perplex our brains.

Tartuffe: Again, Sir, let me say that I've forgiven   45
Damis, and thus obeyed the laws of Heaven;
But I am not commanded by the Bible
To live with one who smears my name with libel.
Cléante: Were you commanded, Sir, to indulge the whim
Of poor Orgon, and to encourage him   50
In suddenly transferring to your name
A large estate to which you have no claim?
Tartuffe: 'Twould never occur to those who know me best
To think I acted from self-interest.
The treasures of this world I quite despise;   55
Their specious glitter does not charm my eyes;
And if I have resigned myself to taking
The gift which my dear Brother insists on making,
I do so only, as he well understands,
Lest so much wealth fall into wicked hands,   60
Lest those to whom it might descend in time
Turn it to purposes of sin and crime,
And not, as I shall do, make use of it
For Heaven's glory and mankind's benefit.
Cléante: Forget these trumped-up fears. Your argument   65
Is one the rightful heir might well resent;
It *is* a moral burden to inherit
Such wealth, but give Damis a chance to bear it.
And would it not be worse to be accused
Of swindling, than to see that wealth misused?   70
I'm shocked that you allowed Orgon to broach
This matter, and that you feel no self-reproach;
Does true religion teach that lawful heirs
May freely be deprived of what is theirs?
And if the Lord has told you in your heart   75
That you and young Damis must dwell apart,
Would it not be the decent thing to beat
A generous and honorable retreat,
Rather than let the son of the house be sent,
For your convenience, into banishment?   80
Sir, if you wish to prove the honesty
Of your intentions . . .
Tartuffe: Sir, it is half-past three.
I've certain pious duties to attend to,
And hope my prompt departure won't offend you.
Cléante (alone): Damn.   85

SCENE II. *Elmire, Cléante, Mariane, Dorine*

Dorine: Stay, Sir, and help Mariane, for Heaven's
                   sake!
    She's suffering so, I fear her heart will break.
    Her father's plan to marry her off tonight
    Has put the poor child in a desperate plight.
    I hear him coming. Let's stand together, now,   5
    And see if we can't change his mind, somehow,
    About this match we all deplore and fear.

SCENE III. *Orgon, Mariane, Dorine, Elmire, Cléante*

Orgon: Hah! Glad to find you all assembled here.
    (*To Mariane.*) This contract, child, contains your happiness,
    And what it says I think your heart can guess.
Mariane (falling to her knees): Sir, by that Heaven which sees me
             here distressed,
    And by whatever else can move your breast,   5
    Do not employ a father's power, I pray you,
    To crush my heart and force it to obey you,
    Nor by your harsh commands oppress me so
    That I'll begrudge the duty which I owe —
    And do not so embitter and enslave me   10
    That I shall hate the very life you gave me.
    If my sweet hopes must perish, if you refuse
    To give me to the one I've dared to choose,
    Spare me at least — I beg you, I implore —
    The pain of wedding one whom I abhor;   15
    And do not, by a heartless use of force,
    Drive me to contemplate some desperate course.
Orgon (feeling himself touched by her): Be firm, my soul. No human
             weakness, now.
Mariane: I don't resent your love for him. Allow
    Your heart free rein, Sir; give him your property,   20
    And if that's not enough, take mine from me;
    He's welcome to my money; take it, do,
    But don't, I pray, include my person too.
    Spare me, I beg you; and let me end the tale
    Of my sad days behind a convent veil.   25
Orgon: A convent! Hah! When crossed in their amours,
    All lovesick girls have the same thought as yours.
    Get up! The more you loathe the man, and dread him,

The more ennobling it will be to wed him.
Marry Tartuffe, and mortify your flesh! 30
Enough; don't start that whimpering afresh.
Dorine: But why . . . ?
Orgon: Be still, there. Speak when you're spoken to.
Not one more bit of impudence out of you.
Cléante: If I may offer a word of counsel here . . .
Orgon: Brother, in counseling you have no peer; 35
All your advice is forceful, sound, and clever;
I don't propose to follow it, however.
Elmire (to Orgon): I am amazed, and don't know what to say;
Your blindness simply takes my breath away.
You are indeed bewitched, to take no warning 40
From our account of what occurred this morning.
Orgon: Madam, I know a few plain facts, and one
Is that you're partial to my rascal son;
Hence, when he sought to make Tartuffe the victim
Of a base lie, you dared not contradict him. 45
Ah, but you underplayed your part, my pet;
You should have looked more angry, more upset.
Elmire: When men make overtures, must we reply
With righteous anger and a battle-cry?
Must we turn back their amorous advances 50
With sharp reproaches and with fiery glances?
Myself, I find such offers merely amusing,
And make no scenes and fusses in refusing;
My taste is for good-natured rectitude,
And I dislike the savage sort of prude 55
Who guards her virtue with her teeth and claws,
And tears men's eyes out for the slightest cause:
The Lord preserve me from such honor as that,
Which bites and scratches like an alley-cat!
I've found that a polite and cool rebuff 60
Discourages a lover quite enough.
Orgon: I know the facts, and I shall not be shaken.
Elmire: I marvel at your power to be mistaken.
Would it, I wonder, carry weight with you
If I could *show* you that our tale was true? 65
Orgon: Show me?
Elmire: Yes.
Orgon: Rot.
Elmire: Come, what if I found a way
To make you see the facts as plain as day?

Orgon: Nonsense.
Elmire: Do answer me; don't be absurd.
    I'm not now asking you to trust our word.
    Suppose that from some hiding-place in here   70
    You learned the whole sad truth by eye and ear —
    What would you say of your good friend, after that?
Orgon: Why, I'd say . . . nothing, by Jehoshaphat!
    It can't be true.
Elmire: You've been too long deceived,
    And I'm quite tired of being disbelieved.   75
    Come now: let's put my statements to the test,
    And you shall see the truth made manifest.
Orgon: I'll take that challenge. Now do your uttermost.
    We'll see how you make good your empty boast.
Elmire (to Dorine): Send him to me.
Dorine: He's crafty; it may be hard   80
    To catch the cunning scoundrel off his guard.
Elmire: No, amorous men are gullible. Their conceit
    So blinds them that they're never hard to cheat.
    Have him come down. (*To Cléante and Mariane.*) Please leave
    us, for a bit.

SCENE IV. *Elmire, Orgon*

Elmire: Pull up this table, and get under it.
Orgon: What?
Elmire: It's essential that you be well-hidden.
Orgon: Why there?
Elmire: Oh, Heavens! Just do as you are bidden.
    I have my plans; we'll soon see how they fare.
    Under the table, now; and once you're there,   5
    Take care that you are neither seen nor heard.
Orgon: Well, I'll indulge you, since I gave my word
    To see you through this infantile charade.
Elmire: Once it is over, you'll be glad we played.
    (*To her husband, who is now under the table.*) I'm going to act
       quite strangely, now, and you   10
    Must not be shocked at anything I do.
    Whatever I may say, you must excuse
    As part of that deceit I'm forced to use.
    I shall employ sweet speeches in the task
    Of making that impostor drop his mask;   15
    I'll give encouragement to his bold desires,
    And furnish fuel to his amorous fires.
    Since it's for your sake, and for his destruction,

That I shall seem to yield to his seduction,
I'll gladly stop whenever you decide   20
That all your doubts are fully satisfied.
I'll count on you, as soon as you have seen
What sort of man he is, to intervene,
And not expose me to his odious lust
One moment longer than you feel you must.   25
Remember: you're to save me from my plight
Whenever . . . He's coming! Hush! Keep out of sight!

SCENE V. *Tartuffe, Elmire, Orgon*

Tartuffe: You wish to have a word with me, I'm told.
Elmire: Yes. I've a little secret to unfold.
Before I speak, however, it would be wise
To close that door, and look about for spies.

Tartuffe goes to the door, closes it, and returns.

The very last thing that must happen now   5
Is a repetition of this morning's row.
I've never been so badly caught off guard.
Oh, how I feared for you! You saw how hard
I tried to make that troublesome Damis
Control his dreadful temper, and hold his peace.   10
In my confusion, I didn't have the sense
Simply to contradict his evidence;
But as it happened, that was for the best,
And all has worked out in our interest.
This storm has only bettered your position;   15
My husband doesn't have the least suspicion,
And now, in mockery of those who do,
He bids me be continually with you.
And that is why, quite fearless of reproof,
I now can be alone with my Tartuffe,   20
And why my heart — perhaps too quick to yield —
Feels free to let its passion be revealed.
Tartuffe: Madam, your words confuse me. Not long ago,
You spoke in quite a different style, you know.
Elmire: Ah, Sir, if that refusal made you smart,   25
It's little that you know of woman's heart,
Or what that heart is trying to convey
When it resists in such a feeble way!
Always, at first, our modesty prevents
The frank avowal of tender sentiments;   30

However high the passion which inflames us,
Still, to confess its power somehow shames us.
Thus we reluct, at first, yet in a tone
Which tells you that our heart is overthrown,
That what our lips deny, our pulse confesses,   35
And that, in time, all noes will turn to yesses.
I fear my words are all too frank and free,
And a poor proof of woman's modesty;
But since I'm started, tell me, if you will —
Would I have tried to make Damis be still,   40
Would I have listened, calm and unoffended,
Until your lengthy offer of love was ended,
And been so very mild in my reaction,
Had your sweet words not given me satisfaction?
And when I tried to force you to undo   45
The marriage-plans my husband has in view,
What did my urgent pleading signify
If not that I admired you, and that I
Deplored the thought that someone else might own
Part of a heart I wished for mine alone?   50
Tartuffe: Madam, no happiness is so complete
As when, from lips we love, come words so sweet;
Their nectar floods my every sense, and drains
In honeyed rivulets through all my veins.
To please you is my joy, my only goal;   55
Your love is the restorer of my soul;
And yet I must beg leave, now, to confess
Some lingering doubts as to my happiness.
Might this not be a trick? Might not the catch
Be that you wish me to break off the match   60
With Mariane, and so have feigned to love me?
I shan't quite trust your fond opinion of me
Until the feelings you've expressed so sweetly
Are demonstrated somewhat more concretely,
And you have shown, by certain kind concessions,   65
That I may put my faith in your professions.
Elmire: (She coughs, to warn her husband.) Why be in such a hurry?
      Must my heart
Exhaust its bounty at the very start?
To make that sweet admission cost me dear,
But you'll not be content, it would appear,   70
Unless my store of favors is disbursed
To the last farthing, and at the very first.
Tartuffe: The less we merit, the less we dare to hope,

And with our doubts, mere words can never cope.
We trust no promised bliss till we receive it;   75
Not till a joy is ours can we believe it.
I, who so little merit your esteem,
Can't credit this fulfillment of my dream,
And shan't believe it, Madam, until I savor
Some palpable assurance of your favor.   80
Elmire: My, how tyrannical your love can be,
And how it flusters and perplexes me!
How furiously you take one's heart in hand,
And make your every wish a fierce command!
Come, must you hound and harry me to death?   85
Will you not give me time to catch my breath?
Can it be right to press me with such force,
Give me no quarter, show me no remorse,
And take advantage, by your stern insistence,
Of the fond feelings which weaken my resistance?   90
Tartuffe: Well, if you look with favor upon my love,
Why, then, begrudge me some clear proof thereof?
Elmire: But how can I consent without offense
To Heaven, toward which you feel such reverence?
Tartuffe: If Heaven is all that holds you back, don't worry.   95
I can remove that hindrance in a hurry.
Nothing of that sort need obstruct our path.
Elmire: Must one not be afraid of Heaven's wrath?
Tartuffe: Madam, forget such fears, and be my pupil,
And I shall teach you how to conquer scruple.   100
Some joys, it's true, are wrong in Heaven's eyes;
Yet Heaven is not averse to compromise;
There is a science, lately formulated,
Whereby one's conscience may be liberated,
And any wrongful act you care to mention   105
May be redeemed by purity of intention.
I'll teach you, Madam, the secrets of that science;
Meanwhile, just place on me your full reliance.
Assuage my keen desires, and feel no dread:
The sin, if any, shall be on my head.   110

Elmire coughs, this time more loudly.

You've a bad cough.
Elmire: Yes, yes. It's bad indeed.
Tartuffe (producing a little paper bag): A bit of licorice may be what
        you need.

COMEDY

Elmire: No, I've a stubborn cold, it seems. I'm sure it
   Will take much more than licorice to cure it.
Tartuffe: How aggravating.
Elmire: Oh, more than I can say.   115
Tartuffe: If you're still troubled, think of things this way:
   No one shall know our joys, save us alone,
   And there's no evil till the act is known;
   It's scandal, Madam, which makes it an offense,
   And it's no sin to sin in confidence.   120
Elmire (having coughed once more): Well, clearly I must do as you
         require,
   And yield to your importunate desire.
   It is apparent, now, that nothing less
   Will satisfy you, and so I acquiesce.
   To go so far is much against my will;   125
   I'm vexed that it should come to this; but still,
   Since you are so determined on it, since you
   Will not allow mere language to convince you,
   And since you ask for concrete evidence, I
   See nothing for it, now, but to comply.   130
   If this is sinful, if I'm wrong to do it,
   So much the worse for him who drove me to it.
   The fault can surely not be charged to me.
Tartuffe: Madam, the fault is mine, if fault there be,
   And . . .
Elmire: Open the door a little, and peek out;   135
   I wouldn't want my husband poking about.
Tartuffe: Why worry about the man? Each day he grows
   More gullible; one can lead him by the nose.
   To find us here would fill him with delight,
   And if he saw the worst, he'd doubt his sight.   140
Elmire: Nevertheless, do step out for a minute
   Into the hall, and see that no one's in it.

SCENE VI. *Orgon, Elmire*

Orgon (coming out from under the table): That man's a perfect
         monster, I must admit!
   I'm simply stunned. I can't get over it.
Elmire: What, coming out so soon? How premature!
   Get back in hiding, and wait until you're sure.
   Stay till the end, and be convinced completely;   5
   We mustn't stop till things are proved concretely.
Orgon: Hell never harbored anything so vicious!

Elmire: Tut, don't be hasty. Try to be judicious.
   Wait, and be certain that there's no mistake.
   No jumping to conclusions, for Heaven's sake!   10

She places Orgon behind her, as Tartuffe re-enters.

SCENE VII. *Tartuffe, Elmire, Orgon*

Tartuffe (not seeing Orgon): Madam, all things have worked out to
   perfection;
   I've given the neighboring rooms a full inspection;
   No one's about; and now I may at last . . .
Orgon (intercepting him): Hold on, my passionate fellow, not so
   fast!
   I should advise a little more restraint.   5
   Well, so you thought you'd fool me, my dear saint!
   How soon you wearied of the saintly life —
   Wedding my daughter, and coveting my wife!
   I've long suspected you, and had a feeling
   That soon I'd catch you at your double-dealing.   10
   Just now, you've given me evidence galore;
   It's quite enough; I have no wish for more.
Elmire (to Tartuffe): I'm sorry to have treated you so slyly,
   But circumstances forced me to be wily.
Tartuffe: Brother, you can't think . . .
Orgon: No more talk from you;   15
   Just leave this household, without more ado.
Tartuffe: What I intended . . .
Orgon: That seems fairly clear.
   Spare me your falsehoods and get out of here.
Tartuffe: No, I'm the master, and you're the one to go!
   This house belongs to me, I'll have you know,   20
   And I shall show you that you can't hurt *me*
   By this contemptible conspiracy,
   That those who cross me know not what they do,
   And that I've means to expose and punish you,
   Avenge offended Heaven, and make you grieve   25
   That ever you dared order me to leave.

SCENE VIII. *Elmire, Orgon*

Elmire: What was the point of all that angry chatter?
Orgon: Dear God, I'm worried. This is no laughing matter.
Elmire: How so?

Orgon: I fear I understood his drift.
    I'm much disturbed about that deed of gift.
Elmire: You gave him . . . ?
Orgon: Yes, it's all been drawn and signed.   5
    But one thing more is weighing on my mind.
Elmire: What's that?
Orgon: I'll tell you; but first let's see if there's
    A certain strong-box in his room upstairs.

ACT V

SCENE I. *Orgon, Cléante*

Cléante: Where are you going so fast?
Orgon: God knows!
Cléante: Then wait;
    Let's have a conference, and deliberate
    On how this situation's to be met.
Orgon: That strong-box has me utterly upset;
    This is the worst of many, many shocks.   5
Cléante: Is there some fearful mystery in that box?
Orgon: My poor friend Argas brought that box to me
    With his own hands, in utmost secrecy;
    'Twas on the very morning of his flight.
    It's full of papers which, if they came to light,   10
    Would ruin him — or such is my impression.
Cléante: Then why did you let it out of your possession?
Orgon: Those papers vexed my conscience, and it seemed best
    To ask the counsel of my pious guest.
    The cunning scoundrel got me to agree   15
    To leave the strong-box in his custody,
    So that, in case of an investigation,
    I could employ a slight equivocation
    And swear I didn't have it, and thereby,
    At no expense to conscience, tell a lie.   20
Cléante: It looks to me as if you're out on a limb.
    Trusting him with that box, and offering him
    That deed of gift, were actions of a kind
    Which scarcely indicate a prudent mind.
    With two such weapons, he has the upper hand,   25
    And since you're vulnerable, as matters stand,
    You erred once more in bringing him to bay.

You should have acted in some subtler way.
Orgon: Just think of it: behind that fervent face,
  A heart so wicked, and a soul so base!   30
  I took him in, a hungry beggar, and then . . .
  Enough, by God! I'm through with pious men:
  Henceforth I'll hate the whole false brotherhood,
  And persecute them worse than Satan could.
Cléante: Ah, there you go — extravagant as ever!   35
  Why can you not be rational? You never
  Manage to take the middle course, it seems,
  But jump, instead, between absurd extremes.
  You've recognized your recent grave mistake
  In falling victim to a pious fake;   40
  Now, to correct that error, must you embrace
  An even greater error in its place,
  And judge our worthy neighbors as a whole
  By what you've learned of one corrupted soul?
  Come, just because one rascal made you swallow   45
  A show of zeal which turned out to be hollow,
  Shall you conclude that all men are deceivers,
  And that, today, there are no true believers?
  Let atheists make that foolish inference;
  Learn to distinguish virtue from pretense,   50
  Be cautious in bestowing admiration,
  And cultivate a sober moderation.
  Don't humor fraud, but also don't asperse
  True piety; the latter fault is worse,
  And it is best to err, if err one must,   55
  As you have done, upon the side of trust.

SCENE II. *Damis, Orgon, Cléante*

Damis: Father, I hear that scoundrel's uttered threats
  Against you; that he pridefully forgets
  How, in his need, he was befriended by you,
  And means to use your gifts to crucify you.
Orgon: It's true, my boy. I'm too distressed for tears.   5
Damis: Leave it to me, Sir; let me trim his ears.
  Faced with such insolence, we must not waver.
  I shall rejoice in doing you the favor
  Of cutting short his life, and your distress.
Cléante: What a display of young hotheadedness!   10
  Do learn to moderate your fits of rage.

In this just kingdom, this enlightened age,
One does not settle things by violence.

SCENE III. *Madame Pernelle, Dorine, Orgon, Mariane, Damis, Cléante, Elmire*

Madame Pernelle: I hear strange tales of very strange events.
Orgon: Yes, strange events which these two eyes beheld.
  The man's ingratitude is unparalleled.
  I save a wretched pauper from starvation,
  House him, and treat him like a blood relation,   5
  Shower him every day with my largesse,
  Give him my daughter, and all that I possess;
  And meanwhile the unconscionable knave
  Tries to induce my wife to misbehave;
  And not content with such extreme rascality,   10
  Now threatens me with my own liberality,
  And aims, by taking base advantage of
  The gifts I gave him out of Christian love,
  To drive me from my house, a ruined man,
  And make me end a pauper, as he began.   15
Dorine: Poor fellow!
Madame Pernelle: No, my son, I'll never bring
  Myself to think him guilty of such a thing.
Orgon: How's that?
Madame Pernelle: The righteous always were maligned.
Orgon: Speak clearly, Mother. Say what's on your mind.
Madame Pernelle: I mean that I can smell a rat, my dear.   20
  You know how everybody hates him, here.
Orgon: That has no bearing on the case at all.
Madame Pernelle: I told you a hundred times, when you were
        small,
  That virtue in this world is hated ever;
  Malicious men may die, but malice never.   25
Orgon: No doubt that's true, but how does it apply?
Madame Pernelle: They've turned you against him by a clever lie.
Orgon: I've told you, I was there and saw it done.
Madame Pernelle: Ah, slanderers will stop at nothing, Son.
Orgon: Mother, I'll lose my temper . . . For the last time,   30
  I tell you I was witness to the crime.
Madame Pernelle: The tongues of spite are busy night and noon,
  And to their venom no man is immune.
Orgon: You're talking nonsense. Can't you realize
  I saw it; saw it; saw it with my eyes?   35

Saw, do you understand me? Must I shout it
Into your ears before you'll cease to doubt it?
Madame Pernelle: Appearances can deceive, my son. Dear me,
We cannot always judge by what we see.
Orgon: Drat! Drat!
Madame Pernelle: One often interprets things away;   40
Good can seem evil to a suspicious eye.
Orgon: Was I to see his pawing at Elmire
As an act of charity?
Madame Pernelle: Till his guilt is clear,
A man deserves the benefit of the doubt.
You should have waited, to see how things turned out.   45
Orgon: Great God in Heaven, what more proof did I need?
Was I to sit there, watching, until he'd . . .
You drive me to the brink of impropriety.
Madame Pernelle: No, no, a man of such surpassing piety
Could not do such a thing. You cannot shake me.   50
I don't believe it, and you shall not make me.
Orgon: You vex me so that, if you weren't my mother,
I'd say to you . . . some dreadful thing or other.
Dorine: It's your turn now, Sir, not to be listened to;
You'd not trust us, and now she won't trust you.   55
Cléante: My friends, we're wasting time which should be spent
In facing up to our predicament.
I fear that scoundrel's threats weren't made in sport.
Damis: Do you think he'd have the nerve to go to court?
Elmire: I'm sure he won't: they'd find it all too crude   60
A case of swindling and ingratitude.
Cléante: Don't be too sure. He won't be at a loss
To give his claims a high and righteous gloss;
And clever rogues with far less valid cause
Have trapped their victims in a web of laws.   65
I say again that to antagonize
A man so strongly armed was most unwise.
Orgon: I know it; but the man's appalling cheek
Outraged me so, I couldn't control my pique.
Cléante: I wish to Heaven that we could devise   70
Some truce between you, or some compromise.
Elmire: If I had known what cards he held, I'd not
Have roused his anger by my little plot.
Orgon (to Dorine, as Monsieur Loyal enters): What is that fellow
looking for? Who is he?
Go talk to him — and tell him that I'm busy.   75

SCENE IV. *Monsieur Loyal, Damis, Elmire, Madame Pernelle, Mariane, Cléante, Orgon, Dorine*

Monsieur Loyal: Good day, dear sister. Kindly let me see
    Your master.
Dorine: He's involved with company,
    And cannot be disturbed just now, I fear.
Monsieur Loyal: I hate to intrude; but what has brought me here
    Will not disturb your master, in any event.   5
    Indeed, my news will make him most content.
Dorine: Your name?
Monsieur Loyal: Just say that I bring greetings from
    Monsieur Tartuffe, on whose behalf I've come.
Dorine (to Orgon): Sir, he's a very gracious man, and bears
    A message from Tartuffe, which, he declares,   10
    Will make you most content.
Cléante: Upon my word,
    I think this man had best be seen, and heard.
Orgon: Perhaps he has some settlement to suggest.
    How shall I treat him? What manner would be best?
Cléante: Control your anger, and if he should mention   15
    Some fair adjustment, give him your full attention.
Monsieur Loyal: Good health to you, good Sir. May Heaven
        confound
    Your enemies, and may your joys abound.
Orgon (aside, to Cléante): A gentle salutation: it confirms
    My guess that he is here to offer terms.   20
Monsieur Loyal: I've always held your family most dear;
    I served your father, Sir, for many a year.
Orgon: Sir, I must ask your pardon; to my shame,
    I cannot now recall your face or name.
Monsieur Loyal: Loyal's my name; I come from Normandy,   25
    And I'm a bailiff, in all modesty.
    For forty years, praise God, it's been my boast
    To serve with honor in that vital post,
    And I am here, Sir, if you will permit
    The liberty, to serve you with this writ . . .   30
Orgon: To — *what?*
Monsieur Loyal: Now, please, Sir, let us have no friction:
    It's nothing but an order of eviction.
    You are to move your goods and family out
    And make way for new occupants, without
    Deferment or delay, and give the keys . . .   35
Orgon: I? Leave this house?

Monsieur Loyal: Why yes, Sir, if you please.
   This house, Sir, from the cellar to the roof,
   Belongs now to the good Monsieur Tartuffe,
   And he is lord and master of your estate
   By virtue of a deed of present date,   40
   Drawn in due form, with clearest legal phrasing . . .
Damis: Your insolence is utterly amazing!
Monsieur Loyal: Young man, my business here is not with you,
   But with your wise and temperate father, who,
   Like every worthy citizen, stands in awe   45
   Of justice, and would never obstruct the law.
Orgon: But . . .
Monsieur Loyal: Not for a million, Sir, would you rebel
   Against authority; I know that well.
   You'll not make trouble, Sir, or interfere
   With the execution of my duties here.   50
Damis: Someone may execute a smart tattoo
   On that black jacket of yours, before you're through.
Monsieur Loyal: Sir, bid your son be silent. I'd much regret
   Having to mention such a nasty threat
   Of violence, in writing my report.   55
Dorine (aside): This man Loyal's a most disloyal sort!
Monsieur Loyal: I love all men of upright character,
   And when I agreed to serve these papers, Sir,
   It was your feelings that I had in mind.
   I couldn't bear to see the case assigned   60
   To someone else, who might esteem you less
   And so subject you to unpleasantness.
Orgon: What's more unpleasant than telling a man to leave
   His house and home?
Monsieur Loyal: You'd like a short reprieve?
   If you desire it, Sir, I shall not press you,   65
   But wait until tomorrow to dispossess you.
   Splendid. I'll come and spend the night here, then,
   Most quietly, with half a score of men.
   For form's sake, you might bring me, just before
   You go to bed, the keys to the front door.   70
   My men, I promise, will be on their best
   Behavior, and will not disturb your rest.
   But bright and early, Sir, you must be quick
   And move out all your furniture, every stick:
   The men I've chosen are both young and strong,   75
   And with their help it shouldn't take you long.
   In short, I'll make things pleasant and convenient,

And since I'm being so extremely lenient,
Please show me, Sir, a like consideration,
And give me your entire cooperation.   80
Orgon (aside): I may be all but bankrupt, but I vow
I'd give a hundred louis, here and now,
Just for the pleasure of landing one good clout
Right on the end of that complacent snout.
Cléante: Careful; don't make things worse.
Damis: My bootsole itches   85
To give that beggar a good kick in the breeches.
Dorine: Monsieur Loyal, I'd love to hear the whack
Of a stout stick across your fine broad back.
Monsieur Loyal: Take care: a woman too may go to jail if
She uses threatening language to a bailiff.   90
Cléante: Enough, enough, Sir. This must not go on.
Give me that paper, please, and then begone.
Monsieur Loyal: Well, *au revoir*. God give you all good cheer!
Orgon: May God confound you, and him who sent you here!

SCENE V. *Orgon, Elmire, Dorine, Cléante, Madame Pernelle, Damis, Mariane*

Orgon: Now, Mother, was I right or not? This writ
Should change your notion of Tartuffe a bit.
Do you perceive his villainy at last?
Madame Pernelle: I'm thunderstruck. I'm utterly aghast.
Dorine: Oh, come, be fair. You mustn't take offense   5
At this new proof of his benevolence.
He's acting out of selfless love, I know.
Material things enslave the soul, and so
He kindly has arranged your liberation
From all that might endanger your salvation.   10
Orgon: Will you not ever hold your tongue, you dunce?
Cléante: Come, you must take some action, and at once.
Elmire: Go tell the world of the low trick he's tried.
The deed of gift is surely nullified
By such behavior, and public rage will not   15
Permit the wretch to carry out his plot.

SCENE VI. *Valère, Elmire, Damis, Orgon, Mariane, Dorine, Cléante,*
Madame Pernelle

Valère: Sir, though I hate to bring you more bad news,
Such is the danger that I cannot choose.
A friend who is extremely close to me

And knows my interest in your family
Has, for my sake, presumed to violate   5
The secrecy that's due to things of state,
And sends me word that you are in a plight
From which your one salvation lies in flight.
That scoundrel who's imposed upon you so
Denounced you to the King an hour ago   10
And, as supporting evidence, displayed
The strong-box of a certain renegade
Whose secret papers, so he testified,
You had disloyally agreed to hide.
I don't know just what charges may be pressed,   15
But there's a warrant out for your arrest;
Tartuffe has been instructed, furthermore,
To guide the arresting officer to your door.
Cléante: He's clearly done this to facilitate
His seizure of your house and your estate.   20
Orgon: That man, I must say, is a vicious beast!
Valère: Quick, Sir; you mustn't tarry in the least.
My carriage is outside, to take you hence;
This thousand louis should cover all expense.
Let's lose no time, or you shall be undone;   25
The sole defense, in this case, is to run.
I shall go with you all the way, and place you
In a safe refuge to which they'll never trace you.
Orgon: Alas, dear boy, I wish that I could show you
My gratitude for everything I owe you.   30
But now is not the time; I pray the Lord
That I may live to give you your reward.
Farewell, my dears; be careful . . .
Cléante: Brother, hurry.
We shall take care of things; you needn't worry.

SCENE VII. *The Officer, Elmire, Dorine, Tartuffe, Mariane, Cléante, Valère,*
Madame Pernelle, Damis, Orgon

Tartuffe: Gently, Sir, gently; stay right where you are.
No need for haste; your lodging isn't far.
You're off to prison, by order of the Prince.
Orgon: This is the crowning blow, you wretch; and since
It means my total ruin and defeat,   5
Your villainy is now at last complete.
Tartuffe: You needn't try to provoke me; it's no use.
Those who serve Heaven must expect abuse.

Cléante: You are indeed most patient, sweet, and blameless.
Dorine: How he exploits the name of Heaven! It's shameless.   10
Tartuffe: Your taunts and mockeries are all for naught;
    To do my duty is my only thought.
Mariane: Your love of duty is most meritorious,
    And what you've done is little short of glorious.
Tartuffe: All deeds are glorious, Madam, which obey   15
    The sovereign prince who sent me here today.
Orgon: I rescued you when you were destitute;
    Have you forgotten that, you thankless brute?
Tartuffe: No, no, I well remember everything;
    But my first duty is to serve my King.   20
    That obligation is so paramount
    That other claims, beside it, do not count;
    And for it I would sacrifice my wife,
    My family, my friend, or my own life.
Elmire: Hypocrite!
Dorine: All that we most revere, he uses   25
    To cloak his plots and camouflage his ruses.
Cléante: If it is true that you are animated
    By pure and loyal zeal, as you have stated,
    Why was this zeal not roused until you'd sought
    To make Orgon a cuckold, and been caught?   30
    Why weren't you moved to give your evidence
    Until your outraged host had driven you hence?
    I shan't say that the gift of all his treasure
    Ought to have damped your zeal in any measure;
    But if he is a traitor, as you declare,   35
    How could you condescend to be his heir?
Tartuffe (to the Officer): Sir, spare me all this clamor; it's growing
    shrill.
    Please carry out your orders, if you will.
Officer: Yes, I've delayed too long, Sir. Thank you kindly.
    You're just the proper person to remind me.   40
    Come, you are off to join the other boarders
    In the King's prison, according to his orders.
Tartuffe: Who? I, Sir?
Officer: Yes.
Tartuffe: To prison? This can't be true!
Officer: I owe an explanation, but not to you.
    (To Orgon.) Sir, all is well; rest easy, and be grateful.   45
    We serve a Prince to whom all sham is hateful,
    A Prince who sees into our inmost hearts,
    And can't be fooled by any trickster's arts.

His royal soul, though generous and human,
Views all things with discernment and acumen;   50
His sovereign reason is not lightly swayed,
And all his judgments are discreetly weighed.
He honors righteous men of every kind,
And yet his zeal for virtue is not blind,
Nor does his love of piety numb his wits   55
And make him tolerant of hypocrites.
'Twas hardly likely that this man could cozen
A King who's foiled such liars by the dozen.
With one keen glance, the King perceived the whole
Perverseness and corruption of his soul,   60
And thus high Heaven's justice was displayed:
Betraying you, the rogue stood self-betrayed.
The King soon recognized Tartuffe as one
Notorious by another name, who'd done
So many vicious crimes that one could fill   65
Ten volumes with them, and be writing still.
But to be brief: our sovereign was appalled
By this man's treachery toward you, which he called
The last, worst villainy of a vile career,
And bade me follow the impostor here   70
To see how gross his impudence could be,
And force him to restore your property.
Your private papers, by the King's command,
I hereby seize and give into your hand.
The King, by royal order, invalidates   75
The deed which gave this rascal your estates,
And pardons, furthermore, your grave offense
In harboring an exile's documents.
By these decrees, our Prince rewards you for
Your loyal deeds in the late civil war,   80
And shows how heartfelt is his satisfaction
In recompensing any worthy action,
How much he prizes merit, and how he makes
More of men's virtues than of their mistakes.
Dorine: Heaven be praised!
Madame Pernelle: I breathe again, at last.   85
Elmire: We're safe.
Mariane: I can't believe the danger's past.
Orgon (to Tartuffe): Well, traitor, now you see . . .
Cléante: Ah, Brother, please,
    Let's not descend to such indignities.
    Leave the poor wretch to his unhappy fate,

And don't say anything to aggravate   90
His present woes; but rather hope that he
Will soon embrace an honest piety,
And mend his ways, and by a true repentance
Move our just King to moderate his sentence.
Meanwhile, go kneel before your sovereign's throne   95
And thank him for the mercies he has shown.
Orgon: Well said: let's go at once and, gladly kneeling,
Express the gratitude which all are feeling.
Then, when that first great duty has been done,
We'll turn with pleasure to a second one,   100
And give Valère, whose love has proven so true,
The wedded happiness which is his due.

Questions about Tartuffe: *Act III, Scene VI*

Focus on Act III, Scene VI — Tartuffe's confession. Make
careful notes on the actions, thoughts, and feelings that need to
be brought to life in the course of this scene. How does Orgon
see Tartuffe? How does Damis see Orgon? How does Orgon see
Damis? Decide what each speaker is for himself and for the
others during these moments, basing decisions on readings of
each speaker's nature. Build up the insides of the appropriate
tones, gestures, and tonal contrasts by which each character's
separateness can be realized from moment to moment. Then
write a paper naming the elements (movements, gestures, expressions, motives) that figure crucially in staging the scene, and
explain why they are all important. Compare your response with
the one that follows.

Note: The following response begins with reading notes and a
list of key elements for close imagining. Such a list can help you
keep track of the wide range of focal points that need attention
when bringing to life any individual scene in a play.

Response

EDITOR'S READING NOTES: Eye and body movements: lots of ups
and downs, very broad stuff. But it starts solemnly. Tartuffe's first
gaze is down. Abashed. Ashamed. Damis is crowing — youthful
and bouncy. Proof at last. Physical excitement, dancing about,

pointing at Tartuffe. Confirmation! See? See? Tartuffe looks forlorn, he's a tree suffering axe blows and making no complaint. Stolid. Do your worst, I deserve it. Then slowly kneels (33), bowed and crushed. Then up (38), then on bended knees (44), then Orgon on *his* knees. Sharp contrasts here: first Tartuffe's sober self-indictment and Orgon made breathless with adoration of Tartuffe's Perfect Virtue. But the deep knee bends, the ups and downs, Damis's bouncy consternation, and at length Tartuffe physically restraining the father — the whole scene is moving toward an explosion of physical action.

Damis's excitability we catch right at the start (I.i.45 — "Good God!"). For Orgon's virtuous reverence, see II.ii.30 ff. Tartuffe's expertise at "playing" the sinner is in sight in III.ii.8–10. "Cover that bosom, girl — I am a helpless sinner and the world is filled with gross temptations . . ."

EDITOR'S KEY ELEMENTS:

1. Tartuffe's initial physical stillness and gravity as contrasted with Orgon's shuttling between fury and pity and Damis's stormy speechlessness
2. The movement within Damis from pleasurable anticipation through relished confirmation to bewilderment, incredulity, rage
3. Orgon's raptness (dazzlement at saintliness) following each of Tartuffe's long speeches
4. The absolute conflicts of perception: Tartuffe as matchless magnanimity (Orgon), Tartuffe as matchless villainy (Damis), Tartuffe as matchless con man (Tartuffe)

EDITOR: We see with Orgon's son as we enter this scene. Damis is triumphant; he's on the verge of I-told-you-so crowing, having just shown his father clear proof of Tartuffe's depravity, thereby presumably awakening Orgon to the absurdity of regarding this man as a model of virtue. Filled with the sense of personal justification, knowing all the cards are his, Damis perches exhilaratedly on the edge of Tartuffe's humiliation.

As Tartuffe speaks, Damis *hears* confession and humiliation. He nods at what he hears, salutes the acknowledgment of guilt.

This is direct confession, is it not? Can anybody miss it? Is it not proof positive that Tartuffe is the greatest villain who has ever existed? Damis swings up hand and arms — what could you expect but this, no? Does the villain not acknowledge that he deserves to be driven off like some base criminal? See? Didn't I tell you? Listen to him! Damis is caught up, smiling in excited, happy relish of this long-awaited downfall of a canting tyrant.

Orgon also is listening — but he's attending to something altogether different from the sound of evil, observing a manner that — to him — cannot communicate wickedness. Orgon is nodding at what *he* hears in the speech, namely beauty and sanctity. For Orgon, Tartuffe's voice is that of a man who, although his moral defects are trivial to the point of nonexistence, is desolated by consciousness of them. Orgon "understands" that Tartuffe's extraordinary conscience drives him to magnify his flaws, to believe his faults are equal to the worst sins, to confess to any and all crimes because he is so powerfully sensitive to his personal failure to live every instant in accordance with lofty religious ideals.

Others less virtuous would defend themselves, would contradict their accusers, would protest in the name of their reputation and good works; but not Tartuffe. See him incline his head as though in guilt ("Yes, Brother, I'm a wicked man," line 2). Feel the heaviness of his torso, the fearful weight of the moral despair in his heart. Orgon is positively stunned by this demonstration of spiritual depth — the sight of a man so mistakenly yet profoundly persuaded of his general guilt that he bares his head to those who would beat him, asking no protection from his persecutors. Orgon is absorbed, awed by the sight of virtue on this scale: to turn away from it under any circumstances would be painful — but to turn away to the loutish noisiness of his son, to be obliged to realize that it is flesh of his flesh that's viciously attacking this saint . . . Too much!

Damis sees his father's response as unbelievable, an impossible, nightmarish joke from which the old man must within the next second wake up. It would be too ridiculous, too absurd for it to go on longer —

But what is this *new* sound coming from the monster Tartuffe?

Believe his story: the boy deserves your trust. (20).

Damis can hear the words — and now he nods frantically, urging his father to attend to the truth they carry. But what Orgon hears is again wholly different: He hears the sound of unbelievably generous forgiveness, sweetness, tenderness ("Yes, my dear son," (29) — magnanimity supreme. Did Jesus himself ever turn his cheek so patiently and self-sacrificingly?

At the sight of Tartuffe kneeling helplessly, seeming actually to welcome the world's scorn, Orgon is *moved*. His rage at Damis softens momentarily; "Have you no heart" (35) is said in almost pleading, choked wonder. Could anyone truly miss the goodness-holiness of this person?

As Damis's "victory" slips out of his fingers, frustration explodes comically inside him. Orgon's effort simultaneously to wreak violence on his son while offering gentle comfort to Tartuffe is, as a physical sight, a comic surprise. The figure at the center of the swirling scene is calm. Amid shouting and abuse — boorishness, churlishness, immoderacy — Tartuffe communicates a kind of tranquil gratitude. To be "exposed," to suffer this disgrace, to be thus publicly condemned is for me a blessing: This is the message sent by his outward serenity.

As for his insides: The chief elements are immeasurable self-confidence, steely scorn, and a gambler's cool. But they are nowhere visible until Act IV, Scene V. What's seen here is a momentarily believable saint — resolute, daring, possessed of dignity on the very brink. We see Tartuffe as Reason embarrassed by the farcical excesses of Orgon and Damis; to bring this scene to life we must imagine him as the very principle of measure and sanity, lawfulness and justice.

Questions about Tartuffe: *Act V, Scene IV*

Focus on Act V, Scene IV — the visit of Monsieur Loyal, the bailiff. Make careful notes on the actions, thoughts, and feelings that need to be brought to life in the course of this scene. Between line 10 and line 56 Dorine reverses her estimate of M. Loyal as "a very gracious man." On what was her original estimate based? Where and when does it change? In what tone does

M. Loyal make his request for the keys to the front door (70–71)? Decide what each speaker is for himself and for the others during the scene, basing decisions on readings of each speaker's nature. Build up the insides of the appropriate tones, gestures, and tonal contrasts by which each character's separateness can be realized from moment to moment. Then write a paper naming the elements (movements, gestures, expressions, motives) that figure crucially in staging the scene, and explain why they are all important.

20

Tragicomedy

CONCEPTS OF ORDER IN TRAGEDY AND COMEDY

Tragedy and comedy are alike in this respect: They tend to assume general agreement within the audience about the difference between good and bad behavior in individuals, about what constitutes success and failure, about right and wrong directions for society at large. No shade of doubt exists in the world of *Macbeth* about the hideousness of the crime with which the title character's descent begins. Murder under any circumstances is a crime; the murder of a guest in one's house is more awful; the murder of the sovereign who has trusted your hospitality is still more unthinkable. Tartuffe's ability to deceive Orgon stems from Orgon's desire to take up a holier-than-thou position before family and friends; Orgon's desire reflects, in turn, overweening pride; the assumption is that everyone agrees ("Blessed are the humble") that pride is a bad thing.

Clarity within the audience about the nature of good and evil — and about the difference between them — is reflected also in the concept of the happy ending (crucial to comedy) and the concept of the restoration of order (often important in tragedy). At the final curtain of a comedy there's general rejoicing that the truly devoted lovers who were wrongly kept apart are at last brought together, or that the truly selfish protagonist who scored triumph after triumph over the decent and innocent is at last brought low. And although tragedies end somberly, their final scenes often point us toward renewal. We understand at the close of *Hamlet* that at least the dead prince's reputation will be

1179

honored in the future, and that a worthy candidate — Hamlet's own — will succeed to the throne. And a similar movement toward reestablishing justice and order seems to begin in Malcolm's last speech in *Macbeth*. Implicit in these endings, as in the firmness of the judgments of crime or folly, is moral consensus — sharply defined, universally accepted conceptions of political, social, and religious order.

CONCEPTS OF ORDER
IN TRAGICOMEDY

In literature, in time, though, all concepts come under questioning. And during the last century and a half, dramatic literature has often asked its questions by mixing genres — setting tragic and comic elements side by side straight through to the end, and refusing to settle whether the work as a whole should be seen as a tragedy or as a comedy. The implication is that the distinction between what's serious and not serious isn't absolute — and also that, within the audience, there is no agreement on a universally valid code of moral and social values. In the two Shakespeare plays in this book, tragicomic elements turn up frequently — for example, in the porter's boozy rambling just after the murder scene in *Macbeth* (II.iii) or in Hamlet's mocking jokes about "the convocation of politic worms" just after the slaying of Polonius (IV.ii.21). But their effect isn't to leave us in doubt about the overall seriousness of both plays' principal action and feeling.

Yet many of the great works of the modern theater — from Henrik Ibsen's *The Wild Duck* to Samuel Beckett's *Waiting for Godot* — suspend the audience in doubt from beginning to end. The reasons for this aren't mysterious. The rate of change in moral codes has immensely increased in our age, and one result is that the concept of a universal moral order is in decline. Political orders and hierarchies have also been transformed. No single conception either of the nature of human distinction or of the proper ends of human society commands everybody's assent. In Anton Chekhov's *The Cherry Orchard*, a family and household of considerable charm faces the destruction of its way of life. The people in question are feckless, true — but they are also kind, sensitive, generous, even in a measure egalitarian. The class and order succeeding them will almost surely lack their grace and perhaps also their moral decency.

And yet their "fall" can't be felt as seamlessly tragic. It's sad — but the notion that it's intensely regrettable can't quickly be accepted. Silliness, laziness, self-indulgence, downright stupidity — these can't be unreservedly approved; the order on which the Ranevskaya household's style of living was based was partly supported by slavery. The order that will replace it is one in which careers are open to the talented. The new order not only improves the quality of life of millions in discernible respects, but it's in the process — if we trust Lopahin's example — of creating a merchant class possessing substantial virtues. Chekhov was sure enough in his own mind that the destruction of the Ranevskayas was no real cataclysm to refer to his play as a comedy. Few who know and love *The Cherry Orchard* have felt much satisfaction with that label. We see the play's tones and feelings as mixed and its concept of order as unsettled. We're undecided about whether the end of this household marks the end or beginning of a civilization, and we therefore describe the play as tragicomic.

Few challenges are more complex than that faced by readers who bring to life one or another of the great nineteenth- and twentieth-century tragicomedies. Evoking them for what they are — simultaneously moving, funny, and mysterious — is among the highest achievements of the active reader's art.

ASKING QUESTIONS ABOUT *THE CHERRY ORCHARD*

The two assignments that follow the play focus on moments during which changes of feeling occur — but the nature of the changes and especially the reasons for the changes don't stand out as unequivocally as they do in *Macbeth* or *Tartuffe*. As active readers, we bring to life the moment-to-moment change or movement of feelings. At times, the feelings may be puzzling or problematic to the characters in the play — feelings of uncertainty or hesitation. And a spirit of uncertainty enters into the very gestures and actions we decide are appropriate.

ANTON CHEKHOV (1860–1904)

The Cherry Orchard
A Comedy in Four Acts

TRANSLATED BY AVRAHM YARMOLINSKY

Lubov Andreyevna Ranevskaya, *a landowner*
Anya, *her seventeen-year-old daughter*
Varya, *her adopted daughter, twenty-two years old*
Leonid Andreyevich Gayev, *Madame Ranevskaya's brother*
Yermolay Alexeyevich Lopahin, *a merchant*
Pyotr Sergeyevich Trofimov, *a student*

Simeonov-Pishchik, *a landowner*
Charlotta Ivanovna, *a governess*
Semyon Yepihodov, *a clerk*
Dunyasha, *a maid*
Firs (pronounced *fierce*), *a man-servant, aged eighty-seven*
Yasha, *a young valet*
A Tramp
Stationmaster, Post Office Clerk, Guests, Servants

The action takes place on Madame Ranevskaya's estate.

ACT I

A room that is still called the nursery. One of the doors leads into Anya's room. Dawn, the sun will soon rise. It is May, the cherry trees are in blossom, but it is cold in the orchard; there is a morning frost. The windows are shut. Enter Dunyasha with a candle, and Lopahin with a book in his hand.

Lopahin: The train is in, thank God. What time is it?
Dunyasha: Nearly two. (*Puts out the candle.*) It's light already.
Lopahin: How late is the train, anyway? Two hours at least. (*Yawns and stretches.*) I'm a fine one! What a fool I've made of myself! I came here on purpose to meet them at the station, and then I went and overslept. I fell asleep in my chair. How annoying! You might have waked me . . .
Dunyasha: I thought you'd left. (*Listens.*) I think they're coming!
Lopahin (listens): No, they've got to get the luggage, and one thing and another . . . (*Pause.*) Lubov Andreyevna spent five years abroad, I don't know what she's like now . . . She's a fine person — lighthearted, simple. I remember when I was a boy of fifteen, my poor father — he had a shop here in the village then — punched me in the face with his fist and made my nose bleed. We'd come into the yard, I don't know what for, and he'd had a drop too much. Lubov Andreyevna, I remember her as if it were yesterday — she was still young

and so slim — led me to the wash-basin, in this very room . . . in the nursery. "Don't cry, little peasant," she said, "it'll heal in time for your wedding. . . ." (*Pause.*) Little peasant . . . my father was a peasant, it's true, and here I am in a white waistcoat and yellow shoes. A pig in a pastry shop, you might say. It's true I'm rich, I've got a lot of money. . . . But when you look at it closely, I'm a peasant through and through. (*Pages the book.*) Here I've been reading this book and I didn't understand a word of it . . . was reading it and fell asleep . . . (*Pause.*)

Dunyasha: And the dogs were awake all night, they feel that their masters are coming.

Lopahin: Dunyasha, why are you so —

Dunyasha: My hands are trembling. I'm going to faint.

Lopahin: You're too soft, Dunyasha. You dress like a lady, and look at the way you do your hair. That's not right. One should remember one's place.

Enter Yepihodov with a bouquet; he wears a jacket and highly polished boots that squeak badly. He drops the bouquet as he comes in.

Yepihodov (picking up the bouquet): Here, the gardener sent these, said you're to put them in the dining room. (*Hands the bouquet to Dunyasha.*)

Lopahin: And bring me some kvass.

Dunyasha: Yes, sir. (*Exits.*)

Yepihodov: There's a frost this morning — three degrees below — and yet the cherries are all in blossom. I cannot approve of our climate. (*Sighs.*) I cannot. Our climate does not activate properly. And, Yermolay Alexeyevich, allow me to make a further remark. The other day I bought myself a pair of boots, and I make bold to assure you, they squeak so that it is really intolerable. What should I grease them with?

Lopahin: Oh, get out! I'm fed up with you.

Yepihodov: Every day I meet with misfortune. And I don't complain, I've got used to it, I even smile.

Dunyasha enters, hands Lopahin the kvass.

Yepihodov: I am leaving. (*Stumbles against a chair, which falls over.*) There! (*Triumphantly, as it were.*) There again, you see what sort of circumstance, pardon the expression. . . . It is absolutely phenomenal! (*Exits.*)

Dunyasha: You know, Yermolay Alexeyevich, I must tell you, Yepihodov has proposed to me.

Lopahin: Ah!

Dunyasha: I simply don't know . . . he's a quiet man, but some-times when he starts talking, you can't make out what he means. He speaks nicely — and it's touching — but you can't understand it. I sort of like him though, and he is crazy about me. He's an unlucky man . . . every day something happens to him. They tease him about it here . . . they call him, Two-and-Twenty Troubles.

Lopahin (listening): There! I think they're coming.

Dunyasha: They *are* coming! What's the matter with me? I feel cold all over.

Lopahin: They really are coming. Let's go and meet them. Will she recognize me? We haven't seen each other for five years.

Dunyasha (in a flutter): I'm going to faint this minute. . . . Oh, I'm going to faint!

Two carriages are heard driving up to the house. Lopahin and Dunyasha go out quickly. The stage is left empty. There is a noise in the adjoining rooms. Firs, who had driven to the station to meet Lubov Andreyevna Ranevskaya, crosses the stage hurriedly, leaning on a stick. He is wearing an old-fashioned livery and a tall hat. He mutters to himself indistinctly. The hubbub off-stage increases. A voice: "Come, let's go this way." Enter Lubov Andreyevna, Anya, and Charlotta Ivanovna, with a pet dog on a leash, all in traveling dresses; Varya, wearing a coat and kerchief; Gayev, Simeonov-Pishchik, Lopahin, Dunyasha with a bag and an umbrella, servants with luggage. All walk across the room.

Anya: Let's go this way. Do you remember what room this is, mamma?

Madame Ranevskaya (joyfully, through her tears): The nursery!

Varya: How cold it is! My hands are numb. (*To Madame Ranev-skaya.*) Your rooms are just the same as they were mamma, the white one and the violet.

Madame Ranevskaya: The nursery! My darling, lovely room! I slept here when I was a child . . . (*Cries.*) And here I am, like a child again! (*Kisses her brother and Varya, and then her brother again.*) Varya's just the same as ever, like a nun. And I recognized Dunyasha. (*Kisses Dunyasha.*)

Gayev: The train was two hours late. What do you think of that? What a way to manage things!

Charlotta (to Pishchik): My dog eats nuts, too.

Pischik (in amazement): You don't say so! (*All go out, except Anya and Dunyasha.*)

Dunyasha: We've been waiting for you for hours. (*Takes Anya's hat and coat.*)

Anya: I didn't sleep on the train for four nights and now I'm frozen . . .

Dunyasha: It was Lent when you left; there was snow and frost, and now . . . My darling! (*Laughs and kisses her.*) I have been waiting for you, my sweet, my darling! But I must tell you something . . . I can't put it off another minute . . .

Anya (listlessly): What now?

Dunyasha: The clerk, Yepihodov, proposed to me, just after Easter.

Anya: There you are, at it again . . . (*Straightening her hair.*) I've lost all my hairpins . . . (*She is staggering with exhaustion.*)

Dunyasha: Really, I don't know what to think. He loves me — he loves me so!

Anya (looking towards the door of her room, tenderly): My own room, my windows, just as though I'd never been away. I'm home! Tomorrow morning I'll get up and run into the orchard. Oh, if I could only get some sleep. I didn't close my eyes during the whole journey — I was so anxious.

Dunyasha: Pyotr Sergeyevich came the day before yesterday.

Anya (joyfully): Petya!

Dunyasha: He's asleep in the bath-house. He has settled there. He said he was afraid of being in the way. (*Looks at her watch.*) I should wake him, but Miss Varya told me not to. "Don't you wake him," she said.

Enter Varya with a bunch of keys at her belt.

Varya: Dunyasha, coffee, and be quick . . . Mamma's asking for coffee.

Dunyasha: In a minute. (*Exits.*)

Varya: Well, thank God, you've come. You're home again. (*Fondling Anya.*) My darling is here again. My pretty one is back.

Anya: Oh, what I've been through!

Varya: I can imagine.

Anya: When we left, it was Holy Week, it was cold then, and all the way Charlotta chattered and did her tricks. Why did you have to saddle me with Charlotta?

Varya: You couldn't have traveled all alone, darling — at seventeen!

Anya: We got to Paris, it was cold there, snowing. My French is dreadful. Mamma lived on the fifth floor; I went up there, and found all kinds of Frenchmen, ladies, an old priest with a book. The place was full of tobacco smoke, and so bleak. Suddenly I felt sorry for mamma, so sorry, I took her head in my arms and hugged her and couldn't let go of her. Afterwards mamma kept fondling me and crying . . .

Varya (through tears): Don't speak of it . . . don't.

Anya: She had already sold her villa at Mentone, she had nothing left, nothing. I hadn't a kopeck left either, we had only just enough to get home. And mamma wouldn't understand! When we had dinner at the stations, she always ordered the most expensive dishes, and tipped the waiters a whole ruble. Charlotta, too. And Yasha kept ordering, too — it was simply awful. You know Yasha's mamma's footman now, we brought him here with us.

Varya: Yes, I've seen the blackguard.

Anya: Well, tell me — have you paid the interest?

Varya: How could we?

Anya: Good heavens, good heavens!

Varya: In August the estate will be put up for sale.

Anya: My God!

Lopahin (peeps in at the door and bleats): Meh-h-h. (*Disappears.*)

Varya (through tears): What I couldn't do to him! (*Shakes her fist threateningly.*)

Anya (embracing Varya, gently): Varya, has he proposed to you? (*Varya shakes her head.*) But he loves you. Why don't you come to an understanding? What are you waiting for?

Varya: Oh, I don't think anything will ever come of it. He's too busy, he has no time for me . . . pays no attention to me. I've washed my hands of him — I can't bear the sight of him. They all talk about our getting married, they all congratulate me — and all the time there's really nothing to it — it's all like a dream. (*In another tone.*) You have a new brooch — like a bee.

Anya (sadly): Mamma bought it. (*She goes into her own room and speaks gaily like a child.*) And you know, in Paris I went up in a balloon.

Varya: My darling's home, my pretty one is back! (*Dunyasha returns with the coffee-pot and prepares coffee. Varya stands at the door of Anya's room.*) All day long, darling, as I go about the house, I keep dreaming. If only we could marry you off to a rich man, I should feel at ease. Then I would go into a convent, and afterwards to Kiev, to Moscow . . . I would spend my life going fron one holy place to another . . . I'd go on and on . . . What a blessing that would be!

Anya: The birds are singing in the orchard. What time is it?

Varya: It must be after two. Time you were asleep, darling. (*Goes into Anya's room.*) What a blessing that would be!

Yasha enters with a plaid and a traveling bag, crosses the stage.

Yasha (finically): May I pass this way, please?

Dunyasha: A person could hardly recognize you, Yasha. Your stay abroad has certainly done wonders for you.

Yasha: Hm-m . . . and who are you?

Dunyasha: When you went away I was that high — (*Indicating with her hand.*) I'm Dunyasha — Fyodor Kozoyedev's daughter. Don't you remember?

Yasha: Hm! What a peach!

He looks round and embraces her. She cries out and drops a saucer. Yasha leaves quickly.

Varya (in the doorway, in a tone of annoyance): What's going on here?

Dunyasha (through tears): I've broken a saucer.

Varya: Well, that's good luck.

Anya (coming out of her room): We ought to warn mamma that Petya's here.

Varya: I left orders not to wake him.

Anya (musingly): Six years ago father died. A month later brother Grisha was drowned in the river. . . . Such a pretty little boy he was — only seven. It was more than mamma could bear, so she went away, went away without looking back . . . (*Shudders.*) How well I understand her, if she only knew! (*Pauses.*) And Petya Trofimov was Grisha's tutor, he may remind her of it all. . . .

Enter Firs, wearing a jacket and a white waistcoat. He goes up to the coffee-pot.

Firs (anxiously): The mistress will have her coffee here. (*Puts on white gloves.*) Is the coffee ready? (*Sternly; to Dunyasha.*) Here, you! And where's the cream?

Dunyasha: Oh, my God! (*Exits quickly.*)

Firs (fussing over the coffee-pot): Hah! the addlehead! (*Mutters to himself.*) Home from Paris. And the old master used to go to Paris too . . . by carriage. (*Laughs.*)

Varya: What is it, Firs?

Firs: What is your pleasure, Miss? (*Joyfully.*) My mistress has come home, and I've seen her at last! Now I can die. (*Weeps with joy.*)

Enter Madame Ranevskaya, Gayev, and Simeonov-Pishchik. The latter is wearing a tight-waisted, pleated coat of fine cloth, and full trousers. Gayev, as he comes in, goes through the motions of a billiard player with his arms and body.

Madame Ranevskaya: Let's see, how does it go? Yellow ball in the corner! Bank shot in the side pocket!

Gayev: I'll tip it in the corner! There was a time, sister, when you and I used to sleep in this very room, and now I'm fifty-one, strange as it may seem.

TRAGICOMEDY

Lopahin: Yes, time flies.
Gayev: Who?
Lopahin: I say, time flies.
Gayev: It smells of patchouli here.
Anya: I'm going to bed. Good night, mamma. (*Kisses her mother.*)
Madame Ranevskaya: My darling child! (*Kisses her hands.*) Are you happy to be home? I can't come to my senses.
Anya: Good night, uncle.
Gayev (kissing her face and hands): God bless you, how like your mother you are! (*To his sister.*) At her age, Luba, you were just like her.

Anya shakes hands with Lopahin and Pishchik, then goes out, shutting the door behind her.

Madame Ranevskaya: She's very tired.
Pishchik: Well, it was a long journey.
Varya (to Lopahin and Pishchik): How about it, gentlemen? It's past two o'clock — isn't it time for you to go?
Madame Ranevskaya (laughs): You're just the same as ever, Varya. (*Draws her close and kisses her.*) I'll have my coffee and then we'll all go. (*Firs puts a small cushion under her feet.*) Thank you, my dear. I've got used to coffee. I drink it day and night. Thanks, my dear old man. (*Kisses him.*)
Varya: I'd better see if all the luggage has been brought in. (*Exits.*)
Madame Ranevskaya: Can it really be I sitting here? (*Laughs.*) I feel like dancing, waving my arms about. (*Covers her face with her hands.*) But maybe I am dreaming! God knows I love my country, I love it tenderly; I couldn't look out of the window in the train, I kept crying so. (*Through tears.*) But I must have my coffee. Thank you, Firs, thank you, dear old man. I'm so happy that you're still alive.
Firs: Day before yesterday.
Gayev: He's hard of hearing.
Lopahin: I must go soon, I'm leaving for Kharkov about five o'clock. How annoying! I'd like to have a good look at you, talk to you . . . You're just as splendid as ever.
Pishchik (breathing heavily): She's even better-looking . . . Dressed in the latest Paris fashion . . . Perish my carriage and all its four wheels . . .
Lopahin: Your brother, Leonid Andreyevich, says I'm a vulgarian and an exploiter. But it's all the same to me — let him talk. I only want you to trust me as you used to. I want you to look at me with your touching, wonderful eyes, as you used to. Dear God! My father was a serf of your father's and grandfather's,

but you, you yourself, did so much for me once ... so much — even more.

Madame Ranevskaya: I can't sit still, I simply can't. (*Jumps up and walks about in violent agitation.*) This joy is too much for me ... Laugh at me, I'm silly! My own darling bookcase! My darling table! (*Kisses it.*)

Gayev: While you were away, nurse died.

Madame Ranevskaya (sits down and takes her coffee): Yes, God rest her soul; they wrote me about it.

Gayev: And Anastasy is dead. Petrushka Kossoy has left me and has gone into town to work for the police inspector. (*Takes a box of sweets out of his pocket and begins to suck one.*)

Pishchik: My daughter Dashenka sends her regards.

Lopahin: I'd like to tell you something very pleasant — cheering. (*Glancing at his watch.*) I am leaving directly. There isn't much time to talk. But I will put it in a few words. As you know, your cherry orchard is to be sold to pay your debts. The sale is to be on the twenty-second of August; but don't you worry, my dear, you may sleep in peace; there is a way out. Here is my plan. Give me your attention! Your estate is only fifteen miles from the town; the railway runs close by it; and if the cherry orchard and the land along the river bank were cut up into lots and these leased for summer cottages, you would have an income of at least twenty-five thousand rubles a year out of it.

Gayev: Excuse me ... What nonsense.

Madame Ranevskaya: I don't quite understand you, Yermolay Alexeyevich.

Lopahin: You will get an annual rent of at least ten rubles per acre, and if you advertise at once, I'll give you any guarantee you like that you won't have a square foot of ground left by autumn, all the lots will be snapped up. In short, congratulations, you're saved. The location is splendid — by that deep river. . . . Only, of course the ground must be cleared . . . all the old buildings, for instance, must be torn down, and this house, too, which is useless, and of course, the old cherry orchard must be cut down.

Madame Ranevskaya: Cut down? My dear, forgive me, but you don't know what you're talking about. If there's one thing that's interesting — indeed, remarkable — in the whole province, it's precisely our cherry orchard.

Lopahin: The only remarkable thing about this orchard is that it's a very large one. There's a crop of cherries every other year, and you can't do anything with them; no one buys them.

Gayev: This orchard is even mentioned in the Encyclopedia.

Lopahin (glancing at his watch): If we can't think of a way out, if we don't come to a decision, on the twenty-second of August the cherry orchard and the whole estate will be sold at auction. Make up your minds! There's no other way out — I swear. None, none.

Firs: In the old days, forty or fifty years ago, the cherries were dried, soaked, pickled, and made into jam, and we used to —

Gayev: Keep still, Firs.

Firs: And the dried cherries would be shipped by the cartload. It meant a lot of money! And in those days the dried cherries were soft and juicy, sweet, fragrant . . . They knew the way to do it, then.

Madame Ranevskaya: And why don't they do it that way now?

Firs: They've forgotten. Nobody remembers it.

Pishchik (to Madame Ranevskaya): What's doing in Paris? Eh? Did you eat frogs there?

Madame Ranevskaya: I ate crocodiles.

Pishchik: Just imagine!

Lopahin: There used to be only landowners and peasants in the country, but now these summer people have appeared on the scene . . . All the towns, even the small ones, are surrounded by these summer cottages; and in another twenty years, no doubt, the summer population will have grown enormously. Now the summer resident only drinks tea on his porch, but maybe he'll take to working his acre, too, and then your cherry orchard will be a rich, happy, luxuriant place.

Gayev (indignantly): Poppycock!

Enter Varya and Yasha.

Varya: There are two telegrams for you, mamma dear. (*Picks a key from the bunch at her belt and noisily opens an old-fashioned bookcase.*) Here they are.

Madame Ranevskaya: They're from Paris. (*Tears them up without reading them.*) I'm through with Paris.

Gayev: Do you know, Luba, how old this bookcase is? Last week I pulled out the bottom drawer and there I found the date burnt in it. It was made exactly a hundred years ago. Think of that! We could celebrate its centenary. True, it's an inanimate object, but nevertheless, a bookcase . . .

Pishchik (amazed): A hundred years! Just imagine!

Gayev: Yes. (*Tapping it.*) That's something . . . Dear, honored bookcase, hail to you who for more than a century have served the

glorious ideals of goodness and justice! Your silent summons
to fruitful toil has never weakened in all those hundred years
(*through tears*) sustaining, through successive generations of
our family, courage and faith, in a better future, and foster-
ing in us ideals of goodness and social consciousness . . .
(*Pauses.*)

Lopahin: Yes . . .

Madame Ranevskaya: You haven't changed a bit, Leonid.

Gayev (somewhat embarrassed): I'll play it off the red in the corner!
Tip it in the side pocket!

Lopahin (looking at his watch): Well it's time for me to go . . .

Yasha (handing a pill box to Madame Ranevskaya): Perhaps you'll
take your pills now.

Pishchik: One shouldn't take medicines, dearest lady, they do
neither harm nor good. . . . Give them here, my valued
friend. (*Takes the pill box, pours the pills into his palm, blows on
them, puts them in his mouth, and washes them down with some
kvass.*) There!

Madame Ranevskaya (frightened.): You must be mad!

Pishchik: I've taken all the pills.

Lopahin: What a glutton!

All laugh.

Firs: The gentleman visited us in Easter week, ate half a bucket of
pickles, he did . . . (*Mumbles.*)

Madame Ranevskaya: What's he saying?

Varya: He's been mumbling like that for the last three years —
we're used to it.

Yasha: His declining years!

*Charlotta Ivanovna, very thin, tightly laced, dressed in white, a lorgnette at her
waist, crosses the stage.*

Lopahin: Forgive me, Charlotta Ivanovna, I've not had time to
greet you. (*Tries to kiss her hand.*)

Charlotta (pulling away her hand): If I let you kiss my hand, you'll
be wanting to kiss my elbow next, and then my shoulder.

Lopahin: I've no luck today. (*All laugh.*) Charlotta Ivanovna, show
us a trick.

Madame Ranevskaya: Yes, Charlotta, do a trick for us.

Charlotta: I don't see the need. I want to sleep. (*Exits.*)

Lopahin: In three weeks we'll meet again. (*Kisses Madame Ranevskaya's hand.*) Good-by till then. Time's up. (*To Gayev.*) Bye-bye.
(*Kisses Pishchik.*) Bye-bye. (*Shakes hands with Varya, then with*

Firs and Yasha.) I hate to leave. (*To Madame Ranevskaya.*) If you make up your mind about the cottages, let me know; I'll get you a loan of fifty thousand rubles. Think it over seriously.

Varya (crossly): Will you never go!

Lopahin: I'm going, I'm going. (*Exits.*)

Gayev: The vulgarian. But, excuse me . . . Varya's going to marry him, he's Varya's fiancé.

Varya: You talk too much, uncle dear.

Madame Ranevskaya: Well, Varya, it would make me happy. He's a good man.

Pishchik: Yes, one must admit, he's a most estimable man. And my Dashenka . . . she too says that . . . she says . . . lots of things. (*Snores; but wakes up at once.*) All the same, my valued friend, could you oblige me . . . with a loan of two hundred and forty rubles? I must pay the interest on the mortgage tomorrow.

Varya (alarmed): We can't, we can't!

Madame Ranevskaya: I really haven't any money.

Pishchik: It'll turn up. (*Laughs.*) I never lose hope, I thought everything was lost, that I was done for, when lo and behold, the railway ran through my land . . . and I was paid for it . . . And something else will turn up again, if not today, then tomorrow . . . Dashenka will win two hundred thousand . . . she's got a lottery ticket.

Madame Ranevskaya: I've had my coffee, now let's go to bed.

Firs (brushes off Gayev; admonishingly): You've got the wrong trousers on again. What am I to do with you?

Varya (softly): Anya's asleep. (*Gently opens the window.*) The sun's up now, it's not a bit cold. Look, mamma dear, what wonderful trees. And heavens, what air! The starlings are singing!

Gayev (opens the other window): The orchard is all white. You've not forgotten it? Luba? That's the long alley that runs straight, straight as an arrow; how it shines on moonlight nights, do you remember? You've not forgotten?

Madame Ranevskaya (looking out of the window into the orchard): Oh, my childhood, my innocent childhood. I used to sleep in this nursery — I used to look out into the orchard, happiness waked with me every morning, the orchard was just the same then . . . nothing has changed. (*Laughs with joy.*) All, all white! Oh, my orchard! After the dark, rainy autumn and the cold winter, you are young again, and full of happiness, the heavenly angels have not left you . . . If I could free my chest and my shoulders from this rock that weights on me, if I could only forget the past!

Gayev: Yes, and the orchard will be sold to pay our debts, strange as it may seem. . . .
Madame Ranevskaya: Look! There is our poor mother walking in the orchard . . . all in white . . . (*Laughs with joy.*) It is she!
Gayev: Where?
Varya: What are you saying, mamma dear!
Madame Ranevskaya: There's no one there, I just imagined it. To the right, where the path turns towards the arbor, there's a little white tree, leaning over, that looks like a woman . . .

Trofimov enters, wearing a shabby student's uniform and spectacles.

Madame Ranevskaya: What an amazing orchard! White masses of blossom, the blue sky . . .
Trofimov: Lubov Andreyevna! (*She looks round at him.*) I just want to pay my respects to you, then I'll leave at once. (*Kisses her hand ardently.*) I was told to wait until morning, but I hadn't the patience . . . (*Madame Ranevskaya looks at him, perplexed.*)
Varya (through tears): This is Petya Trofimov.
Trofimov: Petya Trofimov, formerly your Grisha's tutor . . . Can I have changed so much? (*Madame Ranevskaya embraces him and weeps quietly.*)
Gayev (embarrassed): Don't, don't, Luba.
Varya (crying): I told you, Petya, to wait until tomorrow.
Madame Ranevskaya: My Grisha . . . my little boy . . . Grisha . . . my son.
Varya: What can one do, mamma dear, it's God's will.
Trofimov (softly, through tears): There . . . there.
Madame Ranevskaya (weeping quietly): My little boy was lost . . . drowned. Why? Why, my friend? (*More quietly.*) Anya's asleep in there, and here I am talking so loudly . . . making all this noise. . . . But tell me, Petya, why do you look so badly? Why have you aged so?
Trofimov: A mangy master, a peasant woman in the train called me.
Madame Ranevskaya: You were just a boy then, a dear little student, and now your hair's thin — and you're wearing glasses! Is it possible you're still a student? (*Goes towards the door.*)
Trofimov: I suppose I'm a perpetual student.
Madame Ranevskaya (kisses her brother, then Varya): Now, go to bed . . . You have aged, too, Leonid.
Pishchik (follows her): So now we turn in. Oh, my gout! I'm staying the night here . . . Lubov Andreyevna, my angel, tomorrow morning. . . . I do need two hundred and forty rubles.

Gayev: He keeps at it.
Pishchik: I'll pay it back, dear . . . it's a trifling sum.
Madame Ranevskaya: All right, Leonid will give it to you. Give it to him, Leonid.
Gayev: Me give it to him! That's a good one!
Madame Ranevskaya: It can't be helped. Give it to him! He needs it. He'll pay it back.

Madame Ranevskaya, Trofimov, Pishchik, and Firs go out; Gayev, Varya, and Yasha remain.

Gayev: Sister hasn't got out of the habit of throwing money around. (*To Yasha.*) Go away, my good fellow, you smell of the barnyard.
Yasha (with a grin): And you, Leonid Andreyevich, are just the same as ever.
Gayev: Who? (*To Varya.*) What did he say?
Varya (to Yasha): Your mother's come from the village; she's been sitting in the servants' room since yesterday, waiting to see you.
Yasha: Botheration!
Varya: You should be ashamed of yourself!
Yasha: She's all I needed! She could have come tomorrow. (*Exit.*)
Varya: Mamma is just the same as ever; she hasn't changed a bit. If she had her own way she'd keep nothing for herself.
Gayev: Yes . . . (*Pause.*) If a great many remedies are offered for some disease, it means it is incurable; I keep thinking and racking my brains; I have many remedies, ever so many, and that really means none. It would be fine if we came in for a legacy; it would be fine if we married off our Anya to a very rich man; or we might go to Yaroslavl and try our luck with our aunt, the Countess. She's very, very rich, you know . . .
Varya (weeping): If only God would help us!
Gayev: Stop bawling. Aunt's very rich, but she doesn't like us. In the first place, sister married a lawyer who was no nobleman . . . (*Anya appears in the doorway.*) She married beneath her, and it can't be said that her behavior has been very exemplary. She's good, kind, sweet, and I love her, but no matter what extenuating circumstances you may adduce, there's no denying that she has no morals. You sense it in her least gesture.
Varya (in a whisper): Anya's in the doorway.
Gayev: Who? (*Pauses.*) It's queer, something got into my right eye — my eyes are going back on me. . . . And on Thursday, when I was in the circuit court —

Enter Anya.

Varya: Why aren't you asleep, Anya?

Anya: I can't get to sleep, I just can't.

Gayev: My little pet! (*Kisses Anya's face and hands.*) My child! (*Weeps.*) You are not my niece, you're my angel! You're every-thing to me. Believe me, believe —

Anya: I believe you, uncle. Everyone loves you and respects you . . . but, uncle dear, you must keep still . . . You must. What were you saying just now about my mother? Your own sister? What made you say that?

Gayev: Yes, yes . . . (*Covers his face with her hand.*) Really, that was awful! Good God! Heaven help me! Just now I made a speech to the bookcase . . . so stupid! And only after I was through, I saw how stupid it was.

Varya: It's true, uncle dear, you ought to keep still. Just don't talk, that's all.

Anya: If you could only keep still, it would make things easier for you too.

Gayev: I'll keep still. (*Kisses Anya's and Varya's hands.*) I will. But now about business. On Thursday I was in court; well, there were a number of us there, and we began talking of one thing and another, and this and that, and do you know, I believe it will be possible to raise a loan on a promissory note, to pay the interest at the bank.

Varya: If only God would help us!

Gayev: On Tuesday I'll go and see about it again. (*To Varya.*) Stop bawling. (*To Anya.*) Your mamma will talk to Lopahin, and he, of course, will not refuse her . . . and as soon as you're rested, you'll go to Yaroslavl to the Countess, your great-aunt. So we'll be working in three directions at once, and the thing is in the bag. We'll pay the interest — I'm sure of it. (*Puts a candy in his mouth.*) I swear on my honor, I swear by anything you like, the estate shan't be sold. (*Excitedly.*) I swear by my own happiness! Here's my hand on it, you can call me a swindler and a scoundrel if I let it come to an auction! I swear by my whole being.

Anya (relieved and quite happy again): How good you are, uncle, and how clever! (*Embraces him.*) Now I'm at peace, quite at peace, I'm happy.

Firs (reproachfully): Leonid Andreyevich, have you no fear of God? When are you going to bed?

Gayev: Directly, directly. Go away. Firs, I'll . . . yes, I will undress myself. Now, children, 'nightie-'nightie. We'll consider details tomorrow, but now go to sleep. (*Kisses Anya and Varya.*) I am a man of the 'Eighties; they have nothing good to say of that period nowadays. Nevertheless, in the course of my life I have suffered not a little for my convictions. It's not for nothing that the peasant loves me; one should know the peasant; one should know from which —

Anya: There you go again, uncle.

Varya: Uncle dear, be quiet.

Firs (angrily): Leonid Andreyevich!

Gayev: I'm coming, I'm coming! Go to bed! Double bank shot in the side pocket! Here goes a clean shot . . .

Exits, Firs hobbling after him.

Anya: I am at peace now. I don't want to go to Yaroslavl — I don't like my great-aunt, but still, I am at peace, thanks to uncle. (*Sits down.*)

Varya: We must get some sleep. I'm going now. While you were away something unpleasant happened. In the old servants' quarters there are only the old people, as you know; Yefim, Polya, Yevstigney, and Karp, too. They began letting all sorts of rascals in to spend the night . . . I didn't say anything. Then I heard they'd been spreading a report that I gave them nothing but dried peas to eat — out of stinginess, you know . . . and it was all Yevstigney's doing. . . . All right, I thought, if that's how it is, I thought, just wait. I sent for Yevstigney. . . . (*Yawns.*) He comes. . . . "How's this, Yevstigney?" I say, "You fool . . . (*Looking at Anya.*) Anichka! (*Pauses.*) She's asleep. (*Puts her arm around Anya.*) Come to your little bed. . . . Come . . . (*Leads her.*) My darling has fallen asleep. . . . Come.

They go out. Far away beyond the orchard a shepherd is piping. Trofimov crosses the stage and, seeing Varya and Anya, stands still.

Varya: Sh! She's asleep . . . asleep . . . Come, darling.

Anya (softly, half-asleep): I'm so tired. Those bells . . . uncle . . . dear. . . . Mamma and uncle . . .

Varya: Come, my precious, come along. (*They go into Anya's room.*)

Trofimov (with emotion): My sunshine, my spring!

ACT II

A meadow. An old, long-abandoned, lopsided little chapel; near it, a well, large slabs, which had apparently once served as tombstones, and an old bench. In the background, the road to the Gayev estate. To one side poplars loom darkly, where the cherry orchard begins. In the distance a row of telegraph poles, and far off, on the horizon, the faint outline of a large city which is seen only in fine, clear weather. The sun will soon be setting. Charlotta, Yasha, and Dunyasha are seated on the bench. Yepihodov stands near and plays a guitar. All are pensive. Charlotta wears an old peaked cap. She has taken a gun from her shoulder and is straightening the buckle on the strap.

Charlotta (musingly): I haven't a real passport, I don't know how old I am, and I always feel that I am very young. When I was a little girl, my father and mother used to go from fair to fair and give performances, very good ones. And I used to do the *salto mortale,*° and all sorts of other tricks. And when papa and mamma died, a German lady adopted me and began to educate me. Very good. I grew up and became a governess. But where I come from and who I am, I don't know. . . . Who were my parents? Perhaps they weren't even married. . . . I don't know. . . . (*Takes a cucumber out of her pocket and eats it.*) I don't know a thing. (*Pause.*) One wants so much to talk, and there isn't anyone to talk to. . . . I haven't anybody.

Yepihodov (plays the guitar and sings): "What care I for the jarring world? What's friend or foe to me? . . ." How agreeable it is to play the mandolin.

Dunyasha: That's a guitar, not a mandolin. (*Looks in a hand mirror and powders her face.*)

Yepihodov: To a madman in love it's a mandolin. (*Sings.*) "Would that the heart were warmed by the fire of mutual love!" (*Yasha joins in.*)

Charlotta: How abominably these people sing. Pfui! Like jackals!

Dunyasha (to Yasha): How wonderful it must be though to have stayed abroad!

Yasha: Ah, yes, of course, I cannot but agree with you there. (*Yawns and lights a cigar.*)

Yepihodov: Naturally. Abroad, everything has long since achieved full perplexion.

Yasha: That goes without saying.

Yepihodov: I'm a cultivated man, I read all kinds of remarkable books. And yet I can never make out what direction I should take, what is it that I want, properly speaking. Should I live, or should I shoot myself, properly speaking? Nevertheless, I always carry a revolver about me. . . . Here it is . . . (*Shows revolver.*)

Salto mortale: A standing somersault.

Charlotta: I've finished. I'm going. (*Puts the gun over her shoulder.*) You are a very clever man, Yepihodov, and a very terrible one; women must be crazy about you. Br-r-r! (*Starts to go.*) These clever men are all so stupid; there's no one for me to talk to . . . always alone, alone, I haven't a soul . . . and who I am, and why I am, nobody knows. (*Exits unhurriedly.*)

Yepihodov: Properly speaking and letting other subjects alone, I must say regarding myself, among other things, that fate treats me mercilessly, like a storm treats a small boat. If I am mistaken, let us say, why then do I wake up this morning, and there on my chest is a spider of enormous dimensions . . . like this . . . (*Indicates with both hands.*) Again, I take up a pitcher of kvass to have a drink, and in it there is something unseemly to the highest degree, something like a cockroach. (*Pause.*) Have you read Buckle?° (*Pause.*) I wish to have a word with you, Avdotya Fyodorovna, if I may trouble you.

Dunyasha: Well, go ahead.

Yepihodov: I wish to speak with you alone. (*Sighs.*)

Dunyasha (embarrassed): Very well. Only first bring me my little cape. You'll find it near the wardrobe. It's rather damp here.

Yepihodov: Certainly, ma'am; I will fetch it, ma'am. Now I know what to do with my revolver. (*Takes the guitar and goes off playing it.*)

Yasha: Two-and-Twenty Troubles! An awful fool, between you and me. (*Yawns.*)

Dunyasha: I hope to God he doesn't shoot himself! (*Pause.*) I've become so nervous, I'm always fretting. I was still a little girl when I was taken into the big house. I am quite unused to the simple life now, and my hands are white, as white as a lady's. I've become so soft, so delicate, so refined, I'm afraid of everything. It's so terrifying; and if you deceive me, Yasha, I don't know what will happen to my nerves. (*Yasha kisses her.*)

Yasha: You're a peach! Of course, a girl should never forget herself; and what I dislike more than anything is when a girl don't behave properly.

Dunyasha: I've fallen passionately in love with you; you're edu-cated — you have something to say about everything. (*Pause.*)

Yasha (yawns): Yes, ma'am. Now the way I look at it, if a girl loves someone, it means she is immoral. (*Pause.*) It's agreeable smoking a cigar in the fresh air. (*Listens.*) Someone's coming

---

Buckle: Henry Thomas Buckle (1821–1862), an English historian, author of *History of Civilization in England.*

this way . . . It's our madam and the others. (*Dunyasha embraces him impulsively.*) You go home, as though you'd been to the river to bathe; go by the little path, or else they'll run into you and suspect me of having arranged to meet you here. I can't stand that sort of thing.

Dunyasha (coughing softly): Your cigar's made my head ache.

Exits. Yasha standing near the chapel. Enter Madame Ranevskaya, Gayev, and Lopahin.

Lopahin: You must make up your mind once and for all — there's no time to lose. It's quite a simple question, you know. Do you agree to lease your land for summer cottages or not? Answer in one word, yes or no; only one word!

Madame Ranevskaya: Who's been smoking such abominable cigars here? (*Sits down.*)

Gayev: Now that the railway line is so near, it's made things very convenient. (*Sits down.*) Here we've been able to have lunch in town. Yellow ball in the side pocket! I feel like going into the house and playing just one game.

Madame Ranevskaya: You can do that later.

Lopahin: Only one word! (*Imploringly.*) Do give me an answer!

Gayev (yawning): Who?

Madame Ranevskaya (looks into her purse): Yesterday I had a lot of money and now my purse is almost empty. My poor Varya tries to economize by feeding us just milk soup; in the kitchen the old people get nothing but dried peas to eat, while I squander money thoughtlessly. (*Drops the purse, scattering gold pieces.*) You see there they go . . . (*Shows vexation.*)

Yasha: Allow me — I'll pick them up. (*Picks up the money.*)

Madame Ranevskaya: Be so kind, Yasha. And why did I go to lunch in town? That nasty restaurant, with its music and the tablecloth smelling of soap . . . Why drink so much, Leonid? Why eat so much? Why talk so much? Today again you talked a lot, and all so inappropriately about the 'Seventies, about the decadents. And to whom? Talking to waiters about decadents!

Lopahin: Yes.

Gayev (waving his hand): I'm incorrigible; that's obvious. (*Irritably, to Yasha.*) Why do you keep dancing about in front of me?

Yasha (laughs): I can't hear your voice without laughing —

Gayev: Either he or I —

Madame Ranevskaya: Go away, Yasha; run along.

Yasha (handing Madame Ranevskaya her purse): I'm going, at once. (*Hardly able to suppress his laughter.*) This minute. (*Exits.*)

Lopahin: That rich man, Deriganov, wants to buy your estate. They say he's coming to the auction himself.

Madame Ranevskaya: Where did you hear that?

Lopahin: That's what they are saying in town.

Gayev: Our aunt in Yaroslavl has promised to help; but when she will send the money, and how much, no one knows.

Lopahin: How much will she send? A hundred thousand? Two hundred?

Madame Ranevskaya: Oh, well, ten or fifteen thousand; and we'll have to be grateful for that.

Lopahin: Forgive me, but such frivolous people as you are, so queer and unbusinesslike — I never met in my life. One tells you in plain language that your estate is up for sale, and you don't seem to take it in.

Madame Ranevskaya: What are we to do? Tell us what to do.

Lopahin: I do tell you, every day; every day I say the same thing! You must lease the cherry orchard and the land for summer cottages, you must do it and as soon as possible — right away. The auction is close at hand. Please understand! Once you've decided to have the cottages, you can raise as much money as you like, and you're saved.

Madame Ranevskaya: Cottages — summer people — forgive me, but it's all so vulgar.

Gayev: I agree with you absolutely.

Lopahin: I shall either burst into tears or scream or faint! I can't stand it! You've worn me out! (*To Gayev.*) You're an old woman!

Gayev: Who?

Lopahin: An old woman! (*Gets up to go.*)

Madame Ranevskaya (alarmed): No, don't go! Please stay, I beg you, my dear. Perhaps we shall think of something.

Lopahin: What is there to think of?

Madame Ranevskaya: Don't go, I beg you. With you here it's more cheerful anyway. (*Pause.*) I keep expecting something to happen, it's as though the house were going to crash about our ears.

Gayev (in deep thought): Bank shot in the corner. . . . Three cushions in the side pocket. . . .

Madame Ranevskaya: We have been great sinners . . .

Lopahin: What sins could you have committed?

Gayev (putting a candy in his mouth): They say I've eaten up my fortune in candy! (*Laughs.*)

Madame Ranevskaya: Oh, my sins! I've squandered money away recklessly, like a lunatic, and I married a man who made nothing but debts. My husband drank himself to death on champagne, he was a terrific drinker. And then, to my sorrow, I fell in love with another man, and I lived with him. And just then — that was my first punishment — a blow on the head: my little boy was drowned here in the river. And I went abroad, went away forever . . . never to come back, never to see this river again . . . I closed my eyes and ran, out of my mind. . . . But he followed me, pitiless, brutal. I bought a villa near Mentone, because he fell ill there; and for three years, day and night, I knew no peace, no rest. The sick man wore me out, he sucked my soul dry. Then last year, when the villa was sold to pay my debts, I went to Paris, and there he robbed me, abandoned me, took up with another woman, I tried to poison myself — it was stupid, so shameful — and then suddenly I felt drawn back to Russia, back to my own country, to my little girl. (*Wipes her tears away.*) Lord, Lord! Be merciful, forgive me my sins — don't punish me any more! (*Takes a telegram out of her pocket.*) This came today from Paris — he begs me to forgive him, implores me to go back . . . (*Tears up the telegram.*) Do I hear music? (*Listens.*)

Gayev: That's our famous Jewish band, you remember? Four violins, a flute, and a double bass.

Madame Ranevskaya: Does it still exist? We ought to send for them some evening and have a party.

Lopahin (listens): I don't hear anything. (*Hums softly.*) "The Germans for a fee will Frenchify a Russian." (*Laughs.*) I saw a play at the theater yesterday — awfully funny.

Madame Ranevskaya: There was probably nothing funny about it. You shouldn't go to see plays, you should look at yourselves more often. How drab your lives are — how full of unnecessary talk.

Lopahin: That's true; come to think of it, we do live like fools. (*Pause.*) My pop was a peasant, an idiot; he understood nothing, never taught me anything, all he did was beat me when he was drunk, and always with a stick. Fundamentally, I'm just the same kind of blockhead and idiot. I was never taught anything — I have a terrible handwriting, I write so that I feel ashamed before people, like a pig.

Madame Ranevskaya: You should get married, my friend.

Lopahin: Yes . . . that's true.

Madame Ranevskaya: To our Varya, she's a good girl.

Lopahin: Yes.

Madame Ranevskaya: She's a girl who comes of simple people, she works all day long; and above all, she loves you. Besides, you've liked her for a long time now.

Lopahin: Well, I've nothing against it. She's a good girl. (*Pause.*)

Gayev: I've been offered a place in the bank — six thousand a year. Have you heard?

Madame Ranevskaya: You're not up to it. Stay where you are.

Firs enters, carrying an overcoat.

Firs (to Gayev): Please put this on, sir, it's damp.

Gayev (putting it on): I'm fed up with you, brother.

Firs: Never mind. This morning you drove off without saying a word. (*Looks him over.*)

Madame Ranevskaya: How you've aged, Firs.

Firs: I beg your pardon?

Lopahin: The lady says you've aged.

Firs: I've lived a long time; they were arranging my wedding and your papa wasn't born yet. (*Laughs.*) When freedom came° I was already head footman. I wouldn't consent to be set free then; I stayed on with the master . . . (*Pause.*) I remember they were all very happy, but why they were happy, they didn't know themselves.

Lopahin: It was fine in the old days! At least there was flogging!

Firs (not hearing): Of course. The peasants kept to the masters, the masters kept to the peasants; but now they've all gone their own ways, and there's no making out anything.

Gayev: Be quiet, Firs. I must go to town tomorrow. They've promised to introduce me to a general who might let us have a loan.

Lopahin: Nothing will come of that. You won't even be able to pay the interest, you can be certain of that.

Madame Ranevskaya: He's raving, there isn't any general. (*Enter Trofimov, Anya, and Varya.*)

Gayev: Here come our young people.

Anya: There's mamma, on the bench.

Madame Ranevskaya (tenderly): Come here, come along, my darlings. (*Embraces Anya and Varya.*) If you only knew how I love you both! Sit beside me — there, like that. (*All sit down.*)

Lopahin: Our perpetual student is always with the young ladies.

Trofimov: That's not any of your business.

Lopahin: He'll soon be fifty, and he's still a student!

When freedom came: The serfs were emancipated in 1861.

Trofimov: Stop your silly jokes.

Lopahin: What are you so cross about, you queer bird?

Trofimov: Oh, leave me alone.

Lopahin (laughs): Allow me to ask you, what do you think of me?

Trofimov: What I think of you, Yermolay Alexeyevich, is this: you are a rich man who will soon be a millionaire. Well, just as a beast of prey, which devours everything that comes in its way, is necessary for the process of metabolism to go on, so you too are necessary. (*All laugh.*)

Varya: Better tell us something about the planets, Petya.

Madame Ranevskaya: No, let's go on with yesterday's conversation.

Trofimov: What was it about?

Gayev: About man's pride.

Trofimov: Yesterday we talked a long time, but we came to no conclusion. There is something mystical about man's pride in your sense of the word. Perhaps you're right, from your own point of view. But if you reason simply, without going into subtleties, then what call is there for pride? Is there any sense in it, if man is so poor a thing physiologically, and if, in the great majority of cases, he is coarse, stupid, and profoundly unhappy? We should stop admiring ourselves. We should work, and that's all.

Gayev: You die, anyway.

Trofimov: Who knows? And what does it mean — to die? Perhaps man has a hundred senses, and at his death only the five we know perish, while the other ninety-five remain alive.

Madame Ranevskaya: How clever you are, Petya!

Lopahin (ironically): Awfully clever!

Trofimov: Mankind goes forward, developing its powers. Everything that is now unattainable for it will one day come within man's reach and be clear to him; only we must work, helping with all our might those who seek the truth. Here among us in Russia only the very few work as yet. The great majority of the intelligentsia, as far as I can see, seek nothing, do nothing, are totally unfit for work of any kind. They call themselves the intelligentsia, yet they are uncivil to their servants, treat the peasants like animals, are poor students, never read anything serious, do absolutely nothing at all, only talk about science, and have little appreciation of the arts. They are all solemn, have grim faces, they all philosophize and talk of weighty matters. And meanwhile the vast majority of us, ninety-nine out of a hundred, live like savages. At the least provocation — a punch in the jaw, and curses. They eat disgustingly, sleep in filth and stuffiness, bedbugs everywhere, stench and damp and moral slovenliness. And obviously, the only purpose of all our fine talk is to hoodwink ourselves and others. Show me where the public nurseries are that we've heard so much about, and the libraries. We read about them in novels, but in reality they don't exist, there is nothing but dirt, vulgarity, and Asiatic backwardness. I don't like very solemn faces, I'm afraid of them, I'm afraid of serious conversations. We'd do better to keep quiet for a while.

Lopahin: Do you know, I get up at five o'clock in the morning, and I work from morning till night; and I'm always handling money, my own and other people's, and I see what people around me are really like. You've only to start doing anything to see how few honest, decent people there are. Sometimes when I lie awake at night, I think: "Oh, Lord, thou hast given us immense forests, boundless fields, the widest horizons, and living in their midst, we ourselves ought really to be giants."

Madame Ranevskaya: Now you want giants! They're only good in fairy tales; otherwise they're frightening.

Yepihodov crosses the stage at the rear, playing the guitar.

Madame Ranevskaya (pensively): There goes Yepihodov.
Anya (pensively): There goes Yepihodov.
Gayev: Ladies and gentlemen, the sun has set.
Trofimov: Yes.
Gayev (in a low voice, declaiming as it were): Oh, Nature, wondrous Nature, you shine with eternal radiance, beautiful and indifferent! You, whom we call our mother, unite within yourself life and death! You animate and destroy!
Varya (pleadingly): Uncle dear!
Anya: Uncle, again!
Trofimov: You'd better bank the yellow ball in the side pocket.
Gayev: I'm silent, I'm silent . . .

All sit plunged in thought. Stillness reigns. Only Firs's muttering is audible. Suddenly a distant sound is heard, coming from the sky as it were, the sound of a snapping string, mournfully dying away.

Madame Ranevskaya: What was that?
Lopahin: I don't know. Somewhere far away, in the pits, a bucket's broken loose; but somewhere very far away.
Gayev: Or it might be some sort of bird, perhaps a heron.
Trofimov: Or an owl . . .

Madame Ranevskaya (shudders): It's weird, somehow. *(Pause.)*
Firs: Before the calamity the same thing happened — the owl
screeched, and the samovar hummed all the time.
Gayev: Before what calamity?
Firs: Before the Freedom. *(Pause.)*
Madame Ranevskaya: Come, my friends, let's be going. It's getting
dark. *(To Anya.)* You have tears in your eyes. What is it, my
little one? *(Embraces her.)*
Anya: I don't know, mamma; it's nothing.
Trofimov: Somebody's coming.

A Tramp appears, wearing a shabby white cap and an overcoat. He is slightly drunk.

Tramp: Allow me to inquire, will this short-cut take me to the station?
Gayev: It will. Just follow that road.
Tramp: My heartfelt thanks. *(Coughing.)* The weather is glorious.
(Recites.) "My brother, my suffering brother. . . . Go down to
the Volga! Whose groans . . . ?" *(To Varya.)* Mademoiselle,
won't you spare thirty kopecks for a hungry Russian?

Varya, frightened, cries out.

Lopahin (angrily): Even panhandling has its proprieties.
Madame Ranevskaya (scared): Here, take this. *(Fumbles in her purse.)*
I haven't any silver . . . never mind, here's a gold piece
Tramp: My heartfelt thanks. *(Exits. Laughter.)*
Varya (frightened): I'm leaving. I'm leaving . . . Oh, mamma dear,
at home the servants have nothing to eat, and you gave him a
gold piece!
Madame Ranevskaya: What are you going to do with me? I'm such
a fool. When we get home, I'll give you everything I have. Yer-
molay Alexeyevich, you'll lend me some more . . .
Lopahin: Yes, ma'am.
Madame Ranevskaya: Come, ladies and gentlemen, it's time to be
going. Oh! Varya, we've settled all about your marriage. Congratulations!
Varya (through tears): Really, mamma, that's not a joking matter.
Lopahin: "Aurelia, get thee to a nunnery, go . . ."°
Gayev: And do you know, my hands are trembling: I haven't
played billiards in a long time.

Aurelia . . . go: Translating Hamlet's speech to Ophelia in Shakespeare's *Hamlet,* III.i.136.

Lopahin: "Aurelia, nymph, in your orisons, remember me!"°
Madame Ranevskaya: Let's go, it's almost suppertime.
Varya: He frightened me! My heart's pounding.
Lopahin: Let me remind you, ladies and gentlemen; on the twenty-second of August the cherry orchard will be up for sale. Think about that! Think!

All except Trofimov and Anya go out.

Anya (laughs): I'm grateful to that tramp, he frightened Varya and so we're alone.
Trofimov: Varya's afraid we'll fall in love with each other all of a sudden. She hasn't left us alone for days. Her narrow mind can't grasp that we're above love. To avoid the petty and illusory, everything that prevents us from being free and happy — that is the goal and meaning of our life. Forward! Do not fall behind, friends!
Anya (strikes her hands together): How well you speak! (*Pause.*) It's wonderful here today.
Trofimov: Yes, the weather's glorious.
Anya: What have you done to me, Petya? Why don't I love the cherry orchard as I used to? I loved it so tenderly. It seemed to me there was no spot on earth lovelier than our orchard.
Trofimov: All Russia is our orchard. Our land is vast and beautiful, there are many wonderful places in it. (*Pause.*) Think of it, Anya, your grandfather, your great-grandfather and all your ancestors were serf-owners, owners of living souls, and aren't human beings looking at you from every tree in the orchard, from every leaf, from every trunk? Don't you hear voices? Oh, it's terrifying! Your orchard is a fearful place, and when you pass through it in the evening or at night, the old bark on the trees gleams faintly, and the cherry trees seem to be dreaming of things that happened a hundred, two hundred years ago and to be tormented by painful visions. What is there to say? We're at least two hundred years behind, we've really achieved nothing yet, we have no definite attitude to the past, we only philosophize, complain of the blues, or drink vodka. It's all so clear: in order to live in the present, we should first redeem our past, finish with it, and we can expiate it only by suffering, only by extraordinary, unceasing labor. Realize that, Anya.
Anya: The house in which we live has long ceased to be our own, and I will leave it, I give you my word.

Aurelia . . . remember me: The end of Hamlet's "To be, or not to be" speech, III.i.89–90.

Trofimov: If you have the keys, fling them into the well and go away. Be free as the wind.

Anya (in ecstasy): How well you put that!

Trofimov: Believe me, Anya, believe me! I'm not yet thirty, I'm young, I'm still a student — but I've already suffered so much. In winter I'm hungry, sick, harassed, poor as a beggar, and where hasn't Fate driven me? Where haven't I been? And yet always, every moment of the day and night, my soul is filled with inexplicable premonitions . . . I have a premonition of happiness, Anya. . . . I see it already!

Anya (pensively): The moon is rising.

Yepihodov is heard playing the same mournful tune on the guitar. The moon rises. Somewhere near the poplars Varya is looking for Anya and calling, "Anya, where are you?"

Trofimov: Yes, the moon is rising. (*Pause.*) There it is, happiness, it's approaching, it's coming nearer and nearer, I can already hear its footsteps. And if we don't see it, if we don't know it, what does it matter? Others will!

Varya's voice: "Anya! Where are you?"

Trofimov: That Varya again! (*Angrily.*) It's revolting!

Anya: Never mind, let's go down to the river. It's lovely there.

Trofimov: Come on. (*They go.*)

Varya's voice: "Anya! Anya!"

ACT III

A drawing-room separated by an arch from a ballroom. Evening. Chandelier burning. The Jewish band is heard playing in the anteroom. In the ballroom they are dancing the Grand Rond. Pishchik is heard calling, "Promenade à une paire." Pishchik and Charlotta, Trofimov and Madame Ranevskaya, Anya and the Post Office Clerk, Varya and the Stationmaster, and others, enter the drawing-room in couples. Dunyasha is in the last couple. Varya weeps quietly, wiping her tears as she dances. All parade through drawing-room, Pishchik calling "Grand rond, balancez!" and "Les cavaliers à genoux et remerciez vos dames!" Firs wearing a dress-coat, brings in soda-water on a tray. Pishchik and Trofimov enter the drawing-room.

Pishchik: I'm a full-blooded man; I've already had two strokes. Dancing's hard work for me; but as they say, "If you run with the pack, you can bark or not, but at least wag your tail." Still, I'm as strong as a horse. My late lamented father, who would have his joke, God rest his soul, used to say, talking about our origin, that the ancient line of the Simeonov-Pishchiks was descended from the very horse that Caligula had made a senator. (*Sits down.*) But the trouble is, I have no money. A hungry dog believes in nothing but meat. (*Snores and wakes up at once.*) It's the same with me — I can think of nothing but money.

Trofimov: You know, there *is* something equine about your figure.

Pishchik: Well, a horse is a fine animal — one can sell a horse.

Sound of billiards being played in an adjoining room. Varya appears in the archway.

Trofimov (teasing her): Madam Lopahina! Madam Lopahina!

Varya (angrily): Mangy master!

Trofimov: Yes, I am a mangy master and I'm proud of it.

Varya (reflecting bitterly): Here we've hired musicians, and what shall we pay them with? (*Exits.*)

Trofimov (to Pishchik): If the energy you have spent during your lifetime looking for money to pay interest had gone into something else, in the end you could have turned the world upside down.

Pishchik: Nietzsche, the philosopher, the greatest, most famous of men, that colossal intellect, says in his works, that it is permissible to forge banknotes.

Trofimov: Have you read Nietzsche?

Pishchik: Well . . . Dashenka told me . . . And now I've got to the point where forging banknotes is about the only way out for me . . . The day after tomorrow I have to pay three hundred and ten rubles . . . I already have one hundred and thirty (. . . *Feels in his pockets. In alarm.*) The money's gone! I've lost my money! (*Through tears.*) Where's my money? (*Joyfully.*) Here it is! Inside the lining . . . I'm all in a sweat . . .

Enter Madame Ranevskaya and Charlotta.

Madame Ranevskaya (hums the "Lezginka"): Why isn't Leonid back yet? What is he doing in town? (*To Dunyasha.*) Dunyasha, offer the musicians tea.

Trofimov: The auction hasn't taken place, most likely.

Madame Ranevskaya: It's the wrong time to have the band, and the wrong time to give a dance. Well, never mind. (*Sits down and hums softly.*)

Charlotta (hands Pishchik a pack of cards): Here is a pack of cards. Think of any card you like.

Pishchik: I've thought of one.

Charlotta: Shuffle the pack now. That's right. Give it here, my dear Mr. Pishchik. *Ein, zwei, drei!* Now look for it — it's in your side pocket.

Pishchik (taking the card out of his pocket): The eight of spades! Perfectly right! Just imagine!

Charlotta (holding pack of cards in her hands; to Trofimov): Quickly, name the top card.

Trofimov: Well, let's see — the queen of spades.

Charlotta: Right! *(To Pishchik.)* Now name the top card.

Pishchik: The ace of hearts.

Charlotta: Right! *(Claps her hands and the pack of cards disappears.)* Ah, what lovely weather it is today! *(A mysterious feminine voice which seems to come from under the floor, answers her.)* "Oh, yes, it's magnificent weather, madam."

Charlotta: You are my best ideal.

Voice: "And I find you pleasing too, madam."

Stationmaster (applauding): The lady ventriloquist, bravo!

Pishchik (amazed): Just imagine! Enchanting Charlotta Ivanovna, I'm simply in love with you.

Charlotta: In love? *(Shrugs her shoulders.)* Are you capable of love? *Guter Mensch, aber schlechter Musikant.°*

Trofimov (claps Pishchik on the shoulder): You old horse, you!

Charlotta: Attention please! One more trick! *(Takes a plaid from a chair.)* Here is a very good plaid; I want to sell it. *(Shaking it out.)* Does anyone want to buy it?

Pishchik (in amazement): Just imagine!

Charlotta: Ein, zwei, drei!

Raises the plaid quickly, behind it stands Anya. She curtsies, runs to her mother, embraces her, and runs back into the ballroom, amidst general enthusiasm.

Madame Ranevskaya (applauds): Bravo! Bravo!

Charlotta: Now again! Ein, zwei, drei! (Lifts the plaid; behind it stands Varya bowing.)

Pishchik (running after her): The rascal! What a woman, what a woman! *(Exits.)*

Madame Ranevskaya: And Leonid still isn't here. What is he doing in town so long? I don't understand. It must be all over by now. Either the estate has been sold, or the auction hasn't taken place. Why keep us in suspense so long?

Varya (trying to console her): Uncle's bought it, I feel sure of that.

Trofimov (mockingly): Oh, yes!

Varya: Great-aunt sent him an authorization to buy it in her name, and to transfer the debt. She's doing it for Anya's sake. And I'm sure that God will help us, and uncle will buy it.

Madame Ranevskaya: Great-aunt sent fifteen thousand to buy the

---

Guter Mensch . . . Musikant: A good man, but a bad musician (German).

estate in her name, she doesn't trust us, but that's not even enough to pay the interest. (*Covers her face with her hands.*) Today my fate will be decided, my fate —

Trofimov (teasing Varya): Madame Lopahina!

Varya (angrily): Perpetual student! Twice already you've been expelled from the university.

Madame Ranevskaya: Why are you so cross, Varya? He's teasing you about Lopahin. Well, what of it? If you want to marry Lopahin, go ahead. He's a good man, and interesting; if you don't want to, don't. Nobody's compelling you, my pet!

Varya: Frankly, mamma dear, I take this thing seriously; he's a good man and I like him.

Madame Ranevskaya: All right then, marry him. I don't know what you're waiting for.

Varya: But, mamma, I can't propose to him myself. For the last two years everyone's been talking to me about him — talking. But he either keeps silent, or else cracks jokes. I understand; he's growing rich, he's absorbed in business — he has no time for me. If I had money, even a little, say, one hundred rubles, I'd throw everything up and go far away — I'd go into a nunnery.

Trofimov: What a blessing . . .

Varya: A student ought to be intelligent. (*Softly, with tears in her voice.*) How homely you've grown, Petya! How old you look! (*To Madame Ranevskaya, with dry eyes.*) But I can't live without work, mamma dear; I must keep busy every minute.

Enter Yasha.

Yasha (hardly restraining his laughter): Yepihodov has broken a billiard cue! (*Exits.*)

Varya: Why is Yepihodov here? Who allowed him to play billiards? I don't understand these people! (*Exits.*)

Madame Ranevskaya: Don't tease her, Petya. She's unhappy enough without that.

Trofimov: She bustles so — and meddles in other people's business. All summer long she's given Anya and me no peace. She's afraid of a love-affair between us. What business is it of hers? Besides, I've given no grounds for it, and I'm far from such vulgarity. We are above love.

Madame Ranevskaya: And I suppose I'm beneath love? (*Anxiously.*) What can be keeping Leonid. If I only knew whether the estate has been sold or not. Such a calamity seems so incredible to me that I don't know what to think — I feel lost . . . I could scream . . . I could do something stupid . . . Save me, Petya, tell me something, talk to me!

Trofimov: Whether the estate is sold today or not, isn't it all one? That's all done with long ago — there's no turning back, the path is overgrown. Calm yourself, my dear. You mustn't deceive yourself. For once in your life you must face the truth.

Madame Ranevskaya: What truth? You can see the truth, you can tell it from falsehood, but I seem to have lost my eyesight, I see nothing. You settle every great problem so boldly, but tell me, my dear boy, isn't it because you're young, because you don't yet know what one of your problems means in terms of suffering? You look ahead fearlessly, but isn't it because you don't see and don't expect anything dreadful, because life is still hidden from your young eyes? You're bolder, more honest, more profound than we are, but think hard, show just a bit of magnanimity, spare me. After all, I was born here, my father and mother lived here, and my grandfather; I love this house. Without the cherry orchard, my life has no meaning for me, and if it really must be sold, then sell me with the orchard. (*Embraces Trofimov, kisses him on the forehead.*) My son was drowned here. (*Weeps.*) Pity me, you good, kind fellow!

Trofimov: You know, I feel for you with all my heart.

Madame Ranevskaya: But that should have been said differently, so differently! (*Takes out her handkerchief — a telegram falls on the floor.*) My heart is so heavy today — you can't imagine! The noise here upsets me — my inmost being trembles at every sound — I'm shaking all over. But I can't go into my own room; I'm afraid to be alone. Don't condemn me, Petya . . . I love you as though you were one of us, I would gladly let you marry Anya — I swear I would — only, my dear boy, you must study — you must take your degree — you do nothing, you let yourself be tossed by Fate from place to place — it's so strange. It's true, isn't it? And you should do something about your beard, to make it grow somehow! (*Laughs.*) You're so funny!

Trofimov (picks up the telegram): I've no wish to be a dandy.

Madame Ranevskaya: That's a telegram from Paris. I get one every day. One yesterday and one today. That savage is ill again — he's in trouble again. He begs forgiveness, implores me to go to him, and really I ought to go to Paris to be near him. Your face is stern, Petya; but what is there to do, my dear boy? What am I to do? He's ill, he's alone and unhappy, and who is to look after him, who is to keep him from doing the wrong thing, who is to give him his medicine on time? And why hide it or keep still about it — I love him! That's clear. I love him, love him! He's a millstone round my neck, he'll drag me to the bottom, but I love that stone. I can't live without it. (*Presses Trofimov's hand.*) Don't think badly of me, Petya, and don't say anything, don't say . . .

Trofimov (through tears): Forgive me my frankness in Heaven's name; but, you know, he robbed you!

Madame Ranevskaya: No, no, no, you mustn't say such things! (*Covers her ears.*)

Trofimov: But he's a scoundrel! You're the only one who doesn't know it. He's a petty scoundrel — a nonentity!

Madame Ranevskaya (controlling her anger): You are twenty-six or twenty-seven years old, but you're still a schoolboy.

Trofimov: That may be.

Madame Ranevskaya: You should be a man at your age. You should understand people who love — and ought to be in love yourself. You ought to fall in love! (*Angrily.*) Yes, yes! And it's not purity in you, it's prudishness, you're simply a queer fish, a comical freak!

Trofimov (horrified): What is she saying!

Madame Ranevskaya: "I am above love!" You're not above love, but simply, as our Firs says, you're an addlehead. At your age not to have a mistress!

Trofimov (horrified): This is frightful! What is she saying! (*Goes rapidly into the ballroom, clutching his head.*) It's frightful — I can't stand it, I won't stay! (*Exits, but returns at once.*) All is over between us! (*Exits into anteroom.*)

Madame Ranevskaya (shouts after him): Petya! Wait! You absurd fellow, I was joking. Petya!

Sound of somebody running quickly downstairs and suddenly falling down with a crash. Anya and Varya scream. Sound of laughter a moment later.

Madame Ranevskaya: What's happened? (*Anya runs in.*)

Anya (laughing): Petya's fallen downstairs! (*Runs out.*)

Madame Ranevskaya: What a queer bird that Petya is!

Stationmaster standing in the middle of the ballroom, recites Alexey Tolstoy's "Magdalene,"° to which all listen, but after a few lines, the sound of a waltz is heard from the anteroom and the reading breaks off. All dance. Trofimov, Anya, Varya, and Madame Ranevskaya enter from the anteroom.

Alexey Tolstoy's "Magdalene": A poem contemporary with this play in which Christ appears at a society banquet.

Madame Ranevskaya: Petya, you pure soul, please forgive me . . . Let's dance.

Dances with Petya. Anya and Varya dance. Firs enters, puts his stick down by the side door. Yasha enters from the drawing-room and watches the dancers.

Yasha: Well, grandfather?

Firs: I'm not feeling well. In the old days it was generals, barons, and admirals that were dancing at our balls, and now we have to send for the Post Office Clerk and the Stationmaster, and even they aren't too glad to come. I feel kind of shaky. The old master that's gone, their grandfather, dosed everyone with sealing-wax, whatever ailed 'em. I've been taking sealing-wax every day for twenty years or more. Perhaps that's what's kept me alive.

Yasha: I'm fed up with you, grandpop. (*Yawns.*) It's time you croaked.

Firs: Oh, you addlehead! (*Mumbles.*)

Trofimov and Madame Ranevskaya dance from the ballroom into the drawing-room.

Madame Ranevskaya: Merci. I'll sit down a while. (*Sits down.*) I'm tired.

Enter Anya.

Anya (excitedly): There was a man in the kitchen just now who said the cherry orchard was sold today.

Madame Ranevskaya: Sold to whom?

Anya: He didn't say. He's gone. (*Dances off with Trofimov.*)

Yasha: It was some old man gabbing, a stranger.

Firs: And Leonid Andreyevich isn't back yet, he hasn't come. And he's wearing his lightweight between-season overcoat; like enough, he'll catch cold. Ah, when they're young they're green.

Madame Ranevskaya: This is killing me. Go, Yasha, find out to whom it has been sold.

Yasha: But the old man left long ago. (*Laughs.*)

Madame Ranevskaya: What are you laughing at? What are you pleased about?

Yasha: That Yepihodov is such a funny one. A funny fellow, Two-and-Twenty Troubles!

Madame Ranevskaya: Firs, if the estate is sold, where will you go?

Firs: I'll go where you tell me.

Madame Ranevskaya: Why do you look like that? Are you ill? You ought to go to bed.

Firs: Yes! (*With a snigger.*) Me go to bed, and who's to hand things round? Who's to see to things? I'm the only one in the whole house.

Yasha (to Madame Ranevskaya): Lubov Andreyevna, allow me to ask a favor of you, be so kind! If you go back to Paris, take me with you, I beg you. It's positively impossible for me to stay here. (*Looking around; sotto voce.*) What's the use of talking? You see for yourself, it's an uncivilized country, the people have no morals, and then the boredom! The food in the kitchen's revolting, and besides there's this Firs wanders about mumbling all sorts of inappropriate words. Take me with you, be so kind!

Enter Pishchik.

Pishchik: May I have the pleasure of a waltz with you, charming lady? (*Madame Ranevskaya accepts.*) All the same, enchanting lady, you must let me have one hundred and eighty rubles . . . You must let me have (*dancing*) just one hundred and eighty rubles. (*They pass into the ballroom.*)

Yasha (hums softly): "Oh, wilt thou understand the tumult in my soul?"

In the ballroom a figure in a gray top hat and checked trousers is jumping about and waving its arms; shouts: "Bravo, Charlotta Ivanovna!"

Dunyasha (stopping to powder her face; to Firs): The young miss has ordered me to dance. There are so many gentlemen and not enough ladies. But dancing makes me dizzy, my heart begins to beat fast, Firs Nikolayevich. The Post Office Clerk said something to me just now that quite took my breath away.

Music stops.

Firs: What did he say?

Dunyasha: "You're like a flower," he said.

Yasha (yawns): What ignorance. (*Exit.*)

Dunyasha: "Like a flower!" I'm such a delicate girl. I simply adore pretty speeches.

Firs: You'll come to a bad end.

Enter Yepihodov.

Yepihodov (to Dunyasha): You have no wish to see me, Avdotya

Fyodorovna . . . as though I was some sort of insect. (*Sighs.*) Ah, life!

Dunyasha: What is it you want?

Yepihodov: Indubitably you may be right. (*Sighs.*) But of course, if one looks at it from the point of view, if I may be allowed to say so, and apologizing for my frankness, you have completely reduced me to a state of mind. I know my fate. Every day some calamity befalls me, and I grew used to it long ago, so that I look upon my fate with a smile. You gave me your word, and though I —

Dunyasha: Let's talk about it later, please. But just now leave me alone, I am daydreaming. (*Plays with a fan.*)

Yepihodov: A misfortune befalls me every day; and if I may be allowed to say so, I merely smile, I even laugh.

Enter Varya.

Varya (to Yepihodov): Are you still here? What an impertinent fellow you are really! Run along, Dunyasha. (*To Yepihodov.*) Either you're playing billiards and breaking a cue, or you're wandering about the drawing-room as though you were a guest.

Yepihodov: You cannot, permit me to remark, penalize me.

Varya: I'm not penalizing you. I'm just telling you. You merely wander from place to place, and don't do your work. We keep you as a clerk, but Heaven knows what for.

Yepihodov (offended): Whether I work or whether I walk, whether I eat or whether I play billiards, is a matter to be discussed only by persons of understanding and of mature years.

Varya (enraged): You dare say that to me — you dare? You mean to say I've no understanding? Get out of here at once! This minute!

Yepihodov (scared): I beg you to express yourself delicately.

Varya (beside herself): Clear out this minute! Out with you!

Yepihodov goes towards the door, Varya following.

Varya: Two-and-Twenty Troubles! Get out — don't let me set eyes on you!

(*Exit Yepihodov. His voice is heard behind the door*): "I shall lodge a complaint against you!"

Varya: Oh, you're coming back? (*She seizes the stick left near door by Firs.*) Well, come then . . . come . . . I'll show you . . . Ah, you're coming? You're coming? . . . Come . . . (*Swings the stick just as Lopahin enters.*)

Lopahin: Thank you kindly.

Varya (angrily and mockingly): I'm sorry.

Lopahin: It's nothing. Thank you kindly for your charming reception.

Varya: Don't mention it. (*Walks away, looks back and asks softly*): I didn't hurt you, did I?

Lopahin: Oh, no, not at all. I shall have a large bump, though.

(Voices from the ballroom): "Lopahin is here! Lopahin!"

Enter Pishchik.

Pishchik: My eyes do see, my ears do hear! (*Kisses Lopahin.*)

Lopahin: You smell of cognac, my dear friends. And we've been celebrating here, too. (*Enter Madame Ranevskaya.*)

Madame Ranevskaya: Is that you, Yermolay Alexeyevich? What kept you so long? Where's Leonid?

Lopahin: Leonid Andreyevich arrived with me. He's coming.

Madame Ranevskaya: Well, what happened? Did the sale take place? Speak!

Lopahin (embarrassed, fearful of revealing his joy): The sale was over at four o'clock. We missed the train — had to wait till half past nine. (*Sighing heavily.*) Ugh. I'm a little dizzy.

Enter Gayev. In his right hand he holds parcels, with his left he is wiping away his tears.

Madame Ranevskaya: Well, Leonid? What news? (*Impatiently, through tears.*) Be quick, for God's sake!

Gayev (not answering, simply waves his hand; weeping, to Firs): Here, take these; anchovies, Kerch herrings . . . I haven't eaten all day. What I've been through! (*The click of billiard balls comes through the open door of the billiard room and Yasha's voice is heard*): "Seven and eighteen!" (*Gayev's expression changes, he no longer weeps.*) I'm terribly tired. Firs, help me change. (*Exits, followed by Firs.*)

Pishchik: How about the sale? Tell us what happened.

Madame Ranevskaya: Is the cherry orchard sold?

Lopahin: Sold.

Madame Ranevskaya: Who bought it?

Lopahin: I bought it.

Pause. Madame Ranevskaya is overcome. She would fall to the floor, were it not for the chair and table near which she stands. Varya takes the keys from her belt, flings them on the floor in the middle of the drawing-room, and goes out.

Lopahin: I bought it. Wait a bit, ladies and gentlemen, please, my head is swimming. I can't talk. (*Laughs.*) We got to the auction and Deriganov was there already. Leonid Andreyevich had only fifteen thousand and straight off Deriganov bid thirty thousand over and above the mortgage. I saw how the land lay, got into the fight, bid forty thousand. He bid forty-five thousand. I bid fifty-five. He kept adding five thousands, I ten. Well . . . it came to an end. I bid ninety above the mortgage and the estate was knocked down to me. Now the cherry orchard's mine! Mine! (*Laughs uproariously.*) Lord! God in Heaven! The cherry orchard's mine! Tell me that I'm drunk — out of my mind — that it's all a dream. (*Stamps his feet.*) Don't laugh at me! If my father and my grandfather could rise from their graves and see all that has happened — how their Yermolay, who used to be flogged, their half-literate Yermolay, who used to run about barefoot in winter, how that very Yermolay has bought the most magnificent estate in the world. I bought the estate where my father and grandfather were slaves, where they weren't even allowed to enter the kitchen. I'm asleep — it's only a dream — I only imagine it . . . It's the fruit of your imagination, wrapped in the darkness of the unknown! (*Picks up the keys, smiling genially.*) She threw down the keys, wants to show she's no longer mistress here. (*Jingles keys.*) Well, no matter. (*The band is heard tuning up.*) Hey, musicians! Strike up! I want to hear you! Come, everybody, and see how Yermolay Lopahin will lay the ax to the cherry orchard and how the trees will fall to the ground. We will build summer cottages there, and our grandsons and great-grandsons will see a new life here. Music! Strike up!

The band starts to play. Madame Ranevskaya has sunk into a chair and is weeping bitterly.

Lopahin (*reproachfully*): Why, why didn't you listen to me? My dear friend, my poor friend, you can't bring it back now. (*Tearfully.*) Oh, if only this were over quickly! Oh, if only our wretched, disordered life were changed!
Pishchik (*takes him by the arm; sotto voce*): She's crying. Let's go into the ballroom. Let her be alone. Come. (*Takes his arm and leads him into the ballroom.*)
Lopahin: What's the matter? Musicians, play so I can hear you! Let me have things the way I want them. (*Ironically.*) Here comes the new master, the owner of the cherry orchard. (*Accidentally he trips over a little table, almost upsetting the candelabra.*) I can pay for everything. (*Exits with Pishchik. Madame Ranevskaya, alone, sits huddled up, weeping bitterly. Music plays*

softly. Enter Anya and Trofimov quickly. Anya goes to her mother and falls on her knees before her. Trofimov stands in the doorway.)
Anya: Mamma, mamma, you're crying! Dear, kind, good mamma, my precious, I love you. I bless you! The cherry orchard is sold, it's gone, that's true, quite true. But don't cry, mamma, life is still before you, you still have your kind, pure heart. Let us go, let us go away from here, darling. We will plant a new orchard, even more luxuriant than this one. You will see it, you will understand, and like the sun at evening, joy — deep, tranquil joy — will sink into your soul, and you will smile, mamma. Come, darling, let us go.

ACT IV

Scene as in Act I. No window curtains or pictures, only a little furniture, piled up in a corner, as if for sale. A sense of emptiness. Near the outer door and at the back, suitcases, bundles, etc., are piled up. A door open on the left and the voices of Varya and Anya are heard. Lopahin stands waiting. Yasha holds a tray with glasses full of champagne. Yepihodov in the anteroom is tying up a box. Behind the scene a hum of voices: peasants have come to say good-by. Voice of Gayev: "Thanks, brothers, thank you."

Yasha: The country folk have come to say good-by. In my opinion, Yermolay Alexeyevich, they are kindly souls, but there's nothing in their heads.

The hum dies away. Enter Madame Ranevskaya and Gayev. She is not crying, but is pale, her face twitches and she cannot speak.

Gayev: You gave them your purse, Luba. That won't do! That won't do!
Madame Ranevskaya: I couldn't help it! I couldn't! (*They go out.*)
Lopahin (calls after them): Please, I beg you, have a glass at parting. I didn't think of bringing any champagne from town and at the station I could find only one bottle. Please, won't you? (*Pause.*) What's the matter, ladies and gentlemen, don't you want any? (*Moves away from the door.*) If I'd known, I wouldn't have bought it. Well, then I won't drink any, either. (*Yasha carefully sets the tray down on a chair.*) At least you have a glass, Yasha.
Yasha: Here's to the travelers! And good luck to those that stay! (*Drinks.*) This champagne isn't the real stuff, I can assure you.
Lopahin: Eight rubles a bottle. (*Pause.*) It's devilishly cold here.

Yasha: They didn't light the stoves today — it wasn't worth it, since we're leaving. (*Laughs.*)

Lopahin: Why are you laughing?

Yasha: It's just that I'm pleased.

Lopahin: It's October, yet it's as still and sunny as though it were summer. Good weather for building. (*Looks at his watch, and speaks off.*) Bear in mind, ladies and gentlemen, the train goes in forty-seven minutes, so you ought to start for the station in twenty minutes. Better hurry up!

Enter Trofimov wearing an overcoat.

Trofimov: I think it's time to start. The carriages are at the door. The devil only knows what's become of my rubbers; they've disappeared. (*Calling off.*) Anya! My rubbers are gone. I can't find them.

Lopahin: I've got to go to Kharkov. I'll take the same train you do. I'll spend the winter in Kharkov. I've been hanging round here with you, till I'm worn out with loafing. I can't live without work — I don't know what to do with my hands, they dangle as if they didn't belong to me.

Trofimov: Well, we'll soon be gone, then you can go on with your useful labors again.

Lopahin: Have a glass.

Trofimov: No, I won't.

Lopahin: So you're going to Moscow now?

Trofimov: Yes. I'll see them into town, and tomorrow I'll go on to Moscow.

Lopahin: Well, I'll wager the professors aren't giving any lectures, they're waiting for you to come.

Trofimov: That's none of your business.

Lopahin: Just how many years have you been at the university?

Trofimov: Can't you think of something new? Your joke's stale and flat. (*Looking for his rubbers.*) We'll probably never see each other again, so allow me to give you a piece of advice at parting: don't wave your hands about! Get out of the habit. And another thing: building bungalows, figuring like that is just another form of waving your hands about. . . . Never mind, I love you anyway; you have fine, delicate fingers, like an artist; you have a fine, delicate soul.

Lopahin (embracing him): Good-by, my dear fellow. Thank you for everything. Let me give you some money for the journey, if you need it.

Trofimov: What for? I don't need it.

Lopahin: But you haven't any.

Trofimov: Yes, I have, thank you. I got some money for a translation — here it is in my pocket. (*Anxiously.*) But where are my
rubbers?

Varya (from the next room): Here! Take the nasty things. (*Flings a
pair of rubbers onto the stage.*)

Trofimov: What are you so cross about, Varya? Hm . . . and these
are not my rubbers.

Lopahin: I sowed three thousand acres of poppies in the spring,
and now I've made forty thousand on them, clear profit; and
when my poppies were in bloom, what a picture it was! So, as
I say, I made forty thousand; and I am offering you a loan
because I can afford it. Why turn up your nose at it? I'm a
peasant — I speak bluntly.

Trofimov: Your father was a peasant, mine was a druggist — that
proves absolutely nothing whatever. (*Lopahin takes out his
wallet.*) Don't, put that away! If you were to offer me two
hundred thousand I wouldn't take it. I'm a free man. And
everything that all of you, rich and poor alike, value so
highly and hold so dear, hasn't the slightest power over me.
It's like so much fluff floating in the air. I can get on without
you, I can pass you by, I'm strong and proud. Mankind is
moving towards the highest truth, towards the highest happiness possible on earth; and I am in the front ranks.

Lopahin: Will you get there?

Trofimov: I will. (*Pause.*) I will get there, or I will show others the
way to get there.

The sound of axes chopping down trees is heard in the distance.

Lopahin: Well, good-by, my dear fellow. It's time to leave. We turn
up our noses at one another, but life goes on just the same.
When I'm working hard, without resting, my mind is easier,
and it seems to me that I too know why I exist. But how many
people are there in Russia, brother, who exist nobody knows
why? Well, it doesn't matter. That's not what makes the
wheels go round. They say Leonid Andreyevich has taken a
position in the bank, six thousand rubles a year. Only, of
course, he won't stick to it, he's too lazy. . . .

Anya (in the doorway): Mamma begs you not to start cutting down
the cherry-trees until she's gone.

Trofimov: Really, you should have more tact! (*Exits.*)

Lopahin: Right away — right away! Those men . . . (*Exits.*)

Anya: Has Firs been taken to the hospital?

Yasha: I told them this morning. They must have taken him.

Anya (to Yepihodov who crosses the room): Yepihodov, please find out if Firs has been taken to the hospital.

Yasha (offended): I told Yegor this morning. Why ask a dozen times?

Yepihodov: The aged Firs, in my definitive opinion, is beyond mending. It's time he was gathered to his fathers. And I can only envy him. (*Puts a suitcase down on a hat-box and crushes it.*) There now, of course. I knew it! (*Exits.*)

Yasha (mockingly): Two-and-Twenty Troubles!

Varya (through the door): Has Firs been taken to the hospital?

Anya: Yes.

Varya: Then why wasn't the note for the doctor taken too?

Anya: Oh! Then someone must take it to him. (*Exits.*)

Varya (from adjoining room): Where's Yasha? Tell him his mother's come and wants to say good-by.

Yasha (waves his hand): She tries my patience.

Dunyasha has been occupied with the luggage. Seeing Yasha alone, she goes up to him.

Dunyasha: You might just give me one little look, Yasha. You're going away . . . You're leaving me . . . (*Weeps and throws herself on his neck.*)

Yasha: What's there to cry about? (*Drinks champagne.*) In six days I shall be in Paris again. Tomorrow we get into an express train and off we go, that's the last you'll see of us. . . . I can scarcely believe it. *Vive la France!* It don't suit me here, I just can't live here. That's all there is to it. I'm fed up with the ignorance here. I've had enough of it. (*Drinks champagne.*) What's there to cry about? Behave yourself properly, and you'll have no cause to cry.

Dunyasha (powders her face, looking in pocket mirror): Do send me a letter from Paris. You know I loved you, Yasha, how I loved you! I'm a delicate creature, Yasha.

Yasha: Somebody's coming! (*Busies himself with the luggage, hums softly.*)

Enter Madame Ranevskaya, Gayev, Anya, and Charlotta.

Gayev: We ought to be leaving. We haven't much time. (*Looks at Yasha.*) Who smells of herring?

Madame Ranevskaya: In about ten minutes we should be getting into the carriages. (*Looks around the room.*) Good-by, dear old home, good-by, grandfather. Winter will pass, spring will come, you will no longer be here, they will have torn you down. How much these walls have seen! (*Kisses Anya warmly.*) My treasure, how radiant you look! Your eyes are sparkling like diamonds. Are you glad? Very?

Anya (gaily): Very glad. A new life is beginning, mamma.

Gayev: Well, really, everything is all right now. Before the cherry orchard was sold, we all fretted and suffered; but afterwards, when the question was settled finally and irrevocably, we all calmed down, and even felt quite cheerful. I'm a bank employee now, a financier. The yellow ball in the side pocket! And anyhow, you are looking better, Luba, there's no doubt of that.

Madame Ranevskaya: Yes, my nerves are better, that's true. (*She is handed her hat and coat.*) I sleep well. Carry out my things, Yasha. It's time. (*To Anya.*) We shall soon see each other again, my little girl. I'm going to Paris, I'll live there on the money your great-aunt sent us to buy the estate with — long live Auntie! But that money won't last long.

Anya: You'll come back soon, soon, mamma, won't you? Meanwhile I'll study, I'll pass my high school examination, and then I'll go to work and help you. We'll read all kinds of books together, mamma, won't we? (*Kisses her mother's hands.*) We'll read in the autumn evenings, we'll read lots of books, and a new wonderful world will open up before us. (*Falls into a revery.*) Mamma, do come back.

Madame Ranevskaya: I will come back, my precious.

Embraces her daughter. Enter Lopahin and Charlotta, who is humming softly.

Gayev: Charlotta's happy: she's singing.

Charlotta (picks up a bundle and holds it like a baby in swaddling-clothes): Bye, baby, bye. (*A baby is heard crying.*) "Wah! Wah!" Hush, hush, my pet, my little one. "Wah! Wah!" I'm so sorry for you! (*Throws the bundle down.*) You will find me a position, won't you? I can't go on like this.

Lopahin: We'll find one for you, Charlotta Ivanovna, don't worry.

Gayev: Everyone's leaving us. Varya's going away. We've suddenly become of no use.

Charlotta: There's no place for me to live in town, I must go away. (*Hums.*)

Enter Pishchik.

Lopahin: There's nature's masterpiece!

Pishchik (gasping): Oh . . . let me get my breath . . . I'm in agony.
. . . Esteemed friends . . . Give me a drink of water. . . .
Gayev: Wants some money, I suppose. No, thank you. . . . I'll keep
out of harm's way. (*Exits.*)
Pishchik: It's a long while since I've been to see you, most charming lady. (*To Lopahin.*) So you are here . . . glad to see you, you
intellectual giant. . . . There . . . (*Gives Lopahin money.*) Here's
four hundred rubles, and I still owe you eight hundred and
forty.
Lopahin (shrugging his shoulders in bewilderment): I must be dreaming . . . Where did you get it?
Pishchik: Wait a minute . . . It's hot . . . A most extraordinary
event! Some Englishmen came to my place and found some
sort of white clay on my land . . . (*To Madame Ranevskaya.*)
And four hundred for you . . . most lovely . . . most wonderful . . . (*Hands her the money.*) The rest later. (*Drinks water.*) A
young man in the train was telling me just now that a great
philosopher recommends jumping off roofs. "Jump!" says
he; "that's the long and the short of it!" (*In amazement.*) Just
imagine! Some more water!
Lopahin: What Englishmen?
Pishchik: I leased them the tract with the clay on it for twenty-four
hours. . . . And now, forgive me, I can't stay. . . . I must be
dashing on. . . . I'm going over to Znoikov . . . to Kar-
damanov . . . I owe them all money . . . (*Drinks water.*) Good-
by, everybody . . . I'll look in on Thursday . . .
Madame Ranevskaya: We're just moving into town; and tomorrow
I go abroad.
Pishchik (upset): What? Why into town? That's why the furniture is
like that . . . and the suitcases . . . Well, never mind! (*Through
tears.*) Never mind . . . Men of colossal intellect, these Englishmen . . . Never mind . . . Be happy. God will come to
your help. . . . Never mind. . . . Everything in this world
comes to an end. (*Kisses Madame Ranevskaya's hand.*) If the
rumor reaches you that it's all up with me, remember this old
. . . horse, and say: Once there lived a certain . . . Simeonov-
Pishchik . . . the kingdom of Heaven be his . . . Glorious
weather. . . . Yes . . . (*Exits, in great confusion, but at once returns
and says in the doorway*): My daughter Dashenka sends her regards. (*Exit.*)
Madame Ranevskaya: Now we can go. I leave with two cares weighing on me. The first is poor old Firs. (*Glancing at her watch.*)
We still have about five minutes.

Anya: Mamma, Firs has already been taken to the hospital. Yasha sent him there this morning.

Madame Ranevskaya: My other worry is Varya. She's used to getting up early and working; and now, with no work to do, she is like a fish out of water. She has grown thin and pale, and keeps crying, poor soul. (*Pause.*) You know this very well, Yermolay Alexeyevich; I dreamed of seeing her married to you, and it looked as though that's how it would be. (*Whispers to Anya, who nods to Charlotta, and both go out.*) She loves you. You find her attractive. I don't know, I don't know why it is you seem to avoid each other; I can't understand it.

Lopahin: To tell you the truth, I don't understand it myself. It's all a puzzle. If there's still time, I'm ready now, at once. Let's settle it straight off, and have done with it! Without you, I feel I'll never be able to propose.

Madame Ranevskaya: That's splendid. After all, it will only take a minute. I'll call her at once. . . .

Lopahin: And luckily, here's champagne too. (*Looks at the glasses.*) Empty! Somebody's drunk it all. (*Yasha coughs.*) That's what you might call guzzling. . . .

Madame Ranevskaya (animatedly): Excellent! We'll go and leave you alone. Yasha, *allez!* I'll call her. (*At the door.*) Varya, leave everything and come here. Come! (*Exits with Yasha.*)

Lopahin (looking at his watch): Yes . . .

Pause behind the door, smothered laughter and whispering; at last, enter Varya.

Varya (looking over the luggage in leisurely fashion): Strange, I can't find it . . .

Lopahin: What are you looking for?

Varya: Packed it myself, and I don't remember . . . (*Pause.*)

Lopahin: Where are you going now, Varya?

Varya: I? To the Ragulins'. I've arranged to take charge there — as housekeeper, if you like.

Lopahin: At Yashnevo? About fifty miles from here. (*Pause.*) Well, life in this house is ended!

Varya (examining luggage): Where is it? Perhaps I put it in the chest. Yes, life in this house is ended. . . . There will be no more of it.

Lopahin: And I'm just off to Kharkov — by this next train. I've a lot to do there. I'm leaving Yepihodov here . . . I've taken him on.

Varya: Oh!

Lopahin: Last year at this time it was snowing, if you remember,

but now it's sunny and there's no wind. It's cold, though. . . .
It must be three below.

Varya: I didn't look. (*Pause.*) And besides, our thermometer's
broken. (*Pause. Voice from the yard*): "Yermolay Alexeyevich!"

Lopahin (as if he had been waiting for the call): This minute!

*Exit quickly. Varya sits on the floor and sobs quietly, her head on a bundle of
clothes. Enter Madame Ranevskaya cautiously.*

Madame Ranevskaya: Well? (*Pause.*) We must be going.

Varya (wiping her eyes): Yes, it's time, mamma dear. I'll be able to
get to the Ragulins' today, if only we don't miss the train.

Madame Ranevskaya (at the door): Anya, put your things on.

*Enter Anya, Gayev, Charlotta. Gayev wears a heavy overcoat with a hood. Enter
servants and coachmen. Yepihodov bustles about the luggage.*

Madame Ranevskaya: Now we can start on our journey.

Anya (joyfully): On our journey!

Gayev: My friends, my dear, cherished friends, leaving this house
forever, can I be silent? Can I at leave-taking refrain from
giving utterance to those emotions that now fill my being?

Anya (imploringly): Uncle!

Varya: Uncle, uncle dear, don't.

Gayev (forlornly): I'll bank the yellow in the side pocket . . . I'll be
silent . . .

Enter Trofimov, then Lopahin

Trofimov: Well, ladies and gentlemen, it's time to leave.

Lopahin: Yepihodov, my coat.

Madame Ranevskaya: I'll sit down just a minute. It seems as
though I'd never before seen what the walls of this house
were like, the ceilings, and now I look at them hungrily, with
such tender affection.

Gayev: I remember when I was six years old sitting on that window sill on Whitsunday, watching my father going to church.

Madame Ranevskaya: Has everything been taken?

Lopahin: I think so. (*Putting on his overcoat.*) Yepihodov, see that
everything's in order.

Yepihodov (in a husky voice): You needn't worry, Yermolay Alexeyevich.

Lopahin: What's the matter with your voice?

Yepihodov: I just had a drink of water. I must have swallowed
something.

Yasha (contemptuously): What ignorance!

Madame Ranevskaya: When we're gone, not a soul will be left here.
Lopahin: Until the spring.

Varya pulls an umbrella out of a bundle, as though about to hit someone with it. Lopahin pretends to be frightened.

Varya: Come, come, I had no such idea!
Trofimov: Ladies and gentlemen, let's get into the carriage — it's time. The train will be in directly.
Varya: Petya, there they are, your rubbers, by that trunk. (*Tearfully.*) And what dirty old things they are!
Trofimov (puts on rubbers): Let's go, ladies and gentlemen.
Gayev (greatly upset, afraid of breaking down): The train . . . the station . . . Three cushions in the side pocket, I'll bank this one in the corner . . .
Madame Ranevskaya: Let's go.
Lopahin: Are we all here? No one in there? (*Locks the side door on the left.*) There are some things stored here, better lock up. Let's go!
Anya: Good-by, old house! Good-by, old life!
Trofimov: Hail to you, new life!

Exit with Anya. Varya looks round the room and goes out slowly. Yasha and Charlotta with her dog go out.

Lopahin: And so, until the spring. Go along, friends . . . 'Bye-'bye! (*Exits.*)

Madame Ranevskaya and Gayev remain alone. As though they had been waiting for this, they throw themselves on each other's necks, and break into subdued, restrained sobs, afraid of being overheard.

Gayev (in despair): My sister! My sister!
Madame Ranevskaya: Oh, my orchard — my dear, sweet, beautiful orchard! My life, my youth, my happiness — good-by! Good-by! (*Voice of Anya, gay and summoning*): "Mamma!" (*Voice of Trofimov, gay and excited*): "Halloo!"
Madame Ranevskaya: One last look at the walls, at the windows . . . Our poor mother loved to walk about this room . . .
Gayev: My sister, my sister! (*Voice of Anya*): "Mamma!" (*Voice of Trofimov*): "Halloo!"
Madame Ranevskaya: We're coming.

They go out. The stage is empty. The sound of doors being locked, of carriages driving away. Then silence. In the stillness is heard the muffled sound of the ax striking a tree, a mournful, lonely sound.

Footsteps are heard. Firs appears in the doorway on the right. He is dressed as usual in a jacket and white waistcoat and wears slippers. He is ill.

Firs *(goes to the door, tries the handle):* Locked! They've gone . . . *(Sits down on the sofa.)* They've forgotten me . . . Never mind . . . I'll sit here a bit . . . I'll wager Leonid Andreyevich hasn't put his fur coat on, he's gone off in his light overcoat . . . *(Sighs anxiously.)* I didn't keep an eye on him . . . Ah, when they're young, they're green . . . *(Mumbles something indistinguishable.)* Life has gone by as if I had never lived. *(Lies down.)* I'll lie down a while . . . There's no strength left in you, old fellow; nothing is left, nothing. Ah, you addlehead!

Lies motionless. A distant sound is heard coming from the sky as it were, the sound of a snapping string mournfully dying away. All is still again, and nothing is heard but the strokes of the ax against a tree far away in the orchard.

Questions about The Cherry Orchard: *Act II*

Focus on the following moment in Act II — the appearance of the tramp and its aftermath.

A tramp appears, wearing a shabby white cap and an overcoat. He is slightly drunk.

Tramp: Allow me to inquire, will this short-cut take me to the station?

Gayev: It will. Just follow that road.

Tramp: My heartfelt thanks. *(Coughing.)* The weather is glorious. *(Recites.)* "My brother, my suffering brother . . . Go down to the Volga! Whose groans . . . ?" *(To Varya.)* Mademoiselle, won't you spare thirty kopecks for a hungry Russian?

Varya, frightened, cries out.

Lopahin (angrily): Even panhandling has its proprieties.

Madame Ranevskaya (scared): Here, take this. *(Fumbles in her purse.)* I haven't any silver . . . never mind, here's a gold piece.

Tramp: My heartfelt thanks. *(Exits. Laughter.)*

Varya (frightened): I'm leaving. I'm leaving . . . Oh, mamma dear, at home the servants have nothing to eat, and you gave him a gold piece!

Madame Ranevskaya: What are you going to do with me? I'm such a fool. When we get home, I'll give you everything I have. Yermolay Alexeyevich, you'll lend me some more . . .

Lopahin: Yes, ma'am.

Madame Ranevskaya: Come, ladies and gentlemen, it's time to be going. Oh! Varya, we've settled all about your marriage. Congratulations!

Make careful notes on the actions, thoughts, and feelings that need to be brought to life in the course of this scene. Decide what each speaker is for himself or herself and for the others during these moments, basing decisions on readings of each speaker's nature, and on the appropriate stage action. Consider the following specific questions as you build up your feeling for the tones, gestures, shifts of tone, and movements by which each character's distinctness can be realized.

1. What effect does Gayev's polite answer have on the tramp?
2. What stage action could explain Varya's fright?
3. What other emotions besides fright figure within Varya as she says, "I'm leaving, I'm leaving"?
4. What are Varya's feelings when Madame Ranevskaya promises "when we get back home" to give her "everything"?
5. How should Lopahin say "Yes, ma'am"?
6. What are Varya's feelings when Madame Ranevskaya cries, "Congratulations!"?

Now write a paper naming the elements that figure crucially in staging the scene, and explaining why they are all-important.

Questions about The Cherry Orchard: *Act IV*

Focus on the brief scene in Act IV during which Lopahin and Varya are on stage together with no one else present — the moment Lopahin has scheduled for his marriage proposal.

> *Pause behind the door, smothered laughter and whispering; at last, enter Varya.*
>
> *Varya (looking over the luggage in leisurely fashion):* Strange, I can't find it . . .
>
> *Lopahin:* What are you looking for?
>
> *Varya:* Packed it myself, and I don't remember . . . *(Pause.)*
>
> *Lopahin:* Where are you going now, Varya?
>
> *Varya:* I? To the Ragulins'. I've arranged to take charge there — as housekeeper, if you like.
>
> *Lopahin:* At Yashnevo? About fifty miles from here. *(Pause.)* Well, life in this house is ended!
>
> *Varya (examining luggage):* Where is it? Perhaps I put it in the chest. Yes, life in this house is ended . . . There will be no more of it.
>
> *Lopahin:* And I'm just off to Kharkov—by this next train. I've a lot to do there. I'm leaving Yepihodov here . . . I've taken him on.
>
> *Varya:* Oh!

Lopahin: Last year at this time it was snowing, if you remember, but now it's sunny and there's no wind. It's cold, though. . . . It must be three below.

Varya: I didn't look. (*Pause.*) And besides, our thermometer's bro-ken. (*Pause. Voice from the yard*): "Yermolay Alexeyevich!"

Lopahin (as if he had been waiting for the call): This minute!

Exit quickly. Varya sits on the floor and sobs quietly, her head on a bundle of clothes. Enter Madame Ranevskaya cautiously.

How does Varya behave toward Lopahin as she enters? When does she first look at him? During the last pause in Varya's last speech, where does Lopahin look? Make careful notes on the actions, thoughts, and feelings that need to be brought to life in the course of this scene. Decide what each speaker is for himself or herself and for the other during these moments, basing deci-sions on readings of each speaker's nature. Build up the insides of the appropriate tones, gestures, and tonal contrasts, by which each character's separateness can be realized from moment to moment. Then write a paper naming the elements (movements, gestures, expressions, motives) that figure crucially in staging the scene, and explain why they are all-important. Compare your response with the one that follows the list of key elements.

Note. The following response begins with reading notes and a list of key elements for close imagining. Such a list can help you keep track of the wide range of focal points that need attention when bringing to life a scene in a play.

Response

EDITOR'S READING NOTES: Eye and body movements — Varya: ab-stracted, distracted. Half-searching (the luggage), half-remember-ing or trying to remember — what? Squints, frowns, seems held up by some memory of the thing sought (a memory that won't quite come into focus because after all it's faked), maybe an impatient movement of the hand. What a nuisance, this forgetful-ness of mine! I thought it was right here — Where did I — ? Doesn't act as though she's even aware Lopahin is present. Then discovers him. Surprise! You — ? Oh well, I'm busy, don't bother me, don't interrupt, I'm on an errand . . .

Eye and body movement — Lopahin: he makes one try, one halfhearted attempt to hold her still for a second ("Where are you going now, Varya?"). Eyes on her then, although not quite eye to eye. She won't accept this bid to listen to him — not this fast, anyway. "I?" she says — stops as though arrested by the oddity of being asked a question. Points left index finger at own chest. You mean me? You talking to me? Then very brisk she becomes — and the briskness together with her refusal to answer Lopahin's next question makes him turn away. Probably a shrug goes with "About fifty miles from here."

Earlier and later scenes all have this pattern of patternlessness, discontinuity, fits and starts, brief attentiveness to another person followed by lapses back into self-absorption. Over and over the same. But: This *was* to be a culminating climactic moment. A marriage proposal. There's a current of near-intention back of all the fidgeting and we feel it. But it doesn't quite take hold, too much nervousness for both . . . eagerness not to settle into a feeling . . . . desire not to appear vulnerable. Both act as though this were just one more chance encounter among hundreds — and then everything comes to an end: an awful collapse.

EDITOR'S KEY ELEMENTS:

1. The abrupt sealing off of the household's bustle and flow; sudden silence and enclosure
2. Continuing evasion of eye contact (Varya "examining luggage"; Lopahin surveying room, house, weather outside; Lopahin checking his watch; and so on)
3. Rhythm of engagement and disengagement (stress-packed extended pauses at the edge of the personal, followed by refuge in generalizations, weather talk, and so on)
4. Ragged alternations of pace: Varya at first leisurely, then harried ("Where is it?"). Lopahin veering between on-the-go hustle ("I've a lot to do") and easy, reflective relaxation ("Last year at this time it was snowing")
5. Mounting time pressure, sense of interruption imminent

EDITOR: No moment in the play is as sharply defined beforehand as this one: we're to hear a marriage proposal. Lopahin has just told Madame Ranevskaya that he is ready to propose, Varya has been summoned and presumably told what's coming, champagne glasses are on hand, the two parties are thrust together alone. And the mad activity of the house — music, dancing, packing, card tricks, games, ceaseless parades of visitors — abruptly subsides.

Varya does not enter this stillness as though conscious of being on the verge of a momentous life event. With an effort she gives the impression that she has arrived by happenstance. Her manner is preoccupied; she isn't bent on Lopahin, doesn't seek his glance or await his word. He's been led to expect a young woman who is in readiness as he's in readiness, who's looking for *him*, anticipating his speech. His expectation is that his word is being hung upon, that Varya's focus will be exclusively upon himself. What might he expect her to say or do? Perhaps some hesitant phrase underlining her expectancy (*They said you were looking for me* — ?). Perhaps no word, merely a sustained looking-forward-to glance, followed by eyes cast down. Either or both beginnings would harmonize with his sense of self-importance — and would also confirm for him that his proposal won't surprise her, won't plunge him into awkwardness, difficulty, uncertainty, the unmanageable.

But, disconcertingly, she gives him neither, sets him off balance, suggests by her manner that his presumptions about what's in her mind — about her readiness — could be presumptuous. It is ever so delicate a put-down — but it nudges him backward, transforms (for him) a moment of control into a moment of puzzlement.

So it will go from then on — through their five very brief exchanges. He never altogether loses his assurance that she must be about to attend seriously to him; she for her part never altogether gives up her feigned concentration on the imaginary errand. Tentatively, hesitantly each comes to the borders of the inexpressible lying between them; each hangs fire through more than one pause, as though offering an opportunity to the other — daring the other to touch the subject, to speak personally. It seems each time that now they will reach out, can't postpone it any longer, mustn't postpone it. In this household, who can count on not being interrupted? All she would have to say at her pause (or at his) would be: *It is terrible leaving here.* All he would have to say at her pause (or his own) would be: *Varya, please. Listen for one second.* But no, each time — nothing. They come to the edge, look, wait, turn away.

We can just make out a few reasons for the evasions, the inhibitions. Having struggled up from the peasantry, Lopahin has settled self-protectively on a style of briskness and chaffing as a means of fending off any potential unpleasantness from those who remember his origins. The corollary of his inability to believe he's actually bought this property is an inability to imagine marrying as an equal into the family of the "rightful" owners. When Madame Ranevskaya urges him to propose, he can forget the former differences between them and fully occupy the position he's won for himself. But, as he says, he needs her support. Without it, doubt — obscure, only half-conscious — assails him, buried fear of overreaching, unease at the hint of detachment Varya shows him when she enters.

As for Varya: Her hesitations and evasions might be traced first of all to pride. Not only does the feckless family into which she was adopted provide her with little protection against the world, but they also make light of her efforts to cope with the disaster and suffering their extravagance causes others besides themselves. She is penniless; she loves Madame Ranevskaya; but her adoptive mother nevertheless subjects her — offhandedly and continually — to public humiliation, as in this exchange from Act II:

> *Madame Ranevskaya:* Oh! Varya, we've settled all about your
>   marriage. Congratulations!
> *Varya (through tears):* Really, mamma, that's not a joking matter.

She's drawn to Lopahin, but "he either keeps silent, or else cracks jokes" — and, although nobody else seems to understand this, she herself understands that "I can't propose to him myself." Her family seems ready to throw her at Lopahin; they find her situation funny. (The "smothered laughter and whispering" behind the door just before this encounter with Lopahin shows us that.) Except by creating a certain slight distance — maintaining an initial minimum reserve — how can she keep any measure of self-respect?

We begin, in short, with familiar kinds of sensitivity — familiar modes of pride. Practicalities of some sort necessarily figure in nearly all engagements to marry, but still the heart resists the notion that one's own engagement is a market transaction, an event foreseen, arranged, rendered inevitable by others.

Neither Varya nor Lopahin is a trivial person; each wants a marriage that doesn't outrage the sense of self-worth; both pull back from a situation that seems to deprive them of their freedom, their right to believe in their own personal significance.

And then beyond all this there's the matter of local standards and practices. Who in this household, to this moment, has ever listened fully to another voice? Inspired monologuists — poets, panegyrists, performers — the crowds in this place, even the visiting tramp, are all charmers. But from none of them could you learn how to listen, how to ask a question in such a way as to command attention, how to respond to a question in such a way as to prove you knew what you'd been asked. For one brief interval Varya and Lopahin are sealed off from the hubbub and confusion created by the multiple egos around them, but they're under an awful pressure of time. Somebody's bound to break in on them with a talent show or disappearing act. And, to repeat, there are no models or precedents for true attentiveness anywhere in the household. In a world in which nobody harkens, it's hard to know what harkening would entail. And there's just not enough time for either of these two to begin to learn.

It adds up to amusement first of all, of course. Their pauses are comically balanced against each other. Watching each of them *almost* watch the other, almost dare to seek the other's eye as silence stretches between them — this is funny. At the last possible instant their eyes meet — whereupon comes "the voice from the yard," and all hope ends. Comedy lives on pretense or evasion caught out; we catch Lopahin and Varya in their evasions, and we chuckle at them.

But there's no horselaugh, and we feel an undercurrent of sadness, waste, even desperation. Hateful cruelty, violence are nowhere in evidence; the scale of loss is modest. The fate of whole tribes isn't being settled here, as it is in *Macbeth*. Still, real human damage is being done. Even as we smile, we know that lives are in the process of being destroyed. That this is so is pointless, needless, ridiculous — but it's also actual. It happens before our eyes: people sliding on the banana peel to heartbreak. To imagine the moment in a manner that will allow us to feel the absurdity and still be troubled, even distressed, when, at Lopahin's exit, Varya sinks to the floor, sobbing quietly, "her head on a bundle of clothes": that is, indeed, a high achievement of the reader's art.

21

Plays for Further Study

TENNESSEE WILLIAMS   (1911–1983)

The Glass Menagerie

Nobody, not even the rain, has such small hands.
—*E. E. Cummings*

LIST OF CHARACTERS

Amanda Wingfield, *the mother. A little woman of great but confused vitality clinging frantically to another time and place. Her characterization must be carefully created, not copied from type. She is not paranoiac, but her life is paranoia. There is much to admire in Amanda, and as much to love and pity as there is to laugh at. Certainly she has endurance and a kind of heroism, and though her foolishness makes her unwittingly cruel at times, there is tenderness in her slight person.*

Laura Wingfield, *her daughter. Amanda, having failed to establish contact with reality, continues to live vitally in her illusions, but Laura's situation is even graver. A childhood illness has left her crippled, one leg slightly shorter than the other, and held in a brace. This defect need not be more than suggested on the stage. Stemming from this, Laura's separation increases till she is like a piece of her own glass collection, too exquisitely fragile to move from the shelf.*

Tom Wingfield, *her son. And the narrator of the play. A poet with a job in a warehouse. His nature is not remorseless, but to escape from a trap he has to act without pity.*

Jim O'Connor, *the gentleman caller. A nice, ordinary, young man.*

SCENE: *An alley in St. Louis.*
PART I: *Preparation for a Gentleman Caller.*
PART II: *The Gentleman Calls.*
TIME: *Now and the Past.*

SCENE I

The Wingfield apartment is in the rear of the building, one of those vast hivelike conglomerations of cellular living-units that flower as warty growths in over-

crowded urban centers of lower middle-class population and are symptomatic of the impulse of this largest and fundamentally enslaved section of American society to avoid fluidity and differentiation and to exist and function as one interfused mass of automatism.

The apartment faces an alley and is entered by a fire-escape, a structure whose name is a touch of accidental poetic truth, for all of these huge buildings are always burning with the slow and implacable fires of human desperation. The fire-escape is included in the set — that is, the landing of it and steps descending from it.

The scene is memory and is therefore nonrealistic. Memory takes a lot of poetic license. It omits some details; others are exaggerated, according to the emotional value of the articles it touches, for memory is seated predominantly in the heart. The interior is therefore rather dim and poetic.

At the rise of the curtain, the audience is faced with the dark, grim rear wall of the Wingfield tenement. This building, which runs parallel to the footlights, is flanked on both sides by dark, narrow alleys which run into murky canyons of tangled clotheslines, garbage cans, and the sinister latticework of neighboring fire-escapes. It is up and down these side alleys that exterior entrances and exits are made, during the play. At the end of Tom's opening commentary, the dark tene-ment wall slowly reveals (by means of a transparency) the interior of the ground floor Wingfield apartment.

Downstage is the living room, which also serves as a sleeping room for Laura, the sofa unfolding to make her bed. Upstage, center, and divided by a wide arch or second proscenium with transparent faded portieres (or second curtain), is the dining room. In an old-fashioned what-not in the living room are seen scores of transparent glass animals. A blown-up photograph of the father hangs on the wall of the living room, facing the audience, to the left of the archway. It is the face of a very handsome young man in a doughboy's First World War cap. He is gallantly smiling, ineluctably smiling, as if to say, "I will be smiling forever."

The audience hears and sees the opening scene in the dining room through both the transparent fourth wall of the building and the transparent gauze por-tieres of the dining-room arch. It is during this revealing scene that the fourth wall slowly ascends, out of sight. This transparent exterior wall is not brought down again until the very end of the play, during Tom's final speech.

The narrator is an undisguised convention of the play. He takes whatever license with dramatic convention as is convenient to his purposes.

Tom enters dressed as a merchant sailor from alley, stage left, and strolls across the front of the stage to the fire-escape. There he stops and lights a cigarette. He addresses the audience.

Tom: Yes, I have tricks in my pocket, I have things up my sleeve. But I am the opposite of a stage magician. He gives you illu-sion that has the appearance of truth. I give you truth in the pleasant disguise of illusion. To begin with, I turn back time. I reverse it to that quaint period, the thirties, when the huge middle class of America was matriculating in a school for the blind. Their eyes had failed them, or they had failed their eyes, and so they were having their fingers pressed forcibly down on the fiery Braille alphabet of a dissolving economy. In Spain there was revolution. Here there was only shouting and confusion. In Spain there was Guernica. Here there were disturbances of labor, sometimes pretty violent, in otherwise peaceful cities such as Chicago, Cleveland, Saint Louis. . . . This is the social background of the play.

(Music.)

The play is memory. Being a memory play, it is dimly lighted, it is sentimental, it is not realistic. In memory everything seems to happen to music. That explains the fiddle in the wings. I am the narrator of the play, and also a character in it. The other characters are my mother, Amanda, my sister, Laura, and a gentleman caller who appears in the final scenes. He is the most realistic character in the play, being an emissary from a world of reality that we were somehow set apart from. But since I have a poet's weakness for symbols, I am using this character also as a symbol; he is the long de-layed but always expected something that we live for. There is a fifth character in the play who doesn't appear except in this larger-than-life photograph over the mantel. This is our father who left us a long time ago. He was a telephone man who fell in love with long distances; he gave up his job with the telephone company and skipped the light fantastic out of town. . . . The last we heard of him was a picture post-card from Mazatlán, on the Pacific coast of Mexico, containing a message of two words — "Hello — Good-bye!" and no ad-dress. I think the rest of the play will explain itself. . . .

Amanda's voice becomes audible through the portieres.
(Legend on screen: "Où sont les neiges."°)
He divides the portieres and enters the upstage area.
Amanda and Laura are seated at a drop-leaf table. Eating is indicated by gestures without food or utensils. Amanda faces the audience.
Tom and Laura are seated in profile.
The interior has lit up softly and through the scrim we see Amanda and Laura seated at the table in the upstage area.

Amanda (calling): Tom?
Tom: Yes, Mother.
Amanda: We can't say grace until you come to the table!

Où sont les neiges: Part of a line from a poem by the French medieval writer François Villon; the full line translates, "But where are the snows of Yesteryear?"

Tom: Coming, Mother. (*He bows slightly and withdraws, reappearing a few moments later in his place at the table.*)

Amanda (to her son): Honey, don't *push* with your *fingers*. If you have to push with something, the thing to push with is a crust of bread. And chew — chew! Animals have sections in their stomachs which enable them to digest food without mastica-tion, but human beings are supposed to chew their food before they swallow it down. Eat food leisurely, son, and really enjoy it. A well-cooked meal has lots of delicate flavors that have to be held in the mouth for appreciation. So chew your food and give your salivary glands a chance to function!

Tom deliberately lays his imaginary fork down and pushes his chair back from the table.

Tom: I haven't enjoyed one bite of this dinner because of your constant directions on how to eat it. It's you that makes me rush through meals with your hawklike attention to every bite I take. Sickening — spoils my appetite — all this discus-sion of animals' secretion — salivary glands — mastication!

Amanda (lightly): Temperament like a Metropolitan star! (*He rises and crosses downstage.*) You're not excused from the table.

Tom: I am getting a cigarette.

Amanda: You smoke too much.

Laura rises.

Laura: I'll bring in the blanc mange.

He remains standing with his cigarette by the portieres during the following.

Amanda (rising): No, sister, no, sister — you be the lady this time and I'll be the darky.

Laura: I'm already up.

Amanda: Resume your seat, little sister — I want you to stay fresh and pretty — for gentlemen callers!

Laura: I'm not expecting any gentlemen callers.

Amanda (crossing out to kitchenette. Airily): Sometimes they come when they are least expected! Why, I remember one Sunday afternoon in Blue Mountain — (*Enters kitchenette.*)

Tom: I know what's coming!

Laura: Yes. But let her tell it.

Tom: Again?

Laura: She loves to tell it.

Amanda returns with bowl of dessert.

Amanda: One Sunday afternoon in Blue Mountain — your mother received — *seventeen!* — gentlemen callers! Why, sometimes there weren't chairs enough to accommodate them all. We had to send the nigger over to bring in folding chairs from the parish house.

Tom (remaining at portieres): How did you entertain those gentlemen callers?

Amanda: I understood the art of conversation!

Tom: I bet you could talk.

Amanda: Girls in those days *knew* how to talk, I can tell you.

Tom: Yes?

(Image: Amanda as a girl on a porch greeting callers.)

Amanda: They knew how to entertain their gentlemen callers. It wasn't enough for a girl to be possessed of a pretty face and a graceful figure — although I wasn't slighted in either respect. She also needed to have a nimble wit and a tongue to meet all occasions.

Tom: What did you talk about?

Amanda: Things of importance going on in the world! Never anything coarse or common or vulgar. (*She addresses Tom as though he were seated in the vacant chair at the table though he remains by portieres. He plays this scene as though he held the book.*) My callers were gentlemen — all! Among my callers were some of the most prominent young planters of the Mississippi Delta — planters and sons of planters!

Tom motions for music and a spot of light on Amanda.
Her eyes lift, her face glows, her voice becomes rich and elegiac.
(Screen legend: "Où sont les neiges.")

There was young Champ Laughlin who later became vice-president of the Delta Planters Bank. Hadley Stevenson who was drowned in Moon Lake and left his widow one hundred and fifty thousand in Government bonds. There were the Cutrere brothers, Wesley and Bates. Bates was one of my bright particular beaux! He got in a quarrel with that wild Wainright boy. They shot it out on the floor of Moon Lake Casino. Bates was shot through the stomach. Died in the ambulance on his way to Memphis. His widow was also well-provided for, came into eight or ten thousand acres, that's all. She married him on the rebound — never loved her — carried my picture on him the night he died! And there was that boy that every girl in the Delta had set her cap for! That beautiful, brilliant young Fitzhugh boy from Green County!

Tom: What did he leave his widow?

Amanda: He never married! Gracious, you talk as though all of my old admirers had turned up their toes to the daisies!

Tom: Isn't this the first you mentioned that still survives?

Amanda: That Fitzhugh boy went North and made a fortune — came to be known as the Wolf of Wall Street! He had the Midas touch, whatever he touched turned to gold! And I could have been Mrs. Duncan J. Fitzhugh, mind you! But — I picked your *father!*

Laura (rising): Mother, let me clear the table.

Amanda: No dear, you go in front and study your typewriter chart. Or practice your shorthand a little. Stay fresh and pretty! — It's almost time for our gentlemen callers to start arriving. (*She flounces girlishly toward the kitchenette.*) How many do you suppose we're going to entertain this afternoon?

Tom throws down the paper and jumps up with a groan.

Laura (alone in the dining room): I don't believe we're going to receive any, Mother.

Amanda (reappearing, airily): What? No one — not one? You must be joking! (*Laura nervously echoes her laugh. She slips in a fugitive manner through the half-open portieres and draws them gently behind her. A shaft of very clear light is thrown on her face against the faded tapestry of the curtains.*) (*Music: "The Glass Menagerie" under faintly.*) (*Lightly.*) Not one gentleman caller? It can't be true! There must be a flood, there must have been a tornado!

Laura: It isn't a flood, it's not a tornado, Mother. I'm just not popular like you were in Blue Mountain. . . . (*Tom utters another groan. Laura glances at him with a faint, apologetic smile. Her voice catching a little.*) Mother's afraid I'm going to be an old maid.

(The scene dims out with "Glass Menagerie" music.)

SCENE II

"Laura, Haven't You Ever Liked Some Boy?"

On the dark stage the screen is lighted with the image of blue roses.
    Gradually Laura's figure becomes apparent and the screen goes out.
    The music subsides.
    Laura is seated in the delicate ivory chair at the small clawfoot table.
    She wears a dress of soft violet material for a kimono — her hair tied back from her forehead with a ribbon.

She is washing and polishing her collection of glass.
Amanda appears on the fire-escape steps. At the sound of her ascent, Laura catches her breath, thrusts the bowl of ornaments away, and seats herself stiffly before the diagram of the typewriter keyboard as though it held her spellbound. Something has happened to Amanda. It is written in her face as she climbs to the landing: a look that is grim and hopeless and a little absurd.
She has on one of those cheap or imitation velvety-looking cloth coats with imitation fur collar. Her hat is five or six years old, one of those dreadful cloche hats that were worn in the late twenties, and she is clasping an enormous black patent-leather pocketbook with nickel clasp and initials. This is her full-dress outfit, the one she usually wears to the D.A.R.
Before entering she looks through the door.
She purses her lips, open her eyes wide, rolls them upward, and shakes her head.
Then she slowly lets herself in the door. Seeing her mother's expression Laura touches her lips with a nervous gesture.

Laura: Hello, Mother, I was — (*She makes a nervous gesture toward the chart on the wall. Amanda leans against the shut door and stares at Laura with a martyred look.*)

Amanda: Deception? Deception? (*She slowly removes her hat and gloves, continuing the swift suffering stare. She lets the hat and gloves fall on the floor — a bit of acting.*)

Laura (shakily): How was the D.A.R. meeting? (*Amanda slowly opens her purse and removes a dainty white handkerchief, which she shakes out delicately and delicately touches to her lips and nostrils.*) Didn't you go to the D.A.R. meeting, Mother?

Amanda (faintly, almost inaudibly): — No. — No. (*Then more forcibly.*) I did not have the strength — to go to the D.A.R. In fact, I did not have the courage! I wanted to find a hole in the ground and hide myself in it forever! (*She crosses slowly to the wall and removes the diagram of the typewriter keyboard. She holds it in front of her for a second, staring at it sweetly and sorrowfully — then bites her lips and tears it in two pieces.*)

Laura (faintly): Why did you do that, Mother? (*Amanda repeats the same procedure with the chart of the Gregg Alphabet.*) Why are you —

Amanda: Why? Why? How old are you, Laura?

Laura: Mother, you know my age.

Amanda: I thought that you were an adult; it seems that I was mistaken. (*She crosses slowly to the sofa and sinks down and stares at Laura.*)

Laura: Please don't stare at me, Mother.

Amanda closes her eyes and lowers her head. Count ten.

Amanda: What are we going to do, what is going to become of us, what is the future?

Count ten.

Laura: Has something happened, Mother? (*Amanda draws a long breath and takes out the handkerchief again. Dabbing process.*) Mother, has — something happened?
Amanda: I'll be all right in a minute. I'm just bewildered — (*count five*) — by life. . . .
Laura: Mother, I wish that you would tell me what's happened.
Amanda: As you know, I was supposed to be inducted into my office at the D.A.R. this afternoon. (*Image: A swarm of typewriters.*) But I stopped off at Rubicam's Business College to speak to your teachers about your having a cold and ask them what progress they thought you were making down there.
Laura: Oh. . . .
Amanda: I went to the typing instructor and introduced myself as your mother. She didn't know who you were. Wingfield, she said. We don't have any such student enrolled at the school! I assured her she did, that you had been going to classes since early in January. "I wonder," she said, "if you could be talking about that terribly shy little girl who dropped out of school after only a few days' attendance?" "No," I said, "Laura, my daughter, has been going to school every day for the past six weeks!" "Excuse me," she said. She took the attendance book out and there was your name, unmistakably printed, and all the dates you were absent until they decided that you had dropped out of school. I still said, "No, there must have been some mistake! There must have been some mix-up in the records!" And she said, "No — I remember her perfectly now. Her hand shook so that she couldn't hit the right keys! The first time we gave a speed-test, she broke down completely — was sick at the stomach and almost had to be carried into the wash-room! After that morning she never showed up any more. We phoned the house but never got any answer" — while I was working at Famous and Barr, I suppose, demonstrating those — Oh! I felt so weak I could barely keep on my feet. I had to sit down while they got me a glass of water! Fifty dollars' tuition, all of our plans — my hopes and ambitions for you — just gone up the spout, just gone up the spout like that. (*Laura draws a long breath and gets awkwardly to her feet. She crosses to the Victrola, and winds it up.*) What are you doing?

Laura: Oh! (*She releases the handle and returns to her seat.*)
Amanda: Laura, where have you been going when you've gone
  out pretending that you were going to business college?
Laura: I've just been going out walking.
Amanda: That's not true.
Laura: It is. I just went walking.
Amanda: Walking? Walking? In winter? Deliberately courting
  pneumonia in that light coat? Where did you walk to, Laura?
Laura: It was the lesser of two evils, Mother. (*Image: Winter scene in
  park.*) I couldn't go back up. I — threw up — on the floor!
Amanda: From half past seven till after five every day you mean
  to tell me you walked around in the park, because you
  wanted to make me think that you were still going to Rubicam's Business College?
Laura: It wasn't as bad as it sounds. I went inside places to get
  warmed up.
Amanda: Inside where?
Laura: I went in the art museum and the bird-houses at the Zoo. I
  visited the penguins every day! Sometimes I did without
  lunch and went to the movies. Lately I've been spending most
  of my afternoons in the Jewel-box, that big glass house where
  they raise the tropical flowers.
Amanda: You did all this to deceive me, just for the deception?
  (*Laura looks down.*) Why?
Laura: Mother, when you're disappointed, you get that awful
  suffering look on your face, like the picture of Jesus' mother
  in the museum!
Amanda: Hush!
Laura: I couldn't face it.

Pause. A whisper of strings.
(*Legend: "The Crust of Humility."*)

Amanda (hopelessly fingering the huge pocketbook): So what are we
  going to do the rest of our lives? Stay home and watch the
  parades go by? Amuse ourselves with the glass menagerie,
  darling? Eternally play those worn-out phonograph records
  your father left as a painful reminder of him? We won't have
  a business career — we've given that up because it gave us
  nervous indigestion! (*Laughs wearily.*) What is there left but
  dependency all our lives? I know so well what becomes of
  unmarried women who aren't prepared to occupy a position.
  I've seen such pitiful cases in the South — barely tolerated
  spinsters living upon the grudging patronage of sister's husband or brother's wife! — stuck away in some little mouse-

trap of a room — encouraged by one in-law to visit another — little birdlike women without any nest — eating the crust of humility all their life! Is that the future that we've mapped out for ourselves? I swear it's the only alternative I can think of! It isn't a very pleasant alternative, is it? Of course — some girls *do marry*. (*Laura twists her hands nervously*.) Haven't you ever liked some boy?

Laura: Yes. I liked one once. (*Rises.*) I came across his picture a while ago.

Amanda (with some interest): He gave you his picture?

Laura: No, it's in the year-book.

Amanda (disappointed): Oh — a high-school boy.

(Screen image: Jim as a high-school hero bearing a silver cup.)

Laura: Yes. His name was Jim. (*Laura lifts the heavy annual from the clawfoot table.*) Here he is in *The Pirates of Penzance*.

Amanda (absently): The what?

Laura: The operetta the senior class put on. He had a wonderful voice and we sat across the aisle from each other Mondays, Wednesday, and Fridays in the Aud. Here he is with the silver cup for debating! See his grin?

Amanda (absently): He must have had a jolly disposition.

Laura: He used to call me — Blue Roses.

(Image: Blue roses.)

Amanda: Why did he call you such a name as that?

Laura: When I had that attack of pleurosis — he asked me what was the matter when I came back. I said pleurosis — he thought that I said Blue Roses! So that's what he always called me after that. Whenever he saw me, he'd holler, "Hello, Blue Roses!" I didn't care for the girl that he went out with. Emily Meisenbach. Emily was the best-dressed girl at Soldan. She never struck me, though, as being sincere. . . . It says in the Personal Section — they're engaged. That's — six years ago! They must be married by now.

Amanda: Girls that aren't cut out for business careers usually wind up married to some nice man. (*Gets up with a spark of revival.*) Sister, that's what you'll do!

Laura utters a startled, doubtful laugh. She reaches quickly for a piece of glass.

Laura: But, Mother —

Amanda: Yes? (*Crossing to photograph.*)

Laura (in a tone of frightened apology): I'm — crippled!

(Image: Screen.)

Amanda: Nonsense! Laura, I've told you never, never to use that word. Why, you're not crippled, you just have a little defect — hardly noticeable, even! When people have some slight disadvantage like that, they cultivate other things to make up for it — develop charm — and vivacity — and — *charm!* That's all you have to do! *(She turns again to the photograph.)* One thing your father had *plenty of* — was *charm!*

Tom motions to the fiddle in the wings.
(The scene fades out with music.)

SCENE III

(Legend on the screen: "After the Fiasco — ")
Tom speaks from the fire-escape landing.

Tom: After the fiasco at Rubicam's Business College, the idea of getting a gentleman caller for Laura began to play a more important part in Mother's calculations. It became an obsession. Like some archetype of the universal unconscious, the image of the gentleman caller haunted our small apartment. . . . *(Image: Young man at door with flowers.)* An evening at home rarely passed without some allusion to this image, this specter, this hope . . . Even when he wasn't mentioned, his presence hung in Mother's preoccuppied look and in my sister's frightened, apologetic manner — hung like a sentence passed upon the Wingfields! Mother was a woman of action as well as words. She began to take logical steps in the planned direction. Late that winter and in the early spring — realizing that extra money would be needed to properly feather the nest and plume the bird — she conducted a vigorous campaign on the telephone, roping in subscribers to one of those magazines for matrons called *The Home-maker's Companion*, the type of journal that features the serialized sublimations of ladies of letters who think in terms of delicate cuplike breasts, slim, tapering waists, rich, creamy thighs, eyes like wood-smoke in autumn, fingers that soothe and caress like strains of music, bodies as powerful as Etruscan sculpture.

(Screen image: Glamour magazine cover.)
Amanda enters with phone on long extension cord. She is spotted in the dim stage.

Amanda: Ida Scott? This is Amanda Wingfield! We *missed* you at the D.A.R. last Monday! I said to myself: She's probably suffering with that sinus condition! How is that sinus condition? Horrors! Heaven have mercy! — You're a Christian martyr, yes, that's what you are, a Christian martyr! Well, I just now happened to notice that your subscription to the *Companion's* about to expire! Yes, it expires with the next issue, honey! — just when that wonderful new serial by Bessie Mae Hopper is getting off to such an exciting start. Oh, honey, it's something that you can't miss! You remember how *Gone with the Wind* took everybody by storm? You simply couldn't go out if you hadn't read it. All everybody *talked* was Scarlett O'Hara. Well, this is a book that critics already compare to *Gone with the Wind*. It's the *Gone with the Wind* of the post–World War generation! — What? — Burning? — Oh, honey, don't let them burn, go take a look in the oven and I'll hold the wire! Heavens — I think she's hung up!

(Dim out.)

(Legend on screen: "You think I'm in love with Continental Shoemakers?")

Before the stage is lighted, the violent voices of Tom and Amanda are heard. They are quarreling behind the portieres. In front of them stands Laura with clenched hands and panicky expression.

A clear pool of light on her figure throughout this scene.

Tom: What in Christ's name am I —

Amanda (shrilly): Don't you use that —

Tom: Supposed to do!

Amanda: Expression! Not in my —

Tom: Ohhh!

Amanda: Presence! Have you gone out of your senses?

Tom: I have, that's true, *driven* out!

Amanda: What is the matter with you, you — big — big — IDIOT!

Tom: Look — I've got *no thing*, no single thing —

Amanda: Lower your voice!

Tom: In my life here that I can call my OWN! Everything is —

Amanda: Stop that shouting!

Tom: Yesterday you confiscated my books! You had the nerve to —

Amanda: I took that horrible novel back to the library — yes! That hideous book by that insane Mr. Lawrence.° (*Tom laughs wildly.*) I cannot control the output of diseased minds or

Mr. Lawrence: D. H. Lawrence (1885–1930).

people who cater to them — (*Tom laughs still more wildly.*) BUT I
WON'T ALLOW SUCH FILTH BROUGHT INTO MY HOUSE! No, no, no,
no, no!

Tom: House, house! Who pays rent on it, who makes a slave of
himself to —

Amanda (fairly screeching): Don't you DARE to —

Tom: No, no, *I* mustn't say things! *I've* got to just —

Amanda: Let me tell you —

Tom: I don't want to hear any more! (*He tears the portieres open.*

The upstage area is lit with a turgid smoky red glow.)

*Amanda's hair is in metal curlers and she wears a very old bathrobe, much
too large for her slight figure, a relic of the faithless Mr. Wingfield.*

*An upright typewriter and a wild disarray of manuscripts are on the drop-
leaf table. The quarrel was probably precipitated by Amanda's interruption of his
creative labor. A chair lying overthrown on the floor.*

Their gesticulating shadows are cast on the ceiling by the fiery glow.

Amanda: You *will* hear more, you —

Tom: No, I won't hear more, I'm going out!

Amanda: You come right back in —

Tom: Out, out, out! Because I'm —

Amanda: Come back here, Tom Wingfield! I'm not through talking to you!

Tom: Oh, go —

Laura (desperately): Tom!

Amanda: You're going to listen, and no more insolence from you!
I'm at the end of my patience! (*He comes back toward her.*)

Tom: What do you think I'm at? Aren't I supposed to have any
patience to reach the end of, Mother? I know, I know. It seems
unimportant to you, what I'm *doing* — what I *want* to do —
having a little *difference* between them! You don't think
that —

Amanda: I think you've been doing things that you're ashamed of.
That's why you act like this. I don't believe that you go every
night to the movies. Nobody goes to the movies night after
night. Nobody in their right minds goes to the movies as
often as you pretend to. People don't go the movies at nearly
midnight, and movies don't let out at two A.M. Come in
stumbling. Muttering to yourself like a maniac! You get three
hours' sleep and then go to work. Oh, I can picture the way
you're doing down there. Moping, doping, because you're in
no condition.

Tom (wildly): No, I'm in no condition.

Amanda: What right have you got to jeopardize your job? Jeopardize the security of us all? How do you think we'd manage if you were —

Tom: Listen! You think I'm crazy *about* the *warehouse!* (*He bends fiercely toward her slight figure.*) You think I'm in love with the Continental Shoemakers? You think I want to spend fifty-five *years* down there in that — *celotex interior!* with — *fluorescent* — *tubes!* Look! I'd rather somebody picked up a crowbar and battered out my brains — than go back mornings! I *go!* Every time you come in yelling that God damn *"Rise and Shine!" "Rise and Shine!"* I say to myself "How *lucky* dead people are!" But I get up. I *go!* For sixty-five dollars a month I give up all that I dream of doing and being *ever!* And you say self — *self's* all I ever think of. Why, listen, if self is what I thought of, Mother, I'd be where he is — GONE! (*Pointing to father's picture.*) As far as the system of transportation reaches! (*He starts past her. She grabs his arm.*) Don't grab at me, Mother!

Amanda: Where are you going?

Tom: I'm going to the *movies!*

Amanda: I don't believe that lie!

Tom (*crouching toward her, overtowering her tiny figure. She backs away, gasping*): I'm going to opium dens! Yes, opium dens, dens of vice and criminals' hang-outs, Mother. I've joined the Hogan gang, I'm a hired assassin, I carry a tommy-gun in a violin case! I run a string of cat-houses in the Valley! They call me Killer, Killer Wingfield, I'm leading a double-life, a simple, honest warehouse worker by day, by night a dynamic *czar* of the *underworld, Mother.* I go to gambling casinos, I spin away fortunes on the roulette table! I wear a patch over one eye and a false mustache, sometimes I put on green whiskers. On those occasions they call me — *El Diablo!* Oh, I could tell you things to make you sleepless! My enemies plan to dynamite this place. They're going to blow us all sky-high some night! I'll be glad, very happy, and so will you! You'll go up, up on a broomstick, over Blue Mountain with seventeen gentlemen callers! You ugly — babbling old — *witch.* . . . (*He goes through a series of violent, clumsy movements, seizing his overcoat, lunging to the door, pulling it fiercely open. The women watch him, aghast. His arm catches in the sleeve of the coat as he struggles to pull it on. For a moment he is pinioned by the bulky garment. With an outraged groan he tears the coat off again, splitting the shoulders of it, and hurls it across the room. It strikes against the shelf of Laura's glass collection, there is a tinkle of shattering glass. Laura cries out as if wounded.)*

(Music legend: "The Glass Menagerie.")

Laura (shrilly): My glass! — menagerie. . . . *(She covers her face and turns away.)*

But Amanda is still stunned and stupefied by the "ugly witch" so that she barely notices this occurrence. Now she recovers her speech.

Amanda (in an awful voice): I won't speak to you — until you apologize! *(She crosses through portieres and draws them together behind her. Tom is left with Laura. Laura clings weakly to the mantel with her face averted. Tom stares at her stupidly for a moment. Then he crosses to shelf. Drops awkwardly to his knees to collect the fallen glass, glancing at Laura as if he would speak but couldn't.)*

"The Glass Menagerie" steals in as
(The scene dims out.)

SCENE IV

The interior is dark. Faint light in the alley.

A deep-voiced bell in a church is tolling the hour of five as the scene commences.

Tom appears at the top of the alley. After each solemn boom of the bell in the tower, he shakes a little noise-maker or rattle as if to express the tiny spasm of man in contrast to the sustained power and dignity of the Almighty. This and the unsteadiness of his advance make it evident that he has been drinking.

As he climbs the few steps to the fire-escape landing light steals up inside. Laura appears in night-dress, observing Tom's empty bed in the front room.

Tom fishes in his pockets for the door-key, removing a motley assortment of articles in the search, including a perfect shower of movie-ticket stubs and an empty bottle. At last he finds the key, but just as he is about to insert it, it slips from his fingers. He strikes a match and crouches below the door.

Tom (bitterly): One crack — and it falls through!

Laura opens the door.

Laura: Tom! Tom, what are you doing?
Tom: Looking for a door-key.
Laura: Where have you been all this time?
Tom: I have been to the movies.
Laura: All this time at the movies?

Tom: There was a very long program. There was a Garbo picture and a Mickey Mouse and a travelogue and a newsreel and a preview of coming attractions. And there was an organ solo and a collection for the milk-fund — simultaneously — which ended up in a terrible fight between a fat lady and an usher!

Laura (innocently): Did you have to stay through everything?

Tom: Of course! And, oh, I forgot! There was a big stage show! The headliner on this stage show was Malvolio the Magician. He performed wonderful tricks, many of them, such as pouring water back and forth between pitchers. First it turned to wine and then it turned to beer and then it turned to whiskey. I know it was whiskey it finally turned into because he needed somebody to come up out of the audience to help him, and I came up — both shows! It was Kentucky Straight Bourbon. A very generous fellow, he gave souvenirs. (*He pulls from his back pocket a shimmering rainbow-colored scarf.*) He gave me this. This is his magic scarf. You can have it, Laura. You wave it over a canary cage and you get a bowl of gold-fish. You wave it over the gold-fish bowl and they fly away canaries. . . . But the wonderfullest trick of all was the coffin trick. We nailed him into a coffin and he got out of the coffin without removing one nail. (*He has come inside.*) There is a trick that would come in handy for me — get me out of this 2 by 4 situation! (*Flops onto bed and starts removing shoes.*)

Laura: Tom — Shhh!

Tom: What you shushing me for?

Laura: You'll wake up Mother.

Tom: Goody, goody! Pay 'er back for all those "Rise an' Shines." (*Lies down, groaning.*) You know it don't take much intelligence to get yourself into a nailed-up coffin, Laura. But who in hell ever got himself out of one without removing one nail?

As if in answer, the father's grinning photograph lights up.
(*Scene dims out.*)
Immediately following: The church bell is heard striking six. At the sixth stroke the alarm clock goes off in Amanda's room, and after a few moments we hear her calling: "Rise and Shine! Rise and Shine! Laura, go tell your brother to rise and shine!"

Tom (sitting up slowly): I'll rise — but I won't shine.

The light increases.

Amanda: Laura, tell your brother his coffee is ready.

Laura slips into front room.

Laura: Tom! it's nearly seven. Don't make Mother nervous. (*He stares at her stupidly. Beseechingly.*) Tom, speak to Mother this morning. Make up with her, apologize, speak to her!

Tom: She won't to me. It's her that started not speaking.

Laura: If you just say you're sorry she'll start speaking.

Tom: Her not speaking — is that such a tragedy?

Laura: Please — please!

Amanda (calling from kitchenette): Laura, are you going to do what I asked you to do, or do I have to get dressed and go out myself?

Laura: Going, going — soon as I get on my coat! (*She pulls on a shapeless felt hat with nervous, jerky movement, pleadingly glancing at Tom. Rushes awkwardly for coat. The coat is one of Amanda's, inaccurately made-over, the sleeves too short for Laura.*) Butter and what else?

Amanda (entering upstage): Just butter. Tell them to charge it.

Laura: Mother, they make such faces when I do that.

Amanda: Sticks and stones may break my bones, but the expression on Mr. Garfinkel's face won't harm us! Tell your brother his coffee is getting cold.

Laura (at door): Do what I asked you, will you, will you, Tom?

He looks sullenly away.

Amanda: Laura, go now or just don't go at all!

Laura (rushing out): Going — going! (*A second later she cries out. Tom springs up and crosses to the door. Amanda rushes anxiously in. Tom opens the door.*)

Tom: Laura?

Laura: I'm all right. I slipped, but I'm all right.

Amanda (peering anxiously after her): If anyone breaks a leg on those fire-escape steps, the landlord ought to be sued for every cent he possesses! (*She shuts door. Remembers she isn't speaking and returns to other room.*)

As Tom enters listlessly for his coffee, she turns her back to him and stands rigidly facing the window on the gloomy gray vault of the areaway. Its light on her face with its aged but childish features is cruelly sharp, satirical as a Daumier print.
(Music under: "Ave Maria.")
Tom glances sheepishly but sullenly at her averted figure and slumps at the table. The coffee is scalding hot; he sips it and gasps and spits it back in the cup. At his gasp, Amanda catches her breath and half turns. Then catches herself and turns back to window.

Tom blows on his coffee, glancing sidewise at his mother. She clears her throat. Tom clears his. He starts to rise. Sinks back down again, scratches his head, clears his throat again. Amanda coughs. Tom raises his cup in both hands to blow on it, his eyes staring over the rim of it at his mother for several moments. Then he slowly sets the cup down and awkwardly and hesitantly rises from the chair.

Tom (hoarsely): Mother. I — I apologize. Mother. (*Amanda draws a quick, shuddering breath. Her face works grotesquely. She breaks into childlike tears.*) I'm sorry for what I said, for everything that I said, I didn't mean it.

Amanda (sobbingly): My devotion has made me a witch and so I make myself hateful to my children!

Tom: No, you *don't.*

Amanda: I worry so much, don't sleep, it makes me nervous!

Tom (gently): I understand that.

Amanda: I've had to put up a solitary battle all these years. But you're my right-hand bower! Don't fall down, don't fail!

Tom (gently): I try, Mother.

Amanda (with great enthusiasm): Try and you will SUCCEED! (*The notion makes her breathless.*) Why, you — you're just *full* of natural endowments! Both of my children — they're *unusual* children! Don't you think I know it? I'm so — *proud!* Happy and — feel I've — so much to be thankful for but — Promise me one thing, son!

Tom: What, Mother?

Amanda: Promise, son, you'll — never be a drunkard!

Tom (turns to her grinning): I will never be a drunkard, Mother.

Amanda: That's what frightened me so, that you'd be drinking! Eat a bowl of Purina!

Tom: Just coffee, Mother.

Amanda: Shredded wheat biscuit?

Tom: No. No, Mother, just coffee.

Amanda: You can't put in a day's work on an empty stomach. You've got ten minutes — don't gulp! Drinking too-hot liquids makes cancer of the stomach. . . . Put cream in.

Tom: No, thank you.

Amanda: To cool it.

Tom: No! No, thank you, I want it back.

Amanda: I know, but it's not good for you. We have to do all that we can to build ourselves up. In these trying times we live in, all that we have to cling to is — each other. . . . That's why it's so important to — Tom, I — I sent out your sister so I could discuss something with you. If you hadn't spoken I would have spoken to you. (*Sits down.*)

Tom (gently): What is it, Mother, that you want to discuss?
Amanda: Laura!

Tom puts his cup down slowly.
(Legend on screen: "Laura.")
(Music: "The Glass Menagerie.")

Tom: — Oh. — Laura . . .
Amanda (touching his sleeve): You know how Laura is. So quiet but — still water runs deep! She notices things and I think she — broods about them. (*Tom looks up.*) A few days ago I came in and she was crying.
Tom: What about?
Amanda: You.
Tom: Me?
Amanda: She has an idea that you're not happy here.
Tom: What gave her that idea?
Amanda: What gives her any idea? However, you do act strangely. I — I'm not criticizing, understand *that!* I know your ambitions do not lie in the warehouse, that like everybody in the whole wide world — you've had to — make sacrifices, but — Tom — Tom — life's not easy, it calls for — Spartan endurance! There's so many things in my heart that I cannot describe to you! I've never told you but I — *loved* your father. . . .
Tom (gently): I know that, Mother.
Amanda: And you — when I see you taking after his ways! Staying out late — and — well, you *had* been drinking the night you were in that — terrifying condition! Laura says that you hate the apartment and that you go out nights to get away from it! Is that true, Tom?
Tom: No. You say there's so much in your heart that you can't describe to me. That's true of me, too. There's so much in my heart that I can't describe to *you!* So let's respect each other's —
Amanda: But, why — *why*, Tom — are you always so *restless?* Where do you go to, nights?
Tom: I — go to the movies.
Amanda: Why do you go to the movies so much, Tom?
Tom: I go to the movies because — I like adventure. Adventure is something I don't have much of at work, so I go to the movies.
Amanda: But, Tom, you go to the movies *entirely too much!*
Tom: I like a lot of adventure.

*Amanda looks baffled, then hurt. As the familiar inquisition resumes he becomes
hard and impatient again. Amanda slips back into her querulous attitude toward
him.*

(Image on screen: Sailing vessel with Jolly Roger.)

Amanda: Most young men find adventure in their careers.

Tom: Then most young men are not employed in a warehouse.

Amanda: The world is full of young men employed in warehouses
and offices and factories.

Tom: Do all of them find adventure in their careers?

Amanda: They do or they do without it! Not everybody has a craze
for adventure.

Tom: Man is by instinct a lover, a hunter, a fighter, and none of
those instincts are given much play at the warehouse!

Amanda: Man is by instinct! Don't quote instinct to me! Instinct is
something that people have got away from! It belongs to
animals! Christian adults don't want it!

Tom: What do Christian adults want, then, Mother?

Amanda: Superior things! Things of the mind and the spirit! Only
animals have to satisfy instincts! Surely your aims are somewhat higher than theirs! Than monkeys — pigs —

Tom: I reckon they're not.

Amanda: You're joking. However, that isn't what I wanted to discuss.

Tom (rising): I haven't much time.

Amanda (pushing his shoulders): Sit down.

Tom: You want me to punch in red at the warehouse, Mother?

Amanda: You have five minutes. I want to talk about Laura.

(Legend: "Plans and provisions.")

Tom: All right! What about Laura?

Amanda: We have to be making plans and provisions for her.
She's older than you, two years, and nothing has happened.
She just drifts along doing nothing. It frightens me terribly
how she just drifts along.

Tom: I guess she's the type that people call home girls.

Amanda: There's no such type, and if there is, it's a pity! That is
unless the home is hers, with a husband!

Tom: What?

Amanda: Oh, I can see the handwriting on the wall as plain as I
see the nose in front of my face! It's terrifying! More and
more you remind me of your father! He was out all hours
without explanation — Then *left! Goodbye!* And me with the
bag to hold. I saw that letter you got from the Merchant

Marine. I know what you're dreaming of. I'm not standing here blindfolded. Very well, then. Then *do* it! But not till there's somebody to take your place.

Tom: What do you mean?

Amanda: I mean that as soon as Laura has got somebody to take care of her, married, a home of her own, independent — why, then you'll be free to go wherever you please, on land, on sea, whichever way the wind blows! But until that time you've got to look out for your sister. I don't say me because I'm old and don't matter! I say for your sister because she's young and dependent. I put her in business college — a dismal failure! Frightened her so it made her sick to her stomach. I took her over to the Young People's League at the church. Another fiasco. She spoke to nobody, nobody spoke to her. Now all she does is fool with those pieces of glass and play those worn-out records. What kind of a life is that for a girl to lead!

Tom: What can I do about it?

Amanda: Overcome selfishness! Self, self, self is all that you ever think of! (*Tom springs up and crosses to get his coat. It is ugly and bulky. He pulls on a cap with earmuffs.*) Where is your muffler? Put your wool muffler on! (*He snatches it angrily from the closet and tosses it around his neck and pulls both ends tight.*) Tom! I haven't said what I had in mind to ask you.

Tom: I'm too late to —

Amanda (catching his arms — very importunately. Then shyly): Down at the warehouse, aren't there some — nice young men?

Tom: No!

Amanda: There *must* be — *some.*

Tom: Mother —

Gesture.

Amanda: Find out one that's clean-living — doesn't drink and — ask him out for sister!

Tom: What?

Amanda: For *sister!* To *meet!* Get *acquainted!*

Tom (stamping to door): Oh, my *go-osh!*

Amanda: Will you? (*He opens door. Imploringly.*) Will you? (*He starts down.*) Will you? *Will* you, dear?

Tom (calling back): YES!

Amanda close the door hesitantly and with a troubled but faintly hopeful expression.
(Screen image: Glamour magazine cover.)
Spot Amanda at phone.

Amanda: Ella Cartwright? This is Amanda Wingfield! How are you, honey? How is that kidney condition? (*Count five.*) Horrors! (*Count five.*) You're a Christian martyr, yes, honey, that's what you are, a Christian martyr! Well, I just happened to notice in my little red book that your subscription to the *Companion* has just run out! I knew that you wouldn't want to miss out on the wonderful serial starting in this new issue. It's by Bessie Mae Hopper, the first thing she's written since *Honeymoon for Three.* Wasn't that a strange and interesting story? Well, this one is even lovelier, I believe. It has a sophisticated society background. It's all about the horsey set on Long Island!

(*Fade out.*)

SCENE V

(*Legend on screen: "Annunciation."*) *Fade with music.*
    It is early dusk of a spring evening. Supper has just been finished in the Wingfield apartment. Amanda and Laura in light colored dresses are removing dishes from the table, in the upstage area, which is shadowy, their movements formalized almost as a dance or ritual, their moving forms as pale and silent as moths.
    Tom, in white shirt and trousers, rises from the table and crosses toward the fire-escape.

Amanda (as he passes her): Son, will you do me a favor?
Tom: What?
Amanda: Comb your hair! You look so pretty when your hair is combed! (*Tom slouches on sofa with evening paper. Enormous caption "Franco Triumphs."*) There is only one respect in which I would like you to emulate your father.
Tom: What respect is that?
Amanda: The care he always took of his appearance. He never allowed himself to look untidy. (*He throws down the paper and crosses to fire-escape.*) Where are you going?
Tom: I'm going out to smoke.
Amanda: You smoke too much. A pack a day at fifteen cents a pack. How much would that amount to in a month? Thirty times fifteen is how much, Tom? Figure it out and you will be astounded at what you could save. Enough to give you a night-school course in accounting at Washington U! Just think what a wonderful thing that would be for you, son!

Tom is unmoved by the thought.

Tom: I'd rather smoke. (*He steps out on landing, letting the screen door slam.*)

Amanda (sharply): I know! That's the tragedy of it. . . . (*Alone, she turns to look at her husband's picture.*)

(*Dance music: "All the World Is Waiting for the Sunrise!"*)

Tom (to the audience): Across the alley from us was the Paradise Dance Hall. On evenings in spring the windows and doors were open and the music came outdoors. Sometimes the lights were turned out except for a large glass sphere that hung from the ceiling. It would turn slowly about and filter the dusk with delicate rainbow colors. Then the orchestra played a waltz or a tango, something that had a slow and sensuous rhythm. Couples would come outside, to the relative privacy of the alley. You could see them kissing behind ash-pits and telephone poles. This was the compensation for lives that passed like mine, without any change or adventure. Adventure and change were imminent in this year. They were waiting around the corner for all these kids. Suspended in the mist over the Berchtesgaden, caught in the folds of Chamberlain's umbrella — In Spain there was Guernica! But here there was only hot swing music and liquor, dance halls, bars, and movies, and sex that hung in the gloom like a chandelier and flooded the world with brief, deceptive rainbows. . . . All the world was waiting for bombardments!

Amanda turns from the picture and comes outside.

Amanda (sighing): A fire-escape landing's a poor excuse for a porch. (*She spreads a newspaper on a step and sits down, gracefully and demurely as if she were settling into a swing on a Mississippi veranda.*) What are you looking at?

Tom: The moon.

Amanda: Is there a moon this evening?

Tom: It's rising over Garfinkel's Delicatessen.

Amanda: So it is! A little silver slipper of a moon. Have you made a wish on it yet?

Tom: Um-hum.

Amanda: What did you wish for?

Tom: That's a secret.

Amanda: A secret, huh? Well, I won't tell mine either. I will be just as mysterious as you.

Tom: I bet I can guess what yours is.

Amanda: Is my head so transparent?

Tom: You're not a sphinx.

Amanda: No, I don't have secrets. I'll tell you what I wished for on the moon. Success and happiness for my precious children! I wish for that whenever there's a moon, and when there isn't a moon, I wish for it, too.

Tom: I thought perhaps you wished for a gentleman caller.

Amanda: Why do you say that?

Tom: Don't you remember asking me to fetch one?

Amanda: I remember suggesting that it would be nice for your sister if you brought home some nice young man from the warehouse. I think I've made that suggestion more than once.

Tom: Yes, you have made it repeatedly.

Amanda: Well?

Tom: We are going to have one.

Amanda: What?

Tom: A gentleman caller!

(The Annunciation is celebrated with music.)
Amanda rises.
(Image on screen: Caller with bouquet.)

Amanda: You mean you have asked some nice young man to come over?

Tom: Yep. I've asked him to dinner.

Amanda: You really did?

Tom: I did!

Amanda: You did, and did he — *accept?*

Tom: He did!

Amanda: Well, well — well, well! That's — lovely!

Tom: I thought that you would be pleased.

Amanda: It's definite, then?

Tom: Very definite.

Amanda: Soon?

Tom: Very soon.

Amanda: For heaven's sake, stop putting on and tell me some things, will you?

Tom: What things do you want me to tell you?

Amanda: Naturally I would like to know when he's *coming!*

Tom: He's coming tomorrow.

Amanda: *Tomorrow?*

Tom: Yep. Tomorrow.

Amanda: But, Tom!

Tom: Yes, Mother?

Amanda: Tomorrow gives me no time!

Tom: Time for what?

Amanda: Preparations! Why didn't you phone me at once, as soon as you asked him, the minute that he accepted? Then, don't you see, I could have been getting ready!

Tom: You don't have to make any fuss.

Amanda: Oh, Tom, Tom, Tom, of course I have to make a fuss! I want things nice, not sloppy! Not thrown together. I'll certainly have to do some fast thinking, won't I?

Tom: I don't see why you have to think at all.

Amanda: You just don't know. We can't have a gentleman caller in a pig-sty! All my wedding silver has to be polished, the monogrammed table linen ought to be laundered! The windows have to be washed and fresh curtains put up. And how about clothes? We have to *wear* something, don't we?

Tom: Mother, this boy is no one to make a fuss over!

Amanda: Do you realize he's the first young man we've introduced to your sister? It's terrible, dreadful, disgraceful that poor little sister has never received a single gentleman caller! Tom, come inside! (*She opens the screen door.*)

Tom: What for?

Amanda: I want to ask you some things.

Tom: If you're going to make such a fuss, I'll call it off, I'll tell him not to come.

Amanda: You certainly won't do anything of the kind. Nothing offends people worse than broken engagements. It simply means I'll have to work like a Turk! We won't be brilliant, but we'll pass inspection. Come on inside. (*Tom follows, groaning.*) Sit down.

Tom: Any particular place you would like me to sit?

Amanda: Thank heavens I've got that new sofa! I'm also making payments on a floor lamp I'll have sent out! And put the chintz covers on, they'll brighten things up! Of course I'd hoped to have these walls re-papered. . . . What is the young man's name?

Tom: His name is O'Connor.

Amanda: That, of course, means fish — tomorrow is Friday! I'll have that salmon loaf — with Durkee's dressing! What does he do? He works at the warehouse?

Tom: Of course! How else would I —

Amanda: Tom, he — doesn't drink?

Tom: Why do you ask me that?

Amanda: Your father *did*!

Tom: Don't get started on that!

Amanda: He *does* drink, then?

Tom: Not that I know of!

Amanda: Make sure, be certain! The last thing I want for my daughter's a boy who drinks!

Tom: Aren't you being a little premature? Mr. O'Connor has not yet appeared on the scene!

Amanda: But will tomorrow. To meet your sister, and what do I know about his character? Nothing! Old maids are better off than wives of drunkards!

Tom: Oh, my God!

Amanda: Be still!

Tom (leaning forward to whisper): Lots of fellows meet girls whom they don't marry!

Amanda: Oh, talk sensibly, Tom — and don't be sarcastic! *(She has gotten a hairbrush.)*

Tom: What are you doing?

Amanda: I'm brushing that cow-lick down! What is this young man's position at the warehouse?

Tom (submitting grimly to the brush and the interrogation): This young man's position is that of a shipping clerk, Mother.

Amanda: Sounds to me like a fairly responsible job, the sort of a job *you* would be in if you just had more *get-up*. What is his salary? Have you got any idea?

Tom: I would judge it to be approximately eighty-five dollars a month.

Amanda: Well — not princely, but —

Tom: Twenty more than I make.

Amanda: Yes, how well I know! But for a family man, eighty-five dollars a month is not much more than you can just get by on. . . .

Tom: Yes, but Mr. O'Connor is not a family man.

Amanda: He might be, mightn't he? Some time in the future?

Tom: I see. Plans and provisions.

Amanda: You are the only young man that I know of who ignores the fact that the future becomes the present, the present the past, and the past turns into everlasting regret if you don't plan for it!

Tom: I will think that over and see what I can make of it.

Amanda: Don't be supercilious with your mother! Tell me some more about this — what do you call him?

Tom: James D. O'Connor. The D. is for Delaney.

Amanda: Irish on *both* sides! *Gracious!* And doesn't drink?

Tom: Shall I call him up and ask him right this minute?

Amanda: The only way to find out about those things is to make discreet inquires at the proper moment. When I was a girl in

Blue Mountain and it was suspected that a young man drank, the girl whose attentions he had been receiving, if any girl *was*, would sometimes speak to the minister of his church, or rather her father would if her father was living, and sort of feel him out on the young man's character. That is the way such things are discreetly handled to keep a young woman from making a tragic mistake!

Tom: Then how did you happen to make a tragic mistake?

Amanda: That innocent look of your father's had everyone fooled! He *smiled* — the world was *enchanted!* No girl can do worse than put herself at the mercy of a handsome appearance! I hope that Mr. O'Connor is not too good-looking.

Tom: No, he's not too good-looking. He's covered with freckles and hasn't too much of a nose.

Amanda: He's not right-down homely, though?

Tom: Not right-down homely. Just medium homely, I'd say.

Amanda: Character's what to look for in a man.

Tom: That's what I've always said, Mother.

Amanda: You've never said anything of the kind and I suspect you would never give it a thought.

Tom: Don't be suspicious of me.

Amanda: At least I hope he's the type that's up and coming.

Tom: I think he really goes in for self-improvement.

Amanda: What reason have you to think so?

Tom: He goes to night school.

Amanda (beaming): Splendid! What does he do, I mean study?

Tom: Radio engineering and public speaking!

Amanda: Then he has visions of being advanced in the world! Any young man who studies public speaking is aiming to have an executive job some day! And radio engineering? A thing for the future! Both of these facts are very illuminating. Those are the sort of things that a mother should know concerning any young man who comes to call on her daughter. Seriously or — not.

Tom: One little warning. He doesn't know about Laura. I didn't let on that we had dark ulterior motives. I just said, why don't you come have dinner with us? He said okay and that was the whole conversation.

Amanda: I bet it was! You're eloquent as an oyster. However, he'll know about Laura when he gets here. When he sees how lovely and sweet and pretty she is, he'll thank his lucky stars he was asked to dinner.

Tom: Mother, you mustn't expect too much of Laura.

Amanda: What do you mean?

Tom: Laura seems all those things to you and me because she's ours and we love her. We don't even notice she's crippled any more.

Amanda: Don't say crippled! You know that I never allow that word to be used!

Tom: But face facts, Mother. She is and — that's not all —

Amanda: What do you mean "not all"?

Tom: Laura is very different from other girls.

Amanda: I think the difference is all to her advantage.

Tom: Not quite all — in the eyes of others — strangers — she's terribly shy and lives in a world of her own and those things make her seem a little peculiar to people outside the house.

Amanda: Don't say peculiar.

Tom: Face the facts. She is.

(The dance-hall music changes to a tango that has a minor and somewhat ominous tone.)

Amanda: In what way is she peculiar — may I ask?

Tom (gently): She lives in a world of her own — a world of — little glass ornaments, Mother. . . . *(Gets up. Amanda remains holding brush, looking at him, troubled.)* She plays old phonograph records and — that's about all — *(He glances at himself in the mirror and crosses to door.)*

Amanda (sharply): Where are you going?

Tom: I'm going to the movies. *(Out screen door.)*

Amanda: Not to the movies, every night to the movies! *(Follows quickly to screen door.)* I don't believe you always go to the movies! *(He is gone. Amanda looks worriedly after him for a moment. Then vitality and optimism return and she turns from the door. Crossing to portieres.)* Laura! Laura! *(Laura answers from kitchenette.)*

Laura: Yes, Mother.

Amanda: Let those dishes go and come in front! *(Laura appears with dish towel. Gaily.)* Laura, come here and make a wish on the moon!

Laura (entering): Moon — moon?

Amanda: A little silver slipper of a moon. Look over your left shoulder, Laura, and make a wish! *(Laura looks faintly puzzled as if called out of sleep. Amanda seizes her shoulders and turns her at angle by the door.)* Now! Now, darling, wish!

Laura: What shall I wish for, Mother?

Amanda (her voice trembling and her eyes suddenly filling with tears):
Happiness! Good Fortune!

The violin rises and the stage dims out.

SCENE VI

(Image: High school hero.)

Tom: And so the following evening I brought Jim home to dinner. I had known Jim slightly in high school. In high school Jim was a hero. He had tremendous Irish good nature and vitality with the scrubbed and polished look of white chinaware. He seemed to move in a continual spotlight. He was a star in basketball, captain of the debating club, president of the senior class and the glee club, and he sang the male lead in the annual light operas. He was always running or bounding, never just walking. He seemed always at the point of defeating the law of gravity. He was shooting with such velocity through his adolescence that you would logically expect him to arrive at nothing short of the White House by the time he was thirty. But Jim apparently ran into more interference after his graduation from Soldan. His speed had definitely slowed. Six years after he left high school he was holding a job that wasn't much better than mine.

(Image: Clerk.)

He was the only one at the warehouse with whom I was on friendly terms. I was valuable to him as someone who could remember his former glory, who had seen him win basketball games and the silver cup in debating. He knew of my secret practice of retiring to a cabinet of the washroom to work on poems when business was slack in the warehouse. He called me Shakespeare. And while the other boys in the warehouse regarded me with suspicious hostility, Jim took a humorous attitude toward me. Gradually his attitude affected the others, their hostility wore off, and they also began to smile at me as people smile at an oddly fashioned dog who trots across their paths at some distance.

I knew that Jim and Laura had known each other at Soldan, and I had heard Laura speak admiringly of his voice.

I didn't know if Jim remembered her or not. In high school Laura had been as unobtrusive as Jim had been astonishing. If he did remember Laura, it was not as my sister, for when I asked him to dinner, he grinned and said, "You know, Shakespeare, I never thought of you as having folks!" He was about to discover that I did. . . .

(Light upstage.)
(Legend on screen: "The Accent of a Coming Foot.")
Friday evening. It is about five o'clock of a late spring evening which comes "scattering poems in the sky."
A delicate lemony light is in the Wingfield apartment.
Amanda has worked like a Turk in preparation for the gentleman caller. The results are astonishing. The new floor lamp with its rose-silk shade is in place, a colored paper lantern conceals the broken light fixture in the ceiling, new billowing white curtains are at the windows, chintz covers are on chairs and sofa, a pair of new sofa pillows make their initial appearance.
Open boxes and tissue paper are scattered on the floor.
Laura stands in the middle with lifted arms while Amanda crouches before her, adjusting the hem of the new dress, devout and ritualistic. The dress is colored and designed by memory. The arrangement of Laura's hair is changed; it is softer and more becoming. A fragile, unearthly prettiness has come out in Laura: she is like a piece of translucent glass touched by light, given a momentary radiance, not actual, not lasting.

Amanda (impatiently): Why are you trembling?
Laura: Mother, you've made me so nervous!
Amanda: How have I made you nervous?
Laura: By all this fuss! You make it seem so important!
Amanda: I don't understand you, Laura. You couldn't be satisfied with just sitting home, and yet whenever I try to arrange something for you, you seem to resist it. *(She gets up.)* Now take a look at yourself. No, wait! Wait just a moment — I have an idea!
Laura: What is it now?

Amanda produces two powder puffs which she wraps in handkerchiefs and stuffs in Laura's bosom.

Laura: Mother, what are you doing?
Amanda: They call them "Gay Deceivers"!
Laura: I won't wear them!
Amanda: You will!
Laura: Why should I?
Amanda: Because, to be painfully honest, your chest is flat.
Laura: You make it seem like we were setting a trap.

Amanda: All pretty girls are a trap, a pretty trap, and men expect
them to be. (*Legend: "A Pretty Trap."*) Now look at yourself,
young lady. This is the prettiest you will ever be! I've got to
fix myself now! You're going to be surprised by your mother's
appearance! (*She crosses through portieres, humming gaily.*)

Laura moves slowly to the long mirror and stares solemnly at herself.
*A wind blows the white curtains inward in a slow, graceful motion and with
a faint, sorrowful sighing.*

Amanda (offstage): It isn't dark enough yet. (*She turns slowly before
the mirror with a troubled look.*)

(*Legend on screen: "This Is My Sister: Celebrate Her with Strings!" Music.*)

Amanda (laughing, off): I'm going to show you something. I'm
going to make a spectacular appearance!
Laura: What is it, Mother?
Amanda: Possess your soul in patience — you will see! Something
I've resurrected from that old trunk! Styles haven't changed
so terribly much after all. . . . (*She parts the portieres.*) Now just
look at your mother! (*She wears a girlish frock of yellowed voile
with a blue silk sash. She carries a bunch of jonquils — the legend of
her youth is nearly revived. Feverishly.*) This is the dress in which
I led the cotillion. Won the cakewalk twice at Sunset Hill,
wore one spring to the Governor's ball in Jackson! See how I
sashayed around the ballroom, Laura? (*She raises her skirt and
does a mincing step around the room.*) I wore it on Sundays for my
gentlemen callers! I had it on the day I met your father — I
had malaria fever all that spring. The change of climate from
East Tennessee to the Delta — weakened resistance — I had
a little temperature all the time — not enough to be serious
— just enough to make me restless and giddy! Invitations
poured in — parties all over the Delta! — "Stay in bed," said
Mother, "you have fever!" — but I just wouldn't — I took
quinine but kept on going, going! — Evenings, dances! —
Afternoons, long, long rides! Picnics — lovely! — So lovely,
that country in May. — All lacy with dogwood, literally
flooded with jonquils! — That was the spring I had the craze
for jonquils. Jonquils became an absolute obsession. Mother
said, "Honey, there's no more room for jonquils." And still I
kept bringing in more jonquils. Whenever, wherever I saw
them, I'd say, "Stop! Stop! I see jonquils!" I made the young
men help me gather the jonquils! It was a joke, Amanda and
her jonquils! Finally there were no more vases to hold them,

every available space was filled with jonquils. No vases to hold them? All right, I'll hold them myself! And then I — (*She stops in front of the picture.*) (*Music.*) met your father! Malaria fever and jonquils and then — this — boy. . . . (*She switches on the rose-colored lamp.*) I hope they get here before it starts to rain. (*She crosses upstage and places the jonquils in bowl on table.*) I gave your brother a little extra change so he and Mr. O'Connor could take the service car home.

Laura (with altered look): What did you say his name was?
Amanda: O'Connor.
Laura: What is his first name?
Amanda: I don't remember. Oh, yes, I do. It was — Jim!

Laura sways slightly and catches hold of a chair.
(*Legend on screen: "Not Jim!"*)

Laura (faintly): Not — Jim!
Amanda: Yes, that was it, it was Jim! I've never known a Jim that wasn't nice!

(*Music: Ominous.*)

Laura: Are you sure his name is Jim O'Connor?
Amanda: Yes. Why?
Laura: Is he the one that Tom used to know in high school?
Amanda: He didn't say so. I think he just got to know him at the warehouse.
Laura: There was a Jim O'Connor we both knew in high school — (*Then, with effort.*) If that is the one that Tom is bringing to dinner — you'll have to excuse me, I won't come to the table.
Amanda: What sort of nonsense is this?
Laura: You asked me once if I'd ever liked a boy. Don't you re- member I showed you this boy's picture?
Amanda: You mean the boy you showed me in the year-book?
Laura: Yes, that boy.
Amanda: Laura, Laura, were you in love with that boy?
Laura: I don't know, Mother. All I know is I couldn't sit at the table if it was him!
Amanda: It won't be him! It isn't the least bit likely. But whether it is or not, you will come to the table. You will not be excused.
Laura: I'll have to be, Mother.
Amanda: I don't intend to humor your silliness, Laura. I've had too much from you and your brother, both! So just sit down and compose yourself till they come. Tom has forgotten his key so you'll have to let them in, when they arrive.

Laura (panicky): Oh, Mother — *you* answer the door!

Amanda (lightly): I'll be in the kitchen — busy!

Laura: Oh, Mother, please answer the door, don't make me do it!

Amanda (crossing into kitchenette): I've got to fix the dressing for the salmon. Fuss, fuss — silliness! — over a gentleman caller!

Door swings shut. Laura is left alone.
> *(Legend: "Terror!")*
> *She utters a low moan and turns off the lamp — sits stiffly on the edge of the sofa, knotting her fingers together.*
> *(Legend on screen: "The Opening of a Door!")*
> *Tom and Jim appear on the fire-escape steps and climb to landing. Hearing their approach, Laura rises with a panicky gesture. She retreats to the portieres.*
> *The doorbell. Laura catches her breath and touches her throat. Low drums.*

Amanda (calling): Laura, sweetheart! The door!

Laura stares at it without moving.

Jim: I think we just beat the rain.

Tom: Uh-huh. *(He rings again, nervously. Jim whistles and fishes for a cigarette.)*

Amanda (very, very gaily): Laura, that is your brother and Mr. O'Connor! Will you let them in, darling?

Laura crosses toward kitchenette door.

Laura (breathlessly): Mother — you go to the door!

Amanda steps out of kitchenette and stares furiously at Laura. She points imperiously at the door.

Laura: Please, please!

Amanda (in a fierce whisper): What is the matter with you, you silly thing?

Laura (desperately): Please, you answer it, *please!*

Amanda: I told you I wasn't going to humor you, Laura. Why have you chosen this moment to lose your mind?

Laura: Please, please, please, you go!

Amanda: You'll have to go to the door because I can't!

Laura (despairingly): I can't either!

Amanda: Why?

Laura: I'm *sick!*

Amanda: I'm sick, too — of your nonsense! Why can't you and your brother be normal people? Fantastic whims and behavior! *(Tom gives a long ring.)* Preposterous goings on! Can you give me one reason — *(Calls out lyrically.)* COMING! JUST ONE

SECOND! — why should you be afraid to open a door? Now you answer it, Laura!

Laura: Oh, oh, oh . . . (*She returns through the portieres. Darts to the Victrola and winds it frantically and turns it on.*)

Amanda: Laura Wingfield, you march right to that door!

Laura: Yes — yes, Mother!

A faraway, scratchy rendition of "Dardanella" softens the air and gives her strength to move through it. She slips to the door and draws it cautiously open. Tom enters with the caller, Jim O'Connor.

Tom: Laura, this is Jim. Jim, this is my sister, Laura.

Jim (stepping inside): I didn't know that Shakespeare had a sister!

Laura (retreating stiff and trembling from the door): How — how do you do?

Jim (heartily extending his hand): Okay!

Laura touches it hesitantly with hers.

Jim: Your hand's *cold*, Laura!

Laura: Yes, well — I've been playing the Victrola . . .

Jim: Must have been playing classical music on it! You ought to play a little hot swing music to warm you up!

Laura: Excuse me — I haven't finished playing the Victrola . . .

She turns awkwardly and hurries into the front room. She pauses a second by the Victrola. Then catches her breath and darts through the portieres like a frightened deer.

Jim (grinning): What was the matter?

Tom: Oh — with Laura? Laura is — terribly shy.

Jim: Shy, huh? It's unusual to meet a shy girl nowadays. I don't believe you ever mentioned you had a sister.

Tom: Well, now you know. I have one. Here is the *Post Dispatch.* You want a piece of it?

Jim: Uh-huh.

Tom: What piece? The comics?

Jim: Sports! (*Glances at it.*) Ole Dizzy Dean is on his bad behavior.

Tom (disinterest): Yeah? (*Lights cigarette and crosses back to fire-escape door.*)

Jim: Where are *you* going?

Tom: I'm going out on the terrace.

Jim (goes after him): You know, Shakespeare — I'm going to sell you a bill of goods!

Tom: What goods?

Jim: A course I'm taking.

Tom: Huh?

Jim: In public speaking! You and me, we're not the warehouse type.

Tom: Thanks — that's good news. But what has public speaking got to do with it?

Jim: It fits you for — executive positions!

Tom: Awww.

Jim: I tell you it's done a helluva lot for me.

(Image: Executive at desk.)

Tom: In what respect?

Jim: In every! Ask yourself what is the difference between you an' me and men in the office down front? Brains? — No! — Ability? — No! Then what? Just one little thing —

Tom: What is that one little thing?

Jim: Primarily it amounts to — social poise! Being able to square up to people and hold your own on any social level!

Amanda (offstage): Tom?

Tom: Yes, Mother?

Amanda: Is that you and Mr. O'Connor.

Tom: Yes, Mother.

Amanda: Well, you just make yourselves comfortable in there.

Tom: Yes, Mother.

Amanda: Ask Mr. O'Connor if he would like to wash his hands.

Jim: Aw — no — no — thank you — I took care of that at the warehouse. Tom —

Tom: Yes?

Jim: Mr. Mendoza was speaking to me about you.

Tom: Favorably?

Jim: What do you think?

Tom: Well —

Jim: You're going to be out of a job if you don't wake up.

Tom: I am waking up —

Jim: You show no signs.

Tom: The signs are interior.

(Image on screen: The sailing vessel with Jolly Roger again.)

Tom: I'm planning to change. (*He leans over the rail speaking with quiet exhilaration. The incandescent marquees and signs of the first-run movie houses light his face from across the alley. He looks like a voyager.*) I'm right at the point of committing myself to a future that doesn't include the warehouse and Mr. Mendoza or even a night-school course in public speaking.

Jim: What are you gassing about?
Tom: I'm tired of the movies.
Jim: Movies!
Tom: Yes, movies! Look at them — (*A wave toward the marvels of Grand Avenue.*) All of those glamorous people — having adventures — hogging it all, gobbling the whole thing up! You know what happens? People go to the *movies* instead of *moving!* Hollywood characters are supposed to have all the adventures for everybody in America, while everybody in America sits in a dark room and watches them have them! Yes, until there's a war. That's when adventure becomes available to the masses! *Everyone's* dish, not only Gable's! Then the people in the dark room come out of the dark room to have some adventures themselves — Goody, goody — It's our turn now, to go to the South Sea Island — to make a safari — to be exotic, far-off — But I'm not patient. I don't want to wait till then. I'm tired of the *movies* and I am *about* to *move!*
Jim (incredulously): Move?
Tom: Yes.
Jim: When?
Tom: Soon!
Jim: Where? Where?

(*Theme three: Music seems to answer the question, while Tom thinks it over. He searches among his pockets.*)

Tom: I'm starting to boil inside. I know I seem dreamy, but inside — well, I'm boiling! Whenever I pick up a shoe, I shudder a little thinking how short life is and what I am doing! — Whatever that means. I know it doesn't mean shoes — except as something to wear on a traveler's feet! (*Finds paper.*) Look —
Jim: What?
Tom: I'm a member.
Jim (reading): The Union of Merchant Seamen.
Tom: I paid my dues this month, instead of the light bill.
Jim: You will regret it when they turn the lights off.
Tom: I won't be here.
Jim: How about your mother?
Tom: I'm like my father. The bastard son of a bastard! See how he grins? And he's been absent going on sixteen years!
Jim: You're just talking, you drip. How does your mother feel about it?

Tom: Shhh — Here comes Mother! Mother is not acquainted with my plans!

Amanda (enters portieres): Where are you all?

Tom: On the terrace, Mother.

They start inside. She advances to them. Tom is distinctly shocked at her appearance. Even Jim blinks a little. He is making his first contact with girlish Southern vivacity and in spite of the night-school course in public speaking is somewhat thrown off the beam by the unexpected outlay of social charm.

Certain responses are attempted by Jim but are swept aside by Amanda's gay laughter and chatter. Tom is embarrassed but after the first shock Jim reacts very warmly. Grins and chuckles, is altogether won over.

(Image: Amanda as a girl.)

Amanda (coyly smiling, shaking her girlish ringlets): Well, well, well, so this is Mr. O'Connor. Introductions entirely unnecessary. I've heard so much about you from my boy. I finally said to him, Tom — good gracious! — why don't you bring this paragon to supper? I'd like to meet this nice young man at the warehouse! — Instead of just hearing him sing your praises so much! I don't know why my son is so stand-offish — that's not Southern behavior! Let's sit down and — I think we could stand a little more air in here! Tom, leave the door open. I felt a nice fresh breeze a moment ago. Where has it gone? Mmm, so warm already! And not quite summer, even. We're going to burn up when summer really gets started. However, we're having — we're having a very light supper. I think light things are better fo' this time of year. The same as light clothes are. Light clothes an' light food are what warm weather calls fo'. You know our blood gets so thick during th' winter — it takes a while fo' us to *adjust* ou'selves! — when the season changes. . . . It's come so quick this year. I wasn't prepared. All of a sudden — heavens! Already summer! — I ran to the trunk an' pulled out this light dress — Terribly old! Historical almost! But feels so good — so good an co-ol, y'know. . . .

Tom: Mother —

Amanda: Yes, honey?

Tom: How about — supper?

Amanda: Honey, you go ask Sister if supper is ready! You know that Sister is in full charge of supper! Tell her you hungry boys are waiting for it. *(To Jim.)* Have you met Laura?

Jim: She —

Amanda: Let you in? Oh, good, you've met already! It's rare for a girl as sweet an' pretty as Laura to be domestic! But Laura is, thank heavens, not only pretty but also very domestic. I'm not at all. I never was a bit. I never could make a thing but angel-food cake. Well, in the South we had so many servants. Gone, gone, gone. All vestiges of gracious living! Gone completely! I wasn't prepared for what the future brought me. All of my gentlemen callers were sons of planters and so of course I assumed that I would be married to one and raise my family on a large piece of land with plenty of servants. But man proposes — and woman accepts the proposal! — To vary that old, old saying a little bit — I married no planter! I married a man who worked for the telephone company! — that gallantly smiling gentleman over there! (*Points to the picture.*) A telephone man who — fell in love with long dis-tance! — Now he travels and I don't even know where! — But what am I going on for about my — tribulations! Tell me yours — I hope you don't have any! Tom?

Tom (returning): Yes, Mother?

Amanda: Is supper nearly ready?

Tom: It looks to me like supper is on the table.

Amanda: Let me look — (*She rises prettily and looks through por-tieres.*) Oh, lovely — But where is Sister?

Tom: Laura is not feeling well and she says that she thinks she'd better not come to the table.

Amanda: What? — Nonsense! — Laura? Oh, Laura!

Laura (offstage, faintly): Yes, Mother.

Amanda: You really must come to the table. We won't be seated until you come to the table! Come in, Mr. O'Connor. You sit over there and I'll — Laura? Laura Wingfield! You're keep-ing us waiting, honey! We can't say grace until you come to the table!

The back door is pushed weakly open and Laura comes in. She is obviously quite faint, her lips trembling, her eyes wide and staring. She moves unsteadily toward the table.

(Legend: "Terror!")

Outside a summer storm is coming abruptly. The white curtains billow inward at the windows and there is a sorrowful murmur and deep blue dusk.

Laura suddenly stumbles — She catches at a chair with a faint moan.

Tom: Laura!

Amanda: Laura! (*There is a clap of thunder.*) (*Legend: "Ah!"*) (*Despair-ingly.*) Why, Laura, you *are* sick, darling! Tom, help your sister into the living room, dear! Sit in the living room, Laura — rest on the sofa. Well! (*To the gentleman caller.*) Standing over the hot stove made her ill! — I told her that it was just too warm this evening, but — (*Tom comes back in. Laura is on the sofa.*) Is Laura all right now?

Tom: Yes.

Amanda: What is that? Rain? A nice cool rain has come up! (*She gives the gentleman caller a frightened look.*) I think we may — have grace — now . . . (*Tom looks at her stupidly.*) Tom, honey — you say grace!

Tom: Oh . . . "For these and all thy mercies — " (*They bow their heads, Amanda stealing a nervous glance at Jim. In the living room Laura, stretched on the sofa, clenches her hand to her lips, to hold back a shuddering sob.*) God's Holy Name be praised —

(*The scene dims out.*)

SCENE VII

A Souvenir

Half an hour later. Dinner is just being finished in the upstage area, which is concealed by the drawn portieres.

As the curtain rises Laura is still huddled upon the sofa, her feet drawn under her, her head resting on a pale blue pillow, her eyes wide and mysteriously watchful. The new floor lamp with its shade of rose-colored silk gives a soft, becoming light to her face, bringing out the fragile, unearthly prettiness which usually escapes attention. There is a steady murmur of rain, but it is slackening and stops soon after the scene begins; the air outside becomes pale and luminous as the moon breaks out.

A moment after the curtain rises, the lights in both rooms flicker and go out.

Jim: Hey, there, Mr. Light Bulb!

Amanda laughs nervously.
(*Legend: "Suspension of a Public Service."*)

Amanda: Where was Moses when the lights went out? Ha-ha. Do you know the answer to that one, Mr. O'Connor?

Jim: No, Ma'am, what's the answer?

Amanda: In the dark! (*Jim laughs appreciatively.*) Everybody sit still. I'll light the candles. Isn't it lucky we have them on the table? Where's a match? Which of you gentlemen can provide a match?

Jim: Here.

Amanda: Thank you, sir.

Jim: Not at all, Ma'am!

Amanda: I guess the fuse has burnt out. Mr. O'Connor, can you tell a burnt-out fuse? I know I can't and Tom is a total loss when it comes to mechanics. (*Sound: Getting up: Voices recede a little to kitchenette.*) Oh, be careful you don't bump into something. We don't want our gentleman caller to break his neck. Now wouldn't that be a fine howdy-do?

Jim: Ha-ha! Where is the fuse-box?

Amanda: Right here next to the stove. Can you see anything?

Jim: Just a minute.

Amanda: Isn't electricity a mysterious thing? Wasn't it Benjamin Franklin who tied a key to a kite? We live in such a mysterious universe, don't we? Some people say that science clears up all the mysteries for us. In my opinion it only creates more! Have you found it yet?

Jim: No, Ma'am. All these fuses look okay to me.

Amanda: Tom!

Tom: Yes, Mother?

Amanda: That light bill I gave you several days ago. The one I told you we got the notices about?

Tom: Oh. — Yeah.

(Legend: "Ha!")

Amanda: You didn't neglect to pay it by any chance?

Tom: Why, I —

Amanda: Didn't! I might have known it!

Jim: Shakespeare probably wrote a poem on that light bill, Mrs. Wingfield.

Amanda: I might have known better than to trust him with it! There's such a high price for negligence in this world!

Jim: Maybe the poem will win a ten-dollar prize.

Amanda: We'll just have to spend the remainder of the evening in the nineteenth century, before Mr. Edison made the Mazda lamp!

Jim: Candlelight is my favorite kind of light.

Amanda: That shows you're romantic! But that's no excuse for Tom. Well, we got through dinner. Very considerate of them to let us get through dinner before they plunged us into everlasting darkness, wasn't it, Mr. O'Connor?

Jim: Ha-ha!

Amanda: Tom, as a penalty for your carelessness you can help me with the dishes.

Jim: Let me give you a hand.

Amanda: Indeed you will not!

Jim: I ought to be good for something.

Amanda: Good for something? (*Her tone is rhapsodic.*) *You?* Why,
Mr. O'Connor, nobody, *nobody's* given me this much entertainment in years — as you have!

Jim: Aw, now, Mrs. Wingfield!

Amanda: I'm not exaggerating, not one bit! But Sister is all by her
lonesome. You go keep her company in the parlor! I'll give
you this lovely old candelabrum that used to be on the altar
at the church of the Heavenly Rest. It was melted a little out
of shape when the church burnt down. Lightning struck it one
spring. Gypsy Jones was holding a revival at the time and he
intimated that the church was destroyed because the Episco-
palians gave card parties.

Jim: Ha-ha.

Amanda: And how about coaxing Sister to drink a little wine? I
think it would be good for her! Can you carry both at once?

Jim: Sure. I'm Superman!

Amanda: Now, Thomas, get into this apron!

*The door of kitchenette swings closed on Amanda's gay laughter; the flickering
light approaches the portieres.*

*Laura sits up nervously as he enters. Her speech at first is low and breathless
from the almost intolerable strain of being alone with a stranger.*

(Legend: "I Don't Suppose You Remember Me at All!")

*In her first speeches in this scene, before Jim's warmth overcomes her
paralyzing shyness, Laura's voice is thin and breathless as though she has run up
a steep flight of stairs.*

*Jim's attitude is gently humorous. In playing this scene it should be stressed
that while the incident is apparently unimportant, it is to Laura the climax of her
secret life.*

Jim: Hello, there, Laura.

Laura (faintly): Hello. (*She clears her throat.*)

Jim: How are you feeling now? Better?

Laura: Yes. Yes, thank you.

Jim: This is for you. A little dandelion wine. (*He extends it toward
her with extravagant gallantry.*)

Laura: Thank you.

Jim: Drink it — but don't get drunk! (*He laughs heartily. Laura
takes the glass uncertainly; laughs shyly.*) Where shall I set the
candles?

Laura: Oh — oh, anywhere . . .

Jim: How about here on the floor? Any objections?

Laura: No.

Jim: I'll spread a newspaper under to catch the drippings. I like to sit on the floor. Mind if I do?

Laura: Oh, no.

Jim: Give me a pillow?

Laura: What?

Jim: A pillow!

Laura: Oh . . . (*Hands him one quickly.*)

Jim: How about you? Don't you like to sit on the floor?

Laura: Oh — yes.

Jim: Why don't you, then?

Laura: I — will.

Jim: Take a pillow! (*Laura does. Sits on the other side of the candela-brum. Jim crosses his legs and smiles engagingly at her.*) I can't hardly see you sitting way over there.

Laura: I can — see you.

Jim: I know, but that's not fair, I'm in the limelight. (*Laura moves her pillow closer.*) Good! Now I can see you! Comfortable?

Laura: Yes.

Jim: So am I. Comfortable as a cow. Will you have some gum?

Laura: No, thank you.

Jim: I think that I will indulge, with your permission. (*Musingly unwraps it and holds it up.*) Think of the fortune made by the guy that invented the first piece of chewing gum. Amazing, huh? The Wrigley Building is one of the sights of Chicago. — I saw it summer before last when I went up to the Century of Progress. Did you take in the Century of Progress?

Laura: No, I didn't.

Jim: Well, it was quite a wonderful exposition. What impressed me most was the Hall of Science. Gives you an idea of what the future will be in America, even more wonderful than the present time is! (*Pause. Smiling at her.*) Your brother tells me you're shy. Is that right, Laura?

Laura: I — don't know.

Jim: I judge you to be an old-fashioned type of girl. Well, I think that's a pretty good type to be. Hope you don't think I'm being too personal — do you?

Laura (hastily, out of embarrassment): I believe I *will* take a piece of gum, if you — don't mind. (*Clearing her throat.*) Mr. O'Connor, have you — kept up with your singing?

Jim: Singing? Me?

Laura: Yes. I remember what a beautiful voice you had.

Jim: When did you hear me sing?

(*Voice offstage in the pause.*)

Voice (offstage): O blow, ye winds, heigh-ho,
A-roving I will go!
I'm off to my love
With a boxing glove —
Ten thousand miles away!

Jim: You say you've heard me sing?

Laura: Oh, yes! Yes, very often . . . I — don't suppose you remember me — at all?

Jim (smiling doubtfully): You know I have an idea I've seen you before. I had that idea soon as you opened the door. It seemed almost like I was about to remember your name. But the name that I started to call you — wasn't a name! And so I stopped myself before I said it.

Laura: Wasn't it — Blue Roses?

Jim (springs up, grinning): Blue Roses! My gosh, yes — Blue Roses! That's what I had on my tongue when you opened the door! Isn't it funny what tricks your memory plays? I didn't connect you with the high school somehow or other. But that's where it was; it was high school. I didn't even know you were Shakespeare's sister! Gosh, I'm sorry.

Laura: I didn't expect you to. You — barely knew me!

Jim: But we did have a speaking acquaintance, huh?

Laura: Yes, we — spoke to each other.

Jim: When did you recognize me?

Laura: Oh, right away!

Jim: Soon as I came in the door?

Laura: When I heard your name I thought it was probably you. I knew that Tom used to know you a little in high school. So when you came in the door — Well, then I was — sure.

Jim: Why didn't you *say* something, then?

Laura (breathlessly): I didn't know what to say, I was — too surprised!

Jim: For goodness' sakes! You know, this sure is funny!

Laura: Yes! Yes, isn't it, though . . .

Jim: Didn't we have a class in something together?

Laura: Yes, we did.

Jim: What class was that?

Laura: It was — singing — Chorus!

Jim: Aw!

Laura: I sat across the aisle from you in the Aud.

Jim: Aw.

Laura: Mondays, Wednesdays, and Fridays.

Jim: Now I remember — you always came in late.

Laura: Yes, it was so hard for me, getting upstairs. I had that brace on my leg — it clumped so loud!

Jim: I never heard any clumping.

Laura (wincing in the recollection): To me it sounded like — thunder!

Jim: Well, well, well. I never even noticed.

Laura: And everybody was seated before I came in. I had to walk in front of all those people. My seat was in the back row. I had to go clumping all the way up the aisle with everyone watching!

Jim: You shouldn't have been self-conscious.

Laura: I know, but I was. It was always such a relief when the singing started.

Jim: Aw, yes, I've placed you now! I used to call you Blue Roses. How was it that I got started calling you that?

Laura: I was out of school a little while with pleurosis. When I came back you asked me what was the matter. I said I had pleurosis — you thought I said Blue Roses. That's what you always called me after that!

Jim: I hope you didn't mind.

Laura: Oh, no — I liked it. You see, I wasn't acquainted with many — people. . . .

Jim: As I remember you sort of stuck by yourself.

Laura: I — I — never had much luck at — making friends.

Jim: I don't see why you wouldn't.

Laura: Well, I — started out badly.

Jim: You mean being —

Laura: Yes, it sort of — stood between me —

Jim: You shouldn't have let it!

Laura: I know, but it did, and —

Jim: You were shy with people!

Laura: I tried not to be but never could —

Jim: Overcome it?

Laura: No, I — I never could!

Jim: I guess being shy is something you have to work out of kind of gradually.

Laura (sorrowfully): Yes — I guess it —

Jim: Takes time!

Laura: Yes —

Jim: People are not so dreadful when you know them. That's what you have to remember! And everybody has problems, not just you, but practically everybody has got some problems. You think of yourself as having the only problems, as being the only one who is disappointed. But just look around you and you will see lots of people as disappointed as you are. For instance, I hoped when I was going to high school that I would be further along at this time, six years later, than I am now — You remember that wonderful write-up I had in *The Torch?*

Laura: Yes! (*She rises and crosses to table.*)

Jim: It said I was bound to succeed in anything I went into! (*Laura returns with the annual.*) Holy Jeez! *The Torch!* (*He accepts it reverently. They smile across it with mutual wonder. Laura crouches beside him and they begin to turn through it. Laura's shyness is dissolving in his warmth.*)

Laura: Here you are in *Pirates of Penzance!*

Jim (wistfully): I sang the baritone lead in that operetta.

Laura (rapidly): So — beautifully!

Jim (protesting): Aw —

Laura: Yes, yes — beautifully — beautifully!

Jim: You heard me?

Laura: All three times!

Jim: No!

Laura: Yes!

Jim: All three performances?

Laura (looking down): Yes.

Jim: Why?

Laura: I — wanted to ask you to — autograph my program.

Jim: Why didn't you ask me to?

Laura: You were always surrounded by your own friends so much that I never had a chance to.

Jim: You should have just —

Laura: Well, I — thought you might think I was —

Jim: Thought I might think you was — what?

Laura: Oh —

Jim (with reflective relish): I was beleaguered by females in those days.

Laura: You were terribly popular!

Jim: Yeah —

Laura: You had such a — friendly way —

Jim: I was spoiled in high school.

Laura: Everybody — liked you!

Jim: Including you?

Laura: I — yes, I — I did, too — (*She gently closes the book in her lap.*)

Jim: Well, well, well! — Give me that program, Laura. (*She hands it to him. He signs it with a flourish.*) There you are — better late than never!

Laura: Oh, I — what a — surprise!

Jim: My signature isn't worth very much right now. But some day — maybe — it will increase in value! Being disappointed is one thing and being discouraged is something else. I am disappointed but I'm not discouraged. I'm twenty-three years old. How old are you?

Laura: I'll be twenty-four in June.

Jim: That's not old age.

Laura: No, but —

Jim: You finished high school?

Laura (with difficulty): I didn't go back.

Jim: You mean you dropped out?

Laura: I made bad grades in my final examinations. (*She rises and replaces the book and the program. Her voice strained.*) How is — Emily Meisenbach getting along?

Jim: Oh, that kraut-head!

Laura: Why do you call her that?

Jim: That's what she was.

Laura: You're not still — going with her?

Jim: I never see her.

Laura: It said in the Personal Section that you were — engaged!

Jim: I know, but I wasn't impressed by that — propaganda!

Laura: It wasn't — the truth?

Jim: Only in Emily's optimistic opinion!

Laura: Oh —

(*Legend: "What Have You Done since High School?"*)

Jim lights a cigarette and leans indolently back on his elbows smiling at Laura with a warmth and charm which light her inwardly with altar candles. She remains by the table and turns in her hands a piece of glass to cover her tumult.

Jim (after several reflective puffs on a cigarette): What have you done since high school? (*She seems not to hear him.*) Huh? (*Laura looks up.*) I said what have you done since high school, Laura?

Laura: Nothing much.

Jim: You must have been doing something these six long years.

Laura: Yes.

Jim: Well, then, such as what?

Laura: I took a business course at business college —

Jim: How did that work out?

Laura: Well, not very — well — I had to drop out, it gave me — indigestion —

Jim laughs gently.

Jim: What are you doing now?

Laura: I don't do anything — much. Oh, please don't think I sit around doing nothing! My glass collection takes up a good deal of my time. Glass is something you have to take good care of.

Jim: What did you say — about glass?

Laura: Collection I said — I have one — (*She clears her throat and turns away again, acutely shy.*)

Jim (abruptly): You know what I judge to be the trouble with you? Inferiority complex! Know what that is? That's what they call it when someone low-rates himself! I understand it because I had it, too. Although my case was not so aggravated as yours seems to be. I had it until I took up public speaking, developed my voice, and learned that I had an aptitude for science. Before that time I never thought of myself as being outstanding in any way whatsoever! Now I've never made a regular study of it, but I have a friend who says I can analyze people better than doctors that make a profession of it. I don't claim that to be necessarily true, but I can sure guess a person's psychology, Laura! (*Takes out his gum.*) Excuse me, Laura. I always take it out when the flavor is gone. I'll use this scrap of paper to wrap it in. I know how it is to get it stuck on a shoe. Yep — that's what I judge to be your principal trouble. A lack of confidence in yourself as a person. You don't have the proper amount of faith in yourself. I'm basing that fact on a number of your remarks and also on certain observations I've made. For instance that clumping you thought was so awful in high school. You say that you even dreaded to walk into class. You see what you did? You dropped out of school, you gave up an education because of a clump, which as far as I know was practically nonexistent! A little physical defect is what you have. Hardly noticeable even! Magnified thousands of times by imagination! You know what my strong advice to you is? Think of yourself as *superior* in some way!

Laura: In what way would I think?

Jim: Why, man alive, Laura! Just look about you a little. What do you see? A world full of common people! All of 'em born and all of 'em going to die! Which of them has one-tenth of your good points! Or mine! Or anyone else's, as far as that goes — Gosh! Everybody excels in some one thing. Some in many! (*Unconsciously glances at himself in the mirror.*) All you've got to do is discover in *what!* Take me, for instance. (*He adjusts his tie at the mirror.*) My interest happened to lie in electrodynamics. I'm taking a course in radio engineering at night school, Laura, on top of a fairly responsible job at the warehouse. I'm taking that course and studying public speaking.

Laura: Ohhhh.

Jim: Because I believe in the future of television! (*Turning back to her.*) I wish to be ready to go up right along with it. Therefore I'm planning to get in on the ground floor. In fact, I've already made the right connections and all that remains is for the industry itself to get under way! Full steam — (*His eyes are starry.*) Knowledge — Zzzzzp! Money — Zzzzzzp! — Power! That's the cycle democracy is built on! (*His attitude is convincingly dynamic. Laura stares at him, even her shyness eclipsed in her absolute wonder. He suddenly grins.*) I guess you think I think a lot of myself!

Laura: No — o-o-o, I —

Jim: Now how about you? Isn't there something you take more interest in than anything else?

Laura: Well, I do — as I said — have my — glass collection —

A peal of girlish laughter from the kitchen.

Jim: I'm not right sure I know what you're talking about. What kind of glass is it?

Laura: Little articles of it, they're ornaments mostly! Most of them are little animals made out of glass, the tiniest little animals in the world. Mother calls them a glass menagerie! Here's an example of one, if you'd like to see it! This one is one of the oldest. It's nearly thirteen. (*He stretches out his hand.*) (*Music: "The Glass Menagerie."*) Oh, be careful — if you breathe, it breaks!

Jim: I'd better not take it. I'm pretty clumsy with things.

Laura: Go on, I trust you with him! (*Places it in his palm.*) There now — you're holding him gently! Hold him over the light, he loves the light! You see how the light shines through him?

Jim: It sure does shine!

Laura: I shouldn't be partial, but he is my favorite one.

Jim: What kind of thing is this one supposed to be?

Laura: Haven't you noticed the single horn on his forehead?

Jim: A unicorn, huh?

Laura: Mmm-hmmm!

Jim: Unicorns, aren't they extinct in the modern world?

Laura: I know!

Jim: Poor little fellow, he must feel sort of lonesome.

Laura (smiling): Well, if he does he doesn't complain about it. He stays on a shelf with some horses that don't have horns and all of them seem to get along nicely together.

Jim: How do you know?

Laura (lightly): I haven't heard any arguments among them!

Jim (grinning): No arguments, huh? Well, that's a pretty good sign! Where shall I set him?

Laura: Put him on the table. They all like a change of scenery once in a while!

Jim (stretching): Well, well, well, well — Look how big my shadow is when I stretch!

Laura: Oh, oh, yes — it stretches across the ceiling!

Jim (crossing to door): I think it's stopped raining. (*Opens fire-escape door.*) Where does the music come from?

Laura: From the Paradise Dance Hall across the alley.

Jim: How about cutting the rug a little, Miss Wingfield?

Laura: Oh, I —

Jim: Or is your program filled up? Let me have a look at it. (*Grasps imaginary card.*) Why, every dance is taken! I'll have to scratch some out. (*Waltz music: "La Golondrina."*) Ahhh, a waltz! (*He executes some sweeping turns by himself then holds his arms toward Laura.*)

Laura (breathlessly): I — can't dance!

Jim: There you go, that inferiority stuff!

Laura: I've never danced in my life!

Jim: Come on, try!

Laura: Oh, but I'd step on you!

Jim: I'm not made out of glass.

Laura: How — how — how do we start?

Jim: Just leave it to me. You hold your arms out a little.

Laura: Like this?

Jim: A little bit higher. Right. Now don't tighten up, that's the main thing about it — relax.

Laura (laughing breathlessly): It's hard not to.

Jim: Okay.

Laura: I'm afraid you can't budge me.

Jim: What do you bet I can't? (*He swings her into motion.*)

Laura: Goodness, yes, you can!

Jim: Let yourself go, now, Laura, just let yourself go.

Laura: I'm —

Jim: Come on!

Laura: Trying.

Jim: Not so stiff — Easy does it!

Laura: I know but I'm —

Jim: Loosen th' backbone! There now, that's a lot better.

Laura: Am I?

Jim: Lots, lots better! (*He moves her about the room in a clumsy waltz.*)

Laura: Oh, my!

Jim: Ha-ha!

Laura: Goodness, yes you can!

Jim: Ha-ha-ha! (*They suddenly bump into the table. Jim stops.*) What did we hit on?

Laura: Table.

Jim: Did something fall off it? I think —

Laura: Yes.

Jim: I hope it wasn't the little glass horse with the horn!

Laura: Yes.

Jim: Aw, aw, aw. Is it broken?

Laura: Now it is just like all the other horses.

Jim: It's lost its —

Laura: Horn! It doesn't matter. Maybe it's a blessing in disguise.

Jim: You'll never forgive me. I bet that that was your favorite piece of glass.

Laura: I don't have favorites much. It's no tragedy, Freckles. Glass breaks so easily. No matter how careful you are. The traffic jars the shelves and things fall off them.

Jim: Still I'm awfully sorry that I was the cause.

Laura (smiling): I'll just imagine he had an operation. The horn was removed to make him feel less — freakish! (*They both laugh.*) Now he will feel more at home with the other horses, the ones that don't have horns . . .

Jim: Ha-ha, that's very funny! (*Suddenly serious.*) I'm glad to see that you have a sense of humor. You know — you're — well — very different! Surprisingly different from anyone else I know! (*His voice becomes soft and hesitant with a genuine feeling.*) Do you mind me telling you that? (*Laura is abashed beyond speech.*) You make me feel sort of — I don't know how to put it! I'm usually pretty good at expressing things, but — This is something that I don't know how to say! (*Laura touches her throat and clears it — turns the broken unicorn in her hands.*) (*Even softer.*) Has anyone ever told you that you were pretty?

Pause: Music.

(*Laura looks up slowly, with wonder, and shakes her head.*) Well, you are! In a very different way from anyone else. And all the nicer because of the difference, too. (*His voice becomes low and husky. Laura turns away, nearly faint with the novelty of her emo-*

tions.) I wish that you were my sister. I'd teach you to have some confidence in yourself. The different people are not like other people, but being different is nothing to be ashamed of. Because other people are not such wonderful people. They're one hundred times one thousand. You're one times one! They walk all over the earth. You just stay here. They're common as — weeds, but — you — well, you're — *Blue Roses!*

(Image on screen: Blue Roses.)
(Music changes.)

Laura: But blue is wrong for — roses . . .
Jim: It's right for you — You're — pretty!
Laura: In what respect am I pretty?
Jim: In all respects — believe me! Your eyes — your hair — are pretty! Your hands are pretty! (*He catches hold of her hand.*) You think I'm making this up because I'm invited to dinner and have to be nice. Oh, I could do that! I could put on an act for you, Laura, and say lots of things without being very sincere. But this time I am. I'm talking to you sincerely. I happened to notice you had this inferiority complex that keeps you from feeling comfortable with people. Somebody needs to build your confidence up and make you proud instead of shy and turning away and — blushing — Somebody ought to — ought to — *kiss* you, Laura! (*His hand slips slowly up her arm to her shoulder.*) (*Music swells tumultuously.*) (*He suddenly turns her about and kisses her on the lips. When he releases her Laura sinks on the sofa with a bright, dazed look. Jim backs away and fishes in his pocket for a cigarette.*) (*Legend on screen: "Souvenir."*) Stumble-john! (*He lights the cigarette, avoiding her look. There is a peal of girlish laughter from Amanda in the kitchen. Laura slowly raises and opens her hand. It still contains the little broken glass animal. She looks at it with a tender, bewildered expression.*) Stumble-john! I shouldn't have done that — That was way off the beam. You don't smoke, do you? (*She looks up, smiling, not hearing the question. He sits beside her a little gingerly. She looks at him speechlessly — waiting. He coughs decorously and moves a little farther aside as he considers the situation and senses her feelings, dimly, with perturbation. Gently.*) Would you — care for a — mint? (*She doesn't seem to hear him but her look grows brighter even.*) Peppermint — Life Saver? My pocket's a regular drug store — wherever I go . . . (*He pops a mint in his mouth. Then gulps and decides to make a clean breast of it. He speaks slowly and gingerly.*) Laura, you know, if I had a sister like you, I'd do the

same thing as Tom. I'd bring out fellows — introduce her to them. The right type of boys of a type to — appreciate her. Only — well — he made a mistake about me. Maybe I've got no call to be saying this. That may not have been the idea in having me over. But what if it was? There's nothing wrong about that. The only trouble is that in my case — I'm not in a situation to — do the right thing. I can't take down your number and say I'll phone. I can't call up next week and — ask for a date. I thought I had better explain the situation in case you misunderstood it and — hurt your feelings. . . . (*Pause. Slowly, very slowly, Laura's look changes, her eyes returning slowly from his to the ornament in her palm.*)

Amanda utters another gay laugh in the kitchen.

Laura (*faintly*): You won't — call again?

Jim: No, Laura, I can't. (*He rises from the sofa.*) As I was just explaining, I've — got strings on me, Laura, I've — been going steady! I go out all the time with a girl named Betty. She's a home-girl like you, and Catholic, and Irish, and in a great many ways we — get along fine. I met her last summer on a moonlight boat trip up the river to Alton, on the *Majestic.* Well — right away from the start it was — love! (*Legend: Love!*) (*Laura sways slightly forward and grips the arm of the sofa. He fails to notice, now enrapt in his own comfortable being.*) Being in love has made a new man of me! (*Leaning stiffly forward, clutching the arm of the sofa, Laura struggles visibly with her storm. But Jim is oblivious, she is a long way off.*) The power of love is really pretty tremendous! Love is something that — changes the whole world, Laura! (*The storm abates a little and Laura leans back. He notices her again.*) It happened that Betty's aunt took sick, she got a wire and had to go to Centralia. So Tom — when he asked me to dinner — I naturally just accepted the invitation, not knowing that you — that he — that I — (*He stops awkwardly.*) Huh — I'm a stumble-john! (*He flops back on the sofa. The holy candles in the altar of Laura's face have been snuffed out! There is a look of almost infinite desolation. Jim glances at her uneasily.*) I wish that you would — say something. (*She bites her lip which was trembling and then bravely smiles. She opens her hand again on the broken glass ornament. Then she gently takes his hand and raises it level with her own. She carefully places the unicorn in the palm of his hand, then pushes his fingers closed upon it.*) What are you — doing that for? You want me to have him? — Laura? (*She nods.*) What for?

Laura: A — souvenir . . .

She rises unsteadily and crouches beside the Victrola to wind it up.
(Legend on screen: "Things Have a Way of Turning Out So Badly.")
(Or image: "Gentleman caller waving good-bye! — Gaily.")
*At this moment Amanda rushes brightly back in the front room. She bears a
pitcher of fruit punch in an old-fashioned cut-glass pitcher and a plate of
macaroons. The plate has a gold border and poppies painted on it.*

Amanda: Well, well, well! Isn't the air delightful after the shower?
I've made you children a little liquid refreshment. (*Turns gaily
to the gentleman caller.*) Jim, do you know that song about
lemonade?

"Lemonade, lemonade
Made in the shade and stirred with a spade —
Good enough for any old maid!"

Jim (uneasily): Ha-ha! No — I never heard it.
Amanda: Why, Laura! You look so serious!
Jim: We were having a serious conversation.
Amanda: Good! Now you're better acquainted!
Jim (uncertainly): Ha-ha! Yes.
Amanda: You modern young people are much more serious-
minded than my generation. I was so gay as a girl!
Jim: You haven't changed, Mrs. Wingfield.
Amanda: Tonight I'm rejuvenated! The gaiety of the occasion, Mr.
O'Connor! (*She tosses her head with a peal of laughter. Spills
lemonade.*) Oooo! I'm baptizing myself!
Jim: Here — let me —
Amanda (setting the pitcher down): There now. I discovered we had
some maraschino cherries. I dumped them in, juice and all!
Jim: You shouldn't have gone to that trouble, Mrs. Wingfield.
Amanda: Trouble, trouble? Why it was loads of fun! Didn't you
hear me cutting up in the kitchen? I bet your ears were
burning! I told Tom how outdone with him I was for keeping
you to himself so long a time! He should have brought you
over much, much sooner! Well, now that you've found your
way, I want you to be a very frequent caller! Not just occasional but all the time. Oh, we're going to have a lot of gay
times together! I see them coming! Mmm, just breathe that
air! So fresh, and the moon's so pretty! I'll skip back out — I
know where my place is when young folks are having a —
serious conversation!
Jim: Oh, don't go out, Mrs. Wingfield. The fact of the matter is
I've got to be going.
Amanda: Going, now? You're joking! Why, it's only the shank of
the evening, Mr. O'Connor!

Jim: Well, you know how it is.

Amanda: You mean you're a young workingman and have to keep workingmen's hours. We'll let you off early tonight. But only on the condition that next time you stay later. What's the best night for you? Isn't Saturday night the best night for you workingmen?

Jim: I have a couple of time-clocks to punch, Mrs. Wingfield. One at morning, another one at night!

Amanda: My, but you *are* ambitious! You work at night, too?

Jim: No, Ma'am, not work but — Betty! (*He crosses deliberately to pick up his hat. The band at the Paradise Dance Hall goes into a tender waltz.*)

Amanda: Betty? Betty? Who's — Betty! (*There is an ominous cracking sound in the sky.*)

Jim: Oh, just a girl. The girl I go steady with! (*He smiles charmingly. The sky falls.*)

(*Legend: "The Sky Falls."*)

Amanda (a long-drawn exhalation): Ohhhh . . . Is it a serious romance, Mr. O'Connor?

Jim: We're going to be married the second Sunday in June.

Amanda: Ohhhh how nice! Tom didn't mention that you were engaged to be married.

Jim: The cat's not out of the bag at the warehouse yet. You know how they are. They call you Romeo and stuff like that. (*He stops at the oval mirror to put on his hat. He carefully shapes the brim and the crown to give a discreetly dashing effect.*) It's been a wonderful evening, Mrs. Wingfield. I guess this is what they mean by Southern hospitality.

Amanda: It really wasn't anything at all.

Jim: I hope it don't seem like I'm rushing off. But I promised Betty I'd pick her up at the Wabash depot, an' by the time I get my jalopy down there her train'll be in. Some women are pretty upset if you keep 'em waiting.

Amanda: Yes, I know — The tyranny of women! (*Extends her hand.*) Good-bye, Mr. O'Connor. I wish you luck — and happiness — and success! All three of them, and so does Laura — Don't you, Laura?

Laura: Yes!

Jim (taking her hand): Good-bye, Laura. I'm certainly going to treasure that souvenir. And don't you forget the good advice I gave you. (*Raises his voice to a cheery shout.*) So long, Shakespeare! Thanks again, ladies — Good night!

He grins and ducks jauntily out.
    Still bravely grimacing, Amanda closes the door on the gentleman caller.
Then she turns back to the room with a puzzled expression. She and Laura don't
dare to face each other. Laura crouches beside the Victrola to wind it.

Amanda (faintly): Things have a way of turning out so badly. I
    don't believe that I would play the Victrola. Well, well —
    well — Our gentleman caller was engaged to be married!
    Tom!
Tom (from back): Yes, Mother?
Amanda: Come in here a minute. I want to tell you something
    awfully funny.
Tom (enters with macaroon and a glass of the lemonade): Has the
    gentleman caller gotten away already?
Amanda: The gentleman caller has made an early departure.
    What a wonderful joke you played on us!
Tom: How do you mean?
Amanda: You didn't mention that he was engaged to be married.
Tom: Jim? Engaged?
Amanda: That's what he just informed us.
Tom: I'll be jiggered! I didn't know about that.
Amanda: That seems very peculiar.
Tom: What's peculiar about it?
Amanda: Didn't you call him your best friend down at the ware-
    house?
Tom: He is, but how did I know?
Amanda: It seems extremely peculiar that you wouldn't know
    your best friend was going to be married!
Tom: The warehouse is where I work, not where I know things
    about people!
Amanda: You don't know things anywhere! You live in a dream;
    you manufacture illusions! (*He crosses to door.*) Where are you
    going?
Tom: I'm going to the movies.
Amanda: That's right, now that you've had us make such fools of
    ourselves. The effort, the preparations, all the expense! The
    new floor lamp, the rug, the clothes for Laura! All for what?
    To entertain some other girl's fiancé! Go to the movies, go!
    Don't think about us, a mother deserted, an unmarried sister
    who's crippled and has no job! Don't let anything interfere
    with your selfish pleasure! Just go, go, go — to the movies!
Tom: All right, I will! The more you shout about my selfishness to
    me the quicker I'll go, and I won't go to the movies!

Amanda: Go, then! Then go to the moon — you selfish dreamer!

Tom smashes his glass on the floor. He plunges out on the fire-escape, slamming the door. Laura screams — cut by door.
    Dance-hall music up. Tom goes to the rail and grips it desperately, lifting his face in the chill white moonlight penetrating the narrow abyss of the alley.
    (Legend on screen: "And So Good-Bye . . .")
    Tom's closing speech is timed with the interior pantomime. The interior scene is played as though viewed through sound-proof glass. Amanda appears to be making a comforting speech to Laura who is huddled upon the sofa. Now that we cannot hear the mother's speech, her silliness is gone and she has dignity and tragic beauty. Laura's dark hair hides her face until at the end of the speech she lifts it to smile at her mother. Amanda's gestures are slow and graceful, almost dancelike, as she comforts the daughter. At the end of her speech she glances a moment at the father's picture — then withdraws through the portieres. At close of Tom's speech, Laura blows out the candles, ending the play.

Tom: I didn't go to the moon, I went much further — for time is the longest distance between two places — Not long after that I was fired for writing a poem on the lid of a shoe-box. I left Saint Louis. I descended the steps of this fire-escape for a last time and followed, from then on, in my father's footsteps, attempting to find in motion what was lost in space — I traveled around a great deal. The cities swept about me like dead leaves, leaves that were brightly colored but torn away from the branches. I would have stopped, but I was pursued by something. It always came upon me unawares, taking me altogether by surprise. Perhaps it was a familiar bit of music. Perhaps it was only a piece of transparent glass — Perhaps I am walking along a street at night, in some strange city, before I have found companions. I pass the lighted window of a shop where perfume is sold. The window is filled with pieces of colored glass, tiny transparent bottles in delicate colors, like bits of a shattered rainbow. Then all at once my sister touches my shoulder. I turn around and look into her eyes. . . . Oh, Laura, Laura, I tried to leave you behind me, but I am more faithful than I intended to be! I reach for a cigarette, I cross the street, I run into the movies or a bar, I buy a drink, I speak to the nearest stranger — anything that can blow your candles out! (*Laura bends over the candles.*) — for nowadays the world is lit by lightning! Blow out your candles, Laura — and so good-bye . . .

She blows the candles out.
(The Scene Dissolves.)

ARTHUR MILLER   (b. 1915)

Death of a Salesman
Certain Private Conversations in Two Acts and a Requiem

CHARACTERS

Willy Loman	Uncle Ben
Linda	Howard Wagner
Biff	Jenny
Happy	Stanley
Bernard	Miss Forsythe
The Woman	Letta
Charley	

SCENE: *The action takes place in Willy Loman's house and yard and in various places he visits in the New York and Boston of today.*

Throughout the play, in the stage directions, left and right mean stage left and stage right.

ACT I

A melody is heard, played upon a flute. It is small and fine, telling of grass and trees and the horizon. The curtain rises.

Before us is the Salesman's house. We are aware of towering, angular shapes behind it, surrounding it on all sides. Only the blue light of the sky falls upon the house and forestage; the surrounding area shows an angry glow of orange. As more light appears, we see a solid vault of apartment houses around the small, fragile-seeming home. An air of the dream clings to the place, a dream rising out of reality. The kitchen at center seems actual enough, for there is a kitchen table with three chairs, and a refrigerator. But no other fixtures are seen. At the back of the kitchen there is a draped entrance, which leads to the living-room. To the right of the kitchen, on a level raised two feet, is a bedroom furnished only with a brass bedstead and a straight chair. On a shelf over the bed a silver athletic trophy stands. A window opens onto the apartment house at the side.

Behind the kitchen, on a level raised six and a half feet, is the boys' bedroom, at present barely visible. Two beds are dimly seen, and at the back of the room a dormer window. (This bedroom is above the unseen living-room.) At the left a stairway curves up to it from the kitchen.

The entire setting is wholly or, in some places, partially transparent. The roof-line of the house is one-dimensional; under and over it we see the apartment buildings. Before the house lies an apron, curving beyond the forestage into the orchestra. This forward area serves as the back yard as well as the locale of all Willy's imaginings and of his city scenes. Whenever the action is in the present the actors observe the imaginary wall-lines, entering the house only through its door at the left. But in the scenes of the past these boundaries are broken, and characters enter or leave a room by stepping "through" a wall onto the forestage.

From the right, Willy Loman, the Salesman, enters, carrying two large sample cases. The flute plays on. He hears but is not aware of it. He is past sixty years of age, dressed quietly. Even as he crosses the stage to the doorway of the house, his exhaustion is apparent. He unlocks the door, comes into the kitchen, and thankfully lets his burden down, feeling the soreness of his palms. A word-sigh escapes his lips — it might be "Oh, boy, oh, boy." He closes the door, then carries his cases out into the living-room, through the draped kitchen doorway.

Linda, his wife, has stirred in her bed at the right. She gets out and puts on a robe, listening. Most often jovial, she has developed an iron repression of her exceptions to Willy's behavior — she more than loves him, she admires him, as though his mercurial nature, his temper, his massive dreams and little cruelties, served her only as sharp reminders of the turbulent longings within him, longings which she shares but lacks the temperament to utter and follow to their end.

Linda (hearing Willy outside the bedroom, calls with some trepidation): Willy!

Willy: It's all right. I came back.

Linda: Why? What happened? (*Slight pause.*) Did something happen, Willy?

Willy: No, nothing happened.

Linda: You didn't smash the car, did you?

Willy (with casual irritation): I said nothing happened. Didn't you hear me?

Linda: Don't you feel well?

Willy: I am tired to the death. (*The flute has faded away. He sits on the bed beside her, a little numb.*) I couldn't make it. I just couldn't make it, Linda.

Linda (very carefully, delicately): Where were you all day? You look terrible.

Willy: I got as far as a little above Yonkers. I stopped for a cup of coffee. Maybe it was the coffee.

Linda: What?

Willy (after a pause): I suddenly couldn't drive any more. The car kept going off onto the shoulder, y'know?

Linda (helpfully): Oh. Maybe it was the steering again. I don't think Angelo knows the Studebaker.

Willy: No, it's me, it's me. Suddenly I realize I'm goin' sixty miles an hour and I don't remember the last five minutes. I'm — I can't seem to — keep my mind to it.

Linda: Maybe it's your glasses. You never went for your new glasses.

Willy: No, I see everything. I came back ten miles an hour. It took me nearly four hours from Yonkers.

Linda (resigned): Well, you'll just have to take a rest, Willy, you can't continue this way.

Willy: I just got back from Florida.

Linda: But you didn't rest your mind. Your mind is overactive, and the mind is what counts, dear.

Willy: I'll start out in the morning. Maybe I'll feel better in the morning. (*She is taking off his shoes.*) These goddam arch supports are killing me.

Linda: Take an aspirin. Should I get you an aspirin? It'll soothe you.

Willy (with wonder): I was driving along, you understand? And I was fine. I was even observing the scenery. You can imagine, me looking at scenery, on the road every week of my life. But it's so beautiful up there, Linda, the trees are so thick, and the sun is warm. I opened the windshield and just let the warm air bathe over me. And then all of a sudden I'm goin' off the road! I'm tellin' ya, I absolutely forgot I was driving. If I'd've gone the other way over the white line I might've killed somebody. So I went on again — and five minutes later I'm dreamin' again, and I nearly — (*He presses two fingers against his eyes.*) I have such thoughts, I have such strange thoughts.

Linda: Willy, dear. Talk to them again. There's no reason why you can't work in New York.

Willy: They don't need me in New York. I'm the New England man. I'm vital in New England.

Linda: But you're sixty years old. They can't expect you to keep traveling every week.

Willy: I'll have to send a wire to Portland. I'm supposed to see Brown and Morrison tomorrow morning at ten o'clock to show the line. Goddammit, I could sell them! (*He starts putting on his jacket.*)

Linda (taking the jacket from him): Why don't you go down to the place tomorrow and tell Howard you've simply got to work in New York? You're too accommodating, dear.

Willy: If old man Wagner was alive I'd a been in charge of New York now! That man was a prince, he was a masterful man. But that boy of his, that Howard, he don't appreciate. When I went north the first time, the Wagner Company didn't know where New England was!

Linda: Why don't you tell those things to Howard, dear?

Willy (encouraged): I will, I definitely will. Is there any cheese?

Linda: I'll make you a sandwich.

Willy: No, go to sleep. I'll take some milk. I'll be up right away. The boys in?

Linda: They're sleeping. Happy took Biff on a date tonight.

Willy (interested): That so?

Linda: It was so nice to see them shaving together, one behind the other, in the bathroom. And going out together. You notice? The whole house smells of shaving lotion.

Willy: Figure it out. Work a lifetime to pay off a house. You finally own it, and there's nobody to live in it.

Linda: Well, dear, life is a casting off. It's always that way.

Willy: No, no, some people — some people accomplish something. Did Biff say anything after I went this morning?

Linda: You shouldn't have criticized him, Willy, especially after he just got off the train. You mustn't lose your temper with him.

Willy: When the hell did I lose my temper? I simply asked him if he was making any money. Is that a criticism?

Linda: But, dear, how could he make any money?

Willy (worried and angered): There's such an undercurrent in him. He became a moody man. Did he apologize when I left this morning?

Linda: He was crestfallen, Willy. You know how he admires you. I think if he finds himself, then you'll both be happier and not fight any more.

Willy: How can he find himself on a farm? Is that a life? A farmhand? In the beginning, when he was young, I thought, well, a young man, it's good for him to tramp around, take a lot of different jobs. But it's more than ten years now and he has yet to make thirty-five dollars a week!

Linda: He's finding himself, Willy.

Willy: Not finding yourself at the age of thirty-four is a disgrace!

Linda: Shh!

Willy: The trouble is he's lazy, goddammit!

Linda: Willy, please!

Willy: Biff is a lazy bum!

Linda: They're sleeping. Get something to eat. Go on down.

Willy: Why did he come home? I would like to know what brought him home.

Linda: I don't know. I think he's still lost, Willy. I think he's very lost.

Willy: Biff Loman is lost. In the greatest country in the world a young man with such — personal attractiveness, gets lost. And such a hard worker. There's one thing about Biff — he's not lazy.

Linda: Never.

Willy (with pity and resolve): I'll see him in the morning; I'll have a nice talk with him. I'll get him a job selling. He could be big in no time. My God! Remember how they used to follow him around in high school? When he smiled at one of them their faces lit up. When he walked down the street . . . (*He loses himself in reminiscences.*)

Linda (trying to bring him out of it): Willy, dear, I got a new kind of American-type cheese today. It's whipped.

Willy: Why do you get American when I like Swiss?

Linda: I just thought you'd like a change —

Willy: I don't want a change! I want Swiss cheese. Why am I always being contradicted?

Linda (with a covering laugh): I thought it would be a surprise.

Willy: Why don't you open a window in here, for God's sake?

Linda (with infinite patience): They're all open, dear.

Willy: The way they boxed us in here. Bricks and windows, windows and bricks.

Linda: We should've bought the land next door.

Willy: The street is lined with cars. There's not a breath of fresh air in the neighborhood. The grass don't grow any more, you can't raise a carrot in the back yard. They should've had a law against apartment houses. Remember those two beautiful elm trees out there? When I and Biff hung the swing between them?

Linda: Yeah, like being a million miles from the city.

Willy: They should've arrested the builder for cutting those down. They massacred the neighborhood. (*Lost.*) More and more I think of those days, Linda. This time of year it was lilac and wisteria. And then the peonies would come out, and the daffodils. What fragrance in this room!

Linda: Well, after all, people had to move somewhere.

Willy: No, there's more people now.

Linda: I don't think there's more people. I think —

Willy: There's more people! That's what's ruining this country! Population is getting out of control. The competition is maddening! Smell the stink from that apartment house! And another one on the other side . . . How can they whip cheese?

On Willy's last line, Biff and Happy raise themselves up in their beds, listening.

Linda: Go down, try it. And be quiet.

Willy (turning to Linda, guiltily): You're not worried about me, are you, sweetheart?

Biff: What's the matter?

Happy: Listen!

Linda: You've got too much on the ball to worry about.

Willy: You're my foundation and my support, Linda.

Linda: Just try to relax, dear. You make mountains out of mole-hills.

Willy: I won't fight with him any more. If he wants to go back to Texas, let him go.

Linda: He'll find his way.

Willy: Sure. Certain men just don't get started till later in life. Like Thomas Edison, I think. Or B. F. Goodrich. One of them was deaf. (*He starts for the bedroom doorway.*) I'll put my money on Biff.

Linda: And Willy — if it's warm Sunday we'll drive in the country. And we'll open the windshield and take lunch.

Willy: No, the windshields don't open on the new cars.

Linda: But you opened it today.

Willy: Me? I didn't. (*He stops.*) Now isn't that peculiar! Isn't that a remarkable — (*He breaks off in amazement and fright as the flute is heard distantly.*)

Linda: What, darling?

Willy: That is the most remarkable thing.

Linda: What, dear?

Willy: I was thinking of the Chevvy. (*Slight pause.*) Nineteen twenty-eight . . . when I had that red Chevvy — (*Breaks off.*) That funny? I coulda sworn I was driving that Chevvy today.

Linda: Well, that's nothing. Something must've reminded you.

Willy: Remarkable. Ts. Remember those days? The way Biff used to simonize that car? The dealer refused to believe there was eighty thousand miles on it. (*He shakes his head.*) Heh! (*To Linda.*) Close your eyes, I'll be right up. (*He walks out of the bedroom.*)

Happy (to Biff): Jesus, maybe he smashed up the car again!

Linda (calling after Willy): Be careful on the stairs, dear! The cheese is on the middle shelf! (*She turns, goes over to the bed, takes his jacket, and goes out of the bedroom.*)

Light has risen on the boys' room. Unseen, Willy is heard talking to himself, "Eighty thousand miles," and a little laugh. Biff gets out of bed, comes downstage a bit, and stands attentively. Biff is two years older than his brother Happy, well built, but in these days bears a worn air and seems less self-assured. He has succeeded less, and his dreams are stronger and less acceptable than Happy's. Happy is tall, powerfully made. Sexuality is like a visible color on him, or a scent that many women have discovered. He, like his brother, is lost, but in a different way, for he has never allowed himself to turn his face toward defeat and is thus more confused and hard-skinned, although seemingly more content.

Happy (getting out of bed): He's going to get his license taken away

if he keeps that up. I'm getting nervous about him, y'know,
Biff?

Biff: His eyes are going.

Happy: No, I've driven with him. He sees all right. He just doesn't
keep his mind on it. I drove into the city with him last week.
He stops at a green light and then it turns red and he goes.
(*He laughs.*)

Biff: Maybe he's color-blind.

Happy: Pop? Why he's got the finest eye for color in the business.
You know that.

Biff (sitting down on his bed): I'm going to sleep.

Happy: You're not still sour on Dad, are you, Biff?

Biff: He's all right, I guess.

Willy (underneath them, in the living room): Yes, sir, eighty thousand
miles — eighty-two thousand!

Biff: You smoking?

Happy (holding out a pack of cigarettes): Want one?

Biff (taking a cigarette): I can never sleep when I smell it.

Willy: What a simonizing job, heh!

Happy (with deep sentiment): Funny, Biff, y'know? Us sleeping in
here again? The old beds. (*He pats his bed affectionately.*) All the
talk that went across those two beds, huh? Our whole lives.

Biff: Yeah. Lotta dreams and plans.

Happy (with a deep and masculine laugh): About five hundred
women would like to know what was said in this room.

They share a soft laugh.

Biff: Remember that big Betsy something — what the hell was
her name — over on Bushwick Avenue?

Happy (combing his hair): With the collie dog!

Biff: That's the one. I got you in there, remember?

Happy: Yeah, that was my first time — I think. Boy, there was a
pig! (*They laugh, almost crudely.*) You taught me everything I
know about women. Don't forget that.

Biff: I bet you forgot how bashful you used to be. Especially with
girls.

Happy: Oh, I still am, Biff.

Biff: Oh, go on.

Happy: I just control it, that's all. I think I got less bashful and you
got more so. What happened, Biff? Where's the old humor,
the old confidence? (*He shakes Biff's knee. Biff gets up and moves
restlessly about the room.*) What's the matter?

Biff: Why does Dad mock me all the time?

Happy: He's not mocking you, he —

Biff: Everything I say there's a twist of mockery on his face. I can't get near him.

Happy: He just wants you to make good, that's all. I wanted to talk to you about Dad for a long time, Biff. Something's — happening to him. He — talks to himself.

Biff: I noticed that this morning. But he always mumbled.

Happy: But not so noticeable. It got so embarrassing I sent him to Florida. And you know something? Most of the time he's talking to you.

Biff: What's he say about me?

Happy: I can't make it out.

Biff: What's he say about me?

Happy: I think the fact that you're not settled, that you're still kind of up in the air . . .

Biff: There's one or two other things depressing him, Happy.

Happy: What do you mean?

Biff: Never mind. Just don't lay it all to me.

Happy: But I think if you just got started — I mean — is there any future for you out there?

Biff: I tell ya, Hap, I don't know what the future is. I don't know — what I'm supposed to want.

Happy: What do you mean?

Biff: Well, I spent six or seven years after high school trying to work myself up. Shipping clerk, salesman, business of one kind or another. And it's a measly manner of existence. To get on that subway on the hot mornings in summer. To devote your whole life to keeping stock, or making phone calls, or selling or buying. To suffer fifty weeks of the year for the sake of a two-week vacation, when all you really desire is to be outdoors, with your shirt off. And always to have to get ahead of the next fella. And still — that's how you build a future.

Happy: Well, you really enjoy it on a farm? Are you content out there?

Biff (with rising agitation): Hap, I've had twenty or thirty different kinds of jobs since I left home before the war, and it always turns out the same. I just realized it lately. In Nebraska when I herded cattle, and the Dakotas, and Arizona, and now in Texas. It's why I came home now, I guess, because I realized it. This farm I work on, it's spring there now, see? And they've got about fifteen new colts. There's nothing more inspiring or — beautiful than the sight of a mare and a new colt. And it's cool there now, see? Texas is cool now, and it's spring. And whenever spring comes to where I am, I suddenly get the feeling, my God, I'm not gettin' anywhere! What the hell am I doing, playing around with horses, twenty-eight dollars a week! I'm thirty-four years old, I oughta be makin' my future. That's when I come running home. And now, I get here, and I don't know what to do with myself. (*After a pause.*) I've always made a point of not wasting my life, and everytime I come back here I know that all I've done is to waste my life.

Happy: You're a poet, you know that, Biff? You're a — you're an idealist!

Biff: No, I'm mixed up very bad. Maybe I oughta get married. Maybe I oughta get stuck into something. Maybe that's my trouble. I'm like a boy. I'm not married, I'm not in business, I just — I'm like a boy. Are you content, Hap? You're a success, aren't you? Are you content?

Happy: Hell, no!

Biff: Why? You're making money, aren't you?

Happy (moving about with energy, expressiveness): All I can do now is wait for the merchandise manager to die. And suppose I get to be merchandise manager? He's a good friend of mine, and he just built a terrific estate on Long Island. And he lived there about two months and sold it, and now he's building another one. He can't enjoy it once it's finished. And I know that's just what I would do. I don't know what the hell I'm workin' for. Sometimes I sit in my apartment — all alone. And I think of the rent I'm paying. And it's crazy. But then, it's what I always wanted. My own apartment, a car, and plenty of women. And still, goddammit, I'm lonely.

Biff (with enthusiasm): Listen, why don't you come out West with me?

Happy: You and I, heh?

Biff: Sure, maybe we could buy a ranch. Raise cattle, use our muscles. Men built like we are should be working out in the open.

Happy (avidly): The Loman Brothers, heh?

Biff (with vast affection): Sure, we'd be known all over the counties!

Happy (enthralled): That's what I dream about, Biff. Sometimes I want to just rip my clothes off in the middle of the store and outbox that goddam merchandise manager. I mean I can outbox, outrun, and outlift anybody in that store, and I have to take orders from those common, petty sons-of-bitches till I can't stand it any more.

Biff: I'm tellin' you, kid, if you were with me I'd be happy out there.

Happy (enthused): See, Biff, everybody around me is so false that I'm constantly lowering my ideals . . .

Biff: Baby, together we'd stand up for one another, we'd have someone to trust.

Happy: If I were around you —

Biff: Hap, the trouble is we weren't brought up to grub for money. I don't know how to do it.

Happy: Neither can I!

Biff: Then let's go!

Happy: The only thing is — what can you make out there?

Biff: But look at your friend. Builds an estate and then hasn't the peace of mind to live in it.

Happy: Yeah, but when he walks into the store the waves part in front of him. That's fifty-two thousand dollars a year coming through the revolving door, and I got more in my pinky finger than he's got in his head.

Biff: Yeah, but you just said —

Happy: I gotta show some of those pompous, self-important executives over there that Hap Loman can make the grade. I want to walk into the store the way he walks in. Then I'll go with you, Biff. We'll be together yet, I swear. But take those two we had tonight. Now weren't they gorgeous creatures?

Biff: Yeah, yeah, most gorgeous I've had in years.

Happy: I get that any time I want, Biff. Whenever I feel disgusted. The only trouble is, it gets like bowling or something. I just keep knockin' them over and it doesn't mean anything. You still run around a lot?

Biff: Naa. I'd like to find a girl — steady, somebody with substance.

Happy: That's what I long for.

Biff: Go on! You'd never come home.

Happy: I would! Somebody with character, with resistance! Like Mom, y'know? You're gonna call me a bastard when I tell you this. That girl Charlotte I was with tonight is engaged to be married in five weeks. (*He tries on his new hat.*)

Biff: No kiddin'!

Happy: Sure, the guy's in line for the vice-presidency of the store. I don't know what gets into me, maybe I just have an over-developed sense of competition or something, but I went and ruined her, and furthermore I can't get rid of her. And he's the third executive I've done that to. Isn't that a crummy characteristic? And to top it all, I go to their weddings! (*Indignantly, but laughing.*) Like I'm not supposed to take bribes. Manufacturers offer me a hundred dollar bill now

and then to throw an order their way. You know how honest I
am, but it's like this girl, see. I hate myself for it. Because I
don't want the girl, and, still, I take it and — I love it!
Biff: Let's go to sleep.
Happy: I guess we didn't settle anything, heh?
Biff: I just got one idea that I think I'm going to try.
Happy: What's that?
Biff: Remember Bill Oliver?
Happy: Sure, Oliver is very big now. You want to work for him
again?
Biff: No, but when I quit he said something to me. He put his arm
on my shoulder, and he said, "Biff, if you ever need anything,
come to me."
Happy: I remember that. That sounds good.
Biff: I think I'll go to see him. If I could get ten thousand or even
seven or eight thousand dollars I could buy a beautiful
ranch.
Happy: I bet he'd back you. 'Cause he thought highly of you, Biff.
I mean, they all do. You're well liked, Biff. That's why I say to
come back here, and we both have the apartment. And I'm
tellin' you, Biff, any babe you want . . .
Biff: No, with a ranch I could do the work I like and still be
something. I just wonder though. I wonder if Oliver still
thinks I stole that carton of basketballs.
Happy: Oh, he probably forgot that long ago. It's almost ten years.
You're too sensitive. Anyway, he didn't really fire you.
Biff: Well, I think he was going to. I think that's why I quit. I was
never sure whether he knew or not. I know he thought the
world of me, though. I was the only one he'd let lock up the
place.
Willy (below): You gonna wash the engine, Biff?
Happy: Shh!

*Biff looks at Happy, who is gazing down, listening. Willy is mumbling in the
parlor.*

Happy: You hear that?

They listen. Willy laughs warmly.

Biff (growing angry): Doesn't he know Mom can hear that?
Willy: Don't get your sweater dirty, Biff!

A look of pain crosses Biff's face.

Happy: Isn't that terrible? Don't leave again, will you? You'll find a job here. You gotta stick around. I don't know what to do about him, it's getting embarrassing.

Willy: What a simonizing job!

Biff: Mom's hearing that!

Willy: No kiddin', Biff, you got a date? Wonderful!

Happy: Go on to sleep. But talk to him in the morning, will you?

Biff (reluctantly getting into bed): With her in the house. Brother!

Happy (getting into bed): I wish you'd have a good talk with him.

The light on their room begins to fade.

Biff (to himself in bed): That selfish, stupid . . .

Happy: Sh . . . Sleep, Biff.

Their light is out. Well before they have finished speaking, Willy's form is dimly seen below in the darkened kitchen. He opens the refrigerator, searches in there, and takes out a bottle of milk. The apartment houses are fading out, and the entire house and surroundings become covered with leaves. Music insinuates itself as the leaves appear.

Willy: Just wanna be careful with those girls, Biff, that's all. Don't make any promises. No promises of any kind. Because a girl, y'know, they always believe what you tell 'em, and you're very young. Biff, you're too young to be talking seriously to girls.

Light rises on the kitchen. Willy, talking, shuts the refrigerator door and comes downstage to the kitchen table. He pours milk into a glass. He is totally immersed in himself, smiling faintly.

Willy: Too young entirely, Biff. You want to watch your schooling first. Then when you're all set, there'll be plenty of girls for a boy like you. (*He smiles broadly at a kitchen chair.*) That so? The girls pay for you? (*He laughs.*) Boy, you must really be makin' a hit.

Willy is gradually addressing — physically — a point offstage, speaking through the wall of the kitchen, and his voice has been rising in volume to that of a normal conversation.

Willy: I been wondering why you polish the car so careful. Ha! Don't leave the hubcaps, boys. Get the chamois to the hub-caps. Happy, use newspaper on the windows, it's the easiest thing. Show him how to do it, Biff! You see, Happy? Pad it up, use it like a pad. That's it, that's it, good work. You're doin' all right, Hap. (*He pauses, then nods in approbation for a few seconds, then looks upward.*) Biff, first thing we gotta do when we get

time is clip that big branch over the house. Afraid it's gonna
fall in a storm and hit the roof. Tell you what. We get a rope
and sling her around, and then we climb up there with a
couple of saws and take her down. Soon as you finish the car,
boys, I wanna see ya. I got a surprise for you, boys.

Biff (offstage): Whatta ya got, Dad?

Willy: No, you finish first. Never leave a job till you're finished — remember that. (*Looking toward the "big trees."*) Biff,
up in Albany I saw a beautiful hammock. I think I'll buy it
next trip, and we'll hang it right between those two elms.
Wouldn't that be something? Just swingin' there under those
branches. Boy, that would be . . .

*Young Biff and Young Happy appear from the direction Willy was addressing.
Happy carries rags and a pail of water. Biff, wearing a sweater with a block "S,"
carries a football.*

Biff (pointing in the direction of the car offstage): How's that, Pop,
professional?

Willy: Terrific. Terrific job, boys. Good work, Biff.

Happy: Where's the surprise, Pop?

Willy: In the back seat of the car.

Happy: Boy! (*He runs off.*)

Biff: What is it, Dad? Tell me, what'd you buy?

Willy (laughing, cuffs him): Never mind, something I want you to
have.

Biff (turns and starts off): What is it, Hap?

Happy (offstage): It's a punching bag!

Biff: Oh, Pop!

Willy: It's got Gene Tunney's signature on it!

Happy runs onstage with a punching bag.

Biff: Gee, how'd you know we wanted a punching bag?

Willy: Well, it's the finest thing for the timing.

Happy (lies down on his back and pedals with his feet): I'm losing
weight, you notice, Pop?

Willy (to Happy): Jumping rope is good too.

Biff: Did you see the new football I got?

Willy (examining the ball): Where'd you get a new ball?

Biff: The coach told me to practice my passing.

Willy: That so? And he gave you the ball, heh?

Biff: Well, I borrowed it from the locker room. (*He laughs confidentially.*)

Willy (laughing with him at the theft): I want you to return that.

Happy: I told you he wouldn't like it!

Biff (angrily): Well, I'm bringing it back!

Willy (stopping the incipient argument, to Happy): Sure, he's gotta practice with a regulation ball, doesn't he? (*To Biff.*) Coach'll probably congratulate you on your initiative!

Biff: Oh, he keeps congratulating my initiative all the time, Pop.

Willy: That's because he likes you. If somebody else took that ball there'd be an uproar. So what's the report, boys, what's the report?

Biff: Where'd you go this time, Dad? Gee we were lonesome for you.

Willy (pleased, puts an arm around each boy and they come down to the apron): Lonesome, heh?

Biff: Missed you every minute.

Willy: Don't say? Tell you a secret, boys. Don't breathe it to a soul. Someday I'll have my own business, and I'll never have to leave home any more.

Happy: Like Uncle Charley, heh?

Willy: Bigger than Uncle Charley! Because Charley is not — liked. He's liked, but he's not — well liked.

Biff: Where'd you go this time, Dad?

Willy: Well, I got on the road, and I went north to Providence. Met the Mayor.

Biff: The Mayor of Providence!

Willy: He was sitting in the hotel lobby.

Biff: What'd he say?

Willy: He said, "Morning!" And I said, "You got a fine city here, Mayor." And then he had coffee with me. And then I went to Waterbury. Waterbury is a fine city. Big clock city, the famous Waterbury clock. Sold a nice bill there. And then Boston — Boston is the cradle of the Revolution. A fine city. And a couple of other towns in Mass., and on to Portland and Bangor and straight home!

Biff: Gee, I'd love to go with you sometime, Dad.

Willy: Soon as summer comes.

Happy: Promise?

Willy: You and Hap and I, and I'll show you all the towns. America is full of beautiful towns and fine, upstanding people. And they know me, boys, they know me up and down New England. The finest people. And when I bring you fellas up, there'll be open sesame for all of us, 'cause one thing, boys: I have friends. I can park my car in any street in New England, and the cops protect it like their own. This summer, heh?

Biff and Happy (together): Yeah! You bet!
Willy: We'll take our bathing suits.
Happy: We'll carry your bags, Pop!
Willy: Oh, won't that be something! Me comin' into the Boston stores with you boys carryin' my bags. What a sensation!

Biff is prancing around, practicing passing the ball.

Willy: You nervous, Biff, about the game?
Biff: Not if you gonna be there.
Willy: What do they say about you in school, now that they made you captain?
Happy: There's a crowd of girls behind him everytime the classes change.
Biff (taking Willy's hand): This Saturday, Pop, this Saturday — just for you, I'm going to break through for a touchdown.
Happy: You're supposed to pass.
Biff: I'm takin' one play for Pop. You watch me, Pop, and when I take off my helmet, that means I'm breakin' out. Then you watch me crash through that line!
Willy (kisses Biff): Oh, wait'll I tell this in Boston!

Bernard enters in knickers. He is younger than Biff, earnest and loyal, a worried boy.

Bernard: Biff, where are you? You're supposed to study with me today.
Willy: Hey, looka Bernard. What're you lookin' so anemic about, Bernard?
Bernard: He's gotta study, Uncle Willy. He's got Regents next week.
Happy (tauntingly, spinning Bernard around): Let's box, Bernard!
Bernard: Biff! (*He gets away from Happy.*) Listen, Biff, I heard Mr. Birnbaum say that if you don't start studyin' math he's gonna flunk you, and you won't graduate. I heard him!
Willy: You better study with him, Biff. Go ahead now.
Bernard: I heard him!
Biff: Oh, Pop, you didn't see my sneakers! (*He holds up a foot for Willy to look at.*)
Willy: Hey, that's a beautiful job of printing!
Bernard (wiping his glasses): Just because he printed University of Virginia on his sneakers doesn't mean they've got to graduate him, Uncle Willy!
Willy (angrily): What're you talking about? With scholarships to three universities they're gonna flunk him?

Bernard: But I heard Mr. Birnbaum say —
Willy: Don't be a pest, Bernard! (*To his boys.*) What an anemic!
Bernard: Okay, I'm waiting for you in my house, Biff.

Bernard goes off. The Lomans laugh.

Willy: Bernard is not well liked, is he?
Biff: He's liked, but he's not well liked.
Happy: That's right, Pop.
Willy: That's just what I mean. Bernard can get the best marks in
   school, y'understand, but when he gets out in the business
   world, y'understand, you are going to be five times ahead of
   him. That's why I thank Almighty God you're both built like
   Adonises. Because the man who makes an appearance in the
   business world, the man who creates personal interest, is the
   man who gets ahead. Be liked and you will never want. You
   take me, for instance. I never have to wait in line to see a
   buyer. "Willy Loman is here!" That's all they have to know,
   and I go right through.
Biff: Did you knock them dead, Pop?
Willy: Knocked 'em cold in Providence, slaughtered 'em in
   Boston.
Happy (*on his back, pedaling again*): I'm losing weight, you notice,
   Pop?

Linda enters, as of old, a ribbon in her hair, carrying a basket of washing.

Linda (*with youthful energy*): Hello, dear!
Willy: Sweetheart!
Linda: How'd the Chevy run?
Willy: Chevrolet, Linda, is the greatest car ever built. (*To the boys.*)
   Since when do you let your mother carry wash up the stairs?
Biff: Grab hold there, boy!
Happy: Where to, Mom?
Linda: Hang them up on the line. And you better go down to
   your friends, Biff. The cellar is full of boys. They don't know
   what to do with themselves.
Biff: Ah, when Pop comes home they can wait!
Willy (*laughs appreciatively*): You better go down and tell them
   what to do, Biff.
Biff: I think I'll have them sweep out the furnace room.
Willy: Good work, Biff.
Biff (*goes through wall-line of kitchen to doorway at back and calls
   down*): Fellas! Everybody sweep out the furnace room! I'll be
   right down!

Voices: All right! Okay, Biff.

Biff: George and Sam and Frank, come out back! We're hangin' up the wash! Come on, Hap, on the double! (*He and Happy carry out the basket.*)

Linda: The way they obey him!

Willy: Well, that's training, the training. I'm tellin' you, I was sellin' thousands and thousands, but I had to come home.

Linda: Oh, the whole block'll be at that game. Did you sell anything?

Willy: I did five hundred gross in Providence and seven hundred gross in Boston.

Linda: No! Wait a minute, I've got a pencil. (*She pulls pencil and paper out of her apron pocket.*) That makes your commission . . . Two hundred — my God! Two hundred and twelve dollars!

Willy: Well, I didn't figure it yet, but . . .

Linda: How much did you do?

Willy: Well, I — I did — about a hundred and eighty gross in Providence. Well, no — it came to — roughly two hundred gross on the whole trip.

Linda (without hesitation): Two hundred gross. That's . . . (*She figures.*)

Willy: The trouble was that three of the stores were half closed for inventory in Boston. Otherwise I woulda broke records.

Linda: Well, it makes seventy dollars and some pennies. That's very good.

Willy: What do we owe?

Linda: Well, on the first there's sixteen dollars on the refrigerator —

Willy: Why sixteen?

Linda: Well, the fan belt broke, so it was a dollar eighty.

Willy: But it's brand new.

Linda: Well, the man said that's the way it is. Till they work themselves in, y'know.

They move through the wall-line into the kitchen.

Willy: I hope we didn't get stuck on that machine.

Linda: They got the biggest ads of any of them!

Willy: I know, it's a fine machine. What else?

Linda: Well, there's nine-sixty for the washing machine. And for the vacuum cleaner there's three and a half due on the fifteenth. Then the roof, you got twenty-one dollars remaining.

Willy: It don't leak, does it?

Linda: No, they did a wonderful job. Then you owe Frank for the carburetor.

Willy: I'm not going to pay that man! That goddam Chevrolet, they ought to prohibit the manufacture of that car!

Linda: Well, you owe him three and a half. And odds and ends, comes to around a hundred and twenty dollars by the fifteenth.

Willy: A hundred and twenty dollars! My God, if business don't pick up I don't know what I'm gonna do!

Linda: Well, next week you'll do better.

Willy: Oh, I'll knock 'em dead next week. I'll go to Hartford. I'm very well liked in Hartford. You know, the trouble is, Linda, people don't seem to take to me.

They move onto the forestage.

Linda: Oh, don't be foolish.

Willy: I know it when I walk in. They seem to laugh at me.

Linda: Why? Why would they laugh at you? Don't talk that way, Willy.

Willy moves to the edge of the stage. Linda goes into the kitchen and starts to darn stockings.

Willy: I don't know the reason for it, but they just pass me by. I'm not noticed.

Linda: But you're doing wonderful, dear. You're making seventy to a hundred dollars a week.

Willy: But I gotta be at it ten, twelve hours a day. Other men — I don't know — they do it easier. I don't know why — I can't stop myself — I talk too much. A man oughta come in with a few words. One thing about Charley. He's a man of few words, and they respect him.

Linda: You don't talk too much, you're just lively.

Willy (smiling): Well, I figure, what the hell, life is short, a couple of jokes. (*To himself.*) I joke too much! (*The smile goes.*)

Linda: Why? You're —

Willy: I'm fat, I'm very — foolish to look at, Linda. I didn't tell you, but Christmas time I happened to be calling on F. H. Stewarts, and a salesman I know, as I was going in to see the buyer I heard him say something about — walrus. And I — I cracked him right across the face. I won't take that. I simply will not take that. But they do laugh at me, I know that.

Linda: Darling . . .

Willy: I gotta overcome it. I know I gotta overcome it. I'm not dressing to advantage, maybe.

Linda: Willy, darling, you're the handsomest man in the world —

Willy: Oh, no, Linda.

Linda: To me you are. (*Slight pause.*) The handsomest.

From the darkness is heard the laughter of a woman. Willy doesn't turn to it, but it continues through Linda's lines.

Linda: And the boys, Willy. Few men are idolized by their children the way you are.

Music is heard as behind a scrim, to the left of the house. The Woman, dimly seen, is dressing.

Willy (with great feeling): You're the best there is, Linda, you're a pal, you know that? On the road — on the road I want to grab you sometimes and just kiss the life outa you.

The laughter is loud now, and he moves into a brightening area at the left, where The Woman has come from behind the scrim and is standing, putting on her hat, looking into a "mirror" and laughing.

Willy: Cause I get so lonely — especially when business is bad and there's nobody to talk to. I get the feeling that I'll never sell anything again, that I won't make a living for you, or a business, a business for the boys. (*He talks through The Woman's subsiding laughter; The Woman primps at the "mirror."*) There's so much I want to make for —

The Woman: Me? You didn't make me, Willy. I picked you.

Willy (pleased): You picked me?

The Woman (who is quite proper-looking, Willy's age): I did. I've been sitting at that desk watching all the salesmen go by day in, day out. But you've got such a sense of humor, and we do have such a good time together, don't we?

Willy: Sure, sure. (*He takes her in his arms.*) Why do you have to go now?

The Woman: It's two o'clock . . .

Willy: No, come on in! (*He pulls her.*)

The Woman: . . . my sisters'll be scandalized. When'll you be back?

Willy: Oh, two weeks about. Will you come up again?

The Woman: Sure thing. You do make me laugh. It's good for me. (*She squeezes his arm, kisses him.*) And I think you're a wonderful man.

Willy: You picked me, heh?

The Woman: Sure. Because you're so sweet. And such a kidder.

Willy: Well, I'll see you next time I'm in Boston.

The Woman: I'll put you right through to the buyers.

Willy (slapping her bottom): Right. Well, bottoms up!

The Woman (slaps him gently and laughs): You just kill me, Willy. (*He suddenly grabs her and kisses her roughly.*) You kill me. And thanks for the stockings. I love a lot of stockings. Well, good night.

Willy: Good night. And keep your pores open!

The Woman: Oh, Willy!

The Woman bursts out laughing, and Linda's laughter blends in. The Woman disappears into the dark. Now the area at the kitchen table brightens. Linda is sitting where she was at the kitchen table, but now is mending a pair of her silk stockings.

Linda: You are, Willy. The handsomest man. You've got no reason to feel that —

Willy (coming out of The Woman's dimming area and going over to Linda): I'll make it all up to you, Linda, I'll —

Linda: There's nothing to make up, dear. You're doing fine, better than —

Willy (noticing her mending): What's that?

Linda: Just mending my stockings. They're so expensive —

Willy (angrily, taking them from her): I won't have you mending stockings in this house! Now throw them out!

Linda puts the stockings in her pocket.

Bernard (entering on the run): Where is he? If he doesn't study!

Willy (moving to the forestage, with great agitation): You'll give him the answers!

Bernard: I do, but I can't on a Regents! That's a state exam! They're liable to arrest me!

Willy: Where is he? I'll whip him, I'll whip him!

Linda: And he'd better give back that football, Willy, it's not nice.

Willy: Biff! Where is he? Why is he taking everything?

Linda: He's too rough with the girls, Willy. All the mothers are afraid of him!

Willy: I'll whip him!

Bernard: He's driving the car without a license!

The Woman's laugh is heard.

Willy: Shut up!

Linda: All the mothers —

Willy: Shut up!

Bernard (backing quietly away and out): Mr. Birnbaum says he's stuck up.

Willy: Get outa here!

Bernard: If he doesn't buckle down he'll flunk math! (*He goes off.*)
Linda: He's right, Willy, you've gotta —
Willy (exploding at her): There's nothing the matter with him! You
    want him to be a worm like Bernard? He's got spirit, person-
    ality . . .

*As he speaks, Linda, almost in tears, exits into the living-room. Willy is alone in
the kitchen, wilting and staring. The leaves are gone. It is night again, and the
apartment houses look down from behind.*

Willy: Loaded with it. Loaded! What is he stealing? He's giving it
    back, isn't he? Why is he stealing? What did I tell him? I
    never in my life told him anything but decent things.

*Happy in pajamas has come down the stairs; Willy suddenly becomes aware of
Happy's presence.*

Happy: Let's go now, come on.
Willy (sitting down at the kitchen table): Huh! Why did she have to
    wax the floors herself? Everytime she waxes the floors she
    keels over. She knows that!
Happy: Shh! Take it easy. What brought you back tonight?
Willy: I got an awful scare. Nearly hit a kid in Yonkers. God! Why
    didn't I go to Alaska with my brother Ben that time! Ben!
    That man was a genius, that man was success incarnate! What
    a mistake! He begged me to go.
Happy: Well, there's no use in —
Willy: You guys! There was a man started with the clothes on his
    back and ended up with diamond mines!
Happy: Boy, someday I'd like to know how he did it.
Willy: What's the mystery? The man knew what he wanted and
    went out and got it! Walked into a jungle, and comes out, the
    age of twenty-one, and he's rich! The world is an oyster, but
    you don't crack it open on a mattress!
Happy: Pop, I told you I'm gonna retire you for life.
Willy: You'll retire me for life on seventy goddam dollars a week?
    And your women and your car and your apartment, and
    you'll retire me for life! Christ's sake, I couldn't get past
    Yonkers today! Where are you guys, where are you? The
    woods are burning! I can't drive a car!

*Charley has appeared in the doorway. He is a large man, slow of speech, laconic,
immovable. In all he says, despite what he says, there is pity, and, now, trepidation.
He has a robe over pajamas, slippers on his feet. He enters the kitchen.*

Charley: Everything all right?

Happy: Yeah, Charley, everything's . . .
Willy: What's the matter?
Charley: I heard some noise. I thought something happened. Can't we do something about the walls? You sneeze in here, and in my house hats blow off.
Happy: Let's go to bed, Dad. Come on.

Charley signals to Happy to go.

Willy: You go ahead, I'm not tired at the moment.
Happy (to Willy): Take it easy, huh? (*He exits.*)
Willy: What're you doin up?
Charley (sitting down at the kitchen table opposite Willy): Couldn't sleep good. I had a heartburn.
Willy: Well, you don't know how to eat.
Charley: I eat with my mouth.
Willy: No, you're ignorant. You gotta know about vitamins and things like that.
Charley: Come on, let's shoot. Tire you out a little.
Willy (hesitantly): All right. You got cards?
Charley (taking a deck from his pocket): Yeah, I got them. Someplace. What is it with those vitamins?
Willy (dealing): They build up your bones. Chemistry.
Charley: Yeah, but there's no bones in a heartburn.
Willy: What are you talkin' about? Do you know the first thing about it?
Charley: Don't get insulted.
Willy: Don't talk about something you don't know anything about.

They are playing. Pause.

Charley: What're you doin' home?
Willy: A little trouble with the car.
Charley: Oh. (*Pause.*) I'd like to take a trip to California.
Willy: Don't say.
Charley: You want a job?
Willy: I got a job, I told you that. (*After a slight pause.*) What the hell are you offering me a job for?
Charley: Don't get insulted.
Willy: Don't insult me.
Charley: I don't see no sense in it. You don't have to go on this way.
Willy: I got a good job. (*Slight pause.*) What do you keep comin' in here for?

Charley: You want me to go?

Willy (after a pause, withering): I can't understand it. He's going back to Texas again. What the hell is that?

Charley: Let him go.

Willy: I got nothin' to give him, Charley, I'm clean, I'm clean.

Charley: He won't starve. None a them starve. Forget about him.

Willy: Then what have I got to remember?

Charley: You take it too hard. To hell with it. When a deposit bottle is broken you don't get your nickel back.

Willy: That's easy enough for you to say.

Charley: That ain't easy for me to say.

Willy: Did you see the ceiling I put up in the living-room?

Charley: Yeah, that's a piece of work. To put up a ceiling is a mystery to me. How do you do it?

Willy: What's the difference?

Charley: Well, talk about it.

Willy: You gonna put up a ceiling?

Charley: How could I put up a ceiling?

Willy: Then what the hell are you bothering me for?

Charley: You're insulted again.

Willy: A man who can't handle tools is not a man. You're disgusting.

Charley: Don't call me disgusting, Willy.

Uncle Ben, carrying a valise and an umbrella, enters the forestage from around the right corner of the house. He is a stolid man, in his sixties, with a mustache and an authoritative air. He is utterly certain of his destiny, and there is an aura of far places about him. He enters exactly as Willy speaks.

Willy: I'm getting awfully tired, Ben.

Ben's music is heard. Ben looks around at everything.

Charley: Good, keep playing; you'll sleep better. Did you call me Ben?

Ben looks at his watch.

Willy: That's funny. For a second there you reminded me of my brother Ben.

Ben: I only have a few minutes. (*He strolls, inspecting the place. Willy and Charley continue playing.*)

Charley: You never heard from him again, heh? Since that time?

Willy: Didn't Linda tell you? Couple of weeks ago we got a letter from his wife in Africa. He died.

Charley: That so.

Ben (chuckling): So this is Brooklyn, eh?

Charley: Maybe you're in for some of his money.

Willy: Naa, he had seven sons. There's just one opportunity I had with that man . . .

Ben: I must make a train, William. There are several properties I'm looking at in Alaska.

Willy: Sure, sure! If I'd gone with him to Alaska that time, everything would've been totally different.

Charley: Go on, you'd froze to death up there.

Willy: What're you talking about?

Ben: Opportunity is tremendous in Alaska, William. Surprised you're not up there.

Willy: Sure, tremendous.

Charley: Heh?

Willy: There was the only man I ever met who knew the answers.

Charley: Who?

Ben: How are you all?

Willy (taking a pot, smiling): Fine, fine.

Charley: Pretty sharp tonight.

Ben: Is Mother living with you?

Willy: No, she died a long time ago.

Charley: Who?

Ben: That's too bad. Fine specimen of a lady, Mother.

Willy (to Charley): Heh?

Ben: I'd hoped to see the old girl.

Charley: Who died?

Ben: Heard anything from Father, have you?

Willy (unnerved): What do you mean, who died?

Charley (taking a pot): What're you talkin' about?

Ben (looking at his watch): William, it's half-past eight!

Willy (as though to dispel his confusion he angrily stops Charley's hand): That's my build!

Charley: I put the ace —

Willy: If you don't know how to play the game I'm not gonna throw my money away on you!

Charley (rising): It was my ace, for God's sake!

Willy: I'm through, I'm through!

Ben: When did Mother die?

Willy: Long ago. Since the beginning you never knew how to play cards.

Charley (picks up the cards and goes to the door): All right! Next time I'll bring a deck with five aces.

Willy: I don't play that kind of game!

Charley (turning to him): You ought to be ashamed of yourself!

Willy: Yeah?

Charley: Yeah! (*He goes out.*)

Willy (slamming the door after him): Ignoramus!

Ben (as Willy comes toward him through the wall-line of the kitchen): So you're William.

Willy (shaking Ben's hand): Ben! I've been waiting for you so long! What's the answer? How did you do it?

Ben: Oh, there's a story in that.

Linda enters the forestage, as of old, carrying the wash basket.

Linda: Is this Ben?

Ben (gallantly): How do you do, my dear.

Linda: Where've you been all these years? Willy's always wondered why you —

Willy (pulling Ben away from her impatiently): Where is Dad? Didn't you follow him? How did you get started?

Ben: Well, I don't know how much you remember.

Willy: Well, I was just a baby, of course, only three or four years old —

Ben: Three years and eleven months.

Willy: What a memory, Ben!

Ben: I have many enterprises, William, and I have never kept books.

Willy: I remember I was sitting under the wagon in — was it Nebraska?

Ben: It was South Dakota, and I gave you a bunch of wild flowers.

Willy: I remember you walking away down some open road.

Ben (laughing): I was going to find Father in Alaska.

Willy: Where is he?

Ben: At that age I had a very faulty view of geography, William. I discovered after a few days that I was heading due south, so instead of Alaska, I ended up in Africa.

Linda: Africa!

Willy: The Gold Coast!

Ben: Principally diamond mines.

Linda: Diamond mines!

Ben: Yes, my dear. But I've only a few minutes —

Willy: No! Boys! Boys! (*Young Biff and Happy appear.*) Listen to this. This is your Uncle Ben, a great man! Tell my boys, Ben!

Ben: Why, boys, when I was seventeen I walked into the jungle, and when I was twenty-one I walked out. (*He laughs.*) And by God I was rich.

Willy (to the boys): You see what I been talking about? The greatest things can happen!

Ben (glancing at his watch): I have an appointment in Ketchikan Tuesday week.

Willy: No, Ben! Please tell about Dad. I want my boys to hear. I want them to know the kind of stock they spring from. All I remember is a man with a big beard, and I was in Mamma's lap, sitting around a fire, and some kind of high music.

Ben: His flute. He played the flute.

Willy: Sure, the flute, that's right!

New music is heard, a high, rollicking tune.

Ben: Father was a very great and a very wild-hearted man. We would start in Boston, and he'd toss the whole family into the wagon, and then he'd drive the team right across the country; through Ohio, and Indiana, Michigan, Illinois, and all the Western states. And we'd stop in the towns and sell the flutes that he'd made on the way. Great inventor, Father. With one gadget he made more in a week than a man like you could make in a lifetime.

Willy: That's just the way I'm bringing them up, Ben — rugged, well liked, all-around.

Ben: Yeah? (*To Biff.*) Hit that, boy — hard as you can. (*He pounds his stomach.*)

Biff: Oh, no, sir!

Ben (taking boxing stance): Come on, get to me! (*He laughs.*)

Willy: Go to it, Biff! Go ahead, show him!

Biff: Okay! (*He cocks his fists and starts in.*)

Linda (to Willy): Why must he fight, dear?

Ben (sparring with Biff): Good boy! Good boy!

Willy: How's that, Ben, heh?

Happy: Give him the left, Biff!

Linda: Why are you fighting?

Ben: Good boy! (*Suddenly comes in, trips Biff, and stands over him, the point of his umbrella poised over Biff's eye.*)

Linda: Look out, Biff!

Biff: Gee!

Ben (patting Biff's knee): Never fight fair with a stranger, boy. You'll never get out of the jungle that way. (*Taking Linda's hand and bowing.*) It was an honor and a pleasure to meet you, Linda.

Linda (withdrawing her hand coldly, frightened): Have a nice — trip.

Ben (to Willy): And good luck with your — what do you do?

Willy: Selling.

Ben: Yes. Well . . . (*He raises his hand in farewell to all.*)

Willy: No, Ben, I don't want you to think . . . (*He takes Ben's arm to show him.*) It's Brooklyn, I know, but we hunt too.

Ben: Really, now.

Willy: Oh, sure, there's snakes and rabbits and — that's why I moved out here. Why, Biff can fell any one of these trees in no time! Boys! Go right over to where they're building the apartment house and get some sand. We're gonna rebuild the entire front stoop right now! Watch this, Ben!

Biff: Yes, sir! On the double, Hap!

Happy (as he and Biff run off): I lost weight, Pop, you notice?

Charley enters in knickers, even before the boys are gone.

Charley: Listen, if they steal any more from that building the watchman'll put the cops on them!

Linda (to Willy): Don't let Biff . . .

Ben laughs lustily.

Willy: You shoulda seen the lumber they brought home last week. At least a dozen six-by-tens worth all kinds a money.

Charley: Listen, if that watchman —

Willy: I gave them hell, understand. But I got a couple of fearless characters there.

Charley: Willy, the jails are full of fearless characters.

Ben (clapping Willy on the back, with a laugh at Charley): And the stock exchange, friend!

Willy (joining in Ben's laughter): Where are the rest of your pants?

Charley: My wife bought them.

Willy: Now all you need is a golf club and you can go upstairs and go to sleep. (*To Ben.*) Great athlete! Between him and his son Bernard they can't hammer a nail!

Bernard (rushing in): The watchman's chasing Biff!

Willy (angrily): Shut up! He's not stealing anything!

Linda (alarmed, hurrying off left): Where is he? Biff, dear! (*She exits.*)

Willy (moving toward the left, away from Ben): There's nothing wrong. What's the matter with you?

Ben: Nervy boy. Good!

Willy (laughing): Oh, nerves of iron, that Biff!

Charley: Don't know what it is. My New England man comes back and he's bleedin', they murdered him up there.

Willy: It's contacts, Charley, I got important contacts!

Charley (sarcastically): Glad to hear it, Willy. Come in later, we'll shoot a little casino. I'll take some of your Portland money. (*He laughs at Willy and exits.*)

Willy (turning to Ben): Business is bad, it's murderous. But not for me, of course.

Ben: I'll stop by on my way back to Africa.

Willy (longingly): Can't you stay a few days? You're just what I need, Ben, because I — I have a fine position here, but I — well, Dad left when I was such a baby and I never had a chance to talk to him and I still feel — kind of temporary about myself.

Ben: I'll be late for my train.

They are at opposite ends of the stage.

Willy: Ben, my boys — can't we talk? They'd go into the jaws of hell for me, see, but I —

Ben: William, you're being first-rate with your boys. Outstanding, manly chaps!

Willy (hanging on to his words): Oh, Ben, that's good to hear! Because sometimes I'm afraid that I'm not teaching them the right kind of — Ben, how should I teach them?

Ben (giving great weight to each word, and with a certain vicious audacity): William, when I walked into the jungle, I was seventeen. When I walked out I was twenty-one. And, by God, I was rich! (*He goes off into darkness around the right corner of the house.*)

Willy: . . . was rich! That's just the spirit I want to imbue them with! To walk into a jungle! I was right! I was right! I was right!

Ben is gone, but Willy is still speaking to him as Linda, in nightgown and robe, enters the kitchen, glances around for Willy, then goes to the door of the house, looks out and sees him. Comes down to his left. He looks at her.

Linda: Willy dear? Willy?

Willy: I was right!

Linda: Did you have some cheese? (*He can't answer.*) It's very late, darling. Come to bed, heh?

Willy (looking straight up): Gotta break your neck to see a star in this yard.

Linda: You coming in?

Willy: Whatever happened to that diamond watch fob? Remember? When Ben came from Africa that time? Didn't he give me a watch fob with a diamond in it?

Linda: You pawned it, dear. Twelve, thirteen years ago. For Biff's radio correspondence course.

Willy: Gee, that was a beautiful thing. I'll take a walk.

Linda: But you're in your slippers.

Willy (starting to go around the house at the left): I was right! I was!

(*Half to Linda, as he goes, shaking his head.*) What a man! There
was a man worth talking to. I was right!
Linda (calling after Willy): But in your slippers, Willy!

*Willy is almost gone when Biff, in his pajamas, comes down the stairs and enters
the kitchen.*

Biff: What is he doing out there?
Linda: Sh!
Biff: God Almighty, Mom, how long has he been doing this?
Linda: Don't, he'll hear you.
Biff: What the hell is the matter with him?
Linda: It'll pass by morning.
Biff: Shouldn't we do anything?
Linda: Oh, my dear, you should do a lot of things, but there's
nothing to do, so go to sleep.

Happy comes down the stairs and sits on the steps.

Happy: I never heard him so loud, Mom.
Linda: Well, come around more often; you'll hear him. (*She sits
down at the table and mends the lining of Willy's jacket.*)
Biff: Why didn't you ever write me about this, Mom?
Linda: How would I write to you? For over three months you had
no address.
Biff: I was on the move. But you know I thought of you all the
time. You know that, don't you, pal?
Linda: I know, dear I know. But he likes to have a letter. Just to
know that there's still a possibility for better things.
Biff: He's not like this all the time, is he?
Linda: It's when you come home he's always the worst.
Biff: When I come home?
Linda: When you write you're coming, he's all smiles, and talks
about the future, and — he's just wonderful. And then the
closer you seem to come, the more shaky he gets, and then, by
the time you get here, he's arguing, and he seems angry at
you. I think it's just that maybe he can't bring himself to — to
open up to you. Why are you so hateful to each other? Why is
that?
Biff (evasively): I'm not hateful, Mom.
Linda: But you no sooner come in the door than you're fighting!
Biff: I don't know why. I mean to change. I'm tryin', Mom, you
understand?
Linda: Are you home to stay now?
Biff: I don't know. I want to look around, see what's doin'.

Linda: Biff, you can't look around all your life, can you?

Biff: Just can't take hold, Mom. I can't take hold of some kind of a life.

Linda: Biff, a man is not a bird, to come and go with the spring-time.

Biff: Your hair . . . (*He touches her hair.*) Your hair got so gray.

Linda: Oh, it's been gray since you were in high school. I just stopped dyeing it, that's all.

Biff: Dye it again, will ya? I don't want my pal looking old. (*He smiles.*)

Linda: You're such a boy! You think you can go away for a year and . . . You've got to get it into your head now that one day you'll knock on this door and there'll be strange people here —

Biff: What are you talking about? You're not even sixty, Mom.

Linda: But what about your father?

Biff (lamely): Well, I meant him too.

Happy: He admires Pop.

Linda: Biff, dear, if you don't have any feeling for him, then you can't have any feeling for me.

Biff: Sure I can, Mom.

Linda: No. You can't just come to see me, because I love him. (*With a threat, but only a threat, of tears.*) He's the dearest man in the world to me, and I won't have anyone making him feel unwanted and low and blue. You've got to make up your mind now, darling, there's no leeway any more. Either he's your father and you pay him that respect, or else you're not to come here. I know he's not easy to get along with — nobody knows that better than me — but . . .

Willy (from the left, with a laugh): Hey, hey, Biffo!

Biff (starting to go out after Willy): What the hell is the matter with him? (*Happy stops him.*)

Linda: Don't — don't go near him!

Biff: Stop making excuses for him! He always, always wiped the floor with you. Never had an ounce of respect for you.

Happy: He's always had respect for —

Biff: What the hell do you know about it?

Happy (surlily): Just don't call him crazy!

Biff: He's got no character — Charley wouldn't do this. Not in his own house — spewing out that vomit from his mind.

Happy: Charley never had to cope with what he's got to.

Biff: People are worse off than Willy Loman. Believe me, I've seen them!

Linda: Then make Charley your father, Biff. You can't do that, can you? I don't say he's a great man. Willy Loman never made a lot of money. His name was never in the paper. He's not the finest character that ever lived. But he's a human being, and a terrible thing is happening to him. So attention must be paid. He's not to be allowed to fall into his grave like an old dog. Attention, attention must be finally paid to such a person. You called him crazy —

Biff: I didn't mean —

Linda: No, a lot of people think he's lost his — balance. But you don't have to be very smart to know what his trouble is. The man is exhausted.

Happy: Sure!

Linda: A small man can be just as exhausted as a great man. He works for a company thirty-six years this March, opens up unheard-of territories to their trademark, and now in his old age they take his salary away.

Happy (indignantly): I didn't know that, Mom.

Linda: You never asked, my dear! Now that you get your spending money someplace else you don't trouble your mind with him.

Happy: But I gave you money last —

Linda: Christmas time, fifty dollars! To fix the hot water it cost ninety-seven fifty! For five weeks he's been on straight commission, like a beginner, an unknown!

Biff: Those ungrateful bastards!

Linda: Are they any worse than his sons? When he brought them business, when he was young, they were glad to see him. But now his old friends, the old buyers that loved him so and always found some order to hand him in a pinch — they're all dead, retired. He used to be able to make six, seven calls a day in Boston. Now he takes his valises out of the car and puts them back and takes them out again and he's exhausted. Instead of walking he talks now. He drives seven hundred miles, and when he gets there no one knows him any more, no one welcomes him. And what goes through a man's mind, driving seven hundred miles home without having earned a cent? Why shouldn't he talk to himself? Why? When he has to go to Charley and borrow fifty dollars a week and pretend to me that it's his pay? How long can that go on? How long? You see what I'm sitting here and waiting for? And you tell me he has no character? The man who never worked a day but for your benefit? When does he get the medal for that? Is this his reward — to turn around at the age of sixty-three and find

his sons, who he loved better than his life, one a philandering
bum —

Happy: Mom!

Linda: That's all you are, my baby! (*To Biff.*) And you! What
happened to the love you had for him? You were such pals!
How you used to talk to him on the phone every night! How
lonely he was till he could come home to you!

Biff: All right, Mom, I'll live here in my room, and I'll get a job.
I'll keep away from him, that's all.

Linda: No, Biff. You can't stay here and fight all the time.

Biff: He threw me out of this house, remember that.

Linda: Why did he do that? I never knew why.

Biff: Because I know he's a fake and he doesn't like anybody
around who knows!

Linda: Why a fake? In what way? What do you mean?

Biff: Just don't lay it all at my feet. It's between me and him —
that's all I have to say. I'll chip in from now on. He'll settle
for half my pay check. He'll be all right. I'm going to bed. (*He
starts for the stairs.*)

Linda: He won't be all right.

Biff (turning on the stairs, furiously): I hate this city and I'll stay
here. Now what do you want?

Linda: He's dying, Biff.

Happy turns quickly to her, shocked.

Biff (after a pause): Why is he dying?

Linda: He's been trying to kill himself.

Biff (with great horror): How?

Linda: I live from day to day.

Biff: What're you talking about?

Linda: Remember I wrote you that he smashed up the car again?
In February?

Biff: Well?

Linda: The insurance inspector came. He said that they have
evidence. That all these accidents in the last year —
weren't — accidents.

Happy: How can they tell that? That's a lie.

Linda: It seems there's a woman . . . (*She takes a breath as —*)

⎰ *Biff (sharply but contained):* What woman?
⎱ *Linda (simultaneously):* . . . and this woman . . .

Linda: What?

Biff: Nothing. Go ahead.

Linda: What did you say?

Biff: Nothing. I just said what woman?

Happy: What about her?

Linda: Well, it seems she was walking down the road and saw his car. She says that he wasn't driving fast at all, and that he didn't skid. She says he came to that little bridge, and then deliberately smashed into the railing and it was only the shallowness of the water that saved him.

Biff: Oh, no, he probably just fell asleep again.

Linda: I don't think he fell asleep.

Biff: Why not?

Linda: Last month . . . (*With great difficulty.*) Oh, boys, it's so hard to say a thing like this. He's just a big stupid man to you, but I tell you there's more good in him than in many other people. (*She chokes, wipes her eyes.*) I was looking for a fuse. The lights blew out, and I went down the cellar. And behind the fuse box — it happened to fall out — was a length of rubber pipe — just short.

Happy: No kidding?

Linda: There's a little attachment on the end of it. I knew right away. And sure enough, on the bottom of the water heater there's a new little nipple on the gas pipe.

Happy (angrily): That — jerk.

Biff: Did you have it taken off?

Linda: I'm — I'm ashamed to. How can I mention it to him? Every day I go down and take away that little rubber pipe. But, when he comes home, I put it back where it was. How can I insult him that way? I don't know what to do. I live from day to day, boys. I tell you, I know every thought in his mind. It sounds so old-fashioned and silly, but I tell you he put his whole life into you and you've turned your backs on him. (*She is bent over in the chair, weeping, her face in her hands.*) Biff, I swear to God! Biff, his life is in your hands!

Happy (to Biff): How do you like that damned fool!

Biff (kissing her): All right, pal, all right. It's all settled now. I've been remiss. I know that, Mom. But now I'll stay, and I swear to you, I'll apply myself. (*Kneeling in front of her, in a fever of self-reproach.*) It's just — you see, Mom, I don't fit in business. Not that I won't try. I'll try, and I'll make good.

Happy: Sure you will. The trouble with you in business was you never tried to please people.

Biff: I know, I —

Happy: Like when you worked for Harrison's. Bob Harrison said you were tops, and then you go and do some damn fool thing like whistling whole songs in the elevator like a comedian.

Biff (against Happy): So what? I like to whistle sometimes.

Happy: You don't raise a guy to a responsible job who whistles in the elevator!

Linda: Well, don't argue about it now.

Happy: Like when you'd go off and swim in the middle of the day instead of taking the line around.

Biff (his resentment rising): Well, don't you run off? You take off sometimes, don't you? On a nice summer day?

Happy: Yeah, but I cover myself!

Linda: Boys!

Happy: If I'm going to take a fade the boss can call any number where I'm supposed to be and they'll swear to him that I just left. I'll tell you something that I hate to say, Biff, but in the business world some of them think you're crazy.

Biff (angered): Screw the business world!

Happy: All right, screw it! Great, but cover yourself!

Linda: Hap, Hap!

Biff: I don't care what they think! They've laughed at Dad for years, and you know why? Because we don't belong in this nut-house of a city! We should be mixing cement on some open plain, or — or carpenters. A carpenter is allowed to whistle!

Willy walks in from the entrance of the house, at left.

Willy: Even your grandfather was better than a carpenter. (*Pause. They watch him.*) You never grew up. Bernard does not whistle in the elevator, I assure you.

Biff (as though to laugh Willy out of it): Yeah, but you do, Pop.

Willy: I never in my life whistled in an elevator! And who in the business world thinks I'm crazy?

Biff: I didn't mean it like that, Pop. Now don't make a whole thing out of it, will ya?

Willy: Go back to the West! Be a carpenter, a cowboy, enjoy yourself!

Linda: Willy, he was just saying —

Willy: I heard what he said!

Happy (trying to quiet Willy): Hey, Pop, come on now . . .

Willy (continuing over Happy's line): They laugh at me, heh? Go to Filene's, go to the Hub, go to Slattery's, Boston. Call out the name Willy Loman and see what happens. Big shot!

Biff: All right, Pop.

Willy: Big!

Biff: All right!

Willy: Why do you always insult me?

Biff: I didn't say a word. (*To Linda.*) Did I say a word?

Linda: He didn't say anything, Willy.

Willy (going to the doorway of the living-room): All right, good night, good night.

Linda: Willy, dear, he just decided . . .

Willy (to Biff): If you get tired hanging around tomorrow, paint the ceiling I put up in the living-room.

Biff: I'm leaving early tomorrow.

Happy: He's going to see Bill Oliver, Pop.

Willy (interestedly): Oliver? For what?

Biff (with reserve, but trying, trying): He always said he'd stake me. I'd like to go into business, so maybe I can take him up on it.

Linda: Isn't that wonderful?

Willy: Don't interrupt. What's wonderful about it? There's fifty men in the City of New York who'd stake him. (*To Biff.*) Sporting goods?

Biff: I guess so. I know something about it and —

Willy: He knows something about it! You know sporting goods better than Spalding, for God's sake! How much is he giving you?

Biff: I don't know, I didn't even see him yet, but —

Willy: Then what're you talkin' about?

Biff (getting angry): Well, I said was I'm gonna see him, that's all!

Willy (turning away): Ah, you're counting your chickens again.

Biff (starting left for the stairs): Oh, Jesus, I'm going to sleep!

Willy (calling after him): Don't curse in this house!

Biff (turning): Since when did you get so clean?

Happy (trying to stop them): Wait a . . .

Willy: Don't use that language to me! I won't have it!

Happy (grabbing Biff, shouts): Wait a minute! I got an idea. I got a feasible idea. Come here, Biff, let's talk this over now, let's talk some sense here. When I was down in Florida last time, I thought of a great idea to sell sporting goods. It just came back to me. You and I, Biff — we have a line, the Loman Line. We train a couple of weeks, and put on a couple of exhibitions, see?

Willy: That's an idea!

Happy: Wait! We form two basketball teams, see? Two water-polo teams. We play each other. It's a million dollars' worth of publicity. Two brothers, see? The Loman Brothers. Displays in the Royal Palms — all the hotels. And banners over the ring and the basketball court: "Loman Brothers." Baby, we could sell sporting goods!

Willy: That is a one-million-dollar idea!

Linda: Marvelous!

Biff: I'm in great shape as far as that's concerned.

Happy: And the beauty of it is, Biff, it wouldn't be like a business. We'd be out playin' ball again . . .

Biff (enthused): Yeah, that's . . .

Willy: Million-dollar . . .

Happy: And you wouldn't get fed up with it, Biff. It'd be the family again. There'd be the old honor, and comradeship, and if you wanted to go off for a swim or somethin' — well, you'd do it! Without some smart cooky gettin' up ahead of you!

Willy: Lick the world! You guys together could absolutely lick the civilized world.

Biff: I'll see Oliver tomorrow. Hap, if we could work that out . . .

Linda: Maybe things are beginning to —

Willy (wildly enthused, to Linda): Stop interrupting! *(To Biff.)* But don't wear sport jacket and slacks when you see Oliver.

Biff: No, I'll —

Willy: A business suit, and talk as little as possible, and don't crack any jokes.

Biff: He did like me. Always liked me.

Linda: He loved you!

Willy (to Linda): Will you stop! *(To Biff.)* Walk in very serious. You are not applying for a boy's job. Money is to pass. Be quiet, fine, and serious. Everybody likes a kidder but nobody lends him money.

Happy: I'll try to get some myself, Biff. I'm sure I can.

Willy: I see great things for you kids, I think your troubles are over. But remember, start big and you'll end big. Ask for fifteen. How much you gonna ask for?

Biff: Gee, I don't know —

Willy: And don't say "Gee." "Gee" is a boy's word. A man walking in for fifteen thousand dollars does not say "Gee!"

Biff: Ten, I think, would be top though.

Willy: Don't be so modest. You always started too low. Walk in with a big laugh. Don't look worried. Start off with a couple of your good stories to lighten things up. It's not what you say, it's how you say it — because personality always wins the day.

Linda: Oliver always thought the highest of him —

Willy: Will you let me talk?

Biff: Don't yell at her, Pop, will ya?

Willy (angrily): I was talking, wasn't I?

Biff: I don't like you yelling at her all the time, and I'm tellin' you, that's all.

Willy: What're you, takin' over this house?

Linda: Willy —

Willy (turning on her): Don't take his side all the time, goddammit!

Biff (furiously): Stop yelling at her!

Willy (suddenly pulling on his cheek, beaten down, guilt ridden): Give my best to Bill Oliver — he may remember me. (*He exits through the living-room doorway.*)

Linda (her voice subdued): What'd you have to start that for? (*Biff turns away.*) You see how sweet he was as soon as you talked hopefully? (*She goes over to Biff.*) Come up and say good night to him. Don't let him go to bed that way.

Happy: Come on, Biff, let's buck him up.

Linda: Please, dear. Just say good night. It takes so little to make him happy. Come. (*She goes through the living-room doorway, calling upstairs from within the living-room.*) Your pajamas are hanging in the bathroom, Willy!

Happy (looking toward where Linda went out): What a woman! They broke the mold when they made her. You know that, Biff?

Biff: He's off salary. My God, working on commission!

Happy: Well, let's face it: he's no hot-shot selling man. Except that sometimes, you have to admit, he's a sweet personality.

Biff (deciding): Lend me ten bucks, will ya? I want to buy some new ties.

Happy: I'll take you to a place I know. Beautiful stuff. Wear one of my striped shirts tomorrow.

Biff: She got gray. Mom got awful old. Gee, I'm gonna go in to Oliver tomorrow and knock him for a —

Happy: Come on up. Tell that to Dad. Let's give him a whirl. Come on.

Biff (steamed up): You know, with ten thousand bucks, boy!

Happy (as they go into the living-room): That's the talk, Biff, that's the first time I've heard the old confidence out of you! (*From within the living-room, fading off.*) You're gonna live with me, kid, and any babe you want just say the word . . . (*The last lines are hardly heard. They are mounting the stairs to their parents' bedroom.*)

Linda (entering her bedroom and addressing Willy, who is in the bathroom. She is straightening the bed for him): Can you do anything about the shower? It drips.

Willy (from the bathroom): All of a sudden everything falls to pieces! Goddam plumbing, oughta be sued, those people. I hardly finished putting it in and the thing . . . (*His words rumble off.*)

Linda: I'm just wondering if Oliver will remember him. You think he might?

Willy (coming out of the bathroom in his pajamas): Remember him? What's the matter with you, you crazy? If he'd've stayed with Oliver he'd be on top by now! Wait'll Oliver gets a look at him. You don't know the average caliber any more. The average young man today — (*he is getting into bed*) — is got a caliber of zero. Greatest thing in the world for him was to bum around.

Biff and Happy enter the bedroom. Slight pause.

Willy (stops short, looking at Biff): Glad to hear it, boy.

Happy: He wanted to say good night to you, sport.

Willy (to Biff): Yeah. Knock him dead, boy. What'd you want to tell me?

Biff: Just take it easy, Pop. Good night. (*He turns to go.*)

Willy (unable to resist): And if anything falls off the desk while you're talking to him — like a package or something — don't you pick it up. They have office boys for that.

Linda: I'll make a big breakfast —

Willy: Will you let me finish? (*To Biff.*) Tell him you were in the business in the West. Not farm work.

Biff: All right, Dad.

Linda: I think everything —

Willy (going right through her speech): And don't undersell yourself. No less than fifteen thousand dollars.

Biff (unable to bear him): Okay. Good night, Mom. (*He starts moving.*)

Willy: Because you got a greatness in you, Biff, remember that. You got all kinds a greatness . . . (*He lies back, exhausted. Biff walks out.*)

Linda (calling after Biff): Sleep well, darling!

Happy: I'm gonna get married, Mom. I wanted to tell you.

Linda: Go to sleep, dear.

Happy (going): I just wanted to tell you.

Willy: Keep up the good work. (*Happy exits.*) God . . . remember that Ebbets Field game? The championship of the city?

Linda: Just rest. Should I sing to you?

Willy: Yeah. Sing to me. (*Linda hums a soft lullaby.*) When that team came out — he was the tallest, remember?

Linda: Oh, yes. And in gold.

Biff enters the darkened kitchen, takes a cigarette, and leaves the house. He comes downstage into a golden pool of light. He smokes, staring at the night.

Willy: Like a young god. Hercules — something like that. And the sun, the sun all around him. Remember how he waved to me? Right up from the field, with the representatives of three colleges standing by? And the buyers I brought, and the cheers when he came out — Loman, Loman, Loman! God Almighty, he'll be great yet. A star like that, magnificent, can never really fade away!

The light on Willy is fading. The gas heater begins to glow through the kitchen wall, near the stairs, a blue flame beneath red coils.

Linda (timidly): Willy dear, what has he got against you?
Willy: I'm so tired. Don't talk any more.

Biff slowly returns to the kitchen. He stops, stares toward the heater.

Linda: Will you ask Howard to let you work in New York?
Willy: First thing in the morning. Everything'll be all right.

Biff reaches behind the heater and draws out a length of rubber tubing. He is horrified and turns his head toward Willy's room, still dimly lit, from which the strains of Linda's desperate but monotonous humming rise.

Willy (staring through the window into the moonlight): Gee, look at the moon moving between the buildings!

Biff wraps the tubing around his hand and quickly goes up the stairs.

Curtain

ACT II

Music is heard, gay and bright. The curtain rises as the music fades away. Willy, in shirt sleeves, is sitting at the kitchen table, sipping coffee, his hat in his lap. Linda is filling his cup when she can.

Willy: Wonderful coffee. Meal in itself.
Linda: Can I make you some eggs?
Willy: No. Take a breath.
Linda: You look so rested, dear.
Willy: I slept like a dead one. First time in months. Imagine,

sleeping till ten on a Tuesday morning. Boys left nice and early, heh?

Linda: They were out of here by eight o'clock.

Willy: Good work!

Linda: It was so thrilling to see them leaving together. I can't get over the shaving lotion in this house!

Willy (smiling): Mmm —

Linda: Biff was very changed this morning. His whole attitude seemed to be hopeful. He couldn't wait to get downtown to see Oliver.

Willy: He's heading for a change. There's no question, there simply are certain men that take longer to get — solidified. How did he dress?

Linda: His blue suit. He's so handsome in that suit. He could be a — anything in that suit!

Willy gets up from the table. Linda holds his jacket for him.

Willy: There's no question, no question at all. Gee, on the way home tonight I'd like to buy some seeds.

Linda (laughing): That'd be wonderful. But not enough sun gets back there. Nothing'll grow any more.

Willy: You wait, kid, before it's all over we're gonna get a little place out in the country, and I'll raise some vegetables, a couple of chickens . . .

Linda: You'll do it yet, dear.

Willy walks out of his jacket. Linda follows him.

Willy: And they'll get married, and come for a weekend. I'd build a little guest house. 'Cause I got so many fine tools, all I'd need would be a little lumber and some peace of mind.

Linda (joyfully): I sewed the lining . . .

Willy: I could build two guest houses, so they'd both come. Did he decide how much he's going to ask Oliver for?

Linda (getting him into the jacket): He didn't mention it, but I imagine ten or fifteen thousand. You going to talk to Howard today?

Willy: Yeah. I'll put it to him straight and simple. He'll just have to take me off the road.

Linda: And Willy, don't forget to ask for a little advance, because we've got the insurance premium. It's the grace period now.

Willy: That's a hundred . . . ?

Linda: A hundred and eight, sixty-eight. Because we're a little short again.

Willy: Why are we short?

Linda: Well, you had the motor job on the car . . .

Willy: That goddam Studebaker!

Linda: And you got one more payment on the refrigerator . . .

Willy: But it just broke again!

Linda: Well, it's old, dear.

Willy: I told you we should've bought a well-advertised machine. Charley bought a General Electric and it's twenty years old and it's still good, that son-of-a-bitch.

Linda: But, Willy —

Willy: Whoever heard of a Hastings refrigerator? Once in my life I would like to own something outright before it's broken! I'm always in a race with the junkyard! I just finished paying for the car and it's on its last legs. The refrigerator consumes belts like a goddam maniac. They time those things. They time them so when you finally paid for them, they're used up.

Linda (buttoning up his jacket as he unbuttons it): All told, about two hundred dollars would carry us, dear. But that includes the last payment on the mortgage. After this payment, Willy, the house belongs to us.

Willy: It's twenty-five years!

Linda: Biff was nine years old when we bought it.

Willy: Well, that's a great thing. To weather a twenty-five year mortgage is —

Linda: It's an accomplishment.

Willy: All the cement, the lumber, the reconstruction I put in this house! There ain't a crack to be found in it any more.

Linda: Well, it served its purpose.

Willy: What purpose? Some stranger'll come along, move in, and that's that. If only Biff would take this house, and raise a family . . . *(He starts to go.)* Good-by, I'm late.

Linda (suddenly remembering): Oh, I forgot! You're supposed to meet them for dinner.

Willy: Me?

Linda: At Frank's Chop House on Forty-eighth near Sixth Avenue.

Willy: Is that so! How about you?

Linda: No, just the three of you. They're gonna blow you to a big meal!

Willy: Don't say! Who thought of that?

Linda: Biff came to me this morning, Willy, and he said, "Tell Dad, we want to blow him to a big meal." Be there six o'clock. You and your two boys are going to have dinner.

Willy: Gee whiz! That's really somethin'. I'm gonna knock Howard for a loop, kid. I'll get an advance, and I'll come home with a New York job. Goddammit, now I'm gonna do it!

Linda: Oh, that's the spirit, Willy!

Willy: I will never get behind a wheel the rest of my life!

Linda: It's changing, Willy, I can feel it changing!

Willy: Beyond a question. G'by, I'm late. (*He starts to go again.*)

Linda (calling after him as she runs to the kitchen table for a handkerchief): You got your glasses?

Willy (feels for them, then comes back in): Yeah, yeah, got my glasses.

Linda (giving him the handkerchief): And a handkerchief.

Willy: Yeah, handkerchief.

Linda: And your saccharine?

Willy: Yeah, my saccharine.

Linda: Be careful on the subway stairs.

She kisses him, and a silk stocking is seen hanging from her hand. Willy notices it.

Willy: Will you stop mending stockings? At least while I'm in the house. It gets me nervous. I can't tell you. Please.

Linda hides the stocking in her hand as she follows Willy across the forestage in front of the house.

Linda: Remember, Frank's Chop House.

Willy (passing the apron): Maybe beets would grow out there.

Linda (laughing): But you tried so many times.

Willy: Yeah. Well, don't work hard today. (He disappears around the right corner of the house.)

Linda: Be careful!

As Willy vanishes, Linda waves to him. Suddenly the phone rings. She runs across the stage and into the kitchen and lifts it.

Linda: Hello? Oh, Biff! I'm so glad you called, I just. . . . Yes, sure, I just told him. Yes, he'll be there for dinner at six o'clock, I didn't forget. Listen, I was just dying to tell you. You know that little rubber pipe I told you about? That he connected to the gas heater? I finally decided to go down the cellar this morning and take it away and destroy it. But it's gone! Imagine? He took it away himself, it isn't there! (*She listens.*) When? Oh, then you took it. Oh — nothing, it's just that I'd hoped he'd taken it away himself. Oh, I'm not worried, darling, because this morning he left in such high spirits, it was like the old days! I'm not afraid any more. Did Mr. Oliver see you?

. . . Well, you wait there then. And make a nice impression on him, darling. Just don't perspire too much before you see him. And have a nice time with Dad. He may have big news too! . . . That's right, a New York job. And be sweet to him tonight, dear. Be loving to him. Because he's only a little boat looking for a harbor. (*She is trembling with sorrow and joy.*) Oh, that's wonderful, Biff, you'll save his life. Thanks, darling. Just put your arm around him when he comes into the restaurant. Give him a smile. That's the boy . . . Good-by, dear. . . . You got your comb? . . . That's fine. Good-by, Biff dear.

In the middle of her speech, Howard Wagner, thirty-six, wheels on a small type-writer table on which is a wire-recording machine and proceeds to plug it in. This is on the left forestage. Light slowly fades on Linda as it rises on Howard. Howard is intent on threading the machine and only glances over his shoulder as Willy appears.

Willy: Pst! Pst!
Howard: Hello, Willy, come in.
Willy: Like to have a little talk with you, Howard.
Howard: Sorry to keep you waiting. I'll be with you in a minute.
Willy: What's that, Howard?
Howard: Didn't you ever see one of these? Wire recorder.
Willy: Oh. Can we talk a minute?
Howard: Records things. Just got delivery yesterday. Been driving me crazy, the most terrific machine I ever saw in my life. I was up all night with it.
Willy: What do you do with it?
Howard: I bought it for dictation, but you can do anything with it. Listen to this. I had it home last night. Listen to what I picked up. The first one is my daughter. Get this. (*He flicks the switch and "Roll Out the Barrel" is heard being whistled.*) Listen to that kid whistle.
Willy: That is lifelike, isn't it?
Howard: Seven years old. Get that tone.
Willy: Ts, ts. Like to ask a little favor if you . . .

The whistling breaks off, and the voice of Howard's Daughter is heard.

His Daughter: "Now you, Daddy."
Howard: She's crazy for me! (*Again the same song is whistled.*) That's me! Ha! (*He winks.*)
Willy: You're very good!

The whistling breaks off again. The machine runs silent for a moment.

Howard: Sh! Get this now, this is my son.

His Son: "The capital of Alabama is Montgomery; the capital of Arizona is Phoenix; the capital of Arkansas is Little Rock; the capital of California is Sacramento . . ." (*And on, and on.*)

Howard (holding up five fingers): Five years old, Willy!

Willy: He'll make an announcer some day!

His Son (continuing): "The capital . . ."

Howard: Get that — alphabetical order! (*The machine breaks off suddenly.*) Wait a minute. The maid kicked the plug out.

Willy: It certainly is a —

Howard: Sh, for God's sake!

His Son: "It's nine o'clock, Bulova watch time. So I have to go to sleep."

Willy: That really is —

Howard: Wait a minute! The next is my wife.

They wait.

Howard's Voice: "Go on, say something." (*Pause.*) "Well, you gonna talk?"

His Wife: "I can't think of anything."

Howard's Voice: "Well, talk — it's turning."

His Wife (shyly, beaten): "Hello." (*Silence.*) "Oh, Howard, I can't talk into this . . ."

Howard (snapping the machine off): That was my wife.

Willy: That is a wonderful machine. Can we —

Howard: I tell you, Willy, I'm gonna take my camera, and my bandsaw, and all my hobbies, and out they go. This is the most fascinating relaxation I ever found.

Willy: I think I'll get one myself.

Howard: Sure, they're only a hundred and a half. You can't do without it. Supposing you wanna hear Jack Benny, see? But you can't be at home at that hour. So you tell the maid to turn the radio on when Jack Benny comes on, and this automatically goes on with the radio . . .

Willy: And when you come home you . . .

Howard: You can come home twelve o'clock, one o'clock, any time you like, and you get yourself a Coke and sit yourself down, throw the switch, and there's Jack Benny's program in the middle of the night!

Willy: I'm definitely going to get one. Because lots of time I'm on the road, and I think to myself, what I must be missing on the radio!

Howard: Don't you have a radio in the car?

Willy: Well, yeah, but who ever thinks of turning it on?

Howard: Say, aren't you supposed to be in Boston?

Willy: That's what I want to talk to you about, Howard. You got a minute? (*He draws a chair in from the wing.*)

Howard: What happened? What're you doing here?

Willy: Well . . .

Howard: You didn't crack up again, did you?

Willy: Oh, no. No . . .

Howard: Geez, you had me worried there for a minute. What's the trouble?

Willy: Well, tell you the truth, Howard, I've come to the decision that I'd rather not travel any more.

Howard: Not travel! Well, what'll you do?

Willy: Remember, Christmas time, when you had the party here? You said you'd try to think of some spot for me here in town.

Howard: With us?

Willy: Well, sure.

Howard: Oh, yeah, yeah. I remember. Well, I couldn't think of anything for you, Willy.

Willy: I tell ya, Howard. The kids are all grown up, y'know. I don't need much any more. If I could take home — well, sixty-five dollars a week, I could swing it.

Howard: Yeah, but Willy, see I —

Willy: I tell ya why, Howard. Speaking frankly and between the two of us, y'know — I'm just a little tired.

Howard: Oh, I could understand that, Willy. But you're a road man, Willy, and we do a road business. We've only got a half-dozen salesmen on the floor here.

Willy: God knows, Howard, I never asked a favor of any man. But I was with the firm when your father used to carry you in here in his arms.

Howard: I know that, Willy, but —

Willy: Your father came to me the day you were born and asked me what I thought of the name of Howard, may he rest in peace.

Howard: I appreciate that, Willy, but there just is no spot here for you. If I had a spot I'd slam you right in, but I just don't have a single solitary spot.

He looks for his lighter. Willy has picked it up and gives it to him. Pause.

Willy (with increasing anger): Howard, all I need to set my table is fifty dollars a week.

Howard: But where am I going to put you, kid?

Willy: Look, it isn't a question of whether I can sell merchandise, is it?

Howard: No, but it's a business, kid, and everybody's gotta pull his own weight.

Willy (desperately): Just let me tell you a story, Howard —

Howard: Cause you gotta admit, business is business.

Willy (angrily): Business is definitely business, but just listen for a minute. You don't understand this. When I was a boy — eighteen, nineteen — I was already on the road. And there was a question in my mind as to whether selling had a future for me. Because in those days I had a yearning to go to Alaska. See, there were three gold strikes in one month in Alaska, and I felt like going out. Just for the ride, you might say.

Howard (barely interested): Don't say.

Willy: Oh, yeah, my father lived many years in Alaska. He was an adventurous man. We've got quite a little streak of self-reliance in our family. I thought I'd go out with my older brother and try to locate him, and maybe settle in the North with the old man. And I was almost decided to go, when I met a salesman in the Parker House. His name was Dave Single-man. And he was eighty-four years old, and he'd drummed merchandise in thirty-one states. And old Dave, he'd go up to his room, y'understand, put on his green velvet slippers — I'll never forget — and pick up his phone and call the buyers, and without ever leaving his room, at the age of eighty-four, he made his living. And when I saw that, I realized that selling was the greatest career a man could want. 'Cause what could be more satisfying than to be able to go, at the age of eighty-four, into twenty or thirty different cities, and pick up a phone, and be remembered and loved and helped by so many different people? Do you know? when he died — and by the way he died the death of a salesman, in his green velvet slippers in the smoker of the New York, New Haven and Hartford, going into Boston — when he died, hundreds of salesmen and buyers were at his funeral. Things were sad on a lotta trains for months after that. (*He stands up. Howard has not looked at him.*) In those days there was person-ality in it, Howard. There was respect, and comradeship, and gratitude in it. Today, it's all cut and dried, and there's no chance for bringing friendship to bear — or personality. You see what I mean? They don't know me any more.

Howard (moving away, to the right): That's just the thing, Willy.

Willy: If I had forty dollars a week — that's all I'd need. Forty dollars, Howard.

Howard: Kid, I can't take blood from a stone, I —

Willy (desperation is on him now): Howard, the year Al Smith was nominated, your father came to me and —

Howard (starting to go off): I've got to see some people, kid.

Willy (stopping him): I'm talking about your father! There were promises made across this desk! You mustn't tell me you've got people to see — I put thirty-four years into this firm, Howard, and now I can't pay my insurance! You can't eat the orange and throw the peel away — a man is not a piece of fruit! *(After a pause.)* Now pay attention. Your father — in 1928 I had a big year. I averaged a hundred and seventy dollars a week in commissions.

Howard (impatiently): Now, Willy, you never averaged —

Willy (banging his hand on the desk): I averaged a hundred and seventy dollars a week in the year of 1928! And your father came to me — or rather, I was in the office here — it was right over this desk — and he put his hand on my shoulder —

Howard (getting up): You'll have to excuse me, Willy, I gotta see some people. Pull yourself together. *(Going out.)* I'll be back in a little while.

On Howard's exit, the light on his chair grows very bright and strange.

Willy: Pull myself together! What the hell did I say to him? My God, I was yelling at him! How could I! *(Willy breaks off, staring at the light, which occupies the chair, animating it. He approaches this chair, standing across the desk from it.)* Frank, Frank, don't you remember what you told me that time? How you put your hand on my shoulder, and Frank . . . *(He leans on the desk and as he speaks the dead man's name he accidentally switches on the recorder, and instantly —)*

Howard's Son: ". . . of New York is Albany. The capital of Ohio is Cincinnati, the capital of Rhode Island is . . ." *(The recitation continues.)*

Willy (leaping away with fright, shouting): Ha! Howard! Howard! Howard!

Howard (rushing in): What happened?

Willy (pointing at the machine, which continues nasally, childishly, with the capital cities): Shut it off! Shut it off!

Howard (pulling the plug out): Look, Willy . . .

Willy (pressing his hands to his eyes): I gotta get myself some coffee. I'll get some coffee . . .

Willy starts to walk out. Howard stops him.

Howard (rolling up the cord): Willy, look . . .
Willy: I'll go to Boston.
Howard: Willy, you can't go to Boston for us.
Willy: Why can't I go?
Howard: I don't want you to represent us. I've been meaning to tell you for a long time now.
Willy: Howard, are you firing me?
Howard: I think you need a good long rest, Willy.
Willy: Howard —
Howard: And when you feel better, come back, and we'll see if we can work something out.
Willy: But I gotta earn money, Howard. I'm in no position to —
Howard: Where are your sons? Why don't your sons give you a hand?
Willy: They're working on a very big deal.
Howard: This is no time for false pride, Willy. You go to your sons and you tell them that you're tired. You've got two great boys, haven't you?
Willy: Oh, no question, no question, but in the meantime . . .
Howard: Then that's that, heh?
Willy: All right, I'll go to Boston tomorrow.
Howard: No, no.
Willy: I can't throw myself on my sons. I'm not a cripple!
Howard: Look, kid, I'm busy this morning.
Willy (grasping Howard's arm): Howard, you've got to let me go to Boston!
Howard (hard, keeping himself under control): I've got a line of people to see this morning. Sit down, take five minutes, and pull yourself together, and then go home, will ya? I need the office, Willy. (*He starts to go, turns, remembering the recorder, starts to push off the table holding the recorder.*) Oh, yeah. Whenever you can this week, stop by and drop off the samples. You'll feel better, Willy, and then come back and we'll talk. Pull yourself together, kid, there's people outside.

Howard exits, pushing the table off left. Willy stares into space, exhausted. Now the music is heard — Ben's music — first distantly, then closer, closer. As Willy speaks, Ben enters from the right. He carries valise and umbrella.

Willy: Oh, Ben, how did you do it? What is the answer? Did you
wind up the Alaska deal already?
Ben: Doesn't take much time if you know what you're doing. Just
a short business trip. Boarding ship in an hour. Wanted to
say good-by.
Willy: Ben, I've got to talk to you.
Ben (glancing at his watch): Haven't the time, William.
Willy (crossing the apron to Ben): Ben, nothing's working out. I don't
know what to do.
Ben: Now, look here, William. I've bought timberland in Alaska
and I need a man to look after things for me.
Willy: God, timberland! Me and my boys in those grand outdoors!
Ben: You've a new continent at your doorstep, William. Get out
of these cities, they're full of talk and time payments and
courts of law. Screw on your fists and you can fight for a
fortune up there.
Willy: Yes, yes! Linda, Linda!

Linda enters as of old, with the wash.

Linda: Oh, you're back?
Ben: I haven't much time.
Willy: No, wait! Linda, he's got a proposition for me in Alaska.
Linda: But you've got — *(To Ben.)* He's got a beautiful job here.
Willy: But in Alaska, kid, I could —
Linda: You're doing well enough, Willy!
Ben (to Linda): Enough for what, my dear?
Linda (frightened of Ben and angry at him): Don't say those things to
him! Enough to be happy right here, right now. *(To Willy,
while Ben laughs.)* Why must everybody conquer the world?
You're well liked, and the boys love you, and someday — *(to
Ben)* — why, old man Wagner told him just the other day that
if he keeps it up he'll be a member of the firm, didn't he,
Willy?
Willy: Sure, sure. I am building something with this firm, Ben,
and if a man is building something he must be on the right
track, mustn't he?
Ben: What are you building? Lay your hand on it. Where is it?
Willy (hesitantly): That's true. Linda, there's nothing.
Linda: Why? *(To Ben.)* There's a man eighty-four years old —
Willy: That's right, Ben, that's right. When I look at that man I
say, what is there to worry about?
Ben: Bah!

Willy: It's true, Ben. All he has to do is go into any city, pick up the phone, and he's making his living and you know why?

Ben (picking up his valise): I've got to go.

Willy (holding Ben back): Look at this boy!

Biff, in his high school sweater, enters carrying suitcase. Happy carries Biff's shoulder guards, gold helmet, and football pants.

Willy: Without a penny to his name, three great universities are begging for him, and from there the sky's the limit, because it's not what you do, Ben. It's who you know and the smile on your face! It's contacts, Ben, contacts! The whole wealth of Alaska passes over the lunch table at the Commodore Hotel, and that's the wonder, the wonder of this country, that a man can end with diamonds here on the basis of being liked! *(He turns to Biff.)* And that's why when you get out on that field today it's important. Because thousands of people will be rooting for you and loving you. *(To Ben, who has again begun to leave.)* And Ben! when he walks into a business office his name will sound out like a bell and all the doors will open to him! I've seen it, Ben. I've seen it a thousand times! You can't feel it with your hand like timber, but it's there!

Ben: Good-by, William.

Willy: Ben, am I right? Don't you think I'm right? I value your advice.

Ben: There's a new continent at your doorstep, William. You could walk out rich. Rich! *(He is gone.)*

Willy: We'll do it here, Ben! You hear me? We're gonna do it here!

Young Bernard rushes in. The gay music of the boys is heard.

Bernard: Oh, gee, I was afraid you left already!

Willy: Why? What time is it?

Bernard: It's half-past one!

Willy: Well, come on, everybody! Ebbets Field next stop! Where's the pennants? *(He rushes through the wall-line of the kitchen and out into the living-room.)*

Linda (to Biff): Did you pack fresh underwear?

Biff (who has been limbering up): I want to go!

Bernard: Biff, I'm carrying your helmet, ain't I?

Happy: No, I'm carrying the helmet.

Bernard: Oh, Biff, you promised me.

Happy: I'm carrying the helmet.

Bernard: How am I going to get in the locker room?

Linda: Let him carry the shoulder guards. (*She puts her coat and hat on in the kitchen.*)

Bernard: Can I, Biff? 'Cause I told everybody I'm going to be in the locker room.

Happy: In Ebbets Field it's the clubhouse.

Bernard: I meant the clubhouse. Biff!

Happy: Biff!

Biff (*grandly, after a slight pause*): Let him carry the shoulder guards.

Happy (*as he gives Bernard the shoulder guards*): Stay close to us now.

Willy rushes in with the pennants.

Willy (*handing them out*): Everybody wave when Biff comes out on the field. (*Happy and Bernard run off.*) You set now, boy?

The music has died away.

Biff: Ready to go, Pop. Every muscle is ready.

Willy (*at the edge of the apron*): You realize what this means?

Biff: That's right, Pop.

Willy (*feeling Biff's muscles*): You're comin' home this afternoon captain of the All-Scholastic Championship Team of the City of New York.

Biff: I got it, Pop. And remember, pal, when I take off my helmet, that touchdown is for you.

Willy: Let's go. (*He is starting out, with his arm around Biff, when Charley enters, as of old, in knickers.*) I got no room for you, Charley.

Charley: Room? For what?

Willy: In the car.

Charley: You goin' for a ride? I wanted to shoot some casino.

Willy (*furiously*): Casino! (*Incredulously.*) Don't you realize what today is?

Linda: Oh, he knows, Willy. He's just kidding you.

Willy: That's nothing to kid about!

Charley: No, Linda, what's goin' on?

Linda: He's playing in Ebbets Field.

Charley: Baseball in this weather?

Willy: Don't talk to him. Come on, come on! (*He is pushing them out.*)

Charley: Wait a minute, didn't you hear the news?

Willy: What?

Charley: Don't you listen to the radio? Ebbets Field just blew up.

Willy: You go to hell! (*Charley laughs. Pushing them out.*) Come on, come on! We're late.

Charley (as they go): Knock a homer, Biff, knock a homer!

Willy (the last to leave, turning to Charley): I don't think that was funny, Charley. This is the greatest day of his life.

Charley: Willy, when are you going to grow up?

Willy: Yeah, heh? When this game is over, Charley, you'll be laughing out of the other side of your face. They'll be calling him another Red Grange. Twenty-five thousand a year.

Charley (kidding): Is that so?

Willy: Yeah, that's so.

Charley: Well, then, I'm sorry, Willy. But tell me something.

Willy: What?

Charley: Who is Red Grange?

Willy: Put up your hands. Goddam you, put up your hands!

Charley, chuckling, shakes his head and walks away, around the left corner of the stage. Willy follows him. The music rises to a mocking frenzy.

Willy: Who the hell do you think you are, better than everybody else? You don't know everything, you big, ignorant, stupid . . . Put up your hands!

Light rises, on the right side of the forestage, on a small table in the reception room of Charley's office. Traffic sounds are heard. Bernard, now mature, sits whistling to himself. A pair of tennis rackets and an overnight bag are on the floor beside him.

Willy (offstage): What are you walking away for? Don't walk away! If you're going to say something say it to my face! I know you laugh at me behind my back. You'll laugh out of the other side of your goddam face after this game. Touchdown! Touchdown! Eighty thousand people! Touchdown! Right between the goal posts.

Bernard is a quiet, earnest, but self-assured young man. Willy's voice is coming from right upstage now. Bernard lowers his feet off the table and listens. Jenny, his father's secretary, enters.

Jenny (distressed): Say, Bernard, will you go out in the hall?

Bernard: What is that noise? Who is it?

Jenny: Mr. Loman. He just got off the elevator.

Bernard (getting up): Who's he arguing with?

Jenny: Nobody. There's nobody with him. I can't deal with him any more, and your father gets all upset everytime he comes.

I've got a lot of typing to do, and your father's waiting to sign it. Will you see him?

Willy (entering): Touchdown! Touch — (*He sees Jenny.*) Jenny, Jenny, good to see you. How're ya? Workin'? Or still honest?

Jenny: Fine. How've you been feeling?

Willy: Not much any more, Jenny. Ha, ha! (*He is surprised to see the rackets.*)

Bernard: Hello, Uncle Willy.

Willy (almost shocked): Bernard! Well, look who's here! (*He comes quickly, guiltily, to Bernard and warmly shakes his hand.*)

Bernard: How are you? Good to see you.

Willy: What are you doing here?

Bernard: Oh, just stopped by to see Pop. Get off my feet till my train leaves. I'm going to Washington in a few minutes.

Willy: Is he in?

Bernard: Yes, he's in his office with the accountant. Sit down.

Willy (sitting down): What're you going to do in Washington?

Bernard: Oh, just a case I've got there, Willy.

Willy: That so? (*Indicating the rackets.*) You going to play tennis there?

Bernard: I'm staying with a friend who's got a court.

Willy: Don't say. His own tennis court. Must be fine people, I bet.

Bernard: They are, very nice. Dad tells me Biff's in town.

Willy (with a big smile): Yeah, Biff's in. Working on a very big deal, Bernard.

Bernard: What's Biff doing?

Willy: Well, he's been doing very big things in the West. But he decided to establish himself here. Very big. We're having dinner. Did I hear your wife had a boy?

Bernard: That's right. Our second.

Willy: Two boys! What do you know!

Bernard: What kind of a deal has Biff got?

Willy: Well, Bill Oliver — very big sporting-goods man — he wants Biff very badly. Called him in from the West. Long distance, carte blanche, special deliveries. Your friends have their own private tennis court?

Bernard: You still with the old firm, Willy?

Willy (after a pause): I'm — I'm overjoyed to see how you made the grade, Bernard, overjoyed. It's an encouraging thing to see a young man really — really — Looks very good for Biff — very — (*He breaks off, then.*) Bernard — (*He is so full of emotion, he breaks off again.*)

Bernard: What is it, Willy?

Willy (small and alone): What — what's the secret?

Bernard: What secret?

Willy: How — how did you? Why didn't he ever catch on?

Bernard: I wouldn't know that, Willy.

Willy (confidentially, desperately): You were his friend, his boyhood friend. There's something I don't understand about it. His life ended after that Ebbets Field game. From the age of seventeen nothing good ever happened to him.

Bernard: He never trained himself for anything.

Willy: But he did, he did. After high school he took so many correspondence courses. Radio mechanics, television; God knows what, and never made the slightest mark.

Bernard (taking off his glasses): Willy, do you want to talk candidly?

Willy (rising, faces Bernard): I regard you as a very brilliant man, Bernard. I value your advice.

Bernard: Oh, the hell with the advice, Willy. I couldn't advise you. There's just one thing I've always wanted to ask you. When he was supposed to graduate, and the math teacher flunked him —

Willy: Oh, that son-of-a-bitch ruined his life.

Bernard: Yeah, but, Willy, all he had to do was go to summer school and make up that subject.

Willy: That's right, that's right.

Bernard: Did you tell him not to go to summer school?

Willy: Me? I begged him to go. I ordered him to go!

Bernard: Then why wouldn't he go?

Willy: Why? Why! Bernard, that question has been trailing me like a ghost for the last fifteen years. He flunked the subject, and laid down and died like a hammer hit him!

Bernard: Take it easy, kid.

Willy: Let me talk to you — I got nobody to talk to. Bernard, Bernard, was it my fault? Y'see? It keeps going around in my mind, maybe I did something to him. I got nothing to give him.

Bernard: Don't take it so hard.

Willy: Why did he lay down? What is the story there? You were his friend!

Bernard: Willy, I remember, it was June, and our grades came out. And he'd flunked math.

Willy: That son-of-a-bitch!

Bernard: No, it wasn't right then. Biff just got very angry, I remember, and he was ready to enroll in summer school.

Willy (surprised): He was?

Bernard: He wasn't beaten by it at all. But then, Willy, he disappeared from the block for almost a month. And I got the idea that he'd gone up to New England to see you. Did he have a talk with you then?

Willy stares in silence.

Bernard: Willy?

Willy (with a strong edge of resentment in his voice): Yeah, he came to Boston. What about it?

Bernard: Well, just that when he came back — I'll never forget this, it always mystifies me. Because I'd thought so well of Biff, even though he'd always taken advantage of me. I loved him, Willy, y'know? And he came back after that month and took his sneakers — remember those sneakers with "University of Virginia" printed on them? He was so proud of those, wore them every day. And he took them down in the cellar, and burned them up in the furnace. We had a fist fight. It lasted at least half an hour. Just the two of us, punching each other down the cellar, and crying right through it. I've often thought of how strange it was that I knew he'd given up his life. What happened in Boston, Willy?

Willy looks at him as at an intruder.

Bernard: I just bring it up because you asked me.

Willy (angrily): Nothing. What do you mean, "What happened?" What's that got to do with anything?

Bernard: Well, don't get sore.

Willy: What are you trying to do, blame it on me? If a boy lays down is that my fault?

Bernard: Now, Willy, don't get —

Willy: Well, don't — don't talk to me that way! What does that mean, "What happened?"

Charley enters. He is in his vest, and he carries a bottle of bourbon.

Charley: Hey, you're going to miss that train. (*He waves the bottle.*)

Bernard: Yeah, I'm going. (*He takes the bottle.*) Thanks, Pop. (*He picks up his rackets and bag.*) Good-by, Willy, and don't worry about it. You know, "If at first you don't succeed . . ."

Willy: Yes, I believe in that.

Bernard: But sometimes, Willy, it's better for a man just to walk away.

Willy: Walk away?

Bernard: That's right.

Willy: But if you can't walk away?

Bernard (after a slight pause): I guess that's when it's tough. *(Extending his hand.)* Good-by, Willy.

Willy (shaking Bernard's hand): Good-by, boy.

Charley (an arm on Bernard's shoulder): How do you like this kid? Gonna argue a case in front of the Supreme Court.

Bernard (protesting): Pop!

Willy (genuinely shocked, pained, and happy): No! The Supreme Court!

Bernard: I gotta run. 'By, Dad!

Charley: Knock 'em dead, Bernard!

Bernard goes off.

Willy (as Charley takes out his wallet): The Supreme Court! And he didn't even mention it!

Charley (counting out money on the desk): He don't have to — he's gonna do it.

Willy: And you never told him what to do, did you? You never took any interest in him.

Charley: My salvation is that I never took any interest in anything. There's some money — fifty dollars. I got an accountant inside.

Willy: Charley, look . . . *(With difficulty.)* I got my insurance to pay. If you can manage it — I need a hundred and ten dollars.

Charley doesn't reply for a moment; merely stops moving.

Willy: I'd draw it from my bank but Linda would know, and I . . .

Charley: Sit down, Willy.

Willy (moving toward the chair): I'm keeping an account of everything, remember. I'll pay every penny back. *(He sits.)*

Charley: Now listen to me, Willy.

Willy: I want you to know I appreciate . . .

Charley (sitting down on the table): Willy, what're you doin'? What the hell is goin' on in your head?

Willy: Why? I'm simply . . .

Charley: I offered you a job. You can make fifty dollars a week. And I won't send you on the road.

Willy: I've got a job.

Charley: Without pay? What kind of a job is a job without pay? *(He rises.)* Now, look, kid, enough is enough. I'm no genius but I know when I'm being insulted.

Willy: Insulted!

Charley: Why don't you want to work for me?

Willy: What's the matter with you? I've got a job.

Charley: Then what're you walkin' in here every week for?

Willy (getting up): Well, if you don't want me to walk in here —

Charley: I am offering you a job.

Willy: I don't want your goddam job!

Charley: When the hell are you going to grow up?

Willy (furiously): You big ignoramus, if you say that to me again I'll rap you one! I don't care how big you are! (*He's ready to fight.*)

Pause.

Charley (kindly, going to him): How much do you need, Willy?

Willy: Charley, I'm strapped. I'm strapped. I don't know what to do. I was just fired.

Charley: Howard fired you?

Willy: That snotnose. Imagine that? I named him. I named him Howard.

Charley: Willy, when're you gonna realize that them things don't mean anything? You named him Howard, but you can't sell that. The only thing you got in this world is what you can sell. And the funny thing is that you're a salesman, and you don't know that.

Willy: I've always tried to think otherwise, I guess. I always felt that if a man was impressive, and well liked, that nothing —

Charley: Why must everybody like you? Who liked J. P. Morgan? Was he impressive? In a Turkish bath he'd look like a butcher. But with his pockets on he was very well liked. Now listen, Willy, I know you don't like me, and nobody can say I'm in love with you, but I'll give you a job because — just for the hell of it, put it that way. Now what do you say?

Willy: I — I just can't work for you, Charley.

Charley: What're you, jealous of me?

Willy: I can't work for you, that's all, don't ask me why.

Charley (angered, takes out more bills): You been jealous of me all your life, you damned fool! Here, pay your insurance. (*He puts the money in Willy's hand.*)

Willy: I'm keeping strict accounts.

Charley: I've got some work to do. Take care of yourself. And pay your insurance.

Willy (moving to the right): Funny, y'know? After all the highways, and the trains, and the appointments, and the years, you end up worth more dead than alive.

Charley: Willy, nobody's worth nothin' dead. (*After a slight pause.*) Did you hear what I said?

Willy stands still, dreaming.

Charley: Willy!

Willy: Apologize to Bernard for me when you see him. I didn't mean to argue with him. He's a fine boy. They're all fine boys, and they'll end up big — all of them. Someday they'll all play tennis together. Wish me luck, Charley. He saw Bill Oliver today.

Charley: Good luck.

Willy (on the verge of tears): Charley, you're the only friend I got. Isn't that a remarkable thing? (*He goes out.*)

Charley: Jesus!

Charley stares after him a moment and follows. All light blacks out. Suddenly raucous music is heard, and a red glow rises behind the screen at right. Stanley, a young waiter, appears, carrying a table, followed by Happy, who is carrying two chairs.

Stanley (putting the table down): That's all right, Mr. Loman, I can handle it myself. (*He turns and takes the chairs from Happy and places them at the table.*)

Happy (glancing around): Oh, this is better.

Stanley: Sure, in the front there you're in the middle of all kinds a noise. Whenever you got a party, Mr. Loman, you just tell me and I'll put you back here. Y'know, there's a lotta people they don't like it private, because when they go out they like to see a lotta action around them because they're sick and tired to stay in the house by theirself. But I know you, you ain't from Hackensack. You know what I mean?

Happy (sitting down): So how's it coming, Stanley?

Stanley: Ah, it's a dog's life. I only wish during the war they'd a took me in the Army. I coulda been dead by now.

Happy: My brother's back, Stanley.

Stanley: Oh, he come back, heh? From the Far West.

Happy: Yeah, big cattle man, my brother, so treat him right. And my father's coming too.

Stanley: Oh, your father too!

Happy: You got a couple of nice lobsters?

Stanley: Hundred per cent, big.

Happy: I want them with the claws.

Stanley: Don't worry, I don't give you no mice. (*Happy laughs.*) How about some wine? It'll put a head on the meal.

Happy: No. You remember, Stanley, that recipe I brought you from overseas? With the champagne in it?

Stanley: Oh, yeah, sure. I still got it tacked up yet in the kitchen. But that'll have to cost a buck apiece anyways.

Happy: That's all right.

Stanley: What'd you, hit a number or somethin'?

Happy: No, it's a little celebration. My brother is — I think he pulled off a big deal today. I think we're going into business together.

Stanley: Great! That's the best for you. Because a family business, you know what I mean? — that's the best.

Happy: That's what I think.

Stanley: Cause what's the difference? Somebody steals? It's in the family. Know what I mean? (*Sotto voce.*) Like this bartender here. The boss is goin' crazy what kinda leak he's got in the cash register. You put it in but it don't come out.

Happy (raising his head): Sh!

Stanley: What?

Happy: You notice I wasn't lookin' right or left, was I?

Stanley: No.

Happy: And my eyes are closed.

Stanley: So what's the — ?

Happy: Strudel's comin'.

Stanley (catching on, looks around): Ah, no, there's no —

He breaks off as a furred, lavishly dressed Girl enters and sits at the next table. Both follow her with their eyes.

Stanley: Geez, how'd ya know?

Happy: I got radar or something. (*Staring directly at her profile.*) Oooooooo . . . Stanley.

Stanley: I think that's for you, Mr. Loman.

Happy: Look at that mouth. Oh, God. And the binoculars.

Stanley: Geez, you got a life, Mr. Loman.

Happy: Wait on her.

Stanley (going to The Girl's table): Would you like a menu, ma'am?

Girl: I'm expecting someone, but I'd like a —

Happy: Why don't you bring her — excuse me, miss, do you mind? I sell champagne, and I'd like you to try my brand. Bring her a champagne, Stanley.

Girl: That's awfully nice of you.

Happy: Don't mention it. It's all company money. (*He laughs.*)

Girl: That's a charming product to be selling, isn't it?

Happy: Oh, gets to be like everything else. Selling is selling, y'know.

Girl: I suppose.

Happy: You don't happen to sell, do you?

Girl: No, I don't sell.

Happy: Would you object to a compliment from a stranger? You ought to be on a magazine cover.

Girl (looking at him a little archly): I have been.

Stanley comes in with a glass of champagne.

Happy: What'd I say before, Stanley? You see? She's a cover girl.

Stanley: Oh, I could see, I could see.

Happy (to The Girl): What magazine?

Girl: Oh, a lot of them. (*She takes the drink.*) Thank you.

Happy: You know what they say in France, don't you? "Champagne is the drink of the complexion" — Hya, Biff!

Biff has entered and sits with Happy.

Biff: Hello, kid. Sorry I'm late.

Happy: I just got here. Uh, Miss —

Girl: Forsythe.

Happy: Miss Forsythe, this is my brother.

Biff: Is Dad here?

Happy: His name is Biff. You might've heard of him. Great football player.

Girl: Really? What team?

Happy: Are you familiar with football?

Girl: No, I'm afraid I'm not.

Happy: Biff is quarterback with the New York Giants.

Girl: Well, that is nice, isn't it? (*She drinks.*)

Happy: Good health.

Girl: I'm happy to meet you.

Happy: That's my name. Hap. It's really Harold, but at West Point they called me Happy.

Girl (now really impressed): Oh, I see. How do you do? (*She turns her profile.*)

Biff: Isn't Dad coming?

Happy: You want her?

Biff: Oh, I could never make that.

Happy: I remember the time that idea would never come into your head. Where's the old confidence, Biff?

Biff: I just saw Oliver —

Happy: Wait a minute. I've got to see that old confidence again. Do you want her? She's on call.

Biff: Oh, no. (*He turns to look at The Girl.*)

Happy: I'm telling you. Watch this. (*Turning to The Girl.*) Honey? (*She turns to him.*) Are you busy?

Girl: Well, I am . . . but I could make a phone call.

Happy: Do that, will you, honey? And see if you can get a friend. We'll be here for a while. Biff is one of the greatest football players in the country.

Girl (standing up): Well, I'm certainly happy to meet you.

Happy: Come back soon.

Girl: I'll try.

Happy: Don't try, honey, try hard.

The Girl exits. Stanley follows, shaking his head in bewildered admiration.

Happy: Isn't that a shame now? A beautiful girl like that? That's why I can't get married. There's not a good woman in a thousand. New York is loaded with them, kid!

Biff: Hap, look —

Happy: I told you she was on call!

Biff (strangely unnerved): Cut it out, will ya? I want to say something to you.

Happy: Did you see Oliver?

Biff: I saw him all right. Now look, I want to tell Dad a couple of things and I want you to help me.

Happy: What? Is he going to back you?

Biff: Are you crazy? You're out of your goddam head, you know that?

Happy: Why? What happened?

Biff (breathlessly): I did a terrible thing today, Hap. It's been the strangest day I ever went through. I'm all numb, I swear.

Happy: You mean he wouldn't see you?

Biff: Well, I waited six hours for him, see? All day. Kept sending my name in. Even tried to date his secretary so she'd get me to him, but no soap.

Happy: Because you're not showin' the old confidence, Biff. He remembered you, didn't he?

Biff (stopping Happy with a gesture): Finally, about five o'clock, he comes out. Didn't remember who I was or anything. I felt like such an idiot, Hap.

Happy: Did you tell him my Florida idea?

Biff: He walked away. I saw him for one minute. I got so mad I could've torn the walls down! How the hell did I ever get the idea I was a salesman there? I even believed myself that I'd been a salesman for him! And then he gave me one look and — I realized what a ridiculous lie my whole life has been! We've been talking in a dream for fifteen years. I was a shipping clerk.

Happy: What'd you do?

Biff (with great tension and wonder): Well, he left, see. And the secretary went out. I was all alone in the waiting-room. I don't know what came over me, Hap. The next thing I know I'm in his office — paneled walls, everything. I can't explain it. I — Hap, I took his fountain pen.

Happy: Geez, did he catch you?

Biff: I ran out. I ran down all eleven flights. I ran and ran and ran.

Happy: That was an awful dumb — what'd you do that for?

Biff (agonized): I don't know, I just — wanted to take something, I don't know. You gotta help me, Hap, I'm gonna tell Pop.

Happy: You crazy? What for?

Biff: Hap, he's got to understand that I'm not the man somebody lends that kind of money to. He thinks I've been spiting him all these years and it's eating him up.

Happy: That's just it. You tell him something nice.

Biff: I can't.

Happy: Say you got a lunch date with Oliver tomorrow.

Biff: So what do I do tomorrow?

Happy: You leave the house tomorrow and come back at night and say Oliver is thinking it over. And he thinks it over for a couple of weeks, and gradually it fades away and nobody's the worse.

Biff: But it'll go on forever!

Happy: Dad is never so happy as when he's looking forward to something!

Willy enters.

Happy: Hello, scout!

Willy: Gee, I haven't been here in years!

Stanley has followed Willy in and sets a chair for him. Stanley starts off but Happy stops him.

Happy: Stanley!

Stanley stands by, waiting for an order.

Biff (going to Willy with guilt, as to an invalid): Sit down, Pop. You want a drink?

Willy: Sure, I don't mind.

Biff: Let's get a load on.

Willy: You look worried.

Biff: N-no. (*To Stanley.*) Scotch all around. Make it doubles.

Stanley: Doubles, right. (*He goes.*)

Willy: You had a couple already, didn't you?

Biff: Just a couple, yeah.

Willy: Well, what happened, boy? (*Nodding affirmatively, with a smile.*) Everything go all right?

Biff (takes a breath, then reaches out and grasps Willy's hand): Pal . . . (*He is smiling bravely, and Willy is smiling too.*) I had an experience today.

Happy: Terrific, Pop.

Willy: That so? What happened?

Biff (high, slightly alcoholic, above the earth): I'm going to tell you everything from first to last. It's been a strange day. (*Silence. He looks around, composes himself as best he can, but his breath keeps breaking the rhythm of his voice.*) I had to wait quite a while for him, and —

Willy: Oliver?

Biff: Yeah, Oliver. All day, as a matter of cold fact. And a lot of — instances — facts, Pop, facts about my life came back to me. Who was it, Pop? Who ever said I was a salesman with Oliver?

Willy: Well, you were.

Biff: No, Dad, I was a shipping clerk.

Willy: But you were practically —

Biff (with determination): Dad, I don't know who said it first, but I was never a salesman for Bill Oliver.

Willy: What're you talking about?

Biff: Let's hold on to the facts tonight, Pop. We're not going to get anywhere bullin' around. I was a shipping clerk.

Willy (angrily): All right, now listen to me —

Biff: Why don't you let me finish?

Willy: I'm not interested in stories about the past or any crap of that kind because the woods are burning, boys, you understand? There's a big blaze going on all around. I was fired today.

Biff (shocked): How could you be?

Willy: I was fired, and I'm looking for a little good news to tell your mother, because the woman has waited and the woman has suffered. The gist of it is that I haven't got a story left in my head, Biff. So don't give me a lecture about facts and aspects. I am not interested. Now what've you got to say to me?

Stanley enters with three drinks. They wait until he leaves.

Willy: Did you see Oliver?

Biff: Jesus, Dad!

Willy: You mean you didn't go up there?

Happy: Sure he went up there.

Biff: I did. I — saw him. How could they fire you?

Willy (on the edge of his chair): What kind of a welcome did he give you?

Biff: He won't even let you work on commission?

Willy: I'm out! *(Driving.)* So tell me, he gave you a warm welcome?

Happy: Sure, Pop, sure!

Biff (driven): Well, it was kind of —

Willy: I was wondering if he'd remember you. *(To Happy.)* Imagine, man doesn't see him for ten, twelve years and gives him that kind of a welcome!

Happy: Damn right!

Biff (trying to return to the offensive): Pop, look —

Willy: You know why he remembered you, don't you? Because you impressed him in those days.

Biff: Let's talk quietly and get this down to the facts, huh?

Willy (as though Biff had been interrupting): Well, what happened? It's great news, Biff. Did he take you into his office or'd you talk in the waiting-room?

Biff: Well, he came in, see, and —

Willy (with a big smile): What'd he say? Betcha he threw his arm around you.

Biff: Well, he kinda —

Willy: He's a fine man. *(To Happy.)* Very hard man to see, y'know.

Happy (agreeing): Oh, I know.

Willy (to Biff): Is that where you had the drinks?

Biff: Yeah, he gave me a couple of — no, no!

Happy (cutting in): He told him my Florida idea.

Willy: Don't interrupt. *(To Biff.)* How'd he react to the Florida idea?

Biff: Dad, will you give me a minute to explain?

Willy: I've been waiting for you to explain since I sat down here! What happened? He took you into his office and what?

Biff: Well — I talked. And — and he listened, see.

Willy: Famous for the way he listens, y'know. What was his answer?

Biff: His answer was — *(He breaks off, suddenly angry.)* Dad, you're not letting me tell you what I want to tell you!

Willy (accusing, angered): You didn't see him, did you?

Biff: I did see him!

Willy: What'd you insult him or something? You insulted him, didn't you?

Biff: Listen, will you let me out of it, will you just let me out of it!

Happy: What the hell!

Willy: Tell me what happened!

Biff (to Happy): I can't talk to him!

A single trumpet note jars the ear. The light of green leaves stains the house, which holds the air of night and a dream. Young Bernard enters and knocks on the door of the house.

Young Bernard (frantically): Mrs. Loman, Mrs. Loman!

Happy: Tell him what happened!

Biff (to Happy): Shut up and leave me alone!

Willy: No, no! You had to go and flunk math!

Biff: What math? What're you talking about?

Young Bernard: Mrs. Loman, Mrs. Loman!

Linda appears in the house, as of old.

Willy (wildly): Math, math, math!

Biff: Take it easy, Pop!

Young Bernard: Mrs. Loman!

Willy (furiously): If you hadn't flunked you'd've been set by now!

Biff: Now, look, I'm gonna tell you what happened, and you're going to listen to me.

Young Bernard: Mrs. Loman!

Biff: I waited six hours —

Happy: What the hell are you saying?

Biff: I kept sending in my name but he wouldn't see me. So finally he . . . (*He continues unheard as light fades low on the restaurant.*)

Young Bernard: Biff flunked math!

Linda: No!

Young Bernard: Birnbaum flunked him! They won't graduate him!

Linda: But they have to. He's gotta go to the university. Where is he? Biff! Biff!

Young Bernard: No, he left. He went to Grand Central.

Linda: Grand — You mean he went to Boston!

Young Bernard: Is Uncle Willy in Boston?

Linda: Oh, maybe Willy can talk to the teacher. Oh, the poor, poor boy!

Light on house area snaps out.

Biff (at the table, now audible, holding up a gold fountain pen): . . . so I'm washed up with Oliver, you understand? Are you listening to me?

Willy (at a loss): Yeah, sure. If you hadn't flunked —

Biff: Flunked what? What're you talking about?

Willy: Don't blame everything on me! I didn't flunk math — you did! What pen?

Happy: That was awful dumb, Biff, a pen like that is worth —

Willy (seeing the pen for the first time): You took Oliver's pen?

Biff (weakening): Dad, I just explained it to you.

Willy: You stole Bill Oliver's fountain pen!

Biff: I didn't exactly steal it! That's just what I've been explaining to you!

Happy: He had it in his hand and just then Oliver walked in, so he got nervous and stuck it in his pocket!

Willy: My God, Biff!

Biff: I never intended to do it, Dad!

Operator's voice: Standish Arms, good evening!

Willy (shouting): I'm not in my room!

Biff (frightened): Dad, what's the matter? (*He and Happy stand up.*)

Operator: Ringing Mr. Loman for you!

Willy: I'm not there, stop it!

Biff (horrified, gets down on one knee before Willy): Dad, I'll make good, I'll make good. (*Willy tries to get to his feet. Biff holds him down.*) Sit down now.

Willy: No, you're no good, you're no good for anything.

Biff: I am, Dad, I'll find something else, you understand? Now don't worry about anything. (*He holds up Willy's face.*) Talk to me, Dad.

Operator: Mr. Loman does not answer. Shall I page him?

Willy (attempting to stand, as though to rush and silence the Operator): No, no, no!

Happy: He'll strike something, Pop.

Willy: No, no . . .

Biff (desperately, standing over Willy): Pop, listen! Listen to me! I'm telling you something good. Oliver talked to his partner about the Florida idea. You listening? He — he talked to his partner, and he came to me . . . I'm going to be all right, you hear? Dad, listen to me, he said it was just a question of the amount!

Willy: Then you . . . got it?

Happy: He's gonna be terrific, Pop!

Willy (trying to stand): Then you got it, haven't you? You got it! You got it!

Biff (agonized, holds Willy down): No, no. Look, Pop. I'm supposed to have lunch with them tomorrow. I'm just telling you this so you'll know that I can still make an impression, Pop. And I'll make good somewhere, but I can't go tomorrow, see?

Willy: Why not? You simply —

Biff: But the pen, Pop!

Willy: You give it to him and tell him it was an oversight!

Happy: Sure, have lunch tomorrow!

Biff: I can't say that —

Willy: You were doing a crossword puzzle and accidentally used his pen!

Biff: Listen, kid, I took those balls years ago, now I walk in with his fountain pen? That clinches it, don't you see? I can't face him like that! I'll try elsewhere.

Page's Voice: Paging Mr. Loman!

Willy: Don't you want to be anything?

Biff: Pop, how can I go back?

Willy: You don't want to be anything, is that what's behind it?

Biff (now angry at Willy for not crediting his sympathy): Don't take it that way! You think it was easy walking into that office after what I'd done to him? A team of horses couldn't have dragged me back to Bill Oliver!

Willy: Then why'd you go?

Biff: Why did I go? Why did I go! Look at you! Look at what's become of you!

Off left, The Woman laughs.

Willy: Biff, you're going to go to that lunch tomorrow, or —

Biff: I can't go. I've got no appointment!

Happy: Biff, for . . . !

Willy: Are you spiting me?

Biff: Don't take it that way! Goddammit!

Willy (strikes Biff and falters away from the table): You rotten little louse! Are you spiting me?

The Woman: Someone's at the door, Willy!

Biff: I'm no good, can't you see what I am?

Happy (separating them): Hey, you're in a restaurant! Now cut it out, both of you! (*The Girls enter.*) Hello, girls, sit down.

The Woman laughs, off left.

Miss Forsythe: I guess we might as well. This is Letta.
The Woman: Willy, are you going to wake up?
Biff (ignoring Willy): How're ya, miss, sit down. What do you drink?
Miss Forsythe: Letta might not be able to stay long.
Letta: I gotta get up very early tomorrow. I got jury duty. I'm so excited! Were you fellows ever on a jury?
Biff: No, but I been in front of them! (*The Girls laugh.*) This is my father.
Letta: Isn't he cute? Sit down with us, Pop.
Happy: Sit him down, Biff!
Biff (going to him): Come on, slugger, drink us under the table. To hell with it! Come on, sit down, pal.

On Biff's last insistence, Willy is about to sit.

The Woman (now urgently): Willy, are you going to answer the door!

The Woman's call pulls Willy back. He starts right, befuddled.

Biff: Hey, where are you going?
Willy: Open the door.
Biff: The door?
Willy: The washroom . . . the door . . . where's the door?
Biff (leading Willy to the left): Just go straight down.

Willy moves left.

The Woman: Willy, Willy, are you going to get up, get up, get up, get up?

Willy exits left.

Letta: I think it's sweet you bring your daddy along.
Miss Forsythe: Oh, he isn't really your father!
Biff (at left, turning to her resentfully): Miss Forsythe, you've just seen a prince walk by. A fine troubled prince. A hard-working, unappreciated prince. A pal, you understand? A good companion. Always for his boys.
Letta: That's so sweet.
Happy: Well, girls, what's the program? We're wasting time. Come on, Biff. Gather round. Where would you like to go?
Biff: Why don't you do something for him?
Happy: Me!
Biff: Don't you give a damn for him, Hap?

Happy: What're you talking about? I'm the one who —

Biff: I sense it, you don't give a good goddam about him. (*He takes the rolled-up hose from his pocket and puts it on the table in front of Happy.*) Look what I found in the cellar, for Christ's sake. How can you bear to let it go on?

Happy: Me? Who goes away? Who runs off and —

Biff: Yeah, but he doesn't mean anything to you. You could help him — I can't! Don't you understand what I'm talking about? He's going to kill himself, don't you know that?

Happy: Don't I know it! Me!

Biff: Hap, help him! Jesus . . . help him . . . Help me, help me, I can't bear to look at his face! (*Ready to weep, he hurries out, up right.*)

Happy (starting after him): Where are you going?

Miss Forsythe: What's he so mad about?

Happy: Come on, girls, we'll catch up with him.

Miss Forsythe (as Happy pushes her out): Say, I don't like that temper of his!

Happy: He's just a little overstrung, he'll be all right!

Willy (off left, as The Woman laughs): Don't answer! Don't answer!

Letta: Don't you want to tell your father —

Happy: No, that's not my father. He's just a guy. Come on, we'll catch Biff, and, honey, we're going to paint this town! Stanley, where's the check! Hey, Stanley!

They exit. Stanley looks toward left.

Stanley (calling to Happy indignantly): Mr. Loman! Mr. Loman!

Stanley picks up a chair and follows them off. Knocking is heard off left. The Woman enters, laughing. Willy follows her. She is in a black slip; he is buttoning his shirt. Raw, sensuous music accompanies their speech.

Willy: Will you stop laughing? Will you stop?

The Woman: Aren't you going to answer the door? He'll wake the whole hotel.

Willy: I'm not expecting anybody.

The Woman: Whyn't you have another drink, honey, and stop being so damn self-centered?

Willy: I'm so lonely.

The Woman: You know you ruined me, Willy? From now on, whenever you come to the office, I'll see that you go right through to the buyers. No waiting at my desk any more, Willy. You ruined me.

Willy: That's nice of you to say that.

The Woman: Gee, you are self-centered! Why so sad? You are the saddest self-centeredest soul I ever did see-saw. (*She laughs. He kisses her.*) Come on inside, drummer boy. It's silly to be dressing in the middle of the night. (*As knocking is heard.*) Aren't you going to answer the door?

Willy: They're knocking on the wrong door.

The Woman: But I felt the knocking. And he heard us talking in here. Maybe the hotel's on fire!

Willy (his terror rising): It's a mistake.

The Woman: Then tell him to go away!

Willy: There's nobody there.

The Woman: It's getting on my nerves, Willy. There's somebody standing out there and it's getting on my nerves!

Willy (pushing her away from him): All right, stay in the bathroom here, and don't come out. I think there's a law in Massachusetts about it, so don't come out. It may be that new room clerk. He looked very mean. So don't come out. It's a mistake, there's no fire.

The knocking is heard again. He takes a few steps away from her, and she vanishes into the wing. The light follows him, and now he is facing Young Biff, who carries a suitcase. Biff steps toward him. The music is gone.

Biff: Why didn't you answer?

Willy: Biff! What are you doing in Boston?

Biff: Why didn't you answer? I've been knocking for five minutes, I called you on the phone —

Willy: I just heard you. I was in the bathroom and had the door shut. Did anything happen home?

Biff: Dad — I let you down.

Willy: What do you mean?

Biff: Dad . . .

Willy: Biffo, what's this about? (*Putting his arm around Biff.*) Come on, let's go downstairs and get you a malted.

Biff: Dad, I flunked math.

Willy: Not for the term?

Bigg: The term. I haven't got enough credits to graduate.

Willy: You mean to say Bernard wouldn't give you the answers?

Biff: He did, he tried, but I only got a sixty-one.

Willy: And they wouldn't give you four points?

Biff: Birnbaum refused absolutely. I begged him, Pop, but he won't give me those points. You gotta talk to him before they close the school. Because if he saw the kind of man you are, and you just talked to him in your way, I'm sure he'd come through for me. The class came right before practice, see, and I didn't go enough. Would you talk to him? He'd like you, Pop. You know the way you could talk.

Willy: You're on. We'll drive right back.

Biff: Oh, Dad, good work! I'm sure he'll change it for you!

Willy: Go downstairs and tell the clerk I'm checkin' out. Go right down.

Biff: Yes, sir! See, the reason he hates me, Pop — one day he was late for class so I got up at the blackboard and imitated him. I crossed my eyes and talked with a lithp.

Willy (laughing): You did? The kids like it?

Biff: They nearly died laughing!

Willy: Yeah? What'd you do?

Biff: The thquare root of thixthy twee is . . . (*Willy bursts out laughing; Biff joins him.*) And in the middle of it he walked in!

Willy laughs and The Woman joins in offstage.

Willy (without hesitation): Hurry downstairs and —

Biff: Somebody in there?

Willy: No, that was next door.

The Woman laughs offstage.

Biff: Somebody got in your bathroom!

Willy: No, it's the next room, there's a party —

The Woman (enters, laughing. She lisps this): Can I come in? There's something in the bathtub, Willy, and it's moving!

Willy looks at Biff, who is staring open-mouthed and horrified at The Woman.

Willy: Ah — you better go back to your room. They must be finished painting by now. They're painting her room so I let her take a shower here. Go back, go back . . . (*He pushes her.*)

The Woman (resisting): But I've got to get dressed, Willy, I can't —

Willy: Get out of here! Go back, go back . . . (*Suddenly striving for the ordinary.*) This is Miss Francis, Biff, she's a buyer. They're painting her room. Go back, Miss Francis, go back . . .

The Woman: But my clothes, I can't go out naked in the hall!

Willy (pushing her offstage): Get outa here! Go back, go back!

Biff slowly sits down on his suitcase as the argument continues offstage.

The Woman: Where's my stockings? You promised me stockings, Willy!

Willy: I have no stockings here!

The Woman: You had two bones of size nine sheers for me, and I want them!

Willy: Here, for God's sake, will you get outa here!

The Woman (enters holding a box of stockings): I just hope there's nobody in the hall. That's all I hope. (*To Biff.*) Are you football or baseball?

Biff: Football.

The Woman (angry, humiliated): That's me too. G'night. (*She snatches her clothes from Willy and walks out.*)

Willy (after a pause): Well, better get going. I want to get to the school first thing in the morning. Get my suits out of the closet. I'll get my valise. (*Biff doesn't move.*) What's the matter? (*Biff remains motionless, tears falling.*) She's a buyer. Buys for J. H. Simmons. She lives down the hall — they're painting. You don't imagine — (*He breaks off. After a pause.*) Now listen, pal, she's just a buyer. She sees merchandise in her room and they have to keep it looking just so . . . (*Pause. Assuming command.*) All right, get my suits. (*Biff doesn't move.*) Now stop crying and do as I say. I gave you an order. Biff, I gave you an order! Is that what you do when I give you an order? How dare you cry! (*Putting his arm around Biff.*) Now look, Biff, when you grow up you'll understand about these things. You mustn't — you mustn't overemphasize a thing like this. I'll see Birnbaum first thing in the morning.

Biff: Never mind.

Willy (getting down beside Biff): Never mind! He's going to give you those points. I'll see to it.

Biff: He wouldn't listen to you.

Willy: He certainly will listen to me. You need those points for the U. of Virginia.

Biff: I'm not going there.

Willy: Heh? If I can't get him to change that mark you'll make it up in summer school. You've got all summer to —

Biff (his weeping breaking from him): Dad . . .

Willy (infected by it): Oh, my boy . . .

Biff: Dad . . .

Willy: She's nothing to me, Biff. I was lonely, I was terribly lonely.

Biff: You — you gave her Mama's stockings! (*His tears break through and he rises to go.*)

Willy (grabbing for Biff): I gave you an order!

Biff: Don't touch me, you — liar!

Willy: Apologize for that!

Biff: You fake! You phony little fake! You fake! (*Overcome, he turns quickly and weeping fully goes out with his suitcase. Willy is left on the floor on his knees.*)

Willy: I gave you an order! Biff, come back here or I'll beat you! Come back here! I'll whip you!

Stanley comes quickly in from the right and stands in front of Willy.

Willy *(shouts at Stanley):* I gave you an order . . .

Stanley: Hey, let's pick it up, pick it up, Mr. Loman. (*He helps Willy to his feet.*) Your boys left with the chippies. They said they'll see you home.

A second waiter watches some distance away.

Willy: But we were supposed to have dinner together.

Music is heard, Willy's theme.

Stanley: Can you make it?

Willy: I'll — sure, I can make it. (*Suddenly concerned about his clothes.*) Do I — I look all right?

Stanley: Sure, you look all right. (*He flicks a speck off Willy's lapel.*)

Willy: Here — here's a dollar.

Stanley: Oh, your son paid me. It's all right.

Willy *(putting it in Stanley's hand):* No take it. You're a good boy.

Stanley: Oh, no, you don't have to . . .

Willy: Here — here's some more. I don't need it any more. (*After a slight pause.*) Tell me — is there a seed store in the neighborhood?

Stanley: Seeds? You mean like to plant?

As Willy turns, Stanley slips the money back into his jacket pocket.

Willy: Yes. Carrots, peas . . .

Stanley: Well, there's hardware stores on Sixth Avenue, but it may be too late now.

Willy *(anxiously):* Oh, I'd better hurry. I've got to get some seeds. (*He starts off to the right.*) I've got to get some seeds, right away. Nothing's planted. I don't have a thing in the ground.

Willy hurries out as the light goes down. Stanley moves over to the right after him, watches him off. The other waiter has been staring at Willy.

Stanley *(to the waiter):* Well, whatta you looking at?

The waiter picks up the chairs and moves off right. Stanley takes the table and follows him. The light fades on this area. There is a long pause, the sound of the flute coming over. The light gradually rises on the kitchen, which is empty. Happy appears at the door of the house, followed by Biff. Happy is carrying a large bunch of long-stemmed roses. He enters the kitchen, looks around for Linda. Not seeing her, he turns to Biff, who is just outside the house door, and makes a gesture with his hands, indicating "Not here, I guess." He looks into the living-room and freezes. Inside, Linda, unseen, is seated, Willy's coat on her lap. She rises ominously and quietly and moves toward Happy, who backs up into the kitchen, afraid.

Happy: Hey, what're you doing up? (*Linda says nothing but moves toward him implacably.*) Where's Pop? (*He keeps backing to the right, and now Linda is in full view in the doorway to the living-room.*) Is he sleeping?

Linda: Where were you?

Happy (trying to laugh it off): We met two girls, Mom, very fine types. Here, we brought you some flowers. (*Offering them to her.*) Put them in your room, Ma.

She knocks them to the floor at Biff's feet. He has now come inside and closed the door behind him. She stares at Biff, silent.

Happy: Now what'd you do that for? Mom, I want you to have some flowers —

Linda (cutting Happy off, violently to Biff): Don't you care whether he lives or dies?

Happy (going to the stairs): Come upstairs, Biff.

Biff (with a flare of disgust, to Happy): Go away from me! (*To Linda.*) What do you mean, lives or dies? Nobody's dying around here, pal.

Linda: Get out of my sight! Get out of here!

Biff: I wanna see the boss.

Linda: You're not going near him!

Biff: Where is he? (*He moves into the living-room and Linda follows.*)

Linda (shouting after Biff): You invite him for dinner. He looks forward to it all day — (*Biff appears in his parents' bedroom, looks around, and exits*) — and then you desert him there. There's no stranger you'd do that to!

Happy: Why? He had a swell time with us. Listen, when I — (*Linda comes back into the kitchen*) — desert him I hope I don't outlive the day!

Linda: Get out of here!

Happy: Now look, Mom . . .

Linda: Did you have to go to women tonight? You and your lousy rotten whores!

Biff re-enters the kitchen.

Happy: Mom, all we did was follow Biff around trying to cheer him up! (*To Biff.*) Boy, what a night you gave me!

Linda: Get out of here, both of you, and don't come back! I don't want you tormenting him any more. Go on now, get your things together! (*To Biff.*) You can sleep in his apartment. (*She starts to pick up the flowers and stops herself.*) Pick up this stuff, I'm not your maid any more. Pick it up, you bum, you!

Happy turns his back to her in refusal. Biff slowly moves over and gets down on his knees, picking up the flowers.

Linda: You're a pair of animals! Not one, not another living soul would have had the cruelty to walk out on that man in a restaurant!

Biff (not looking at her): Is that what he said?

Linda: He didn't have to say anything. He was so humiliated he nearly limped when he came in.

Happy: But, Mom, he had a great time with us —

Biff (cutting him off violently): Shut up!

Without another word, Happy goes upstairs.

Linda: You! You didn't even go in to see if he was all right!

Biff (still on the floor in front of Linda, the flowers in his hand; with self-loathing): No. Didn't. Didn't do a damned thing. How do you like that, heh? Left him babbling in a toilet.

Linda: You louse. You . . .

Biff: Now you hit it on the nose! (*He gets up, throws the flowers in the wastebasket.*) The scum of the earth, and you're looking at him!

Linda: Get out of here!

Biff: I gotta talk to the boss, Mom. Where is he?

Linda: You're not going near him. Get out of this house!

Biff (with absolute assurance, determination): No. We're gonna have an abrupt conversation, him and me.

Linda: You're not talking to him!

Hammering is heard from outside the house, off right. Biff turns toward the noise.

Linda (suddenly pleading): Will you please leave him alone?

Biff: What's he doing out there?

Linda: He's planting the garden!

Biff (quietly): Now? Oh, my God!

Biff moves outside, Linda following. The light dies down on them and comes up on the center of the apron as Willy walks into it. He is carrying a flashlight, a hoe, and a handful of seed packets. He raps the top of the hoe sharply to fix it firmly, and then moves to the left, measuring off the distance with his foot. He holds the flashlight to look at the seed packets, reading off the instructions. He is in the blue of night.

Willy: Carrots . . . quarter-inch apart. Rows . . . one-foot rows. (*He measures it off.*) One foot. (*He puts down a package and measures off.*) Beets. (*He puts down another package and measures again.*) Lettuce. (*He reads the package, puts it down.*) One foot — (*He breaks off as Ben appears at the right and moves slowly down to him.*) What a proposition, ts, ts. Terrific, terrific. 'Cause she's suffered, Ben, the woman has suffered. You understand me? A man can't go out the way he came in, Ben, a man has got to add up to something. You can't, you can't — (*Ben moves toward him as though to interrupt.*) You gotta consider, now. Don't answer so quick. Remember, it's a guaranteed twenty-thousand-dollar proposition. Now look, Ben, I want you to go through the ins and outs of this thing with me. I've got nobody to talk to, Ben, and the woman has suffered, you hear me?

Ben (standing still, considering): What's the proposition?

Willy: It's twenty thousand dollars on the barrelhead. Guaranteed, gilt-edged, you understand?

Ben: You don't want to make a fool of yourself. They might not honor the policy.

Willy: How can they dare refuse? Didn't I work like a coolie to meet every premium on the nose? And now they don't pay off? Impossible!

Ben: It's called a cowardly thing, William.

Willy: Why? Does it take more guts to stand here the rest of my life ringing up a zero?

Ben (yielding): That's a point, William. (*He moves, thinking, turns.*) And twenty thousand — that is something one can feel with the hand, it is there.

Willy (now assured, with rising power): Oh, Ben, that's the whole beauty of it! I see it like a diamond, shining in the dark, hard and rough, that I can pick up and touch in my hand. Not like — like an appointment! This would not be another damned-fool appointment, Ben, and it changes all the aspects. Because he thinks I'm nothing, see, and so he spites me. But the funeral — (*Straightening up.*) Ben, that funeral will be massive! They'll come from Maine, Massachusetts, Vermont, New Hampshire! All the old-timers with the strange license plates — that boy will be thunder-struck, Ben, because he never realized — I am known! Rhode Island, New York, New Jersey — I am known, Ben, and he'll see it with his eyes once and for all. He'll see what I am, Ben! He's in for a shock, that boy!

Ben (coming down to the edge of the garden): He'll call you a coward.

Willy (suddenly fearful): No, that would be terrible.

Ben: Yes. And a damned fool.

Willy: No, no, he mustn't, I won't have that! *(He is broken and desperate.)*

Ben: He'll hate you, William.

The gay music of the boys is heard.

Willy: Oh, Ben, how do we get back to all the great times? Used to be so full of light, and comradeship, the sleigh-riding in winter, and the ruddiness on his cheeks. And always some kind of good news coming up, always something nice coming up ahead. And never even let me carry the valises in the house, and simonizing, simonizing that little red car! Why, why can't I give him something and not have him hate me?

Ben: Let me think about it. *(He glances at his watch.)* I still have a little time. Remarkable proposition, but you've got to be sure you're not making a fool of yourself.

Ben drifts off upstage and goes out of sight. Biff comes down from the left.

Willy (suddenly conscious of Biff, turns and looks up at him, then begins picking up the packages of seeds in confusion): Where the hell is that seed? *(Indignantly.)* You can't see nothing out here! They boxed in the whole goddam neighborhood!

Biff: There are people all around here. Don't you realize that?

Willy: I'm busy. Don't bother me.

Biff (taking the hoe from Willy): I'm saying good-by to you, Pop. *(Willy looks at him, silent, unable to move.)* I'm not coming back any more.

Willy: You're not going to see Oliver tomorrow?

Biff: I've got no appointment, Dad.

Willy: He put his arm around you, and you've got no appointment?

Biff: Pop, get this now, will you? Everytime I've left it's been a fight that sent me out of here. Today I realized something about myself and I tried to explain it to you and I — I think I'm just not smart enough to make any sense out of it for you. To hell with whose fault it is or anything like that. *(He takes Willy's arm.)* Let's just wrap it up, heh? Come on in, we'll tell Mom. *(He gently tries to pull Willy to left.)*

Willy (frozen, immobile, with guilt in his voice): No, I don't want to see her.

Biff: Come on! *(He pulls again, and Willy tries to pull away.)*

Willy (highly nervous): No, no, I don't want to see her.

Biff (tries to look into Willy's face, as if to find the answer there): Why don't you want to see her?

Willy (more harshly now): Don't bother me, will you?

Biff: What do you mean, you don't want to see her? You don't want them calling you yellow, do you? This isn't your fault; it's me, I'm a bum. Now come inside! (*Willy strains to get away.*) Did you hear what I said to you?

Willy pulls away and quickly goes by himself into the house. Biff follows.

Linda (to Willy): Did you plant, dear?

Biff (at the door, to Linda): All right, we had it out. I'm going and I'm not writing any more.

Linda (going to Willy in the kitchen): I think that's the best way, dear. 'Cause there's no use drawing it out, you'll just never get along.

Willy doesn't respond.

Biff: People ask where I am and what I'm doing, you don't know, and you don't care. That way it'll be off your mind and you can start brightening up again. All right? That clears it, doesn't it? (*Willy is silent, and Biff goes to him.*) You gonna wish me luck, scout? (*He extends his hand.*) What do you say?

Linda: Shake his hand, Willy.

Willy (turning to her, seething with hurt): There's no necessity to mention the pen at all, y'know.

Biff (gently): I've got no appointment, Dad.

Willy (erupting fiercely): He put his arm around . . . ?

Biff: Dad, you're never going to see what I am, so what's the use of arguing? If I strike oil I'll send you a check. Meantime forget I'm alive.

Willy (to Linda): Spite, see?

Biff: Shake hands, Dad.

Willy: Not my hand.

Biff: I was hoping not to go this way.

Willy: Well, this is the way you're going. Good-by.

Biff looks at him a moment, then turns sharply and goes to the stairs.

Willy (stops him with): May you rot in hell if you leave this house!

Biff (turning): Exactly what is it that you want from me?

Willy: I want you to know, on the train, in the mountains, in the valleys, wherever you go, that you cut down your life for spite!

Biff: No, no.

Willy: Spite, spite, is the word of your undoing! And when you're down and out, remember what did it. When you're rotting somewhere beside the railroad tracks, remember, and don't you dare blame it on me!

Biff: I'm not blaming it on you!

Willy: I won't take the rap for this, you hear?

Happy comes down the stairs and stands on the bottom step, watching.

Biff: That's just what I'm telling you!

Willy (sinking into a chair at the table, with full accusation): You're trying to put a knife in me — don't think I don't know what you're doing!

Biff: All right, phony! Then let's lay it on the line. (*He whips the rubber tube out of his pocket and puts it on the table.*)

Happy: You crazy —

Linda: Biff! (*She moves to grab the hose, but Biff holds it down with his hand.*)

Biff: Leave it there! Don't move it!

Willy (not looking at it): What is that?

Biff: You know goddam well what that is.

Willy (caged, wanting to escape): I never saw that.

Biff: You saw it. The mice didn't bring it into the cellar! What is this supposed to do, make a hero out of you? This supposed to make me sorry for you?

Willy: Never heard of it.

Biff: There'll be no pity for you, you hear it? No pity!

Willy (to Linda): You hear the spite!

Biff: No, you're going to hear the truth — what you are and what I am!

Linda: Stop it!

Willy: Spite!

Happy (coming down toward Biff): You cut it now!

Biff (to Happy): The man don't know who we are! The man is gonna know! (*To Willy.*) We never told the truth for ten minutes in this house!

Happy: We always told the truth!

Biff (turning on him): You big blow, are you the assistant buyer? You're one of the two assistants to the assistant, aren't you?

Happy: Well, I'm practically —

Biff: You're practically full of it! We all are! And I'm through with it. (*To Willy.*) Now hear this, Willy, this is me.

Willy: I know you!

Biff: You know why I had no address for three months? I stole a
suit in Kansas City and I was in jail. (*To Linda, who is sobbing.*)
Stop crying, I'm through with it.

Linda turns away from them, her hands covering her face.

Willy: I suppose that's my fault!
Biff: I stole myself out of every good job since high school!
Willy: And whose fault is that?
Biff: And I never got anywhere because you blew me so full of
hot air I could never stand taking orders from anybody!
That's whose fault it is!
Willy: I hear that!
Linda: Don't, Biff!
Biff: It's goddam time you heard that! I had to be boss big shot in
two weeks, and I'm through with it!
Willy: Then hang yourself! For spite, hang yourself!
Biff: No! Nobody's hanging himself, Willy! I ran down eleven
flights with a pen in my hand today. And suddenly I stopped,
you hear me? And in the middle of that office building, do
you hear this? I stopped in the middle of that building and I
saw — the sky, I saw the things that I love in this world. The
work and the food and time to sit and smoke. And I looked at
the pen and said to myself, what the hell am I grabbing this
for? Why am I trying to become what I don't want to be?
What am I doing in an office, making a contemptuous,
begging fool of myself, when all I want is out there, waiting
for me the minute I say I know who I am! Why can't I say that,
Willy? (*He tries to make Willy face him, but Willy pulls away and
moves to the left.*)
Willy (with hatred, threateningly): The door of your life is wide
open!
Biff: Pop! I'm a dime a dozen; and so are you!
Willy (turning on him now in an uncontrolled outburst): I am not a
dime a dozen! I am Willy Loman, and you are Biff Loman!

*Biff starts for Willy, but is blocked by Happy. In his fury, Biff seems on the verge of
attacking his father.*

Biff: I am not a leader of men, Willy, and neither are you. You
were never anything but a hard-working drummer who
landed in the ash can like all the rest of them! I'm one dollar
an hour, Willy! I tried seven states and couldn't raise it. A
buck an hour! Do you gather my meaning? I'm not bringing

home any prizes any more, and you're going to stop waiting for me to bring them home!

Willy (directly to Biff): You vengeful, spiteful mutt!

Biff breaks from Happy. Willy, in fright, starts up the stairs. Biff grabs him.

Biff (at the peak of his fury): Pop, I'm nothing! I'm nothing, Pop. Can't you understand that? There's no spite in it any more. I'm just what I am, that's all.

Biff's fury has spent itself, and he breaks down, sobbing, holding on to Willy, who dumbly fumbles for Biff's face.

Willy (astonished): What're you doing? What're you doing? *(To Linda.)* Why is he crying?

Biff (crying, broken): Will you let me go, for Christ's sake? Will you take that phony dream and burn it before something happens? *(Struggling to contain himself, he pulls away and moves to the stairs.)* I'll go in the morning. Put him — put him to bed. *(Exhausted, Biff moves up the stairs to his room.)*

Willy (after a long pause, astonished, elevated): Isn't that — isn't that remarkable? Biff — he likes me!

Linda: He loves you, Willy!

Happy (deeply moved): Always did, Pop.

Willy: Oh, Biff! *(Staring wildly.)* He cried! Cried to me. *(He is choking with his love, and now cries out his promise.)* That boy — that boy is going to be magnificent!

Ben appears in the light just outside the kitchen.

Ben: Yes, outstanding, with twenty thousand behind him.

Linda (sensing the racing of his mind, fearfully, carefully): Now come to bed. Willy. It's all settled now.

Willy (finding it difficult not to rush out of the house): Yes, we'll sleep. Come on. Go to sleep, Hap.

Ben: And it does take a great kind of a man to crack the jungle.

In accents of dread, Ben's idyllic music starts up.

Happy (his arm around Linda): I'm getting married, Pop, don't forget it. I'm changing everything. I'm gonna run that department before the year is up. You'll see, Mom. *(He kisses her.)*

Ben: The jungle is dark but full of diamonds, Willy.

Willy turns, moves, listening to Ben.

Linda: Be good. You're both good boys, just act that way, that's all.

Happy: Night, Pop. (*He goes upstairs.*)

Linda (to Willy): Come, dear.

Ben (with greater force): One must go in to fetch a diamond out.

Willy (to Linda, as he moves slowly along the edge of the kitchen, toward the door): I just want to get settled down, Linda. Let me sit alone for a little.

Linda (almost uttering her fear): I want you upstairs.

Willy (taking her in his arms): In a few minutes, Linda. I couldn't sleep right now. Go on, you look awful tired. (*He kisses her.*)

Ben: Not like an appointment at all. A diamond is rough and hard to the touch.

Willy: Go on now. I'll be right up.

Linda: I think this is the only way, Willy.

Willy: Sure, it's the best thing.

Ben: Best thing!

Willy: The only way. Everything is gonna be — go on, kid, get to bed. You look so tired.

Linda: Come right up.

Willy: Two minutes.

Linda goes into the living-room, then reappears in her bedroom. Willy moves just outside the kitchen door.

Willy: Loves me. (*Wonderingly.*) Always loved me. Isn't that a remarkable thing? Ben, he'll worship me for it!

Ben (with promise): It's dark there, but full of diamonds.

Willy: Can you imagine that magnificence with twenty thousand dollars in his pocket?

Linda (calling from her room): Willy! Come up!

Willy (calling into the kitchen): Yes! Yes. Coming! It's very smart, you realize that, don't you, sweetheart? Even Ben sees it. I gotta go, baby. 'By! 'By! (*Going over to Ben, almost dancing.*) Imagine? When the mail comes he'll be ahead of Bernard again!

Ben: A perfect proposition all around.

Willy: Did you see how he cried to me? Oh, if I could kiss him, Ben!

Ben: Time, William, time!

Willy: Oh, Ben, I always knew one way or another we were gonna make it, Biff and I!

Ben (looking at his watch): The boat. We'll be late. (*He moves slowly off into the darkness.*)

Willy (elegiacally, turning to the house): Now when you kick off, boy, I want a seventy-yard boot, and get right down the field under the ball, and when you hit, hit low and hit hard, because it's important, boy. (*He swings around and faces the audience.*) There's all kinds of important people in the stands, and the first thing you know . . . (*Suddenly realizing he is alone.*) Ben! Ben, where do I . . . ? (*He makes a sudden movement of search.*) Ben, how do I . . . ?

Linda (calling): Willy, you coming up?

Willy (uttering a gasp of fear, whirling about as if to quiet her): Sh! (*He turns around as if to find his way; sounds, faces, voices, seem to be swarming in upon him and he flicks at them, crying.*) Sh! Sh! (*Suddenly music, faint and high, stops him. It rises in intensity, almost to an unbearable scream. He goes up and down on his toes, and rushes off around the house.*) Shhh!

Linda: Willy?

There is no answer. Linda waits. Biff gets up off his bed. He is still in his clothes. Happy sits up. Biff stands listening.

Linda (with real fear): Willy, answer me! Willy!

There is the sound of a car starting and moving away at full speed.

Linda: No!

Biff (rushing down the stairs): Pop!

As the car speeds off, the music crashes down in a frenzy of sound, which becomes the soft pulsation of a single cello string. Biff slowly returns to his bedroom. He and Happy gravely don their jackets. Linda slowly walks out of her room. The music has developed into a dead march. The leaves of day are appearing over everything. Charley and Bernard, somberly dressed, appear and knock on the kitchen door. Biff and Happy slowly descend the stairs to the kitchen as Charley and Bernard enter. All stop a moment when Linda, in clothes of mourning, bearing a little bunch of roses, comes through the draped doorway into the kitchen. She goes to Charley and takes his arm. Now all move toward the audience, through the wall-line of the kitchen. At the limit of the apron, Linda lays down the flowers, kneels, and sits back on her heels. All stare down at the grave.

REQUIEM

Charley: It's getting dark, Linda.

Linda doesn't react. She stares at the grave.

Biff: How about it, Mom? Better get some rest, heh? They'll be closing the gate soon.

Linda makes no move. Pause.

Happy (deeply angered): He had no right to do that. There was no necessity for it. We would've helped him.

Charley (grunting): Hmmm.

Biff: Come along, Mom.

Linda: Why didn't anybody come?

Charley: It was a very nice funeral.

Linda: But where are all the people he knew? Maybe they blame him.

Charley: Naa. It's a rough world, Linda. They wouldn't blame him.

Linda: I can't understand it. At this time especially. First time in thirty-five years we were just about free and clear. He only needed a little salary. He was even finished with the dentist.

Charley: No man only needs a little salary.

Linda: I can't understand it.

Biff: There were a lot of nice days. When he'd come home from a trip; or on Sundays, making the stoop; finishing the cellar; putting on the new porch; when he built the extra bathroom; and put up the garage. You know something, Charley, there's more of him in that front stoop than in all the sales he ever made.

Charley: Yeah. He was a happy man with a batch of cement.

Linda: He was so wonderful with his hands.

Biff: He had the wrong dreams. All, all, wrong.

Happy (almost ready to fight Biff): Don't say that!

Biff: He never knew who he was.

Charley (stopping Happy's movement and reply. To Biff): Nobody dast blame this man. You don't understand: Willy was a salesman. And for a salesman, there is no rock bottom to the life. He don't put a bolt to a nut, he don't tell you the law or give you medicine. He's a man way out there in the blue, riding on a smile and a shoeshine. And when they start not smiling back — that's an earthquake. And then you get yourself a couple of spots on your hat, and you're finished. Nobody dast blame this man. A salesman is got to dream, boy. It comes with the territory.

Biff: Charley, the man didn't know who he was.

Happy (infuriated): Don't say that!

Biff: Why don't you come with me, Happy?

Happy: I'm not licked that easily. I'm staying right in this city, and I'm gonna beat this racket! (*He looks at Biff, his chin set.*) The Loman Brothers!

Biff: I know who I am, kid.

Happy: All right, boy. I'm gonna show you and everybody else that Willy Loman did not die in vain. He had a good dream. It's the only dream you can have — to come out number-one man. He fought it out here, and this is where I'm gonna win it for him.

Biff (with a hopeless glance at Happy, bends toward his mother): Let's go, Mom.

Linda: I'll be with you in a minute. Go on, Charley. (*He hesitates.*) I want to, just for a minute. I never had a chance to say good-by.

Charley moves away, followed by Happy. Biff remains a slight distance up and left of Linda. She sits there, summoning herself. The flute begins, not far away, playing behind her speech.

Linda: Forgive me, dear. I can't cry. I don't know what it is, but I can't cry. I don't understand it. Why did you ever do that? Help me, Willy, I can't cry. It seems to me that you're just on another trip. I keep expecting you. Willy, dear, I can't cry. Why did you do it? I search and search and I search, and I can't understand it, Willy. I made the last payment on the house today. Today, dear. And there'll be nobody home. (*A sob rises in the throat.*) We're free and clear. (*Sobbing more fully, released.*) We're free. (*Biff comes slowly toward her.*) We're free . . . We're free . . .

Biff lifts her to her feet and moves out up right with her in his arms. Linda sobs quietly. Bernard and Charley come together and follow them, followed by Happy. Only the music of the flute is left on the darkening stage as over the house the hard towers of the apartment buildings rise into sharp focus, and —

The Curtain Falls

**ATHOL FUGARD, JOHN KANI,
and WINSTON NTSHONA**

The Island

CHARACTERS
John ⎱
Winston ⎰ *two prisoners*

SCENE I

Centre stage: a raised area representing a cell on Robben Island. Blankets and sleeping-mats — the prisoners sleep on the floor — are neatly folded. In one corner are a bucket of water and two tin mugs.

The long drawn-out wail of a siren. Stage-lights come up to reveal a moat of harsh, white light around the cell. In it the two prisoners — John stage-right and Winston stage-left — mime the digging of sand. They wear the prison uniform of khaki shirt and short trousers. Their heads are shaven. It is an image of back-breaking and grotesquely futile labour. Each in turns fills a wheelbarrow and then with great effort pushes it to where the other man is digging, and empties it. As a result, the piles of sand never diminish. Their labour is interminable. The only sounds are their grunts as they dig, the squeal of the wheelbarrows as they circle the cell, and the hum of Hodoshe, the green carrion fly.

A whistle is blown. They stop digging and come together, standing side by side as they are handcuffed together and shackled at the ankles. Another whistle. They start to run . . . John mumbling a prayer, Winston muttering a rhythm for their three-legged run.

They do not run fast enough. They get beaten . . . Winston receiving a bad blow to the eye and John spraining an ankle. In this condition they arrive finally at the cell door. Handcuffs and shackles are taken off. After being searched, they lurch into their cell. The door closes behind them. Both men sink to the floor.

A moment of total exhaustion until slowly, painfully, they start to explore their respective injuries . . . Winston his eye, and John his ankle. Winston is moaning softly and this eventually draws John's attention away from his ankle. He crawls to Winston and examines the injured eye. It needs attention. Winston's moaning is slowly turning into a sound of inarticulate outrage, growing in volume and violence. John urinates into one hand and tries to clean the other man's eye with it, but Winston's anger and outrage are now uncontrollable. He breaks away from John and crawls around the cell, blind with rage and pain. John tries to placate him . . . the noise could bring back the warders and still more trouble. Winston eventually finds the cell door but before he can start banging on it John pulls him away.

Winston (calling): Hodoshe!

John: Leave him, Winston. Listen to me, man! If he comes now we'll be in bigger shit.

Winston: I want Hodoshe. I want him now! I want to take him to the office. He must read my warrant. I was sentenced to Life brother, not bloody Death!

John: Please, Winston! He made us run . . .

Winston: I want Hodoshe!

John: He made us run. He's happy now. Leave him. Maybe he'll let us go back to the quarry tomorrow. . . .

Winston is suddenly silent. For a moment John thinks his words are having an effect, but then he realizes that the other man is looking at his ear. Winston touches it. It is bleeding. A sudden spasm of fear from John who puts a hand to his ear. His fingers come away with blood on them. The two men look at each other.

Winston: Nyana we Sizwe!°

Nyana we Sizwe: Brother of the land.

In a reversal of earlier roles Winston now gets John down on the floor of the cell so as to examine the injured ear. He has to wipe blood and sweat out of his eyes in order to see clearly. John winces with pain. Winston keeps restraining him.

Winston *(eventually):* It's not too bad. (*Using his shirt-tail he cleans the injured ear.*)

John *(through clenched teeth as Winston tends his ear):* Hell, *ons was gemoer vandag!*° (*A weak smile.*) News bulletin and weather forecast! Black Domination was chased by White Domination. Black Domination lost its shoes and collected a few bruises. Black Domination will run barefoot to the quarry tomorrow. Conditions locally remain unchanged — thunderstorms with the possibility of cold showers and rain. Elsewhere, fine and warm!

Winston has now finished tending John's ear and settles down on the floor beside him. He clears his nose, ears, and eyes of sand.

Winston: Sand! Same old sea sand I used to play with when I was young. St. George's Strand. New Year's Day. Sand dunes. Sand castles. . . .

John: *Ja,*° we used to go there too. Last . . . (*Pause and then a small laugh. He shakes his head.*) The Christmas before they arrested me, we were down there. All of us. Honeybush. My little Monde played in the sand. We'd given her one of those little buckets and spades for Christmas.

Winston: Ja.

John: Anyway, it was Daddy's turn today. (*Shaking his head ruefully.*) *Haai,*° Winston, this one goes on the record. 'Struesgod! I'm a man, brother. A man! But if Hodoshe had kept us at those wheelbarrows five minutes longer . . . ! There would have been a baby on the Island tonight. I nearly cried.

Winston: Ja.

John: There was no end to it, except one of us!

Winston: That's right.

John: This morning when he said: "You two! The beach!" . . . I thought, Okay, so it's my turn to empty the sea into a hole. He likes that one. But when he pointed to the wheelbarrows, and I saw his idea . . . ! (*Shaking his head.*) I laughed at first. Then I wasn't laughing. Then I hated you. You looked so stupid, *broer!*°

Winston: That's what he wanted.

---

ons was gemoer vardag: We were fucked over today.   *Ja*: Yes.   *Haai*: An exclamation of surprise.   *broer*: Brother.

John: It was going to last forever, man! Because of *you*. And for *you*, because of *me*. *Moer!*° He's cleverer than I thought.
Winston: If he was God, he would have done it.
John: What?
Winston: Broken us. Men get tired. Hey! There's a thought. We're still alive because Hodoshe got tired.
John: Tomorrow?
Winston: We'll see.
John: If he takes us back there . . . If I hear that wheelbarrow . . . of yours again, coming with another bloody load of . . . eternity!
Winston (with calm resignation): We'll see.

Pause. John looks at Winston.

John (with quiet emphasis, as if the other man did not fully understand the significance of what he had said): I *hated* you Winston.
Winston (meeting John's eyes): I hated *you*.

John puts a hand on Winston's shoulder. Their brotherhood is intact. He gets slowly to his feet.

John: Where's the *lap*?
Winston: Somewhere. Look for it.
John: Hey! You had it last.

Limping around the cell looking for their wash-rag.

Winston: Haai, man! You got no wife here. Look for the rag yourself.
John (finding the rag beside the water bucket): Look where it is. Look! Hodoshe comes in here and sees it. "Whose *lappie* is that?" Then what do you say?
Winston: "It's his rag, sir."
John: Yes? Okay. "It's my rag, sir." When you wash, use your shirt.
Winston: Okay, okay! "It's our rag, sir!"
John: That will be the bloody day!

John, getting ready to wash, starts to take off his shirt. Winston produces a cigarette butt, matches, and flint from their hiding-place under the water bucket. He settles down for a smoke.

Shit, today was long. Hey, Winston, suppose the watch of the chap behind the siren is slow! We could still be there, man!

Moer: Literally means "womb," equivalent in force to "fuck" or "fucking."

(*He pulls out three or four rusty nails from a secret pocket in his trousers. He holds them out to Winston.*) Hey there.

Winston: What?

John: With the others.

Winston (taking the nails): What's this?

John: Necklace, man. With the others.

Winston: Necklace?

John: Antigone's necklace.

Winston: *Ag*, shit, man!

Slams the nails down on the cell floor and goes on smoking.

Antigone! Go to hell, man, John.

John: Hey, don't start any nonsense now. You promised. (*Limps over to Winston's bed-roll and produces a half-completed necklace made of nails and string.*) It's nearly finished. Look. Three fingers, one nail . . . three fingers, one nail . . . (*Places the necklace beside Winston who is shaking his head, smoking aggressively, and muttering away.*) Don't start any nonsense now, Winston. There's six days to go to the concert. We're committed. We promised the chaps we'd do something. This *Antigone* is just right for us. Six more days and we'll make it.

He continues washing.

Winston: Jesus, John! We were down on the beach today. Hodoshe made us run. Can't you just leave a man . . . ?

John: To hell with you! Who do you think ran with you? I'm also tired, but we can't back out now. Come on! Three fingers. . . .

Winston: . . . one nail! (*Shaking his head.*) *Haai . . . haai . . . haai!*

John: Stop moaning and get on with it. Shit, Winston! What sort of progress is this? (*Abandoning his wash.*) Listen. Listen! Number 42 is practising the Zulu War Dance. Down there they're rehearsing their songs. It's just in this *moer* cell that there's always an argument. Today you want to do it, tomorrow you don't want to do it. How the hell must I know what to report to the chaps tomorrow if we go back to the quarry?

Winston is unyielding. His obstinacy gets the better of John, who eventually throws the wash-rag at him.

There! Wash!

John applies himself to the necklace while Winston, still muttering away in an undertone, starts to clean himself.

How can I be sure of anything when you carry on like this?
We've still got to learn the words, the moves. Shit! It could be
so bloody good, man.

*Winston mutters protests all the way through this speech of John's. The latter
holds up the necklace.*

Nearly finished! Look at it! Three fingers . . .
Winston: . . . one nail.
John: Ja! Simple. Do you still remember all I told you yesterday?
Bet you've bloody forgotten. How can I carry on like this? I
can't move on, man. Over the whole bloody lot again! Who
Antigone is . . . who Creon is . . .
Winston: Antigone is mother to Polynices . . .
John: Haai, haai, haai . . . shit, Winston! (*Now really exasperated.*)
How many times must I tell you that Antigone is the sister to
the two brothers? Not the mother. That's another play.
Winston: Oh.
John: That's all you know! "Oh." (*He abandons the necklace and fishes
out a piece of chalk from a crack in the floor.*) Come here. This is
the last time. 'Struesgod. The last time.
Winston: Ag, no, John.
John: Come! I'm putting this plot down for the last time! If you
don't learn it tonight I'm going to report you to the old men
tomorrow. And remember, *broer,* those old men will make
Hodoshe and his tricks look like a little boy.
Winston: Jesus Christ! Learn to dig for Hodoshe, learn to run for
Hodoshe, and what happens when I get back to the cell?
Learn to read *Antigone!*
John: Come! And shut up! (*He pulls the reluctant Winston down
beside him on the floor. Winston continues to clean himself with the
rag while John lays out the "plot" of Antigone.*) If you would just
stop moaning, you would learn faster. Now listen!
Winston: Okay, do it.
John: Listen! It is the Trial of Antigone. Right?
Winston: So you say.
John: First, the accused. Who is the accused?
Winston: Antigone.
John: Coming from you that's bloody progress. (*Writing away on
the cell floor with his chalk.*) Next the State. Who is the State?
Winston: Creon.
John: King Creon. Creon is the State. Now . . . what did Antigone
do?

Winston: Antigone buried her brother Eteocles.

John: No, no, no! Shit, Winston, when are you going to remember this thing? I told you, man, Antigone buried Polynices. The traitor! The one who I said was on *our* side. Right?

Winston: Right.

John: Stage one of the Trial. (*Writing on the floor.*) The State lays its charges against the Accused . . . and lists counts . . . you know the way they do it. Stage two is Pleading. What does Antigone plead? Guilty or Not Guilty?

Winston: Not Guilty.

John (trying to be tactful): Now look, Winston, we're not going to argue. Between me and you, in this cell, we know she's Not Guilty. But in the play she pleads Guilty.

Winston: No, man, John! Antigone is Not Guilty . . .

John: In the play . . .

Winston (losing his temper): To hell with the play! Antigone had every right to bury her brother.

John: Don't say "To hell with the play." We've got to do the bloody thing. And in the play she pleads Guilty. Get that straight. Antigone pleads . . .

Winston (giving up in disgust): Okay, do it your way.

John: It's not my way! In the play . . .

Winston: Guilty!

John: Yes, Guilty!

Writes furiously on the floor.

Winston: Guilty.

John: Stage three, Pleading in Mitigation of Sentence. Stage four, Sentence, State Summary, and something from you . . . Farewell Words. Now learn that.

Winston: Hey?

John (getting up): Learn that!

Winston: But we've just done it!

John: I've just done it. Now *you* learn it.

Winston (throwing aside the wash-rag with disgust before applying himself to learning the "plot"): Learn to run, learn to read . . .

John: And don't throw the rag there! (*Retrieving the rag and placing it in its correct place.*) Don't be so bloody difficult, man. We're nearly there. You'll be proud of this thing when we've done it. (*Limps to his bed-roll and produces a pendant made from a jam-tin lid and twine.*) Look. Winston, look! Creon's medallion. Good, hey! (*Hangs it around his neck.*) I'll finish the necklace while you learn that. (*He strings on the remaining nails.*) Jesus, Winston! June 1965.

Winston: What?

John: This, man. *Antigone.* In New Brighton. St. Stephen's Hall. The place was packed, man! All the big people. Front row . . . dignitaries. Shit, those were the days. Georgie was Creon. You know Georgie?

Winston: The teacher?

John: That's him. He played Creon. Should have seen him, Winston. Short and fat, with big eyes, but by the time the play was finished he was as tall as the roof.

Onto his legs in an imitation of Georgie's Creon.

"My Councillors, now that the Gods have brought our City safe through a storm of troubles to tranquillity . . ." And old Mulligan! Another short-arsed teacher. With a beard! He used to go up to the Queen . . . (*Another imitation.*) "Your Majesty, prepare for grief, but do not weep."

The necklace in his hands.

Nearly finished!

Nomhle played Antigone. A bastard of a lady that one, but a beautiful bitch. Can't get her out of my mind tonight.

Winston (indicating the "plot"): I know this.

John: You sure?

Winston: This! . . . it's here. (*Tapping his head.*)

John: You're not bullshitting, hey? (*He rubs out the "plot" and then paces the cell.*) Right. The Trial of Antigone. Who is the Accused?

Winston: Antigone.

John: Who is the State?

Winston: King Creon.

John: Stage one.

Winston (supremely self-confident): Antigone lays charges . . .

John: NO, SHIT, MAN, WINSTON!!!

Winston pulls John down and stifles his protests with a hand over his mouth.

Winston: Okay . . . okay . . . listen, John . . . listen . . . The State lays charges against Antigone.

Pause.

John: Be careful!

Winston: The State lays charges against Antigone.
John: Stage two.
Winston: Pleading.
John: What does she plead? Guilty or Not Guilty?
Winston: Guilty.
John: Stage three.
Winston: Pleading in Mitigation of Sentence.
John: Stage four.
Winston: State Summary, Sentence, and Farewell Words.
John (very excited): He's got it! That's my man. See how easy it is, Winston? Tomorrow, just the words.

Winston gets onto his legs. John puts away the props. Mats and blankets are unrolled. The two men prepare for sleep.

John: Hell, I hope we go back to the quarry tomorrow. There's still a lot of things we need for props and costumes. Your wig! The boys in Number Fourteen said they'd try and smuggle me a piece of rope from the jetty.
Winston: Ja, I hope we're back there. I want to try and get some tobacco through to Sipho.
John: Sipho?
Winston: Back in solitary.
John: Again!
Winston: Ja.
John: Oh hell!
Winston: Simon passed the word.
John: What was it this time?
Winston: Complained about the food I think. Demanded to see the book of Prison Regulations.
John: Why don't they leave him alone for a bit?
Winston: Because he doesn't leave them alone.
John: You're right. I'm glad I'm not in Number Twenty-two with him. One man starts getting hard-arsed like that and the whole lot of you end up in the shit.

Winston's bed is ready. He lies down.

You know what I'm saying?
Winston: Ja.
John: What?
Winston: What "What"?
John: What am I saying?
Winston: Haai, Johnny, man! I'm tired now! Let a man . . .
John: I'm saying Don't Be Hard-Arsed! You! When Hodoshe

opens that door tomorrow say "*Ja, Baas*" the right way. I don't want to be back on that bloody beach tomorrow just because you feel like being difficult.

Winston (wearily): Okay, man, Johnny.

John: You're not alone in this cell. I'm here too.

Winston: Jesus, you think I don't know that!

John: People must remember their responsibilities to others.

Winston: I'm glad to hear you say that, because I was just going to remind you that it is your turn tonight.

John: What do you mean? Wasn't it my turn last night?

Winston (shaking his head emphatically): Haai, haai. Don't you remember? Last night I took you to bioscope.°

John: Hey, by the way! So you did. Bloody good film too. "Fastest Gun in the West." Glenn Ford.

Whips out a six-shooter and guns down a few bad-men.

You were bullshitting me a bit though. How the hell can Glenn Ford shoot backwards through his legs. I tried to work that one out on the beach.

He is now seated on his bed-roll. After a moment's thought he holds up an empty mug as a telephone-receiver and starts to dial. Winston watches him with puzzlement.

Operator, put me through to New Brighton, please . . . yes, New Brighton, Port Elizabeth. The number is 414624. . . . Yes, mine is local . . . local. . . .

Winston (recognizing the telephone number): The Shop!

He sits upright with excitement as John launches into the telephone conversation.

John: That you Scott? Hello, man! Guess who! . . . You got it! You bastard! Hell, shit, Scott, man . . . how things with you? No, still inside. Give me the news, man . . . you don't say! No, we don't hear anything here . . . not a word. . . . What's that? Business is bad? . . . You bloody undertaker! People aren't dying fast enough! No, things are fine here. . . .

Winston, squirming with excitement, has been trying unsuccessfully to interrupt John's torrent of words and laughter. He finally succeeds in drawing John's attention.

Winston: Who else is there? Who's with Scott?

bioscope: Cinema.

John: Hey, Scott, who's there with you? . . . Oh no! . . . call him to the phone, man. . . .
Winston: Who's it?
John (ignoring Winston): Just for a minute, man, please, Scott. . . .

Ecstatic response from John as another voice comes over the phone.

Hello there, you beautiful bastard . . . how's it, man? . . .
Winston: Who the hell is it, man?
John (hand over the receiver): Sky!

Winston can no longer contain his excitement. He scrambles out of his bed to join John, and joins in the fun with questions and remarks whispered into John's ear. Both men enjoy it enormously.

How's it with Mangi? Where's Vusi? How are the chaps keeping, Sky? Winston? . . . All right, man. He's here next to me. No, fine, man, fine, man . . . small accident today when he collided with Hodoshe, but nothing to moan about. His right eye bruised, that's all. Hey, Winston's asking how are the punkies doing? (*Big laugh.*) You bloody lover boy! Leave something for us, man!

John becomes aware of Winston trying to interrupt again: to Winston.

Okay . . . okay. . . .
(*Back to the telephone.*) Listen, Sky, Winston says if you get a chance, go down to Dora Street, to his wife. Tell V. Winston says he's okay, things are fine. Winston says she must carry on . . . nothing has happened . . . tell her to take care of everything and everybody. . . . *Ja.* . . .

The mention of his wife guillotines Winston's excitement and fun. After a few seconds of silence he crawls back heavily to his bed and lies down. A similar shift in mood takes place in John.

And look, Sky, you're not far from Gratten Street. Cross over to it, man, drop in on number thirty-eight, talk to Princess, my wife. How is she keeping? Ask her for me. I haven't received a letter for three months now. Why aren't they writing? Tell her to write, man. I want to know how the children are keeping. Is Monde still at school? How's my twin baby, my Father and Mother? Is the old girl sick? They mustn't be afraid to tell me. I want to know. I know it's an effort to write, but it means a lot to us here. Tell her . . . this was another day. They're not very different here. We were down on the beach. The wind was blowing. The sand got in our eyes. The sea was rough. I couldn't see the mainland properly. Tell them that maybe tomorrow we'll go to the quarry. It's not so bad there. We'll be with the others. Tell her also . . . it's starting to get cold now, but the worst is still coming.

Slow fade to blackout.

SCENE II

The cell, a few days later. John is hidden under a blanket. Winston is in the process of putting on Antigone's wig and false breasts.

John: Okay?
Winston (still busy): No.
John: Okay?
Winston: No.
John: Okay?
Winston: No.

Pause.

John: Okay?

Winston is ready. He stands waiting. John slowly lifts the blanket and looks. He can't believe his eyes. Winston is a very funny sight. John's amazement turns into laughter, which builds steadily. He bangs on the cell wall.

Hey, Norman. Norman! Come this side, man. I got it here. *Poes!°*

John launches into an extravagant send-up of Winston's Antigone. He circles "her" admiringly, he fondles her breasts, he walks arm in arm with her down Main Street, collapsing with laughter between each "turn." He climaxes everything by dropping his trousers.

Speedy Gonzales! Here I come!

This last joke is too much for Winston who has endured the whole performance with mounting but suppressed anger. He tears off the wig and breasts, throws them down on the cell floor, and storms over to the water bucket where he starts to clean himself.

Winston: It's finished! I'm not doing it. Take your Antigone and shove it up your arse!

Poes: Cunt.

John (trying to control himself): Wait, man. Wait. . . .

He starts laughing again.

Winston: There is nothing to wait for, my friend. I'm not doing it.

John: Please, Winston!

Winston: You can laugh as much as you like, my friend, but just let's get one thing straight, I'm *not* doing Antigone. And in case you want to know why . . . I'm a man, not a bloody woman.

John: When did I say otherwise?

Winston: What were you laughing at?

John: I'm not laughing now.

Winston: What are you doing, crying?

Another burst of laughter from John.

There you go again; more laughing! Shit, man, you want me to go out there tomorrow night and make a bloody fool of myself? You think I don't know what will happen after that? Every time I run to the quarry . . . "Nyah . . . nyah. . . . Here comes Antigone . . . Help the poor lady! . . ." Well, you can go to hell with your Antigone.

John: I wasn't laughing at you.

Winston: Then who were you laughing at? Who else was here that dressed himself as a lady and made a bloody fool of himself?

John (now trying very hard to placate the other man): Okay Winston. Okay! I'm not laughing any more.

Winston: You can go to hell with what you're saying.

John: Look, Winston, try to understand, man . . . this is Theatre.

Winston: You call laughing at me Theatre? Then go to hell with your Theatre!

John: Please, Winston, just stop talking and listen to me.

Winston: No! You get this, brother, . . . I am not doing your Antigone! I would rather run the whole day for Hodoshe. At least I know where I stand with him. All *he* wants is to make me a "boy" . . . not a bloody woman.

John: Okay, okay. . . .

Winston: Nothing you can say . . .

John (shouting the other man down): Will you bloody listen!

Winston (throwing the wash-rag down violently): Okay. I'm listening.

John: Sure I laughed. *Ja . . . I laughed.* But can I tell you why I laughed? I was preparing you for . . . stage fright! You think I don't know what I'm doing in this cell? This is preparation for stage fright! I know those bastards out there. When you get in front of them, sure they'll laugh . . . Nyah, nyah! . . . they'll laugh. But just remember this brother, nobody laughs forever! There'll come a time when they'll stop laughing, and that will be the time when our Antigone hits them with her words.

Winston: You're day-dreaming, John. Just get it into your head that I'm not doing Antigone. It's as simple as that.

John (realizing for the first time that Winston needs to be handled very carefully): Hey, Winston! Hold on there, man. We've only got one more day to go! They've given us the best spot in the programme. We end the show! You can't back out now.

Winston: You think I can't? Just wait and see.

John: Winston! You want to get me into trouble? Is that what you want?

Winston: Okay, I won't back out.

John (delighted with his easy victory): That's my man!

Winston (retrieving the wig and false breasts off the floor and slamming them into John's hands): Here's Antigone . . . take these titties and hair and play Antigone. I'm going to play Creon. Do you understand what I'm saying? Take your two titties. . . . I'll have my balls and play Creon. (*Turns his back on a flabbergasted John, fishes out a cigarette-butt and matches from under the water bucket, and settles down for a smoke.*)

John (after a stunned silence): You won't make it! I thought about that one days ago. It's too late now to learn Creon's words.

Winston (smoking): I hate to say it, but that is just too bad. I am not doing Antigone.

John is now furious. After a moment's hesitation he stuffs on the wig and false breasts and confronts Winston.

John: Look at me. Now laugh.

Winston tries, but the laugh is forced and soon dies away.

Go on.

Pause.

Go on laughing! Why did you stop? Must I tell you why? Because behind all this rubbish is me, and you know it's me. You think those bastards out there won't know it's you? Yes, they'll laugh. But who cares about that as long as they laugh in the beginning and listen at the end. That's all we want them to do . . . listen at the end!

Winston: I don't care what you say John. I'm not doing Antigone.

John: Winston . . . you're being difficult. You promised. . . .

Winston: Go to hell, man. Only last night you tell me that this Antigone is a bloody . . . what you call it . . . legend! A Greek one at that. Bloody thing never even happened. Not even history! Look, brother, I got no time for bullshit. Fuck legends. Me? . . . I live my life here! I know why I'm here, and it's history, not legends. I had my chat with a magistrate in Cradock and now I'm here. Your Antigone is a child's play, man.

John: Winston! That's Hodoshe's talk.

Winston: You can go to hell with that one too.

John: Hodoshe's talk, Winston! That's what he says all the time. What he wants us to say all our lives. Our convictions, our ideals . . . that's what he calls them . . . child's play. Everything we fucking do is "child's play" . . . when we ran that whole day in the sun and pushed those wheelbarrows, when we cry, when we shit . . . child's play! Look, brother, . . . I've had enough. No one is going to stop me doing Antigone. . . .

The two men break apart suddenly, drop their trousers, and stand facing the wall with arms outstretched. Hodoshe calls John.

Yes, sir!

He then pulls up his trousers and leaves the cell. When he has left, Winston pulls up his trousers and starts muttering with savage satisfaction at the thought of John in Hodoshe's hands.

Winston: There he goes. Serves him right. I just hope Hodoshe teaches him a lesson. Antigone is important! Antigone this! Antigone that! Shit, man. Nobody can sleep in this bloody cell because of all that bullshit. Polynices! Eteocles! The other prisoners too. Nobody gets any peace and quiet because of that bloody Antigone! I hope Hodoshe gives it to him.

He is now at the cell door. He listens, then moves over to the wig on the floor and circles it. He finally picks it up. Moves back to the cell door to make sure no one is coming. The water bucket gives him an idea. He puts on the wig and, after some difficulty, manages to see his reflection in the water. A good laugh, which he cuts off abruptly. He moves around the cell trying out a few of Antigone's poses. None of them work. He feels a fool. He finally tears off the wig and throws it down on the floor with disgust.

Ag voetsek!°

Ag voetsek: Go to hell.

Hands in pockets he paces the cell with grim determination.

I'm not going to do it. And I'm going to tell him. When he comes back. For once he must just shut that big bloody mouth of his and listen. To me! I'm not going to argue, but 'struesgod that . . . !

The wig on the floor. He stamps on it.

Shit, man! If he wants a woman in the cell he must send for his wife, and I don't give a damn how he does it. I didn't walk with those men and burn my bloody passbook in front of that police station, and have a magistrate send me here for life so that he can dress me up like a woman and make a bloody fool of me. I'm going to tell him. When he walks through that door.

John returns. Winston is so involved in the problem of Antigone that at first he does not register John's strangely vacant manner.

Listen, *broer*, I'm not trying to be difficult but this Antigone! No! Please listen to me, John. 'Struesgod I can't do it. I mean, let's try something else, like singing or something. You always got ideas. You know I can sing or dance. But not Antigone. Please, John.

John (quietly): Winston . . .

Winston (still blind to the other man's manner): Don't let's argue, man. We've been together in this cell too long now to quarrel about rubbish. But you know me. If there's one thing I can't stand it's people laughing at me. If I go out there tomorrow night and those bastards start laughing I'll fuck up the first one I lay my hands on. You saw yourself what happened in here when you started laughing. I wanted to *moer* you, John. I'm not joking. I really wanted to. . . . Hey, are you listening to me? (*Looking squarely at John.*)

John: Winston . . . I've got something to tell you.

Winston (registering John's manner for the first time): What's the matter? Hodoshe? What happened? Are we in shit? Solitary?

John: My appeal was heard last Wednesday. Sentence reduced. I've got three months to go.

Long silence. Winston is stunned. Eventually . . .

Winston: Three . . .

John: . . . months to go.

Winston: Three. . . .

John: Ja. That's what Prinsloo said.
Winston: John!

Winston explodes with joy. The men embrace. They dance a jig in the cell. Winston finally tears himself away and starts to hammer on the cell walls so as to pass on the news to other prisoners.

Norman! Norman!! John. Three months to go. *Ja.* . . . Just been told. . . .

Winston's excitement makes John nervous. He pulls Winston away from the wall.

John: Winston! Not yet, man. We'll tell them at the quarry tomorrow. Let me just live with it for a little while.
Winston: Okay, okay. . . . How did it happen?

He pulls John down to the floor. They sit close together.

John: Jesus, I'm so mixed up, man! *Ja* . . . the door opened and I saw Hodoshe. Ooo God, I said to myself. Trouble! Here we go again! All because of you and the noise you were making. Went down the corridor straight to Number Four . . . Solitary and Spare Diet!! But at the end, instead of turning right, we turned left into the main block, all the way through it to Prinsloo's office.
Winston: Prinsloo!
John: I'm telling you. Prinsloo himself, man. We waited outside for a little bit, then Hodoshe pushed me in. Prinsloo was behind his desk, busy with some papers. He pulled out one and said to me: "You are very lucky. Your lawyers have been working on your case. The sentence has been reduced from ten years, to three."
Winston: What did Hodoshe say?
John: Nothing. But he looked unhappy.

They laugh.

Hey, something else. Hodoshe let me walk back here by myself! He didn't follow me.
Winston: Of course. You are free.
John: Haai, Winston, not yet. Those three months . . . ! Or suppose it's a trick.
Winston: What do you mean?
John: Those bastards will do anything to break you. If the wheelbarrows and the quarry don't do it, they'll try something else. Remember that last visit of wives, when they lined up all the

men on the other side. . . . . "Take a good look and say goodbye! Back to the cells!"

Winston: You say you saw Prinsloo?

John: Prinsloo himself. Bastard didn't even stand up when I
walked in. And by the way . . . I had to sign. *Ja!* I had to sign a
form to say that I had been officially told of the result of my
appeal . . . that I had three months to go. *Ja.* I signed!

Winston (without the slightest doubt): It's three months, John.

John (relaxing and living with the reality for the first time): Hell,
Winston, at the end of those three months, it will be three
years together in this cell. Three years ago I stood in front of
that magistrate at Kirkwood — bastard didn't even look at
me: "Ten years!" I watched ten years of my life drift away like
smoke from a cigarette while he fidgeted and scratched his
arse. That same night back in the prison van to the cells at
Rooihel. First time we met!

Winston: *Ja.* We had just got back from our trial in Cradock.

John: You, Temba, . . .

Winston: Sipho. . . .

John: Hell, man!

Winston: First time we got close to each other was the next
morning in the yard, when they lined us up for the vans. . . .

John: And married us!

They lock left and right hands together to suggest handcuffs.

Winston: Who was that old man . . . remember him? . . . in the
corner handcuffed to Sipho?

John: Sipho?

Winston: *Ja,* the one who started the singing.

John (remembering): Peter. Tatu Peter.

Winston: That's him!

John: Hell, it comes back now, man! Pulling through the big
gates, wives and mothers running next to the vans, trying to
say goodbye . . . all of us inside fighting for a last look
through the window.

Winston (shaking his head): Shit!

John: Bet you've forgotten the song the old man started?

*Winston tries to remember. John starts singing softly. It is one of the Defiance
Campaign songs. Winston joins in.*

Winston (shaking his head ruefully): By the time we reach Humansdorp though, nobody was singing.

John: Fuck singing. I wanted to piss. Hey! I had my one free hand
on my balls, holding on. I'd made a mistake when we left the
Rooihel. Drank a gallon of water thinking of those five
hundred miles ahead. Jesus! There was the bucket in the
corner! But we were packed in so tight, remember, we
couldn't move. I tried to pull you but it was no bloody good.
So I held on — Humansdorp, Storms River, Blaaukrantz . . .
held on. But at Knysna, to hell with it, I let go!

*Gesture to indicate the release of his bladder. Winston finds this enormously
funny. John joins in.*

You were also wet by then!

Winston: Never!

John: Okay, let's say that by George nobody was dry. Remember
the stop there?

Winston: Ja. I thought they were going to let us walk around a bit.

John: Not a damn! Fill up with petrol and then on. Hey, but what
about those locals, the Coloured prisoners, when we pulled
away. Remember? Coming to their cell windows and shouting . . . "Courage, Brothers! Courage!" After that . . . ! Jesus, I
was tired. Didn't we fall asleep? Standing like that?

Winston: What do you mean standing? It was impossible to fall.

John: Then the docks, the boat. . . . It was my first time on one. I
had nothing to vomit up, but my God I tried.

Winston: What about me?

John: Then we saw this place for the first time. It almost looked
pretty, hey, with all the mist around it.

Winston: I was too sick to see anything, *broer.*

John: Remember your words when we jumped off onto the jetty?

Pause. The two men look at each other.

Heavy words, Winston. You looked back at the mountains . . .
"Farewell Africa!" I've never forgotten them. That was three
years ago.

Winston: And now, for you, it's three months to go.

*Pause. The mood of innocent celebration has passed. John realizes what his good
news means to the other man.*

John: To hell with everything. Let's go to bed.

Winston doesn't move. John finds Antigone's wig.

We'll talk about Antigone tomorrow.

John prepares for bed.

Hey, Winston! I just realized. My family! Princess and the children. Do you think they've been told? Jesus, man, maybe they're also saying . . . three months! Those three months are going to feel as long as the three years. Time passes slowly when you've got something . . . to wait for. . . .

Pause. Winston still hasn't moved. John changes his tone.

Look, in this cell we're going to forget those three months. The whole bloody thing is most probably a trick anyway. So let's just forget about it. We run to the quarry tomorrow. Together. So let's sleep.

SCENE III

The cell, later the same night. Both men are in bed. Winston is apparently asleep. John, however, is awake, rolling restlessly from side to side. He eventually gets up and goes quietly to the bucket for a drink of water, then back to his bed. He doesn't lie down, however. Pulling the blanket around his shoulders he starts to think about the three months. He starts counting the days on the fingers of one hand. Behind him Winston sits up and watches him in silence for a few moments.

Winston (with a strange smile): You're counting!
John (with a start): What! Hey, Winston, you gave me a fright, man. I thought you were asleep. What's the matter? Can't you sleep?
Winston (ignoring the question, still smiling): You've started counting the days now
John (unable to resist the temptation to talk, moving over to Winston's bed): Ja.
Winston: How many?
John: Ninety-two.
Winston: You see!
John (excited): Simple, man. Look . . . twenty days left in this month, thirty days in June, thirty-one in July, eleven days in August . . . ninety-two.
Winston (still smiling, but watching John carefully): Tomorrow?
John: Ninety-one.
Winston: And the next day?
John: Ninety.
Winston: Then one day it will be eighty!
John: Ja!

Winston: Then seventy.

John: Hey, Winston, time doesn't pass so fast.

Winston: Then only sixty more days.

John: That's just two months here on the Island.

Winston: Fifty . . . forty days in the quarry.

John: Jesus, Winston!

Winston: Thirty.

John: One month. Only one month to go.

Winston: Twenty . . . (*holding up his hands*) then ten . . . five, four, three, two . . . tomorrow!

The anticipation of that moment is too much for John.

John: NO! Please, man, Winston. It hurts. Leave those three months alone. I'm going to sleep!

Back to his bed where he curls up in a tight ball and tries determinedly to sleep. Winston lies down again and stares up at the ceiling. After a pause he speaks quietly.

Winston: They won't keep you here for the full three months. Only two months. Then down to the jetty, into a ferry-boat . . . you'll say goodbye to this place . . . and straight to Victor Verster Prison on the mainland.

Against his will John starts to listen. He eventually sits upright and completely surrenders himself to Winston's description of the last few days of his confinement.

Life will change for you there. It will be much easier. Because you won't take Hodoshe with you. He'll stay here with me, on the Island. They'll put you to work in the vineyards at Victor Verster, John. There are no quarries there. Eating grapes, oranges . . . they'll change your diet . . . Diet C, and exercises so that you'll look good when they let you out finally. At night you'll play games . . . Ludo, draughts, snakes and ladders! Then one day they'll call you into the office, with a van waiting outside to take you back. The same five hundred miles. But this time they'll let you sit. You won't have to stand the whole way like you did coming here. And there won't be handcuffs. Maybe they'll even stop on the way so that you can have a pee. Yes, I'm sure they will. You might even sleep over somewhere. Then finally Port Elizabeth. Rooihel Prison again, John! That's very near home, man. New Brighton is next door! Through your cell window you'll see people moving up and down in the street, hear the buses roaring. Then one night you won't sleep again, because you'll be counting.

Not days, as you are doing now, but hours. And the next morning, that beautiful morning, John, they'll take you straight out of your cell to the Discharge Office where they'll give you a new khaki shirt, long khaki trousers, brown shoes. And your belongings! I almost forgot your belongings.

John: Hey, by the way! I was wearing a white shirt, black tie, grey flannel trousers . . . brown Crockett shoes . . . socks? (*A little laugh.*) I can't remember my socks! A check jacket . . . and my watch! I was wearing my watch!

Winston: They'll wrap them up in a parcel. You'll have it under your arm when they lead you to the gate. And outside, John, outside that gate, New Brighton will be waiting for you. Your mother, your father, Princess and the children . . . and when they open it . . .

Once again, but more violently this time, John breaks the mood as the anticipation of the moment of freedom becomes too much for him.

John: Stop it, Winston! Leave those three months alone for Christ's sake. I want to sleep.

He tries to get away from Winston, but the latter goes after him. Winston has now also abandoned his false smile.

Winston (stopping John as he tries to crawl away): But it's not finished, John!

John: Leave me alone!

Winston: It doesn't end there. Your people will take you home. Thirty-eight, Gratten Street, John! Remember it? Everybody will be waiting for you . . . aunts, uncles, friends, neighbours. They'll put you in a chair, John, like a king, give you anything you want . . . cakes, sweets, cool drinks . . . and then you'll start to talk. You'll tell them about this place, John, about Hodoshe, about the quarry, and about your good friend Winston who you left behind. But you still won't be happy, hey. Because you'll need a fuck. A really wild one!

John: Stop it, Winston!

Winston (relentless): And that is why at ten o'clock that night you'll slip out through the back door and make your way to Sky's place. Imagine it, man! All the boys waiting for you . . . Georgie, Mangi, Vusumzi. They'll fill you up with booze. They'll look after you. They know what it's like inside. They'll fix you up with a woman. . . .

John: NO!

Winston: Set you up with her in a comfortable joint, and then leave you alone. You'll watch her, watch her take her clothes off, you'll take your pants off, get near her, feel her, feel it. . . . *Ja*, you'll feel it. It will be wet. . . .

John: WINSTON!

Winston: Wet *poes*, John! And you'll fuck it wild!

John turns finally to face Winston. A long silence as the two men confront each other. John is appalled at what he sees.

John: Winston? What's happening? Why are you punishing me?

Winston (quietly): You stink, John. You stink of beer, of company, of *poes*, of freedom. . . . Your freedom stinks, John, and it's driving me mad.

John: No, Winston!

Winston: Yes! Don't deny it. Three months time, at this hour, you'll be wiping beer off your face, your hands on your balls, and *poes* waiting for you. You will laugh, you will drink, you will fuck and forget.

John's denials have no effect on Winston.

Stop bullshitting me! We've got no time left for that. There's only two months left between us. (*Pause.*) You know where I ended up this morning, John? In the quarry. Next to old Harry. Do you know old Harry, John?

John: Yes.

Winston: Yes what? Speak, man!

John: Old Harry, Cell Twenty-three, seventy years, serving Life!

Winston: That's not what I'm talking about. When you go to the quarry tomorrow, take a good look at old Harry. Look into his eyes, John. Look at his hands. They've changed him. They've turned him into stone. Watch him work with that chisel and hammer. Twenty perfect blocks of stone every day. Nobody else can do it like him. He loves stone. That's why they're nice to him. He's forgotten himself. He's forgotten everything . . . why he's here, where he comes from.

That's happening to me John. I've forgotten why I'm here.

John: No.

Winston: Why am I here?

John: You put your head on the block for others.

Winston: Fuck the others.

John: Don't say that! Remember our ideals. . . .

Winston: Fuck our ideals. . . .

John: No Winston . . . our slogans, our children's freedom. . . .

Winston: Fuck slogans, fuck politics . . . fuck everything, John.

Why am I here? I'm jealous of your freedom, John. I also want to count. God also gave me ten fingers, but what do I count? My life? How do I count it, John? One . . . one . . . another day comes . . . one. . . . Help me, John! . . . Another day . . . one . . . one. . . . Help me, brother! . . . one. . . .

John has sunk to the floor, helpless in the face of the other man's torment and pain. Winston almost seems to bend under the weight of the life stretching ahead of him on the Island. For a few seconds he lives in silence with his reality, then slowly straightens up. He turns and looks at John. When he speaks again, it is the voice of a man who has come to terms with his fate, massively compassionate.

Nyana we Sizwe!

John looks up at him.

Nyana we Sizwe . . . it's all over now. All over. (*He moves over to John.*) Forget me. . . .

John attempts a last, limp denial.

No, John! Forget me . . . because I'm going to forget you. Yes, I will forget you. Others will come in here, John, count, go, and I'll forget them. Still more will come, count like you, go like you, and I will forget them. And then one day, it will all be over.

A lighting change suggests the passage of time. Winston collects together their props for Antigone.

Come. They're waiting.
John: Do you know your words?
Winston: Yes. Come, we'll be late for the concert.

SCENE IV

The two men convert their cell-area into a stage for the prison concert. Their blankets are hung to provide a makeshift backdrop behind which Winston disappears with their props. John comes forward and addresses the audience. He is not yet in his Creon costume.

John: Captain Prinsloo, Hodoshe, Warders, . . . and Gentlemen! Two brothers of the House of Labdacus found themselves on opposite sides in battle, the one defending the State, the other attacking it. They both died on the battlefield. King Creon, Head of the State, decided that the one who had defended the State would be buried with all religious rites due to the noble dead. But the other one, the traitor Poly-nices, who had come back from exile intending to burn and destroy his fatherland, to drink the blood of his masters, was to have no grave, no mourning. He was to lie on the open fields to rot, or at most be food for the jackals. It was a law. But Antigone, their sister, defied the law and buried the body of her brother Polynices. She was caught and arrested. That is why tonight the Hodoshe Span, Cell Forty-two, pre-sents for your entertainment: "The Trial and Punishment of Antigone."

He disappears behind the blankets. They simulate a fanfare of trumpets. At its height the blankets open and he steps out as Creon. In addition to his pendant, there is some sort of crown and a blanket draped over his shoulders as a robe.

My People! Creon stands before his palace and greets you! Stop! Stop! What's that I hear? You, good man, speak up. Did I hear "Hail the King"? My good people, I am your *servant* . . . a happy one, but still your servant. How many times must I ask you, implore you to see in these symbols of office nothing more, or less, than you would in the uniform of the humblest menial in your house. Creon's crown is as simple, and I hope as clean, as the apron Nanny wears. And even as Nanny smiles and is your happy servant because she sees her charge . . . your child! . . . waxing fat in that little cradle, so too does Creon — your obedient servant! — stand here and smile. For what does he see? Fatness and happiness! How else does one measure the success of a state? By the sumptuous-ness of the palaces built for its king and princes? The magnif-icence of the temples erected to its gods? The achievements of its scientists and technicians who can now send rockets to the moon? No! These count for nothing beside the fatness and happiness of its people.

But have you ever paused to ask yourself whose respon-sibility it is to maintain that fatness and happiness? The answer is simple, is it not? . . . your servant the king! But have you then gone on to ask yourself what does the king need to maintain this happy state of affairs? What, other than his silly crown, are the tools with which a king fashions the happiness of his people? The answer is equally simple, my good people. The law! Yes. The law. A three-lettered word, and how many times haven't you glibly used it, never bother-ing to ask yourselves, "What then is the law?" Or if you have,

then making recourse to such clichés as "the law states this
. . . or the law states that." The law states or maintains
nothing, good people. The law defends! The law is no more
or less than a shield in your faithful servant's hand to protect
YOU! But even as a shield would be useless in one hand, to
defend, without a sword in the other, to strike . . . so too the
law has its edge. The penalty! We have come through difficult times. I am sure it is needless for me to remind you of
the constant troubles on our borders . . . those despicable
rats who would gnaw away at our fatness and happiness. We
have been diligent in dealing with them. But unfortunately
there are still at large subversive elements . . . there are still
amongst us a few rats that are not satisfied and to them I
must show this face of Creon . . . so different to the one that
hails my happy people! It is with a heavy heart, and you shall
see why soon enough, that I must tell you that we have caught
another one. That is why I have assembled you here. Let what
follows be a living lesson for those among you misguided
enough still to harbour sympathy for rats! The shield has
defended. Now the sword must strike!
> Bring in the accused.

*Winston, dressed as Antigone, enters. He wears the wig, the necklace of nails, and
a blanket around his waist as a shirt.*

> Your name!

Winston: Antigone, daughter of Oedipus, sister of Eteocles and
Polynices.

John: You are accused that, in defiance of the law, you buried the
body of the traitor Polynices.

Winston: I buried the body of my brother Polynices.

John: Did you know there was a law forbidding that?

Winston: Yes.

John: Yet you defied it.

Winston: Yes.

John: Did you know the consequences of such defiance?

Winston: Yes.

John: What did you plead to the charges laid against you? Guilty
or Not Guilty?

Winston: Guilty.

John: Antigone, you have pleaded guilty. Is there anything you
wish to say in mitigation? This is your last chance. Speak.

Winston: Who made the law forbidding the burial of my brother?

John: The State.

Winston: Who is the State?

John: As King I am its manifest symbol.

Winston: So you made the law.

John: Yes, for the State.

Winston: Are you God?

John: Watch your words, little girl!

Winston: You said it was my chance to speak.

John: But not to ridicule.

Winston: I've got no time to waste on that. Your sentence on my life hangs waiting on your lips.

John: Then speak on.

Winston: When Polynices died in battle, all that remained was the empty husk of his body. He could neither harm nor help any man again. What lay on the battlefield waiting for Hodoshe to turn rotten, belonged to God. You are only a man, Creon. Even as there are laws made by men, so too there are others that come from God. He watches my soul for a transgression even as your spies hide in the bush at night to see who is transgressing your laws. Guilty against God I will not be for any man on this earth. Even without your law, Creon, and the threat of death to whoever defied it, I know I must die. Because of your law and my defiance, that fate is now very near. So much the better. Your threat is nothing to me, Creon. But if I had let my mother's son, a Son of the Land, lie there as food for the carrion fly, Hodoshe, my soul would never have known peace. Do you understand anything of what I am saying, Creon?

John: Your words reveal only that obstinacy of spirit which has brought nothing but tragedy to your people. First you break the law. Now you insult the State.

Winston: Just because I ask you to remember that you are only a man?

John: And to add insult to injury you gloat over your deeds! No, Antigone, you will not escape with impunity. Were you my own child you would not escape full punishment.

Winston: Full punishment? Would you like to do more than just kill me?

John: That is all I wish.

Winston: Then let us not waste any time. Stop talking. I buried my brother. That is an honourable thing, Creon. All these people in your state would say so too, if fear of you and another law did not force them into silence.

John: You are wrong. None of my people think the way you do.

Winston: Yes they do, but no one dares tell you so. You will not sleep peacefully, Creon.

John: You add shamelessness to your crimes, Antigone.

Winston: I do not feel any shame at having honoured my brother.

John: Was he that died with him not also your brother?

Winston: He was.

John: And so you honour the one and insult the other.

Winston: I shared my love, not my hate.

John: Go then and share your love among the dead. I will have no rats' law here while yet I live.

Winston: We are wasting time, Creon. Stop talking. Your words defeat your purpose. They are prolonging my life.

John (again addressing the audience): You have heard all the relevant facts. Needless now to call the state witnesses who would testify beyond reasonable doubt that the accused is guilty. Nor, for that matter, is it in the best interests of the State to disclose their identity. There was a law. The law was broken. The law stipulated its penalty. My hands are tied.

Take her from where she stands, straight to the Island! There wall her up in a cell for life, with enough food to acquit ourselves of the taint of her blood.

Winston (to the audience): Brothers and Sisters of the Land! I go now on my last journey. I must leave the light of day forever, for the Island, strange and cold, to be lost between life and death. So, to my grave, my everlasting prison, condemned alive to solitary death.

Tearing off his wig and confronting the audience as Winston, not Antigone.

Gods of our Fathers! My Land! My Home!

Time waits no longer. I go now to my living death, because I honoured those things to which honour belongs.

The two men take off their costumes and then strike their "set." They then come together and, as in the beginning, their hands come together to suggest handcuffs, and their right and left legs to suggest ankle-chains. They start running . . . John mumbling a prayer, and Winston a rhythm for their three-legged run.

The siren wails.

Fade to blackout.

Further Thoughts on Writing about Literature

All good writing about stories, poems, or plays originates in strong responses to individual texts. It's true that most literature papers written for college courses contain a certain amount of relatively impersonal matter — for example, plot or situation summaries meant to refresh the reader's memory of events and speakers. It's also true that minding your literary manners — observing the rules and conventions for literary essays that have developed over the years — will make your papers more effective. When you quote from a text, for example, the quotation should bear directly on the point you are making, and you yourself should make clear to your reader why the passage helps you prove that point. (Rules about footnote form and other conventions of documentation can be found in handbooks or manuals of style such as the *MLA Handbook for Writers of Research Papers*.)

But first-class literary essays call for more than observance of rules. At the core of every first-rate paper — as its basic source material — lies personal response. And it follows that improving yourself as a writer about literature means sharpening your ability to describe, explain, and justify your own responses.

There are various ways of working toward this end, and none involves obeying formulas or hunting for quick fixes. Improvements occur gradually as individual writers learn more about three closely related matters:

1. How to generate sequences of questions that clarify the lines of personal response.

2. How to recognize, keep track of, and label the significant details of a reading experience.
3. How to use the revision of early notes and drafts as a means of achieving more precise, more appropriate responses.

GENERATING QUESTIONS ABOUT PERSONAL RESPONSE

Do I or don't I like it? For many this is the only question that comes to mind when they finish reading a work of literature — and it is, undeniably, an important question. But producing an interesting and illuminating paper about a literary text demands that this question be redefined in ways that allow you to move from mere thumbs-up or thumbs-down opinionizing to positions that can be stated and supported with reasoned argument and evidence. For your papers to be genuinely stimulating either to write or to read, they need to locate and explain the grounds on which your approval and disapproval is based. And more often than not, in the course of your effort to do this, the issue of whether you like or dislike the work will be transformed. A fresh subject will emerge that will permit you to make a closer approach, in your own thinking, to the responses you actually had while reading and rereading.

The process of redefinition through which the fresh subject is produced requires personal inventiveness. A textbook such as *Close Imagining* can suggest questions, but the suggestions can only be useful if, as you work with them, you begin to see ways of framing new questions tightly linked to your own experience of the text. One sensible way of rephrasing the question Do I like John Updike's "Snowing in Greenwich Village"? (see p. 19) would be to shift the question to personal experience of a character. For example: Do I find Richard Maple or Rebecca Cune a likable person? The answer to this question suggests a way to step back to *self*-interrogation. What makes him or her attractive or unattractive to me?

Probing in this direction, you turn to particular passages to which you remember having had a strong response. You ask, What caused this response? And that query generates a whole new set of questions and answers. What does Richard Maple think of himself at this moment? Is his self-estimate correct? If it's incorrect, does the author help me to understand why? Is the author's judgment of the character one that I can live with? Does his judgment seem shrewd and penetrating, off the mark, misconceived? Why so? A series of questions evolving in this fashion often has the power to open up aspects of response to a character that at first were fuzzy or unfocused. Time and again the effect of this process is to bring to light a fresh problem that seems, as soon as you glimpse it, to provide a kind of entryway to the aspects of the reading experience that mattered most to you.

Look back at the first student response to a text in *Close Imagining* (p. 27). The student began with a question about what was taking place in Richard Maple at the climax of the story, but that question quickly induced others: How can I account for his behavior? Why does he think and feel as he does about Rebecca? The writer decided that the reasons for Richard's thoughts and feelings lay in certain evasions and failures of understanding, and that to understand the evasions it's necessary to think about both the situation of the relatively newly married and the human tendency to blame others for behavior about which we feel guilty. The paper took shape as an inquiry into the complex feelings and motives of a married man full of anxiety.

We may or may not agree with this writer's conclusions. Certainly we need more evidence than the paper supplies that Richard actually has many "doubts" about his marriage and his wife. But the paper does engage with significant details of the behavior presented — Richard's impulse to blame Rebecca — and the writer is clearly working to bring feelings to life. The moral issue that surfaces as a result of this effort is far from trivial.

RECOGNIZING SIGNIFICANT DETAILS

The early chapters of *Close Imagining* had a lot to say about the process of taking notes on one's responses — generating fresh questions, sorting out the ideas and feelings aroused by the details, keeping track of the main elements of the reading experience. A major part of the effort behind every successful paper on a work of literature goes into locating significant, supporting detail and deciding how to use it to clarify your ideas. What is a significant detail, and how can it be recognized? There are several answers. A significant detail can be an action that helps you to define a relation between the beginning and end of a text, or between two scenes that at first glance seem unconnected, or between two quite different characters, or between any of numberless other elements of the text. On the one hand, a significant detail can be a bit of behavior or talk that the author doesn't comment on explicitly but that you seem to know precisely how to interpret the instant you encounter it. On the other hand, a significant detail can be a bit of behavior or talk that the author doesn't comment on but that you find yourself puzzling over, uncertain of the meaning yet convinced that it must be interpreted if you're to arrive at an appropriate response to the text as a whole.

Reread the second student response to "Snowing in Greenwich village" (p. 28), and this problem of significant detail may become clearer. This paper is organized as a commentary on significant details of two different kinds. In the opening paragraph the writer focuses on an action that is repeated at the beginning and end of the story — removing a coat. The writer asks and answers questions about the meaning of this action. How does the repetition function in the structure of the story? What does it tell us about Richard's feelings?

The writer also singles out a bit of speech — Rebecca's swearing — on which the author does not directly comment. What does the hero think when he hears Rebecca say "hot as hell"? What conclusion does he reach about her state of mind?

The likelihood is strong that the writer of this paper, like most of us, did not arrive at complete, or even partial, certainty about the significance of the details in question on the first reading of the story. Often we return repeatedly to details that intrigue us without quite knowing what questions to pose about them. Often we probe with questions that remain imprecise for several readings — until we realize, sometimes suddenly, that a detail we can interpret as an answer to a related, specific, and revealing question lies straight before us. The writer of the second paper *may* have decided at once that the key to Richard's guess about what is going on in Rebecca's mind lies in Rebecca's "hot as hell." But that decision could also have been reached slowly, after more than one reading and considerable pondering.

In short, significant details don't leap out at us tagged and flagged; we *create* their significance, in our interaction with the author, as we work to bring the story to life by writing about it.

REVISING RESPONSES

Implicit in everything just said is that the effective student writer is engaged almost ceaselessly, from start to finish, in processes of revision. Questions undergo constant change. Passages that were provisionally interpreted one way are re-examined from different perspectives. Answers that at first seemed satisfactory are shot down as more intensive analysis discloses their weaknesses. *All this activity occurs in writing.* Few people on earth are capable of conducting in their heads the imaginative and deliberative work that goes into a successful paper about a story, poem, or play. The only way this work can be done is in writing; by no other means can changes of perception, alternative readings, and tentative new interpretations be compared, rephrased, rejected, interfused, harmonized.

Many student writers experience difficulty with their papers because of confusion about the purpose of — the need for — revision. Some make the mistake of assuming that revising a first draft amounts merely to checking spelling, punctuation, and grammar, or making sure that paragraphs are connected. Others think of revision as a matter primarily involving the *start* of the writing process — the moment when the writer rejects one opening sentence, begins another, rejects that, and settles on a third. Admittedly, the problem of getting started is a serious one. For a reminder of what it is like, consider the drafts of a lead sentence that were saved by the student whose paper about Ben Jonson's "Inviting a Friend to Supper" appears on p. 559:

> "Inviting a Friend to Supper" strikes the reader most obviously as an open informal invitation to a party complete with food, drink, and company.

> The tone of "Inviting a Friend to Supper" first simply
> suggests to the hearer as an
>
> The tone of "Inviting a Friend to Supper" sugg
>
> "Inviting a Friend to Supper" sounds, at first, as
>
> The initial tone or attitude suggested to the reader of
> "Inviting a Friend to Supper"
>
> The voice first heard by the reader of "Inviting a
> Friend to Supper" is that of an apparently mild, unassuming
> host inviting and trying to persuade a hesitant, wished-for
> guest to come to an informal dinner party.

In fact, revision needs to be understood as the process through which, at every stage of the paper — beginning, middle, and end — writers refine their responses to the text: discover, develop, and analyze their response so that nothing in it is disproportionate to or incompatible with the actual experience of the text they now have as readers. (An example of a disproportionate response is that of the reader of Thomas Hardy's "The Slow Nature," [p. 33], who wrote that Mistress Damon had no feeling for her husband.) When engaged in this process of revision, writers stretch their reflective and imaginative powers. By looking hard at their initial reactions (as set forth in first drafts and notes), by moving back and forth between those reactions and the specific passages in the text that seem to have given rise to them, by focusing on elements of those passages that don't square with what the first notes or drafts say about them, writers bring to bear both on their own writing and on the text the strongest and most disciplined resources of their minds and feelings.

Often a paper gives the impression that the revision process hasn't been launched until fairly late; reflections toward the close of the paper represent a clear advance on those at the beginning, but the writer seems not to realize that the beginning and end of the paper are inconsistent. The clarity achieved in the course of thinking out the draft of the paper isn't recognized for what it should be: the starting point for a whole fresh description of response. Look again at the student paper about the Jonson poem. It starts by describing the speaker as a "self-abasing, humble man," implicitly criticizes him for having a "too highly piled humility," and claims that the speaker may well see himself as "contemptible" in the eyes of the person he's inviting. But the paper also asserts that the tone keeps changing, and that the speaker moves from "humility to the grand manner" and at length to something better than either: "The audience hears finally neither the voice of an artificially genuflecting man nor the voice of a stodgy pedant but the voice of someone hoping that all his friends and acquaintances, whatever their particular tastes, will enjoy an unrestrained, unrestricted moment of fraternity." What about the possibility that the alleged changes of tone are in fact only shifts in the reader's understanding of the tone? The paper nicely illustrates the shifts of perspective that are common as active imaginers bring texts to life. The second draft shows the writer bringing her perceptions into clearer and more consistent relationship with each other and communicating fuller understanding of her original response.

At the end of "Inviting a Friend to Supper" we see that the host is a fundamental believer in what he describes as the "simple word" that neither "make[s] us sad next morning, or affright[s] / the liberty that we'll enjoy tonight." There won't be any bemoaning of man's fate or moralizing about his nature at my party--so concludes our host. And the audience hears finally neither the voice of an artificially genuflecting man nor the voice of a stodgy pedant but the voice of someone hoping that all his friends and acquaintances, whatever their particular tastes, will enjoy an unrestrained, unrestricted moment of fraternity. Accept or don't accept, as you wish. That is the tone. The attitude toward the invited guest is one of liking but also of self-respect.

It may not seem that way at first. In the opening lines the voice seems to be that of an apparently mild, unassuming person inviting and trying to persuade a hesitant, wished-for guest to come to his dinner party. "It is the fair acceptance, sir, creates / the entertainment perfect, . . ." The speaker seems to put himself down as a person of "poor house" and (according to him) little objectively visible worth, trying to squeeze out an acceptance from a grave, skeptical man. Also he, the speaker, offers many enticements. Is he trying to bribe the guest into coming? He moves from tempting his guest with a simple salad to tempting him with game aplenty. And there will be more than game. Instead of pheasant there will be some light good-time larking around ("And though fowl now be scarce, yet there are clerks, / The sky not falling, think we may have larks").

But we soon see that the host is continually changing his tactics, not the tone. He moves from humility to the grand manner but always with a playful reserve for larking around. If the suggestion of a full table provokes no response, what will? Virgil, Tacitus, Livy? The listener hears: "You want lofty discourse, you got it." A little Virgil or Livy over steak? A little Greek theater and beer? There isn't any real abasement but just an attempt to say-- in as many playful ways as possible--that I'd really like you to come, and we'll have a fine time.

A fully revised, worked-through paper at no point leaves the impression that the writer is shooting from the hip. The paper establishes that contrasting viewpoints and perspectives have been weighed and adjusted to each other. Steadily, intensely, the writer has gone back over both the later text and the text of early drafts, asking whether the words in those drafts exactly fit the writer's *present* experience and understanding of the text. The combination of reading and writing has brought the reader fully and continuously into the work as an active imaginer; a rich and complex response is sustained throughout.

THE FUNCTIONS OF RESTRAINT:
A NOTE ON TASTE

What finally distinguishes — for reader and writer alike — more satisfying from less satisfying papers? No universally acceptable answer to that question can be supplied. And it isn't really desirable that writers, readers, students, and teachers sit down to hammer out a code of standards. As this book has often emphasized, the appropriateness of literary responses can't be judged in a vacuum, can't be separated from either historical and social circumstance or from personal backgrounds and beliefs.

This doesn't mean that no yardsticks exist for measuring the seriousness or scrupulosity of a reading. Papers that substantiate claims — that give reasons for their conclusions — are more impressive than those that don't. So, too, are papers that work out their own contradictions and that seek to be comprehensive, taking into account both the evidence that supports the reader's conclusions and details that inconveniently complicate the matter. Papers that are marked by genuinely personal engagement — evident strength of feeling for the pertinent issues, characters, language — obviously inspire more enthusiastic attention than do those with a distinct let's-get-this-over-with air.

In responding to others' work, discussing it in and out of class, it's helpful to know the basis of personal tastes and to be able to explain them to others. As the editor of *Close Imagining*, I have had occasion to read each of the responses (including my own) to John Updike's "Snowing in Greenwich Village" many times. I know which of those responses I like best — the third — and I know why. I like the third paper because the writer doesn't rush to generalizations, doesn't turn up the volume too high, checks the tendency many of us have to believe that at every moment human beings are in the grip of large, unambiguous feelings. Writer 5 think that "the air is rife with sexual excitement" and "guilt," and that "the courting ritual has begun." Writer 4 imagines Rebecca Cune as nervous, as wanting "to seduce Richard," and as fearing "rejection." They and the other writers seem to me too categorical about the feelings at this moment in the story, too determined to see the world in terms of momentous, clear-cut choices, insufficiently open to the truth that we can simultaneously want, half-want, and not want something to happen. The third writer's account isn't hazy or indefinite in its evocation of the moment, but it does avoid heavy overstatement, keeping in mind throughout the indeterminacy of much that happens in our emotional lives. According to my taste, the third paper is a pleasing, delicately imagined piece of writing.

But would a similar response seem as appropriate to a crisis moment in *Antigone* or *Macbeth?* How will this reader perform when grand passions — feelings that are powerful and unambiguous — need to be brought to life? If we strive to emulate Writer 3, may we not handicap ourselves as close imaginers of the heroic, confrontational moments common in the work of Sophocles or Shakespeare?

The answer, of course, is that no single model of response can be invoked as everywhere appropriate. Our goal as readers and writers is to develop our own variousness — our capacity to adapt our sympathies and intellects to a wide range of demands. The best way to think about improving ourselves as writers of papers about literature is to relate that work to a far larger project: general self-development, both emotional and intellectual. We have returned to the theme with which this book began: By bringing texts to life through reading and writing, we expand the possibilities of the self.

Glossary of
Literary Terms

Accent Same as **stress**, the emphasis placed on a given syllable in a line, compared with the emphasis given to surrounding syllables.

Accentual meter See **meter**.

Alexandrine A line of **verse** written in **iambic hexameter**, containing six iambic feet. Thomas Hardy uses alexandrines in "The Convergence of the Twain."

Allegory A literary work that readers follow on at least two levels: One level is that of a narrative involving recognizable **characters** and events; another level is that of a discourse in which the characters and events represent moral, political, religious, or other ideas or meanings.

Alliteration In poetry the repetition of identical consonant sounds, usually at the beginnings of words, in words appearing near each other in a written work, as in this line from T. S. Eliot's "Gerontion": "*B*listered in *B*russels, *p*atched and *p*eeled in London."

Internal alliteration The repetition of consonant sounds in the middle or at the ends of words that appear near each other in a written work, as in the following lines from Emily Dickinson:

> The *F*ingers grew too cold
> To a*ch*e — and li*k*e a S*k*ater's Broo*k* —

Allusion A reference to a **character**, event, place, or object in literature, history, or art that triggers, in readers who recognize it, an emotional response.

Ambiguity An arrangement of words that invites readers to hold in mind more than one interpretation.

Anapest   See meter.

Anapestic meter   See meter.

Antagonist   A character or force opposing, or in conflict with, the **protagonist** (main character) of a narrative. The antagonist may be another character, some natural or intangible force, or something within the protagonist's own character.

Anticlimax   An insignificant, trivial, often sudden conclusion to a series of significant events; an unsatisfying **resolution** occurring either after, or in place of, a conventional **climax**.

Antihero   A **protagonist** in some works of modern **fiction** and **drama** who lacks traditional heroic qualities. Krapp in Samuel Beckett's play *Krapp's Last Tape* is an example.

Apostrophe   A **figure of speech** that entails addressing someone absent, dead, or otherwise unable to hear or respond. The **speaker** may also be addressing an abstraction or something inanimate, as when John Keats apostrophizes an urn in his "Ode on a Grecian Urn."

Approximate rhyme   See rhyme.

Aside   A direct communication to the audience by a character in a play who is not alone onstage. By theatrical **convention** the words spoken, although audible everywhere, are understood by the audience to be heard only by them.

Assonance   In poetry the repetition of identical vowel sounds in nearby words that end in different consonant sounds, as in the line "And the green freedom of a cockatoo" from Wallace Stevens's "Sunday Morning." (If the final consonant is the same — as in *name* and *fame* — the result is **rhyme** rather than assonance.)

Ballad   A **narrative poem** written in four-line **stanzas**, or **quatrains**, characterized by simple language, dramatic action, **dialogue**, and repetition, often in the form of a **refrain**. "The Twa Corbies" is an example of a traditional Scottish ballad.
Ballad stanza   A four-line **stanza**, usually rhyming *abcb*, which alternates lines of iambic **tetrameter** with lines of iambic **trimeter**.
Literary ballad   Also called **art ballad**. A ballad with known authorship (John Keats's "La Belle Dame sans Merci," for example), as opposed to early folk ballads, most of which were anonymous and were intended to be sung.

Blank verse Poetry written in unrhymed **iambic pentameter**. Shakespeare's plays are largely written in blank verse.

Burlesque A theatrical entertainment, often humorous and bawdy, involving comic scenes, striptease acts, and song and dance.

Carpe diem Latin for "seize the day." A term used to describe literature, especially poetry, that stresses the idea that since beauty and life are fleeting, they should be enjoyed now, while they last. Robert Herrick's "To the Virgins, to Make Much of Time" is a classic expression of this theme.

Catharsis A feeling of purgation or emotional release. The term derives from Aristotle's observations on **tragedy** and originally referred to the feeling thought to follow reading or watching an effective tragedy.

Cesura (or caesura) In poetry, a strong pause or break within a line, usually indicated by a comma or period, as in "I listened, ‖ motionless and still" from William Wordsworth's "The Solitary Reaper."

Character Any person who appears in a narrative or dramatic work. (See Chapter 2.)

    Round character A complicated, unpredictable figure; often such a character develops during the course of the story.

    Stereotype A **stock character** whose qualities, beliefs, and behavior conform to familiar **conventions**.

    Stock character A familiar character type such as the absent-minded professor or the evil stepmother.

Chorus In Greek **tragedy**, a group of actors who speak in unison, commenting on the events without otherwise taking part in the play.

Classical unities In **drama**, the principles governing action, time, and place in a particular play. According to critics who value the unities as strict guidelines, any **subplot** should be directly related to the main action, the entire play should take place during the course of one day, and the action should all occur in one place. The first two principles are derived from the observations of Aristotle.

Cliché Any phrase or idea used so often that it has become trite and consequently has lost its effectiveness (its evocative or descriptive powers).

Climax The turning point of the action in a conventional narrative; the point up to which the **rising action** and tension of the story lead.

Closed couplet   See **couplet**.

Colloquial English   See **diction**.

Comedy   A type of **drama** in which characters initially suffer ill fortune but ultimately overcome the various obstacles that stand between them and the play's happy ending. (See Chapter 19.)

Common meter   See **meter**.

Conceit   In poetry, an intricate, extended **metaphor**. In "The Canonization," for example, John Donne makes an ingenious comparison between two lovers and the legendary phoenix.

Conflict   The struggle or clash between the **protagonist** (main **character**) and the **antagonist** of a narrative. The conflict propels the **rising action**, which leads toward the **climax** of the story and then to the **resolution**.

Connotation   The overtones and associations of a word or words in a given context, as distinguished from literal meanings.

Consonance   In poetry, the use of words with identical beginning and/or ending consonant sounds and different vowel sounds, as *weed* and *wide* or *father* and *feather*.

Convention   Any feature of a literary work that has become standardized over time. Examples range from the stage **aside** to the **sonnet** as a poem that always has fourteen lines.

Couplet   In poetry, two successive lines, usually employing **end rhyme**, as in Shakespeare's "Devouring Time, blunt thou the lion's paws":

> Yet do thy worst, old Time; despite thy wrong,
> My love shall in my verse ever live young.

Closed couplet   Two successive rhymed lines that contain a syntactically and grammatically complete statement.

Heroic couplet   Two successive rhymed lines of **iambic pentameter**, which are often but not always **closed**. Alexander Pope's "An Essay on Man" is composed in heroic couplets, one of which reads as follows:

> Created half to rise, and half to fall;
> Great lord of all things, yet a prey to all.

Crisis Same as **climax**.

Dactyl See **meter**.

Dactylic meter See **meter**.

Decorum Literary propriety, or that which is considered appropriate language for a given **character** or subject, or appropriate content for a given type of literary work.

Denotation The literal meaning, or dictionary definition, of a word.

Denouement French for "the untying of a knot." Same as **resolution**.

Deus ex machina Literally, "god from the machine." Any unexpected or contrived device used to resolve a **plot** happily.

Dialogue The spoken words of **characters** in a narrative.

Diction The kind of words chosen by a writer and the ways in which those words are arranged. Also, the writer's choice of a level of language (formal, slang, other).
    Colloquial English Informal, conversational speech; the language as it is spoken casually.
    Poetic diction Fancy language (*whither* for *where*) once thought to enhance poems.

Dimeter See **meter**.

Drama A play written in prose or **verse** that tells a story and portrays **characters** through action, emotions, and **dialogue**. Also, events or **situations** involving **conflicts** of forces.

Dramatic irony See **irony**.

Dramatic monologue A poem in which the **speaker** reveals his or her thoughts and insights (to the reader or to another **character** in the poem) in an extended speech. Robert Browning often used this form. See his "Soliloquy of the Spanish Cloister" and "My Last Duchess." (See also **soliloquy**, from which the dramatic monologue derives.)

Elegy A formal, reflective poem on a solemn theme, most often lamenting the death of someone significant to the poet.

End rhyme See **rhyme**.

End-stopped line A line of poetry that is syntactically complete and ends in a full pause, usually with a punctuation mark, as this line from Robert Frost's "Once by the Pacific": "The shattered water made a misty din."

Enjambment   The running-on of one line of poetry into the next. The lines are not separated by punctuation, and the logical and grammatical sense of the first line is completed in the line that follows, as in this example from William Blake's "A Poison Tree":

> In the morning glad I see
> My foe outstretched beneath the tree.

Epic   A long **narrative poem** (Homer's *Iliad* or Milton's *Paradise Lost*, for example) that documents the adventures of a hero or heroine and is written in an elevated style. Epics usually cover vast territory and time and often treat the origins of new cultures and civilizations. Gods and demons sometimes observe the action or even participate in it.

Epigram   A concise, witty saying or poem, often satirical in tone.

Epigraph   An inscription on the title page of a book or at the beginning of a chapter. T. S. Eliot begins "The Love Song of J. Alfred Prufrock" with an epigraph from Dante's *Inferno*.

Euphony   A smooth, pleasant sound, created by careful choice and arrangement of words.

Fable   A brief tale, often using animals as characters, with a clear moral.

Falling meter   A **meter**, such as **trochaic** or **dactylic**, that moves from stressed to unstressed syllables.

Farce   A short, humorous play, emphasizing action, coarse wit, exaggeration, and unlikely **situations**.

Feminine rhyme   See rhyme.

Fiction   A novel or story rooted more in the author's imagination than in literal fact.

Figurative language   Language employing **figures of speech**, such as **irony, metaphor,** and **simile**.

Figure of speech   Words and phrases used in ways that alter their literal meanings or otherwise deviate from standard patterns of conversational or written language. **Hyperbole, irony, metaphor, metonymy, oxymoron, personification, simile,** and **synecdoche** are all figures of speech.

First-person point of view   See **point of view.**

Flashback   A device used in a narrative to present events that occurred at a time chronologically prior to that in which the story is being told.

Foot   In poetry, the unit used to measure **meter.** A foot usually consists of one stressed syllable and one or more unstressed syllables.

Free verse   Poetry that has no prescribed metrical structure or **rhyme scheme** but instead uses other patterns, such as the natural rhythms and pauses of speech.

Vers libre   Literally, "free verse." A movement begun in the late nineteenth century by poets in revolt against the strictures of formal poetry.

Genre   A "kind," "type," or "form" of literature, such as **drama, fiction,** essay, and poetry. There are genres within each genre as well; for example, the genres of **tragedy** and **comedy** within the genre of drama.

Gesture   In **drama,** actions and movements used as a means of expression by the **characters.**

Haiku   A Japanese poetic form admired for highly concentrated evocations of feeling. It consists of three lines; the first and last lines have five syllables each and the middle line has seven.

Heroic couplet   See **couplet.**

Hexameter   See **meter.**

Hubris (or hybris)   Excessive pride or ambition. In classical **tragedy,** hubris is often the **tragic flaw** that leads to the **protagonist's** downfall.

Hyperbole   Exaggeration or overstatement elaborated into a **figure of speech.**

Iamb   See **meter.**

Iambic meter   See **meter.**

Iambic pentameter   See **meter.**

Ideology   The beliefs, values, assumptions, ideals, and goals of a particular group or culture.

Image   The verbal representation of a sensory impression or experience.

In medias res Latin for "in the midst of things." The literary device of starting a narrative in the middle of an unexplained action.

Innocent narrator See **narrator**.

Interior monologue A device used to reveal a character's inner thoughts and emotions without having the character speak them aloud. At first encounter interior monologues usually appear ungrammatical, illogical, repetitious, and chaotic in nature.

Internal alliteration See **alliteration**.

Internal rhyme See **rhyme**.

Irony A **figure of speech** built on a contrast between literal meaning and intended meaning.
  Dramatic irony Occurs when there is a gap between what a character perceives to be true and what the audience knows to be true.
  Situational irony The opposite, more or less, of what the reader expects to happen.

Italian sonnet See **Petrarchan sonnet**.

Leitmotif A recurring word, phrase, image, idea, or situation in a work that has a unifying effect and may clarify meanings of the words.

Limerick A type of humorous verse with a set form of five lines, rhyming *aabba*. Limericks are often nonsensical or bawdy.

Literary ballad See **ballad**.

Lyric A brief songlike poem expressive of strong personal feeling.

Masculine rhyme See **rhyme**.

Melodrama A type of **drama** marked by the presence of sensationalism, **sentimentality**, and contrived happy endings, and by the absence of convincing **characters**.

Metaphor A **figure of speech** in which one thing is said to be another.
  Mixed metaphor A metaphor or succession of metaphors in which incompatible elements are compared, usually by mistake, as in "she flew off the handle into a tangent" or "he stormed into the room under a full head of steam."

Meter The regular rhythmic patterns in poetry, measured in units called feet. Examples for the different meters described in this entry are from Samuel Taylor Coleridge's poem "Metrical Feet."

Accentual meter Meter that is measured by **stresses** instead of by feet; the same number of stresses appear in each line, although the number of lightly stressed words and syllables may vary.

Anapest A foot consisting of two unstressed syllables followed by a stressed one (as in *ĭntĕrrúpt* and *cŏmprĕhénd*).

Anapestic meter Meter in which most of the feet are anapests: "Wĭth ă leáp ănd ă boúnd thĕ swĭft Ánăpĕsts thróng."

Common meter The meter found in hymns, which traditionally feature four-line **stanzas** with alternating lines of *iambic tetrameter* and iambic **trimeter**, and the **rhyme scheme** *abab*.

Dactyl A foot consisting of a stressed syllable followed by two unstressed syllables (as in *téndĕrly̆* and *míghtĭĕst*).

Dactylic meter Meter in which most of the feet are dactyls: "Ĕvĕr tŏ cóme ŭp wĭth Dácty̆l trĭsýllăblĕ."

Dimeter A line consisting of two feet.

Hexameter A line consisting of six feet.

Iamb A foot consisting of an unstressed syllable followed by a stressed syllable (as in *ĭndéed*).

Iambic meter Meter in which most of the feet are iambs: "Ĭámbĭcs márch frŏm shórt tŏ lóng."

Iambic pentameter A line consisting of five iambic feet; for example, the first line from Shakespeare's sonnet "Thăt tíme ŏf yéar thŏu máy̆st ĭn mé bĕhóld."

Octameter A line consisting of eight feet.

Pentameter A line consisting of five feet. The most commonly used line in English poetry.

Pyrrhic foot A foot consisting of two unstressed syllables.

Quantitative meter Meter in which feet are measured by the duration of sound instead of by stress. This meter was common in classical Greek and Latin poetry.

Spondee A foot consisting of two equally (or almost equally) stressed syllables, as in "nót nów."

Tetrameter A line consisting of four feet.

Trimeter A line consisting of three feet.

Trochaic meter Meter in which most of the feet are trochees: "Tróchĕe trĭps frŏm lóng tŏ shórt."

Trochee A foot consisting of a stressed syllable followed by an unstressed syllable (as in "brókĕn" and "wátch ĭt").

Metonymy A **figure of speech** in which one item is evoked by use of a term designating another. For example, "The *bench* [meaning the "judge"] ruled against him."

Mixed metaphor See **metaphor.**

Morality play A medieval **drama** (*Everyman*, for example), that is allegorical in form and focused on moral issues.

Motivation The inner forces causing **characters** to act as they do.

Mystery play A medieval play (*The Last Judgment* or *The Resurrection*, for example) that dramatizes biblical events, such as the birth or death of Jesus.

Myth A story by which a particular culture or society explains why things are the way they are.

Naive narrator See **narrator.**

Narrative poem A poem that tells a story. (See *ballad* and *epic*.)

Narrator (in drama) A **character** in some plays who introduces and comments on the action by speaking directly to the audience. In Tennessee Williams's *Glass Menagerie*, Tom occasionally acts as the narrator.

Narrator (in fiction) The person ostensibly telling the story.

 Innocent narrator See **naive narrator.**

 Naive narrator An unsophisticated or innocent character who is unaware of, or does not fully understand, the implications of the story he or she is telling. Larry in Frank O'Connor's "My Oedipus Complex" is a somewhat naive narrator.

 Unreliable narrator A narrator whose knowledge, perceptions, and judgment cannot be trusted and cannot be assumed to be perceptions the author shares. Naiveté is one form of unreliability, but narrators may also be unreliable because of limited intelligence or because they do not have enough emotional distance to tell their stories objectively (for example, the narrator of Charlotte Perkins Gilman's "The Yellow Wallpaper").

Near rhyme See **rhyme.**

Octameter See **meter.**

Octave An eight-line **stanza**. Also, the first eight lines of a Petrarchan (or Italian) **sonnet**.

Ode A relatively long **lyric** poem, complex in form and elevated in language. See Percy Bysshe Shelley's "Ode to the West Wind" and John Keats's "Ode to a Nightingale" and "Ode on a Grecian Urn."

Omniscience See **point of view.**

Onomatopoeia The use of words that seem to sound like the things they stand for. *Bowwow* is an onomatopoeic word.

Overstatement See **hyperbole.**

Oxymoron A **figure of speech** consisting of two words that seem to cancel each other; a type of **paradox,** as "bright darkness."

Parable A brief story that illustrates a moral or teaches a religious lesson.

Parados In ancient Greek **drama,** the first **ode** sung by the **chorus** as they enter the orchestra. Also, aisles on either side of the orchestra, which actors used to enter and exit.

Paradox A **situation** or statement that appears to be self-contradictory yet carries a truth worth weighing.

Parody A critical imitation of another literary work, sometimes funny, at its best scathing.

Pentameter See **meter.**

Peripeteia A sudden plot **reversal** sharply altering the **protagonist's** prospects.

Persona Originally, a mask worn by actors in classical **tragedy.** In criticism, persona refers to the "mask" (in the form of the **narrator** or **speaker**) a writer uses in a literary work.

Personification The attribution of animate, human characteristics to inanimate objects or abstractions, as when Emily Dickinson portrays death riding in a carriage in "Because I could not stop for Death — "

Petrarchan sonnet Also called **Italian sonnet.** A fourteen-line poem divided into an **octave** (rhyming *abbaabba*) and a **sestet** (which may follow one of several **rhyme schemes**). The sonnet is usually written in **iambic pentameter.** John Milton's "On the Late Massacre in Piedmont" follows this form.

Plot The events, actions, and reactions composing a narrative, and the order in which they occur. A conventional plot includes a **conflict, climax** or crisis, and **resolution.**

Poetic diction   See **diction.**

Point of view   The perspective from which a story is narrated or told. (See Chapter 13.)

First-person point of view   Involves a **narrator** who uses the pronoun *I* in telling a story he or she participated in or observed.

Third-person point of view   Like **first person**, can belong to a narrator who is either a participant or an observer, but a third-person narrator tends to stand at a greater distance from events and characters than does an "I" narrator.

Omniscience   Literally, "all-knowingness." An omniscient point of view entails a **third-person** narrator who purports to know everything and has access to the thoughts, feelings, and actions of any and all **characters.**

Selective omniscience   Also called **limited omniscience.** The **third-person** narrator of a story using selective omniscience speaks from a perspective close to or identical with everything that **character** knows and feels.

Prologue   An introduction or preface to a literary work. Originally, the action or speech at the beginning of a Greek **tragedy.**

Prose poem   A short composition written in prose but achieving poetic effect through the use of **figurative language, imagery, internal rhyme,** and **rhythm.**

Prosody   The study of sound and the rhythmic elements in poetry, including **diction, meter, rhythm,** and **stress.**

Protagonist   The main **character** of a narrative, whose personality and temperament are defined in part by the way he or she reacts to events in the story and the way he or she deals with **conflict.**

Pun   A play on words involving two words that sound the same, or similar, but have different meanings. For example, when Hamlet talks about the skull of a land buyer, he puns on the word *fine*: "Is this the fine of his fines, and the recovery of his recoveries, to have his fine pate full of fine dirt?" (V.i.96–97).

Pyrrhic foot   See **meter.**

Quantitative meter   See **meter.**

Quatrain   A four-line **stanza.**

Recognition   The coming to knowledge (often self-knowledge) of a **character** in a literary work. A recognition often occurs as the result of a personal or **plot reversal.**

Refrain   A word, phrase, line, or group of lines that is repeated during the course of a poem, usually at the end of a **stanza.**

Resolution   The point in a narrative occurring after the **climax,** when the **conflict** is resolved.

Reversal   A dramatic change in a **character's** luck or in the plot of a literary work. (Also called **peripeteia.**)

Rhyme   The repetition of very similar or identical sounds in stressed syllables of different words, usually at the ends of poetic lines.

Approximate rhyme   Same as **near rhyme.**

End rhyme   Rhymes that occur at the ends of lines, as in this example from Langston Hughes's "Harlem (A Dream Deferred)":

> Maybe it just sags
> like a heavy *load*
>
> Or does it ex*plode?*

Feminine rhyme   Also called **double rhyme.** Rhymes that occur in two consecutive syllables, stressed and unstressed, respectively (as in *weeping* and *seeping*).

Internal rhyme   Rhymes that occur in the middle of lines. They can be in consecutive lines or within the same line, as in "whose *breasts* still bear the *stress*" (Adrienne Rich, "Diving into the Wreck").

Masculine rhyme   Also called **single rhyme.** A rhyme that occurs between two single, stressed syllables, either the final or only syllables of the rhyming words, as in up*set* and re*gret,* or *break* and *take.*

Near rhyme   Rhymes in which the final consonants of the words are the same, but the vowel sounds are slightly different, so that the words no longer match precisely, as in Emily Dickinson's lines

> After great pain, a formal feeling *comes* —
> The Nerves sit ceremonious, like *Tombs* —

Rhyme scheme The sequence of rhyming words in a particular **stanza**, poem, or type of poem. By **convention** the sequence is coded by letters of the alphabet. For example, the rhyme scheme of the *octave* in the *Petrarchan sonnet* is *abbaabba*.

Rhyme scheme See **rhyme**.

Rhythm The recurrence of sounds and *stresses* in a written or spoken work.

Rising action The events or action in a narrative that lead up to the **climax** or crisis.

Rising meter Meters, such as **iambic** and **anapestic**, that move from unstressed to stressed syllables.

Rondel A French verse form of thirteen or fourteen lines featuring a **refrain** and a fixed **rhyme scheme**.

Round character See **character**.

Run-on line A line of **verse** that is incomplete in itself and depends on the subsequent line to finish its meaning and syntax. See **enjambment**.

Satire A literary form that uses humor (often mocking or derisive) to attack a particular individual or institution, or human vices and follies generally.

Scansion A method for determining the rhythm of a poem by dividing lines into feet, locating and marking **stresses**, and noting regularities and variations in the general pattern.

Scene In **drama**, a unit into which acts are divided, often marked by the entrance (and subsequent exit) of a major **character**. A shift in scene can also signify a shift in time or location.

Selective omniscience See **point of view**.

Sentimentality Indulgence without sufficient or appropriate cause in sloshy emotions.

Sestet A six-line **stanza**. Also, the last six lines of a **Petrarchan sonnet**.

Sestina A poem of thirty-nine lines, containing six **sestets** and a final three-line **stanza**. Sestinas do not rhyme but follow a complicated set of rules governing the repetition of certain words at certain points throughout the poem.

Setting The time and place at which a literary work occurs.

Shakespearean sonnet Also called *English sonnet*. A four-teen-line poem containing three **quatrains** and a **couplet**, rhyming *abab/cdcd/efef/gg*.

Simile A **figure of speech** in which one thing is said to be like another; a form of comparison generally using the word *like* or *as*. (See Chapter 9 for simile in poetry.)

Situation The precise events and circumstances in which **characters** find themselves at the beginning — or at any specific point — of a narrative in poetry or prose.

Situational irony See **irony**.

Social drama Drama that explores social issues, such as the situation of women (see the work of Henrik Ibsen) or the success myth in America (see the work of Arthur Miller).

Soliloquy A speech that a **character** (usually alone onstage) delivers either to himself or herself or to the audience for the purpose of revealing his or her thought and feelings.

Sonnet A fourteen-line **lyric** poem usually written in **iambic pentameter** and following a set **rhyme scheme**. See **Petrarchan sonnet** and **Shakespearean sonnet**.

Speaker In poetry, the person who is ostensibly telling, or narrating, the poem. As with the **narrator** in **fiction**, the speaker should be distinguished from the actual author.

Spondee See **meter**.

Stanza A structural unit in **verse**; a grouping of two or more lines either on the basis of length, **meter**, and **rhyme scheme** or on the basis of conventional meaning.

Stereotype See **character**.

Stock character See **character**.

Stream of consciousness The attempt to depict a **character**'s inner flow of thought and associations unstructured by logic and grammar.

Stress The emphasis placed on a given syllable in a line of poetry, compared with the emphasis given to surrounding syllables.

Style The embodiment in words of an author's individu-

ality. Style involves numberless personal decisions about every·
thing from **point of view** to **diction** to choice of subject.

Subplot   A secondary **plot** in a narrative or dramatic work
that, by likeness or contrast, comments on the main plot.

Suspense   The quality of tension in a narrative generated by
the reader's uncertainty about the **resolution** of **conflicts**. (See
Chapter 14.)

Syllabic verse   Poetry that is measured by the number of
syllables in a line instead of by the number of **feet** or **stresses**.

Symbol   An object, event, or action that suggests meanings
beyond its literal meaning. (See Chapters 10 and 16).

Synecdoche   A **figure of speech** in which a part is used to
represent the whole, or vice versa, as in "wheels" for a car.

Syntax   The grammatical order in which words are put to·
gether in a phrase, sentence, or line of **verse** or **dialogue**.

Tercet   A three-line **stanza**.

Terza rima   A three-line **stanza** with an interlocking *rhyme
scheme* of *aba/bcb/cdc*, and so on. See Percy Bysshe Shelley's "Ode to
the West Wind" for an example.

Tetrameter   See **meter**.

Theater of the absurd   The term for a mode of twentieth-
century **drama** that assumes that the universe is incomprehensi·
ble and that human life is meaningless.

Theme   The reader's name for the central meaning of a lit·
erary work.

Third-person point of view   See **point of view**.

Tone   The expression of the author's (or **speaker's** or **narra·
tor's**) attitude toward the audience addressed or toward his or her
material. (See Chapter 7 for tone in poetry.)

Tragedy   A type of **drama** in which **characters** of distinction
and significant position suffer ill fortune, usually leading to
catastrophe. (See Chapter 18.)

Tragic flaw   In classical **tragedy**, the weakness that leads to
the **protagonist's** downfall.

Tragic irony   See **irony**.

Tragicomedy A play blending elements of **tragedy** and **comedy**, usually possessing a serious **theme** and **tone**, and ending happily. (See Chapter 20.)

Trimeter See **meter.**

Trochaic meter See **meter.**

Trochee See **meter.**

Unreliable narrator See **narrator.**

Vaudeville Stage entertainment popular in the early twentieth century that included animal acts and comic turns as well as performances by singers, acrobats, dancers, and magicians.

Verse Poetry in general, as opposed to prose. Also, a single line of poetry.

Vers libre See **free verse.**

Villanelle A French verse form of nineteen lines composed of five **tercets** followed by a **quatrain,** featuring a set **rhyme scheme.** Dylan Thomas's "Do not go gentle into that good night" is an example.

Acknowledgments (continued from page iv)

W. H. Auden. "Musée des Beaux Arts," copyright 1940 and renewed 1968 by W. H. Auden. Reprinted from *W. H. Auden: Collected Poems*, edited by Edward Mendelson, by permission of Random House, Inc. and Faber and Faber Ltd. "Petition," copyright 1934 and renewed 1962 by W. H. Auden. Reprinted from *The English Auden: Poems, Essays and Dramatic Writings, 1927–1939* by W. H. Auden, edited by Edward Mendelson, by permission of Random House, Inc. and Faber and Faber Ltd.

James Baldwin. "Sonny's Blues" from *Going to Meet the Man*. Copyright © 1948, 1951, 1957, 1958, 1960, 1965 by James Baldwin. Reprinted by permission of Doubleday & Company, Inc.

Toni Cade Bambara. "The Lesson" from *Gorilla, My Love* by Toni Cade Bambara. Copyright © 1972 by Toni Cade Bambara. Reprinted by permission of Random House, Inc.

John Barth. "Lost in the Funhouse" by John Barth. Copyright © 1967 by *Atlantic Monthly Company* from the book *Lost in the Funhouse*. Reprinted by permission of Doubleday & Company.

Samuel Beckett. *Krapp's Last Tape*. Copyright © 1957 by Samuel Beckett. Copyright © 1958, 1959, 1960, 1986 by Grove Press, Inc. Reprinted by permission from Grove Press, Inc. and Faber and Faber Limited.

Wendell Berry. "The Peace of Wild Things," copyright © 1968 by Wendell Berry. Reprinted from his volume *Openings* by permission of Harcourt Brace Jovanovich, Inc.

John Berryman. "Dream Song 14" from *77 Dream Songs* by John Berryman. Copyright © 1959, 1962, 1963, 1964 by John Berryman. Reprinted by permission of Farrar, Straus and Giroux, Inc.

Elizabeth Bishop. "At the Fishhouses," "Filling Station," "Questions of Travel," and "The Armadillo" from *The Complete Poems, 1929–1979* by Elizabeth Bishop. Copyright 1947, 1955, 1956, 1957; copyright renewed 1974, 1979 by Elizabeth Bishop. These poems originally appeared in *The New Yorker*. Reprinted by permission of Farrar, Straus and Giroux, Inc.

Gwendolyn Brooks. "The Lovers of the Poor" and "We Real Cool" reprinted by permission of the author.

Anton Chekhov. "The Lady with the Pet Dog" and *The Cherry Orchard* from *The Portable Chekhov*, edited and translated by Avrahm Yarmolinsky. Translation copyright 1947, © 1968 by The Viking Press, Inc. Copyright renewed © 1975 by Avrahm Yarmolinsky. Reprinted by permission of Viking Penguin Inc. "The Bishop" © Ronald Hingley 1975. Reprinted from *The Oxford Chekhov*, translated and edited by Ronald Hingley, vol. 9 (1975), by permission of Oxford University Press.

Caryl Churchill. *Light Shining in Buckinghamshire*, copyright © Caryl Churchill Ltd., 1978, 1985. Reprinted by permission of the author. CAUTION: All rights whatsoever in this play are strictly reserved and application for performances etc. should be made before rehearsal to Margaret Ramsay Ltd., 14A Goodwin's Court, St. Martin's Lane, London WC2N 4LL, England. No performance may be given unless a license has been obtained.

Amy Clampitt. "A New Life" from *What the Light Was Like* by Amy Clampitt. Copyright © 1985 by Amy Clampitt. "Balms" from *The Kingfisher* by Amy Clampitt. Copyright © 1980 by Amy Clampitt. Both poems reprinted by permission of Alfred A. Knopf, Inc.

Countee Cullen. "Incident" from *On These I Stand* by Countee Cullen. Copyright 1925 by Harper & Row, Publishers, Inc. Reprinted by permission of Harper & Row, Publishers, Inc.

E. E. Cummings. "a salesman is an it that stinks Excuse," copyright 1944 by E. E. Cummings; renewed 1972 by Nancy T. Andrews. Reprinted from *Complete Poems, 1913–1962* by E. E. Cummings by permission of Harcourt Brace Jovanovich, Inc.

C. Day-Lewis. "Sheepdog Trials in Hyde Park" from *The Gate*. Reprinted by permission of A. D. Peters & Co. Ltd.

Emily Dickinson. "I heard a Fly buzz — when I died," "I like to see it lap the Miles," "After great pain a formal feeling comes," " 'Twas warm — at first — like Us," "There's a certain Slant of light," "A Bird came down the Walk," and "Because I could not stop for

Death" from *Complete Poems of Emily Dickinson*, edited by Thomas H. Johnson. Copyright 1914, 1929, 1935, 1942 by Martha Dickinson Bianchi; copyright © renewed 1957, 1963 by Mary L. Hampson; reprinted by permission of Little, Brown and Company. Also, reprinted by permission of Harvard University Press and the Trustees of Amherst College from *The Poems of Emily Dickinson*, edited by Thomas H. Johnson. Cambridge, Mass.: The Belknap Press of Harvard University Press. Copyright 1951, © 1955, 1979, 1983 by the President and Fellows of Harvard College.

Deborah Eisenberg. "What It Was Like, Seeing Chris" from *Transactions in a Foreign Currency* by Deborah Eisenberg. Copyright © 1985 by Deborah Eisenberg. Reprinted by permission of Alfred A. Knopf, Inc.

T. S. Eliot. "The Love Song of J. Alfred Prufrock," "Gerontion," and "Journey of the Magi" from *Collected Poems, 1909–1962* by T. S. Eliot. Copyright 1935, 1936 by Harcourt Brace Jovanovich, Inc.; copyright © 1964 by T. S. Eliot. Reprinted by permission of Harcourt Brace Jovanovich, Inc. and Faber and Faber Limited.

William Faulkner. "Barn Burning," copyright 1939 and renewed 1967 by Estelle Faulkner and Jill Faulkner Summers. Reprinted from *Collected Stories of William Faulkner* by permission of Random House, Inc.

Robert Frost. "After Apple-Picking," "The Oven Bird," "Spring Pools," "Design," "Once by the Pacific," and "The Silken Tent" from *The Poetry of Robert Frost*, edited by Edward Connery Lathem. Copyright © 1969 by Holt, Rinehart and Winston, Inc. Copyright © 1962 by Robert Frost. Copyright © 1975 by Lesley Frost Ballantine. Reprinted by permission of Henry Holt and Company.

Athol Fugard, John Kani, and Winston Ntshona. *The Island*, copyright © 1973 and 1974 by Athol Fugard, John Kani, and Winston Ntshona. Published by arrangement with Theatre Communications Group, Inc., New York. CAUTION: Professionals and amateurs are hereby warned that these plays, being fully protected under the Copyright Laws of the United States of America and all other countries of the Berne and Universal Copyright Conventions, are subject to a royalty. All rights including, but not limited to, professional, amateur, recording, motion picture, recitation, lecturing, public reading, radio and television broadcasting, and the rights of translation into foreign languages are expressly reserved. Particular emphasis is placed on the question of readings and all uses of these plays by educational institutions, permission for which must be secured from the authors' representative: Esther Sherman, William Morris Agency, 1350 Ave. of the Americas, New York, NY 10019; (212) 586-5100.

Tess Gallagher. "The Hug" from *Willingly* (Graywolf Press, 1984). Reprinted by permission of Graywolf Press.

Louise Glück. "Labor Day," copyright © 1968 by Louise Glück. From *Firstborn* by Louise Glück, first published by the Ecco Press in 1968. Reprinted by permission of the Ecco Press.

Jorie Graham. "Over and Over Stitch" from *Hybrids of Plants and Ghosts* (in the Princeton Series of Contemporary Poets). Copyright © 1980 by Princeton University Press. Reprinted by permission of Princeton University Press.

Wallace Gray. Excerpt from *Homer to Joyce* (pp. 64–67) by Wallace Gray reprinted with permission of Macmillan Publishing Company. Copyright © 1985 by Wallace Gray.

Michael Harper. "Martin's Blues" from *History Is Your Own Heartbeat* by Michael Harper. Copyright © 1971 by Michael Harper. Reprinted by permission of the author and the University of Illinois Press.

Seamus Heaney. "Digging" from *Poems, 1965–1975* by Seamus Heaney. Copyright © 1966, 1969, 1972, 1975, 1980 by Seamus Heaney. Reprinted by permission of Farrar, Straus and Giroux, Inc., and by permission of Faber and Faber Limited from *Death of a Naturalist* by Seamus Heaney.

Anthony Hecht. "Lizards and Snakes" from *The Hard Hours* by Anthony Hecht. Copyright © 1967 by Anthony Hecht. Reprinted with the permission of Atheneum Publishers, a division of Macmillan, Inc.

Ernest Hemingway. "Hills Like White Elephants" from *Men Without Women*. Copyright 1927 by Charles Scribner's Sons; copyright renewed © 1955 by Ernest Hemingway. Reprinted with the permission of Charles Scribner's Sons, a division of Macmillan, Inc.

A. E. Housman. "Eight O'Clock," copyright 1922 by Holt, Rinehart and Winston, Inc. Copyright 1950 by Barclays Bank Ltd. Reprinted from *The Collected Poems of A. E. Housman* by permission of Henry Holt and Company.

Langston Hughes. "Harlem (A Dream Deferred)," copyright 1951 by Langston Hughes. Reprinted from *The Panther and the Lash: Poems of Our Times* by Langston Hughes, by permission of Alfred A. Knopf, Inc. "Dream Boogie" and "Ballad of the Landlord" from *Montage of a Dream Deferred* by Langston Hughes, copyright 1951 by Langston Hughes. Copyright renewed 1979 by George Houston Bass. Reprinted by permissiom of Harold Ober Associates Incorporated.

Ted Hughes. "View of a Pig" from *New Selected Poems* by Ted Hughes. Copyright © 1960 by Ted Hughes. Reprinted by permission of Harper & Row, Publishers, Inc. and by Faber and Faber Limited from *Lupercal* by Ted Hughes.

Henrik Ibsen. *A Doll's House*, Michael Meyer, translator, from *Ghosts and Three Other Plays* (1966). Copyright © 1966 by Michael Meyer. Reprinted by permission of Harold Ober Associates Incorporated. This play is fully protected, in whole, in part or in any form under the copyright laws of the United States of America, the British Empire including the Dominion of Canada, and all other countries of the Copyright Union, and is subject to royalty. All rights including motion picture, radio, television, recitation and public reading are strictly reserved. For professional rights and amateur rights, all inquiries should be addressed to the author's agent: Robert A. Freedman Dramatic Agency, Inc., 1501 Broadway, New York, NY 10036.

Shirley Jackson. "The Lottery" from *The Lottery* by Shirley Jackson. Copyright 1948, 1949 by Shirley Jackson. Copyright renewed © 1976, 1977 by Laurence Hyman, Barry Hyman, Mrs. Sarah Webster, and Mrs. Joanne Schnurer. Originally apeared in *The New Yorker*. Reprinted by permission of Farrar, Straus and Giroux, Inc.

Randall Jarrell. "The Woman at the Washington Zoo" from *The Woman at the Washington Zoo*. Copyright © 1960 by Randall Jarrell. Reprinted with the permission of Atheneum Publishers, a division of Macmillan, Inc. "The Lost Children" and "Well Water" from *The Lost World* by Randall Jarrell. Copyright © Randall Jarrell 1965. Reprinted with permission of Macmillan Publishing Company.

James Joyce. "Araby" from *Dubliners* by James Joyce. Copyright 1916 by B. W. Huebsch. Definitive text copyright © 1967 by the Estate of James Joyce. Reprinted by permission of Viking Penguin Inc.

Franz Kafka. "The Metamorphosis" from *The Penal Colony* by Franz Kafka, translated by Willa and Edwin Muir. Copyright © 1948, 1976 by Schocken Books Inc. Reprinted by permission of Schocken Books Inc.

Jamaica Kincaid. "In the Night" from *At the Bottom of the River* by Jamaica Kincaid. Copyright © 1978, 1979, 1981, 1982, 1983 by Jamaica Kincaid. Originally appeared in *The New Yorker*. Reprinted by permission of Farrar, Straus and Giroux, Inc.

Galway Kinnell. "Cells Breathe in the Emptiness" from *Flower Herding on Mount Monadnock* by Galway Kinnell. Copyright © 1964 by Galway Kinnell. Reprinted by permission of Houghton Mifflin Company.

Philip Larkin. "Coming" and "Church Going" from *The Less Deceived* by Philip Larkin, published by the Marvell Press, England. Reprinted by permission. "The Whitsun Weddings" from *The Whitsun Weddings* by Philip Larkin. Reprinted by permission of Faber and Faber Limited.

D. H. Lawrence. "Snake," "Tortoise Gallantry," "Humming Bird," and "Piano" from *The Complete Poems of D. H. Lawrence*, edited by Vivian De Sola Pinto and F. Warren Roberts. Copyright © 1964, 1971 by Angelo Ravagli and C. M. Weekley, Executors of the Estate of Frieda Lawrence Ravagli. "Odour of Chrysanthemums" from *The Complete Short Stories of D. H.*

Flannery O'Connor. "The Artificial Nigger," copyright 1955 by Flannery O'Connor; renewed 1983 by Regina O'Connor. Reprinted from *A Good Man Is Hard to Find* by Flannery O'Connor by permission of Harcourt Brace Jovanovich, Inc.

Frank O'Connor. "My Oedipus Complex," copyright 1950 by Frank O'Connor. Reprinted from *Collected Stories* by Frank O'Connor, by permission of Alfred A. Knopf, Inc. and Joan Daves.

Mary Oliver. "The Truro Bear" from *Twelve Moons* by Mary Oliver. Copyright © 1978 by Mary Oliver. First appeared in *The Ohio Review*. Reprinted by permission of Little, Brown and Company, Inc. "Milkweed" reprinted from *Dream Work* by Mary Oliver, copyright © 1986 by Mary Oliver. Reprinted by permission of the Atlantic Monthly Press.

Sylvia Plath. "Mushrooms," copyright © 1960 by Sylvia Plath. Reprinted from *The Colossus and Other Poems* by Sylvia Plath, by permission of Alfred A. Knopf, Inc. and Olwyn Hughes from *The Collected Poems of Sylvia Plath*, © Ted Hughes 1965, 1981. "Balloons," "Lady Lazarus," and "The Arrival of the Bee Box" from *The Collected Poems of Sylvia Plath*, edited by Ted Hughes. Copyright © 1963 by Ted Hughes. Reprinted by permission of Harper & Row, Publishers, Inc. for U.S. rights, and by permission of Olwyn Hughes from *The Collected Poems of Sylvia Plath*, © Ted Hughes 1965, 1981 for Canadian rights.

Ezra Pound. "The River Merchant's Wife: A Letter" from *Personae* by Ezra Pound. Copyright 1926 by Ezra Pound. Reprinted by permission of New Directions Publishing Corporation.

John Crowe Ransom. "Bells for John Whiteside's Daughter," copyright 1924 by Alfred A. Knopf, Inc. and renewed 1952 by John Crowe Ransom. Reprinted from *Selected Poems*, Third Edition, Revised and Enlarged by John Crowe Ransom, by permission of Alfred A. Knopf, Inc.

Henry Reed. "Naming of Parts" from *A Map of Verona* by Henry Reed. Reprinted by permission of Henry Reed and Jonathan Cape Ltd.

Adrienne Rich. "The Middle-Aged," "Living in Sin," and "Diving into the Wreck" reprinted from *The Fact of a Doorframe: Poems Selected and New, 1950–1984* by Adrienne Rich, by permission of W. W. Norton & Company, Inc. Copyright © 1984 by Adrienne Rich. Copyright © 1975, 1978 by W. W. Norton & Company, Inc. Copyright © 1981 by Adrienne Rich.

Edwin Arlington Robinson. "Mr. Flood's Party" from *Collected Poems* by Edwin Arlington Robinson. Copyright 1921 by Edwin Arlington Robinson, renewed 1949 by Ruth Nivison. Reprinted with permission of Macmillan Publishing Company.

Theodore Roethke. "Elegy for Jane," copyright 1950 by Theodore Roethke; "The Minimal," copyright 1942 by Theodore Roethke; "Cuttings," copyright 1948 by Theodore Roethke, and "Cuttings (Later)," copyright 1948 by Theodore Roethke from *The Collected Poems of Theodore Roethke*. Reprinted by permission of Doubleday & Company, Inc.

Anne Sexton. "For My Lover, Returning to His Wife" from *Love Poems* by Anne Sexton. Copyright © 1967, 1968, 1969 by Anne Sexton. Reprinted by permission of Houghton Mifflin Company.

William Shakespeare. *Macbeth* by William Shakespeare, edited by Alfred Harbage. Copyright 1956 by Penguin Books, Inc. Copyright renewed © 1984 by Viking Penguin Inc. Reprinted by permission of Viking Penguin Inc. *Hamlet, Prince of Denmark* by William Shakespeare, edited with notes by Willard Edward Farnham. Copyright © 1957 by Penguin Books Inc.; copyright renewed 1985 by Diana Farnham O'Hehir, Anthony E. Farnham, and Nicholas H. Farnham. Reprinted by permission of Viking Penguin Inc.

Dave Smith. "The Spring Poem" from *Cumberland Station*. Copyright © 1976 by Dave Smith. Reprinted by permission of the author and the University of Illinois Press.

Sophocles. *Antigone* from *Sophocles: The Three Theban Plays*, translated by Robert Fagles with notes by Bernard Knox. Copyright © 1977, 1979, 1982 by Robert Fagles. Annotations copyright © 1982 by Bernard Knox. Reprinted by permission of Viking Penguin, Inc. This play in its printed form is designed for the reading public only. All dramatic rights in it are fully protected by copyrights and no public or private performances — professional or amateur — and no public readings for profit may be given without the written permission of

Index of
First Lines

Index of
Authors and Titles